SPORTS AND RECREATIONAL ACTIVITIES

TWELFTH EDITION

Dale Mood
Professor
Department of Kinesiology
University of Colorado, Boulder

Frank F. Musker
Formerly Professor of Physical Education,
Boston University; Supervisor of Physical Education,
Peabody Public Schools, Peabody, Massachusetts

Judith E. Rink
Associate Professor,
Department of Physical Education,
University of South Carolina,
Columbia, South Carolina

Boston Burr Ridge, IL Dubuque, IA Madison, WI New York San Francisco St. Louis
Bangkok Bogotá Caracas Lisbon London Madrid
Mexico City Milan New Delhi Seoul Singapore Sydney Taipei Toronto

WCB/McGraw-Hill
A Division of The **McGraw-Hill** *Companies*

SPORTS AND RECREATIONAL ACTIVITIES, TWELFTH EDITION

This book is printed on recycled, acid-free paper containing 10% postconsumer waste.

1 2 3 4 5 6 7 8 9 0 QPD/QPD 9 3 2 1 0 9 8

ISBN 0-07-092111-3

Vice president and editorial director: *Kevin T. Kane*
Publisher: *Edward E. Bartell*
Executive editor: *Vicki Malinee*
Developmental editor: *Patricia A. Schissel*
Senior marketing manager: *Pamela S. Cooper*
Project manager: *Sheila M. Frank*
Senior production supervisor: *Sandra Hahn*
Coordinator of freelance design: *Michelle D. Whitaker*
Senior photo research coordinator: *Lori Hancock*
Supplement coordinator: *Tammy Juran*
Compositor: *GAC Indianapolis*
Typeface: *10/12 Caledonia*
Printer: *Quebecor Printing Book Group/Dubuque, IA*

Freelance cover designer: *Paul Uhl; Design Associates*
Cover illustration: *Steve Hunter*

The credits section for this book begins on page 663 and is considered an extension of the copyright page.

1520–7919

www.mhhe.com

Consultants

HEALTH-RELATED PHYSICAL FITNESS

James Morrow, Professor and Chair
Department of Kinesiology, Health Promotion and Recreation
University of North Texas
Denton, TX 76203

GROUP-EXERCISE AEROBIC DANCE

Mary Yoke
29 Blueberry Lane
Stormville, NY 12582

ARCHERY

Frank Thomas, Senior Lecturer
Department of Kinesiology
Texas A&M University
College Station, TX 77843

BACKPACKING

Jeff Steffen, Associate Professor
Department of Physical Education
University of Wisconsin-LaCrosse
LaCrosse, WI 54601

BADMINTON

Donald C. Paup, Professor
Department of Exercise Science
George Washington University
Washington, D.C. 20052

BASKETBALL

James D. LaPoint, Associate Professor
Department of Health, Sport, and Exercise Sciences
University of Kansas
Lawrence, KS 66045

and

March Krotee, Professor
School of Kinesiology and Leisure Studies
University of Minnesota
Minneapolis, MN 55455

BICYCLING

Tom Swensen, Assistant Professor
Department of Exercise & Sport Science
Ithaca College
Ithaca, NY 14850

BOWLING

Rosemary McMahan, Assistant Professor
Department of Physical Education and Sports Studies
University of Georgia
Athens, GA 30602

DANCE: RECREATIONAL, CONCERT, CULTURAL

Cynthia Noble, Associate Professor
Department of Visual & Performing Arts
Springfield College
Springfield, MA 01109

FENCING

Anne Klinger, Professor Emerita
Department of Physical Education
Clatsop Community College
Astoria, OR 97103

FIELD HOCKEY

Karen Weaver, President
College Sport Services
2100 Susquehanna Rd.
Abington, PA 19001

GOLF

A. Craig Fisher, Professor & Chair
Department of Exercise and Sport Science
Ithaca College
Ithaca, NY 14850

GYMNASTICS

Lindy Franzini, Owner & Head Coach
Gymnastics Institute of Colorado
360 South Potomac Street
Aurora, CO 80012

JOGGING

Don Torok, Assistant Professor
Department of Health Sciences, Program of Exercise Science and Wellness
Florida Atlantic University
Davie, FL 33314

KARATE

Rick Schmidt, Associate Professor
School of Health, Physical Education, and Recreation
University of Nebraska
Lincoln, NE 68588

KAYAKING AND CANOEING

Peter Werner, Professor
Department of Physical Education
University of South Carolina
Columbia, SC 29208

LACROSSE

David Urick, Head Coach
Georgetown University
Washington, D.C. 20057

MOUNTAINEERING

Stephan Greenway, Instructor
Boulder Rock Club
Boulder, CO 80301

ORIENTEERING

Jerry Andrew, Lecturer
Department of Health and Kinesiology
Texas A&M University
College Station, TX 77843

RACQUETBALL, PADDLEBALL, AND HANDBALL

Gene Ezell, Professor
Department of Exercise Science and Health Promotion
University of Tennessee
Chattanooga, TN 37403

RUGBY

Christian Averill, Managing Editor
Rugby Press
2350 Broadway
New York, NY 10024

SKIING: ALPINE

Richard Rokos, Head Ski Coach
Department of Athletics
University of Colorado
Boulder, CO 80309

SKIING: CROSS-COUNTRY

George Atkinson, Director
School of General Studies
Northeastern University
Boston, MA 02115

and

Bob Fitzpatrick, Coach
Cambridge Sports Union Junior Nordic Ski Team
Leicester, MA 01524

SKIN AND SCUBA DIVING

Mark Jellison
Scuba Joe, Incorporated
Boulder, CO 80301

SOCCER

James D. LaPoint, Associate Professor
Department of Health, Sport, and Exercise Sciences
University of Kansas
Lawrence, KS 66045

and

March Krotee, Professor
School of Kinesiology and Leisure Studies
University of Minnesota
Minneapolis, MN 55455

SOFTBALL

Jimmy Disch, Associate Professor and Chair
Department of Human Performance and Health Sciences
Rice University
Houston, TX 77251

SPEEDBALL

Laura deGhetaldi, Lecturer
Department of Kinesiology
University of Colorado
Boulder, CO 80309

SPRINGBOARD DIVING

Gerald DeMers, Associate Professor and Aquatic Director
Department of Physical Education and Kinesiology
California Polytechnic State University
San Luis Obispo, CA 93407

SWIMMING

Joel Stout, Instructor
Department of Kinesiology, Health Promotion, and Recreation
University of North Texas
Denton, TX 76203

TABLE TENNIS

Seth Pederson, Communications Director
USA Table Tennis
One Olympic Plaza
Colorado Springs, CO 80909

TEAM HANDBALL

James D. LaPoint, Associate Professor
Department of Health, Sport, and Exercise Sciences
University of Kansas
Lawrence, KS 66045

and

March Krotee, Professor
School of Kinesiology and Leisure Studies
University of Minnesota
Minneapolis, MN 55455

TENNIS

Randy Hyllegard, Assistant Professor
Department of Physical Education
Western Illinois University
Macomb, IL 61455

TOUCH AND FLAG FOOTBALL

Randy Bonnette, Assistant Professor
Department of Physical Education
University of New Mexico
Las Cruces, NM 88011

TRACK AND FIELD

Al McDaniels, Track Coach
Department of Athletics
University of Nevada
Las Vegas, NV 89154

VOLLEYBALL

Linda Delk, Head Volleyball Coach
Department of Athletics
University of Northern Colorado
Greeley, CO 80631

WATER POLO

Clint Bell, Water Polo Coach
Recreation Center
University of Colorado
Boulder, CO 80309

WEIGHT TRAINING

Dwight Robinson
Department of Kinesiology
University of Colorado
Boulder, CO 80309

WRESTLING

Gerald Landwer, Professor
Department of Kinesiology
University of Nevada
Las Vegas, NV 89154

Contributors

DISC SPORTS

Joe Jacobs, Assistant Professor
Department of Physical Education
Winthrop University
Rock Hill, SC 29730

IN-LINE SKATING

Liz Miller, Certified Instructor
P. O. Box 1115
Danville, CA 94526

Contents

Preface

PURPOSE OF THE BOOK

The purpose of the twelfth edition of *Sports and Recreational Activities* is to provide current fundamental knowledge about a broad spectrum of physical activities. The physiological, psychological, and social benefits of participation in physical activities have long been proclaimed by physicians, physical educators, and recreation directors, and it appears that their advice is receiving the public's attention. Most evidence suggests that the number of people engaging in regular physical activity is higher than in the past, although it is still considerably lower than the goals set by national health agencies. There is some evidence that the number of people in the United States participating in regular physical activity might actually be declining after several years of increase. For reasons of safety, enjoyment, and motivation, it is important that participants start out correctly and that they are exposed to a variety of possibilities. We believe that participation in physical activities can enrich the quality of life and that use of the basic concepts provided in this book will promote this enrichment.

Sports and Recreational Activities is written for two groups of readers—participants and instructors (or instructors-to-be). People who decide to embark on a personal program of sports and recreation can benefit from this book's excellent overview of forty-two popular physical activities. Physical educators, recreation leaders, playground directors, and camp counselors, no matter how well trained, seldom have the time to learn the fundamentals of the many activities covered in this book. For these instructors or students who will become instructors, the book should serve as a valuable resource when they are called upon to teach an unfamiliar activity.

In most cases, each chapter includes a brief historical perspective of the activity, information about the selection and care of required equipment, a digest of the basic rules, a discussion of the fundamental skills and techniques required, ideas about strategies, safety concerns, a list of teaching considerations, terminology, and selected references. Armed with this knowledge both the participant and the instructor should find increased enjoyment in physical activities.

CHANGES IN THE TWELFTH EDITION

The revision process for this edition was extensive. Although much about sports and recreational activities remains constant over the years, there also is much that changes. For example, we have updated the text to reflect the invention of new equipment, changes in the rules, the discovery of new techniques, and the increase in available references, including, for the first time, Web sites. The increasing participation of women in sports and recreational activities has brought about many rule changes during recent years (consider basketball, for example). The conversion of various dimensions to metric units and the simple need to update photographs as new apparel becomes available are other reasons revision is necessary. Along with these updating needs, many other changes have been made in this twelfth edition to make it a more useful book.

CHAPTER CONSISTENCY

Particular attention has been given to present this wealth of diverse material as consistently as possible from chapter to chapter. In general and where appropriate, each chapter proceeds from behavioral objectives, to history, to equipment and facilities, to rules and etiquette, to fundamental skills and techniques, to strategies, to teaching considerations, and finally to ancillary information such as a glossary, suggested readings, and audiovisual materials.

NEW ILLUSTRATIONS

Many new photographs and drawings have been added and others replaced or modified to illustrate the latest developments in technique and instruction. If a picture is worth a thousand words, then the hundreds of illustrations in the book provide an efficient method for communicating a great deal of information. However, it is not always a simple task to obtain just the right photograph or drawing to capture the intent. A great deal of effort was spent on improving the illustrations for this edition so that the reader can truly "see" the nuances of each activity.

NEW CHAPTERS

Two new chapters have been added to the twelfth edition of *Sports and Recreational Activities.* The new chapters cover disc sports and in-line skating. The popularity of these activities is spreading across the country, warranting their inclusion in this book. In addition, to highlight the importance of participation in physical activities for healthful reasons, the physical fitness chapter has been moved to follow the introduction.

Each chapter has been revised to include only the latest rules and regulations. Photos and illustrations have also been updated to include current and easy-to-follow pictures and drawings. Additionally, you will find:

- References to 1996 Olympic achievements throughout
- New information on *extreme sports* in chapter 1
- A completely revised chapter on physical fitness, adding focus on health-related fitness
- New drill activities throughout, especially in the chapters on racquetball, paddleball and handball, track and field, volleyball, and water polo
- A revised chapter on aerobic dance, recognizing the current shift to group exercise
- Expanded sections on mountain and trail biking in the bicycling chapter, due to increased popularity of these activities
- Increased information on specific training schedules in the jogging chapter
- A new section on the international scale of river difficulty in the chapter on kayaking and canoeing
- A new section on backboard and ball machine use in the tennis chapter
- Revisions within the chapter on weight training to shift the focus to noncompetitive weight training
- Numerous relevant Web site resources in the end-of-chapter reference sections

ANNOTATED REFERENCES

Recognizing that a book such as this cannot present every facet of every activity, we present a list of suggested readings for each chapter. Beginning in the ninth edition and continuing through this edition, we have provided a short annotation for many of these references. This will allow readers who wish further details about an activity to select readings that are germane to their particular interests.

VIDEOTAPES

New to the tenth and continuing and updated for the twelfth edition is information at the end of most chapters specifying where relevant videotapes may be found. Videotapes of talented performers and of classic events are being used for instructional purposes at an increasing rate. We hope this additional resource will continue to prove helpful.

APPENDIX MATERIAL

Appendix A contains some playing field and court dimensions, and we have listed in Appendix B a guide for converting metric and English units.

INSTRUCTOR'S MANUAL

An instructor's manual has been prepared for use with the twelfth edition. It includes chapter outlines, test questions, and suggestions for discussion. The chapter outlines can be used to obtain a quick synopsis of the chapter contents. They are useful for organizing class lectures and could be reproduced for students as study guides. Objective test questions (true–false, matching, and multiple choice) are provided only as a source of ideas from which an instructor may build a valid examination over the factual materials presented in each chapter. It is much better, from a validity viewpoint, for each instructor to build his or her own examination than to rely only on the suggested questions in the instructor's manual. The suggestions for discussion include questions that can be used either as essay questions on examinations or as stimuli for discussions. They generally require the student to demonstrate comprehension of the chapter information by applying learned material for summarizing important concepts contained in the chapter.

ACKNOWLEDGMENTS

A book with as diverse and broad a scope as this is obviously the result of the work and ideas of many people. We wish to thank all the consultants and contributors, with a special tip of the hat to Joe Jacobs and Liz Miller for their contributions of the new chapters on disc sports and in-line skating, respectively.

Special thanks go to the officials of the various sporting goods companies and publishers for giving us permission to reproduce many drawings and photographs.

We also want to thank Karen Ruder of Castleton State College, and Robert Kauffman of Frostburg State University, for reviewing this twelfth edition and providing us with valuable feedback.

We wish to express our gratitude to Pat Schissel, Sheila Frank, and all the other folks at WCB/McGraw-Hill for providing feedback and guidance and for keeping us to our deadlines. Their suggestions and gentle reminders are much appreciated.

Dale P. Mood
Frank F. Musker
Judith E. Rink

1 Introduction

There is almost unanimous agreement that optimum health is our most prized possession. Schopenhauer, the German philosopher, expressed this idea when he remarked, "The greatest of follies is to neglect one's health for any other advantage of life."

To improve and maintain optimum health, it is necessary for people of all ages to participate in physical exercise. However, there is wide variation in the types of exercises recommended for different age groups.

A good example of the importance of exercise in maintaining health is the emphasis placed on it in the health regimen of presidents of the United States. Recent White House physicians have included such exercises as walking, jogging, hiking, golfing, swimming, and horseback riding, in addition to close medical supervision, in the presidents' conditioning programs. The most recent large-scale endorsement for physical activity is a 1996 document titled *Physical Activity and Health: A Report of The Surgeon General*. This report, produced by the U.S. Department of Health and Human Services, the U.S. Centers for Disease Control and Prevention, and the U.S. Surgeon General, advocates that all Americans increase their physical activity levels.

In addition to the value of exercise in maintaining optimum health, there are often social and recreational benefits as well. In this age of increased leisure time these benefits are becoming even more important than in the past.

Although in many high schools, colleges, and universities students are required to participate in physical education classes, several institutions have eliminated this requirement and instituted an elective program. In a large percentage of these cases the number of students taking physical activity classes has remained constant or even increased.

There is little doubt that, in addition to students on college campuses, the number of adults participating in sports and recreational activities in the United States has increased dramatically in recent years. However, this number is still far short of goals set by national health agencies.

Ironically, the number of children being exposed to high-quality, daily physical activity in physical education programs in the public schools has been decreasing for many years. Local economic shortfalls are the primary cause for this phenomenon, and the trend has public health officials concerned. A large amount of scientific evidence is now available to demonstrate that early and continued participation in physical activity can significantly improve the overall health of this country. The mechanism to provide this exposure (physical education in the public schools) is available but is currently being curtailed. This may prove to be very shortsighted in the long run.

The increase in activity participation noted among adults can be attributed to an increase in the amount of leisure time available to most Americans. We have shorter work weeks and more and longer vacations than in the past. In addition, sports and recreational facilities have become increasingly abundant and accessible to larger and more diverse segments of the population.

The increased leisure time, however, does not explain why Americans choose to use this time engaged in sports and recreational activities; it merely provides the opportunity

to do so. Likewise, increased facilities reflect only that larger segments of the population choose to participate, but they do not supply a reason for this choice.

A great number of theories have been proposed by educators, sociologists, medical personnel, and others to explain why we engage in physical activity. These theories are diverse yet contain many overlapping concepts. The satisfaction of creative desires, expression of inherent animal instincts, use of excess energy, preparation for other types of life situations, and exposure to risk to provide excitement are a few of the concepts that have been proposed.

People have become increasingly aware of several benefits of physical activity, particularly in the physiological and health areas. Some of these benefits and relevant considerations are presented in chapter 2, "Health-Related Physical Fitness." In addition to the physiological benefits, the following are other areas believed to be affected positively by participation in sports and recreational activities.

PSYCHOLOGICAL FACTORS

Many life situations are conducive to producing tension and emotional stress, resulting in worry, anxiety, fear, frustration, and the like. Although the evidence is not as definite because the factors involved are more difficult to measure, there is some indication that exercise under the proper conditions can be helpful in improving emotional stability and mental fitness, just as it aids in developing physical fitness. Participation in an interesting sport takes the mind off other things and prevents it from dwelling on problems. Exercise also helps release emotions through socially approved channels. It is a means of satisfying certain primitive urges that all people have, and it provides for self-expression. Experiencing success in developing skills and participating in a physical activity are excellent means of developing confidence and reaping satisfaction that comes from successful accomplishment. Through individual activities such as archery, bowling, running, swimming, gymnastics, and golf, it is possible to compete against oneself as well as against others. The personal gains and achievements possible through participation in physical activities have been shown to be related positively to motivation and self-confidence.

Although participation in almost any sport or any physical activity involves a degree of risk, an interesting phenomenon, sometimes called "extreme sports," has recently emerged. In about the mid 1980s, inline skates (see chapter 16) began to replace standard roller skates, and now over 25 million people in the United States inline-skate at least once a year. In 1995 nearly 7 million mountain bikes were sold. About 200 indoor climbing gyms now exist or are planned. Large increases in the number of people who snowboard, skydive, and mountain climb have been recorded in the 1990s. Some TV sports networks have broadcast extreme sports competitions, and mountain biking and halfpipe snowboarding appeared in the 1998 Winter Olympics.

Whether or not this increase in risky sports is a passing fancy or a historical trend is difficult to determine at this time. Certainly for now there is an undisputed increase in the participation and interest in the psychological trait of risk taking through involvement in dangerous physical activities. See the Web site listed at the end of this chapter for additional information about extreme sports.

KNOWLEDGE

A dominant factor in the American way of life is the ability of the average citizen to know about and understand sports, if not as a participant, then as a spectator. Therefore, it is beneficial to learn the rules and strategies of various sports. In addition, knowledge of etiquette, safety, equipment, history, values, techniques, and other factors can enhance the enjoyment of watching or participating in team, dual, or individual activities.

SOCIAL VALUES

An important aspect of education is providing a program of activities to help in the socialization of the individual. Because we are living in an age of social conflict, it is highly important that teachers use every means possible to instill positive social habits in their students. A program of physical activities offers unlimited opportunities for developing broad social understandings. In fact, initial contacts between previously distant cultures or societies are sometimes made through a common interest in sports.

One facet of common social interests of Americans is shown by the wide publicity given to sports through radio and television, sports pages of newspapers, magazines, and discussions between individuals of all ages. There is possibly no better way to learn how to get along with and to live with others than through participation in sports and physical activities. In these settings the individual must show the same qualities that are necessary for successful and happy living in a democratic society. To be most successful, courtesy, self-control, initiative, cooperation, and loyalty must be acquired. The experience of being both a follower and a leader can be gained. Successful participation in sports implies that the participant must learn to be a good sport and to give credit where it is due, regardless of who wins or loses. Participation in team games, particularly, teaches the individual to work with others to the best advantage of the team and to control emotions.

People are often motivated by the social instinct of belonging. One way the desire to associate with others can be satisfied is through participation in physical activities. The congenial atmosphere of sports presents the opportunity to develop friendships that may have lasting value.

RECREATION

Technology has liberated us from much physical work, and recreation has assumed an important place in modern life as a result of the increasing amount of leisure time available to all.

It is evident that people can use leisure time constructively or destructively. One of the aims of a physical activities program is to teach the wise use of leisure time. People should be made aware of the vital place that wholesome recreation, and especially sports, can play in the full enjoyment of life.

Recreation, to be helpful, need not be elaborate or expensive. Many of the simple forms of recreation available to all are the most satisfying and of the greatest help in maintaining physical, mental, and emotional health.

FACTORS ASSOCIATED WITH A PHYSICAL ACTIVITY PROGRAM

To profit most from participation in sports and physical activities, a number of things should be considered.

Training and Conditioning

Some physical educators and sports directors make a distinction between "conditioning" and "training." Conditioning is usually considered to be related to such things as proper eating, resting, relaxing, sleeping, and exercising regularly, as well as working toward the improvement of skills in a particular activity. Training, on the other hand, is considered by some to be the practice of certain movements by constant repetition until a skill is established or mastered. An example of this would be attempting to improve—and master to the greatest possible extent—skills required in such sports as swimming, golf, tennis, or track. The meanings of the words "training" and "conditioning" overlap, for gains in one generally lead to increases in the other.

Recent evidence suggests that the amount of physical activity required to enjoy **health** benefits may be less than originally believed. To improve and maintain a reasonably modest level of physical fitness, it is necessary to participate in vigorous physical activities at regular intervals. It is generally recommended by the American College of Sports Medicine that a minimum one should participate in a moderately intense physical activity for 30 minutes at least three times per week. To reach this state, it is best to begin with mild exercise and to increase the intensity gradually during subsequent periods. This is recommended to prevent undue stress and strain on muscles. The duration of exercise periods should be governed by the response of the individual to exercise and past training periods. Other factors, such as age and physical condition, will dictate the initial intensity and duration of exercise periods. To develop the greatest overall muscular efficiency, one should participate in activities that require some use of all the major muscles of the body. Many sports require repeated use of a limited set of muscles; thus, it is best to take part in a wide variety of sports.

However, epidemiologists examining the **health** benefits of physical activity (defined mainly as living longer and

with a higher quality of life) have determined that even modest participation is valuable. Indications are that 30 minutes per day of rather modest energy expenditure (even if it takes the form of 3 bouts of 10 minutes each) produce health benefits such as reduced risk of heart disease and increases in longevity. The value of an activity as simple as taking a brisk walk periodically has been determined to be an important predictor of improved health. It is unwise to engage in any strenuous activity before the body is in condition for it. To **improve** the condition of the body requires application of a stress or overload. However, to **maintain** a particular state of physical condition requires less intense activity than is required to get to that level. It is also generally accepted that if participation is discontinued the degree of physical condition will decline at about the same rate required to build it.

Good physical conditions is sufficient for participation in most sports. However, it must be kept in mind that certain sports require special training. Age makes a difference in conditioning and training; younger people can train and condition more rapidly than older people.

Physical Examination

No one should participate in prolonged and strenuous physical activity without first having a complete medical examination by a physician. A medical examination including an exercise stress test is so important that it cannot be overemphasized, especially after the age of 40, and regular examinations should be repeated periodically throughout life. The results of medical examinations show that most people do not need to restrict physical activity; however, if certain defects are present, such as a defective heart, participation in unrestricted strenuous exercise can be very damaging.

Precautions

It should be apparent that an exercise program needs to be structured to fit each individual. Beginning level of fitness, medical condition, interests, age, and availability of facilities are examples of factors to be considered.

Before one engages in strenuous physical activity, common sense dictates that there should be a period of gradual **warming up** and stretching of the muscles to eliminate some of the danger of muscle injury. Large-muscle groups, including the arms, legs, and trunk, should be warmed up first. In fact, they should receive major attention throughout the warming-up and limbering-up period.

It is usually recommended that vigorous and strenuous physical activity be tapered off. Sudden and complete relaxation after vigorous exertion without tapering off can cause dizziness, nausea, and even fainting if the exercise has been particularly strenuous. Giving the body processes a chance to slow down gradually is a precautionary measure observed by practically all champion athletes.

There are good reasons for **tapering off** following vigorous or strenuous exercise. During exercise the heart rate speeds up to keep the muscles supplied with sufficient oxygen and nutrients. The increased heart rate sends the arterial blood into the veins. Because the venous system has no forceful mechanism like the heart to help move blood back to the heart, the action of muscles must be depended on to help the return flow of blood. When the veins fill with blood, the pressure of contracting muscles produces a pumping action on the thin-walled veins to propel the blood back toward the center of the body. If vigorous exercise ends abruptly, the heat continues for a time to send extra amounts of arterial blood to the muscles. Because the muscles are suddenly inactive, there is not sufficient force for returning the extra blood to the heart. Consequently, the extra blood tends to pool in the muscles, and the imbalance may leave some organs with an inadequate supply of blood. During the tapering-off process following strenuous exercise, the muscles continue to squeeze blood from the extremities of the body back into the main circulation.

Regardless of the care taken in beginning training and conditioning for sports, muscles may become sore and stiff. Mild exercise, in cases of this sort, helps the pumping action of the heart that is necessary to bring blood to the sore muscle and thereby speeds up the carrying away of waste products.

Another precaution is **avoidance of overexertion.** Excess emotional stress can greatly add to the seriousness of overexertion. The ability to recuperate after strenuous exercise is a good guide at any age to the amount and extent of exercise to participate in at one time. The recovery should be reasonably prompt. However, if the breathing and heart rate are still greatly accelerated 10 minutes after exercise, and if there is marked fatigue or weakness after a few hours of rest or a sense of definite fatigue the day following, the exercise likely has been too severe or prolonged.

As a last precaution following strenuous exercise, an adequate **cooling-off period** should follow the tapering-off process. From 3 to 6 minutes should elapse between tapering off and entering the shower. Otherwise, the warm water will prevent loss of heat from the body and it will continue to perspire. Heavy perspiration following a shower and dressing may cause chilling, with the same results as chilling after being drenched by a cold rain.

Of course, local and environmental conditions may require other precautions. For example, physical activity in very warm temperatures requires attention to fluid replacement and core body temperature. Acclimation to unusually high altitudes may be required before engaging in strenuous physical activity. In most cases, common sense should be used to prevent discomfort or injury.

Rest and Sleep

Sufficient rest and sleep are necessary for maintenance of good physical, mental, and emotional health. Although it is thought that the average person needs 8 to 9 hours of sleep each night, the amount varies with the individual and with age. Growing children require more sleep than adults. Some people require more sleep than others who have similar activity levels. Regularity in rest and sleep is very important. If one is not getting sufficient rest and sleep, participation in strenuous and vigorous physical activities can be more harmful than helpful. It is recommended that each individual learn to judge the amount of sleep and rest necessary to maintain physical and mental alertness and a feeling of well-being.

Diet and Nutrition

A balanced diet based on the food pyramid is necessary for maintenance of good nutrition. Nutrition is basic to physical, mental, and emotional health. Those who participate in physical activity usually require more food than those who lead sedentary lives. Participation in physical activities requires energy, and food is the main source of energy for the body. Replacement of fluid and electrolytes lost through physical activity is also important.

It is usually best not to eat heavy meals before strenuous physical activity, especially if emotional stress is present, as in a competitive activity. It is difficult for the body to digest and assimilate food under such circumstances.

Finally, together with exercise, diet is a controlling factor in body weight. Exercise is sometimes helpful in weight reduction, however, the number of calories eliminated through exercise is minimal when compared with the number of calories that can be eliminated through a sensible diet. If the overweight person uses exercises to reduce weight and then refrains from overeating, the exercise can be helpful.

Clothing and Cleanliness

Proper clothing is important when participating in sports. It is essential to change from street clothes to sports clothing when participating in vigorous activities that will cause perspiration and body odor. Even sports clothing can become so soiled by dirt and perspiration that they become objectionable to others. Therefore, it is important to have sufficient sports clothing and to keep it clean as possible. It is particularly important that shoes and socks be selected properly. Gymnasium or other sports shoes should fit properly to safeguard the feet. Blisters form easily if shoes or socks do not fit properly. Clothing that fits too tightly or that may hinder performance should be avoided.

A shower should be taken after participation in vigorous physical activity for both hygienic and social reasons. Showers not only cleanse the skin, but also reduce chances of infection. Some people like a warm shower followed by a short, cold shower; others prefer that water temperature be tapered from warm to comfortably cool. Prolonged hot showers are not recommended because they interfere with the body's ability to recover from the changes in blood flow brought on by the exercise.

Injuries and Illness

People often ask whether they should participate in physical activities during or following periods of mild illness, such as colds, flu, and other infectious diseases. In most cases it is best to refrain from participation in physical activities during any illness caused by infection.

Care should be given to even slight injuries received while participating in physical activities. Small scratches and cuts should be treated as soon as possible. Any cut or scratch that seems to have become infected should have the attention of a physician immediately. Various infections can be contracted in gymnasiums and shower rooms. Participants should be careful in taking showers and drying in the dressing rooms to avoid "athlete's foot." Serious sprains and bruises should be treated with immediate first aid and then examined by a physician.

Safety

Sports and physical activities should be as safe as possible. Participants should take every precaution to prevent injury to themselves and to others. Equipment and rules and regulations of games and sports generally are designed to protect players as much as possible. Some sports (e.g., football) and activities require special protective equipment, and playing them without protective equipment risks serious injury.

The beginner in certain sports should recognize that some advanced activities may be dangerous to attempt. For example, a beginner attempting advanced tumbling stunts would be in danger of injury because of a lack of skill. Everyone should give attention to safety, because a high percentage of the injuries and deaths from accidents can be prevented.

REFERENCE

Physical activity and health: A report of the surgeon general. 1996. Atlanta: U.S. Department of Health and Human Services, Centers for Disease Control and Prevention, National Center for Chronic Disease Prevention and Health Promotion.

WEB SITE

Information about extreme sports: http://www.charged.com

Health-Related Physical Fitness

After completing this chapter, the reader should be able to:

- Understand the importance of physical activity and how it relates to health, quality of life, and total well-being
- Define and identify the components of health-related physical fitness
- Develop an activity or training program that will increase aerobic endurance, positively influence body composition, and increase muscular strength and endurance and flexibility
- Assess one's health-related physical fitness

The term *physical fitness* means many things to people. For some, it conjures up visions of a large muscular "Adonis" weight lifter whose rippling muscles testify of the great shape he or she is in. Others envision a marathon runner, a lean individual who has trained to run great distances and has a physique quite different from that of the weight lifter. Actually, neither of these individuals is the best illustration of physical fitness. Rather, a physically fit individual is one who can conduct the functions of daily life without undue stress on the body and, perhaps more importantly, has a healthy body and is not at risk for disease as a result of his or her fitness level or physical inactivity. Thus, the term often used today for physical fitness is *health-related physical fitness* (HRPF). This chapter will focus on HRPF: how it differs from the historical definition of physical fitness, the components of HRPF, how to achieve HRPF, and the scientific literature defining how one can develop HRPF and maintain it throughout life. The science of epidemiology—the study of diseases, their causes, and their impact on society—has been widely used in the past fifty years to illustrate the relationship between a physically inactive lifestyle and increased morbidity and mortality. Many diseases can be said to be hypokinetic in origin because they result from physically inactive lifestyles. The scientific literature was so supportive of the relationship between physical inactivity and disease that the U.S. Department of Health and Human Services, the U.S. Centers for Disease Control and Prevention, and the U.S. Surgeon General released a document entitled *Physical Activity and Health: A Report of the Surgeon General* (1996) summarizing this influence and calling for national dedication to increasing the physical activity levels of all Americans.

Our understanding of the importance of exercise or physical activity and its impact on quality of life can be traced back at least as far as Hippocrates (460–370 B.C.), who stated that "eating alone will not keep a man well; he must also exercise." Over the years, attention to fitness components and the reported lack of fitness has often been associated with times of war, when individuals were found to be unfit for military service. However, those individuals' "unfitness" really had little to do with fitness as it is perceived today. For example, many were declared unfit for military service because of poor eyesight, flat feet, or syphilis. Also, historically, "physical fitness" tests measured a number of characteristics that were greatly influenced by genetics (e.g., speed, agility, quickness) and thus were not easily modifiable. HRPF components are trainable and modifiable and, most importantly, are related to health, disease, and quality of life.

EXERCISE OR PHYSICAL ACTIVITY?

For years the focus about physical fitness was on "exercise." The phrases "No pain, no gain" and "maximum performance" expressed common expectations about what was necessary for becoming fit. However, research by exercise physiologists has given us more accurate knowledge of how to develop physical fitness in healthy adults. The American College of Sports Medicine (ACSM), a professional organization with a membership of over 15,000 physiologists, physicians, and physical and health educators, created guidelines for achieving fitness in healthy adults. These guidelines are presented in table 2-1. Note the term used is *fitness.* The guidelines also suggest that different levels of *physical activity* can achieve a health benefit. The ACSM states, "It is now clear that lower levels of physical activity than recommended by this position statement may reduce risk for certain chronic degenerative diseases and yet may not be of sufficient quantity or quality to improve [aerobic fitness]. . . . ACSM recognizes the potential health benefits of regular exercise performed more frequently and for a longer duration, but at lower intensities than prescribed [for aerobic fitness]" (ACSM 1990). Physical activity can be exercise, but scientific evidence indicates that physical activity need not be at the intensity necessary for being physically "fit" to achieve a health benefit. Pate et al. published a statement in 1995 about the health benefits of moderate levels of physical activity.

This chapter will illustrate activities that result in improved quality of life and protection against disease.

Table 2-1. AMERICAN COLLEGE OF SPORTS MEDICINE RECOMMENDED QUANTITY AND QUALITY OF EXERCISE FOR DEVELOPING AND MAINTAINING CARDIORESPIRATORY AND MUSCULAR FITNESS IN HEALTHY ADULTS

1. Frequency of training should be 3 to 5 days per week.
2. Intensity of training should be at 60 to 90 percent of maximum heart rate[a] or 50 to 85 percent of maximum oxygen uptake or maximum heart rate reserve[b].
3. Duration of training should be 20 to 60 minutes of continuous aerobic activity. However, duration and intensity interact, so that if you have increased intensity, the duration need not be as great, and if you have lower intensity, the duration should be longer.
4. The mode of exercise should use large muscle groups and be continuous, rhythmic, and aerobic in nature (e.g., walking, running, cycling, dancing, rope skipping, stair climbing, swimming).
5. Strength training should be conducted with large muscle groups at least 2 days per week. Moderate-intensity exercises should include one set of 8 to 12 repetitions of 8 to 10 different strength movements.

Source: ACSM 1990.
[a]Maximum heart rate can be estimated as 220 − your age. For example, a 20-year-old has a maximum heart rate of about 200 beats per minutes (i.e., 220 − 20 = 200).
[b]Maximum heart rate reserve is calculated as the difference between resting and maximum heart rate. A percentage of this value is then added to the resting heart rate to estimate exercise heart rate.

Table 2-2. ORGANIZATIONS WITH STATEMENTS OR POSITION PAPERS ON THE POSITIVE EFFECTS OF PHYSICAL ACTIVITY ON HEALTH AND/OR QUALITY OF LIFE

American Academy of Pediatrics
American Cancer Society
American College of Sports Medicine
American Diabetic Association
American Heart Association
International Federation of Sports Medicine
International Society and Federation of Cardiology
Royal College of Physicians
Surgeon General of the United States
U.S. Centers for Disease Control and Prevention
World Health Organization

Table 2-3. DISEASES RELATED TO PHYSICAL INACTIVITY

Cancer (particularly rectal)
Depression, anxiety, and mood (mental health)
Diabetes
Heart disease
Hypertension (high blood pressure)
Obesity
Osteoporosis
Stroke

Certainly, people who are physically fit (i.e., have achieved higher levels of fitness as a result of greater-intensity exercise) are generally healthy. However, we will provide evidence and steps that you can take that will improve your HRPF, your health status, and your quality of life without turning you into a muscle-rippling weight lifter or a marathoner.

Many professional organizations have developed position statements on the important role that physical activity plays in health. Some of these organizations are listed in table 2-2. A list of the diseases known to be related to levels of physical activity is presented in table 2-3.

COMPONENTS OF HEALTH-RELATED PHYSICAL FITNESS

The three major components of HRPF are aerobic capacity, body composition, and musculoskeletal development (muscular strength and endurance, and flexibility). We will consider each of these components and why they are important to HRPF.

Aerobic Fitness

The term *aerobic fitness* is often used synonymously with the term physical fitness. Aerobic fitness is probably the aspect most commonly agreed to be a part of physical fitness. Essentially, aerobic capacity is the maximum amount of oxygen your body can extract from inspired air and utilize at maximal exercise. Many studies have shown a relationship between aerobic capacity and a number of health factors. For example, persons who are aerobically fit are less likely to prematurely die due to heart disease, and they are less likely to have a stroke, develop diabetes, be overweight, have high blood pressure, or develop certain cancers. Your aerobic capacity is related to the frequency, intensity, duration, and type of exercise or physical activity in which you engage. A "dose response" to the level of physical activity has been demonstrated. The term *dose response* refers to the fact that as you increase your "dose" (amount) of aerobic exercise, you can expect better health outcomes and quality of life.

Figure 2-1 illustrates the findings from six studies on the dose response resulting from increased physical activity. You can increase the "dose" in a number of ways. You can increase the frequency, intensity, and/or duration of the aerobic exercise that you do. However, this does not mean that you must do a great deal of exercise to have a health benefit. To the contrary, because many individuals have relatively sedentary lifestyles (approximately 30% of American adults—40 million people—reportedly engage in no leisure-time physical activity), the greatest benefit in risk reduction is often seen as people move from the lowest level of fitness to the next level of fitness. Figure 2-2 shows that, for males and females, the relative risk of mortality

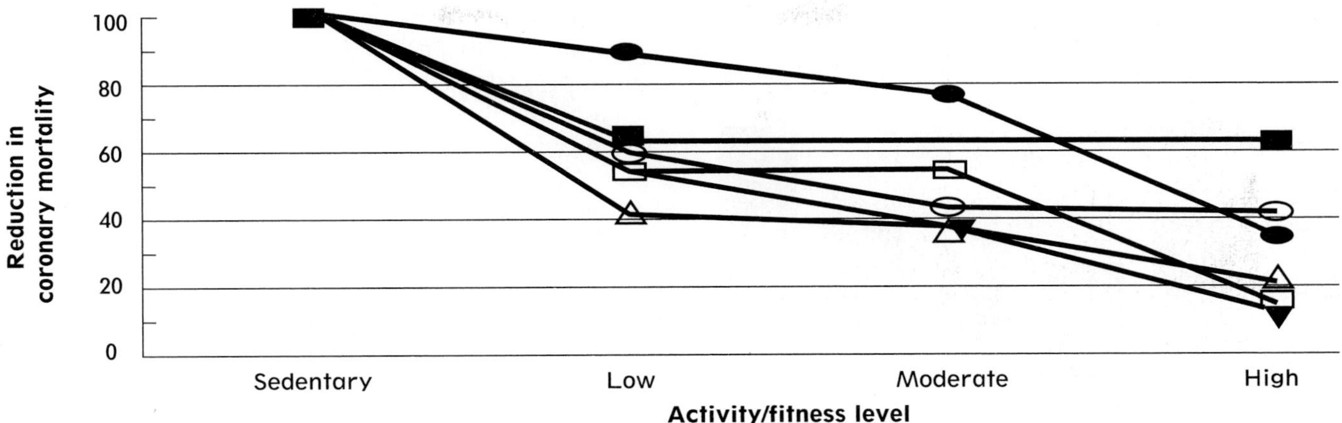

Figure 2-1. Results from six studies illustrating the dose response effect on reduction in coronary mortality associated with increased physical activity/fitness level. (Source: Blair and Connelly 1996. Reprinted with permission from *Research Quarterly for Exercise and Sport,* Vol 67, No. 2, 193–205, copyright 1996 by the American Alliance for Health, Physical Education and Dance, 1900 Association Drive, Reston, VA 20191.)

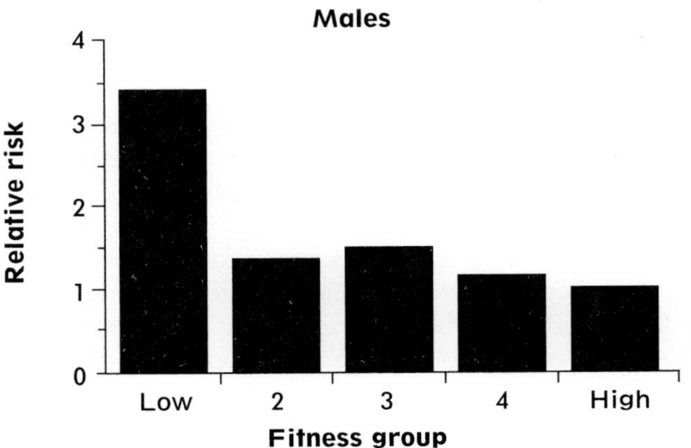

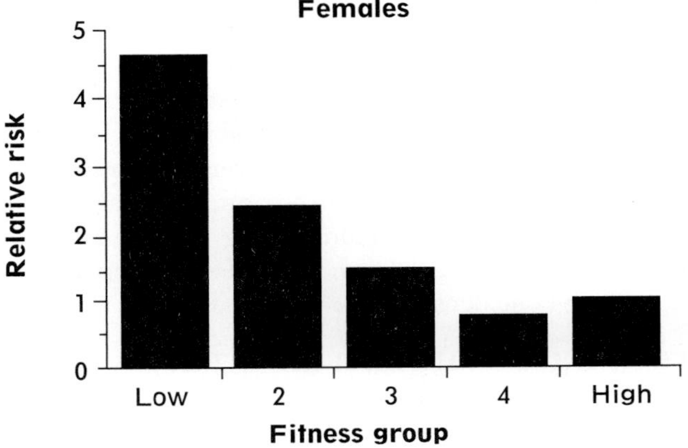

Figure 2-2. Age-adjusted all-cause death rates per 10,000 person-years of follow-up. (Source: Blair et al. 1989.)

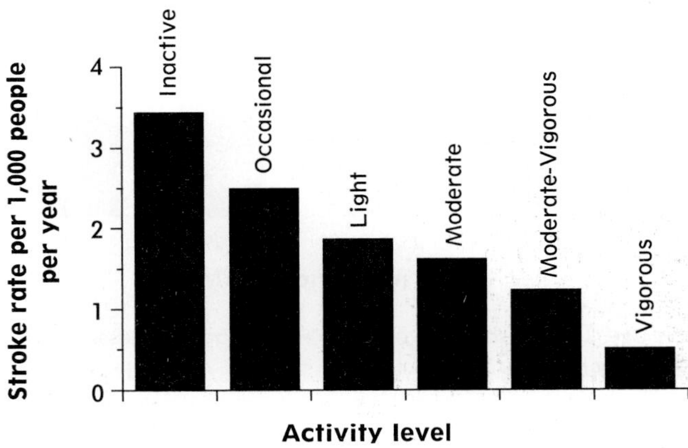

Figure 2-3. Age-adjusted reductions in stroke rate per 1,000 people per year.

from all causes of death declines as one moves to a higher level of fitness. Figure 2-3 presents similar information for prevention of stroke in persons who are physically active.

Body Composition

The body composition aspect of HRPF refers to the amount and relative distribution of fat in your body. Americans of all ages are now carrying more fat than their ancestors of just a few decades ago. Excessive body fatness is related to a variety of negative health consequences, including heart disease, hypertension, and diabetes. Figure 2-4 illustrates the risk associated with increased body fatness. Figure 2-4 essentially indicates that as one's relative fatness increases (measured by body mass index, described later in the assessment section of this chapter), the risk of developing coronary heart disease also increases. There are conflicting research results about the relationship between body size and various diseases. Suffice it to say that

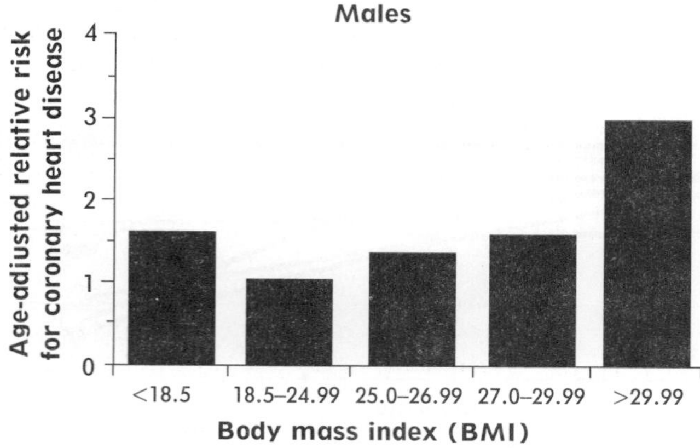

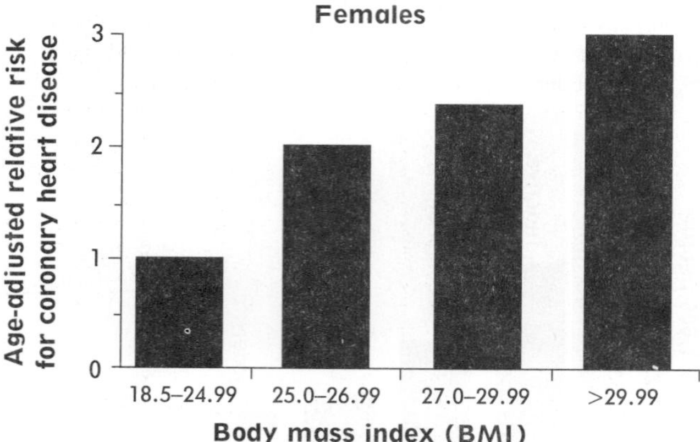

Figure 2-4. Association between relative body fatness and coronary heart disease.

increased weight is associated with some notable diseases (e.g., high blood pressure and diabetes). Recent evidence indicates that even those who are overweight are at reduced risk if they are physically fit. This suggests that physical fitness plays a more important role than body weight alone in some disease development (see Barlow et al. 1995, and Blair et al. 1996).

It is important to realize that it is not weight alone that is the risk factor. One's body can be "compartmentalized" into several different components. One model suggests three body compartments: fat, lean (muscle and bones), and other tissues (e.g., organs). If a person has a high weight but the weight is largely lean tissue, the health risks associated with the high weight might not be as great as if the weight were made up of a higher percentage of fat. An additional consideration is how the weight is distributed on the body. Individuals whose weight is stored in the waist have a greater risk of disease than those whose body fat is stored throughout their body or in the hips. Waist/hip girth values greater than .95 for males and .85 for females are associated with increased risk of disease. You will learn more about this in the assessment section later in this chapter.

Musculoskeletal Fitness

The arguments for health risk reduction are not as great for the musculoskeletal component. The primary reason musculoskeletal fitness is included in HRPF is because one needs sufficient muscular strength to conduct daily activities. Certainly muscles that are trained increase in size (hypertrophy) and strength. That is, the musculoskeletal aspect of HRPF is largely "functional" in nature because sufficient musculoskeletal strength permits one to conduct daily activities requiring some degree of strength and endurance. There are, however, two important health-related aspects to sufficient strength and endurance. Many fitness tests contain items of abdominal strength and endurance because of the theoretical relationship between abdominal strength and reduced risk of low back pain. This relationship has not been well supported in the scientific literature, but from theoretical and physical therapeutic perspectives, abdominal strength and endurance are important to holding the spine in correct alignment. Another area where strength is important is the development of strong bones. Much attention has been directed at the development of osteoporosis in women. Osteoporosis is becoming more important as a health consequence because people are living longer and thus disease has a longer time to have an effect on people. Both males and females suffer from osteoporosis, but it is found much more frequently in females. A good protection against the development of osteoporosis as you age is to have strong, solid bone tissue when you are young. Everyone's bones become less dense as they age. It is important to develop as much bone tissue as possible so that when the deterioration begins, it will take longer for the bone to "demineralize" and reach the "fracture threshold" where it is more easily broken. Although dietary supplements have been suggested for increasing bone density, another good way to help develop bone density is to stress the muscles connecting the bones. As these muscles are stressed, the bones connected to them are also stressed and become more fully developed. For example, a tennis player's dominant arm is more dense than the nondominant arm, because the dominant arm is used much more during practice and play. Thus, stressing bones through physical exertion is a means of creating bone density.

TRAINING FOR HEALTH-RELATED PHYSICAL FITNESS

A few overall guidelines must be considered when training for health-related fitness. These are presented in table 2-4. Additionally, there are guidelines that are specific to each component of health-related fitness. Recall that the focus here is on improving one's health and decreasing risk of disease, not on making you an Olympic athlete. Thus, the guidelines provided herein can result in improved health status. As indicated in tables 2-5 and 2-6, increased levels of physical activity will improve your health and quality of life.

Table 2-4. GENERAL PRINCIPLES FOR HEALTH-RELATED PHYSICAL FITNESS TRAINING

Specificity
Training must be specific to the type of effect desired. Aerobic training will improve aerobic capacity. Strength training will improve strength. Flexibility training will improve flexibility. Additionally, strength and flexibility training must be specific to the muscle group or joint that you wish to train.
Overload principle
An improvement in fitness level is achieved when the system (aerobic, musculoskeletal, or flexibility) is required to go beyond its current capacity. That is, the fitness level is increased as one progressively increases the "load" placed on the body as training occurs. If you are happy with your current level of fitness, keep doing what you are doing. If you would like to increase your level of fitness, you will have to progressively overload your system to improve your fitness level.
Progressive resistance
Improvements in fitness levels are best achieved through progressive increases in the amount of work conducted. The work may be aerobic or muscular in nature. One should begin at a comfortable level and then gradually increase the amount of energy expended in the activity.
Reversibility principle
Unfortunately, this principle simply means that if you stop training or being physically active, your body will revert back to a deconditioned state.

Aerobic Fitness

Becoming aerobically fit does not require spending money to join a club or buying expensive workout clothes. Many simple lifestyle changes can help you improve your aerobic fitness level. The key point is to accumulate a minimum of 30 minutes of moderate-intensity physical activity nearly every day of the week. Lifestyle changes such as walking during lunch, parking farther from the entrance at work or the store, or taking the stairs can help improve your health. Household tasks (gardening and raking leaves, moving furniture, caring for children, etc.) that cause an increase in your metabolic rate will have a positive effect on your aerobic fitness. A suggested aerobic training program is presented in table 2-7.

Body Composition

You don't just "train" to maintain your body composition characteristics within a healthy range. Changes in your body weight and composition are a function of "caloric balance." You are in caloric balance if the number of calories you ingest from food is equal to the number of calories that you expend through simply being alive plus the number of calories you expend in physical activity. If you take in more calories than you expend, you are in a "positive caloric balance" and you will gain weight (and fat). If you expend more calories than you take in, you are in a "negative caloric balance" and you will lose weight. It is as simple as that. If nothing else changed in your life for the next year except that you expended an extra 50 calories per day through physical activity (walking for about 7 to 8 minutes) and you decreased your caloric intake by 50 calories per day (the approximate number of calories in one cookie), you would lose 10 pounds of fat in one year. Your negative caloric balance would be approximately 100 calories per day for 365 days (or 36,500 calories for the year), and it takes about 3,500 calories to gain a pound of fat (positive caloric balance) or to lose a pound of fat (negative caloric balance). Unfortunately, most people don't pay sufficient attention to their caloric balance; as a result, most people gain about 45 pounds of fat from age 20 to age 45! However, their total

Table 2-5. RECOMMENDATION FROM THE CENTERS FOR DISEASE CONTROL AND PREVENTION AND THE AMERICAN COLLEGE OF SPORTS MEDICINE

Every U.S. adult should accumulate 30 minutes or more of moderate-intensity physical activity on most, preferably all, days of the week.

Source: Pate et al. 1995.

Table 2-6. SUMMARY STATEMENT OF THE NIH CONSENSUS DEVELOPMENT PANEL ON PHYSICAL ACTIVITY AND CARDIOVASCULAR HEALTH

All Americans should engage in regular physical activity at a level appropriate to their capacity, needs and interest. Children and adults alike should set a goal of accumulating at least 30 minutes of moderate-intensity physical activity on most, and preferably all, days of the week. Most Americans have little or no physical activity in their daily lives, and accumulating evidence indicates that physical inactivity is a major risk factor for cardiovascular disease. However, moderate levels of physical activity confer significant health benefits. Even those who currently meet these daily standards may derive additional health and fitness benefits by becoming more physically active or including more vigorous activity.

Source: "Physical Activity and Cardiovascular Health" 1996.

Table 2-7. AEROBIC TRAINING PROGRAMS

Warm-up portion	10 to 15 minutes of flexibility and general calisthenics
Activity portion	
For health benefit	20 to 30 minutes of moderate to vigorous physical activity
For fitness benefit	15 to 20 minutes of vigorous activity according to the ACSM guidelines presented in table 2-1
Cool-down portion	10 to 15 minutes of flexibility activities

weight might not change that much. As they decrease their physical activity, their lean tissue is replaced by fat tissue. As the fat level increases, the risk of developing disease increases. A good goal is to attempt to lose one pound of weight every year after you reach age 25. You don't really plan to lose a pound each year (ultimately, you might disappear!)—the point is to make lifestyle changes and decisions that result in your being aware of your caloric balance so that you can maintain your weight throughout adulthood and not reach a state where your weight causes you to be at an increased risk for degenerative diseases.

An important point to note regarding weight loss is that "spot reduction" does not work. Often you will hear of people who attempt to lose inches around the abdomen or inches off the hips by purchasing special equipment or engaging in special "fad" diets. Unfortunately, most of these devices and diets do not work. The key is to develop and maintain lifestyle changes that you can live with. Working specific muscle groups to lose fat in that particular body area will simply not work. It certainly will increase the muscular strength in that body part, but the best way to lose body fat is through general aerobic conditioning that results in a negative caloric balance. This will result in fat being removed from wherever it is stored in the body.

Musculoskeletal Fitness

The principles of specificity, overload, and progression are most important in the development of musculoskeletal strength and endurance and flexibility. Specific exercises must be completed with body segments to effect changes in musculoskeletal fitness. A few definitions are necessary for you to understand a strength training program:

repetition maximum (RM) The maximum weight that can be lifted a specific number of times. For example, 1-RM is the maximum amount of weight that can be lifted one time while 10-RM is the maximum amount of weight that can be lifted 10 times.

repetitions (reps) You might conduct 10 repetitions of a specific exercise.

set The number of times you complete the repetitions. You might conduct 3 sets of 10-RM.

A key concept is to begin the activity with weights that you can lift and slowly increase the number of sets and repetitions until you reach the level of strength and endurance you desire. Generally, higher weights lifted with fewer repetitions results in greater strength development, and lower weights lifted with a higher number of repetitions results in increased muscular endurance. There are many types of weights to choose from (e.g., free weights, machines, constant resistance), and each type of weight equipment can be used to increase muscular strength and endurance. Table 2-8 provides an example of a training program for improving musculoskeletal fitness.

Similar training concepts can be used for flexibility training. Start slowly by moving the joint of interest through its unrestricted range of motion. Gradually add to the amount of movement that you do and attempt to increase the range of motion over a period of weeks. For example, a common flexibility movement is to touch one's toes. You may attempt this exercise in either a standing or a sitting position. However, your first attempts might result in your being able to reach only somewhere near your ankles. Flex and hold this position for 5 to 10 seconds and then relax. Repeat this for 8 to 10 repetitions. Over a period of a few weeks, you will see increased flexibility, resulting in your ability to reach farther toward your toes. Flexibility is an area particularly vulnerable to the reversibility principle. It is easy to lose flexibility if you don't continue to practice the movements.

GETTING STARTED WITH AND MAINTAINING HEALTHY LIFESTYLE HABITS

Starting a physical activity, diet, or exercise program is not easy. Sticking with a program is not easy. The dropout rates for such programs are significant. A key factor in continu-

Table 2-8. MUSCULOSKELETAL STRENGTH AND ENDURANCE TRAINING PROGRAM

Training for muscular strength				
Weeks	**Frequency**	**Sets**	**Repetitions**	**Resistance**
1–3	2 days/week	2/session	6–10 set	12-RM
4–20	3 days/week	3/session	6–10 set	6-RM
21+ (maintenance)	3 days/week	3/session	6–10 set	6-RM
Training for muscular endurance				
Weeks	**Frequency**	**Sets**	**Repetitions**	**Resistance**
1–3	2 days/week	2/session	15/set	40% 1-RM
4–20	3 days/week	3/session	15+/set	60% 1-RM
21+ (maintenance)	1–2 days/week	3/session	15+/set	60% 1-RM

Source: From Howley and Franks 1997. Adapted by permission from E.T. Howley and B.D. Franks, 1997, *Health Fitness Instructor's Handbook*, 3rd ed. (Champaign, IL: Human Kinetics), 308.

ing your exercise program is to determine what you can currently do and then choose activities that you know you can and will continue. Starting too quickly can result in increased fatigue and/or injury, and this results in lack of motivation. The program you start must match your needs, if you are to begin, continue, and then maintain healthy lifestyle behaviors. This is true no matter what the behavior change, whether physical activity, diet, smoking, seatbelt wearing, or flossing your teeth. Intervention strategies for motivating individuals to engage in physically active lifestyles must be consistent with the individual's desires and current levels of interest. Much research has been conducted on "stages of change" in order to create intervention strategies consistent with individual goals and objectives. Table 2-9 illustrates stages of change related to physical activity. Note that individuals at each of these stages will need to be motivated differently, and the intervention strategy that might work for one group of people could well be ineffective for another group.

ASSESSMENT OF HEALTH-RELATED PHYSICAL FITNESS COMPONENTS

Aerobic Fitness

Aerobic fitness is best assessed through a treadmill test where you are taken to maximum performance and the maximum amount of oxygen that you can extract and utilize is measured. Unfortunately, because of the equipment and expertise needed, such a test is generally unavailable to most individuals. Thus, field tests of aerobic fitness have been developed. The most popular of these tests involves measuring the time it takes you to complete a specific distance (e.g., 1 mile) or the amount of distance you can cover in a specific time (e.g., 12 minutes). Table 2-10 provides results of a 1-mile walk/run test and evaluative categories for performance on the test. Table 2-11 provides similar information for the 12-minute walk/run.

Table 2-9. STAGES OF READINESS TO CHANGE

Precontemplation
I do not exercise/walk regularly and I do not intend to start in the near future.

Contemplation
I do not exercise or walk regularly, but I have been thinking of starting.

Preparation
I am trying to start to exercise or walk regularly, or I exercise/walk infrequently.

Subaction
I am doing vigorous exercise less than 3 times per week or moderate exercise less than 5 times per week.

Action for moderate physical activity
I have been doing moderate exercise more than 5 times per week (or more than 2.5 hours per week) for the last 1 to 6 months.

Maintenance for moderate physical activity
I have been doing moderate exercise more than 5 times per week (or 2.5 hours per week) for more than 7 months.

Action for vigorous physical activity
I have been doing vigorous exercise 3 to 5 times per week for 1 to 6 months.

Maintenance for vigorous physical activity
I have been doing vigorous exercise 3 to 5 times per week for 7 or more months.

Table 2-10. NORMATIVE DATA FOR 1-MILE WALK TEST

Subjects aged 30–69 years		
Rating	**Males**	**Females**
Excellent	<10:12	<11:40
Good	10:13–11:42	11:41–13:08
High average	11:43–13:13	13:09–14:36
Low average	13:14–14:44	14:37–16:04
Fair	14:45–16:23	16:05–17:31
Poor	>16:24	>17:32
Subjects aged 18–30 years		
Percentile[a]	**Males**	**Females**
90	11:08	11:45
75	11:42	12:49
50	12:38	13:15
25	13:38	14:12
10	14:37	15:03
Poor	>16:24	>17:32

Source: Jackson, Solomon, and Stusek 1992. Reprinted with permission from *Research Quarterly for Exercise and Sport*, Vol 63, No. 1, A52, copyright (1992) by the American Alliance for Health, Physical Education, Recreation and Dance, 1900 Association Drive, Reston, VA 20191.

[a]A percentile represents the percentage of people who score at this value or poorer. For example, if you are a male who completes the 1-mile walk test in 11:08, you scored better than 90 percent of the males who completed the test.

Table 2-11. FITNESS LEVEL DETERMINATION BASED ON DISTANCE (IN MILES) COVERED IN 12 MINUTES

Males	**Age**			
Fitness level	**29 or under**	**30–39**	**40–49**	**50+**
Excellent	>1.65	>1.60	>1.55	>1.45
Good	1.50–1.65	1.45–1.60	1.40–1.55	1.30–1.45
Fair	1.30–1.50	1.30–1.45	1.25–1.40	1.15–1.30
Poor	1.20–1.30	1.20–1.30	1.15–1.25	1.05–1.15
Very poor	<1.20	<1.20	<1.15	<1.05
Females	**Age**			
Fitness level	**29 or under**	**30–39**	**40–49**	**50+**
Excellent	>1.35	>1.30	>1.25	>1.20
Good	1.20–1.35	1.20–1.30	1.10–1.25	1.05–1.20
Fair	1.10–1.20	1.05–1.20	1.00–1.10	0.95–1.05
Poor	0.95–1.10	0.95–1.05	0.90–1.00	0.85–0.95
Very poor	<0.95	<0.95	<0.90	<0.85

Table 2-12. CALCULATING BODY MASS INDEX (BMI)

Weight (lb)	Height (in) 48	49	50	51	52	53	54	55	56	57	58	59	60	61	62	63	Weight (kg)
100	30.6	29.3	28.2	27.1	26.1	25.1	24.2	23.3	22.5	21.7	20.9	20.2	19.6	18.9	18.3	17.8	45.5
105	32.1	30.8	29.6	28.4	27.4	26.3	25.4	24.5	23.6	22.8	22.0	21.3	20.5	19.9	19.2	18.6	47.7
110	33.6	32.3	31.0	29.8	28.7	27.6	26.6	25.6	24.7	23.9	23.0	22.3	21.5	20.8	20.2	19.5	50.0
115	35.2	33.7	32.4	31.2	30.0	28.8	27.8	26.8	25.8	24.9	24.1	23.3	22.5	21.8	21.1	20.4	52.3
120	36.7	35.2	33.8	32.5	31.3	30.1	29.0	27.9	27.0	26.0	25.1	24.3	23.5	22.7	22.0	21.3	54.5
125	38.2	36.7	35.2	33.9	32.6	31.4	30.2	29.1	28.1	27.1	26.2	25.3	24.5	23.7	22.9	22.2	56.8
130	39.8	38.1	36.6	35.2	33.9	32.6	31.4	30.3	29.2	28.2	27.2	26.3	25.4	24.6	23.8	23.1	59.1
135	41.3	39.6	38.0	36.6	35.2	33.9	32.6	31.4	30.3	29.3	28.3	27.3	26.4	25.6	24.7	24.0	61.4
140	42.8	41.1	39.5	37.9	36.5	35.1	33.8	32.6	31.5	30.4	29.3	28.3	27.4	26.5	25.7	24.9	63.6
145	44.3	42.5	40.9	39.3	37.8	36.4	35.0	33.8	32.6	31.4	30.4	29.3	28.4	27.5	26.6	25.7	65.9
150	45.9	44.0	42.3	40.6	39.1	37.6	36.2	34.9	33.7	32.5	31.4	30.4	29.4	28.4	27.5	26.6	68.2
155	47.4	45.5	43.7	42.0	40.4	38.9	37.5	36.1	34.8	33.6	32.5	31.4	30.3	29.3	28.4	27.5	70.5
160	48.9	47.0	45.1	43.3	41.7	40.1	38.7	37.3	35.9	34.7	33.5	32.4	31.3	30.3	29.3	28.4	72.7
165	50.5	48.4	46.5	44.7	43.0	41.4	39.9	38.4	37.1	35.8	34.6	33.4	32.3	31.2	30.2	29.3	75.0
170	52.0	49.9	47.9	46.6	44.3	42.6	41.1	39.6	38.2	36.9	35.6	34.4	33.3	32.2	31.2	30.2	77.3
175	53.5	51.4	49.3	47.4	45.6	43.9	42.3	40.8	39.3	37.9	36.7	35.4	34.2	33.1	32.1	31.1	79.5
180	55.0	52.8	50.7	48.8	46.9	45.1	43.5	41.9	40.4	39.0	37.7	36.4	35.2	34.1	33.0	32.0	81.8
185	56.6	54.3	52.1	50.1	48.2	46.4	44.7	43.1	41.6	40.1	38.7	37.4	36.2	35.0	33.9	32.8	84.1
190	58.1	55.8	53.5	51.5	49.5	47.7	45.9	44.3	42.7	41.2	39.8	38.5	37.2	36.0	34.8	33.7	86.4
195	59.6	57.2	55.0	52.8	50.8	48.9	47.1	45.4	43.8	42.3	40.8	39.5	38.2	36.9	35.7	34.6	88.6
200	61.2	58.7	56.4	54.2	52.1	50.2	48.3	46.6	44.9	43.4	41.9	40.5	39.1	37.9	36.7	35.5	90.9
205	62.7	60.2	57.8	55.5	53.4	51.4	49.5	47.7	46.1	44.5	42.9	41.5	40.1	38.8	37.6	36.4	93.2
210	64.2	61.6	59.2	56.9	54.7	52.7	50.7	48.9	47.2	45.5	44.0	42.5	41.1	39.8	38.5	37.3	95.5
215	65.7	63.1	60.6	58.2	56.0	53.9	51.9	50.1	48.3	46.6	45.0	43.5	42.1	40.7	39.4	38.2	97.7
220	67.3	64.6	62.0	59.6	57.3	55.2	53.2	51.2	49.4	47.7	46.1	44.5	43.1	41.7	40.3	39.1	100.0
225	68.8	66.0	63.4	60.9	58.6	56.4	54.4	52.4	50.5	48.8	47.1	45.5	44.0	42.6	41.2	39.9	102.3
230	70.3	67.5	64.8	62.3	59.9	57.7	55.6	53.6	51.7	49.9	48.2	46.6	45.0	43.5	42.2	40.8	104.5
235	71.9	69.0	66.2	63.7	61.2	58.9	56.8	54.7	52.8	51.0	49.2	47.6	46.0	44.5	43.1	41.7	106.8
240	73.4	70.4	67.6	65.0	62.5	60.2	58.0	55.9	53.9	52.0	50.3	48.6	47.0	45.4	44.0	42.6	109.1
245	74.9	71.9	69.0	66.4	63.8	61.5	59.2	57.1	55.0	53.1	51.3	49.6	47.9	46.4	44.9	43.5	111.4
250	76.4	73.4	70.5	67.7	65.1	62.7	60.4	58.2	56.2	54.2	52.4	50.6	48.9	47.3	45.8	44.4	113.6
Height (m)	1.22	1.24	1.27	1.30	1.32	1.35	1.37	1.40	1.42	1.45	1.47	1.50	1.52	1.55	1.57	1.60	

Body Composition

There are a number of ways to determine your level of body fatness and the risk associated with your level of fatness. Three ways are described in this chapter.

The first is assessment of your body mass index (BMI). BMI is a measure of weight relative to height. If two people are the same height, the person who weighs more generally is at greater risk for developing disease, if the extra weight consists of body fat and not lean tissue. BMI is calculated by dividing your weight in kilograms by your height in meters squared (wt in kg/ht in m^2). Use table 2-12 to determine your BMI and table 2-13 to determine the category into which your BMI places you.

A second simple test is to determine your waist-to-hip ratio. A higher waist-to-hip ratio correlates with greater risk for cardiovascular disease. Use the landmarks provided in table 2-14 to measure your waist-to-hip ratio and then determine if you are at increased risk. Recall that males are at increased risk if the waist-to-hip ratio is greater than .95 and females are at greater risk when the ratio is greater than .85.

The third method of determining your body composition is the estimation of body fatness from measures of the fat levels that underlie the skin. Skinfold measures of sub-

Table 2-13. INTERPRETING BODY MASS INDEX

Category	BMI
Desirable	20–25
Grade 1 obesity	25–29.9
Grade 2 obesity	30–40
Morbid obesity	>40

Source: Jequier 1987.

Table 2-12 (Continued) CALCULATING BODY MASS INDEX (BMI)

Weight (lb)	Height (in) 64	65	66	67	68	69	70	71	72	73	74	75	76	77	78	Weight (kg)
100	17.2	16.7	16.2	15.7	15.2	14.8	14.4	14.0	13.6	13.2	12.9	12.5	12.2	11.9	11.6	45.5
105	18.1	17.5	17.0	16.5	16.0	15.5	15.1	14.7	14.3	13.9	13.5	13.2	12.8	12.5	12.2	47.7
110	18.9	18.3	17.8	17.3	16.8	16.3	15.8	15.4	14.9	14.5	14.2	13.8	13.4	13.1	12.7	50.0
115	19.8	19.2	18.6	18.0	17.5	17.0	16.5	16.1	15.6	15.2	14.8	14.4	14.0	13.7	13.3	52.3
120	20.6	20.0	19.4	18.8	18.3	17.8	17.3	16.8	16.3	15.9	15.4	15.0	14.6	14.3	13.9	54.5
125	21.5	20.8	20.2	19.6	19.0	18.5	18.0	17.5	17.0	16.5	16.1	15.7	15.2	14.9	14.5	56.8
130	22.4	21.7	21.0	20.4	19.8	19.2	18.7	18.2	17.7	17.2	16.7	16.3	15.9	15.4	15.1	59.1
135	23.2	22.5	21.8	21.2	20.6	20.0	19.4	18.9	18.3	17.8	17.4	16.9	16.5	16.0	15.6	61.4
140	24.1	23.3	22.6	22.0	21.3	20.7	20.1	19.6	19.0	18.5	18.0	17.5	17.1	16.6	16.2	63.6
145	24.9	24.2	23.5	22.8	22.1	21.5	20.8	20.3	19.7	19.2	18.7	18.2	17.7	17.2	16.8	65.9
150	25.8	25.0	24.3	23.5	22.9	22.2	21.6	21.0	20.4	19.8	19.3	18.8	18.3	17.8	17.4	68.2
155	26.7	25.8	25.1	24.3	23.6	22.9	22.3	21.7	21.1	20.5	19.9	19.4	18.9	18.4	17.9	70.5
160	27.5	26.7	25.9	25.1	24.4	23.7	23.0	22.4	21.7	21.2	20.6	20.0	19.5	19.0	18.5	72.7
165	28.4	27.5	26.7	25.9	25.1	24.4	23.7	23.1	22.4	21.8	21.2	20.7	20.1	19.6	19.1	75.0
170	29.2	28.3	27.5	26.7	25.9	25.2	24.4	23.8	23.1	22.5	21.9	21.3	20.7	20.2	19.7	77.3
175	30.1	29.2	28.3	27.5	26.7	25.9	25.2	24.5	23.8	23.1	22.5	21.9	21.3	20.8	20.3	79.5
180	31.0	30.0	29.1	28.3	27.4	26.6	25.9	25.2	24.5	23.8	23.2	22.5	22.0	21.4	20.8	81.8
185	31.8	30.8	29.9	29.0	28.2	27.4	26.6	25.9	25.1	24.5	23.8	23.2	22.6	22.0	21.4	84.1
190	32.7	31.7	30.7	29.8	28.9	28.1	27.3	26.6	25.8	25.1	24.4	23.8	23.2	22.6	22.0	86.4
195	33.5	32.5	31.5	30.6	29.7	28.9	28.0	27.3	26.5	25.8	25.1	24.4	23.8	23.2	22.6	88.6
200	34.4	33.4	32.3	31.4	30.5	29.6	28.8	28.0	27.2	26.4	25.7	25.1	24.4	23.8	23.2	90.9
205	35.3	34.2	33.2	32.2	31.2	30.3	29.5	28.7	27.9	27.1	26.4	25.7	25.0	24.4	23.7	93.2
210	36.1	35.0	34.0	33.0	32.0	31.1	30.2	29.4	28.5	27.8	27.0	26.3	25.6	25.0	24.3	95.5
215	37.0	35.9	34.8	33.7	32.8	31.8	30.9	30.0	29.2	28.4	27.7	26.9	26.2	25.5	24.9	97.7
220	37.8	36.7	35.6	34.5	33.5	32.6	31.6	30.7	29.9	29.1	28.3	27.6	26.8	26.1	25.5	100.0
225	38.7	37.5	36.4	35.3	34.3	33.3	32.4	31.4	30.6	29.7	28.9	28.2	27.4	26.7	26.1	102.3
230	39.6	38.4	37.2	36.1	35.0	34.0	33.1	32.1	31.3	30.4	29.6	28.8	28.1	27.3	26.6	104.5
235	40.4	39.2	38.0	36.9	35.8	34.8	33.8	32.8	31.9	31.1	30.2	29.4	28.7	27.9	27.2	106.8
240	41.3	40.0	38.8	37.7	36.6	35.5	34.5	33.5	32.6	31.7	30.9	30.1	29.3	28.5	27.8	109.1
245	42.1	40.9	39.6	38.5	37.3	36.3	35.2	34.2	33.3	32.4	31.5	30.7	29.9	29.1	28.4	111.4
250	43.0	41.7	40.4	39.2	38.1	37.0	35.9	34.9	34.0	33.1	32.2	31.3	30.5	29.7	29.0	113.6
Height (m)	1.63	1.65	1.68	1.70	1.73	1.75	1.78	1.80	1.83	1.85	1.88	1.91	1.93	1.96	1.98	

Source: Morrow et al. 1995.

Table 2-14. MEASURING AND INTERPRETING YOUR WAIST-TO-HIP RATIO

Use a metal or nonstretching tape measure. Be certain that measures are taken horizontal to the floor.
The waist measure is a horizontal measure taken between the navel and the lowest portion of the breastbone.
The hip measure is a horizontal measure taken at the largest circumference of the buttocks/hip area.
Divide the waist circumference by the hip circumference.
Males are at greater risk for cardiovascular disease when the ratio is greater than .95.
Females are at greater risk for cardiovascular disease when the ratio is greater than .85.

cutaneous fat obtained by using skinfold calipers (see figure 2-5) are used to estimate total percent body fat. Because males and females generally store their fat in different places, different sites are used in males and females to assess skinfold fat. Measurements are taken for males at the chest, abdomen, and thigh (see figure 2-6), while measures for females are taken at the triceps, suprailium, and thigh. Figure 2-7 illustrates how these measures are obtained. Table 2-15 can then be used to estimate your total body fatness. You can then use table 2-16 to evaluate your body fatness.

Musculoskeletal Fitness

It is difficult to measure strength and flexibility, because of the specificity of the associated movements. See the

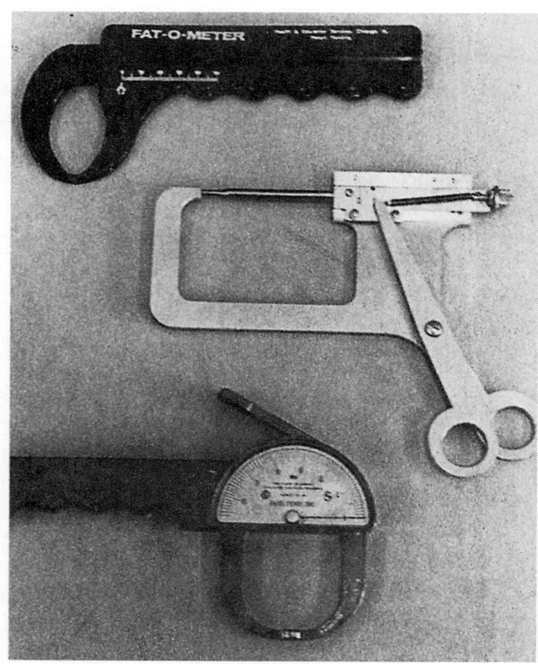

Figure 2-5. Skinfold calipers.

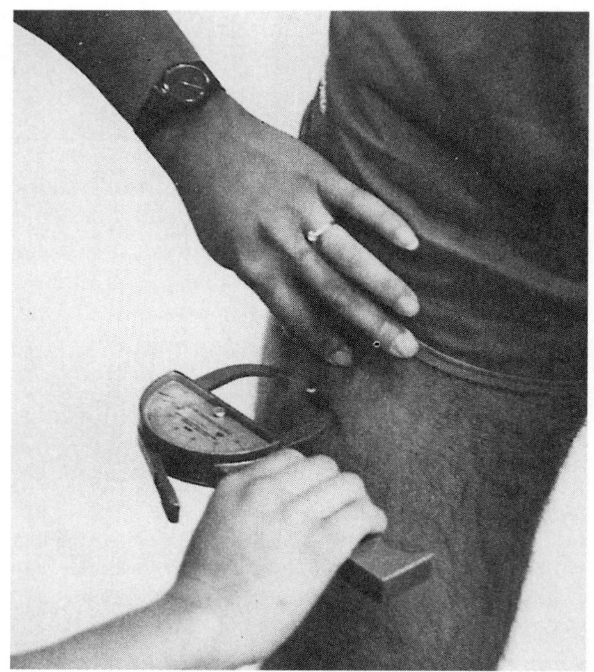

Figure 2-6. Skinfold measure taken at the thigh.

Male sites

Chest
A measure taken diagonally, halfway between the front of the armpit and the nipple

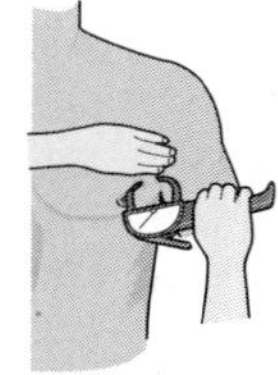

Abdominal
A vertical measure taken 2 cm lateral to the umbilicus

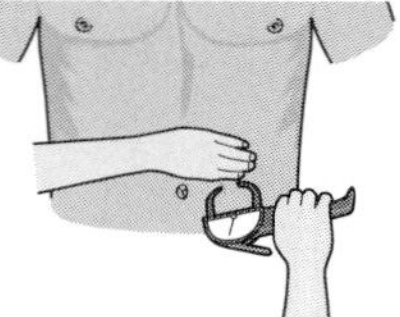

Thigh
A vertical measure taken at the midpoint of the right thigh, with the leg relaxed and knee slightly bent

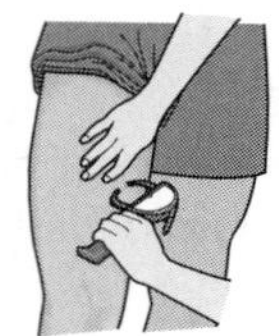

Female sites

Triceps
A vertical measure taken on the back of the upper arm halfway between the elbow and "point" of the shoulder, with the arm extended and the elbow relaxed

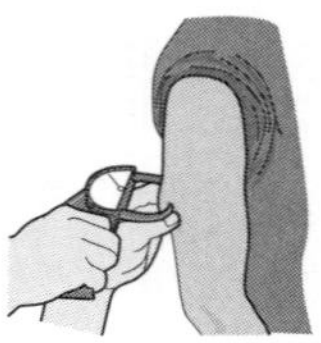

Suprailium
A diagonal measure taken above the hip at an imaginary vertical line extending down from the front of the armpit

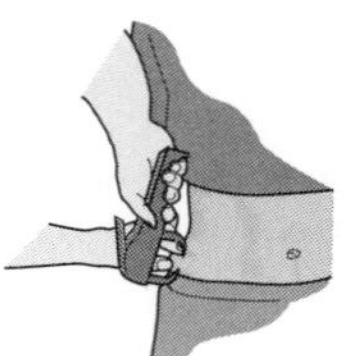

Thigh
A vertical measure taken at the midpoint of the right thigh, with the leg relaxed and the knee slightly bent

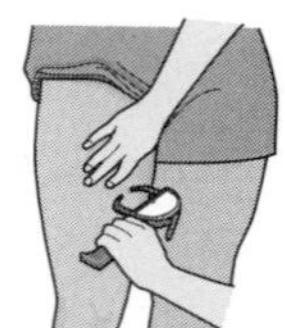

Figure 2-7. Descriptions of skinfold measurements.

Table 2-15. CONVERTING SKINFOLDS TO PERCENT FAT—MALES—SUM OF CHEST, ABDOMINAL, AND THIGH SKINFOLDS

	Age to the last year								
Sum of skinfolds (mm)	Under 22	23 to 27	28 to 32	33 to 37	38 to 42	43 to 47	48 to 52	53 to 57	Over 58
8–10	1.3	1.8	2.3	2.9	3.4	3.9	4.5	5.0	5.5
11–13	2.2	2.8	3.3	3.9	4.4	4.9	5.5	6.0	6.5
14–16	3.2	3.8	4.3	4.8	5.4	5.9	6.4	7.0	7.5
17–19	4.2	4.7	5.3	5.8	6.3	6.9	7.4	8.0	8.5
20–22	5.1	5.7	6.2	6.8	7.3	7.9	8.4	8.9	9.5
23–25	6.1	6.6	7.2	7.7	8.3	8.8	9.4	9.9	10.5
26–28	7.0	7.6	8.1	8.7	9.2	9.8	10.3	10.9	11.4
29–31	8.0	8.5	9.1	9.6	10.2	10.7	11.3	11.8	12.4
32–34	8.9	9.4	10.0	10.5	11.1	11.6	12.2	12.8	13.3
35–37	9.8	10.4	10.9	11.5	12.0	12.6	13.1	13.7	14.3
38–40	10.7	11.3	11.8	12.4	12.9	13.5	14.1	14.6	15.2
41–43	11.6	12.2	12.7	13.3	13.8	14.4	15.0	15.5	16.1
44–46	12.5	13.1	13.6	14.2	14.7	15.3	15.9	16.4	17.0
47–49	13.4	13.9	14.5	15.1	15.6	16.2	16.8	17.3	17.9
50–52	14.3	14.8	15.4	15.9	16.5	17.1	17.6	18.2	18.8
53–55	15.1	15.7	16.2	16.8	17.4	17.9	18.5	19.1	19.7
56–58	16.0	16.5	17.1	17.7	18.2	18.8	19.4	20.0	20.5
59–61	16.9	17.4	17.9	18.5	19.1	19.7	20.2	20.8	21.4
62–64	17.6	18.2	18.8	19.4	19.9	20.5	21.1	21.7	22.2
65–67	18.5	19.0	19.6	20.2	20.8	21.3	21.9	22.5	23.1
68–70	19.3	19.9	20.4	21.0	21.6	22.2	22.7	23.3	23.9
71–73	20.1	20.7	21.2	21.8	22.4	23.0	23.6	24.1	24.7
74–76	20.9	21.5	22.0	22.6	23.2	23.8	24.4	25.0	25.5
77–79	21.7	22.2	22.8	23.4	24.0	24.6	25.2	25.8	26.3
80–82	22.4	23.0	23.6	24.2	24.8	25.4	25.9	26.5	27.1
83–85	23.2	23.8	24.4	25.0	25.5	26.1	26.7	27.3	27.9
86–88	24.0	24.5	25.1	25.7	26.3	26.9	27.5	28.1	28.7
89–91	24.7	25.3	25.9	26.5	27.1	27.6	28.2	28.8	29.4
92–94	25.4	26.0	26.6	27.2	27.8	28.4	29.0	29.6	30.2
95–97	26.1	26.7	27.3	27.9	28.5	29.1	29.7	30.3	30.9
98–100	26.9	27.4	28.0	28.6	29.2	29.8	30.4	31.0	31.6
101–103	27.5	28.1	28.7	29.3	29.9	30.5	31.1	31.7	32.3
104–106	28.2	28.8	29.4	30.0	30.6	31.2	31.8	32.4	33.0
107–109	28.9	29.5	30.1	30.7	31.3	31.9	32.5	33.1	33.7
110–112	29.6	30.2	30.8	31.4	32.0	32.6	33.2	33.8	34.4
113–115	30.2	30.8	31.4	32.0	32.6	33.2	33.8	34.5	35.1
116–118	30.9	31.5	32.1	32.7	33.3	33.9	34.5	35.1	35.7
119–121	31.5	32.1	32.7	33.3	33.9	34.5	35.1	35.7	36.4
122–124	32.1	32.7	33.3	33.9	34.5	35.1	35.8	36.4	37.0
125–127	32.7	33.3	33.9	34.5	35.1	35.8	36.4	37.0	37.6

(continued)

Table 2-15 (Continued) CONVERTING SKINFOLDS TO PERCENT FAT—FEMALES—SUM OF TRICEPS, SUPRAILIUM, AND THIGH SKINFOLDS

	Age to the last year								
Sum of skinfolds (mm)	Under 22	23 to 27	28 to 32	33 to 37	38 to 42	43 to 47	48 to 52	53 to 57	Over 58
23–25	9.7	9.9	10.2	10.4	10.7	10.9	11.2	11.4	11.7
26–28	11.0	11.2	11.5	11.7	12.0	12.3	12.5	12.7	13.0
29–31	12.3	12.5	12.8	13.0	13.3	13.5	13.8	14.0	14.3
32–34	13.6	13.8	14.0	14.3	14.5	14.8	15.0	15.3	15.5
35–37	14.8	15.0	15.3	15.5	15.8	16.0	16.3	16.5	16.8
38–40	16.0	16.3	16.5	16.7	17.0	17.2	17.5	17.7	18.0
41–43	17.2	17.4	17.7	17.9	18.2	18.4	18.7	18.9	19.2
44–46	18.3	18.6	18.8	19.1	19.3	19.6	19.8	20.1	20.3
47–49	19.5	19.7	20.0	20.2	20.5	20.7	21.0	21.2	21.5
50–52	20.6	20.8	21.1	21.3	21.6	21.8	22.1	22.3	22.6
53–55	21.7	21.9	22.1	22.4	22.6	22.9	23.1	23.4	23.6
56–58	22.7	23.0	23.2	23.4	23.7	23.9	24.2	24.4	24.7
59–61	23.7	24.0	24.2	24.5	24.7	25.0	25.2	25.5	25.7
62–64	24.7	25.0	25.2	25.5	25.7	26.0	26.7	26.4	26.7
65–67	25.7	25.9	26.2	26.4	26.7	26.9	27.2	27.4	27.7
68–70	26.6	26.9	27.1	27.4	27.6	27.9	28.1	28.4	28.6
71–73	27.5	27.8	28.0	28.3	28.5	28.8	29.0	29.3	29.5
74–76	28.4	28.7	28.9	29.2	29.4	29.7	29.9	30.2	30.4
77–79	29.3	29.5	29.8	30.0	30.3	30.5	30.8	31.0	31.3
80–82	30.1	30.4	30.6	30.9	31.1	31.4	31.6	31.9	32.1
83–85	30.9	31.2	31.4	31.7	31.9	32.2	32.4	32.7	32.9
86–88	31.7	32.0	32.2	32.5	32.7	32.9	33.2	33.4	33.7
89–91	32.5	32.7	33.0	33.2	33.5	33.7	33.9	34.2	34.4
92–94	33.2	33.4	33.7	33.9	34.2	34.4	34.7	34.9	35.2
95–97	33.9	34.1	34.4	34.6	34.9	35.1	35.4	35.6	35.9
98–100	34.6	34.8	35.1	35.3	35.5	35.8	36.0	36.3	36.5
101–103	35.3	35.4	35.7	35.9	36.2	36.4	36.7	36.9	37.2
104–106	35.8	36.1	36.3	36.6	36.8	37.1	37.3	37.5	37.8
107–109	36.4	36.7	36.9	37.1	37.4	37.6	37.9	38.1	38.4
110–112	37.0	37.2	37.5	37.7	38.0	38.2	38.5	38.7	38.9
113–115	37.5	37.8	38.0	38.2	38.5	38.7	39.0	39.2	39.5
116–118	38.0	38.3	38.5	38.8	39.0	39.3	39.5	39.7	40.0
119–121	38.5	38.7	39.0	39.2	39.5	39.7	40.0	40.2	40.5
122–124	39.0	39.2	39.4	39.7	39.9	40.2	40.4	40.7	40.9
125–127	39.4	39.6	39.9	40.1	40.4	40.6	40.9	41.1	41.4
128–130	39.8	40.0	40.3	40.5	40.8	41.0	41.3	41.5	41.8

Source: Pollack, Schmidt, and Jackson 1980. Reprinted with permission. © American Society of Contemporary Medicine & Surgery. (Michael L. Pollack, PhD; Donald H. Schmidt, MD; and Andrew S. Jackson, PE. Measurement of Cardio-Respiratory Fitness and Body Composition in the Clinical Setting. *Comp Ther.* 1980; 6(9): 12–27.

weight-lifting guidelines in chapter 41 for more information. However, tables 2-17 and 2-18 provide normative data that are expressed relative to one's body weight and for upper-body endurance.

A variety of tests can measure abdominal strength and endurance. One widely used test is to determine the number of sit-ups one can perform in 1 minute. To start the test, lie supine on the floor with the knees flexed so that the angle between the thighs and the calves is about 90 degrees. Cross your arms in front of your chest and place your hands on the opposite shoulders. A partner should hold your feet to keep them in contact with the floor (see figure 2-8). When timing starts, do as many sit-ups as you can in 1 minute. The sit-up is performed by touching the elbows to the thighs, with the arms maintaining contact with the chest, and returning to the starting position with the middle of the back touching the floor. Use table 2-19 to interpret your results.

Table 2-16. INTERPRETING PERCENT BODY FAT

Males

	Age (years)					
Rating	**18–25**	**26–35**	**36–45**	**46–55**	**56–65**	**66+**
Very lean	4–7	8–12	10–14	12–16	15–18	15–18
Lean	8–10	13–15	16–18	18–20	19–21	19–21
Leaner than average	11–13	16–18	19–21	21–23	22–24	22–23
Average	14–16	19–21	22–24	24–25	24–26	24–25
Fatter than average	18–20	22–24	25–26	26–28	26–28	25–27
Fat	22–26	25–28	27–29	29–31	29–31	28–30
Overfat	28–37	30–37	30–38	32–38	32–38	31–38

Females

	Age (years)					
Rating	**18–25**	**26–35**	**36–45**	**46–55**	**56–65**	**66+**
Very lean	13–17	13–18	15–19	18–22	18–23	16–18
Lean	18–20	19–21	20–23	23–25	24–26	22–25
Leaner than average	21–23	22–23	24–26	26–28	28–30	27–29
Average	24–25	24–26	27–29	29–31	31–33	30–32
Fatter than average	26–28	27–30	30–32	32–34	34–36	33–35
Fat	29–31	31–35	33–36	36–38	36–38	36–38
Overfat	33–43	36–48	39–48	40–49	39–46	39–40

Source: Reprinted from *Y's way to physical fitness,* 3rd ed., with permission of the YMCA of the USA, 101 N. Wacker Drive, Chicago, IL 60606.

Table 2-17. NORMATIVE DATA ON STRENGTH TESTS (1-RM LB/LB BODY WEIGHT)

Males

	Age (years)				
Rating	**20–29**	**30–39**	**40–49**	**50–59**	**60+**
Excellent	>1.26	>1.08	>0.97	>0.86	>0.78
Good	1.17–1.25	1.01–1.07	0.91–0.96	0.81–0.85	0.74–0.77
Average	0.97–1.16	0.86–1.00	0.78–0.90	0.70–0.80	0.64–0.73
Fair	0.88–0.96	0.79–0.85	0.71–0.77	0.65–0.69	0.60–0.63
Poor	<0.87	<0.78	<0.71	<0.64	<0.59

Females

	Age (years)				
Rating	**20–29**	**30–39**	**40–49**	**50–59**	**60+**
Excellent	>0.78	>0.66	>0.61	>0.54	>0.55
Good	0.72–0.77	0.62–0.65	0.57–0.60	0.51–0.53	0.51–0.54
Average	0.59–0.71	0.53–0.61	0.48–0.56	0.43–0.50	0.41–0.50
Fair	0.53–0.58	0.49–0.52	0.44–0.47	0.40–0.42	0.37–0.40
Poor	<0.52	<0.48	<0.43	<0.39	<0.36

Based on norms from *The Physical Fitness Specialist Manual,* The Cooper Institute for Aerobics Research, Dallas, Texas, revised 1988; used with permission.

Table 2-18. NORMATIVE DATA FOR BENCH PRESS ENDURANCE TEST

Males (80 pounds with 30 repetitions per minute)						
	Age (years)					
Rating	18–25	26–35	36–45	46–55	56–65	66+
Excellent	45–38	43–34	40–30	35–24	32–22	30–18
Good	34–30	30–26	28–24	22–20	20–14	14–10
Above average	28–25	25–22	22–20	17–14	14–10	10–8
Average	22–21	21–18	18–16	13–10	10–8	8–6
Below average	20–16	17–13	14–12	10–8	6–4	<5
Poor	13–9	12–9	10–8	6–4	4–2	<3
Very poor	<9	<6	<6	<3	0	0
Females (35 pounds with 30 repetitions per minute)						
	Age (years)					
Rating	18–25	26–35	36–45	46–55	56–65	66+
Excellent	50–36	48–33	46–28	42–26	34–22	26–18
Good	32–28	29–25	25–21	22–20	20–16	14–12
Above average	25–22	22–20	20–17	17–13	15–12	11–9
Average	21–18	18–16	14–12	12–10	10–8	8–5
Below average	16–13	14–12	11–9	9–6	7–4	4–2
Poor	12–8	9–5	8–4	5–2	3–1	<3
Very poor	5–1	<3	<3	<2	0	0

Source: Reprinted from *Y's way to physical fitness*, 3rd ed., with permission of the YMCA of the USA, 101 N. Wacker Drive, Chicago, IL 60606.

Table 2-19. ONE-MINUTE SIT-UP NORMS

Males	Age			
Fitness level	29 or under	30–39	40–49	50+
Excellent	>60	>45	>42	>38
Good	48	37	32	26
Fair	40	23	20	15
Poor	25	18	15	10
Very poor	<18	<12	<10	<6
Females	Age			
Fitness level	29 or under	30–39	40–49	50+
Excellent	>50	>40	>35	>25
Good	40	34	26	20
Fair	32	15	10	7
Poor	20	12	6	3
Very poor	<12	<8	<2	<1

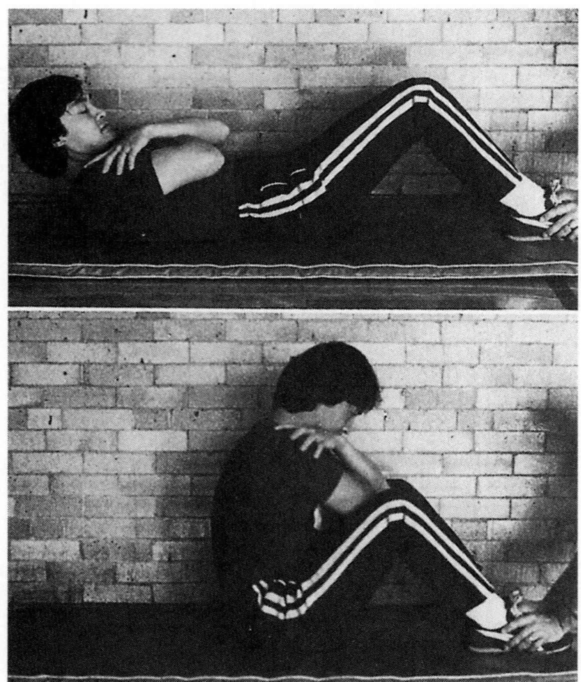

Figure 2-8. Sit-up test.

Likewise, flexibility can be measured in many different ways because of its specificity to body part and joint. A commonly used test is the sit-and-reach test. A special piece of equipment is needed for this test (see figure 2-9). To perform the test, remove your shoes and sit down with your feet against the board and your legs fully extended. Extend your arms forward with one hand on top of the other with the palms facing downward and fingertips even.

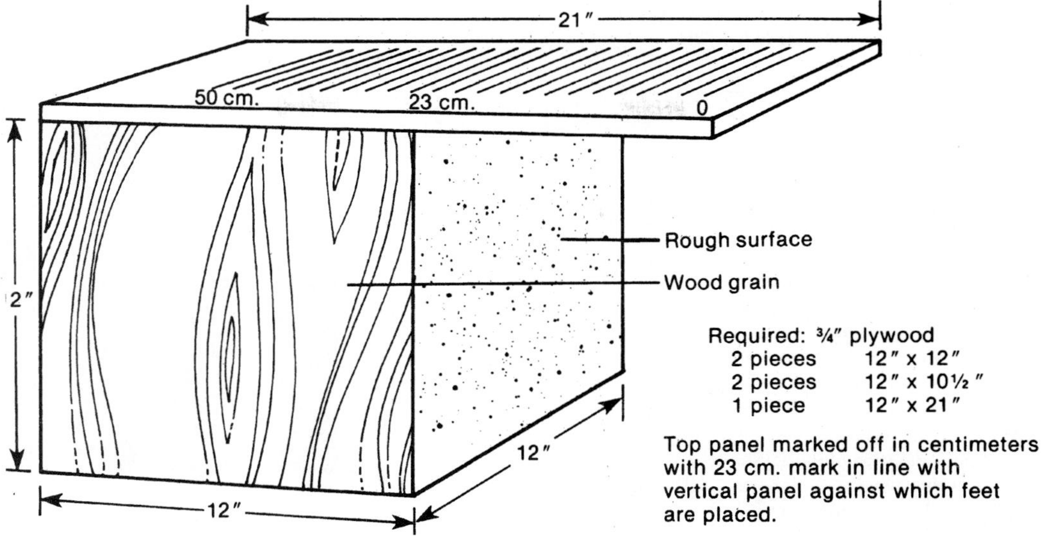

Figure 2-9. Apparatus necessary for sit-and-reach test.

Reach as far forward as possible while keeping your knees straight. Repeat four times and hold the maximum reach on the fourth trial for 1 second. The score is the farthest reach achieved, to the nearest centimeter. When performing this test, do not use a forceful bobbing motion; use a smooth forward slide. Compare your results with the norms presented in table 2-20.

IT'S NEVER TOO EARLY OR TOO LATE TO START

Some might believe that they have been deconditioned, overweight, or inflexible for so long that it is useless to begin a physical activity program. Quite the contrary, it is never too early or too late to start. Evidence indicates that elementary school age children can be trained to increase their aerobic fitness, body composition, and muscular strength. Table 2-21 has guidelines for physical activity in children and adolescents that were developed as a result of a national consensus conference. Note the similarity those guidelines have with those suggested for adults in terms of daily physical activity levels. Similarly, research conducted on octogenarians indicates that they too can show increases in functional capacity with training.

Figure 2-10 shows results from a study on patients at the Cooper Clinic in Dallas, Texas, indicating the changes in disease risk from one physical examination to another. At the first examination, these adults had a specific risk factor (e.g., were physically inactive, smoked, had high cholesterol, had high blood pressure, or high fat level). Upon returning for their second examination, they were no longer at risk, because they had changed the risk behavior (i.e., were physically active, no longer smoked, had normal cholesterol, had normal blood pressure, or no longer had excessive body fatness). Note that the individuals who had the greatest risk reduction for all-cause mortality were those who were physically inactive at the first visit but were then physically active at the second visit. Physically active at the second visit did not mean that they were marathoners or highly trained runners. They had simply increased their fitness as a result of increased physical activity from the lowest 20 percent to somewhere in the upper 80 percent of people. This suggests that just being out of the lowest 20 percent of people in terms of aerobic fitness level had a significant health benefit.

Table 2-20. SIT-AND-REACH NORMS (IN CENTIMETERS)

Males	**Age**			
Fitness level	**29 or under**	**30–39**	**40–49**	**50+**
Excellent	>42	>48	>48	>43
Good	36	43	41	38
Fair	30	23	25	20
Poor	16	18	13	13
Very poor	<10	<12	<8	<5
Females	**Age**			
Fitness level	**29 or under**	**30–39**	**40–49**	**50+**
Excellent	>42	>53	>53	>48
Good	38	50	48	46
Fair	32	36	30	30
Poor	22	30	25	23
Very poor	<18	<20	<15	<15

Table 2-21. A CONSENSUS ON PHYSICAL ACTIVITY GUIDELINES FOR ADOLESCENTS

Physical Activity Guidelines for Adolescents. The health-related rationale for optimizing physical activity during adolescence is twofold: first, to promote physical and psychological health and well-being during adolescence; second, to enhance future health by increasing the probability of remaining active as an adult.

Guideline 1: All adolescents should be physically active daily or nearly every day, as part of play, games, sports, work, transportation, recreation, physical education, or planned exercise, in the context of family, school, and community affairs.

Adolescents should do a variety of physical activities as part of their daily lifestyles. These activities should be enjoyable, involve a variety of muscle groups, and include some type of weight-bearing activities. The intensity or duration of the activity is probably less important than the fact that energy is expended and a habit of daily activity is established. Adolescents are encouraged to incorporate physical activity into their lifestyles by doing such things as walking up stairs, walking or riding a bicycle for errands, having conversations while walking with friends, parking at the far end of parking lots, or doing household chores.

Guideline 2: In addition to daily lifestyle activities, three or more sessions per week of activities lasting 20 minutes or more at a time, that require moderate to vigorous levels of exertion, are recommended.

Moderate to vigorous activities are those that require at least as much effort as brisk or fast walking. A diversity of activities that use large muscle groups are recommended as part of sports, recreation, chores, transportation, work, school physical education, or planned exercise. Examples include brisk walking, jogging, stair climbing, basketball, racquet sports, soccer, dance, swimming laps, skating, strength (resistance) training, lawn mowing, strenuous housework, cross-country skiing, and cycling.

Source: Sallis and Patrick 1994. Reprinted by permission from J.F. Sallis and K. Patrick, 1994, "Physical Activity Guidelines for Adolescents: Consensus Statements," Pediatric Exercise Science, 6(4): 306–308.

Many of the other chapters in this text can help you develop skills for remaining active throughout your life. Not everyone likes to swim, or run, or jog. Choose an activity that you like and that will help you remain physically active throughout your life. It will improve your health, quality of life, and general well-being.

INTERNET RESOURCES

Table 2-22 provides a list of World Wide Web sites related to health-related physical fitness. Visit these sites regularly; many of them are updated as new evidence is obtained about the relationship between physical activity and health, quality of life, and total well-being.

TEACHING CONSIDERATIONS

1. Health-related physical fitness can be taught as a separate unit or integrated into other units of a school or broad-based program. Long-lasting effects, in terms of attitudes and habits, are probably best achieved when a concern for fitness is imparted in

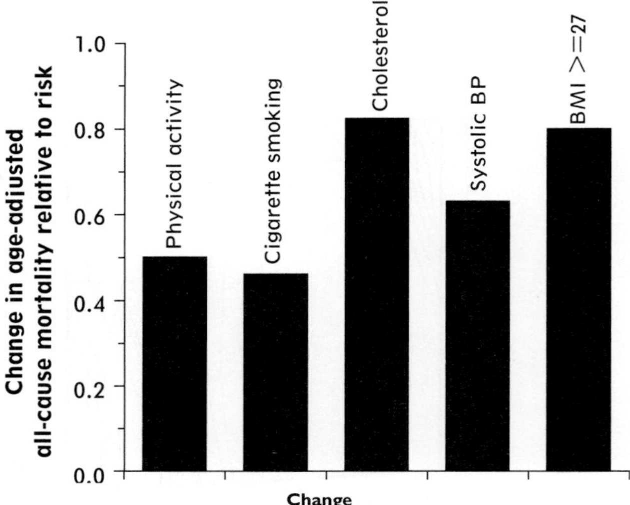

The graph indicates the decrease in all-cause mortality risk when participants made one of the following changes in lifestyle behaviors:
Inactive became active
Smokers became nonsmokers
Cholesterol changed from high to normal range
Blood pressure changed from high to normal range
Body mass index (BMI) changed from high to desirable range

Figure 2-10. Reduction in relative risk for all-cause mortality with change in risk behavior.

Table 2-22. INTERNET SOURCES ASSOCIATED WITH HEALTH-RELATED PHYSICAL FITNESS

American College of Sports Medicine
www.acsm.org

American Heart Association
www.amhrt.org

Centers for Disease Control and Prevention
www.cdc.gov

Duke University Diet and Fitness Center
dmi-www.mc.duke.edu/dfc/home.html

Food Pyramid Guide
www.ganesa.com/food/foodpyramid.html

Global Health Network
www.pitt.edu/HOME/GHNet/GHNet.html

National Coalition for Promoting Physical Activity
www.ncppa.org

National Institute of Arthritis and Musculoskeletal and Skin Diseases
www.nih.gov/niams

National Osteoporosis Foundation
www.nof.org

Physical Activity and Health: A Report of the Surgeon General
www.cdc.gov/nccdphp/sgr/sgr.htm

Physical Activity and Health Network (PAHNet)
info.pitt.edu/~pahnet/

Shape Up America
www.shapeup.org/sua

U.S. Department of Agriculture: Food and Nutrition Information Center
www.nal.usda.gov/fnic

programs active enough to both develop and maintain fitness.
2. Teach the "why" as well as the "how-to" of fitness components. Make instruction activity-based as well as information-based.
3. The most effective programs for older students teach how to assess, design, and conduct personal programs of fitness.
4. Use preassessment and postassessment to gear the program to individuals and to assess both their and the program's effectiveness. Share information with the student about personal progress and where the student is relative to program and individual goals.
5. Plan lessons to include work in more than one aspect of fitness.
6. Use recovery time from exercise to teach concepts.
7. Promote responsibility. Encourage work on fitness outside of class and give students the ability to design fitness programs using a variety of exercise types.
8. Testing should be only a small part of the program. Reduce testing time by assigning partners or station work where possible.
9. Choose ways to conduct activities that promote maximum participation. Use space, equipment, and time maximally.
10. Be sure that activities are being done correctly.
11. Be familiar with information on exercises that can be harmful.

GLOSSARY

aerobic exercise Activity that uses the oxygen system. Typically the aerobic system is used when continuous physical activity lasts longer than approximately 4 or 5 minutes.

aerobic fitness Fitness that positively influences the cardiorespiratory system so that one's endurance level is increased.

body composition The analysis of the body into fat, lean, and tissue components.

body max index (BMI) The ratio of weight in kilograms to height in meters squared.

chronic diseases Diseases that develop over time.

epidemiology The study of diseases, their causes, and their impact on society.

duration The length of an exercise or physical activity session.

exercise frequency The number of times per week that an individual exercises.

exercise intensity The vigor or energy level of physical activity. Often measured in terms of heart rate during the activity.

health-related physical fitness Physical fitness based on components that have been shown to be related to health, quality of life, and reduced disease.

hypertension High blood pressure.

hypertrophy Enlargement of muscle cells.

hypokinetic diseases Diseases that result from physical inactivity.

lean body mass Muscle, bone, and other nonfat tissues of the body.

maximum heart rate reserve The difference between maximum heart rate and resting heart rate.

maximum heart rate The maximum heart rate that one can achieve at maximum exercise. Usually estimated as 220 minus one's age.

musculoskeletal fitness Fitness that positively influences the muscular system to increase muscular strength and endurance and joint flexibility.

obesity Excessive amount of body fat.

osteoporosis Demineralization of bone, resulting in bones that are less dense and, as a result, more easily broken.

overload principle Imposing a greater than normal stress on one or more body systems.

reversibility The fact that increases in fitness level are not fixed and will reverse if the person does not continue to train to maintain or further increase fitness level.

RM Repetition maximum. 1-RM is the maximum amount of weight that can be lifted 1 time. 10-RM is the maximum amount of weight that can be lifted 10 times.

skinfold measurements Assessment of subcutaneous fat by measuring a fold of skin as an indicator of underlying fat.

specificity The concept of distinctiveness as it relates to a particular influence of physical activity or exercise.

REFERENCES

American College of Sports Medicine. 1990. Position stand: The recommended quantity and quality of exercise for developing and maintaining cardiorespiratory and muscular fitness in healthy adults. *Medicine and Science in Sports and Exercise.* 22:265–74.

Blair, S. N. 1993. C. H. McCloy research lecture: Physical activity, physical fitness, and health. *Research Quarterly for Exercise and Sport,* 64:365–76.

Golding, L., Myers, C., and Sinning, W. 1989. *Y's way to physical fitness.* Champaign, Ill.: Human Kinetics.

Howley, E. T., and Franks, B. D. 1997. *Health fitness instructor's handbook* (3d ed.). Champaign, Ill.: Human Kinetics.

Jackson, A., Solomon, J., and Stusek, M. 1992. One-mile walk test: Reliability, validity, and norms for young adults [Abstract}. *Research Quarterly for Exercise and Sport,* 63:A52.

Jequier, E. 1987. Energy, obesity, and body weight standards. *American Journal of Clinical Nutrition,* 45:1035–47.

Morrow, J. R., Jr., Jackson, A. W., Disch, J. G., and Mood, D. P. 1995. *Measurement and evaluation in human performance.* Champaign, Ill.: Human Kinetics.

Pate, R. R., Pratt, M., Blair, S. N., Haskell, W. L., Macera, C. A., Bouchard, C., Buchner, D., Ettinger, W., Heath, G. W., King, A. C., Kriska, A., Leon, A. S., Marcus, B. H., Morris, J., Paffenbarger, R. S., Jr., Patrick, K., Pollock, M. L., Rippe, J. M., Sallis, J. F., and Wilmore, J. H. 1995. Physical activity and public health: A recommendation from the Centers for Disease Control and Prevention and the American College of Sports Medicine. *Journal of the American Medical Association,* 273: 402–07.

Physical activity and cardiovascular health: NIH consensus development panel on physical activity and cardiovascular health. 1996. *Journal of the American Medical Association,* 276:241–46.

Pollack, M. L., Schmidt, D. H., and Jackson, A. S. 1980. Measurement of cardiorespiratory fitness and body composition in the clinical setting. *Comprehensive Therapy,* 6(9):12–27.

Sallis, J. F., and Patrick, K. Physical activity guidelines for adolescents: Consensus statement. *Pediatric Exercise Science,* 6:302–14.

SUGGESTED READINGS

Allsen, P. E., Harrison, J. M., and Vance B.: *Fitness for life,* ed 6, Dubuque, Iowa, 1997, W. C. Brown. Contains information on how to appraise, design, and write a fitness program for specific lifestyles and initial levels of fitness.

American College of Sports Medicine. 1993. Physical activity, physical fitness, and hypertension. *Medicine and Science in Sports and Exercise.* 25:i–x.

American College of Sports Medicine. 1995. ACSM position stand on osteoporosis and exercise. *Medicine and Science in Sports and Exercise.* 27:i–vii.

American Diabetes Association. 1990. Technical review: Exercise and NIDDM. *Diabetes Care,* 13:785–89.

American Heart Association. 1992. Statement on exercise: Benefits and recommendations for physical activity programs for all Americans: A statement for health professionals by the Committee on Exercise and Cardiac Rehabilitation of the Council on Clinical Cardiology, American Heart Association. *Circulation,* 88:1402–05.

Barlow, C. E., Kohl, W. H., III, Gibbons, L. W., and Blair, S. N. 1995. Physical fitness, mortality and obesity. *International Journal of Obesity,* 19:S41–S44.

Bjorntorp, P., Sjostrom, L., and Sullivan, L. 1979. The role of physical exercise in the management of obesity. In *The treatment of obesity* ed. J. F. Munro (pp. 123–38). Baltimore: University Park Press.

Blair, S. N., and Connelly, J. C. 1996. How much physical activity should we do? The case for moderate amounts and intensities of physical activity. *Research Quarterly for Exercise and Sport,* 67:193–205.

Blair, S. N., Kampert, J. B., Kohl, W. H., III, Barlow, C. E., Macera, C. A., Paffenbarger, R. S., Jr., and Gibbons, L. W. 1996. Influences of cardiorespiratory fitness and other precursors on cardiovascular disease and all-cause mortality in men and women. *Journal of the American Medical Association,* 276:205–10.

Blair, S. N., Kohl, H. W., III, Barlow, C. E., Paffenbarger, R. S., Jr,., Gibbons, L. W., and Macera, C. A. 1995. Changes in physical fitness and all-cause mortality: A prospective study of healthy men and women. *Journal of the American Medical Association,* 273:1093–98.

Blair, S. N., Kohl, H. W., III, Paffenbarger, R. S., Jr., Clark, D. G., Cooper, K. H., and Gibbons, L. W. 1989. Physical fitness and all-cause mortality: A prospective study of healthy men and women. *Journal of the American Medical Association,* 262:2395–2401.

Bouchard, C., Shephard, R. J., and Stephens, T., eds. 1994. *Physical activity, fitness, and health: International proceedings and consensus statement.* Champaign, Ill.: Human Kinetics.

Calfas, K. J., Long, B. J., Lovato, C. Y., and Campbell, J. 1994. Physical activity and its determinants before and after college graduation. *Medicine, Exercise, Nutrition, and Health,* 3:323–34.

Caspersen, C. J., Powell, K. E., and Christensen, G. M. 1985. Physical activity, exercise, and physical fitness: Definitions and distinctions for health-related research. *Public Health Reports,* 100:126–31,

Corbin, C. B., and Lindsay R. *Concepts of fitness and wellness with laboratories,* ed 2, Dubuque, Iowa, 1997, W. C. Brown/McGraw Hill.

Daniel, E. A guidebook for fitness/wellness/personal health, Englewood CO, 1997, Morton Publishing Company. Contains directions to 152 web sites covering 34 topics about fitness, wellness and personal health.

DeBusk, R. F., Stenestrand, U., Sheehan, M., and Haskell, W. L. 1990. Training effects of long versus short bouts of exercise in healthy subjects. *American Journal of Cardiology,* 65:1010–13.

DiPietro, L. 1995. Physical activity, body weight, and adiposity: An epidemiologic perspective. *Exercise and Sport Science Reviews,* 23:275–303.

Drinkwater, B. 1993. Exercise in the prevention of osteoporosis. *Osteoporosis International,* 1:S169–S171.

Fiatarone, M. A., O'Neill, E. F., Ryan, N. D., Clements, K. M., Solares, G. R., Nelson, M. E., Roberts, S. B., Kehayias, J. J., Lipsitz, L. A., and Evans, W. J. 1994. Exercise training and nutritional supplementation for physical frailty in very elderly people. *New England Journal of Medicine,* 330:1769–75.

Floyd, P. et al.: *Wellness: A lifetime commitment,* Winston-Salem, N.C., 1993, Hunter Textbooks.

Getchell, B.: *Physical fitness: a way of life,* ed 4, New York, 1992, Macmillan. Includes a variety of physical-activity programs, beginning to advanced, that are safe, reasonable, and effective. Self-assessment tests and guidelines are also included.

Greenberg, J., Dintiman, G., and Myers, B. *Physical fitness and wellness,* Needham Heights, MA, 1995, Allyn & Bacon. Specific attention is paid to behavior change and motivational strategies.

Hawkins, J., and Weigle, S.: *Walking for fun and fitness,* Englewood, Colo, 1992, Morton Publishing.

Healthy people 2000: Midcourse review and 1995 revisions. 1995. Washington, D.C.: U.S. Department of Health and Human Services, Public Health Service.

Healthy people 2000: National health promotion and disease prevention objectives, full report, with commentary. 1990. DHHS Publication Number (PHS)91-50212. Washington, D.C.: U.S. Department of Health and Human Services, Public Health Service.

Hockey, R.V.: *Physical fitness: the pathway to healthful living,* ed 8, 1996, Dubuque, Iowa, W. C. Brown/McGraw Hill. Provides scientific yet practical information on the importance of exercise and fitness. Written to enable readers to evaluate their levels of fitness and then design and implement a personal program to achieve optimal fitness.

Hoeger, W., and Hoeger, S.: *Lifetime physical fitness and wellness,* ed 3, Englewood, Colo, 1992, Morton Publishing.

Hoeger. W., and Hoeger, S.: *Fitness and wellness,* ed 2, Englewood, Colo, 1990, Morton Publishing.

Howley, E. and Franks, D. *Health fitness instructor's handbook,* ed 2, Champaign IL, 1992, Human Kinetics.

Jaglal, S. B., Kreiger, N., and Darlington, G. 1993. Past and recent physical activity and risk of hip fracture. *American Journal of Epidemiology,* 138:107–18.

Kayman, S., Bruvold, W., and Stern, J. S. 1990. Maintenance and relapse after weight loss in women: Behavioral aspects. *American Journal of Clinical Nutrition,* 52:800–07.

Katch, F., and McArdle, W.: *Nutrition, weight control and exercise,* ed 2, Philadelphia, 1991, Lea & Febiger. Contains information on optimum nutrition for exercise and sport, evaluation of body composition, strength training, and cardiovascular health and aging.

King, H., and Kriska, A. M. 1992. Prevention of type II diabetes by physical training: Epidemiology considerations and study methods. *Diabetes Care,* 15:1794–99.

Kriska, A. M., and Bennett, P. H. 1992. An epidemiological perspective of the relationship between physical activity and NIDDM: From activity assessment to intervention. *Diabetes/Metabolism Reviews,* 8:355–72.

Kuczmarski, R. J. 1992. Prevalence of overweight and weight gain in the United States. *American Journal of Clinical Nutrition,* 55:495S–502S.

Kusinitz, I., and Fine, M.: *Your guide to getting fit,* ed 2, Palo Alto, Calif, 1991, Mayfield Publishing. A guide designed to help individuals create individualized physical-fitness programs.

Lee, I-M., Manson, J. E., Hennekens, C. H., and Paffenbarger, R. S., Jr. 1993. Body weight and mortality: A 27-year follow-up of middle-aged men. *Journal of the American Medical Association,* 270:2823–28.

Leslie, D., ed.: *Mature stuff: physical activity for the older adult,* Reston, Va, 1990, American Alliance for Health, Physical Education, Recreation, and Dance.

Marcus, B. H., Eaton, C. A., Rossi, J. S., and Harlow, L. L. 1994. Self-efficacy, decision-making, and stages of change: An integrative model of physical exercise. *Journal of Applied Social Psychology,* 24:489–508.

Marcus, B. H., Rakowski, W., and Rossi, J. S. 1992. Assessing motivational readiness and decision making for exercise. *Health Psychology,* 11:257–61.

McCauley, E., and Randolph, D. 1995. Physical activity, aging, and psychological well-being. *Journal of Aging and Physical Activity,* 3:67–96.

McGlynn, G.: *Dynamics of fitness,* ed 4, Dubuque, Iowa, 1996, W. C. Brown/McGraw Hill.

Miller, D., and Allen, T.: *Fitness: a lifetime commitment,* ed 5, Needham Heights, MA, 1995, Allyn & Bacon.

Nieves, J. W., Grisson, J. A., and Kelsey, J. L. 1992. A case-control study of hip fracture: Evaluation of selected dietary variables and teenage physical activity. *Osteoporosis International,* 2(3):122–27.

Nutrition and your health: Dietary guidelines for Americans (4th ed.) 1995. Washington, D.C.: U.S. Department of Agriculture, U.S. Department of Health and Human Services.

Paffenbarger, R. S., Jr., Hyde, R. T., Wing, A. L., Lee, I-M., and Kampert, J. B. 1993. The association of changes in physical activity level and other lifestyle changes with mortality among men. *New England Journal of Medicine,* 328:538–45.

Physical activity and health: A report of the surgeon general. 1996. Atlanta: U.S. Department of Health and Human Services, Centers for Disease Control and Prevention, National Center for Chronic Disease Prevention and Health Promotion.

Powell, K. E., and Blair, S. N. 1994. The public health burdens of sedentary living habits: Theoretical but realistic estimates. *Journal of the American Medical Association,* 248:1073–76.

Prentice, W.: *Fitness for college and life,* Dubuque IA, 1997, W. C. Brown/McGraw Hill. Designed for students in general fitness and conditioning courses.

Rejeski, W. J., Brawley, L. R., and Schumaker, S. A. 1996. Physical activity and health-related quality of life. *Exercise and Sport Sciences Reviews,* 24:71–108.

Seidell, J. C., Verschuren, W. M. M., van Leer, E. M., and Kromhout, D. 1996. Overweight, underweight, and mortality: A prospective study of 48,287 men and women. *Archives of Internal Medicine,* 156:958–63.

Sharkey, B.J.: *Physiology of fitness,* ed 3, Champaign, Ill, 1990, Human Kinetics. Covers aerobic fitness, muscular training, weight control, cardiovascular health, flexibility, and other topics.

Shephard, R. J., and Shek, P. N. 1995. Cancer, immune function, and physical activity. *Canadian Journal of Applied Physiology,* 20:1–25.

Spindt, G., Monti, W., and Hennessy, B.: *Moving for life,* Dubuque, Iowa, 1991, Kendall/Hunt Publishing.

Stokes, R., et al.: *Fitness: the new wave,* Winston-Salem, N.C., 1992, Hunter Textbooks.

Williams, C., et al.: *Personal fitness: looking good/feeling good,* Dubuque, Iowa, 1992, Kendall/Hunt Publishing.

Williams, M.: *Lifetime fitness and wellness: a personal choice,* ed. 4, Dubuque, Iowa, 1996, W. C. Brown/McGraw Hill. Organized around the premise that with the information it contains, the reader can design and implement a healthy lifestyle. Aerobic exercise, nutrition, relation of flexibility to prevention of lower-back pain, and stress reduction are some of the topics covered.

Group-Exercise Aerobic Dance

After completing this chapter, the reader should be able to:

- Recognize the benefits associated with regular participation in group exercise
- Organize and design a safe and effective group exercise class, including the sequencing of activities
- Select appropriate music, movement patterns, and exercises for a group exercise program

HISTORY

The activity referred to as aerobic dance is undergoing a change, mostly a broadening of the definition. The focus is less on the spandex, thong leotard, dance imagery and more on inclusion of the general population, including men, seniors, and overweight individuals.

Group exercise may be defined as exercise in a class-type setting where participants are all following a format predetermined by a group exercise instructor. Group exercise is usually, but not always, performed to music. Group exercise may include a wide variety of class formats as well as varying modes of exercise such as aerobic dance, step aerobics, slide aerobics, stationary indoor cycling, water exercise, muscle conditioning, and flexibility work.

Aerobic dance, defined as continuous and rhythmic movement to music, was introduced by Jackie Sorenson in 1969. The combination of vigorous dance steps and exercises performed to popular music in a group setting soon became one of the fastest growing leisure activities in the United States. Today more than 25 million exercise enthusiasts participate in this multimillion dollar industry. Virtually every community offers some form of aerobic dance class. Even home exercisers can participate in this physically demanding activity by following popular group exercise leaders on television programs and videotapes.

Aerobic dance has evolved from rigidly choreographed dance routines intended for female participants to freestyle routines that incorporate random combinations of dance, sport, and exercise movements designed to attract men and women. In 1990 step aerobics was introduced, and by 1996 participation in step aerobics exceeded participation in either low or high impact aerobic dance (American Sports Data Inc. and Fitness Products Council). In addition, participation continues to grow in other group exercise modalities such as slide, water fitness, and indoor cycling.

Professional fitness associations are helping meet the demand for qualified instructors. Organizations such as the International Association of Fitness Professionals and the Aerobic and Fitness Association of America (AFAA) provide their members with services that include subscriptions to exercise journals, access to fitness conventions and workshops, and opportunities to become certified as a group exercise instructor.

BENEFITS OF GROUP-EXERCISE AEROBIC DANCE

Group exercise is an excellent activity for developing overall physical fitness. Balancing the health-related components of fitness, group exercise can improve a participant's flexibility, strength, cardiovascular fitness, and body composition. The rhythmic movements performed to music also help develop coordination and balance. In addition, exercising in a group setting provides opportunities for social interactions not afforded by many other aerobic activities (figure 3-1).

FACILITY

The ideal setting for conventional group exercise includes:

1. Good ventilation with a room temperature of 60° to 70° F.
2. A floor that will absorb shock while controlling lateral motions of the foot and providing adequate traction. A hardwood sprung floor is an ideal aerobic dance surface.
3. Space for each participant to move comfortably. A good guide is enough space for each participant, with arms outspread, to take two large steps in any direction without touching anyone.
4. Acoustics that allow the instructor's voice to be heard over the music.
5. For large groups, a raised platform for the instructor.
6. Mirrors to help participants observe and correct their posture and exercise positions.

Other settings include shallow or deep water pools and outdoor courses for walking and in-line skating.

Figure 3-1. Aerobics dance class.

EQUIPMENT

Equipment needs vary according to the type of facility and the size of the class. Most programs require a sound system and a collection of audiotapes or CDs. A wireless microphone for the instructor may be necessary if the class is in a large space. Many other possibilities for equipment and/or props are available, such as steps (benches), slides, rubber tubes or bands, hand weights (1- to 10-pound dumbbells are commonly used), ankle weights, stability balls, mats, stretch straps, jump ropes, boxing gloves and/or tape, spinning cycles, water mitts, noodles, wings, and water steps.

APPAREL AND SHOES

Participants should wear lightweight, well-ventilated clothing. Cotton fabrics are recommended because they absorb moisture while allowing air to circulate through the material. Many of the fabrics used for exercise apparel are made of cotton blends. Knee-length tights or fitness shorts worn with a leotard or T-shirt provide the greatest comfort and mobility. Cotton socks will help absorb perspiration and reduce the likelihood of blisters. Participants should be encouraged to layer their clothing in cool facilities and remove outer garments (such as a warm-up suit) as the body temperature rises with increased levels of activity.

Shoes are perhaps the most important item worn by the participants in aerobic dance and step classes. Because certain high-impact aerobic dance and step moves can generate vertical forces on the feet of up to four times one's body weight, participants need to select a shoe designed to help absorb these impacts: A well-constructed aerobic shoe has a sole adequately cushioned, especially under the ball of the foot, to help absorb the shock of forefoot movements characteristic of most aerobic steps. Proper support and stability are particularly important for lateral movements. The traction provided by the shoe should match the surface on which activities are being performed. For example, less traction is needed on a carpeted surface while greater traction is necessary on a hardwood floor. Finally, a shoe should be selected for its durability, flexibility, and lightweight characteristics.

FUNDAMENTAL SKILLS AND TECHNIQUES

Components of a Typical Group Exercise Class

A well-designed format for group exercise consists of:

1. Warm-up and prestretch (10 minutes)
2. Aerobic activity (20 to 30 minutes)
3. Cool-down (2 to 5 minutes)
4. Strength work (5 to 10 minutes)
5. Final stretch (5 to 10 minutes)

Warm-up and prestretch

The purpose of the warm-up is to increase blood flow to the muscles, increase the rate of oxygen exchange between blood and muscles, increase the speed and force of muscle contraction, increase muscle elasticity as well as the flexibility of tendons and ligaments, and reduce the risk of cardiac abnormalities. Movements during the warm-up should include rhythmic, full-range-of-motion exercises designed to prepare the body for movements used during the aerobic segment. The initial warm-up should concentrate on large movements for the shoulders, arms, and legs. A warm-up routine might consist of shoulder rolls, arm circles, marches, step touches, and toe and heel raises. After the muscles have been warmed, static stretching exercises should be performed to increase joint range of motion. Stretching positions should be held for at least 10 seconds, paying special attention to muscles of the shoulders, chest, hips, low back, thighs, calves, and feet.

Aerobic activity

The purpose of the aerobic segment is to improve cardiovascular endurance. The physiological benefits of aerobic activity include increased heart and lung efficiency and decreased body fat. Aerobic benefits are achieved by using prolonged and continuous movement of the large muscles. Ideally, the aerobic segment of class will last 20 to 30 minutes, performed at an intensity of 50 to 85 percent of the heart rate reserve.

To determine appropriate exercise intensity, participants need to determine their resting heart rates (RHR) and then calculate their target heart rate zones. Upon waking in the morning, the RHR can be determined by lightly placing the middle and index finger on either the carotid artery (at the neck) or the radial artery (on the thumb side of the wrist) and counting the number of beats occurring in 60 seconds. The target heart rate zone is then calculated by completing Karvonen's formula twice, once to establish the 50 percent value and again to establish the 85 percent value. The target heart rate zone lies between these two values. The formulas are:

$$[(220 - \text{age} - \text{RHR}) \times 0.5 \text{ (training percentage)} + \text{RHR}] \div 6 \text{ (to provide a 10-second heart rate)} = 50\% \text{ value}$$

$$[(220 - \text{age} - \text{RHR}) \times 0.85 + \text{RHR}] \div 6 = 85\% \text{ value}$$

For example, the target heart rate zone for a 40-year-old person with a resting heart rate of 72 beats per minute would be 21 to 27.

$$[(220 - 40 - 72) \times 0.5 + 72] \div 6 = 21.0$$

$$[(220 - 40 - 72) \times 0.85 + 72] \div 6 = 27.3$$

Exercise heart rate is taken for 10 seconds at the end of the aerobic segment (heart rate should be taken more frequently than this for beginners) and should be within the target zone (figure 3-2). Participants above the target heart rate can reduce the intensity of exercise in a land-based aerobic or step class by keeping the feet closer to the floor, by decreasing the amount of arm movement, or by minimizing the extent of traveling. Conversely, exercise intensity can be increased by lifting the feet higher off the floor, by increasing the amount of arm motion, or by adding directional movement.

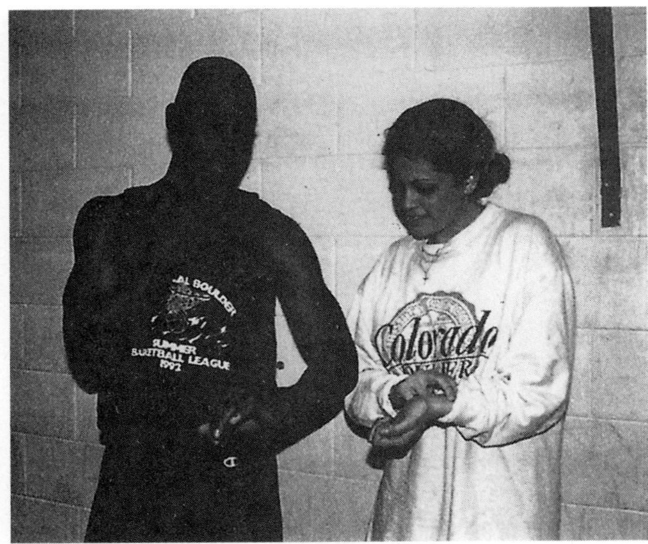

Figure 3-2. Taking the exercise heart rate.

The aerobic segment of an aerobic or step class consists of movement patterns choreographed to music. Movement patterns can be extremely varied, ranging from calisthenic exercises such as jumping jacks to dance movements such as leaps and lunges. Instructors can enhance their movement repertoire by using steps common to other dance forms, including jazz, modern, folk, and ballet, or by borrowing movement patterns used in sports and games, such as basketball dribbling.

Common basic steps used in aerobic dance include jogs, marches, hops, jumps, knee lifts, kicks, twists, step touches, jumping jacks, and lunges. These steps can be varied by changing the rhythm (half time, double time) or the direction of movement (forward, backward, sideways, diagonally, or in circles) or by adding arm positions to accompany the leg movements (figures 3-3 and 3-4). Common moves used in step aerobics include the basic step (up, up, down, down), V step, travel step with alternating lead, over the top, lift step, lunge, L step, repeater, and turn step. There are several possible approaches to the step: front, side, end, corner, top, and astride.

Steps can be combined into movement patterns in several ways. Routines can be rigidly choreographed, repeating the same movements each time the routine is performed. Choreographed routines help participants become secure with a movement sequence, allowing them to concentrate on the intensity of exercise and correct exercise positions. However, choreographed routines require a great deal of preparation by the instructor and can take extra class time to teach. Many instructors prefer to use a freestyle approach to combine movement patterns with music. Rather than using routines, instructors using the freestyle technique select movements in a random fashion,

Figure 3-3. Leg kick.

Figure 3-4. Knee lift.

building combinations of step patterns as the music progresses. When skillfully led, participants enjoy the movement variety associated with the freestyle method. If, however, the step patterns are too complex for the group, participants may be unable to maintain appropriate exercise intensity as they struggle with unexpected and unfamiliar movements.

Freestyle choreography can be taught using a linear progression or by sequencing movement patterns into combinations. A linear progression is defined as a movement that advances into another, changing only one variable at a time, such as the leg or arm movement, the direction of movement, or the rhythm. This type of freestyle choreography is easy to follow, especially for beginners. The following is an example of a linear progression in traditional aerobic dance:

Base movement: 4 knee lifts in place (8 counts)
Add arms: Overhead presses (8 counts)
Add direction: Travel forward with 4 knee lifts and overhead presses (8 counts)
Change direction: Travel backward with 4 knee lifts and overhead presses (8 counts)
Change arms: Arm curls while traveling forward and backward with knee lifts (16 counts)
Change legs: 4 step kicks with arm curls traveling forward and backward (16 counts)
Change arms: Chest presses with step kick traveling forward and backward (16 counts)

Notice that only one variable was added or changed whenever a new movement was introduced.

Freestyle movements can also be sequenced into combinations. A combination is defined as two or more movement patterns that are sequenced together and repeated in a cycle. The following is an example of two simple combinations:

Combination 1
- 4 knee lifts traveling forward while pressing the arms overhead (8 counts)
- 4 step kicks traveling backward while curling the arms down and up (8 counts)

Combination 2
- 8 jogs forward with alternating arm curls (8 counts)
- 4 jumping jacks backward with hand claps (8 counts)

Combination 1 can be taught and repeated several times before combination 2 is introduced. Combination 2 can then be added to combination 1, producing a more interesting and challenging sequence of movements.

The first aerobic routine following the warm-up should be performed at a moderate pace to give the cardiovascular system ample time to adjust to the increasing demands of exercise. As the class progresses through the aerobic segment, the intensity and music tempo should be increased. Participants should be instructed to adjust the intensity of their movements to correspond with their level of cardiovascular fitness.

Cool-down

The purpose of the cool-down is to gradually lower the heart rate toward normal, prevent excessive pooling of blood in the lower extremities, and promote removal of metabolic waste products from the muscles. Slow but continued rhythmic contraction of the leg muscles is important to help return the blood from the lower extremities to the heart. A cool-down of 2 to 5 minutes can consist of walking around the room while gently swinging the arms or doing a slow aerobic routine.

It is wise to take a recovery heart rate at the end of the cool-down. A decrease in recovery heart rate over time is a measure of improved cardiovascular fitness. For comparative purposes, the recovery heart rate must be taken the same number of minutes following the end of the aerobic segment. A record sheet for recording exercise and recovery heart rates is useful for observing the progress of participants.

Strength exercises

Muscular strength is important for preventing injuries by helping the participant maintain proper alignment and body mechanics. It is therefore important to strengthen the muscles that help maintain good posture and aid in the proper execution of aerobic dance routines and floor exercises. Weak upper back muscles (upper trapezius and rhomboids) contribute to rounded shoulders, while weak abdominals can lead to a swayback posture. Aggravated by vigorous movements on the feet, these anatomical deviations can result in neck, shoulder, and low back pain. Therefore, it is prudent to strengthen the upper back muscles and abdominals in each class session. Rowing exercises and prone shoulder raises can be used to strengthen the upper back while curl-ups, diagonal curls, reverse curls, and pelvic tilts will help strengthen the abdominals.

It is also important to strengthen muscles of the shins (tibialis anterior). One of the most common injuries reported in aerobics is shinsplints. Although there are many causes for shin pain, a typical problem results from a muscle imbalance between the strong calf muscles (gastrocnemius), which contract vigorously for a prolonged period of time during the aerobic dance segment, and the weak shin muscles, which are used less frequently during class. Various forms of toe tapping, walking on the heels, and ankle flexion with light weights or rubber bands can help to strengthen tibialis anterior muscles.

If time allows, instructors can include strength exercises for other parts of the body. These include side leg lifts for the hip abductors and adductors, leg curls and lifts for the hamstrings and gluteals, knee extensions for the quadriceps, arm curls for the biceps, elbow extensions for the triceps, one-arm bent-over rows for latissimus dorsi, and lateral raises for the deltoids. Muscular strength is achieved by overloading the muscle with adequate resistance so that the student can complete 8 to 12 repetitions of an exercise. Surgical tubing, elastic bands, or weights can provide appropriate resistance. In addition, holding a contraction for 5 seconds at different points in the movement pattern can provide added resistance to the muscles. To continue strength gains, the resistance for each exercise should be increased when participants can comfortably complete three sets of 8 to 12 repetitions.

To encourage controlled movements during the strength exercises, music tempos should be moderately paced and participants should be instructed to adjust the tempo (half time or double time) and the number of repetitions required to meet their personal levels of strength. To encourage proper exercise technique, the instructor should move around the room and provide appropriate exercise cues while observing and critiquing performance.

Final stretch

The purpose of the final stretch is to improve overall flexibility, which helps maintain good posture and proper body mechanics throughout the day. Stretching after a vigorous exercise session is often easier than stretching before because the joints are well lubricated and the temperature of the muscles is increased following the aerobic workout. It is best to perform these stretches on the floor, allowing participants an opportunity to relax and concentrate on each stretch. The final stretch is most effective when performed to slow background music that does not have a strong beat. Flexibility exercises, held for 10 to 30 seconds, should include stretches for muscles of the low back, hip flexors, calves (Achilles tendinitis is a common injury in step aerobics), hamstrings, chest, shoulders, and neck (figures 3-5 and 3-6).

Low, moderate, and high impacts

In the past, most aerobic dance routines consisted of high-impact movements, including variations of jogs, hops, and jumps. High-impact aerobics (HIA), characterized by movements that require both feet to leave the floor frequently, can produce vertical forces of up to four times the weight of the body. Researchers reporting on injuries suf-

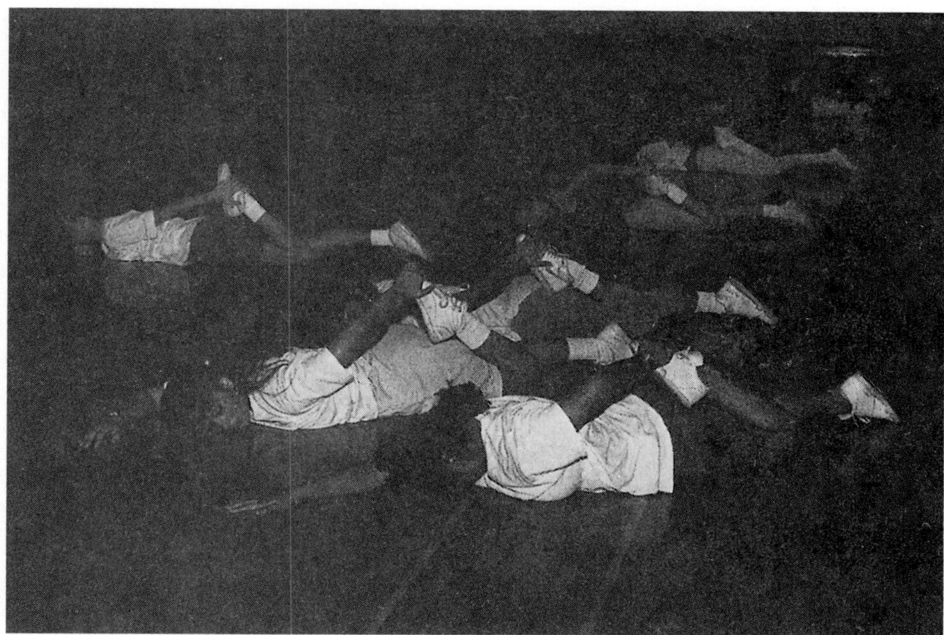

Figure 3-5. Quadriceps stretch.

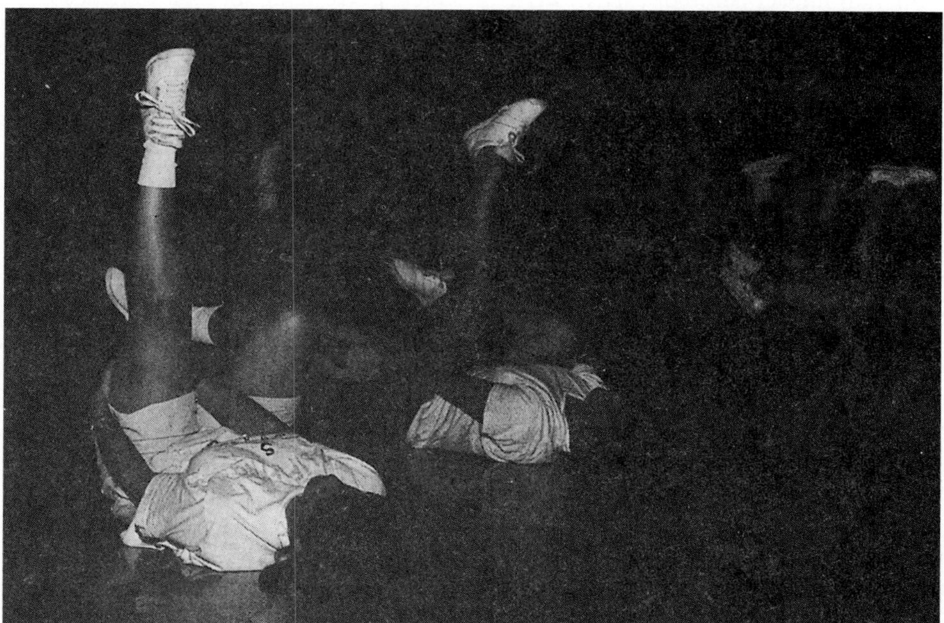

Figure 3-6. Hamstrings stretch.

fered by aerobic dancers found a fairly high incidence of injury to the shins, feet, knees, and lower back. Although the injuries were seldom serious enough to require medical attention, concern that high-impact movements were in part responsible for these aches and pains led to the development of a new form of aerobic dance called low-impact aerobics (LIA). LIA, characterized by movements that use a wide base of support while keeping one foot on the floor at all times, has not been without its share of unique problems and injuries.

In an attempt to stay close to the floor during LIA, the use of a wide base of support and the extreme lowering and raising of the center of gravity produces a great deal of prolonged and often extreme knee flexion. This can result in a number of knee injuries for individuals already suffering from structural knee problems. In addition, the larger arm movements used to maintain exercise intensity during LIA have resulted in shoulder injuries among participants using uncontrolled arm-flinging motions.

Generally, LIA is not recommended for anyone who complains of knee discomfort during prolonged knee flexion or for well-conditioned individuals who are unable to achieve appropriate intensity levels using low-impact movements. On the other hand, HIA is generally not recommended for individuals who are deconditioned, especially if they are obese; for women in the latter stages of pregnancy; for anyone who is susceptible to injuries related to impact shock, such as shinsplints; or for individuals who are uncomfortable with high-impact steps, such as people suffering from incontinence. To accommodate individual differences in each class, many programs use a combination of high- and low-impact steps throughout the aerobic routines. This results in a decrease in the number of high-impact steps being performed.

A compromise that combines the best elements of HIA and LIA is called moderate-impact aerobics (MIA). MIA movements require that one foot remain on the floor most of the time, as in LIA, although the base of support is narrower and the center of gravity is lifted up and down as in HIA. MIA steps are therefore characterized by a springlike motion. All MIA movements should begin by lifting the body upward, rising onto the balls of the feet. Each step should be completed by gently pressing the heels against the floor. The advantages of MIA include less-prolonged and -extreme knee flexion than often associated with LIA, and smaller vertical impacts than found in many HIA movements.

Other aerobic training modes

Traditionally the aerobic segment of an aerobic dance class consisted of continuous exercise. Today interval and circuit training have become common in both aerobics and step.

Aerobic interval training involves high-intensity work bouts (near maximal heart rate) followed by active rest or recovery periods of an equal length of time. Exercise and rest intervals vary from 1 to 3 minutes in length and are repeated 5 to 12 times during the aerobic segment of class. Because interval training requires high-intensity exercise during the work bouts, high-impact or propulsive movements such as jumps are commonly choreographed to fast-paced music. During the active rest, moderately paced movements such as walks and step touches are performed. Due to the fast-paced, high-intensity nature of interval training, this activity is recommended only for the more advanced participant. Interval training is associated with more physical pain than is experienced in continuous forms of training, because more metabolic waste products are produced and accumulated in the muscles during the near-maximal efforts of the activity.

Circuit training is another popular technique used in aerobic dance programs. A circuit consists of a specified number of exercise stations used to promote all-around physical fitness. The emphasis is on development of muscular strength and endurance, cardiovascular endurance, flexibility, and sometimes coordination and balance. Most circuits have 10 to 20 stations. Each area is posted with a sign indicating the task to be completed. Participants are instructed to remain at a station for a set amount of time (30 to 60 seconds) and move to the next station on command. The circuit moves in a clockwise or counterclockwise direction and can be repeated two to three times. Many other creative formats are possible. For example, cardio/strength intervals are popular. This type of class might alternate a 4-minute cardio segment (either step or aerobic dance) with a 4-minute muscle-conditioning segment. The muscle-conditioning segments might include squats and standing side leg lifts, unilateral bent-over rows and triceps extensions, overhead presses, biceps curls, and abdominal work. An advantage of this type of format is the increased amount of total work accomplished.

TEACHING CONSIDERATIONS

Patterns of Class Organization

Group exercise class should be arranged so that everyone can hear the instructor's verbal cues and see the demonstrations. Above all, it is important that the instructor be able to observe all class participants. In a typical class, the instructor stands at the front of the room with the participants facing forward. The disadvantage of this system is that the advanced participants usually stand at the front of the room while the less skilled stay at the back. The instructor cannot clearly observe those who are in greatest need of feedback. To resolve this problem, the instructor can periodically move from the front of the room to the back or the sides, asking participants to turn and face the instructor. A system of rotation is another effective way of observing class participants. At the end of each song the teacher instructs the participants to rotate. The front line moves to the back of the room while every other line moves forward one row. Other patterns of class organization include circle formations (where the instructor stands at the center) and movement patterns that travel from one end of the floor to the other.

Cuing

Cuing is a very important part of teaching group exercise, particularly when the moves must be performed to music. Participants depend on the instructor's verbal and nonverbal cues for every step they take. Each anticipatory verbal cue should be brief and called on the preceding measure, giving ample time to move smoothly from one step to the next. Instructors can use a combination of types of anticipatory cuing, including footwork cuing (indicates whether to move the right or left foot), directional cuing (refers to the direction of movement: forward, backward, left, or right), rhythmic cuing (indicates the correct rhythm of the routine, such as slow or quick), numerical cuing (refers to counting the rhythm, such as "one, two, three, and four"), and step cuing (indicates the name of the step, such as "step touch"). Initially participants will be most dependent on footwork, directional, and numerical cuing. Once they become somewhat skilled and learn the names of each step or movement pattern, the participants will rely more on step cues and pay most attention to nonverbal cues, such as hand signals indicating direction. In addition to anticipatory cues, skilled instructors provide educational cues (or information), safety and alignment cues, and motivational cues. An example of an educational cue would be "This exercise is for your lats, which are *here*" (instructor points to her own lats). "Be sure to control the movement on the way down to minimize stress to the joints" is an example of a safety cue. "Terrific!" and "I like the way you're all concentrating on good form!" are motivational cues.

When leading most aerobic routines, the instructor should face the class and use mirroring techniques (the instructor moves to the left when the class moves to the right). To avoid potential collisions between students, instructors should begin lateral movements to the same side each time. Most instructors prefer moving first to the right and then to the left.

Music

Music provides the timing and style for exercise movements. In addition, it adds fun, variety, and excitement to class. The tempo, or rate of speed, at which music is played determines the progression and intensity of exercise. Instructors can determine the tempo of the music by counting the beats per minute (bpm). Over the years, the following guidelines have been adopted by instructors for selecting appropriate music tempo for land-based aerobic classes:

Warm-up, prestretch, and cool-down: 120 to 140 bpm
Floor exercise: 110 to 130 bpm
Aerobic activity: 130 to 160 bpm (LIA); 144 to 160 bpm (HIA)
Step aerobics: 120 to 128 bpm
Final stretch: under 100 bpm

Instructors must be cautious when using fast music tempos (more than 150 bpm). To avoid uncontrolled movements, participants should be encouraged to use the arms through a small range of motion and take short steps. Because beginners are not proficient enough to perform fast movements under control, they should not be expected to exercise to fast-paced music. When using music with fast tempos, instructors should be aware that participants with long arms and legs need more time than participants with short limbs to cover the same spatial area. For example, people with short arms can raise them above their heads more quickly than people with long arms. Tall participants should therefore be encouraged to bend their arms in order to keep in time with fast music. The most efficient way to use music in class is to record a 40- to 60-minute audiotape that includes music for the warm-up, prestretch, aerobic segment, cool-down, floor exercises, and final stretch. However, instructors reproducing and playing music in an aerobic dance class should be familiar with the copyright laws. The Copyright Act of 1976 states that a person wishing to play copyrighted music for a "public performance" must obtain permission from the copyright owner. Using music during a group exercise class constitutes a public performance. Because it would be time-consuming to obtain permission from the copyright owner of each piece of music used in a class, instructors can save valuable time by joining performing rights societies (ASCAP and BMI). These societies have been assigned the nondramatic rights of copyright owners and grant their members permission to play the music of numerous artists. Under the "fair use" doctrine, instructors teaching in the public schools or at institutions of higher education may be exempt from having to obtain copyright permission. It is wise, however, for instructors to consult with an attorney to determine if their use of music qualifies as "fair use."

Developing music tapes can be one of the most time-consuming tasks for the instructor. To save valuable time and to stay current with popular music selections, instructors can subscribe to a number of music services that provide complete audiotapes for all segments of many different types of classes (see the Resources section at the end of this chapter).

SAFETY CONCERNS

To ensure the safety of class participants, instructors should comply with the following guidelines:

1. Screen participants for common anatomical problems, such as kyphosis, lordosis, and excess pronation of the feet. Also evaluate them for tight or weak muscles. Early detection and correction of such problems can reduce the risk of injuries.
2. Encourage appropriate body alignment throughout the class period. Proper posture includes: head up, shoulders back, chest up, buttocks tucked under the hips, and knees relaxed.
3. Avoid or minimize the use of the following potentially harmful exercise positions: (a) sustained and unsupported forward flexion in a standing position, (b) unsupported forward flexion in a standing position with rotation, (c) trunk rotation against a fixed axis, (d) neck hyperextension, (e) fast head circles, (f) the

yoga plough, (g) deep knee bends, (h) hurdler stretch, (i) hyperextension of the elbows and knees, (j) straight-leg sit-up, (k) double leg raises, and (l) side leg lifts supported on the knees and hands or elbows.

4. Avoid ballistic stretching. Static stretching is effective and tends to be safer than bobbing or bouncing techniques.
5. Insist that participants wear shoes during the aerobic segment of class.
6. Be aware of the placement of class members to avoid collisions during rapid movements across the floor.
7. Encourage participants to control the placement of their arms, avoiding any flinging motions. Shoulder injuries are becoming increasingly common in aerobic dance and step.
8. Avoid having the participants keep their arms at or above shoulder level for a prolonged period of time. This increases blood pressure, places stress on the tendons and muscles of the shoulder, and increases heart rate in a manner not beneficial to increased cardiovascular conditioning.
9. Avoid prolonged and excessive deep knee flexion. Make sure the knees of participants remain over the first and second toes.
10. Be cautious of lateral movements on carpeted surfaces. The added friction associated with carpet can result in ankle inversion sprains.
11. Avoid impact on concrete surfaces.
12. Reduce the risk of common musculoskeletal injuries during aerobic activity by progressing slowly and by not exceeding intensity levels of 85 percent of heart rate reserve, exercise durations of 30 minutes, and exercise frequencies of 4 days per week on alternate days.
13. Avoid too many consecutive movements on one foot, such as dozens of hops.
14. Avoid rapid changes of direction.
15. Participants should avoid staying on the balls of their feet for extended periods of time. The lowering of the heels to the floor provides additional shock absorption for the feet.
16. Face the class as often as possible to effectively observe everyone's performance.
17. Do not allow the participants to hold their breath while performing strength exercises. Encourage them to exhale on exertion.
18. Control the movement of hand and ankle weights at all times.
19. Be aware of exercise restrictions and modifications for special populations. For example, people with high blood pressure should not perform isometric contractions and should avoid keeping the arms above shoulder level for extended periods of time.
20. Platform height: deconditioned participants should begin on 4 inches, highly skilled and experienced steppers can use up to 10 inches. The knee joint should not flex deeper than 90 degrees when the knee is fully loaded.
21. When stepping up, lean from the ankles and not the waist, to avoid excessive stress on the lumbar spine.
22. Contact the platform with the entire sole of the foot. To avoid Achilles tendon injury, do not allow the heel to land over the edge of the platform.
23. Step close to the platform (no more than one shoe length away) and allow the heels to contact the floor to help absorb shock. On lunges and repeaters, do not push the heel into the floor.
24. Change the leading foot after no more than 1 minute.
25. Do not perform propulsion steps (both feet off the floor or platform at the same time) for more than 1 minute at a time. Propulsion steps result in higher vertical impact forces and are considered an advanced technique.
26. Do not perform more than five consecutive repeaters on the same leg.
27. It is recommended that weights be reserved for the strength segment of a step training class, due to the increased potential for shoulder joint injury when weights are rapidly moved through a large range of motion. (Reebok International 1993).

GLOSSARY

aerobic dance Continuous and rhythmic movement to music intended to improve cardiovascular fitness.

choreographed routine Formally arranged step patterns taught in the same sequence each time the routine is performed to the same music.

circuit training A form of exercise that promotes all-around physical fitness by incorporating various stations involving strength, aerobic, and agility activities.

combination Two or more movement patterns that are sequenced together and repeated in a cycle.

continuous training A form of aerobic training that requires the continuous performance of moderate to vigorous movement over a specified period of time.

cuing Verbal and nonverbal techniques that inform participants of upcoming movements, safety, alignment and increase motivation.

duration of exercise The total time of each exercise session.

flexibility The range of motion possible at a joint.

freestyle routine Aerobic movements performed in a random fashion, building combinations of step patterns as the music progresses.

frequency of exercise The total number of exercise sessions per week.

HIA (high-impact aerobics) An aerobic dance style characterized by movement that frequently requires both feet to leave the floor simultaneously.

intensity of exercise A form of aerobic and anaerobic training that involves performing a series of high-intensity work bouts alternating with active rest periods.

linear progression A movement that advances into another, changing only one variable at a time, such as the leg or arm movement, the direction of movement, or the rhythm.

LIA (low-impact aerobics) An aerobic dance style that minimizes the amount of vertical impacts by keeping one foot on the floor at all times while covering a larger spatial area with the feet and arms.

MIA (moderate-impact aerobics) An aerobic dance style requiring that one foot remain on the floor most of the time while lifting the body high onto the balls of the feet and then gently pressing the heels to the floor.

muscular strength Maximum force exerted by a muscle or muscle group against resistance.

step aerobics An aerobic mode performed to music utilizing a 4- to 10-inch step bench.

target heart rate zone The number of heart beats per specified period of time necessary to achieve aerobic benefits while minimizing possible musculoskeletal injury.

tempo Rate of speed music is played, determined by counting the number of beats per minute (bpm).

REFERENCES

IHRSA/American Sports Data Health Club Trend Report, American Sports Data Inc, Hartsdale, NY. 1996.

Step Manual, 1993, Reebok International, Reebok University Press Publisher, Boston, MA.

SUGGESTED READINGS

Aerobic and Fitness Association of America; Jordan, P., ed. 1995. *Fitness theory and practice,* Sherman Oaks, Calif.: HDL Publishing.

Casten, C., and Jordan, P. 1990 *Aerobics today.* St Paul: West.

Cotton, R. ed. 1993. *Aerobics instructor manual.* San Diego: American Council on Exercise/Reebok.

Francis, L. 1993. *Keeping fit with aerobic dance.* Dubuque, Iowa: WCB/McGraw-Hill.

Kan, E., and Kraines, M. 1991. *Keep moving! It's aerobic dance.* Palo Alto, Calif.: Mayfield.

Kennedy, C., and Legel, D. 1992. *Anatomy of an exercise class.* Champaign, Ill.: Sagamore.

Kravitz, L. 1986. *Anybody's guide to total fitness.* Dubuque, Iowa: Kendall/Hunt.

Mazzeo, K.S. 1992. *Aerobic dance: A way to fitness* (3d ed.). Englewood, Colo.: Morton. Includes an explanation of the "mirroring" presentation style of photography used in the book and how the written and spoken cues match what the reader sees. Also provides tear-out charts.

Mazzeo, K.S. 1996. *Fitness through aerobics and step training* (2d ed.). Englewood, Colo.: Morton. An abridged version of *Aerobic dance: a way to fitness.*

Mazzeo, K.S., and Mangili, L.M. 1993. *Step training plus.* Englewood, Colo.: Morton.

Spitzer, T., and Hoeger, W. 1990. *Physical fitness: The water aerobics way.* Englewood, Colo.: Morton.

Stanforth, D., and Ellison, D. 1997. *Aerobic dance exercise.* Dubuque, Iowa: WCB/McGraw-Hill.

Stanforth, D., and Ellison, D. 1997. *Aerobic dance exercise.* St. Louis: Mosby.

RESOURCES

Aerobic dance associations

Aerobic and Fitness Association of America (AFAA), 15250 Ventura Blvd, Suite 310, Sherman Oaks, CA 91403.

American Council on Exercise, 5820 Oberlin Dr., Suite 102, San Diego, CA 92121.

International Dance Exercise Association (IDEA), 6190 Cornerstone E, Suite 204, San Diego, CA 92121.

Reebok Professional Instructor Alliance (a free service to aerobic dance instructors), 100 Technology Center Dr., Stoughton, MA 02072.

Films and videotapes

Brick, L. *How to teach aerobics.* Brick Bodies, 212 W Padonia Rd., Titonium, MD 21093.

Dantzler, S. *Aerobics!!! The ultimate fat-burning workout.* Athletic Institute, 200 Castlewood Dr., North Palm Beach, FL 33408.

Kooperman, S. *Chicago jazz'd funk: instructor training video.* Sara's City Workout, 1876 N Sheffield, Chicago, IL 60614.

Ottis, R. *Sportsmoves: instructor video.* Ottis Training Organization, P.O. Box 402203, Austin, TX 78704.

Twombly, G. *Creative instructors aerobics.* 2314 Naudian St., Philadelphia, PA 19146.

Music services

The Aerobic Beat, 7985 Santa Monica Blvd., Suite 109, Los Angeles, CA 90046.

David Shelton Productions, P.O. Box 310, Mendon, UT 84325.

Dynamix, 733 W. 40th St., Suite 10, Baltimore, MD 21211

Fitnet, 1131 Harbor Bay Parkway, Suite 121, Alemeda, CA 94501.

Mix Music International, P.O. 2452, Kankakee, IL 60901.

Muscle Mixes, 623 N Hyer Ave., Orlando, FL 32803.

MusicFlex, P.O. Box 140435, Queens, NY 11414

Power Productions, 1303 S. Swaner Rd., Salt Lake City, UT 84104

SportsMusic, Box 769689, Roswell, GA 30076

Music performing rights societies

ASCAP, 1 Lincoln Plaza, New York, NY 10023.

BMI, 320 W 57th St., New York, NY 10019.

Archery

After completing this chapter, the reader should be able to:

- Recognize and select appropriate archery equipment
- Understand rules and scoring procedures
- Describe the best technique for stringing the bow
- Describe the steps involved in shooting
- Identify and use proper safety procedures
- Instruct a group of students in the fundamentals of archery
- Recognize and use archery terms correctly

HISTORY

The bow and arrow is one of the oldest mechanical weapons and remains the weapon of many aboriginal peoples in certain parts of the world. The bow and arrow was first used by primitive peoples for hunting. It was the chief weapon of the American Indians, both for hunting and for war. It was used as a weapon by the Egyptians in overthrowing Persia and in many other wars.

With the development of gunpowder and firearms in comparatively recent times, the bow and arrow has been retired to the realm of sport. In this capacity it has sporadically interested groups in various parts of the world, particularly in England and the United States, but archery has not flourished to the same extent as many other sports.

The earliest archery contest, The Ancient Scorton Arrow, was created by the Ancient Scorton Arrow Society in England in 1673. This tournament is still in existence.

In the United States the first archery club, the United Bowmen of Philadelphia, was organized in 1828. The first tournament was held in Chicago in 1879, and tournaments sponsored by this club are still being held.

The formation of the Federation Internationale de Tir à l'Arc (FITA) in 1931 gave a great boost to target archery. A demonstration sport in the 1900 and 1904 Olympics, archery was given full status in 1908, and then was dropped after the 1920 games. Through the efforts of FITA, archery was reinstated as a gold medal sport in the 1972 Olympic Games. Since this time the United States has done extremely well in archery competition, winning the individual men's gold medal at every Olympic Games with the exception of the 1980 Games in Moscow, which the United States boycotted (gold won by Tomi Poikolainen) and the 1992 Games (gold won by Sebastian Flute). Beginning the winning tradition for the U.S. men was John Williams, 1972 gold medalist. Darrell Pace won in 1976 and 1984, and Jay Barrs placed first in 1988. The 1996 Olympic Games held in Atlanta, Georgia, were a huge success for U.S. archery. Justin Huish won the individual gold medal and was joined by Richard "Butch" Johnson and Rod White to win the team gold. The U.S. women archers dominated the 1972 Olympic Games (Doreen Wilbur, gold medalist) and 1976 Olympic Games (Luann Ryon, gold medalist); but since the boycott of the 1980 Moscow Olympics (won by Keto Losaberidze, USSR), dominance has shifted to the South Korean women.

A new shooting format was used at the 1996 Olympic Games in order to increase public awareness and gain television viewer support for archery. The format includes an elimination round, which was first introduced by FITA in 1986. The current Olympic system includes a 72-arrow ranking score shot at 70 meters. Because the new Olympic format allows for only 64 men and 64 women to attend the Games, each archer is ranked according to the 72-arrow score and placed in a bracket, then shoots the first round of the eliminations (3 ends of 6 arrows for a possible score 180). The elimination bracket continues to work in the same way (3 ends of 6 arrows) until the semifinals, where the format changes to matches of 4 ends of 3 arrows with an alternating shot format.

In 1971, the College Division of the National Archery Association was founded in order to coordinate and promote collegiate archery throughout the United States. A national tournament is hosted and rotated each year throughout the United States. For more information on the College Division of the NAA, contact the NAA (One Olympic Plaza, Colorado Springs, CO 80909).

Today archery continues to hold interest for several reasons: (1) the introduction of the elimination round and head-to-head competition, (2) development of more efficient bows, arrows, and other archery equipment, and (3) the fascination many people find in the activities possible for the archer, ranging from target shooting, clout, field shooting, and novelty shoots to the hunting of small and large game.

EQUIPMENT

The Bow

The two types of bows most commonly used are the recurve bow (figure 4-1) and the compound bow (figure 4-2). The compound bow's pulley system and its sophisticated weighting, balancing, and sighting devices have completely revolutionized the sport of archery. Of course, these advances have increased the cost of the sport substantially, so the recurve bow is still popular, especially among beginners and Olympic hopefuls.

One should select a bow that one can pull back to full draw and hold steady while aiming. This is determined by the weight of the bow—that is, the number of pounds of pull it takes to pull the arrow to its full length. Proper bow weight varies with the age, sex, and strength of the archer. These are general recommendations for bow weights: teenage girls, 20 to 25 pounds (9 to 11.25 kg); teenage boys, 20 to 30 pounds (9 to 13.5 kg); women, 20 to 30 pounds (9 to 13.5 kg); and men, 25 to 40 pounds (11.25 to 15 kg).

The proper length of the bow is related to the length of the draw.

Draw length (inches)	Recommended bow length (inches)
24 or less (61 cm or less)	60 to 64 (152 to 163 cm)
25 to 26 (63.5 to 66 cm)	65 to 66 (165 to 168 cm)
27 to 28 (68.6 to 71.1 cm)	67 to 68 (170 to 173 cm)
29 or more (73.7 cm or more)	69 to 70 (175 to 178 cm)

Today's bows are made of fiberglass, wood, fiberglass-laminated wood, carbon, synthetic foam, ceramic, and aluminum alloy. Bow prices run from around $20 for a child's bow to $2,000 for a top-of-the-line target bow. Several bowmakers supply both recurve and compound bows costing around $200 that make respectable beginner bows.

Strings are usually made of Dacron or Fast Flight. Dacron strings are still used in most school and camp programs and in some compound bows. Most serious archers use Fast Flight, which gives a more consistent brace height and is as durable as Dacron.

Points to consider when selecting a bow

1. Purpose: Will the bow be used for target shooting, hunting, or both?
2. Shooting right- or left-handed: See the section below on eye dominance.
3. Bow weight: Select a bow that can be held without straining.
4. Limbs: Make sure they are straight, not twisted.

Eye dominance

Most coaches believe that an archer's potential is increased if he or she shoots with the hand on the same side as the dominant eye. Eye dominance must be determined if the archer chooses to shoot with both eyes open. If the archer

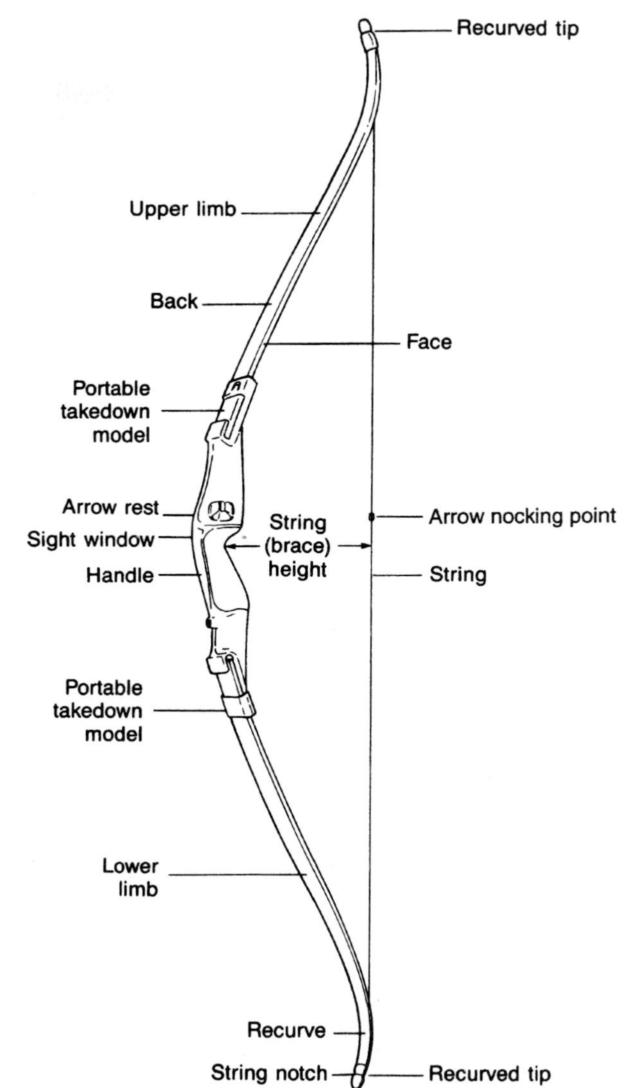

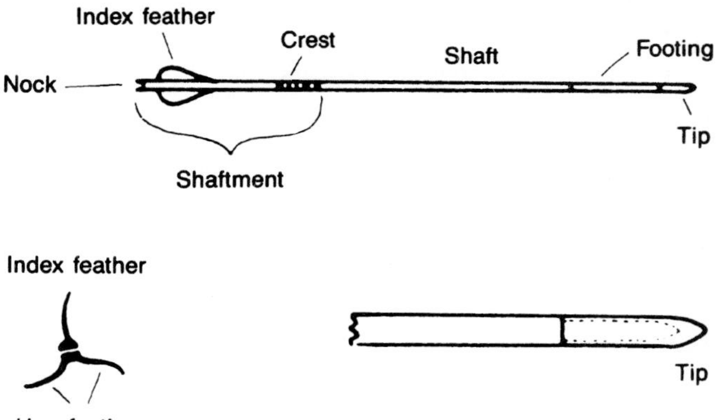

Figure 4-1. Parts of the bow and arrow..

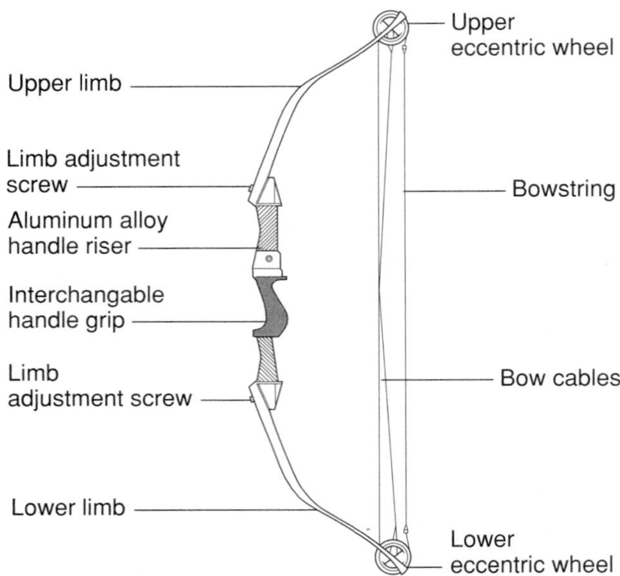

Figure 4-2. Compound bow.

Figure 4-3. Eye dominance.

chooses to shoot with one eye closed, eye dominance is not a determining factor in shooting right- or left-handed and the archer should shoot on the side he or she is accustomed to using. If the archer is unable to keep an eye closed, a patch can be used to cover the eye.

To determine eye dominance, stretch your arms out to their full length. Put your hands together to form a hold between the thumb and fingers (figure 4-3). Aim at a spot while keeping both eyes open. Bring your hands toward your face, continuing to aim at the same spot. When your hands reach your face, the opening will be in front of your dominant eye.

The Arrow

Arrows are made of four types of material: wood, fiberglass, aluminum, or carbon graphite. Arrows made of wood are the most inexpensive, but they are rarely straight and they warp easily. Fiberglass arrows are much straighter and more durable than wood. They can take quite a bit of abuse and still be in good shape, which makes them a good choice for beginners.

For serious archers, aluminum and carbon graphite arrows are the most logical choice. These arrows are straighter and lighter and can be matched to suit each archer's individual needs. These characteristics increase the flight speed of the arrows and allow for better flight out of the bow. Aluminum and carbon graphite arrows are more expensive and possibly less durable than wood and fiberglass, but for the experienced archer the benefits of shooting this type of arrow outweigh the consequences.

The arrow is one of the most important pieces of equipment in archery, so be sure to select the type of arrow that works best for you. If you need help, ask a staff person at an archery pro shop to advise you on arrow selection or use an arrow chart to determine what size arrow will best meet your needs.

When selecting arrows, there are three factors to consider: arrow length, arrow spine, and the type of vane or fletching. To determine arrow length, draw an oversized arrow to full draw. The arrow should be marked in 1-inch increments. Select the arrow length that is closest to 1 inch past the back of the bow.

"Arrow spine" refers to the stiffness of the arrow shaft. Arrows with different spines will fly differently when shot from the same bow. When you have a choice of spines, consult an arrow spine chart to determine the best selection. Experimentation will allow you to find the arrow length, spine, and point size that work best for you.

Once you have selected the arrow size, you must determine whether to use vanes or feathers and what size is best. Feathers are most suited to indoor archery because they stabilize the arrow's flight more quickly than vanes and reduce the arrow's speed, which causes them to drift in the wind when used outdoors. Vanes are made of several types of plastic and are best suited for outdoor shooting. Vanes do not stabilize arrows as well as feathers, but they help arrows fly much faster. Both feathers and vanes come in a variety of sizes, so experimentation will be necessary to find what works best for you.

Protective Devices

Finger protection (see figure 4-4) is necessary for all archers. Without it, the archer's shots will be inaccurate and painfully executed. There are two types of finger pro-

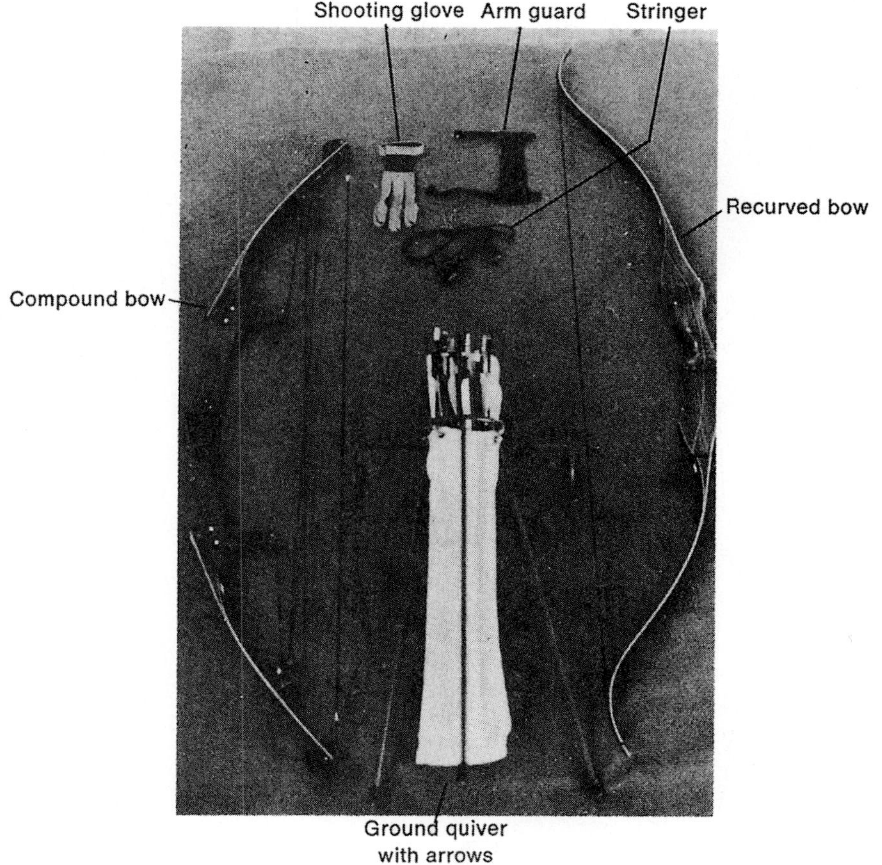

Figure 4-4. Archery equipment.

tection: (1) the finger tab, leather tab patterned to fit the index, middle, and ring fingers; and (2) the shooting glove, similar to an ordinary glove without the thumb and little finger. A compound bow may be shot with a mechanical release aid. The arm guard protects the forearm of the bow arm from string contact.

The Target

Homemade targets and stands are usually considered the least expensive and best option for beginning archers.

The tripod stand should consist of three pine boards, 3 inches × 1 inch × 6 feet (7.5 cm × 2.5 cm × 1.8 m) long. It should incline backward about 10 to 15 degrees from the vertical (figure 4-5).

The target butt is approximately 4 feet (1.2 m) in diameter and 4 or 5 inches (10–12.5 cm) thick. It is constructed from rye straw or marsh hay wound tightly in a coil and held firmly together with tarred cord. Ethafoam targets have recently been used in target shooting due to their light weight, durability, and easy maneuverability.

The target face is made with heavy reinforced paper. Five colored circles are painted on the face with two

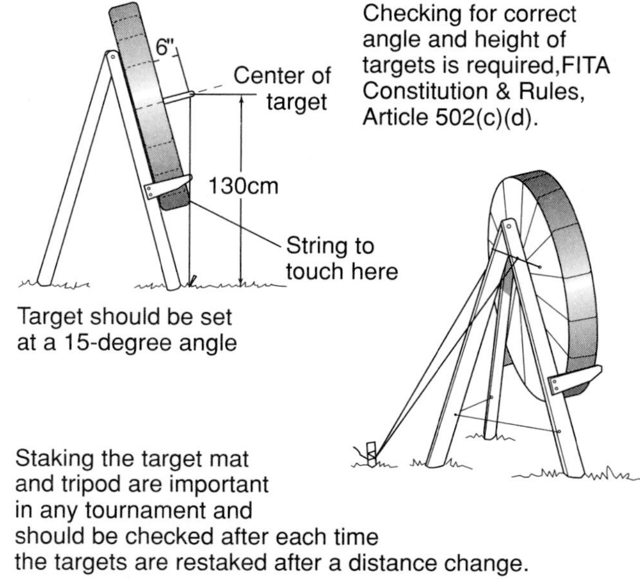

Figure 4-5. Target height and angle.

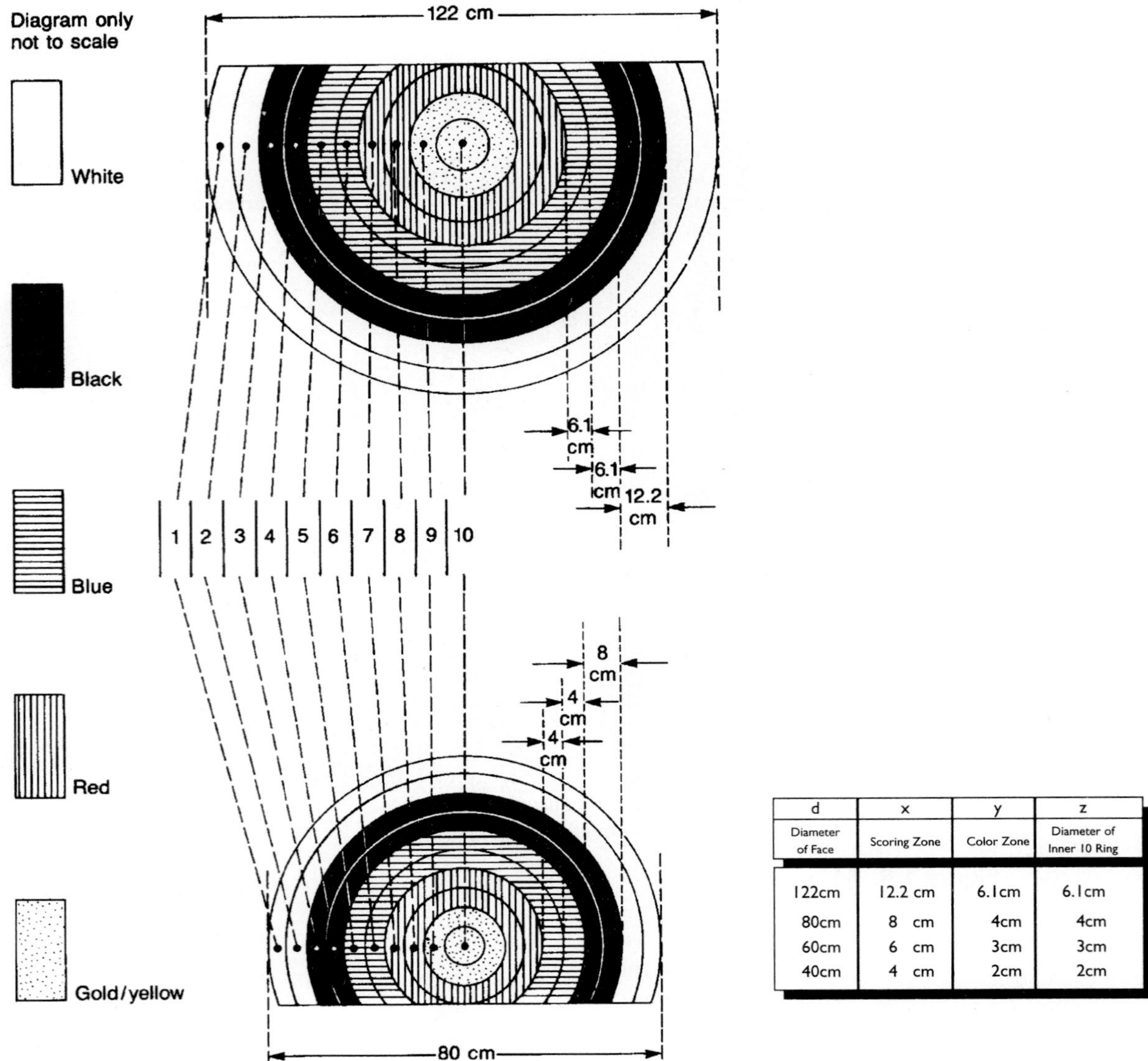

d	x	y	z
Diameter of Face	Scoring Zone	Color Zone	Diameter of Inner 10 Ring
122cm	12.2 cm	6.1cm	6.1cm
80cm	8 cm	4cm	4cm
60cm	6 cm	3cm	3cm
40cm	4 cm	2cm	2cm

Figure 4-6. Ten-ring target. (To convert centimeters to inches, multiply centimeters by 0.4.)

scoring rings being represented by each color. The center is painted gold, followed by red, blue, black, and white circles. The target should be hung so that the exact enter of the gold circle is 4 feet from the ground. Different sizes of target faces are used for different distances (figure 4-6).

RULES (USA)

The three major organizations governing the sport of archery are the National Archery Association (NAA), the National Field Archery Association (NFAA), and the International Bowhunters Organization (IBO).

NAA tournaments are conducted under FITA international rules, which place limitations on the equipment used. See table 4-1 for various types of tournaments. For example, a release aid and sight magnification may be used by compound shooters but not by recurve shooters. Compound shooters are also limited to a 60-pound maximum draw weight.

The NFAA tournament structure also includes many classifications and categories (such as limited and unlimited) that govern the equipment each archer may add to the bow.

Tournaments conducted by the IBO involve competitions that simulate hunting. Various categories, including types of bows and age separation, are used.

Crossbow archers shoot in competitions organized by the National Crossbow Association; they do not compete officially against recurve or field shooters.

Table 4-1. TARGET ROUNDS

FITA round	Number of arrows	Distance (m)	Face (cm)	FITA round	Number of arrows	Distance (m)	Face (cm)
Men and intermediate	36	90	122	New Olympic round			
boys	36	70	122	(64 individuals			
	36	50	80	seeded 1 to 64)			
	36	30	80	Round of			
Women and	36	70	122	64	18†	70	122
intermediate girls	36	60	122	32	18	70	122
	36	50	80	16	18	70	122
	36	30	80	8	12‡	70	122
Junior metric round	36	60	122	4	12	70	122
	36	50	122	2	12	70	122
	36	40	80	Indoor FITA round I§	30	18	40
	36	30	80	Indoor FITA round II§	30	25	60
Cadet metric round	38	45	122	Miniature round (indoor)‖	60	15	2 ft.
	36	35	122	Range round (indoor)‖	60	#	2 ft.
	36	25	80	Junior scholastic round‖	24	30††	122
	36	15	80		24	20††	122
900 m round: men,	30	60	122	Columbia round‖	24	50††	122
women, intermediate	30	50	122		24	40††	122
boys and girls	30	40	122		24	30††	122
Junior 900 m round	30	50	122	Junior Columbia round‖	24	40††	122
	30	40	122		24	30††	122
	30	30	122		24	20††	122
Cadet 900 m round	30	40	122	Clout round**			
	30	30	122	Men and intermediate	36	165††	—
	30	20	122	boys			
Easton 600 m round*	20	60	122	Women and	36	125††	—
	20	50	122	intermediate girls			
	20	40	122	Junior and Cadet boys	36	110††	—
Collegiate 600 m round*	20	50	122	and girls			
	20	40	122				
	20	30	122				

*Four ends of five arrows per end at each distance.
†Three ends of six arrows.
‡Two ends of six arrows.
§Arrows are shot in ends of three arrows, and scoring is tallied after each end. A 2½-minute limit is allowed for each end.
‖Not an official NAA round, but may be used in school or camp tournaments.
#Sixty arrows from a single distance of 50, 40, 30, or 20 m (55, 44, 33, or 22 yards).
**The clout target is circular, 14.5 m (48 feet) in diameter, divided into five concentric scoring zones each 1.22 m (4 feet) in width. The target may be marked on the ground, or the scoring lines may be determined by steel tape or nonstretch cord marked off at the dividing lines. The center is marked with a white marker, not more than 36 inches (90 cm) nor less than 30 inches (75 cm) square, standing perpendicular to the ground. Scoring values of each scoring zone from the center outward are 9, 7, 5, 3, 1.
††Yards

SCORING

According to FITA, in an outdoor tournament, six arrows are shot before scoring. The number of arrows shot before each scoring period is referred to as an "end." And end in an indoor tournament consists of three arrows. An arrow hitting the wrong target counts as a shot, but its score is forfeited. An arrow that has fallen within the reach of the archer (without moving the feet) can be shot for score. However, it is counted as a scoreless shot if it falls beyond the archer's reach.

An arrow that cuts two colors is always given the higher value of the two, even if the greater part of the arrow is in the ring of lower value. In tournament shooting, all arrow holes are marked when arrows are pulled from the target. If an arrow rebounds or passes through the target mat, the score is recorded as that of the unmarked hole. Scores are always listed with the highest score first, awarding 10, 9(gold), 8, 7(red), 6, 5(blue), 4, 3(black), and 2, 1(white) points for each arrow shot. Arrows must remain in the target until all are scored.

SAFETY PRECAUTION WHILE SHOOTING IN GROUPS

Each archer may approach the shooting line following two blasts of a whistle. The arrows are shot after one blast of a whistle. Each archer backs away from the shooting line, and all arrows may be retrieved when the whistle is blown three times. The cycle begins again when all archers are behind the shooting line and the whistle is blown two times. More than three blasts of the whistle means that a dangerous situation exists and the archers should stop shooting immediately and remove all arrows from their bows.

NAA TOURNAMENT SHOOTING

In NAA outdoor tournaments, arrows are shot and scored at four distances (six ends of 6 arrows at each distance.) Men shoot at 90 m, 70 m, 50 m, and 30 m. Women shoot at 70 m, 60 m, 50 m, and 30 m. A perfect score for 144 arrows is 1,440.

In an NAA indoor tournament, arrows are shot and scored at 18 m. Ten ends of 3 arrows are shot for a possible score of 300. A tournament consists of four rounds being shot for a possible total score of 1,200.

Both male and female archers are classified as follows:

Adult	18 years old and older
FITA Competitive	Anyone younger than 18 wishing to shoot adult distances
Intermediate	15–18 years old
Junior	12–15 years old
Cadet	less than 12 years old

The distances shot in a tournament vary according to the division in which you shoot.

Field Shooting

Because of the vast increase in bow hunting in this country, the National Field Archers' Association of Redlands, California, sponsors a type of tournament and practice range called field shooting. Fourteen or 28 targets of different sizes are placed at random over a course with both hills and valleys.

Groups of four archers shoot a "field round" and advance from target to target. Targets are black and white and have bull's-eye that counts 5 points and an outer ring that counts 3 points. Four arrows are shot at each target. The archer with the highest score is the winner.

FUNDAMENTAL SKILLS AND TECHNIQUES

Stringing the Bow

The safest way to string a bow is to use a bow bracer, often called a "bow stringer" (figure 4-7) A bow bracer is a length of braided cord with leather cups that fit over the tips of the bow limbs. To string the bow, place the top loop of the string over the top limb and slide it down until the bottom loop can be placed in the grooves of the lower limb. Then place the leather caps of the bow bracer over the tips of the limbs. Hold the bow parallel to the ground with the back of the bow facing up. The bow bracer cord should be on the ground. Step on the cord and pull the bow up. Guide the upper loop along the limb and slip it into the grooves at the end of the limb. Let the bow down slowly, and check to see if the loops are securely in the grooves.

Figure 4-7. Stringing the recurved bow.

Checking the Bow After Stringing

Make sure that the loop is slipped completely into the notch and that the bowstring is centered. The distance from the string to the deepest part of the handle should measure about 8½ to 9½ inches (21.6 to 24.1 cm), which may be measured roughly by making a fist and letting the thumb extend perpendicularly from it. This is called the fistmele or brace height.

Unstringing (Unbracing) the Bow

The process is exactly the same as stringing, except that the string is pulled out of the notch, and the loop is slid down over the upper limb.

PREPARATION FOR THE DRAW

Stance

The archer stands astride the shooting line in such a way that the body is perpendicular to the line. The bow arm is held at a 90-degree angle to the body and pointed directly toward the target. The archer's feet should be spread about

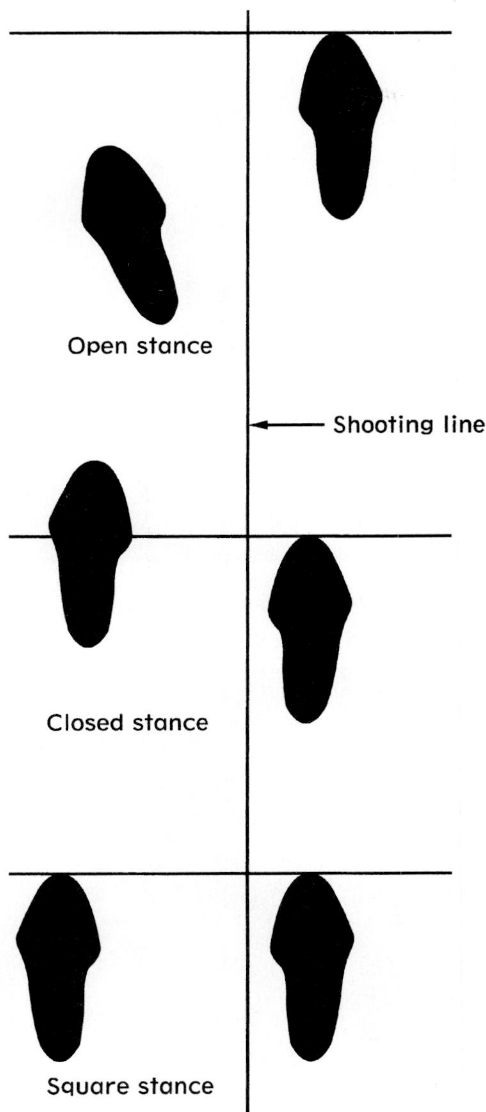

Figure 4-8. Three types of shooting stances.

shoulder-width apart and the body and head should be held in a normally erect, comfortable position. This posture should allow for a complete absence of tension. Three types of stances are shown in figure 4-8. Choose the stance that feels most comfortable to you. Beginners usually start with the open or square stance.

Possible errors in stance

1. Both feet on the same side of the line
2. Feet too close or too far apart
3. Too much weight on one foot

Position of the Bow Hand

As you raise the bow to shooting position, allow the hand to bend at the wrist so that the pressure of the bow is against

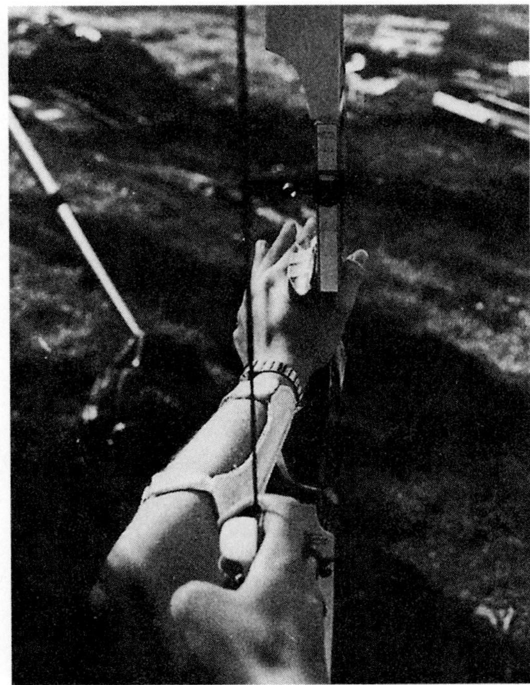

Figure 4-9. Bow-hand position.

the part of the palm just inside the base of the thumb. Allow the thumb and fingers to encircle the bow very lightly—just enough to keep it from falling. Never tightly grip or squeeze the bow (figure 4-9).

Position of the String Hand

For best release of the arrow, begin by hooking the first, second, and third fingers of the drawing hand onto the string. The index finger should be above the arrow and the other two fingers below it with the first joint of each finger wrapped around the string.

NOCKING

For best clearance, make sure that the index feather (odd colored) is perpendicular to the string, pointing away from the bow on a recurve bow. On a compound bow, the index feather position varies according to what type of arrow rest is being used. A nock locator used as a reference point is placed on the string at a position such that the arrow will make a 90-degree angle when placed on the string. The nock locator should be tight against the string, and the arrow should be nocked below the nock locator (see figure 4-10).

THE DRAW AND TRANSITION PERIOD

To begin the draw, the bow arm should be lifted to the desired shooting positions, followed by a simultaneous pushing of the elbow arm and pulling with the string arm.

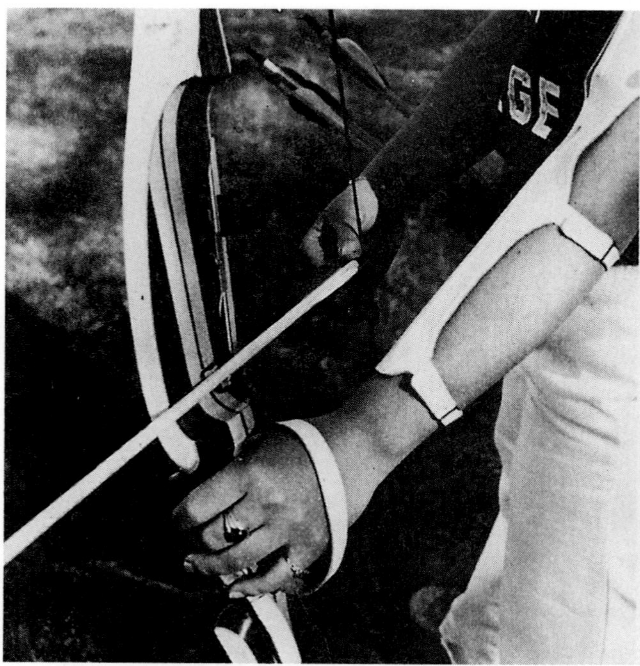

Figure 4-10. Correct nocking position.

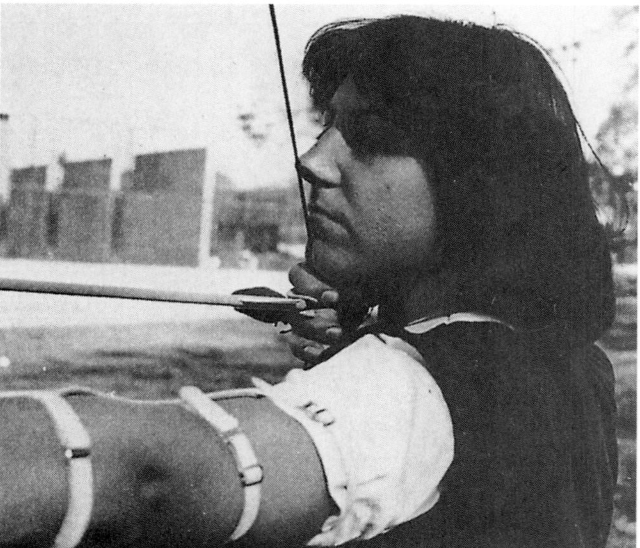

Figure 4-11. Anchor position (low, or under-the-chin, anchor).

As the draw is made, equal pressure should be placed on the bow arm and string arm.

At full draw, the bow arm should be raised to shoulder height, and the elbow should have as little bend as possible. In sight shooting, the string hand is brought back to the face with the index finger placed under the chin in constant motion along the jawbone. The string bisects both the chin and the nose for additional reference points (figure 4-11). A consistent transition period is one of the most important phases in becoming a good archer. At full draw, the elbow of the string arm should be in line with the arrow.

In point-of-aim shooting, the string hand is brought back to the face; the string passes the nose to the side, and the index finger is locked in place under the cheekbone (figure 4-12).

Possible errors in the draw

Bow arm:

1. Elbow straight or hyperextended
2. Elbow bent too much
3. Left shoulder hunched

String arm:

1. Anchor point too far forward, too high, or below the chin
2. Some part of the hand other than the end segment of the forefinger or the string touches the anchor point
3. Elbow too high or too low

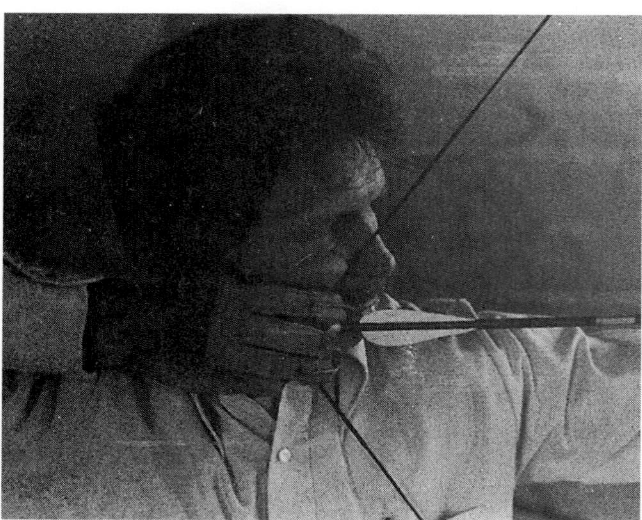

Figure 4-12. High anchor point for field shooting with point of aim.

Aim, Release, and Follow-Through

Point of aim

Point of aim is a satisfactory method of aiming for the beginner, although sights may be used. With any bow and arrow, there is only one distance at which a person may shoot and hit the center of the target by aiming directly at it while using point of aim. This will vary with the weight of the bow and with the length and weight of the arrow (figure 4-13). In order that the arrows may be grouped on the target at distances farther or closer than this point-blank range, the archer must use some auxiliary object in the background or foreground. This auxiliary object is known

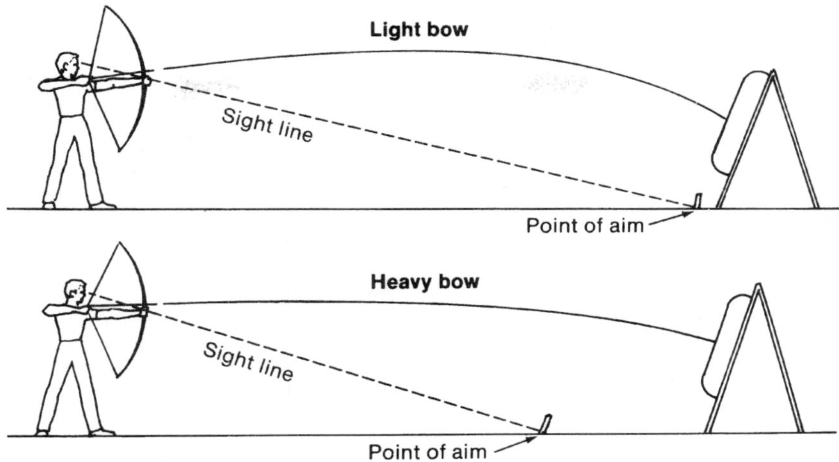

Figure 4-13. Effect of weight of bow upon point of aim.

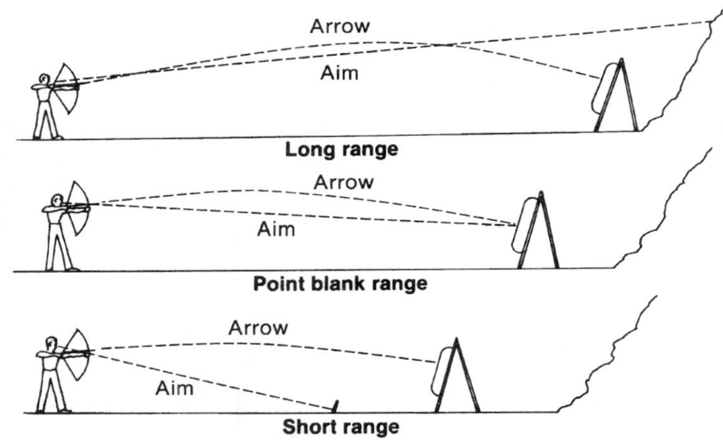

Figure 4-14. Theory of the point of aim.

as the *point of aim*. At the completion of the draw, the point of the arrow should appear to be somewhere near the point of aim. The left hand is then moved slowly and steadily until the point of aim appears to be resting exactly on top of the point of the arrow (figure 4-14).

At the instant the aim is adjusted to your satisfaction, release the string by allowing the fingers to quit holding. But allow only the fingers to relax; the muscles of the string shoulder and back must keep pulling, and the muscles of the bow arm and shoulder must remain steady until the arrow has hit the target.

Note the location of the group formed by the arrows that were properly shot. If they are high on the target, the point of aim must be lowered or brought toward the archer. If they are low on the target, the point of aim must be raised or moved toward the target. If the point of aim is in proper line and they group to the right or left or scatter over the target, check for faults other than in point of aim.

Possible errors in aiming and releasing

1. Shift in position
2. Both arms and shoulders relaxed at the moment of release
3. Point of aim not reached before releasing string
4. Point of aim to the right or left of a line directly between the archer and the center of the target
5. Aiming with the nondominant eye
6. Sighting with both eyes
7. "Wrong arrow" used

Range finder

A device used for recording the established point of aim is called a "range finder." It might be a piece of wood about 6 inches (15.3 cm) long. To record the point of aim, hold the finder at arm's length (figure 4-15) toward the target, with the bull's-eye appearing just over the top of it. With the finder in this position, move the thumb up the stick

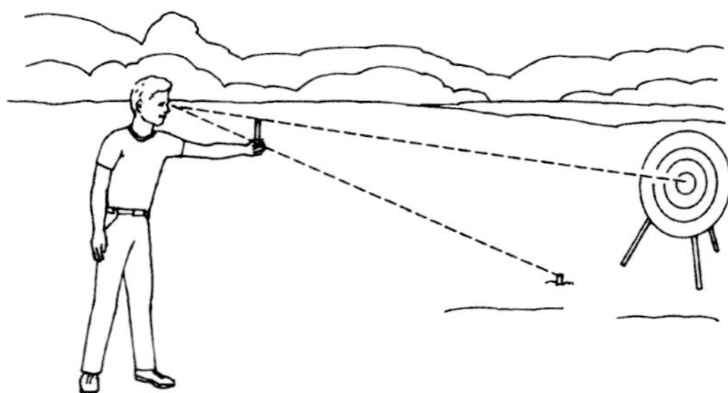

Figure 4-15. The range finder.

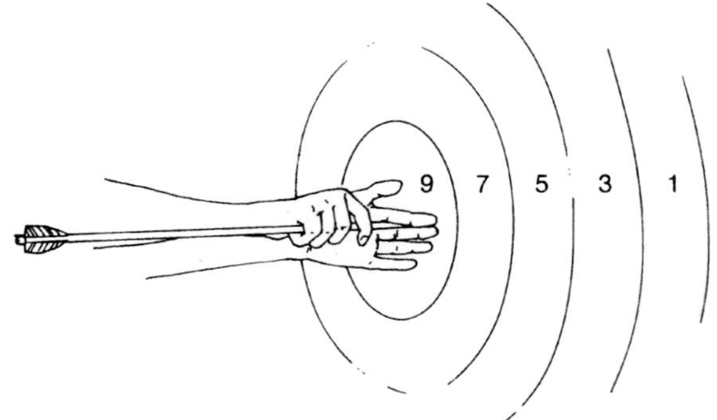

Figure 4-16. Drawing the arrow from the target.

until it is in line with the point of aim already established. At this point place a mark on the stick. In future shooting at the same distance, the point of aim can be reestablished by sighting through the mark recorded on the finder.

Bow sight (freestyle)

A device that is used for sighting and is attached to the back of the bow is termed a *bow sight*. It has vertical and horizontal adjustments and is good for all ranges. In use, the line of vision is through the sight to the center of the target. For a right-handed archer (one who draws the string back with the right hand), the left eye should be closed and the sight should be placed by the target's center. For a left-handed archer, the right eye is closed.

Pin sight

One of the most economical types of bow sights today is the pin sight, in which the shooter uses masking tape or weather stripping with one or two large pins for sighting. Other shooters may use a tongue depressor held to the bow by adhesive tape and a pin or matchstick for sighting.

When adjusting the sight:

1. Always start about 10 yards (9.14 m) from the target.
2. Set the pin about 4 inches (10 cm) above the arrow rest. Sight through the pin to the yellow of the target.
3. Shoot a group of 3 arrows. If the arrows land high on the target, set the pin higher; if they are low, set the pin lower. Always move the pin in the direction the arrows are missing.
4. After resetting the pin, try again. Aim at the gold (yellow) and shoot.
5. When changing distances, adjust the pin sight. As the archer moves away from the target, the pin sight should be moved closer to the grip of the bow.

Drawing Arrows from the Target

The back of one hand is placed against the target in such a way that the arrow is between the first and second fingers (figure 4-16). Grasp the arrow close to the target with the other hand and pull the arrow from the target. Care must be taken to draw the arrow straight out so that it will not be bent, or kinked. After being drawn out, drop the arrow on the ground, leaving the hand free for removing the remaining arrows. If an arrow penetrates to where the feathers have entered the target, it must be drawn on through the back of the target to prevent roughing or stripping off the feathers. If the arrow has penetrated one of the wooden legs or the wooden support of the target, it should be loosened with a pair of pliers before removal. At times, arrows that miss the target slither along the ground and into the grass. These must be pulled from the point end, much in the same manner as removing an arrow that has penetrated the target past the feathers. When looking for arrows that have missed the target, keep your eyes on the ground so you do not step on an arrow and break it.

SAFETY PRECAUTIONS

Archery contains certain elements of danger if participants become careless. Proper conduct while shooting or taking care of equipment off the range is exceedingly important. Safety rules are as follows:

1. Do not go to the target while others are shooting. All participants should retrieve arrows at the same time.
2. When finished shooting, step back three paces and wait.
3. Draw an arrow only when directed at the target.
4. Shoot at targets only from the shooting line.
5. Remember that bows and arrows are not toys.
6. Faithfully obey the starting and stopping signals.
7. While shooting, be certain that there is an adequate backstop behind the target or, if there is no backstop, that the area is clear behind target.
8. Never leave bows and arrows unguarded where children or careless persons might handle them.
9. Never shoot straight up into the air under any circumstance.
10. Never shoot with a faulty bow or arrow or permit others to do so.
11. Never take chances or be careless.

12. Do not pinch the arrow between the thumb and finger to shoot. Always use three fingers for drawing the arrow, so you cannot accidentally release the arrow.

TEACHING CONSIDERATIONS

1. Teach safety procedures with no flexibility and with strong consequences for any rule infractions. Establish and use consistent signals.
2. When teaching students, have the bows strung before the first class so that time is not wasted on this procedure and students get an opportunity to shoot during the first class period.
3. Assign bows and arrows to students the first day that they will use the entire unit unless adjustments need to be made.
4. Teach stringing and unstringing of bows on the second day.
5. Give students the whole idea of the skill before breaking it down into parts. This can be done through demonstration or the use of audiovisual aids with a description of cues during the demonstration.
6. Practice stance, draw, and aim without an arrow, establishing clearly that the string is not to be released. Practice until each of these aspects is done correctly and with proper from. Do not continue until students have mastered the basics of each of these principles. Walk through each step, if need be, one step at a time until mastered. In large classes use partners for feedback on:
   a. Straddling the line.
   b. Raising the bow with the bow weight on the palm of the hand.
   c. String-hand position using the first three fingers and whole first joint.
   d. Level, straight pathway of elbow as it draws string back (9 o'clock position).
   e. Slightly flexed elbow on bow arm.
   f. Correct transition period.
7. When students have mastered these steps, add nocking arrow, draw, anchor, aim, and release. Walk students through each step using cues before going to self-paced practice. Reemphasize rules for stepping in front of the shooting line before students release any arrows.
8. Teach students how to retrieve arrows and how to score arrows at one target before directing them to retrieve and score their own arrows.
9. Reemphasize point of aim and form after students have had an opportunity to shoot an end.
10. Help students analyze their errors in form based on clustering of arrows after enough practice results in consistent errors.
11. In longer units develop skills for shooting rounds and add novelty shooting (balloons, golf archery, etc.).

GLOSSARY

addressing the target Assuming the proper stance; ready to shoot. Feet should straddle the shooting line.

archer's golf An archery game simulating golf; sometimes played on a golf course.

arm guard A protective cover for the lower part of the bow arm.

back The side of the bow away from the body and facing the target.

belly The inside of the bow; the side facing the string.

bow arm The arm that is extended in preparation for release.

bow sight A device attached to the bow used to assist in aiming.

brace To loop the string in the nock when stringing the bow.

broadhead An arrow point used for shooting live game.

butt Any object against which the face is placed.

cast The distance an arrow may be shot.

clout shooting Usually 36 arrows shot at a 48-foot (14.5 m) target placed or marked on the ground, 120 or 140 yards (108 m or 126 m) for women and 180 yards (162 m) for men.

Columbia round A women's round consisting of 24 arrows shot at 55, 44, and 33 yards (50, 40, and 30 m).

crest The marks identifying the arrow.

double round A round shot twice in succession.

drift The motion of the arrow caused by wind or weather.

end Usually the shooting of 6 arrows, either in succession or in two groups of three.

eye The string loop.

face The front of the target.

field captain Usually the tournament director.

fistmele The height of the fist with the thumb raised (brace height).

fletch To place feathers on an arrow.

flight shooting The contest of distance shooting.

grouping Shooting a group of arrows close together on the target.

head The pile tip of the arrow.

hen feathers The two similar-colored feathers.

hit To strike the target anywhere.

in Second unit to be shot in a round.

index feather That feather of an arrow set at a right angle to the nock; the odd-colored feather.

instinctive shooting Shooting without the aid of any sighting device.

jerking Jolting caused by too much recoil of the shooting hand on release.

Junior Columbia round For boys and girls; 24 arrows shot at each of 33 and 22 yards (30 and 20 m).

Junior Scholastic round For boys and girls; 24 arrows shot at each of 33 and 22 yards (30 and 20 m).

keeper A piece of binding used to keep the loose end of the string fastened to the unstrung bow.

lady paramount Woman directing a tournament.

let fly To release an arrow.

limbs Upper and lower parts of the bow.

loose The release of the bowstring after the draw.

low strung Less than a fistmele between the string and bow.

miniature round Indoor shooting; 60 arrows shot from 16.7 yards (15 m) on a 2-foot (60 cm) target.

nock The groove at the end of the arrow.

nocking point The point on the string at which the arrow is placed.

out First unit to be shot in a round.
overbowed Using a bow too heavy in draw weight.
perfect end To put 6 shots in the gold.
petticoat On the target face but outside the rings; beyond the white ring. If hit, no score is given.
pin sight A device on the bow to help in aiming.
point of aim The auxiliary object used in hitting the center of the target when the archer is not at point-blank range.
point-blank range The single distance where the true aim is on the bull's-eye.
point The metal tip of the arrow.
quiver A device to hold arrows.
range Shooting distance.
range finder A device used to determine various distances.
range round Indoor shooting; 60 arrows shot from a single distance—55, 44, 33, or 22 yards (50, 40, 30, or 20 m).
reflexed bow A bow with limbs that curve out.
release To shoot an arrow.
round To shoot a definite number of arrows at specific distances.
roving Shooting a given number of arrows at targets placed at varied distances over an outside course.
Scholastic round Twenty-four arrows shot at each of 44 and 33 yards (40 and 30 m).
self arrow An arrow made from one piece of wood.
self bow A bow made from one piece of wood, as opposed to a composite bow.
serving The thread wrapped around the bowstring.
shaft The long center part of the arrow.
shaftment The part of the arrow holding the crest and feathers.
shooting line The line where one stands to shoot; the archer straddles this line.
shooting tab A protective device for fingers.
sight An aiming device that enables the archer to aim directly at the gold.
snake An arrow lost in deep grass.
spine A characteristic of the arrow's strength and flexibility.
spot Aiming center.
stringing To place the string on the bow and make it ready to shoot.
stroke Shooting position.
tackle Archery equipment.
tassel A bunch of fabric or a piece of cloth to wipe off wet arrows.
timber "Heads up"; a call of warning that an arrow is to be released. Used in field archery.
toxophilite One who has studied and mastered the art of shooting.
trajectory The flight of the arrow; the path that the arrow takes.
underbowed Using a bow that is too light in draw weight.
unit A 14-target course, including all official shots.
vane A plastic feather on an arrow.
wand shoot Shooting at an upright stick.
weight The number of pounds it takes to fully draw a bow.
windage The adjustment on the sight for right and left errors.
wobble Erratic motion of an arrow as it travels in flight.

SUGGESTED READINGS

Addison, C. 1989. *Archery technique*. Boston: American Press.

Chase, C. 1997. *Archery: Guidelines to excellence*. Dubuque, Iowa: Eddie Bowers. Focuses on the archer on the shooting line. Written from the perspective of an experienced field archer.

Clark, J. 1992. *Lifetime sports*. Dubuque, Iowa: Eddie Bowers. The chapter on archery discusses history, benefits, terminology, rules, equipment, skill fundamentals, error correction, drills, games, and skills.

Haywood, K. M., and Lewis, C. F. 1989. *Archery: Steps to success*. Champaign, Ill.: Human Kinetics.

Haywood, K. M., and Lewis, C. F. 1989. *Teaching archery*. Champaign, Ill.: Human Kinetics.

McKinney, W. C., and McKinney, M. W. 1997. *Archery*. 2d ed. Dubuque, Iowa: Wm. C. Brown. Includes information on the latest tackle and techniques for target archery, bow hunting, and bow fishing, plus a brief introduction to the rich heritage of archery in literature, art, and history. Contains a unique chapter on physical conditioning for archers and more than 130 illustrations.

National Field Archery Association. 1993. *Official handbook of field archery*. Palm Springs, Calif.: National Field Archery Association.

RESOURCES

Films and Videotapes

Archery, by Fred Schuette. Basic skills, nock, anchor and release, aiming, pregap, and sight methods. Sports Video, 745 State Circle, P. O. Box 1941, Ann Arbor, MI 48106.

Archery right on, 16 mm film, sound, color. Archery from caveman to the Olympics. A complete overview. Fred Bear Sports Club Film Library, 25921 W Eight Mile Rd, Detroit, MI 48235.

Archery videos: bows and arrows; Bull's-eye archery; How to tune your compound bow; You should know. Available from "How To" Sport Videos, P.O. Box 5852, Denver, CO 80217.

The best of the best, 16 mm film. Free loan. Scenes from the 1976 Olympic Games. Fred Bear Sports Club Film Library, 25921 W Eight Mile Rd, Detroit, MI 48235.

Men's archery or Women's archery. Three loop films each, depicting the 7 steps of shooting form. Athletic Institute, 200 Castlewood Dr, North Palm Beach, FL 33408.

Olympic archery/the inner contest. Scenes from the 1976 Montreal Olympics. Archery Manufacturers' Organization, c/o S.G.M.A., 200 Castlewood Rd, North Palm Beach, FL 33408. Free loan: Modern Talking Picture Service, 2323 New Hyde Park Rd, New Hyde Park, NY 11042.

On target for fun: archery skills and techniques demonstrated by Olympic medal winners, Athletic Institute, 200 Castlewood Dr, North Palm Beach, FL 33408.

A return to the Olympics. Shows beginners to advanced archers preparing for the Olympic Games. Archery Manufacturers' Organization, c/o S.G.M.A., 200 Castlewood Dr, North Palm Beach, FL 33408.

7 steps to gold. Rental $10. John Williams, 1972 Olympic gold medalist, demonstrates the seven basic steps. Covers freestyle and instinctive methods. Orange County Film Service, 2111 S Standard, Santa Ana, CA 92707.

25th world archery championships. Shows international archers competing for world championship titles at Valley Forge, Pa. Fred Bear Sports Club Film Library, 25921 W Eight Mile Rd, Detroit, MI 48235.

Several hunting films are available from Fred Bear Sports Club Film Library, 25921 W Eight Mile Rd, Detroit, MI 48235.

Backpacking

After completing this chapter, the reader should be able to:

- Select and care for proper backpacking equipment
- Plan a safe backpacking trip
- Recognize the importance of conditioning and safety in backpacking
- Understand trail etiquette
- Teach a group of beginners the fundamentals of backpacking

HISTORY

Throughout history people have carried loads on their backs as a basic means of transporting the necessities of life. With the introduction of horses, wagons, railroads, motor vehicles, airplanes, and other more efficient forms of transportation, the need to carry loads over long distances has disappeared. The backpacker of today transports basic necessities in primitive fashion as a means of independence, recreation, and fun. With only a minimum of equipment and a little knowledge, the hiker can reach places that are inaccessible by any other form of transportation. The rewards to the backpacker are magnificent scenery, solitude, and a sense of awe inspired by the magnitude of natural surroundings. There is a great thrill and feeling of accomplishment in "doing it the hard way." There is challenge in the unknown and adventure on the trail. With a reasonable amount of preparation, any person in normal health who is willing to exert the effort can enjoy the vigorous life of the backpacker. To move about freely in the wilderness is to experience the adventures of our heritage and to learn of some of the most important lessons Earth has to offer.

EQUIPMENT

Modern backpacking equipment is highly efficient and well designed to minimize the weight that must be carried. It is also rather expensive, and a full outfit may call for an investment of several hundred dollars. Such an investment calls for judicious scrutiny of all items before purchase, and it may be found that alternatives to large cash outlays can be achieved. If at all possible, equipment of the desired type should be borrowed, or perhaps rented, to find out whether it lives up to expectations. Only the necessary pieces of equipment should be bought at first, and additions can be made as experience and resources allow.

Hiking Boots, Socks, and Gaiters

Good-quality leather hiking boots are essential for the serious backpacker. All sorts of footgear may be seen on the trail, even sandals; but good boots offer protection and comfort (figure 5-1). The boot selected should be sufficiently durable to last over many miles and should have a sole that will withstand wear from rocks and gravel and provide traction for walking on nearly every surface encountered. Most boots manufactured today have soles made of a synthetic rubber product known as Vibram, which is very durable. Lightweight hiking shoes also offer protection at a reasonable cost and decreased break-in time.

Beginners tend to buy boots that are heavier and more expensive than necessary; a reputable outfitter selling quality merchandise can be of great help. It is extremely important that boots fit properly and that they be long enough so that the toes do not contact the front of the boot while walking downhill. Proper fitting procedure should include standing on a slant board to check toe position. A good indication of a proper fit is when the toes do not contact the end of the boot after kicking a solid object several times. In all instances, boots must be well broken in before attempting to hike on the trail. They should be worn at every opportunity before making a long hike, to make sure

Figure 5-1. Backpacking foot gear.

that they will not cause blisters. Opinions vary regarding the best way to break in boots, but wearing them frequently is recommended. To increase wear and comfort of boots, a protective waterproofing should be applied to the exterior surface. This will prolong the life of the leather and keep feet dry.

Socks are important companion pieces to boots, and most hikers use two pairs. The inner pair is usually lightweight wool, polypropylene, or a similar material to wick moisture away from the feet. The outer pair is usually a heavyweight wool to provide cushioning of the feet within the boots. Clean socks should be worn every day, and at least one extra set of socks is needed. They can usually be laundered and dried at night, or pinned to the outside of the pack if they are not dry when it is time to start hiking.

Nylon or Gore-Tex gaiters will assist in keeping debris such as dirt and snow from entering into the top of the boots. Gaiters usually have side or rear zippers to allow the wearer to put them on or take them off without having to remove the boot.

Sandals or lightweight tennis shoes are often overlooked as a campsite alternative. After a long day of hiking, a pair of sandals allow the hiker to air out the feet and dry out the boots at the same time. Sandals or tennis shoes do not offer enough support for carrying heavy loads, but they do have a function around the campsite.

Packs

The pack (figure 5-2) is a major investment and should meet the needs of the person using it. The frame size should be matched to the individual. The pack size, or volume capacity, should be determined by the length and type of the anticipated trips. The volume may vary from 3,500 to 7,000 cubic inches (57.4 to 114.7 cu/dm). Pack prices will vary with size and quality. A quality pack of 5,400 cubic inches (88.6 cu/dm) will cost between $200 and $250.

Traditional packs are mounted on external frames. It should be possible to remove the pack from the frame in case one wants to use the frame for carrying loads other than the pack. Frames are made of lightweight metal, usually tubular aluminum alloy.

Internal frame packs are a popular choice for serious backpackers. Internal stays are sewn into the material of the pack to provide strength and shape. Often the stays can be removed and shaped to conform to the contours of the back. Internal frame packs should be equipped with compression straps to allow the user to adjust the size of the pack.

Both internal and external frame packs should come equipped with well-padded shoulder, waist, and sternum straps. Shoulder straps should be fully adjustable and allow the wearer to secure a heavy load to the shoulders without slipping. A sternum strap allows the wearer to connect the shoulder straps in the front to prevent the pack from slipping from side to side. A padded, adjustable waist belt will allow the wearer to bear much of the weight of the pack on his or her hips. The amount of weight distributed between the hips and shoulders is a matter of personal preference and can be adjusted while hiking.

Generally, heavy items are placed near the top in external frame packs. Internal frame packs carry easier with heavy items placed in the middle section near the back of the hiker. Lighter items, such as sleeping bag or clothes, are best stored near the bottom of the pack. For convenience, items used frequently should be stored near the top.

The packsack is often made of nylon or a tough Cordura fabric. Inspection of the stitching and seams is an important consideration. The number of stitches per inch reflects the strength of the seams; generally, the more stitches, the greater the strength. Weak seams can pull apart under the stress of heavy loads. The seams should also be taped or waterproofed, from the inside, with a seamsealer.

A

B

Figure 5-2. Internal and external frame packs. **A,** Back view; **B,** Front view.

Packs are usually loaded from the top, but access from the side or bottom is an option some manufacturers incorporate. Additional accessories, such as detachable side packs and storm flaps, will allow the wearer easier access to commonly used items and will increase the pack's waterproofness.

The choice between an internal or external frame should be based on comfort and purpose. External frame packs are preferred for durability. Internal frame packs are preferred for extended expeditions involving climbing and skiing.

Rucksacks or daypacks, which allow the hiker to carry basic essentials on short excursions from camp, are helpful. Some packs have detachable tops that convert to fannypacks for this purpose. This saves space and weight.

Clothing

The major requirements for clothing used for backpacking are that it be comfortable and adequate for temperatures likely to be encountered on the trail. Much backpacking is done in fairly cool climates, and wool or pile clothing is usually welcome at night and in the early morning. In some instances a set of long underwear or polypropylene tights can provide extra warmth during the day and be a sleeping garment at night. Wool has an advantage over most other materials in that it will maintain some of its insulating qualities when wet. Pile or fleece will wick away moisture faster than wool and is substantially lighter. Clothes made of cotton or a cotton blend are the least desirable. Cotton is a poor insulator when it is wet and it dries slowly. It is usually best to "layer" clothing and adjust the number of layers to suit the temperature and degree of physical activity. When layering, it is best to put insulating materials next to the body and cover with a nylon or Gore-Tex shell. Down jackets and vest are lightweight and highly efficient in retaining body heat, but they lose their insulating qualities when wet.

Some type of adequate rainwear is necessary if rain is likely to be encountered, and it should be compatible with other clothing worn. Lightweight rain suits that protect the wearer from the elements are available. Some types of rain suits are made of materials that permit body moisture to accumulate inside; "breathable" fabrics eliminate this problem. Rain chaps—sleeves that cover the legs and tie to the belt—are often used with a rain parka or poncho. The poncho is a large waterproof sheet of fabric or plastic with a hole in the middle through which the head is thrust to form a cloak-type garment. The poncho may also double as a ground cloth to prevent absorption of ground moisture by the sleeping bag or tent. Lightweight plastic raincoats or jackets likely to tear easily should be avoided, as they may fail at the time they are most needed.

For cooler weather, a wool watch cap or pile ski hat is advisable. Approximately 50 percent of the body heat can be lost through the head, neck, and ears if uncovered. Also, such a hat can be worn while sleeping if the sleeping bag does not cover the head. In extremely cold weather a glove or mitten system that includes a synthetic fleece lining separate from a nylon or Gore-Tex shell allows for increased warmth and protection.

Clothing for warmer hiking conditions should be made of lightweight synthetic material, such as polypropylene. This will allow perspiration to wick away from the hiker's body during exercise. Care should be taken to protect the skin from the sun with sunscreen or maximum coverage with clothes. Hats with broad bills and bandanas to protect the hiker's neck from the sun are advisable. Long-sleeve T-shirts and underwear will protect the skin from the sun, as well as from insects. Additional mosquito netting may be necessary for the head and neck in some environments.

It is wise to include in the clothing some reflective material that can be seen in the dark when a light shines on it. This could be very important if a member of the party becomes lost.

Sleeping Bags

The memories of minor discomforts of a hard day's hiking can be quickly erased by a good night's sleep. A sleeping-bag adequate for low temperatures encountered will contribute to such a night. Sleeping bags come in all sizes and shapes and with several types of insulation. Remember that no sleeping bag generates heat; it only serves to stop heat loss from one's body. The mummy-style bag is probably most popular with backpackers. Down is often selected for its insulating value. However, down loses its efficiency when wet, and it is then of little value to stop heat loss. The synthetic fibers used for insulating sleeping bags, such as Dacron, Hollofil II, Polarguard, Fiberfil II, and Hollowbound II, are almost as efficient as down and have the advantage of being less influenced by moisture. However, synthetic-insulation-filled bags are approximately 30 percent heavier than down bags of equivalent warmth. Regardless of whether the sleeping bag is filled with down or synthetic fibers, it should never be stored tightly stuffed or rolled. Such storage will compress and break the insulating fibers. Sleeping bags should not be stored in stuff sacks. Most sleeping bag covers are made of ripstop nylon and are available in numerous colors. Although color is of little importance for other than aesthetic purposes, a light, tough cover that will permit body moisture to escape is essential. Sleeping bag covers should never be made of waterproof material, as large amounts of body moisture will collect in the bag and cause rapid heat loss. Often a bivouac sack is used to provide warmth and protection to a sleeping bag.

In the campsite, sleeping bags should be allowed to breathe. Rolling your bag out early in the evening allows the bag to regain its original insulating qualities. Likewise, hanging your bag in a tree in the morning allows the moisture that has accumulated from your body to evaporate.

Sleeping Pads and Air Mattresses

In addition to a ground cloth to prevent ground moisture from being absorbed by the sleeping bag or tent floor, some means of blocking heat loss through the ground is desirable. This can be accomplished through the use of a foam sleeping pad or air mattress. Most regular air mattresses will not block heat loss as well as foam pads, but air mattresses can be purchased that are specially designed for backpacking. The two basic types of foam pad are of closed-cell or open-cell construction. Closed-cell pads need no additional cover and can serve as ground cloths, but open-cell pads will absorb moisture and a ground cloth is needed. Foam pads enclosed in waterproof material offer added protection from wetness.

Tents and Shelters

One of the heavier items frequently carried in a backpack is a small tent, usually made of ripstop nylon or similar lightweight material, with aluminum poles and stakes (figure 5-3). In some situations, no shelter at all may be needed, but it is highly advisable to have some sort of covering to remain dry during rain or snow. A lightweight tarp (or tube tent) is the choice of some hikers, while others prefer a tent. The tarp works well in light rain, but it is not nearly as effective as a tent in avoiding mosquitoes or other insects.

It is advantageous if the tent has a waterproof floor to serve as a moisture barrier and to eliminate the need for carrying a special ground cloth. The walls and roof of some tents are also made of waterproof material, which causes moisture to condense inside the tent, usually near the top. A more desirable arrangement is a tent with waterproof floor and walls and a roof of material porous enough for moisture to escape. This makes an additional covering necessary, that is, a tent fly stretched over the entire top of the tent (figure 5-4).

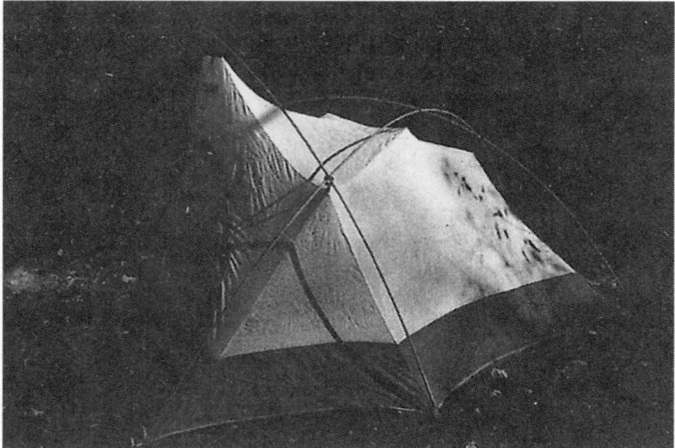

Figure 5-3. Backpacking tent.

Figure 5-4. Backpacking tent with fly.

Tents are often described as "two-person," "three-person," and so on. The prospective buyer should always see the tent set up before buying, to make sure that space in the tent is as extensive as described. Most two-person tents provide barely enough space for two average-sized people and little or no room for packs or other gear. Tents traditionally have an A-frame shape, but there are many options to choose from. Geodesic-shaped tents are popular for backpacking in extreme weather. I-pole-shaped tents with no floor are a popular choice when weight is a critical factor. Vestibules will provide additional room for cooking and storage.

Tent seams should be well stitched, with reinforcement at points of strain. The typical tent designed for backpacking weighs 5 to 10 pounds (2.3 to 4.5 kg), depending on size, type of material, and weight of poles and stakes. Tent closures should fit tightly and are usually of the zipper type. It is important that zippers are of high quality. Mosquito netting that closes tightly is a must if the tent flaps are to be left open in warm weather. Regardless of the weather, the tent should be secured to the ground with stakes to prevent it from blowing away if a high wind develops.

Cooking and Eating Equipment

Many types of cooking and eating utensils are available at most outfitters. Cooking kits are designed for lightweight and compactness (figure 5-5). Pots and pans should fit into one another to decrease volume required. The pots and pans should be of thick-enough aluminum to resist collapsing. Fry pans coated or treated with Teflon will increase menu choices and ease of cleanup. Pots require sturdy handles and lids that also can be used with the fry pan. A pair of rubber-coated channel locks make a great universal pot holder.

Figure 5-5. Cooking and eating utensils.

Stainless steel or heavy plastic tableware is adequate. Heavy plastic is lighter than steel and will not stick to your lips in extremely cold weather. Heavy plastic plates or bowls are preferred over metal for serving. Food cools quickly when served on metal. Connecting the spoon and bowl with a utility cord will keep your personal serving set together. Insulated plastic cups with a lid will keep drinks warm, will not burn your lips, and will reduce camp spills. Additional cookware—such as a large spoon, spatula, funnel, and heavy aluminum foil—may be desirable. Experience will assist the hiker in deciding what type of equipment to take. After a few trips, such selection will pose no problem.

Trail Stoves

Most backpackers prefer to cook over an open fire, and where this is possible, it offers maximum enjoyment of the outdoors. The cooking fire should be kept small, and wood that will provide coals should be used where possible. Most woods found in mountain country are softwoods and burn rather quickly with almost no coals. Cooking pots blacken as a result of cooking over such fires, but such blackening in no way affects the quality of cooking, and it may actually increase the ability of the pot to absorb heat. If it is desirable to keep a cooking utensil bright and shiny, a coating of soap on the outside before using it over the open fire will help prevent permanent blackening.

However desirable the open cooking fire may be, there are places and times when such fires are not permitted, such as in areas of high danger of forest fire or where fuel is unavailable. In an attempt to minimize the impact on the wilderness, many backpackers are carrying small trail stoves (figure 5-6). As the number of campers increases, the restrictions on open fires will also increase. The use of stoves will thus increase in popularity as our concern for the environment increases. Most such stoves are lightweight and very efficient at all altitudes. Trail stoves burn several types of fuel, including white gasoline, kerosene, compressed propane gas, or butane gas. Other fuels such as Sterno or hexamine may be used, but these usually deliver considerably less heat. In the case of butane fuel, the fuel tank must be kept above freezing for effective use. This may make it necessary for the hiker to sleep with the fuel tank to have usable fuel to cook breakfast! Transporting stoves and fuels can be dangerous, and they should always be stored in the pack properly. Liquid fuel, such as white gasoline, should be transported only in metal bottles designed for that purpose. Fuel bottles should be carried in an outside pocket of the pack so that leaks can be observed in time to prevent the pack from becoming a torch through accidental ignition. Be sure to carry a stove repair kit and to try out the stove before an overnight trip. In extreme climates, an aluminum wind shield will increase the efficiency of the camp stove.

Whenever a fire is used, extreme care must be taken to make sure that only those things are burned that are intended to be burned. Burnable materials must be removed from proximity to open fires, and every fire must be "dead out" before leaving the campsite. Garbage that will burn should be consumed completely by the fire, and all traces of the fire should be removed. Items that will not burn completely should be packed and placed in a proper receptacle at the end of the trip. Let no one say, and say it to your shame, that all was beauty here until *you* came! It is the mark of the conscientious backpacker to "camp without a trace" and to protect the surroundings for the future enjoyment of others.

Figure 5-6. Three types of trail stoves.

Pocket Equipment

Several items should be carried in the hiker's pants pockets. A reserve supply of wooden matches, enclosed in a waterproof container, should be carried in the pocket, in addition to a supply in the pack. A folding pocketknife should also be carried, and special effort must be made to know the whereabouts of the knife at all times. Knives are probably the most "losable" items carried, and they are also one of the most important.

A small whistle should also be carried in the pants pocket, to use as an emergency signal if needed. The whistle can be heard over greater distances than the voice, and the whistle will still make noise long after the sound production of the vocal cords has been diminished to a whisper. In areas unfamiliar to the hiker, a compass should also be carried in the pocket.

These items must be carried on the person in the event that the pack is lost. They are of prime importance to survival in an emergency and must be kept readily available in a location separate from the pack.

Equipment Selection

The prospective backpacker with limited funds will be forced to make many careful choices when buying equipment. It is generally better to buy fewer items of good quality than to buy a larger number of items and compromise on quality. Again, it is advisable to borrow or rent equipment and actually use it before investing in an item intended for long-term service. Gaps in noncritical equipment can be filled in with simple makeshift gear until further knowledge is gained and the right equipment is bought.

The following list is offered to aid the novice in planning equipment purchase. The list is intended to present equipment needed in most areas of the United States, but additions or deletions may be appropriate depending on local conditions. Always consider quality of construction, weight, bulk, and durability. Remember, there are no equipment stores in the wilderness!

Backpacking Checklist

Backpack with rain cover

Personal equipment
shirts
pants
socks
raingear
boots
underwear
synthetic jacket
synthetic pants
pullover
parka
windpants
hat
gloves/mittens

Bedroom
sleeping bag
sleeping pad
tent with fly
groundcloth
stakes

Kitchen
stove
fuel bottles
cooking pot/frying pan
plastic bowl/spoon
mug
water filter
water bottles
dish scrubber

Food
breakfast
lunch
supper
trail food
drinks
emergency foods

Miscellaneous items
first aid
flashlight with extra bulb and batteries
matches/lighter
map/compass
repair kit
camera
nylon cord
notebook/pencil
trash bags
whistle/mirror
sunglasses
insect repellent
lip balm
sunscreen
personal toilet articles
pocket knife
watch
prescription medicine
contacts
towel
camp sandals/shoes

Always check with land managers or experienced backpackers from the area where you plan to backpack, to determine special equipment needs.

PLANNING THE TRIP

Where To Go

A major decision confronting the hiker planning a trip is the selection of a suitable area. One of the great features of backpacking is the freedom it offers, within limits of particular areas. Many people enjoy the "bushwhack," that is, cross-country travel in any direction desired without confinement to established trails. In areas where this is permitted, it can offer solitude that may not be attainable otherwise. The beginning packer will quickly find that characteristics of the landscape may make the bushwhack difficult and that established trails offer better routes. Generally it is considered best to stick to existing trails until experience has been gained that would benefit the hiker in the cross-country venture. Some areas of the country have become well known for excellent trails and beautiful scenery, so much so that agencies in charge of many areas have been forced to establish a quota system that permits a limited number of people on a trail at a given time. Otherwise, the trails literally become worn out from excessive use and the abuse of overcrowding in campsite areas. Persons wishing to hike in such areas should determine whether permits are required and make application, if needed. Most areas open for backpacking are public-use areas and include land controlled by state parks, the U.S. Forest Service, the National Park Service, conservation departments, or similar agencies. Many of the controlling agencies publish information about their respective areas and will furnish it on request. When selecting an area, you should consider the nature of the terrain, existing trails, area rules, and the availability of such things as water and places to camp. Established trails originate at a place called a trailhead, and parking facilities are usually provided for at least a limited number of vehicles. If plans call for the trip to end at the same place it begins, it may be desirable to leave vehicles at that point. Should it end at some other access to the trail, it will be necessary to enlist the aid of someone to deliver hikers to the start of the of the hike and pick them up at its end.

For first-timers, a good approach is to camp out in the backyard, using the equipment to be taken on the trail. Thus, if something goes badly, experience can be gained without the discomfort or danger of being miles from home. Another good idea is to make a short overnight hike near home to "shake down" equipment and determine its adequacy. The things that the hiker can carry will be limited; needed things not carried will be unavailable, and things carried and not needed only add useless weight to the pack. There is no substitute for an actual trial to determine those things that must be taken and those that are better left at home.

Checklists

One of the most valuable things that the beginner can do is make a list of things that are to be taken on the trip and check them off as the pack is loaded. This helps avoid leaving a critical item of equipment at home and brings organization to the process of preparation.

Food

An adequate supply of food is essential. The planner must realize that energy expenditure in hiking is much greater than in normal daily activities, and thus appetites are often much greater than normal on the trail. Certainly a good practice for the novice is to take what seems to be an adequate amount of food and then add a little more. A matter for prime consideration is the weight of the food. Much of the weight of most food is water, and any process to reduce water contained in food will aid in reducing the total load to be carried.

The major area where weight can be reduced is food, and dehydrated foods of some sort are essential if the trip is to be of more than a few days' duration. Well-prepared foods are available that have been freeze-dried or have had the major portion of water removed by some other process. Wide choices are available from the typical outfitter. The major hindrance to such foods is their high cost. Freeze-dried foods may be the only resource for long trips, but many equally nutritious foods that weigh only slightly more can be purchased at a supermarket. Pretrip activities should include a visit to a supermarket to find dry foods that suit the palates of the persons involved. When such foods are selected, they should be removed from their bulky commercial wrappings and repackaged into smaller, space-saving units. Preparation instructions should be retained for each item.

One means of food acquisition often espoused by backpackers is "living off the land." Not only is this uncertain, but it may be impossible because of low availability of natural food or local regulations that prohibit it. It is true that in some areas the diet may be supplemented by fish, berries, and sometimes fruit, but the wise packer will take an adequate supply of food along until sufficient experience is gained to be able to forage effectively.

The amount of food necessary will be dictated by the length, climate, and strenuousness of the trip. Cold weather and difficult terrain add to caloric needs. An "average" woman on an "average" hike might require 2,500 to 3,000 calories per day. An "average" man might require about 3,500 to 4,000 calories per day. Teenagers are likely to require twice as much.

Menus

Although some hikers detest any sort of formal organization, it will aid the beginner to take a written plan for each meal to be eaten on the trip. Changes can always be made, but it may be difficult to determine the amount of food needed without such a specific plan. When food is purchased, a good procedure is to group the items to be eaten at each specific meal. Then each of these groups should be placed in a plastic bag and labeled according to its intended time of consumption, such as "breakfast Saturday" or "supper Sunday." Such organization may not appeal to everyone; but it will ensure an orderly approach to the problem of providing adequate meals. Although unusual diets will probably not cause significant problems over a few days, the general procedure should be to follow the same guidelines in meal planning as one would at home; that is, plan a balanced diet that contains a variety of foods. Because energy expenditure will be high, a diet containing large portions of carbohydrates is desirable, but other food elements should not be neglected. The consumption of small amounts of water at frequent intervals along the trail will aid in preventing fatigue.

Trail Food

It is usually desirable to plan lunches that require little or no cooking. In addition, most hikers find it advantageous to eat small amounts of high-energy foods during the course of the day's hike. A favorite is a mixture called "gorp." The origin of this word is obscure; it is sometimes said to mean "good old raisins and peanuts." Whatever the origin of the term, the mixture is often a creation of art. Depending on the taste of the preparer, it may include such items as dried fruit, chocolate, nuts of various kinds, cereals, and any other food that is high in energy but that will not become sticky when warm.

Water

Water is essential for the hiker, and it should be consumed frequently. There is a tendency for the inexperienced hiker to drink less water than is desirable, and effort may be necessary to ensure adequate consumption. It is better to drink more than is needed than to chance becoming dehydrated. This is particularly true in hot weather, and regular water stops should be planned.

Powdered sport drinks or electrolytes will help reduce lost minerals and reduce cramping. Water that is not needed is excreted by normal body processes, and the better choice is to consume more than is needed rather than too little.

Sources of safe water along the trail may be difficult to find, but proper pretrip planning involving use of available maps, trail guidebooks, and local inquiries can make this task easier. *Giardia lambliea* can cause sever diarrhea, flatulence, bloating, and dehydration. Take precautions to purify your water as recommended to kill or remove giardia and other bacteria and viruses.

In some instances water must be carried for long distances; in others, it may be readily available from springs, streams, or lakes. Where the safety of water is questionable, it should be treated with chemicals carried in the pack. Commercial preparations, such as halazone, are available from drugstores and outfitters. It is always advisable to check the date on the container of such preparations, as their effective life is limited. The amount of treated water consumed should always be in accordance with instructions on the container. Equally effective treatment can be accomplished with materials readily available in the typical household. Tincture of iodine may be used at the rate of 3 drops per quart of clear water (double the amount if the water is not clear). The chemical should be thoroughly dissolved in the water by vigorous shaking, and the treated water should then be left to stand for at least 30 minutes before being consumed. Although there will be a slight taste of the chemical used, it will be far better to drink treated water than to contract gastrointestinal disorders or other serious maladies. On extended expeditions, a commercial water filter may be desirable. These filters mechanically remove impurities from the water with ceramic filters. These filters are expensive and considered a luxury, even by experienced backpackers.

Maps and Guidebooks

Local guidebooks are of great help in assessing terrain and general physical characteristics of the area selected for hiking. They give many features of the land areas represented, including elevations, contours, water sources, campsites, area histories, and much more. Maps can be purchased from many outfitters, and if not available locally they may be obtained from the Geological Survey and Water Resources Agency in each state. For information on maps of areas east of the Mississippi River, contact the Geological Survey Office in Washington, D.C.; for areas west of the Mississippi, contact the Geological Survey Office in Denver. Index maps of each state are available; maps for specific areas may be ordered after consulting the index map. The use of maps and a compass is discussed in detail in chapter 22 of this book.

Loading the Pack

Once all of the items to be taken are assembled, they should be placed in the pack in some sort of order related to their function. Generally, lighter and noncrushable items are loaded near the bottom of the pack, and heavier items should be loaded near the top and close to the front. It is important to keep the greater portion of weight high on the back near the shoulders. Items that are likely to be used frequently or those that might be needed quickly should be placed in the side pockets on the pack to avoid the process of unpacking when the item is needed. Certainly rainwear should be readily accessible, and many packs provide special pockets for rainwear and maps. The most effective organization of the pack involves the use of multiple stuff sacks—for example, extra clothes in a blue stuff sack, food in a red stuff sack, etc.

Try to keep the basic pack unit to a weight of 25 pounds or less. This weight includes all necessities—such as pack, tent, sleeping bag, and the like—and excludes expendable items, primarily food. The total maximum weight carried may vary considerably from one person to another, but a general rule of thumb is for the total weight to be carried not to exceed one third the body weight of the person carrying it. This is a *heavy* load, and the beginner will do well to limit the load to a considerably lower weight.

First-Aid Kit

A first-aid kit should be a basic part of the backpacker's equipment. Commercially prepared kits are available, but a satisfactory one can be put together from items readily available from a local drugstore. The following is a suggested list of items for such a kit:

- antiseptic
- Band-Aids (several sizes, including extra-large)
- sterile gauze pads
- moleskin
- adhesive tape
- lip balm
- tweezers
- needle
- safety pins
- triangular bandage
- snakebite kit
- anaphylactic shock kit (if appropriate)
- other items as anticipated needs may indicate (such as personal medications, extra contact lenses, etc.)

ON THE TRAIL

Conditioning and Safety

It is important that the hiker be in good physical condition and able to walk for extended periods while carrying a pack.

Conditioning before the hike will improve stamina and make the process more enjoyable. Conditioning should be accomplished over a reasonable period of time and may include walking, jogging, and similar activities that promote overall conditioning. In any event the hiker should build up to the activity and not attempt greater distances than can be covered in the time allotted. Enjoyment, not exhaustion, is the objective. During the first few miles of a hike, it is wise to start slowly and "warm up" to the task. This is especially advisable if there is considerable increase in altitude in the first portion of the trail.

Particular care must be given to the feet, and at the first sight of irritation, action must be taken. The first warning is a burning sensation, often on the heel or toes. When this warning signal occurs, *stop*! Continued walking will quickly result in a blister, and the hiker may be "crippled" with the hike hardly started. Boot and socks should be removed and the area of irritation inspected. A moleskin plaster may be applied over the area affected. This material, available at drugstores, has a smooth surface to reduce friction and an adhesive backing that causes it to stick to skin. After applying moleskin, the hiker can apply foot powder and replace socks and boot, paying close attention to the way the foot feels after walking is resumed. It is much better to avoid blisters than to treat them, but if one occurs, it should be taken care of at once. A Band-Aid and powder can be applied if the blister is small. Opening the blister should be avoided if possible. If the blister must be opened, this should be done with a needle that has been heated until the point is red hot and sterilized. The skin should be disturbed as little as possible, antiseptic applied, and the spot covered with a Band-Aid or similar dressing. It may be necessary to delay hiking a day or so if blisters become severe, and care must be taken to avoid infection and otherwise making them worse. Applications of a commercial preparation of benzoin (Tuf-Skin) several days in advance of the trip will help to toughen the skin on the feet and reduce the likelihood of blisters.

When hiking in groups, there are usually some individuals who wish to walk faster than others. It is irritating to walk behind a person who walks slower than you do, and it is good to let the sprinters pass—but keep the party together! One rule is to keep the person behind you in sight by looking back frequently and stopping to rest when the group gets spread farther than is desirable. Although it may cause some irritation on the part of those who wish to walk faster, a sure way to keep the group together is to put the slowest hiker in front and allow no one to pass. Some experienced packers make solo hikes into deep wilderness areas, and once in a while one remains there permanently. A much safer arrangement is to hike with at least one partner and to know the whereabouts of each other at all times. The "buddy system" allows one person to go for help in case of serious emergency.

Falls are a primary source of injury to backpackers, and precautions should be taken to avoid unnecessary risks. A broken leg or sprained ankle is no fun at any time, and on the trail deep in a wilderness area it becomes a serious problem. Travel over ice, wet rocks, and loose rocks poses special problems and should not be attempted without special knowledge and training. Each hiker must be responsible for her or his own safety and be ready to assist others.

A trip control plan (TCP) should be left with someone before starting to locate a hiker in an emergency and to enable emergency aid to be directed to the proper place if it should become necessary. TCPs should be as specific as possible, including information on mileage, elevation gain or loss, anticipated travel time, and identification of landmarks and probable campsites. Most established trails have some sort of registration procedure, either at a ranger station or a drop box a short distance up the trail from the trailhead. A good plan is to have someone start looking for you if you are not in contact with them at a specified time. In the event of a delay that is not an emergency, the party with whom you have the arrangement should be notified of your safety as soon as possible.

Extra precaution should be observed when descending trails, especially near the end of a trip, when fatigue is most evident and mishaps are most likely to occur. During downhill travel, hazards may be more likely to be hidden by vegetation, and loose rocks, rotten logs, and other dangers may appear without warning. Lightning in the mountains poses an extremely dangerous threat, and in the event of an electrical storm, hikers should retreat to the lowest available area, avoiding high ridges and lone trees.

Trail Pests

The degree of irritation caused by trail pests is usually inversely proportional to the size of the pest. The uninitiated hiker may fear mountain lions, grizzly bears, and other wild creatures, but mosquitoes, black flies, "no see-ums," and similar insects can cause far more discomfort than larger animals. Generally, it must be understood that it is the hiker who is the interloper in any confrontation with an animal. Most animals wish only to be left alone. Snakes are often feared, but most are harmless. Small garter snakes frequent springs in some mountain ranges, but they are there for the same purpose as the packer: to get a cool drink. Rattlesnakes are dangerous, and most can be avoided by careful observation during walking and especially when sitting down beside the trail or reaching along a rocky ledge. A good insect repellent will help considerably in dealing with insects, and common sense should prevail in dealing with other animals. No animal should be teased or antagonized. Remember, you are the intruder in the animal's home!

Personal Hygiene

Habits of personal hygiene should not vary markedly from those practiced at home. It is important to maintain personal cleanliness, and although baths may not be taken as regularly as at home, they may be even more necessary. Small mountain streams should not be used as bathtubs or as a place to wash dishes or clothes. The water is usually cold, and the aquatic balances that influence fish and other life can be easily affected. Water can be heated in the cooking pot and used for washing clothes or for bathing. Use biodegradable soap, because the soil can break it down much more rapidly than ordinary soaps. Soapy water should not be discarded where it can run into a stream. The idea of washing socks and cooking in the same pot may not be attractive to some, but the matter of weight makes it essential to leave the wash basin at home. A thorough rinsing and boiling of water in the pot after use for washing will make it safe and ready for the next meal. Thorough rinsing of the pot is essential, because soap acts as a strong laxative if ingested.

Good toilet habits should be practiced, including depositing fecal material in a small hole at least 50 feet (15 m) from the trail and at least 100 feet (30 m) from any surface water and covered with 6 inches (15.2 cm) of soil near other organic life.

Trail Etiquette

All travelers on the trail have the same rights and privileges, and all should respect other travelers. On a narrow trail let faster hikers pass by simply stepping off the trail and greeting them cordially. In many areas horse pack trains use the same trails as backpackers, and often the packers do not rate very highly with the horse wrangler. Even though the packhorses see hikers frequently, they are sometimes "spooked" by them. If you see a pack train approaching or one overtakes you, move off the trail at least 20 feet (6 m) on the downhill side and stand quietly as the animals pass. Sudden movement or loud noise may cause horses to bolt and may result in runaways or horses falling down the side of the mountain.

Campsites

On some trails camping may be permitted in designated areas only. It is important to adhere to such regulations to prevent damage to the surroundings and to keep the area in a near natural state for others who will follow. When camping is unrestricted, it is convenient if the campsite can be located near water. Level ground is also desirable, but it may be difficult to find in some areas. Fires must be used with great discretion, and the campsite must be made as natural as possible before leaving. Fires must be completely extinguished and the fire scar covered. All garbage that will not burn completely must be packed out. Backpackers are the self-appointed guardians of the wilderness, and they must use it with the least possible damage and leave no evidence of their presence in the area. Popular phrases such as "low impact camping," "carry in, carry out" and "take pictures and leave only footsteps," should guide hikers in campsite management.

Hypothermia

The greatest killer of people in the outdoors is hypothermia. This condition occurs when the body core temperature falls below normal. Unless the condition is reversed, death results. Hypothermia is not freezing to death! Most often hypothermia occurs when the outdoor temperature is between 30 and 50°F. Hypothermia may be a problem at lower temperatures, but usually a person prepares more effectively for such situations. Sudden changes in weather may occur, and hikers caught unprepared in cold rainstorms are prime candidates for hypothermia. The combination of wet clothing and exposure to wind most frequently causes the problem. Such conditions remove heat from the body surface faster than it can be generated by normal body functions, and the decrease in temperature results. The hiker should be familiar with windchill factors.

It is extremely important that early symptoms of hypothermia—continued shivering, loss of alertness, and loss of control of the hands—be recognized and treated immediately. All of these things occur without the victim being aware of what is happening. The four basic defenses against hypothermia are these:

1. Stay dry and out of the wind.
2. If chilling has already started, get out of the wind and rain, give up objectives for the day, if necessary, and "hole up" in a sheltered spot. Erect a tent and take advantage of such natural shelter as may be available.
3. Detect hypothermia by checking party members for uncontrolled shivering, slurred speech, memory lapses, stumbling, drowsiness, and apparent exhaustion.
4. Treat hypothermia as follows: Get the victim to shelter, strip off his or her wet clothes and put on dry ones, get the victim into a warm sleeping bag, give warm drinks, and, if at all possible, build a fire. Keep the victim awake, and, if necessary, place the victim in a sleeping bag with another person, both naked (bare skin contact will generate additional body heat). Remember, *think* hypothermia and be prepared to deal with it at the first sign of difficulty. Don't wait!

Heat Stress

Another problem that can confront the hiker is heat stress. Precautions should be taken to avoid heat exhaustion and heat stroke, but it is equally important to recognize their symptoms and to treat them if they occur.

Heat is eliminated from the body by conduction, convection, radiation, and evaporation. The most important process for regulation of body temperature is sweating, which promotes cooling through evaporation. While hiking, some heat is lost through perspiration, but it is minimal. Evaporation of sweat is influenced by the relative humidity, wind velocity, and outside temperature. High humidity is especially troublesome, because it reduces the rate of evaporation that can take place.

The steps of prevention, recognition, and treatment of heat stress are as follows:

1. Carry and ingest adequate amounts of liquid and salt to prevent depletion of these basic body requirements.
2. Ensure adequate rest and opportunity for cooling. Take frequent rest stops in shady areas.
3. Detect heat exhaustion from such symptoms as fatigue, muscle cramps, abdominal pain, and nausea. The pulse will be normal, the skin will be moist and pale, and there might not be an increase in temperature, although more commonly there will be. The tongue and mouth will be dry, and the hiker will feel weak and uncoordinated and may appear mentally dull.
4. Treat heat exhaustion by moving the hiker to a cool area, replenishing the liquid content of the body. Electrolytes or sport drinks will replace fluids and minerals simultaneously.
5. Detect heat stroke from such symptoms as fever; a rapid pulse rate; hot, dry, flushed skin; involuntary limb movements; and possible unconsciousness.
6. Treat heat stroke immediately by lowering body temperature through use of cold water, fanning, and massaging the limbs. Seek medical help as soon as possible.

TEACHING CONSIDERATIONS

Only instructors with a great deal of experience in backpacking and wilderness first aid should guide others on a trip. Training is advisable through an organization such as the National Outdoor Leadership School in Lander, Wyoming. Having adequate training is particularly important when backpacking in wilderness areas where help in emergency situations is not likely to be available. All instructors should consider the conditioning and experience of their group in planning a trip and should not consider more than casual day trips with unconditioned, unprepared, or ill-equipped backpackers.

GLOSSARY

A-frame A triangle-shaped tent.

benzoin A commercial preparation used in advance to toughen the skin of the feet.

biodegradable soap A type of soap that should be used when backpacking because the soil can break it down very quickly.

bivouac A temporary camp.

bivouac sack An external covering for the sleeping bag.

campsite An area for sleeping and/or fire building. On some trails, camping may only be permitted in designated areas.

checklist A list of things that are to be taken. This is critical so that nothing is left behind.

dead out The condition every fire must be in before leaving the campsite.

external frame pack A pack with a frame on the outside of the pack sack.

first-aid kit A kit that contains all the immediate remedies for the hazards encountered along the trail.

fleece Synthetic fabric that adds insulation and dries fast.

foam sleeping pad A pad used for blocking heat loss through the ground.

gaiters Nylon or cloth anklets used to keep snow and dirt from falling into boots.

geodesic dome A dome-shaped tent.

giardiasis/giardia A waterborne disease.

gorp A high-energy food eaten during the course of the day's hike; "good old raisins and peanuts."

halazone A product used to treat water where its safety is questionable. Can be purchased in drugstores.

heat stress A common problem that confronts the hiker. High humidity is especially troublesome.

hip belt A padded waist belt.

hypothermia A condition that occurs when the body core temperature falls below normal. It is the greatest killer of people in the outdoors.

I-pole tent A lightweight tent with one pole in the middle.

internal frame pack A pack with the frame enclosed in the pack sack.

liquid fuel One source of fuel for camping; should be kept in a metal container and carried in a pocket on the outside of the pack.

loft The thickness of a sleeping bag.

maps Guides for assessing the terrain and general physical characteristics of the area selected for hiking.

menus Written plans for food consumption for each meal.

moleskin Bandaging material to prevent blisters.

mummy-style bag A sleeping bag adequate for temperatures encountered and most popular with hikers.

pack A compartmentalized bag mounted on a metal frame.

pile A soft fabric made from polyester.

rain chaps Sleeves that cover the legs and may be tied to the belt.

seam sealer A special glue used to waterproof material where seams come together.

sternum strap Nylon straps that connect shoulder straps of the pack.

storm flap Panel of material on a garment or tent that prevents moisture and wind from getting in.

stuff sack A nylon bag with drawstring closure.

trail etiquette Observance of respect for other travelers.

trailhead A place where established trails originate.

trail pests Animals that may cause discomfort or danger; remember that the hiker is the interloper in any confrontation with an animal and that good insect repellent will help deal with insects.

trip control plan (TCP) A detailed description of the trip, including departure and return times, and route description.

vestibule An extension of the tent that secures to the front or back.

SUGGESTED READINGS

Fletcher, C. 1991. *The complete walker.* New York: Knopf.

Ford, P., and Blanchard, J. 1993. *Leadership and administration of outdoor pursuits.* State College, PA.: Venture.

Goll, J. 1992. *The camper's pocket handbook: A backcountry traveler's companion.* Merrillville, Ind.: ICS Books.

Hampton, B., and Cole, D. 1995. *Soft paths.* Mechanicsburg, Penn.: Stackpole Books.

Hatton, M. 1992. *Lightweight camping: A four-seasons source book.* Fresno, Calif.: Thompson Educational.

Meier, J. 1993. *Backpacking.* 2d ed. Reston, Va.: American Alliance for Health, Physical Education, Recreation and Dance. Presents a history of national scenic and historic trails, and lists suggested equipment, clothing, and menu items.

Olson, L. 1990. *Outdoor survival skills.* Chicago: Chicago Review Press.

Seaburg, E., and Dudley, E. 1994. *Hiking and backpacking.* Champaign, Ill.: Human Kinetics.

RESOURCES

Dupont Fibrefill Marketing Division, Centre Road Bldg, Wilmington, DE 19898. For information on Hollowfil II, Quallowfil, and Thermolite.

Mountain Equipment Co-op, 1655 W Third Ave, Vancouver, BC Canada V6J 1K1. For a general catalog of outdoor clothing and gear.

Patagonia, 1609 Babcock St, P. O. Box 8900, Bozeman, MT 59715. For information on Patagonia products.

WL Gore, Rte 213, P.O. Box 1220, North Elkton, MD 21921. For information on Gore-Tex.

Films and filmstrips

Backpacking, filmstrip. American Camping Association, Bradford Woods, 5000, State Hwy 67 N, Martinsville, IN 46151.

Camping, filmstrip. American Camping Association, Bradford Woods, 5000, State Hwy 67 N, Martinsville, IN 46151.

Camping education, 16 mm film. Rand McNally, P. O. Box 7600, Chicago, IL 60680.

Badminton

After completing this chapter, the reader should be able to:

- Appreciate the versatility of the game of badminton
- Know the important considerations for selecting and caring for badminton equipment
- Understand the rules and scoring procedures of the game
- Describe the correct grip, wrist action, ready position, footwork, strokes, and shots
- Understand badminton strategy and etiquette
- Instruct a group of students in the fundamentals of badminton
- Emphasize skill, stamina, and athletic ability necessary for badminton competition
- Recognize and use badminton terms correctly

HISTORY

A game with some sort of racquet and a feathered object goes far back into history. A game similar to badminton (shuttlecock kicking) was played in China as early as the fifth century A.D. and there is mention of the game as long ago as the twelfth century in the Royal Court records of England.

Battledore shuttlecock was popular in the era of King James I, so it is not surprising that the game was played by early English settlers in the United States.

The portrait "Young Prince Sulkonsik" by Adam Mangoki, who lived during the 1700s, shows young members of the Royal Family of Poland holding a shuttlecock and racquet with a stance similar to that used by a modern expert preparing to serve. A portrait by Jean Simeon Chardin (1699–1779) hanging in the Uffizi Gallery in Florence depicts a girl with a racquet and shuttle.

"Portrait of Master Stephen Crossfield" hangs in the Metropolitan Museum of Art, New York. Painted by American William Williams (1727–1791), it depicts a young man holding a battledore (racquet) and shuttlecock.

It is generally accepted that the modern game of badminton, involving court boundaries and a winning objective, was named when a group of British army officers home on leave from India around 1873 played the game at Badminton, the country estate of the Duke of Beaufort in Gloucestershire, England. In 1878 the Badminton Club of New York City was founded. Records in the New York City Museum of History substantiate that this is the oldest organized badminton club in the world. The club was the leading social rendezvous in New York for 25 years. Such names as Astor, Roosevelt, Rockefeller, and Vanderbilt appeared on the membership list. Badminton had its heyday in the United States in the 1930s, when thousands of players, including famous athletes and Hollywood stars, enjoyed the game.

The American Badminton Association was founded in 1936, and in 1977 changed its name to the United States Badminton Association.

The second organized badminton club was founded in Ireland in 1899. This organization was a founding member of the International Badminton Federation (IBF) in 1934. (The first badminton played internationally was a match between England and Ireland in Dublin in 1903.) The original IBF included nine national badminton organizations. By 1939 the tally had risen to 15; today there are more than 130 member organizations worldwide. The Thomas Cup competition for men's teams was started in 1948; the Uber Cup competition for women's teams was started in 1956. Strangely, no European country has yet won either trophy. Malaysia, Indonesia, and China have split the 18 competitions for the men's trophy. The Uber Cup was won 3 times by the United States between 1956 and 1964. The other 12 cups have been held by China, Japan, and Indonesia. The Thomas and Uber Cups are now staged every even year. The Sudirman Cup, world mixed team championship, initially held in 1989, is staged every odd year and has been won by Indonesia, Korea, and China. Additional international competition is provided by the Asian games, the British Commonwealth games, the South East Asian games, and the Pan American games. In 1977 the first official world championship was held in Malmo, Sweden; tournaments are now scheduled every odd year.

Badminton was a demonstration sport in the 1972 Olympics and an exhibition sport at the 1988 Olympics. In 1992 it was a full medal sport for the first time at Barcelona, Spain. At these Olympic games the sport was dominated by the Asian teams with Indonesia, Korea, and China winning all the medals. In 1996 Denmark won the men's singles gold medal with Indonesia, China, and Korea winning four medals each and Malaysia winning two. All U.S. competitors were eliminated in the first or second rounds. Badminton is now part of the U.S. Olympic Festival.

CARRYOVER VALUES

Badminton offers fun and fitness for everyone. It is a sport that is easy to learn but difficult to master. A beginning player receives pleasure and exercise immediately, and an advanced player can get an extremely vigorous workout by playing just one game with an equally skilled opponent. Research studies of movement show that a badminton player uses more arm action in one match than the average baseball pitcher does in a nine-inning baseball game. Also, a top-flight badminton player runs more in one match than a running back or end does in a 60-minute football game.

Badminton is a family sport, played by women, men, and children. Adaptability to small areas, indoors and outdoors, at a minimal cost provides an opportunity for everyone to participate. For advanced players who wish to compete, tournament play is available almost anywhere in the United States. Tournaments sponsored by local badminton clubs (there are over 250) sanctioned by the U.S. Badminton Association provide tournament competition for juniors, women's singles, men's singles, women's doubles, men's doubles, mixed doubles, senior men's singles, senior doubles (men's and women's), and senior mixed doubles. In addition, most tournaments provide play for persons aged 40 years and older. The United States has junior (18 and under), adult (19 to 39), senior (40+), masters (50+), grand masters (60+), and golden masters (70+) championships.

SELECTION AND CARE OF EQUIPMENT

In all sports, good equipment is a prerequisite to good play. Badminton is no exception. For the beginner, good used equipment is often preferable to cheap new equipment.

The Racquet

1. Most racquets are constructed of aluminum, steel, or various blends of carbon, graphite, ceramic, or boron. The carbon graphite racquets are popular among advanced players because they are very light and powerful.
2. Weight depends on the strength of the individual and the feeling of comfort with the racquet.
   a. Most good racquets are between 3 and 4 ounces (86 to 114 g).
   b. Smaller players should select light racquets for better maneuverability.
3. Racquets should be evenly balanced or slightly lighter in the head.
   a. Doubles players usually prefer lighter racquets because quicker shots are possible.
   b. Point of balance is normally 11 to 13½ inches (27.5 to 33.8 cm) from the bottom of the handle.
4. Handle (grip):
   a. Size depends on size of hand.
   b. Normal racquet grips vary between 3½ and 3⅝ inches (8.8 to 9.1 cm) in circumference.
   c. The player should try several sizes and pick the one that feels best.
5. Strings:
   a. Nylon is relatively immune to moisture, inexpensive, longer lasting than gut, and preferred for class use and beginners because of its serviceability and cost.
   b. Gut is expensive, less durable than nylon, not moisture proof, and requires special care. Synthetic gut is preferred by advanced and tournament players because of its resiliency and playability.
   c. Gut and nylon are normally strung at tensions from 14 to 20 pounds (6.4 to 9 kg).
6. Care of the racquet:
   a. Frayed strings should be replaced before they break to prevent loosening of string tension.
   b. Racquets should be kept away from extreme heat or extreme cold.

Shuttlecocks

Shuttles are made either of goose feathers or nylon. There are several kinds of feather shuttles, and the price varies depending on the quality of the feathers and construction of the shuttle. Feather shuttles are usually used for tournaments, but because of feather breakage, these shuttles usually last only one or two games. Feathers can be pointed or rounded on the tip. The feather shuttle should be kept in a moist environment to prevent the feathers from drying out. This can be done by wrapping a moist towel around the tube 24 hours before use or by placing a damp paper towel in the end of the tube. Nylon shuttles are best for class use because they last several weeks and require no special environment, although they also last longer if humidified.

The International Badminton Federation has defined the correct speed of a shuttlecock. Recorded in the IBF Statute Book, Law 4 states: "A shuttlecock shall be deemed to be of correct pace if, when a player of average strength strikes it with a full underhand stroke from a spot immediately above one back boundary line in a line parallel to the sidelines, and at an upward angle, it falls not less than 1 foot (30 cm) and not more than 2½ feet (75 cm) short of

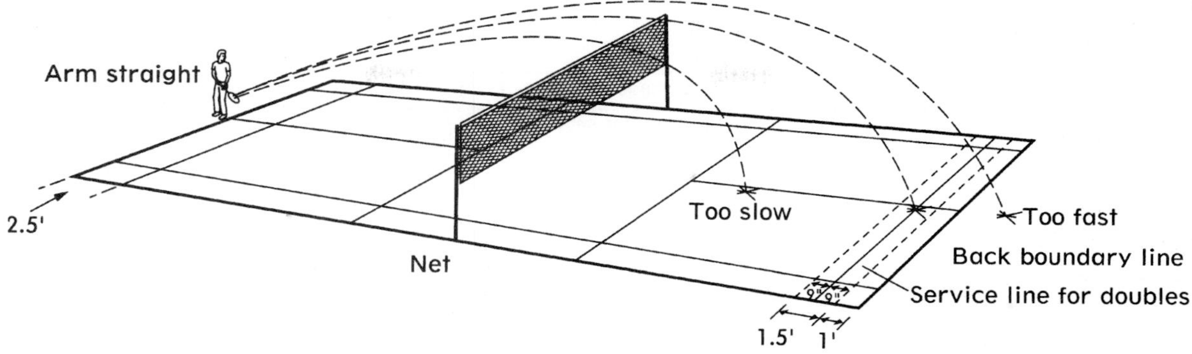

Figure 6-1. Testing the speed of shuttlecocks. They should land within 9 inches (22.5 cm) of either side of the service line for doubles.

the other back boundary line." This statement needs to be further explained for those not accustomed to testing shuttles. The problem is to determine the shuttle speed at the particular time and place. The manufacturer has previously determined the speed by weighing the shuttle. The measure of weight is by grains (approximately ⅙ ounce). Shuttles weigh 73 to 85 grains.

In making the test (figure 6-1), attention should be given to the point of contact of the shuttle and the racquet. It should be directly above the back boundary line.

The distance between the long service line for doubles and the back boundary line is 2½ feet (75 cm). A shuttle of correct pace will fall within 9 inches (22.5 cm) of either side of the doubles service line when tested properly.

Students and teachers of badminton should know how to test a shuttle and should test those in use. When ordering shuttles, whether feathered or nylon, indicate a shuttle speed to suit the particular time (winter, summer), altitude, and area of the country (north, east, south, west) in which they are to be used. The speed of the shuttle determines the type of game that results. It requires an undue amount of effort and strain to clear a slow shuttle overhead from back line to back line; to clear a backhand the length of the court is almost impossible. The game becomes one of brute force, and the stronger person will prevail. The game should be one of speed, finesse, deception, control, and power.

The Net and Standards

The net is 5 feet 1 inch (1.53 m) in height from the surface of the court at the post. The posts are placed on the side boundary lines of the court and should be sufficiently firm to keep the net stretched. Where this is not practicable, some method must be used for indicating the position of the side boundary line where it passes under the net, such as by the use of a thin post or strip of material, not less than 1½ inches (3.75 cm) in width, fixed to the side boundary line and rising vertically to the net cord. On a court marked for doubles, it should be placed on the side boundary line of the doubles court, regardless of whether singles or doubles are being played.

The net is made of fine natural cord or artificial fiber of a dark color and an even thickness not exceeding ⅝ to ¾ inch (1.6 to 1.9 cm) mesh. It should be firmly stretched from post to post and is 2 feet 6 inches (75 cm) in depth. The top of the net is 5 feet (1.5 m) from the floor at the center and 5 feet 1 inch (1.53 m) at the posts, and it is edged with 3-inch (7.5 cm) white tape doubled and supported by a cord or cable run through the tape and strained over and flush with the top of the posts.

HOW TO LAY OUT A COURT

If two or more courts are laid out side by side, a minimum of 4 feet (1.3 m) should be allowed between them. In laying out a home court in the backyard, either tape or dry lime can be used for the boundary lines. For the gymnasium, the boundary lines are defined by white or yellow lines 1.5 inches (3.8 cm) wide. In laying out a badminton court at home, the singles and doubles courts can be combined. The doubles playing court is the same length (13.4 m) as the singles playing court, but is 0.92 m wider.

The ceiling height of a court used for international competitive play is a minimum of 30 feet (9 m) from the floor over the full court (figure 6-2).

RULES

The object of the game is to hit the shuttlecock back and forth across the net with the racquet without permitting it to touch the ground, attempting to hit the shuttlecock into the opposing court so that it cannot be returned.

Scoring

The doubles and men's singles games consist of 15 points. When the score is 13 all, the side that first reached 13 has

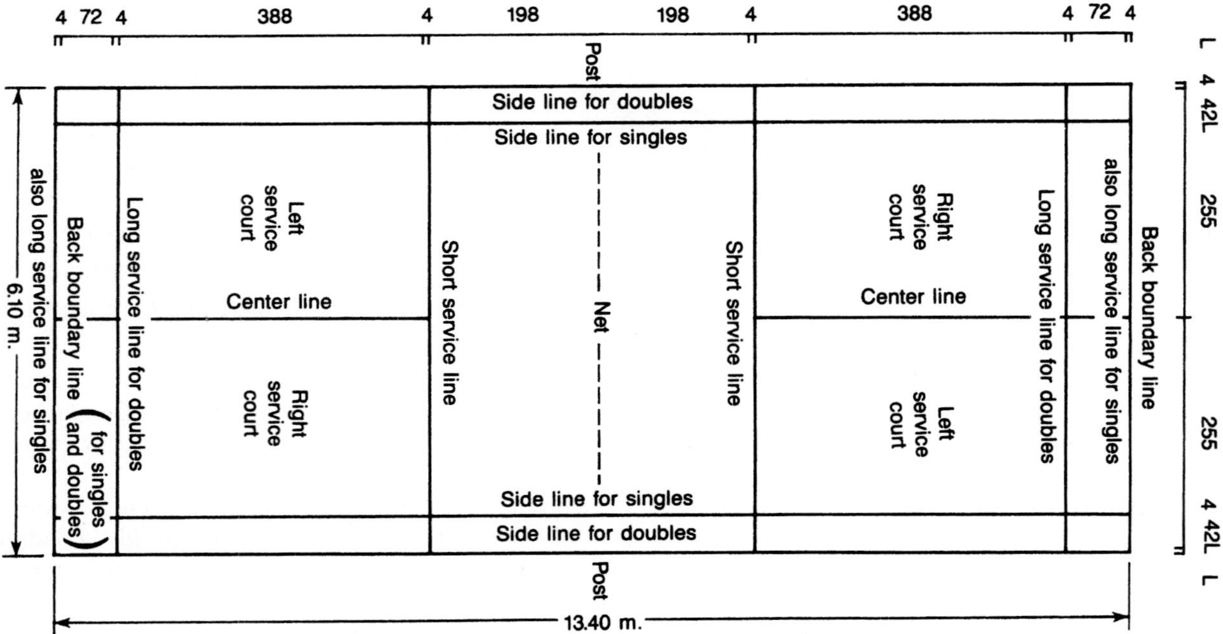

Figure 6-2. Double and single badminton court dimensions.

the option of "setting" the game to 5; and if the score becomes 14 all, the side that first reached 14 has the option of setting the game to 3. If a game is not set at 13 all, it can later be set at 14 all. After a game has been set, the score is called "love all," and the side that first scores 5 or 3 points (whichever set has been exercised) wins the game. In either case the option to set the game must be made before the next service is delivered, after the score has reached 13 all or 14 all.

The women's singles games consists of 11 points. When the score is 9 all, the player who first reached 9 has the option of setting the game to 3; or when the score is 10 all, the player who first reached 10 has the option of setting the game to 2. If a game is not set at 9 all, it can later be set at 10 all.

The opposing sides contest the best of three games. The players change ends at the start of the second game and also at the start of the third game (if any). In the third game, the players change ends when the leading score reaches 8 in a game of 15 points or 6 in a game of 11 points. When it has been agreed to play only one game, the players change ends as provided for the third game.

If players forget to change ends, the ends are changed as soon as the mistake is discovered and the existing score stands.

Faults

A fault made by a player of the side that is in (has the serve) puts the serve out; if made by a player whose side is out, it counts a point to the in side.

It is a fault:

1. If, in serving, the shuttle at the instant of being struck is higher than the server's waist, or if at the instant of the shuttle being struck, the shaft of the racquet is not pointing sufficiently downward that the whole head of the racquet is discernibly below the whole of the server's hand holding the racquet (figure 6-3).
2. If, in serving, the shuttle falls into the wrong service court (into the one not diagonally opposite the server) or falls short of the short service line, beyond the long service line, or outside the side boundary lines of the service court into which service is in order.
3. If the server's feet are not in the service court from which service is at the time being in order, or if the feet of the player receiving the service are not in the service court diagonally opposite until the service is delivered.
4. If, before or during the delivery of the service, any player makes preliminary feints or otherwise intentionally balks (tries to deceive) the opponent, or if any player deliberately delays serving the shuttle or getting ready to receive it, so as to obtain an unfair advantage.
5. If, either in service or play, the shuttle falls outside the boundaries of the court, or passes through or under the net, or fails to pass the net, or touches the roof or side walls, or touches the person or dress of a player. A shuttle falling on a line is deemed to have fallen in the court or service court of which such line is a boundary.

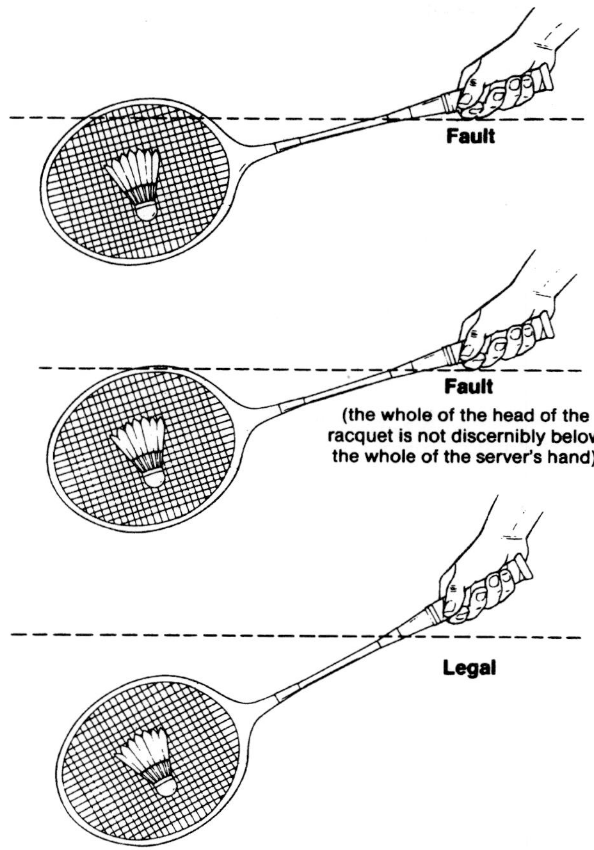

Figure 6-3. Delivery of service.

6. If the shuttle in play is struck before it crosses to the striker's side of the net. The striker may, however, follow the shuttle over the net with the racquet in the course of the stroke.
7. If, when the shuttle is in play, a player touches the net or its supports with racquet, person, or dress.
8. If the shuttle is held on the racquet (that is, caught or slung) during the execution of a stroke, or if the shuttle is hit twice in succession by the same player with two strokes, or if the shuttle is hit by a player and partner successively.
9. If a player obstructs an opponent.

General

The server may not serve until the opponent is ready, but the opponent is deemed to be ready if a return of the service is attempted.

The server and the player served to must stand within the limits of their respective service courts (as bounded by the short and long service lines and the center and side lines), and some part of both feet of these players must remain in contact with the surface of the court in a stationary position until the service is delivered. A foot on or touching a line in the case of either the server or the receiver is held to be outside the service court. The respective partners may take up any position, provided they do not unsight or otherwise obstruct an opponent.

If, in the course of service or rally, the shuttle touches and passes over the net, the stroke is valid and play continues. It is a good return if the shuttle, having passed outside either post, drops on or within the boundary lines of the opposite court. A "let" may be given by the umpire for any unforeseen or accidental hindrance.

If, in service or during a rally, a shuttle, after passing over the net, is caught in or on the net, it is a let.

If the receiver is faulted for moving before the service is delivered or for not being within the correct service court, and at the same time the server is also faulted for service infringement, it is considered a let.

When a let occurs, the play since the last service does not count and the player who last served serves again.

If the server in serving misses the shuttle completely, it is a fault; but if the shuttle is touched by the racquet, a service is delivered.

If a player has the chance of striking the shuttle when quite near the net, an opponent must not extend the racquet near the net. A player may, however, hold up the racquet for protection to avoid being hit in the face if this action does not result in obstructing the opponent's stroke.

It is the duty of the umpire to call "fault" or "let" should either occur, without appeal being made by the players, and to give a decision on any appeal regarding a point in dispute, if made before the net service, and also to appoint line judges and service judges at the umpire's discretion. The umpire's decision is final, but the decision of a line judge or service judge should be upheld. This does not preclude the umpire also from faulting the server or receiver.

Singles Play

The players serve from and receive service in their respective right-hand service courts only when the server's score is 0 or an even number of points, with the service being delivered from and received in their left-hand service courts when the server's score is an odd number of points. Setting the game does not affect this sequence.

Both players change service courts after each point has been scored.

Doubles Play

After it has been decided which side is to have the first service, the player in the right-hand service court of that side commences the game by serving to the player in the service court diagonally opposite. If the latter play returns the shuttle before it touches the ground, it is to be returned by one of the in (serving) side and then returned by one of the out (receiving) side, and so on, until a fault is made or the shuttle ceases to be in play. If a fault is made by the in side, its right to continue serving is lost, as only one player of the side beginning a game is entitled to do so, and the opponent in the right-hand service court then becomes the server; but if the service is not returned or the fault is made by the out side, the in side scores a point. The in-side players then change from one service court to the other, the service now being from the left-hand service court to the player in the service court diagonally opposite. So long as a side remains in, service is delivered alternately from each service court into the one diagonally opposite, the change being made by the in side when, and only when, a point is added to its score.

The first service of a side in each inning is made from the right-hand service court. A service is delivered as soon as the shuttle is struck by the server's racquet. The shuttle is thereafter in play until it touches the floor or playing surface or until a fault or let occurs. After the service is delivered, the server and the player served to may take up any position they choose on their side of the net, regardless of boundary lines.

Only the player served to may receive the service; however, should the shuttle touch or be struck by his or her partner, the in side scores a point. No player may receive two consecutive services in the same game.

Only one player of the side beginning a game is entitled to serve in its first innings. In all subsequent innings each partner has the right, and they serve consecutively. The side winning a game always serves first in the next game, but either of the winners may serve and either of the losers may receive the service.

If a player serves out of turn or from the wrong service court and the serving side wins the rally, it is a let, provided that such let is claimed and allowed or ordered by the umpire before the next service is delivered.

If a player of the out side standing in the wrong service court is prepared to receive the service when it is delivered and the receiving side wins the rally, it is a let, provided that such let is claimed and allowed or ordered by the umpire before the next service is delivered.

If, in either of the previous cases, the side at fault loses the rally, the mistake stands and the player's position is not corrected.

Should a player inadvertently change sides incorrectly and the mistake is not discovered until after the next service has been delivered, the mistake stands, a let cannot be claimed or allowed, and the player's position is not corrected.

FUNDAMENTAL SKILLS AND TECHNIQUES

Grip of the Racquet

1. Forehand grip: The handle of the racquet is held as if the player were shaking hands with the racquet (figure 6-4 A, B).
2. Backhand grip: Similar to the forehand grip except that the hand is rotated slightly to the left and the thumb is placed flat against the side bevel for additional power. The changing of grips during play becomes somewhat automatic (figure 6-4 C, D).
3. The racquet should be held at the extreme end of the handle with the third, fourth, and fifth fingers together (not spread).
4. A standard grip may be secured by placing the racquet, as the player normally would, in front of the body, with the playing surface perpendicular to the floor and then grasping the racquet as one would grip the handle of a hatchet.
5. The standard grip can be used for both forehand and backhand strokes.
6. The hand, wrist, and arm should be entirely relaxed, but the fingers should tighten on the handle just before the racquet contacts the shuttle.
7. Compared to other racquet sports, the badminton racquet is gripped by the fingers and not held in the palm of the hand.

Wrist Action

1. Wrist action is used to disguise intentions. A simple flick of the wrist aids not only in directing the shuttle, but also in sending the opponent in the wrong direction, since the flight is concealed until the last fraction of a second.
2. In starting all shots, the player should keep the racquet well back by cocking the wrist. The racquet's forward swing should not be checked; follow-through is important.

Ready Position and Footwork

To move properly on a badminton court, the player must start from a constantly maintained "ready position." The ideal starting position on the court is approximately a step and a half from the short line and straddling the center line. The player who does not reach this ideal position on the court before the opponent hits the shuttle should stop and react to where the shuttle is hit. A player should never be moving as the opponent is hitting the shuttle.

The correct stance is similar to that of a baseball infielder expecting a grounder. Weight should be on the balls of the feet, with the feet far enough apart to ensure stable balance. The body should be ready to spring in any direction. The knees should be slightly bent. The racquet head should be held at about shoulder height, comfortably away from the body.

In the ready position the feet are in the 12 o'clock position (figure 6-5). To cover the court properly, the player should be ready to move quickly to the 1 o'clock, 3 o'clock and 5 o'clock positions for a forehand stroke. Movement to the right, for a forehand stroke, at these positions on the

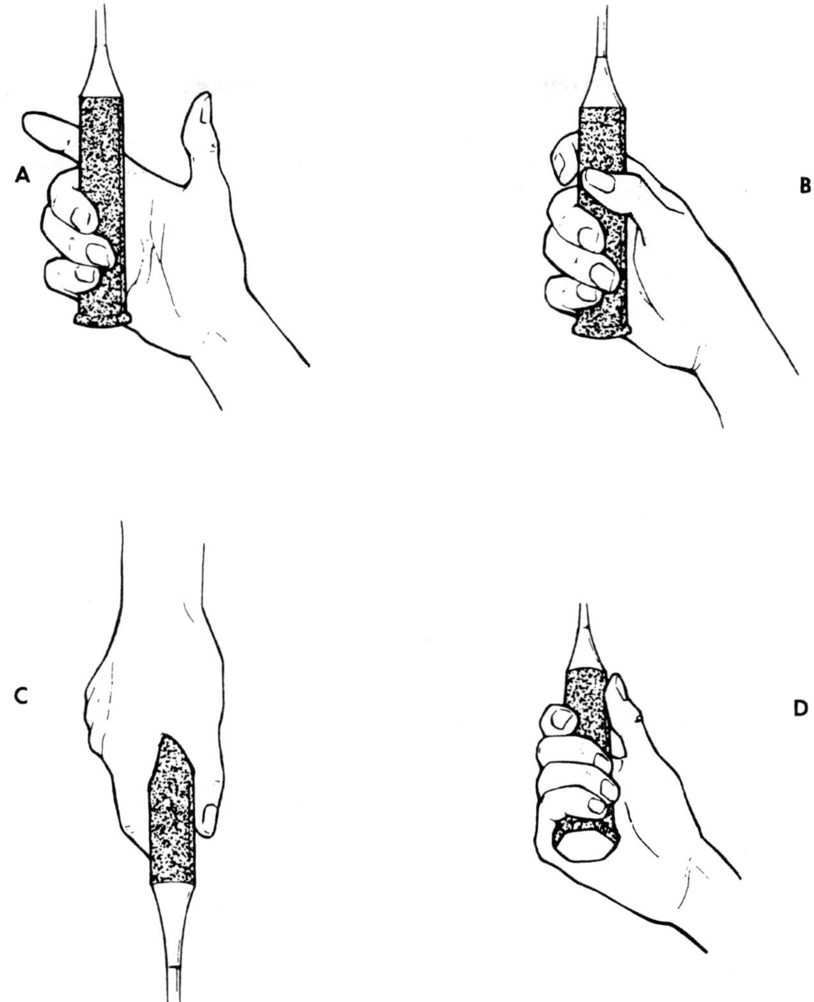

Figure 6-4. Gripping the racquet (right-handed player).

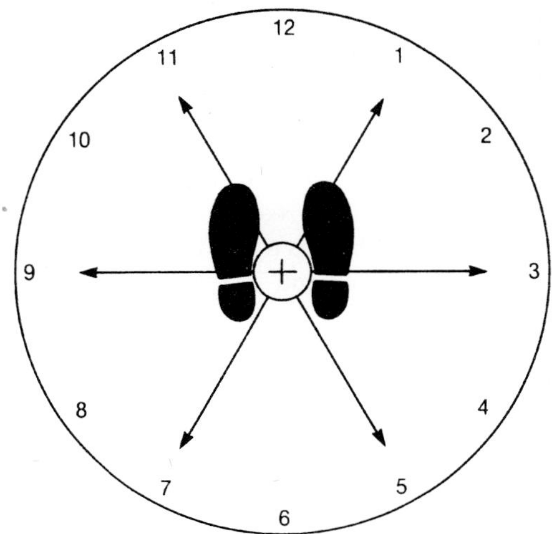

Figure 6-5. Footwork.

court involves moving the body's center of gravity in the direction of the shuttle. For the backhand stroke the player should be ready to move to the 7 o'clock, 9 o'clock, and 11 o'clock positions.

STROKES

The badminton strokes consist of overhead, sidearm, and underhand swinging patterns from both the forehand and backhand sides of the body. The in-front-of-the-body stroke is hit with the backhand swinging pattern. The serves and all other shots are executed with these stroking patterns and are identified by height and location of shuttle trajectory (figure 6-6).

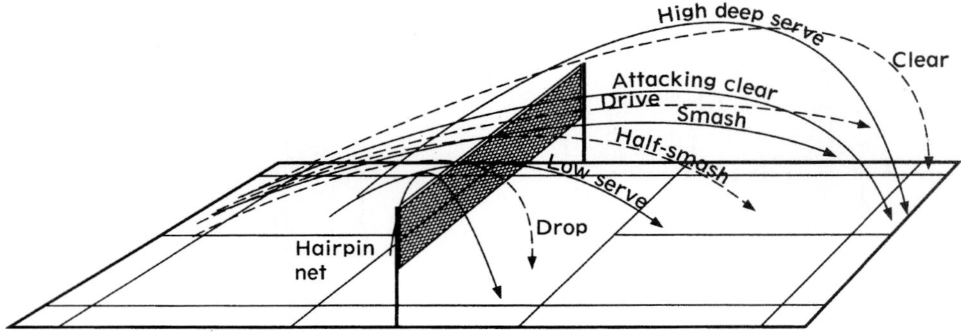

Figure 6-6. Badminton strokes.

Service

High, deep serve

The high, deep serve is an underhand forehand serve hit high so that the shuttle will land in deep court, near the backline.

1. Starting position: Feet in stride position with left foot in front for right-handed players. Shift weight to the rear on backswing, then forward as racquet comes forward. Both feet must remain in contact with the court; "stepping" is a fault.
2. A full backswing is made with the wrist cocked.
3. The wrist is uncocked just before contact.
4. Follow-through: Shuttle contact is made well in front of the body, not at the side. On the follow-through of the underhand stroke, the racquet carries over the left shoulder.

Low, short serve

The low, short serve should be made in such a manner that the shuttle barely clears the net, is on a downward trajectory the moment it passes over the net, and lands close to the short line in the opponent's court.

All basic techniques for the low, short serve—starting position, body rotation, shift in weight, and so on—are the same as for the deep, high serve except:

1. This is a "push" type of serve, accomplished with the wrist remaining almost fully cocked throughout the serve, with little rotation of the forearm.
2. The server should attempt to contact the shuttle as close to the waist height as possible to achieve the desired flat trajectory.

Drive serve

The drive serve is comparable to hitting a line drive in baseball. This serve can be driven at the opponent preferably to hit just below shoulder level.

Basic techniques for the drive serve—starting position, body rotation, and so on—are the same as for the deep, high serve except:

1. The wrist is partially uncocked at contact with the shuttle and the upper arm extends toward the net.
2. Inasmuch as the racquet does not go beyond half cock, there is not a complete follow-through in a full arc, as in the high, deep serve.

Forehand Overhead Strokes

Forehand overhead shots begin with the player's weight on the back foot, followed by shifting of weight from the right to the left foot. Body rotation occurs here. During the shots, the forearm is rotated counterclockwise to produce power at the instant of contact.

Defensive clear shot

1. The racquet is angled slightly back from the perpendicular to attain a high trajectory (figure 6-7 A).
2. Contact with the shuttle is high and over the player's right shoulder (or head).
3. The player should hit the shuttle high and deep and assume proper court position as a receiver.

Attacking clear shot

1. This is the same shot as the defensive clear, except the head of the racquet is almost perpendicular to the floor on contact with the shuttle, giving it a flattened trajectory (figure 6-7 B).
2. This is a quick, hard hit used primarily to place the shuttle deep and out of reach of the opponent.
3. The object of this shot is to get the shuttle past an out-of-position opponent.

Smash

1. Deception on this put-away, or kill, shot is accomplished by making it appear that the return will be a clear or drop.
2. The body should be facing the net on completion of the shot.
3. One should lead with the elbow as the body rotates. The arm should be straight on contact with the shuttle.

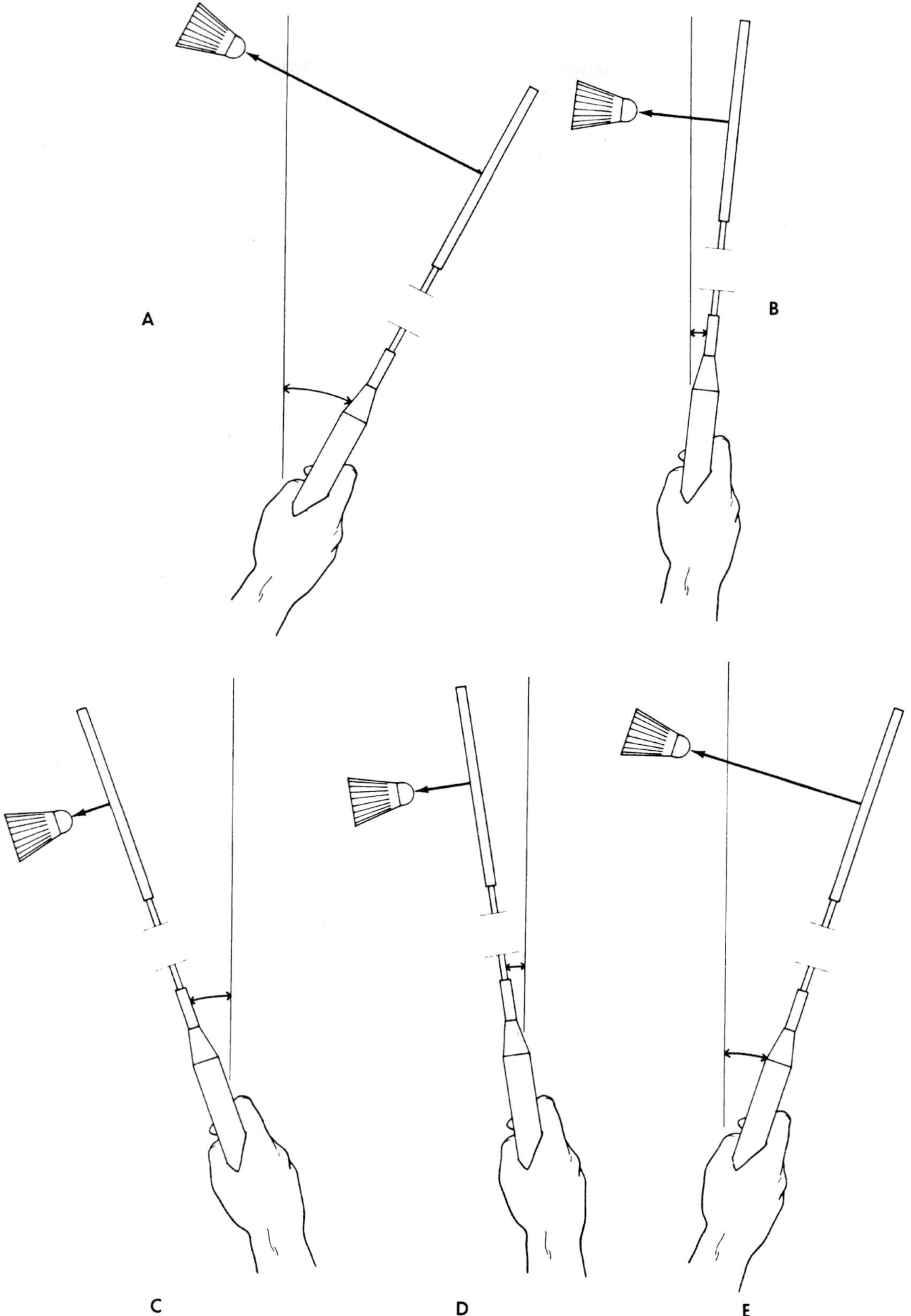

Figure 6-7. Racquet contact points for various shots. **A,** Contact point for defensive clear. **B,** Contact point for attacking clear. **C,** Contact point for smash. **D,** Contact point for fast drop. **E,** Contact point for loop drop.

4. This shot is an extension of the overhead clear, except contact is made with the shuttle farther in front of the body and the angle of the racquet is slightly forward (figure 6-7 C).
5. Vigorous forearm rotation just before contact provides the velocity for the smash.

Drop

1. For a fast drop, the racquet is held at approximately the same angle as for the smash at contact. It should be hit like a smash, except with a softer touch (figure 6-7 D).
2. For a loop drop, the racquet angle is similar to that of a defensive clear (figure 6-7 E).

Backhand Overhead Strokes

The player's back is to the net. The forearm is bent toward the chest with the elbow leading for the "ready" position. On striking the shuttle, the arm is extended and the forearm is simultaneously rotated in a clockwise direction. The angles at contact, the placement of the shuttle in the opponent's court, and the use of backhand overhead shots are the same as for forehand overhead shots, except the contact point is 2 to 3 feet (60 to 90 cm) to the side of the body rather than over the right shoulder (or head).

Drive Strokes

The shuttle is hit quickly, forehand or backhand, on a flat trajectory. The forearm drive action is similar to that of throwing a baseball sidearm.

1. In both forehand and backhand, one should lead with the elbow and hit from a cocked position.
2. The arm should be straight on contact with the shuttle.

Underhand Clear Stroke

The player swings up and through with the wrist in a cocked position, using the same mechanics as in a high, deep serve.

Net Strokes

Net shots require a delicate stroke. The racquet, therefore, does not need to be held as firmly as it is in other shots.

1. Contact the shuttle as near the top of the net as possible.
2. Use arm movement with wrist remaining cocked instead of forearm rotation. This applies to both forehand and backhand net shots.
3. Stretch and reach for the shuttle.

Around-the-Head Strokes

Such strokes are within an arc around the head, above the shoulder, and on the left side of the body.

1. Body faces net, with weight on left foot at contact.
2. Right leg swings forward at completion of stroke.
3. Basic stroke is accomplished through a rotation motion.
4. The angle of the racquet at the time the shuttle is hit determines whether a clear, smash, or drop shot can be executed.

STRATEGY

Singles

1. Serve long unless opponent is playing back for just such a serve; in that case, serve short to take advantage of opponent's poor position.
2. Base use of long or short serve on opponent's strengths and weaknesses.
3. Return a high serve with a drop or clear shot.
4. Use an attacking clear or drive shot for a low serve; or if it can be reached before falling too far below the net, use a net shot.
5. Use down-the-line smashes or smash at opponent's right hip or shoulder.
6. Return a smash with a drop to the point on the court farthest from the point at which the smash was made.
7. Drive down the sidelines.
8. Play your position; do not try to outguess your opponent.
9. Take advantage of your opponent's weaknesses, but not to the extent that such repeated effort improves the weakness.
10. Alternate shots deep in court with drop shots to make the opponent run further to return the shuttle. Once out of position, hit a smash to win the point.

Doubles

1. Play formations:
   a. Side by side: Each person is responsible for half the court, from front to back. Disadvantages are that it is hard to run from the net to the back court and make a good smash or a good attacking shot, and returns to the center cause confusion as to who will hit them. This is the best defensive position.
   b. Front and back: One person plays the front court and one the back, with the front player taking all net shots and any other shot that can be returned with a better shot than the partner can deliver. Although this is a popular formation for doubles, a disadvantage is the resulting poor defense against smashes and drives down the sidelines. This is the best attacking formation.
   c. Combination: This formation combines the best features of the other two. The partners rotate in a counterclockwise circle, so that the backcourt player need never return for a backhand shot in

the near court. When the team using this formation is on the attack, the players should be playing front and back; when on defense, they should be playing side by side.

2. Play shots that will give an opening for your partner on his or her return. Do not hit short clears, which may leave your partner open to an attack from the opponents.
3. Serve low and short, preferably to the comer formed by the center line and short service line.
4. Smash long serves, but occasionally use a drop shot.
5. Rush forward on short serves.
6. Do not play too close to the net. A position around the short service line is best for playing the net.
7. If servers are playing in front-and-back formation, the best return of a low serve is a shot down the sidelines to about half court.
8. Almost all high, deep shots should be returned with smash shots directed between the center line and the opponent playing straight ahead in a side-by-side defense. When in the front and back attacking formation, this smashing strategy generally forces a return directed to the forecourt player, who can hit a winning shot.

CONDITIONING FOR BADMINTON

When badminton players are of equal skill, whether novice or advanced, fitness becomes an important factor in deciding the winner. To increase stamina, strength, and speed, the fitness training program for badminton players must consist of drills and play patterns that simulate actual play patterns used in competition.

Three general categories of fitness training programs based upon the demands of the sport should be followed:

1. *Traditional fitness training*. This involves wind sprints, running, rope skipping, circuit weight training, and calisthenics—some examples are listed below:
   a. Wind sprints: 6 sets of very high intensity exercise; 10 seconds of exercise with 30-second recovery periods.
   b. Running: 6 to 8 sets of relatively high intensity exercise; 30 seconds of exercise with 60-second recovery.
   c. 1 set of continuous aerobic exercise (run/cycle/jump rope); 10 to 60 minutes at 120 skips/minute.
   d. Weight training or circuit weight training: These are exercises using various machines (e.g., Universal Gym, Nautilus) or free weights to work trunk, lower body, and upper body major muscle groups. Badminton players should emphasize toe raises, leg flexion and extension, trunk flexion and extension, triceps extension, forearm, wrist, and shoulder exercises.
2. *Shadow drills*. Shadow drills are running and jumping exercises designed to simulate play patterns and improve balance, footwork, and court speed as well as fitness. For maximum benefit the player should carry a badminton racket and simulate the execution of a badminton shot at each court position. Shadow drills can be set patterns or can be directed by the instructor and use the same time periods as wind sprints (10-second drill/30-second rest; 30-second drill/60-second rest; 1- to 3-minute drill/2- to 3-minute rest). The instructor uses hand signals to direct the player about the court at the fastest rate at which the player can maintain good balance.
3. *Pressure training*. These are continuous high-intensity badminton playing drills that require the player to move to all areas of the court, either in set patterns or in variation, to return a shuttle hit by the instructor or other players. Pressure training fitness programs become more effective as the player's skill increases to a level where long rallies can be played without making an error.

WARMING UP AND COOLING DOWN FOR BADMINTON

Warm-up for badminton consists of low-intensity exercise with gradually increasing activity over a period of 3 to 5 minutes until the player begins to sweat. Stretching exercises can be introduced at this time to increase or maintain player flexibility. The player can then do calisthenics, lunges, jumps, and racquet swinging exercises. These activities can be done off the court. Once the player moves onto the court, the warm-up consists of skill activities in which the player hits a variety of clears, drops, and smashes with power and accuracy.

Stretching exercises are recommended following a hard workout or competition to maintain or improve flexibility and/or prevent muscle soreness. Stretching exercises can *also* be done as the last portion of the warm-up if the player has low flexibility or is recovering from an injury. One to three sets of static stretching (no bobbing) of 20- to 30-seconds' duration are recommended.

BADMINTON ETIQUETTE

Sportsmanship is the foremost courtesy. Be gracious; never needle an opponent. If in doubt about a boundary decision, call it in favor of the opponent; the opponent, if a good sport, will disagree. If fouling occurs at the net, one should call it on oneself.

Hand a shuttle over to an adjoining court player at the end of a rally. Thank a player when your shuttle is returned.

Do not delay in calling a foul.

Do not play indifferently against an inferior opponent.

Wear appropriate clothing, especially shoes that do not mark the floor.

TEACHING CONSIDERATIONS

1. For school-age populations, establish the grip and ready position as well as a basic underhand and overhead shot. It is not necessary to teach specialized shots until students can keep the shuttlecock going continuously across the net cooperatively with these basic shots.
2. Begin with singles, even if it means using half a court for practice.
3. Design experiences to have students change the placement, force levels, and trajectory of the shuttlecock from these basic shots. For example:
   a. Move your opponent from the net to the back line (up-and-back strategy using drop shots and clears).
   b. Tape four 3 foot by 3 foot squares in each of the back corners of the court. Have students practice getting the shuttlecock inside the squares or give each student an extra point if the shuttlecock lands inside the square during game play.
   c. Start working with your partner cooperatively. On the fourth hit back and forth, one of the partners calls "Now," and the object of the game should be to make the other person "miss" by hitting the shuttlecock forward and back, left and right, or hitting it hard to the opponent.
4. Teach the short and high deep serve.
5. After minimal amounts of practice of a skill in basic conditions, put that skill back in the context of game play. Students can perform many badminton shots efficiently and effectively without having to execute the shot using correct form. Correct form allows the shot to be disguised in a game (for example, drop shot and smash).
6. Introduce competitive play and stress placement of shuttlecock away from opponent. Introduce the clear and drop shots as students attempt to place the shuttlecock in front of the service line and near the back boundary. Practice the specialized skills and put them back into the game. Modify the games, if need be, by giving extra points for points won using one of these shots.
7. Begin doubles play with side-by-side strategies. Introduce combination up and back and side by side as soon as students are consistently returning to their home base position after being pulled out of position defensively.
8. Design warm-up activities that include combinations of skills using both forehand and backhand strokes.

GLOSSARY

alley The 1.5-area on the sides of the court between the singles and doubles sidelines.

around-the-head A stroke hit from the backhand side of the body with a forehand stroking pattern.

backhand Strokes hit on the side of the body opposite to the racquet hand (left side of the body for right-handed players).

base Ready position to which players try to return after each shot.

bird Slang term for a shuttlecock or shuttle. The object hit back and forth over the net.

carry (sling, throw) A shot in which the shuttle slides across the face of the racket and is misdirected from the intended shot. Since 1981 this shot is legal if hit unintentionally.

clear (lob) A shot hit high and deep to the opponent's backcourt.

combination doubles formation Partners play side-by-side on defense and up-and-back on offense.

cross-court A shot hit diagonally from one side of the court to the other.

defense A situation in which your opponent has the opportunity to hit a smash at you.

doubles A game played with two players on each side.

drive A sidearm stroke hit so as to land between the opponent's short service line and the back boundary line.

drop shot A shot hit from any position that passes close to the net and lands in the opponent's front court (in front of the short service line).

even court The side of the court corresponding to the right service court.

fault A violation of the rules. (See Law 14.)

forehand Strokes hit on the racket side of the body.

game A badminton game is played to 15 in all events except women's singles, which is played to 11 points, unless the game has been set. (See Rule 7; Scoring.)

grip (a) The covering of the racket handle, usually leather. (b) The positioning of the hand in holding the racquet handle.

half-court shot A shot hit down the sideline that lands in the opponent's court midway between net and back baseline.

IBF International Badminton Federation, governing body for international competition.

kill (put-away, winner) A smash hit to win the rally.

let An incident that requires the replay of a rally. (See Rules 12 and 17.)

long serve A high serve directed toward the receiver's back baseline.

match The best two out of three games.

mixed doubles A game contested with a male and female on each team.

net shot A shot played to the opponent's forecourt, dropping close to the net.

odd court The side of the court corresponding with the left service court.

offense A player or team on the attack or with the opportunity to smash.

overhead Strokes hit above head height.

power shots Shots that are hit very hard; clears, drives, and smashes.

racquet The implement used to strike the shuttle.

rally The exchange of shot during play or during warm-up.

receiver The player who receives the service.

server The player who hits the serve.

service The act of putting the shuttle in play to begin a rally.

service court The singles or doubles court boundary into which the service must be delivered.

setting A method of extending the game when tied near the end of the game. (See Rule 7.)
short serve A serve hit just over the net to land near the short service line. The primary serve in doubles.
shot A clear, drive, drop, or smash that has been hit from one of the stroking positions.
shuttlecock (shuttle, bird) The object hit back and forth over the net.
side-by-side formation A doubles defensive formation in which the players play side-by-side in the midcourt.
smash A hard overhand shot hit with a downward angle.
stroke The basic hitting patterns from which all shots are executed.
Thomas Cup An international men's team competition held every two years.
toss Before a match begins, players "toss" a coin, spin a racket, or hit a shuttle to determine who will serve and defend court end.
Uber Cup An international women's team competition held every two years.
underhand A stroke in which the shuttle is contacted below the waist and in front of the body.
up-and-back formation A doubles formation providing the best attack positioning. Classic mixed-doubles positioning with the women in the forecourt and the man in the backcourt.
USA badminton The national governing body for badminton in the United States (formerly Badminton USA).
winner (see *kill, put-away*)

SUGGESTED READINGS

Ballou, R. B. 1998. *Badminton for beginners*. Englewood, Colo.: Morton. W for beginners, but also discusses intermediate and advanced skills.

Bloss, M. V. 1994. *Badminton*. 7th ed. Dubuque, Iowa: Wm. C. Brown.

Chadwick, G., and Schoppe, D. 1994. *Championship badminton drills*. P.O. Box 3327, Manhattan Beach, Calif. Extensive lists of drills for the novice through the championship player.

Chafin, M. B., and Turner, M. 1988. *Badminton everyone*. Winston-Salem, N.C.: Hunter Textbooks. Contains material on techniques, strategies, rules, and terminology. Also includes tips for students, hundreds of illustrations, and chapter quizzes.

Clark, J. 1991. *Seven lifetime sports*. Dubuque, Iowa: Eddie Bowers. The chapter on badminton contains information on history, benefits, terminology, rules, equipment, skill fundamentals, error corrections, drills, games, and skills tests.

Grice, T. 1995. *Badminton: Steps to success*. Champaign, Ill.: Human Kinetics.

Poole, J., and Poole, J. 1996. *Badminton*. 4th ed. Prospect Heights, Ill.: Waveland Press. Includes a step-by-step summary of mechanics for each movement, latest developments in equipment and mechanics, and drills.

Sweeting, R., and Wilson, J. 1991. *Badminton: Basic skills and drills*. Mountain View, Calif.: Mayfield. Provides step-by-step instruction in the basics of the game while emphasizing tactics and techniques. Contains more than 100 line drawings.

U.S. Badminton Association. *Official rules of play (USBA handbook)*. USBA, One Olympic Plaza, Colorado Springs, CO 80909.

Wadood, T., and Tan, K. 1990. *Badminton today*. St. Paul, Minn.: West. Includes more than 150 photographs and 60 figures depicting skills, strategies, drills, and fitness training. An instructor's manual is available.

RESOURCES

Films And Videotapes

Badminton Instructional Video Tapes, 817-23rd St., NW, Wash. D.C. 20052. (1) Grip, Footwork, Serves; (2) Basic Strokes (3) Basic Strategy.

Badminton Movies. Louisville Badminton Supply, 9411 Westport Road, Louisville, KY 40222.

Badminton: Winning Fundamentals, HL Corporation, P.O. Box 3327, Manhattan Beach, CA.

Selected Highlights of the 1973 U.S. Open Amateur Championships. Travelers Insurance Companies, 1 Tower Square, Hartford, CT 06115.

USBA Video Library (rental of videocassettes of national and international events, weight training, International Badminton Federation instructional video's). USA Badminton, One Olympic Plaza, Colorado Springs, CO 80909. (719) 578-4808, Fax. (719) 578-4507. E-mail: usab2004@rmi.net. USBA Home page: http://mid1.external.hp.comm/stanb/usba/usba.html.

Magazines

Badminton USA. USA Badminton, One Olympic Plaza, Colorado Springs, CO 80909.

World Badminton. The International Badminton Federation, 4 Manor Park, Mackenzie Way, Cheltenham, Gloucestershire, England GL51 9TX.

Basketball

After completing this chapter, the reader should be able to:

- Tell the history of the game of basketball
- Explain the basic rules of the game and the slight differences that exist between the men's and women's game
- Demonstrate the fundamental skills of passing, dribbling, and shooting
- Explain the general principles of offensive and defensive strategy
- Instruct a group of students in the basic skills of basketball

HISTORY

Basketball was introduced in 1891 by Dr. James A. Naismith, then physical education director at the YMCA College in Springfield, Massachusetts. The first official game was not played until 1892. Basketball was principally designed as a game to create interest in the gymnasium during the winter months.

A peach basket was first used as the hoop. After each score the ball had to be taken out of the basket before play could be resumed.

The game spread rapidly to the nation's playgrounds, community centers, gymnasiums, schools, and colleges. Today nearly every boy and girl learns to play basketball.

In 1899 women formulated their own rules, and in 1901 the first women's *Basketball Guide* was published.

Men's Olympic Basketball History

Although basketball was included as a demonstration sport in the 1904 St. Louis Olympic Games, it was not finally adopted until 1936. The United States defeated Canada (19 to 8) for the gold medal in the 1936 Berlin Games, but the game was played outdoors on a clay court in the rain. The United States dominated Olympic basketball by winning the gold medal in 1948 (65 to 21 over France), 1952 (36 to 25 over U.S.S.R.), 1956 (85 to 55 over U.S.S.R.), 1960 (81 to 57 over U.S.S.R.), 1964 (73 to 59 over U.S.S.R.), and 1968 (65 to 50 over Yugoslavia). The United States lost for the first time in Olympic history in the famous final game of the 1972 Munich Olympics when the Soviet team, after protesting, was awarded the chance to replay the final 3 seconds of the game and won 50 to 49. In 1976 the United States regained the gold medal by defeating Yugoslavia 95 to 72. Yugoslavia defeated Italy 86 to 77 in 1980, the year the United States boycotted the Moscow Olympics. In Los Angeles (1984) the U.S. team once again claimed the gold medal by defeating Spain 96 to 65. In the 1988 Seoul Olympics the U.S. men's team had its worst finish ever by claiming the bronze medal.

To compensate for their third-place finish in 1988, the U.S. men's team elected to allow professional players from the National Basketball Association to try out for the Olympic team. This team, known as the "Dream Team," was composed of 11 professional players and one collegiate player. The American team defeated Croatia 117 to 85 to win the gold medal in the Barcelona Olympics in 1992. In the 1996 Summer Olympics, held in Atlanta, Georgia, the U.S. men's team, known as Dream Team 2, composed of NBA players, easily won the gold medal. Yugoslavia and Lithuania won the silver and bronze, respectively.

Women's Olympic Basketball History

Women's basketball was added to the Olympics in 1976, and the gold medal was claimed by the Soviets, with the U.S. team picking up the silver medal. In 1980 the Soviet women defeated Bulgaria 104 to 73. The U.S. women's team won its first gold medal by defeating Korea 85 to 55 in 1984 and its second straight gold medal with a victory over Yugoslavia in 1988. In the 1992 Olympics in Barcelona, Spain, the U.S. women's team defeated Cuba 88 to 74 for the bronze medal. In the Atlanta Olympic Games, the U.S. women's team captured the gold medal. Brazil won the silver and Australia the bronze.

The game of basketball has flourished at all levels of competition, including youth, high school, college, and professional. The number of girls and young women participating in these leagues has increased dramatically. In the summer and fall of 1997, two new professional leagues for women (WNBA and ABL) emerged. The number of spectators attending these games indicates that women's professional basketball in the United States may have been finally accepted on a permanent basis.

COURT AND EQUIPMENT

The playing court is a rectangular surface free from obstructions, having maximum dimensions for college of 94 x 50 feet (28.65 x 15.24 m) and for high school of 84 x 50 feet (25.60 x 15.24 m) (figure 7-1). However, many courts

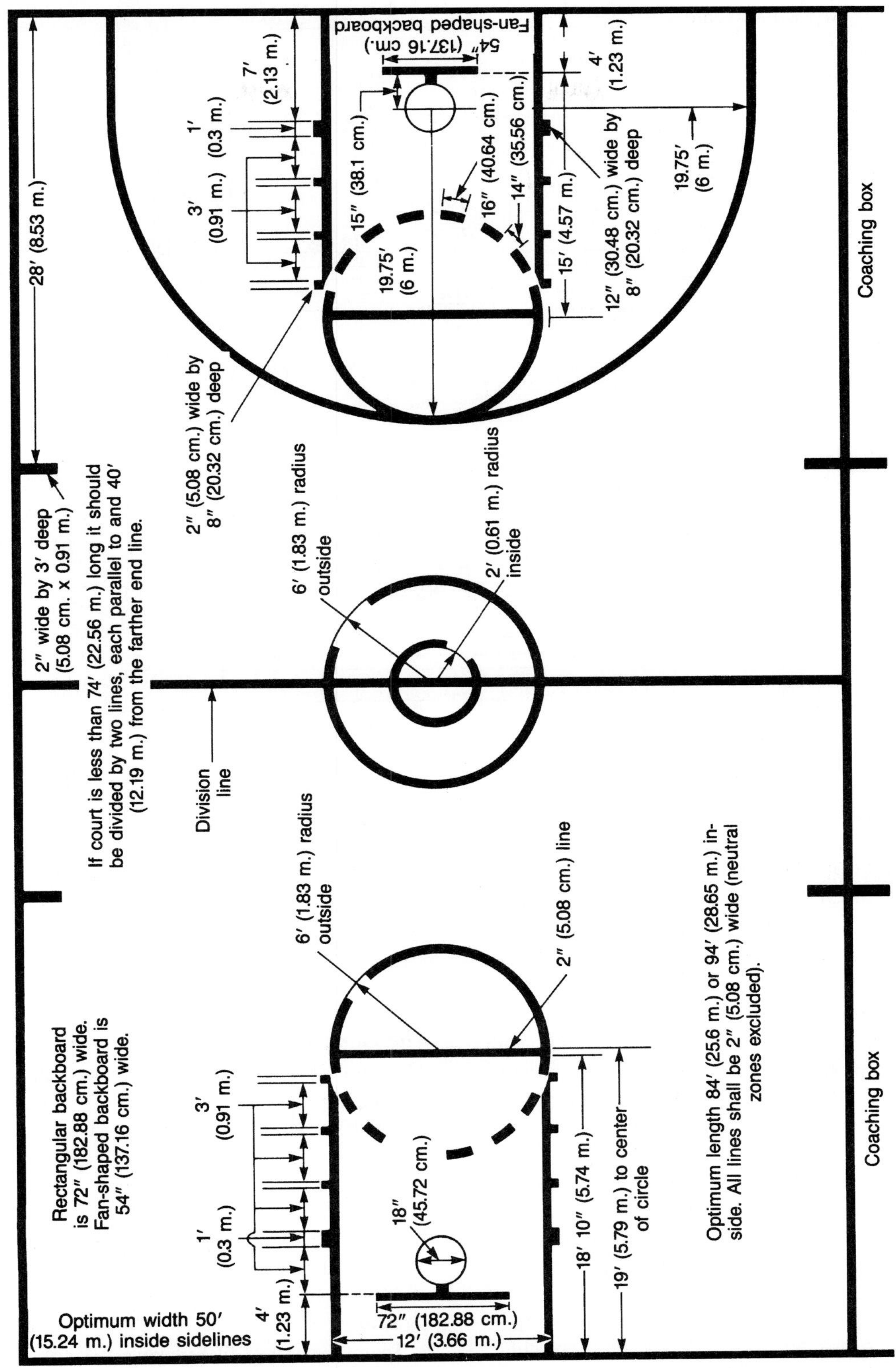

Figure 7-1. Basketball court for men and women. Left end shows large backboard for college games; right end shows small backboard for high school games. For the broken semicircle in the free throw lane, it is recommended that there be eight marks 16 inches (40.64 cm) long and seven spaces 14 inches (35.56 cm) long. There should be a minimum of 3 feet (0.91 m) and preferably 10 feet (3.05 m) of unobstructed space outside the court. If this is impossible, a narrow broken 1-inch (2.54 cm) line should be marked inside the court parallel with and 3 feet (0.91 m) inside the boundary. Three point line is 19.75 feet (6 m) from the basket for high school and college courts.

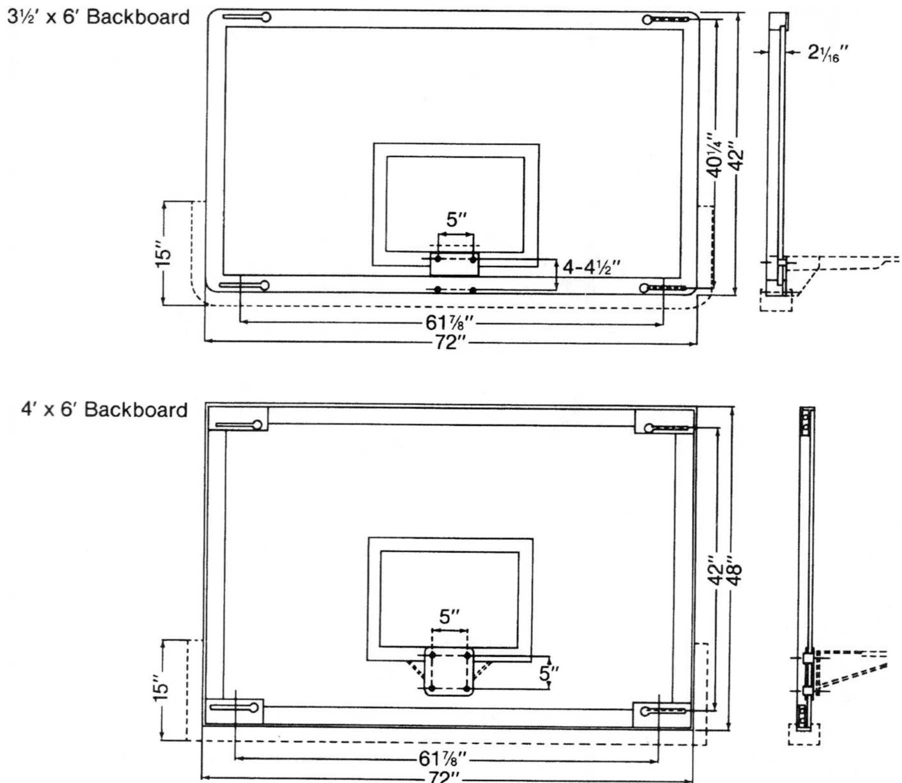

Figure 7-2. Basketball goals.

are smaller. The court dimensions are the same for men's and women's basketball.

The backboard, 6 feet (1.83 m) wide and 4 feet (1.22 m) high (smaller for high school), is located at the center of each end of the court 4 feet (1.22 m) in from the end line and 9 feet (2.74 m) above the floor. It can be made of hardwood, metal, or glass (figure 7-2).

The basket is an open hammock net, suspended from the backboard on a metal ring 18 inches (45.7 cm) in diameter, which must be 6 inches (15.2 cm) from the rigid surface to which it is fastened and 10 feet (3.05 m) above the floor.

The ball is spherical, and the one used by men measures 30 inches (76.2 cm) in circumference. The ball used by women is 28.5 to 29.0 inches (72.4 to 73.7 cm) in circumference.

Foot comfort and protection should be a primary concern of both coach and player. Shoes and socks that fit well and that are designed for use by basketball players help avoid unnecessary injuries and discomfort, including blisters, sprained ankles, and bruised heels.

GENERAL RULES

Rules governing the game are revised each year by the joint Basketball Rules Committee, representing the Amateur Athletic Union (AAU), National Association for Girls and Women in Sport (NAGWS), National Collegiate Athletic Association (NCAA), Young Men's Christian Association (YMCA), National Federation of State High School Associations (NFSHSA), Canadian Amateur Basketball Association, USA Basketball, and chartered boards of officials.

The Game

The home team provides the game ball, and traditionally the visiting team is given the choice of end of court for the first half. If a neutral court is used, a coin toss determines home team and choice of ends. The teams change sides of the court at halftime. Half of the court is the frontcourt of one team and the backcourt of the other team.

The ball is passed, thrown, bounced, handed, or otherwise moved among players of one team, with the intent of scoring a basket and preventing the other team from scoring.

Teams consist of five players: two forwards, two guards, and one center. Generally the forwards play closest to the basket, the guards play farthest from their team's basket, and the center plays between the forwards and the guards. At higher levels of competition, the players are referred to by numbers as well as by positions: point guard (1), shooting guard (2), small or wing forward (3), power forward (4), and center (5).

The game is started with a jump ball between any two opponents (usually the centers) at center court. After each field goal the ball is put into play by the team not scoring, from the out-of-bounds area behind the basket at which the score was made.

After a free throw awarded because of a personal foul, the ball is put into play by the opponent from behind the opponent's basket. If the free throw is the result of a technical foul, the ball is put into play from out of bounds at midcourt by the free thrower's team.

A player is out of bounds if he or she touches the floor on or outside the boundary line. If a player causes the ball to pass over the boundary line, the ball is put into play by an opposing player from that spot. Any player can make the throw-in. The player throwing the ball in must stand out-of-bounds where the referee designates, may take one lateral step to the left or right, jump up or take two or more steps backward, and may use either one or two hands to make the throw-in, which must be completed within 5 seconds.

Rules Common to Men's and Women's Basketball

1. Numbers must be worn by players on front and back.
2. A jump ball is taken following a double foul.
3. The hand is considered to be a part of the ball on tie balls, shots, dribbles, interceptions, and the like.
4. The penalty for a violation is loss of possession of the ball.
5. The following are not considered dribbles:
   a. Successive tries for goals
   b. Fumbles
   c. Attempts to gain control of the ball by:
      (1) Tapping it from the control of another player
      (2) Tapping it from the reach of another player
      (3) Blocking a pass and recovering the ball
      (4) Blocking a shot and recovering the ball
6. During a free throw, players from the defensive team shall occupy both lane spaces adjacent to the end line.
7. On jump balls, opponents are entitled to alternate positions around the restraining circle if they so indicate before the official is ready to toss the ball.
8. On jump balls, the players must hold their established positions around the restraining circle until the ball has been tossed,
9. After the opening jump ball to start the game, any jump ball situation results in the teams' alternating possession of the ball. The team losing the opening jump ball is awarded the first possession, with teams alternating possessions for the rest of the game.
10. The game clock is stopped after successful field goals in the last minute of the game and the last minute of any overtime period, with no substitutions allowed during this stoppage.

Rule Differences

It must be pointed out that there are basic differences between high school and college rules and regulations. At the high school level, for example, there is no shot clock used.

Two important differences in the rules for college men's and women's basketball are:

1. Use of a 30-second shot clock in women's basketball and a 35-second clock in men's basketball. After securing possession of the ball, the offensive team must attempt a shot at the basket before the time clock goes to zero or give up possession of the ball.
2. In men's basketball the ball must be advanced into the frontcourt within 10 seconds, but in women's basketball (with the shorter, 30-second clock) there is no such rule.

Violations Common to Men's and Women's Basketball

1. Taking more than one step with the ball without passing, shooting, or dribbling
2. Kicking the ball with the foot or lower leg
3. Stepping out of bounds with the ball
4. The center's leaving the circle before the ball is tipped in beginning play
5. Staying in one's own free-throw lane for more than 3 seconds
6. Failure to observe free-throw regulations
7. Failure to inbound the ball within 5 seconds
8. Double dribbling
9. Moving the ball into the backcourt once it has been advanced to the frontcourt (over-and-back)
10. Technical fouls include:
    a. Taking time out too often
    b. Failure of substitutes to report to proper officials
    c. Unsportsman-like conduct
    d. Use of illegal numbers or uniforms
    e. Touching the backboard or rim illegally
11. Personal fouls include:
    a. Charging
    b. Blocking
    c. Pushing
    d. Holding
    e. Tripping
    f. Hacking or kneeing

When a violation is committed, the ball is given to the opponents out-of-bounds. When a foul is committed, the opponents may be given a free throw, an opportunity to make two free throws if the first one is made, or the ball out-of-bounds. The decision as to which of these options is awarded depends on the particular foul committed, the level of play (high school or college), and the number of fouls that the offending team has previously committed. A player fouled in the act of shooting gets two free throws. If the basket is made, one free throw is awarded and the basket is counted. Only personal fouls disqualify a player. A player is allowed only four personal fouls; a fifth sidelines the player for the remainder of the game.

Officials

The officials include a referee, an umpire, three timekeepers, and two scorers (one timekeeper and one scorer are assistants). The third timekeeper runs the 30- or 35-second shot clock. At the men's college division 1A level, there are three officials utilized to referee the game. There is a referee and two umpires. Because of the speed of the players and the complexity of the offenses and defenses, many high school state associations have adopted the three-officials system.

Scoring

Two points are awarded for each basket from the floor, and one point is awarded for each free throw. Three points are awarded for field goals made from outside the three-point line.

Coaching Box

A coaching box is outlined outside the side of the court on which the officials' table and players' benches are located. The area is bounded by the endline extended, the sideline, the midcourt marker extended, and the players' bench. The endline and midcourt mark lines are 3 feet (0.9 m) long and 2 inches (5 cm) wide, and their color contrasts with that of the midcourt mark line and endline.

DURATION OF GAME

College men and women play for two halves of 20 minutes each, with a 15-minute rest at halftime. If the score is tied at the end of the game, as many 5-minute periods as needed to break the tie are played.

High school teams play four quarters of 8 minutes each, with a 10-minute halftime rest and 1 minute between quarters. If the score is tied at the end of the fourth quarter, as many 3-minute periods as needed to break the tie are played.

FUNDAMENTAL SKILLS AND TECHNIQUES

Passing

Passing is the key to successful basketball. A team must be able to handle, control, and move the ball downcourt quickly and accurately to create scoring opportunities.

First, learn to catch as well as pass. When the ball is thrown to you, spread your fingers but keep them relaxed. When the ball hits your fingers, let your arms give slightly toward the body. When the ball is under control, finger it into passing position by placing your hands on each side of the ball so that you can get it away quickly or get set for a shot.

Some practical hints

1. Remember that the cause of most fumbling is holding the arms too stiffly while catching.
2. Watch the ball all the way into your hands.
3. Do not fight the ball; that is, do not pass until you have full control of the ball.
4. Stay relaxed, and try not to rush passes.
5. Keep your head up, and use peripheral vision to spot any free teammate.
6. When a teammate calls for the ball, check the position of the defender before making a pass, and make the pass to the side farthest from the defender.
7. Move toward a pass rather than away from it.
8. Passes to moving teammates should lead them so they do not have to slow down or reverse direction.
9. When some mastery in controlling the ball has been gained, learn to pass with deception—for example, looking one way and passing another or faking high and passing low.
10. Rely on "split vision," actually looking straight ahead but seeing the receiver out of the corner of your eye.
11. Do not pass blindly.

Chest or push pass

Hold the ball with both hands, elbows close to the body, fingers spread with thumbs pointed inward. Step toward the receiver and whip the ball with a strong wrist snap and push of thumbs and fingers, making the arms follow through in the direction of the pass (figure 7-3).

Flip pass

A pass that can be used when there is to be a close exchange of the ball is a flip pass. This pass is executed by flipping or almost handing the ball to a teammate when the defense is applying heavy pressure. The person making the pass should try to position the body between the defensive player and the teammate to whom the pass is being made. To allow the other player the best chance to catch the ball, it should be flipped up softly. This passing technique is very effective in getting the ball to a teammate who is driving to the basket off a screen set by another player.

Bounce pass

A bounce pass can be executed with either one or two hands and is often used to get the ball past a defensive player between the passer and the teammate who is to receive the pass. For the two-handed bounce pass, hold the ball in much the same manner as for the chest pass except somewhat lower, about waist high. Then push the ball out and down with enough force and at such an angle that the ball bounces to the teammate. The one-hand bounce pass

Figure 7-3. Chest pass.

is often executed directly from the dribble. The bounce pass should only be used for short passes and it should travel between one half and three quarters of the distance in the air.

Two-hand overhead pass

Hold and throw the ball with both hands. Bring the ball well above and slightly behind the head with both hands and release it with a strong wrist snap and extension of the arms. Arms and hands follow through in the direction of the pass (figure 7-4).

Off-the-dribble pass

This pass can be used by players who have mastered the dribble. In this pass the player will see the open teammate and, without stopping to pick the ball up, make a pass with the dribbling hand. This pass gets the ball to the open player before the defense can react, and it is very effective in fast-break situations.

Baseball pass

Shift the ball in front of the waist to the throwing hand, turn the opposite side of the body in the direction of the pass, and then whip the ball back, as in an infield throw. Step toward the receiver and throw the ball with a full arm motion and wrist snap. Permit the fingers to follow through without a twist so that the movement does not cause the ball to curve (figure 7-5).

One-hand hook pass

With the opposite side turned in the direction of the receiver, bring the ball from the hips, up and back. Cradle the ball on the wrist with the fingers well spread behind it for control, and throw it with a hook motion of the arm and strong wrist action over the head, following through with the hand (figure 7-6).

Pivoting

Pivoting is a skill used to elude an opponent when a player has the ball. A forward pivot is executed by keeping one foot in place on the floor and moving the other forward and across the foot in place (figure 7-7). A reverse pivot is executed by keeping one foot in place and moving the other backward in a semicircle.

Dribbling

Learn to dribble with the body low for protection and the head up. Dribble with the hand farthest from the defender,

Figure 7-4. Two-hand overhead pass. **A,** Midway; **B,** End.

Figure 7-5. Baseball pass.

Figure 7-6. One-hand hook pass.

Figure 7-7. Pivot and pass.

Figure 7-8. Fake right.

and use the body to protect the ball. Spread the fingers and relax the wrist and fingers. Control the ball with the fingers, pushing it down and forward; do not bat it.

Keep the ball low, below the waist. Avoid a high-bounce dribble. The ball can be moved downcourt faster by passing than by dribbling, so never dribble when you can pass.

Up-and-under fake pass and dribble

Stand for the shot in front of the opponent and go through the motion of bringing the ball up for a jump shot. As the guard closes in or leaps to block the shot, duck low and drive past to one side, dribbling with the hand farthest from the opponent.

Fake pass and dribble

Hold the ball waist high on receiving it; then fake to the right with the ball and head. As the guard goes in that direction, turn quickly to the left and cross-step with the right foot and dribble the ball on the left side with the left hand, which is farthest from the guard (figure 7-8).

Shooting

Basic mechanics of shooting

Shooting is a fundamental, learned skill. To become a good shooter, a player should know the basic mechanics of the shot and become aware of the common shooting faults. The following shooting methods can be practiced by looking into a mirror. Do not be afraid to look at the wrist action and follow through until a natural release can be attained. This is the reason it is wise to shoot off a wall or backboard; striving for accuracy should not be the primary objective until the smooth release has been learned.

Before becoming involved in the mechanics of shooting, the player should have a fundamental knowledge of the basket and the point at which to aim. Good shooters do not follow the flight of the ball with their eyes; they concentrate on the basket during the entire shooting process. Coaches and teachers vary in their opinions on what part of the basket the shooter should look at. Some believe the front rim should be the focal point, while others suggest focusing on the back of the rim. In selecting either method, it might be wise to analyze the ball-basket relationship.

Figure 7-9 illustrates that two regulation basketballs will fit through the basket at the same time. This suggests that looking at the approximate center of the basket would be the best because you can compensate for your margin of error in the following manner: If the shot is short, the ball can still be put in by aiming for the center. If the shot is slightly long, the ball can be put in by glancing off the back lip of the rim. If long by a large margin, the player can put the ball in off the backboard (figure 7-10).

Front view of shooting positions (figure 7-11). *A*, The ball should be rolled off the fingertips with a backspin effect. The backspin will cause the ball to become dead upon impact with the rim. *B*, The wrist should be cocked with the ball resting on the fingers and not touching the inside palm of the hand. *C*, The elbow should be on line to the target area. A slight lateral shift of the elbow, if comfortable, should be permitted for some shooters. *D*, The opposite hand should be placed on the ball in a position that is comfortable. However, this hand should not interfere with the shooting motion. *E*, The eyes should be focused on the basket. Watch for the common fault of following the ball. *F*, The shoulders should be squared off to the basket.

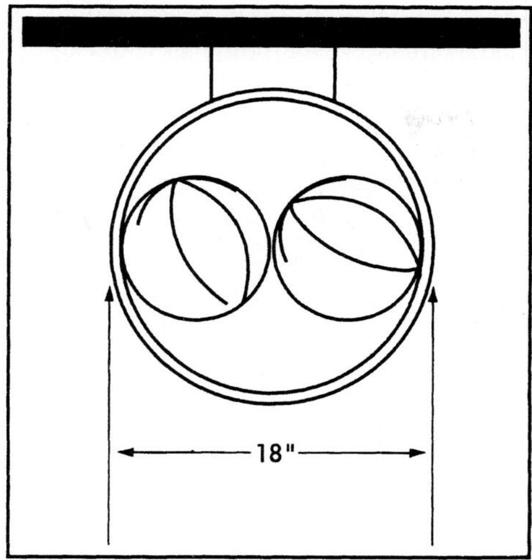

Figure 7-9. Basket size.

Figure 7-10. Aiming the shot.

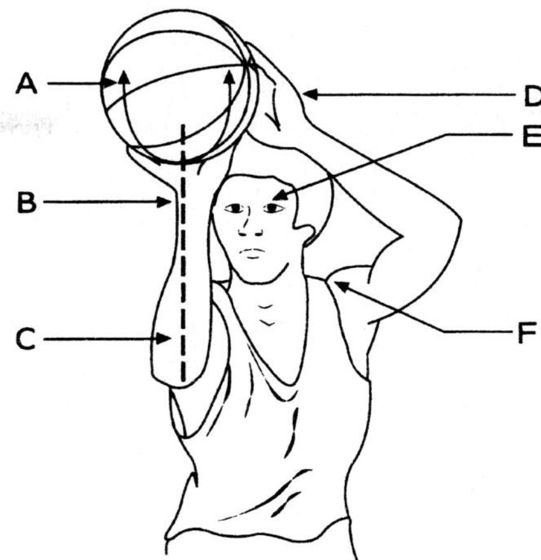

Figure 7-11. Front view of the shooting positions. See text for details.

Figure 7-12. Shot from the side. See text for details.

Shot from the side (figure 7-12). *A*, The edge of the ball should be approximately on line with the shooting elbow. *B*, The off-hand should be placed on the ball in a position that is comfortable to the shooter, but it should not interfere with the shot motion. *C*, The ball should rest on the fingertips. *D*, The eyes should be focused on the basket during all phases of the shot, especially the release. *E*, The shoulders should be squared away with the basket.

View of shot from behind shooter (figure 7-13). *A*, The fingers should be spread, with the ball leaving the shot hand with a reverse spin. The ball should leave the area between the first and second fingers last to ensure the proper backspin. *B*, The spread of the thumb and first finger should be in the form of a V. *C*, The wrist should be cocked. *D*, The shooter's forearm should be in line with the basket. *E*, The ball should be released in a position over the shooting eye and on line with the target. The shot should be a natural motion without actually aiming the ball.

Release action (figure 7-14). *A*, The ball should be rolled off the finger. *B*, The wrist should be coiled. *C*, The eyes should remain focused on the rim. *D*, The release should preferably be over the shooting eye so that concentration will not be broken, with the ball passing through the sight of the shooter. *E*, After the release the follow-through should be emphasized. The shooter should think of reaching inside the rim with the shot hand on the follow-through. *F*, The elbow should be pointing to the basket.

Jump shot

The jump shot is the most common one in basketball. It is often executed from a dribble, but players should be able to accomplish it in almost any situation. Come to a stop from the dribble and execute a controlled jump. At the same time, bring the ball overhead, with the shooting hand behind and the elbow of the shooting arm under the ball and the other hand in front. At the peak of the leap, remove the balance hand and release the ball with extension of the right forearm and good wrist extension (figure 7-15).

One-hand set shot

Hold the ball chin high with both hands, the fingers spread along the sides and slightly behind the ball, the thumbs directed inward behind the ball, and the feet close together with one slightly ahead of the other. Turn the ball so that the shooting hand is behind and under the ball. Bend the knees, bring the ball up, removing the left hand if shooting with the right, and shoot with a strong wrist action and extension of the arm, letting the feet come off the floor, and follow through. At the high school level many players

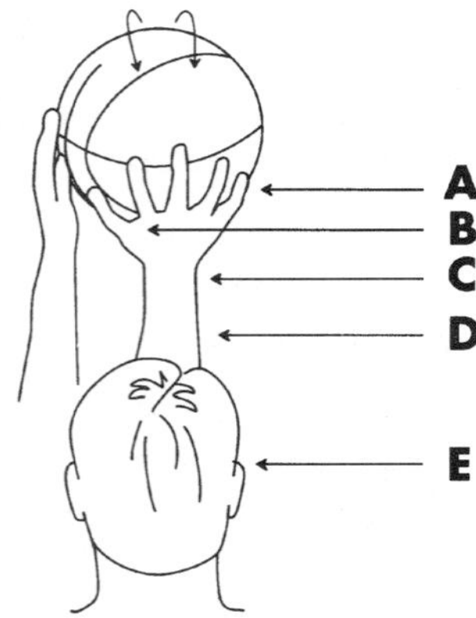

Figure 7-13. View of shot from behind the shooter. See text for details.

Figure 7-14. The release action. See text for details.

Figure 7-15. Jump shot.

Figure 7-16. One-hand set shot.

employ this shooting technique when attempting the longer three-point shot (figure 7-16).

Lay-up shot

Stop dribbling when the right foot is on the floor, step with the left foot, bring up the right knee and jump off the left foot, leap high into the air, shifting the ball to the shooting hand, and raise the shooting hand as high as possible above and in front of the head. Release the ball off the fingertips, laying it softly against the backboard (figure 7-17). *Note*: Use both hands to bring the ball up for the shot and do not remove the balancing hand too soon.

Hook shot

Hold the ball high with both hands, bring the ball to the right side opposite the basket, and remove the balance hand (left). Shoot with a full sweep of the right arm, keeping the arm perfectly straight. In starting the shot, take a short step with the left foot away from the basket and take off on it. The ball is released farthest from the guard, making the shot difficult to block (figure 7-18).

Defense

There are two principal types of defense: one-on-one and zone. In one-on-one defense, each player is responsible for one opponent. In zone defense, each player is responsible for a certain area, or zone.

One of the main reasons for using a zone defense is to tightly guard the opponent's free-throw-line area to prevent drives for easy lay-up shots. All players shift on

Figure 7-17. Lay-up shot.

defense as the ball moves, to cut off passing lanes to the basket. It is considered strategically sound to use a zone defense when:

1. You are playing on a small floor.
2. Your team is in foul trouble.
3. You have an exceptional rebounder you want to keep near the opponent's basket.
4. The opponents have a height advantage.
5. The opponents have a weak outside shooting.
6. The opponents have an exceptional player or two that your best defenders cannot handle one-on-one.

Stance

The feet should be in a forward stride position, knees and hips slightly bent, and the back straight. If the left arm is raised and the right arm extended to the side, the left foot should be forward. If the right arm is up, the right foot should be forward. From this position one should be able to quickly move in any direction.

Role of defensive player

A defensive player should attempt to position the body between the opposing player and the player's own basket. If a pressing defense is being used, the defensive player should get into position so that one arm and hand are in the

Figure 7-18. Hook shot.

passing lane, between the ball and the player being guarded.

Objectives of defensive players

1. To harass the opponent by playing in close and moving arms in a distracting manner
2. To block the shot by staying with the ball as the opponent attempts to throw it (do not jump too soon)
3. If the opponent holds the ball unprotected, to tie up the ball by grabbing it
4. To knock an unprotected ball out of the opponent's hands
5. To steal a ball that is being dribbled
6. To deflect a ball that is being passed by an opponent to a teammate
7. To intercept a passed ball

Player-to-player and zone defenses

For students just learning the game of basketball, it is important to understand the differences between a player-to-player defense and a zone defense. In a player-to-player defense each player is responsible for guarding an opposing player wherever he or she goes on the court. This is a very effective type of defense if the players are in excellent physical condition. Another advantage is that players can be matched up to guard an opposing player of the same approximate height, as well as the same position. For example, a guard versus guard, forward versus forward, and center versus center. When a team does not have a good matchup against the other team in terms of speed, height, rebounding skill, and shooting skills, it might be best to use a zone defense.

In a zone defense each player is responsible for guarding a certain area of the court, rather than an opposing team player. The primary emphasis in a zone is on the ball, not the player. It does not matter where the opposing players move to, each defensive player covers a prescribed area of the court. Four popular zone defenses are the 2-1-2, 2-3, 1-3-1, and the 1-2-2. The defensive zone assignments for each of these configurations are shown in figure 7-19.

A. *2-1-2 zone defense.* This is a zone defense that applies most of the defensive pressure in and around the free-throw line. It forces the offensive team to move the ball to the side positions for open shots at the basket.
B. *2-3 zone defense.* This is a defense that puts three tall players around the basket, forcing the offense to take shots from farther out. If you do not have three tall players, select players that are above-average jumpers and rebounders.
C. *1-3-1 zone defense.* In this defensive set-up you are forcing the offensive team to play the ball over the top of the defense, hoping to force a bad pass, resulting in a turnover.
D. *1-2-2 zone defense.* A pressure-type defense that forces the opposing team to set up their offense farther out from the basket. You might need to utilize shorter, more active players to make this zone work.

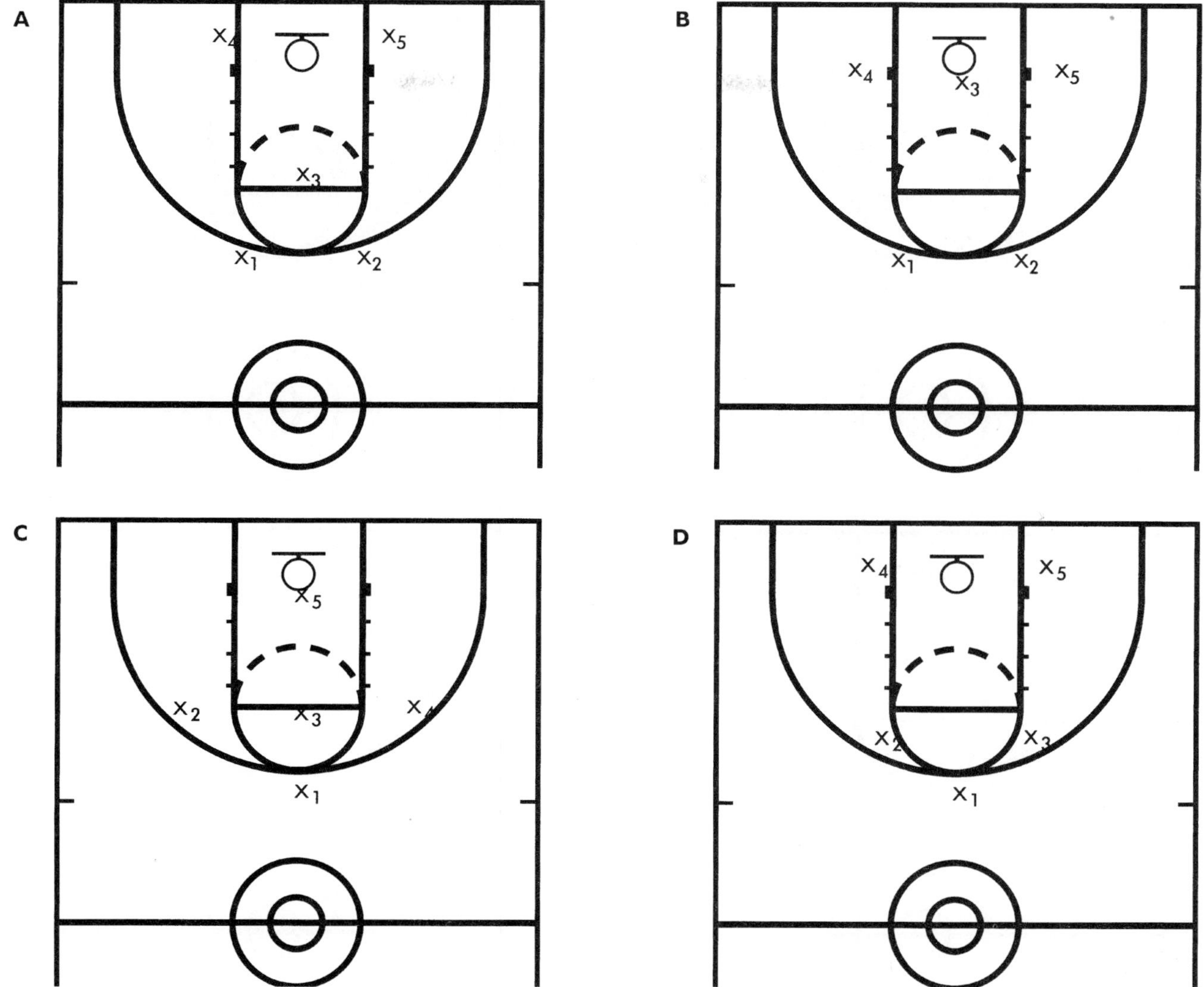

Figure 7-19. Basic defensive positions. **A,** 2-1-2 zone defense; **B,** 2-3 zone defense; **C,** 1-3-1 zone defense; **D,** 1-2-2 zone defense.

Offense

Offensive tactics will vary with the defensive play patterns employed by an opposing team throughout a single game of basketball. One type of offensive tactic must be employed to meet a 2-1-2, 2-3, 1-3-1, or a 3-2 zone defense and another type to meet a player-to-player defense.

The most common method of offense against the zone defense is to use quick, sharp passing with the intent of penetrating the zone and forcing an opposing player out of an assigned position. Other tactics commonly used are mismatching (1-3-1 offense against a 2-1-2 defense) and overloading (putting an extra offensive player in a weakly defended area of the zone).

Basic maneuvers against the player-to-player defense are the give-and-go and the pick-and-roll. The intent is to screen a defensive player and then get the ball to the open offensive player. Spontaneous player-to-player offense, called freelancing, is quite common, but it is more common to use sets of plays.

Basic offensive formations

When determining the best offensive patterns to use, it is important to be aware of the abilities of the personnel on the team. Extensive details about complex offensive formations are beyond the scope of this text, but the top college teams in the United States use what is called a "motion offense." This is an advanced and complicated system wherein players have the opportunity to freelance in the offensive area. However, there are some basic concepts that are important. As the players move about, they are constantly looking to

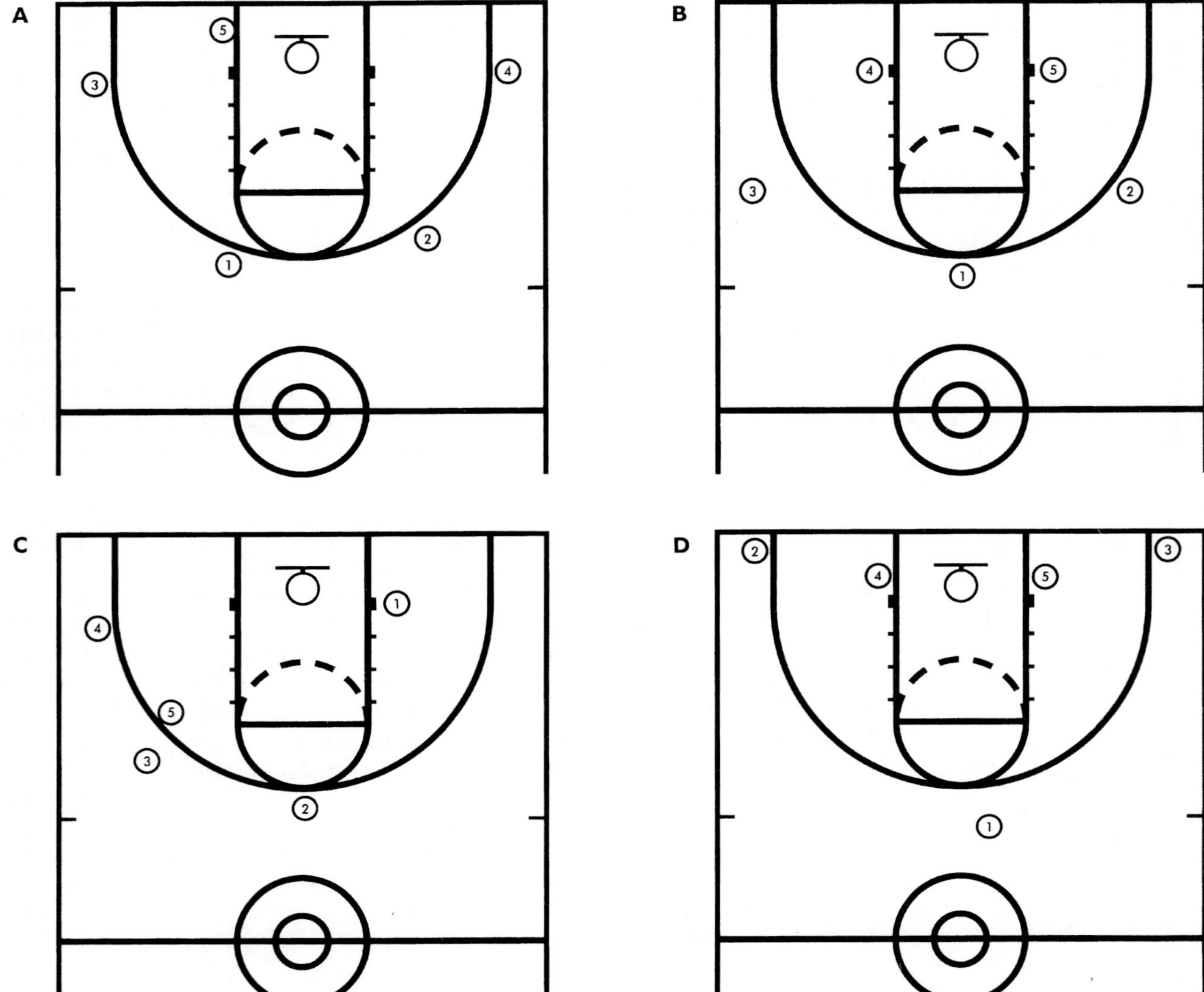

Figure 7-20. Basic offensive formations. **A,** Single-post offense; **B,** Double-post; **C,** Shuffle offense; **D,** Flex offense.

screen for one of their teammates to allow an open shot or a drive to the basket. They always look for the easy pass and try to get the ball to a teammate who has a closer shot at the basket. This offensive system is built on a very strong team concept: All players contribute to the offensive attack. The scoring and the assists in this system will be distributed more evenly among the players than in the single- or double-post offenses, where one or two players are called on to do a majority of the scoring.

The alignments for four basic offensive formations are shown in figure 7-20.

A. *Single-post offense*. This offense is designed for a team that has one tall center who can work around the basket area. This player should be a reasonably good shooter close to the basket.
B. *Double-post offense*. This set-up is similar to the single post, except that you have two tall players to operate around the basket.
C. *Shuffle offense*. This offense relies on quick, accurate passes, with players passing in one direction then moving in the opposite direction to set a screen for a teammate.
D. *Flex offense*. This type of offense spreads the defensive players out much more, allowing for many screens to create open shots.

TIPS TO REMEMBER

1. Dribble only when necessary to set up a shot or pass.
2. Move the ball by passing rather than dribbling. It is faster.

3. Practice being able to pass and catch the ball with no wasted motion. This is essential to an effective offense.
4. Improve your shooting percentage by developing a consistent shooting form and concentration.
5. Become proficient at lay-ups and other short-range, high-percentage shots before working on more difficult shots.
6. Practice most often those shots you expect to get in games as a result of your team's offensive patterns.
7. Be aware of floor balance. Your team should always have one or more rebounders when a shot is taken and one player back on defense to prevent an easy fast-break basket by the opponents.
8. Make an extra effort to get the inside position on opponents at both ends of the court to improve your rebounding.
9. Learn to position yourself on defense so as not to lose sight of either the ball or the person being guarded.
10. Work on proper physical conditioning. It is as important to be able to get from one end of the court to the other and back again as it is to play good offense and defense.
11. Stay in condition year-round. Injuries result from inactivity followed by hard workouts with little or no adjustment period.
12. Remember that basketball is a team sport. The best individual players do not always make the best team players. Good team players develop an ability to help others play at their peak performance.

TEACHING CONSIDERATIONS

1. For younger learners use smaller and lighter balls to develop basic skills.
2. Develop individual skills of dribbling for control of the object in simple conditions first (in one spot; moving forward, to the left, to the right, and backward; changing speed and level of dribble; stopping and starting; and dribbling to avoid others or objects).
3. Develop passing skills in a stationary position first, varying the level of pass. As soon as some degree of proficiency has been established, practice passing to a moving receiver, varying the distance and adding the pass on the move. Emphasize quick passes and the idea of the lead pass (passing the ball ahead of the moving receiver).
4. Combine dribbling and passing skills with an emphasis on a smooth transition from one skill to another (pass to a dribble and dribble to a pass). Add several players and emphasize cutting into a space to receive a pass in cooperative group work.
5. Teach basics of the foul shot, set shot, and lay-up. Combine the set shots and lay-up with combinations of dribble and pass as soon as basic proficiency in simple conditions has been established.
6. Begin offensive and defensive play with one-on-one situations. Teach students defensive positions to get the ball from a dribbler and offensive strategies to maintain possession.
7. Beginners should spend adequate time in two-on-two and three-on-three situations to learn about basketball as a "space" game. Offense must be able to create space and opportunities for passes, and defense must be able to close up space and passing opportunities. Teaching focus should be on the person with the ball, the receiver, as well as the person without the ball on offense. On defense the focus should be on cutting off angles of opportunity for the offense.
8. With large groups of learners decrease the amount of space for game play, particularly when less than five-on-five work is being developed.
9. Manipulate the rules to bring out better play (e.g., no dribbling, three passes) and to encourage continuous play (e.g., be flexible when calling traveling, eliminate foul shots and jump balls).
10. Consider introducing zone defense as a concept of defending space. Three defensive players can constitute a zone defense. Add different patterns of zone defense as the number of defensive players increases.
11. Mix some game play with skill work in each lesson once a unit gets started. Progress with skills over the unit. Do not establish units that do all the basic skill development in the first few lessons and all the play in the last few lessons.
12. See figure 7-21 for official signals.

GLOSSARY

alternate-possession rule The rule where any jump ball situations after the opening jump ball result in each team gaining possession of the ball. The team losing the opening jump ball will be awarded the first possession, with teams alternating possession for the rest of the game.

assist A pass or handoff resulting in a basket by a teammate.

backboard The surface of wood, metal, or glass to which the basket is affixed, used to carom shots into the basket.

backcourt The half of the court away from the basket under attack; the guards are often called backcourt players.

basket (*a*) The iron hoop through which goals are scored; (*b*) a field goal.

bench The reserve strength of a team, apart from the starting five players.

blocking A foul by a defensive player who blocks the legal path of an offensive player.

center jump The method of putting the ball into play at the beginning of a game by having the referee toss up the ball between the rival centers.

Figure 7-21. Official basketball signals.

charging A foul by an offensive player who runs into a defensive player who has established legal court position.

dribble To bounce and control the ball continuously with one hand while walking or running. To double dribble is to stop and then resume dribbling, which is a violation.

dunk To leap to or above the basket and stuff the ball through the hoop. Such a movement with great vigor is called a "slam dunk."

fast break A style of offense in which a team attempts to race to the offensive basket before the defense can get set.

field goal A basket scored from the floor.

free throw An unobstructed shot from the foul line, worth one point, awarded as a penalty for a foul by the opposing team.

free-throw lane The area on the floor bounded by the free-throw line, the end line under the basket, and two connecting lines forming a 12-foot (3.6 m) (collegiate) or 18-foot (5.4 m) (professional) lane; also called "foul lane."

free-throw line A line, 15 feet (4.5 m) from the basket, behind which the shooter must stand in attempting a free throw; also called "foul line."

frontcourt The half of the court in which a basket is under attack.

give and go A play in which one player passes to a teammate and drives toward the basket to receive a pass for a lay-up.

handoff Handing the ball to a teammate (instead of passing it).

held ball Simultaneous possession of ball by opposing players, leading to use of the alternate-possession rule.

hook shot A sweeping, one-handed field goal attempt, with the shooter's back at least partially to the basket.

hoop (*a*) The rim of the basket; (*b*) a basket or score.

jump ball A means of putting the ball into play by having an official toss it upward between two players. This only occurs at the start of the game.

jump shot A field goal attempt in which the ball is released at the top of a vertical jump; also called a "jumper."

lay-up A shot from alongside the basket, using the backboard as a guide.

offensive foul A personal foul committed by a member of the offensive team, usually not involving a free throw as part of the penalty.

palming An illegal means of carrying the ball along while dribbling.

personal foul Any of a variety of body-contact fouls; five, or in professional ball, six personals disqualify the player who commits them.

pick A legal method of providing shooting room for a teammate by taking a position that "picks off," or blocks, a defensive player.

pick-and-roll A maneuver in which a player moves suddenly (rolls) toward the basket for a pass from the teammate for whom a pick has been set.

pivot A position taken by a player with his/her back to the basket, at the head or alongside the free-throw lane, from which he/she can spin and shoot or hand off to teammates moving past him/her toward the basket; also the floor area where pivot play is feasible.

player-to-player defense A style of team defense in which each is assigned to a specific opponent to guard anywhere on the court.

post A position on the offensive end of the court where the player places him or herself just outside of the free throw lane. Low post means the player is closer to the basket, while high post means the player is closer to the free throw line.

press A style of defense in which offensive players are closely guarded and harried. A "full-court press" is applied all over the floor; a "half-court press" only after the ball is brought across the midcourt line.

rebound A shot that caroms off the basket or backboard and remains in play, to be recovered by either team.

set shot A field goal attempted from a stationary position with both feet on the floor when the player releases the ball. This shot is usually taken relatively far from the basket.

steal Capture of the ball from the hands of a player by the defender; an intercepted pass.

switch A defensive technique in which players who have player-to-player assignments switch responsibilities with each other as their offensive players cross paths.

technical foul A foul imposed for misbehavior or some technical rule infraction. The penalty is a free throw plus possession of the ball for the offended team.

ten-second rule The requirement that a team bring the ball across the midcourt line within 10 seconds after gaining possession.

three-pointer A field goal made by a player who is fouled in the act of shooting, plus the free throw that is made; also a basket scored from outside the three-point line on the court.

three-second rule The restriction against offensive players taking up set positions within the free-throw lane for more than 3 seconds.

tip-in A field goal made by tipping the ball into the basket while airborne for a rebound.

trailer A player who follows behind his/her teammates on a fast break as a passing option if they are unable to get off a shot.

trap Convergence of two or more defenders on a ball handler to force a turnover or steal.

traveling Illegally moving the ball by violating the dribbling rules.

turnover Loss of possession of the ball without attempting a field goal.

twenty-four second rule In the National Basketball Association (NBA) the requirement that a team make a field goal attempt within 24 seconds after gaining possession of the ball; in international amateur competition the limit is 30 seconds; in college basketball the limit is 35 seconds for men and 30 seconds for women.

violation Any infraction not classified as a foul. The penalty is loss of possession of the ball.

zone A style of team defense in which each player is assigned to guard a designated floor area, rather than a specific opponent.

SUGGESTED READINGS

American coaching effectiveness program: Rookie coaches basketball guide. 1991. Champaign, Ill.: Human Kinetics. Provides beginning coaches with detailed information about the responsibilities of a coach.

American Sport Education Program. 1995. *Coaching youth basketball*. Champaign, Ill.: Human Kinetics.

Brittenham, G. 1996. *Complete conditioning for basketball*. Champaign, Ill.: Human Kinetics. Reveals the strength and conditioning drills of professional teams.

Head-Summitt, P., and Jennings, D. 1996. *Basketball*. 2d ed. Dubuque, Iowa: WCB/McGraw-Hill. Discusses basic terms, skills, rules, strategies, and team play.

Isaacs, L. 1993. *Basketball everyone*. Winston-Salem, N.C.: Hunter Textbooks. Designed specifically for the college activity program. Assumes minimal knowledge and playing ability.

Krause, J. 1990. *Basketball resource guide*. 2d ed. Champaign, Ill.: Human Kinetics.

Krause, J. 1991. *Basketball skills and drills*. Champaign, Ill.: Human Kinetics. Part I focuses on individual basketball skills. Part II focuses on general team offensive and defensive principles.

Lieberman-Cline, N., and Roberts, R. 1995. *Basketball for women: Becoming a complete player*. Champaign, Ill.: Human Kinetics. Deals with the mental approach and presents tips for skill development. Discusses Nancy Lieberman's playing experiences.

National Basketball Conditioning Coaches Association. 1997. *NBA power training*. Champaign, Ill.: Human Kinetics. Provides an inside look at the power and conditioning exercises of professional basketball teams.

NCAA official basketball rules. College Athletics Publishing Service, Shawnee Mission, Kansas.

Pauletto, B. 1994. *Strength training for basketball*. Champaign, Ill.: Human Kinetics.

Paye, B. 1996. *Playing the post: Basketball skills and drills*. Champaign, Ill.: Human Kinetics. Provides detailed information about how to play the post position. Includes a good number of player drills.

Wilkes, G. 1998. *Basketball*. 7th ed. Dubuque, Iowa: WCB/McGraw-Hill. Discusses essential basketball skills, information on offensive and defensive patterns of play, strategy, rules of the game, and sportsmanship.

Williams, J., and Williams, S. 1993. *Youth league basketball*. Indianapolis: Masters Press. Helpful teaching techniques for coaches and parents at all levels of youth play.

Wissell, H. 1994. *Basketball: Steps to success*. Champaign, Ill.: Human Kinetics. Provides an easy-to-use, self-paced program for expanding and refining basketball skills and strategies.

Wooden, J. 1988. *Practical modern basketball*. 3d ed. Riverside, N.J.: Macmillan. Stresses the fundamentals and appropriate teaching methods. Contains extensive photographs and illustrations, as well as multiple drills and techniques.

Wootten, M. 1992. *Coaching basketball*. Champaign, Ill.: Human Kinetics. Breaks down sophisticated techniques into practical skills, strategies, and drills.

RESOURCES

Videotapes

Coach to coach: the ultimate clinic on the art of coaching. The top coaches of the NBA lead in-depth clinics on their areas of expertise. West One Video, 1935 Bailey Hill Rd, Eugene, OR 97405.

A wide selection of videos is available from the following distributors:

Cambridge Health and Physical Education, P.O. Box 2153, Charleston, WV 25328. Videos include: "Basketball of the 90s" series (7 videos), including *Beginning basketball with Henry Bibby*, Lute Olson's *Developing the big man* and *Developing the perimeter player* and Tara Vanderveer's *Building a championship offense* and *Building a championship defense*; Steve Alford's *50 minute all American workout*; *Pistol Pete's homework basketball* (4 videos); *Coach Doug Noll's instructional free-throw shooting*; *Bob Hurley's championship basketball* (2 videos); Spud Webb's *Reach for the skies*; Rick Pitino's *Learn the up-tempo game* (4 videos); and ESPN's *Teaching kids basketball*.

"How To" Sports Videos, P.O. Box 5852, Denver, CO 80217. Makes available 45 videos on skills, strategies, famous coaches' tips, drills, and plyometrics.

Human Kinetics, P.O. Box 5076, Champaign, Illinois 61825-5076. 10 videos covering all aspects of playing and coaching basketball.

Karol Video, 22 Riverview Dr, Wayne, NJ 07470. Provides 10 individual NCAA instructional videos, including three on women's basketball.

Sysko's Basketball Books and Videos, 30 W Main St, P.O. Box 6, Benton, WI 53803. Distributes more than 300 books and videos on all aspects of basketball, including its own *Feeder system* (2 videos), by Coach Jerry Petitgoue.

Computer Software

Krause, J., and Brennan, S. 1998. *Basketball resource guide*. Champaign, Ill.: Human Kinetics.

Davis, C. 1995. *The coach's edge: Player visualization software*. The Coach's Edge, Lawrence, Kansas.

Bicycling

After completing this chapter, the reader should be able to:

- Explain how to select the proper size bicycle and how to adjust it correctly
- Explain which kind of cycling equipment is required to ride safely and comfortably
- Demonstrate how to start, steer, shift, and stop a bicycle
- State the rules of the road and execute them for maximum safety when road riding
- State the rules of the trail and execute them for maximum safety when mountain biking
- List basic training skills that enhance bicycling enjoyment

HISTORY

The first bicycles, developed in the 1800s, were unlike today's machines. They did not move well and were almost impossible to stop. They were heavy, crude, and inefficient. When approaching a corner, the rider had to dismount and turn the bike around by hand because there was no way to steer it. Needless to say, these first bicycles were not used for transportation.

However, even those first cumbersome contraptions did have a simple advantage over walking: they used muscle power to move horizontally rather than vertically. When walking, energy is expended to fight gravity by moving the body up in order to move the legs out to take a step. This upward movement is wasted because it is not in the direction we wish to go.

When we stand up, muscles must be tensed and bones compressed to support body weight. This muscle tension expends energy even though no motion takes place. Walking triples the load on the legs. By sitting on a seat or board with two wheels attached to it, we save much of the expended vertical energy lost through standing muscle tension. Thus, the first bicyclists could sit on a seat and pedal the bike with their feet and glide along to their destination, using less energy than walking requires.

One of the first changes made to the bicycle was to increase the size (circumference) of the front wheel, a change that increased the distance the bike traveled with each pedal stroke. High wheelers, or "ordinaries" or "penny-farthings," as they were called, were in use from 1870 to 1885.

The development of the chain-driven-rear-wheel "safety bicycle," which first appeared in 1885, was the most important bicycle innovation. As the name implies, this type of bike is inherently safer because it does not have a huge front wheel. This design, still in use today, also removed the restriction of direct drive from pedals to wheels. Perhaps the most significant change to the bicycle since the introduction of the safety design was the addition of the derailleur in the 1930s. A derailleur enables one to select different gear ratios while pedaling, which permits the proper matching of pedal rate with changes in the terrain. For example, if the pitch of the road suddenly increases, one can shift the bike to a lower, easier gear. Before the development of the derailleur, most bikes had only one gear; today, high-performance road bikes have 18 gears and mountain bikes (MTB) have up to 27 gears.

The bicycle of today (figure 8-1) is a remarkably lightweight, efficient, versatile, and economical machine. In many countries it is used as the primary mode of transportation.

Cycling as an Olympic event has changed a great deal over the years, for the most part because of changes in equipment. In the 1896 Olympics six cycling events, including a 12-hour race, were held. In the 1900 Olympics in Paris there was only one cycling event. In 1908 in London the first cycling events on a banked 500 m oval track were conducted. European nations—especially England, France, and the Netherlands—provided the best cyclists in the early Olympics. Until 1984 no U.S. cyclist had won a medal since 1908. With professional cycling increasing in popularity and attracting the finest Western European cyclists, the Eastern European countries and the Soviet Union began winning most of the medals after 1960. If the Soviet Union had not boycotted the 1984 Olympics, it would have probably brought a very strong cycling team to the Los Angeles games. However, the Soviet absence contributed to the success of the U.S. cycling team, which came somewhat as a surprise.

The success of the U.S. cycling team at the 1984 Olympics, where it won several medals in both the sprint and road race events, provided a needed boost for U.S. cycling. Also, the success of the U.S. riders Greg LeMond,

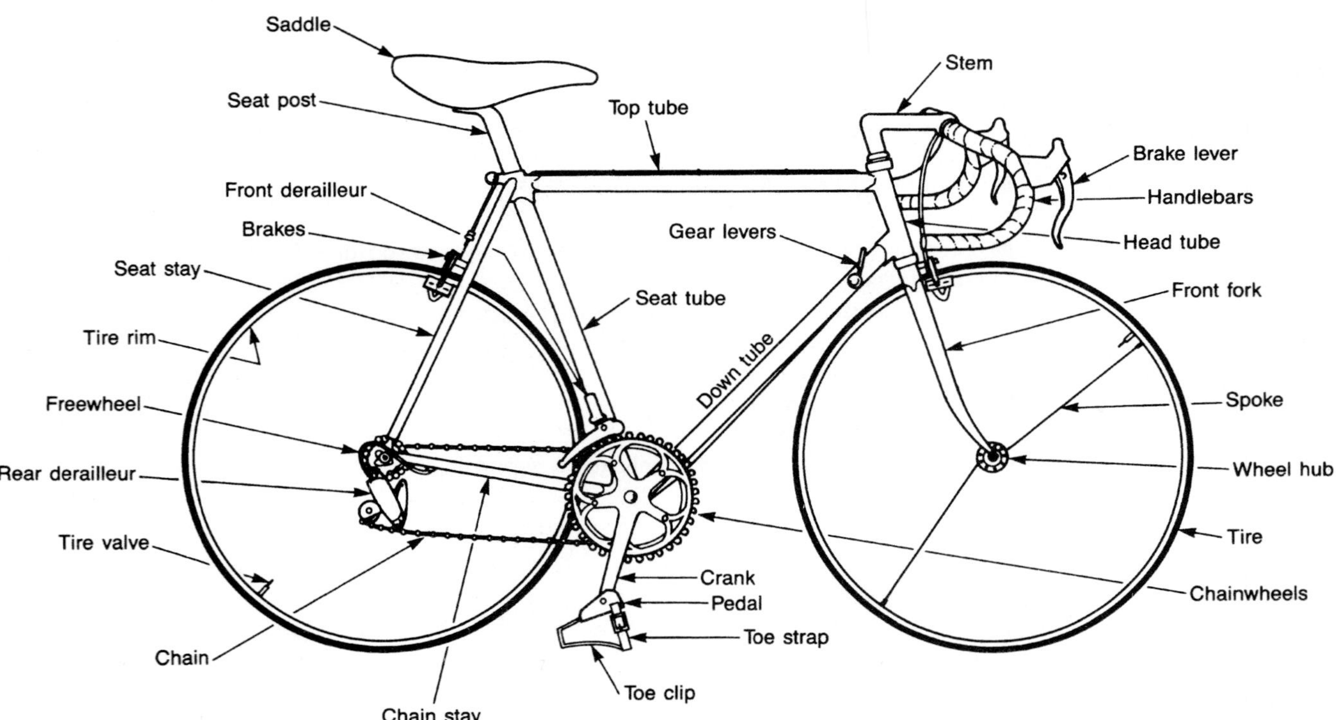

Figure 8-1. Modern bicycle.

Lance Armstrong, and Bobby Julich in the professional road-racing circuit has also increased interest in the sport. In 1989 LeMond staged an incredible performance to win the 2000-mile Tour de France stage race by 8 seconds! In addition to this win, LeMond also won the 1989 World Road Championship and the 1990 Tour de France. Lance Armstrong won the 1996 Tour Dupont and became the first U.S. rider to win a European classic, a traditional one-day race that typically covers about 300 km (186 miles) and climbs many hills or runs over stretches of ancient, muddy cobblestone roads. Bobby Julich, meanwhile, placed 17th in the 1997 Tour de France, the highest placing since LeMond's win in 1990.

Perhaps the greatest changes in professional and Olympic cycling over the last ten years have been the development of a professional mountain bike racing circuit and the inclusion of mountain biking and of professional off-road and road racers in the Olympics. These changes to the Games first occurred in the 1996 Atlanta Olympics. As with other Olympic sports that have allowed professionals to compete, the cycling professionals won the majority of the 1996 Olympic cycling events, including the men's and women's road and mountain bike race, road time trials, and nearly all the track races, which consisted of more than ten events for both genders combined.

THE BICYCLIST

Posture

One of the most important considerations in choosing a bicycle is its fit. A bicycle that does not fit will be uncomfortable and will not handle correctly. Most people believe that the bicyclist sits on the seat, pushes with the legs, bends the back, and steers with the hands. In reality, the cyclist straddles the seat, spins the pedals, leans forward from the hips, and steers by leaning. The basic components of a correct cycling posture include bike size; saddle height, tilt, and fore-aft positioning; and handlebar height and stem length.

Bike Size and Saddle Positioning

To check the basic frame size of a road bike, straddle it and lift it until the top tube touches the crotch. If the bicycle is the proper size, there should be 1 to 2 inches (2.5 to 5.1 cm) of clearance between the tires and the ground. In contrast, when sizing a mountain bike, there should be about 20 to 30 cm (7.5 to 12 inches) between the tires and the ground when the top tube is lifted against the crotch. The saddle should be positioned so that it is just possible to place the heels on the pedals at the bottom position and pedal backward without rocking the hips. A final check for saddle height is the angle between the upper and lower leg

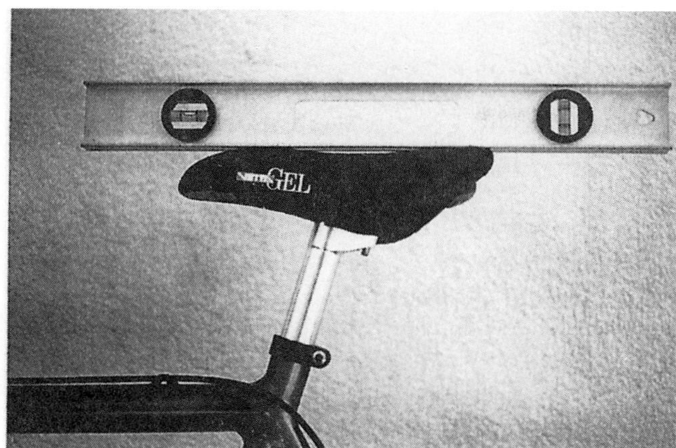

Figure 8-2. Proper saddle tilt.

Figure 8-3. Positioning of the cleat. Notice the ball of the foot is directly over the pedal spindle when the pedal is in the 3 o'clock position and is pointed nearly straight ahead.

when the leg is fully extended and fixed to the pedal; the angle should be between 20 and 30 degrees.

After adjusting the saddle height, one needs to adjust saddle tilt and fore-aft positioning because they are important factors for attaining a proper bike posture. Saddle tilt is an easy adjustment; all you have to do is make sure the saddle is level from the tip to the back. To check the tilt, place a level across the top of the saddle and adjust accordingly by loosening the nut that affixes the saddle to the seat post (figure 8-2). If the saddle is tilted backward (with the tip higher than the back of the saddle), you may experience discomfort and numbness in the crotch while riding. If the saddle is tilted forward (with the tip lower than the back), you will slide off the front of the saddle while pedaling, which greatly increases neck, shoulder, and upper-arm fatigue.

Unlike the saddle tilt adjustment, fore-aft positioning is a bit tricky. First you have to adjust your cycling shoes precisely, a procedure that is extremely personalized, although there are two rules of thumb that serve as a good starting point: Position the cleat so that the ball of your foot lies directly over the pedal axle and make sure your foot is pointing straight ahead, in the so-called neutral position (figure 8-3). Most people do not need to have their shoes pointed inward (pigeon-toed) or outward (duck-foot), positions that often increase the risk of knee injury.

After setting up your cleats, you can then adjust the fore-aft position of your saddle. The first part of this adjustment is to find the area on the inside of your knee where the thigh bone and lower leg meet. You should be able to feel a small indentation in this area—the joint line of the knee—when your leg is fully extended (figure 8-4). Mark this indentation with a big *X*. Next, sit on your saddle and place your feet on the pedals, rotating them to the 9 and 3 o'clock positions; the foot of the marked leg should be at 9 o'clock. (It helps to lean against a wall, door jam, or friend for this procedure.) Once accomplished, drop a plumb line from the mark on your leg to the pedal. The line will bisect the pedal axle if your fore-aft positioning is correct. If not, move your saddle forward or backward by loosening the nut that affixes the saddle to the seat post.

Figure 8-4. A plumb line dropped from the joint line of the knee past the crank arm when the pedals are at 3 and 9 o'clock position bisects the pedal spindle.

The final aspects of attaining proper bike posture are setting handle bar height and choosing stem length. A good rule of thumb for handle bar height is that the bars should be about 1 inch (25 cm) lower than the tip of your saddle. To check stem length, sit on the saddle, reach forward, and place your hands on the hooks or drops of a road handle bar or the handle bar grips of a mountain bike. (Again, it helps to lean on a wall, door jam, or friend.) If the handle bars obscure your view of the front hub while you are so positioned, the stem length is correct. If not, you will need a longer or shorter stem. It is a good idea to check stem length when you purchase a bike; most shops will replace the stem free at this time.

Clothing

A great deal of specialized clothing is available today, designed and manufactured with racing and long-distance bicycling in mind. Cycling shorts are made from stretchable Lycra and are chamois lined to prevent saddle chafe and sores. Some are anatomically designed; that is, they are curved to fit the cyclist in the seated position.

Cycling jerseys are made with special fabrics that wick moisture from the skin. This keeps a bicyclist cooler in the summer and warmer in the winter. In addition, they have long zippers in the front for added ventilation and pockets in the back for carrying identification, spare tire tubes (flats are common), and energy snacks.

A bottle is fitted to the frame and its contents are used to replace body fluids. Fingerless gloves, worn by many bicyclists, can be used to rub bits of glass off tires and protect the palms of the hands should a fall occur.

Special cycling shoes are also worn. These shoes have hard soles that distribute the forces generated from pedaling over a larger area of the foot, a characteristic that reduces foot discomfort and fatigue. Cycling shoes also have cleats of various forms (the form depending on the type of pedal you have). Cleats allow for a better interface between the foot and the pedal, which increases pedaling efficiency for all types of riding. In addition, many cleated mountain biking shoes contain rubber spikes on the toe and heel, which provide the cyclist with additional traction if it becomes necessary to dismount to make it up a hill.

Lightweight bicycling helmets are available in most bicycle shops. The newer ones, made of Styrofoam with a thin plastic coating, are well ventilated and very light, weighing only about 8 ounces.

Whereas cycling shorts and jerseys are relatively unimportant to the short-distance rider, all cyclists should wear a helmet. Almost all deaths and most serious injuries incurred in cycling accidents are caused by head injuries. Where there is the chance of the head striking an immovable object—as in football, hockey, auto racing, and other contact sports—protective headgear can save a life (figure 8-5).

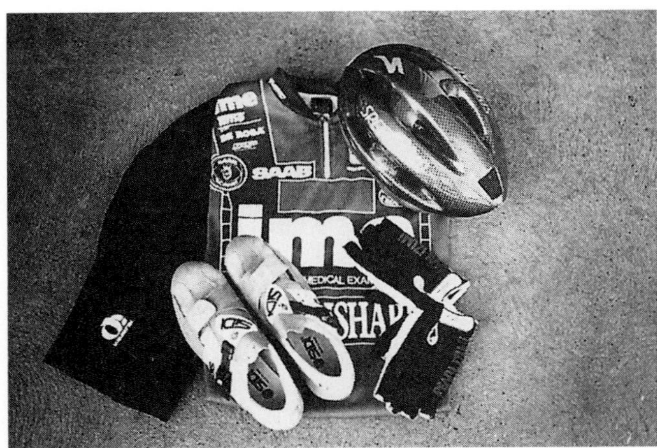

Figure 8-5. Bicycling clothing.

Saddle Selection

Because the rider does not sit on the seat but straddles it, the saddle (seat) is a prop for the pelvic bones. It is important that chafing be avoided, because the legs will be in constant motion. Therefore, the best saddle is smooth, flexible, and just wide enough for good support but not wide enough to chafe.

Most saddles today are made of flexible plastic covered with foam and leather and are quite comfortable. Women will probably find a saddle designed for wider pelvic bones to be more comfortable than a conventional saddle. The less expensive vinyl-covered saddles are often too hard, and they do not absorb moisture. A mattress saddle with springs is only satisfactory for riding short distances in an upright position. It may feel better at first, but the longer the ride, the more uncomfortable it gets.

Pedaling Technique

The mark of a good bicyclist is the smooth, steady way in which she or he pedals the bike. The foot must be placed on the pedal so it can push the pedal as far around the circle as possible. To do this, you use the foot as a lever with the ankle as fulcrum while pedaling on the ball of the foot. At the bottom of the circle, the heel is up and the toe is down. At the top of the circle, the heel is down and the toe is up, thus pulling the pedal back. This is called "ankling." Smooth ankling is achieved only by using cycling shoes equipped for clipped or clipless pedals, but this technique should be practiced even if tennis shoes or rubber pedals are used.

The feet should rotate the pedals at a rhythmic, constant pace (cadence), twice as fast as walking, A slow cadence is 60 revolutions per minute; 80 is normal; and 90 to 100 is racing pace.

Care of Equipment

Before starting a ride of any distance, be sure to give the bicycle a quick safety check. Grip the brake levers and make sure that the brakes work. Look for worn brake blocks and loose cables. Make sure the handlebars, seat, and wheels are not loose and see that the wheels are true—that is, they do not wobble from side to side when you spin them (they do not rub the brake pads). Check the tires for the proper pressure and for worn or cut places. Underinflated tires greatly increase rolling resistance and increase the chance of damaging the rims. Lubricate the chain if necessary. Make sure to have a spare tube, tire irons, and a pump. Taking a few moments before a ride could save a long walk home, but more importantly, it could prevent an accident.

Tires

Tires fail more frequently than any other part of a bicycle. Knowing how to change tires and fix flats will save a lot of time and money.

There are two kinds of bicycle tires. The most common type—"wired-on," or clinchers—are so named because of the wire bead that seals the tires to the rim. The other kind, used almost exclusively by racers, are "tubulars," which are glued on to the wheel rim.

Changing wired-on tires is not difficult, and with a little practice one can become proficient. If a spare tube, some tire irons, and a pump are carried, a flat tire should never cause a delay of more than a few minutes.

Tubes within the tires also come in two types (actually, it is the valves that are different), so it is important that the tire pump carried fits the type of valve on the bike. Schrader valves are large and thick, like automobile valves. Presta valves are narrow and require the little button on the valve tip to be unscrewed to use them. Each takes a different hand pump to fill with air.

Types of Bicycles

There are many different types of bicycles, each designed for a different purpose. *Road racing bikes* feature drop handlebars and short wheelbases and are lightweight (figure 8-6). *Touring bikes* are equipped for carrying loads: They have heavy-duty wheels, luggage rack attachments, and "granny gears" for climbing steep hills. *Mountain bikes* have wide, knobby tires and rugged construction; they were originally designed for use on dirt roads and trails, but their upright posture and ease of use have made them popular in cities as well (figure 8-7). The *cycle-cross bike* is a road racing bike fitted with knobby tires and ridden with mountain biking cleats and pedals over off-road courses that force the rider to dismount and run frequently. This late fall sport is very popular in Europe and is growing in popularity in the United States. *Track bikes* have the same frame design as road bikes but do not have brakes. They also have a fixed gear or single speed that is set up so that the rider cannot stop pedaling unless the bike is brought to a complete standstill. These bikes are raced only on specialized banked tracks. *BMX (Bicycle Motor Cross)* bikes have small wheels, a fixed gear, and a coaster brake, and are ridden in a sprint-like fashion around 400 m (× ¼ mile) dirt tracks that contain many small hills. This sport is popular among children and young adults, many of whom have gone on to great success in other cycling sports. John Tomac, a premier U.S. off-road racer in the 1990s, started with BMX racing. *Commuter bikes* are average "around-

Figure 8-6. Road racing bike.

Figure 8-7. Fully suspended mountain bike.

town" vehicles that come in all shapes and sizes. Often equipped with fenders and reflectors, they provide reliable transportation and recreation.

BASIC MANEUVERS

Starting

Grasp the top of the handlebars and swing a leg over the seat to straddle the bicycle. Backpedal until one pedal is forward and high. Place the ball of the foot on the high pedal and kick off with the other foot. This will start the bicycle moving. Place the other foot on its pedal and ease the crotch backward up onto the saddle.

Stopping

Apply the brakes to slow down. Put the pedals in the high and low positions, transfer your weight to the low pedal, and slide forward and off the seat. Remove the foot from the high pedal and reach for the ground while slowing to a stop. Just before the stop, turn the front wheel away from the free foot to tip the bicycle. If timed correctly, the bicyclist will stop and lean onto the free foot just as it touches the ground. Backpedal to the starting position.

Steering

Steering is accomplished more by leaning than by turning the handlebars. This effect can best be tested by walking along, pushing the bike forward, and holding onto only the saddle. A slight tip to the left or right will naturally turn the front wheel in the same direction. This action occurs when the bicyclist is in the saddle. The hands and arms on the handlebars primarily support the body's upper torso.

Gear Shifting

The premise of variable bicycle gear ratios on multispeed bikes is that the bicyclist is most efficient when pedaling at a constant rate in revolutions per minute. (One revolution is two complementary strokes, one from the left leg and one from the right.) Inasmuch as the bicyclist faces variable conditions during the ride, it would be impossible to keep a constant pace with only one gear. For example, the average bicyclist would be unable to keep the same pace going uphill as on the flat. Other variable conditions include wind and weight carried. Shifting gears allows the optimum in mechanical efficiency.

Shifting gears on a bicycle has become very easy—almost foolproof—since the advent of index, or "click," shifting in the mid 1980s. To shift, you simply move the gear lever—be it incorporated in the brake lever (see figure 8-6), on the down tube, or on the handle bars (thumb shifters) (see figure 8-7)—until a click is heard. If the derailleur cables are properly tensioned and the frame is aligned, the bike will now be in a new gear. It is as easy as that. Sometimes it helps to reduce pedaling force so as to facilitate the shift, but this is usually unnecessary except in extreme situations, such as shifting while riding at a low pedal frequency on a steep incline. In general, it is best to anticipate the shift, that is, shift before the pedal cadence drops dramatically. It is wise to practice shifting on a flat, lightly traveled road so you can shift smoothly and safely in all situations.

Braking

Use both brakes to stop safely by applying pressure first to the rear brake and then to the front brake. Gradually brake harder until coming to a stop or until the rear wheel starts to skid. If this happens, let up on both brake levers until the wheels start to turn again.

Never use only the rear brake in traffic. It cannot provide enough deceleration to stop in the event of trouble. Also never brake hard with only the front brake, as you may be thrown forward over the handlebars. Be careful when riding in rain. The brakes will not work until the brake blocks wipe the rims dry. Riding on steel rims in wet weather is much more dangerous than riding on alloy rims. In any case, remember to leave extra distance for stopping as it takes much longer to slow down with wet steel rims than with wet alloy rims.

RULES OF THE ROAD

The rules of the road for bicyclists are the same as for automobile drivers. Automobile drivers cooperate with each other within the rules of the road, and motorists usually cooperate with bicyclists who obey these rules. Conflict arises when bicyclists or motorists, through ignorance or design, act unreasonably on the roadway.

Where to Ride on the Roadway

Bicyclists have a right to a safe corridor along the road. Care must be taken, however, not to interfere with other users of the road. Courtesy toward others will pay in increased respect and safety. Bicycles are vehicles, and the following are recommended rules governing the place of bicycles on the roadway. Unfortunately, some people do not recognize bicycles as legitimate vehicles. This belief often results in actions inconsistent with standard traffic engineering practice and commonsense rules of behavior in traffic situations.

When riding on a road of standard width, the bicyclist should ride inside the traffic lane at the right-hand side of the road. Cars will usually have ample room to pass within or nearly within this lane. On roads that are too narrow to permit safe passing either within the lane or over the centerline, the bicyclist should ride in the center of the right lane. If riding as fast as or faster than the other traffic, use the lane as if operating a car. Do not weave in and around parked cars.

Never ride on the left side of the street, facing traffic. Very few bicyclists are hit by overtaking cars. Instead, the greatest number of car-bicycle collisions are caused by wrong-way riding. When approaching a motorist from an unexpected spot, the bicyclist could be hit without being seen. Riding on the wrong side of the road also causes bicycle-bicycle collisions. Bicyclists usually occupy the right portion of the roadway; but going in the wrong direction, there exists a risk of a head-on collision with another bicyclist.

It is important not to ride in the motorist's blind spot, especially when approaching intersections or driveways, where a motorist might make a right turn. Overtake on the right only when the cars are stopped or are barely moving. Never overtake on the right where it is possible for the motorist to make a right turn, and never overtake on the right when the road is too narrow to do so safely.

Right Turns

Make a right turn in the same manner as a car does: from the farthest right of the roadway.

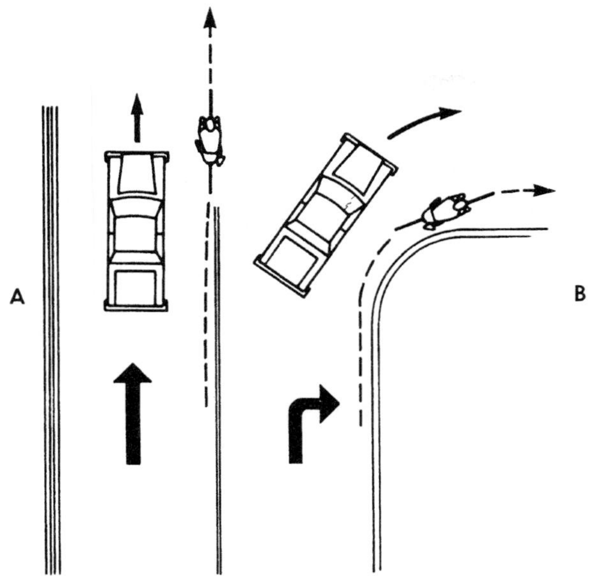

Figure 8-8. Right turns. See text for details.

Some roads have right-turn-only lanes. When riding in the right-hand portion of a right-turn-only lane, the bicyclist must turn right (figure 8-8B). If the bicyclist attempts to go straight through, he or she could be hit by a motorist legally turning right. When a bicyclist encounters a right-turn-only lane but does not wish to follow it, the alternative is to merge to the left and ride on the right-hand edge of the next straight-through lane (figure 8-8A). Merge left by looking over your left shoulder before changing the path of travel. Change lanes only when overtaking traffic has cleared or slowed to allow you to move over.

Left Turns

Never attempt a left turn from the right side of the street. The bicyclist stands a good chance of being hit by an overtaking car by making a left turn in front of it. To make a safe left turn, the bicyclist must follow the same procedure as an automobile driver. The first step is to merge left. Look back over your shoulder for overtaking cars. It may help to signal, but the look is mandatory. Never signal without looking. A signal is a matter of courtesy; the look is a matter of life and death. After looking over the left shoulder for overtaking cars, move into the left lane if the way is clear. When occupying a left-turn-only lane, ride at the *right* edge of the lane (figure 8-9A). This will allow motorists to also occupy the lane and turn simultaneously when the way ahead is clear. If the lane is not a left-turn-only lane, stay as close to the centerline of the road as possible (figure 8-9B). This will allow motorists who wish to go straight through to pass on the right while the bicyclist is waiting for the oncoming traffic to clear.

After completing a left turn, you should turn into the right lane of the new street. But before doing this, check for traffic in that lane. Remember to check for oncoming traffic that may make a right turn on red and enter the inside lane just as the bicyclist does.

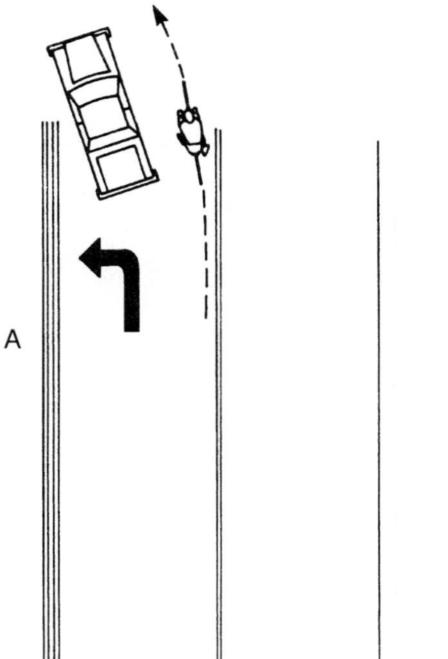

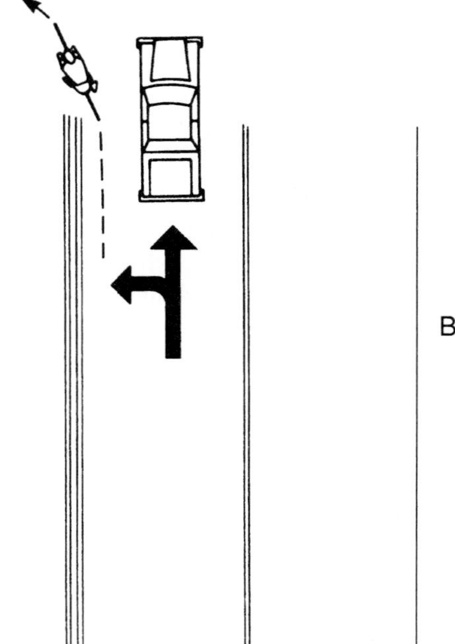

Figure 8-9. Left turns. See text for details.

Sometimes on multilane streets the traffic is so heavy that it is not possible to make a left-hand turn in the manner described. If this happens, it is best to use pedestrian rules, ride to the far corner of the intersection, and turn the bicycle in the proper direction and wait for the light to change. At an intersection without a signal, wait for the traffic to clear in all directions.

RULES OF THE TRAIL

With the increasing popularity of the mountain bike and off-road riding, it is imperative that you follow a few simple rules when trail riding. In so doing you will insure the safety of all trail users, while also helping to preserve the trail. To start, only ride where it is legal to ride. Some trails are closed and to ride on these may mobilize public sentiment against any trails being open to off-road riding. Once on the trail, **always** yield to hikers and horses. Be especially careful around the latter, as they are easily spooked by bikes. While on the trail do not leave it to take a short cut, as this cuts new trails and increases erosion, which could lead to trail closures. In the same light, ride through the edges of large puddles rather than around them, as riding around them increases the size of the puddle. If there are too many puddles because of a lot of rain, then do not ride, as a saturated trail is susceptible to damage. Another way to minimize trail damage is to stay in control of your bike, that is, do not skid around the turns on a steep downhill. When skidding around turns, you may not be able to stop if a hiker or horse is around the bend. Finally, volunteer to maintain the trails that you use. Responsible trail use and frequent trail maintenance means that you will always have trails to ride on.

SAFETY

Statistics show that in the majority of bicycle accidents the rider simply falls off the bicycle for some reason. The most frequent serious injury resulting from a fall is a cranial contusion. For this reason it is imperative that you always wear a helmet when road or off-road riding. The remainder of accidents are collisions with automobiles, fixed objects, and other bicyclists. This implies that the greatest cause of accidental injury is inept bicyclists.

First, it is important to know how to ride a bicycle. The bicyclist should adopt riding procedures that are reasonable and proper, always be observant, recognize potential problems, and be able to cope in emergency situations. Second, it is important to operate a bicycle as a vehicle. This provides operating procedures that are predictable and expected by drivers of automobiles and by other bicyclists. Because of unexpected turning and crossing maneuvers into streets from bike paths and sidewalks, it is much safer to ride a bicycle in the street than in these off-street facilities.

Studies have shown that experienced, active bicyclists, such as those who belong to organized clubs, have one-sixth to one-seventh the accident rate of other bicyclists. It appears that—in the case of bicycling, at least—a little learning is truly a dangerous thing.

In addition, all cyclists should be self-sufficient on every ride. The road cyclists should carry a working pump, spare inner tube, patch kit with fresh glue, a piece of tire casing to fix a torn sidewall, and money for food and a phone call. The off-road cyclists should carry the same things as a road cyclist, plus a few tools, as mechanical failure is more common off-road. Tools should include a chain breaker, a few extra chain links, and chain lube; allen and box-end wrenches suitable to your bike's needs; and a screwdriver.

BICYCLING ACTIVITIES

Safe and proper bicycling offers a lifetime of enjoyment and fitness. Social and other benefits are also possible by joining a local bicycle club. Bicycle club members can supply a wealth of knowledge and are happy to help newcomers become more knowledgeable and more skillful bicyclists. Usually club members are aware of the latest equipment. On club rides the novice can rapidly learn what others spent years finding out: where the best rides are, bicycling techniques that make riding easier, and favorite lunch stops.

There are many types of cycling clubs, including road racing, touring, and off-road (figures 8-10 and 8-11). Check with a local bicycle shop to find out about club activities.

Figure 8-10. Bicycle touring.

Figure 8-11. Bicycle racing.

The novice is wise to investigate joining a touring club. Touring clubs usually have three levels of rides: short, medium, and long, or easy, moderate, and strenuous. Initially pick an easy ride and go with the club.

BASIC TRAINING TIPS AND RIDING SKILLS

Before beginning a ride, stretch lightly (chapter 3 provides some basic stretching techniques applicable to cycling). In addition to stretching, you may also want to perform some basic strength training exercises (see chapter 41), especially for the legs, the lower back, and the abdomen. If you lift, give yourself a day to recover before riding. Stretching and strength training help reduce the risk of injury. Once on the bike, start easily. Only after you are warmed up should you begin to ride at a fast speed. Moderation is especially important if going on a long ride, as novice riders frequently ride too fast at the start of a ride, only to fade at the end because they "hit the wall."

If you are thinking about racing, obtain one of the books on training listed in the suggested readings section. These books provide a wealth of knowledge on road or off-road training and race strategy. If you like to tour or ride for recreation, it is advisable to vary your riding style from day to day. For example, on some days ride a bit longer than usual, on other days take a shorter but faster ride than usual. The shorter, faster rides can be broken down into intervals, which can vary based on time. You might do a 10-minute fast stretch or two 5-minute fast stretches, and so on. You might want to do a few sprints or hill climbs. By varying ride speed and duration, you improve different aspects of your fitness, which ultimately increases your riding pleasure by making it easier to ride into a headwind or climb a hill climb. Regardless of how you ride, be methodical: do not add too many hard sessions or even long slow rides without adequate preparation.

To further enhance riding pleasure, it is important to acquire a few skills, such as hill climbing, riding into the wind, and drafting. To climb a hill well, it is imperative that you have the proper gear ratio. If your easiest gear is too big, then climbing a hill will be like lifting too much weight. The gear ratio you need depends on the gradient and length of the climb. Long, gradual climbs can be handled with a mixture of in and out of the saddle riding. Choose a gear at the base of the hill that allows you to maintain a good cadence of 70 to 90 RPM. If cadence drops, shift to an easier gear if you have one; otherwise, it is time to stand and pedal out of the saddle. Periodically when pedaling uphill in the saddle, you may want to shift to a harder gear (one or two gears higher—the chain moves down the rear sprocket) and stand for a few hundred meters to utilize a few other muscles and relieve some pressure on the quadriceps. Short, steep climbs of about 1 to 2 km (.6 to 1.25 miles) require you to shift to one of your lowest gears as soon as you begin the ascent. If you have only two chain rings up front (a double crank), then stand and pedal out of the saddle with a cadence of 65 to 80 RPM, much like walking your bike up the hill. If off-road or touring, you will probably have three chain rings up front (a triple crank), so you may have a gear ratio small enough to allow you to pedal fairly comfortably in the saddle. The primary consideration off-road is traction. If you stand, the rear wheel can slip, causing a dismount, which means you might finish the hill walking rather than riding.

As with riding up long, gradual hills, you should maintain a good cadence into the wind. This might require you to shift to an easier gear. The prime consideration with riding hills or into the wind is effort, not speed. You will have to slow down. Do not make the mistake of maintaining speed, as riding into a hard wind or up a hill with a high gear wears you out quickly, sapping valuable energy reserves that you might need later. A big energy saver when riding into the wind, or anywhere for that matter, is drafting. When drafting, ride about 15 to 30 cm (6 to 12 inches) behind the rider in front of you. By doing this, you reduce your effort at the lead rider's expense by about 30 percent, that is, it is easier to go faster or farther. When drafting, pay close attention to the task: keep hands on the brake hoods or levers and eyes focused on the road in front of the lead rider, not his or her rear wheel. In so doing you can anticipate when the lead rider will have to alter course or speed, which permits proactive rather than reactive riding. Drafting takes practice but it is an essential skill, one that allows experienced riders and beginners to ride together enjoyably.

TEACHING CONSIDERATIONS

1. Define the purpose of the instruction in terms of road or off-road riding.

2. Check equipment for safety and fit.
3. Teach bicycle safety and etiquette. For cyclists who do not have a license to drive a car, spend some time practicing the rules of the road. Use videotapes of different driving conditions, if necessary. Take students out on the road with no traffic to practice until hand signals and understanding of the rules of the road become automatic.
4. Combine more lecture-type material with opportunities for activity.
5. Provide opportunities to cycle. Where possible, conduct these activities in the environment to be used by the student. Choose less heavily traveled areas or less technical trails to begin practice and then move to more demanding areas.
6. Design an obstacle course in a parking lot for improving bike handling skills. The course can contain cones for steering or logs for jumping depending on class emphasis.
7. Hold a 5-mile time trial, starting individual cyclists at 30-second intervals.
8. When planning initial trips, organize a buddy system.
9. Do not take large groups of cyclists into heavy traffic.
10. Have students play "bumper-bike" on a grassy field. The students ride *slowly* and bump into each other on a grassy field, which teaches them how to handle bikes in tight situations.

GLOSSARY

bicycle clothing Special clothing, such as chamois-lined shorts, that prevent saddle chafe and sores.

brake hoods Rubber portion of the brake lever/shift lever mechanism. A good place to rest your hands while cycling.

braking Bringing the bicycle to a stop by using both brakes properly.

clincher tires Tires that have either a wire or kevlar bead, which holds the tire to the rim. Kevlar is more expensive, but much lighter. The lighter weight aids acceleration, which makes for a livelier ride.

double crank A crank assembly that has two chain rings up front. Found on road racing and recreational bikes.

drafting Following closely behind the lead rider to reduce energy expenditure.

gear shifting (derailleur) Varying the gear ratios on multispeed bikes; the bicyclist is most efficient when pedaling at a constant rate of revolutions per minute.

helmet Lightweight headgear designed for bicycle riding.

presta valve European bike tire valve that has small knob at the end of the valve stem. The knob must be screwed out to inflate tire.

rear sprocket The cogs on the rear wheel. The big cogs are the low gears and the little cogs are the high gears. Part of the freewheel on older bikes and the freehub on newer bikes.

RPM The number of revolutions per minute the crank-arms turn. A higher cadence or RPM is generally better than a low one.

rules of the road Rules that apply to both cyclists and automobile drivers.

rules of the trail Always yield to hikers and horses, stay on the trail, stay in control, and ride where it is legal. Do not rim puddles and skid around bends in the trail on downhills. Maintain trails: be a builder as well as a user.

saddle A smooth leather seat just wide enough for good support and not so wide as to chafe.

safety check Checking that the parts of the bicycle are in good working order before a ride.

shrader valve Bike tire valve that is similar to one found in automobile tires in the United States.

steering Guiding the bicycle more by leaning than turning the handlebars.

tools for the trail Chain breaker, chain links, and chain lube; allen and box-end wrenches suitable to your bike's needs; pump; spare tire, patch kit, and a piece of tire casing to repair tire sidewall; screwdriver.

tools for the road Pump; spare tire, patch kit, and piece of tire casing to repair tire sidewall; a few dollars for food and some change for a phone call.

triple crank A crank assembly that has three chain rings up front. Found on touring and mountain bikes.

SUGGESTED READINGS

Abt, S. 1989. *In high gear*. Mill Valley, Calif.: Bicycle Books. A colorful account of professional bicycle racing.

Bicycle Magazine. 1986. *Complete guide to bicycle maintenance and repair*. Emmaus, Pa.: Rodale Press. Puts basic bicycle repair and maintenance within the rider's reach. With many illustrations and photographs, it provides clear step-by-step instructions for almost any repair.

Browder, S. 1983. *American biking atlas and touring guide*. New York: Workman.

Burke, E. 1992. *Cycling health and physiology*. Brattleboro, Vt.: Vitesse Press.

Burke, E. 1996. *High-tech cycling.* Champaign, IL: Human Kinetics. This book provides cutting-edge information on how to enhance road and mountain bike performance. It covers riding, position, biomechanics, cadence, injuries, strength training and nutrition.

Burke, E., and Newsom, M. 1988. *Medical and scientific aspects of cycling*. Champaign, Ill.: Human Kinetics.

Burney, S. 1996. *Cycle-cross.* Boulder, CO: VeloPress. This book provides a complete guide to cycle-cross racing.

Clark, J. 1995. *Mountain biking the national parks.* San Francisco: Bicycle Books. This guide shows where mountain biking in the U. S. national parks is permitted. It covers the parks most suitable for sustainable trail riding.

Friel, J. 1997. *The cyclists training bible,* ed. 2. Boulder, CO: VeloPress.

Gould, T. 1992. *Mountain bike racing.* San Francisco: Bicycle Books.

Kienholz, M., and Pawlak, R. 1996. *Cycling in cyberspace.* San Francisco: Bicycle Books. This book provides a thorough listing of the various on-line sites containing cycling related information.

Maffetone, P. 1996. *Training for endurance.* Stamford, NY: David Barmore Productions.

Mountain Bike Magazines's Complete Guide to Mountain Bike Skills. 1996. Emmaus, PA: Rodale Press. This book is designed to help all riders perform better on the trail, from beginners to experts.

Newby-Fraser, P. 1995. *Peak fitness for women*. Champaign, IL: Human Kinetics.

Phinney, D., and Carpenter, C. 1992. *Training for cycling*. New York: Perigee Books.

Snowling, S., and Evans, K. 1990. *Bicycle mechanics*. 2d ed. Champaign, Ill.: Human Kinetics.

Watson, G. 1990. *The Tour de France and its heroes*. Boulder, Colo.: Venonews Books. An account of the heroes of the tour during the 1980s.

Zinn, L. 1996. *Zinn and the art of mountain bike maintenance.* Boulder, CO: VeloPress.

Periodicals

Bicycling, published eleven times per year by Rodale Press, Box 7308, Red Oak, IA 51591-0308.

Bicyclists, published eight times a year by Peterson Publishing, P.O. Box 52712, Boulder, CO 80322-8712.

Cycle Sport, published monthly by Cycle Sport USA, 704 Hennepin Ave, Minneapolis, MN 55403. European publication, which provides the best English language coverage of professional road racing.

Mountain Bike Magazine, published eleven times a year by Rodale Press, Box 7308, Red Oak, IA 51591-0308.

VeloNews, published twenty times a year by Inside Communications, Box 21450, Boulder, CO 80308-4450. Large newspaper format. Provides coverage of professional mountain and road bike racing, covers amateur racing, training tips, and lists 45 race events.

RESOURCES

Films and Videos

Anybody's bike video (bike repair), *Lessons in cycling*, *Mountain biking*, and *The complete cyclist* are all available from Cambridge Physical Education and Health, P.O. Box 2153, Charleston, WV 25328.

Lessons in Cycling, 1991. This video from Velo covers all aspects of road racing. www.velocatalogue.com. Velo, 1830 N. 55th Street, Boulder, CO 80301-2700.

Only one road. AAA Foundation for Traffic, Falls Church, VA.

Performance Mountain Biking, 1996. This video from Velo covers all aspects of mountain bike racing. www.velocatalogue.com. Velo, 1830 N. 55th Street, Boulder, CO 80301-2700.

Surviving the Trail, 1993. This video from Velo covers all aspects of mountain bike maintenance on the trail. www.velocatalogue.com. Velo, 1830 N. 55th Street, Boulder, CO 80301-2700.

World Cycling Productions, 704 Hennepin Ave, Minneapolis, MN 55403. They sell videos that cover all the major professional races in Europe.

Bowling

After completing this chapter, the reader should be able to:

- Display a knowledge of the rules of bowling
- Demonstrate the correct grip, stance, approach, and delivery in bowling
- Identify three styles of delivery
- Instruct a group of students in the fundamentals of bowling
- Recognize and use bowling terminology correctly

HISTORY

Bowling can be traced back in history about 7000 years, which easily establishes it as one of the oldest games known. Archaeologists trace its origin to the ancient Egyptians, with evidence of crudely shaped implements being used.

The game of modern tenpins had its inception in northern Italy, being derived from variations played by the ancients. The Italians called their game "bowls." Rounded stones without finger holes and held in the open hand were used as balls.

In the thirteenth century the game spread to Germany, The Netherlands, and England where it was known as "ninepins." The playing area was known as the bowling green because the game was usually played on grass. In 1623 Dutch settlers introduced the game to America as ninepins. It was first played on grass or clay and later on a single wide board. The game attracted considerable interest, and people bet extensively on it. Laws banning ninepins were passed in several states in the 1840s. Later, to circumvent the law, a Dutchman added one more pin and called it "tenpins."

In 1895 the American Bowling Congress* was organized, and it formulated rules governing alleys, balls, and pins. Bowling is so popular in the United States that it can safely be said that it has more enthusiasts today than almost any other sport. It is estimated that nearly 60 million people bowl.

In recent years high school officials formulated the American High School Bowling Congress (AHSBC).† The Women's International Bowling Congress (WIBC) was formed before the AHSBC.

Colleges and universities often include lanes in their student recreation centers, and in many colleges bowling is a popular course in the physical education curriculum.

Contests on television have done much to increase the popularity of bowling; it became a demonstration sport in the 1988 Olympics.

*2200 N Third St, Milwaukee, WI 53212
†5301 S 76th St, Greendale, WI 53129

SOCIAL VALUES

Bowling is a sport that appeals to everyone: weak or strong, young or old, men and women. It requires the learning of comparatively few skills. It requires only a change of shoes and no special uniform. One can bowl during lunchtime, after work, or in the evening, which is appealing to the average American. It requires no great strength; rather, rhythm, relaxation, and coordination are the essentials. Once mastered, it is an art. Around the bowling alley, social intercourse is pleasurable and tensions seem to disappear. There is always the challenge, as in golf, to turn in a better score. One can play alone for enjoyment or easily join a local team. Bowling, because it uses many muscles, is one of the best recreational sports skills, and it is relatively inexpensive.

EQUIPMENT AND FACILITIES

In bowling, ten wooden or plastic pins are set in a triangular position at the far end of a wooden runway called a "lane" (figure 9-1). The lane is 60 feet (18.3 m) long from the No. 1 pin to the foul line. It is about 42 inches (1.1 m) wide. On each side of the lane a channel approximately 9 inches (22.5 cm) wide runs from the foul line to the pit, behind the pins. Behind the foul line is the approach, which must not be less than 15 feet (4.6 m) long. The pit must have a drop of at least 9½ inches (23.8 cm) from the lane floor.

Pins are set 12 inches (30 cm) apart from center to center (figure 9-2). A pin is 15 inches (37.5 cm) in height, with a base diameter of 2¼ inches (5.6 cm). It is typically constructed of clear, hard maple.

Balls are constructed of Bakelite or of a hardened rubber substance. The circumference is not more than 27 inches (67.5 cm), and the official ball weighs from 10 to 16 pounds (4.54 to 7.26 kg). Balls usually have three bored holes for the bowler's fingers to aid in holding and accurately delivering the ball. Special balls with four or five finger holes are now available.

Other forms of bowling—such as duckpins, barrel pins, and candlepins—involve the use of small pins and small

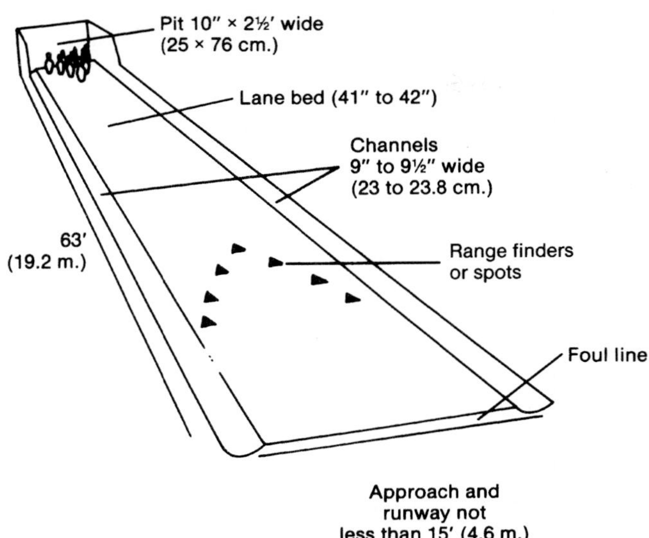

Figure 9-1. The lane.

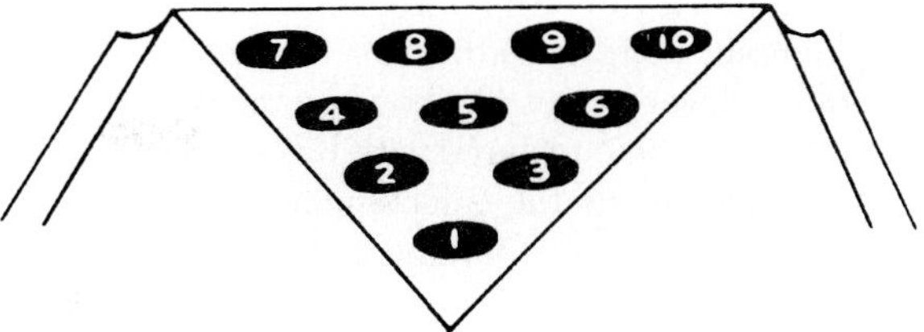

Figure 9-2. Positions of pins and their numbers.

balls. The fundamentals of all these games are essentially the same. In duckpins three balls are rolled per frame.

RULES

In general, a game of American tenpins consists of 10 frames. A player delivers two balls in each of the first nine frames unless a strike is scored. In the tenth frame a player delivers three balls if a strike or spare is scored. Specifically:

1. The bowler is allowed to roll two balls from behind the foul line down the lane at the pins in an attempt to knock down all the pins. If all the pins are knocked down with the bowler's first ball, it is called a "strike" (shown on the scorecard as an X in the upper righthand corner of the frame in which it was made), and it is not necessary to roll the second ball.
2. A spare is made when a player bowls down all the pins with two balls in any frame; it is designated by a slash (/) in the upper right-hand corner of the frame in which it is made. The count in such a frame is left open until the player bowls the first ball in the succeeding frame, when the number of pins knocked down thereby is added to the 10 earned by the spare, and the total is credited.
3. Pins that are knocked down by another pin rebounding in the play from the side partition or rear cushion are counted as pins down, except where pins rebound off the body, arms, or legs of a human pinsetter. Pins that are bowled off the lane bed, rebound, and remain standing on the lane are counted as pins standing. A pin knocked down by a human or mechanical pinsetter does not count and must be replaced on the spot where it stood before delivery of the ball.
4. A foul occurs when the bowler permits any part of the foot, hand, or arm, while in contact with the lane, to rest on or extend beyond the foul line, or if at any time after the ball leaves the hands and passes over the foul line, the bowler permits any part of the body to come in contact with the lane, division boards, wall, or uprights that are on or beyond the foul line.
5. No count is made on a foul ball, and any pins that are knocked down or displaced by it are respotted. A foul ball counts as a ball bowled by the player.

League Bowling

1. Two adjoining lanes are used in all games of league or tournament play, and the bowling of 10 complete frames on the pair of lanes on which the game was started constitutes an official game. The members of the contesting teams successively and in regular order bowl one frame on one lane, the next frame on the other lane, alternating each frame until the game is completed. Each player bowls two balls in every frame, except where a strike is made.
2. No pins may be conceded, and only those actually knocked down may be counted. Every frame must be completed at the time the player is bowling in regular order.
3. When a strike is made in the tenth frame, the bowler is then permitted to bowl two more balls on the same lane. When a spare is made in the tenth frame, the bowler is permitted to bowl one more ball on the same lane.
4. In case of a tie game, each team bowls one complete frame on the same lane on which its tenth frame was bowled, bowling and scoring said extra frame in the same manner as the tenth frame. If, at the completion of the first extra frame, a tie still exists, teams change lanes for any additional frames that may be required to determine the winner.
5. Every ball delivered, unless it is declared a dead ball by the umpire, is counted against the player. If, when rolling at a full frame, it is discovered after the ball has been delivered that one or more pins are misplaced, the ball and resulting pinfall are counted. It is the duty of each player to look at the pins before

bowling and, if the setup is not satisfactory, to request that the pins be respotted.

6. Should a player by mistake bowl on the wrong lane or out of turn or be interfered with by another bowler or spectator, or should the ball come in contact with any obstacle on the lanes, then the ball is called a dead ball by the umpire and is immediately rebowled.
7. Pins that are knocked down or displaced by a ball that leaves the lane before reaching the pins, or from a ball rebounding from the rear cushions, do not count and they are immediately respotted. Removal or interference with pins by a human pinsetter before they stop rolling is cause for the umpire to order the pins respotted.

SCORING

Although many newer bowling establishments now provide automatic scoring by computer, considerable enjoyment is added to the game if each participant is able to keep score accurately. A perfect score is 300 points. To score the game, the results for each frame are recorded, and the cumulative total for the 10 frames is the final score. In each frame the total number of pins knocked down in two tries is recorded except when a strike or spare is made. In the case of a strike, the score for the frame is 10 (marked with an X in the small square) plus the count of the next two balls bowled. In the case of a spare, the score for the frame is 10 plus the number of pins knocked down with the next ball. If a foul is committed, the score for that ball is not counted. If the foul occurs on the first ball, all pins are reset and the next ball is scored as the second ball of that frame. The correct method of scoring a game (called a line) is illustrated in figure 9-3.

Tips to Remember

1. A strike followed directly by a frame that includes a spare = 20 pins.
2. A spare followed directly by a frame in which a strike is recorded = 20 pins.
3. The highest total pin count that may be added to a preceding frame = 30 pins.

Sample game scoring

Frame 1. The bowler, on the first ball, knocks down eight pins. An 8 is placed in the first square of the first frame. On the second ball, the bowler fails to hit either of the two remaining pins. The miss is indicated by a dash (—), which is called an "error." The bowler totals the number of pins knocked down with both balls and places the score 8 in the first frame.

Frame 2. The bowler knocks down seven pins with the first ball in this frame and places a 7 in the first square to indicate the number of pins scored. The bowler gets the remaining three pins with the second ball and thus places the symbol for a spare (/) in the second square. The second frame cannot be scored until the results of the first ball of the third frame are known.

Frame 3. Six pins are knocked down with the first ball in the third frame. The score of 6 is added to the 10 gotten in the second frame to give a total of 16. The running score in the second frame is 8 (first frame) plus 16, or 24. Three pins are knocked down with the second ball, giving a total of nine pins for the third frame. The running score in the third frame is 24 + 9, or 33.

Frame 4. Unfortunately, the bowler rolls the first ball of the fourth frame into the gutter. This is recorded in the first square as a G (gutter ball) or — (miss), which has a zero value. The second ball of this frame knocks down all 10 pins. However, as this is the second ball, it is scored as a spare. The running score in the fourth frame cannot be scored until the first ball of the fifth frame has been delivered.

Frame 5. The bowler crosses the foul line while delivering the first ball. Although the bowler knocks down nine pins, a zero score is received for the first ball because a foul has been committed. The fourth frame can now be scored. The score for the fourth frame is 10 plus 0, or 10. The running score in the fourth frame is 43. The foul is indicated by placing an F in the first square. The pins are then reset and the bowler delivers the second ball, which knocks down nine pins. A 9 is placed in the second square, and 9 is added to the score of the previous frame to give a running score of 52 in the fifth frame.

Frame 6. The bowler knocks down all 10 pins with the first ball. This is indicated by placing an X in the first square. The running score cannot be recorded as a strike but is scored by adding 10 to the number of pins knocked down with the next two balls bowled.

Frame 7. The bowler again makes a strike with the first ball. The bowler now has two consecutive strikes, or a "double." The player cannot yet score the sixth or seventh frame.

Frame 8. In this frame the bowler gets seven pins with the first ball rolled and records the 7 in the first square. Now the score for the sixth frame can be computed. This score is 10 (strike in frame 6) plus 10 (strike in frame 7) plus 7 (number of pins gotten with the first ball in the eighth frame), or 27. The running score in the sixth frame is 52 plus 27, or 79. The second ball in frame 8 knocks down two pins, recorded by a 2 in the second square. Now

Frames	1	2	3	4	5	6	7	8	9	10	TOTAL
	8 –	7 /	6 3	– /	F 9	X	X	7 2	8 –	9 / 5	
Name	8	24	33	43	52	79	98	107	115	130	130

Figure 9-3. Sample method of scoring.

the seventh-frame score can be computed. It is 10 plus 7 plus 2, or 19; the running scored is 98 in the seventh frame and 107 in the eighth frame.

Frame 9. In this frame the first ball delivered hits the headpin (No. 1 pin) squarely, and a "split" results. The No. 7 and No. 10 pins remain standing. The split is indicated by encircling the 8, shown in the first square of the ninth frame. The second ball misses both pins and a miss (error) is indicated by the dash (—) in the second square. The ninth frame score of 8 is added to the running score of 107 to give a total of 115 in the ninth frame.

Frame 10. The bowler gets a spare with the second ball. Because this is the tenth frame, the bowler is entitled to another ball. The extra ball knocks down 5 pins, giving a score of 15 for the tenth frame. The 15 is added to the ninth frame's running score of 115 to give a total score of 130.

FUNDAMENTAL SKILLS AND TECHNIQUES

Ball Selection

Select a ball, not too heavy or too light, that fits the fingers comfortably. A comfortable fit is essential to good delivery. Select a ball with finger holes that are neither too narrow nor too wide for finger spread, that is, from thumb to fingers. A good method to determine finger span is to insert the thumb into the thumb hole up to the second joint, or about four-fifths of its length, then lay the hand flat on the surface of the ball with the fingers spread over the holes. The knuckle joints of the fingers should extend about ¼ inch beyond the inside near edge of the finger hole. This allows for proper looseness or slack, which is essential for a comfortable grip. This slack, or play, between the palm and the ball should be about ¼ inch. This is the recommended method of fitting a regular ball; it does not apply to fingertip or semifingertip balls.

Grip

The three-finger grip (conventional) is the most commonly used and is recommended for beginners and young bowlers. It causes less strain on the wrist and arms, and the popular hook ball can be delivered better with this grip than with others. If a person has an excessively weak grip, a four- or five-hole ball is recommended. Bowling balls supplied by bowling establishments are nearly always three-hole balls (figure 9-4).

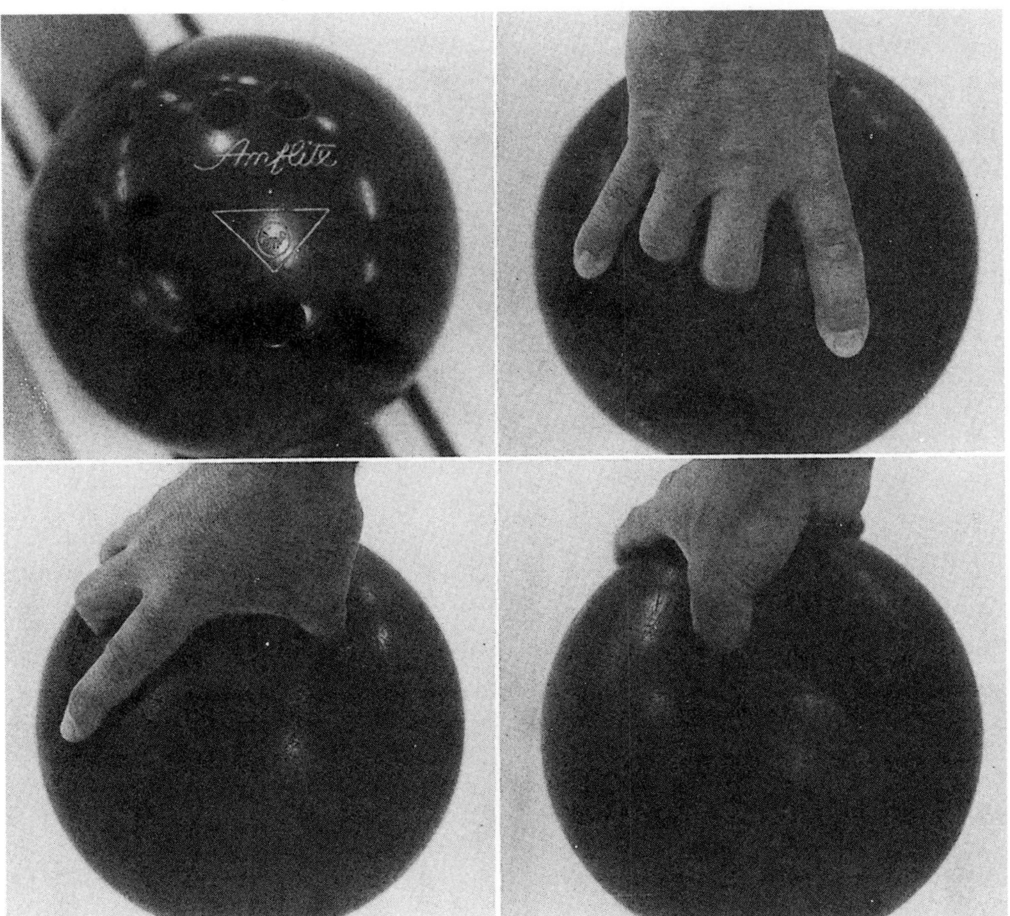

Figure 9-4. Conventional grip.

Figure 9-5. The stance.

Figure 9-6. The push-away.

When the ball is released, the thumb should come out of the hole first.

Stance

The bowler assumes a stance with the body facing the pins, erect or slightly crouched, about 15 feet (4.57 m) back of the foul line (figure 9-5). The left foot is slightly in front of the right. The ball is held in the right hand, waist high. Some bowlers hold it higher, with the idea of aiming, resting the weight of the ball on the left hand.

Footwork

The most essential and fundamental skills confronting the beginning bowler are footwork, balance, and rhythm. Bowlers take three, four, or five steps before delivering the ball. There are many good bowlers using each style. The least acceptable style is the three-step approach due to the difficulty in timing with the arm movements. Probably the most popular among bowlers, because timing with the arms is more natural, is the four-step approach. However, each bowler should experiment until he or she finds the number of steps that fit. After this is accomplished, the bowler is ready to synchronize the footstep pattern with the arm movements while delivering the ball. The result of this practice is rhythm and timing. You should practice footwork so that the feet move parallel to each other, remaining on the same board on which they start. Practice a fast walk, a slow run, or gliding movement, rather than the walk or run. To find the correct starting spot in the approach, starting from the foul line, step off the number of steps desired and add 6 inches (15 cm).

Delivery and Approach to Foul Line

There are many styles of delivery. Usually the ball is carried anywhere from chest high to waist high and may be carried in the center of the body or in front of the right shoulder. In general, the approach has four phases: push-away, swing, forward swing, and release of the ball.

The bowler starts the approach toward the foul line by pushing the ball slightly down and away from the body so that it is extended outward between chest and waist height (figure 9-6). During this movement a step forward with the right foot is taken if the bowler is using the four-step delivery. If a five-step delivery is used, the left foot starts first. The push-away places the ball forward about waist high, and the weight of the ball and gravity give the impetus in making the backward swing arc that is the next phase in the series of movements (figure 9-7).

In executing this arc, the bowler should not carry the ball too far backward at the end of the arc but end a little above waist high. The ball is now poised in readiness to

Figure 9-7. The backswing.

Figure 9-8. The forward swing.

gain momentum from this pendulum swing downward and forward smoothly for the release and follow-through (figure 9-8).

Release

If the bowler has achieved perfect timing, the ball should be coming forward in its well-executed arc just as the last step (left foot) is being taken. The body weight should be perfectly balanced over this last step with the left foot (figure 9-9).

With continued practice the series of arm and feet movements blend into a graceful, coordinated, rhythmic pattern.

The approach starts slowly and accelerates toward the end. The last step must stop short of the foul line (see rules). The ball should contact the lane about 12 to 16 inches (30 to 40 cm) beyond the foul line.

Follow-Through

At the finish of the arm movement, the bowler's left foot will be in front, the right foot balanced on the floor like a rudder behind, and the bowling arm extended forward and upward in the follow-through so essential in many sports skills. The final movement of the approach is an easy sliding glide that is controlled to stop about 2 to 4 inches (5 to 10 cm) short of the foul line (figure 9-10).

The bowler's posture at the finish should be smooth, easy, and relaxed, with a bend at the knees and very little at the hips. The opposite arm is used as an aid to balance. A straight ball should be rolled smoothly onto the alley beyond the foul line and about 6 to 8 inches (15 to 20 cm) from the right channel. For a hook or curve ball this distance will vary depending on the amount of curve.

Delivery

The skill techniques just described are common to all delivery styles. The bowler is now confronted with the choice of three styles of delivery: straight ball, hook, and curve (figure 9-11). The beginner should first try the straight ball. It is the easiest delivery to accomplish, and positive results are seen in a short amount of time. Once comfortable with the straight ball, the bowler should experiment with the hook. The hook ball is the most efficient and is used by almost all professional bowlers.

Straight Ball

To throw a straight ball, the thumb is placed on top of the ball in a 12 o'clock position (figure 9-12A) directed at the headpin so that the ball will roll in a straight line. The most universal approach is from the right corner of the lane, so that the aim is directed in a diagonal crosslane path between the No. 1 and No. 3 pins.

Figure 9-9. Release.

Hook Ball

The hook ball is the most effective of all bowling styles for producing strikes. This style is universal with high-scoring teams. The technique recommended for the beginner's hook ball is as follows: The thumb is placed at the 10 o'clock position, so that the V formed by the thumb and forefinger points down the lane (figure 9-12B). In a natural hook the wrist and/or fingers do not turn or rotate. The thumb's coming out first allows the fingers to lift their side of the ball, and a hook results. The ball is released near the right channel. The aim is at the 3-6 pocket. The ball then rolls with a forward motion and breaks sharply toward the left at the 1-3 pocket (figure 9-11). With the ball coming in at such a sideward angle, the pins are effectively swept off the lane. Unlike other styles, the hook ball, even thinly hitting the head pin, leaves few single pins remaining and few splits. There is no question of the effectiveness of the hook ball, and it can be mastered with practice.

Curve Ball

The curve ball is not recommended for beginners because of its inconsistency and the difficulty in controlling it. Much practice is required for its mastery (figure 9-11).

The technique is as follows: On the backswing the wrist is rotated to the right, and on the forward swing to the left, which gives the ball a wide, sweeping curve (figure 9-12C and D). The release is the same as for the hook ball. The

Figure 9-10. The follow-through.

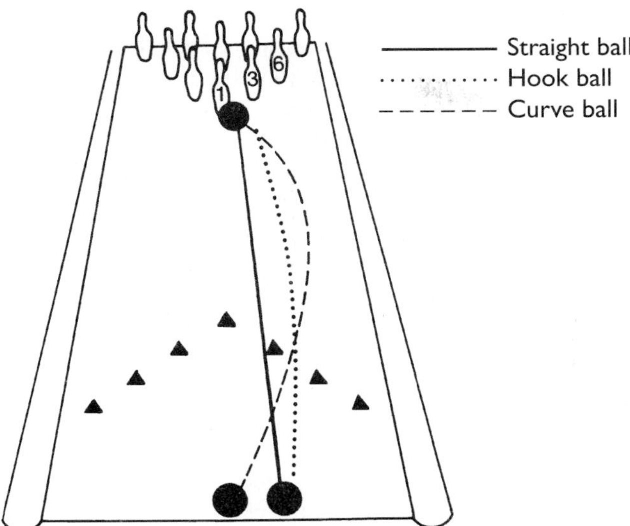

Figure 9-11. Types of deliveries.

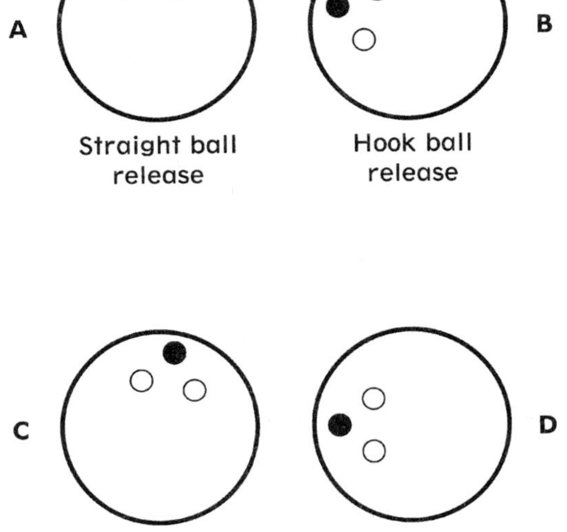

Figure 9-12. Grips for various types of delivery. See text for details.

ball is laid down near the center of the lane. The follow-through is forward.

Aim

There are two methods of aiming: at the pin and at the spot. The most effective balls are rolled to hit the 1-3 pocket. For the beginner, the pin method is best—that is, aiming at the pin or pocket one desires the ball to hit. The eyes should be focused on that area throughout the entire delivery and follow-through (figure 9-13).

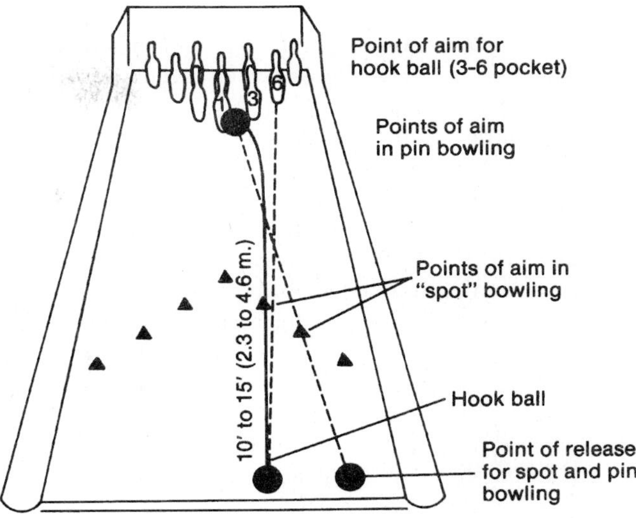

Figure 9-13. Point of aim for various shots.

In the spot method the bowler usually aims to roll the ball over a definite spot on the lane or over an imaginary line from the foul line down the lane to coincide with the pin or pocket desired to be hit. To aid the spot bowler, most lanes have triangularly shaped spots located at specific distances from the foul one (see figure 9-1).

POSSIBLE ERRORS AND CORRECTIONS

Possible errors	Corrections
Ball travels directly to right or left gutter when released.	Keep the ball close to your body on backswing and forward swing.
Ball does not have adequate speed.	Increase the speed of your approach or push the ball higher as you complete the push-away.
Bowler releases ball too late or too soon.	Release the ball as it reaches the right knee (for right-handed bowler).
Path of the ball is inconsistent.	Keep shoulders square to the pins and the sliding or forward foot pointed toward the target. Follow-through should be toward target.
Bowler fails to start approach with the correct foot.	For the four-step approach, right-handers should start with the right foot. Left-handers should start with the left foot.
Bowler frequently fouls.	Make the first step in your approach very short.
Bowler lofts the ball.	Bend more at the knees than at the waist at point of release.
Ball falls from bowler's hand during swing.	Check size of finger holes and length of span.

TIPS TO REMEMBER

1. Develop an even speed in rolling all shots, and use whichever speed develops the most accuracy and consistency.
2. Concentrate on the spot desired to be hit.
3. Relax.
4. Be sure that the approach is not too fast or too slow.
5. Do not force a delivery; let the weight of the ball do the work. The arm merely serves as a pendulum.
6. In rolling the straight ball, be sure that the fingers are behind the ball when it is released, to prevent the ball from curving.
7. Learn to let the thumb come out of the hole first.
8. Hold the wrist firm when releasing the ball.
9. Lay the ball on the lane smoothly.
10. In follow-through, let the arm continue in the direction of the pins.

BOWLING FOR SPARES

Spare bowling is extremely critical for good scores and requires practice to obtain accuracy and confidence. Improvement in bowling is directly related to mastering the techniques for picking up spares. The following points are important to this aspect of the game:

1. Determine the key pin (usually the one closest to the bowler) and where it must be hit to get the most action-reaction to pick up the remaining pins.
2. Use the three basic alignments for the remaining pins:
   a. Center position for center pins
   b. Left position for right-side pins
   c. Right position for left-side pins
3. Roll the same style of ball for the spare as used for the first ball of the frame.
4. Concentrate harder on the second ball than the first, as there is less opportunity for pin action and less margin for error.

TEACHING CONSIDERATIONS

1. Basics of bowling can be taught in a gymnasium without real balls by using softballs and a target area. Stance, footwork, approach, and delivery can be effectively practiced before going to the lanes.
2. If needed, lanes can be set up inside the gymnasium using hard rubber bowling balls, 2 × 4s, and plastic pins.
3. If lanes are available for instruction, begin with selection of the ball. Teach stance, delivery, and approach with proper footwork without using the ball. Then add the ball. Concentrate on the push-away action.
4. Teach a four-step approach and straight ball as the basic style. This can be modified later for individuals as needed.
5. Begin practice without the pins set up, and initially disregard foul-line infractions. Add rule infractions as learners develop consistency in the coordination and rhythm of their delivery and are placing, rather than dropping, the ball onto the alley.
6. Once pins are set up, the instructor may vary the approach to strike and spare bowling. Some instructors effectively teach strike bowling by setting up only the 1-3 pins and encouraging pin bowling at the 1-3 pocket. Students will not be successful unless they hit the pocket most desirable for strike bowling. Eventually all pins should be set up, and both strike and spare bowling strategies need to be communicated and practiced.
7. Several students can be involved on one lane by charting the path of the *first ball* rolled in each frame for each other. This is a good exercise for evaluating consistency. Students would have to be given pencils and diagrams of the lanes. Evaluating the diagrams would help the instructor correct problems.
8. All aspects of scoring do not have to be introduced until learners are using two balls to get down all the pins. All students should be expected to learn how to score.
9. Spot bowling can be introduced to advanced beginners once consistency and some success in pin bowling has been achieved.
10. Introduce spare bowling by setting up different spare combinations with pins in front of the learner and having the learner make decisions about which pin to hit and where to hit it.
11. Based on the students' previous bowling scores, compute their handicaps and put them into teams for a tournament. All groups will be equal, regardless of skill level, with the use of handicaps. If time permits, alternate instruction with actual games so students are bowling games early in the unit and are still receiving instruction throughout the unit.

GLOSSARY

ABC American Bowling Congress.
AHSBC American High School Bowling Congress.
anchor The last bowler on a team.
approach That part of the lane, or runway, on which the bowler takes steps to proceed to the delivery point, the foul line.
average Total number of pins credited to a bowler divided by the number of games bowled in one season in a sanctioned league.
baby split The 3-10 split for right-handed bowlers and the 2-7 split for left-handed bowlers.
backup ball A ball delivered in such a manner as to curve toward the arm that delivered the ball. For a right-handed bowler the ball curves to the right.
bedposts The 7-10 split.
big four The 4-6-7-10 split.

blind score Score for an absent bowler. This is usually the average minus 10 pins.
blow Same as error or miss.
box Same as frame.
Brooklyn or crossing over Hitting the headpin and adjacent pin on the opposite side of the lane from which the bowler released the ball on the delivery.
channel Another name for "gutter."
cherry Knocking down one or more of the front pins in a spare and leaving others standing.
convert To make a spare.
double Two consecutive strikes.
error A complete failure to knock down any remaining pins after the first ball is rolled.
foul The act of touching the foul line with the foot or hand. If a foul is made on the first throw, all 10 pins are respotted; if it occurs on the second throw, only the pins knocked down with the first ball count.
frame The box on the score sheet in which the scores are recorded. Ten frames constitute a game.
gutter Trough, or channel, on each side of a lane.
gutterball A ball that falls off the lane into the gutter.
handicap System used to equalize competition.
headpin The No. 1 pin.
hook A ball that is caused to curve from outside in on its way to the pins.
kingpin The No. 5 pin.
lane The alley bed.
leave Pins left standing after the first ball has been rolled.
lift An upward motion given to the ball by the fingers during the release.
line A complete game recorded in the 10 frames across the score sheet.
loft Throwing the ball onto the lane rather than placing it down near the foul line.
mark A strike or spare.
open frame Failure to achieve a strike or spare in a frame.
perfect game A score of 300.
pitch Angle at which holes are drilled into the bowling ball.
pocket The gap between the No. 1 and No. 3 pins for right-handed bowlers and between the No. 1 and No. 2 pins for left-handed bowlers.
rack The trough holding the balls beside the runway.
return The ball returned from the pit to the bowler by way of a trough alongside or under the alley.
setup The arranging of 10 pins in regular formation.
sleeper A pin that is hidden behind another pin.
spare Bowling down all pins with two balls in any one frame.
strike Bowling down all pins with the first ball rolled.
striking out Rolling strikes for any part of a remainder of a game.
tandem Any two pins in a spare formation arranged one behind the other.
triple or turkey Three consecutive strikes at any time in a game.
WIBC Women's International Bowling Congress.

SUGGESTED READINGS

ABC bowling guide. Current edition. American Bowling Congress, 2200 N. Third St., Milwaukee WI 53212

Ange-Traub, C. 1998. *Bowling*. 8th ed. Dubuque, Iowa: WCB/McGraw-Hill. Provides readers with all the basics, including up-to-date information on equipment and advanced techniques.

Blassingame, C., and Cross, T. 1991. *Success in bowling*. Dubuque, Iowa: Kendall/Hunt. A very practical workbook approach to bowling, with pages included for notes and chapter reviews.

Borden, F. 1997. *Bowling*. Dubuque, Iowa: WCB/McGraw-Hill.

Clark, J. 1991. *Seven lifetime sports*. Dubuque, Iowa: Eddie Bowers. The chapter on bowling contains information on history, benefits, terminology, rules, equipment, skill fundamentals, error corrections, drills, games, and skills test.

Edginton, C. 1993. *Bowling*. Dubuque, Iowa: Eddie Bowers. Features a step-by-step approach to the game of bowling, and discusses techniques, strategies, lane markers, pin placements, and scoring.

Grinfields, V., and Hulstrnad, B. 1996. *Right down your alley*. 4th ed. Englewood, Colo.: Morton. Contains advice on how to improve bowling efficiency, accuracy, and consistency, and how to correct common errors.

Johnson, C. 1994. *Bowling*. Scottsdale, Ariz.: Gorsuch, Scarisbrick. Includes sections on special games, the psychological side of bowling, and checklists for form and team play. Contains 37 photographs and numerous illustrations.

Mackey, R. 1993. *Bowling*. 5th ed. Mountain View, Calif.: Mayfield. A concise bowling handbook that discusses auditory and visual cues to help students acquire basic skills when practicing on their own.

Martin, J. L., Tandy, R. E., and Ange-Traub, C. E. 1990. *Bowling*. 5th ed. Dubuque, Iowa: Wm. C. Brown. Presents the fundamental skills needed to be a good bowler and introduces special bowling events. Covers both basic and advanced bowling skills, and explains common faults and their remedies.

Strickland, R. H. 1996. *Bowling: Steps to success*. 2d ed. Champaign, Ill.: Human Kinetics.

Strickland, R. H. 1996. *Teaching bowling: Steps to success*. 2d ed. Champaign, Ill.: Human Kinetics.

Women's International Bowling Congress. Current edition. *Rules for WIBC, Inc., sanctioned leagues*. WIBC, Columbus, Ohio.

RESOURCES

Videotapes

Earl Anthony on beginning bowling. RMI Media Productions, 2807 W 47th St, Shawnee Mission, KS 66205.

ESPN's teaching kids bowling, Let's bowl with Dick Weber, and Don Johnson's a pro's guide to better bowling. These three videos available from Cambridge Physical Education and Health, P. O. Box 2153, Charleston, WV 25328.

Let's bowl with Dick Weber, The bowling masters, and Bowling with Marshall Holman and John Petraglia. Karol Video, 22 Riverside Dr, Wayne, NJ 07470

A pro's guide to better bowling, vols 1 and 2, each 60 min. "How To" Sport Videos, P.O. Box 5852, Denver, CO 80217.

Six bowling videos available from Sports Video, Champions on Film, 745 State Circle, P.O. Box 1941, Ann Arbor, MI 48106.

Web Site

Complete Bowlingindex: http://www.bowlingindex.com/

Dance: Recreational, Concert and Cultural Forms

After completing this chapter, the reader should be able to:

- Distinguish among various forms of dance and appreciate their development
- Demonstrate the fundamentals of movement
- Understand how elements of movement (space, time, and force) and creativity apply to modern dance
- Organize and teach square dancing
- Organize and teach folk dancing
- Recognize forms of social dancing

Dance offerings today at all academic levels are increasingly broad in scope and rich in content. On the national level, the diversity of dance programming makes generalization difficult. Curriculum frameworks for dance exist in both physical education and the arts, and are mandated at the state level. They have changed substantially over the past few decades. One significant shift has been toward framing dance as cultural activity, relating it to social studies and humanities curricula. Another has been to teach dance at the elementary level using Rudolf Laban's movement concepts and developmental theory.

School programs often include two broadly defined types of dance: recreational forms and concert (performance) forms. The first category might include international folk dance (world dance), social (ballroom), square dance, hip-hop (club dance), and country line dance. These types of dance are done largely for health benefits, socialization, and the enjoyment of participants. They are primarily leisure activities having some aspects of cultural appreciation.

By contrast, concert dance forms can be distinguished by using the body and movement as a means of communication, usually with an audience. In concert dance, with its emphasis on performance outcomes, the process of making and performing dances is central. Students can be taught the basic skills for creating and performing their own dances. The goals of dance performance are varied: they may be to entertain, inform, educate, enlighten, or provoke an audience. In most cases, however, the primary goals are aesthetic rather than recreational. Although modern dance and creative dance (movement education) are the forms most frequently taught in schools, ballet and jazz dance are sometimes included.

The growth of participation in recreational dance forms is indicated by the proliferation of clubs, classes, performances, festivals, conferences, publications, and videos. Recreational forms of dance undergo regular changes in popularity from time to time. Over the past decade, there have been many changes in vogue, from break dance, to country line dance, to tango and lambada, to Irish step dancing. Many dances experience a resurgence of popularity after a period of decline—for instance, disco, tap, and swing dance have all had renewed interest in the past decade.

As a nonverbal means of communication, dance can quickly transcend barriers of language and promote cultural understanding. In fact, international folk dance has been used in American education since the beginning of the century to enhance cross-cultural understanding. At the community level, dance often plays an important part in the affirmation of cultural identity, shared history, and values. Ethnic communities throughout the United States regularly host festivals, parades, and special events designed to celebrate and strengthen culture, share it with others, educate children, and enhance political presence. In many of these cultural events, dance plays a key role.

Experts in dance education, supported by Howard Gardner's theories of multiple intelligences identifying bodily-kinesthetic intelligence, tend to recommend creative dance and modern dance as important foundations in dance education in the early years. These forms emphasize body awareness, fundamental elements of movement, problem solving, creativity, and self-expression. This is the best time to involve boys (who are often not encouraged to dance in American culture) as they quickly find it exciting, challenging, and gratifying to participate in dance. Only in later years should there be an emphasis on technical skill, style, and mastering more complex choreography, without sacrificing the creative component of dance making. In this schema, each type of dance potentially has a special contribution to make.

It is quite possible to develop a wide and deep appreciation of dance through reading, and watching dance in performance or on film and video. However, only through active participation in dance does one develop the bodily-kinesthetic knowledge needed for teaching or fully understanding any kind of dance. Specialized training is needed for any teacher who wishes to integrate dance activities into the curriculum. College courses in dance are offered for those majoring in dance, physical education, and elementary education. Professional development workshops in dance are useful for educators who wish to expand their teaching competencies.

As a subject area, dance is malleable and can be successfully introduced or adapted within almost any context. Dance programming is most effective when determined by assessing the needs of a particular population. However, it often happens that a dance program, once established, shifts its focus as it grows. One common sequence is that dance is first introduced perhaps for recreational purposes, but as participants increase their dance knowledge, ability, and self-confidence, performance opportunities are sought out as a natural and satisfying culmination.

HISTORY OF DANCE

People have always danced. They have used some form of rhythmic movement as a part of their life experience from the beginning of time. Scholars argue that dance is one of the first forms of human communication. History indicates that dance has been used in worship, as part of ritualistic ceremonies connected to important rites of passage, for entertainment, for socialization, for education, for healing, in preparation for war, and as means of expressing ideas and emotions. Recent research, conducted worldwide, defines dance as cultural activity and reveals the rich and varied forms of dance in different cultures.

Concert forms

MODERN DANCE

At the turn of this century in the United States, a new form of dance was created. Five pioneers rebelled against the styles of dance imported from Europe (ballet, social dance, and musical revues) and set out to forge a new form of dance befitting American culture and spirit. The results were the beginning of modern dance.

Isadora Duncan, considered by many to be the first modern dancer, retreated from the artificial movements, rigid style, and royal court settings of ballet. She explored free and natural movements generated from the center of the body (solar plexus). She also shed the restrictive clothing and many corsets of Victorian-era women. She danced barefoot, in loose and flowing Greek-inspired tunics.

An American contemporary of Duncan was Loie Fuller, who experimented with lighting, props, and fabric to create illusions on stage. Both artists struggled to find success in the United States, but were immediately embraced by European audiences that better understood their artistic contributions.

Following closely upon Duncan and Fuller came Ruth St. Denis and Ted Shawn, who reintroduced theatricality and technique into dance and founded the first school for modern dance in Los Angeles in 1915, the Denishawn school. A major contribution of Ted Shawn's was bringing men into American modern dance, and founding Jacob's Pillow, a modern dance retreat in the Berkshires of Massachusetts that is an international showcase for dance.

The Denishawn company helped to promote the young art form by making thirteen cross-country performance tours in the 1920s while the school provided training for future teachers and performers. These included three pioneers of the second generation of modern dancers: Martha Graham, Charles Weidman, and Doris Humphrey. All three of these artists established themselves in New York City in the late 1920s, where they taught, performed, created new choreographies, and eventually opened schools.

The fifth pioneer to contribute to the development of modern dance in this country and to musical theater was a German dancer, teacher, and choreographer, Hanya Holm. Holm represented the best of the German tradition in modern dance, which began with Rudolf von Laban in the early 1900s and was furthered by the great German expressionist dancer Mary Wigman. The German and American modern dance forms originated at almost the same time, but Germany's was disrupted by World War II when many German dancers emigrated to the United States or England.

During the 1930s, New York City became the hub for modern dance and modern art. During this period at Bennington College in Vermont, many college teachers of physical education participated in dance classes taught by these outstanding artists and in turn taught dance to the students in their classes, in effect spreading modern dance ideas and technique throughout the nation. As a result, today many universities house a dance department either within physical education or the arts. Dance has become a professional orientation for many students who eventually become teachers, performers (in television, film, or on stage), choreographers, dance therapists, and scholars.

Modern dance has a special contribution to make because it is founded on the fundamentals of all movement and can be effectively used with people of all ages. It is of great importance in total education because it involves the individual mentally, physically, emotionally, and spiritually. Ultimately it stresses individualism, creativity, and development of personal choreographic style (see figure 10-1).

FUNDAMENTALS OF MOVEMENT

An understanding of the fundamentals of movement is an important element in the education of a dancer. The fundamentals are a language of movement with a distinct vocabulary, structure, and conceptual framework.

Figure 10-1. Modern dance students improvise.

Theorists through the years have attempted to articulate the basis of movement for purposes of studying, analyzing, and teaching dance. Rudolf Laban spent his entire career developing a conceptual and practical framework for penetrating the complexities of movement. His ideas have been widely incorporated in dance and physical education programs throughout the United States, Canada, and Europe.

Laban observed that every movement has three interconnected aspects: body, space, and effort.

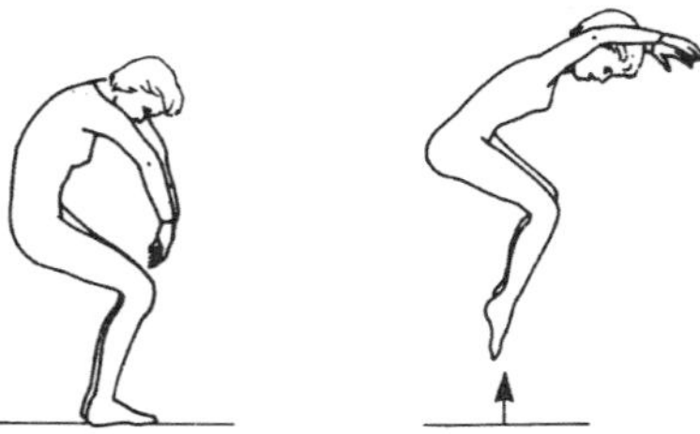

Figure 10-2. Flexion.

Body

Laban suggested that there are at least six basic body actions: weight shift, gesture, traveling (locomotion), jumping, turning, and balancing. Weight shift is any movement that causes the body to transfer weight from one part to another. The most obvious example is stepping. Another example might be shifting weight from one hip to another in a seated position.

Gesture is defined as any non-weight-bearing movement, such as flexion, extension, rotation, bending, stretching, reaching, collapsing, or spiraling. See figures 10-2 and 10-3.

Traveling causes the body to move from one location in general space to another. There are many ways to travel, and they might include some of the other body actions. Examples of ways of locomoting include walking (with different body parts), running, rolling, crawling, creeping, and sliding.

Figure 10-3. Extension.

When considering just foot patterns in traveling, there are only five possible ways to transfer the weight of the body using the feet:

walk, run. or leap (figure 10-4) transfer of weight from one foot to the other foot.
hop (figure 10-5) Transfer of weight from one foot to the same foot.
jump (figure 10-6). Transfer of weight from two feet to two feet.
assemble Transfer of weight from one foot to two feet.
sissonne Transfer of weight from two feet to one foot.

With the exception of walk and run, the rest of these patterns are aerial. They can only be performed with a push-off and landing component.

Once the five basic weight transfers are mastered, it is easy to see how all other dance steps are simply combinations or variations of them. The following dance steps are commonly found in many dance forms:

gallop Combination of a leap and a walk. The leap, the first part of the movement, is rhythmically long, and the walk onto the other foot is rhythmically short.
skip Combination of a walk and a hop. The movement is performed on the same foot. The step, which is the first part of the movement, is rhythmically long, and the hop, the second part of the movement, is short.
slide Combination of two walking steps. The forward step, or the first part of the movement, is rhythmically long, and the second step, in which the other foot is brought up to the forward foot and the weight placed on it, is rhythmically short.
two-step Combination of two quick steps followed by one slow step.
schottische Combination of three walks and a hop. Each movement is rhythmically the same length as the others. The hop creates a fun variation on weight transfer.
step-hop Combination of a walk followed by a hop on the same leg. The first and second parts of the movement are rhythmically equal.

In particular, the skip, slide, and gallop have an identical rhythmic pattern and can easily be linked together in dance combinations. Adding changes of direction or floor pattern (see the section on space) can make for interesting and delightful challenges.

Turning is defined as a change of body facing. Turns can be performed to varying degrees ranging from one-eighth of a turn to multiple turns.

Balancing is momentary stillness in movement, where the body finds dynamic equilibrium and the shape of the body takes on heightened importance.

The basic body actions can be used quite effectively as a starting point for making dance combinations. For example, a teacher might easily create an interesting dance combination using the following sequence: perform a gesture while also shifting weight, followed by some type of traveling pattern, climaxing in a turning jump, and resolving with a balancing shape. This phrase would be both challenging and fun for students to perform.

Figure 10-4. Leap.

Figure 10-5. Hop.

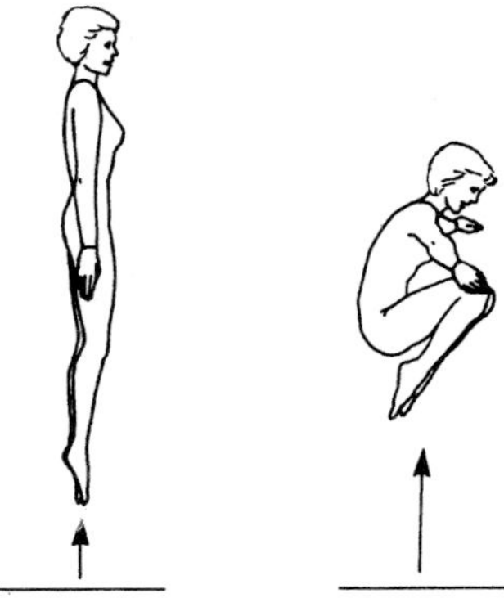

Figure 10-6. Jump.

Space

Dancers inhabit space and also shape it with their bodies. Therefore, a knowledge of the basic space elements is a necessary part of dance education. The basic elements of space include personal space, general space, directions, levels, floor patterns, and shape.

Personal space is defined as the area directly around the body that can be reached without stepping or traveling. (Laban termed it "kinesphere." Educators who teach young children sometimes refer to it as a "space bubble.") Individuals can never leave their personal space, it travels with them when they move through general space. Teaching students to have an awareness of personal space has many advantages, not the least of which is empowering students to create a large enough personal space away from others for their bodies to move freely and safely.

Dance, like all movement, must take direction in space. It is possible for the dancer to move forward, backward, up, down, side right, side left, and diagonally. Exploring directions in space can easily lead to creating interesting patterns of movement, particularly if other ideas are included, such as levels (up and down), facing changes (turns), rhythm (fast and slow), and floor patterns (pathways).

Floor patterns are spatial pathways taken by a dancer while traveling. Some common floor patterns are linear, curved, zigzag, and spiral.

Dancers, teachers, and choreographers, to be creative, must consider how space can be used to full advantage. A dance must be well placed in the space or area in which the dancer is moving. This usually means that the dancer uses all areas fully (unless this would violate the intention of the dance), by traveling toward or away from all sides of the room.

Effort: Movement Qualities

Movement qualities are related to the dynamics and expressive aspects of movement. A dancer can intentionally use energy in different ways to color or shade movement deeply altering the effect it has upon the viewer.

Laban and F. C. Lawrence observed that human movement reveals the inner attitude of the mover through the presence of different movement qualities. They identified four effort factors: time, space, weight, and flow.

Time relates to the speed of movement. Movement can be performed slowly in a sustained, leisurely, legato fashion, expressing an indulgent attitude toward time. It can also be performed quickly, with suddenness and an attitude of urgency.

Space relates to the focus of the dancer. It can be indirect and flexible, attending to a wide span of overapping foci. Or it can be direct and pinpointed to a very specific focus.

Weight pertains to an active use of body weight. Light is experienced as resisting gravity, decreasing pressure, and moving delicately. Strong is increasing pressure, power, and forcefulness. A passive use of body weight leads to collapse and heaviness.

Flow is experienced as greater or lesser amounts of bodily tension. A free-flow movement is one that is difficult to restrict or stop; it has a sense of ongoingness. A bound movement is one that is easy to stop; it has a sense of holding back.

By exploring all the efforts singly and in combinations, dance students learn a wide range of expressive possibilities.

Aileene Lockhart categorized movement qualities in a different way, using the mechanical properties and release of energy into the various parts of the body as criteria. She classifies movement qualities into swinging, sustaining, percussing, suspending, vibrating, and collapsing.

Swinging is the most frequently used and naturally occurring of the body's movements. Swings are characterized by a slight impulse, a giving away to gravity, and a pause prior to repetition. These movements convey feelings of freedom, openness, and ease.

Sustained movement is even, smooth, and free of sudden and sharp actions. This requires maximum muscular control. Sustained movement elicits feelings of calmness, self-control, restraint, and sometimes mystery.

Sharp, aggressive movements in which energy appears and disappears quickly symbolize percussive movement quality. Emotions of vigor, explosiveness, directness, and aggressiveness are evoked through percussive movement.

Movement is described as suspended when two opposing forces are equated. The instant at the peak of a leap when the upward force and the force of gravity are equal is an example of this movement quality. It is used to express anticipation, ecstasy, and breathlessness.

Vibrating movement results from quickly recurring, small percussive movements. It is characterized by intermittent spurts of energy within a limited range. Most commonly this quality of movement is used to denote fear or rage.

Collapsing movements occur when muscular tension in the body is released and gravity is permitted to take over. This can be accomplished in a gradual and controlled manner or suddenly. Emotions such as acquiescence, resignation, and helplessness are elicited through this movement quality.

Rhythm and Its Relationship to Dance

Rhythm is what makes the world go around; it is the pulsation of the universe, the foundation of the world. We would not and could not be alive today if rhythm was not a part of us. The beating of our hearts and exhalation of air from our lungs are excellent examples of rhythm. Changing of seasons, patterns in rock formations on the coast, stars in the heavens, tides, and patterns of trees and flowers are all rhythmic examples given to us by nature. We also find rhythm in the pattern of our lives. These rhythmic patterns may be seen in changes in the fashion world, politics, economics, and in the many social changes that come upon us during a lifetime.

Rhythm, by definition, is a series of pulsations that can be even or uneven, weak or strong. These are grouped in small groups of time. Some rhythmic elements a dancer is concerned with are:

accent Stress or force of movement that can vary from very strong and hard to light and weak.
phrase A group of several meters giving a feeling of unity and completion to the rhythmic sentence and movement pattern.
underlying beat Constant pulsation that takes place throughout the dance. This beat is divided into units, thus designating the meter or time in which the dance is performed.

Modern dance may be performed with or without accompaniment, but in either case the above rhythmic elements are always present and must be taken into consideration.

Technique

Modern dance technique develops control of the body and a kinesthetic awareness and increases the range of movement. Warm-up exercises prepare the body for the more demanding work to follow. Patterns in place develop strength and flexibility, alignment, and balance and expand the movement vocabulary. Combinations using the length of the studio develop a sense of air or lightness, timing, and a culmination in actually "dancing" all that has preceded. Each section is a preparation for the next.

To teach dance rather than a series of exercises to music, the leader must be technically skilled to the level of competent demonstration. Phrasing must be clear, with interesting rhythmic variations. Many kinds and variations of movement must be presented to increase the beginner's vocabulary of movement. A dance class is conducted in the same way whether students are taking a class for fun, career preparation, or body development. Students should dance in class as if they were on stage, with total concentration and intensity.

All individuals can be creative in movement to some degree, if only because we are creative in movement in the way we go about our daily tasks. Modern dance develops further the individual's creativity in movement. In a modern dance class the student learns to explore movement and then to solve movement problems. The student learns to improvise, or move on the spur of the moment without any previous plan, and then to plan a dance pattern or dance study. This study usually is based on some element of the dance the student is studying at the time: qualities of movement, one or several space elements, rhythmic elements, or various forms of axial or locomotor movements. Last, the dancer is prepared to create a composition. This composition has a theme or idea and has a beginning, a development, a climax, and an ending.

Sources of inspiration for creativity in modern dance come from the world around us. A dance study may be based on an idea, emotion, interesting design, or another art form, such as music, poetry, literature, painting, or sculpture, or it may be centered around an everyday experience or even a sports event. In planning a dance composition or study, the dancer should develop the idea in a personal, perhaps unusual or unexpected manner, but always keeping the main idea present. Also remember that in planning a dance composition, all the elements of time, space, force, and the various types of movement and design, whether symmetric or asymmetric, are to be used and to be seen. In a dance composition there must be unity and harmony as well as variety and contrast and yet repetition for emphasis. The ending of one movement should be the beginning of the next. If this is accomplished, a smooth transition of movement and thought will take place, and the composition will relate a well-developed idea and not a series of unrelated and unstructured events.

The following are suggestions or sources of inspiration in composing a dance:

1. Select an experience, such as shopping on a crowded Saturday afternoon at Christmastime. Show accomplishment as well as failure by stylizing the movements with changes in level and dimension.
2. Imagine you are caught in a very small tunnel and cannot find your way out. Express your reactions and fears in a movement pattern.
3. Find a unique way to greet a friend you have not seen for some time. Plan the sequence of movements in relation to various qualities of movement.
4. Draw an interesting design of heavy and light curves, circles, and wiggly lines. Then create a dance sequence to interpret the design.
5. Select a game or a sport. Analyze part of the movement patterns used in the sport. Stylize them as to success and failure based on changes in tempo.
6. Choose a simple gesture, such as opening or closing a door. Do it as many different ways as you can and relate each to a different character study, such as a fearful, shy individual; a fast-moving, egocentric individual; a tough tomboy; or a demure old lady.

In composing a dance, the dancer must explore over and over again the various movement patterns possible until one is found that the dancer likes and is comfortable performing. This takes practice. Movements must be clear and set well in space. Rhythmic changes must be exact and well defined. This is a mental, physical, and emotional challenge, but the final outcome is well worth the effort, because that is when the complete expression and discovery of the individual are realized.

BALLET

History

Ballet technique emerged from court dances of the sixteenth century. The basic steps were codified by Beauchamps at the Royal Academy of Dance in Paris in

Figure 10-7. Ballet class.

the seventeenth century. In the early nineteenth century Carlo Blasis published two books that described the theories and procedures of that day. His descriptions are the basis of ballet training of the intervening years and of today. Ballet moved through a period of acclaim in the eighteenth and early nineteenth centuries, but public interest declined in the latter part of the nineteenth century. When Serge Diaghilev's Ballet Russe, a group of émigrés from Russia, went to Paris in 1909, western Europe was astonished by the artistic daring and innovation of Russian ballet. This created renewed interest throughout the Western world. Although it only functioned for 20 years, in that time it transformed ballet into a vital art form.

By the 1940s the United States could claim two major companies, Ballet Theatre (later changed to American Ballet Theatre), and the New York City Ballet. Since that time ballet has flourished throughout the United States, with many ballet companies active today, including a large number of civic and regional groups.

Ballet in Education

Today ballet is much more frequently a part of the secondary school dance program than in the past. The highly disciplined training builds a strong technique (figures 10-7 and 10-8). Youngsters are most responsive to ballet, much to the surprise of some teachers who have been hesitant to include it in the school dance offerings. As in all other aspects of dance, the caliber of the teaching will determine the eagerness and enthusiasm of the students, the amount of progress made, and the suitability of the form in the total dance offerings.

JAZZ

History

Jazz dance grew out of the African heritage, the Irish clog dance, minstrel shows, vaudeville, social dances, and other sources. It is truly American in origin. Syncopation makes jazz rhythmically stimulating.

Jazz Dance in Education

Jazz in the educational setting ranges from clichéd movements or steps taken from disco dancing to work that is original and varied, exciting for the movement style as well as the rhythm. It is changing continually because of its strong relationship to contemporary popular culture.

The way jazz is taught determines whether it will be a limited movement opportunity or an opportunity to improve and expand technique and to explore movement in this exuberant style.

TAP DANCING

History

Tap dancing is an American dance form that originated from the merging of African, Irish, and English cultures. It began in the southern United States when blacks and whites copied each other's dance styles, and developed further in the mid 1800s in northern urban settings. Tap dance was made popular through touring minstrel shows and later during the vaudeville tours; however, blacks and whites were segregated as performers, which lead to the peculiar use of blackface characterization (white performers blackening their faces to imitate African American performers.)

Figure 10-8. Ballet practice.

A combination of Irish jig, English clog dancing, and African-based dance steps mixed with complex African rhythms distinguish tap dancing from all other forms of dance. The earliest forms were flat-footed and used the edges of the foot in a style called "buck and wing." The 1900s brought about a new and complex set of steps that were more rhythmic, smooth, and steady. Tap dancing became extremely popular during these times through vaudeville shows, on showboats and especially Broadway stage in Ziegfeld Follies and other shows. In the 1920s and 1930s, Bill "Bojangles" Robinson invented and popularized a new style of tap dancing that was up on the toes, elegant, and rhythmically very precise.

Tap dancing reached a zenith during the 1930s on Broadway and in Hollywood musical films, when enormous productions were mounted, sometimes employing hundreds of tap dancers. Many of these shows and films are now considered "classics" in the history of American entertainment. Some examples are the opulent art deco films of Busby Berkeley, the romantic films of Fred Astaire and Ginger Rogers, and the films of Gene Kelly, which blend athleticism with tap dancing. During the 1960s and 1970s, tap dance experienced a period of decline in popularity, with the exception of a few masters like Honi Coles who kept performing and teaching throughout the United States and Europe.

In the 1980s a revival of interest in tap dancing as a form of recreation and entertainment led to reconstruction of many Broadway classics such as *Singin' in the Rain, On Your Toes, Showboat*, and *42nd Street*, and the making of new films such as *White Nights* and *Tap*. Other new shows such as *Sophisticated Ladies, A Chorus Line, The Tap Dance Kid*, and *Jelly's Last Jam* featured new talented artists like Gregory and Maurice Hines, and Savion Glover.

In the 1990s, enormous, sustained public interest in shows like the traditional Irish step-dancing production *Riverdance*, percussion-filled *Stomp*, and Broadway's *Bring in Da Noise, Bring in Da Funk* have fueled the success of many similar shows such as Australian *Tap Dogs* and the spin-off of *Riverdance, Lord of the Dance*.

Tap Dance in Education

Tap-dancing instruction began in public schools around the early 1900s. Today there are hundreds of teachers, primarily in private dance studios and recreation centers, who continue to teach this art form. Since the late 1970s there has been a sustained public interest in tap-dance instruction, which has recently been boosted by the growing interest in its parent form of traditional Irish step dancing.

Tap dance has a standardized vocabulary, as do ballet, jazz, and modern dance. The marked difference between these forms is that tap dancing might be considered drumming with the feet. Mastering precise rhythmic patterns and a sense of musicality are an important part of the art form. It is recommended that children begin creative forms of dance before moving on to tap dancing which requires sophisticated control of the feet and balance.

Recreational forms

All recreational dance involves people moving together and enjoying the group or partner as well as the rhythmic movement. These forms are an ideal coeducational activity, as they provide an easy, casual basis for mixing and working together. There are dances suitable for every age level.

A major stimulus to the growth of recreational dance has been the development of good recordings. Having appropriate, inexpensive music readily available eliminates the cost and trouble of an accompanist. Moreover, authentic music is motivating to beginning dancers. They can tape music for home practice and small parties. Where once only large groups could afford dance music, now the individual can bring an "orchestra" home for a family swing lesson.

If teachers, recordings, and dances are up to date, students can move readily from the classroom to local clubs and recreational classes for leisure enjoyment. Some teachers take their classes to community dances or require attendance once during the semester to increase the likelihood of participation after graduation.

Fun is part of any recreational dance class from the first day. There is no long period of learning before the student can enjoy the satisfaction of accomplishment. At the same time, challenging new figures, steps, or dances should constantly be presented, as should more complicated combinations or more intricate rhythms. The range of skill possible in recreational dance forms is extremely wide.

Limitations of space preclude discussion of all the types of recreational dance, and new variations are constantly becoming popular. For example, country-western round dance, country-western swing, and round dancing are currently very popular. Thus, only square dancing is presented in detail; folk and social dances are introduced briefly.

AMERICAN SQUARE DANCE

History

The American square dance (figure 10-9) had its beginning in England with the English country dance, a dance form that developed among the people in rural districts. In the early 1600s the dance did not enjoy tremendous popularity, especially in larger cities. The impetus that propelled it into prominence came in 1651 when John Playford published the first English country dance book. Most of the dances compiled for this publication were known as "longways," or what the French later called *contre* dances. In the contre, participants arranged themselves in two lines facing each other. Through various sequences of movements, dancers moved from one position in the line to the next or from one line to the other.

Before the introduction of Playford's book, the dances of the royal court had been in vogue. These dances sometimes contained intricate dance steps and suggested a romantic or flirtatious attitude on the part of participants. To understand the significance of Playford's publication in regard to the people's choice of dances, it is necessary to investigate the conditions that prevailed in England during the early part of the seventeenth century.

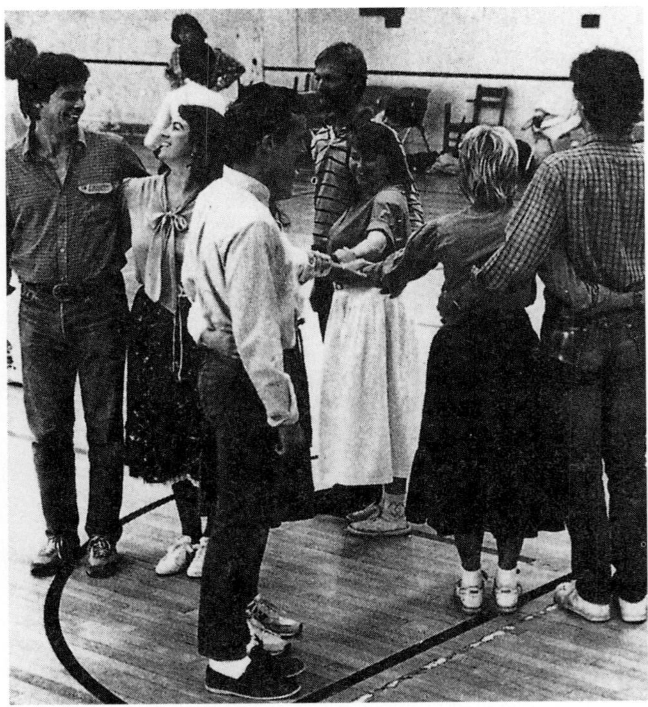

Figure 10-9. Square dancers doing a left-hand square.

Segments of England's population had been agitating for change in government. This led to civil war and the eventual beheading of the king. Before this event a group of Puritans, who had been urging separation of church and state, managed to sail to America in an attempt to set up its own government. As evidence of the desire for a government of their own and as a sign of their rebellion, the Puritans and other sympathetic groups refused to participate in the dances of the court, preferring the more simple English country dances. Playford, a Puritan, attempted to meet this need with his publication. Not only was his book accepted with great acclaim among England's discontented, but it also met with favor in America.

From this beginning the American square dance evolved. Instead of the pomp and circumstance attending the dances of the court and the social etiquette marked by favors given to the most prestigious persons at a dance, participants took their places in lines according to their order of arrival. Gone was the intricate, delicate footwork, and in its place was a steady, even movement of the feet to each beat of the music. The flirtatious attitude among participants of the court dances was replaced by emphasis on movement patterns and the coordination of all dancers in an attempt to work together to effect these patterns of movement. The dance emphasized the cohesiveness of the people and stressed democracy in action. Today the American square dance is still based on these principles.

From its beginning, the American square dance has exemplified the ideals on which the country was founded and that its citizens have attempted to realize in the intervening years. It is the folk dance of North America, not only because it has been a part of the culture since its colonial beginnings, but also because the essence of the dance reflects the philosophy and values of its people.

In the early 1700s the French, who had also found enjoyment in the longways, introduced the square formation. It was believed that the contre did not allow for sufficient activity or excitement. The French realized that they could effect figures similar to those used in the contre in the square formation, thereby assuring more activity for all participants. The new style of dance that emerged as a result of this innovation was called the *cotillion*.

The advent of the French Revolution added further innovations to the cotillion. A faster tempo and more intricate dance steps grew out of the cultural changes taking place in France. People were demanding change and excitement, and they found an outlet in their dance.

By the mid 1800s the cotillion no longer satisfied the people. Its rather short, simple movement patterns were not enough to sustain interest. All facets of the culture were becoming more complicated, and it was inevitable that the dance should also articulate this growing complexity. The French combined five to six cotillions into one dance for greater intricacy in dancing. The French *quadrille* became popular in England and the United States soon after its inception.

The first American innovation to the dance came with the introduction of the "caller." It is the caller who sets the American square dance apart from all other dances and that provides the major justification for labeling it the American folk dance. Before the advent of the caller in the early 1800s (during or soon after the War of 1812) participants memorized each dance. However, with a caller presiding over the dance program, it was possible to perform a new, unfamiliar dance as long as one knew its "basics" or dance patterns (circle, dos-a-dos, promenade, and such). This change heralded a new method of learning how to dance. Sequences of basics no longer needed to be committed to memory. The patter call evolved as an adjunct to this concept. The caller would make up dances as he or she went along. This introduced the element of anticipation—not knowing what will be called next—that has drawn many people to the square dance over the years. Participants rely on their knowledge of basics, listening ability, coordination, timing, and rhythm to complete a dance successfully.

In the mid to late 1800s the singing call emerged. Currently popular music was used (the practice when choreographing new dances), and a figure was developed by the choreographer in which there was an exchange of partners. This figure was constructed in such a way that if repeated three more times dancers would be back with their original partners in their home positions.

In the late 1800s the waltz, polka, and other couple dances became overwhelmingly popular in Europe and in the eastern United States. Consequently, ballroom dancing took over as the favorite form of social dancing in the cities, and the contre and square dances were eliminated from the dance program. In the eastern United States, the American square dance receded into small towns.

Meanwhile, it was enjoying tremendous popularity in the West. The visiting-couple figure predominated, as did rhyming patter depicting life on the plains. However, by the early 1900s ballroom dancing became popular in the newly formed cities of the West, and here, too, square dancing became associated with the small town, the roundups, and the granges.

Little change occurred in the American square dance from the early 1900s until after World War II. For the most part, those who participated in dancing were content to perform the dances of yesteryear. A study of the evolution of the American square dance shows that change in the dance has occurred during times of social unrest and political upheaval. Thus, it was inevitable that World War II would precipitate a new style of American square dance.

During the war, United Service Organizations, church groups, and other organizations presented social activities for service personnel. The square dance seemed a logical activity to inspire congenial social cohesiveness among strangers. After the war many of the young men who had enjoyed this experience turned to calling to provide hometown neighbors with a similar experience. Overnight, it seemed, the American square dance gained tremendous popularity, and with this popularity came many changes in the dance.

The wave of popularity grew in the West and quickly spread eastward. In southern California in 1941 there were approximately 10 clubs and 5 callers. By November 1948 there were some 30 callers and 75 square dance clubs. Six months later, in May 1949, the number had risen to some 400 active groups in the same area. By the end of 1950 there were an estimated 50,000 square dancers in Los Angeles alone and five million in the nation.

By the time the wave of popularity hit the east coast in the late 1940s and the early 1950s, a new dance style—the modern American square dance—had developed. There were few differences in dancing from one section of the country to the other. For this reason, dance historians believe it was at this point that the square dance finally emerged as the national dance—the American folk dance.

The square dance as it developed from the 1940s to the 1970s is vastly different from the square dance of the early twentieth century. From some 10 or 12 basic movements prior to 1940, there are now over 800. Twenty or more new singing calls are released each month from the 15 or so commercial square dance record companies now in existence. One to two years' instruction is required to prepare participants for community dancing. The simple visiting-couple figure of the Western square dance is no longer performed. Instead, the line, posting, and star-thru figures are used, along with the traditional circle formation. Participants learn to perform basics, not dances. They rely on their ability to listen to the calls; to coordinate their movements with each other; to time each basic correctly while dancing; to move to the beat, tempo, and phrasing of the music; and to space their steps appropriately for the various formations and basics used in the dancing.

It is estimated that some 6 to 10 million people belong to square dance clubs in the United States. For many, square dancing takes up at least two evenings a month; while for others, dancing two or three evenings a week is not unusual. The American folk dance knows more participants than any other national folk dance. It continually changes as the culture changes. It is a vibrant, living folk dance articulating the values of its people.

Objectives of Square Dancing

1. To provide satisfaction and pride by giving the participant a new ability.
2. To promote gracefulness.
3. To develop coordination.
4. To help develop self-discipline.
5. To help develop good timing and rhythm.
6. To provide an opportunity to learn to relax with the opposite sex.
7. To provide an opportunity to develop emotional and social values.
8. To provide an activity that will promote togetherness and fun for everyone.

Square Dance Formation

The square dance is performed by sets of four couples. The woman is always situated to the right of the man. The couple in front of the caller is couple 1. Couple 3 faces couple 1. These two couples are the *head* couples unless otherwise designated. Couple 2 is to the right of 1. Couple 4 is opposite 2. Couples 2 and 4 are the *side* couples. Home position is the starting position. If a mistake is made by a couple while performing a figure, "Square the set" is called, and all couples return to their starting positions.

Relative Position of Partners

The woman on the man's right is always his *partner;* the one to his left is his *corner.* The man to the woman's left is her *partner*; the man to her right is her *corner*. During the dance the man may be separated from his starting partner. If he is separated and the word *partner* is called, he must take the woman who at that time is to his right. Partners hold hands whenever possible.

Shuffle Step

The dance should be performed in a light-footed, lively shuffle step, with the dancers changing from one basic to another. One step is taken on each beat, or count. The feet slide forward on the floor. When moving to the right, as in "Circle right," dancers step right foot to the side, then left foot in front of the right. They continue this sequence with toes pointed toward the center of the circle.

Square Dance Composition

basics Individual movements—for example, "Go forward and back."
dance Enough figures to take a couple through a song.
figure A group of phrases, usually 64 counts, in which the couples start at and return to home position.
name of square dance Usually the main figure—for example, "Ducking for the Oyster" or "Taking a Peek." The dance can be identified by the name of the music to which it is danced.
phrase A number of basics making 8 or 16 counts.

Starting the Dance

The call "Honor your partner" starts the dance. Participants bow first to their corners and then to their partners.

Fundamental Skills of the Square Dance

allemande left Eight counts. The man joins left hand or arm with whomever allemande is to be made. Both then shuffle counterclockwise around each other, back to starting position.
around that couple, take a peek Sixteen counts forward and back. Couple 1 faces Couple 2. Couple 1 goes forward, splits, goes past Couple 2, peeking at each other, and then backs up to starting position. The call may be for heads or for sides to take a peek.
balance Dancers take two steps back from partner and curtsy.
balance and swing Couples balance, then take two steps forward, joining hands or arms, and rotate twice around each other.
circle Eight beats halfway; 16 beats all the way. Designated dancers join hands, turn slightly in the direction designated, and shuffle-step around. This may be to the left or to the right. The call may be for women, for men, or for everybody.
dive for the oyster Sixteen counts. First and second couples face by shuffling together. All hold hands and circle halfway to the left. Second couple joins hands and raises arms while the first couple goes four steps under and four steps back. Again all join hands and circle halfway around and back to starting position.
dos-a-dos (pronounced doe-see-doe) Eight counts. Partners, corners, or opposites shuffle forward, go back to right of each other past each other's right arm, go back to back, and then back out to starting position.

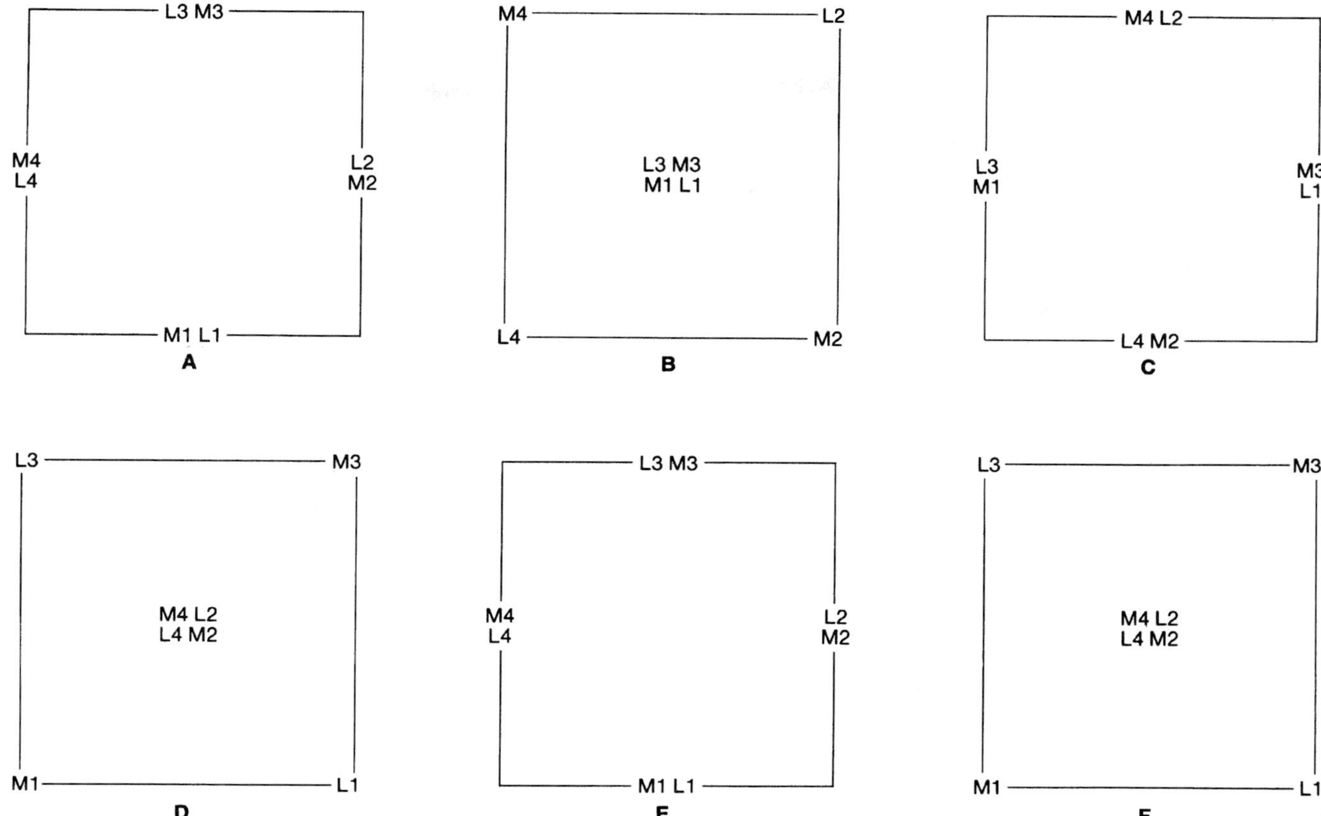

Figure 10-10. Grand square. See text for details.

forward and back Eight beats, or counts. Designated couples take four steps toward the center of the circle and then four steps back out.

grand right and left Eight counts halfway; 16 counts all the way. Partners face each other and hold right hands. They walk by each other and take the opposite hand of the dancer they are facing. They advance around the circle, alternating from side to side until they meet. Men go counterclockwise; women advance clockwise.

grand square Thirty two counts. Simultaneously all dancers walk a small square in their corner of the full square (figure 10-10A). Couples 1 and 3 walk forward four steps, meeting in the center of the set, while partners in Couples 2 and 4 face each other and walk four steps backward to the outside corners of the set (figure 10-10B). Partners in Couples 1 and 3 face each other with backs to side walls, join inside hands and walk back four steps (they will now be in home position of Couples 2 and 4); at the same time, man 4 and woman 2 and man 2 and woman 4 face each other and walk four steps forward to arrive at original home position of Couples 1 and 3 (figure 10-10C). They continue this sequence as shown in figure 10-10D and 10-10E, at which point all couples should be back in their home positions. The entire sequence is then reversed (first four counts shown in figure 10-10F) by beginning with Couples 2 and 4 walking to the center while Couples 1 and 3 move backward to the outside corners of the set.

ladies' chain Eight counts. Women, heads or sides, shuffle across the set, touching right hands as they pass each other in the center of the circle. They then extend their left hands to the men. The men take the women's left hands with their left hands, place their right hands on the women's waists, and all turn counterclockwise to home and starting position.

promenade Eight counts halfway; 16 counts all the way. Pairs take right hands as though shaking hands and position themselves side by side, facing counterclockwise with the man on the inside of the circle and the woman on the outside. The man reaches under his right arm with his left hand and grasps the woman's left hand. They then shuffle-step together around the circle.

right and left thru Eight counts halfway; 16 counts all the way. Two couples face each other. Couples extend their right hands to the persons opposite them and pass them on the right, then immediately give their left hands to each other, and men put their right arm around their ladies to courtesy-turn them around to face each other (couples have exchanged places).

right hand round the partner Eight counts. Partners face each other holding right hands and go around each other moving in a clockwise direction, then return to starting position. This basic is opposite to allemande left (and is sometimes called allemande right).

sashay round your corner Eight counts. Using sideward sliding steps and always facing the center, the man goes to the left, outside and around his corner, and returns to his original position.

seesaw round your own Eight counts. The man uses sideward sliding steps to the right, outside and around his corner, returning to his original position.

star Eight counts. Designated partners extend designated hands into the center of the circle and shuffle around in an inner circle one full circle, returning to starting position. Dancers may be called to do a right or left star.

weave the ring Eight counts halfway; 16 counts all the way. Same movement as the grand right and left except hands do not touch.

Construction of the Figure

"Bow to your corner, bow to your partner, and all join hands"

Circle to the left halfway	8 counts
All go forward and back	8 counts
Circle right halfway	8 counts
Circle to the left all the way	16 counts
Circle to the right all the way	16 counts
All go forward and back	8 counts
	64 counts

"Bow to your corner, bow to your partner"

Dos-a-dos your corner	8 counts
Dos-a-dos	8 counts
All join hands and circle left	16 counts
Heads go forward and back	8 counts
Sides go forward and back	8 counts
All join hands and circle right	16 counts
	64 counts

"Take a peek"

Circle left all the way	16 counts
Heads "take a peek" round the couple on the right	16 counts
Sides "take a peek" round the couple on the right	16 counts
Circle right all the way	16 counts
	64 counts

Music for Square Dancing

Patter, or hoedown, music

Patter music is used for timing and rhythm. It usually does not have a familiar melody, and as a rule it is used to teach the basic skills.

Singing call

Singing call music has a definite melody, and there is a specific set of figures written for it. Examples of singing calls are: *Oh Johnny!, Hot Time in the Old Town Tonight, Hello, Dolly!, Cabaret, Buffalo Girls*, and *Pop Goes the Weasel*.

FOLK DANCE

Folk dances (figure 10-11) are traditional dances, part of the cultural heritage of a group, nation, or religion. They developed as ethnic dances in which ordinary folk participated. In contrast, some ethnic dances evolved as art forms danced by highly skilled performers.

Sources

Folk dances are international. Some had their start as a means of celebrating some special occasion, such as the harvest, a wedding, or a feast day. Others grew out of work practices, religious ceremonies, or military customs. But most evolved as recreational pastimes, a means of having fun.

Because folk dances are "of the people," they often are changed "by the people." Someone may add a clap here or a turn there to make a dance more enjoyable. Others follow along, and the change thus spreads. This continues today. There may be a local variation on almost any dance, but basic styles, steps, and formations tend to endure and give each dance its special flavor.

Forms

Folk dances take many forms. In some, individuals dance alone without touching anyone else. In others the individual is in a line or circle or broken circle (with a leader at one end) in contact with those on either side. Neighbors may join hands, hook arms, put hands to shoulders or about the waist, or just interlace little fingers. Sometimes they wear loose belts that are grasped by dancers on either side, especially in line dances for men where the action is very vigorous.

Dances for two, three, six, or eight are more structured. Group formations vary from short lines to single circles, double circles, parallel lines, squares, stars, and even triangles. In dances for partners there is a definite dance position or way they relate to each other—for example, closed (facing and close as for ballroom dance), open (side by side), shoulder-waist (man's hands at the woman's waist and her hands on his shoulders), and butterfly (partners facing, hands joined, and arms outstretched at shoulder height).

Currently, nonpartner dances for any number seem to be most popular. They are quickly organized and make it easy for anyone to join the group. They suit the casual atmosphere of many folk gatherings. Couple and group dances take more organization to get started, and some persons may be left out.

Basic Dance Steps

Basic movements used in folk dances are walking (or stepping), running, leaping, jumping, hopping, skipping, slid-

Figure 10-11. Folk dance students practice a line dance.

ing, and galloping. Traditional folk dance steps are composed of combinations of these basic movements put to various rhythms. Following are brief descriptions of some common folk dance steps. ("Close" means to bring the feet together and step, and *L* is left, *R* is right.)

two-step (2/4 or 4/4 meter) The rhythm is quick, quick, slow as the last count is held.

step	close	step	hold
L	**R**	**L**	

polka (2/4 meter) The hop is quick, coming on the pick-up beat just before count 1. The rhythm changes from the two-step to ah, quick, quick slow.

hop	step	close	step
L	**R**	**L**	**R**

schottische (4/4 meter) Four movements on four counts with a steady rhythm. Sometimes the action is step, close, step, hop; sometimes runs are used in place of steps.

step	step	step	hop
L	**R**	**L**	**L**

waltz box (3/4 meter) Six steps on six counts (two measures of music) with an even rhythm. The rhythm is slow, slow, slow.

step forward	side	close
L	**R**	**L**
step backward	side	close
R	**L**	**R**

mazurka (3/4 meter) Three actions on three counts in even time. Styling includes sweeping the left foot backward across the right shinbone on the hop.

step	close	hop
L	**R**	**R**

Combinations of the basic movements changing direction, rhythm, and style appear in amazing variety in the hundreds of folk dances recorded and performed. The steps described here are a small sampling that have become set through frequent use.

Regional Dance Characteristics

The following brief highlights point up some regional differences in dance styling. There is much fascinating material available (see sources listed) in this area for the student dancer.

England. Country dances for couples moving with light, springy, running steps have a smooth, gliding effect. With arms hanging freely and bodies erect, the dancers interweave in interesting patterns.

Germany. Couple dances with regular patterns, such as waltzes, polkas, and schottisches, are typical. Also there are dances featuring intricate clapping sequences and much slapping of the body with rhythmic precision.

Greece. Common are broken-circle dances led by a man waving his handkerchief to signal step changes. He improvises with much flamboyance as the line keeps the basic step. Often the women are in separate lines and are much more restrained in their movements.

Hungary. Sudden changes in tempo, clicking of the heels, stamping of feet, and individual improvisation are part of such dances as the csárdás.

Ireland. Intricate, exact footwork characterizes Irish solo dances, such as jigs and hornpipes. Reels call for simpler, more gliding steps.

Israel. Religious dances express hope, joy, and courage. National dances serve to unify the many ethnic groups in Israel, blending movements from Europe, Asia, and the Mideast. The use of circle formations in Israeli dances reflects the strength of their ties. Accomplished choreographers create new dances based on traditional steps and forms. The hora is Israel's national dance.

Mexico. Fast footwork with crisp stamping and heel-toe tapping gives excitement to flirtatious couple dances. Action centers in the legs and feet as the man clasps his hands behind his back and the woman holds her full skirt.

Scandinavia. Smoothly turning couple dances are typical. Best known is the Swedish hambo. There are also vigorous dances for men and some clowning, light-hearted dances.

Scotland. To traditional bagpipe music, precise Scottish dancers perform with toes pointed, bodies erect, and hands carefully placed. Flings, reels, schottisches, and sword dances are familiar.

Yugoslavia. Most typical is the kolo, with a leader waving his handkerchief to signal step changes. The many kolos are as varied as the diverse Slavic peoples of this country. Some are quiet, some are bouncy, and some are lively and noisy as the dancers punctuate their steps with exuberant shouts.

SOCIAL DANCE

Popular couple dances without set patterns are classified as social or ballroom dances (figure 10-12). They have a casual, relaxed quality not possible in patterned dances. Each couple moves independently of others, and in some dances partners are quite independent of each other, improvising at will. But most social dances are characterized by the man leading and the woman partner following whatever steps, styling, and rhythmic variations he chooses and indicates.

Sources

Formal social dancing began with the European court dances of the Renaissance. Dance masters were employed to develop and teach proper steps to the aristocracy. Today dancers and dance teachers continually invent new steps and styles. Popular music, films, television, and stage shows have all inspired new dances that have swept the United States.

The social dances of one era tend to become the folk dances of later eras. Whenever pleasing combinations begin to be repeated and take set forms, the dance can be recorded and copied by others. The waltz, polka, schottische, and mazurka were all early social dances. Only the waltz continues as a modern ballroom dance, although the polka appears occasionally in the ballroom. The Charleston of the Roaring Twenties already is appearing in folk dance books. Some of the current fad dances may well have the same fate in time. Continual change seems to be the only certainty in popular social dancing. However, set standards and required steps are spelled out for establishing dance forms, especially those used in dance competitions.

Figure 10-12. A social dance: the fox trot.

Basic Steps

"Anyone who can walk to music can dance!" This common introduction to a social dance class points up the fact that every form of social dance is based on walking steps. Differences of style and rhythm and patterns set to distinctive music distinguish the different forms. A few variations on the basic steps that are common to all forms include:

balancing Taking a long step followed by two closes. Often the shift of weight is minimal on the closes.

closing Stepping one foot next to the other and transferring the weight. Steps may be forward, backward, or sideways.

hesitating Pausing by touching the free foot to the floor without transferring weight.

pivoting Rotating in either direction. Dancers may stay in place or travel on a pivot.

rocking Staying in place stepping forward and back or from side to side.

Social dance forms

To indicate the rhythmic patterns of the common social dances listed below, the symbol *S* indicates slow and the symbol *Q* indicates a quick step.

Fox-trot. The fox-trot is an American dance evolving from a trotting dance performed by Harry Fox in a Ziegfeld show in 1913. Present forms tend to be smooth, with dancers gliding around the dance floor with little up-and-down motion. Fox-trots may be dreamy and slow or quick and light. They can be adapted to in-place dancing in a small space or be expansive where space permits (one step *QQQQ*, two step *QQS*, magic step *SSQQ*).

Swing. From the lindy of the 1920s and the jitterbug of the 1930s comes our modern swing. The basic step is still the six-count lindy with variations. Though the music may be bouncy, good swing dancers smoothly execute the individual turns, exchanges, and position variations typical of Eastern swing. On the West Coast a slower, more complicated swing form has developed.

Waltz. The oldest ballroom dance form and the first to be danced in closed (or waltz) position, the waltz was considered shocking when first introduced to Americans in the early nineteenth century. Previously it was the rage in Vienna, with Strauss waltzes filling the air. It probably originated in seventeenth-century Germany. The name comes from a German word meaning "to revolve," and turning with smooth, gliding steps continues to be characteristic of waltzing (*SSS*).

Cha-cha. A Cuban dance growing out of the earlier mambo in the mid 1950s, this dance is characterized by three quick steps. The dancers often are apart, allowing much freedom of movement around the basic "step, step, cha, cha, cha," of the dance. The Latin rhythm is catchy and distinctive (*SSQQQ*).

Rumba. The rumba was introduced to the United States from Cuba in 1930. Like the cha-cha, action is from the waist down, with a subtle swaying of the hips resulting from careful knee and foot action. The dancers weave interesting patterns as they change positions in this relatively restrained Latin dance (*SQQ*).

Tango. From Argentina this "dance with a stop," as it was called, came by way of Europe to the United States in 1913. Characterized by sudden changes of direction interrupting the catlike slow steps, the tango is a distinctive form with its many fan (flaring) and corté (dipping) steps (*SSQQS*).

Samba. From Brazil comes this bouncy, vibrant dance. It involves much knee action, with the dancers' bodies resembling a swinging pendulum as they sway and turn. It was introduced to the United States at the New York World's Fair in 1939 (*QQS*).

Contemporary dances. Always of interest to students are the currently popular dances. Now and then one endures to find its way into dance literature. For some years, through the 1960s and 1970s, discotheque, no-contact, partner dances were the fad. Then the line hustle came along, and there was no partner at all, just individuals doing essentially the same steps at the same time. At present there is a resurgence in the popularity of ballroom and couple dancing. New steps come out regularly, with studios competing to create interesting combinations. These are enjoyable, stimulating dances that add a contemporary spice to the classroom scene.

TEACHING CONSIDERATIONS

Square Dance

1. Explain the activity and let participants hear a recording of the fundamentals.
2. Use a chalkboard, draw a "set," explain positions: home, head, sides, partner, corner.
3. Explain what is meant by "Honor your partner," and have students practice: bow to the corner, bow to your partner.
4. Teach the class the shuffle step. Have them perform and repeat it until all students do this well. Have them hold hands, go forward and backward, and circle right and left.
5. Explain and demonstrate the beat, or count, of the square dance, and explain how square dances are phrased. Play a recording and let the class hear the beats and phrases as you count.
6. Teach each basic until all participants are familiar with the mechanics and the call and until they react quickly.

Folk and Social Dances

1. If possible, provide students with the opportunity to see the dance performed with the music.
2. With complex step patterns, teach the basic step directly (not necessarily in the appropriate group formation). Slow down the speed, if needed, using word cues (e.g., step, close, step, hold). Increase speed of practice until it approaches correct speed. Add the music to practice. Allow sufficient individual practice to have the step be automatic before using the group formation of the dance.
3. With complex group formations (folk dance), teach the chorus first and then other patterns. Walk through parts of the dance with the students—first slowly, then more quickly, and then with the music—before adding parts to the whole.
4. Repeat parts as new ones are added.
5. Keep the atmosphere and learning climate informal, but stress good technique. The dances are more enjoyable that way.
6. As the number of dances students learn increases, provide opportunities for review. Try not to have whole lessons of just new dances.
7. Intersperse giving regional information with learning dances (folk dance).
8. Use the names for the steps to provide later transfer to other dances that use the same steps.
9. Use mixers to provide opportunities for students to dance with different partners.

SUGGESTED READINGS

General

Ambrosio, N. 1994. *Learning about dance: An introduction to dance as an art form and entertainment.* Dubuque, Iowa: Kendall/Hunt.

Cass, T. 1993. *Dancing through history.* Needham Heights, Mass.: Allyn & Bacon.

Haynes, E. 1993. *An introduction to the teaching of dance.* 2d ed. Pennington, N.J.: Princeton Book Publishers.

Humphrey, D. 1992. *The art of making dance.* Pennington, N.J.: Princeton Book Publishers.

Kraus, R. G. 1991. *The history of dance in art and education.* 3d ed. Englewood Cliffs, N.J.: Prentice Hall.

Laban, R. 1963. *Modern educational dance.* London: MacDonald & Evans.

Laban, R. 1966. *The mastery of movement.* London: MacDonald & Evans.

McGreavy-Nichols, S., and Scheff, H. 1995. *Building dance: A guide to putting movements together.* Champaign, Ill.: Human Kinetics.

Minton, S. C. 1986. *Choreography.* Champaign, Ill.: Human Kinetics. Contains suggestions on selecting accompaniment, designing costumes, and planning lighting.

Minton, S. C. 1989. *Body and self.* Champaign, Ill.: Human Kinetics. Designed to teach you how to move more gracefully, exercise without injury, detect habitual movement patterns, and create more imaginative movements.

Concert forms

Anderson, J. 1992. *Ballet and modern dance*. 2d ed. [CITY: PUBLISHER].

Bartenieff, I. 1988. *Body movement: Coping with the environment*. New York: Gordon & Breach.

Bloom, L. A., and Chaplin, L. T. 1988. *The moment of movement*. Pittsburgh: University of Pittsburgh Press.

Cheney, G. 1989. *Basic concepts in modern dance: A creative approach*. Princeton, N.J.: Princeton Book Publishers.

Hammond, S. 1992. *Ballet basics*. 3d ed. Mountain View, Calif.: Mayfield.

Hawkins, A. M. 1991. *Moving from within: A new method for dance making*. Chicago: A Capella Books.

Joyce, M. 1994. *First steps in teaching creative dance to children*. 2d ed. Mountain View, Calif.: Mayfield.

Laban, R., and Lawrence, F. C. 1947. *Effort*. London: MacDonald & Evans.

Minton, S., and Campbell, K. 1991. *Modern dance: Body and mind*. 2d ed. Englewood, Colo.: Morton. Aimed at the beginning student, this book uses more than 125 illustrations to describe the kinesiologic basis of dance movement and provide an understanding of the relationships between technique, improvisation, and composition.

Penrod, J., and Plastino, J. 1990. *The dancer prepares: Modern dance for beginners*. Mountain View, Calif.: Mayfield. Introduces students to the techniques, combinations, and vocabulary of modern dance.

Schlaich, J., and Dupont, B. 1993. *The art of teaching dance*. Reston, Va.: American Alliance for Health, Physical Education, Recreation and Dance.

Recreational forms

General

Harris, J., Pittman, A., and Waller, M. S. 1988. *Dance a while*. 6th ed. New York: Macmillan.

Land, C. 1995. *Christy Lane's complete book of line dancing*. Champaign, Ill.: Human Kinetics.

Stinson, S. 1988. *Dance for young children: Finding magic in movement*. Reston, Va.: American Alliance for Health, Physical Education, Recreation and Dance.

Social dance

Wright, J. 1992. *Social dance: Steps to success*. Champaign, Ill.: Human Kinetics.

Wright, J. 1996. *Social dance instruction*. Champaign, Ill.: Human Kinetics.

Square dance

Casey, B. 1985. *The complete book of square dancing and round dancing*. Garden City, N.Y.: Doubleday.

Schild, M. M. 1987. *Square dancing everyone.* Winston-Salem, N.C.: Hunter Textbooks. Covers the background and development of square dance, resource materials, singing call drills, basics of clogging, and a checklist of basic square dance movements.

Tap and jazz dance

Kraines, M., and Kan, E. 1990. *Jump to jazz: A primer for the beginning jazz student*. 2d ed. Mountain View, Calif.: Mayfield.

Lapoint-Crump, J., and Staley, K. 1992. *Discovering jazz dance: America's energy and soul*. Dubuque, Iowa: WCB/McGraw-Hill.

Marx, T. 1983. *Tap dance*. Englewood Cliffs, N.J.: Prentice Hall.

Periodicals

Dance Teacher Now, SMW Communications, 3020 Beacon Blvd., West Sacramento, CA 95691.

Dancemagazine, 33 W 60th St., New York, NY, 10023.

Journal of Physical Education, Recreation and Dance, American Alliance for Health, Physical Education, Recreation and Dance, 1900 Association Dr., Reston, VA 22091.

Sets in Order, National Square Dance Magazine, 462 N. Robertson Blvd., Los Angeles, CA 90048.

RESOURCES

Dance Instructions and Recordings

American Alliance for Health, Physical Education, Recreation and Dance, 1900 Association Dr., Reston, VA 22091. Provides books, tapes, films, lesson plans, and resource guides for all types of dance.

World of Fun, 819 NW 92nd St., Oklahoma City, OK 73114. Offers a complete collection of beginner folk dance instructions and records for children and adults.

World Tone Music, 230 Seventh Ave., New York, NY 10011. Offers extensive collections of audiotapes and records, some with instructions, for teaching folk and square dances.

Videotapes

Many videotapes are available for preview, rental, or sale from the following organizations or libraries:

American Alliance for Health, Physical Education, Recreation and Dance, 1900 Association Dr., Reston, VA 22091. Titles include: *Dance design: shape and time; Dance design: motion; Dance design: space; Preparing to dance*; and *Sources for dance*.

Cambridge Physical Education and Health, P.O. Box 2153, Charleston, WV 25328. Titles include: *Learn to dance* (3 videos), *Let's learn how to dance* (12 videos), and *You can dance* (9 videos).

Home Vision, P.O. Box 800, Concord, MA 01742.

"How To" Sports Videos, P.O. Box 5852, Denver, CO 80217. *Social dance aerobics* (5 videos), *Learn to dance* (3 videos).

Kimbo Educational, P.O. Box 477K, Long Beach, NJ 07740. Distributes many records, audiocassettes, filmstrips, and videotapes.

Media for the Arts, 360 Thames St., Newport, RI 02840.

Princeton Book Company/Dance Book Club, P.O. Box 57, Pennington, NJ 08534.

Sports Video, 745 State Circle, P.O. Box 1941, Ann Arbor, MI 48106. *Ballet class: intermediate and advanced and tap dancing for beginners*.

University of California, Extension Media Center, 2176 Shattuck Ave., Berkeley, CA 94704. Provides titles for preview, rental, or purchase.

University of Rochester, Dance Film Archive, Rochester, NY 14627. Provides videos for rental or purchase.

Frederic H. Weiner, 1325 Second Ave., New Hyde Park, NY 11040.

Disc Sports: Ultimate and Disc Golf

After completing this chapter, the reader should be able to:

- Appreciate the versatility of the games of ultimate and disc golf
- Demonstrate the correct grip, stance, approach, and delivery of three throwing styles
- Display a knowledge of the rules and strategy for ultimate and disc golf
- Display a knowledge of the variety of skills, sports, and games associated with throwing and catching discs
- Instruct a group of students in the fundamentals of ultimate and disc golf

Ultimate and disc golf are two extraordinary examples of modern-day sport evolving from the use and popularity of a commercial toy product. The invention of the flying disc, which only after many years later came to be called Frisbee, is credited for the development of these two sports.* Ultimate and disc golf are the most popular of flying disc sports, others being Guts, Discathon, and Freestyle. Both sports require players to throw a Frisbee or disc toward targets—moving players in ultimate, and, pole mounted baskets in disc golf. The discs come in a variety of sizes, shapes, and weights. Each sport involves players moving and changing positions to prepare themselves and execute throws. Both ultimate and disc golf invite players to compete in various versions of games and activities where the skills needed to be successful are easily acquired. Rules are simple and easy to follow and may be easily modified to extend or reduce the complexity of the skill or the physical challenge of the sport. Few popular sports today appeal to such a diversity of players regardless of age, size, or physical or intellectual ability.

HISTORY

The games of ultimate and disc golf are modern examples of hybrid sports that appeal to players because the play in each game requires a combination of physical and mental skills. Ultimate combines the playing skills of soccer and football; disc golf resembles the play of traditional golf. Learning to throw the disc for distance and accuracy is the main skill component needed to be successful in both sports.

The histories of both ultimate and disc golf began with the invention of the plastic flying disc, originally called the "Pluto Platter," by Fred Morrison in 1949. This prototype was derived from earlier handcrafted models by Morrison and Warren Fancioni in 1948. Morrison sold the rights to this flying disc to a leading toy manufacturer, Wham-O, Inc., in 1955, which in turn developed and marketed its own model by 1957. In 1959, Wham-O instituted the trademark label, and the ever-popular name *Frisbee* for all such flying discs, then began selling them in stores across the country. Wham-O is reported to have renamed its flying disc Frisbee after observing Yale University students playing catch with metal pie pans from the Frisbie Pie Company. When a thrown pie pan veered too close to people passing by, the players would yell "Frisbie!" The evolution of the sports of ultimate and disc golf developed along similar paths in that the flying disc was the instrument of play and each player was the prime mover and individual performer of each disc throw. However, the inception of each sport is unique, with its own history, rules, styles of play, equipment, players, and separate sport associations that exist today.

Disc Golf

Wham-O continued to market versions of the Frisbee, experimenting for a number of years with sizes, shapes, and aerodynamic designs. Ed Headrick became CEO of Wham-O Toys in 1964 and is credited with finding, in the years to follow, new applications and formalizing the game of disc golf from an unorganized activity. The original version of the game of disc golf developed during these years. In 1975 Headrick designed and invented the Disc Pole Hole to serve as the fixed target for aiming disc golf shots. The first Disc Pole Hole and, subsequently, first disc golf course were in Oak Grove Park in La Canada, California. Ed Headrick is known as the "father of disc golf" and has personally designed over two hundred disc golf courses around the world. His visions and ambitions for disc golf were to improve a park's environment by designing an activity that might deter vandalism and loitering and provide a fun sport in pleasant surroundings that would appeal to all people, including people with mental and physical impairments.

In 1976, only three disc golf courses existed in the United States. Since that time, over five hundred new

*Frisbee is a term often associated with flying discs and is a registered trademark of Wham-O, Inc.

courses have been installed in at least forty-eight states (figures 11-1 and 11-2). The evidence of its growing popularity accounts for having at least one hundred new disc golf courses installed since 1992. Disc golf courses are most prevalent in Texas and California, with the DeLaveaga Disc Golf Course in Santa Cruz, California, on the West Coast, and the Winthrop Lakefront Disc Golf Course in Rock Hill, South Carolina, on the East Coast, considered by some players to be among the best in the world. Disc golf courses can be designed to conform to a variety of geographical locations and land forms, including forests, deserts, and mountains, making them challenging and appealing to all players. The widespread popularity of disc golf has expanded internationally. There are more than a hundred disc golf courses in Canada, Europe, and Japan.

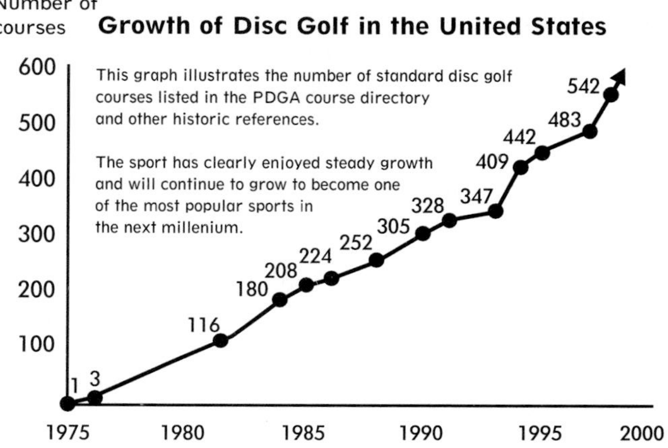

Figure 11-1. The growth of disc golf.

Many local park and recreation departments have capitalized on this recreational trend and installed disc golf courses for less than it might cost to install one lighted tennis court. A typical 18-hole disc golf course might cost less than $10,000, where one lighted tennis court could cost twice that amount. The revenue generated in disc golf could come from sales of golfing discs, user fees to play the course, and entry fees from sponsored tournaments. The phase-in installation process for disc golf holes and minimal maintenance costs for grounds and target baskets are attractive to community parks and recreation departments with budget constraints. The cost for players is remarkably inexpensive; with virtually indestructible golfing discs costing less than $10 each. Experienced players will carry with them during play a disc golf bag that might hold a dozen or more discs designed differently for different types of throws. For example, a "driving" disc is aerodynamically designed to throw farther than a "putting" disc for short accurate tosses.

The typical disc golf hole has a tee area, similar to traditional golf, a fairway and rough, hazards, out-of-bounds, and a "hole" consisting of a five-foot-tall durable galvanized steel basket. The basket is mounted on a metal pole and consists of a circular top plate or rim with hanging chains arranged above a circular metal basin. The chains act to catch the disc and then drop down in the basin.

Playing disc golf is much like playing traditional golf. The objective is to take as few attempts (throws) as possible to land your disc into the basket. A disc golf course may be laid out with different length holes sporting various trees,

Figure 11-2. Disc golf course locations.

bushes, and other hazards along the fairway to call for strategy and variation in the type of throws taken by the player approaching the hole. Novice players will attempt their most basic shots with a standard delivery style which they feel confident will keep the disc straight and go far. However, more experienced players will select a particular disc of size or weight and, using their own particular delivery style, make a throw toward the target with a particular design to maximize air flight and roll distance on the ground.

The game of disc golf appeals to many players because it is both fun and challenging. It can be learned and played by individuals from any economic or cultural background. Equally inviting to the young and old, male and female, physically talented and physically limited, and novice and expert players, it is recognized as a lifelong sport where one can enjoy the outdoors, walk for exercise, throw for accuracy, and find a challenge in every toss. Disc golf is fast becoming a popular sport that brings people together for fun and recreation.

Paralleling the popularity of disc golf has been the growth of its official organizing association, the Professional Disc Golf Association (PDGA) founded in 1984 and now numbering over 10,000 members. PDGA annually sponsors over 175 tournaments worldwide with over $300,000 in prize money.

Ultimate

In 1968, the first version of the game of ultimate, at that time called Ultimate Frisbee, was played at Columbia High School in Maplewood, New Jersey. Students arranged in teams passed the disc from one end of the field to the other to score a goal. Much like football and soccer, the team in possession of the disc was on offense. The team trying to intercept passes or throws was on defense. In 1998, in tribute to the inception of Ultimate Frisbee at this school, the Thirtieth Anniversary Maplewood Ultimate Frisbee Tournament was held. The first reported collegiate game of ultimate was held in 1972, with Rutgers University playing Princeton University. The first collegiate championship was held in 1974 with eight colleges participating. Since 1979, when Tom Kennedy founded the Ultimate Players Association (UPA), ultimate has become an international sport and is developing in a way that may lead to it becoming an Olympic sport. The UPA has more than 10,000 members and acts as the official international governing body for the sport of ultimate.

Ultimate is a very active team sport that requires a great deal of running in addition to throwing and catching skills. It can be enjoyed by players of almost any skill level and physical ability. The action of the game involves players for the team with possession of the disc running to an open space and catching a disc thrown to them. It is a noncontact sport involving a team on offense advancing the disc down the field, much like football, toward its opponent's end zone. The disc can be passed forward and backward between teammates, much like soccer, as long as each pass is caught in the air by a teammate. A dropped pass or missed catch reverses possession of the disc to the other team, and the team that previously held possession now becomes defenders. The action of the defensive team is to cover offensive players and knock down or intercept throws made by the offense. An incomplete pass, whether knocked down by the defense or simply not caught by an offensive teammate, results in a turnover, with the defensive team now on offense. Throughout a game, turnovers have teams changing form offense to defense very quickly.

Players agree that the appeal of the sport is in generating speed and force in the act of throwing and releasing a disc using smooth and graceful form, with the result being a uniquely flying disc. Selecting different types of shots and using various strategies gives players a feeling of artistic control and thrill of athletic accomplishment. The added elements of throwing to specific targets to score, inviting cooperation from teammates, and competition with other players define both ultimate and disc golf as sport.

SOCIAL VALUES

Ultimate and disc golf have been tremendously popular with youth in recreational programs and school settings, and more recently with coed students in collegiate recreational and intramural sports. Public park directors frequently report that disc golf courses are popular in their communities and deter vandalism and unwelcome individuals. They also report that players are environmentally conscientious, careful to respect the trees, bushes, flowers, and grounds, and are often seen picking up their trash and the trash of other park users.

Both ultimate and disc golf invite the use of basic and elementary motor skills, making either sport a proper choice as a developmental activity. With only minor modifications to the rules, procedures, and facilities of either sport, individuals with particular mental and physical conditions and limitations can have fun and be successful. Both sports have social value, combining cooperation and competition in proper balance to be considered fun, physically challenging, and socially rewarding for all players. Camaraderie would seem essential for playing and practicing disc sports, yet many of the skills for both games can be rehearsed individually, or with partners and teams. In both sports, the "spirit of the game" involves players acting as their own referees to enforce the rules of play and etiquette and display sportsmanship and respect for other players in the true spirit of competition.

FUNDAMENTAL SKILLS AND TECHNIQUES REQUIRED

Many people associate "playing Frisbee" with unstructured fun and imagine people at beaches, parks, and picnics

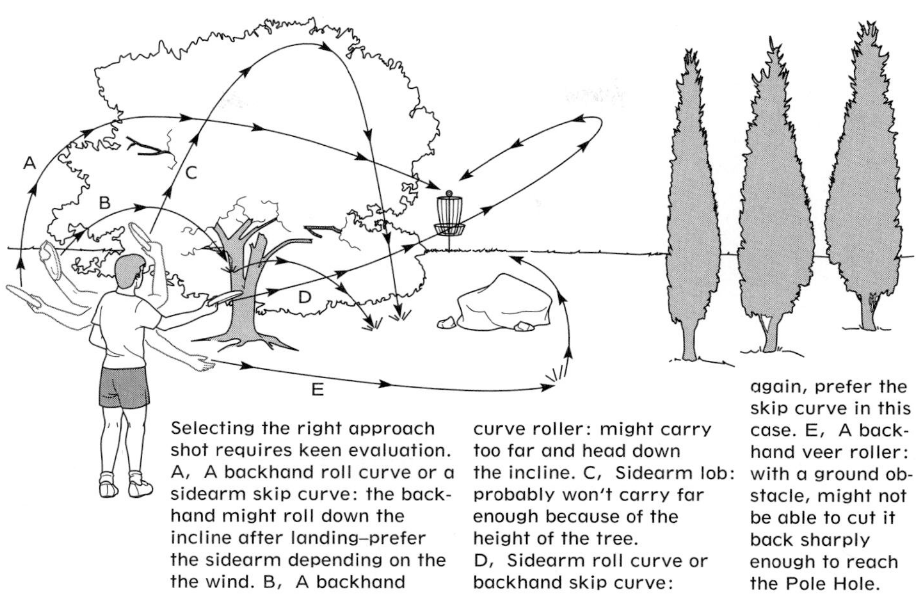

Selecting the right approach shot requires keen evaluation. A, A backhand roll curve or a sidearm skip curve: the backhand might roll down the incline after landing–prefer the sidearm depending on the the wind. B, A backhand curve roller: might carry too far and head down the incline. C, Sidearm lob: probably won't carry far enough because of the height of the tree. D, Sidearm roll curve or backhand skip curve: again, prefer the skip curve in this case. E, A backhand veer roller: with a ground obstacle, might not be able to cut it back sharply enough to reach the Pole Hole.

Figure 11-3.

engaged in a loosely organized activity. For this reason many beginners may be challenged to remain focused and attentive to the detail required to be capable of competent play in these sports. Once provided with the proper instruction and direction on the fundamental skills and techniques for throwing and catching the disc, it is important that players experiment with their own personal technique and perfect their own unique style.

The situations and circumstances that arise during play in ultimate and disc golf often require a little inventiveness and imagination from a player who is called to execute a throw around or over other players and obstacles (figure 11-3). The development of the ability to execute these throws is dependent upon body coordination and consistent mental concentration. The key to successful throws in either sport is the total development and use of the body's lever systems to project the disc by generating force and imparting spin onto the disc. Before describing the three major styles of throws, we will introduce some basic terminology. This terminology is accompanied by a discussion of hand positions and grips, body positioning and stance, typical disc flight patterns, and catching skills.

Hand Positions and Grips

Hand positioning for the three most basic grips on a disc is simple yet critical. To identify the disc, remember to think of the top as the part having the label or logo inscribed; the bottom then is underneath and does not have a logo. The circular span of the disc is referred to as the flight plate with a center and rim, the top part of the rim called the lip, and the bottom part of the rim called the edge.

To learn the first basic grip (figure 11-4) grab the disc with your thumb on the topside with your index finger stretched out along the lip and your remaining fingers fanned out underneath (as if to fan yourself). In this manner you have positioned your hand for the most elementary of throwing styles, referred to as the cross-body backhand. The degree to which one fans out the underside finger is individual; however, closing the fingers down toward the edge and cupping the rim enables the thrower to generate greater force. A minor modification of dropping your index finger off the rim and curling it partially below the edge produces the Berkeley grip, now preferred by most players. Many players experiment with this grip and throwing style first because it is recognized easily in other players and is chosen by most players as the most forceful and accurate of all throwing styles.

A second basic grip used for the sidearm or forehand style is called the two-finger grip (figure 11-5). Grasp the disc with your middle finger positioned underneath and along the inside edge of the disc, with your thumb on the topside. Your index finger should lie neatly on top of your middle finger for support while your ring finger and small finger are cupped into the palm of your hand. A variation of this grip is to cup your middle finger into your palm as well and place only the index finger along the inside edge of the disc.

The third basic grip to be introduced is used for the overhand style throw (figure 11-6). Grasp the disc with your thumb on the underside edge of the disc with your index finger extended along the outer rim. The rest of your fingers are fanned out across the top of the disc. If you are

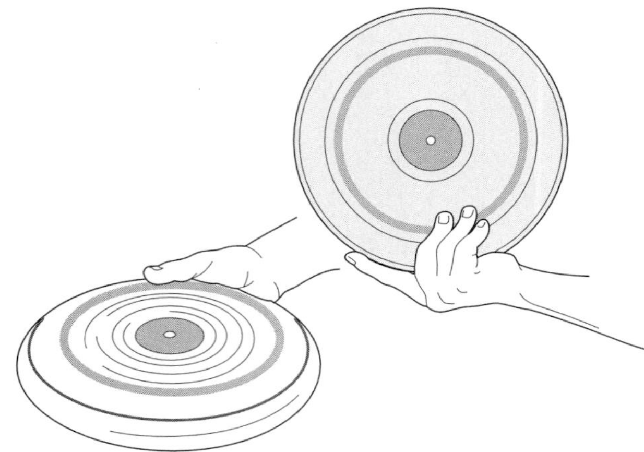

Figure 11-4.

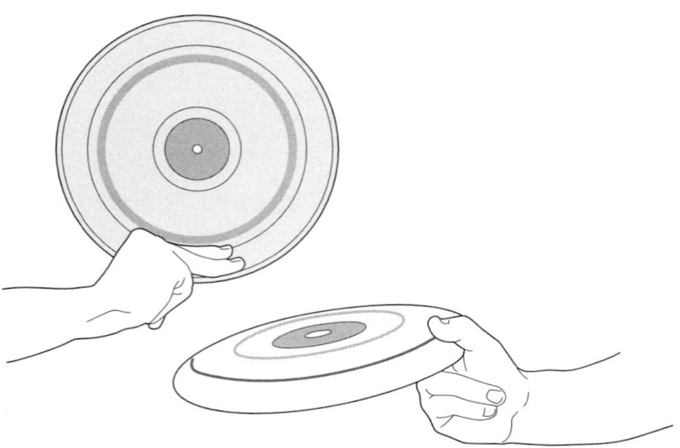

Figure 11-5.

able to follow these descriptions and practice them on a disc, you will notice that the first two grips are underhanded with your thumb on the topside of the disc positioned skyward, while the last grip, the overhand, has your thumb on the underside of the disc facing the ground.

Body Positioning and Stance

To simplify discussions of left side and right side for right- or left-handed throwers, the terms on-side and off-side are introduced. On-side always refers to the side of the body that is handling the disc. The other side then is the off-side. When the on-side arm initiates a throw or makes a catch on the off-side, it is said to be cross-body. This may help you understand why the most easily recognized and most popular throwing style is called the cross-body backhand. The disc is positioned on the off-side of the body, and the action of throwing brings the arm across the body. Both sidearm and overhand styles are on-side. It might be argued that the arm will cross the body during the action of throwing

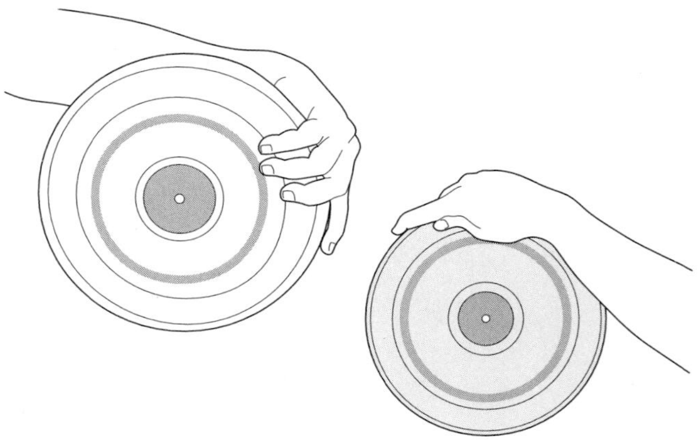

Figure 11-6.

sidearm or overhand styles, but one must note that the disc is positioned on-side to initiate the throw.

Stance is important to generate force and angle of delivery. A throw facing square to a target is in a facing stance, and if facing away from a target is in a blind stance. The blind stance is used in ultimate, or for trick throws and stunts. Useful of understanding throwing style are the terms open stance and closed stance. An open stance, as is used for sidearm throws, has the arm and hand positioned away from the body in the cocked position as the throw is initiated. The closed stance, used for backhand style throws, has the arm and hand tucked inside and close to the body as the throw is initiated.

Disc Flight Patterns

Think of the disc in flight as divided into four quarters. Regardless of how much spinning the disc does, the front or forward quarter is referred to as the "nose." The back quarter is the "tail," and the lateral or side quarters are the "shoulders." During the flight, the angle of the nose to the tail is called the attack angle. A nose up position, with the nose above the tail, is considered a negative attack angle, and the disc will tend to stall before dropping. Conversely, a positive attack angle, with the nose down or below the tail, will cause the disc to dive forcefully without slowing or losing speed.

In each flight there is a skip shoulder and a roll shoulder, which are directly related to the direction of spin on the disc. The side or shoulder of disc that is spinning forward during flight (imagine that being the left side for a right-hand thrower) is the skip shoulder. Upon striking the ground surface, given enough force and speed, the disc may bounce or skip (figure 11-7). The side or shoulder of a disc that is spinning backward during flight is the roll shoulder. Upon striking the ground surface it will likely roll with enough force and speed. These terms remain constant for every flight except a boomerang flight. At the apex of its

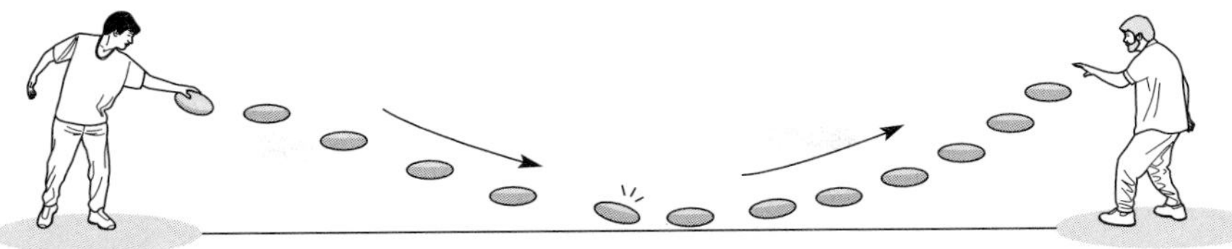

Figure 11-7.

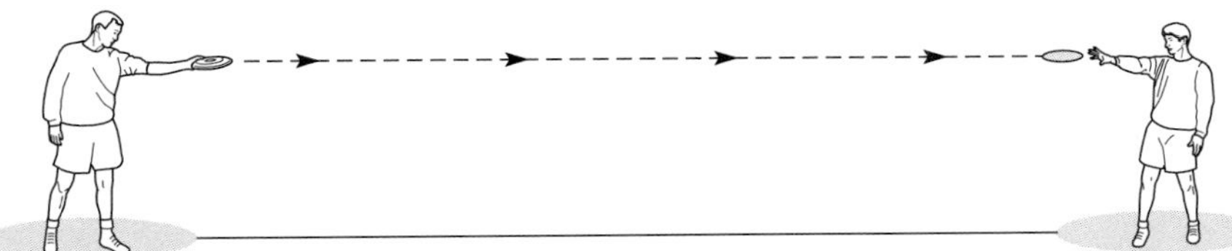

Figure 11-8.

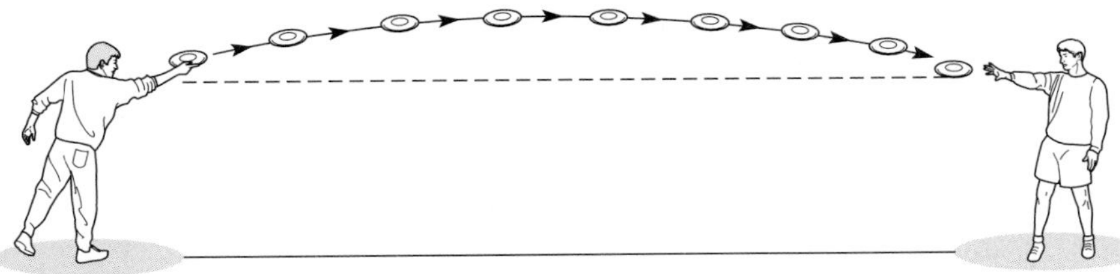

Figure 11-9.

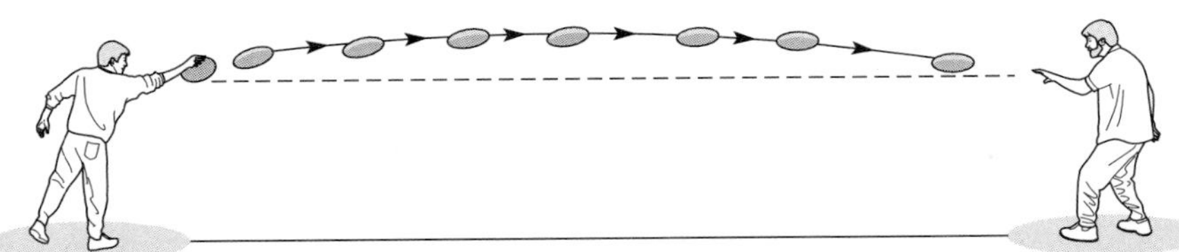

Figure 11-10.

outward motion, as the disc stalls and begins retreating toward the thrower, the nose becomes the tail, the tail becomes the nose, and the skip and roll shoulders switch sides as well.

Once in flight, the disc tends to display a definite tendency in flight pattern. Basically straight and level flights (figure 11-8) remain that way, while curving flights continue curving in the same direction, in more or less dramatic fashion. While it is convenient to refer to curving throws as curving either "right" or left," in each case the curve should be properly designated as skip curve or roll curve depending on which shoulder of the disc the curving the motion is headed. For example, a right-handed thrower who uses a cross-body backhand style will observe a throw curving to the right in its downward flight as a roll curve (figure 11-9). This makes sense because upon striking the ground the tendency of the disc is to roll. If that same thrower with the same throwing style observes a throw curving or bending left, it is a skip curve (figure 11-10).

One other flight worth mentioning is called the hover (or floater) flight (figure 11-11). As one might imagine, at some point, usually toward the end of its flight, a disc will slow down and stall before descending. At that point before it begins to drop, it is said to be hovering or floating. Even with a hover flight, the descending action may curve in one direction or the other. For the sake of simplicity, it is still considered a hover flight because of its predominant attitude.

Beginners often throw discs where the flight curves in an extreme fashion and "turns over" the disc. In most cases where this occurs the skip shoulder is lifting towards a vertical position caused by the combination of excessive arm

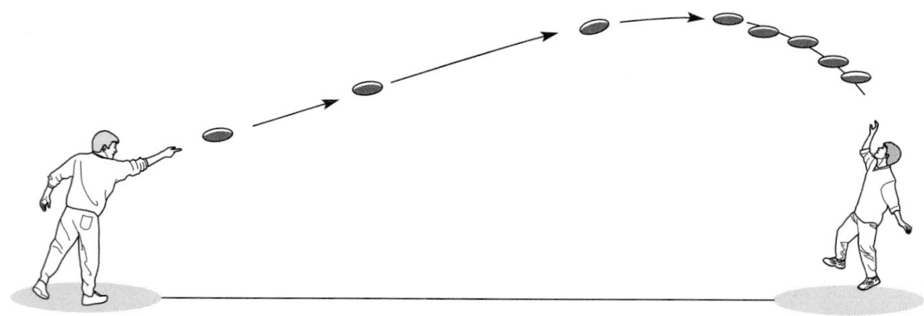

Figure 11-11.

action and minimal wrist action. Some degree of skip shoulder lifting is part of almost every flight, but practice is required to minimize excessive lifting action. With practice, this correction feature used to compensate for excessive skip shoulder lifting and the tendency of the disc to turnover is called hyzer. By determining the exact angle of flight and angling the skip shoulder slightly away from the direction it will lift, the delivery should compensate for the lifting action. In one sense, the term *hyzer* refers to the correction or adjustment for lifting; in another sense, it is used simply to mean the angle of delivery.

Adjustments for lifting are critical, because prior to and at the moment of release, the positions of both the wrist and the disc, combined with the amount of pressure used to grasp the disc, determine the characteristics of the flight. The pressure on the disc produced by one's grasp at the moment of release may be called the pinch point. To minimize excessive lift, and reduce the likelihood of wobble or unstable flight, both wrist and disc must pivot around the pinch point on the same level plane as the disc snaps out of one's grasp. In addition, the wrist and disc must be in the same alignment with the angle of flight. The throw must first visualize the angle of flight and attempt to keep the wrist and disc on the same plane at the moment of delivery. Achieving this co-planar alignment can be visualized with a basically flat throwing motion using a backhand or sidearm delivery. If the desired flight path is a flat level throw, and the arm motion, as well as the wrist and disc, are basically flat and level, the likelihood of wobble or flutter is minimized.

Catching Skills

There is an art to catching as there is an art to throwing. In fact, there are almost as many styles for catching a disc as there are for throwing one. Intuitively, most players understand that a successful catch entails reading the flight of the disc and tracking it to position oneself within reach of it during descent. Once within reach, the skill of eye-hand coordination is combined with cupping the hand and grasping the disc with a "giving" or retreating action of the arm. This action means simply bringing the catching motion in line with the motion of the disc and avoiding a tense and rigid posture of the arm and body as the catch is made. It is important as well to position oneself to catch the disc between the farthest reach of the outstretched hand and one's body. This sets up the receiving motion of the arm and hand to be moving toward the body as opposed to away from the body. The following pointers will be helpful in developing better catching skills.

A catch, by definition, is anytime the flight of the disc is arrested by a player. Essentially, the cupping action of the hand to form a "C" between the thumb and the fingers is how a true catch is made. Determining whether to catch the disc with the thumb in a down position where the thumb will grasp the underside of the disc, or in the up position with the thumb on the topside, is a matter of adjusting to the height at which the disc is received. Generally, one should be able to visualize catching low throws with a thumb-up position and high throws with a thumb-down position. Develop this skill using both hands together, then the dominant hand alone, and lastly, the nondominant hand alone. A catch made between both hands held flat with fingers extended, as if to clamp down from the top and up from the bottom, is a trap. A trap can also occur between a hand and another part of the body. Additionally, one can develop skills referred to as discwork, where manipulating the flight of the disc during flight will set up a catch. Examples of this are tipping, brushing, or slapping the disc to slow down its action, or fingertipping the disc with the tip of one's finger to control its spinning action and make a catch.

Regardless of catching method, the first challenge is to move to be in position to make a catch. The secret to success in this skill is in the ability to read the flight of the incoming disc and react quickly with footwork, balance, and body positioning. There is much visual information to be used even prior to the disc's flight, beginning with the body position and throwing action of the thrower. The direction of spin on the disc is determined by the releasing action of the thrower's wrist and hand, so it is important to immediately recognize the thrower's style of delivery and associate it with direction of spin and the typical flight pattern.

The spin direction of the incoming disc is important as you decide which hand and what method you will use to catch the disc. It is helpful to know whether the disc will spin into or out of the palm of your hand. A disc spinning out of your hand or way from you will require you to close your grasp more quickly and firmly. Though developing an eye for reading the spin direction quickly is beneficial, the exact amount of pressure applied by the hand and fingers during a catch must be experimented with and practiced in order to improve on this skill.

The height, angle of attack, angle of delivery, and speed of the incoming disc must also register immediately with the receiver as positioning action is taken. Adjustments for height can be made by advancing toward or retreating away from the disc. The angle of attack (nose to tail) helps you determine if and how much a disc will rise, hover, fall, and drop. The hyzer (shoulder-to-shoulder) angle controls the lateral curve of the flight. In each flight, the disc has the tendency to continue this flight pattern, often with more or less emphasis, depending on wind variation. Experienced players will include reading the wind conditions as a determining feature for both throwing and catching. As one might imagine, the speed of the incoming disc is greatly affected by wind direction. Disc speed at the moment of catch is also determined by the distance between the catcher and the thrower and the amount of force generated by the throw. The beginner should be experimenting with applying various amounts of force in throwing as well as learning to catch discs thrown at various speeds.

Being knowledgeable about the basic principles of grip, stance, and flights of throws, and having added to that an appreciation for some catching skills, we can move on toward developing an understanding of throwing and delivery styles. Familiarity with the terminology introduced above will aid in the understanding and appreciation of the following three major styles of throws; the cross-body backhand, the sidearm or forehand, and the overhand.

The Cross-Body Backhand

To throw a disc using the cross-body backhand style, grip the disc with your thumb on the topside and your fingers fanned out on the underside (figure 11-4). As introduced earlier, the index finger may run along the rim or slightly bend and partially curl beneath the edge. Novice throwers may spread the fingers underneath apart for stability, but then curl them up to the rim as their proficiency develops. The degree of firmness with which to grasp the disc must be experimented with individually; usually a firm but relaxed grip is required.

The stance and approach used for a step throw is the basic delivery skill that the novice must practice, after which the full walk-up or run-up delivery can be developed. To execute the step throw, position your throwing shoulder toward the target and place your feet along the line of the intended flight; this is basically a closed position (figure 11-12). With most of your weight on your rear foot from the target, curl your throwing arm, shoulders, and hips behind you. As you step forward down the target line and your weight transfers to the lead foot, release your hips, then shoulders, then arms, wrist, and disc. The transfer of weight to the lead foot is timed to immediately precede the beginning action of releasing your hips. With practice, a smooth, graceful, and powerful delivery can be developed. To generate maximum throwing force and use full-body action, a walk-up or run-up approach initiates the throw. The forward momentum of the walk or run approach must be controlled and applied to the torque action of the legs and hips. Immediately prior to the weight transfer step, the trailing leg should be planted behind the throwing side leg. With the weight on this backside leg, the hips, shoulders, and throwing arm should be rotated back. As the lead foot steps forward and the weight transfer begins, the hips, shoulders, and arm should release and rotate forward toward a natural follow-through. Foot placement must be practiced and perfected to achieve complete balance and full momentum (figure 11-13).

Figure 11-12.

To achieve success throwing discs with different flights using this throwing style, it is important to recognize that body motion and arm action constitute only part of the throw. Indeed, every throw is critically dependent on the angle of the forearm and wrist at the release point, and the amount of additional force imparted on the disc using wrist flexion or extension.

Setting up for the cross-body backhand throw involves cocking the wrist in a accented flexed position and timing the release from that position with the pressure and release of the fingers on the disc. One should attempt to release the disc flatly, at first, with an easy and smooth motion.

Figure 11-13. Cross-body backhand delivery motion.

Note the way the arm, wrist, and fingers feel during each attempt and make subtle corrections in a trial-and-error fashion. Experiment with finger placement and pressure, wrist action, and arm motion between each throw.

A skip curve thrown by a right-hander will curve left from the intended target line, whereas a roll curve will curve right. Remember, the direction of the curve, either right or left of the target, is related to which shoulder the disc is curving toward. In most throws, it is well to intend to have some degree of curve during flight. The amount of curve is determined by a sensitive adjustment, either lowering or raising, of the angle of the skip or roll shoulder. Again, this adjustment is the hyzer. To correct for excessive roll curve, where the skip shoulder is lifting toward vertical, you must experiment with hyzer, or the degree of angle of the skip shoulder during delivery. An excessive roll curve taken to its extreme results in a turnover, which can be corrected for in the delivery by angling the skip shoulder slightly away from the direction of lift.

The hover throw can be practiced by attempting to throw a basically straight shot with the nose of the disc elevated. This shot is intended to slow down and stall out at some point during flight then drop down over the target. This feature is useful in both ultimate and disc golf.

Skip shots and roll shots that strike and move along the ground are not applicable for ultimate, but are extremely useful for disc golf, and they must be practiced by the disc golfer. With the right purpose and intention, skipping a shot toward a target or rolling a shot down a fairway makes perfect sense. In the right situation, using a throw that exaggerates the angle of the skip or roll shoulder during delivery will produce the skip or roll shot. Although the angle of the shoulder appears to be the critical element of the shot, the player must be able to recognize and predict the effect of the ground or surface on the action of the disc.

The Sidearm or Forehand

The sidearm and forehand throws are one in the same, keeping in mind that the natural forward throwing motion of the arm can be delivered from the same various arm angles used for throwing in other sports. Similar to a pitcher's delivery in baseball, the arm can come forward and through in a flat or sidearm position, directly over the top of the shoulder as in tomahawk motion, or somewhere in between, often referred to as a three-quarter delivery. In all cases, the forward throwing motion of the arm is initiated by the shoulder muscles of that arm, while the delivery and release is led by the elbow then followed by the wrist and hand.

The sidearm grip uses the middle finger and index finger on the underside of the disc with the thumb on top (figure 11-5). The thrower may position the middle finger against the rim together with the index finger, or spread the index finger toward the middle of the disc. An index finger only (underneath) is another grip variation. The amount of pressure applied by the fingers must conform to the extent that the disc can be held level at release while the wrist is allowed to snap freely and forcefully. The hand and wrist are cocked backward as the arm retreats behind the body. Forward arm motion and arm speed, along with wrist flexion, are primarily responsible for the force exerted in this throw.

Again, a step throw for the sidearm or forehand relies upon the weight transfer from the back foot to the front foot during delivery. Both feet should be positioned along the line of the intended flight, with the front foot stepping forward and slightly open to the target during delivery (figure 11-14). This footwork is accompanied by leg, hip, trunk, and shoulder rotations that open up to the target as the arm comes forward toward release. To set up for this throw, the thrower must be able to turn away from the target the shoulders and hips, and coil the upper body to generate rotational force and momentum. The stepping motion and weight transfer must be practiced and timed to coincide with the releasing action of the hips, shoulder, and

Figure 11-14. Sidearm stance and delivery.

Figure 11-15. Sidearm delivery motion.

arm. Easy and rhythmic throwing action should be practiced at varying distances to establish comfort and control. Added force and additional arm speed should be practiced after a natural motion is established (figure 11-15).

To generate optimum force and speed for this delivery style, as well as for others, a walk-up or run-up approach during delivery can be added. Again, it is important to maintain balance and rhythm and stay relaxed through acceleration to generate as much force as possible into the last moment of release. All energy generated by added footwork must be timed and directed into the last act of releasing the throw. Toward the final step in this approach, many players will use a short hop to plant the weight on to the back foot to begin uncoiling the body. They quickly follow by stepping and shifting the weight forward to the front foot, releasing the hips and shoulders, and accelerating the arm forward.

For the disc to adopt the best angle of delivery upon release from the hand, it is critical to have the wrist and disc maintain a level posture. To enable this positioning to take place, the forearm should also approximate a level posture. For the forearm be in a level posture, the arm must approach the release point from a sideways position versus a three-quarter or over the top position. Hence, most forehand throws are of the sidearm delivery. The action of positioning the arm toward vertical during delivery increases the likelihood of a rolling curve to the point where the disc will turn over. A forehand throw where the arm and disc are released in nearly vertical position, a tomahawk position, is observed to produce a turnover where the disc flies most of its flight upside down. This throwing style is effective for both distance and accuracy and should be experimented with and practiced.

For the most part, however, a sidearm throw, keeping the forearm, wrist, and disc level during delivery, will achieve great distances and can be thrown with accuracy. It is critical to snap the wrist quickly and forcefully at the release point, otherwise the throw suffers from an excessive roll curve, where the skip shoulder lifts toward vertical and the flight of the disc descends rapidly.

The thrower must experiment with pressure applied and location (pinch point) of the thumb and fingers to hold the disc level. Practicing the snapping action of the wrist while holding the disc in place will afford additional control and sense of adjustment. At the release point, where in fact the wrist does snap, the arm should temporarily freeze or stop moving forward as the wrist, hand, and fingers release the disc. This freezing action, while brief and momentary, will inhibit any form of a long or extended follow-through. Developing throwers must practice throwing level flights by controlling the lifting action of either shoulder of the disc. Correcting for excessive lifting action was discussed under disc flight patterns.

The release point will determine the direction the disc flies out of the hand. Minor adjustments produce major changes in direction. The amount of spin imparted on the disc can act to stabilize the disc during flight. Generally, a

Figure 11-16. Overhand stance and delivery.

wobbly disc is the result of insufficient force applied by the snap of the wrist. The sidearm delivery can generate skip curves, roll curves, skip shots, and roll shots.

For skip curves and skip shots, maintaining an open stance improves the chance to angle the skip shoulder down and produce the desired results. An observant thrower will notice that successfully throwing skip curves and skip shots requires the arm motion to be more inside or closer to the body during delivery than with a straight shot or roll curve. The roll curve, then, will likely position the arm outside and away from the body to allow the roll shoulder to maintain a down position. The roll shot takes the disc to near vertical position with the roll shoulder very much in the down position. The flight paths of the roll curve can be varied from sharp and steep to soft and wide, with both paths exaggerated or compromised by wind conditions. The action from the roll shot (roller) obviously depends on ground surface conditions as well as the force, angle, and impact with which the disc strikes the ground.

The Overhand

The overhand delivery style might appear unorthodox at first and feel quite different from the first two styles of delivery mentioned. As noted earlier, the grip for this throw is different from the other three by placing the thumb on the underneath side of the disc with the fingers spanned out over the top of the disc (figure 11-6). Most throwers prefer to place their index finger along the outside of the rim of the disc for better feel and control. With the disc held in this grip, as the arm retreats during the backswing, the wrist is fully cocked.

The position of the body has the feet aligned with the intended flight of the disc and the opposite shoulder pointed toward the target. As the backswing is started, the shoulders and hips rotate into a closed position. With the weight back on the rear foot, the body is coiled, cocked, and ready. The release begins with a step and transfer of weight on to the lead foot, followed by the immediate release of the hips and shoulders. As the arm comes around to make the throw, arm speed is generated toward the release point. It is important to maintain the forearm in a level position as wrist snap and release occur. It is helpful to learn this throw by practicing a delivery with the motion of the arm and wrist occurring at shoulder height. This enables the thrower to prematurely set the forearm in a level position (figure 11-16).

Much force can be generated from a properly timed and coordinated release of the body and arm, but, as in other throws, a walk-up or run-up approach can greatly increase the amount of force. Much like the forehand throw from over the top, a short hop to set the weight on to the rear foot will start the momentum forward, and precede the release of the rotational action from the hips and shoulders. At the release point, with the forearm fairly level, the wrist will extend forcefully from the cocked position. From start to finish, a full-body motion delivery is the most effective and least stressful. A disc diving downward sharply, as in an extreme roll curve, is evidence that the wrist and forearm were not held in a level position during release.

Straight shots and hover flights are fairly easily performed if position of the forearm, wrist, and disc are virtually preset, level, and co-planar with the angle of flight the thrower is attempting to achieve. A roll curve can easily be thrown with the overhand delivery by simply modifying the arc of the throwing arm. Skip curves and skip shots are executed by simply dropping the angle of the arm from shoulder level to waist level as the arm proceeds through delivery and into release position.

ULTIMATE

General Description

Ultimate combines throwing and catching skills with simple strategies and a great deal of running. Generally, almost any number of individuals can play in a game, given teams of equal numbers and ability and a playing area large enough to accommodate them. Typically, ultimate is played by two seven-person teams. The rectangular playing field has an end zone at each end. Teams are posed against each other, with the offensive team in possession of the disc, attempting to advance the disc toward its opponent's end zone to score.

The object of the game is to score goals by passing the disc among teammates. A goal is scored if a pass from a teammate is caught in the end zone. One point is awarded for each goal. A player may not run with the disc. Upon catching a throw, a player must come to a stop and establish a pivot foot immediately. The disc may be thrown in any direction to players positioned anywhere in the field of play. A careful and controlled offensive team will throw the disc among its players, much like soccer and lacrosse, as it advances downfield toward the opponent's end zone. Because running with possession of the disc is not permitted, unlike in soccer and lacrosse, the ability to throw accurately and to catch successfully while moving and avoiding defenders is most important. Intentional physical contact, including pushing, shoving, tripping, and blocking, is not permitted. Shielding a teammate from a defender by positioning oneself between the players, and setting picks, are also illegal.

The defensive team attempts to prevent the opponents from reaching their end zone by guarding and covering the opponent's players and trying to knock down or intercept throws, or by causing an errant throw to be made. Two basic defensive strategies are zone or one-on-one coverage. Ultimately, possession of the disc when it is in the air is up for grabs. Once a disc thrown by the offense is intercepted, missed, knocked down, or lands on the ground, the defense immediately takes possession at that spot and goes on offense. They now proceed in the other direction to advance the disc toward their opponent's end zone. Once the game has started and a disc is "in play," it remains in play until a goal is scored and a restart ensures. The first team to score 21 points is declared the winner.

Play is continuous even as offense and defense exchange possession. There is no offsides, so any player positioned within the field of play by either team at any given moment is legal. Possession is reversed whenever a throw lands out of bounds or a member of the offensive team commits a foul on a member of the defense. In a friendly game of ultimate, players call their own fouls and referees are not used. However, for UPA-sanctioned competition, official observers are used to act as mediators for contested calls. What is unique to the sport of ultimate is the "spirit of the game." Players observe elements of etiquette, sportsmanship, and camaraderie not always found in other competitive team sports.

Field/Equipment

1. The field of play is a rectangular area measuring 70 yards in length and 40 yards in width, with end zones 25 yards deep.
2. The perimeter lines are not considered part of the playing field and are out of bounds.
3. Any flying disc acceptable to both teams may be used.
4. Players for opposing teams are identified by any method agreeable by both teams.

Abridged Rules

Starting and restarting play

1. Initial possession: A coin toss, or any other method acceptable to both teams, decides which team receives the initial throw-off and/or which end of the field to defend initially. To begin the second half of the game, the throw-off will be made by the team that received the initial throw-off to start the game.
2. The throw-off: A throw-off is used to begin play in each half, and to restart play after a goal is scored. Each team must line up on its respective goal line. The receiving team must indicate its readiness to receive a throw before the disc is thrown by the opposing team. Any player for the offensive team may elect to make the throw-off, and any player on the receiving team may elect to catch the throw-off. The throw-off must land and remain in the field of play. At this point, whether the disc is caught in the air or not by a member of the receiving ream, possession will begin with the receiving team at that spot. No member of the throwing team may touch the disc before the receiving team has had a chance to put the disc in play. After a goal is scored, the teams switch end zones; the team that was scored upon walks to the other goal line and the scoring team lines up for the throw-off.
3. The check: When play is interrupted, the player who was in possession of the disc retains possession at the spot where he or she was located when play was halted. All other players remain at their respective locations. The defender covering that thrower will hand the disc back to the thrower to resume play.

Offense

1. Thrower: The disc is advanced toward the end zone by passing. Passes may be made in any direction. The thrower must establish a pivot foot, as in basketball, in attempting to pass in any direction and in any fashion. If the thrower takes steps, or the pivot foot is "lifted," traveling may be called by the defender and play is immediately halted. This violation results in a turnover, and a "check" is called; the player called for traveling hands the disc over to the defender at that spot. A throw-off that goes out of bounds is put in play at either a spot at the sideline where the disc crossed out of bounds or at a spot in the middle of the field, perpendicular to the point where the throw-off crossed out of bounds. The thrower establishes a pivot foot at either point to begin play.
2. Receiver: After catching a pass, a receiver is allowed the fewest number of steps, usually three, to come to a complete stop and establish a pivot foot. In situations where a pass is caught near the sideline or the end zone line, the receiver's first point of contact with the ground determines where the pass was caught and whether it is ruled in or out of bounds or a goal or not. If the catch is good and the player's momentum takes him or her out of bounds or over the goal line, the player must return to the point of contact with the ground, and play resumes without a check.

Defense

1. Marker: A marker is the defender, who may guard the thrower but must allow the thrower to pivot and must maintain a distance equal to the diameter of a disc away from the thrower at all times. Therefore, hitting

or slapping a disc out of the hands of the thrower or receiver is illegal. The thrower cannot maintain possession of the disc indefinitely, and the marker, at any time, can initiate a 10-second stall count by counting 10 seconds aloud. If the thrower has not released the disc within the 10-second count, a turnover is called by the defender and a check ensues.

2. General: Double-teaming is not permitted in guarding the thrower. However, defenders against receivers may position themselves in any manner they feel is best suited to defend against the pass.
3. Basic strategies are zone defenses and one-on-one coverage.

Fouls and violations

Fouls are the result of physical contact between opposing players. A foul can be called only by the player who has been fouled and must be announced by calling out "Foul!" loudly and immediately after the infraction. A foul may be called by either an offensive or a defensive player. Once a foul is called, play is immediately halted. If the foul is called by a defensive player, the disc goes back to the thrower in possession before the foul occurred and a check is called before play resumes, unless a turnover occurs, in which case possession reverts to the defensive team. If the foul is called by an offensive player, play resumes at the point of infraction unless the pass is completed. In both cases, a check is called before play ensues.

Miscellaneous

1. Substitutions: Unlimited substitution is allowed but only after a goal is scored or for an injured player.
2. Dispute/confusion: If there is a dispute or confusion on the field, play is halted and the issue is resolved before a check is called to restart the game.
3. Length of game: The length of game can be adjusted according to constraints. An official game is to 21, although teams may agree to any number of goals necessary to win, preferably before the game begins.

Teaching Considerations

1. Before providing lengthy instruction on learning the fundamental skills and techniques used in playing ultimate, it may be helpful to have the rules of the game and basic procedures of play discussed and demonstrated. Players might associate greater relevance to variations in throwing styles and deliveries by experiencing or visualizing the variety of game situations and circumstances.
2. Throwing and catching skills improve with guided instruction and feedback. Initially, helping students find success with one basic style of throwing and catching might be the primary objective. With confidence in one skill, a student might be less apprehensive about trying other skills. Conversely, students might rely too much on one successful style and need to be encouraged and challenged to develop versatility.
3. Throwing and catching drill must accompany playing time. Correct and repeated practice is necessary for continued improvement of basic skills. Several drills are described below, but instructors are encouraged to invent drills to challenge their particular learners as well as accommodate students with physical and mental limitations.
4. Drill work for throwing off a pivot foot under various conditions must be practiced. Faking, pivoting, and throwing with low and high release points goes beyond the basic skills of throwing and catching.
5. Beginners might initially prefer games where the thrower is a greater distance from the defender than in regular play.

DRILLS

1. Rapid thrower drill: Space one player as thrower about 5 yards from the remaining players, who form a line of receivers. Receivers have the discs to begin the drill. The first player in line tells the thrower the intended pass route, gives a short, accurate toss to the thrower, and runs the pass route. The thrower throws to the player in motion, and the next receiver steps up to the line and does the same. After catching or retrieving the throw from the thrower, the receiver returns to the line. After several times through the line, a new thrower is installed.
2. Throw-spin-throw drill: Identify one player as thrower in the middle of two groups of receivers lined up and facing a different direction from each other. The thrower has two discs on the ground next to him or her. On the command "Go!", the first receiver in each line takes off running as the thrower grasps one disc, sets up and throws, then spins and grabs the other disc, sets up and makes a throw to the second receiver.
3. Guard drill: A modified version of Drill #1. The receiver who runs a pass route becomes a defender and shadows the next receiver before returning to the line.
4. Triangular and circle throwing: Players are arranged in either formation. Each player uses alternate throwing styles to a player positioned to the left or right in the group. Modifications: catch only in dominate hand or nondominant hand; sidearm, and cross-body backhand delivery styles must follow catches made in the thumb-up position. Overhand deliveries follow catches made in the thumb-down position.

DISC GOLF

General Description

Disc golf is played like traditional golf. However, instead of hitting a ball with a club into a hole, you throw a flying disc and hit a target. The layout for a disc golf course is very similar to a regular golf course. There is a tee area or designated starting point for every hole from which your first throw to the target is made. The target, in disc golf, is a five-foot-high metal pole supporting a circular metal basket consisting of hanging chains and a catch basin. To land "in the hole," the disc must be thrown into, and remain within, the basket. The object of the game is to take as few throws as possible to get from the tee area to the hole. Generally, a course is laid out with nine or eighteen holes. Each hole presents a challenge to avoid trees, bushes, and other obstacles as the disc golfer proceeds down the fairway from the tee to the hole.

Disc golf presents an interesting challenge for disc throwers. The course layout, and wind and ground surface conditions, make it nearly impossible to simply throw straight shots down the fairway. The disc golfer must often elect to throw discs that fly both long and straight or short and curve or roll and skip along the ground. As the distance from the tee to the target is covered, accuracy takes on greater importance, until the final shot is taken, which must fall in the basket.

Practice for disc golf can take the form of throwing at any target (e.g., fence post, telephone pole) without having to have an actual course on which to play. Players can "make up holes as they go" and find it equally challenging and fun. Beginners must learn to develop consistency and control in disc throwing as well as power for long-distance throws.

Field/Equipment

Disc golf courses are laid out like traditional golf courses with nine or eighteen holes, each of which is composed of a tee-off area, a fairway, out-of-bounds areas, a hole or target, and obstacles and hazards. Holes are of varying distances with a predetermined average number of strokes to hit the target (par). Typically, most holes on a disc golf course are par 3, with few labeled par 4 or 5. Without an official course, players can invent their own course using a park or field for fairways and boundaries, and trees, bushes, fenceposts, and telephone poles for targets. The cost to play is minimal; many courses are free to the public, and flying discs retail for under $10. There are no other requirements of a player except a throwing arm with which to propel the disc toward the target, and the means to get from one throw to the next.

Play

Disc golf has adopted common courtesy rules of play that are similar to those for regular golf. With more than one player playing, players throw one at a time. It is inappropriate to distract or interfere with another player's throw by any means. Players are not permitted to handle other players' discs. Each player should make her or his throw, then wait in turn for the remaining players to throw. After all players have thrown, all proceed to their discs and prepare for the next throw.

Typically, the player whose throw has landed farthest away from the hole will be the first to throw again. Therefore, other players must remain behind and out of the way of the throw as they take their turns. To begin a new hole, the player who has scored the fewest number of throws on the last hole will throw first, and so on. Players record their own scores for each hole on a score card.

From one throw to the next, each player must mark the spot where the disc has landed, and make the next throw from behind that mark. Many disc golfers use a marker disc to place on the ground immediately in front of and touching the disc where it landed. With the location marked, the disc is picked up and the thrower prepares for the next throw, which must be taken with one foot planted behind and within close proximity to the marker disc. If a walk-up or run-up approach is used from the tee or in the fairway, the plant foot must be as close to touching the marker disc as possible. The follow-through action can carry the throw past the market disc, without penalty, except for throws of less than 10 meters.

For any throw to the target from within 10 meters, the plant foot must be positioned behind the marker and the other foot must remain behind a line perpendicular to the intended line of flight. Any follow-through motion that causes a player to touch the ground in front of this perpendicular line is a violation and results in a one-stroke penalty and rethrow. A player may be warned one time concerning a putting infraction without penalty, although a rethrow must be taken if the illegal putt was successful.

Accurate foot placement on lies and tees is required and is self-policing. However, other players may inform a player of the violation and the ruling of a one-stroke penalty and rethrow after the first warning.

Abridged Rules and Procedures

Practice throws are not permitted. Each player is allowed a maximum of thirty seconds to prepare and make a throw to the target once the playing area is cleared and the previous player has thrown. This rule is self-policing, but other players may inform a player of the violation and the ruling of a one-stroke penalty and rethrow after the first warning.

If a throw comes to rest above ground in a tree or bush or some other permanent feature of the course, the subsequent throw must be made from a marker directly below the elevated spot but no closer to the hole.

If a throw lands out-of-bounds, where boundaries are clearly determined and enforced, the disc is brought in-bounds at the point where it left the in-bounds area, and a one-throw penalty is assessed. Other hazards, including ponds, lakes, and other fenced-off or restricted areas, are played similarly to out-of-bounds areas.

If a disc lands within bounds in an unplayable area due to standing water, muddy grounds, or manmade objects, the subsequent throw must be made from a marker positioned directly next to the area but no closer to the hole.

Teaching Considerations

1. The fundamental skills and techniques used in playing disc golf include the introduction and practice of various throwing styles and deliveries. It can be helpful for students to have the rules of the game and basic procedures of play discussed and demonstrated as many of these skills are practiced. Players might associate increased relevance to variations in throwing styles and deliveries by experiencing or visualizing the variety of game situations and circumstances.
2. Throwing skills improve with experimentation, guided instruction, and feedback. Helping students develop proficiency with one basic style of throwing is the first objective. A student who has developed confidence in one type of delivery might be encouraged to experiment with other styles. On the other hand, students might rely too much on one successful style and need to be encouraged and challenged to develop versatility.
3. Throwing drill work must accompany playing time. Correct and repeated practice conducted on and off a playing course is necessary for continued improvements of basic skills. Instructors are encouraged to invent challenging tasks and play scenarios for students as well as accommodate students with physical and mental disabilities.

GLOSSARY

approach shot Any shot in disc golf thrown with the purpose of gaining putting position.

attitude The angle of the disc with reference to the shoulder axis. Nose up is called positive attitude. Nose down is called negative attitude.

backhand A cross-body throw with the thumb on top of the disc and the fingers on the underside.

barrel roll Exaggerated turnover in flight.

basket The target in disc golf.

bend A curve steep enough to have a pronounced peak.

Berkeley grip A backhand grip with the forefinger hooked around the rim and the other fingers curled back and beneath the edge.

bogey Hitting a target in disc golf in one throw over par.

bomb A long downfield pass in ultimate.

brush A glancing slap on a disc in flight.

birdie Hitting a target in disc golf in one throw under par.

check A momentary delay in game during ultimate where the defender holds the disc as players get settled before handing the disc over to the offense.

closed stance The throwing position for a backhand.

cross-body Any catch or throw made with the arm reaching across the chest.

delivery The entire throwing motion.

defection Any change in the course of the disc's flight caused by contact with the disc's lip.

dip Any sudden drop during a disc's flight, particularly when the disc rises afterward.

disc golf hole A standardized golf hole and target.

discwork Any move or action of the body or hand to control a disc.

drop A missed catch in ultimate that falls to the ground.

eagle Hitting a target in disc golf in two throws under par.

edge The bottom-most portion of the rim of the disc.

facing stance A throwing position in which the thrower faces directly toward the target.

fairway The playing area considered in-bounds on each hole in disc golf.

fan grip A backhand grip with the forefinger along the rim and the other fingers spread out on the flight plate.

flight axis An imaginary line through the center of a flying disc from nose to tail.

flight plate The surface of a disc from rim to rim.

floater A hovering disc.

give and go A passing technique used in ultimate in which one player, after completing a short pass, sprints to catch a return pass.

glide phase The most nearly level portion of flight in the descent of a throw.

hover A type of flight in which the disc has little or no forward momentum and descends slowly.

hyzer (1) The tendency of a disc to rotate around its flight axis (most discs lift slightly at the roll shoulder). (2) The degree to which this tendency must be compensated for in the angle of release to produce the desired flight.

lie The spot where a disc comes to rest after being thrown in disc golf.

lip The outside rim of a disc.

marker A defensive player in ultimate who is guarding an offensive player in possession of the disc.

marker disc A mini-disc used in disc golf to mark the spot where a throw landed.

move Any act of throwing, controlling, or catching a disc, often used to refer to a series of discwork tricks as well.

multiple skips A steep skip flight that results in two or more skips.

normal curve A term sometimes used for a skip curve.

nose The leading edge of a disc in flight.

open stance The throwing position for forehand and overhand throws.

out-of-bounds The area beyond the field of play in both disc golf and ultimate, marked with boundary lines or otherwise, where a disc or player is considered out of play.

pancake (1) Trapping the disc between both hands. Also called a sandwich trap. (2) The flattening out motion of an upside-down lob throw.

par The predetermined average number of throws the tournament players in disc golf take to hit the target on each hole.

pick-up Any technique used to retrieve a disc from the ground.

propulsion Any technique used to impart spin to a disc.

rim The outer portion of a disc—the lip, rim, and edge.

roll curve A curved flight in which the roll shoulder is lower so that the disc tends to roll when it lands.

roll shoulder The shoulder of the disc that spins back toward the thrower.

set-up (1) Any method to impart spin on a disc without propulsion. (2) To get in position for a particular move.
shadow To guard or defend a receiver in ultimate.
shoulder axis An imaginary line through the center of a flying disc from roll shoulder to skip shoulder.
shoulders The sides of a disc in flight, 90 degrees from the nose or tail.
sidearm A forehand throw usually made with the middle finger underneath and against the inside edge of a disc with the thumb on top of the disc.
skip curve A curved flight in which the skip shoulder is lower so that the disc tends to skip when it lands.
spin axis An imaginary line through the center of the disc perpendicular to the flight plate.
stability The property of a disc to maintain flight at the angle of release—the ability to resist turnover.
stall A portion of some flights during which the disc loses forward momentum.
stalling A defensive call in ultimate when the passer is taking too much time; followed by a countdown.
stroke (1) Any throw in disc golf. (2) The forward-moving portion of the delivery.
tacking A disc's holding its course across a wind.
tail The rear end of a disc in flight.
tee-box The designated area in disc golf for taking the first throw for each hole.
throw-off The arrangement of teams in ultimate on their respective end zone lines and subsequent first throw by one team to the other.
tipping Control of a disc by finger contact with the flight plate.
touch Appropriate speed and spin in the act of putting in disc golf.
trap A type of catch in which the disc is stopped between any two parts of the body or even a part of the body and another surface.
turnover (1) Rotation of a flying disc about the flight axis. (2) A discwork technique in which the disc is turned from upside down to rightside up or vice versa.
wrist flip An overhand throw made with the thumb on the belly and the fingers fanned out on top.

ACKNOWLEDGMENT

The contents of this chapter contain information that has been copied and reproduced from earlier writings. Permission has been obtained to use all such material. The assistance provided by Dan "Stork" Roddick has been instrumental in the assembly of this information.

SUGGESTED READINGS

Roddick, D., and Boda, T. 1992. The *discourse,* 4th ed, San Gabriel, Calif.: Wham-O Sports Promotion. A basic introduction to skills that describes additional sporting contests and proficiency test formats for various skill levels. Copies of this publication can also be purchased through mail-order supply houses of disc sporting goods.

Tips, C., and Roddick, D. 1979. *Frisbee sports and games.* Millbrae, Calif.: Celestial Arts.

World Flying Disc Federation. Current edition. *The official rules of flying disc sports.* World Flying Disc Federation, 655 Rim Road, Pasadena, CA 91107. Copies of this publication can also be purchased through mail-order supply houses of disc sporting goods.

NEWSPAPER/JOURNAL ARTICLES

Altmyer, D. 1996. Disc golf fever: Will your park catch it? *Outdoor Recreation*, 1997. (National Recreation and Park Association), August.

Jenkins, C. 1997. Throw caution to the wind, flip a disc on Frisbee golf course? *The News and Observer* (Raleigh, N.C.), Sunday, June 29.

Prichard, O. 1997. Disc golf taking flight as recreational sport in mid-Iowa. *The Daily Tribune* (Ames, Iowa), Friday, July 5.

Schmid, S. 1995. Par for the course, *Athletic Business,* September.

U.S. Kids: Discover disc golf. *U.S. Kids: A Weekly Reader Magazine*, 6 (7), Oct/Nov 1993.

Walters, J. 1993. A sport for the disc-erning. *Sports Illustrated*, June 14.

RESOURCES

Freestyle Players Association, P.O. Box 2612, Del Mar, CA 92014.

Professional Disc Golf Association (PDGA), 65 Front St. West, Suite 0116-24, Toronto, Ontario, Canada M5J 1E6.

Ultimate Players Association (UPA), 3595 E. Fountain Blvd., Suite J2, Colorado Springs, CO 80910.

United States Disc Sports, c/o Bob Verish, 8550 Tujunga Valley Street, Sunland, CA 91040.

World Flying Disc Federation (WFDF), c/o Dan Roddick, 655 Rim Rd., Pasadena, CA 91107

Books, Films and Videotapes

Distributors

Circular Productions, P.O. Box 793, Austin, TX 78767-0792

Discovering the World, Box 911, La Mirada, CA 90637.

Disc Golf World, P.O. Box 4474, Overland Park, KS 66204

Professional Disc Golf Association , 65 Front St. West, Suite 0116-24, Toronto, Ontario, Canada M5J 1E6.

The Wright Life, 200 Linden, Fort Collins, CO 80524.

Ultimate Stuff, C Associates, P.O. Box 14520, Washington, DC 20003.

Wham-O Sports Promotion, 3830 Del Amo Blvd., Suite 101, Torrance, CA 90501.

Web Sites

WFDF: http://www.uka.de/~thgries/wfdf/
UPA: http://www.upa.org/~upa/
PDGA: http:www.discgolf.com/pdga/pdga.html
PDGA course directory: http//home.netscape.com/people/bfitler/pdgadir/
AOL: Keyword "Sports Boards," select "Other Sports" then "Flying disc sports"
USENET, go to rec.sport.disc or you can receive batch mailings by sending your subscription request which includes the word "subscribe" and your internet address to: ultimate-request@doe.carleton.ca

Fencing

After completing this chapter, the reader should be able to:

- Describe the historical development of fencing
- Differentiate between the various fencing weapons
- Cite the basic rules of the sport
- Demonstrate fundamental fencing skills
- Execute basic offensive and defensive fencing tactics
- Teach beginning fencing students using proper techniques, terminology, and safety skills

HISTORY

Fencing can be defined as the art and sport of swordplay. Its fascinating history begins with primitive people who engaged in crude forms of fencing almost as soon as they could fashion weapons. In the fourteenth century, Germany attempted to make dueling a sport rather than a deadly combat. Prospective members of German university fraternities stood trial by sword, and a scar on the cheek was a sign of manhood.

The first fencing schools were established in Spain in the fifteenth century and in Italy in the sixteenth century. Students traveled long distances to enroll in these schools and learn the secrets of the masters.

The invention of gunpowder rendered the sword ineffective as a major weapon of warfare. Dueling became an individual way to avenge insults or restore honor, rather than a means of mass combat.

In the eighteenth century, further influences on the development of fencing as a sport were the creation of protective equipment and the outlawing of dueling to the death throughout most of Europe.

Different types of swords were created by the Italians, French, and Germans, finally culminating in the modern fencing weapons: foil, épée, and saber. Schools of fencing instruction flourished throughout Europe. Heavy swords were replaced by lighter weapons to obtain greater speed, dexterity, and precision. Thus, this formerly deadly method of combat was converted into an internationally popular modern sport stressing skill, precision, and concentration.

Fencing has been an Olympic sport since the modern Olympics began in 1896. It will continue to be part of the Olympic scene, and fencing has become an international sport at many other events such as the Pan-American Games and the World Games.

The French and Italians won most of the fencing medals from the early Olympic years through the 1960s. Edoardo Mangiarotti of Italy amassed an amazing total of 13 medals (6 gold, 5 silver, and 2 bronze) between 1932 and 1956. Since the 1960s, Olympic fencing has been dominated by Eastern European and Soviet fencers, although the 1996 Olympics were again dominated by France (7 medals) and Italy (6 medals).

The United States has not fared well in the Olympics. Peter Westbrook's bronze medal in the saber in 1984 was the first individual medal the United States had won since 1960. In the 1996 Olympics in Atlanta, Georgia, the United States had one finalist, Ann Marsh, who placed seventh in the women's individual foil. In the team events, the U.S. men's and women's teams placed tenth in foil and eighth in épée, and the men's saber team placed ninth.

Fencing is important in a modern program of physical education and recreation. It demands a high level of physical conditioning and concentration. Fencing has long traditions of sportsmanship and honor. Fencing is suitable for all ages, both sexes, and physically challenged individuals. It can be enjoyed on many levels; the beginner will find as much satisfaction in a correctly executed action as will an expert in fencing a challenging bout. The rules permit men and women to fence all three weapons, and to fence each other in competition.

The new professional fencing league, which gets under way in 1998, will offer monetary rewards for fencers choosing to go professional. Information on the league is included at the end of this chapter.

OBJECT OF FENCING

The object of fencing is to win a bout by scoring five clean touches on an opponent's valid target area, which differs for each of the three weapons. If neither fencer scores five touches during the six minutes allotted for the bout, the winner is the fencer having the higher number of valid hits against the opponent. If the bout is tied when time expires, fencing continues without time restriction until one fencer scores a touch. In the foil and épée, the touch must be scored with the tip of the blade. In the saber, the tip and edges of the blade may be used to score.

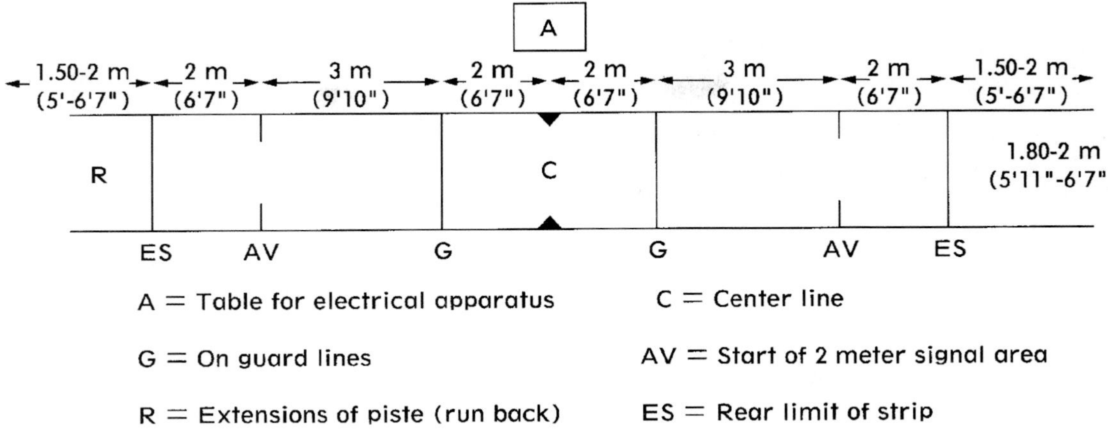

Figure 12-1. Regulation strip (called a "piste"), for all three weapons.

EQUIPMENT

1. Competition uniforms, made of nylon and/or Kevlar. For class, heavy duck is the best choice, both for price and durability.
2. Mask, with a sewn-in bib, to protect the face and neck.
3. For women, plastic breast shields, similar to ones worn by soccer players, or metal breast protectors. Women's jackets are provided with pockets to house protectors.
4. Soft leather glove that extends over the cuff of the jacket.
5. For saber, an elbow guard of leather or composite material (recommended).
6. Foil, épée, or saber, depending on what weapon is being taught.
7. Mats: the strips on which bouts take place. These should be 5 feet 11 inches to 6 feet 7 inches (1.8 m to 2 m) in width and 45 feet 11 inches (13.8 m) in length. Five parallel lines are drawn across the strip. The center line, which is a broken line across the strip, two solid on-guard lines, and two solid rear-limit lines. Additionally, the last two meters of the strip before the rear-limit lines must be clearly distinguishable—if possible, by a different color from the strip—to enable fencers to identify their position on the strip. (See figure 12-1.)

ABRIDGED RULES OF FENCING

In the United States, the governing body of fencing is the United States Fencing Association.

There are two types of competition, team and individual. A team consists of three persons. Each contestant fences a bout with each of the three opponents, for a total of nine bouts. The first team to win five bouts is considered the winner of the match.

In individual competition, many formats are used. Round-robin and single and double elimination are common formats.

General Procedures

1. When competition is nonelectric (now rare except in classes), the bout is judged by a jury of four judges and a head referee, a timer, and a scorer.
2. In nonelectric competition, fencers change ends of the strip after three touches have been scored, unless one fencer is left-handed, in which case the judges change ends of the strip. After the bout ends, each fencer *must* shake hands with the opponent. Refusal to do so results in expulsion from the tournament.
3. When the competition is scored electronically, the only officials needed are the referee, timer, and scorer.
4. The referee calls "Fencers ready" and then starts the action with a call of "Fence," and stops the action with a call of "Halt." The referee then applies the rules of right of way to decide who has scored the touch. The referee also assesses any penalties.
5. The clock runs only between "Fence" and "Halt." The timer signals when one minute remains in the

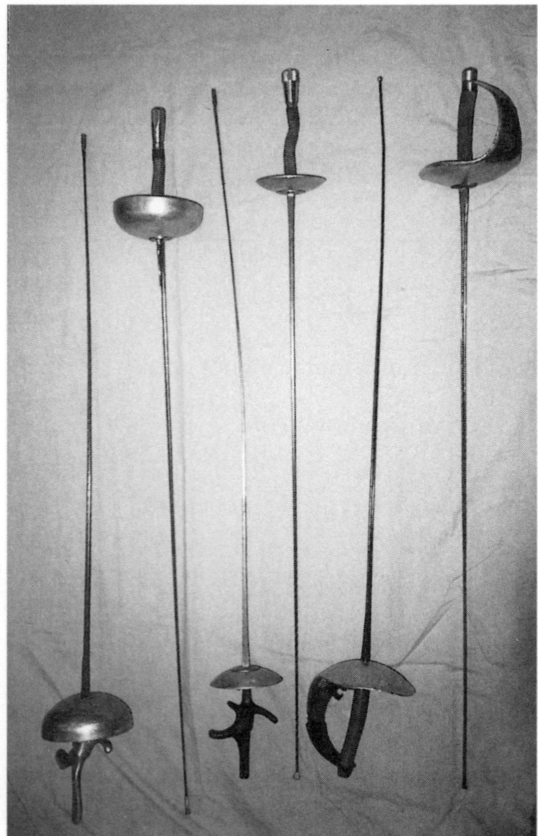

Figure 12-2. The fencing weapons. Standard weapons are depicted point down, electric weapons point up. Left to right: Electric épée, standard épée, electric foil, standard foil, electric saber, standard saber. Note that the electric foil is a pistol grip for a left-hander. The electric épée and saber are for a right-hander.

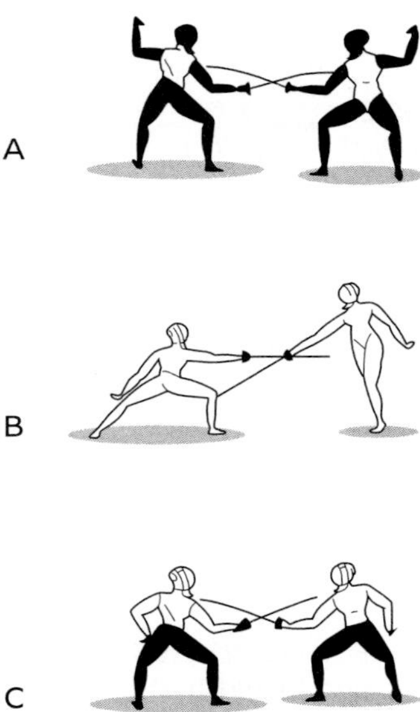

Figure 12-3. Legal targets for each weapon. Note that the legal target is the white portion of the figure. A, legal target in foil. B, legal target in épée. C, legal target in saber.

bout. Fencers may ask the referee the amount of time remaining in the last minute whenever the clock is stopped.

Method of Play

Fencers salute each other, then come on guard and wait for the command "Fence." They move up and down the strip, maintaining a safe distance from each other until one decides to attack. If the attack succeeds, the referee halts the bout and awards the touch. If the attack is blocked or parried by the fencer on the defense, the fencer who parried may then elect to attack, which is called a "riposte."

Modern Fencing Weapons

Foil

The foil (figure 12-2) is the basic weapon of fencing. It is a thrusting weapon. The maximum weight of the foil is 17.64 ounces (500 g), and its maximum length 33 inches (82.5 cm). A foil consists of a blade and the hilt. The blade is steel, quadrangular, and has three sections—the forte (the strongest third of the blade), the middle third, and the foible (the weakest, most flexible part of the blade, which ends in a buttonlike tip). The hilt is composed of the bell guard, usually referred to as the "guard," which is circular and concave to protect the hand, the thumb pad, the handle, and the pommel. Handles, or grips, are of varying types. They may be wood, cord wrapped, molded metal, or plastic. They may be straight or specially fashioned to suit the individual. The pommel is the weighted counterbalance to the back end of the foil. It screws into the tang (the section of the blade that fits into the handle) and holds the weapon together.

The target in foil fencing includes the trunk from the collar to the groin lines in front or to a horizontal line passing across the tops of the hip bones in the back (figure 12-3).

The scoring area in foil is covered by a conductive garment called a "lame." To be valid, touches in foil must:

1. Arrive on the target as the result of a thrusting action clearly and cleanly with the point, never with the side of the blade.
2. Be in accordance with certain conventions, or rules of order, called "right of way" or "privilege of attack."

Right of way is established by extending the weapon arm with the point of the foil clearly threatening the valid target of the opponent. The opponent (defender) must block (called a "parry") the thrust by the attacker. If the parry is successful, the defender may then extend his or her arm and attack, (called a "riposte"). These actions continue until one of the fencers successfully outwits the other and scores a touch.

In foil, touches made on the head, arms, or legs are called "off-target" and are not counted as valid. The referee will stop the bout for off-target touches, then restart the fencers from the point where the off-target touch occurred.

When both fencers are touched simultaneously, the touch is awarded to the one who has the right of way. If neither fencer has the right of way, no touch is awarded.

The first person scoring five touches within 5 minutes wins the bout. If the time runs out and the score is tied, fencing continues without time restriction until one fencer scores a touch.

Épée

The épée (figure 12-2) is also a thrusting weapon. Heavier and more rigid than the foil, it weighs 27 ounces (770 g) and has a maximum length of 43.2 inches (108 cm). The target for épée includes every portion of the body (figure 12-3).

Épée has no right-of-way convention. If both fencers are touched simultaneously (double touch), each is awarded a touch. If the score is tied after time expires, the bout continues until one fencer scores a single touch. Additionally, when the score is tied and time runs out, the score on the scoresheet remains 5–5, no matter how many touches are scored, and one fencer is credited with a victory and one with a defeat.

Saber

The saber (figure 12-2) is a weapon with cutting edges along the entire front and one-third of the back of the blade. Cuts as well as thrusts are valid.

The saber has a maximum weight of 17.5 ounces (500 g) and a maximum length of 41.2 inches (103 cm).

The saber target includes the head, arms, hands, and torso above a horizontal line drawn through the greater trochanter (hip bone) (figure 12-3).

Saber has the same right-of-way convention as foil and is scored the same way.

FUNDAMENTAL SKILLS AND TECHNIQUES

In fencing, the student must learn to coordinate movement of all body parts with the weapon. In addition, the student must also acquire a keen sense of distance and speed and the ability to think on the move and change tactics as the situation requires. The best definition of fencing is chess at 100 miles (160 km) an hour.

The French Grip

The convex side of the curve of the handle should be placed in the palm at the heel of the thumb. The thumb is placed on the top of the broad surface of the handle, close to the circular guard. The tip of the index finger is placed on the opposite side of the handle so that the foil is controlled with the thumb and forefinger. The other three fingers curl around the handle so that the fingertips rest on the concave surface and press the handle firmly against the base of the thumb. The wrist is held slightly flexed and supinated so that the pommel rests flat against the wrist in such a manner that when the forearm is extended the foil will form a straight line toward the opponent's target (figure 12-4).

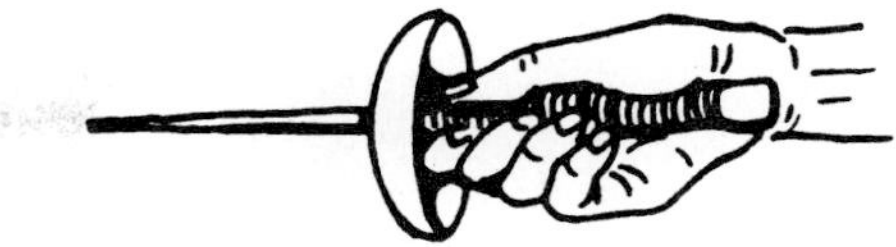

Figure 12-4. The French grip (top view).

On Guard

The on-guard position provides the best balance and efficiency in performing either offensive or defensive movements when advancing, retreating, or directly attacking. In this position, the body offers the smallest possible target.

Using the proper grip, the weapon arm is extended toward the opponent, the elbow flexed in an obtuse angle and held closely in line with the body. The hand is about level with the lower sternum, the weapon pointing slightly upward, directly toward the opponent's chest (figure 12-5).

In the on-guard position, the feet are placed approximately shoulder width apart and form a right angle, heels in line. The body weight is distributed evenly over both feet. The knees are bent so that they extend over the instep of each foot. The torso is held erect, with the dominant side and toe of the leading foot facing the opponent. The head is erect and turned to face the opponent. The non-dominant arm is raised behind so that the upper arm is horizontal, the forearm vertical, and the hand completely relaxed behind the head (figure 12-5).

Advance and Retreat

Advancing and retreating are the basic movements from the on-guard position. To advance, the forward foot is first moved forward and the other foot follows. To retreat, the rear foot is moved back and then the forward foot is moved back. The steps are short, varying from a few inches to about 1 foot (30 cm). The legs remain in the on-guard position, with the knees flexed. The purpose of the advance is to get within attacking distance of an opponent; the purpose of the retreat is to get out of reach of an opponent.

Figure 12-5. The fencer on the right is in the foil on-guard position. the fencer on the left is in the épée on-guard position.

Another advancing step used is a jump, called the "ballestra." In this jump, both feet leave the floor at the same time and regain contact with the floor at the same time. A jump back is sometimes used for retreating.

Thrust

To obtain the right of way, the thrust, which is the extension of the weapon arm, must precede all attacks. With the weapon held in the on-guard position, the arm is extended quickly but smoothly from the elbow. Be careful not to lock the elbow or elevate or hunch the shoulder. The point of the weapon should now be slightly lower than the hand and directed at the center of the chest of the opponent. When the tip of the blade lands, no additional pushing or jabbing should take place. Allow the hand to relax and lift very slightly as the hit is made so that the point of the weapon will bend down into the target and not upward, which could cause injury.

Lunge

The proper execution of the lunge is vital. The lunge is the method most often used to make a touch against an opponent. It is executed from the on-guard position and preceded by a thrust. After the thrust, the back leg gives a powerful push by extending fully, as the front leg lifts slightly from the ground. The front leg is driven forward by the push of the back leg and lands firmly, with the knee bent. The front knee should form a right angle, with the thigh parallel to the floor and the knee directly above the ankle. The back foot remains in place. Simultaneously with the lunge, the back arm extends fully (figure 12-6).

Recovery from Lunge

To recover to the on-guard position, bend the left leg and simultaneously push back with the right, then bring the forward foot back quickly to the on-guard position. The back arm, by being brought back into its original on-guard position, also aids in recovery from the lunge. During recovery the body should remain low.

It is sometimes necessary to recover forward to take up ground given by an opponent who is retreating from a lunge. This action simply involves bringing the rear foot to the on-guard position. This enables the attacker to defend if the attack has failed, to attack again, or to retreat if the opponent counterattacks.

Line

Before discussing attacks or defense, the concept of line must be addressed. For purposes of offense and defense, the target is divided into four areas called "lines." Historically, these lines are as follows:

Line 6: The line outside the defender's blade and higher than the defender's hand when the hand is in the on-guard position

Line 8: The line outside the defender's blade and lower than the defender's hand when the hand is in the on-guard position

Line 4: The line inside the defender's blade and higher than the defender's hand when the hand is in the on-guard position.

Line 7: The line inside the defender's blade and lower than the defender's hand when the hand is in the on-guard position.

Line 6 is the established on-guard line. Any line that is guarded is described as "closed"; any unguarded line is

Figure 12-6. The lunge. Note the lamé (metallic jacket) on the fencer on the right, which clearly defines the legal foil target.

described as "open." For example, in an on-guard 6 position, the 6 line is closed and lines 4, 7, and 8 are open. At any one time three lines will always be open. The attacker tries to attack to open lines only. "Changing the line" is an offensive move in which the attacker moves the blade from a guarded, or covered, line to an open line in the hope of making a touch.

SIMPLE ATTACKS

A simple attack is a single movement without feint or previous threat to an opponent's open line. The three main types of simple attacks are the straight attack, the disengage, and the cutover.

Straight Attack

The lunge, already described, is also referred to as a "straight attack."

Disengage

The disengage is accomplished by passing the point of the attacker's weapon around the bell guard of the defender's weapon, thereby changing from a closed line into an open line. The arm must be kept extended during the disengage to avoid losing the right of way, and the defender must not be allowed to parry the blade. The movement is V-shaped and is executed by the hand and fingers. The fingers are relaxed and allow the foil to drop below the bell guard and move to the open line. Then the fingers are tensed to bring the point of the foil back to the same level above the bell guard. The weapon is kept close to the opponent's weapon to keep the movement small. It may be necessary to do more than one disengage to find the open line if the defender is a fast parrier. The disengage can be used with or without a lunge.

Cutover

This simple attack is the opposite of the disengage: The tip of the weapon is passed over the tip of the defender's blade when the defender is defending in the high line, or under the defender's tip when defending in the low line. The action is executed by sharply lifting the tip of the weapon over the point of the defender's weapon, using the wrist and fingers only, not the whole forearm. The arm is extended as the weapon passes over the tip and forward toward the target. The cutover is principally used when a defender has lowered the weapon tip or used pressure with the weaker part of the blade against the forte (the part of the blade that is between the middle and the hilt—the strongest part of the blade) of the attacker's blade.

COMPOUND ATTACKS

Compound attacks are composed of more than one action. The first action is usually a feint, designed to draw a response from the opponent.

The Beat

The beat is a quick sharp blow by the middle of the attacker's blade to the weak part of the opponent's blade to make an opening or feint before an attack.

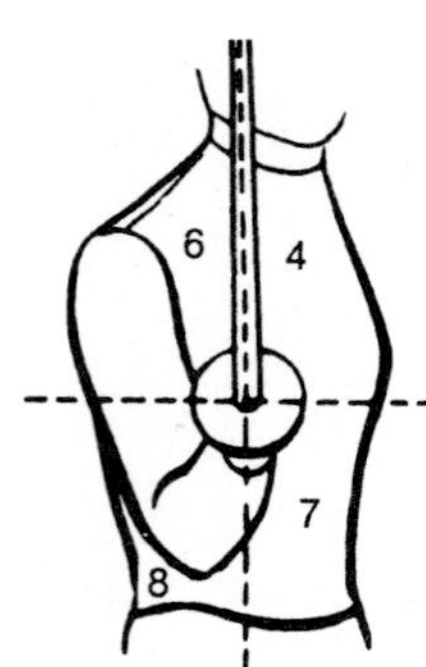

Figure 12-7. The four areas of the target.

The One-Two (or Double Disengage)

The attacker makes a disengage, as previously described, hoping that the defender will attempt to parry If the defender responds with a simple parry, the attacker avoids the blade contact and makes a second disengage back to the original line. Ideally, an attack occurs with the second disengagement.

The Doublement (Double)

The double also begins with a disengage, again hoping to draw a parry from the defender. If the defender responds with a circular parry, the attacker follows the defender's bell guard; that is, the defender passes the blade tip over and around the defender's bell guard to complete the attack in the line of the first disengage.

DEFENSE

Parries are lateral or circular defensive movements executed to deflect the attacker's blade so that a touch is not scored. When an attack is made, the defender moves the blade to a position that closes the target line being attacked. Parries of 4 and 6 are the most common parries because most attacks, especially at the beginning level, are made to the high target lines. For example, if the attack is directed to the 4 line, the defender uses the fingers to move the weapon just enough to cover the 4 area. If the attack is directed to the 6 line, the defender's blade is moved to cover the 6 area.

The parry is executed by placing the forte (strongest part of the blade) in contact with the opponent's foible (the part of the blade that is between the middle and the tip—the weakest part of the blade) in such a manner that the attacker's blade is deflected from the target. After parrying, the defender makes an immediate counterattack. The counterattack is usually a simple extension of the weapon arm, called a "riposte."

The target for defense is divided as for offense. The weapon hand must protect the four major areas, or lines. Parries are named for the line they protect. The parries are:

Parry 6: The point of the weapon is directed at the opponent's chest level, the weapon arm is bent at the elbow, and the hand is below the level of the point (figure 12-8A).

Parry 4: As in parry 6, except that the high inside of the target is covered. Note that the blade remains in line with the opponent's target to permit an immediate riposte (figure 12-8B).

Parry 8: The weapon protects the flank. The hand is above the point that is about knee level in height (figure 12-8C).

Parry 7: As in 8, except the blade is shifted to cover the inside low line (figure 12-8D).

Points to remember in parrying

1. The arm must be bent. Parries cannot be made with a straight arm.
2. Keep the lateral movements of the blade extremely small so that multiple parries can be made quickly.
3. Do not advance when parrying.
4. Keep the blade in line with the opponent's target while parrying.
5. Parry only hard enough to deflect the blade. Do not continue to push on the opponent's blade after parrying. Lighter parries permit quicker ripostes.

BASIC STRATEGY

To succeed in fencing, you must plan your moves. Before fencing an opponent, watch him or her to ascertain any weaknesses. Is the fencer right- or left-handed? Tend to be offense oriented or rely on defense? Have good or bad footwork? Move up and down the strip or tend to stay in one place? What is his or her favorite attack? What could you do to stop that attack from scoring? What would be the most effective attack against this particular opponent?

FENCING ETIQUETTE

1. Show respect for opponent by stopping the attack when he or she waves the back hand and calls for the referee to stop the bout.
2. Show a high level of fair play throughout the match. Call a "touch" on yourself whenever there is a question. Also call "off-target" when you hit an opponent in a nonlegal area.
3. Be totally familiar with the competition rules.
4. Acknowledge all touches.
5. Refuse all questionable scores.
6. Respect the decisions of the judges.
7. Always salute the opponent, the jury, and the referee before a bout.
8. If an opponent drops a weapon, withhold an attack until it has been recovered.
9. Shake hands with the opponent after the bout and thank the referee for presiding.

TIPS TO REMEMBER

Fencing weapons are used quite differently from weapons in other sports. In fencing, the weapon is used for thrusting

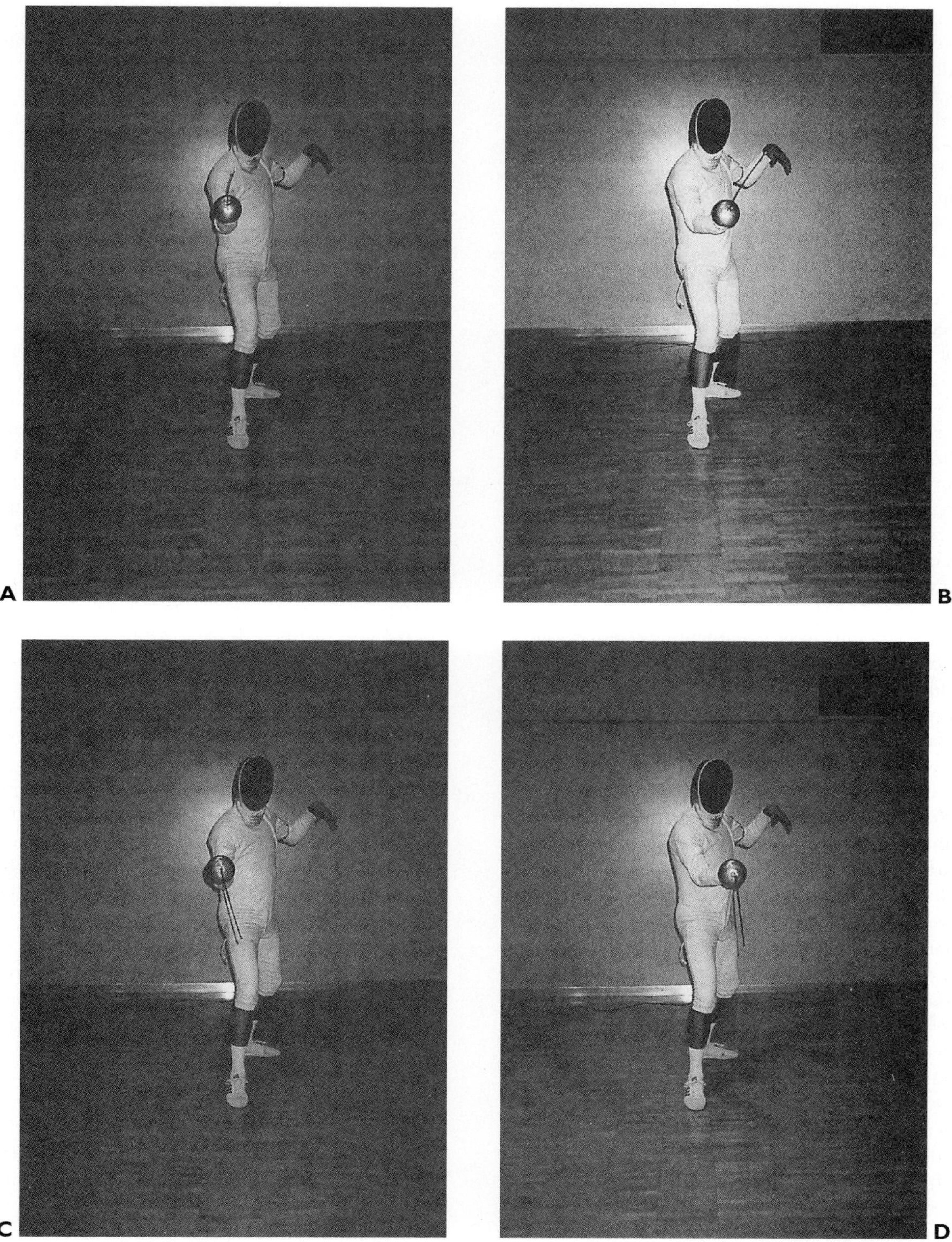

Figure 12-8. **A,** Parry 6; **B,** Parry 4; **C,** Parry 7; **D,** Parry 8.

rather than for hitting or swinging. Thus, it is essential for the beginners to learn the fundamental skills, because they are not skills that beginners ordinarily are accustomed to or carryovers from other sports. Fencing is a game of leverage. The defender uses the strong part of the weapon against the weak part of the attacker's blade and vice versa.

Although fencing places a premium on quickness, speed of reaction, finesse, agility, and dexterity, the sport has become increasingly aggressive, and therefore requires both strength and endurance conditioning.

TEACHING CONSIDERATIONS

1. Emphasize safety at all times. Follow the basic safety rule of fencing: Never point a weapon at someone not wearing a mask.
2. Always carry a weapon with the point toward the floor.
3. Make sure the weapon bends upward in the middle and down at the tip, to avoid dangerous hits.
4. Do not teach fencing to students who are likely to engage in horseplay or off-task behavior that could be dangerous.
5. Begin each class with students checking jackets for rips or tears, masks for dents, rust, or loose bibs, and weapons for wear on rubber/plastic tips.
6. Insist that students wear sweatpants and gloves, and that women also wear chest protectors, such as those worn for soccer. Tennis shoes are a must. Street clothes, especially with pockets, cannot be permitted.
7. After safety checks, begin by reviewing the previous lesson. Students need to repeat fencing basics over and over.
8. Teach only one or two new skills per session. Keep class interesting by devising drills that build mental skills as well as physical ones.
9. Don't permit rough or sloppy fencing.
10. Use the foil to teach basics. Begin with the grip and on-guard position. Then teach advance and retreat. Conditioning exercises and stretching might be necessary for students who experience muscle soreness from these activities.
11. All attacks can be practiced at a wall target first, with the four target areas clearly outlined. Then a passive defense can be added, with the defender responding first in a predictable manner, and then in an unpredictable one. Do not move on until students have the fine control of the foil necessary to make the practice safe.
12. Practice the lunge until the sequence of point thrust, extension of the back leg, kick of the front leg, and recovery are natural actions.
13. Specify the area of attack, parry, and riposte (for example, attack line 4 and defender parry 4 and riposte). Initially, specify the sequence of offensive and defensive roles; later move to self-initiated roles.
14. Practice all possible combinations of offensive and defensive sequences. Develop fencing terminology so that communication can take place.
15. As soon as students have a sufficient repertoire of offensive and defensive moves, include some periods of bouting, limiting the actions permitted.
16. Encourage students to learn to referee, as this will help them articulate the actions they see and develop their sense of right of way.

SUGGESTED DRILLS

1. Practice all footwork without blades until students are competent to practice these moves with weapons.
2. In leader-follower mode, two students practice footwork skills. The follower and leader try to keep an on-guard distance between them.
3. Ghost fencing—practice all action sequences without weapons. For example, when the leader makes a lunge, the follower must parry and then riposte. Practicing all sequences without weapons insures the correct reaction when weapons are used. This enhances both skill and safety.
4. In the on-guard position, the leader extends the blade toward the follower. The follower walks onto the point so that both learn that the touch is not painful. Try this drill with the advance and lunge also. Be sure blades bend correctly.
5. Practice the lunge against a partner. The partner should not permit a touch if the lunge is incorrectly made (figure 12–9).
6. To develop distance sense, allow one fencer to have a foil and one to be unarmed. The fencer with the foil initiates an attack from a stationary position. The unarmed one moves back only far enough to make the attacker miss. Additionally, this drill will develop reaction time and increase lunge speed.
7. Practice parries by placing the foil in correct parry position and letting the partner attack this position. If the parry is correct, the line will be closed and the partner will not be able to score a touch. Adjust position until this goal is achieved.
8. Place a penny or small coin under the heel of the front leg when fencer is in the on-guard position. On the lunge, the coin should shoot across the floor if the heel is kept close to the ground. If the front foot is lifted too high during the lunge, the coin will remain in place.
9. Use cones, gym lines, or a whistle to make fencers change directions quickly.
10. Tennis balls can be used to learn the correct method of making the thrust before lunging. Place a ball on the upturned slightly cupped hand. By extending the arm, toss the ball to a partner. Do this while advancing and retreating. Add the lunge to the drill.

GLOSSARY

absence of blade Blades are not engaged.

advance Move forward to gain ground.

attack Initial offensive action made by extending the arm and threatening the opponent's valid target.

attack of second intention Attack intended to be parried, so that the attacker may parry the riposte and score on the counter-riposte.

attack on the blade An attack used to move the opponent's blade off target by striking it sharply or pressing on it. The beat, press, and glide are considered attacks on the blade.

attack on the preparation A counterattack made during an opponent's preparation. To be valid the attack must land before the opponent's final movement begins, or the opponent must miss the target (see figure 12-10).

ballestra or **jump lunge** A forward or backward movement employing a jump before the lunge.

beat attack An attempt to create an opening for an attack by giving a sharp blow to the opponent's blade.

Figure 12-9. Practicing the lunge.

blade parts:

- **foible** Weak and flexible portion of the blade, comprising the third of the blade nearest the tip.
- **forte** Strong, inflexible third of the blade nearest the guard.
- **middle** Middle third of the blade.

bout A contest between two individuals.

circular parry A parry made in line opposing an attack—for example, the defender parries the attack by using a circular motion rather than a lateral motion, thus encircling the attacking blade.

compound attack An attack made up of more than one movement (e.g., a double disengage)

counterattack Offensive or offensive-defensive action made in response to the offensive action of the opponent (figure 12-10).

engagement Crossing and touching of weapons.

épée A type of fencing where touches are made with the point of a long, stiff weapon anywhere on the full body of the opponent. Épée is not governed by right-of-way conventions, and both fencers may score a touch during a fencing action.

fencing time The time required to perform one simple fencing action.

feint A movement of the blade designed to draw a parry or other reaction from the opponent.

fleche An offensive movement made by crossing the back foot in front of leading foot, usually followed by a short run (figure 12-11).

foil A type of fencing where touches are made with the point of a light, flexible weapon against a limited target on the opponent. The target consists of the torso, front and back, and excludes all other body areas. Touches falling on nontarget areas stop the bout and fencing is restarted at the point on the strip where the off-target touch occurred. Foil is governed by right-of-way conventions; only one fencer may score a touch as a result of a fencing action.

jury Four judges and the referee, who conduct the fencing bout.

match The aggregate of bouts fenced between members of two teams.

off-target Landing on an opponent in an area that is not a valid target area.

Figure 12-10. Counterattack.

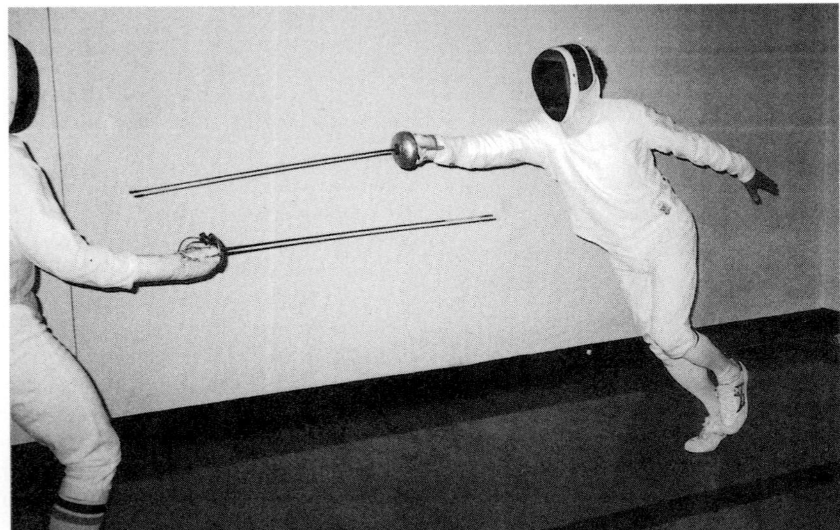

Figure 12-11. Fleche.

on guard The position taken by a fencer signaling a readiness to fence.

parry A defensive action made with the weapon to prevent a touch being scored.

pommel The metal piece at the end of the weapon that holds it together.

referee Director of a bout.

remise Following an attack, the defender does not riposte. The attacker may merely move the weapon so the point is replaced in the target area.

retreat To move backward to open the distance from an opponent.

right of way The right to attack. Established by a fencer who first extends the weapon arm with the point threatening a valid target.

riposte An offensive action of the fencer who has parried an attack.

saber A type of fencing where touches are made by the point or side of the weapon against the limited target on the opponent. The target consists of the entire body above a horizontal line between the top of the folds formed by the thigh and trunk of a fencer in an on-guard position. Touches on the nontarget portions of the body do not stop the action or nullify subsequent touches. Saber is governed by right-of-way conventions; only one fencer may score a touch as a result of a fencing action.

simple attack An attack made in one motion, without preliminary feints. The three simple attacks are straight thrust, cutover, and disengage.

SUGGESTED READINGS

Bower, M., ed. 1996. *Foil fencing.* 8th ed. Dubuque, Iowa: Brown and Benchmark. Descriptions of basic positions, techniques, and strategies for the beginning foilist. Also offensive and defensive drills, conditioning exercises, and bouting strategies. Good illustrations and glossary.

Evangelista, N. 1996. *Art and science of fencing.* Indianapolis, IN: Masters Press. History of fencing, types of equipment, specific techniques for all weapons. Highly readable.

Garret, M. 1994. *Foil, sabre, and épée fencing*. University Park, PA: Pennsylvania State University Press. A good resource for all three weapons.

Gaugler, W. 1992. *The science of fencing.* Bangor, Maine: Laureate Press. Classic Italian technique, 150 photos. For beginning or advanced fencers, all three weapons are covered.

Nadi, A. 1995. *On fencing*. Bangor, Maine: Laureate Press. Reprint of the famous classic work by possibly the greatest swordsman of our time. Philosophical as well as practical.

Werner, D. 1996. *Fencer's start up: A beginner's guide to traditional and sport fencing*. Start-Up Sports/Tracks. Especially written for beginners. Explains what it's like to learn to fence. All three weapons are covered. Two hundred photographs.

Westbrook, P. 1996. *Harnessing anger: The way of an American fencer*. New York, NY: Stories Press. Peter Westbrook's own story of how he overcame his inner-city background of adversity and used his anger to help him become a six-time Olympian—and a legend in the sport.

RESOURCES

Fencing Associations

Professional Fencing League, 18 Main St., Mechanicville, NY 12118. (518-366-5790). Journal and latest information on newly formed professional fencing league. Tournament schedules available. Web site: http://www.profence.com/fanclub.html

United States Fencing Association, 1 Olympic Plaza, Colorado Springs, CO 80909 (phone 719-578-4511; fax 719-632-5737). Web site: http://www.usfa.org E-mail: USFencing@aol.com. National governing body of fencing. Publishes *American Fencing Magazine*. Keeps all official records, has access to videotapes of Olympics and other competitions, and teaching videos.

Veteran Fencers Quarterly, 3075 Overlook Place, Clearwater, FL 34620 (phone 813-535-3404; fax 813-531-5766). E-mail: zippydav@aol.com. Voice of the veteran fencer. Interesting contrast to *American Fencing*.

Current Videos

Sabre Seminar with Fencing Master Nazlimov; Seminar in Épée, Foil, and Sabre. Each of these videos is available through the USFA.

Field Hockey

After completing this chapter, the reader should be able to:

- Describe the history and development of field hockey
- Be aware of important equipment selection and care considerations
- Understand the rules of field hockey and related games
- Execute the correct grip, dribble, strokes, and ball control skills
- Understand basic defensive and offensive strategies and formations
- Demonstrate fundamentals to a group of students
- Recognize and use field hockey terms correctly

HISTORY

About 2500 years ago the early Greeks and other ancient nations played a game very similar to our present-day hockey. Centuries later the game was being played in France and was called "hoquet." Then the English began to play it under the name "hokay." The game became generally known as hockey with its English spelling and pronunciation. However, later—when ice hockey, a similar game played on ice, became popular—the game of hockey was called "field hockey," and so it remains today.

Between 1880 and 1890 field hockey was played exclusively by men in England, France, and other European countries and is still popular with them. In the United States, men tried the game, but it met with little favor.

A group of women who formerly lived in England formed the Livingston Association—a field hockey club—on Staten Island, New York, about this time, but it was short-lived. Then in 1901 Constance M. K. Applebee, of the British College of Physical Education, demonstrated the game of field hockey during a visit to Radcliffe College. She recommended it as a health-building form of combative recreation for college women. Miss Applebee was then invited to several Eastern women's colleges (Smith, Vassar, Wellesley, Bryn Mawr, and Mount Holyoke), and on each campus field hockey was accepted with great favor. Women's teams were formed, and the first interclass contest was held in 1902.

The women enjoyed the game so much that they adopted it and revised the rules to make them uniform and suitable for women's play. In 1920 an American women's team traveled to England, and later an English team visited the United States to play games in Philadelphia, New York, Boston, and Baltimore, thereby establishing field hockey as an international game.

In 1922 the United States Field Hockey Association (USFHA) was formed in Philadelphia to govern the sport for women, its purpose being to advance the interests of hockey for women and girls. The game's popularity spread rapidly among schools, colleges, and clubs.

In 1927 the worldwide interest in field hockey brought about the International Federation of Women's Hockey Associations (IFWHA), and tournaments were held in Philadelphia and Denmark.

In 1963 the USFHA hosted 18 of the 25 IFWHA member nations. Plans were made for this federation to meet every four years for conference games and discussion of international rules and hockey problems.

The next conference was held in Cologne, Germany, in 1967, with the format unchanged. The first unofficial IFWHA World Championship was held in 1971 in Auckland, New Zealand. The Netherlands won the tournament, and the United States finished eighth. The first official World Championship was held in Edinburgh, Scotland, in 1975. England won the title, and the United States finished eleventh.

The second World Championship was held in Vancouver, Canada, in 1979. The United States improved to an amazing third in world standings. The Netherlands finished first and West Germany second.

The Fédération Internationale de Hockey (FIH)—until 1930 a men's group—controls Olympic hockey and has well over fifty members. Members conduct world championships between Olympics for both men and women. The IFWHA and the FIH united in 1981 to form a single international governing body.

With women's hockey introduced into the Olympics for the first time in 1980, a combined committee from both world organizations was formed to organize the methods, standards, and procedures for qualifying. The team from Zimbabwe won the round-robin tournament (six teams) to capture the first women's field hockey Olympic gold medal. The decision of the United States to boycott the Moscow Olympics cost the U.S. team the chance to compete, which they had earned in the 1979 World Championship. The appearance of both the men's and women's field hockey teams in the 1984 Olympics marked the first time in 28 years for them in this competition together. Although they had been ranked among the top six teams in the world in the early 1980s, it nevertheless came as a mild surprise when the women's field hockey team took the bronze medal in the 1984 Olympics by winning a stroke-off against Australia to break the tie for third place.

In 1988 the men's team from Great Britain won the Olympic gold medal, as did the women's team from Australia. The U.S. women's team finished eighth. In 1992 the men's team from Germany and the women's team from Spain won gold medals at the Barcelona Olympic Games. The U.S. teams did not qualify. At the Centennial Olympic Games in Atlanta, the United States was guaranteed a spot in the 1996 Games by virtue of being the host country. The women secured their highest Olympic finish since 1984, finishing fifth out of eight, but disappointment was evident as the team had hoped to win a medal in front of the large home crowds. The men's team was more competitive than in previous Olympic experiences, but was unable to win a game and finished twelfth out of twelve teams. The men's Olympic champion was the Netherlands, and the women's Olympic Champion was Australia.

Men's field hockey is popular around the world and has been in the Olympics since 1908. India and Pakistan dominated for years, but Germany, the Netherlands, and Australia have emerged as consistent world-class teams. The U.S. men's team has never been an influence in world competition. While most of the world focuses on producing a strong men's and women's team, the U.S. has struggled with a lack of a true player development system for male field hockey players. There are no college programs, and there are only limited club team opportunities for men to play their sport on a year round basis. The U.S. team has made strides with additional Olympic funding and access to facilities, but it has a smaller development pool of young athletes than other nations one-tenth their size.

In 1974, the USFHA sponsored a national collegiate championship for the very first time. Powerhouses such as West Chester State College, Ursinus College, and Lock Haven University were perennially the best collegiate teams. With the advent of athletic scholarships in 1975, slowly the composition of the tournament field changed. Larger schools, such as Penn State University, the University of Maryland, and the University of Massachusetts, began to dominate the championship scene. Field hockey championships were held from 1975 to 1981 under the direction of the AIAW (Association of Intercollegiate Athletics for Women). In 1982, the NCAA (National Collegiate Athletic Association) integrated women's sports into its traditional all-male championship structure. Women's field hockey national champions are now named in NCAA Division I, II, and III. In the 1990s, collegiate dynastics have been established by Old Dominion University and the University of North Carolina at the Division I level, Lock Haven and Bloomsburg University at the Division II level, and the College of New Jersey and William Smith College at the Division III level.

The NCAA now sponsors championships for women in Divisions I, II, and III. Over 225 colleges play around the country, with the highest concentration being east of the Mississippi River.

Indoor hockey is now quite popular in the winter months. Played by six players (five plus a goalkeeper), the game produces high scoring and lots of end-to-end action. The USFHA now sponsors national tournaments for adult men, women, colleges, and high school girls. While still not up to the level of European competition, the United States has seen a growth in this particular version of the sport.

GENERAL DESCRIPTION

The official game is played by two teams of 11 players on a grass field or artificial surface. Each player has a stick with which to propel and receive the ball. Each team attempts to put the ball into the opponent's goal, which is defended by a goalkeeper, the only player with special privileges and equipment.

The game should be modified in a variety of ways for youngsters, physical education classes, and intramural sports for maximum participation and fun. Games having two, three, or four players on each team in limited space, using cones as goals, are appropriate in these situations.

EQUIPMENT

Sticks

The implement for propelling and receiving the ball in field hockey is a stick (figure 13-1), which is commonly divided into two parts—the handle and the head—for discussion and selection purposes. The head, which is the playing part of the stick, is curved and must be flat on the left side and rounded on the right. Only the flat side may be used to play the ball. It is referred to as the "face" of the stick. The handle is thin and round for a comfortable grip. The handle is generally covered with toweling, rubber, or leather; the head of the stick is uncovered and is usually made of mulberry. The legal maximum stick weight is 23 ounces (644 g) for women and 28 ounces (784 g) for men; the minimum is 12 ounces (336 g). Most players choose a stick weighing 18 to 21 ounces (504 to 588 g). All sticks are "right-handed" only and thus cannot be played on the right side of the body.

The thin handle is preferred so that the stick's weight is in the head. The heavier the head, the easier it is to hit hard, but the more difficult it is to quickly and deftly maneuver the ball. The length can vary from 30 to 38 inches (0.77 to 0.97 m). Most high school and adult players should use 35-inch (0.9 m) sticks. Youngsters and junior high players use 30- to 34-inch (0.77 to 0.87 m) sticks. If the stick is slightly too long, the player can choke down a little.

Care of the stick includes treating the head with linseed oil and replacing the covering when it wears out and becomes uncomfortable. To prevent drying and warping,

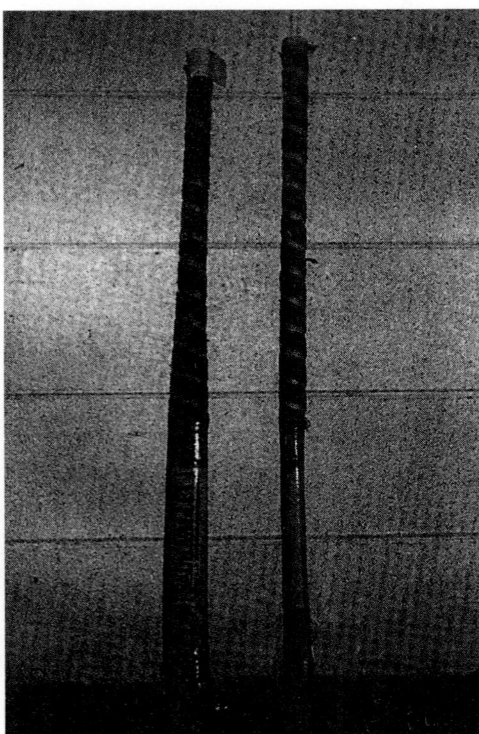

Figure 13-1. Hockey sticks.

the sticks should be stored in a horizontal position in a well-ventilated place.

Ball

The official ball is made of a hard polyurethane composition. The circumference is not more than 9¼ inches (23.1 cm) or less than 8¹³⁄16 inches (22 cm), and the weight is between 5½ and 5¾ ounces (157 to 164 g).

Shin Guards

Many types of leg protectors are available. Most are plastic with light padding inside. Like soccer guards, they fit comfortably into knee socks, and some have elastic straps that fit around the calf of the leg. Sockguards, ¾-inch (1.9 cm) foam rubber inserts in the sock, are popular. Players should wear shin guards to prevent injury.

Shoes

Cleated shoes are best for play on grass. The cleats may be rubber or plastic but not metal. On hard surfaces basketball shoes are recommended. Turf shoes are now available for play on artificial turf.

Clothing

The traditional uniform for males is shorts, shirt, and socks. For females it is a kilt, shirt, and socks. The goalkeeper plays in ice-hockey-style shorts and/or Lycra pants with a long-sleeve goalkeeping jersey of a contrasting color.

Figure 13-2. Goalkeeper's equipment.

Goalkeeper's Equipment (figure 13-2)

Pads. The goalkeeper needs to protect the legs up to midthigh. High-density foam pads have recently been introduced, and they provide great protection while enhancing mobility. Some players still rely on canvas or bamboo-style pads, but these do not provide nearly the protection nor quickness of foam pads.

Kickers. These are pads that fit over and around the shoe. High-density foam is also being used for kickers, which dramatically increases the protection of the foot from a hard shot. They are strapped behind and around the foot.

Gloves. Gauntlet-style gloves or ice hockey gloves are commonly used. The left palm is heavily padded, while the right palm is thinner to allow a comfortable grip on the stick. Recently, high-density foam "blockers" have been designed to allow for even more hand protection. Now goalkeepers can redirect the ball away from the goal cage rather than actually catching the ball.

Upper-body protectors. Shoulders, arms, chest, and stomach are all areas that should be protected. Lycra padded "pullover" protection, as well as fitted padding, are a necessary extension of harder shots and a more active goalkeeper. This equipment should always be used.

Throat protectors. They are made of foam that wraps around the neck like a collar. They are recommended for advanced players.

Helmets. Helmets are now required at nearly every level of play. They are similar to ice hockey helmets and have a full faceguard. Some keepers wear custom fitted face masks, but these are usually way beyond the typical budget.

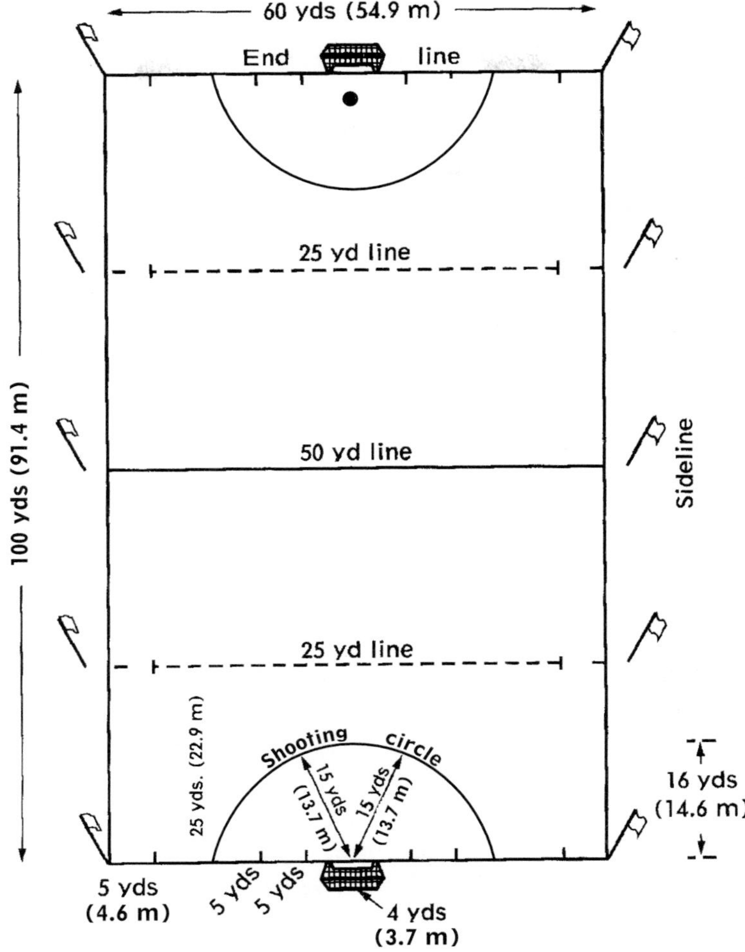

Figure 13-3. Plan of field of play.

DIMENSIONS OF FIELD

The hockey field (figure 13-3) is a little wider than a football field (100 × 60 yards) (91.4 × 54.9 m), with a goal at each end. Goalposts are 4 yards (3.7 m) apart and 7 feet (2.13 m) high, joined by a crossbar. The goal is enclosed by a net or wire screen supported by two additional posts 4 to 6 feet (1.2 to 1.8 m) behind the goal. A half-circle having a 15-yard (13.7 m) radius is drawn in front of each goal cage to designate the scoring area. A smaller field can be used for junior play.

RULES

Basic Rules

The game is played by two teams of no more than 11 players each. One player is designated goalkeeper.

Time of play varies according to the level of competition, but no more than two halves of 35 minutes each, with a 5-minute halftime, are played. To play-off a tie, up to two 15-miunute overtimes are played. If after the first 15 minutes the score is still tied, a second sudden-death period is played. If no goals are scored in the sudden-death period, the game can go into a stroke-off to determine a winner.

Pass-Back

To start the game or to resume play after halftime and after each goal is scored, a pass-back is played at the center of the field. The pass-back for the start of the game is made by a player of the team that did not make the choice of ends, after halftime by a player of the opposing team, and after a goal has been scored by a player of the team that the goal was scored against. Teams may cross the center-line at first touch. The pass-back may not be directed over the centerline.

Players other than the player making the pass-back must be in their own half of the field. Players on the opposing team must be at least 5 yards (4.6 m) from the ball. The clock is stopped on the official's signal for a goal and restarted on the official's whistle for a pass-back.

Coin toss

The captains toss a coin for choice of start or ends. The winner of the toss has the choice either of possession of the ball at the start of the game or of which end of the field to attack in the first half. The loser of the toss has the option not selected by the winner of the toss.

Scoring

Putting the whole ball over the goal line into the opponent's goal is a score. The ball must be touched by a member of the attacking team in the circle to count. Except in the case of a direct free hit, side-in, or long hit, the ball must first be touched by another player of the team in possession for the goal to count. Each goal counts 1 point.

Fouls

A player may not:

1. Play the ball with the round side of the stick.
2. Raise the stick in a dangerous way.
3. Propel the ball with any part of the body.
4. Play dangerously—that is, wildly or deliberately hit into an opponent or uncontrollably raise the ball.
5. Interfere in any way with an opponent's stick.
6. Trip, charge, shove, or interfere with any opponent's person or clothing.
7. Use the hand to stop or catch the ball.

Goalkeepers play by the same rules except that they may play the ball with their feet and may give an aerial ball slight impetus forward. Goalkeepers lose these privileges if they leave the circle.

No foul should be called when the fouled team is able to maintain an advantage and has the same or better opportunities than it had prior to the foul.

Penalties

1. When the foul occurs *outside the circle*, the opponents get a free hit from the spot where the foul occurred. An intentional, flagrant foul inside the 25-yard line results in a penalty corner.
2. When the foul occurs *inside the circle by an attacker*, the defenders have a free hit anywhere in the circle.
3. When the foul occurs *inside the circle by a defender*, the attackers have a penalty corner.
4. When a foul is committed *inside the circle by a defender, and a certain goal was prevented*, a penalty stroke is awarded to the attackers.

Offside

In 1996, the offsides rule was eliminated in field hockey, dramatically changing the defensive styles and scoring opportunities for the attach and expanding the role of the goalkeeper.

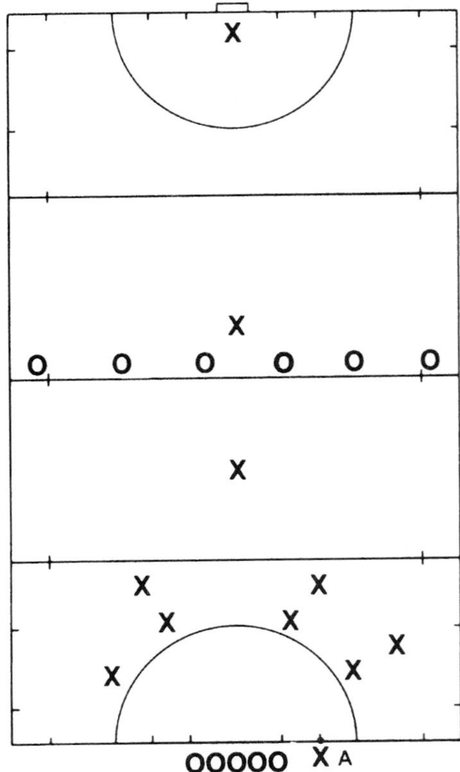

Figure 13-4. Field hockey penalty corner.

Free hit

The free hit is taken on the spot by any member of the fouled team. An exception is when the offense fouls in the circle. In this case the defense may take the free hit anywhere in the circle.

The ball should be motionless, and the striker may use any legal stoke. The ball may not be raised, At the moment the free hit is taken, no player of the opposing team may be within 5 yards (4.6 m) of the ball. However, should the umpire consider that a player is standing within 5 yards in order to gain time, the free hit is not delayed.

For a free hit awarded to the attacking team for a breach of rules within 5 yards of the circle, at the moment when the free hit is taken both teams must be 5 yards off of the ball. After a free hit is taken, the striker may not touch the ball again until it is touched by someone else.

Penalty corner

1. The corner hitter (Player XA in figure 13-4 hits or pushes the ball along the ground from a spot no closer than 10 yards (9.1 m) from the near goalpost on the side of the team's choosing. Lifting the ball is a foul. The hitter may straddle the endline. The player may not touch the ball again until it is touched by someone else.

2. Any of XA's teammates may be receivers. No member of the team may have any part of the body or stick in the circle until the ball is hit. No member may be closer than 5 yards (4.6 m) to the corner hitter. The receiver must control the ball before shooting, and passes or deflections must be controlled before the shot is taken unless a defender touches the ball. In college and international competition the ball must be stopped dead.
3. The defending team may have no more than five players on the endline. The remaining six must go to the 50-yard (45.5 m) line. Their bodies and sticks must be behind the line until the ball is hit; then they may move to defend. No defender may be closer than 5 yards to the corner hitter.

Penalty stroke

The penalty stroke is between the goalkeeper and any member of the fouled team:

1. The goalkeeper is not permitted any change in dress or equipment. The keeper must have part of the feet on the goal line and may not move them until the ball is stroked. At the moment the ball is stroked, the goalkeeper may use all legal means to prevent the ball from going into the goal. The goalkeeper need not clear the ball.
2. The stroker is 7 yards (6.4 m) from the center of the goal line. The stroker may push, flick, or scoop but may not hit. The stroker lines up with the feet behind the ball and is permitted one stride prior to stroking the ball. Dragging or lifting the back foot is not considered a step unless it passes the front foot before the ball is shot. The ball may be touched only once, and the attacker must execute smoothly and continuously with no faking or deception. When the whistle blows, the attacker has 5 seconds to execute the stroke.
3. All other players of both teams shall be beyond the nearer 25-yard (22.9 m) line.
4. A successful goal is followed by a pass-back. An unsuccessful shot gives the defending team a 16-yard (14.6 m) hit opposite the center of the goal line.

Out-of-bounds

1. When the ball goes out-of-bounds *over the sideline*, the opponents receive a side-in.
2. When the defending team unintentionally sends the ball over the endline from within its 25-yard (22.9 m) area, a long hit shall be taken by the attacking team. A player from the attacking team shall hit the ball from a spot on the end line within 5 yards (4.6 m) of the corner flag nearest to the side where the ball crossed the goal line.
3. When the ball is hit *over the endline by the attack*, a 16-yard (14.6 m) hit is awarded to the defense.

Side-in

Any member of the team may push or hit the ball into play from the spot where it went out-of-bounds. The player's feet may straddle the sideline. At the moment the side-in is taken, players on the opposing team must be 5 yards (4.6 m) away. After taking a hit-in, the player may not touch the ball again until it is touched or has been played by another player of either team. The side-in must be kept on the ground.

16-yard hit

The ball is hit from any spot not more than 16 yards (14.6 m) from the endline opposite the point where the ball went out of bounds. All rules of the free hit apply here.

Fouls on push-in or free hits

1. When the foul is by the hitter, the opponents are awarded a hit-in or free ht on the same spot. The exception is a foul by a player taking a free hit in the circle, in which case the opponents are awarded a penalty corner.
2. When the foul is by the opposition, the play is repeated only if the foul gives the opposition an advantage.

Fouls on penalty corners

1. When the foul is on the attacking team on a penalty corner, the defense has a free hit anywhere in the circle or 1 yard (0.91 m) outside the circle in line with where the foul occurred.
2. When the foul is by the defense, the play is repeated only if the violation gives the opposition an advantage.

Rules for Indoor Hockey

The rules are generally the same as for field hockey unless noted otherwise. Two exceptions are that no lifted balls (except on a goal) and no back swing strokes are allowed. The game is played by two teams of six players. Each half lasts a maximum of 20 minutes.

Starting and restarting the game

At the start of the game a pass-back is made by the player of the team winning the toss, and after a goal it is made by a member of the team scored against. The pass may or may not be forward. All players must be in their half of the court, and no one except the passer may be closer than 3.3 yards (3 m) from the ball. No player shall cross the centerline until the ball is pushed.

Playing area

The court is rectangular, 43.8 × 21.9 yards (40 × 20 m). When possible, sideboards 4 inches wide and inclined slightly inward will surround the area.

Circle

The circle measures 10 yards (9.4 m) instead of 15 yards (14.1 m). On narrower-than-regulation playing areas the

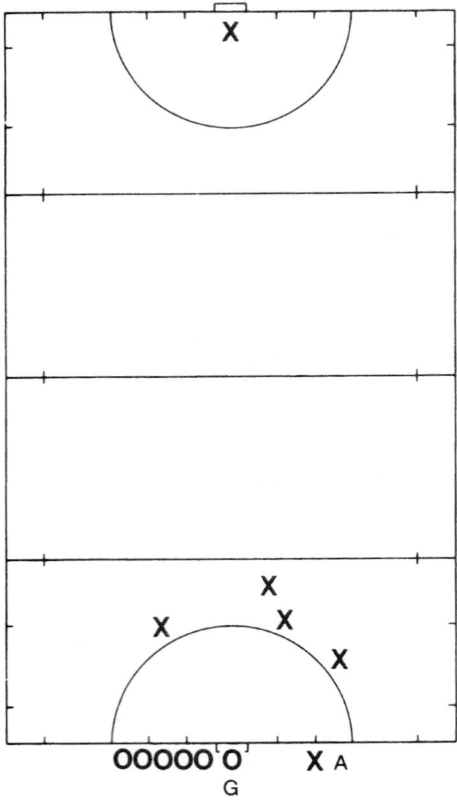

Figure 13-5. Indoor hockey penalty corner.

circles will meet the sideline. Penalty corner marks will be 6.6 yards (6 m) from the goalposts, and the penalty stroke will be 6.6 yards (6 m) from the center of the goal mouth.

Fouls

A player may not:

1. Hit or play the ball in the air.
2. Take part in the play while lying on the ground unless the player is the goalkeeper.
3. Hit the ball.
4. Lift the ball outside the circle.

Free pushes

Free hits are referred to as "free pushes." All players must be at least 3.3 yards (3 m) from the pusher.

Penalty corners

Offense.

1. The pusher is 6.6 yards (6 m) from the near goalpost.
2. No one may be within 3.3 yards (3 m) of the pusher.
3. The half or game shall be prolonged to complete a penalty corner. The corner is over when the ball leaves the circle or a goal is scored.

Defense. All players may defend, but they are on the endline opposite the side of the pusher. No player other than the goalkeeper is allowed in the goal (figure 13-5).

Out-of-bounds over the sideboards

Any ball that goes over the sideboards is put in play by a member of the opposite team 1.1 yards (1 m) from the sideboards but not in the circle. No one may be within 3.3 yards (3 m) of the pusher.

Out-of-bounds over the endlines

No matter who sends the ball over, the defending team gets a free push inside the circle. The exception is when a defender deliberately sends the ball over the endboard or makes no effort to keep it in play; then a penalty corner is awarded.

FUNDAMENTAL SKILLS AND TECHNIQUES

Stickwork

Key focal points

1. Grip: left hand at top; V of thumb and forefinger down the side of the stick; right hand comfortably wrapped around the stick midway down (figure 13-6).
2. Eyes should be focused on a point about 2 yards (1.8 m) in front of the ball, but *scanning* is important—you need to be able to see 180 degrees around you. Looking up is also important!
3. Forehand dribbling: The ball should be positioned off the right front foot, slightly out to the side. There are two types of forehand side dribbles: close and loose.
   a. Close: The ball rests against the stick at all times—no tapping! This is to be done in traffic, and you *always* need to be ready for a sudden change of direction.
   b. Loose: The ball stays within 3 feet (0.9 m) of stick; stick angle goes backward to a 45-degree angle *underneath* the ball; hands slide up the stick. The ball is pushed more in front of the right foot.
4. Backhand dribbling: The left hand controls the ball: the right hand is off the stick. Be sure to make the grip change by rotating your top hand one quarter turn to the left. The ball is in front of left shoulder, outside of the left foot. Be careful not to let the ball drop behind your left shoulder—it's obstruction!

Spin Move

1. Your plan should be to end up with possession in a space with time to make a good pass or dodge. Don't roll into traffic!
2. Begin your move by taking the ball on a slight angle toward one foot of your defender. You need to initiate your spin *well ahead* of the defender because you cannot make contact (no bump and run!), and you need to create the space for your body to move into.

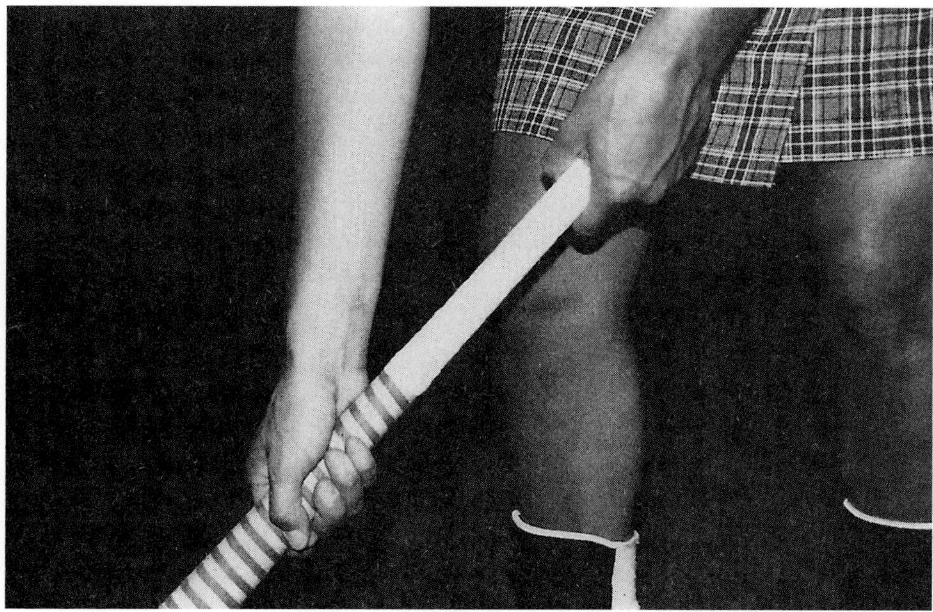

Figure 13-6. Grip.

3. Protect the ball with your body as you roll. More importantly, keep the ball ahead of your feet as you move so you don't get stuck.
4. Finish by going on a 45-degree angle to space—and look up!

Dribble

The ultimate objective is for each player to develop a rhythm and harmony between self and the ball, at speed, over varying distances, and against all kinds of opposition. The dribble (figure 13-7) is needed to gain ground, to set up a pass by drawing an opponent, and to beat or dodge an opponent. In open field the straight dribble (the ball moves in a straight line) is best. Before passing or beating an opponent, the Indian, or zigzag, dribble (the ball moves ahead but in dong so it alternately moves diagonally left and right) is best because it is quicker and can be more deceptive.

Grip

Straight dribble. The back of the left hand now faces obliquely up and over the right shoulder. The back of the right hand faces backward.

Zigzag dribble. When the ball is moved left, the back of the left hand faces the same as in the straight dribble. When the ball is moved right, the back of the left hand faces the ground. The back of the right hand faces right throughout the dribble.

Wrists and arms

Straight dribble. The left wrist and forearm are a straight extension of the stick. The arm is at 90 degrees at the elbow, which is 10 to 12 inches (25 to 30 cm) from the body. The right wrist is hyperextended, and the right arm is straight.

Zigzag dribble. This is the same as the straight dribble except the left arm is almost straight out in front of the body and the right wrist is straight.

Body and head

Straight dribble. The body is slightly left of and behind the ball, and the center of gravity is slightly lower than when running without the ball. The head is up as often as possible for increased vision.

Zigzag dribble. The procedure is the same as in the straight dribble except the body is directly behind the ball. In a one-on-one play the player swerves downfield rather than run in a straight line. Lifting the head frequently is essential.

Feet and legs

Straight dribble. Both feet are slightly left of and behind the ball. With balance, one can run quite fast without losing the ball.

Zigzag dribble. Both feet are directly behind the ball; the player runs fast, with sudden changes of pace and direction to get around opponents quickly.

Stick

Straight dribble. The stick is angled across the body at 45 degrees. The top of the handle is opposite the left thigh. The face of the stick faces the direction in which the player is moving and is ahead of and slightly to the right of the right foot.

Figure 13-7. Dribble.

Zigzag dribble. The stick is angled straight out in front of the body. The left hand grip rotates one-quarter turn counterclockwise to accommodate the reverse stick. When moving the ball left, the face of the stick faces diagonally left. When moving the ball right, the stick is turned over and the toe is down, moving the ball diagonally right. Playing the ball with the toe down is referred to as "reverse stick." The stick is turned by the left hand through a relaxed right hand. The back of the right hand faces right throughout every move of the stick in the zigzag dribble.

Ball

Straight dribble. The ball is 14 to 18 inches (35 to 45 cm) in front of and slightly to the right of the right foot. It is propelled forward in a series of short taps, imparted principally by the right hand.

Zigzag dribble. The ball moves alternately left and right diagonally 14 to 18 inches (35 to 45 cm) out in front of the body. The ball should not be allowed to get outside either foot.

Common faults

1. The wrist bends so that the forearm, wrist, and stick no longer form a straight line.
2. The player fails to keep the stick at 45 degrees away from the feet.
3. The ball is too close to the feet.
4. The eyes become riveted to the ball. The player no longer scans the field for options.

Push

The push (figure 13-8) is used for passing over short distances. It is characterized by the absence of a backswing, which allows for quickness in execution and disguising the direction of the pass until the last instant.

Grip

Using the continental grip, the back of the left hand faces obliquely up over the right shoulder. With the traditional grip the back of the left hand faces the intended direction of the pass. The back of the right hand faces backward. Unless player is very strong, the right hand is halfway or farther down the stick.

Wrists and arms

The hands work together in a common motion. Beginners tend to use a shovel motion rather than a dragging motion.

Body and head

The body is inclined forward with the head over the ball. The left shoulder faces the intended direction of the pass. The body weight is back on the right foot before the push. The weight shifts to the left foot as the right hand and wrist push the ball. The body on the follow-through is low and at full stretch.

Feet and legs

The left foot is forward a little more than shoulder's width from the right foot. The feet are parallel and slightly angled. The legs are bent, and the right leg extends on the

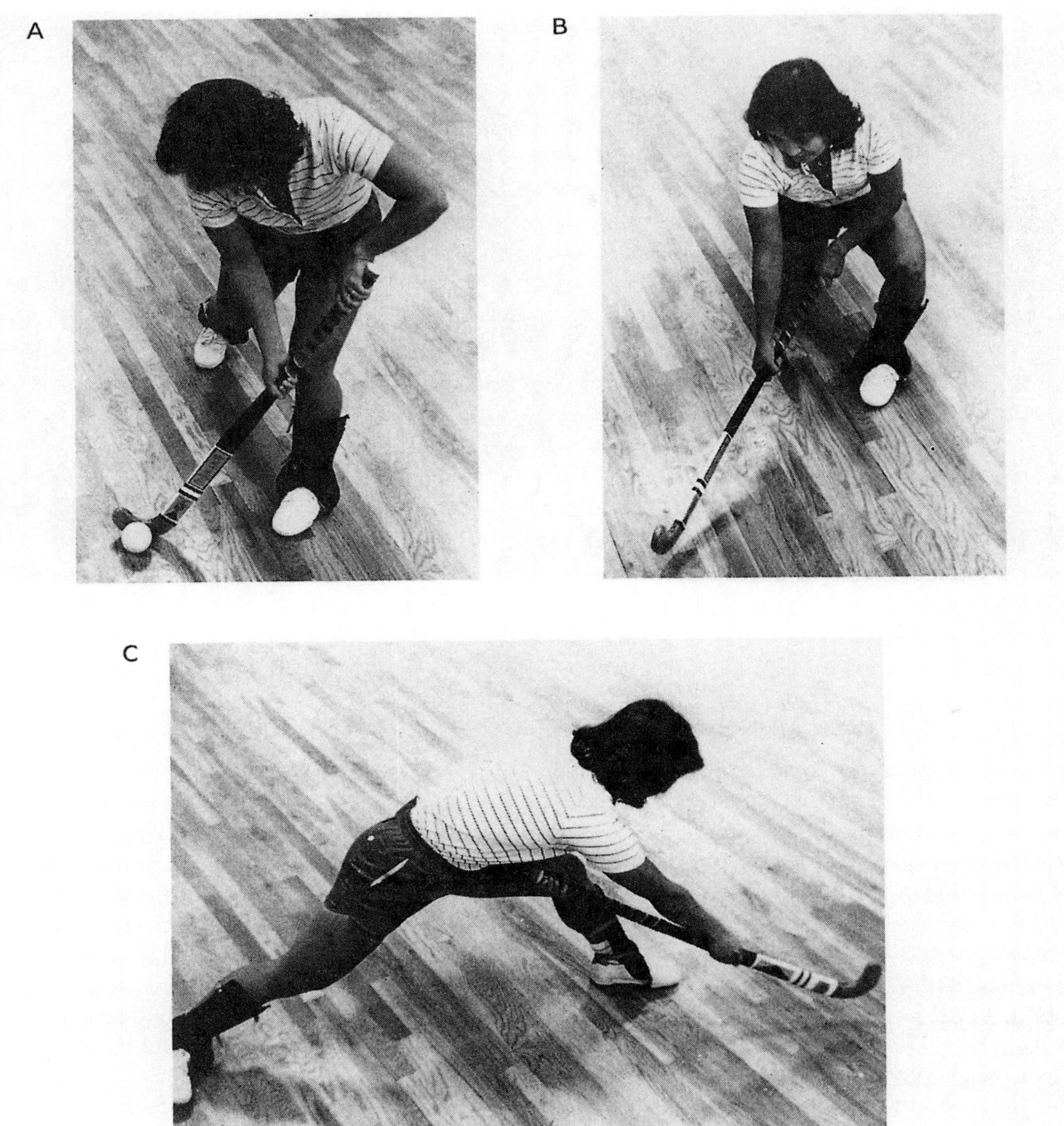

Figure 13-8. Push. **A** and **B,** Front views. **C,** Side view.

follow-through. The ball starts slightly behind the midline of the body.

Stick

The stick is angled about 45 degrees across the body, with the handle slightly ahead of the head of the stick. The face of the stick is directly behind and on the ball. The stick follows through the ball in the direction of the push as far as possible.

Common faults

1. The player is unable to coordinate weight transfer.
2. The left shoulder is not brought around.
3. The stick is held vertically instead of angled.
4. The hands do not work together, moving across the body.
5. The player fails to follow through.
6. The right foot is forward.

Receiving Skills

Ball control is the ability to bring any ball coming at you from any direction under control—to "catch" it. The ball's speed is deadened on the face of the stick. Ultimately, players should be able to play the ball immediately upon receiving it.

Figure 13-9. Ball control. Ball coming from the left.

Figure 13-10. Ball control. Ball coming from the right.

Grip

Ball coming toward the player. Both hands are relaxed enough to absorb the ball and stop it dead. A 45-degree angle is sometimes used to "trap" the ball.

Ball coming from left. Allow the ball to come across your body and receive it off your right foot. The stick is stationary (figure 13-9).

Ball coming from right. Allow the ball to come across your body and receive it off your left foot. The stick is stationary (figure 13-10).

In receiving any ball, the right hand, which is comfortably down the stick, is very relaxed so that it can move the face of the stick behind the ball and then act as the major factor in cushioning the ball and preventing deflections.

Wrists and arms

Ball coming toward the players. The left wrist and forearm are straight extensions of the stick, with the left elbow bent at 90 degrees. The right wrist is hyperextended, and the right arm is comfortably straight.

Ball coming from left. The left wrist and arm are straight extensions of the stick. The right wrist and arm are straight.

Ball coming from right. Taking the ball midstride, both arms and wrists are the same as when the ball is coming toward the players. Taking the ball reverse stick, both arms and wrists are the same as when the ball is coming from the left.

Body and head

When receiving any ball, the player must concentrate enough to see the ball make contact on the face of the stick.

Ball coming toward the player. The body is behind and slightly left of the ball.

Ball coming from left. The body is inclined forward.

Ball coming from the right. Taking the ball midstride, the body twists 90 degrees right from the waist to face the oncoming ball. Taking the ball reverse stick is the same as when the ball is coming from the left.

Feet and legs

Except when taking a ball from the right in midstride, the feet must be sufficiently behind the ball to prevent overrunning it.

As in other sports, players must be prepared to go to meet the ball or the pass will be intercepted.

Stick

When fielding any ball and at the moment of contact, the face of the stick must squarely meet the ball. The face of the stick must be inclined slightly toward the ball to trap it and keep it on the ground.

Ball coming toward the player. The stick is angled 45 degrees across the front of the body. The handle is opposite the left thigh, and the head is on the ground forward of and slightly right of the right foot.

Ball coming from left. The stick is angled forward in front of the right foot. The toe is up.

Ball coming from the right. Taking the ball midstride, the stick is angled across the body with the handle slightly higher than and left of the left knee, and the head of the stick is on the ground out from but between the feet. In reverse stick the stick is angled forward opposite the left foot with the toe down.

Ball
The ball, after contact with the stick, is in position to be dribbled, pushed, hit, or shot. Deflections and rebounds are acceptable as long as they are not dangerous.

Common faults
1. The face of the stick is not square to the oncoming ball.
2. The left wrist is bent.
3. The right hand is too tight, so the player does not feel the ball on the stick.
4. The player moves the stick into the ball rather than absorbing its speed.
5. The top of the stick is not angled forward, creating upward deflections.

Hit
The hit moves the ball far, hard, and decisively to any part of the field. It is a necessary complement to the push because it allows for the big game by opening up and spreading the play. A "good ball" is a hard, accurate pass that hugs the ground and can be handled by the receiver. Although the following are components of the hit, successful execution is one action; that is, the backswing, downswing, hit, and follow-through combine in one continuous motion (figure 13-11).

Grip
Preliminary. The traditional grip is used with the back of the left hand facing the intended direction of the pass. The right hand is directly under and touching the left, with the back facing right. The *V* formed by the thumb and index fingers on both hands are in line with the toe of the stick. In most cases the right hand slides up to the left, but some prefer to slide the left hand down. Quickness, not power, is gained.

Backswing. The same grip is used.

Hit and follow-through. The hands grip tighter at contact.

Wrists and arms
Preliminary. Wrists and arms are straight and out from the body.

Backswing. The stick is brought back with the arms and wrists, which do not touch any part of the body. The wrists are about waist height, firmly cocked, so that the head of the stick is higher than the wrists. The arms move together on the backswing with the right arm rotated and slightly bent. The right elbow points back, about 6 inches (15 cm) away from the body. Hands are 5 to 7 inches (12.5 to 17.5 cm) off the hip. The toe of the stick should point up at the end of the backswing.

Hit and follow-through. Transfer the weight from the right foot to the left on the downswing with the left foot (even with the ball at contact). The arms, wrists, hip rotation, and weight transfer provide a strong hit. The muscles of the arms and wrists, like all muscles, must be tensed on impact but relaxed on the backswing and follow-through. Follow through until the arms are parallel to the ground.

Body and head
The head is over the ball throughout.

Preliminary. The body is turned so that the left shoulder faces the intended direction of the pass.

Backswing. The weight is shifted to the rear foot.

Hit and follow-through. The weight is shifted to the front foot just before the stick makes contact with the ball. The force of the swing should naturally bring the body through in the direction of the hit.

Feet and legs
Preliminary. The feet are about shoulder-width apart and pointed at right angles to the direction of the hit. The left foot is ahead of the right. The legs need to be firm, strong, and slightly flexed.

Backswing. Same feet and leg positions are used. A slight hip rotation is important.

Hit and follow-through. At impact the leg muscles must be tense but not rigid, with the knees slightly bent.

Stick
Preliminary. The flat side of the stick is placed directly behind the ball, facing the intended direction of the pass.

Backswing. The stick goes straight back, not behind the right shoulder. The toe is above the wrists and pointing slightly upward.

Hit and follow-through. The stick is vertical at impact, and it clearly continues in the direction of the hit until the head reaches waist height and there is no more upward movement. The toe is again pointing slightly upward.

Ball
Preliminary. The ball is a comfortable distance from the body and is slightly behind the left foot at the moment of impact due to the step.

Hit. After being struck by the middle of the face of the stick, the ball should travel smoothly along the ground.

Common faults
1. Choppy, lofted, or sliced hits because of poor arm and hip synchronization.
2. Topping the ball because of not keeping the eyes on the ball throughout the hit.
3. The left shoulder is not around far enough, causing misdirection.

Figure 13-11. Hit. **A,** Backswing. **B,** Contact. **C,** Follow-through.

4. The arms are too tight in on the body, restricting their movement.
5. The right elbow is bent, weakening and making the hit awkward.
6. Only the wrists or only the arms are used.
7. Failure to follow through.
8. Carrying the stick in a backswing position for several yards, thus telegraphing intentions.
9. Trying to "overhit" the ball.

Flick

The flick is a lofted stroke that is used to score goals and to clear over the opponents. The basics are the same as the push, with the following differences:

1. The stick must not only be behind the ball but also slightly under it.
2. The ball is positioned slightly more forward just prior to the flick.

3. The right shoulder and elbow drop behind the ball on a 45-degree angle to enhance the height of the flick.

Tackle

The tackler wants to dispossess the opponent of the ball. If that is not possible, the player can, by the pressure exerted, force passes that can be intercepted by teammates.

Jab

The stick is held with a "frying pan" grip. The tackler attempts to jab underneath the ball and pop it over the dribbler's stick. The tackler needs to pull the stick back immediately and protect the feet. Body position for this tackle is square and in front of the dribbler.

Block

The player is square with and in front of the dribbler. The defender uses the length of the stick on the forehand or backhand side to "block" space and take the ball away. Both hands should be used to tackle, and the weight should be balanced evenly on both feet.

Common Faults

1. Having center of gravity too high.
2. Hitting opponent's stick or leg.
3. Not being forceful enough on the ball.
4. Overcommitting.

Passing

Passing is the heart of the game. It is the intentional movement of the ball by two teammates. Passes eliminate defenders.

Techniques

1. Pushing and hitting for delivering the ball.
2. Controlling or fielding skills to receive the ball.

Players without the ball

To receive a pass, teammates without the ball must take the initiative and get free of their opponents so they can receive a pass. Making short, hard cuts at speed is one way to lose an opponent.

Player with the ball

The passer makes the pass when he or she is sure there is no opponent in or close to the line of the intended pass. If the path of the pass is clear, then the passer must send the ball *accurately and properly paced* to a teammate. A ball hit too hard will go by the teammate, and too soft a hit gives the opponent time to move in and intercept. To make an accurate pass, the passer must assess the teammate's speed and direction so that the receiver does not break stride. The passer must time the pass. Players who get free without the ball do not have much time before the defender recovers. If the passer is slow to recognize the moment the teammate is free, the pass will be late and likely intercepted. Conversely, the passer must recognize when to hold the ball momentarily because the teammate is getting free and will be available in a few steps. If the passer passes too soon, the teammate will not be there. Good vision, timing, and accuracy are important for successful passing.

Passing strategies

Upfield pass (figure 13-12A). When possible, passes should always go to an open teammate closer to the goal than the player with the ball. Upfield passes will be at a variety of angles.

Through pass (figure 13-12B). This is the ultimate upfield pass. It runs parallel to the sideline and is very penetrating because it eliminates two defenders.

Square pass (figure 13-12C). This pass gains no field position because it runs parallel to the endline. It should not be used if there is any chance of an interception. The square pass is best used in a "give and go" (figure 13-12D). This passing combination is most often associated with basketball, but it is equally useful and effective in field hockey. The player with the ball takes it close to an opponent. The player "gives" a square pass to a teammate and "goes" quickly to the open space behind the opponent for a return pass.

Back pass. Passing backward will often open up the field of play and allow the team to change the point of attack.

Shooting. Scoring a goal should be viewed as the final pass. It is a ball that goes by the goalkeeper into the goal.

BASIC DEFENSE

Simply stated, defense is the team not in possession of the ball. When the opponents have possession, the players on the defending team in the vicinity of the ball actively attempt to get it while their teammates not immediately involved move back into the best defensive position in case the ball suddenly shifts. Pressure, marking, and covering are the basic principles in defense (figure 13-13).

Pressure. Pressure must be exerted against the opponent with the ball in such a way that a tackle is possible if ball control is lost. If a tackle is not possible, pressure reduces the passing angles.

Marking. Defense must be such that opposing attack players without the ball cannot receive the ball or are under instant pressure if they do. To mark effectively, the defender must be goalside and ballside of the opponent and the defender must be able to see both the opponent and the ball. The farther the opponent is from the ball, the less tightly the defender has to mark.

Covering. At the point of attack where the opponent with the ball is pressured and nearby teammates are marked, there is space behind the defenders. A player must be

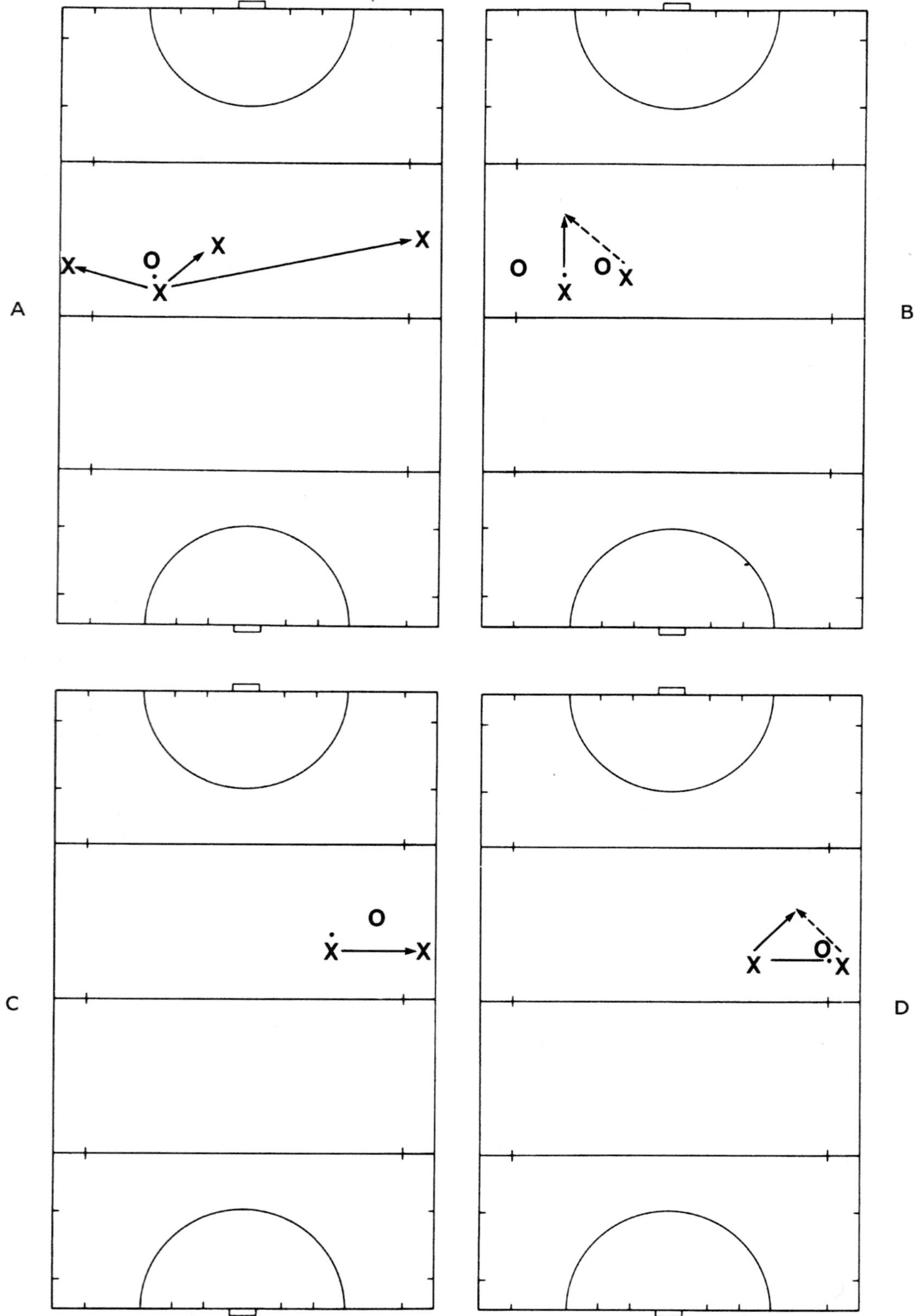

Figure 13-12. Passing strategies. **A,** Upfield pass. **B,** Through pass. **C,** Square pass. **D,** Give and go.

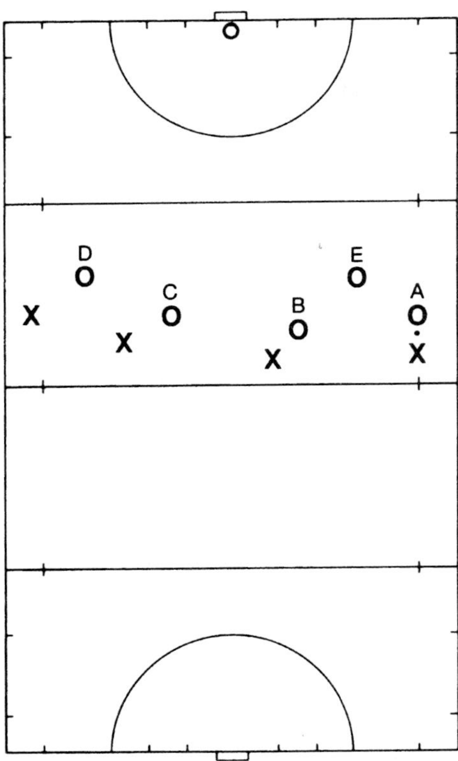

Figure 13-13. Defense. OA is pressuring; OB, OC, and OD are marking. OE is covering.

assigned to cover this space should a pass suddenly come through or an opponent get by.

BASIC OFFENSE

The offense is the team with the ball. At the moment a player gets the ball, every teammate thinks offense and the players in the vicinity of the ball become active participants in the attack.

Principles of Offense

Movement off the ball. The key to successful attacks is players without the ball seeking open space. The player with the ball should have a minimum of two open teammates to whom to pass.

Width. Crowding is one of the biggest problems in all team sports. The first move a player should make is wide—to the sidelines. This forces the defender into a decision. Does the defender go with the ball carrier or stay in position? By spreading out and stretching the defense, the ball carrier will be able to receive the ball and have some space to work with.

Depth. This principle encourages an uneven distribution of attack players rather than a straight line. This provides more passing opportunities for the player with the ball.

STATIC SITUATIONS

Free Hit

Offensively, the first priority is to take a free hit quickly, before the other team sets up. If this is not possible, the player can delay slightly to give teammates a chance to organize. Movement by the receivers and deception by the passer are essential. Usually a short pass is most effective, and a long pass should only be used if a player is wide open.

Defensively, against the free hit, the team must recover quickly and set themselves up so there is no outlet for the free hit.

Side-in

Essentially, tactics of the side-in are the same as in the free hit. Offensively, it is important to keep possession of the ball, and the pusher should not make a back or square pass if there is any chance of interception.

Penalty Corner

Offense. The player who hits-in must be able to accurately and smoothly hit the ball to the shooter. The shooter should be the player with the greatest ability to hit hard, accurately, and quickly. On the college and international levels a "stick stopper" is employed to provide a dead stop for the shooter. This is very common on artificial surfaces. The other forwards are in a position to get a goal from a goalkeeper's rebound. At least three defenders should be in a backup position should the ball come out of the circle. Tactically, it is best to take the penalty corner on the left because the shot on goal is to the weak side (left) of the onrushing defender, making it difficult to stop.

Defense. The fastest player should go to the shooter, hoping to get the ball or at least disrupting the shooter's rhythm and concentration. Two players, one on each side, come out a step behind to get any deflections or dodges. One defender covers and one comes out on the opposite side from the corner in case the ball suddenly shifts. No one should block the goalkeeper, who comes out to reduce the angle of the shot.

GOALKEEPING

The goalkeeper is the last line of defense. The goalkeeper needs the qualities of agility, quickness, strength, and power and the ability to anticipate. If all these qualities are evident but there are signs, no matter how small, of lack of courage, aggression, or confidence, the player is not meant to be a goalkeeper.

Skills

Stopping and clearing. With the advent of high-density foam pads, goalkeepers will redirect 90 percent of all shots coming at them. The old days of "controlling" a ball and then clearing it (i.e., stop and clear) are gone, as keepers

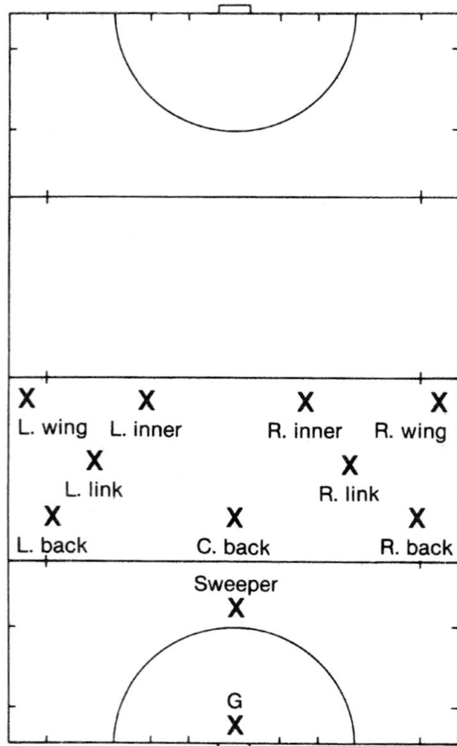

Figure 13-14. The 4-2-3-1 system.

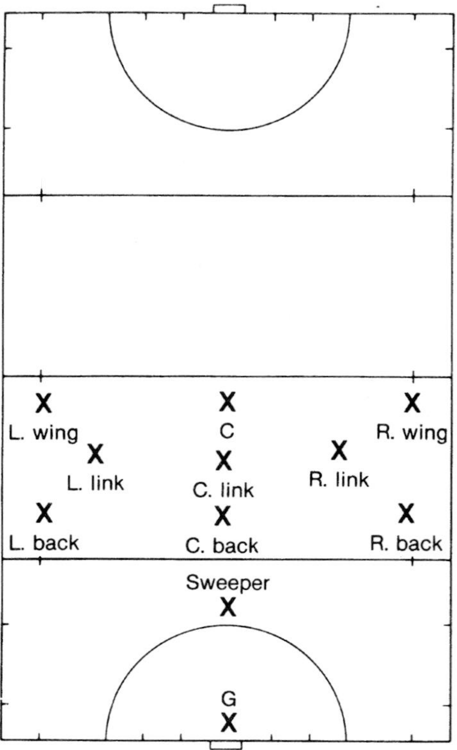

Figure 13-15. The 3-3-3-1 system.

try to stay balanced and clear the ball at the same time (one-time clearing).

Aerial balls. Goalkeepers are forced to use their hands standing up as well as lying down. Most balls are immediately redirected away from the play. The keeper may not cover the ball at any time (as goalies are permitted to do in ice hockey).

Tactics

The basic tactic for goalkeepers is to take the shooting angles away from the forward. By coming off the goal line and being directly between the ball and goal, the goalkeeper reduces the shooter's opportunity for scoring, and the goalkeeper's chance for success is greater.

FORMATIONS

Other than the goalkeeper, whose position remains stable, the players can be arranged in any manner. It is now more common to employ a system where two or three defenders or attackers are made midfielders or links who play both offense and defense (figure 13-14, top high school system, and figure 13-15, top college or international system). It is thought that the defense is tighter and more secure and that the offense is more varied and unpredictable. Generally speaking, the team needs a sweeper, whose job it is to cover and to chase down through balls and take on breakaway forward. The team needs three backs, whose job is primarily defense; two or three midfielders, who play about 60 percent defense and 40 percent offense; and three or four forwards, who are primarily responsible for scoring.

PROGRAM

General

All players must have equipment they can handle. A stick that is too long or heavy forces the player to compensate, producing bad technique. In the early stages it is not important for beginners to know all parts of every technique. The techniques can be learned and improved by making minor adjustments to many children's games. All kinds of tag, relays, obstacle courses, "keep away," and "steal the bacon" types of games are useful and fun.

Small Games and Competitions

In the beginning, the game can be played one versus one and then gradually moved up to two versus two, three versus three, and so on. Interspersed with even sides should be uneven sides, such as two versus one, three versus two, and the like, to work on specific group play and to give one team a good chance of succeeding. These types of games contain all the skills and tactics of 11 versus 11, but they

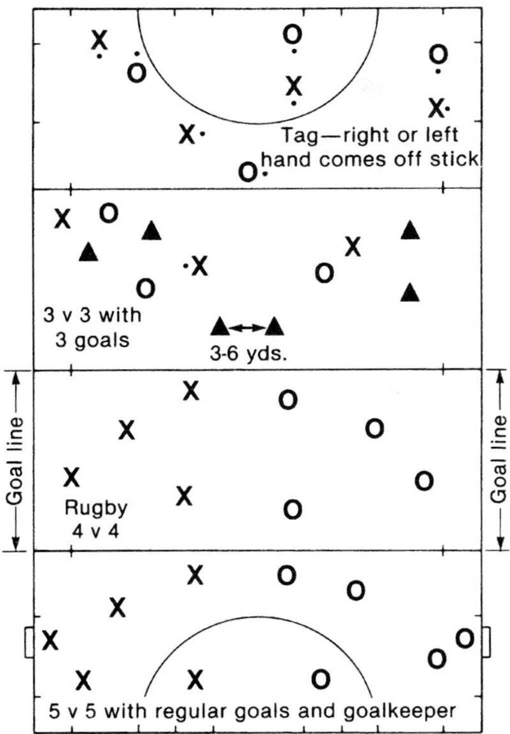

Figure 13-16. Small games and competition.

permit the players many more opportunities with the ball (figure 13-16).

Scoring

The scoring objectives in these small games and competitions are many and varied.

1. No goals—"keep away"—object is to see which team can achieve the highest number of consecutive passes.
2. One, two, or multiple goals (cones) placed on the lines or indiscriminately in the playing area where scoring can come from either side, with or without goalkeepers.
3. Regulation goals, with or without goalkeepers, in limited space, depending on number of players.
4. Rugby—successfully having possession of the ball over any part of a line up to 25 yards (22.9 m) long. This game is excellent for spreading play. Players should think of that line as if it were the edge of the circle. If they control the ball over the line, then they can be certain they would have had a shot on goal.
5. Be creative.

FLOOR HOCKEY

Floor hockey is a popular game and is an excellent lead-in to field hockey. It is a combination of ice hockey and basketball, is strenuous, is ideal for boys and girls, and can be taught in a short time. However, the stick usage is very different in floor hockey, as a player can use both sides of the stick and can only use one side in field hockey. Players need to be shown the differences in stick length and curve as well.

For safety, participants should play the puck, not the opponents. The stick must be carried below the waist at all times, and body checking is not allowed.

A basketball court can be used as the playing area, and either a puck or a floor hockey ball can be used. The midcourt line of the basketball court is the center line. The basketball midcourt jump circle is the center circle, in which play always begins (after a goal or penalty). The goal area should not exceed 58 × 46 inches (1.45 × 1.15 m); hockey nets are recommended. A restraining line 5 feet (1.52 m) from the front of the goal and 4 feet (1.22 m) on each side of the goal defines the goal box.

Each team consists of six players. One is the goalkeeper, who can stop shots with the stick, feet, or hands. One is the center, who is the only player allowed to move full court and is the offensive leader. The stick of the center must be striped with black tape. Two players are defensive and cannot go past the center line, and their main task is to keep the puck out of their half of the floor. Two players are forwards, who work with the center player on offense. These two players cannot go into their defensive half of the court.

The game consists of three periods, each 8 minutes in length, with 5-minute rest periods between them. A flip of a coin determines which team gets the puck to begin the game. Whichever team is behind gets the puck to start the second and third periods. Play begins with the referee's whistle. The center of the team in possession of the puck begins play with a pass. The center must have at least one foot inside the center circle during this pass, and all other players must be outside the 10-feet (3.05 m) restraining circle.

The clock begins when the puck is touched by any player following the center pass and runs continuously, except for a roughing foul, a misconduct call, or the scoring of a goal. Any player that accumulates a total of five fouls or a combination of three roughing fouls and a misconduct must be substituted for immediately. Free substitution is allowed at any time.

TEACHING CONSIDERATIONS

1. Passing, fielding, and dribbling work should dominate practice sessions for beginners working alone and with partners for maximum practice opportunities. Combine dribbling and passing as soon as possible. Be firm about safety rules regarding use of the stick. Do not forget to help fielders receiving a pass from the right to adjust to using only one side of the stick.
2. As soon as some degree of ball control has been achieved, work with two-on-one situations to emphasize opening up space, quickpasses, dodging, tackling and

defensive and offensive strategy. Two-on-one experiences can be designed as a "keep-away" situation or as two offensive players shooting against a goalie.

3. All essential skills and strategies can be taught in five-on-five games or practice situations of four-on-three or five-on-three. It is critical that hockey be learned as a "space" game, and reduced numbers make basic strategies easier for the beginner to utilize. Games with fewer numbers also give more practice opportunities. Teach how to avoid defense and how to defend with few players.
4. Save specialty situations (e.g., penalty corner) for more advanced players. These tend to slow the game down.
5. Be strict in calling safety violations, but be more flexible for beginners on fouls such as off-sides and obstruction.

GLOSSARY

ball control Maneuvering or maintaining possession of the ball.

clear Removing the ball from the scoring area.

cover Defender stationed behind a teammate challenging for ball so that the defender will be in a position should the teammate be beaten.

defender A player whose major contribution is to get the ball from the opponents; prevents opponents from scoring.

dribble Individual technique of moving and maintaining control of the ball with short taps off the end of the stick.

fielding Absorbing the ball's speed on the end of the stick so that it is immediately under control.

flick Push that is lofted; primarily a shot for getting the ball out of danger.

forwards Primarily offense; the first line of the attack.

goal (1) The unit of scoring; (2) the cage on the end line into which a team tries to put the ball.

hit Stroke used for moving the ball over great distances and for shooting.

links Midfielders; play both offense and defense.

marking (1) Defender playing close enough to an opponent to prevent opponent from receiving a pass; (2) defender close enough to tackle or pressure an opponent immediately upon receiving the ball; (3) one-on-one defense.

pass Intentional moving of the ball from one teammate to another.

pressure Decreasing the time and space that an attacking player has in which to pass or dribble.

push The stroke used for short passes; there is no preliminary action before release, making it the quickest pass.

reverse stick Playing the ball with the toe of the stick down.

score Goal; the final pass.

square Pass that goes parallel to endline to a teammate moving forward and taking it on the run.

sweeper Free defender who covers and roams behind defense, picking up all through passes and taking on forward with ball who gets free.

system Arrangement of players on the field.

tactics Thinking level of play; the outwitting of opponents.

through pass Pass that goes parallel to sideline between opponents.

timing Releasing a pass at the right moment; involves good judgement of the positions of teammates and opponents.

weak side (1) The left side of the player; (2) the side of the field away from the ball.

zigzag dribble Controlling ball in front of body and propelling it forward in a zigzag pattern; ball is moved alternately with a regular dribble and reverse stick.

SUGGESTED READINGS

Hockey coach: The official manual of the Hockey Association. 1992. London: Hodder & Stoughton.

Rulebook for outdoor and indoor hockey. 1992. Colorado Springs: United States Field Hockey Association.

United States Field Hockey Association manual for coaches. 1992. Colorado Springs: United States Field Hockey Association.

Working rules of the game of hockey. 1992. London: Charles Mitchell.

RESOURCES

Longstreth Sporting Goods. Major U.S. supplier of current books, videos, and magazines from around the world. Contact: Longstreth Sporting Goods, P.O. Box 475, Parkerford, PA 18457; 800-322-7022.

United States Field Hockey Association. Various coaching publications and up-to-date rule books. Contact: USFHA, One Olympic Plaza, Colorado Springs, CO 80909; 303-578-4567.

Films and Videotapes

Field hockey, by Vonnie Gros. A 26-minute videotape available from Sports Video, 745 State Circle, P.O. Box 1941, Ann Arbor, MI 48106.

Field hockey: The basic skills. Available from Longstreth Sporting Goods, P.O. Box 475, Old Schnylkill Rd., Parkerford, PA 18457.

Field hockey: The basics. A 45-minute videotape available from "How To" Sports Videos, P.O. Box 5852, Denver, CO 80127.

Goalkeeping techniques. 15 minutes. American Alliance for Health, Physical Education, and Recreation, 1900 Association Dr., Reston, VA 22091-1599.

Hockey for coaches, 5 videotapes. Available through Reedswain, Inc., 62 Byers Rd., Chester Springs, PA 19425.

Hockey—Improve your game, by All England Women's Hockey Association. 60 minutes. American Alliance for Health, Physical Education, Recreation and Dance, 1900 Association Dr., Reston, VA 22091-1599.

Hockey strokes—Fundamentals of the game, by Scottish Women's Association. 40 minutes. American Alliance for Health, Physical Education, Recreation and Dance, 1900 Association Dr., Reston, VA 22091-1599.

Hockey—The skills revolution. Available through the United States Field Hockey Association, 1750 E Boulder St., Colorado Springs, CO 80909.

Web Sites

F.I.H. (Fédération Internationale de Hockey): www.fihockey.com

I.O.C. (International Olympic Committee): www.olympic.org

Field hockey information changes on a regular basis, and the reader is encouraged to contact the above suppliers for the latest resource materials

14 Golf

After completing this chapter, the reader should be able to:

- Recognize the values and benefits of participation in golf
- Select proper golf equipment and explain the use for each club
- Practice proper technique in executing the basic golf swing and the several specialized shots
- State the rules of golf and be familiar with the etiquette of the game
- Teach a group of beginning students the fundamentals of golf
- Use properly the many colorful terms associated with golf

Golf is one of the most challenging and fascinating of modern sports. The thrill of striking a ball well over 200 yards (183 m) and the satisfaction of successfully executing the soft touch needed for a 4-foot (1.2 m) putt are of lasting pleasure. Whether one learns to play golf for relaxation and fun or aspires to achieve a high competitive level is the privilege of the individual. Few sports offer playing fields with such great variety and beauty as golf courses.

HISTORY

The game of golf is one of the most ancient of the modern sports. Historians do not agree on its origin, but it appears certain that golf was played in Scotland more than 500 years ago. As early as 1457 the Scottish Parliament ordained that golf should not be played because it was detracting from the practice of archery, which was deemed necessary for defensive purposes. Old paintings and drawings show that similar games were also played about that time in The Netherlands, Belgium, and France. The Dutch term *kolf,* meaning a "club," is considered by some to have given rise to the name of the present-day game. Regardless of how much Scotland invented on its own and how much it borrowed from others, it appears certain that Scotland was the source from which the game as it is known today spread to all parts of the world. St. Andrews in Fife, Scotland, is believed to be the oldest existing golf course.

Courses, or links, of the early days differed greatly from those of today. Golf was then distinctly a seaside game, played over stretches of land that linked the seashore with tillable lands farther inland. It was this condition that led to calling the scene of play "links," which in fact means a seaside golf course.

The location of holes followed no definite plan. The landscape was partially covered by bushes, trees, and the like. Open areas were chosen as finishing points or putting greens. No official number of holes was adopted as standard for a round of play until 1858, when 18 holes were designated as a round.

Golf clubs were organized in the United States in the closing years of the eighteenth century, but the game as we know it today had its start in the United States approximately 90 years ago. A few clubs were started in the eastern United States, and the rapid increase in popularity since then has greatly increased the number of private and municipal courses. Today class instruction in golf is found in most high schools and colleges. Colleges and universities often own and operate golf courses; high schools use private and municipal courses. In recent years television coverage of major golf events has done much to stimulate interest in the game. In fact, in many urban areas of the country the number of golf courses is insufficient to accommodate the demand. In 1980 the National Golf Foundation indicated that if a new golf course were built every day until the year 2000, there would still be a shortage. In 1989 they revised this statement to suggest that if five new courses were built every day until 2000, there would still be a shortage. It has been estimated that more than 25 million Americans golf, playing nearly 500 million rounds per year.

There are at least 15,000 golf courses and 16,000 golf driving ranges in the United States. Many people become enthusiasts and start playing golf as a result of experience on a driving range.

Golf today is no longer a game for those with a high income. It is played by individuals from a variety of economic backgrounds and includes the young and the old, duffers as well as masters.

Truly, golf is a sport that offers a life-long source of pleasure. One or two well-timed and well-directed shots often serve as the catalyst that causes the player to return for another round.

The social aspects of golf include the following: It encourages excellent compatibility of mixed groups; it clears and freshens the mind by diversion of interest; it brings urban dwellers into sunshine and nature; it provides restful activity for the working individual; the golfer is pitted against self as well as against opponents; each hole is a separate contest and challenge; and the game is played by people of all ages, sizes, and builds. As recreation, golf is one of the most desirable of all sports.

GENERAL DESCRIPTION

Eighteen holes make up the typical golf course. The first, ninth, tenth, and eighteenth holes are generally near the clubhouse. Any multiple of nine holes can be played, and each hole varies in length and general layout. Hazards are generally placed to penalize a poor shot. The object is to score as few strokes as possible for each hole. Play starts at the tee between two markers, continues along the fairway, which is generally bounded by rough, and finishes at the green, which is often surrounded by bunkers. The ball is rolled into the hole marked by the pin, or flagstick.

EQUIPMENT

The United States has contributed in large share to improvements in golf equipment—for example, the type of ball in use today; the steel-, graphite-, and titanium-shafted clubs; the peg tee; and utility clubs such as the sand wedge.

Clothing

Dress should be comfortable and in accord with local custom on the course played. Many courses have clothing restrictions (e.g., no T-shirts or jeans allowed).

Spiked golf shoes are an important part of a player's golfing equipment. However, if they are not available, a pair of tennis shoes will suffice. Recently, soft spikes have become mandatory at many courses because they cause less damage to the greens than metal spikes.

Clubs

It is not necessary to have the most expensive set of golf clubs on the market to enjoy playing golf and to play it satisfactorily. On the other hand, one should not handicap one's game by playing with inferior equipment. Purchasing clubs that are suitable to your characteristics and that are made by a dependable manufacturer is a sound policy for assurance of satisfaction and long wear.

Golf clubs come in a variety of lengths, weights, shaft flexibility, and other features (figure 14-1). Club length is usually determined by a person's height, and club weight is often selected on personal preference in relation to feel. Usually, the faster the swing, the less whip you should have in your club shafts. Ask your golf teacher or club professional for advice on the type of clubs to purchase.

Starter set

The beginning golfer need not invest in an expensive, complete set of clubs. Options include purchasing a set of used clubs or a starter set. The advantages of purchasing a set of used clubs rather than a starter set are usually in the quality and number of clubs obtained for a comparable cost. In either case, the minimum clubs to start with include a 3 wood; a putter; and the 3, 5, 7, and 9 irons.

Woods

The three common woods are the driver, or No. 1 wood; the No. 3 wood; and the No. 5 wood (figure 14-2). They have longer shafts and weigh more than the iron clubs and, consequently, can give more distance than an iron club having a similar loft, or tilt, to the club face. Seldom are woods constructed of wood now; metal heads are the norm today. However, these clubs are still referred to as "woods."

It is difficult to state precisely the distance any individual can hit the golf ball, because there are so many variables (e.g., experience, gender, age). However, below are estimates of the distances one might expect.

Driver. This club is usually used to hit off the tee when long distances are required. Males typically drive the ball 180 to 260 yards (165 to 238 m); females typically drive the ball 150 to 220 yards (137 to 201 m).

No. 3 wood. This club is usually used off the fairway or when accuracy off the tee is more important than distance. Males typically hit the ball 165 to 240 yards (151 to 219 m); females typically hit the ball 140 to 210 yards (128 to 192 m).

No. 5 wood. This club is usually used off the fairway or on some par-3 holes. Males typically hit the ball 150 to 215 yards (137 to 197 m). Females typically hit the ball 130–190 yards (119–174 m).

Irons

Irons are used from the fairway or from the tee on short holes. The player selects the proper iron according to the distance required (figure 14-3). For various irons and distances achieved with each, see figures 14-3 and 14-4.

Putter. This club is used for putting on the green or from just off the green. Putters are manufactured in a great variety of styles and are chosen on the basis of individual preference.

Pitching or sand wedge. These clubs are used for short approaches from the rough and fairways, less than 125 yards (114 m), and as a trouble club from tall rough or sand traps. They are very versatile when properly used.

Golf Balls

Golf balls are made by many manufacturers. Their construction varies from a solid, one-piece ball to a ball developed from a small, hard core wound with rubber bands and sealed with a durable cover.

Ball preference is left up to individual feel and style of play. The better players usually prefer a wound ball of higher compression, whereas beginners often use a one- or two-piece ball with a durable cover that does not cut easily. One should have several balls in the golf bag when going out to play.

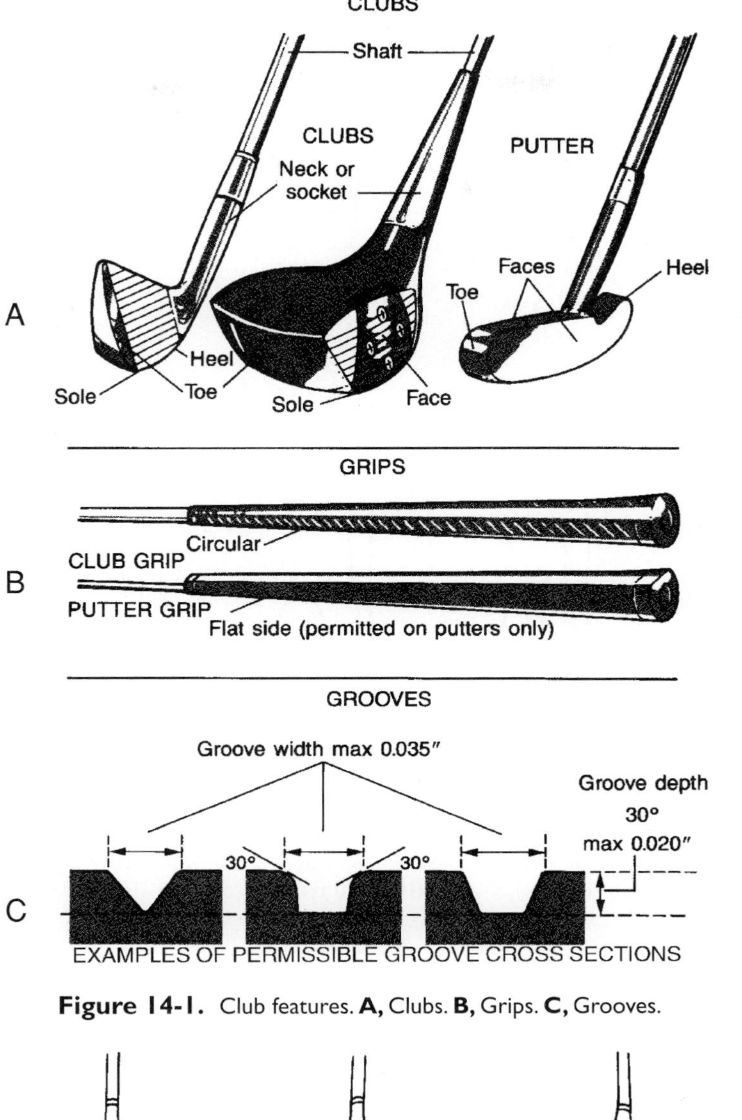

Figure 14-1. Club features. **A,** Clubs. **B,** Grips. **C,** Grooves.

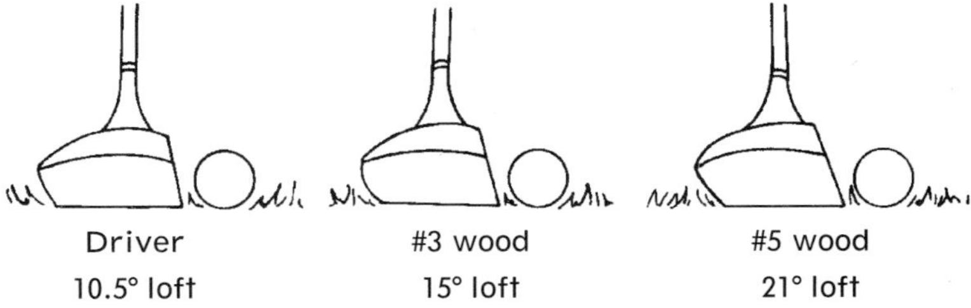

Figure 14-2. The woods.

Plastic balls may be used for the gymnasium, small field, or backyard practice.

THE COURSE

A golf course is actually built and constructed to best conform to the contours of the land. A complete golf course consists of 18 holes, which requires not less than 100 acres. In many communities 9-hole or 18-hole courses are constructed on less acreage with shorter holes that require less time to play. Par-3 courses, on which 18 holes can be played in 3 hours or less, are becoming increasingly popular.

A well-constructed golf course is architecturally planned so that each hole differs from the rest, yet certain elements are common to all.

Each hole is composed of a tee and tee markers, fairway, rough, trees, boundary, sand bunkers and sometimes water

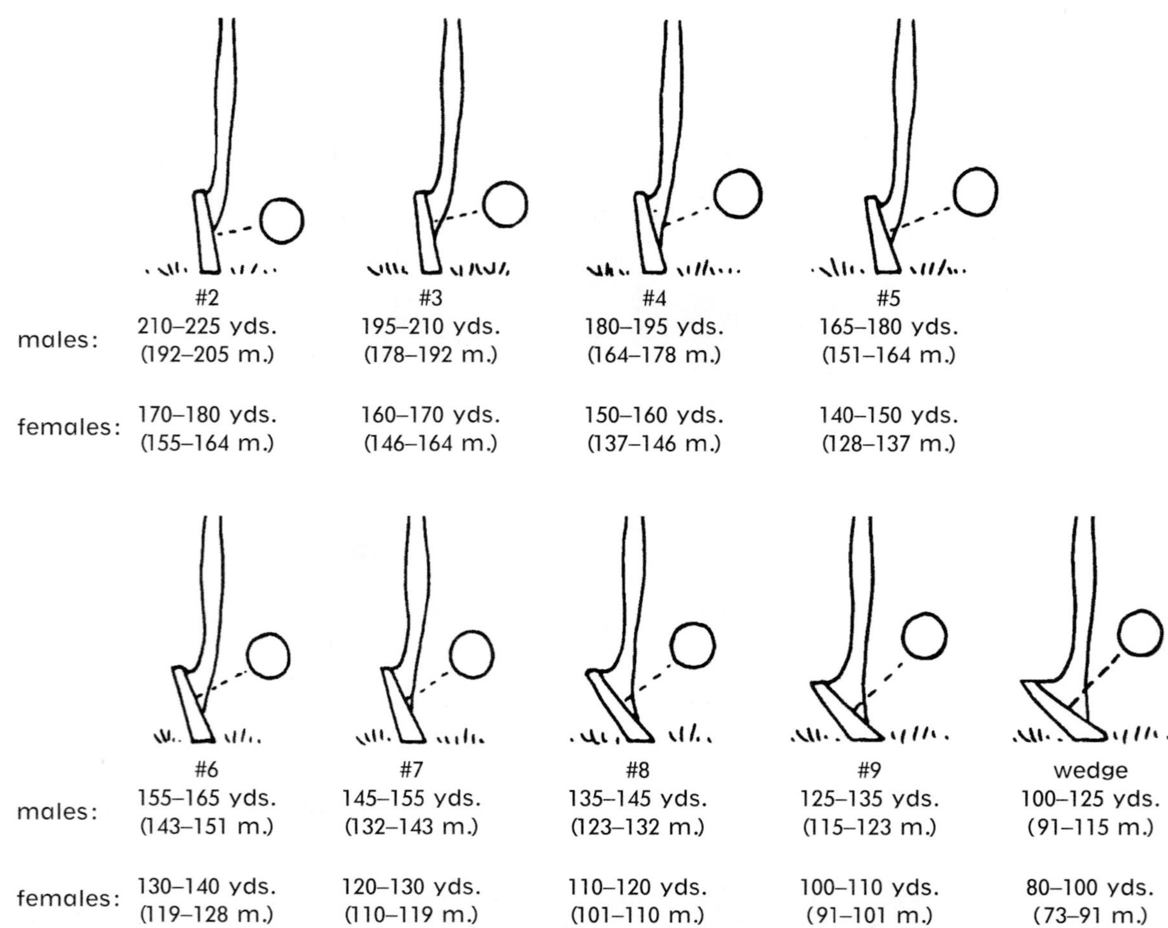

Figure 14-3. Various irons showing angle of pitch of each club and approximate distance obtained by experienced golfers.

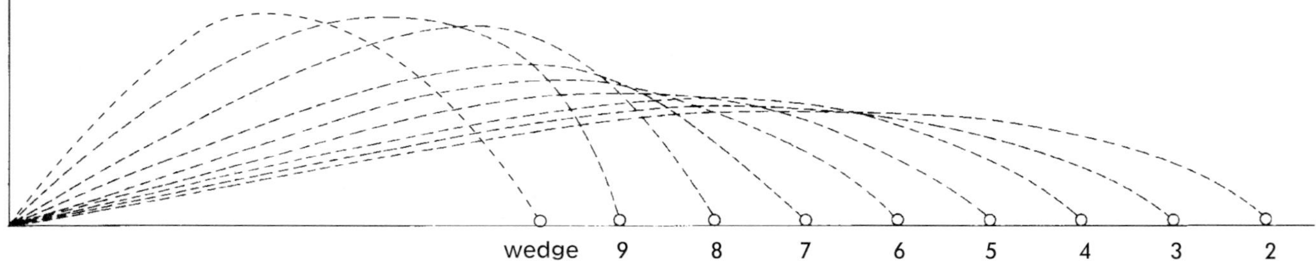

Figure 14-4. Trajectory or flight of ball using the same swing with each iron (male golfer).

hazards, and a green, cup, and flag. The shape and size of the greens, as well as the placing of bunkers and water hazards, are left to the creativity of the golf course architect (figure 14-5).

Par is determined by the distance of the hole from the middle of the tee down the middle of the fairway to the middle of the green. Holes up to 250 yards (229 m) are usually designated as par 3, holes from 251 to 470 yards (230 to 430 m) as par 4, and holes from 471 to 600 yards (431 to 549 m) as par 5. Par 3 is a score usually obtained by reaching the green in one shot and rolling the ball into the cup with two putts. On a par 4, the golfer should reach the green in two; and on a par 5, reach it in three. A championship course usually has a par of 72, or an average of four strokes per hole. A typical course has four par-3 holes, 10 par-4 holes, and four par-5 holes.

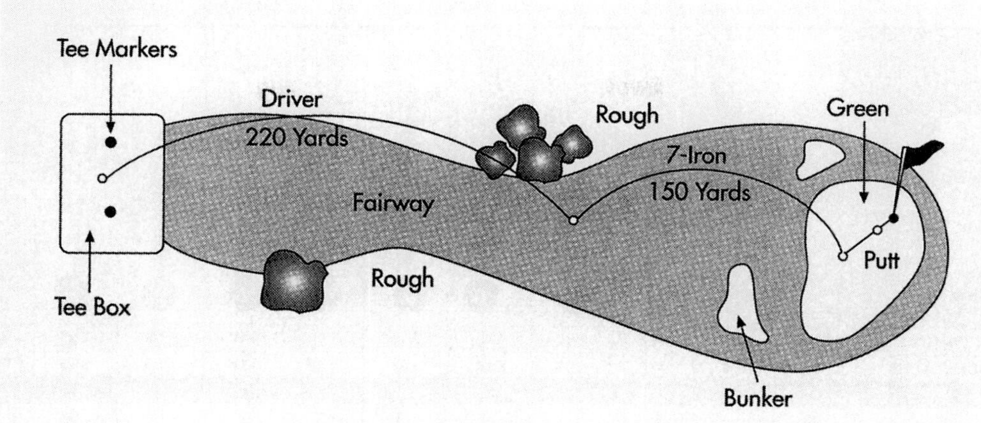

Figure 14-5. Example of 375 yard par-4 hole.

Par for women differs somewhat from that for men, depending on the difficulty of each hole as to distance, hazards, and the like.

Refer to the sample scorecard (figure 14-6) with regard to par with men and women, distances of each hole, and hole handicap (a ranking of the holes by difficulty).

FACILITIES FOR PRACTICE

1. Outdoor driving range and putting green.
2. Any large room, preferably a gymnasium.
3. Two or three large pieces of canvas hung in front of a wall with fish netting along the sides to form a cage-type setup.
4. Mats from which to hit.
5. Clubs and balls (plastic balls may be used if nets are not available).
6. A large rug with short nap for putting.
7. Putting cups for individual putting (water glasses can be used).

FUNDAMENTAL SKILLS AND TECHNIQUES

Because certain clubs and types of shots fall into natural groupings, the following material has been arranged to take advantage of these categories. For the left-handed player, it will be necessary to reverse the techniques presented here because consideration has been given only to the right-handed player.

The Golf Grip

1. Ten-finger grip; sometimes used by players with small, weak hands or extremely short fingers (figure 14-7).
2. Interlocking grip; preferred by some players who like a solid feel (figure 14-8).
3. Overlapping, or Vardon, grip (figure 14-9); the most popular grip, used by most players (described here).

One opens the left hand, and with the thumb and fingers together, places the club diagonally across the hand from the middle joint of the index finger across the heel of the hand. The hand closes over the club so that it is held by the fingers. The *V* formed by the thumb and index finger should point approximately to the right shoulder. When the club is held in the position of address, you should see the first three knuckles of the fingers. The thumb is above, one quarter turn over the club, with the pad of the thumb on the grip of the club formed by the first and second fingers on the left hand. The correct rotation of the left hand allows cocking of the wrist at the peak of the backswing. It also allows the left arm to deal a backhand blow to the ball. At this point the player should try swinging the club head with only the left arm, watching that the arm remains comfortably straight and that the wrist cocks at the top of the backswing.

To place the right hand in position, the grip should first contact the middle joint of the right forefinger. When the hand is closed, this forefinger knuckle must be on the right side of the grip, never under it. Then one closes the hand, placing the thumb to the left, diagonally across the shaft so that it helps the forefinger to grip. The feel of the club head is controlled mainly by the fingers, giving more power and control. The left thumb should fit snugly into the palm of the right hand. The little finger of the right hand should be wrapped around the crevice formed by the first two fingers of the left hand (overlapping grip).

It should be emphasized that, regardless of the grip used, the back of the left hand and the palm of the right should face squarely toward the target.

Stance

For various foot positions, see figure 14-10.

Square stance. The feet, knees, hips, and shoulders are parallel to the line of flight. This stance is used for almost all long shots of both woods and irons because it allows free

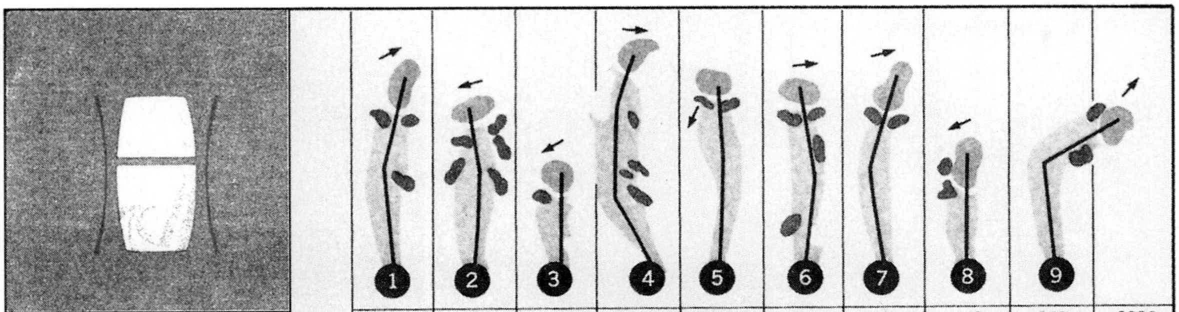

	1	2	3	4	5	6	7	8	9	
MENS TEES (WHITE)	457	357	187	525	341	374	340	148	353	3082
CHAMPIONSHIP TEES	474	371	199	543	362	388	352	180	369	3240
PAR	5	4	3	5	4	4	4	3	4	36
HANDICAP	7	15	1	11	13	3	9	17	5	
LADIES TEES (RED)	406	342	174	485	343	349	334	141	342	2916
PAR	5	4	3	5	4	4	4	3	4	36
HANDICAP	7	3	5	1	15	11	9	17	13	

PLAYERS ARE FORBIDDEN TO ENTER WALLED DRILLING ISLANDS, INDIVIDUAL FENCED WELL SITES, OR TO CROSS OVER CHAIN-LINK FENCE • U.S.G.A. rules shall govern all play except as modified by the following local rules. LOCAL RULES: • Ball may be dropped two club lengths from staked trees—no penalty. • Drop off all paved paths and roads—no penalty. • Walled drilling islands are out of bounds. • Wire fenced well sites—if within orange staked area drop straight behind point where ball lay and hole, no limit to distance behind—no penalty. • Water hazards: holes 3, 6, 10, 14, 15. • Rock drainage ditches—when rock interferes with stance or swing, drop two club

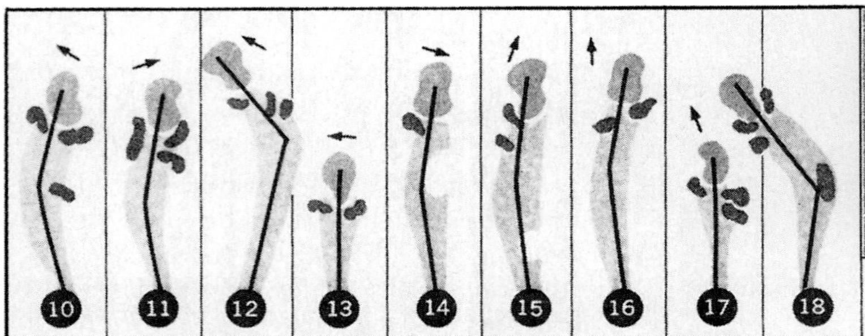

COURSE RATING
CHAMPIONSHIP TEES 70.1
MENS TEES 68.0

DATE ____________

PLAYER ____________

ATTEST ____________

10	11	12	13	14	15	16	17	18	IN	TOTAL	HDCP	NET	
404	348	487	166	366	363	375	178	439	3116	6198			
411	369	506	184	380	381	394	203	466	3294	6534			
4	4	5	3	4	4	4	3	5	36	72			
2	10	14	16	6	8	4	12	18					
383	340	418	149	351	347	358	155	441	2942	5858			
4	4	5	3	4	4	4	3	5	36	72			
4	14	2	18	10	12	8	16	6	LADIES COURSE RATING 72.4				

lengths—no penalty. • Out of bounds defined by white stakes or green stakes—white tops: No. 4 only—out of bounds right side as staked. • Driving range Out of Bounds as staked. COURSE RULES: • Players will at all times observe the rules of Golf etiquette. • Practicing prohibited anywhere on course. • Replace turf and fix ball marks on greens. • Keep electric carts off tees and 30 ft. from greens. • Keep electric carts on paths and designated areas. • Keep pull carts off tees, areas between traps and greens, and 10 ft. from greens. Lateral water hazard: Hole No. 4.

Figure 14-6. Typical scorecard.

movement of either side of the body. The knees are slightly bent, the toes turned slightly outward, and the weight evenly distributed. The arms hang downward from the shoulders and away from the body but not forward. The body curves naturally, but not sharply, forward. The eyes are on the ball.

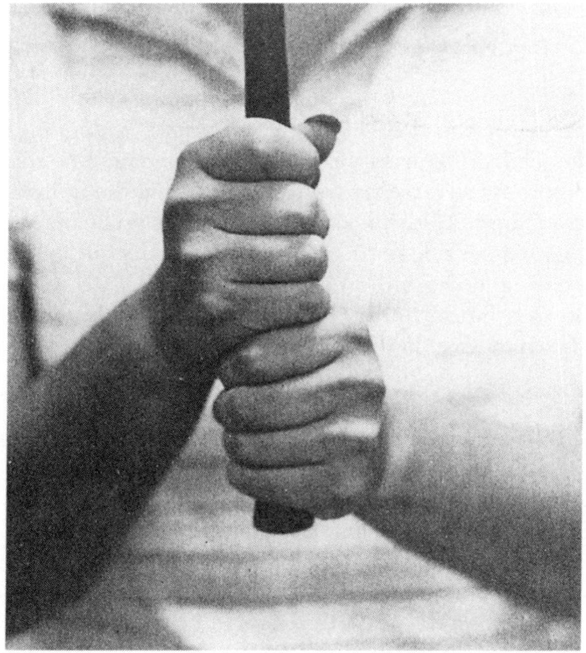

Figure 14-7. Ten-finger grip.

Open stance. The left foot is withdrawn slightly from the line of flight, but the knees, hips, and shoulders remain square. This stance is used rarely for wood shots but more often for the shorter iron shots. It tends to restrict the turning and pivoting of the left side, but allows a better follow-through. This stance encourages the fade, or slice, but can result in increased distance.

Closed stance. The right foot is withdrawn slightly from the line of flight, but the knees, hips, and shoulders remain square. This stance is often used for wood shots and encourages a draw, or hook.

Swing

For progressive steps in the golf swing see figure 14-11.

Tempo

Maintaining an even tempo is one of the most important aspects of developing a proper golf swing. A player who is able to maintain good rhythm and smoothness throughout the swing will be able to develop an efficient and consistent golf swing. Most beginners attempt to hit the ball too hard, which results in an improper tempo or an uneven rhythm and causes many faults. In fact, as a variable, strength is much less important than proper tempo and clubhead speed in the successful golf swing. Beginning golfers should strive to achieve a consistent tempo or rhythm in all shots attempted. Often a simple key such as saying "Back," "Wait," and "Through" or "one, two, three" on the backswing and "One, two, three" on the downswing and follow-through will help to develop the rhythm necessary for

A

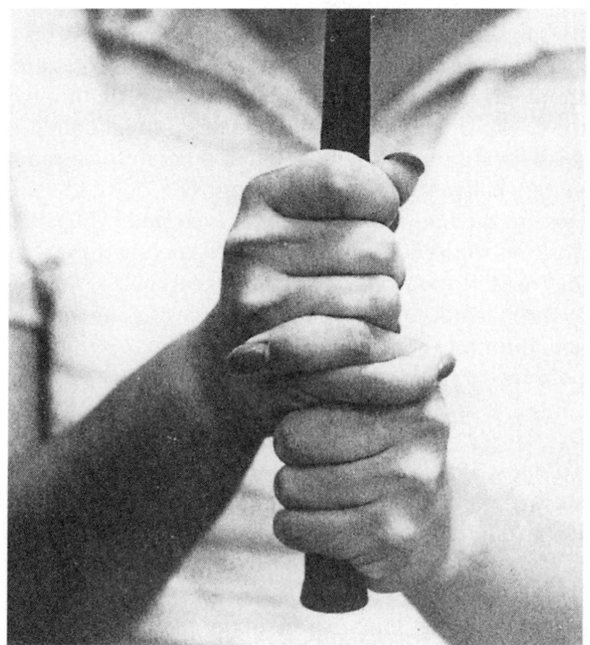

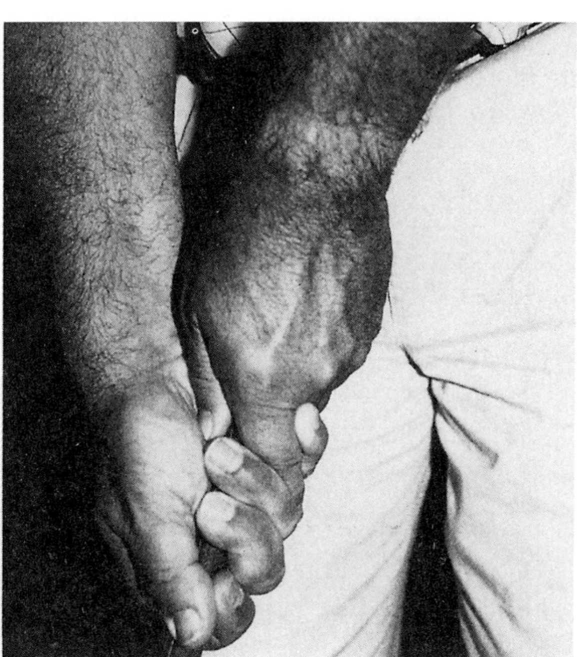

B

Figure 14-8. A, Interlocking grip (back view). **B,** Interlocking grip (front view).

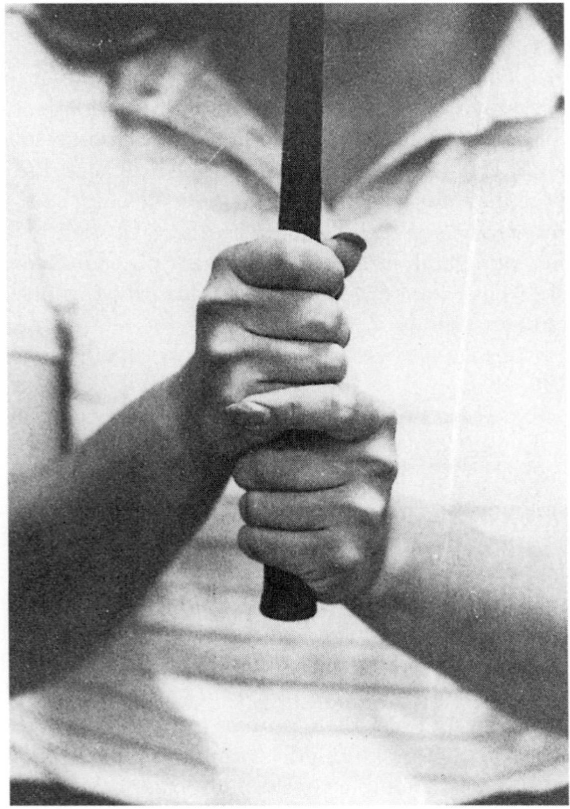

Figure 14-9. Overlapping grip.

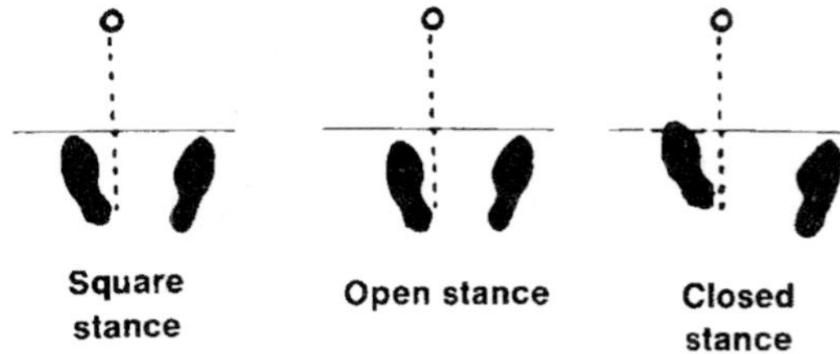

Figure 14-10. Various foot positions.

success. Once the idea of tempo is understood and accomplished, the beginner will have the necessary basis for the development of a sound golf swing. Without proper rhythm, it is difficult to hit the ball correctly and much power is wasted. In general, the golf swing is developed by gradually increasing the speed. The golfer should begin slowly, then accelerate on the downswing, keeping a continuous rhythm throughout. It takes approximately the same time to take the club from the address to the top of the backswing as it does to complete the downswing and the follow-through.

Selecting the Target

The first step the golfer should take in preparing to hit the ball is to select a target. Often the ball will not end up precisely at the target or along the intended target line, but it is difficult to realize the ideal shot unless the target is selected beforehand.

Addressing the Ball

When addressing the ball, the player takes the proper grip and places the head of the club on the ground, with the sole of the club parallel to the turf. The feet should be placed approximately shoulder-width apart or in a relative position for the club used—for example, wider for the longer clubs. The arms should fall naturally from the shoulders and not so far away from the body that the individual is stretching. For the woods, the ball is generally placed in line with the inside portion of the left heel. As the length of the club and the required distance decrease, the ball is addressed farther to the right of the left foot but seldom farther back than in the center of the stance.

Waggle

The waggle is a preliminary movement that takes a variety of forms, depending on individual preference. It is designed to help the golfer relax, adjust the grip, check alignment, and get ready to begin the swing. Usually, it involves slight body movement and the lifting of the club head several inches to check balance and position. When the golfer feels ready, there is a slight hesitation before the beginning of the full swing. This preliminary move tends to ease tension in preparation for the shot.

Backswing

Before beginning the swing, the golfer must fix his or her eye on the ball. The swing is started with a rotation of the shoulder and hips, which starts the club head moving to the back. The left arm should be kept straight and the club head low to the ground. The wrists begin to cock approximately halfway back on the swing. The right elbow is kept close to the body, and the weight is shifted from a balanced position to the right foot. The left knee is turned inward, and the left foot rolls to the right, keeping the left heel low to the ground. At the top of the backswing the left shoulder is pointing at the ball and club is parallel to the ground and pointing toward the target.

Downswing

To make a smooth change of direction, the downswing is started with the left leg. The left foot comes down flat to the ground, and the knees and hips are moved forward toward the target. The knees are bent slightly to allow freedom of movement as the weight is shifted from the right side to the left. There should be a feeling of pulling from the left side. The wrists should remain cocked until the arms are parallel with the ground. The left leg straightens,

Figure 14-11. Progressive steps of swing.

and the left side becomes firm to provide a strong hitting position. At impact there should be a straight line from the ball or club head through the hands to the left shoulder. The head must remain stationary and the eyes remain focused on the ball after contact is made.

Follow-through

After impact the right arm becomes just as straight as the left arm was on the backswing. The head rises naturally, but does not move forward as the right shoulder comes under. Both arms should be stretched out as far as possible toward the target. The wrists will begin to turn over after the arms have reached their limit, finishing with the hands high above the head.

Swing plane

When the golfer takes the club back from the ball, the club should come slightly inside the line of flight, maintaining a plane that will run back approximately between the shoulders and neck. One of the keys to a successful golf swing is to maintain this same plane on the downswing. To accomplish this, the golfer must maintain the proper sequence of body movements. The swing is started with the legs and hips, then the arms come into play, then the wrists begin cocking. This same order must be maintained on the downswing if the plane is not to be broken. The downswing starts with the legs and hips, then the arms come into play, and next the wrists uncock so that they are straight at the point of contact. This sequence will enable the golfer to swing from slightly inside the line of flight out through the ball, maintaining proper control of the shot. Any deviations from this sequence will allow the club head to break the plane and will cause inconsistency or initiate numerous faults or problems with the flight of the ball. This sequence and having the clubhead square to the intended line of flight at impact are the two most important factors in a successful golf swing.

Common errors

The following are errors often made by beginners when learning the golf swing:

1. Swaying or moving the head to the right instead of pivoting the body over the ball.
2. Backswing that is too fast, eliminating good tempo and throwing the golfer off balance.
3. Bending the left arm.
4. Raising the left shoulder.
5. Backswing with a too flat or too horizontal plane.
6. Raising the head from its original position.
7. Pausing too long or not long enough at the top of the swing.
8. Rushing the downsizing.
9. Uncocking the wrists too soon, which throws off the proper sequence and usually casts the club outside the correct plane.
10. Hitting too hard with the right hand, which drops the right shoulder, causing contact behind the ball.
11. Relaxing the wrists at the moment of impact or slowing the downswing, impeding proper rhythm or tempo.
12. Failing to complete the follow-through with the hands held high.
13. Hitting at the ball rather than swinging the club at the target.

Short swing

One of the consistent factors in golf is that it is not necessary to learn a different swing for each club. The plane varies slightly with the length of the club; however, there is no difference in what has to be learned to attempt the swing. When a shot requires less distance than produced by the shortest club in the bag, a shorter swing must be executed. The short swing is a breakdown of the full swing, and the distance of the shot is commensurate with the length of the backswing. If a half swing is required for a particular shot, then the golfer uses less body turn and less wrist action than in the full swing, where the wrist break is not completed until the club is brought to the top of the swing. The shorter the swing, the less wrist action and body movement occur. The follow-through is the same as in the backswing. A one-quarter backswing requires a one-quarter follow-through; a one-half backswing requires a one-half follow-through; and so on. The rest of the fundamentals are exactly the same as described for the full swing. The golfer should practice short swings of various lengths to determine how far the ball will travel and to obtain the correct feel for the distance required. Regardless of the distance of the shot, the club head must be accelerated through the ball.

Pitch Shot

The pitch shot (figure 14-12) is usually executed with a No. 9 iron, pitching wedge, or sand wedge. This shot will fly high and is used to hit the ball over a bunker or hazard of some type and will stop on the green with very little roll. The stance should be square or slightly open, with the length of the backswing determined by the distance needed as described for the short swing. Some golfers prefer to choke down on the club for greater control, particularly for shorter shots. Inasmuch as the swing is shorter, body movement is kept to a minimum, there is little wrist cock, and the left arm is straight throughout the swing. It is important that the follow-through be carried the same distance as the backswing, with care taken not to make any special effort to meet or hit the ball hard.

Tempo is just as important in the short swing or pitch shot as it is in the full swing. Regardless of the distance of the shot, it is important that one hit down through the ball and not try to scoop the ball into the air. The club is designed to give the proper lift to the ball.

Figure 14-12. Pitch shot.

Figure 14-13. Chip shot.

The Chip Shot

The chip shot (figure 14-13) is usually executed with a No. 7 iron and is effective when the golfer has an open shot to the pin and does not have to hit over any type of hazard.

The stance is similar to that for the pitch shot, with slightly more weight forward at the address. The less-lofted club face will allow the ball to travel low and run much farther than the pitch shot. Again, the distance of the shot is determined by the length of the backswing, and the follow-through should be commensurate with the backswing. One should practice taking the club back various distances to determine the proper length of the backswing for the distance required. Club selection for this shot is usually determined by selecting the club that will allow the ball to hit as close to the edge of the green as possible and roll the remainder of the way to the cup. A short chip can be executed in a manner similar to a putting stroke. Again, the key to the chip shot is proper tempo and rhythm, with care not to chop at the ball with an uneven tempo.

Putting

Putting is individual in nature, although there are certain aspects of the stroke that must be maintained, regardless of the golfer's style or the type of putter used. For examples of the many styles and designs in which putters are manufactured, see figure 14-14. The stance may be wide, narrow, open, or closed, depending on individual preference. However, there must be no body or head movement, and the putter blade should be taken straight back in line with the direction required for a straight-through motion toward the hole. Figures 14-15 and 14-16 display two types of putting stances that can be used. The following description of

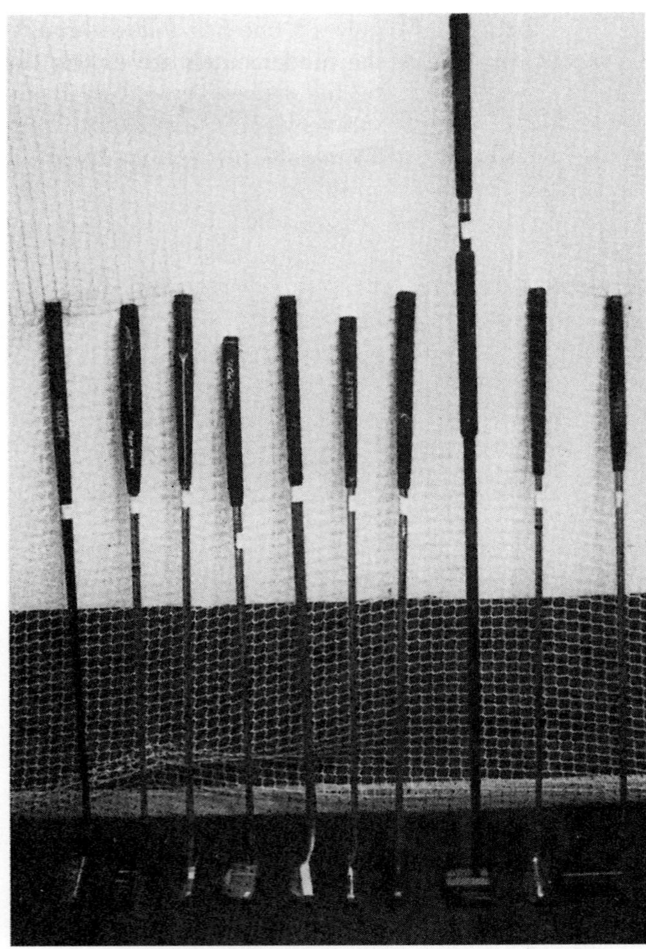

Figure 14-14. Putters.

putting can be used as a guide; however, technique can be varied according to personal preference. The distance of the putt is determined by the length of the backswing. A shorter putt requires a shorter backswing and a longer putt a longer backswing, but the tempo must be consistent throughout.

Stance

1. The stance is fairly upright, with the neck and shoulders bent slightly.
2. The feet are 8 to 12 inches (20 to 30 cm) apart.
3. The stance is square.
4. The weight is balanced.
5. The left arm is kept close to the torso.
6. The right forearm is close to the right thigh.
7. The ball is at the left instep.

Grip

1. The back of the left hand and the palm of the right hand are square to the line.
2. Both thumbs are directly on top of the grip.

Swing (see box)

1. The swing is short and low to the ground.
2. It is in line with the intended roll of the ball.
3. It is completely relaxed, slow, and steady.
4. There are no body or head movements.
5. The club head follows through.
6. The ball should be struck firmly enough to reach the hole.

Figure 14-15. Upright putting stance.

Figure 14-16. Crouched putting stance.

Reading the green

1. The player sights the hole from behind the ball to determine the angle of roll, more commonly called the break.
2. The player checks the grass to determine whether the putt will be with or against the grain. A lighter color indicates the intended path is with the grain, which allows the ball to roll faster.

Sand Bunkers

Properly executing the bunker shot can save the golfer many strokes. To control this shot, the player must hit the sand about 2 inches behind the ball and let the sand throw the ball out of the trap. The distance the ball travels is relative to the distance hit behind the ball. The object is not to bury the club but to continue to swing smoothly through the sand under the ball, with a strong follow-through and finish.

General principles

1. Because sand traps vary from deep, soft sand to shallow, hard clay and sand, each shot is different.
2. The trap is entered from the lowest point so as not to destroy the bank or unduly disturb the surface.
3. The player positions his or her feet and then moves them back and forth in order to sink into the sand and have a firm stance.
4. In addressing the ball, one should not touch the sand with the club head until the ball is hit.
5. On leaving the trap, all irregularities made in the sand should be covered by smoothing them out with the club head or rake.

The explosion shot (figure 14-17)

1. The grip, stance, and swing are about the same as for the short, high approach.
2. The stance is open, with the feet fairly close together and well-set in the sand.
3. The grip must be firm but not tense.
4. The swing must be fairly long, upright, and U-shaped.
5. The club head must not stop in the sand because sand pushed ahead of the club with cause the ball to rise. The follow-through should be definite and powerful.
6. The amount of sand taken, or the distance back of the ball that the club head enters the sand, determines the distance the ball will travel. Thus the closer one is to the green, the more sand one must take.

Sidehill lies

When playing from sidehill lies, the golfer must adjust the stance and ball replacement to conform to the contour of the ground. The golfer should avoid trying to overswing and should first take one or two practice swings to become familiar with the changes in swing feel.

General principles

1. Do not overswing
2. Play for accuracy
3. Allow the club head to follow the contour of the ground

Uphill

1. There is a tendency to pull or hook, so aim to the right
2. Stand close to the ball with the feet almost together
3. Put more weight on the right foot
4. Play the ball forward of the normal position in stance

Downhill

1. There is a tendency to slice, so aim to the left
2. On a steep slope avoid wood clubs, because it is difficult to achieve a rise

1 2 3

Figure 14-17. The explosion shot.

3. Play the ball back of the normal position in stance
4. Weight is naturally more on the left foot, which will restrict the action of the pivot to the left. Shift the weight to the right foot

Ball below feet

1. There is a strong tendency to slice, so play to the left
2. The weight is on the toes, so open the stance somewhat
3. Avoid topping by moving the grip closer to the top end of the club and concentrating on staying down until after the ball is contacted
4. Do not pivot as much as on level ground; more of a U-shaped swing is natural

Ball above feet

1. The tendency is to pull or hook, so play to the right
2. Hold the club short
3. Swing slowly; a fast swing will throw you back, causing you to top the ball
4. There is a tendency to toe the ball with the club, so play it close

Playing from the Rough

When playing from the rough, set yourself firmly with a slightly open stance. The club should be brought back in a more upright motion. Hit down through the ball and finish the swing strongly. Be sure to select the club with enough loft to get the ball out of the rough. This is the primary objective.

General principles

1. Do not press in trying for too much distance
2. Use the U-shaped swing

CHECKPOINTS FOR THE GOLF SWING

1. The overlapping grip
   a. Left hand is gripped with fingers to form V over right shoulder
   b. Right hand is not too far under shaft; the V formed should point over right shoulder
   c. The thumbs are placed on the side of the shaft
   d. The little finger of the right hand overlaps the first finger of the left hand
2. The stance
   a. Square: Both feet are equidistant from the line of flight
   b. Open: The left foot is a little farther from the line of flight than the right foot
   c. Closed: The right foot is farther away from the line of flight than the left foot
3. The swing
   a. Pick target
   b. Backswing
      i. Fix the eye on the ball; determine the proper position of the head
      ii. Start back with rotation of shoulder and hips
      iii. Keep the left arm straight
      iv. Keep the club head low to the ground
      v. Begin to cock the wrists approximately halfway back on the swing
      vi. Keep the right elbow close to the body
      vii. Shift weight from left foot to right foot
      viii. At top of backswing the left shoulder will be pointing at the ball and the club will be parallel to the ground, pointing toward the target
   c. Downswing
      i. Start with the left leg
      ii. Left foot comes down flat to the ground
      iii. Shift weight from right foot to left foot
      iv. Bend the knees to allow freedom of movement
      v. There is a feeling of pulling from the left side
      vi. Uncock the wrists when the hands are parallel with the ground
      vii. At the moment of impact the ball, the hands, and the left shoulder are almost in a straight line
      viii. The left leg straightens and becomes firm
   d. Follow-through
      i. The right arm is just as straight as the left was on the backswing
      ii. The head rises naturally with the pulling of the right shoulder
      iii. The grip must be firm but not tight throughout the swing
      iv. Arms are stretched out as far as possible
      v. The wrists will begin to turn over after the arms have reached the limit
      vi. Finish with the hands high
4. Suggestions for putting
   a. Keep the putter blade flat on the ground
   b. Keep toes parallel with the line of flight
   c. Putt the ball off the left foot
   d. Keep the blade low to the ground
   e. Use no body or head action at any time

3. Play the shot safely rather than gamble on a "lucky one"
4. Open the face of the club slightly to cut the grass better and to give a quicker rise in long grass
5. Each rough position will differ from the last, so judge each one individually

RULES

1. The ball must be played as it lies except as outlined by the rules. Local rules may permit preferred lies, or "winter rules," in which case the ball may be moved with the club head, provided that it is not moved nearer the hole.
2. The ball must be fairly struck with the head of the club.
3. The player whose ball is farthest from the hole plays first.
4. If a ball goes out of bounds, the player must play the next stroke at the spot from which the ball was last struck. If the stroke was played from the tee, the ball may be teed; in all other cases it must be dropped. The penalty is loss of stroke and distance. (Add 2 strokes to score for the hole.) If any part of the ball lies in-bounds, the ball remains in play.
5. In match play, if a player's ball knocks the opponent's ball into the hole, the opponent shall be considered to have holed out on the last shot. A ball that has been moved by an opponent's ball may be left at that point or replaced in its original spot. In stroke play, the ball moved must be replaced as near as possible to its original spot. The golfer playing the putt has the right to ask the opponent to mark the ball.

   The player has the option of having the flagstick attended or removed. If the putted ball strikes an attended flagstick or a person attending the flagstick in stroke play, there is a 2-stroke penalty. In match play, if the flagstick is held by an opponent or an opponent's caddy, the opponent loses the hole. If it is held by the player's caddy, the player loses the hole.

   Note: If a ball is believed to be out of bounds, a provisional ball may be played before the golfer leaves the point from which the first ball was played.
6. Irregularities of surface that might in any way affect the player's stroke may not be removed or pressed down by the player, any partner, or caddies. However, ball marks on a green may be repaired before putting.
7. A player may not move, bend, or break anything fixed or growing before striking at a ball in play. This applies to holding branches out of the way and to trampling weeds to improve the lie of the ball.
8. A ball lying or touching an obstruction, such as clothing, lumber, vehicles, ground under repair, and the like, may be lifted and dropped away from such

an object without penalty but may not be moved closer to the hole. The ball is dropped by holding it in front of the body and with the arm parallel to the ground.

9. If a player's stroke is interfered with by any object such as just mentioned, the ball may be moved two club lengths, no nearer the hole, without penalty.
10. When a ball lies in a hazard, nothing shall be done that can in any way improve its lie; the club may not touch the ground in addressing the ball or during the backswing; nor may anything be touched or moved by the player before the ball is struck.
11. If a ball lies or is lost in a recognized water hazard (whether the ball lies in water or not, or in casual water in a hazard) the player may drop a ball, under penalty of 1 stroke, either behind the hazard, keeping the spot at which the ball crossed the margin of the hazard between himself or herself and the hole, or in the hazard, keeping the spot at which the ball entered the water between himself or herself and the hole. If the ball was played from the teeing ground, a ball may be teed under the penalty of 1 stroke, as near as possible to the spot from which the original ball was played. If a ball lies or is lost in casual water (unintentional hazard), the player may drop a ball without penalty on dry ground as near as possible to the spot where the ball lay but not nearer to the hole.
12. A golfer may have no more than 14 clubs when playing.
13. A ball is considered lost if not found within 5 minutes.

ETIQUETTE

Students should study golf etiquette carefully and govern their conduct accordingly. Golf developed as a mannerly game, and it still remains so. One should play the game by the rules without exception.

1. There may be no more than four persons in one party, and each person must have a set of clubs.
2. No one should move or talk or stand close to or directly behind the ball or the hole when a player is making a stroke.
3. On the putting green, the player whose ball lies nearest the hole should hold the pin while other players putt.
4. No player should play until golfers playing ahead are out of range.
5. Players looking for a lost ball should allow other players coming up to pass them. They should signal to the players following them to pass, and having given such a signal, should not continue their play until these players have passed ahead and are out of range.
6. A player should see that any turf cut or displaced (a divot) by him or her is at once replaced and *pressed down*.
7. No practice shots should be attempted on any part of the course when other golfers are following.
8. Slow players should allow a faster group to play through.
9. Local course rules should be observed.
10. All shots should be played according to the rules of the game.
11. The player farthest away from the hole plays or putts first.
12. A player should avoid walking ahead of partners or opponents.
13. The tee shot must be played from between or slightly behind the markers.
14. If any person on the course is in danger of being hit by your shot, "Fore" should be called as a warning.
15. The golf bag should always be kept off the green.
16. Footprints in a sand trap should be smoothed out after a shot.
17. When holding the flag on the green, a player should stand so that a shadow does not fall across the cup.
18. When all players have holed out, the party leaves the putting green immediately for oncoming players.
19. When one member of a twosome, threesome, or foursome has lost a ball, all members of the group should help look for it.
20. Above all, players should be courteous.

Golf teaches the highest principles of etiquette and consideration for others. The game is no longer enjoyable when rules are broken at random. Golf etiquette is easily understood and, when correctly observed, affords pleasure and enjoyment of the game.

TEACHING CONSIDERATIONS

1. The basic swing is usually introduced with a No. 5 iron as a full swing. It is advisable to practice without the ball until basic form is established. Golf whiffle balls are useful once the ball is introduced. This enables students to get a great deal of practice with limited equipment. Repetition is critical. Nets to hit into prevent time being wasted chasing balls.
2. As soon as possible, give students a target and distance goal to swing toward so that maximum force can be attained and the importance of form can be established.
3. Introduce woods and other irons as only slight variations of the basic swing. Emphasize the basic elements as well as critical differences between use of the woods and other irons. One wood and a No. 9 or wedge are all that are necessary for basic instruction before learners are

introduced to playing a hole (or toward a distance target area).

4. Teach principles of putting, but permit variations in style.
5. After learners have had experience with a wood, several irons, and putting, introduce concepts regarding the short swing, pitch and chip shots, and strategies for different lies. Each of these situations should be practiced separately, not just alluded to in instruction.
6. If possible, have learners go to a golf course before the end of the unit and not just as a culminating event. Prepare them for a particular course and review golf etiquette and rules. Learners will return to instruction highly motivated and willing to share their experiences and problems when they have had an opportunity to actually play golf.
7. Emphasize safety considerations at the beginning of the golf unit. Be strict about the movement patterns allowed on the field or in the gymnasium. For example, some golfers will finish hitting their allotment of balls before others, and the tendency for those already finished is to collect their balls. This places these golfers in the line of fire from those still hitting. Also, be strict about maintaining an appropriate distance from other golfers, on all sides.

GLOSSARY

ace Making the hole in one stroke
addressing the ball Placing the body and club in position to stroke the ball.
approach shot A shot played to the green.
apron The area immediately surrounding the green.
away Ball farthest from the hole, to be played first.
banana ball Slang term for "slice."
birdie Making a hole in 1 stroke less than par.
bogey A score of 1 over par on any hole.
bunker Hazard, usually artificial, of exposed ground or sand.
caddie Assistant to the player, who watches the ball, carries the clubs, and the like.
carry The distance the ball travels through the air.
casual water Not a permanent water hazard. A ball lying in casual water may be lifted without penalty.
clubs Implements used to propel the ball.
course rating Comparative course difficulty.
cup Hole into which the ball is played.
dead Ball does not roll after flight.
divot Slice of turf cut out with club.
driver No. 1 wood.
eagle Two under par for any hole.
face Contact surface of the club head.
fairway The mowed or well-kept part of the area between the tee and the green.
flagstick Indicates the position and sometimes the number of hole. The flagstick is in the hole.
fore Warning signal that a ball is approaching another player.
foursome Four people playing as a group.
fringe See **apron.**
green Short-cropped grass around a hole.
grip Handle of the club or method of grasping.
gross score Actual score shot by a player in stroke play.
halved Tied score on a hole or in a complete game.
handicap Strokes given to a player to enable him or her to shoot a score of par, computed on the basis of the difference between the player's average score and par.
hazard Natural or unnatural obstacle on a course.
head Part of club used for hitting.
heel Inside part of the club head at base of shaft.
hole The cup into which the ball is rolled.
hole high A shot hit the correct distance to the green but not on target.
hole out Final stroke for a hole.
holed A ball is "holed" when it is in the cup.
honor Right to play first from a tee by low score on the previous hole.
hook A shot that curves to the left if hit by a right-handed golfer.
iron A club with an iron head.
lie Position of the ball on the course.
links The entire course.
loft The elevation of a shot or angle of the club face.
match A game.
match play Competition played on a hole-by-hole basis.
medal play Competition based on total strokes per round (also called "stroke play").
par Expected score for a hole; a set number of strokes
penalty stroke A stroke added to the score of a player or team for a rules violation.
pin The flagstick in the hole marking it.
play through When faster players are allowed to advance through slower players.
press Too much tensing of muscles or swinging too hard. Also, slight forward movement of the hands before putting or swinging the club.
pull-shot A shot hit diagonally to the left (right-handed golfer).
push-shot A shot hit diagonally to the right (right-handed golfer).
rim the cup A ball that rolls around the edge of the cup without falling in rims the cup.
rough Rough ground and long grass off the fairway.
round Any series of holes, generally 18.
sandy Successful one-putt following a bunker shot.
shaft The stick that holds the club head.
slice The ball curves to the right (right-handed golfer).
stance Position of the feet.
stroke Act of swinging at the ball even though it may be missed.
swing through A focus point a golfer uses prior to hitting the ball.
tee An elevation, generally a wooden peg, on which the ball is placed and from which it is to be driven.
teeing ground Starting point for each hole; a designated area between markers.
toe Front portion of the club head away from the shaft.
topped A ball hit above the center that rolls on the ground.
trap Usually a sand pit in the fairway and around the green.
up The number of holes or strokes by which one leads an opponent.

up and down Successful one-putt following a pitch or chip shot.

waggle Preliminary movements with the club as the ball is addressed.

whiff A swing that misses the ball.

wood A club with a wooden head.

SUGGESTED READINGS

Ballingall, P. 1995. *101 essential tips: Golf.* New York: Dorling Kindersley. Covers all aspects of golf, including grip and swing fundamentals, playing the game, special conditions, and clothing and equipment. This book is a handy reference to all aspects of the game.

Burr, B. 1997. *Golf for lefties.* Indianapolis: Masters Press. A book written with the left-handed golfer in mind. Covers the entire game from driving to putting.

Ewers, J. R. 1989. *Golf.* Glenview, Ill.: Scott, Foresman. Geared for beginning and intermediate golfers. The book contains practice drills, methods for correcting errors, and advice on how to choose a golf course.

Fahey, T. D. 1995. *Basic golf.* Mountainview, Calif.: Mayfield. Presents the fundamentals of golf with an overview of the history, rules, equipment, and fundamentals. Golf-specific conditioning and golf-related injuries are discussed briefly.

Fisher, A. G. 1992. *Golf: Your turn for success.* Boston: Jones & Bartlett. Covers basic skills, rules, etiquette, specialty shots, practice and improvement techniques, mental aspects of the game, and tournament play.

Flick, J. 1997. *On golf: Lessons from America's master teacher.* New York: Villard. The author does not believe in the mechanical approach to golf but offers enough mechanics to be instructional. The book is inspirational, instructional, and entertaining.

Frank, J. A. 1994. *Golf secrets.* New York: Lyons & Burford. Offers tee-to-green solutions for golf's toughest problems. The content is useful to both beginning and advanced golfers.

Heuler, O. 1995. *Perfecting your golf swing: New ways to lower your score.* New York: Sterling. Full-color photographs and expert advice on all aspects of the game, including warm-up exercises and common faults. The book is written for all golfers, from beginners to experts.

How to play better golf. 1991. London: Ward Lock. Comprehensive instruction manual written by a distinguished team of PGA golf professionals. The book covers fundamentals, solutions to common faults, and choice of equipment.

Leadbetter, D. 1993. *David Leadbetter's faults and fixes.* New York: HarperCollins. Offers solutions to eighty of the most common problem areas in golf. The author identifies a weakness and then offers drills and exercises to eliminate it.

Leadbetter, D. 1990. *The golf swing.* Lexington, Mass: Stephen Greene Press. Presents an organized and systematic way of accelerating the learning process. Shows how a sound swing can be developed in a step-by-step manner, highlighted by 250 color illustrations.

Mackenzie, M. M. 1990. *Golf: The mind game.* New York: Dell. Provides over thirty situation-specific exercises to help readers deepen their awareness of their emotional and intellectual barriers to learning and performing. The book is a good companion to skill learning because it shows readers how to capitalize on their inner resources—confidence, consistency, and concentration.

Owens, D., and Bunker, L. K. 1995. *Golf: Steps to success.* 2d. ed. Champaign, Ill.: Human Kinetics. Provides more than eighty drills and practice techniques for golfers of all abilities. The book offers a sequential program of lessons and drills, including performance goals, key points to remember while performing, and skill progressions. Instructor guide available.

Rankin, J. 1995. *A woman's guide to better golf.* Chicago: Contemporary Books. Offers a combination of mechanical advice, gleaned from the author's many years of competitive golf, and practical suggestions specifically targeted to today's woman golfer. The book covers the spectrum of the setup, full swing, short game, putting, sand play, strategy, and trouble shots.

Rotella, B. 1996. *Golf is a game of confidence.* New York: Simon & Schuster. Filled with anecdotes and inspirational instruction. Focuses on the most important skill a golfer can have—the ability to think confidently. More relevant for intermediate and advanced players.

Rotella, B. 1995. *Golf is not a game of perfect.* New York: Simon & Schuster. Emphasizes the mental approach to the game once the basic skills are learned. More relevant for intermediate and advanced players.

United States Golf Association. 1996. *1997 rules of golf.* Far Hills, N.J.: United States Golf Association. Official rules of the game.

Whitworth, K. 1990. *Golf for women.* New York: St. Martin's Press. Illustrated with 120 instructional photographs, the book is simple enough for a beginner, but offers advice and techniques useful for advanced players. Fundamentals covered include driving, long iron play, trouble shots, chipping, putting, and bunker shots.

Wiren, G. 1991. *The PGA manual of golf.* New York: Simon & Schuster. Covers everything from selection of equipment to preshot routines, and from golf exercises and physical training to the mental side of the game. Also included are hundreds of sequence shots of the game's best players.

Golf Magazines

Golf Digest, 800-PAR-GOLF.

Golf Magazine, 800-876-7726. Both are available on the newsstand or by subscription. Articles cover all facets of the game, from fundamentals to travel.

RESOURCES

Audiovisual

Golfworks, 4820 Jackson Rd., Newark, OH 43055

"How To" Sports Videos, P.O. Box 5852, Denver, CO 80217

Professional Golf Association, 100 Ave. of the Champions, P.O. Box 12458, Palm Beach Gardens, FL 33410

Sports Video, 745 State Circle, P.O. Box 1941, Ann Arbor, MI 48106

CD-ROM

Fundamentals of a model swing, deluxe edition (Windows). Offers step-by-step instructions on how to master the perfect swing with over 8½ hours of drills and instruction.

Golf tips: Breaking 100 (DOS). Basic fundamentals for beginning and intermediate golfers.

Gymnastics and Tumbling

After completing this chapter, the reader should be able to:

- Appreciate the historical development of gymnastics and tumbling
- Understand the importance of safety and spotting techniques
- State the basic rules for dual-meet competitions in gymnastics
- Explain fundamental skills in vaulting, pommel horse, parallel bars, high bar, still rings, floor exercise, uneven parallel bars, and balance beam
- Demonstrate fundamental skills and techniques in tumbling activities
- Teach basic gymnastics and tumbling skills safely

Gymnastics

HISTORY

The word *gymnastics* means "naked art" and comes from the early Greeks. It is believed that the Chinese were the first to develop activities that resembled gymnastics. The Greeks worked *with* an apparatus rather than on it, whereas the Romans used an apparatus in the form of a wooden horse on which to practice in preparation for combat. The word *gymnasium* is also a Greek word and means the ground or place for gymnastic performances.

Johann Basedow (1723–90) was the first European to teach organized gymnastic exercises. Johann Guts Muths (1759–1839), the "great-grandfather of gymnastics," published the first book on gymnastics.

After the Napoleonic victories over the Germans, a plan for building up the national strength of Germany was formulated by Frederick Jahn during the period from 1810 to 1852. Jahn is credited with introducing the parallel bars, the horizontal bar, the side horse with pommels, and the vaulting buck. He wanted the Germans to be united to protect themselves, so he took the boys of Berlin to nearby woods on hikes and there they invented these different types of apparatus. In 1842, ten years before Jahn's death, formally structured gymnastics was introduced into the German public school.

Mats were first used in Copenhagen, Denmark, when the Military Gymnastic Institute was opened to train teachers in gymnastics.

Around 1850 a wave of German immigration brought gymnastics clubs to the United States, where they were called Turner Societies.

In 1865 the American Turners established a Normal College of the American Gymnastic Union for training gymnastic teachers.

Gymnastics, through these Turner Clubs, YMCAs, schools, and colleges, became well established in the United States. Heavy apparatus, such as parallel bars, uneven parallel bars, vaulting horse, horizontal bar, side horse, rings, and balance beams, is the equipment used in most schools, colleges, clubs, and YMCA gymnasiums; the more elementary jungle gyms, teeter-totters, slides, rings, and swings are used in parks and community centers.

Gymnastics in modern usage and competition generally refers to body movements on apparatus and tumbling on mats.

The use of apparatus in American public schools and colleges was impeded by three factors:

1. Around 1800 Dio Lewis introduced exercises that did not require apparatus, and the schools accepted them enthusiastically.
2. The Swedish influence around 1900 emphasized calisthenics.
3. Between World War I and World War II, gymnastics did not occupy its rightful place in the total program of high schools and colleges in the United States. The trend was toward mild recreational activities for the majority, and strenuous competition was encouraged only for a few.

Following World War II the pendulum swung back to resistive forms of exercise, including gymnastics. Today there is considerable emphasis on competitive gymnastics in the secondary schools, YMCAs, private gymnastics clubs, and colleges throughout the United States.

Noteworthy developments were the organization of the National Association of American Gymnastic Coaches in 1946 and the National Gymnastic Clinic in 1951. The current ruling body for gymnastics is USA Gymnastics (USAG).

Participation in gymnastics has increased dramatically in recent years. This increase is probably in part due to the impact of the televised Olympic games, during which names such as Olga Korbut, Nadia Comaneci, Kurt Thomas, and Mary Lou Retton became familiar. The tremendous success of the 1984 U.S. Olympic gymnastics team will undoubtedly continue this trend. Because the strong Soviet team was not present at the 1984 Los Angeles Olympics, the first American gold medal in gymnastics since 1932 was won by the men's team. Mary Lou Retton's gold medal in the all-around event was the first individual Olympic gymnastics medal of any kind to be won by an American woman. By winning the team gold, all-around silver (Peter Vidmar); pommel horse gold (Vidmar); parallel bars gold (Bart Connors), silver (Mitch Gaylord), and bronze (Tim Dagget); and rings bronze (Mitch Gaylord), the 1984 U.S. men's team by far surpassed any previous U.S. gymnastics success. But perhaps the most dramatic moment of the 1984 summer Olympics came when Mary Lou Retton "stuck" her vault for a rare perfect score of 10 to win the all-around event. This highlight capped the best U.S. women's gymnastics performance ever with a team silver medal, vault silver (Mary Lou Retton), uneven parallel bars silver (Julianne McNamara) and bronze (Mary Lou Retton), balance beam bronze (Kathy Johnson), and floor exercise silver (Julianne McNamara) and bronze (Mary Lou Retton).

The Soviet men and women returned to the 1988 Olympic games with outstanding teams. Both won the team gold medal and most of the individual medals. The U.S. men's team finished a disappointing eleventh, and the women's team finished fourth, with Phoebe Mills capturing the only individual medal (a bronze on the beam).

The women's bid for the team bronze was crushed by a controversial 0.5-point penalty assessed by the head of the technical committee. In fact, many tremendous gymnastic performances were overshadowed by such controversies and questions about judging. Forty perfect scores of 10 were awarded to 14 gymnasts, and in the men's pommel horse a three-way tie for the gold was awarded.

In the 1992 Olympics the former USSR team, then called the Unified team, won the men's and women's team gold. The U.S. men's team finished sixth; the women's team finished third. The highlight for the U.S. men's team was a first place finish on the high bar by Trent Dimas. Shannon Miller was the best performer of the women's team, earning second in the all-around and a silver and two bronze medals for individual events.

Although the 1996 Olympic Games in Atlanta were somewhat disappointing for the U.S. men's team (the only medal they won was a silver in the parallel bars by Jair Lynch), it was spectacular for the U.S. women's team. Dominique Dawes won the bronze medal in floor exercise, Amy Chow tied for the silver in the uneven parallel bars, and Shannon Miller captured the gold on the balance beam—and the team gold was won by the United States women, just edging out the Russian team.

SAFETY RULES

1. Apparatus should be inspected regularly to detect faults, make proper adjustments, and remove hazards.
2. Accidents on apparatus rarely "just happen." They are usually caused by carelessness.
3. An adequate number of clean mats should be placed around the apparatus. To extend their wear, mats should be carried, not dragged. To prevent landing injuries, especially to ankles, mats should not be overlapped when placed around the apparatus. They should be folded and put away when not in use.
4. Strength and skill are built progressively; the need for progression from the simple to the more complex must be recognized.
5. Instructors should master the art of spotting through instruction and by practicing with supervision.
6. Magnesium chalk on the hands will help prevent slipping. To prevent hand tearing, wearing leather grips should be encouraged.
7. Horseplay should be absolutely forbidden in the gymnastics area.
8. Flexibility and stretching exercises are essential before and after practicing stunts. Strength development is also an important feature of any gymnastics program.

SPOTTING

Spotting is such an important safety and teaching skill that it deserves special attention. It involves the supporting, catching, or adjusting of the performer to aid in the completion of a stunt and to prevent possible injury from landing incorrectly. Spotting can aid the performer in "getting the feel" of a stunt or sequence of stunts. It is accomplished by hand spotting or with specialized equipment such as spotting belts. The most important purpose of spotting is for safety and to prevent injury, especially of the head, neck, and spine. Whether for teaching or for safety, the spotter should (1) know what the gymnast is about to perform, (2) know what and when possible mishaps might occur, (3) know what must be done to execute the spot and when the spot must occur, and (4) be strong enough to assist if needed. Directions for spotting are given with many of the stunts described. Where required, the spot (•) shown on the figures illustrating most of the skills indicates the point(s) at which the instructor should offer assistance.

DUAL-MEET COMPETITION

Competition rules for high schools are written by the National Federation of State High School Associations. The USAG writes rules for competitions in colleges and clubs.

Order of competition

Men

The events, in order of competition, for a dual meet are floor exercise, pommel horse, still rings, long-horse vaulting, parallel bars, and high bar. Usually a 2-minute warm-up period is allowed after the start in championship meets; however, none is permitted in dual meets.

Number of entries. Each team shall be limited to a maximum of six entries per event. Four of the men must be designated as all-around contestants. A gymnastics team shall be limited to 12 men.

Women

For women the order of events in competition is vaulting, uneven parallel bars, balance beam, and floor exercise.

Number of entries. The number of gymnasts from each team to compete in each event should exceed the number of scores that will count for the final team totals (for example, five entries using three scores per team or four entries using three scores per team).

Score

The best three scores for each team in each gymnastics event are totaled to determine the team's score for that event. This includes the all-around score. The event scores are totaled to determine the final team score.

Judges

Four judges plus one superior judge conduct the competition. Each of the four judges flashes a score based on 10 points, 4 points for composition and 6 points for execution. Then the low and high scores are dropped and the other two averaged. If the middle two scores are too far apart, the superior-judge's score is added to the average of these two scores and this sum is then divided by two to get the final score.

EQUIPMENT

1. Pommel horse
2. Long horse
3. Parallel bars
4. Uneven parallel bars
5. Horizontal bars
6. Still rings
7. Balance beam
8. Mats
9. Carbonate of magnesium
10. Emery paper to clean bars
11. Springboard
12. Floor exercise area: 40 × 40 feet (12 × 12 m)

FUNDAMENTAL SKILLS AND TECHNIQUES

The gymnastic exercises presented here are basic movements primarily for developmental purposes. Advanced stunts and routines may be found in other sources.

Vaulting

In all gymnastics events except vaulting, several stunts and movements are linked to produce a routine. In vaulting, a single stunt is performed and judged.

The vaulting event is slightly different for men and women. For men, the long horse over which the vaults are made is approximately 53 inches (1.35 m) in height, and the vaults are made over the length of the horse. In women's competition the vaults are made across the width of the horse, which is approximately 43 inches (1.09 m) in height.

Figure 15-1. Squat vault.

The vaults described and illustrated in this chapter are fundamental and seldom used in anything but the most elementary gymnastics competition. On the other hand, they are fun to learn and in some cases require courage to try the first time. The use of a springboard is optional with the vaults presented here.

Squat vault

Use a two-foot takeoff, and as the hands contact the horse, push downward; as the body begins to lift, pull the knees to the chest. When the body clears the horse, extend the body. At the landing, flex at the knees, bring the arms forward for balance, and finish by standing as if at attention (figure 15-1). The spotter should stand in front of the horse (to the left or the right).

Flank vault

This is also called the "side vault." Use a two-foot takeoff and vault so that the side of the body passes over the horse. Keep the legs extended and the toes pointed. Land in a partial knee bend with the arms extended to the side (figure 15-2).

Face vault

Use a two-foot takeoff and pass the body over the horse by doing a quarter turn so that the body faces the horse as it passes over it. Land with the side to the horse, with one hand on the horse and the other extended to the side (figure 15-3).

Rear vault

In this vault the rear (back) of the body passes over the end of the horse. If the vault is a rear vault to the right, the body makes a quarter turn to the right and passes over the horse in this position. After the body passes over the horse,

Figure 15-2. Flank vault.

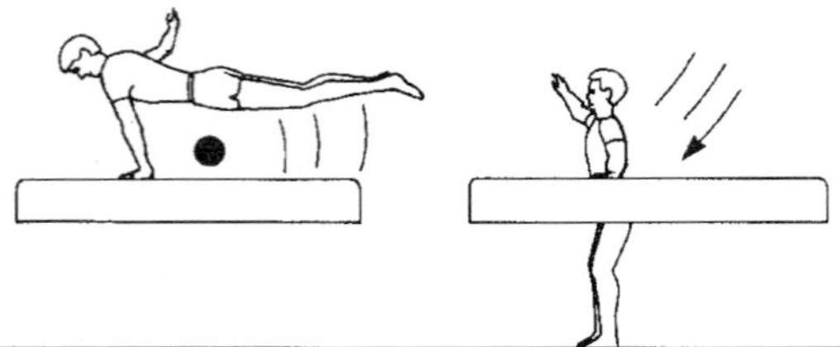

Figure 15-3. Face vault.

place the left hand on the horse and extend the right to the side (figure 15-4).

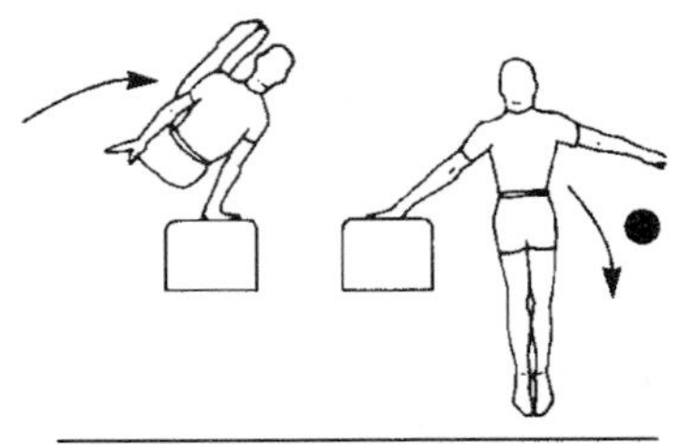

Figure 15-4. Rear vault.

Straddle vault

Do not stop on top of the horse, but pass the body completely over it. Keep the head up. This vault should be spotted closely.

The spotter stands in front of the horse and grabs both upper arms of the vaulter. As the vaulter comes forward over the horse, the spotter moves backward (figure 15-5).

Figure 15-5. Straddle vault.

Stoop vault

The stoop vault is the same as the squat vault except that the legs are kept straight rather than tucked as the body passes over the horse. This requires more height, and a vaulting board should be used. A spotter should stand in front of the horse and to one side of the performer. The spotter should grasp and lift the near shoulder and use the other arm to help lift the performer's hips as they pass over the horse (figure 15-6).

Pommel Horse

As with vaulting, the stunts described here are not normally seen in gymnastics competition, but are rather fundamental to this apparatus and are lead-up activities to more advanced stunts.

Squat to rear support

Use a two-foot takeoff and pass over the horse by lifting the hips high, keeping the head up, and bringing the knees between the arms. After the feet pass over the horse, the legs point straight down and the rear of the vaulter is supported by the horse (figure 15-7).

Feint left or right

Do this from the front support. Swing the leg up and over the end of the horse, either the right side (the croup) or the left side (the neck). If the right leg passes over the horse, turn the face to the left; if the left leg passes over the horse, turn to the right. Keep the arms fully extended, legs stiff,

Figure 15-6. Stoop vault.

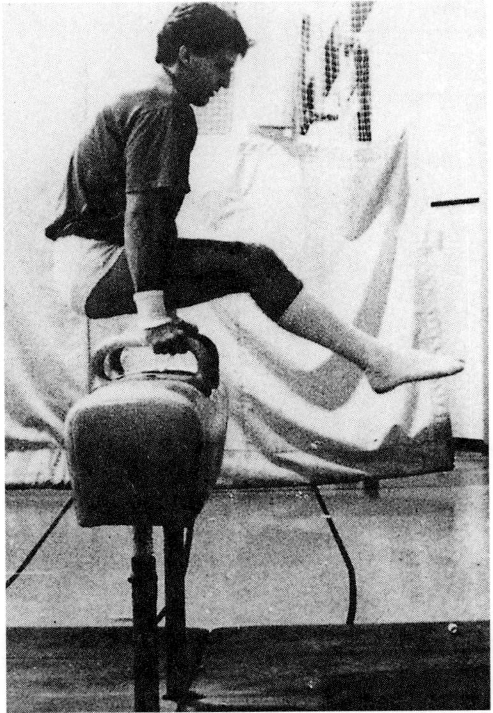

Figure 15-7. Squat to rear support.

and toes pointed. Pass the leg over the horse and then bring it back (figure 15-8).

Cut left or right

From the front leaning support, pass the leg over the end of the horse and under one hand. To accomplish this, the weight of the body must be transferred to the opposite hand. Attempt to keep both arms and legs extended (figure 15-9).

Right flank to rear support, reverse flank left to front support

If the weight is kept over the horse as the flank is performed, the catch to the rear support is not difficult. To perform the reverse flank, put all the weight on the right

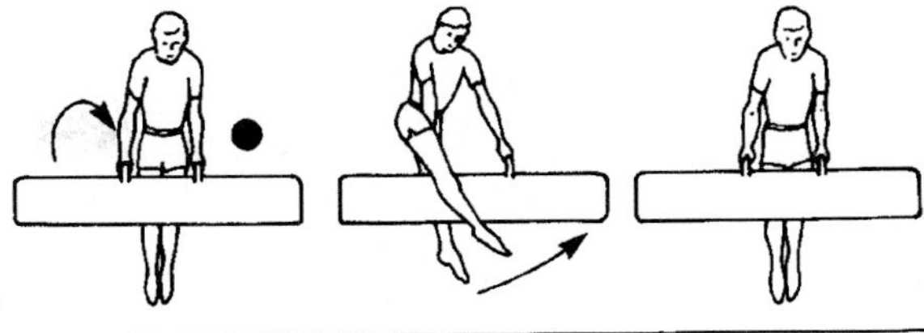

Figure 15-8. Feint left or right.

Figure 15-9. Cut left or right.

arm. The secret of the vaults and catch is proper weight distribution (figure 15-10).

One-half alternating single-leg circles and return

Jump to a support, lean to the left, and lift the right leg and arm. Bring the right leg forward, and replace the right hand on the right pommel. Lean on the right hand, lift the left leg and arm, swing the left leg forward, and replace the left hand on the left pommel. The performer should now be in a rear support position. Shift both legs to the right, separate them as the right arm is lifted, and return the right leg to its original position. Finally, lean on the right hand as the left leg is returned to its original position (figure 15-11).

Parallel Bars

Run and jump to cross support

Take the jump as in the dive and roll. Land in the forward-leaning position and then swing forward. *Spot for a collapse on the backswing.* Spot under the bar on the chest if a collapse takes place (figure 15-12).

Hand traveling

1. Hand over hand, walk forward the length of the bars. Keep the chest out, head up, back arched, and toes pointed (figure 15-13).
2. Hop the length of the bars in a straight-arm support position. In this hop forward, the hands are moved simultaneously.
3. Riding a bicycle with the legs increases the difficulty (figure 15-14).

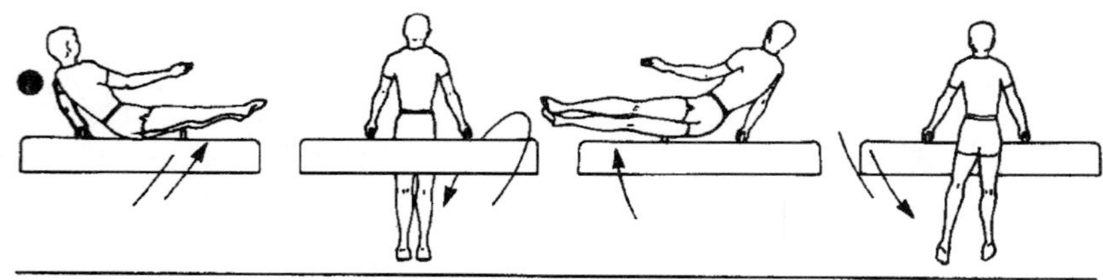

Figure 15-10. Flank right to rear support, reverse flank left to front support.

Figure 15-11. One-half alternating single-leg circles and return.

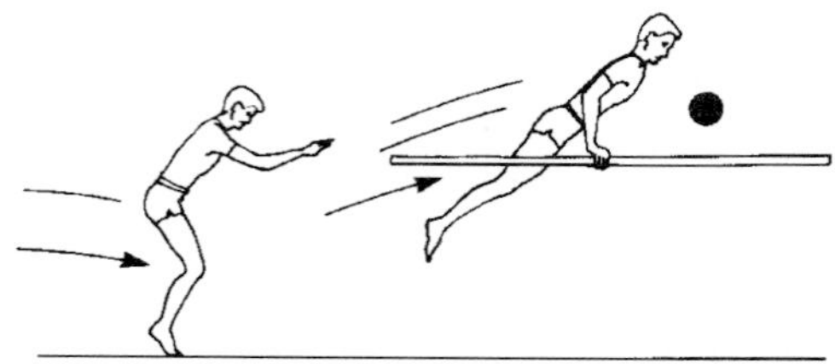

Figure 15-12. Run and jump to cross support.

Intermediate swing

From a cross-support position in the center of the bars, start to swing the body from the shoulders forward and backward. Learn to balance the center of body weight over the hand supports by learning back when the legs are moving back.

Intermediate swing with hop

In doing the intermediate swing, keep the arms extended, flex the body on the front swing, and extend it to the back

Figure 15-13. Hand traveling.

swing. The hop is executed on the front swing. *Spot this for a possible collapse right after the catch* (figure 15-15).

Forward swinging dips

1. Swing from the shoulders.
2. At the end of the rear swing, flex the arms, keeping the back arched and head up (figure 15-16).
3. Swing forward in a bent-arm position so that the chin is even with the bars in the middle of the swing.
4. At the front end of the swing, straighten the arms and shoot the feet forward.

Hip rise

Swing forward vigorously in the upper-arm hang. Approaching the front end of the swing, pull forward with the arms and then push up to a cross support (figure 15-17).

Back roll from sitting position

From a straddle-seat position in the center of the bar, grip the bar behind the back with the thumbs in. Spread the flexed elbows to make rockers. Slowly roll backward to a straddle-seat position.

Figure 15-14. Bicycle riding.

Shoulder balance

Be in the center of the bar and extend elbows to be level with the shoulders. The forearms should be flexed at the elbow, with the hands on the bar. Flex the knees and place the feet on the bars for support. Roll the hips up first, then the legs, and arch the back to maintain balance. If you start to fall backward, keep the elbows well spread and swing downward, using the upper arms as rockers. *Always have a spotter on each side when practicing this* (figure 15-18).

Dismounts

From a cross support at the center of the bars, execute one of the following dismounts over either bar:

1. Rear vault dismount, in front of hands (figure 15-19).
2. Front vault dismount behind hands.
3. Side vault dismount facing outward, in front of the hands.

From the outside cross seat on one bar, execute a rear vault over the other bar.

Short underswing dismount

Stand under the bar; jump up and grasp the bar. From a hang position, pull the body up over the bar to a front rest, drop the trunk backward, and at the same time pike at the hips and raise the legs (straight at knees) forward until the ankles are at the bar. As the body swings downward under the bar, shoot the feet forward and pull backward and upward with the arms, shooting out forward to stand on the mat.

Single- and double-leg cut

Single-leg cut. At the end of the forward swing, push back and cut off. *Keep the head back so that the face does not hit*

Figure 15-15. Intermediate swing with hop.

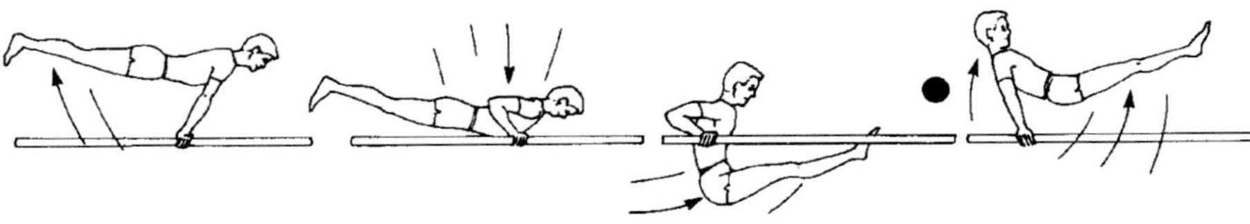

Figure 15-16. Forward swinging dips.

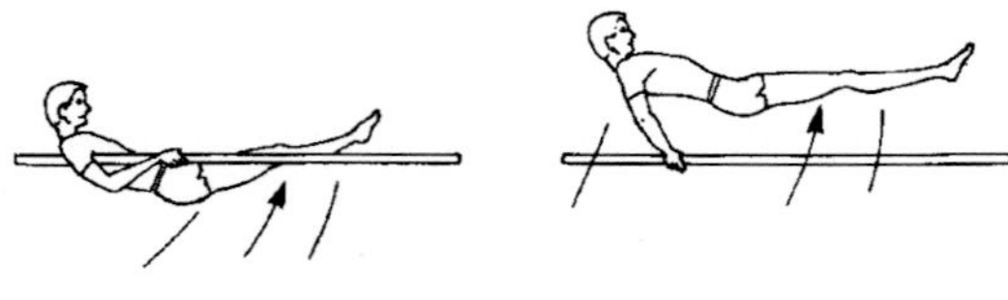

Figure 15-17. Hip rise.

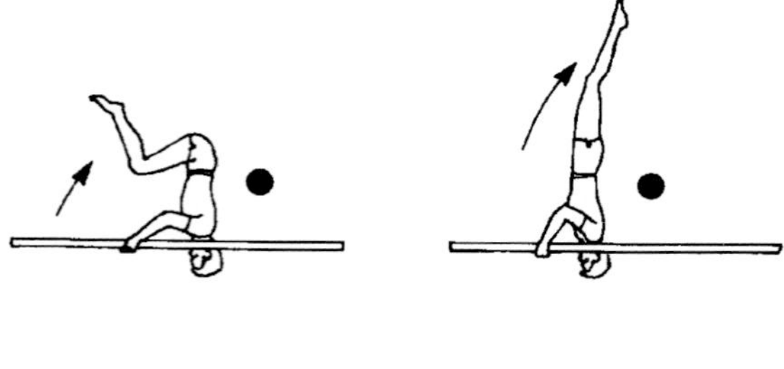

Figure 15-18. Shoulder balance.

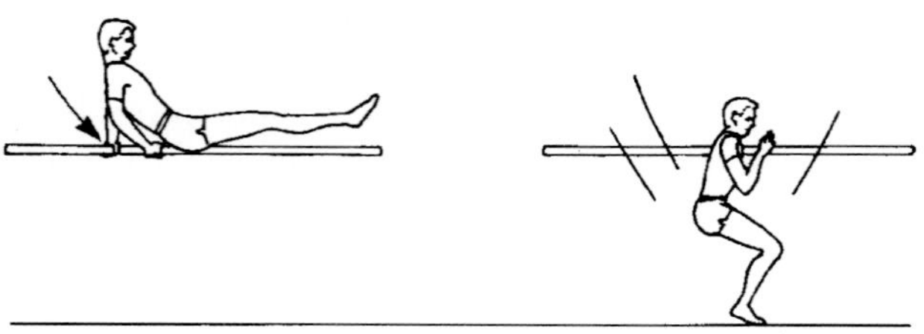

Figure 15-19. Rear vault dismount.

the bar. Spot this on both shoulders from the back. The backward lean before the cut-off is very important (figure 15-20).

Double-leg cut. Apply the same principle as in the single-leg cut-off. Cut off with both legs. Use the same spotting technique as for the single-leg cut-off. Lean back just before the cut-off (figure 15-21).

Split-off

This is nothing but a straddle vault. Be sure to keep the head up. Do not raise the hips too high. *Spot this forward on the chest and shoulders* (figure 15-22).

High Bar

Swing

Execute a short underswing from the hang and dismount.

Chins

1. Use the ordinary grasp and pull up to the chest six times.
2. Use the wide grasp and pull up to the back of the neck four times.

Figure 15-20. Single-leg cut.

Figure 15-21. Double-leg cut.

3. One hand grasps the bar and the other hand grasps the wrist of the chinning arm. Chin two times.
4. One hand grasps the bar and the other hand grasps the bicep of the chinning arm.

Skin the cat over the bar

From a hang position, pull the legs up through the hands and then over the bar; do not allow the body to swing.

Skin the cat

From a hang position, bring the legs up through the arms and over the head until the feet point toward the floor. Return to original position.

Monkey hang

From a hang position, bring the legs up through the arms and over the head until the feet point toward the floor. Release one arm, swing a complete turn on one arm, and then regrasp the bar.

Seat swing-up from swing

Pull the legs up through the hands and then over the bar. Arch the back and quickly pull the body up over the bar

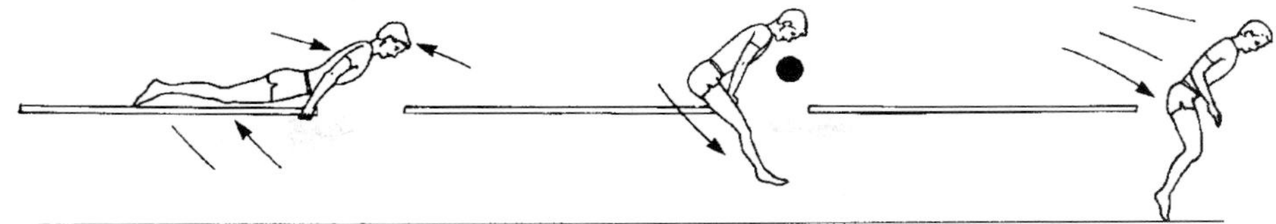

Figure 15-22. Split-off.

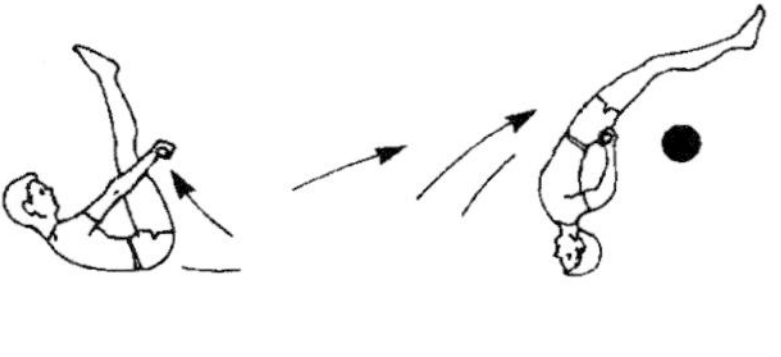

Figure 15-23. Seat swing-up from swing.

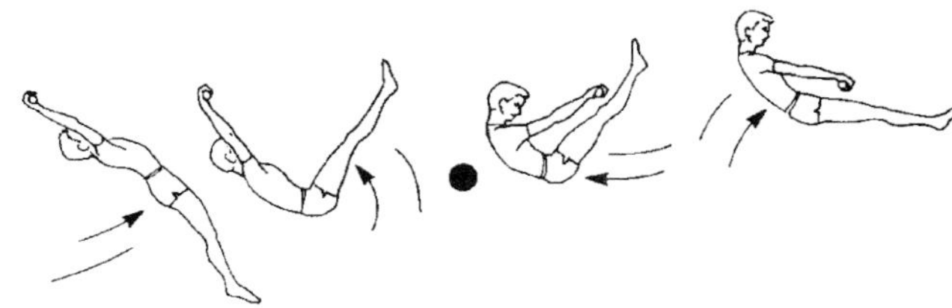

Figure 15-24. Kip, or upstart.

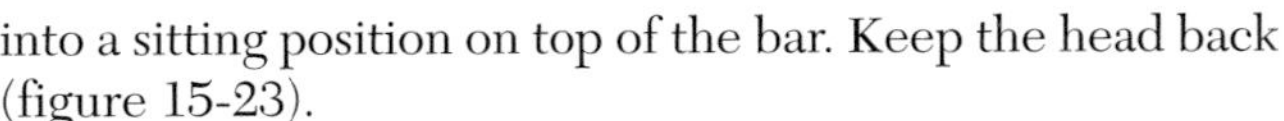

into a sitting position on top of the bar. Keep the head back (figure 15-23).

Kip, or upstart

Stress arching the back at the front of the swing. As the extended body approaches the height of the swing, bring the ankles to the bar. As the hips start to drop in the backswing, shoot the legs up, out, and down. Press down and in with the shoulder muscles. Get a little wrist motion when going above the bar. Do not push away from the bar. Force the shoulders well forward (figure 15-24).

Single-knee mount

From a hang position with an ordinary grasp, swing one knee over and hook it on the bar, inside the arms, using either leg. Swing the free leg downward and backward and pull in with the arms, mounting to a cross seat on the top of the bar.

Hand and knee circles

From a cross-riding seat on the bar (one leg on each side of the bar) and with a forward grip (thumbs in direction circle is made), reach back with the rear leg and swing it downward hard and forward. The other leg is hooked at the knee over the bar, and a complete circle backward around the bar is made. The spotter assists at the upper arm.

Crotch circles

From a side-riding seat and an ordinary grasp, fall backward to start the circle. When the body is under the bar, flex and pull on the arms somewhat to complete the circle. This circle can also be executed forward with the reverse grasp, with the thumbs in the direction of the circle. This can also be performed sideways from a cross-riding seat, the hands grasping in front. Dismount with a short underswing.

Cast

From a hang position with a regular grasp, pull up to a half chin, lean the shoulders and head back, and at the same time raise the legs, holding the knees and ankles stretched and together. Shoot the legs forward and upward, at the same time extending the elbows. As the legs swing upward and shoot outward, also shoot the body forward by pushing on the elbows for a big swing (figure 15-25). Practice this swing several times. Spot in case the hands slip off.

Heel circle forward with reverse grip

Sit on top of and grasp the bar with a reverse or undergrip. Keep the legs extended, extend the arms, and raise the hips backward until the heels rest on the bar. Keep this position and let the body drop. Slightly alter the hand and leg relationship. Start the hip extension. Drive the legs over the bar. Return to a sitting position (figure 15-26). Spot on back to the sitting position.

Uprise

A requisite for this skill is a good cast. After the cast, swing down and back in an extended posture. At the end of the back swing, pike, raise the back and shoulders, and lift the body above the bar by pushing down with the hands. Place the body weight over the bar by leaning over the bar and arching. Come to the front-leaning support (figure 15-27).

Hip circle forward

Pull over to a front-leaning support. Push down with the arms and raise the body so that the thighs rest on the bar. With the head held up, fall forward, keeping the thighs in contact with the bar. Hold this position. Shorten the radius

Figure 15-25. Cast.

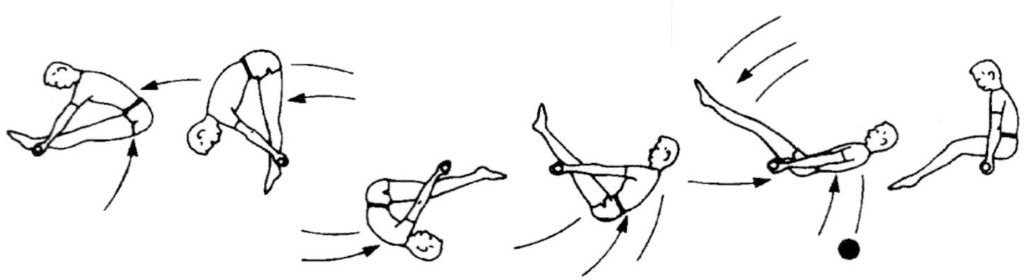

Figure 15-26. Heel circle forward with reverse grip.

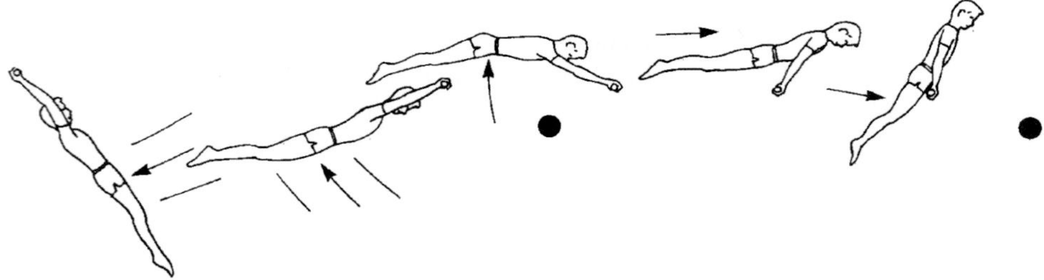

Figure 15-27. Uprise.

on the upswing by forcing the head forward and bending the arms. Come to a rest over the bar.

Cast to handstand

Practice this first on the low bar with both grips. Assume a front-leaning support position. Slightly flex the arms so that the bar contacts the lower abdomen, and swing the legs under the bar as the body leans forward. Forcefully hyperextend the body and push with the arms as the body weight remains over the bar (figure 15-28).

Half giant swing

Use the overgrip (palms down). Start cast as for a handstand, but push back. Swing down fully extended. At the 5 o'clock position, break at the waist and come to a rest on the bar (figure 15-29). The spotter can assist by pushing on the back.

Still Rings

Double front cut-off

From a pike hang position, rotate the body forward vigorously, bending the elbows, and at the same time bring the separated legs, with the knees bent, down across the elbows. Immediately afterward, while still rotating forward, release the rings and land standing on the mat (figure 15-30). The spotter can assist in the upward rotation.

Straddled fly-away

From a bent-arm hang, swing the legs and hips upward vigorously, spreading the legs held straight until the crotch is astride the wrists. While the body still has momentum, release the rings and land in a standing position (figure 15-31). Spot the lift of the hips and the front of the shoulder through the landing.

Front roll with arms flexed

This is a good stunt for the weight lifter, the bodybuilder, or the student who has been working apparatus for quite a while. It takes strength. Use a low ring to spot. Jump to the cross-support position. Lower the shoulders and raise the hips. Do not turn the hands as you perform this first move. As the body falls over, supinate the hands. Do not let the shoulders drop. As the body turns forward, pull up as high as possible and pronate the hands. This move should bring the weight above the rings and on the arms. Now perform a push-up. Spot by lifting the performer above the rings (figure 15-32).

Shoulder stand

Lower the rings to about 3 feet (0.91 m) from the floor. Now stand up on a chair or stool. Grasp the rings from the inside. Raise the hips slowly as the shoulders are lowered. On the first couple of tries, steady the body by locking the

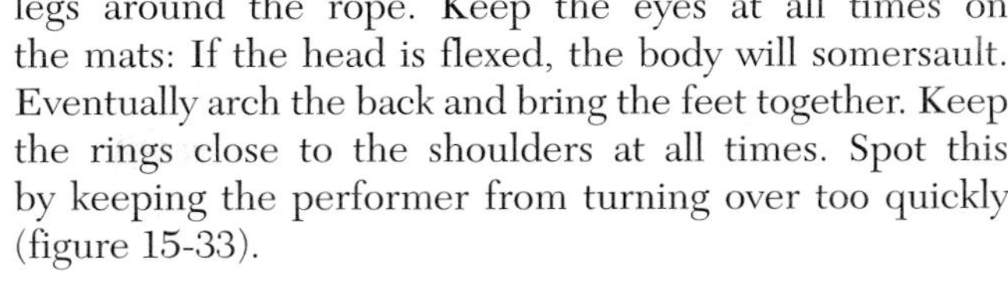

legs around the rope. Keep the eyes at all times on the mats: If the head is flexed, the body will somersault. Eventually arch the back and bring the feet together. Keep the rings close to the shoulders at all times. Spot this by keeping the performer from turning over too quickly (figure 15-33).

Muscle-up

Grasp the rings with the false, or high, grip. The body should be suspended on the wrists. Execute a pull-up as high as the chest. As the height of the pull-up is completed, the feet should be raised to about a 30-degree angle. Now drop the legs down and pronate the hands as the arms are inwardly rotated. This action should place you above the rings. Now push up, arch the back, and hold the head up. Spot this by helping to lift the performer above the difficult level (figure 15-34).

Kip

Put the rings down to chest height. Grasp them from the outside. Now take a half step backward. Lift one leg and then the other into the pike position. Swing forward, and on the backward swing extend rapidly at the waist as you push down with the hands. Force the head and shoulders forward and up. This action should place the body in a cross-support position. Spot this in the middle of the back through the waist extension (figure 15-35).

Figure 15-28. Cast to handstand.

Figure 15-29. Half giant swing (overgrip).

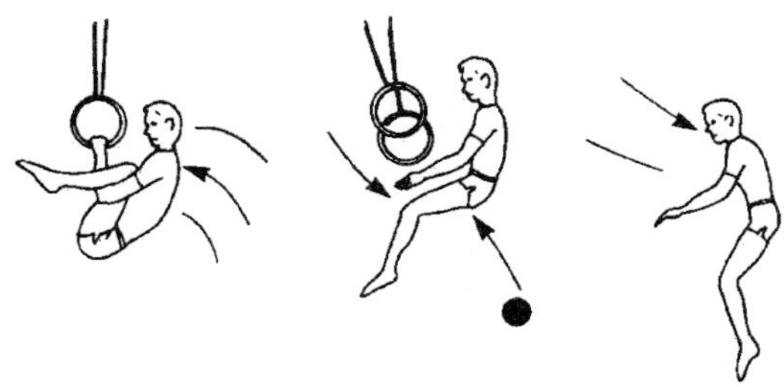

Figure 15-30. Double front cut-off.

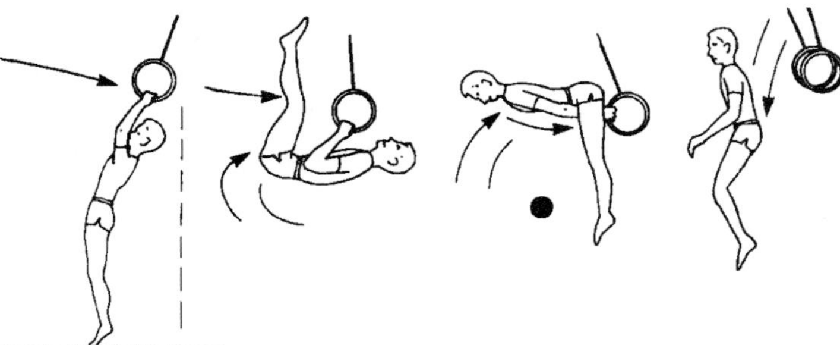

Figure 15-31. Straddled fly-away.

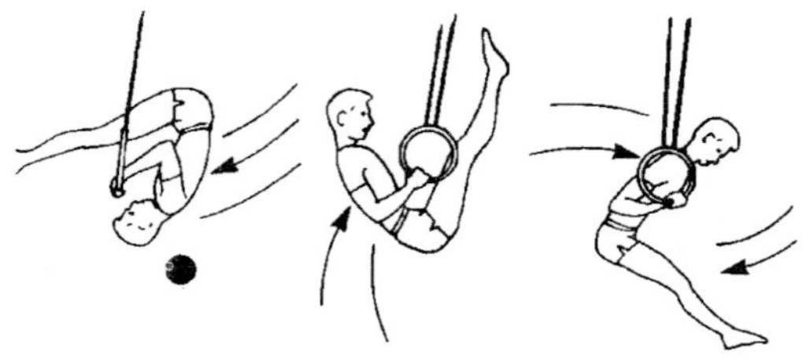

Figure 15-32. Front roll with arms flexed.

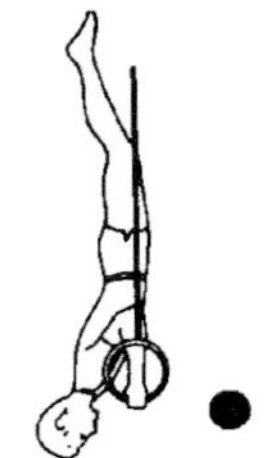

Figure 15-33. Shoulder stand.

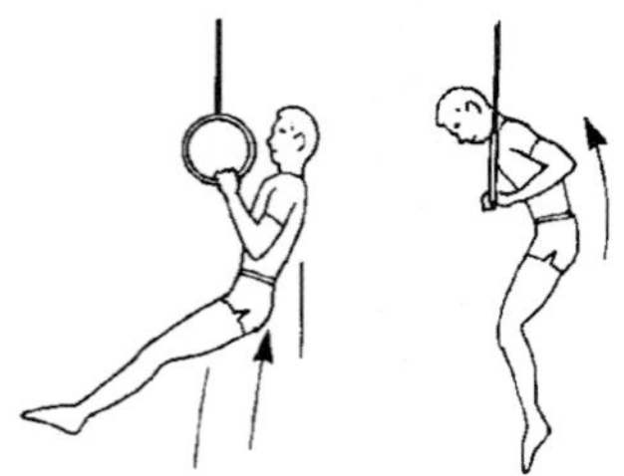

Figure 15-34. Muscle-up, or pull- and push-up.

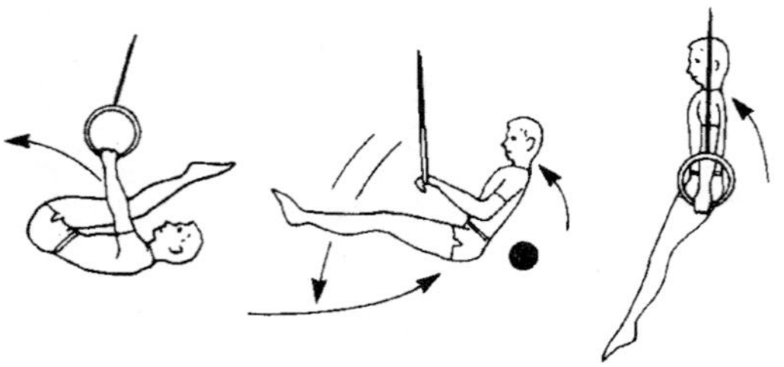

Figure 15-35. Kip.

Standing back, or reverse, cut-off

This is not a difficult stunt to master. The important thing is the timing. The level of the rings should be just above the head. Grasp the rings from the outside. While holding the rings, fall off balance, pull up to a half bend, throw the head back, and flex rapidly at the waist. Hold on as the body rotates until you can see the mat, and then release the hands. Spot with the spotter's right hand over the performer's left arm and on the chest, the left hand in the small of the back to turn the performer (figure 15-36).

Reverse uprise, or back kip

Study the figures closely. On the forward swing, go into the pike. Immediately, without a swing in the pike position, lift the hips above the rings by quickly pulling up. Now, without losing momentum, hyperextend the head and shoulders. Push down forcefully with the hands. End in a cross-support position. This is accomplished most easily with the false grip. Spot this under the shoulders (figure 15-37).

Uprise

The important move in this stunt is from the pike to hyperextension. The hips should drop out of the pike first. After the hips drop, whip the legs back and then up. Push down hard with the hands, and bring the body to rest in the cross position (figure 15-38). Spot a possible overthrow.

Floor Exercise

High-level competition in floor exercise is performed on "spring floors" made of certain types of wood, special springs, ethafoam, and covered by carpet. Those floors cover an area 40 × 40 feet (12.2 × 12.2 m). This event in high schools and recreation facilities is often performed on wrestling mats.

Floor exercise contains dance movements, including leaps and poses, elements of dance combinations, acrobatics, and tumbling grouped in rhythmic and harmonious patterns. Through these and other movements, the gymnast explores tempo, height, distance, mood, direction, and precision of form. The basic elements of form are balance,

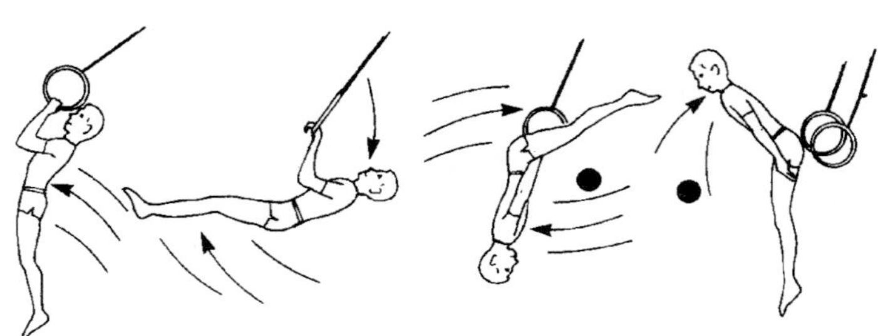

Figure 15-36. Standing back, or reverse, cut-off.

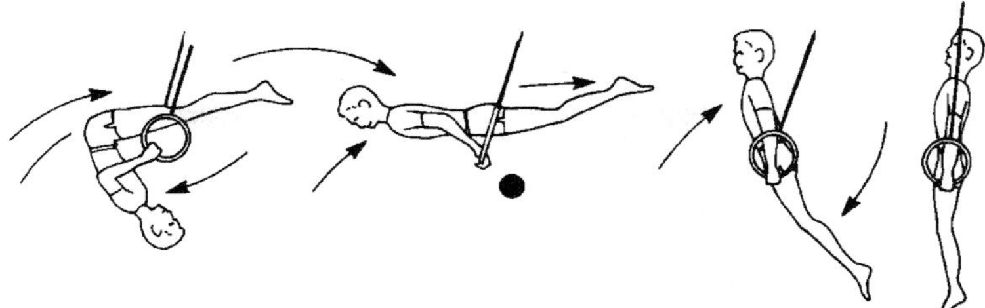

Figure 15-37. Reverse uprise, or back kip.

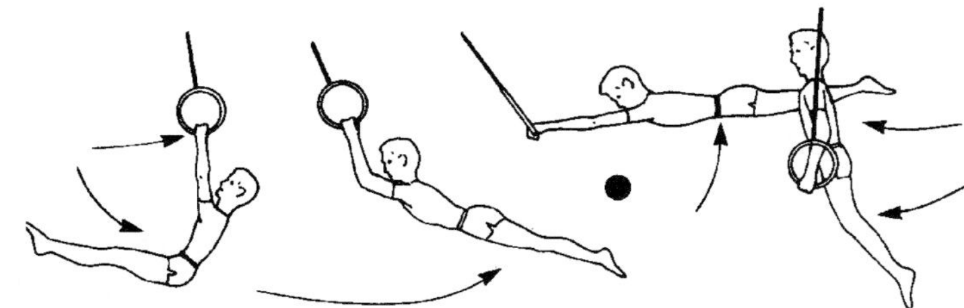

Figure 15-38. Uprise.

good body alignment, and full body extension (including pointed toes).

The routines, which are performed to music for women and without music for men, generally begin and end with a sequence of tumbling. The main part, or body, of the routine consists of dance movements, balances, flexibility stunts, and one or two additional tumbling passes.

The gymnast tries to create an artistic image. The composition is developed into a coherent pattern showing a change of pace, vitality, expression, individuality, and originality.

A great part of an individual's success involves adhering to an established and well-defined routine that includes elements that are not too difficult for the performer. Once the routine is composed, it must be practiced consistently.

Learning methods

The elementary movements and combinations must be adapted not only to the age and sex of the students but also to their mental and physical abilities.

1. Learn skills first—simple, fundamental, elementary movements. A spotter should be nearby to assist.
2. Combine various skills into series; combine dance steps and tumbling and make them into a simple routine.
3. Set routines to music for women gymnasts.
4. Warm up properly with stretching and flexibility exercises before trying the routine.

A few movements that may be used in a floor exercise routine are described below.

Toe rise, or stand

Take a standing position. Rise up on your toes and extend your arms sideward and back with the palms of your hands facing down and out, chest up, shoulders down. Lower your heels to the floor as you drop your arms at your sides to return to a full stand (figure 15-39). This activity is often practiced as an ankle strengthener.

Figure 15-39. Toe rise, or stand.

Body wave

Start with the body partially flexed—knees, hips, back, and head. Balance on the toes, with arms reaching forward but

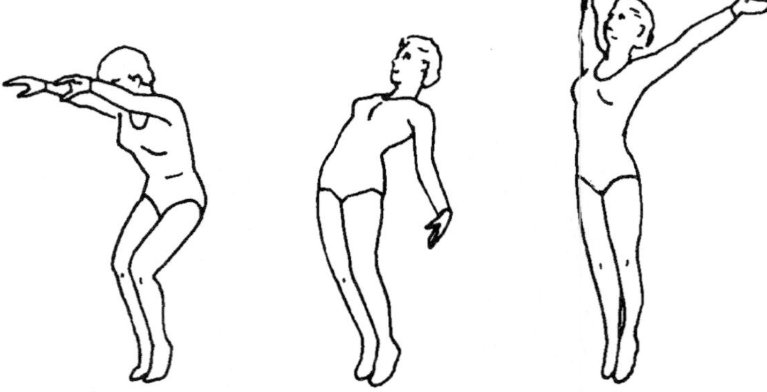

Figure 15-40. Body wave.

Figure 15-41. Split.

relaxed; then hyperextend the body and drop the arms down and back and the head forward. Last, extend the head, raise the body tall, and elevate the arms (figure 15-40).

Split

Stand with one leg ahead of the other, and slowly lower the body downward into a split (figure 15-41).

One-leg balance

Take a standing position. Raise one leg to the side as high as possible. Grasp the instep of your raised leg with one hand and extend the other arm to a horizontal or upward position (figure 15-42).

Front scale

Take a standing position. Raise one leg backward and upward as the chest moves forward. As you balance on one foot, extend your arms horizontally in front of you. Keep your head up and arch your back (figure 15-43).

Figure 15-42. One-leg balance.

Arabesque

Take a standing position. Raise one leg horizontally backward. Balance on one foot and hold your arms out to the side and slightly back for balance. (One arm may be raised, the other one out to the side.) Allow your body to lean slightly forward and at the same time keep your head and chest almost vertical (figure 15-44).

Figure 15-43. Front scale.

Figure 15-44. Arabesque.

Handstand

Place your hands on the mat, shoulder-width apart, with your fingers pointing forward. Keep your arms straight, head up, and eyes forward. Kick upward. Extend the shoulders and hold stomach and buttocks tight. Do not arch the back (figure 15-45). The spotter should catch the calf of the leg on the kick-up and place the beginner in a good handstand position.

Figure 15-45. Handstand.

Figure 15-46. Back walkover.

Back walkover

From a standing position with the arms raised over the head, bring one leg (extended) up parallel with the floor. As the hips shift forward, reach back, arch the back, and place the hands with the fingers pointing forward on the mat. As the hands contact the mat, kick the leg that was originally raised and push with the other leg to complete the walkover. Spot by kneeling on the side of the raised leg, support the performer's back with an extended right arm, and use the left hand to assist the movement of the raised leg during the kicking portion of the stunt (figure 15-46).

Figure 15-47. Front walkover.

Figure 15-48. Valdez to handstand.

Front walkover

Take a standing position. Go into a handstand with the legs split (figure 15-47). Shift the shoulders back as the lead foot continues over to the floor. Land on one foot. As the hips shift forward, lift your hands off the floor, bring your body to an upright position, and then bring your other foot to the floor.

Valdez to handstand

Sit on the floor. Place one hand on the floor in back of your hip. Raise your other arm shoulder high and turn the palm of that hand upward. Bend one leg so that the sole of your foot is on the floor near your seat and your knee is near your chest. Extend the other leg. (A Valdez can be done on the same arm with either leg bent. For some it is easier to have the bent leg on the same side and the supporting arm.) From this position, push with the support bent leg to lift the hips upward, raise your arm overhead and directly to the rear with the head following the arc of the arm thrown upward. (The hand is twisted, but the throw is directly back.) Lift the extended leg upward. (The move will be on one plane with one dimension—a straight line back like a flip-flop.) Speed is picked up with a vigorous leg push and a strong head and arm throw. Keep the head between the arms for straight, clean lines and correct body position. A handstand is assured with an extended head throw (figure 15-48). A spotter should assist with the leg push.

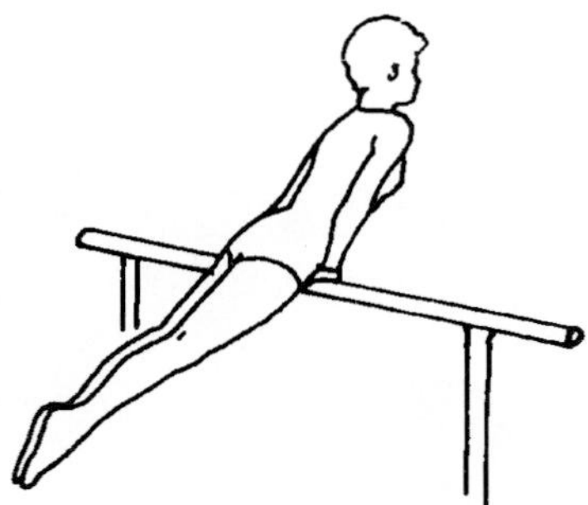

Figure 15-49. Jump to front-leaning support.

Figure 15-50. Back pullover.

Uneven Parallel Bars

One of the last pieces of apparatus to be added to the sport of gymnastics was the uneven parallel bars. The routines performed on this apparatus are a cross between those performed on the horizontal bar and those on the parallel bars. Originally the routines included predominately pretty, graceful positions, but over the years the event has become one of fast, powerful swinging movements. The following stunts and their explanations are basic to more complex stunts but still require much time and practice to master.

Jump to front-leaning support

Stand facing the low bar. With the hands on the bar in an overgrip, jump so that the body comes to rest on a straight-arm support (figure 15-49).

Back pullover

Grasp the low bar with an overhand grip. Kick one leg (extended) forward while pulling the hips toward the bar with the hands. Bring the legs together and rotate around the bar to a front support position (figure 15-50). A spotter

Figure 15-51. Cast to dismount.

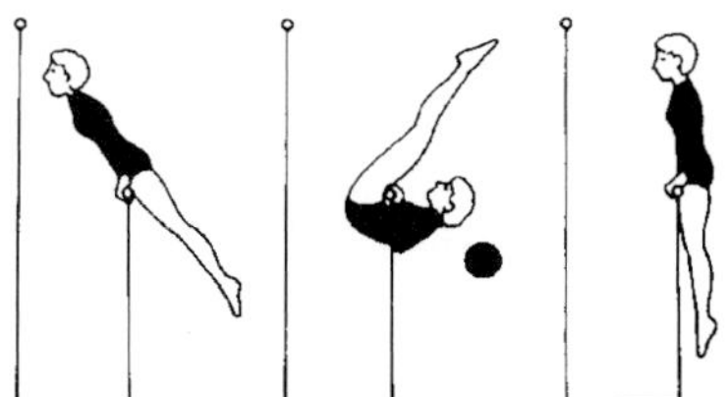

Figure 15-52. Back hip circle.

should help by pushing the hips and upper legs over the bar as well as supporting the back.

Cast to dismount

Start in a front support position on the low bar (facing the high bar), with an overhand grip. Pike at the waist around the low bar. Push back with the heels and against the bar with the thighs while pushing down on the bar with the arms. Continue to grip the bar until the body is parallel with the floor. As the descent from this position begins, push away from the bar, extending at the shoulders, release the grip, and land on the feet facing the bar (figure 15-51).

Back hip circle

Start from a front support position. Push away (cast) and then return to the bar. As the hips touch the bar, they allow the body to pike slightly at the waist and lean back with the shoulders as the legs come forward around the bar. Rotate around the bar and extend from the pike as the rotation is completed. Learn this stunt on the low bar before trying it on the high bar, and use a spotter during the learning phase (figure 15-52). The spotter should help keep the hips to the bar.

Forward mill circle

Start with one leg on either side of the bar (stride support) and an underhand grip (palms forward). Lift the body as high and as far forward as possible. As the rotation begins, extend the upper body out from the bar as far as possible. At the bottom of the downswing, curve the body slightly forward to shorten the radius and continue the rotation until the starting position is reached (figure 15-53).

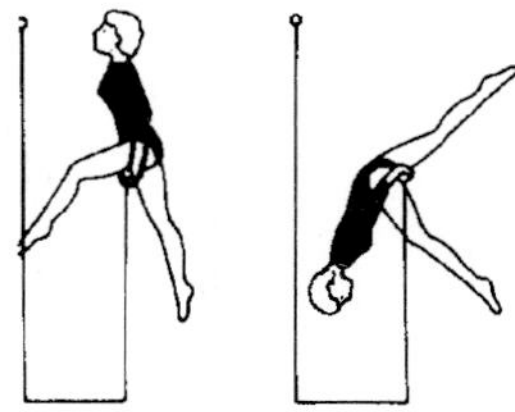

Figure 15-53. Forward mill circle.

Figure 15-54. Front hip circle.

Figure 15-55. Single-leg stem rise.

Front hip circle

Use an overhand grip and start in the front support position. Lean forward while pushing against the bar to extend the upper body. As the bottom of the downswing is reached, begin to pike slightly at the waist and pull against the bar to shorten the radius for the upswing. Continue the rotation until the original starting position is attained (figure 15-54). The spotter should assist with upswing.

Single-leg stem rise

Start by sitting on the low bar and grasping the high bar with an overhand grip. Flex one leg and place that foot on the low bar while raising the other leg (extended) to the high bar. Pull with the arms, push against the low bar with the support foot, and extend the straightened leg up against the high bar. Finish in a support position on the high bar (figure 15-55).

Glide kip

Facing the low bar and about 3 feet (0.9 m) away from it, jump upward with the hips as the upper body reaches for

Figure 15-56. Glide kip.

the bar. Grasp the bar with straight arms and begin the downswing with a pike at the hips. As the rotation continues, straighten at the hips so that an extended position is attained. As the height of the forward swing is reached, immediately pike at the hips and bring the legs to the bar, creating a pike position. Immediately "shoot the legs up the bar" as the body extends and the arms push down on the bar. Finish with a front support position on the bar (figure 15-56).

Balance Beam

Routines on the balance beam involve many of the stunts that are performed in floor exercise except that they must be accomplished on a beam only 4 inches (10.2 cm) wide and approximately 16 feet (4.88 m) long. The routine on the beam must be continuous and smooth and include tumbling, dance-type movements, and not more than three static, or balance, positions.

After mounting the beam (sometimes with the use of a spring board) various tumbling stunts (described later in this chapter) are interspersed with locomotor combinations. The routine is completed with some form of dismount. The routine performed in competition has a minimum and a maximum time limit.

Any number of sequences can be developed from the positions illustrated in figure 15-57.

Tumbling

Tumbling is the art of manipulating the body in feats of skill without the use of apparatus. Tumbling maneuvers include rolls, somersaults, twists, springs, balances on hands, and manipulation of the body in unusual positions.

From primitive times and through all stages of development, people have nurtured the desire to learn new ways to move the body. Tumbling offers such an outlet.

HISTORY

The earliest historical records—in the form of painting, sculpture, and literature—indicate that tumbling was connected with the dance, a most fundamental activity. Tumblers of early times had an important influence on entertainment and the theater, and in Greece and Rome tumblers entertained at private dinner parties and social occasions. Tumbling was also popular during the Middle Ages.

The word *tumble* is Teutonic in origin and means to dance violently or to dance with posturing, balancing, and contortions. The terms used by other nationalities have similar spelling, and embody the same activities of somersaulting, rolling, and contorting the body.

There is no question that springboard diving in swimming pools and rebound tumbling on the trampoline have been influenced by the tumbling art.

EQUIPMENT

A firm, padded, nonslippery mat is all that is necessary. Gymnastics slippers and a proper gymnasium uniform are adequate.

FUNDAMENTAL SKILLS AND TECHNIQUES

Tumbling provides an excellent means for developing agility, poise, balance, and coordination as well as being helpful in developing physical fitness. Success in learning new skills gives the individual self-confidence, courage, and determination.

A great number of stunts and tumbling skills can be learned. Those presented are individual, elementary, and fundamental and form a basis to advance to the more difficult skills. A vast number of companion (or pairs) exercises can be introduced into a program. Pyramid building can also be used. Also a routine in which several of the single stunts presented can be done in progression is an enjoyable and rewarding exercise.

Lead-Up Developmental Exercises

Animal walks (figures 15-58 to 15-65) should be used as part of the conditioning program. The snail drag is especially good for developing the upper body.

First-Level Stunts

Beginning tumblers should never work without a spotter. Use safety belts when necessary. See that mats are always in place.

The following are considered progressive-ability stunts of the first level of proficiency.

Figure 15-57. Balance beam; pass-through positions.

Figure 15-58. Galloping dog. Run on all fours.

Figure 15-60. Crab walk. Belly up.

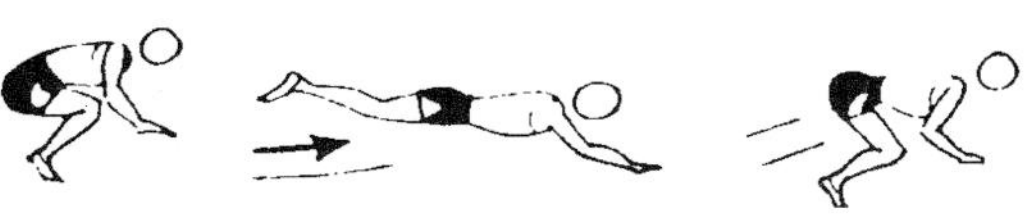

Figure 15-59. Frog hop. Dive to hands and land in squat.

Figure 15-61. Elephant walk. Keep knees stiff and spread feet.

Spinal rock. Keep the head up, grasp the shins, pull tight, and rock (figure 15-66).

Forward roll. Reach forward, take the weight on the hands, duck the head well under, round the back, roll, and tuck (figure 15-67).

Forward roll to back. Place the hands on the mat, complete the forward roll, but do not lift the head after passing over it (figure 15-68).

Backward roll over shoulder. Lie supine on the mat, place the right hand down by the side and the left arm out to the side, turn the head to the right, and bring the knees up and over the left shoulder. Land on the knees (figure 15-69).

Backward roll. Begin in a squat position with the hands next to the ears. Make the back round and roll to the rear. Keep the chin tucked to the chest and the knees together throughout the movement.

Backward roll, pike. Bend forward with the knees stiff, place the hand behind the thighs, drop back to the seat, raise the legs, and roll straight over the head (figure 15-70).

Backward extension roll. Start as for the backward roll pike, but when the weight is on the shoulders, shoot the legs to the ceiling and push hard with the hands (figure 15-71). The spotter may grab the feet and lift.

Football roll. Spread the feet apart, bend over, and place the left hand on the mat. Reach under the left arm with the right. Drop to the right shoulder, roll over, and roll across the back from the right shoulder to the left hip. Get up on the left knee, and then step up on the right foot (figure 15-72).

Tripod. Make a triangle with the head and hands. Slowly place the knees on the elbows (figure 15-73).

Headstand. Be sure that the head and hands form a good triangle. Place the forehead, not the top of the head, on the mat. Raise the hips by straightening the back. Now raise the legs slowly (figure 15-74).

Figure 15-62. Wet-cat footwalk. Walk on three limbs and shake one.

Figure 15-63. Bear walk. Same as elephant walk but with feet together.

Figure 15-64. Kangaroo hop, or donkey kick. Place hands on mat, kick feet in air, and land in squat position with hands still on mat. Reach forward and repeat.

Figure 15-65. Snail drag. Keep legs inactive and drag body with arms.

Figure 15-66. Spinal rock.

Figure 15-67. Forward roll.

Figure 15-68. Forward roll to back.

Figure 15-69. Backward roll over shoulder.

Figure 15-70. Backward roll, pike.

Figure 15-71. Backward extension roll.

Figure 15-72. Football roll.

Figure 15-73. Tripod.

Figure 15-74. Headstand.

Figure 15-75. Flying angel.

Figure 15-76. Cartwheel.

Figure 15-77. Cheststand on partner.

Flying angel. Bottom performer lifts the top performer over the body slowly. Top performer then arches the back and raises the head (figure 15-75).

Cartwheel. Begin in a standing position with the side of the body facing down the length of the mat and the arms extended overhead. Rock back on the back leg and then the forward leg. Place the front hand down on the mat. As the other hand comes over, place it on the mat in line with the first hand. At the same time push with the front leg and swing the back leg up and over the body. Keep the head up and watch the hands as they are placed on the mat. When the stunt is completed, the performer should be facing the same way as at the start (figure 15-76).

Cheststand on partner. Place the chest on the back of the partner, grasp the upper arm and thigh, kick slowly into position, hold tight, and arch the back slightly (figure 15-77).

Two high. The important move here is the hand position. The top performer stands in back of the bottom performer. The bottom performer reaches over the shoulders with the palms up. The top performer places the palms in the bottom performer's hands. Holding this hand position, the two face each other. The position now should be like shaking hands with the left hands, right hands over the head. The top performer places the left foot on the bottom performer's left thigh. This is done from the side with the toe of the top performer pointing in toward the middle of the bottom performer's body. As the bottom performer pulls with the right hand, the top performer steps up on the shoulder (figure 15-78). The spotter should stand in front.

Handstand support. Keep the head down, looking at the floor, as you kick up. The catcher should stand to the side to prevent being kicked in the face (figure 15-79).

Headstand in hands. Place the forehead in the hands and the forearms on the mat. Kick up slowly (figure 15-80).

Figure 15-78. Two high.

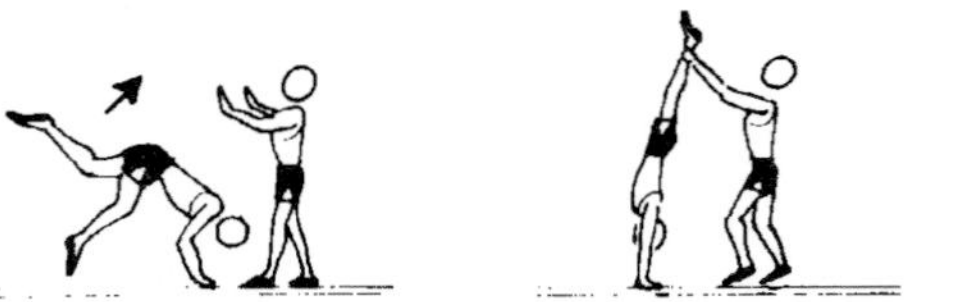

Figure 15-79. Handstand support.

Figure 15-80. Headstand in hands.

Figure 15-81. Triple roll.

Figure 15-82. Headspring over mat.

Second-Level Stunts

The following are exercises for those who have advanced to a more progressive level of tumbling skill. They represent the second level of proficiency.

Triple roll. From the three-performer lying position, the middle performer rolls to the left, and the performer on the left springs from the hands and knees over the middle performer, landing in the middle. The middle performer always rolls under and executes only one full turn and comes to rest on hands and knees. This is repeated from left to right (figure 15-81).

Headspring over mat. The best way to learn this is to do a flexed handstand. Let the body fall off balance. Just as the balance is lost, kick hard and push with the hands (figure 15-82). The spotter kneels in front (to the side) and places a hand on the performer's back.

Double roll with partner. Hold onto each other's ankles. Flex the knees and place the feet on the floor close to the thighs. Spread the knees apart so that the performer on top can duck the head and roll. This is important. Each person should work hard to help the other performer (figure 15-83).

Figure 15-83. Double roll with partner.

Figure 15-84. Fish dive.

Figure 15-85. Dive cartwheel.

Figure 15-86. Tiger stand.

Figure 15-87. Mule kick.

Fish dive. Take a standing position. Kick either foot backward and upward and jump off the other foot. Land on the hands, with the feet over the head (handstand position). Now bend the arms and let the body down, rolling from the chest to the knees. Flex at the waist and push hard with the hands until the weight is back over the feet. Lift the body to the squat stand (figure 15-84).

Dive cartwheel. To do this stunt properly, start with a run of a few steps, finish with a short hop, dive about 5 feet (1.5 m) and do a cartwheel (figure 15-85).

Tiger stand. Try to keep the upper arm perpendicular to the floor and kick up slowly (figure 15-86).

Mule kick. The best way to start this is from the handstand. Slightly bend the knees and bend the arms. Snap the legs downward and push hard with the arms. This is the true landing position: body bent forward and arms reaching backward and upward. Immediately use the lift of the arms, and jump back up into the handstand position. As the jump is made, keep the head down (figure 15-87).

Round-off. Facing the far end of the mat, take several running steps and do a skip step. Throw the arms forward and downward and place the front hand on the mat. The second hand is then placed in front and slightly forward (not on the same line) of the first hand. At the same time

Figure 15-88. Round-off.

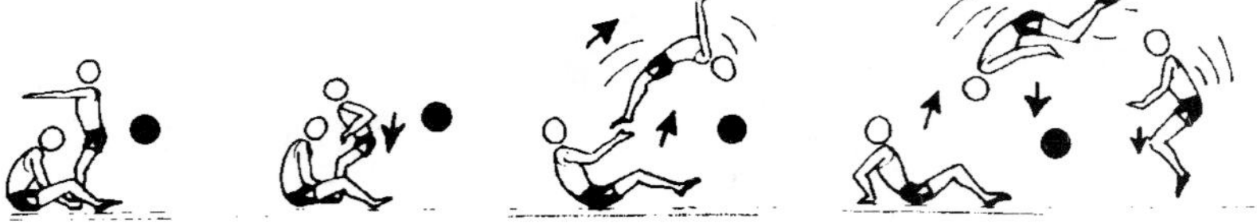

Figure 15-89. Pitch-back flip.

Figure 15-90. Pitch from belly.

Figure 15-91. Kip from mat.

push with the front leg and drive the other leg upward. As the legs come overhead, bring them together, turn the body and finish with a mule kick. At the finish, the performer should be facing the opposite direction from the start (figure 15-88).

Fifteen-second handstand. Kick into a good balance and lock. Keep the head in line and use the fingers. Point the toes and tighten the muscles through the hips.

Pitch-back flip. The top performer stands in the palms of the bottom performer. On the count of three, the top performer throws the arms straight for the ceiling and jumps with all his or her strength. The top performer then throws the head back and forcibly brings the knees up to give rotation. As the top performer jumps, the bottom performer lifts straight up and sits back to prevent being kicked in the face. The thing to watch for in this stunt is the overthrow. Be sure to have a spotter or safety belt. This is very important. Never attempt this skill without spotting (figure 15-89).

Pitch from belly. This is a handspring with the assistance of the bottom performer. The top performer places the stomach on the bottom performer's feet. The feet are placed in a V—heels together, toes apart. The bottom performer pulls the top performer forward, and as all the top performer's weight is felt, the bottom performer pulls the top performer's upper body forward and pushes hard with the feet. As the top performer's weight passes over, the bottom performer pushes with the hands. It is important to have at least one spotter assisting so that the top performer does not overthrow (figure 15-90).

Kip from mat. While in the lying position, place the hands over the shoulders on the floor and roll back until the weight is on the back of the head and shoulders. As the body is rolled forward slightly, shoot the legs up in the air and push hard with the hands. The legs should go up and forward (figure 15-91). The spotter should kneel and put a hand on the back in case an assist is needed.

Rollover kip from mat. Start this as a forward roll. Immediately on contact of the shoulders with the floor or mat, kip as in the preceding exercise (figure 15-92). The spotter may have to lift.

Headspring. This is executed from the top of the head. Place the head on the mat with the hands slightly forward. Keep the knees flexed as the body falls off balance. As the body rolls past center, kick hard as in the kip and push hard with the hands (figure 15-93). The spotter may have to support and lift.

Front handspring. Take about a 5-yard (4.6 m) run, hop, and whip the hands to the mat. Kick one foot hard backward and upward and push hard with the other. Keep the head up and the arms extended. As the legs pass over the head, give a little kick, flex at the wrist, and land on the feet (figure 15-94).

Back flip. Stand with the arms outstretched. Drop the arms down, and flex the knees to about a quarter knee bend. Throw the arms up just short of vertical as hard and

Figure 15-92. Rollover kip from mat.

Figure 15-93. Headspring.

Figure 15-94. Front handspring.

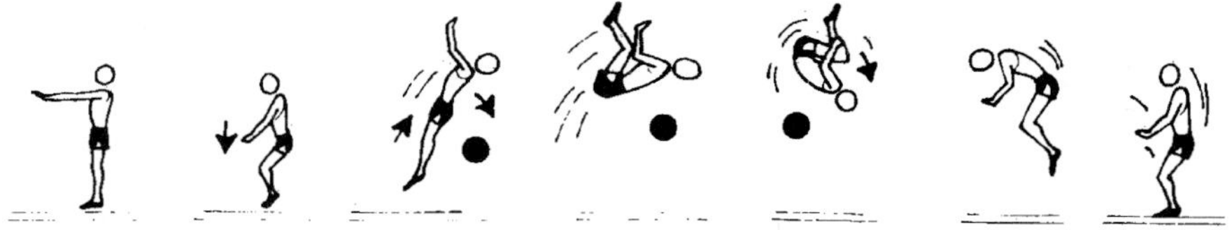

Figure 15-95. Back flip.

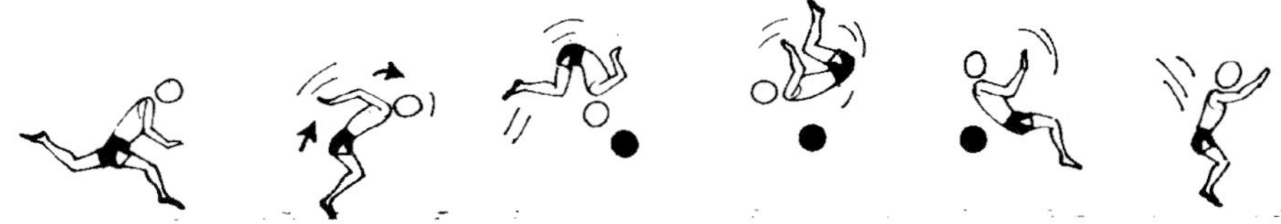

Figure 15-96. Front flip.

fast as possible so that the body is lifted off the floor. Jump with the arm lifted as high as possible. Throw the head back and bring the knees up to the chest. Tuck and let out. This should never be done without a spotter. The overhead mechanic should be used (figure 15-95).

Front flip. There are many different ways to throw this stunt, but the best is the two-arm backward-upward lift. Take two or three running steps. Use a two-foot take-off. From the take-off, which is executed in a one-quarter forward bend, jump hard and throw the arms with much force backward and upward. Roll over in the air into a tight tuck, and let out. Beginners can learn this by landing on two or three loosely rolled mats (figure 15-96). Spotting can be done with a hand belt.

Back handspring. This is performed as though sitting on a chair. Sit with the back straight, and swing the arms down and back. Keep the feet flat on the floor. Just as the body falls off balance, whip the arms over the head and throw the head back. As the arms are thrown back, reach for the floor and throw the belly to the ceiling. Snap to the feet (figure 15-97). Two spotters should use a hand belt or teach using an overhead belt.

TEACHING CONSIDERATIONS

1. Although the apparatus activities described in this chapter are basic to more-advanced skills, they require physical abilities not developed in many students. Particular amounts of arm strength, abdominal strength, and flexibility are necessary in many cases for students to be able to learn these skills successfully. Teachers must choose either to develop these prerequisites or to modify downward the

Figure 15-97. Back handspring.

expectations for learning. Students who attempt skills for which they do not have the prerequisite abilities create safety problems.

2. Many tumbling skills are basic to apparatus work. Because of this, many teachers choose to teach tumbling skills at first or build in tumbling skills with apparatus work. Tumbling skills permit more activity practice for larger numbers of students.
3. Checklists of skills on apparatus that go from simple to complex are often helpful for students to know what to work on and also for teachers to evaluate student progress. The emphasis must be on good form and not merely getting through an action.
4. It is often helpful to introduce a piece of apparatus to the whole group, but then use stations of different apparatus to practice. Teachers can make the decision to be at one or two stations for a period or to rotate as needed. Stations can be organized so that groups rotate at a signal from the teacher, or individuals can move freely from one station to another. Situations without teacher supervision can be assigned to a "group captain" who is a competent spotter.
5. Some students can perform some skills without spotters. Aerial skills in particular should be performed with trained spotters or should not be performed without the teacher. Instruction should continuously emphasize control of movement. Crashes and abandonment of control should never be permitted.
6. It is often desirable to have a culminating experience involving performance in gymnastics units toward which students can work. Students can choose one or two events and work to put sequences together. They can practice even the simplest moves until they perform them with smooth transitions and good form.

SUGGESTED READINGS

Cooper, P., and Trnka, M. 1994. 3d ed. Needham Heights, Mass.: Allyn & Bacon. *Teaching basic gymnastics: A coeducational approach.* For the beginning student, this book covers the basic skills of teaching gymnastics. Skills, safety, spotting, and teaching techniques are included.

Cornelius, W. L. 1983. *Gymnastics*. Englewood, Colo.: Morton Publishing. Provides gymnastics progression from individual skills and short combinations to compulsory routines for men. Also contains material on equipment and strength and flexibility programs.

Fodero, J., and Furblur, E. 1989. *Creating gymnastics pyramids and balances.* Champaign, Ill.: Human Kinetics.

Gula, D. 1990. *Dance choreography for competitive gymnastics.* Champaign, Ill.: Human Kinetics. Uses combinations of dance steps to create complete choreographed sequences for floor and beam routines.

Lihs, H. 1990. *Teaching gymnastics.* Boston: American Press. Written primarily for preparing physical educators for the special demands of teaching gymnastics.

National Collegiate Athletic Association. 1997. *Official gymnastics rules.* Phoenix: College Athletics Publishing Service.

Rookie coaches gymnastics guide. 1992. Champaign, Ill.: Human Kinetics. This complete resource for the entry-level coach is prepared by the American Coaching Effectiveness Program.

Ryser, O., and Brown, J. 1990. *A manual for tumbling and apparatus.* 8th ed. Dubuque, Iowa: WCB/McGraw-Hill.

Turoff, F. 1991. *Artistic gymnastics: A comprehensive guide to performing and teaching skills for beginners and advanced beginners.* Dubuque, Iowa: WCB/McGraw-Hill.

RESOURCES

Films and Videotapes

Gymnastics films or videotapes can be obtained from the following:

American Alliance for Health, Physical Education, Recreation and Dance, 1900 Association Dr., Reston, VA 22091.

Cambridge Physical Education and Health, P.O. Box 2153, Charleston, WV 25328. *NCCA gymnastics videos* (4 tapes), *Gymnastics exercise for men and women* (2 tapes), *Foundations of gymnastics excellence* (4 tapes), and *Gymnastics fun with Bela Karolyi.*

"How To" Sports Video, P.O. Box 5852, Denver, CO 80127. Twelve videos, including three on beginning, intermediate, and advanced tumbling.

Sports Video: Champions on Film, 745 State Circle, P.O. Box 1941, Ann Arbor, MI 48106. Eight videos, including one each featuring the men's and women's USSR gymnastics team.

United States Gymnastic Federation, P.O. Box 7686, Fort Worth, TX 76111.

Web Site

USA Gymnastics: http://www.usa-gymnastics.org/membership/

16 In-line Skating

After completing this chapter, the reader should be able to:

- Appreciate the history, disciplines, and values of in-line skating
- Appreciate the significance, and teach all aspects, of in-line safety
- Select and maintain in-line skates and protective gear
- Introduce beginning skaters to a positive first-time experience
- Demonstrate and describe balance improvement drills
- Properly teach beginning and intermediate striding, turning, and stopping skills

HISTORY

Because in-line skating is such a convenient form of exercise and recreation, and is so easy to learn, the number of nonathletes attracted to the sport exploded in the mid 1990s. Today, people of all ages are eager to gain its many recreational, social, and health benefits. Though others tinkered with placing wheels in a single row in the 1800s, modern-day in-lines were born in the early 1980s in the garage of an inventive athlete. An ice hockey enthusiast in Minnesota named Scott Olson designed the prototypes for today's in-line skates so he could use them for dry-land cross training. He and his friends enjoyed those early models so much, they started skating for fun as well as hockey practice, and soon the recreation began to spread. With the infusion of cash from some forward-thinking investors, Rollerblade, Inc., was launched and so were the first mass-produced in-line skates.

Before long, skiers, bicyclists, speed skaters, rowers, and many other athletes began to cross-train on in-lines. In the 1990s this recreational boom generated several new competitive sports: extreme downhill trials, endurance and short-track speed events, street and ramp ("vert") competitions, and, of course, roller hockey, to name the most popular (figure 16-1).

DISCIPLINES

Recreational/Fitness

Approximately 90 percent of the world's in-line skaters participate primarily for pleasure and fitness. Though recreational skating is attractive to people of all ages, according to a demographic breakdown of U.S. participants in a 1969 survey by SGMA/American Sports Data, the average recreational skater is 31 years old and most likely a white-collar professional. Of these, 56.9 percent are male.

Because the fluid in-line stride delivers nonimpact cardiovascular, body composition, and muscular benefits, in-line workouts are ideal for those who are interested in building and maintaining healthy bodies through sustained physical effort. Striding upright along a bike path at 8 to 12 mph, a skater can easily benefit from a workout that is comparable to biking. With practice, better balance makes it possible to assume a more aerodynamic stance and achieve a longer range of motion in the stroke; this style of skating increases the exertion to a level that compares to running.

Aggressive

Young skaters, especially boys, are often drawn to the thrills of launching off a ramp, doing aerial stunts on a quarter- or half-pipe, and curb grinding. Besides

Figure 16-1. Recreational in-line skating.

specialized equipment (or free access to public structures), aggressive skating demands precise footwork, excellent balance, and more than a little endurance, in every sense of the word.

Freestyle

Freestyle in-line skating includes everything from line dancing to performance figure skating. Recreational skates remain the favorite footwear, especially on the street. However, with the 1997 model year, the first skates specifically designed for off-ice figure skating appeared on the market, complete with leather boots and a rolling toe stop that emulates the pick used for launching into jumps or spins. Look for this discipline to grow as a result.

Roller Hockey

Girls as well as boys are attracted to the fast action and excitement of roller hockey. Novices who give it a try report that the excitement generated by team dynamics, stick handling, and competitive play add up to a shorter learning curve for all striding and maneuvering skills. Players begin to think on their feet instead of about their feet. As for gear, each nongoalie player needs a hockey stick, protective gloves, a face shield and mouthpiece, hockey pants, shin guards, shoulder pads, and, for males, a jock strap and cup. Goalies need even more protective gear.

Skate to Ski

The U.S. Ski Team and the Professional Ski Instructors Association (PSIA) discovered in-lines as a dry-land performance training program that improved the team's slalom skiing technique. Skaters who cross-train with ski poles not only become better, more centered snow skiers, they also learn how to manage both climbing and descending steeper asphalt hills.

Speedskating

In-line racing entered this decade on the urethane wheels of both ice and quad speedskating converts. It tends to cater to the elite athlete, due in part to the expense of lightweight custom boots, precision bearings, five-wheel frames, and new or like-new wheels. Some race promoters have begun to add nonpro events such as fun rolls to their venues, which gives interested amateurs a taste of the race.

VALUES

- Because pavement is easy to find in any town and equipment is compact, in-line skating is one of the most portable and versatile forms of fitness and recreation.
- In-line skating improves balance, strengthens every muscle from the lower back to the knees, and stimulates the upper body.
- The in-line learning curve is relatively short compared to other balance sports.

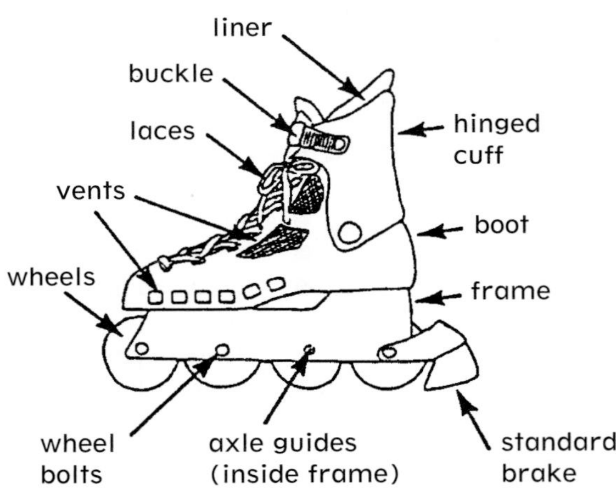

Figure 16-2. In-line skate components. (Source: From Liz Miller, 1998. *Get Rolling.* Ragged Mountain Press. Reproduced with permission of The McGraw-Hill Companies.)

- Used for aerobic workouts, a fast pace with long strides produces a training heart rate without the high-impact penalty of joint stress.
- Used for cross-training, in-line skating can be used to complement specific and repetitive workouts geared toward improved sport-related performance.
- In-line skating is sociable, drawing participants together where the pavement quality is best. Combine fresh air, time to play, and healthy bodies, and friendships blossom naturally.
- Skating is just plain fun.

EQUIPMENT AND FACILITIES

Skates

Encourage students who don't own their own equipment to rent from a reputable skate shop that you have already checked out. They'll come to class in gear designed to deliver a positive first experience. When asked for advice, warn them not to shop at a toy or discount department store because the quality of mass-market gear is inevitably horrendous. Cheap gear invariably leads to a disappointing introduction to the sport (figure 16-2).

Shopping tips

- For children, purchase a model that comes with two boot liners, allowing it to accommodate four full sizes. These are made by the top manufacturers and retail for about $75.
- Adults should spend no less than $175 (list price) to get a decent skate. At the other end of the spectrum, avoid high-end hockey or five-wheel speedskates. These are too expensive and require better skills than a beginner will have for months (and usually a heel brake is not an option) (figure 16-3).

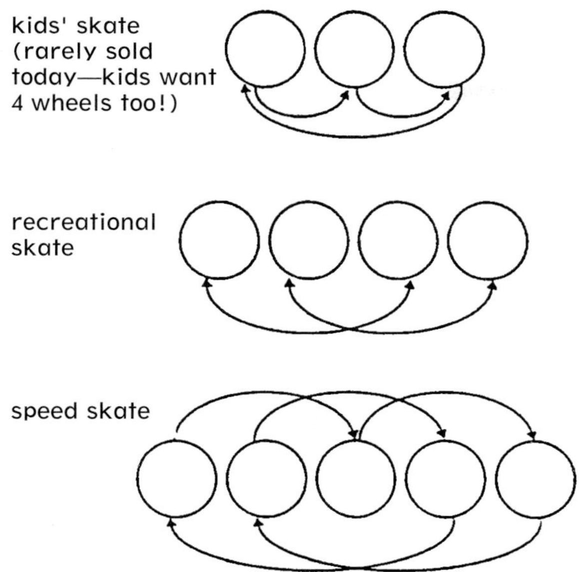

Figure 16-3. Types of in-line skates.

- Novices should purchase a skate with a high, molded-plastic cuff and at least one buckle at the top for good ankle stabilization.
- When trying on skates, wear a pair of thin athletic socks manufactured specifically for athletic activity. Wear the same socks for skating to "wick" moisture away from the foot.
- Cuff-activated braking technology (such as Rollerblade, Inc.'s ABT, Bauer's Force Multiplier, the GEM brake) is a godsend for beginners because they aren't required to balance on one foot in order to stop: all eight wheels remain on the ground.
- Ladies' skate models are available from the better manufacturers. They usually compensate for the lower position of a woman's calf muscle and her narrower Achilles tendon. If the tag doesn't differentiate genders, the skate is probably made to fit men but sold as unisex.

Skate features

Fit. For the best performance, in-lines should fit snugly but without discomfort. With straight knees, the toes should lightly touch the end of the boot. Conversely, in the flexed hip and knee skating stance, the toes should pull away from the end of the boot as the shins press forward against the tongue. When striding, the heel should be cupped by the boot so it doesn't slide up and away from the sole.

Plastic vs. soft boots. Molded plastic ski-style boots offer the best stability and ankle support, and tend to be less costly than soft-boot skates. Suede and mesh boots may be slightly less supportive unless they contain an interior hinged cuff, but if correctly fit, they remain more comfortable for a long day of skating.

Vents. Cutouts in a plastic boot increase air flow, reduce perspiration, and make the skate lighter.

Buckles or laces. All-buckle models are easier to get on and off; at a minimum one top buckle delivers solid ankle support. Laces allow the close custom fit required by speed skaters or a game of fast-action in-line hockey. Velcro "power straps" can be purchased to add ankle support and keep the laces tight on lace-only recreational skates.

Liners. The foam-padded liners inside plastic in-line boots are replaceable. All good-quality skates feature performed insoles, which are easily replaced with custom insoles.

Frames. Four-wheel frames are best for recreational, hockey, and artistic skating, and five-wheelers are built for stability at high speeds and to maximize the benefits of longer, more powerful strides. At the specialty end, frames can be equipped with "grind plates" to facilitate rail and curb grinding, or manufactured using the strong, lightweight composites used by speedskaters.

Bearings. ABEC1 precision-rated bearings are the standard on lower-end recreational skates. ABEC3 or ABEC5 are used by fitness and speed skaters and as upgrades for recreational skates. High-performance bearings might also feature removable shields to allow access to the inner balls and race, so that soaking in a solvent removes the grit that causes friction and loss of performance.

Wheels. A new skate's wheels feature the core type, hardness, profile, and diameter deemed to be best suited to the features of the skate on which they are mounted. Before shopping for replacement wheels, be sure you know the maximum wheel size the skate's frames can accommodate (found in the owner's manual).

- Standard wheel **diameters** are: 60 mm for children's skates, 72 mm for hockey and entry-level recreational skates, 78 mm for fitness, and 80 mm for racing. The size is usually printed on the side of the wheel. Wheels in the low 60s and below are used on aggressive skates.
- The **profile** is the wheel's shape where it meets the road. Race wheels have the narrowest profile to reduce road drag. Recreation and fitness wheels are slightly wider to deliver a good grip on a variety of pavement surfaces. Hockey wheels are wider still to ensure stability and quick-turning maneuverability.
- Hardness, measured by **durometer** rating, dictates a wheel's shock absorption and grip qualities and is designated by a number ranging from 75 to 101 followed by the letter "A." Although softer wheels grip better and reduce vibrations, they also wear out faster than harder ones.
- The **core** (also known as the hub) is a hard substance that the wheel's urethane bonds to, providing torsional stability and a solid seat for the bearings. Vented cores keep bearings cooler at high speeds. Smaller aggressive-style wheels have no core at all, or the core might be hidden inside to provide better impact handling.

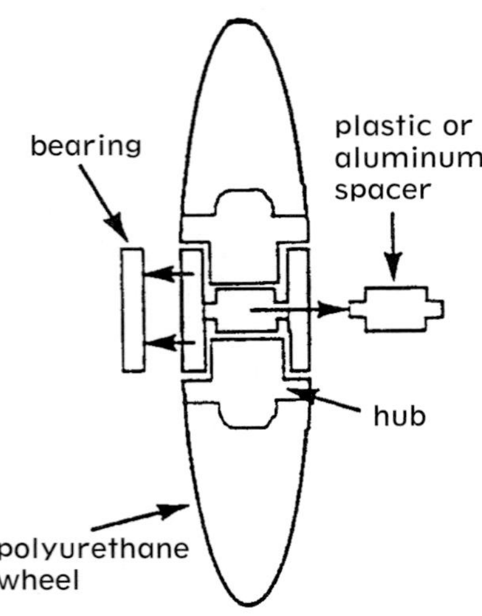

Figure 16-4. The in-line skate wheel.

Skate Maintenance

Preventive maintenance is as simple as proper skate storage. The boot liners become warm and moist after half an hour of skating, and the tongue can easily dry out in an unnatural shape. To prevent the resulting discomfort, carefully arrange the tongue in its proper position, then buckle or lace the boot closed to keep it there. This is even more important for long-term (winter) storage.

Replace the brake pad once it is worn down to one-third inch or less. On most models, this is a simple matter of unscrewing the brake from the frame and inserting a new one. Usually the brake cannot be removed without also removing the rear wheel.

With time, wheels eventually begin to wear flat under the arch side of the foot. When rotating skate wheels, swap those with the most wear (usually the front and rear) with wheels with the least wear. A scheme that works for most wear patterns is to trade wheel #1 with wheel #3, and wheel #4 with wheel #2. At the same time, flip the wheels so that the worn-off side is mounted facing the outside ankle. During the process, wipe mud and dust from the boot, the inside of the wheel frame, and the outsides of the bearings (figure 16-4).

Eventually, even with regular wipe-downs, bearings can become noticeably slower due to rust or extended use. This is when they are ready to be replaced. (However, for a low-end skate model, upgrading with new bearings is one way to improve performance.) Depending on the skater, environment, and preferred activity, this can occur any time within one to three years after the skates were purchased. Meanwhile, unless speedskating is the primary activity, it is not necessary to be concerned with interior bearing maintenance, although some skaters find the mechanics of the process just too fascinating to resist.

Helmet

Skate-specific helmets are offered by several manufacturers, usually providing lower coverage for the back of the head. A bicycle helmet works fine, however. No matter what the sport, the helmet should carry the ANSI or SNELL impact rating sticker. A new N-94 standard was introduced in the mid 1990s to add an additional rating that withstands a series of impacts. This has been adopted by several aggressive skating helmet makers.

Wrist Guards

Wrist guards offer abrasion protection for the palms, and plastic splints on the front and back prevent the wrist from hyperextending during crash landings.

Knee and Elbow Pads

A thick knee pad offers the best protection for a forward fall where the skater's entire body weight strikes the ground at the knees first. Elbow pads should be thick enough to take the full body weight in a sideways fall. Sleeved, slip-on pads stay in place better than those that strap on with hook and loop fasteners alone.

SAFETY CONSIDERATIONS

Basic Skills

To ensure safety, the new skater absolutely must learn how to turn to avoid danger, fall properly, and use the heel brake to slow and stop. First-day skaters can learn to stride and turn on their own, but rarely learn how to use the heel brake without qualified instruction. Until they do, they remain either widely uncomfortable or ignorantly confident.

The International In-line Skating Association (IISA) has standardized in-line skating teaching techniques worldwide through its Instructor Certification Program. Anybody planning to teach in-line skating to beginners or on a continuing basis should acquire the first level of certification beforehand. Instructor candidates can achieve certification by attending weekend ICP clinics in various locations: Level 1 certifies the candidate to teach beginning skills; Level 2 certifies for intermediate skills; and Level 3 certifies instruction in a specialized discipline (e.g., aggressive, speedskating, in-line hockey).

Protective Gear

The vast majority of in-line injuries can be prevented by wearing protective gear. The Consumer Product Safety Commission recommends that, at minimum, everyone should wear a helmet and wrist guards on every skate outing. Those items, plus knee and elbow pads, are a must for emergency stopping maneuvers, hills, and such aggressive moves as ramp skating and riding stairs. Street hockey should be played with all available safety gear; it doesn't take long to find out why.

Attitude

Unfortunately, the skaters least likely to wear protective gear have the greatest tendency to engage in high-risk behavior. According to a year-long study by the Centers for Disease Control and Prevention (CDC) using the National Electronic Injury Surveillance System, male skaters were treated 30 percent more than females during the study period; for teens, the injury ratio leaped to 90 percent males.

The rules of the road should be prepared as class materials to educate every student about essential trail etiquette and safety habits. The following is one version distributed by the International In-line Skating Association.

RULES OF THE ROAD

Skate Smart

- Always wear your helmet, wrist guards, knee and elbow pads.
- Learn the basics: speed control, turning, braking, and stopping.
- Keep all of your equipment in safe condition.

Skate Legal

- Observe all traffic regulations; on skates, you must obey the laws for wheeled vehicles.
- Skate with, not against, the flow of traffic.
- Don't "skitch." Never allow yourself to be towed by a motorized vehicle or bicycle.

Skate Alert

- Always skate in control.
- Stay away from water, oil, debris, sand, and uneven or broken payment.
- Avoid areas with heavy traffic.
- Avoid wearing headphones or anything that makes it hard to hear.

Skate Polite

- Skate on the right side of the path and call out a warning before you pass on the left.
- Yield to pedestrians.
- Quit stroking to make room for passing cyclists (and avoid catching a skate in their spokes)!
- Be a goodwill ambassador for in-line skating.

FUNDAMENTAL SKILLS AND TECHNIQUES

Every in-line skating move involves one or more of the fundamental in-line skills: balance, pressure, upper body rotation and edging. **Balance** starts from what is known as the ready position—a centered, bent-knee stance with weight evenly distributed over the feet. **Pressure** applied to alternate or both skates causes strides, turns, and virtually all other skating dynamics. Varying degrees of upper body **rotation** aid in turning when combined with **edging** or tipping the skates onto the outside, inside or corresponding (both left or both right) wheel edges.

Figure 16-5. Ready position.

For the purpose of instruction without reference to right and left, the **support leg** is the one that is used for balance, while the **action leg** is stroking or performing other maneuvers.

Before You Roll

Skating stances

Standing on dry lawn or another nonrolling surface, practice the following in-line body positions.

Ready position. (figure 16-5) The in-line ready position is the same centered semicrouch that is used for tennis and skiing, among many other sports. Well-bent knees are the most important component of a balanced ready position, resulting in a platform of stability from which the skater can respond by moving in any direction, depending on the situation. With knees already straight, the usual upward response of a startled beginner often leads to a backward fall. Bent knees are also necessary to achieve stroke effectiveness. With straight knees, stroke power and efficiency are limited to the few inches the skate can remain in contact with the pavement.

1. Place feet shoulder-width apart.
2. Raise both hands to waist level and within peripheral vision.
3. Flex the ankles, knees, and hips to sink a few inches, keeping shoulders over hips and hips over heels. When looking downward (discouraged except for this test), the knee pads should block sight of the toes.
4. Eyes up, clasp hands under the chin and sink until the elbows contact the knees. This is the aerodynamic tuck and extreme knee bend used by speedskaters; it

Figure 16-6. A-frame stance.

is still a balanced ready position because the body weight is evenly distributed fore and aft over the arches. The ready position test when stroking in a tuck is "nose over knees, knees over toes."

5. Regain an upright stance and practice the following in-line stances standing still.

A-frame. Ready position with feet wider than shoulder width, skates tipped onto inside edges (figure 16-6).

V-stance. Ready position with heels nearly touching and toes pointed out at a 45-degree angle.

A-stance. Ready position with toes nearly touching and heels pointed out a 45-degree angle.

Scissors stance. Ready position with knees together, weight 75 percent over supporting leg, action skate parallel and advanced 6 to 12 inches, all wheels touching the pavement.

Balance and edging. Starting from the ready position, pick up one foot at a time, tip both skates onto corresponding edges, and touch the toes. Make a small hop or two (if on lawn).

How to Fall and Get Up

A controlled fall early in the lesson builds confidence in the protective gear and reduces the trepidation that can restrict some students' ability to progress.

1. In the ready position, reach toward your toes.
2. Fingers raised, reach forward along the pavement until your knee pads topple to it, then finish by landing on your hands.
3. Tap both knee and elbow pads on the pavement hard enough to test the cushion. In a real skating situation, when you feel a fall coming, do your best to twist around and get your hands near your knees so you will land where the most padding is.

There are two ways to get up from the pavement. Weaker or overweight skaters will require the second method.

Method 1

1. Start from "all fours," on hands and knees.
2. Lift one knee and place the skate of that foot on the pavement, close to your other knee.
3. Tighten up the gap between the upright skate and the knee still on the ground, to reduce the chance of rolling as you rise.
4. Now, leading with the head, rise straight up in one fluid motion. For added stability, place both hands on the raised knee and push down.

Method 2

1. Start from "all fours."
2. Lift one knee and place the skate of that foot on the pavement, with the knee wedged at an outward angle.
3. Place both palms on the pavement between the knees, not in front of them.
4. Using the hands for support, raise the second knee and place that skate flat on the pavement, close to the first.
5. Push the hips up first, and then follow with the head and upper body.

The Safe T

This skill allows the skater to stand stationary without rolling.

1. Starting from the ready position, place the skate without a brake (usually the left) so that its heel is tucked into the arch of the other. This places the feet in a T position.
2. With weight evenly distributed and knees bent, shift skates if necessary until they feel locked together.

Beginning Stride, Turn, and Stop

The V Walk

The purpose of this drill is to start the skater moving forward, transferring the weight from one skate to the other with the feet in proper stride position. Practice it on a non-rolling surface first.

1. Starting from the V stance with toes pointing outward, take tiny steps forward.
2. Shift the weight from right to left between each short step, keeping the toes pointed out and heels as close together as possible.

Stride 1 (the beginning stride)

1. Building on the V walk, start pushing against the back skate's inside edge as the weight is shifted onto the front skate. That pressure results in a short glide. The combination of pressure and glide becomes a stride.

Figure 16-7. The beginning stride-start.

Figure 16-8. The beginning stride-small steps.

2. Keep strides short at first to maintain balance and a slow speed. Relax into a coasting ready position if the speed picks up too much for comfort.
3. Resist the temptation to bend forward at the waist, a common beginner's reaction that diminishes with a few hours of skating. Expect some back and lower-leg stiffness the day after this first foray (figures 16-7 and 16-8).

Heel brake stop

Excellent heel brake technique is essential for recreational, skate-to-ski, and fitness skaters who must deal with hills, intersections, and traffic and often must share multi-use trails with an unpredictable crowd. Hockey and aggressive skaters manage to survive with T stops, lunge stops, and power slides, because in most cases they stick to fairly flat terrain. Speedskaters sacrifice brakes for the sake of speed, and rely on T stops, agility, and sheer luck for downhills.

Unfortunately, the heel brake is not as easy to use as it looks. Simply raising the toe of the braking skate is not effective because the upper body tends to keep moving when the feet stop. For best results, the skater must learn how to push the brake ahead instead of down, which is not exactly intuitive.

To get a feeling for how cuff-activated brakes work, lower the brake very close to the ground. Once you are confident you can engage it properly, raise the brake slightly so that doesn't interfere with other skills.

The heel brake stop is a four-phased movement: from coasting ready position to scissors stance glide to light brake drag to dropping the hips.

Practice the scissors stance standing still before progressing to the rolling version. Besides serving as an approach for heel brake stops, this is the best position to glide safely and easily over nasty patches of pavement, because the wheels form a longer platform that provides better front-to-back stability.

1. Assume the ready position, with knees well bent, feet shoulder-width apart.
2. Shift your weight to the supporting leg, keeping the braking skate in place.
3. Moving *only* your brake leg from the knee down, push that skate forward. It won't go very far if your supporting knee is straight. From the side view, your lower legs should form a triangle over the pavement surface.
4. Make sure your skates are parallel (no more than four inches apart) so your toes are both pointing forward.

- **Note for cuff-activated brake users:** A wide scissors stance causes the calf muscle to move the cuff of the skate backward, which moves the brake arm down, which automatically engages the brake with all four wheels still on the ground.

You need to be able to coast for at least ten feet in order to learn how to stop with the heel brake. Later, this phase lasts just long enough to assume a good preparatory ready position.

1. Stride to gain a moderate speed (fast enough to stay in balance, slow enough to prevent fear).
2. **Phase 1:** Relax into a coasting ready position with hands waist high and in view.
3. **Phase 2:** Assume the scissors stance. Retain 75 percent of the body weight on the support leg (the one without the brake). Hold steady and continue to roll. Regain speed and practice the scissors stance roll until it feels balanced, making sure to keep feet close together and both toes pointing the same direction.
4. **Phase 3:** Engage the brake and lightly drag it on the pavement. Repeat several times, starting from the scissors stance. Try to hear and prolong the light contact, but don't bother trying to stop yet.
   - **Standard brake:** Lift the toe of the brake skate until the rubber touches the pavement. Let it drag audibly but only very lightly on the pavement. If necessary, drop your toe to regain balance, then lift and drag again. Touch and then raise the brake several times over a long coast. Repeat until you can roll several feet while dragging the brake lightly. Remember to keep the brake ahead of your upper body.
   - **Cuff-activated brakes:** Press the big toe in the braking skate downward onto the pavement as you scissors that boot ahead, making sure to sink over the opposite knee rather than leaning forward over the brake. Feel the drag, and then retract the skate back under you. If the brake doesn't touch the ground when you scissors, lower the brake pad and/or shift more of your body weight to the support leg.
5. Once you are able to brake lightly in a straight line, gradually increase the brake pressure by pushing the pad further ahead. The only way to do this is to bend the support leg's knee.
6. **Phase 4:** To assertively finish the stop, drop your hips as though sitting down, as you "squirt" the brake forward at the same time. Start with an upright torso, so that as the force of the stop pulls your shoulders forward, they have someplace to go. Resist that pull by tightening up the abdominal muscles.
7. Quickly straighten up to avoid loss of balance.

To gain the most effective and instinctive heel brake skill, make many practice stops on a line, and use the light drag as a speed control mechanism on gentle hills, making occasional full stops.

A-frame turn

Turning is a result of pressure along the curved sides of the skate wheels, known as edging.

1. Stride to gain a moderate speed.
2. Starting from a coasting ready position, push your skates into a wide A-frame stance.
3. Rotate head, shoulders, hands, and hips toward the left, and press against the inside edge of the right skate at the same time, keeping the body weight evenly distributed over both skates. A turn to the left results.
4. Rotate the upper body to the right and pressure the left skate to make a right turn.

Advanced Beginning Stride, Turn, and Stop

Stride 2 (the basic stride)

The difference between Stride 1 and Stride 2, the basic stride, is added pressure at push off and a longer glide.

1. Stride to gain a moderate speed.
2. With torso upright, lower your hips closer to your heels by bending your knees. The stiff, lurching stride commonly seen in beginners results from bending forward at the waist, which straightens the knees.
3. Try to prolong the duration of each glide by counting "one-two-three-four" before starting a new stroke.
4. Attempt to recover the stroking leg fully beneath the hips before returning it to the pavement to begin a new stroke. This may prove difficult for first-time skaters who are nervous or lacking in balance.

A fun drill to improve balance and coordination at this point is to have students skate in a large circle and respond to called-out instructions (e.g., play "Simon Says"). Direct them to coast in the ready position, touch their knees, toes, and then the pavement one hand at a time, if possible (getting upright in between calls). Allow them to rebuild speed as needed and use A-frame turns to turn the corners if skating in an oval pattern. Finally, from a coast, have them lift one skate and coast as far as possible on the other, an excellent balance drill and preparation for heel brake expertise.

Parallel turn

The graceful parallel turn is made on one outside and one inside skate edge (corresponding edges). It is a core hockey skill and valuable for maneuvering in tight situations. This skill does not come easily to most first-day skaters because it requires the confidence and balance that comes with at least twenty hours on in-lines.

The parallel turn is easier to learn on a slight slope—such as the drainage gutter in a parking lot—with a marker or object to swerve around.

1. Stride to gain a moderate speed, approaching the marker with arms outstretched.
2. Scissors the left skate forward and tuck your right knee behind the left.
3. In one assertive motion, shift your weight back onto the right tucked-under skate, while twisting head, shoulders, hands, and hips 180 degrees toward the

Figure 16-9. The swizzle.

left. This twisting action forces the upper body across the left skate so that pressure is applied to the outside of the left skate's back wheel.

4. Weight is now distributed 75 percent on the right supporting skate and 25 percent on the back wheel of the inside action skate. The upper body is tilted toward the center of the turn. Trust centrifugal force and seek its swinging pull.
5. Both skates will curve to the left, tilted onto their left edges. Straighten out once you have made a turn of at least 90 degrees.
6. Practice tightening up the turn until you can swerve close to the mark but still clear it; see if you can make a 180-degree parallel turn.

Swizzle

The swizzle improves balance because it requires the skater to stay properly centered over both skates; it is a building block for learning how to make slalom turns and also introduces the concept of pushing to the side with the heel wheels to improve stroke efficiency (figure 16-9).

1. Standing in a V stance, put both knee pads together and push them two or three inches forward, letting the skates tilt onto the inside edges. The knees are bent into a "coiled" position.
2. With the torso upright, push outward against both heels; as the legs uncoil and heels separate, forward propulsion results, in an A-frame stance. The more abrupt the push, the faster and farther the roll.
3. Keeping most of your weight over the heels, steer the knees and toes into a pigeon-toed position.
4. Use your inner thigh muscles to pull the skates close together under your hips.
5. Once both skates are back under the hips, rotate toes and knees outward again to achieve a new V stance.
6. Move the chest and knees forward to make another short, quick push against both heels to start a new swizzle, rising immediately after. Find the rhythm: sink to coil and push, rise to lighten the pressure so you can steer the skates back together.

Spin stop

The spin stop evolves out of the basic A-frame turn.

1. Stride to gain a moderate speed.
2. Begin a left A-frame turn by pressuring the right skate and rotating the upper body left.
3. Momentarily shift your weight to the right skate, so you can lift the left skate's heel wheel (not the whole skate) and aggressively rotate the left knee out and heel in. Keep the knees wide and the weight of the upper body between them.
4. As soon as your left heel is under your left hip (meaning both knees are pointed outward), return it quickly to the pavement and balance your weight evenly between both thighs. A counterclockwise spin stop results.

Intermediate Stride, Turn, and Stops

Forward crossover

Crossovers (figure 16-10) are used to maintain or even gain speed through a corner. This skill presents a significant balance challenge, because it requires the skater to lean the upper body and center of gravity momentarily outside the stable space between both feet. Crossover turns are easier to learn on a marked circle about 15 to 20 feet in diameter, such as those found on school playgrounds. Alternatively, place an object on the pavement that can serve as the center marker.

1. Approach one of the circles at a moderate speed, traveling in a clockwise direction.
2. Outstretch both arms and rotate the upper body toward the center of the circle. Imagine that you are hugging the circle, right hand over the line ahead of you and left hand behind.
3. Begin a glide on the left skate. Relax the left ankle so the left skate tips onto its outside edge. Combined with the upper body rotation, this forces the upper body to tilt into the circle slightly.

Figure 16-10. Forward crossover.

4. Return the right skate to the pavement directly in front of the left, on the perimeter of the circle. Lift and advance the left skate, and return it to the pavement further up the perimeter of the circle.
5. As you continue skating in a circle, gradually try to cross the right skate farther over the left skate. Beware: the more successfully you cross the right skate over the left, the faster you'll go. Stop stroking and coast if you find yourself moving too fast for comfort or begin to feel dizzy.

Backward swizzle

The easiest version of backward skating is nothing more than linked backward swizzles. Before starting any backward skating session, be sure the pavement is entirely clean of debris. Glance over your shoulder frequently as you practice.

1. Standing still on the pavement, assume the A-stance with toes toughing and heels angled out. The knees are bent into a "coiled" position.
2. Push outward against both skates' toe wheels in one quick swipe. As the legs uncoil and the toes separate, rearward propulsion results. The more abrupt the push, the faster and farther you roll.
3. Before your skates reach a full A-frame width, stand tall to further lighten the load on your heel wheels. At the same time, pull your heels together.
4. Once you've steered your skates back under your hips, rotate your heels outward again to achieve a new A-stance.
5. Lower your hips over both skates to begin another quick outward push against the toes. Rise as you uncoil so you can bring your heels back in.
6. Get your skates back under your hips before you begin a push, and press your toe wheels straight out to the sides, not behind you; otherwise, you'll topple forward when you push!

Backward movement

1. Begin a series of rhythmic backward swizzles.
2. At the moment of the narrowest A-stance, shift most of your weight to the left skate. At the same time, begin a half-swizzle by pressuring only the right skate. The right skate begins its arc to the side.
3. Before the right skate passes behind your right hip, shift your weight onto it and begin to press the left skate into a half swizzle in a quick swiping motion. Make sure you keep both skates in constant contact with the ground, but apply the pressure with the toe wheels.
4. Continue alternating feet until you can get a short glide from each half swizzle.

Slalom turn

A close relative of the parallel turn, slaloms, too, are the result of turning on corresponding edges: Link a series of parallel turns on a wide slope and they become slaloms. Besides a thrilling way to embrace the pull of gravity, slaloms deliver speed control on wide downhill terrain as well as a near-perfect cross-training exercise for avid alpine-style skiers.

The two prerequisites to learning slaloms are good heel brake skills and the ability to perform parallel turns in both directions. Slalom turns are best learned on a very gentle grade, with a long, flat run-out. Lacking a slope, stroke hard to build up speed before performing drills, or, if available, skate with a strong tail wind.

1. At slalom speed, begin coasting in the ready position.
2. Looking toward the left side of the "run," scissors the left skate forward to initiate a parallel turn to the left, with weight one-third distributed over the left skate's outside edge and two-thirds over the right skate's inside edge.
3. Mid turn (when both skates are 45 degrees across the direction of travel), rotate head, hands, and shoulders to the right, . . .

4. . . . scissors the right skate forward, tip onto both right corresponding edges, and swap the weight distribution so the most pressure is on the left (outside, downhill) skate.
5. Continue linking turns until the momentum or gravitational pull dies.

Once you are able to rhythmically link consecutive turns in both directions:

1. Sink into each turn by bending the knees as the skates tip onto the new corresponding edges. The resulting increased pressure on both uphill edges is what aids in speed control.
2. To initiate the next turn, rise and "uncoil" at the moment of weight shift.
3. As you drill, begin to phase out the parallel turn's upper body rotation as much as possible, and instead, allow the edging, tipped skates to generate slalom turns.
4. Practice making both big and small turns to feel the difference this makes in speed reduction. Tighter arcs deliver better speed control.

Lunge turn

Lunge turns are used in a fast-moving game of hockey or to make a wide turn at the bottom of a hill. Lunge turns are similar to parallel turns except that the skater's weight is more over the advanced skate than the behind skate (figure 16-11).

Place an object down or mark the pavement for an imaginary corner.

1. Starting from at least twenty feet away, approach the mark at high speed.
2. About three feet before you pass your mark, assertively scissors the left skate forward and turn your head and upper body toward the direction of the turn.
3. Sink into a wide, low lunge as you enter the turn, making sure to center your chest over the left knee as you transfer most of your weight to that skate, tipping it onto its outside edge. The trailing leg carries enough weight to maintain pressure, with the knee slightly bent.
4. Allow centrifugal force to provide balance while both skates tip onto their left edges and press into the arc of the turn.
5. Close the gap between your skates and straighten up to resume forward momentum in the new direction.

Stride 3 (the power stride)

The skater who has achieved a competent basic stride is ready to learn a stronger, more efficient stroke. Stride 3 combines aerodynamics, proper use of the arms, stride angle and duration, and stroke initiation from the action skate's outside edge.

Figure 16-11. Lunge turn.

- **Aerodynamics**: Standing still with feet shoulder-width apart, fold your hands together, place your knuckles under your chin and touch your elbows to your knees. This is the most aerodynamic tuck used by serious speedskaters. Besides reduced wind resistance, the tuck's deep knee bend results in powerful, long strokes. Recreational and fitness skaters don't need to get quite this low. It takes most people months of practice to work up to maintaining a tuck position without back pain.
- **Arms**: The arm swing is strictly front-to-back, with arms close by your sides. The armswing starts with the thumb close to the nose (bent elbow) and ends with the little finger pointing skyward (straight arm). For maximum energy conservation, both arms are held close to the body with hands in the small of the back. To achieve this level of balance, start training with just one arm out of play.
- **Stride angle and duration**: When the support leg is bent into the tuck's deeper angle, the duration of each

stroke can be longer and stronger because the stroking skate maintains pressure on the pavement until the leg is fully extended. The stroke is pushed straight out to the side with all wheels in contact with the pavement, focusing pressure on the heel wheel.

- **Outside edge**: To further maximize each stroke, the recovered skate is placed back on the pavement beyond the midline of the direction of travel, touching down on its outside edge. The stroke, now lengthened by 1 to 3 inches, also gains power as it is pulled across the midline, and rolled onto its inside edge to finish with a standard pushing stroke.

Find a training location that allows unhindered and fast skating for long distances. It's easier to learn Stride 3 by focusing on just one leg at first. Once you can consistently perform it on one side, switch the focus to the opposite leg, then try it on both.

1. Begin skating at a fast pace in a moderate tuck, making long strokes with the heel wheel pressing outward, not back. Swing the arms from front to back.
2. Begin landing just one skate on its outside edge beyond the midline of the direction of travel; this is Stride 3. Skate normally with the other leg (using Stride 2).
3. Seek a feeling of pressure along the outside edge of your stroking foot each time that skate hits the pavement; feel the short pull as it rolls from its outside to its inside wheel edges and begins a push.

180-degree transitions

Forward-to-backward

1. From a forward rolling coast at a moderate pace, begin a counterclockwise spin stop, riding the right skate while pivoting on the left toe wheel.
2. The moment the left heel wheel returns to the pavement (heel-to-heel with the right skate), shift your weight to the left.
3. Make the right skate parallel with the left by means of a quick pivot on the right toe wheel, finishing with the weight equally balanced on both skates.
4. Complete the transition by pushing off into a backward stroke.

Backward-to-forward

1. From a backward rolling coast, look over the right shoulder and, at the same time, push the right skate outward into a backward half swizzle. The weight shifts to the left skate.
2. As the hips rotate sideways to the direction of travel, lift and rotate the right skate until the toe is pointing toward the direction of travel, then step forward onto it.
3. Utilize the pressure still on the left skate's inside edge to push smoothly off into a forward glide on the right skate.

Learn the following two versions of the 180-degree transition using raised arms as rotation and spotting guides; relax the arms when spotting is no longer needed. Try both movements standing still first.

Forward-to-backward pivot

1. From a forward rolling coast at a moderate pace, raise both outstretched hands to shoulder height—left hand straight ahead, right hand behind—lined up with the direction of travel.
2. Eyes on your left hand, pivot on both skates' *toe* wheels to rotate your hips, toes, and knees clockwise 180 degrees.
3. Return the heels to the pavement. Eyes and hands do not move during the entire movement. For best results, keep your knees bent and your upper body movements smooth as you rotate the lower body.

Backward-to-forward pivot

1. From a backward rolling coast at a moderate pace, raise both outstretched hands to shoulder height—left hand straight ahead, right hand behind—lined up with the direction of travel. Without moving the positions of your arms, look over your shoulder at your right hand.
2. Eyes on your right hand, pivot on both skates' *heel* wheels to rotate your hips, toes, and knees clockwise 180 degrees.
3. Return the toes to the pavement. Eyes and hands do not move during the entire movement. For best results, keep your knees bent and your upper body movements smooth as you rotate the lower body.

Advanced Stops

T-stop

Skaters who have good one-footed balance are ready to try the T-stop. Be aware that relying on this as your only stopping method can use up perfectly good wheels in a hurry. A heel brake is cheaper to replace and is more effective tool when stopping really counts.

In the following T-stop drills, the support leg is the one bearing most of your weight, and the action leg is the one handling the braking activity.

1. Begin coasting in your best ready position at a moderate speed.
2. Scissors your support leg forward slightly and transfer all of your weight to it as you . . .
3. . . . quickly lift and rotate the action skate a full 90 degrees and return all wheels to the pavement a few inches behind and perpendicular to the support skate's heel.
4. Curve your hips forward over your supporting skate in a slight lunge to better leverage the back skate's pressure and reduce knee stress.

5. Gradually increase the pressure on the dragging wheels by pulling the action skate closer to the balance skate.
6. Repeat the T-stop at progressively faster approaches while attempting to shorten the distance it takes your body to stop. For best results, practice stopping on a line.

Lunge stop

The lunge stop is used extensively in roller hockey.

1. Skating forward at a moderate speed, fix your eyes on an object or mark on the pavement fifteen feet ahead.
2. Begin a lunge toward the left, keeping your eyes fixed on the mark ahead of you.
3. Chest over the left knee, begin to arc the right, trailing skate into the turn. As it swings past, begin transferring pressure from the lunging left leg onto the sharply angled wheels of the right skate.
4. Just before the right skate crosses between you and the mark on the pavement, begin to rise slightly from the lunge. This adds more pressure and friction to the extended braking leg.

Backward power slide

The power slide is used for stopping when skating backward. When accomplished correctly, this move ends in a lunge with the braking skate extended in the direction of travel, low on its inside wheel edges. Do not attempt to use the power slide to stop yourself in a high-speed emergency.

This drill uses the left leg as the support leg and the right leg as the action (braking) leg. Hips and shoulders begin facing away from the direction of travel, and finish rotated sideways 90 degrees.

1. Using your favorite backward skating method, relax into a moderate-paced coast. Look over your right shoulder and spot an object or mark on the pavement fifteen feet behind, in the direction of travel.
2. Drop your chest over the left knee and begin to arc the right skate out to the side and back, at the same time transferring pressure to its inside wheel edges.
3. Begin to rise from over the left leg so that you can increase the pressure on the braking leg's inside edge. Reach maximum pressure just before the right skate crosses between you and the mark on the pavement. This friction is what causes the stop.

TEACHING STRATEGIES, CONSIDERATIONS

Teaching Locations

A safe location for teaching first-time skaters is crucial. Beginners need a level, traffic-free environment for practicing their first strokes. Ideally, the first few moments on skates should be spent on carpeting or dry grass. The best outdoor site is a smooth concrete game court (basketball or tennis without the net) with a dry lawn nearby. Fine-grade asphalt parking lots are good, as long as auto traffic is blocked off.

Warning: The lesson site will be marked with harmless black stripes after heel brake practice.

Hills are the bane of the new in-line skater, and beginners should avoid them entirely until they learn how to use the heel brake or some other stopping method effectively. Even parking lots offer more than enough thrill, because, visible to the eye or not, there is always a drainage slope.

That said, a slight slope a short distance from the beginner area is a wonderful way to empower skaters near the end of a stopping lesson by having them first drag the brake lightly for speed control and, on the next pass, stop completely at a designated spot mid-slope.

Student Age and Previous History

As a rule, the most successful beginners have several hours experience in ice or quad-style roller skating. Alpine or cross country skiing are the next best previous experience because the student is already used to the gliding/sliding feeling. Lacking these, any sport that requires centered balance will help the beginner, whether it is cycling, gymnastics, snowboarding, or riding a horse. Even if it's been years since the last participation, the balance learned in the past can still be reactivated for skating. Thanks to better balance, which leads to better confidence, these students progress swiftly on the first day of instruction.

Young children and adults without a solid balance background require extra attention and tips on improving balance. For the average beginning skater, the initial awkwardness gives way to improved balance and coordination after about twenty hours on skates, as long as the time span is no greater than six months.

Enhancing the Beginner Experience

For many beginning skaters, especially those over 30 years old, the fear of falling is the biggest hurdle. Add self-doubt, self-consciousness in front of others, lapses in concentration, or negative thoughts, and anxious novices tend to become even more awkward and prone to injury. Here are some ways to give the beginner a better sense of control:

- **Focus on safety**. Stress the benefits of wearing *all* protective gear, and learning how stop with the heel brake. Make sure the student takes a controlled practice fall early in the lesson.
- **Reduce variables**. Stick with one teaching location for every skating session. Suggest that skaters practice on their own at one location until skills and confidence grow.
- **Encourage repetition**. Repeated drills build a foundation for more advanced skills later on, and this is one sport where repetition is rarely boring. To keep the learning curve in a strong upward arc, novices should practice no less than twice a week for several weeks. In

many cases, they can progress beyond the basics without further instruction just by getting out on the pavement for hours of play.

- **Suggest club membership**. Observation and emulation are great teachers. To find out where other skaters gather, inquire at the local skate shops about skating clubs, weekly group skates, and hockey leagues.

GLOSSARY

A-frame stance A balanced, upright stance with skates positioned parallel and wider than shoulder width.

A-stance A version of the ready position where the toes are nearly touching and the heels are angled out.

ABEC A bearing precision rating system developed by the Annular Bearing Engineering Council: an ABEC5 bearing spins faster than an ABEC1.

action leg The leg that performs the work for a given movement, as opposed to the balance leg, which provides support.

axle guide The plastic frame inserts that can be rotated in some skate models to allow rockering the wheels or lengthening the wheel base.

balance One of the four fundamentals of skating, balance on in-lines is achieved through proper stance using the ready position. The result is better equilibrium and confidence for learning new skills.

bearings The hardware that makes a smooth-spinning wheel (two per wheel), using small ball bearings that roll in a track called the race.

carving The act of riding one or both sets of wheel edges around the curved arc of a turn, commonly used in describing slalom turns.

center edge The place on the wheel that is in contact with the pavement when the skate is perpendicular to the surface.

center line The imaginary line that bisects the path of travel.

coasting ready position The rolling stance that results after the skater strides to attain a moderate speed (enough momentum to ensure good balance) and then relaxes into a balanced ready position.

coned The shaved-off state of a wheel that is worn on one side, indicating the wheel needs to be flipped over and rotated or replaced.

core See **hub.**

corresponding edges The outside edge of the right skate's wheels corresponds to the inside wheel edges of the left skate, and vice versa. When both skates are tipped in the same direction, they are said to be on corresponding edges.

cross-training Using in-line skating workouts to enhance performance for another sport, and vice versa.

cuff The portion of the in-line skate that encases the ankle, usually plastic.

cuff-activated brake A braking system utilizing an arm connected at the top to the boot's hinged cuff, with a brake attached at the bottom. The brake automatically engages when the skate is pushed forward and the cuff angles back, allowing the skater to keep all four wheels in contact with the pavement.

diameter The measurement that determines wheel sizes, usually marked on the side of the wheel in millimeters.

durometer A rating system used to classify in-line wheel hardness, usually printed on the side of the wheel with a two-digit number followed by the letter *A*. The higher the number, the harder the wheel.

edges The portion of the wheel that contacts the pavement. There are three edges on a skate's wheels: the inside edge, the outside edge, and the center edge.

edging The act of tipping the skate onto the outside or inside edge to perform skating movements. Edging is one of the four fundamental elements of skating.

fall line On a hill, the direction with the most gravitational pull.

footbed The replaceable insole of the skate boot liner.

gliding The period of time when the skate rolls on the pavement after a stroke.

grinding Landing on the skate's wheel frame between the wheels to perform tricks like sliding across the edge of a tree planter or down stairway banister; also performed in special apparatus during aggressive skating competitions.

half-swizzle A forward or backward swizzle performed with one action leg only; the other leg remains the support leg. Also known as scooters or sculling.

hub A hard substance that the wheel's urethane bonds to, providing torsional stability and a solid seat for the bearings.

inside edges The sides of the wheels below the foot's arch.

outside edges The sides of the wheels below the outside of the foot.

polyurethane The plastic material used to manufacture in-line wheels.

pressure The application of pressure is one of the four fundamentals of skating. Pressure application results in a wide range of skating skills when it is combined with rotation, weight transfer, and edging.

profile The wheel's shape when viewed from the edge. Wide profiles result in quick-turning, slower skates; the narrowest-profile wheels are used for speed.

race The track inside a bearing around which the balls roll.

ready position The balanced alignment of the body that results in equilibrium and confidence. Feet are shoulder-width apart. Shoulders, hip joints, and arches are balanced along an invisible line that runs from head to foot. Knees and hips are flexed, hands and arms are at waist height within sight.

recovery The act of lifting the skate that has just finished a stride and returning it to the proper position to push off into a new stride.

rockered A wheel configuration where the center wheels are slightly lower than the end wheels, giving the skater more turning maneuverability (used in hockey and figure skating).

rotation Rotary motion is one of the four fundamentals of skating. Upper-body rotation is used to help skaters learn most turning skills.

safe-T The locked stance used for standing still, where one heel is rolled up against the other skate's arch.

shield The exterior cover on the side of a bearing; can be permanent or removable for maintenance.

skitching Hitching a ride by grabbing onto a moving vehicle. Don't do it!

spacer The metal or plastic spacer that sits within a wheel between the bearings.

Stride 1 The beginning stride, a variation that consists of short strokes with toes pointed out duck-fashion, used to introduce beginners to the glide and stride.

Stride 2 The basic in-line stride used for forward propulsion.

Stride 3 The power stride, a variation that combines an aerodynamic body position with an enhanced stroke and arm swing to maximize power and efficiency (used by fitness skaters and speedskaters).

striding The result of combining stroking and gliding.

stroking The leg action that propels the skater in forward or backward movement.

support leg The leg that provides support and bears the most weight during movements that require independent legwork. Sometimes referred to as the balance leg.

T-stop A stopping method accomplished by dragging one skate's wheels across the pavement perpendicular to the direction of travel.

V-stance A version of the ready position where the heels are nearly touching and the toes are pointed out.

wheelbase The length of a skate's wheel contact with the pavement.

wheel frame The chassis attached to the sole of the in-line boot into which the wheels are bolted (custom frames can be purchased for some skate models).

RESOURCES

Organizations

Aggressive

Aggressive Skaters Association (ASA), 171 Pier Ave., Suite 247, Santa Monica, CA 90405, Todd Shays, Executive Director, 310-399-3436, Fax: 310-581-3552, www.aggroskate.com/asa; asa@aggroskate.com

Camps

Camp Santa Rosa c/o Snoopy's Gallery, 1665 West Steel Ln., Santa Rosa, CA 95403, Jill Schulz, 800-959-3385, Fax: 707-546-0391

Woodward Camp, Box 93, Rte. 45, Woodward, PA, 16882, 814-349-5633, Fax: 814-349-5643, www.woodwardcamp.com/in-line.htm; office@woodwardcamp.com

Freestyle

USA Roller Skating (USAC/RS), 4730 South St. (P.O. Box 6579), Lincoln, NE 68506-0578, Andy Seeley, Sports Information Director, 402-483-7551, Fax: 402-483-1465, www.usacrs.com; sk8sid@aol.com

Hockey

National Roller Hockey LLC (NARCH), 3830 Broadway, Suite 35, Boulder, CO 80304, 309-786-8764, Fax: 303-546-0581, Kdluff@aol.com

Roller Hockey International (RHI), 13070 Fawn Hill Dr., Grass Valley, CA 95945, Larry King, President, 916-272-7825, Fax: 916-274-1115

Roller Hockey International~Amateur (RHI~A), 249 E. Ocean Blvd., Suite 800, Long Beach, CA 90802, Michele Massy, Vice President, 310-628-0524, Fax: 800-884-7442

USA Hockey In-line, 4965 N. 30th St., Colorado Springs, CO 80919, Brian Williams, In-line Manager, 719-559-5500, Fax: 719-599-5994, www.usahockey.com; brianw@usahockey.com

Hybrid sports

National In-line Basketball League (NIBBL), 135 Rivington St., Suite 3F, New York, NY 10002, 212-539-1132, www.nibbl.com

Roller Soccer International Federation, P.O. Box 423318, San Francisco, CA 94142-3318, Zack Phillips, 415-864-6879 or 888-475-7727, www.rlrscr.com/html; RSIF@rlrscr.com

WindSkate, Inc., P.O. Box 3081, Santa Monica, CA 90403, Jamie Budge, 310-453-4808, www.windskate.com

In-line Trade

International In-line Skating Association (IISA), 3720 Farragut Ave., Suite 400, Kensington, MD 20895, Gil Clark, Executive Director, 301-942-9770, or 301-942-9771, www.iisa.org; iisahq@erols.com

IISA Government Relations Committee, 3720 Farragut Ave., Suite 400, Kensington, MD 20895, Laura Poellet, Director, 301-942-9770

IISA Sport and Competition Council (SCC), 1507 Walnut St., Philadelphia, PA 19102, Bob Gollwitzer, Director, 301-942-9770, www.fwcc.com; iisa/scc@fwcc.com

IISA, National Skate Patrol Division, 3720 Farragut Ave., Suite 400, Kensington, MD 20895, John Reich, Director, 301-942-9770

IISA/ICP Instructor Certification Program, 201 N. Front St., Suite 306, Wilmington, NC 28401, Kalinda Mathis, Director, 910-762-7004, Fax: 910-762-9477, www.iisa.org; iisaicp@aol.com

National Sporting Goods Association (NSGA), 1699 Wall St., Mt. Prospect, IL 60056, Larry Weindruch, 847-439-4000, Fax: 847-439-0111, www.nsgachicagoshow.com; nsga1699@aol.com

Roller Skating Association International, 6905 Corporate Dr., Indianapolis, NE 46278, Katherine McDonell, Executive Director, 317-347-2626, Fax: 317-347-2636, www.rollerskating.org/; rsa@oninternet.com

Sporting Goods Manufacturers Association (SGMA), 200 Castlewood Dr., North Palm Beach, FL 33408-5696, Mike May, Director of Communications, 561-840-1165, Fax: 561-863-8984, www.sportlink.com; mmsgma@aol.com

USA Roller Skating, US Amateur Confederation of Roller Skating, 4730 South St. (P.O. Box 6579), Lincoln, NE 68506-0578, Jean Stanek, Sports Information Director, 402-483-7551, Fax: 402-483-1465, www.usacrs.com; sk8sid@aol.com

Slalom

In-line Slalom Skaters International (ISSI), 28 Paragon Lane, Stamford, CT 06905, Pete Beatty, 203-357-0225 or 888-sk8works

Speedskating

Amateur Speedskating Union (ASU), 1033 Shady Lane, Glen Ellyn, IL 60137, Shirley Yates, Executive Secretary/Treasurer,

630-790-3230, Fax: 630-790-3235, jeffrey@mit.edu; http://web.mit.edu/jeffrey/speedskating/asu.html

National In-line Racing Association (NIRA), 4708 E. 4th Pl., Tulsa, OK 74112, Joe Cotter, Executive Director, 800-758-6472 or 800-SK8 NIRA, Fax: 918-627-3504

USA In-line Racing (USA/IR), P.O. Box 162055, Altamonte Springs, FL 32716, Dan Lind, Executive Director, 407-682-2328, www.usain-line.org/; tjmartin@sprintmail.com

Trail Advocates

Intermodal Surface Transportation Efficiency Act (ISTEA), 1506 21st St. NW, Suite 200, Washington, DC 20036, 202-463-8405

Rails-to-Trails Conservancy, HQ, 1100 17th St. NW, 10th Floor, Washington, DC 20036, 202-331-9696 or 800-888-7747, ext 11, Fax: 202-331-9680

Publications

Powell, M. and Svensson, J. 1993. *In-line skating*. Champaign Ill.: Human Kinetics. Contains 100 photographs and diagrams and step-by-step instructions for in-line skating fundamentals.

Aggressive, Box Magazine, 2025 Pearl St., Boulder, CO 80302, 800-804-8885

Daily Bread, P.O. Box 82146, San Diego, CA 92138-2146, sanford@well.com, 619-270-6656

Box Magazine, 2025 Pearl St., Boulder, CO 80302, 800-804-8885

Scum Magazine, 1004 Durham Dr., Austin, TX 78753, Havoc@utxvms.cc.utexas.edu, 512-834-8604 or 512-634-4108

X SK8 Magazine, 2200 Wilson Blvd., Box 102-178, Arlington, VA 22201, xsk8mag@aol.com, 703-522-XSK8

Fitness

Nottingham, S., and Fedel, F. 1997. *Fitness in-line skating*. Champaign, Ill.: Human Kinetics. To order: 800-747-4454

Bradley, C. 1994. *Skate fit: The complete in-line skating workout*. New York: ABA, Inc. To order: 800-376-5551

Humphrey, R. 1996. *Rollerdancing: A workout on skates.* San Francisco: Movement in Motion Productions (606 Head St., San Francisco, CA 94132)

Fitness and Speedskating Times, 2401 NE 15th Terrace, Pompano Beach, FL 33064, SpeedSk8in@aol.com, 954-782-5928

Fitness Skater, Straight Line Communications, Inc., 12327 Santa Monica Blvd., Suite 202, Los Angeles, CA 90025, 310-442-6660

Hockey

Hockey Player, P.O. Box 1007, Okemus, MI 48805, hockeymag@aol.com, 800-403-6397 or 517-347-1172

Roller Hockey Magazine, P.O. Box 16027, North Hollywood, CA 91695, 310-442-6660 or 800-576-5537, Fax: 310-442-6663

USA Hockey in-line Magazine, 1775 Bob Johnson Dr., Colorado Springs, CA 80906, brianw@usahockey.com, 719-576-8724

In-line Trade

in-line Retailer, 2025 Pearl St., Boulder, CO 80302, Annemink@aol.com, 303-440-5111, Fax: 303-440-3313, www.in-linemag.com

Recreational

Miller, L. 1996. *California in-line skating: The complete guide to the best places to skate.* San Francisco: Foghorn Press. To order: 800-FOGHORN

Gear up! Guide to in-line skating. Published by IISA/ICP. Free booklet describes the sport, safety aspects, equipment, and IISA programs, 800-567-5283

Global Skate Magazine, 16478 Beach Blvd., #361, Westminster, CA 92683, gskate30@aol.com, 714-979-7791

in-line Magazine, 2025 Pearl St., Boulder, CO 80302, www.ilinemag.com,Annemink@aol.com, 303-541-3678

In-line Skater Magazine, 13645 Beta Rd., Dallas, TX 75244, skater@flc.mhs.compuserve.com, 972-851-1700, www.xcscx.com/skater

Time Out Magazine, 40575 California Oaks Rd., #D2255, Murrieta, CA 92562, 909-677-0464

Speedskating

Fitness and Speedskating Times, 2401 NE 15th Terrace, Pompano Beach, FL 33064, SpeedSk8in@aol.com, 954-782-5928

Jogging

After completing this chapter, the reader should be able to:

- State the guidelines for starting a jogging program
- Select and care for proper jogging equipment, particularly shoes
- Demonstrate correct running form
- Construct a proper training schedule according to one's goals
- Prevent and treat jogging injuries
- Teach fundamental jogging principles and skills

The popularity of jogging as a fitness activity has steadily progressed over the last 30 to 40 years. During the early 1960s most organized jogging activities were directed by the YMCA, boys clubs, or college physical education programs. The physiological benefits of jogging were not widely known until a scientific study by Dr. Kenneth H. Cooper (Major, USAF Medical Corps) demonstrated a positive correlation between heart rate and oxygen consumption. He suggested a variety of types of exercise and explained how each helped build one's cardiorespiratory fitness. Cooper differentiated activities based upon the primary energy source required during their performance and substantiated the major role that aerobic activities, such as jogging, play in increasing cardiorespiratory fitness.

As the American public became increasingly fitness conscious, the high visibility of successful U.S. athletes such as Frank Shorter, Bill Rogers, Alberto Salazar, Mary Decker, and Joan Benoit Samuelson helped stimulate interest in jogging and running. The emergence of a number of running magazines and the writings of such authors as Dr. David Costill, Bill Bowerman, and George Sheehan helped to present the benefits of jogging to the increasingly fitness-conscious American public. The media also has helped to increase the visibility and popularity of running events. Some of these events have emerged to draw national attention and thousands of participants. With this push, jogging moved into the mainstream of American pastime activities.

Jogging may attract some individuals as a means of improving health and reducing the risk of heart disease. Others may be looking for a means of losing weight or reducing stress in their daily lives. And yet others find that jogging builds self-esteem and makes them feel good. Some are attracted to the social atmosphere often associated with many running events and participating in a type of activity where there is the potential to challenge oneself and others. Whatever the reason, jogging facilitates the improvement of one's quality of life.

GETTING STARTED

Jogging is usually defined as running slowly at a comfortable pace of about 9 to 12 minutes per mile. Running is an individual activity, so some will be able to run farther and faster than others with about the same effort. A good guideline for the beginning runner is to utilize the talk test: run just fast enough so that you are still able to carry on a conversation.

Running need not be a form of self-torture. To have a successful running experience, a sensible program should be initiated. The following guidelines are applicable to almost everyone:

1. Consult your physician before initiating any type of exercise program. This guideline increases in importance with an increase in age. You should answer the questions found in a general preparticipation health screening form, such as the Physical Activity Readiness Questionnaire (PAR-Q), before beginning a moderately intensive exercise program such as jogging. A diagnostic exercise test is generally not essential for apparently healthy men under 40 years of age and women under 50 if the exercise program is going to begin at the moderate intensity level. This means exercising at 60 to 74 percent of one's maximal heart rate (see the general suggestion section), an RPE (rating of perceived exertion of 11 to 13 (very light to somewhat hard), or 40 to 60 percent of $\dot{V}O_2max$ (maximum oxygen capacity). Exercising at this level should be well within the individual's cardiorespiratory capacity and sustainable for about 60 minutes.
2. Start slowly. If you overdo, your first day will probably be your last.
3. Be consistent. Set up a practical routine, and stick with it for at least 6 to 8 weeks. Jogging every other day gives the body time to recover from the previous workout.
4. Listen to your body. It will reveal your limits. Try not to become overly competitive and exceed those limits. If you become sore, back off for a day or two.

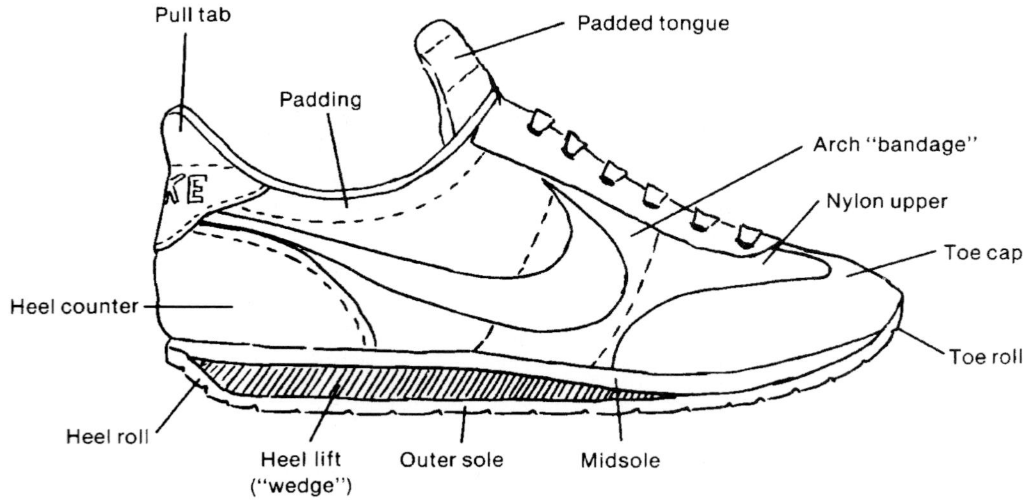

Figure 17-1. Anatomy of a running shoe.

5. Take walking breaks frequently during the first few runs. Warm up and cool down by walking.
6. Get a pair of comfortable, properly fitting shoes (see next section). Clothing will be dictated by common sense and experience.
7. Do not always gear your schedule to how far you can run. Try using time as a guideline and increase your total time by no more than 10 percent per week. Start with as little as 5 minutes of walking and 5 minutes of easy running. Increase the time slowly, trying not to strain. By gearing your program to time, you allow the body to work to its own limits. Disappointment will not be part of your program when you fail to cover a set number of miles or kilometers.

Running can be enjoyable if it is done with a positive frame of mind.

SHOE SELECTION

Individual needs and requirements vary greatly from runner to runner, so one type of shoe cannot be recommended for everyone. Some things to be considered in your shoe selection are: comfort and shock absorption, body size and running-style mechanics, and skill and competitive level.

The running shoe (figures 17-1 and 17-2) is designed to provide protection while leaving running motion unencumbered, so keep in mind that proper selection of a training shoe is essential for avoiding injuries while ensuring maximum performance and comfort.

Checking the wear on the soles of your shoes will usually give you some good information about your normal gait. The soles will provide you with information about whether you are an overpronator or underpronator. If you are an overpronator, your feet roll excessively inward and your shoes will wear on the inside of your heels. Look for a straight or slightly curve-lasted shoe. If you are an underpronator, you don't roll inward or you land and run on the balls of your feet and the wear will be on the outside of the shoes. Look for a shoe that has good shock absorption, curved or semicurved last with a slip-lasted construction.

Figure 17-2. Running shoes.

When selecting shoes, there are some terms that you should be familiar with: The *shape,* or *last,* of a shoe is its basic construction shape, which will affect its fit and support characteristics. There are four different lasts: (1) *straight*: gives the most support; preferred by the overpronator; (2) *slightly curved*: gives good medial (arch area) support; (3) *semicurved*: gives some medial support with

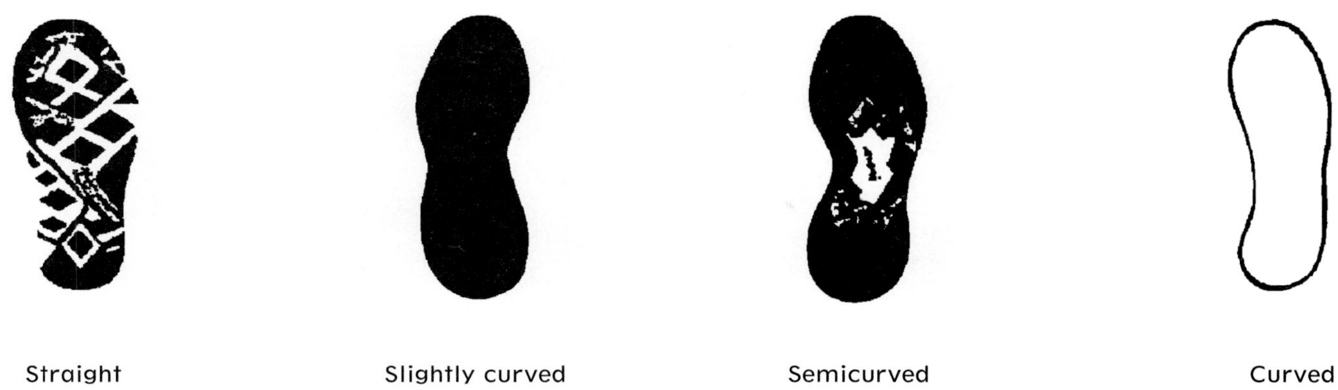

Figure 17-3. Various running shoe shapes.

greater inflare (the sole of the shoe becomes narrower only on the inner arch side); and (4) *curved*: has greatest inflare; very flexible, with the least amount of medial support; usually found in lightweight trainers or racing flats. See figure 17-3 for examples of the different shapes.

There are also three styles of shoe construction: (1) *slip-lasted*: stitched together on the underside; provides good flexibility; (2) *board-lasted*: has a cardboard or cardboard-like material cemented over the midsole; provides good stability and support for orthotics; and (3) *combination lasting*: board-lasted in the rear of the foot for stability and slip-lasted in the forefoot for flexibility.

The best place to start is with a running shoe specialist, one who offers a wide variety of brands and models. Try on several varieties and lace them up for a run. Check the shoes for minor defects (which are common in this age of mass production), and then take them out for a short run. Take your time in making a selection.

If you have orthotics, be sure that they fit in the shoes. You may have to pull out the sockliner to make room for them. You should also be sure to wear the same type of socks that you normally run in when selecting your shoes. You should have about a thumb's width between the toe of the shoe and your longest toe for a proper fit. Shoes that are too tight or too large will lead to blisters and will be uncomfortable.

Set your own requirements, keeping these questions in mind: Are you heavy on your feet, or do you run lightly with good form? What type of terrain will you run on (trails, roads, or grass)? Are you strictly a fun runner, or are you training for a specific distance or time? Find the shoes that fit your needs and buy the pair that fits your feet best.

Width sizing has become popular with the expansion of the running-shoe market in the past few years. Price is also a factor, but one should remember that high cost does not ensure a good fit or quality.

A good pair of shoes are a runner's most critical investment (outside of time), yet they are not a cure-all. The anatomy of your foot may call for something not offered by today's mass-produced shoes. If you cannot find shoes that fit comfortably, you may need to seek professional help from a qualified podiatrist or orthopedist.

Reserve your running shoes for running. Using them for casual wear causes different wear patterns, which will affect the life of the shoe.

Beginners should purchase a pair of training shoes. They offer more cushioning than a racing shoe. Always remember that it is important to wear high-quality socks when jogging. Socks capable of wicking moisture away from the feet are a must.

RUNNING FORM

Many people believe long-distance running requires little or no skill. Simple observation of different runners shows that some seem to float along almost effortlessly, whereas others pound along, struggling with each step and exhibiting contorted expressions. The obvious difference is cardiovascular conditioning, but technique and efficiency of movement are also involved to a great extent and require skill and practice.

Distance running is a natural activity, so a runner should do what comes naturally, as long as it is mechanically sound. The slower a runner travels, the easier it is to get away with poor form. Problems arise when the tempo is increased and mechanical inefficiencies become compounded by the increase in speed.

Foot Placement

The slower you go, the flatter the landing. Try to land lightly and gently; do not pound. As you run faster, you move higher on the foot, toward the toes. All runners land first on the outside edge of the foot, then roll inward. This absorbs shock. The precise point of contact varies with speed.

Stride

Stride is a function of speed. The short stride is more economical and also slower. As the pace increases, so does the

Figure 17-4. Good running form.

Figure 17-5. Runner who is "sitting."

length of stride. Keep in mind that you should lead with the knee first. The foot should follow and extend to meet the ground. Do not overstride; keep your feet under you. The point of foot contact should be directly under the knee, with the knee slightly flexed.

Body Carriage

Run tall and with a straight back (figure 17-4). The head should remain level. Do not look at the sky or at your feet, but instead out in front of you about 10 to 15 feet (3 to 4.5 m). This approach ensures an erect, balanced running stance. The head should be in line with the trunk and the trunk in line with the legs.

The hips should be directly over the legs. Try not to "sit" or lean forward. A runner tends to "sit" when fatigue sets in, and this leads to a shorter, mechanically inefficient stride (figure 17-5).

The arms should play an active role in running. They are there for balance and driving and should not be ignored. Arms help the legs go faster as long as they remain rhythmic. Hold the hands loosely cupped and relaxed, palms turned inward. Bend the elbow 90 degrees and bring the arms parallel to each other, slightly inward but not across the midline of the chest. The hands should swing back, but not past the midline of the trunk. When a runner starts to fatigue, the hands and arms are no longer relaxed and they are much closer to the body. This is the time to drop the arms to your side and shake them out.

The best time to practice technique is during a short afternoon run. Stride six times over 50 to 60 yards (45 to 55 m) on a smooth, grassy surface, concentrating on any problem. Have someone watch you run several times and then make suggestions. All runners have innocent quirks in running styles that are their trademarks. If these quirks do not affect mechanical efficiency, they should be left alone.

TRAINING

Along with the increase in the number of joggers in the country, there has been a large increase in the availability of races in which to participate. Almost every weekend, a run is sponsored by some organization. Some are for serious runners, some for fun, some for raising money for charitable causes, and some for recognizing local traditions. Although, it is possible to be a jogger and never enter a race, these events are motivational, much like the recital that piano teachers use to motivate students to continue practicing. These races also can be enjoyable social events. If you desire to enter a race, it shouldn't be done without advance preparation and training for the event's demands.

The word *training*, like the word *jogging*, can be ambiguous. The difference is sometimes artificial. Training indicates effort toward completing a specific distance or race; jogging is usually done on a more casual basis for fitness or health reasons.

There are several methods of starting training. Most are fairly simple. There are guiding principles, terminology, and systems of training for the beginning racer or jogger.

Fundamental Principles of Training

Four major components are necessary for the development of cardiorespiratory fitness: *mode of the exercise* (e.g., jogging or running); *frequency* (how often you do the activity; generally three time per week is the minimum); *intensity* (how hard you are working, or percentage maximum heart rate; generally 50 to 90 percent of maximum heart rate); and *duration* (length of time of workout; generally more than 20 minutes).

Stress. The body must adapt to stress if it is to improve its general condition. Training stimulates the type of stress the body will encounter during a race. A fine line separates training from stress and strain during the run.

Overload. Overload means taking on a little more work than is comfortable. It should be done for brief periods at first, perhaps every other day. Stretch your limits gradually. If done too quickly, it can result in injury or at least soreness.

Specificity of training. Training must resemble the type of race you are preparing for in both speed and distance.

Consistency. Body systems get into shape by regular training. Do not do a super workout one day and then be unable to walk the next. Be consistent.

Recovery. The body must be given adequate time to rejuvenate itself. Continuous hard training will bring you down eventually. Rest is just as important as exercise.

Pacing. Establish a long-view approach toward running. Both in races and training, focus on gradual improvement. At first, improvement comes quickly as mileage piles up. *Remember:* More does not always mean better.

Running surfaces. The surface that you run on will influence the amount of force that your body must absorb. Running on cement provides the greatest amount of stress. Cement has very little give and is very hard on the legs. Running on paved roads is a little less stressful than cement. Most modern running tracks are a little softer than running on the roads. A dirt or cinder track, grass, or a wood-chipped trail would provide the least amount of stress on the legs. Stay away from running in the sand along a beach, if you are just beginning. This type of surface is generally very uneven and requires a great deal of extra energy. The same would be true of trying to run in the snow. This surface can be very dangerous even with shoes that have excellent tread. Changing the type of surface that you run on can provide your legs with some needed stress relief. Selecting the proper surface can make your training program more enjoyable and reduce the possibility of injuries. Remember that as you increase your total time running, you are also increasing the amount of stress on your body.

Training Schedules

Individualize your training schedule. Find a system that fits your lifestyle and makes your running a part of you for the rest of your life. Keep yourself happy and eager. It is important to keep in mind that every workout should begin with an easy warm-up, followed by 10 to 15 minutes of static stretching, jogging, a cool-down, and some additional stretching. Do not increase your weekly mileage by more than 5 to 10 percent at one time. You will find that small increases are much easier for the body to handle than large increases. Undertrain rather than overtrain.

Another point that may help lessen the potential for injury in your training program is to reduce your training volume every fourth week. This will give your body a little better chance to recover and adapt to the training.

The warm-up and cool-down are very important parts of your workout. Before the muscles of the body are ready to begin an increased level of use, there must be sufficient time for the muscles to warm up and to increase the blood flow to these muscles. After 5 to 10 minutes of easy moving, you should spend an equal period of time in static stretching to increase or help maintain flexibility. A static stretch should be taken to the point where you can feel the stretch, but not to the point of pain. After holding the stretch for 10 to 20 seconds, relax and repeat the stretch 2 to 4 times. One generally starts with the larger muscle groups and works toward the smaller muscles (see the section "Beneficial Stretches and Resistance Training" for examples). A short period of time stretching should help reduce the potential for muscle strains and soreness. By the same token, the cool-down after a workout, where there is a gradual decrease in the level of activity, allows the body a period of recovery. The cool-down allows the muscle pump to keep the blood circulating and helps disperse a large portion of the built-up metabolites. Culminating the workout with a short stretching period will again help to increase one's flexibility.

Three different programs (beginner, intermediate, and advanced) are provided here as guides for developing your own jogging program. Each program will have a different focus and level of fitness required for successful completion. Remember to keep the goals for your jogging program realistic and practical. It should be fun and something that you look forward to.

Beginner program

The beginner program assumes that you have not had any prior training or have not trained for the last 6 months. Keep in mind that you want to find a level area to begin your jogging program. Running up and down hills in the beginning of a program may place too much stress on your joints and ligaments. If you are very overweight or your cardiovascular fitness is extremely low, you may want to begin with a 4- to 6-week walking program before starting to jog.

The beginner program starts with a combination of walking and easy jogging done every other day. You can use a number of different methods (time, distance, steps) to monitor your training program. Select the one that is easiest for you and use it to guide your program.

Counting steps. When counting steps, it is easier to count only the number of times that one foot strikes the ground. Start with 5 to 10 jogging steps, followed by 5 to 10 walking steps. Repeat this cycle for 20 to 30 minutes. Be sure to monitor your heart rate and keep it at the lower end of your target heart rate (the method for determining your target heart rate is presented later in this chapter) or keep in mind the "talk test." This activity should not be labored activity. In the second week, increase the jogging to 15 to 20 steps, followed by 5 to 10 walking steps, for a total of 20 to 30 minutes. By week 3 you should be able to jog for 25 to 40 steps, followed by 5 to 10 walking steps, for the full 20 to 30 minutes. In each succeeding week try to increase the time that you jog before having to add the short walking segment. In a few months, you should be able to go a full 20 to 30 minutes without any walking and start working to increase the intensity of the runs.

Time. Start with 10 to 15 seconds of jogging, followed by 10 to 15 seconds of walking. Repeat this cycle for 20 to 30 minutes. Follow the same guidelines as mentioned above. In the second week, increase the jogging to 20 to 30 seconds, followed by 10 to 15 seconds of walking, for a total of 20 to 30 minutes. By week 3 you should be able to jog for 30 to 40 seconds, followed by 10 to 15 seconds of walking, for the full 20 to 30 minutes. In each succeeding week try to increase the time that you jog before having to add the short walking segment.

Distance. This method requires that you have an area that is marked off for distances. This could be a running track, or a street with driveways, or telephone poles along the road. Start with jogging a specific distance, followed by walking for the same distance. You could start by jogging from one driveway to the next and then walking until you reached the next. Repeat this cycle for 20 to 30 minutes. Again, follow the same guidelines as given above. In the second week, increase the distance that you jog, followed by the same walking distance as used in week 1, for a total of 20 to 30 minutes. By week 3 you should be able to jog for three driveways, followed by walking for one driveway, for the full 20 to 30 minutes. In each succeeding week try to increase the distance that you jog before having to add the short walking segment. In a few months, you should be able to go a full 20 to 30 minutes without any walking and start working to increase the intensity of the runs.

Intermediate program

The program for an intermediate jogger incorporates different training methods (table 17-1). Training is carried out 4 days a week for 30 to 60 minutes per workout. This type of program is for someone who is interested in participating in an occasional road race in the 5K to 10K range. The program is based upon a 12-week preparation period for a road race, but the basic pattern can be used for longer or shorter preparation periods. The program for each week starts with a workout day, followed by a day off, followed by two consecutive days of training, followed by another day off, followed by a day of training, and finally a day off. The first 3 weeks are directed toward building a running base. The runs should not be hard, but work at a level where you can carry on a conversation throughout the run (the "talk test"). Use the fourth week as a recovery week.

The next 4-week cycle adds to the base that has already been created and adds some faster-paced runs into the workout schedule (table 17-2). Now is a good time to introduce some "fartlek" training (see "Types of Training Systems") and some faster-paced repeats into your workout schedule. Alternating between a fast and a slow pace is repeated throughout the workout. The 400 m repeats (6 to 10) are done at a faster pace than you are normally accustomed to running. Each repeat is followed by an easy jog for the same distance.

The last 4 weeks of the 12-week program introduce some intervals and longer, faster-paced running (table 17-3). The duration of the runs will not increase, but the intensity will be at a slightly higher level. The intervals should be 800 to 1200 m at a 5K-race pace, with a 4- to 5-minute recovery between each interval. The high-intensity runs should vary in length, but over 800 m, and a little slower than your 5K-race pace. The recovery time between high-intensity runs should be rather short (1 to 1½ minutes).

By the time you finish this 12-week program, you should be able to finish a 5K or 10K road race.

Advanced program

A program for the advanced jogger—one who has been training for months and who is now interested in preparing

Table 17-1. INTERMEDIATE TRAINING PROGRAM: FIRST FOUR-WEEK CYCLE

Training day	Week 1 time	Week 2 time	Week 3 time	Week 4 time
Day 1	20 minutes	22 minutes	25 minutes	20 minutes
Day 2	20 minutes	25 minutes	30 minutes	25 minutes
Day 3	20 minutes	20 minutes	25 minutes	20 minutes
Day 4	30 minutes	35 minutes	40 minutes	35 minutes

Table 17-2. INTERMEDIATE TRAINING PROGRAM: SECOND FOUR-WEEK CYCLE

Training day	Week 5 time	Week 6 time	Week 7 time	Week 8 time
Day 1 fartlek workout	25 minutes	27 minutes	30 minutes	25 minutes
Day 2	20 minutes	25 minutes	30 minutes	20 minutes
Day 3 400 m repeats	25 minutes (6 x 400)	30 minutes (8 x 400)	35 minutes (10 x 400)	20 minutes (6 x 400)
Day 4	40 minutes	45 minutes	50 minutes	35 minutes

Table 17-3. INTERMEDIATE TRAINING PROGRAM: THIRD FOUR-WEEK CYCLE

Training day	Week 9 time	Week 10 time	Week 11 time	Week 12 time
Day 1 Intervals	25 minutes (5 x 800)	27 minutes (6 x 1000)	30 minutes (6 x 800)	25 minutes (5 x 1000)
Day 2	20 minutes	25 minutes	30 minutes	20 minutes
Day 3 High-intensity runs	25 minutes (6 x 1000)	30 minutes (5 x 1200)	35 minutes (4 x 1600)	20 minutes (Easy)
Day 4	40 minutes	45 minutes	50 minutes	Race

for a 10- to 26.2-mile (marathon) run (16.1 to 42.3 km)—will now increase the number of days of training and the total time and mileage. The overall program can be based upon time or a combination of time and mileage, with more than one workout per day.

A time-and-mileage program might look like this:

Sunday. Long, easy run of 15 miles (24 km) or 1½ hours on a relatively flat terrain.

Monday. *Morning*: Easy 40 minute run. *Evening*: Brisk 45-minute run, followed by 8 to 10 strides on grass. Stretch and cool down. Do abdominal exercises.

Tuesday. *Evening*: Medium to hard 1-hour run on fairly hilly terrain. Start easy, finishing with a long, hard, sustained pace. Be sure to cool down.

Wednesday. *Morning*: Easy run of 3 to 5 miles (5 to 8 km). *Evening*: 40-minute run, according to the way you feel.

Thursday. *Morning*: 40-minute run. *Evening*: Fartlek workout over hills, changing the pace often; 1 hour total time.

Friday. *Evening*: Brisk 45-minute run.

Saturday. Try to find a race over 3 miles (4.8 km). Set a predetermined goal. Experiment with pace. *Afternoon*: Easy run of 4 to 5 miles (6.5 to 8 km).

This sample workout is equal to about 70 miles (113 km) a week, adequate even for a marathon of less than 3 hours.

In a time-based program, each week has one long run, a day of rest, and the other five days done at a comfortable pace. For the 14 weeks leading up to a long run or marathon, you should alternate the length of the long run to allow you to increase your mileage slowly and give you time to recover during the following week. The typical training program is illustrated in table 17-4.

You are now ready for a marathon during the next week. You should make sure to run easily during the first 3 days of the week and possibly take 2 days off before the race or, instead, run very easily. Some extra carbohydrates in your diet before a race of this length would also be beneficial. Using time as the basis for your program will allow you to individualize your training and respond to the way your body feels. If you feel good, cover more miles. If you need more time to recuperate, run fewer total miles. Get to know your fatigue symptoms because continual overstress will result in a reverse training effect. Table 17-5 provides an approximate race pace projection guide for different race distances if one were to maintain the same race pace throughout the entire race.

Beneficial Stretches and Resistance Training

There are a number of good stretches and some basic resistance training exercises that can easily be added to your program. These exercises can help you develop a little additional flexibility and strength to aid you in this new endeavor. It is a good idea to do your stretching after you have warmed your muscles up and after your cool-down. Each stretch should be held for 10 to 30 seconds and repeated a second time. Hold the stretch to the point where you can feel the stretch, but not to the point of pain. Try to stretch the larger muscles first and then move to the smaller muscle groups. It is a good idea to stretch every day. Here are some stretches that should help with your running program:

1. Lower back
2. Upper back
3. Groin
4. Hamstring
5. Hurdlers
6. Quads
7. Lower leg
8. Calf
9. Shoulders
10. Triceps
11. Ankle
12. Neck

Your resistance exercises should be done after your workout is completed. Some of these exercises require only the use

Table 17-4. ADVANCED TRAINING PROGRAM: TIME-BASED

	Time		
Week number	Days 1 to 5	Day 6	Day 7
1	25–35 minutes	60 minutes	Rest
2	25–35 minutes	90 minutes	Rest
3	25–35 minutes	60 minutes	Rest
4	25–35 minutes	110 minutes	Rest
5	25–35 minutes	60 minutes	Rest
6	25–35 minutes	130 minutes	Rest
7	25–35 minutes	60 minutes	Rest
8	25–35 minutes	150 minutes	Rest
9	25–35 minutes	60 minutes	Rest
10	25–35 minutes	170 minutes	Rest
11	25–35 minutes	60 minutes	Rest
12	25–35 minutes	180 minutes	Rest
13	25–35 minutes	60 minutes	Rest
14	25–35 minutes	75 minutes	Rest

Table 17-5. RACE PACE PROJECTIONS

Min/mile	5,000 m	10,000 m	Half marathon	Marathon
6:00	18:36	37:12	1:18:36	2:37:12
6:30	20:09	40:18	1:25:09	2:50:18
7:00	21:42	43:24	1:31:42	3:03:24
7:30	23:15	46:30	1:38:15	3:16:30
8:00	24:48	49:36	1:44:48	3:29:36
8:30	26:21	52:42	1:51:21	3:42:42
9:00	27:54	55:48	1:57:54	3:55:48
9:30	29:27	58:54	2:04:27	4:08:54
10:00	31:00	1:02:00	2:11:00	4:22:00
10:30	32:33	1:05:06	2:17:33	4:35:06
11:00	34:06	1:08:12	2:24:06	4:48:12
11:30	35:39	1:11:18	2:30:39	5:01:18
12:00	37:12	1:14:24	2:37:12	5:14:24

of one's own body, or some homemade implements. You don't have to purchase any expensive equipment to get some results. These resistance exercises will add a little strength without muscle bulk. If you need some weights, you can fill plastic milk containers with water or sand. Start with a small amount and gradually add more as your strength increases. Strive to do one to two sets of 10 to 15 repetitions of each exercise unless otherwise advised. These exercises are generally done only 2 to 3 times per week, with a day of rest between each workout. Try these out.

1. Sit-ups: Work up to 35. These can be done every day or every other day.
2. Push-ups: Work up to 25. These can be done every day or every other day.
3. Lunges: Forward. Step forward and extend so that your front knee is at a 90-degree angle. Don't extend so far forward that your knee extends beyond 90 degrees.
4. Lunges: Backward. Step backward and extend so that your front knee is at a 90-degree angle. Don't extend so far backward that your knee extends beyond 90 degrees.
5. Squats: Do not go beyond a 90-degree bend in your knees.
6. Overhead presses.
7. Upright rows.
8. Arm curls.
9. Tricep extensions with bike tube or towel.
10. Leg curls with bike tube.
11. Leg extensions with bike tube.

Types of Training Systems

Long, slow distance (LSD). In this method of training a runner concentrates on running longer and farther, with little attention to speed. At least 95 percent of the time you should be able to converse and feel comfortable while on a training run. Keep pulse rate and respiration well within your limits. Do all things in moderation.

Fartlek. *Fartlek* is a Swedish word meaning "speed play." The basic principle is to change the pace endlessly by charging hills, stretching out going downhill, accelerating to a sprint, striding, jogging, and walking. Try to let changes in pace occur naturally, such as when forced to stop at an intersection or pausing to admire the mountain scenery. Do it off the track on uneven and changing terrain. Fartlek is not a long, easy distance run in the country with a 50-yard burst thrown in every mile!

Interval training. This method of training has five basic components: (1) distance of each fast run, (2) interval or recovery between the fast runs, (3) number of repetitions to be run, (4) duration of each run, and (5) activity done between each run (walking, jogging, or complete rest). When trying to build endurance, run longer training runs with shorter rest periods or jog for recovery. To sharpen and become faster, run as fast as or faster than race pace, with almost complete rest for recovery. Interval training can bring quick results, but unless it is used in conjunction with a good endurance base, the results can be quickly wiped out by illness or injury. Intervals should not be added to your program until after you have put in at least 6 to 8 weeks of training.

Hard-easy-hard. This is more a philosophy toward running and training. The body must be given the opportunity to recuperate after being placed under stress. There should be days when the activity is varied or when little or no training is done. Supplemental activities such as swimming, cycling, or weight training may be incorporated.

Hill running. Most runners believe that hills should be an integral part of the training routine. Hill work is actually speed work in disguise, in that the heart rate is elevated and resistance work is done. Few runners enjoy hills, and many fear them when they are part of a race. However, by placing them on your training schedule you may gain not only strength but confidence. Hill running does require that you adjust your normal stride length. During uphill running, you want to shorten your stride and lean forward slightly. During downhill running you need to lengthen your stride and run "tall." Because of the force producing braking action of the striking leg, pain in the lower back, hip, or knee can result from downhill running. Downhill running should be done like sprinting or fast striding. Keep yourself balanced with the hips into the running action. Do not "sit." Land on the ball of the foot. Keep the arms in rhythm.

SAFETY MEASURES AND CONSIDERATIONS

There are a number of different factors to be aware of when participating in any type of exercise program. First you must know how to recognize and prepare for different environmental factors during exercise. You need to recognize the potential dangers of both heat and cold. The cold can usually be dealt with by wearing several layers of clothing to wick the water away from the body's surface and protect you from the wind. Heat is not always as easy to deal with because of the relative humidity. You must be prepared to take in fluids (generally water) at the rate of 150 to 250 ml every 15 minutes during high temperatures and high humidity. This will help reduce the possibility of dehydration during the workout. You should consider drinking another 500 ml of fluids for every pound lost during a run. Older adults and children need to be especially concerned with fluid replacement because they are less tolerant of the heat. By the time you become thirsty, the body has already lost about 1 percent of its weight. In addition to drinking fluids, you should wear light-colored clothing when exercising in the heat because dark-colored clothing retains more heat and increases the heat load on the body.

Other safety precautions to keep in mind include:

1. Always run facing traffic if you are running alongside a road, and wear some type of reflective apparel.
2. Always carry some form of identification in case an accident happens.
3. Never run alone at night or in areas that are not well lighted. Change your running routes and times; do not become too predictable.
4. Be aware of your general environment and other individuals around you. Listening to music while you run may be a great motivator, but music that is so loud that you can't hear what is going on around you can be dangerous.
5. Watch for animals, especially dogs. It is usually best to slow down and keep any dog in sight. If necessary, let a dog know that you want no part of it by yelling "No!" or "Get Back!" If that fails, you may have to use some type of weapon (stick, stone, or spray).
6. Be considerate of others: Move out of the inside lanes of a track so that faster runners will not run you over; move to the side of a sidewalk when other runners are approaching from the opposite direction; and let others in front of you know beforehand that you are going to pass them from behind.
7. Stay away from secluded areas and try to find a training partner. This will be good motivation for both of you.

INJURIES

Most running experts suggest that a stretching routine before and, perhaps more importantly, after jogging can reduce injuries. If you start your jog easily, the initial stretching may not be as important, but a warm-down routine is important. This is true not only for limbering up but also to keep muscles constricting and pumping blood back to the heart. Even with adequate stretching, warming up, and cooling down, injuries will occur to most runners. Most runners try to ease through their injuries by taking time off or running easier for a while.

Minor irritations are a way of life for most runners. As one disappears, another arises; but they are usually not serious enough to make the runner give up the sport.

There are those who, through their own ignorance, are unwilling to heed the signs of trouble indicated by those minor irritations. Their excuse for avoiding medical attention is that the physician usually tells them to stop running for a while. However, the number of injuries to the lower limbs is on the rise and cannot be dismissed. Injuries present real problems, and the runner should seek a sensible solution based on fact rather than on hit-or-miss guesswork.

Problems with muscles or tendons are usually associated with fatigue or an aching pain. Burning or shooting pain may indicate nerve irritation. A consistent burning pain is probably caused by inflammation. Other injuries include blisters, bone spurs, Morton's toe, muscle strain and tears, plantar fascia inflammation, and sciatic nerve problems.

It is necessary to isolate the location of an injury and determine the type of pain and its depth and point of maximum tenderness. Also important to note are: How did the pain start? Was it from new shoes or running a long way on roads or sharp downhills? Did you have a proper warm-up? Did you make unusual demands on your body?

Most injuries can be attributed to simple overuse or overstress. During training, the foot can strike the ground 5,000 times in 1 hour—a tremendous amount of stress for the leg to sustain. This stress is magnified by the fact that each step is responsible for generating about three to four times your body weight with each step. Unless you take a sensible approach to training, your legs will be unable to withstand this stress.

Biomechanical deformities, structural susceptibilities, and postural malformations that may not be evident in everyday walking can show themselves as injury when the runner has been overstressed. Add to this, poor running shoes, improper training methods, and poor running surfaces, and the runner is a risk for injuries.

The overuse syndrome usually is evidenced by shin splints. Achilles tendinitis, chondromalacia of the knee, stress fractures, or bursitis. This syndrome can be treated by proper training, which includes a well-organized stretching program with a hard-easy approach to training. A well-planned conditioning period, proper shoes, and varied running surfaces all contribute to lessening the problems of overuse.

The knee is a common area of injury because it is a vulnerable hinge joint that takes most of the punishment inflicted by hard surfaces. The bottom edge of the kneecap is often irritated, a condition medically termed *chondromalacia.* This condition indicates joint instability and usually affects the hyaline cartilage on the joint side of the kneecap. It can be a result of excessive rotation of the knee at foot strike. The best way to prevent this injury is by stabilizing the foot with heel or arch supports and by strengthening the quadriceps, or thigh muscles, through weight training.

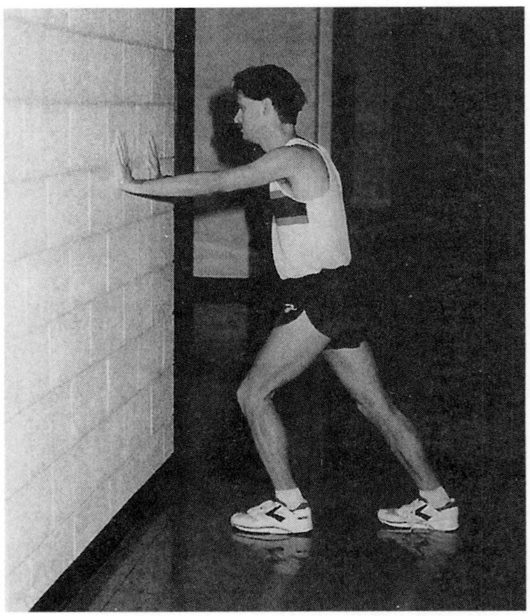

Figure 17-6. Inclined wall push-up (Achilles tendon stretch).

The Achilles tendon connects the heel bone and the calf muscles. It is synonymous with vulnerability. Running tends to shorten this tendon and cause inflexibility and tightness. The best way known to prevent this is to stretch before and after a run. The inclined wall push-up is a good exercise to specifically work on the Achilles tendon (figure 17-6). One method of reducing the stress placed on the affected tendon is to place a ¼-inch lift in the running shoes.

The term *shinsplints* is a catchall for lower-leg problems. Shinsplints is a symptom, not a condition. It is primarily a swelling along the lower front of the legs and is usually a muscular problem. It results from (1) improper shoes, (2) insufficient shock absorption, (3) excessive training on hard surfaces, concrete, or all-weather tracks, (4) lack of flexibility, or (5) poor running form. Runners who suffer the least from shinsplints are those who keep their feet and knees in line with their hips. Other potential causes include an imbalance between an overly strong calf muscle and weak anterior, or front, muscles. Soreness in the shins can be a common complaint of the beginning runner. The legs are not used to this type of muscular activity and should be given time to adjust.

Cryotherapy, or ice treatment, has been used for all of these problems with excellent results for many years. The primary effect of cold—vasoconstriction (decrease in size of blood vessels)—takes place in the first few minutes of application. This is strictly a reflex action, with an accompanying decrease in the capillary blood pressure and an increase in the arterial blood pressure. Ice is used for the first 24 to 48 hours in acute muscular-skeletal injuries. The secondary effect is vasodilation, an increase in the rate of blood flow to the injured area. Massive hyperemia (blood congestion) is produced because of the increase in blood flow, with the peripheral blood vessels being constricted and the deeper blood vessels being dilated. (In contrast, with heat application there is dilation, with stagnation of blood in the area.) Cold also produces an anesthetic effect: a decrease in the spasticity of the muscles and an increase in the blood flow rate, rather than a gross increase in the circulation.

There are several methods of cold application. Crushed or shaved ice works best and produces a colder solution. A slush solution with a cold towel also works well. A massage with a frozen cup of ice is best for the knee and similar joint areas. The surface temperature when using ice treatments should be no higher than 55° F (31° C).

Remember: When ice therapy is first induced, the shock of the cold will cause an aching sensation. The skin will become numb in about 3 minutes and then redden. Therapy should be terminated at this point and repeated later.

One other method that can be used to either prevent or rehabilitate injuries is *cross-training:* use of multifaceted modes of training, either as an addition to or a temporary replacement for the activity. For the jogger there are many modes of training that can be added to a program to add variety and to offset some of the stress of jogging. Cycling, swimming, cross-country skiing, roller-blading, stepping machines, and pool running all offer a change of pace for the jogger. Some will find that the use of these non-weight-bearing activities allows them the opportunity to maintain their aerobic activities during times of recovery from overuse or injury.

These are some of the most common types of injuries, preventive measures, and simple methods of treatment. If a problem persists, seek advice of a qualified podiatrist or orthopedic surgeon.

GENERAL SUGGESTIONS

1. Do everything in moderation.
2. Start out by improving your cardiovascular efficiency. Work up gradually to at least a 30-minute jog three times per week.
3. Use the hard-easy-hard approach, allowing your body time to recuperate. Understrain rather than overstrain.
4. Learn to calculate and measure your target heart rate (THR) and train at a pace to elicit this heart rate. THR is really a range, and the object is to keep your heart rate in this range while jogging. THR can be calculated by subtracting your age from the value of 220. The resulting value is an estimate of your maximum heart rate. Multiply this value by 0.70 and by 0.85 to obtain the two end points of the THR range, which is appropriate for young adults in good health. These percentages would be lower for older adults. For example, the estimated maximum heart rate for a 20-year-old is 200 (220 − 20). Multiplying this value by 0.70 and 0.85 results in a THR range of 140 to 170 beats per minute. Jogging at a pace to elicit a heart rate between these two values will produce a training effect over time. The use of a heart rate monitor makes it easy to keep your intensity level within your desired target range. Most of these monitors will make a sound when your heart rate exceeds or falls below the training limits that you set.
5. Keep an accurate record of your mileage or time. Find out how much stress your body can handle comfortably. Take your pulse before getting out of bed and about 1 or 2 hours after your evening workout. Place the numbers on a graph. This will allow you to see the progress being made toward cardiovascular efficiency.
6. The recovery phase is also important to the jogger. It will take between 3 and 5 hours for the heart rate to return to its preexercise level. By taking your pulse 1 to 2 hours after evening workouts, you will begin to see what type of adaptation your body is making to running stress.
7. Eat sensibly. With an increase in calorie expenditure, expect an increase in appetite. Eat a well-balanced diet. Be wary of fad diets.
8. Take fluids early if you are planning to run more than 1 hour, especially in warm weather. Water seems to work best for everyone. Be prepared and do not overextend yourself—whatever your goal!
9. Vary the training program.
10. Run with someone. Making your jogging sessions enjoyable through social interaction will help ensure that you stick with them.

TEACHING CONSIDERATIONS

1. Instructional programs for groups must deal with two major factors:
   a. For clear training effects to be achieved, students must exercise at least 3 days a week, a minimum of 30 minutes, for at least 5 to 6 weeks.
   b. Individuals will start at different levels of ability and will have different target goals.
2. If programs do not meet for the length of time required, additional work outside of the instructional period should be included.
3. Some type of preassessment should be used to determine beginning levels of students. Several tests using time (a 12-minute run-walk) or heart rate for a given work load are available. Programs should then be designed on this basis.

4. Heart rate is the best simple indictor of workload. Teach students how to calculate their target heart rates. Before set training programs are established, teach pacing for this rate. Begin increasing students' distance according to heart rate on a weekly basis. Have them keep records of progress. Give each student a target distance and time for the end of the program if possible.
5. Use the jogging experience to teach about the effects of exercise on the body and lifestyle of the student. Students are interested in this information. Jogging units can be combined with physical fitness experiences.
6. Provide a lot of encouragement, slow down overeager beginners, and be alert to adverse physical reactions. Become part of the class if possible.
7. Encourage students to be sensitive to their body to determine limits.
8. Begin your class instruction in an area that is easy to monitor—such as on a running track or large grassy field. When selecting this area, consider the potential problems and safety concerns that might arise. Do not select areas where students must cross roadways or encounter automobile traffic. You might want to consider a short loop for the beginners and a longer loop for the more advanced students, but keep in mind that you want to be able to visually monitor the whole class. Stay away from areas where your students must run along bushes or behind buildings.

GLOSSARY

aerobic Running that allows a near-normal breathing pattern; literally, "with oxygen."
anaerobic Running involving labored breathing; literally, "without oxygen."
endurance Ability to run for a long time; created by long, slow, easy running.
fartlek A style of training employing frequent changes of pace; from the Swedish word meaning "speed play."
fast distance Steady training running at slightly less than maximum speed.
interval training A formalized training program alternating fast running with rest periods.
lactic acid Chemical by-product of anaerobic, or oxygen-debt, running that produces fatigue.
long distance More than 6 miles (10 km).
marathon 26 miles, 385 yards (42.25 km); Olympic distance.
middle distance 880 yards to 6 miles (800 to 10,000 m).
overdistance Longer than one's racing distance.
oxygen debt Running faster than one's normal breathing pattern can sustain body needs; shortness of breath.
pace Average rate at which a distance is run.
recovery Rebuilding energy after a hard effort.
repetitions Series of runs with recovery breaks between, as in interval training.
resistance Body's ability to withstand stress.
specificity The principle that physiologic preparation for an activity must include training very similar to that activity.
steady state Maximum rate at which the body can operate aerobically.
training Running program designed to increase the level of fitness and improve a runner's performance in racing.

SUGGESTED READINGS

Anderson-Jordan, T. 1983. *Distance running*. Ames, Iowa: Championship Books.
Bompa, T. O. 1990. *Theory and methodology of training: The key to athletic performance*. Dubuque, Iowa: Kendall/Hunt.
Bowerman, W. J., and Freeman, W. H., 1991. *High-performance training for track and field.* Champaign, Ill: Human Kinetics.
Brown, R. L., and Henderson, J. 1994. *Fitness running*. Champaign, Ill.: Human Kinetics.
Campbell, D. 1994. *Jogging*. 2d ed. Boston: American Press.
Cavanagh, P. 1990. *Biomechanics of distance running*. Champaign, Ill.: Human Kinetics.
Cooper, K. H. 1970. *The new aerobics*. New York: M. Evans.
Cooper, K. H. 1982. *The aerobics program for total health and well-being.* New York: M. Evans.
Costill, D. L. 1978. *A scientific approach to distance running*. Los Altos, Calif.: Tafnews Press.
Daniels, J., Fitts, R., and Sheehan, G. 1978. *Conditioning for distance runners.* New York: Wiley.
Derderian, T. 1996. *Boston marathon*. Champaign, Ill.: Human Kinetics.
Drinkwater, B. 1986. *Female endurance athletes*. Champaign, Ill.: Human Kinetics.
Evans, M. 1997. *The endurance athlete's edge*. Champaign, Ill.: Human Kinetics.
Galloway, J. 1983. *Jeff Galloway's book of running*. Atlanta: Phidippides.
Greene, L., and Pate, R. 1997. *Training for young distance runners*. Champaign, Ill.: Human Kinetics.
Hawkins, J., and Hawkins, S. 1996. *Walking for fun and fitness*, 2d ed. Englewood, CO: Morton Publishing.
Henderson, J. 1996. *Better runs: 25 years' worth of lessons for running faster and farther.* Champaign, Ill.: Human Kinetics.
Henderson, J. 1997. *Marathon training*. Champaign, Ill.: Human Kinetics.
Higdon, H. 1979. *On the run from dogs and people*. Chicago: Chicago Review Press.
Lynch, J. 1987. *The total runner: A complete mind-body guide to optimal performance*. Englewood Cliffs, N.J.: Prentice Hall.
Lydiard, A. 1978. *Running the Lydiard way*. Mountain View, Calif.: Anderson/World.
Martin, D. E., and Coe, P. 1997. *Better training for distance runners*. Champaign, Ill.: Human Kinetics.
Micheli, L. J. 1996. *Healthy runner's handbook*. Champaign, Ill.: Human Kinetics.
Moran, G. T., and McGlynn, G. H. 1997. *Cross-training for sports*. Champaign, Ill.: Human Kinetics.
Newsholme, E. A., Leech, T., and Duester, G. 1994. *Keep on running: The science of training and performance*. New York: Wiley.
Niles, R. 1997. *Time-saving training for multisport athletes*. Champaign, Ill.: Human Kinetics.

Noakes, T. D. 1991. *Lore of running*. Champaign, Ill.: Human Kinetics.

Pollock, M. L., Wilmore, J. H., and Fox, S. M., III. 1978. *Health and fitness through physical activity*. New York: Wiley.

Rosato, F. 1995. *Jogging and walking for health and fitness*, 3rd ed. Englewood, CO: Morton Publishing.

Rudner, R. 1995. *Walking*. Champaign, IL: Human Kinetics.

Samuelson, J. B. 1995. *Joan Samuelson's running for women*. Emmaus, Pa.: Rodale Press.

Sandrock, M. 1996. *Running with the legends*. Champaign, Ill.: Human Kinetics.

Scaff, J., and Gordon, J. 1979. *Your first marathon*. Lafayette, Calif.: Running Wild.

Seiger, L., and Hesson, J. 1998. *Walking for Fitness*, 3rd ed. Dubuque, IA: WCB/McGraw-Hill.

Sheehan, G. A. 1978. *Medical advice for runners*. Mountain View, Calif.: Anderson/World.

Sleamaker, R., and Browning, R. 1996. *Serious training for endurance athletes*. Champaign, Ill.: Human Kinetics.

Sparks, K., and Kuehls, D. 1996. *The runners book of training secrets*. Emmaus, Pa.: Rodale Press.

Subotnick, S. I. 1977. *The running foot doctor*. Mountain View, Calif.: Anderson/World.

Subotnick, S. I. 1979. *Cures for common running injuries*. Mountain View, Calif.: Anderson/World.

Tanser, T. 1997. *Train hard, win easy: The Kenyan way*. Mountain View, Calif.: Track & Field News.

Ungerleider, S. 1996. *Mental training for peak performance*. Emmaus, Pa.: Rodale Press.

RESOURCES

Videotapes

Coaching by the experts: Track and field running events. Champaign, Ill.: Human Kinetics, 1990. 48-minute videotape.

Organizations and Newsletters

American Running and Fitness Association, 1150 S. Washington St. #250, Alexandria, VA 22314. (1-800-776-2732) Web: http://www.rrca.org

Peak Running Performance, P.O. Box 3000, Dept. PRP, Denville, NJ 07834 (new subscriptions) or 1-800-551-5558 or Peak Running Performance web site: http://www.peakrun.com

Running Research News, P.O. Box 27041, Lansing, MI 48909. (517-393-3150).

Runner's World Online: http://www.runnersworld.com

Team Oregon: Links to online publications: http://www.teamoregon.com/~teamore/publications/mags html#Research Pubs.

Training distance runners—A primer, by Jack Daniels. Gatorade Sports Science Institute, Chicago, IL, 1989.

USA Track & Field, 1 RCA Dome, Suite 140, Indianapolis, IN 46225: http://www.usaldr.org

Web Sites

The World Wide Web provides a new area where information can easily be attained, but some web sites do change their addresses (URL) or completely disappear. Hopefully most of the sites listed below will still be around, but if not use your search engine to find a new site.

1. http://www.usatf.org/. This is the site of USA Track and Field, the national governing body for track and field, long-distance running, and race walking in the United States.
2. http://www.runnersworld.com/calendar/marca197.html Extensive list of marathons, including dates and contact names and addresses, maintained by *Runner's World* magazine.
3. http://sunsite.unc.edu/drears/running/running.html The Running Page has links to many running resources.
4. http://fox.nstn.ca/~dblaikie/index.html Ultramarathon World is a site for really long distance runners maintained by David Blaikie.
5. http://www.research.digital.com/CRL/personal/tuttle/gbtc/home.html Greater Boston Track Club</A>. Homepage of prominent Boston track club, which has boasted such members as Bill Rodgers, Greg Meyer, Alberto Salazar, and Pete Pfitzinger.
6. http://www.catalog.com/webrun/running/running.html WebRunner is a site devoted to running in the southeast United States.
7. http://www.ontherun.com On the Run is a running and racing news site from the northwest United States.
8. news:rec.running This is a usenet group for discussion of running.
9. http://www.medacess.com/fitness/onestep.htm An Introduction to Running: One Step At A Time provides general guide on how to get started.
10. http://s2.com/html/etj/etj.html Endurance Training Journal
11. http://www.lava.net/~marathon/TRL.html The Running Life is an electronic magazine.
12. http://home.netone.com/~woodyg3/runiche.html Runner's Niche is an electronic magazine.
13. http://www.clark.net/pub/pribut/spsport.html This site is about running injuries; by Stephen M. Pribut, D.P.M., F.A.A.P.S.M.
14. http://www.med.und.nodak.edu/depts/sportmed/dsmhome1.htm From the Division of Sports Medicine at the University of North Dakota.
15. http://www.halhigdon.com The site for Hal Higdon, a collection of columns by a senior writer for Runner's World Magazine.
16. http://www.runningnetwork.com The Running Network is a site that features various regional publications across the United States.
17. http://www-rohan.sdsu.edu/dept/coachsci/intro.html This site contains "Coaching Science Abstracts" of current research articles.

Karate

After completing this chapter, the reader should be able to:

- Appreciate the rich tradition behind this martial art
- Be familiar with the types of karate training
- Understand the ranking system used in karate
- Practice the etiquette and safety precautions of karate
- Explain the physical and psychological principles of karate

HISTORY

The martial art of karate as it is known today began in the late nineteenth and early twentieth centuries in Okinawa and Japan. Its origin as a system of self-defense, however, dates back many centuries. Legend relates how a Buddhist priest named Bodhidharma (Daruma) traveled overland from India to China around A.D. 525 to instruct monks of the Liang dynasty at the Shaolin Temple regarding the tenets of Buddhism. There he taught the monks a combination of Indian fistfighting and yoga that eventually became known as the kung-fu system of Shaolin-tsu (Shaolin "fist-way"). As the art spread throughout China, many styles and systems appeared.

As cultural trade increased, the fighting techniques of China were carried to other Asian countries, the most significant of which was Okinawa. It was here that the empty-handed fighting systems of China were combined with the empty-handed fighting systems of Okinawa (known as *te*) and a rough form of karate was developed.

It was not until the twentieth century, when Gichin Funakoshi (an Okinawan karate instructor and school teacher) introduced Okinawa-te to Japan, that it acquired the name *karate*. It is important to note that the original Chinese characters that made up the name *karate* translated as "Chinese hands." Mr. Funakoshi is credited with substituting for the first character, *kara* (meaning "Chinese"), that of *kara* (meaning "empty"). The latter means not only empty-handed or weaponless fighting but also keeping one's spirit of inner self hollow (meaning both selflessness and unselfishness).

Karate was introduced into the Okinawan middle-school system in 1905, where it became a required part of the physical education curriculum. It was not until the years between 1917 (in Kyoto at the Butokuden-Hall of Martial Virtues) and 1923 (at the national Athletic Exhibition in Tokyo) that karate began to spread into the universities in Japan, where the art received its greatest impetus. Following World War II, from 1945 to 1965, many U.S. servicemen studied karate, judo, and other martial arts in Japan. On their return to the United States a number of these servicemen opened martial arts schools. Here, too, the martial arts spread rapidly, and today they are practiced by thousands of students.

Today there are more than a hundred styles of karate. The word *style* here refers to a specific system or tradition in the way that karate and other forms of empty-handed combat are taught. Generally, styles of karate and other forms of empty-handed combat can be classified according to national systems, such as Japanese, Korean, Chinese, and Okinawan. Under each of these national systems there are many different styles today. Table 18-1 provides an overview of some of the major styles of empty-handed combat taught throughout the world today.

PRONUNCIATION OF JAPANESE

To better understand the terms used in this chapter, it is necessary to provide a short explanation of some of the relevant Japanese terms.

In the Japanese language, each syllable consists of a vowel or of a vowel and a consonant, except for the syllabic *n* and the letters *k*, *p*, *t*, and *s* when they occur as the first

Table 18-1. MAJOR STYLES OF EMPTY-HANDED COMBAT

Japanese	Okinawan	Korean	Chinese
Shotokan	Goju-ryu	Tae Kwon Do	T'ai Chi Ch'uan
Wado-ryu	Isshin-ryu		Siu-Lum
Shito-ryu	Shorei-ryu	Hapkido	Hsing-I
Goju-ryu	Shorin-ryu	Tang Soo Do	Wing Chun
Kyokushinkai	Uechi-ryu	Taekyon	Hop Gar

letter of a double consonant. In pronouncing Japanese, each syllable receives approximately equal stress and time.

Vowels

There are only five vowel sounds in Japanese:

- *a* sounds like "ah" as in f**a**ther (not the *a* in back or gate)
- *i* sounds like "ee" as in mach**i**ne (not the *i* in hit or flight)
- *u* sounds like "oo" as in gl**ue** (not the *u* in cut)
- *e* sounds like "eh" as in m**e**t (not the *e* in free)
- *o* sounds like "oh" as in r**o**pe (not the *o* in pot)

Long vowels

Long vowel sounds are important in the pronunciation of Japanese because the meaning of some words will change according to the length of the vowel. For example, *o-ba-san* (aunt) and *o-ba-a-san* (grandmother) are distinguished by the length of the vowel *a*.

Short vowels

The vowels *u* and *i* are sometimes short—that is, they are not voiced (not pronounced) at all when they appear between unvoiced consonants (*f, h, k, p, s, ch, sh*) or when *u* appears at the end of a sentence after an unvoiced consonant. Examples:

u between two voiced consonants:

su:

desu ka?	(is it?)	sounds like deska
sukoshi	(a little)	sounds like skoshi
suki	(like)	sounds like ski

ku:

kushami (sneeze) sounds like kshami

tsu:

tsukue (desk) sounds like tsuke

fu:

futatsu (two) sounds like ftatsu

i between two unvoiced consonants:

shi:

shite (doing) sounds like shte

chi:

chikai (near) sounds like chkai

ki:

kitte	(stamp)	sounds like ktte
Kippu	(ticket)	sounds like kppu

hi:

hitori (one person) sounds like htori

u at the end of a sentence:

Hon desu. (It is a book.) sounds like Hon des

Consonants

Most Japanese consonants are pronounced almost the same as English consonants, except for the following:

- *f* is made by blowing air between the lip, without letting the lower lip touch the teeth. The sound produced is approximately halfway between the *h* sound and the *f* sound of English.
- *g* is hard, like the g in *go* or *get* (not the g in generation or judgment).
- *n* is sometimes considered to be a full syllable itself (without any vowel). It sounds something like the *ng* in *singer* or *ping-pong*, but without the slightest hint of a g sound.
- *r* is pronounced between the *l* and *d* sounds of English. It is a flap-*r*, in which the tip of the tongue briefly touches the roof of the mouth just behind the teeth.
- *ch* is pronounced like the *ch* in church.
- *ts* is pronounced like the final *ts* in *cuts*.

Double Consonants

- *kk* is pronounced like the *kk* in *bookkeeper*. The first *k* (*p, t, tch,* or *s*) is a momentary pause (silence) equivalent in time to the pronunciation of one syllable of Japanese; the second *k* (*p, t, tch,* or *s*) is pronounced as usual.
- *pp* is pronounced like the *p* sounds connecting two words in English such as "flip past" (not like the *pp* in a single word such as *supper*).
- *tt* is pronounced like the *t* sounds connecting two words in English such as "flight time" (not like the *tt* in a single word such as *butter*).
- *tch* is a variation of the *tt* sound, the pronunciation of *ch* in Japanese begins with the *t* sound.
- *ss* is pronounced like the *s* sounds connecting two words in English, such as "less shame" or "let's sing."

THE MEANING OF KARATE-DO

The modern Japanese martial arts of karate and judo are practiced the world over as forms of sport competition, self-defense, physical education, and aesthetics. However, their primary focus is to serve as systems of self-cultivation and to transmit the ideals, norms, and behaviors associated with the traditional cultural setting of the martial arts. These include loyalty, bravery, and the acceptance of physical and mental hardships through disciplined training. Of paramount importance is the development of a strong fighting spirit.

The martial arts are considered to be both physical and mental disciplines that focus on self-cultivation through a combative mode. The *do* suffix in the words *karate-do* and *judo* suggests that they are philosophical paths or ways to travel throughout one's life in the pursuit of self-perfection of character. Japanese culture is replete with such activities. Those more familiar to the Westerner include the tea ceremony (*chado*), calligraphy (*shodo*), and Zen meditation. The martial arts, however, serve as a unique system of *seishin*

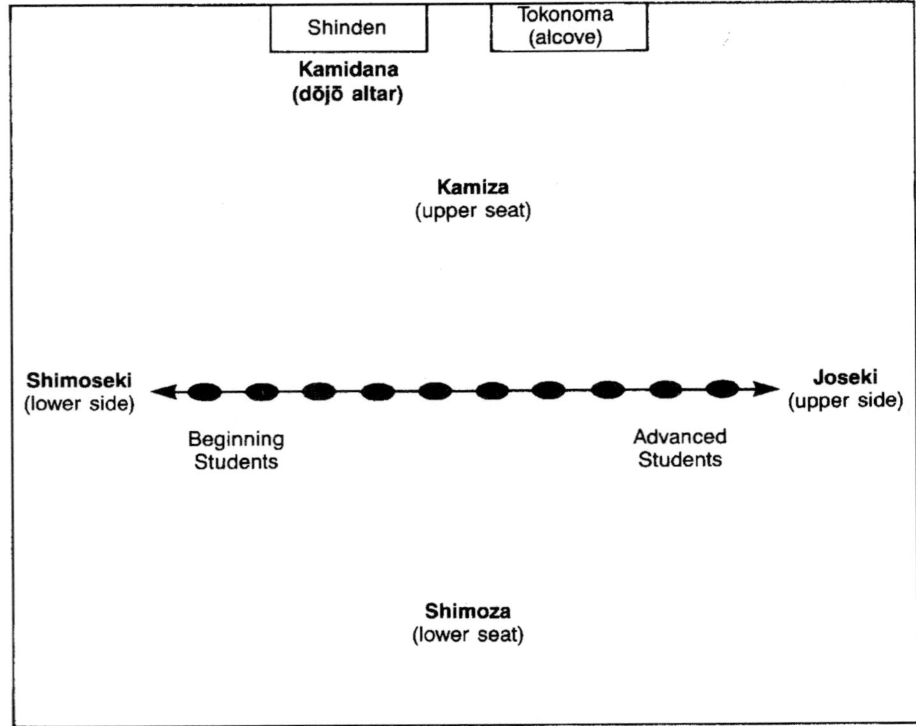

Figure 18-1. Dojo schematic.

kyoiku (spiritual education) through a combative mode. The highest aim of all of the martial arts such as karate-do, kendo, judo, kyudo, and aikido is to develop one's character through physical, mental, and moral education.

DOJO

Every *dojo* (martial arts training hall) is arranged so that there is a front and back wall and an upper and lower side (see figure 18-1). The point of reference for training activity and etiquette is the front wall (*shomen*). At the front wall in most traditional dojos, there is a Shinto or Buddhist diety shelf (*kamidana*). It is the kamidana specifically that serves as the focal point for all training activity and etiquette. In place of the kamidana, many dojos outside of Japan elect to place either a national flag or a picture of the founder of their particular karate style on the front wall. Some dojos also have a *tokonoma*, or a special place on the front wall in which may be placed a fine sword or a piece of calligraphy (*kakemono*) depicting a martial arts training concept.

The upper seat in the dojo is known as the *kamiza*, while the lower seat in the dojo is known as the *shimoza*. The kamiza is the approximate location that the teacher occupies at the beginning and end of class for formal salutation. The shimoza is the location where the students line up before and after class for the same purpose. Generally, the higher-ranking students line up toward the right, or *joseki*, side of the dojo, and the lower-ranking students line up toward the left, or the *shimoseki*, side.

Ideally, a dojo should be clean, simple, and without ostentatious display of trophies or other encumbrances. The floor should be of smooth wood and should be thoroughly cleaned by all students at the end of each training period.

UNIFORM

The uniform worn while training is called the *karate-gi*. It consists of a jacket, pants, and a belt that is about 8 feet long. Most traditional dojos require the karate-gi to be white, although there are exceptions. While the belt primarily serves to keep the jacket closed, its color also denotes level of expertise.

Karategi are manufactured in light-, medium-, and heavy-weight material and are available in a variety of costs and sizes. It is important that it fit somewhat loosely and not restrict movement while training. Table 18-2 illustrates the most common sizes available.

RANKING SYSTEM USED IN KARATE

Karate uses the *kyu-dan* system to rank its exponents in terms of proficiency, knowledge, and experience. The *kyu* ranks, also known as the *mudansha* (ungraded) ranks,

Table 18-2. KARATE UNIFORM SIZE CHART

Size	Measurements for children	Jacket length	Pants length	Belt length
0	under 4′9″ (1.45 m) <150 lbs	28″ (71 cm)	26.5″ (67 cm)	77″ (1.96 m)
1	4′10″–5′3″ (1.47–1.60 m) 106–120 lbs	30.5″ (77 cm)	29″ (74 cm)	79.5″ (2.02 m)
2	5′4″–5′6″ (1.63–1.68 m) 121–135 lbs	36″ (91 cm)	31.5 (80 cm)	88″ (2.24 m)
3	5′7″–5′9″ (1.70–1.75 m) 136–165 lbs	38″ (97 cm)	34″ (86 cm)	95.5″ (2.43 m)
4	5′10″–6′0″ (1.78–1.83 m) 166–200 lbs	39.5″ (100 cm)	37.5″ (95 cm)	102″ (2.59 m)
5	6′1″ (1.85 m) 200+ lbs	40″ (102 cm)	39″ (99 cm)	111″ (2.82 m)
6		50.5″ (128 cm)	41.5″ (105 cm)	120″ (3.05 m)

begin with either the tenth, ninth, or eighth kyu for beginners and proceed up to the first kyu (usually designated in most dojos by the brown belt. The *dan* ranks, also known as the "yudansha" (graded) ranks, begin with the first-degree black belt (*shodan*) and progress up to the tenth-degree black belt (*judan*). In most traditional dojos it takes four to five years to achieve the rank of first-degree black belt if a karateka trains three to five times per week with no breaks in training. Belt colors most often used in the mudansha class include white, orange, blue, purple, green, red, and brown. The black belt is used to denote those in the yudansha class. The Japan Karate Federation (JKF) uses the ranking system shown in table 18-3.

It is considered axiomatic in most karate circles that to progress from one martial arts rank to a higher one, the practioner must demonstrate significant improvement in both martial arts skill and technique as well as character. This necessitates that karateka pursue not only physical training, but academic training as well, if they are to acquire the requisite skill and knowledge required for their rank. In addition, examinees are tested on *kihon* (basics), *kata* (formal exercises), and *kumite* (sparring). More advanced karateka must demonstrate sufficient skill in *tameshiwari* (board breaking) and self-defense. Some schools require that advanced karateka demonstrate technical proficiency in the use of a traditional martial arts weapon. The highest yudansha levels require that the karateka produce a written thesis or completed research on some aspect of martial arts theory or practice.

In addition to the kyu and dan ranks given in karate, karateka may also be awared one of three honorary titles after reaching the rank of *yondan* (fourth-degree black belt). The three special titles are those of *renshi* (instructor), *kyoshi* (teacher), and *hanshi* (master). Refer to table 18-3 for the requirements for these titles.

A head instructor of a style of karate is usually referred to as *kancho* (literally, "building chief"). *Shihan* (master) is the term of address usually given to those of fifth-degree black belt or higher. *Sensei* (teacher) is the term of address given to those black belts who head an individual dojo or who have the primary responsibility of teaching within a dojo. *Sempai* (senior) is the term usually given to the more experienced and higher-ranking students within a group, while the term *kohai* (junior) is used to designate those karateka of lower rank and lesser experience. It is important to note that while the terms *Sensei*, *sempai*, and *shihan* are used as formal forms of address, *kohai* is never used in this manner.

KARATE TRAINING

Karate training is generally divided into three basic aspects: kihon, kata, and kumite. Kihon (basics) training consists of fundamental practice in the execution of blocks, punches, strikes, kicks, stances, stepping, and body-shifting techniques. Generally, these are performed by karateka (practitioners of karate) on an individual basis or during group practice. Kata training consists of learning and executing prearranged traditional routines of attack and defense against imaginary opponents. Most schools require karateka to learn two to three kata per rank for advancement purposes. Kumite training consists of learning and executing basic, intermediate, and advanced levels of fighting. Basic sparring, sometimes referred to as "one-attack fight," or *yakusokugeiko* ("promise" practice), consists of two opponents executing basic attack and defense techniques against prearranged targets.

Kihon (Fundamental Practice)

1. *Blocking techniques*: These are employed to defend vital areas of the body against punches, strikes, and kicks primarily by deflecting them from their intended target of attack. The more common techniques include the down block, the middle forearm chest block, the high block, and the knife-hand block (figure 18-2).

Table 18-3. KARATE RANKING SYSTEM*

Rank	Age	Title
Ju-Dan (10th) over 10 years after Ku-Dan	70 years or over	Hanski (master)† over 15 years after Kyoshi 55 years old or over
Ku-Dan (9th) 10 years after Hachi-Dan	60 years or over	
Hachi-Dan (8th) 8 years after Shichi-Dan	50 years or over	Kyoshi (teacher)† over 10 years after Renshi 40 years old or over
Shichi-Dan (7th) 7 years after Roku-Dan	42 years or over	
Roku-Dan (6th) over 5 years after Go-Dan	35 years or over	Renshi (instructor)† over 2 years after 5th Dan 35 years old or over
Go-Dan (5th) over 3 years after Yo-Dan	under 35 years	
Yo-Dan (4th) over 3 years after San-Dan	under 35 years	
San-Dan (3rd) over two years after Ni-Dan	under 35 years	No formal title
Ni-Dan (2nd) over 1 year after Sho-Dan	under 35 years	No formal title
Sho-Dan (1st) at least three years‡	under 35 years	No formal title
Ikkyu (1st Brown) Nikyu (2nd Brown) Sankyu (3rd Brown) Yonkyu (4th class) Gokyu (5th class) Rokkyu (6th class) Shichikyu (7th class) optional Hachikyu (8th class) optional	No age specified	Kyu (below brown identified by different colors) However, all kyus are considered white relative to the black belt

*Ranking system adopted by the Federation of All Japan Karate-Do Organizations (FAJKO) on March 27, 1971.
†Title may not be given irrespective of how high the rank; awarded for exceptional achievement and outstanding character.
‡Daily practice.

2. *Punching and striking techniques*: These are used to attack vital areas of the body. The two basic techniques are the lunge punch (or straight punch) and the reverse punch. Basic striking techniques include the ridge-hand strike, knife hand strike, and elbow strike (figure 18-3).
3. *Kicking techniques*: The front, round, side, and back kicks comprise the basic kicking techniques used in karate. Like the punching and striking techniques, these may be delivered to vital target areas in attack or counterattack modes (figure 18-4).
4. *Stances*: For the karateka, strong stances (tachikata) and combative postures (kamaekata) serve as the foundations from which to deliver strong offensive and defensive techniques. Some of the more common stances used in karate include the front stance, back stance, rooted stance, horse-riding stance, free-fighting stance, and cat-leg stance (figure 18-5).
5. *Stepping and body-shifting techniques*: Stepping techniques allow the karateka to move from one position to another for attack and defense purposes. During basic practice the front stance is used to execute many of the attacking techniques while the back stance and rooted stance are used to execute many defensive techniques.

Figure 18-2. Blocking techniques. **A,** route of downward block. **B,** Route of forearm block against body attack. **C,** Route of upper block against head attack.

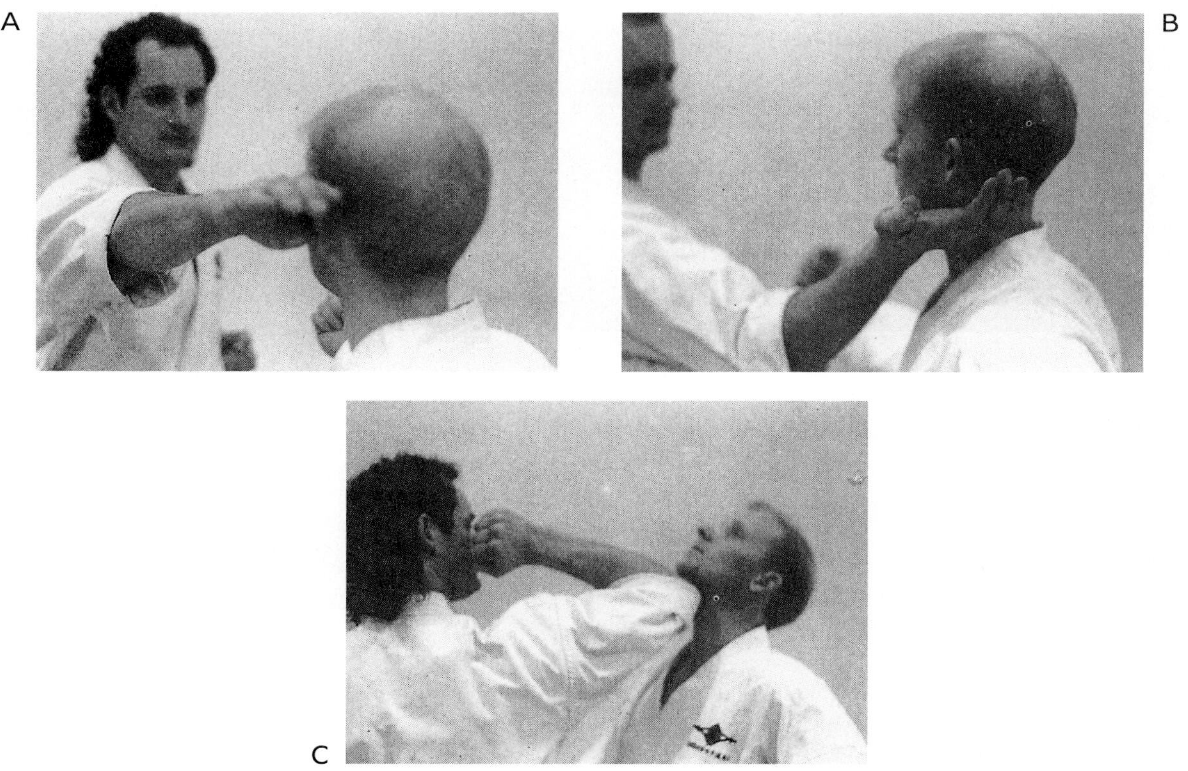

Figure 18-3. Punches and strikes. **A,** Ridge hand strike. **B,** Knife hand strike. **C,** Elbow strike.

Kata (Practice of Forms)

Kata are exercises of offensive and defensive techniques arranged in formal sequences and executed against imaginary opponents. They are loosely analogous to compulsory floor routines in gymnastics. Formulated and transmitted down through the ages by past true masters of the art of karate, they consist of a number of movements that must be performed in a strict sequence with correct power,

Figure 18-4. Kicking techniques. **A,** Route of side thrust kick. **B,** Route of side snap kick. **C,** Route of roundhouse kick.

A B C

D E F

Figure 18-5. Karate stances. **A,** Front stance. **B,** Back stance. **C,** Rooted stance. **D,** Horse-riding stance. **E,** Free-fighting stance. **F,** Cat-leg stance.

Table 18-4. NAMES OF KATA PRACTICED IN THE SHOTOKAN KARATE TRADITION

Name of Kata	Meaning of Kata	Outstanding feature(s)
Ten-no Kata	"Form of the universe"	Basic attack and defense techniques
Taikyoku	"Chaos" or "Void"	Fundamental stances, blocks, and punches
Heian	"Peaceful"	Comprehensive techniques that, when mastered, should be "comfortable" in most basic self-defense situations
Bassai Sho and Dai	"To penetrate a fortress"	Strong movements intended to change disadvantage into advantage by employing differing degrees of power and rapidly switching blocks
Kanku Sho and Dai	"To view the sky"	Variation of fast and slow technique, jumping
Jion	name of originator	Turning, shifting, various stepping patterns
Jutte (sometimes "Jitte")	"Ten hands"	Fast and slow movements, high and low body positions, reversal of body positions
Empi	"Flying swallow"	Fast and slow movements, high and low reversal of body positions
Hangetsu	"Cresent" or "Half moon"	Coordinating stepping and breathing with circular arm and leg movements
Gankaku	"Crane on a rock"	Balancing on one leg, side kick and back fist
Chinte	"Small hands"	Small, but powerful, hand blocks and strikes
Unsu	"Cloud hand"	Strong forceful arm and hand blocks with stances and high-level ridge-hand strikes
Sochin	"Preservation of peace among men"; "immovable"	Low, powerful movements in stances
Nijushi	"24 hands"	Strong blocking and striking techniques
Tekki	"Iron horse"	Strong hand and leg techniques from horse stance
Jion	named after Chinese monk who visited Okinawa	Multiple hand punches, strong hand and foot techniques

speed, focus, rhythm, and movement interpretation. Historically, they represent a condensation of the fighting knowledge of the master who developed the kata. Kata were originally designed to have no unnecessary movements. Each movement in the kata had a very specific combative application. As the karateka practices each kata, the vast amount of information within the kata, under the guidance of a knowledgeable teacher, gradually begins to reveal itself to the practitioner.

In performing kata, execution of techniques must not be rigid and robotic, but must effectively contrast the active (do) and passive (sei) elements of the kata to demonstrate proper rhythm and fluidity of human motion. Years of practice are required to master even the most basic kata. Figure 18-6 shows an example of a kata known as Heian Yondan.

Japanese karate kata are traditionally divided into the two styles of Okinawan karate from which they were derived, the Shorin-ryu and the Shorei-ryu. Kata from the Shorin-ryu tradition emphasize movements that are light and flexible, while those of the Shorei-ryu tradition emphasize movements that are strong and powerful. Generally, kata were commonly named by the originator according to a particular technique, movement, or philosophical meaning of the kata itself. At other times, the kata were assigned the name of the originator. Table 18-4 lists the Japanese names and meanings of some of the kata that are practiced by karateka who train in the Shotokan tradition of karate-do.

Kumite (Free-Fighting)

Kumite, or free-fighting, is the application of skills learned in kihon and kata practice to practical fighting and self-defense situations. This aspect of karate training allows karateka to practice their fighting skills against one another. Beginning karateka train to execute all attacking and counterattacking techniques with maximum power and speed and stop just short (*Sun-dome* = about 3 cm) of actual contact to prevent intentional injury. More-advanced karateka, after undergoing disciplined training and conditioning, are allowed to make light contact to restricted target areas during kumite. Kumite teaches the concepts of proper distancing and timing, the proper moment to initiate an attack or defense, and recognition of different offensive and defensive maneuvers made by an opponent. Additionally, it is necessary to master effective body shifting (*taisabaki*) techniques and quick-witted changing techniques (*henka waza*).

Kumite is arbitrarily categorized into basic, intermediate, advanced, and specialized levels. Basic kumite, also called *yakusoku* or "promise" (agreement to attack only a predesignated target area) kumite, consists of *sanbon* (three-step) kumite, *gohon* (five-step) kumite, and *ippon* kumite (one-attack fight). In sanbon or gohon kumite the attacking karateka attacks either three to five times consecutively to the *jodan* (upper level), *chudan* (middle level), or *gedan* (lower level) with a lunge-punch-front stance technique while the defending karateka steps backward in a

Figure 18-6. Heian Yondan.

Figure 18-6. *(continued)*

Figure 18-6. *(concluded)*

front stance at the same time executing the appropriate high, middle, or low blocking technique. On the last block, the defending karateka counters with a reverse punch technique.

In the initial attack in ippon kumite (one-attack fight), the offensive karateka launches a prearranged attack to the face with a lunge-punch-front stance technique while the defending karateka steps to the rear in a defensive stance (usually an immovable stance or a back stance) and executes a counteroffensive technique. It is important here for the offensive karateka to hold position after the attack so that the defending karateka has time to deliver a counteroffensive technique with good form. In the second attack, the offensive karateka executes a lunge-punch-front stance technique to the middle level and the defending karateka counters with an appropriate counteroffensive technique. In the third attack, the offensive karateka launches a prearranged front-kick-front stance attack and the defending karateka again counters with an appropriate counteroffensive technique. At the completion of the first high, middle, and low attack-counter sequence, both karateka change roles to gain equal practice in attack and defense training.

Ippon jiyu kumite (one-attack fight from fighting stance position) is performed almost like ippon kumite. Two exceptions are that both karateka use a free-fighting stance position and the attacking karateka instantaneously returns to the original preattack position after attack delivery so that the defending karateka does not have time to counter the initial attack.

Jiyu kumite allows both karateka to move about at will and execute offensive and defensive maneuvers as opportunities arise. Again, as in the other forms of kumite, all punches, kicks, and strikes are stopped just short of contact to avoid injury. When training in a karate dojo (training hall), the kumite usually continues until one karateka scores what is considered to be a decisive blow on the opponent. A decisive blow is one in which good technique, posture, timing, balance, and power can be demonstrated. In competitive sport matches, kumite bouts usually last for a designated period (e.g., 3 or 5 minutes) or number of points scored (e.g., one to three).

Specialized free-fighting may include activities such as circle fighting (*enjin*) kumite or seated free-fighting (suwari geiko) kumite. In enjin kumite, one karateka is located in the center of a circle of six to eight other karateka. Each karateka on the circle takes turns in rapidly attacking the karateka in the center with a strong technique. The karateka in the center is responsible for avoiding, blocking, and countering each attack. In suwarigeiko kumite, two karateka face each other about 1 m apart in a formal Japanese kneeling posture known as *seiza*. The offensive and defensive karateka follow the same sequence of attack and defense as in ippon kumite, described previously.

ETIQUETTE

Proper behavior in the dojo is considered to be the hallmark of a martial art that is taught within traditional contexts. Dojo protocol and etiquette create a teaching and learning environment that is conducive to disciplined training according to Japanese customs and traditions. Rituals followed within the dojo have a purpose, and it is not one of religious conversion. They serve to establish decorum, develop an attitude conducive to disciplined training, prepare for the learning process, and show respect for the karate tradition.

There is agreement among practitioners regarding the general behavior that is allowed when visiting or training in any dojo. It is customary not to wear shoes on the training surface even if you are in everyday clothes. Prior to beginning a training session, karateka should present themselves with a clean body and clean *karategi* (uniform). This shows respect for those you are going to train with and for your martial art. While training, it is inappropriate to wear jewelry, watches, or the like. Your training uniform must always be kept neat and clean. It is important to bow when entering and leaving a dojo, before and after training with an opponent, and before and after speaking with an instructor or senior student. Acts of profanity, loud talking, laughing, socializing, and misconduct are out of place. When in the dojo one should use the time to either train or meditate. Karate and other martial arts begin and end with courtesy.

SAFETY

Because the martial art of karate is a combative activity, safety is extremely important. Following a few basic rules will reduce the potential for injuries. When attacking or counterattacking during kumite, one must remember to stop all techniques just short of contact. It is recommended that karateka, especially beginners, use protective equipment to cover the shins, forearms, and hands when engaged in free-fighting. It is strongly encouraged that one wear a protective mouthguard and refrain from wearing eyeglasses or hard contact lenses when sparring. If eyeglasses are worn, it is important to wear some type of associated protective device. Keeping toenails and fingernails trimmed and not wearing jewelry during training will also reduce injury.

CONDITIONING

Karate involves the balanced use of almost all major muscle groups. Speed, power, flexibility, balance, agility, and reaction time are important components of training sessions. Although practicing kihon, kata, and kumite provides an adequate conditioning stimulus to the body, supplemental conditioning such as jogging, cycling, swimming, and weight training will enhance cardiorespiratory fitness, muscular strength, endurance, flexibility, and body composition.

Serious karateka make extensive use of the *makiwara* (straw-wrapped punching board) and the heavy bag to develop precision and power in performing effective punches, strikes, and kicks. Use of these two pieces of training equipment helps karateka develop the focus necessary in tensing and relaxing muscles during various techniques.

PHYSICAL AND PSYCHOLOGICAL PRINCIPLES

Being successful at karate requires an understanding and application of fundamental physical and psychological principles to training. The proper use of speed, strength, technique, balance, timing, distance, and focus is necessary to effectively use karate skills.

Tachikata (Importance of Stances)

To maintain balance, the center of gravity must be within the base of support. There are times in karate when you need a stable stance and times when you need an unstable stance. Stable stances are needed to strike with force or when you are receiving a strong attack. Unsatble stances are required when it is necessary to change your stance and move rapidly from one position to another.

Chikara (Power)

The ability to generate power is necessary in karate. Because power is a product of speed and strength, it is important to emphasize both of these in training. Energy generated from the slower but larger and more powerful muscles of the hips and trunk should be coupled with those of the smaller, weaker, but faster, muscles of the extremities to generate maximum power in blocking, punching, striking, and kicking.

Kime (Focus)

The ability to focus (*kime* means "to penetrate the spirit") your technique results from contracting muscles at the moment you make contact with your target. At the same time, it is important to exhale forcefully to help augment the power generated.

Kiai (Spirit Cry)

Associated with karate is the traditional spirit cry known as the *kiai*! Kiai represents a willful activation and union of the karateka's vital energy and should not be misconstrued as merely "shouting."

Koshi Kaiten (Hip Rotation)

The importance of the lower central torso region in generating power and maintaining stability in karate and other martial arts cannot be overemphasized. This region, known as the *seika tanden*, is the focal point of thought and motion. Without effectively employing the hips in karate techniques, there can be no true power.

Jun Kaiten (Regular Hip Rotation)

Jun kaiten is a motion that occurs when the direction of rotation and direction of technique are the same. As an example, when the hips are rotated to the left, the right fist is used for punching. When the hips are rotated to the right, the left arm may be used for an outward-to-inward block.

Gyaku Kaiten (Reverse Hip Rotation)

Gyaku kaiten is a motion that occurs when the direction of rotation and direction of the technique are opposite to one another. In this motion the hips rotate to the right and the technique is executed to the left. As an example, reverse rotation is used in executing the down block, middle block, and knife-hand block.

Kokyu (Use of Proper Breathing)

As a general rule, when attempting to generate power to execute any technique, it is necessary to exhale forcefully only about two thirds of the air from the lungs. In doing so, less time is needed to refill the lungs prior to the next technique. Additionally, exhaling all the air from the lungs may weaken the power of a technique.

Mizu No Kokoro (Mind Like Water)

Mizu no kokoro refers to the need to make the mind calm and serene, like an undisturbed body of water. Just as undisturbed water accurately reflects objects, so does the undisturbed mind accurately reflect that which it sees. A composed mind, devoid of distractions and apprehensions, will accurately reflect the physical and mental posture of the opponent and will be able to respond with appropriate offensive and counteroffensive techniques. Conversely, if the surface of the water is disturbed, the images it reflects will also be disturbed. In like manner, if the mind is preoccupied with thoughts of attack, defense, or apprehension, it will not be able to anticipate the opponent's intensions and thus create an opportunity for the opponent to attack.

Tsuki No Kokoro (Mind Like the Moon)

Just as moonlight shines equally on everything within its range, the karateka can be constantly aware of the totality of the opponent's movements and intentions. Clouds that block out the light of the moon are similar to nervousness and distractions that interfere with the interpretation of your opponent's intentions. This makes it impossible to find openings in your opponent's defenses to deliver an effective attack or counterattack. When watching an opponent, a karateka should envision looking at a distant mountain (*enzan no metsuke*). This ensures that the opponent's entire body, as well as the background, is in the field of vision. Better detection of the relative motion of the opponent's technique is then possible.

Ma (Timing)

Ma deals with the principle of correct timing in attack and defense situations.

Maai (Combative Engagement Distance)

Maai is the principle of correct distancing in delivering offensive and defensive techniques. For training, distancing is generally divided into close, middle, and far distance. Opponents practice modifying techniques so that they can be used at these ranges.

Kuzushi (Off-Balancing)

Kuzushi refers to unbalancing your opponent, either psychologically or physically, to create an opening for an attack or counterattack.

Tsukuri (Fitting In)

Tsukuri refers to "fitting in," or closing the combative engagement distance between you and your opponent with an appropriate technique.

Kake (the Attack)

Kake is the attack or counterattack in a combative situation.

Ki, Ken, Tai Ichi (Spirit, Sword, and Body Are One)

This combative concept comes from Japanese swordsmanship and indicates that for a technique to be effectively employed, one's resolute will, proper technique, and body must all be used simultaneously.

Suki (Opening)

Suki refers to a physical or psychological "opening" in your opponent through which to deliver an attack or counterattack.

Waza o Hodokoso Koki (Proper Moment to Attack)

Closely related to the concept of suki is that of *waza o hodokoso koki*, which is the psychological moment to execute an effective technique. Generally, there are four instances in which a karateka may deliver a technique against an opponent. These are (1) at the start of the opponent's technique, (2) when the attack comes, (3) when the opponent's mind is motionless, and (4) when creating an opening in your opponent.

Kobo Ichi (Appropriateness of Attack)

Kobo ichi refers to the appropriate timing of offensive and defensive techniques. Three levels of timing are recognized:

1. *San no sen*: to take the initiative with one's attack.
2. *Tai no sen*: to take the initiative when the enemy attacks.
3. *Go no sen*: to take the initiative later. This is not the same as engaging in defensive karate. It refers to setting up or leading an opponent into a situation in which you have an advantage.

Zanshin (Remaining Heart)

Zanshin translates literally as "remaining heart" or "remaining mind." It refers to the psychological domination or awareness remaining or "lingering" over an opponent, even after an offensive or counteroffensive technique has been completed.

RULES FOR SPORT COMPETITION

The martial art of karate is an international sport and is practiced in almost every country of the world. In most karate tournaments karateka may participate in either kata or kumite competition, or both. The specific rules under which karateka compete in sport competition vary according to the sponsoring organization. Some of the major organizations under whose auspicies international and national karate sport competition is held are the Japan Karate Federation (JKF) in Japan, the FMK (*Fédération Mondiale de Karate—also known as the World Karate Federation or WKF*) in France, and the World Karate Confederation (WKC) in Switzerland. In the United States, karate sport competition is held under several different organizations including the United States of America–National Karate-do Federation (USA-NKF), which is a member of the U. S. Olympic Committee and is the U.S. representative to the WKF; the United States Karate Federation (USKF), which is associated with the WKC; and the Amateur Athletic Union (AAU), which has a separate membership with the WKC. There are, however, a multitude of national and international karate organizations and styles that have no affiliation with the aforementioned bodies and who host their own competitions.

Kata competition takes the form of individual and team matches. Team matches usually consist of three contestants, either all male or all female. The individual kata competition consists of solo performance in separate female and male divisions. Kata are judged according to correct sequence of movements (*embusen*), good form, proper body rhythm (*unsoku*), proper speed (*waza no kamkyu*), development of power, proper tension and relaxation of techniques (*karada no shin-shuku*), correct breathing, continuity (*renzokusei*), and awareness of imaginary opponents (*waza no imi*). They must be executed with competence and must demonstrate a clear understanding of the kata *bunkai* (practical applications). Contestants are expected to perform compulsory (*shitei*) and self-selected (*tokui*) kata.

Kata competition is organized into three rounds. The first round selects sixteen contestants, the second round selects eight contestants, and the third round selects the winner and final placings. Each kata judge displays the score by means of points on a card held in the hand. To minimize ties generally, scoring is held to between 5 and 7 points in the first round, between 6 and 8 points on the second round, and between 7 and 9 points on the final round. Deductions for a momentary hesitation in a smooth

Table 18-5. ONE BASIS FOR AWARDING POINTS IN KATA COMPETITION

Perfect	10
Excellent	9
Very good	8
Good	7
Average	6
Fair	5
Poor	4
Very poor	3

performance, an inappropriate pause in the kata, and instabilities range from (−0.1 to −0.4 points). If the contestant loses balance completely or falls, a disqualification will result. In some scoring systems each judge (the number of which may vary according to the rules used) awards a score, and the highest and lowest scores are deleted; the remainder of the scores are added together to form a total score. Deductions ranging from −0.1 to −1.0 points may be made in each area. The karateka with the highest total score at the end of the competition is declared the winner. One of the point systems used to judge kata is shown in table 18-5.

Kumite competition is divided into team and individual matches. The individual match may be divided into weight or rank divisions and open category. Weight divisions are divided into bouts, with a "bout" being competition between opposing pairs of team members. Duration of the kumite bout is defined as three minutes or 3 points for senior male kumite (both teams and individuals) and two minutes for women and junior bouts. The result of a bout is determined by either contestant scoring three *ippon* (1 full point for each ippon awarded), six *waza-ari* (6.5 points), or a combination of the two totaling *sanbon*, or obtaining a decision, or by *hansoku* (foul), *shikkaku* (disqualification), or *kiken* (renunciation) imposed against a contestant. An ippon is awarded when a valid strike is delivered to a valid target area (head, neck, face, abdomen, chest, back, and sides). A valid strike consists of a technique that is delivered with good form (*shisei*), correct technique (*kohon waza*), correct fighting attitude, vigorous and correct application of power (*chikara no kyojaku*), perfect finish (*zanshin*), speed (*waza no kamkyu*), and proper timing (*ma*) and distance (*maai*). The actual kumite consists of a free exchange of punches, blocks, strikes, and kicks employing rapidly changing offensive and counteroffensive movements until one karateka scores an effective "hit" (stopped just short of actual contact) against a valid target area. The competition area (*shiaijo*) is generally a flat surface, preferably a wood floor, with an area of about 8 meters square. Located within the match area itself are usually two judges (*fukushin*), one referee (*shushin*), and one arbitrator (*kansa*).

Target Areas of the Human Body

Effective attacks and counterattacks are aimed at a vital target area. In self-defense, this means that the technique delivered will strike an area in such a way as to cause the assailant to quit the assault. In sport competition, it means that if the technique were to make contact, it would cause the opponent to quit the assault also. Figure 18-7 shows the most common target areas of the body against which techniques may be delivered to disable an assailant.

GLOSSARY

Japanese/English

Tachikata (stances)

fudo-dachi Immovable stance.
hachiji-dachi Open-leg stance.
hangetsu-dachi Half-moon stance.
heiko-dachi Parallel stance.
heisoku-dachi Attention stance.
jiyu-dachi Free-fighting stance.
kiba-dachi Horse stance.
kokutsu-dachi Back stance.
kosa-dachi Cross-legged stance.
neko-ashi-dachi Cat-leg stance.
renoji-dachi L-stance.
sanchin-dachi Hourglass stance.
shiko-dachi Square stance.
shizentai-dachi Natural stance.
sochin-dachi Diagonal straddle-leg stance.
teiji-dachi T-stance.
uchi-hachiji-dachi Inverted open-leg stance.
yoi-dachi Preparatory stance.
zenkutsu-dachi Front stance.

Ukewaza (blocking techniques)

age-uke Rising block.
gedan-barai Downward block.
haishi-uke Back-hand block.
juji-uke X-block
kake-uke Hooking block.
kakiwake-uke Reverse wedge block.
kakuto-uke Bent-wrist block.
keito-uke Chicken-head wrist block.
morote-sukui-uke Two-hand scooping block.
morote-tsukami-uke Two-hand grasping block.
morote-uke Augmented forearm block.
nagashi-uke Sweeping block.
osae-uke Pressing block.
otoshi-uki Dropping block.
seiryuto-uke Ox-jaw block.
shuto-uke Knife-hand block.
sokumen-awase-uke Side two-hand block.
soto-uke Outside block.
sukui-uke Scooping block.
teisho-awase-uke Combined palm-heel block.
tekyubi-uke Wrist-hook block.
tsukami-uke Grasping block.
uchi-uke Inside block.

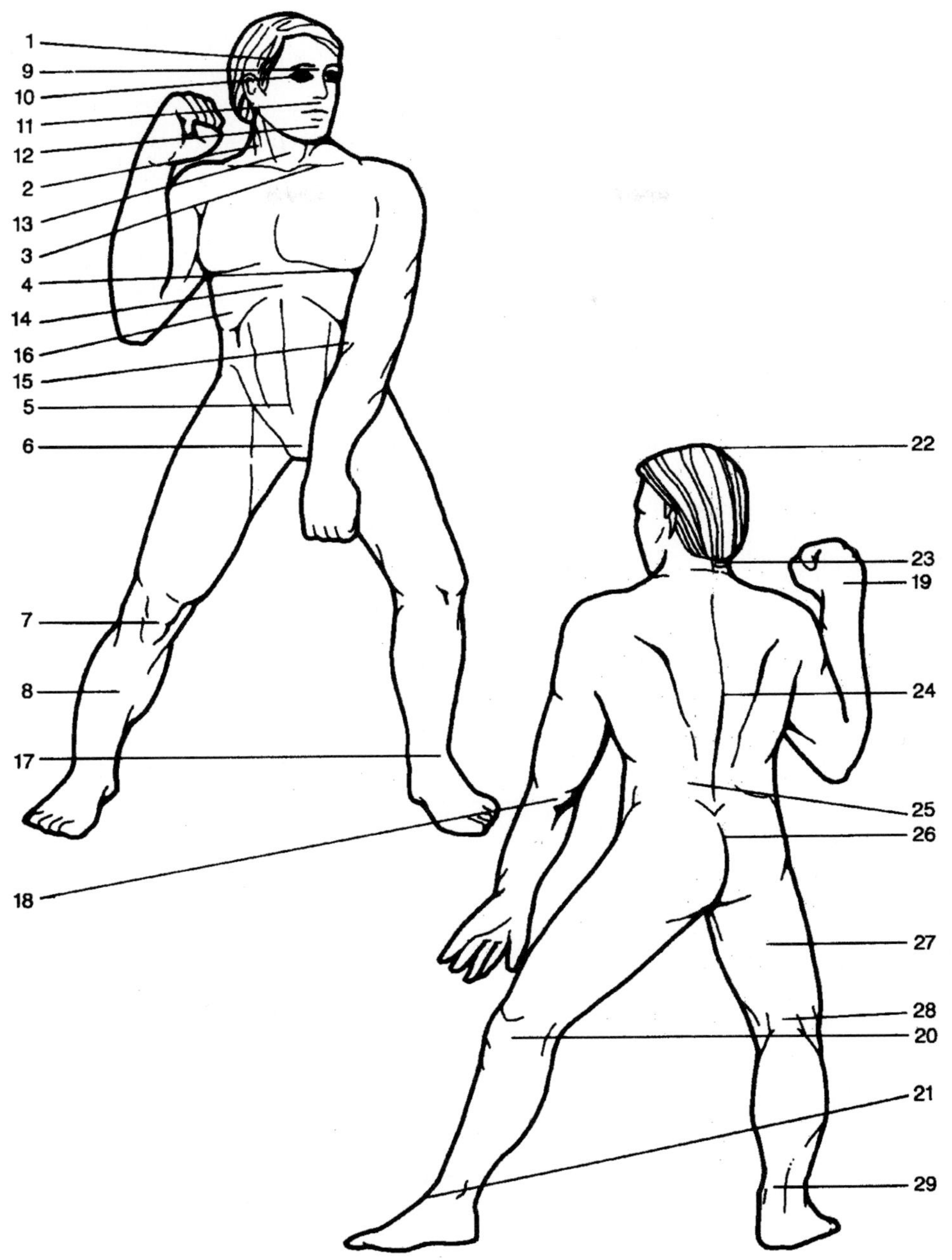

1. Chin
2. Side of neck
3. Collarbone
4. Armpit
5. Abdomen
6. Testicles
7. Knee
8. Shin
9. Bridge of nose
10. Eye
11. Just below nose
12. Chin
13. Throat
14. Solar plexus
15. Front of elbow
16. Ribs
17. Ankle
18. Back of elbow
19. Wrist
20. Side of knee
21. Instep
22. Skull
23. Back of neck
24. Center of back
25. Kidneys
26. Coccyx
27. Back of thigh
28. Back of knee
29. Achilles tendon

Figure 18-7. Target areas.

Tsukiwaza (punching techniques)

age-zuki Rising punch.
awase-zuki U-punch.
choku-zuki Straight punch.
dan-zuki Consecutive punching.
gyaku-zuki Reverse punch.
hiraken-zuki Fore-knuckle fist straight punch.
hasami-zuki Scissors punch.
heiko-zuki Parallel punch.
ippon-ken-zuki One-knuckle fist straight punch.
kagi-zuki Hook punch.
kizami-zuki Jab punch.
morote-zuki Double-fist punch.
nagashi-zuki Flowing punch.
nakadaka ippon ken Middle-finger one-knuckle fist.
oi-zuki Lunge, or chase, punch.
seiken choku-zuki Fore-fist straight punch.
tate-zuki Vertical fist punch.
teisho-zuki Palm-heel punch.
ura-zuki Close punch.
yama-zuki Mountain punch.

Keriwaza (kicking techniques)

age-uke-kake-uke Upper block (reverse foot).
ashibo-kake-uke Leg-hooking block.
ashikubi-kake-uke Ankle-hooking block.
fumikiri Cutting kick.
fumikomi Stomping kick.
gyaku-mawashi-geri Reverse round kick.
mae-geri Front kick.
mae-tobi-geri Jumping front kick.
mawashi-geri Round kick.
mikazuki-geri Crescent kick.
nidan-geri Double jump kick.
sokutei-mawashi-geri Circular sole kick.
sokutei-osae-geri Pressing sole block.
tobi-geri Jumping kick.
yoki-tobi-geri Jumping side kick.

Uchiwaza (striking techniques)

empi-uchi Elbow strike.
haishu-uchi Back-hand strike.
haito-uchi Ridge-hand strike.
hiji-uchi Elbow strike.
kentsui-uchi Bottom-fist strike.
nukite Spear hand.
riken-uchi Back-fist strike.
shuto-uchi Knife-hand strike.
tettsui-uchi Bottom-fist strike.
uraken-uchi Back-fist strike.

Commands and directions

hajime Begin.
hidari Left.
mae Front.
mawatte Turn.
migi Right.
modotte Return to original position.
narande Line up.
otagai ni rei Bow to each other.
rei Bow.
seiretsu Line up by rank.
sensei ni rei Bow to teacher.
shomen ni rei Bow to the front of the dojo.
ushiro Back.
yame Stop.
yasume Relax.
yoi Ready.

Other important terms

aite Opponent.
dan Black-belt rank.
dojo Martial arts school.
embusen Kata performance line.
enjin kumite Circle fight.
jiyu kumite Free-fighting.
kamae Posture.
kancho Building chief ("chief instructor of organization").
karate Empty hand.
kata Formal exercise.
kiai Spirit cry.
kihon Basic exercise.
kohai Junior.
kumite Sparring.
kyu Colored-belt rank.
makiwara Punching post.
mokuso Meditation.
nagewaza Throwing technique.
obi Belt.
okyu teate First aid.
osotu-gari Major outside leg sweep.
osu Greeting that shows respect.
ouchi-gari Major inside leg sweep.
renzuki Alternate punching.
ryu Tradition.
sanbon-kumite Three-step sparring.
seiza Formal sitting position.
sempai Senior.
senjin kumite Line fight.
sensei Teacher.
shihan Master.
shotokan Pine-sea style ("kan" translates here as "building").
suki Opening.
suwari-geiko Seated sparring.
teki Enemy.
tori Attacker.
uke Defender.
ukemi Falling practice.

SUGGESTED READINGS

Egami, S. 1980. *The heart of karate-do*. Tokyo: Kodansha.
Kim, D., and Leland, T.W. 1975: Karate. 2d ed. Dubuque, Iowa: Wm. C. Brown.
Nishiyama, H., and Brown, R.C. 1965. *Karate*. Rutland, Vt. Charles E. Tuttle.
Sawyer, M. *Karate for everyone*. 1985. Winston-Salem, N.C.: Hunter Textbooks Inc. Written for the college karate class,

this text discusses origins, conditioning tips on self-protection, and safety considerations.

Schmidt, R. J. and Hesson, J. 1988. *Karate: A sport for life*. Glenview, Ill.: Scott, Foresman. Suitable for individual and group instruction, this book contains an overview of the sport, basic skill sequences, and a description of forms of competition. Also contains a pronunciation guide.

RESOURCES

Videotapes

Karate aerobics and Martial arts, (5 videos), two titles available from Cambridge Physical Education and Health, P.O. Box 2153, Charleston, WV 25328.

Kayaking and Canoeing

After completing this chapter, the reader should be able to:

- Describe the history and development of canoeing and kayaking
- Select and care for proper equipment
- Describe and execute fundamental canoeing and kayaking techniques
- Practice proper safety procedures
- Practice boating etiquette
- Instruct a group of students in basic canoeing and kayaking techniques

HISTORY

Canoeing and kayaking have evolved over hundreds of years. The first boating vessels were probably single logs or logs strapped together (rafts). With the use of fire and primitive tools, crafts such as the dugout canoe emerged. Natives from Central America, the Fiji Islands, Africa, the Solomon Islands, and Indian tribes in North America used the dugout canoe for travel, trade, and war.

The canoe and kayak can be traced to the Indian tribes and Eskimos of North America. In areas where trees were scarce, frame-and-skin craft were constructed. A wooden or bone frame was designed to form the gunwales, keel, and ribs; and the skins of buffalo, moose, or cattle were sewn together and stretched over the frame. Seams were sealed with pitch or tallow. In the north-central parts of the United States and Canada, where trees were plentiful, bark from birch trees was stretched over a wooden frame.

Decked (covered) boats were used by Eskimos mainly in Alaska and Greenland. These boats were called "kayaks" or "umiaks." Kayaks were smaller, for one person, and were paddled with double-blade paddles. Umiaks were larger, up to 30 feet (9.14 m), and were paddled by up to eight paddlers using single-blade paddles. Open boats were called "canoes." Canoes for one person were 12 to 17 feet (3.7 to 5.2 m) long, while those built up to 30 feet (9.14 m) long could carry more people. They were mainly paddled with single-blade paddles. Sometimes poles were used for steering and navigating upstream.

The canoe and kayak were a primary source of transportation. They were used for hunting and for transporting furs to trading centers. When the settlers from Europe and Great Britain came to North America, they often had the help of Indians in facilitating travel. Canoes were fast, had good maneuverability on the water, and were lightweight for portaging between lakes or rivers. Many French immigrants—known as *voyageurs*—settled in the Canadian North and found the adventurous life of hunting and trapping more attractive than clearing land and farming. They adopted the Indian lifestyle and became expert canoeists.

Unlike voyageurs, other European settlers employed the Indians to help them. Samuel de Champlain, Jacques Marquette, Louis Joliet, Lewis and Clark, and others had Indian guides and used Indians to paddle canoes. Therefore, paddling expertise was never attained by these explorers.

In time, Western settlement of the United States and Canada evolved from frontier to settlements of farmers and ranchers to a more urban society. As a result, the art of canoeing nearly disappeared. In 1900 over two thirds of the population lived in the country, and the demands of farming left little time for leisure. Later, railroads and automobiles further lessened the canoe's importance as a means of transportation. Between 1920 and 1940 both Canada and the United States changed from being two-thirds rural to three-fourths urban, which led to the near disappearance of canoeing and kayaking in North America.

Interestingly, Europeans who traveled in the United States and Canada saw the canoe or kayak and popularized it as sport in their countries. In 1865 John MacGregor made his famous thousand-mile trip throughout England and Europe in the *Rob Roy.* Because the *Rob Roy* and others like it were closed or decked boats, kayaking became known as canoeing throughout Europe. Because of the influence of French fur trappers who preferred more open Indian style vessels, the term *un canadien,* or "a Canadian," became a popular name for the canoe, and it is still used throughout Europe. Whitewater paddling in Europe was pursued as a leisure activity, and Europeans have dominated international canoe and kayak racing throughout the twentieth century.

The resurgence of canoeing and kayaking in North America was influenced primarily by recreational pursuits. Sport fishing in the North became popular, and fishermen hired Indian guides to paddle their canoes. However, the sport was fishing, not canoeing. The real impetus for recreational paddling was in summer camps for children. Private camps, YMCA camps, military academies, and the like have done an excellent job of teaching the basics of flat-

Figure 19-1. Canoeing rivers offers many recreational opportunities.

water canoeing for several generations. However, with rules such as "No standing in the canoe" and "Don't shoot the rapids," little was done to develop whitewater techniques until the mid-1970s. From the late 1930s through the early 1970s canoe and kayak building was limited to two or three models by two companies, Old Town and Grumman. Canoes were usually made of wood strips and aluminum.

The development of such synthetics as fiberglass, acrylonitrile butadiene styrene (ABS), and Kevlar, along with a maturing of social, economic, and environmental values, has resulted in a growing popularity of canoeing and kayaking (figure 19-1). Although the popularity of flat-water boating has stabilized, participation in whitewater canoeing and kayaking continues to increase. Interest in sea kayaking promises to lead the industry in the 1990s. In states with coastal waters or large inland bodies of water, sea kayaks provide opportunities for exploring saltwater marshes and intercoastal waterways, whale and dolphin watching, and cruising barrier islands in open expanses of water with some degree of stability.

Play-boating, hotdogging, and freestyle are also being explored by canoeists and kayakers. As people gain expertise in controlling their vessels, there is always an urge to test the limits of what can be done, just as in skiing, surfing, and rock climbing. As a result, the art of quick turning by laying a boat on its side, pirouettes, and the like is continually evolving.

With the expansion of interest in canoeing and kayaking, Americans have also returned to racing to be competitive with the Europeans. In the 1988 Olympics Greg Barton won the first U.S. gold medal in flat-water kayaking. The first World Whitewater Competition in the United States took place on the Savage River in Maryland in 1989, after being held in Europe for decades. Kathy Hearn, Davey Hearn, Jon Lugbill, and others have led the resurgence of whitewater slalom racers. In the 1992 Olympics in Barcelona, Spain, Joe Jacobi and Scott Strausbaugh became the first Americans to win a gold medal in whitewater competition. Dana Chladex also won a bronze medal in women's solo canoe for the United States. The 1996 Olympics in Atlanta had venues in both flat-water canoeing and kayaking, as well as in downriver and slalom whitewater canoeing and kayaking. The whitewater events were held on the Ocoee River in southeastern Tennessee. Once again the Europeans dominated the events, although Dana Chladek from the United States won a silver medal in women's singles kayak.

VALUES

Whereas most outdoor recreation and sports develop muscles of the lower limbs, canoeing and kayaking primarily develop muscles of the back, abdomen, shoulders, and arms. It is an excellent aerobic activity because most canoe and kayak outings last for at least half an hour and many take from half a day to several days. Canoeing and kayaking may begin as recreational activities or as a sports interest. As skill is developed, the number of options become almost limitless. One can canoe or kayak solo or with a partner. Canoeing and kayaking can offer solitude as well as the companionship of groups. Canoeing and kayaking are done by both sexes and by people of all ages.

The versatility of canoes and kayaks is amazing. One can paddle on the smallest creek, river, lake, or even the sea. After developing skill in a selected vessel, it is possible to combine paddling with picture taking, sightseeing, fishing, hunting, bird watching, and the like. If one wishes to become competitive, there is flat-water racing or whitewater slalom and down river racing competition. Competition varies from citizens races (friendly, novice racing) to Olympic events.

EQUIPMENT

Paddles, boats, personal gear, and clothing have changed greatly in recent years. Natural materials in clothing and boats have given way to synthetics, which have brought about changes in the sport.

In the past, equipment such as an aluminum canoe served many purposes. Today specialized equipment exists for different boating and paddling styles. Because the diversity of equipment can be overwhelming, asking instructors or boat outfitters appropriate questions concerning equipment and gear will enhance the chance of making good choices.

CLOTHING

On a hot summer day you may be comfortable in a swimsuit or a cotton shirt and shorts. However, during the spring or fall and on cold-water rivers or lakes, always consider the prospect of hypothermia.

Layering clothes increases warmth and comfort. A wicking layer next to the body transfers moisture from the skin to the outer layers. Silk and polypropylene serve this purpose. Absorbing material should be the middle layer. Wool, pile, and bunting moves moisture to the outer layer. The outer layer protects against wind and water and is usually made of nylon or Gore-tex. Although it may not be necessary to wear all these clothes at all times, harsh weather conditions should always be considered. Clothes not needed immediately should be packed in a dry bag. Wet suits and dry suits are often worn by paddlers in extreme conditions.

Shoes should also be considered. Entry, exit, and portage conditions cannot always be predicted. Old sneakers, hiking boots, river shoes, and booties are all choices. Many accidents have been caused by poor traction or stepping on cut glass. It is important to protect the feet from injury.

Other personal choices are hats and sunglasses. Hats help keep the body warm and protect the eyes from the sun's glare. Sunglasses protect eyes from glare and from harmful ultraviolet rays.

ACCESSORY GEAR

Accessories for canoeing and kayaking include paddles, life vests, flotation devices, spray covers, first-aid kits, and rescue equipment. Next to choosing a proper canoe or kayak, the choice of a paddle is the most critical. Paddles are constructed of wood, fiberglass, carbon fiber, plastic, or aluminum. Grips are either pear-shaped or T-shaped. Shafts are straight or angled from 5 to 15 degrees. Blade width may vary from 6 to 9 inches (15.2 to 22.9 cm) or more. Length is determined by the paddler's height and whether the paddle will be used from a sitting or kneeling position. When standing, a canoe paddle should be long enough to come up approximately to the chin of a person. High-performance paddles are light and expensive, but sometimes not very durable. Paddles used on rugged, remote trips should be durable. Aluminum shafts are light and durable, but they may feel cold to bare hands. Beginning paddlers usually use whatever the outfitter provides, but as one becomes serious about canoeing or kayaking, one must learn about the available choices before buying.

Paddlers should always wear a U.S. Coast Guard–approved life vest for adequate buoyance, physical protection, and warmth (figure 19-2). Type III and Type V personal flotation devices (PFDs) are most commonly used. Persons in paddle-decked boats (kayaks, C-1s, etc.) or open boats in difficult rivers with a probability of capsizing should use helmets. Helmets have a plastic or fiberglass shell with a liner to cushion blows.

Type I PFD - Off-Shore Life Jacket
Best for open, rough or remote water, where rescue may be slow coming.
Advantages - Floats you the best.
Turns most unconscious wearers face-up in water. Highly visible color.
Disadvantages - Bulky

Type II PFD - Near Shore Buoyant Vest
Good for calm, inland water, or where there is a good chance of fast rescue.
Advantages - Turns some unconscious wearers face-up in water. Less bulky, more comfortable than Type I PFD.
Disadvantages - Not for long hours in rough water.
Will not turn some unconscious wearers face up in water.

Type III - Flotation Aid
For calm, inland water, or where there is good chance of fast rescue.
Advantages - Generally the most comfortable type for continuous wear. Designed for general boating or the activity that is marked on the device.
Disadvantages - Wearer may have to tilt head back to avoid going face-down. In rough water, a wearer's face may often be covered by waves.
Not for extended survival in rough water.

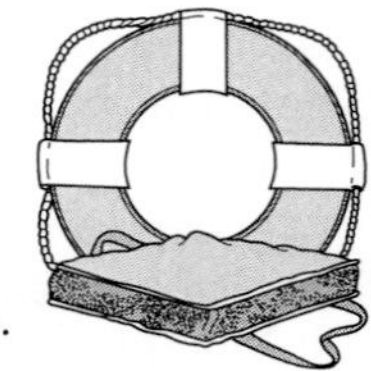

Type IV PFD - Throwable Device
For calm, inland water with heavy boat traffic, where help is always nearby.
Advantages - Can be thrown to someone.
Good back-up to wearable PFDs.
Some can be used as seat cushion.
Disadvantages - Not for unconscious persons.
Not for nonswimmers or children.
Not for many hours in rough water.

Type V PFD - Special Use Devices
For special uses or conditions such as rough whitewater canoeing and kayaking, boardsailing, etc.
Advantages - High level of flotation.
Good for continuous wear.
Turns most unconscious wearers face-up in the water.
Disadvantages - Approved for limited use.

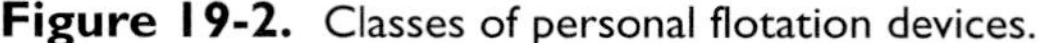

Figure 19-2. Classes of personal flotation devices.

Flotation is necessary for canoes and kayaks so that they will not sink when swamped. Many aluminum and fiberglass canoes have flotation in sealed compartments in the bow and stern. Closed boat flotation includes airbags and Ethafoam or Styrofoam walls that also prevent the deck from collapsing on the boater's legs in the case of a pin. Open-boat flotation may include inflatable air bags, Styrofoam blocks, and tire inner tubes. Extra flotation causes greater displacement of water when the boat is capsized, making rescue easier.

Spray covers and spray skirts are used in some canoeing conditions and most kayaking conditions to keep water from entering the vessel. Spray covers and skirts must release reliably, but not prematurely, under normal boating conditions so the paddler can get free of the boat.

First-aid equipment is a must for all boaters. The extent of readiness depends on the qualifications of the personnel in the group and the nature of the trip. Long-distance or wilderness trips require additional readiness. At a minimum, a first-aid kit should contain dressings, ointments, disinfectants, pain medication, emergency phone numbers, and health forms for each participant.

Rescue equipment is important for unexpected emergencies. Throw lines or rescue bags are often necessary for rescuing people or boats. "Painter lines" on canoes and grab loops on kayaks are helpful in rescue because they allow a person to get away from the boat while still maintaining contact. Other rescue equipment could include pulley-and-rope systems and repair kits for remote travel.

BOATS

The characteristics of canoes and kayaks vary widely. Paddlers can select boats geared to their strength, body size, and purpose (racing, touring, or pleasure). The most important features of canoes, kayaks, and paddles are shown in figure 19-3.

Length

The overall length of a boat is the distance from one end to the other. If the width remains the same, an increase in length will increase the speed and tracking ability of the craft.

Width (Beam)

Width is measured at two points for canoes: the molded beam and the waterline. The molded-beam width is the distance between the tops of the two sides. The narrower this width, the easier it is to paddle because the canoeist does not have to reach out as far. The waterline width is the widest point that a boat rests in the water. More weight added to a boat will generally increase its waterline width. Kayak width is measured at the widest point. Whitewater models generally are widest near the middle. This allows for increased maneuverability. Touring and downriver kayaks are widest somewhat back of the middle. This increases straight-line tracking ability, but inhibits maneuverability.

Depth

In a canoe, depth is measured at the centerline from the gunwale down. A taller boat deflects spray and waves, but may catch more wind than one with less depth. A shallow boat minimizes wind resistance, but increases the probability of shipping water. Depth in a kayak influences the amount of room for the legs.

Rocker

The rocker is the shape of the hull along the underwater keel line (figure 19-4). A straight keel line improves tracking ability. Turning is made easier (less drag) when a rocker is added.

Flare and Tumblehome

Flare and *tumblehome* are terms used to refer to the shape of the boat above the waterline (figure 19-5). Flared sides provide increased stability. Boats with tumblehome have less molded beam width than waterline width. When boats with tumblehome are leaned extremely, stability is decreased dramatically.

Symmetry

Symmetry refers to the shape of the boat from front to back at the waterline (figure 19-6). Symmetry affects a boat's movement through the water and its ability to turn. Symmetrical boats are used for quick maneuverability. Asymmetrical boats usually lengthen and streamline the shape of the bow to increase the efficiency of passage through the water. In asymmetrical boats directional control is increased, but turning ability is decreased.

Vees, Arches, and Flat Bottoms

Vees, arches, and *flat bottoms* are terms used to describe the bottom shape of the boat (figure 19-7). Flat-bottom boats tend to be very stable. Rounded hulls are initially less stable than flat bottoms if they have flare. They have good stability and are forgiving, however, when the boat is leaned. The greater the boat's V shape, the better the directional ability but the poorer its stability.

Volume

Volume indicates the fullness of a boat's shape and how much weight it can carry. High-performance vessels for racing have low volume. Medium-volume boats can carry some gear and are suited for general recreational paddling. High-volume boats can carry more than 200 pounds and are used for extended travel.

Boat Types

Canoes are classed into two divisions: tandem (for two people) and solo. Each division has several classes based on the purposes for which the canoe may be used. Within the tandem division the casual-recreation, day-tripper, touring, and downriver boats are the most popular. Casual-recreation canoes are generally built with cost as a primary consideration, along with low maintenance, casual storage, and safety (figure 19-8A). Performance is not a primary consideration. Tripper and touring canoes have a medium volume (figure 19-8B). They are designed to carry two paddlers with gear, yet have low profiles, are lightweight for portability, and are fairly quick in the water. Downriver canoes are valued primarily for their directional integrity or fast straight-ahead paddling (figure 19-8C). They are good performers in waters ranging from millponds and open bays to nontechnical class II and class II whitewater rivers. Competition cruising, whitewater play boat, whitewater slalom, and Olympic

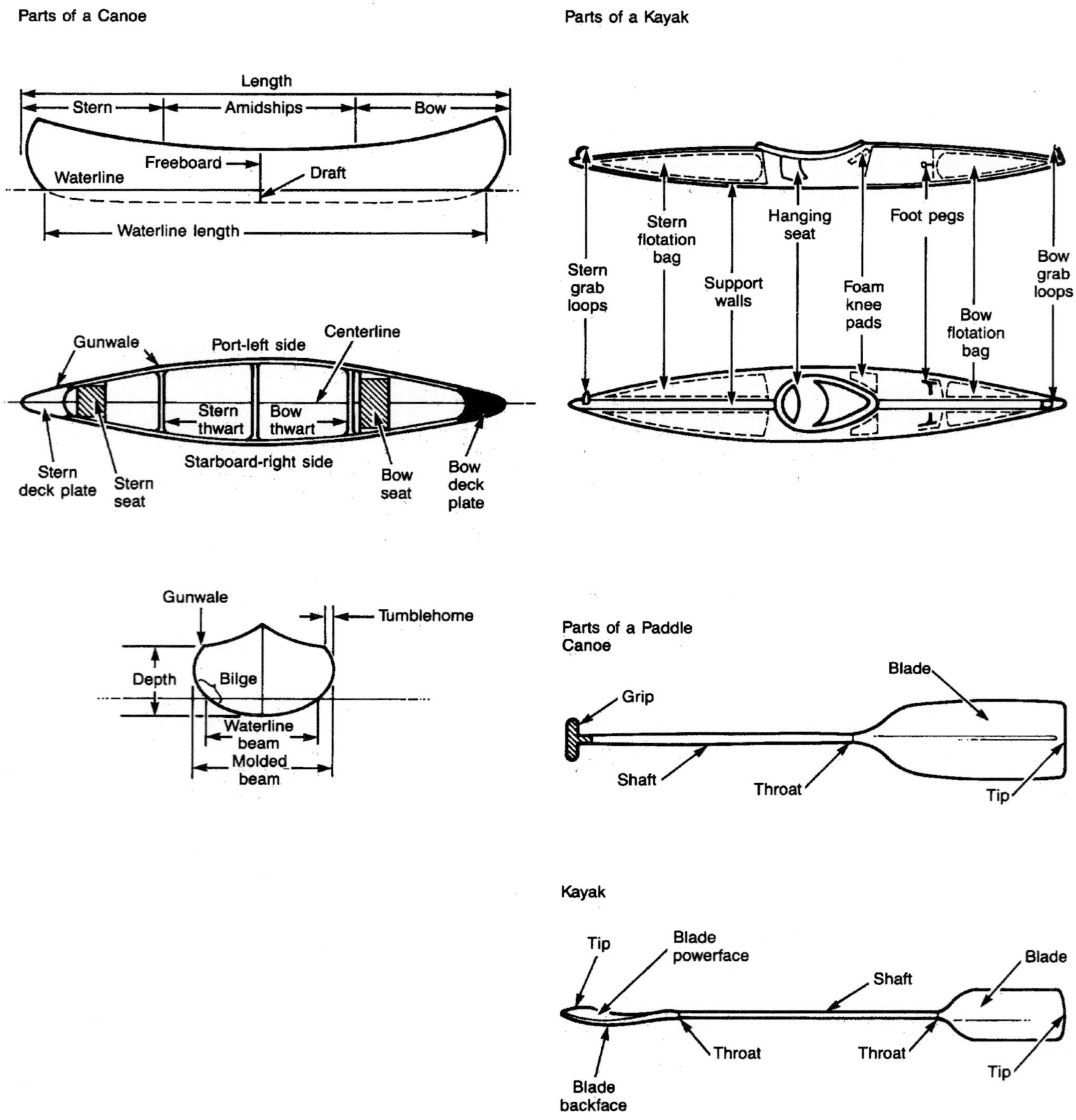

Parts of a Canoe

Parts of a Kayak

Parts of a Paddle Canoe

Kayak

Figure 19-3. Features of canoes, kayaks, and paddles.

flat-water are further types of tandem canoes used for racing in various conditions.

Solo canoes are the second division of canoes. Types of solo canoes are cruising, racing, sport, whitewater, and Olympic flat-water (figure 19-9). Cruising canoes are designed for the traveler. Sport canoes are ideal for day-tripping or "just messing around" on a lake or millpond. They combine maneuverability and directional integrity.

Kayaks also have many designs (figure 19-10). They include casual recreation, touring, sea kayak, downriver, whitewater slalom, whitewater play boat, squirt, and Olympic flat-water. Casual-touring kayaks are primarily touring boats,

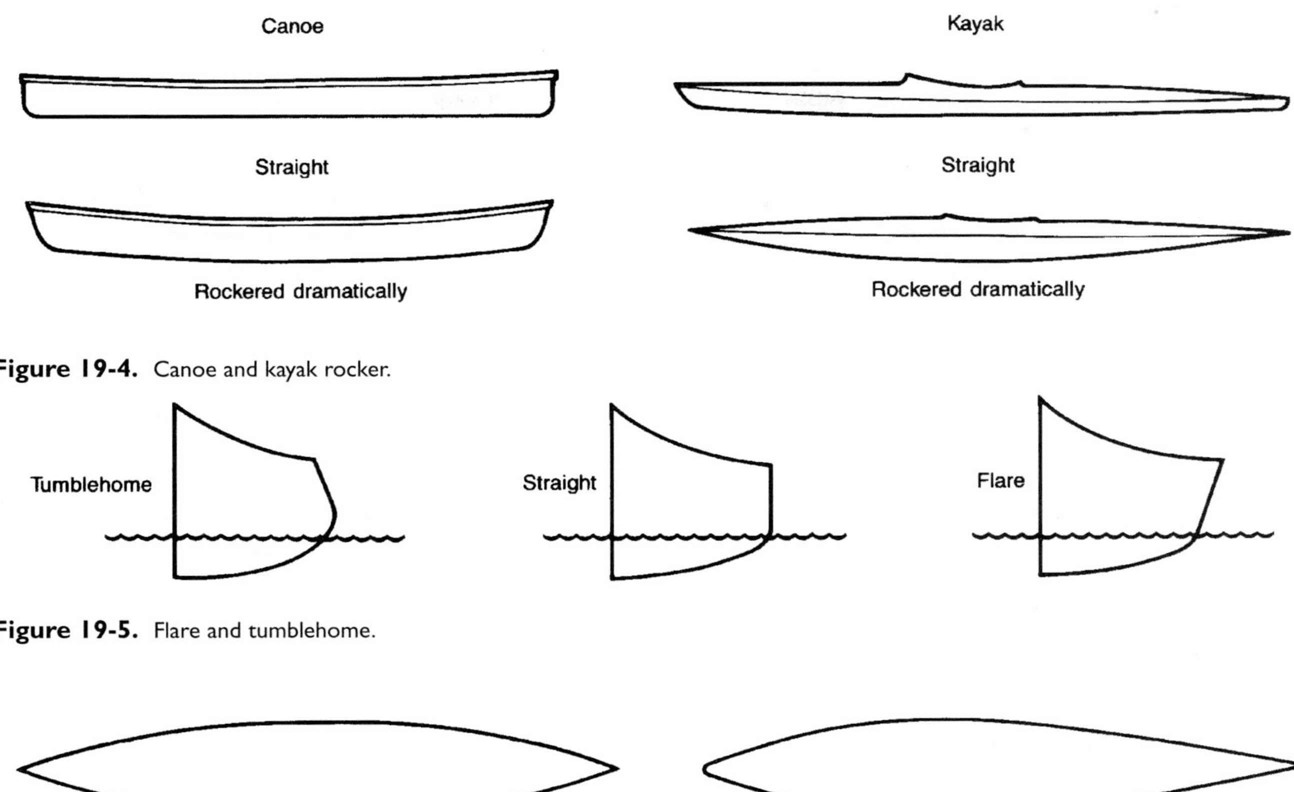

Figure 19-4. Canoe and kayak rocker.

Figure 19-5. Flare and tumblehome.

Figure 19-6. Symmetry.

but they will handle nicely in moderate whitewater. Touring kayaks are high-volume boats designed to carry generous loads with compromising handling qualities or moderately rough water. Sea kayaks are long, high-volume boats designed to cover long stretches of unpredictably rough open water with comparative ease. Because of the interest in exploring the open water and coastline, this is the fastest growing segment of the kayak industry. The remaining kayaks are generally for racing or recreation in whitewater.

GENERAL RULES AND WATER ETIQUETTE

Be Kind to Others

There is an old rule that good friends or spouses should never paddle together because of disagreements over route selection, fault for capsize, and so on. Communicate with your partner. Help or compensate for your partner. Offer assistance when asked. Don't be loud and obnoxious. Don't hog the best practice place, view, and the like.

Stay with Your Group

If you are in a group, paddle as fast or as slow as the rest while maintaining a reasonable distance between boats. Getting too far ahead or behind puts you in a position to get lost, reduces the safety of the group as a whole, and generally causes ill feeling toward you. If necessary, break your group into two units—one faster, one slower.

Respect Others' Property

Make sure you have permission to put your boats in the water and take them out. When stopping along a lake or river to eat, rest, or sleep, get permission and respect the trees, animals, fences, and land. Don't litter; and when you can, clean up the litter of others.

Follow Established Rules

The U.S. Coast Guard and other governing bodies, such as the American Whitewater Affiliate of the American Canoe Association, have rules for safety on the water. Know and follow them. Some general rules are:

1. Boats propelled by oars or paddles have the right-of-way over motorboats.
2. In a crossing situation the boat to the right has the right-of-way.
3. Use the universal river signals to communicate to others (figure 19-11).

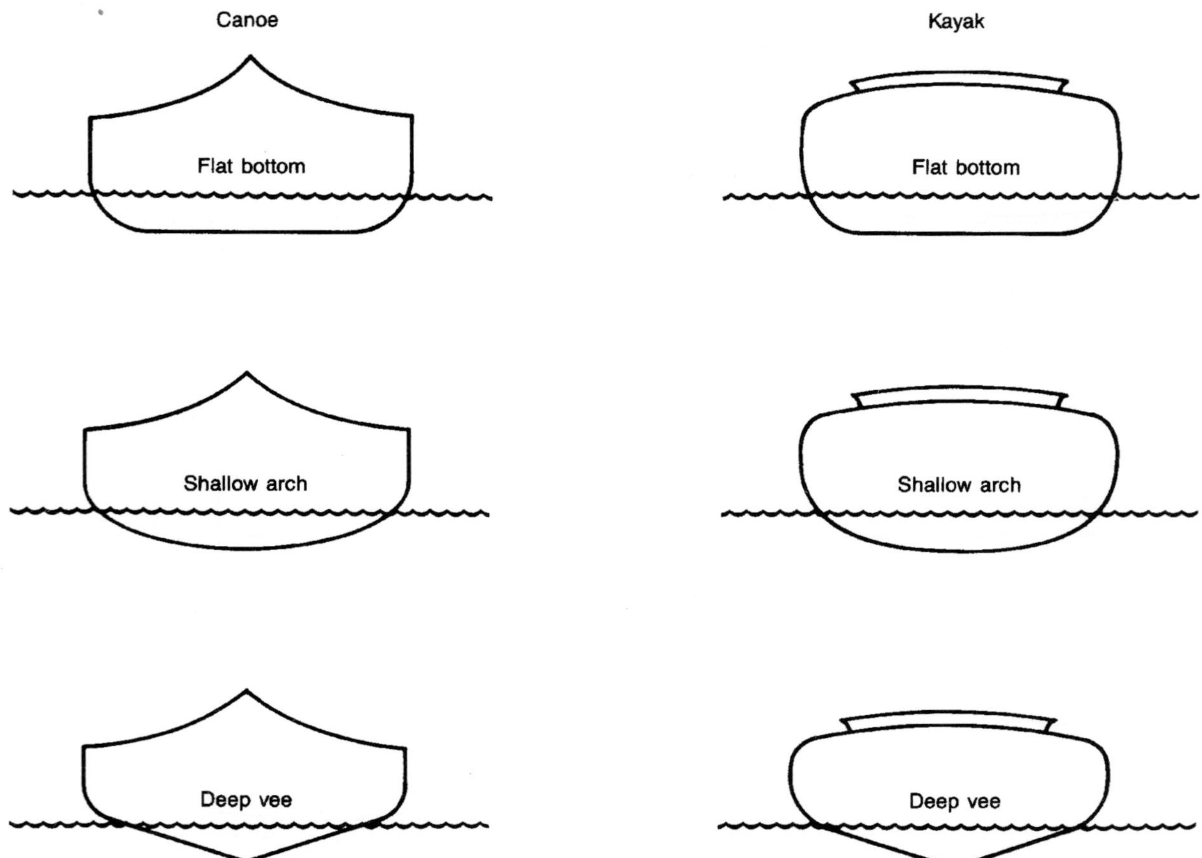

Figure 19-7. Vees, arches, and flat bottoms.

FUNDAMENTAL SKILLS AND TECHNIQUES

Orienting the Paddler to the Boat

Canoes and kayaks are lightweight and shallow-draft crafts. They are sensitive to weight distribution (fore and aft as well as side to side). The key is to keep the center of gravity (CG) over the base of support (BS). In a canoe the base of support may be thought of as that part of the canoe that is in direct contact with the water. As weight of packs or paddlers is added to a canoe or kayak, there is a potential for both the CG and BS to shift fore, aft, or to one side.

Maintaining balance in a canoe or kayak is regulated by keeping the CG over the BS and by keeping the CG as low as possible. A sudden change in trim caused by an outside force—such as a wave, collision, or by leaning to one side—results in a shift where the CG may begin to fall outside the BS. If this happens, it is necessary to use a righting action called a "hip flip" to recenter the CG over the BS. As one leans the canoe to the left, for example, the left gunwale lowers and comes close to the water. If one continues to lean left, the CG may fall outside the base of the canoe, causing it to capsize. To guard against this, the canoeist can shift his or her weight to the right knee while simultaneously shifting the hips to the right, thereby rebalancing or leveling the canoe again, bringing the CG over the BS.

The recommended position for canoe paddling is kneeling. This offers a low center of gravity with three points of contact with the canoe. The knees are spread wide with the buttocks resting against the seat, or thwart. One can also perform the righting action (hip flip) from this position quite well. Other paddling positions—sitting, high-kneel, or standing—are possible. However, each causes the canoeist to have a higher CG relative to the BS and should not be tried until one has a feel for the canoe and has become competent in basic paddling strokes.

Kayakers always sit in their vessel with their legs out in front. To get a good fit, or to "wear the kayak," the knees should be bent up and out to fit snugly on the upper walls of the kayak. Foot braces should be adjusted so the balls of the feet press against the braces. This snug fit gives a low CG and allows a good hip flip for maintaining stability.

A good stability drill is to get into position in the boat, lean slightly to one side, and then flip the hips back under to correct the BS and regain equilibrium. Another good

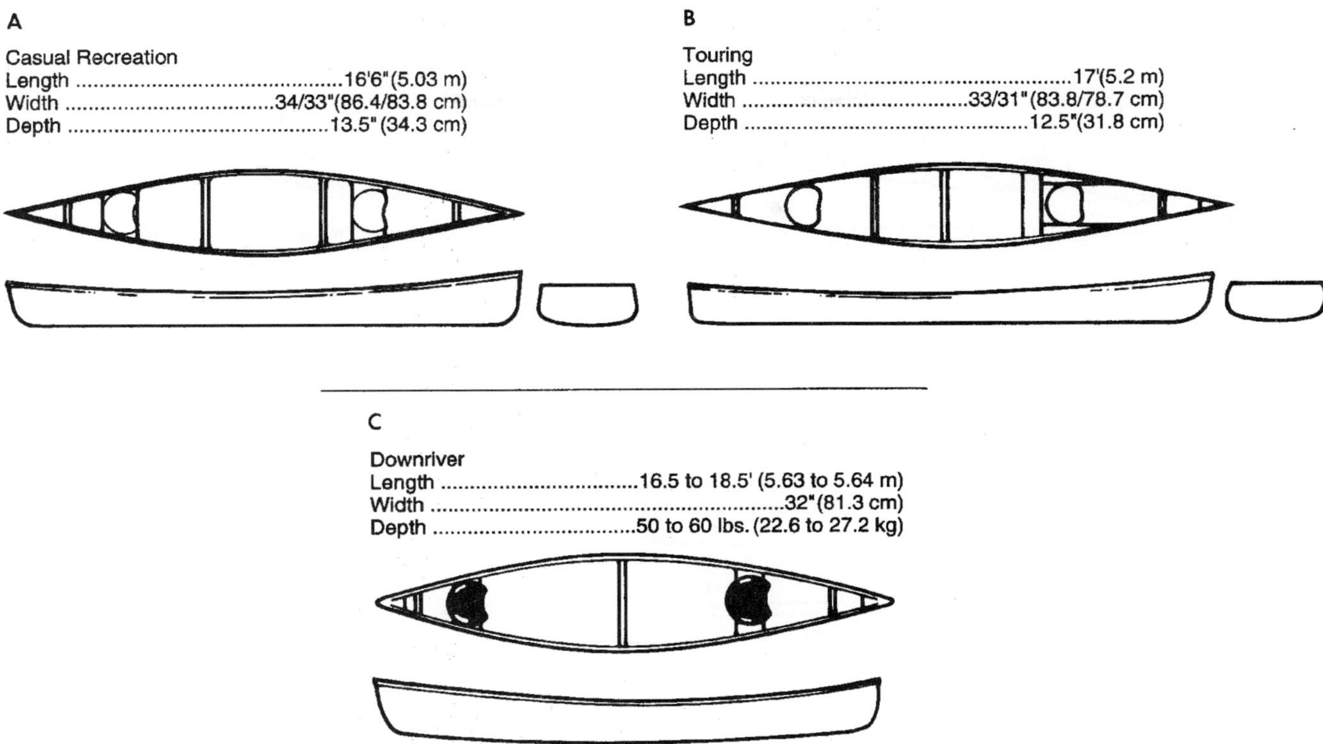

Figure 19-8. Types of tandem canoes.

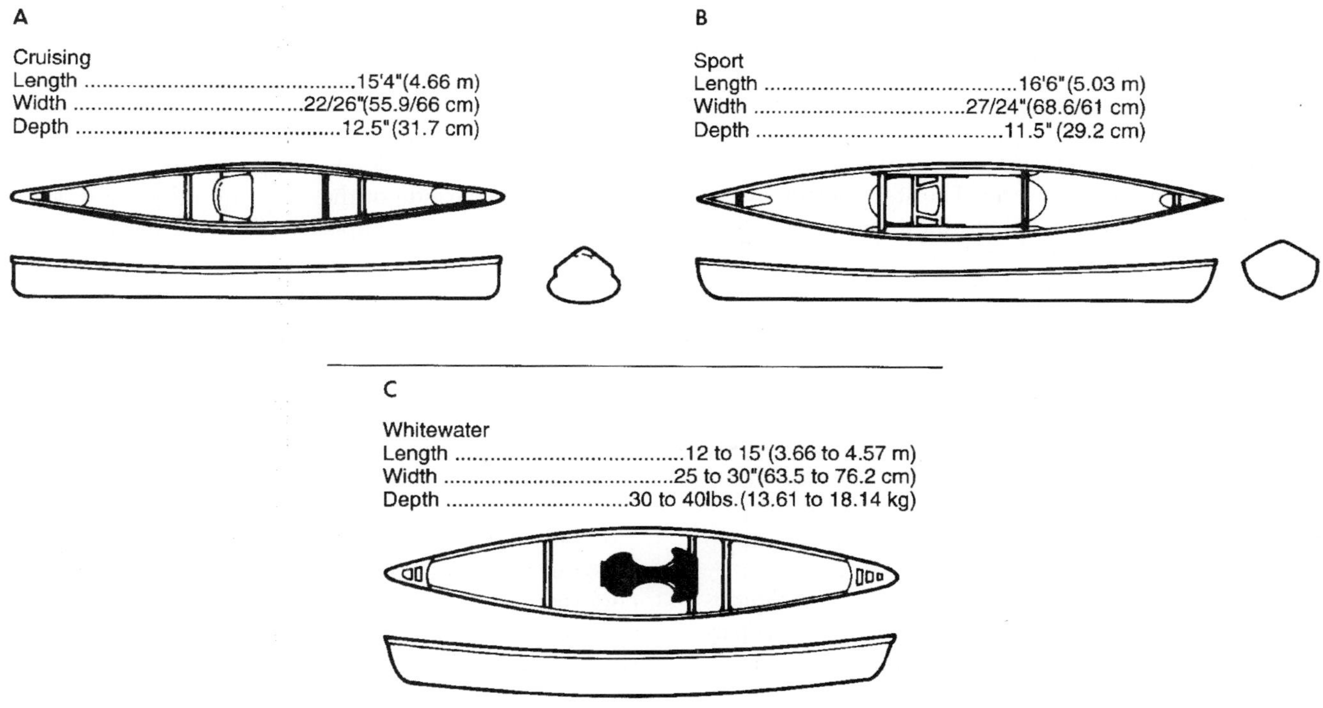

Figure 19-9. Types of solo canoes.

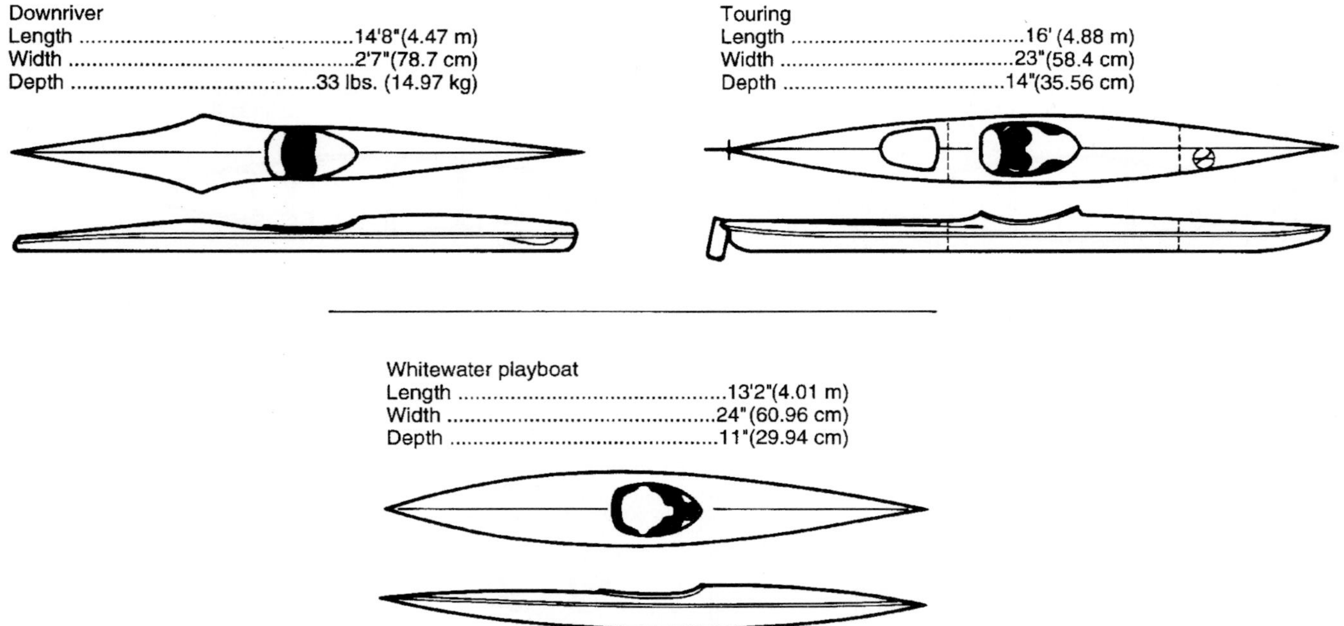

Figure 19-10. Types of kayaks.

stability drill is to rock from side to side while keeping the navel, shoulders, and head in a centered position. In both instances paddlers can get a good feel for the boat and learn that by making adjustments the craft can maintain stability under changing conditions.

Correct launching and docking (getting in and out) of canoes and kayaks are essential to a successful experience. Canoes may be boarded end-first, with the canoe perpendicular to shore, or from the side, with the side parallel to shore. When two people board a canoe, the bowman usually boards first to maintain trim. The stern person assists by straddling the canoe and holding the gunwales. The bow person places the first foot on the center, or keelline of the canoe while keeping the weight centered over the leg on the bank or dock. Next, while keeping low by bending at the hips and knees, the hands grasp each of the gunwales. Then the trail leg is brought into the canoe, at which time the canoeist assumes the kneeling position to assist the stern person in getting in (figure 19-12). When getting out, the process is reversed. Launching and docking a canoe from a position parallel to the dock involves the same procedures. Step into the center. Grasp both gunwales. Keep your weight low (figure 19-13).

Getting into and out of a kayak, with its tiny cockpit, is more of a challenge. The best way is to place the kayak parallel and next to shore. Place the paddle across the kayak, just behind the cockpit, with one of the blades lying flat on shore for support. With the hand nearest the kayak, grip the junction of the kayak paddle and the cockpit to keep the boat steady. While keeping your weight leaning toward shore, place the leg nearest the kayak just to the front of the seat (figure 19-14). Follow it with the other leg. Then lower yourself into the seat, being careful not to scrape your shins across the top of the cockpit. Exiting is a reversal of this process.

In both canoeing and kayaking it may be necessary to perform what is called a wet entry and exit. The exit part is easy. In a canoe, rather than jumping out or capsizing, it is safer to place both hands on one gunwale, maintain contact and slip over the side of the canoe into the water. When doing a wet entry it is important for a partner or another canoe to provide support and assistance. With this assistance being provided from the opposite side, place both hands on the gunwale, perform a scissors kick to gain lift, and push up with the arms into a support position with the hips near the gunwale. Next, swing the legs one at a time over the gunwale and into the canoe. Staying low through this process is important. A wet exit from a kayak is accomplished by capsizing, removing the skirt from the cockpit rim with a pulling action, and carefully withdrawing the hips and legs from the boat. After righting the kayak and approaching it diagonally from the rear, a wet entry can be performed by placing both hands on the cockpit and using the arms to pull up onto the back deck of the kayak in straddle position. Then, by placing both hands behind the hips, both legs are lifted simultaneously (bilaterally) and smoothly back into the kayak and slid back down into a sitting position.

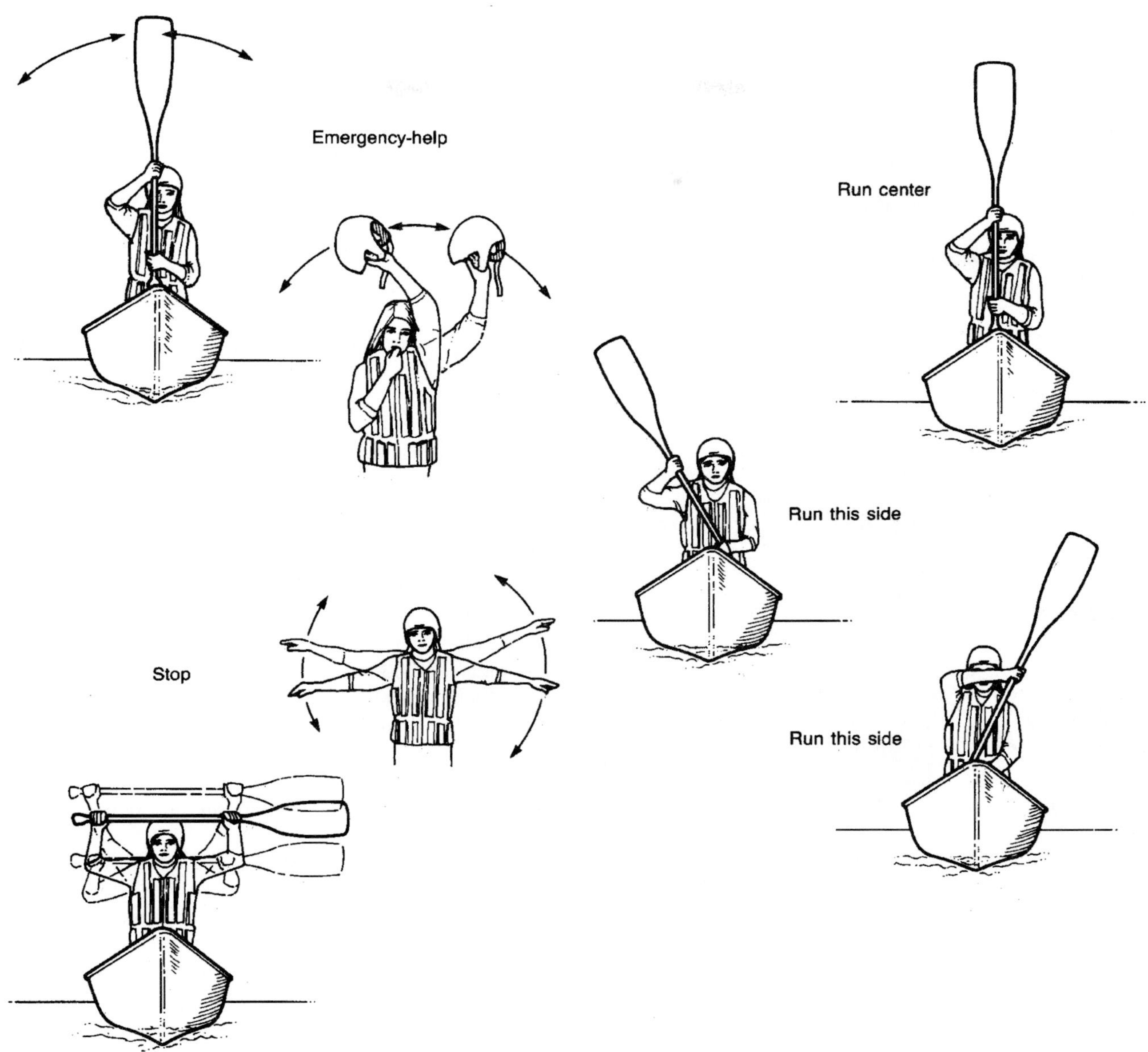

Figure 19-11. Universal river signals.

Mechanics of Paddling

There are three major types of canoe and kayak strokes: power strokes; turning, lateral, or corrective strokes; and bracing strokes. Power strokes primarily provide forward or reverse momentum. Turning and lateral strokes pivot the boat or make it go sideways, while corrective strokes adjust the path of the boat to keep it on a straight course. Bracing strokes provide stability for the craft.

Strokes are also divided into onside and offside strokes. Onside strokes are executed on the selected paddling side. Offside strokes are executed on the other side. There are two phases to all strokes. The *propulsion phase* is the application of force on the paddle against the water. The *recovery phase* is the return of the paddle to a "catch" position, where the blade is braced against the water, ready to begin the propulsion phase. Recoveries can be feathered above the water or sliced through the water.

Strokes can be dynamic or static. A dynamic stroke moves the blade actively against the current. A static stroke is a fixed-position stroke used to turn or veer the boat. Static strokes require the boat to be moving faster than the current to be effective.

Figure 19-12. Launching.

Figure 19-13. Launching parallel to dock.

Figure 19-14. Launching the kayak.

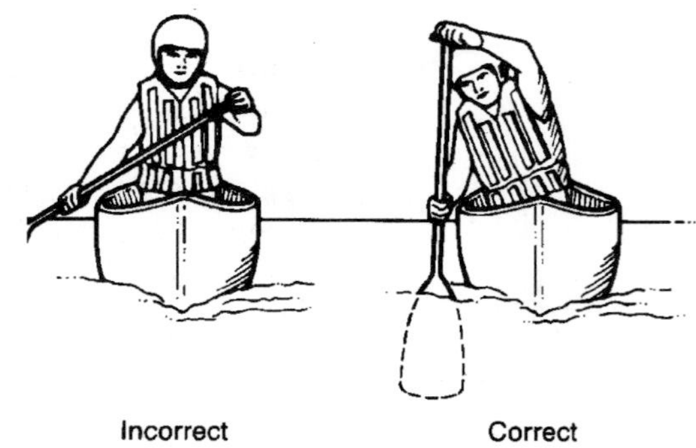

Figure 19-15. Paddle position for linear motion.

Paddling strokes utilize leverage to gain propulsion through the water. With a firm grip of the top hand, the paddler reaches in a chosen direction with the bottom hand to propel the load (canoe/kayak) through the water (forward, backward, sideways, or turning). As the paddle blade enters the water one can think of it like placing it in molasses or cement. While there is some slippage of the paddle through the water, the resulting muscular action on the paddle propels the craft in the desired direction. Speed and range of motion are gained at the blade end of the paddle. Mechanical advantage is the result. In selected strokes such as the J and pry, or push-away, the paddler can attempt to use the middle of the shaft against the gunwale of the canoe and transfer the power of the stroke directly to the canoe, as in rowing with an oar, and make the stroke more effective.

The power face is that side of the blade that is pressed against the water during a forward stroke. The back face is the reverse side of the paddle and is pressed against the water during a backstroke. Turning, lateral, correcting, and bracing strokes will be identified according to whether they use the power face or back face of the paddle for execution.

To establish linear motion in a canoe or kayak, it is best to have the paddle in a vertical position and follow a straight path parallel to the keel line of the boat (figure 19-15). To establish rotary motion (figure 19-16) in a vessel, it is best to apply force to the paddle as far forward, or aft, of midships as possible to establish an arc around a pivot point.

Newton's Third Law of Motion states that for every action there is an equal and opposite reaction. In paddling, the action is the application of force to the blade. The reaction is the movement of the craft in the opposite direction. To go forward, pull the water back. To go to the right, push or pull the water to the left.

The most powerful stroking action is accomplished with the arms in a relatively fixed, straight, extended position and by using the large, strong muscles of the back and torso. This concept is called "torso rotation" (figure 19-17).

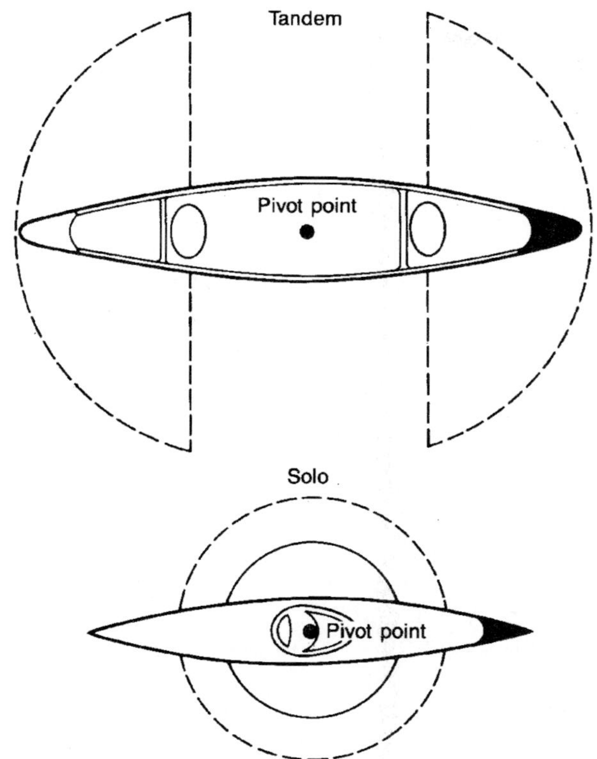

Figure 19-16. Rotary motion.

During the recovery phase the shoulder of the onside arm is rotated forward to "coil" the body. During the power phase the torso is unwound.

Three types of wind and water resistance that can affect a craft are frontal, surface, and eddy resistance (figure 19-18). Frontal resistance occurs where the force of wind or water strikes a craft first. It exerts the greatest pressure against a boat. Surface resistance occurs when the wind or water slides along the craft. Eddy resistance is created when a craft displaces wind or water at its widest point. The resulting vacuum is filled in by an unstable whirl of displaced water. An understanding of these resistances helps paddlers determine which stroke to use in a given situation. For example, corrective strokes are most effective in the eddy resistance end. When paddling forward, the stern person can best steer the craft. When paddling backward, the bow person can best steer the craft.

Paddling Strokes

Power strokes

Forward. The forward stroke is used in solo and tandem canoeing and kayaking. For clarity, the forward canoe stroke is discussed separately from the kayak stroke.

In the catch position the body is wound tightly with the bottom, or shaft, arm reaching as far forward as possible. Both arms are relatively straight. The top, or control, arm is across the midline of the body to allow the paddle to be vertical in the water. The torso remains fairly upright, with no more than a 20-degree bend (figure 19-19). Lunging and straightening the back causes the canoe to bob in the water. The propulsion phase of the stroke involves unwinding the torso. The arms remain relatively straight, with the most movement occurring at the shoulder nearest the paddle as it unwinds like a spring. The power of the stroke occurs during the first 5 to 7 inches (13 to 18 cm). Thus, a short stroke with the recovery beginning when the paddle is beside the hip is important. During recovery, the blade should be angled to cut through the air like a knife to reduce air resistance.

The forward kayaking stroke involves a push-pull action against the paddle (figure 19-19). Paddlers punch out with their upper arm as the lower arm pulls back. Rotating the body with torso rotation, as in the forward canoe stroke, is also important. Exit and recovery begins when the lower hand reaches the hip. The paddle blade is removed from the water by lifting the wrist and elbow to shoulder level. This action promotes a clean exit and a quick recovery for the next stroke.

Common inefficiencies include failing to submerge the blade fully, leaning forward (lunging), making the stroke too long, and sweeping the blade in an arc rather than pulling vertically parallel to the keel line. Keeping a boat on a straight course requires timing and power, which may be elusive at first.

Back. The backstroke for canoes and kayaks retraces the forward stroke with the same body techniques. The catch position is just behind the hip nearest the blade and the power phase ends when the upper hand is near the shoulder. The back face of the paddle blade is used. Beginners should look over one shoulder to see where they are going.

Turning, lateral, and corrective strokes

J stroke. When using the forward stroke, a canoe will begin to veer off course to the soloist's or stern person's off paddling side. For this reason a corrective stroke is needed to keep the vessel on track. The J stroke (figure 19-20) is used for this. It is not a kayaking stroke.

The initial part of the J stroke, including the catch and beginning of the propulsion phase, resembles the forward stroke. A vertical paddle shaft and torso rotation are keys to success. However, as the paddle comes back to the hip, departure from the forward stroke begins. Rather than an immediate recovery, the paddle, or shaft, hand grasps the gunwale and simultaneously cups the shaft, creating an anchor point and a first-class lever. The top, or control hand, with the paddle shaft in a vertical position (blade under the boat), rotates the thumb downward to present the power face of the paddle to a vertical position, facing away from the canoe. In this position the paddler uses the

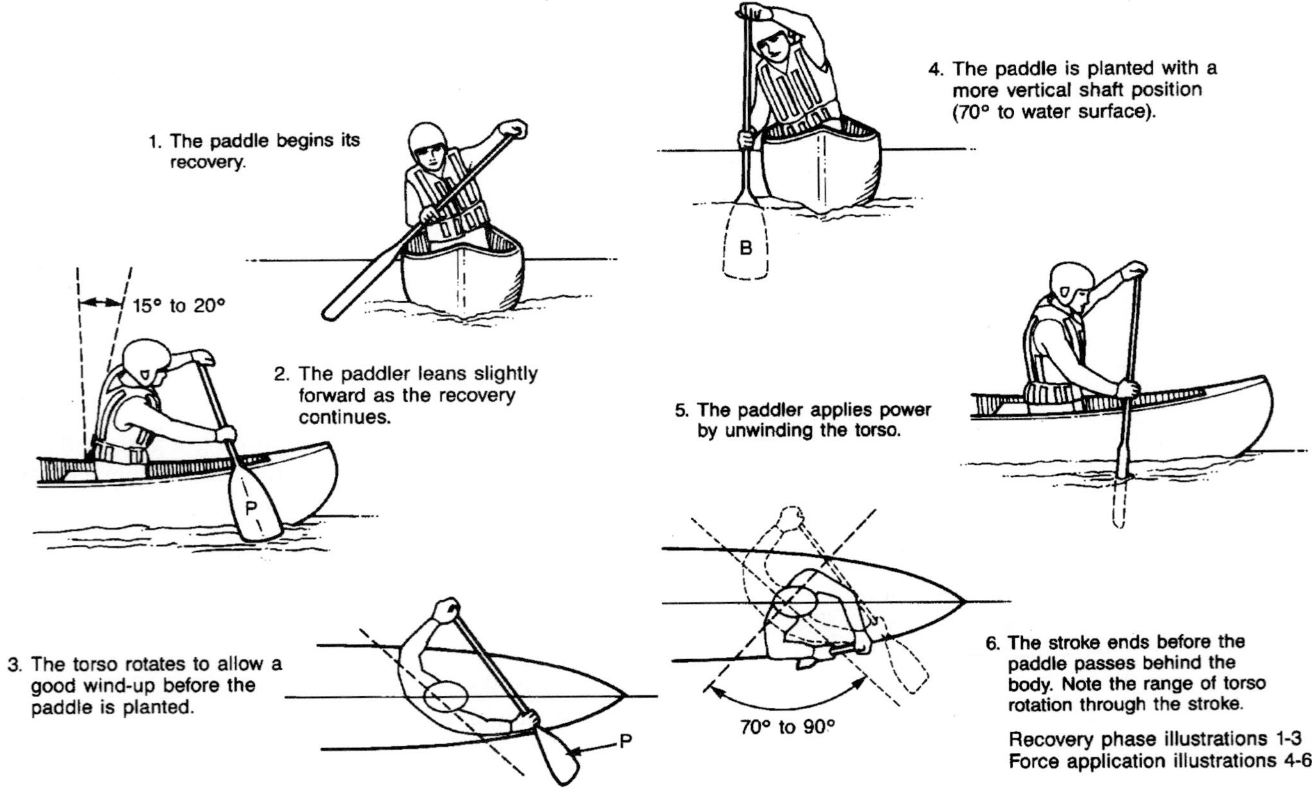

Figure 19-17. Torso rotation in forward stroke.

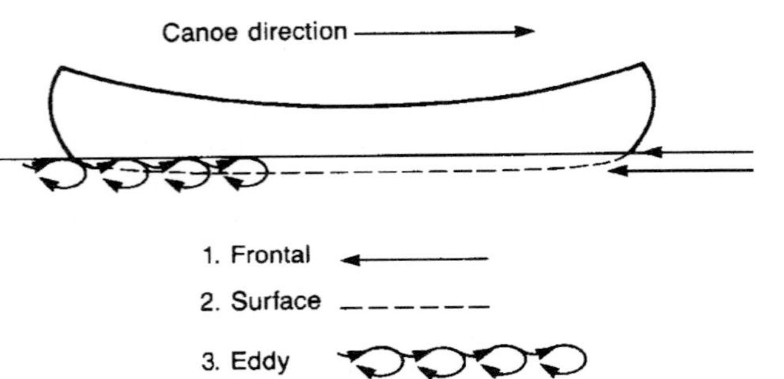

Figure 19-18. Three types of resistance.

control hand to curve the blade sideways away from the canoe, which corrects the veer and puts the canoe back on track.

This movement is rather quick yet powerful, allowing the paddler to keep an uninterrupted pace, or stroke rate. The use of the J stroke will vary according to factors such as solo or tandem paddling and strength/weight ratio of the tandem pair. Sometimes it is used every stroke in combination with the forward stroke; at other times it is used every two to four strokes. The trick is to gauge its use to anticipate and counteract the effects of veering.

Draw stroke. The draw stroke is used in canoeing and kayaking to move a boat laterally or to turn a boat, depending on the conditions under which it is applied. The basic draw stroke (figure 19-21) is performed at a right angle to the paddler's side. With the arms making a C shape and the paddle in a vertical position extended out and away from the boat, the paddle is inserted fully into the water. The boat is then pulled to the blade. Most of the force is provided by the lower, or shaft, arm as it pulls into the hip. The hip simultaneously is thrust toward the paddle blade, thereby moving the boat back under the paddler's center of gravity. The stroke ends with the blade parallel to and near the boat. The recovery is initiated with a backward slicing action of the blade above the water or a knifing action of the blade through the water back to the catch position.

Variations on the draw stroke include performing a stationary draw or a dynamic draw (several in a row). The stationary draw is used when the boat has built up some speed and the paddler wants to use one powerful stroke to shift the boat sideways to his or her onside or to initiate a turning action. The dynamic draw is used for lateral or turning maneuvers requiring continuous action or where the boat has no forward momentum. If the draw is used from midships, lateral movement will occur. If the paddler is posi-

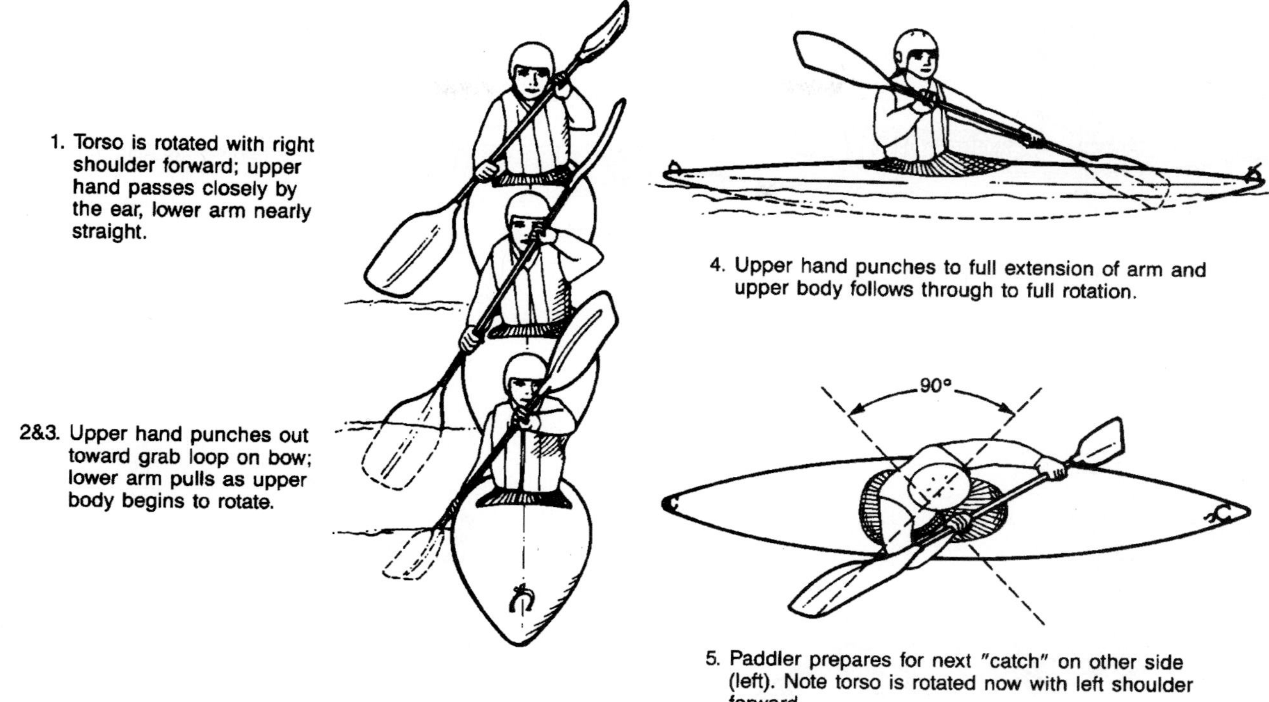

Figure 19-19. Forward stroke—kayak.

Figure 19-20. J stroke.

tioned fore or aft or lowers the top hand fore or aft, the draw can be used to turn the boat. Other variations of the draw stroke are bracing strokes and the Duffek stroke, which will be discussed later.

Cross draw. The cross draw (figure 19-22) requires the paddler to lift the paddle across the boat to the offside. The body and arms are twisted to face the offside. The top hand is kept stationary at or near the armpit. The paddling action is done entirely by the lower arm. The hand on the shaft is palm down. The grip palm faces forward. The power face of the paddle blade is in a vertical position and is pulled toward the bow. Recovery is above the water. The stroke is used as an alternate to the pry stroke. It is used to turn or move the canoe laterally. It may be used dynamically or from a static position.

Pry stroke. The pry, sometimes called the "push-away," moves the canoe in the opposite direction of the draw. It moves the boat to the paddler's offside and can be used to turn or move the boat laterally, depending on where the force is applied and whether the canoeist is paddling solo or in tandem. The pry is not a kayak stroke.

To execute the pry (figure 19-23), place the paddle in a vertical position with the shaft in contact with the gunwale. The bottom hand holds the paddle and simultaneously cups the gunwale to stabilize the paddle, making it a first-class lever. The top hand, knuckles out, pulls sideways toward the midline of the body. A short, quick, powerful action is used with the back face of the paddle used for the stroke. The recovery can be out of or through the water. In each case the paddle is knifed or sliced back to the catch position.

The pry can be used dynamically (several in a row) or singly. It can be used in combination with other strokes, such as a forward stroke into a pry.

Sweep strokes. Sweep strokes, as the name implies, are wide-sweeping arcs of the paddle. Solo sweeps in a canoe or kayak involve a 180-degree arc and are called "one-half sweeps" (figure 19-24). Tandem sweeps are intended to account for one's position in a boat and thus cover 90 degrees and are referred to as "one-fourth sweeps" (figure 19-25).

Unlike previous strokes in which the paddle was in a vertical position, the paddle position is low and angular.

Figure 19-21. Basic draw stroke.

Figure 19-22. Cross draw.

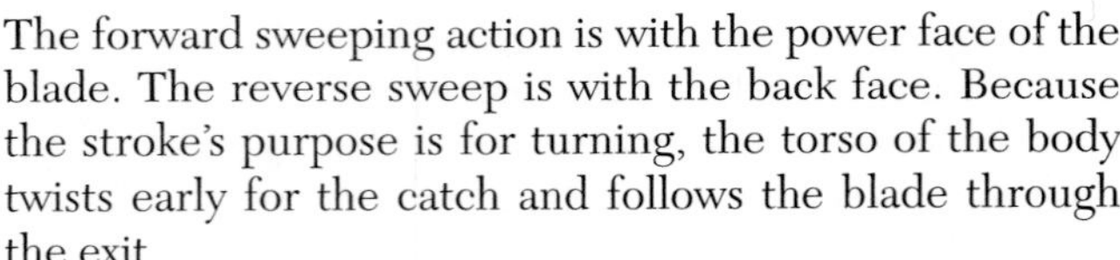

Figure 19-23. Pry stroke.

The forward sweeping action is with the power face of the blade. The reverse sweep is with the back face. Because the stroke's purpose is for turning, the torso of the body twists early for the catch and follows the blade through the exit.

When performed from a solo position at midships, a forward sweep enters at the 12 o'clock position and exits at the 6 o'clock position as the paddler follows with the torso, head, and arms until the shoulders are parallel to the keel line. The forward sweep turns the boat to the paddler's offside. The reverse sweep for a solo boater begins at the 6 o'clock position, ends at the 12 o'clock position, and turns the boat to the paddler's onside.

When paddling tandem, the bow paddler's arcs are from the 12 o'clock position to the 3 o'clock position (or to the 9 o'clock position). The stern paddler's strokes are from the 3 o'clock position (or the 9 o'clock position) to the 6 o'clock position. If the bow does a forward one-fourth sweep and the stern does a reverse one-fourth sweep, the canoe will turn in one direction. If the bow does a reverse one-fourth sweep and the stern does a forward one-fourth sweep, the boat will turn in the opposite direction.

Duffek. The Duffek stroke is a turning stroke. It was first used in kayaking, but it can be used in canoeing by a solo paddler or by the bow paddler when tandem canoeing. The purpose of the Duffek is to make a 180-degree turn to enter or exit currents and eddies or to turn behind a solid object, such as a dock or pier. Because the boat has forward momentum, a sweep stroke (forward or backward) is used to initiate the turn.

A left turn in kayaking, for example, would be initiated by a forward sweep on the right. The Duffek would then be executed on the turning side, or left side (figure 19-26). In many ways the Duffek is like the stationary draw. The paddle is vertical in the water. However, in the catch position the blade is opened until it broaches the current. The

Figure 19-24. One-half sweep.

Figure 19-25. One-fourth sweep.

wrists are cocked to present the power face of the paddle perpendicular to the boat. As the boat turns around the paddle, which is acting as a fulcrum, or anchor, the wrists uncock. Other important aspects of the Duffek are a turning of the torso so that one can see the stern at the beginning of the stroke. The top arm is also kept as low as possible (across the forehead). The lower arm is bent, relaxed, and extended slightly forward and over the boat. All of these factors are important to prevent shoulder dislocation. A cross Duffek, like a cross draw, can be executed in canoeing on the canoeist's offside.

Bracing strokes

High brace. Bracing strokes are used to right a vessel and prevent capsizing (figure 19-27). The high brace is a variation of the draw stroke. The power face of the blade is used on the water. Instead of drawing the boat to the paddle from a vertical position, there is more of an angle to the blade. This allows for part of the force to be applied in a downward direction, giving the paddler time to regain balance and reposition the CG inside the boat by thrusting the near hips toward the paddle and moving the boat back within one's base.

Low brace. The low brace is used in canoeing and kayaking to lean the boat into turns and to correct an impending capsizing (figure 19-28). In the low brace, lay the back face of the paddle flat in the water behind the hips. The position of the knuckles of both the grip and shaft hands is down. The elbow of the shaft hand is above the paddle. From the entry position, the blade is simultaneously pushed down and swept to the side, perpendicular to the boat. A quick push down on the paddle will cause the boat to roll to the opposite side, allowing the paddler to regain balance. In an extreme crisis the head and torso can be put into the water and the boat brought around the knees and hips (hip flip). The body is brought back aboard (over the vessel) only at the end of the recover, just as in an Eskimo roll.

Eskimo roll. The Eskimo roll is an advanced maneuver used mostly in turbulent whitewater conditions. Because the potential for danger always exists, the Eskimo roll should be learned carefully in calm water first. The Eskimo roll, or modified C-to-C roll, is a two-part process using a sweep stroke combined with a hip snap (figure 19-29). The forward sweep brings the paddler's body from under the boat and up to the water's surface in a C position. Then the lower body can snap the boat upright with a hip snap (a high brace maneuver) to the second C position.

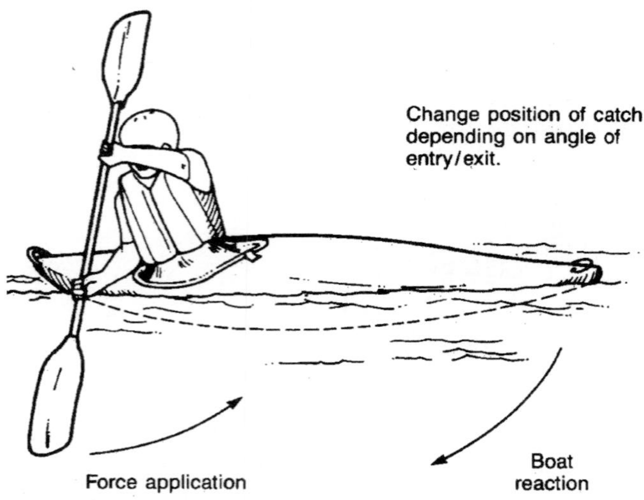

Figure 19-26. Duffek stroke.

Calm-Water Practice of Maneuvers

Boat maneuvers in ponds, lakes, and slow-moving rivers involve moving in a straight line, moving sideways, spins, and U turns (figure 19-30). Each involves one or more of the strokes previously discussed. The choice of a stroke is often dependent on whether one is in a canoe or a kayak and whether one is paddling solo or tandem.

Spins

Spins are discussed first because they can be taught to a group of people and executed under various practice conditions while allowing the group to remain in one place. Spins, full or partial, are used when moving around a bend in a river or positioning around another object, such as a boat or a dock.

From a kayak or from a solo position in a canoe, a forward one-half sweep will turn the bow to the offside of the stroke. A reverse one-half sweep will move the bow to the onside of the stroke. From a tandem paddling position, several combinations of strokes will spin the canoe. If both people draw, the canoe will turn to the onside (figure 19-31A). If both paddlers pry, the canoe will turn to the offside. If the bow paddler executes a forward one-fourth sweep while the stern does a reverse one-fourth sweep, the canoe will spin to the offside (figure 19-31B). If the bow does a reverse one-fourth sweep and the stern does a forward one-fourth sweep, the canoe will spin to the outside.

Moving sideways

Moving laterally in a canoe or kayak is helpful to pull up beside another boat or the shore or to move sideways to

Figure 19-27. High brace.

Figure 19-28. Low brace.

avoid an object, such as a rock or branch in the water (figures 19-32 and 19-33).

In kayak or solo canoe paddling, drawing to the right or left from midships will move the boat sideways in the direction of the onside, or paddling side (figure 19-34). Use of a pry or cross draw will move the boat to the offside (figure 19-35). In tandem paddling, the use of opposite strokes (draw/pry) will move the boat sideways (figure 19-36).

Moving in a straight line

Moving in a straight line (or tracking) is most often the intent of paddling. Going forward is the obvious choice because it is the most powerful and efficient stroke. Also, you can see where you are going!

In a kayak, forward movement occurs with the power stroke on alternate sides (figure 19-37). Remembering that the boat and paddle are bilaterally symmetrical, equal amounts of force should be applied on each side to enhance going straight ahead. In a solo canoe the J stroke is preferred to go forward. Sometimes a C stroke is used, which is in essence a draw moving directly into a J stroke. Both C and J strokes prevent a canoe from veering to the paddler's offside (figure 19-38). When tandem canoeing, the bow person uses a forward power stroke. The stern paddler uses a forward stroke with a J or forward one-fourth sweep as needed to keep the boat moving in a straight line (figure 19-39).

At times one may also want to go backward—for example, backing away from shore, another boat, or from danger.

In a kayak one uses a backstroke on alternating sides (figure 19-40). In a solo canoe one uses a backstroke in combination with a reverse J because the steering is now done at the bow (eddy) end of the canoe (figure 19-41). In tandem paddling the stern person does the backstroke, while the bow person steers with a reverse J (figure 19-42).

U-turns

A U-turn (an abrupt 180-degree turn) in flat-water paddling, though not an essential skill, can be taught to develop proficiency in using combinations of strokes. However, the value of a U-turn becomes apparent when you need to stop behind a rock (eddy turn) or reenter the current (peel out).

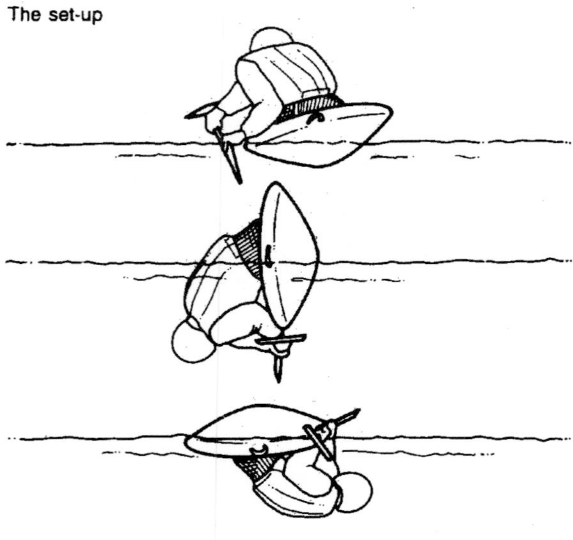

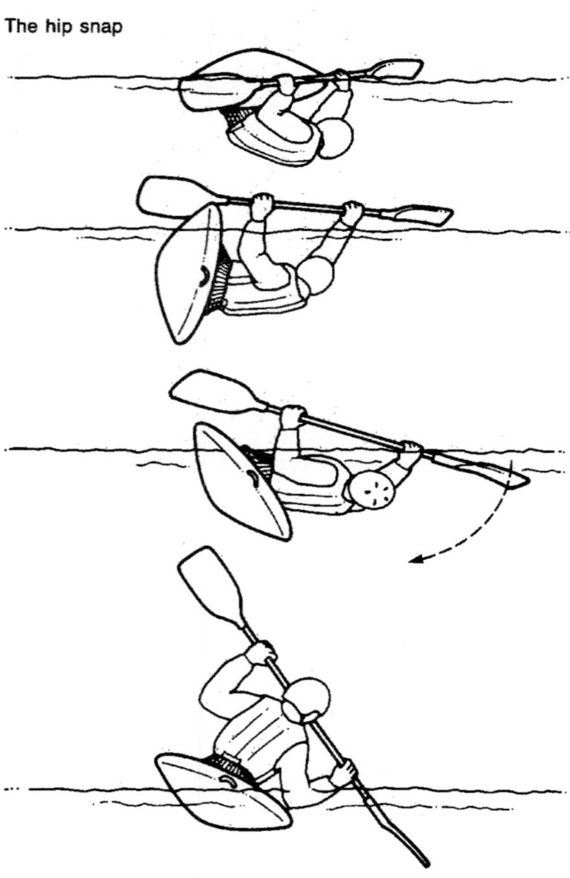

Figure 19-29. Eskimo roll.

Figure 19-30. Learning stroke technique on a flatwater pond.

In a kayak, a U-turn is done with a sweep on the outside to initiate the turn and carry the momentum forward. Then a Duffek is executed on the inside of the turn. In solo canoe paddling, the choice of strokes depends on the side of the turn. To turn to the onside, combine a reverse sweeping low brace and follow with a Duffek and forward stroke (figure 19-43). To turn to the offside, combine a forward stroke followed by a cross Duffek (figure 19-44). In tandem paddling, to turn to the onside the stern uses forward one-fourth sweeps while the bow uses a Duffek followed by a forward stroke. To turn to the offside, the stern uses a reverse sweeping low brace while the bow uses a cross Duffek followed by a cross forward stroke (figure 19-45).

Possible Errors and Corrections

Possible Errors	**Corrections**
Canoe veers to the stern paddler's offside.	Stern paddler must make a more effective J stroke—paddle blade must be vertical at the end of the stroke, and the blade must push the water sideways away from the canoe.
Canoe gradually turns in a sweeping curve.	Make sure in the power paddling strokes that the paddle is held vertically and that the paddle follows a straight pathway back rather than the curved path of the gunwale line.
Path of the canoe makes an S pattern through the water.	Anticipate changes of direction, don't overcorrect in one direction or the other.
Canoe appears to bob up and down in the water.	Entry and exit of the paddle stroke must be corrected—avoid reaching too far forward and pushing down on the water and pulling up at the end of the stroke while lifting water.

(continued on p. 291)

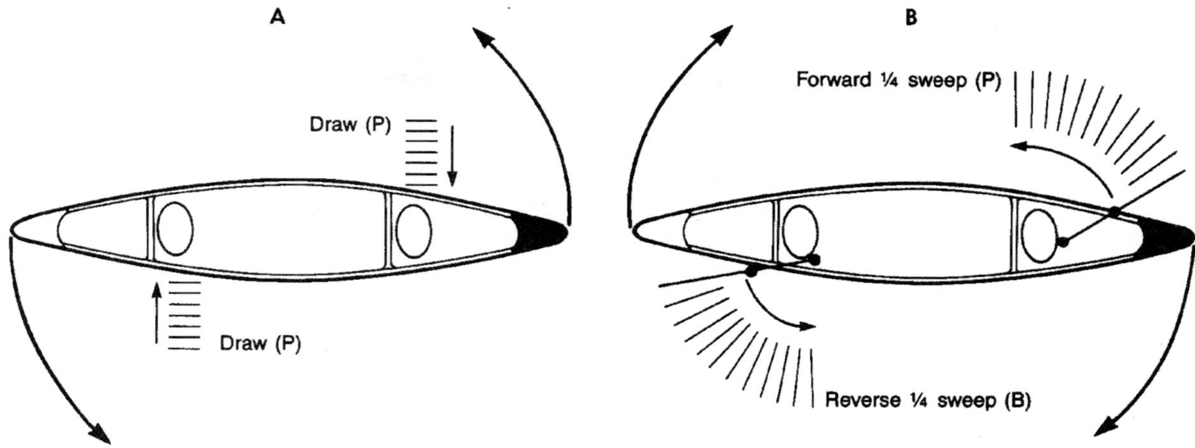

Figure 19-31. Spins.

Figure 19-32. Canoeists using proper ferry technique to run laterally across the river.

Figure 19-33. Sideslipping technique allows canoeists to negotiate rock formations.

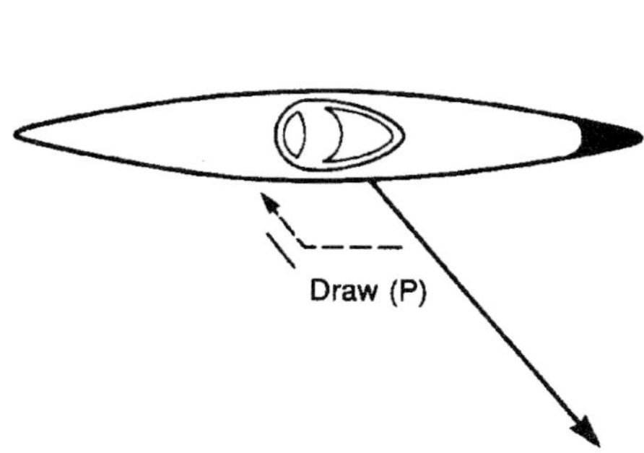

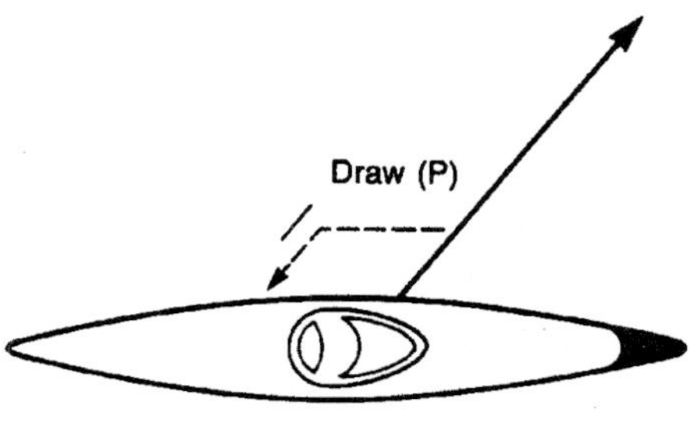

Figure 19-34. Moving sideways by drawing.

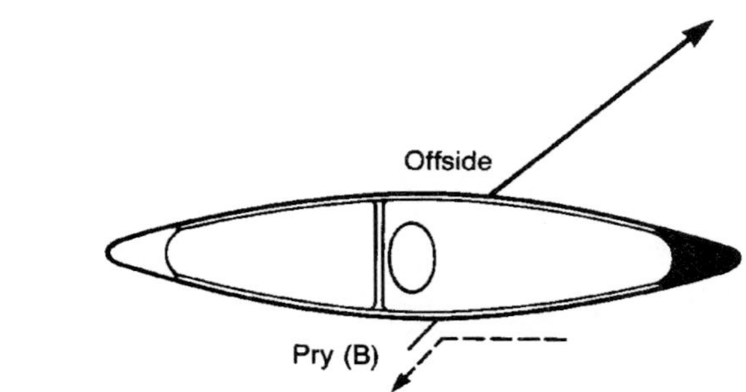

Figure 19-35. Moving sideways using a pry.

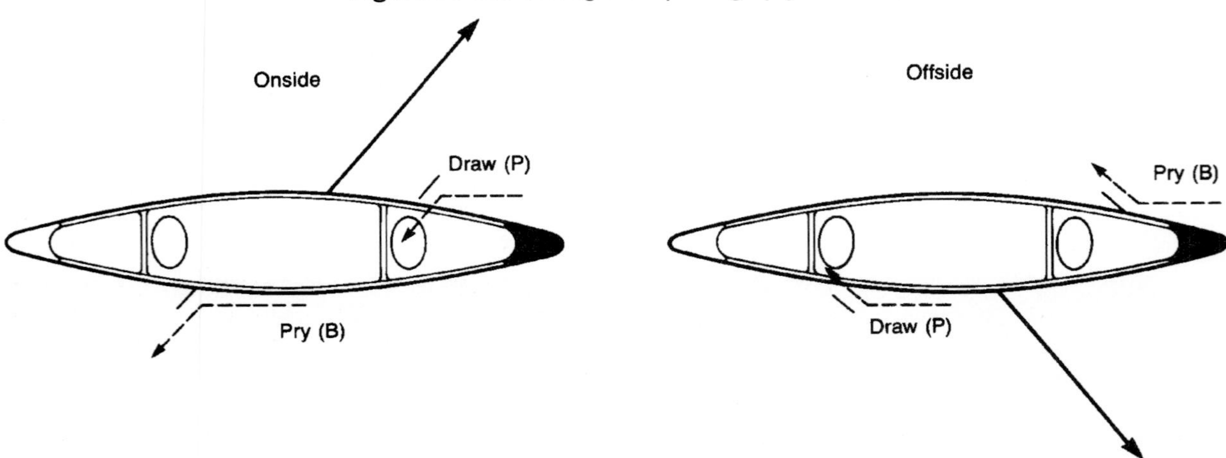

Figure 19-36. Moving sideways in tadem paddling.

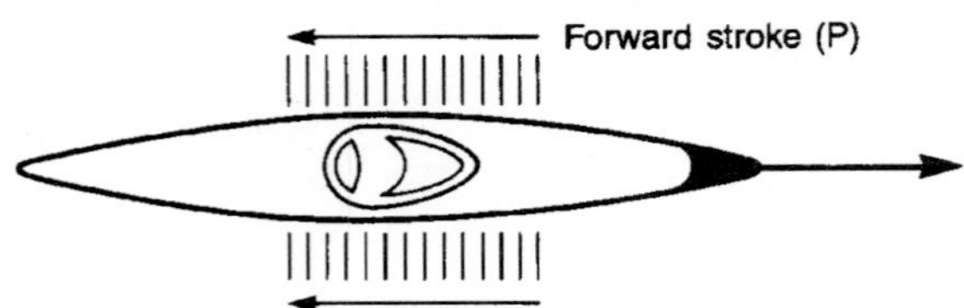

Figure 19-37. Moving forward in a kayak.

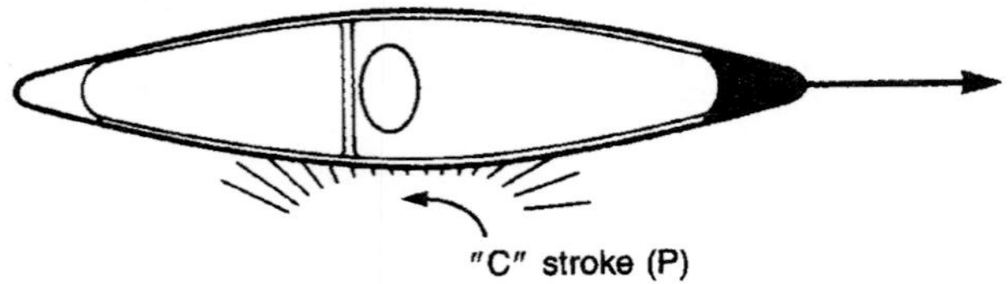

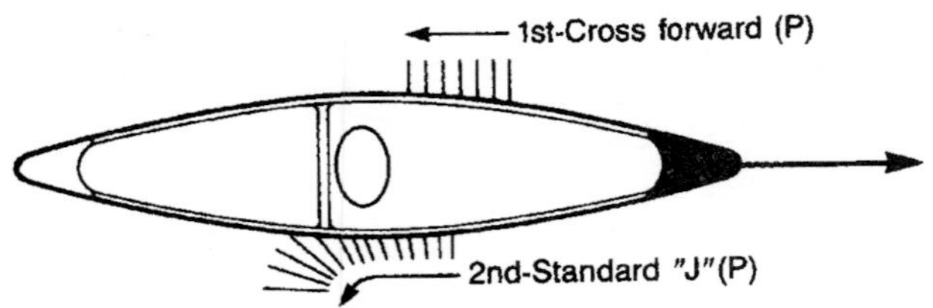

Figure 19-38. Moving forward when solo in a canoe.

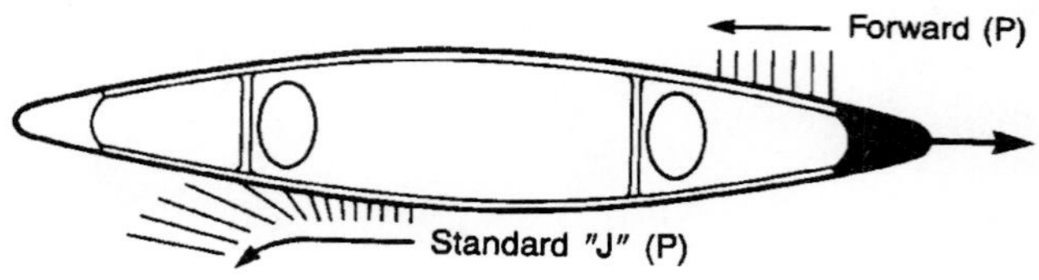

Figure 19-39. Moving forward when tandem in a canoe.

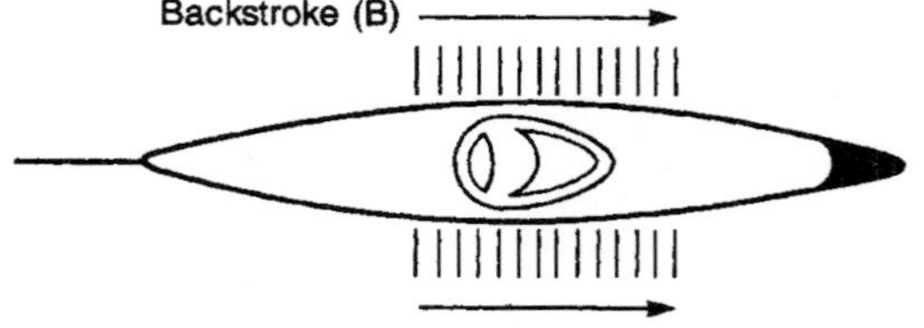

Figure 19-40. Moving backward in a kayak.

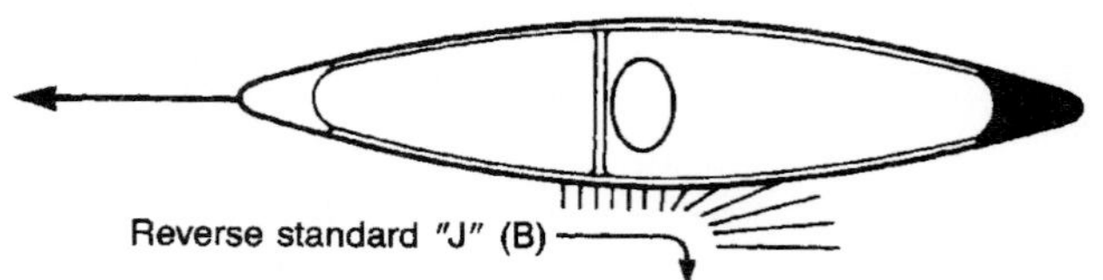

Figure 19-41. Moving backward when solo in a canoe.

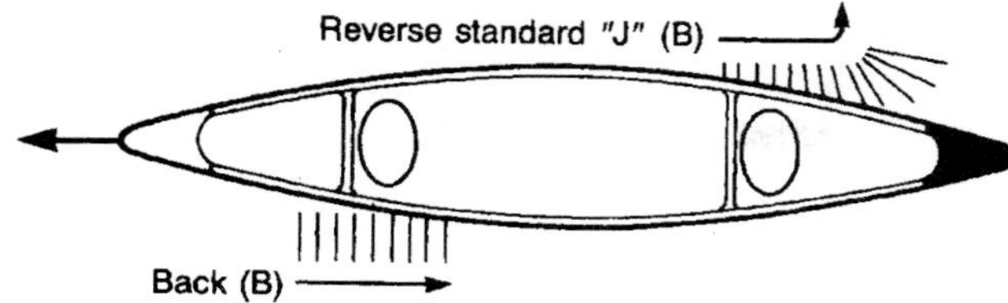

Figure 19-42. Moving backward when tandem in a canoe.

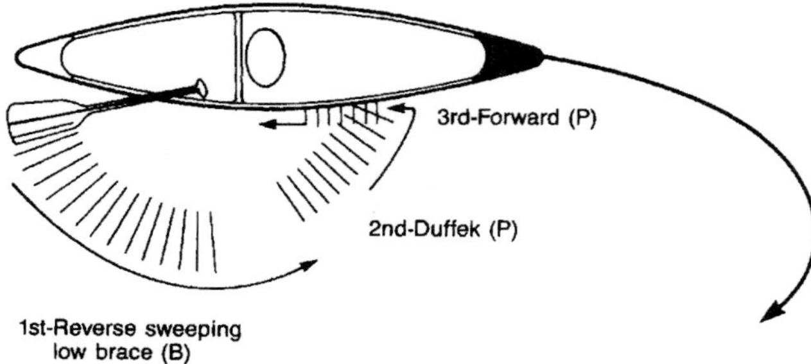

Figure 19-43. Onside U-turn.

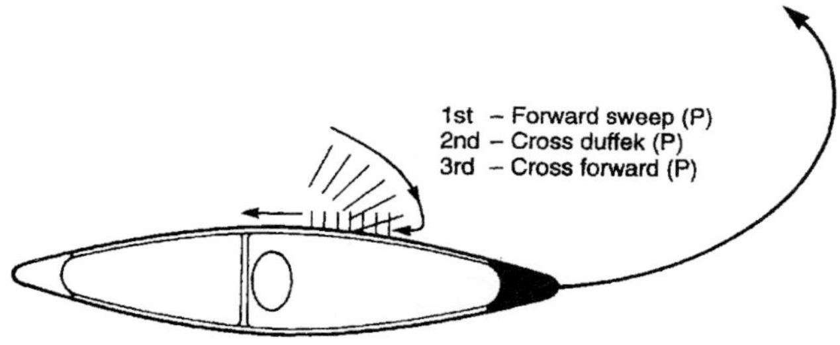

Figure 19-44. Offside U-turn.

Possible Errors	Corrections
Turning strokes are ineffective, resulting in slow turns.	Make sure that the draw and pry strokes are done with the paddle vertical in the water—the paddle must push/pull the water directly sideways.
Ferry maneuvers are ineffective.	Paddlers must establish a proper angle to the river current and flow of the water—maintain a slight angle in the direction of movement.
Eddy turns are ineffective.	Paddlers must enter the turn with proper speed, at a 45-degree angle, and lean into the turn.
Peel-outs are ineffective.	The bow of the canoe must re-enter the downstream current, the appropriate Duffek maneuver must be made in the downstream current, and paddlers must lean into the turn.

Rescue

Principles of rescue

Swamping or capsizing a canoe or kayak on flat water may be caused by wind, waves, wake from powerboats, a paddler's poor balance, or improper trim from improper loading. If a boat does capsize, paddlers must evaluate the situation and determine a course of action. The following guidelines should be observed:

1. Alert other boaters that your boat has capsized.
2. Victims should initiate self-rescue procedures immediately and be ready to accept assistance from others.
3. Other paddlers can assist in the rescue when it is safe to do so.
4. Paddlers not involved in the rescue should keep their distance and continually evaluate the rescue in the event that more help is needed.

There are rescue priorities to help reduce confusion in a potentially hazardous situation. The first priority is saving the paddler in the water. Once in the water, the paddler should initiate self-rescue procedures. Paddlers of decked boats should attempt an Eskimo roll. Once boaters are out of their craft, they should swim to safety if danger exists. If a paddler has a partner, he or she should establish visual and voice contact. Capsized paddlers, after assessing the situation, may elect to stay with their boat and attempt to get back into it using procedures described later. They may choose to swim with their equipment to shore if it is close enough. Boats and other equipment should be rescued only when it is safe to do so.

The second priority in rescue operations is recovering the swamped boat. Paddlers can try a self-rescue of the boat or, when the other paddlers are available, use group rescue techniques.

The third priority in rescue operations is obtaining other equipment. Objects such as shoes, gear bags, and coolers should be tied in loosely in flat-water situations. They will then bob in the water until paddlers are safe and the boat has been righted. Equipment can then be brought on board again.

Self-rescue

Paddlers can rescue a swamped craft in deep water without assistance from other boats using a Capistrano flip or a shake-out technique. The Capistrano flip is accomplished by ducking under the capsized canoe and coming up in the air pocket. In unison, the paddlers use a scissors kick and a forceful lifting action to one side to push the craft above the water and roll it upright. A shake-out is done while the boat remains upright. One paddler pushes down on an end of the canoe while also pushing forward. The end must then be lifted before the water flows back in. Another way to accomplish the shake-out is to rock the canoe from side to side and then quickly pull up on the gunwale before

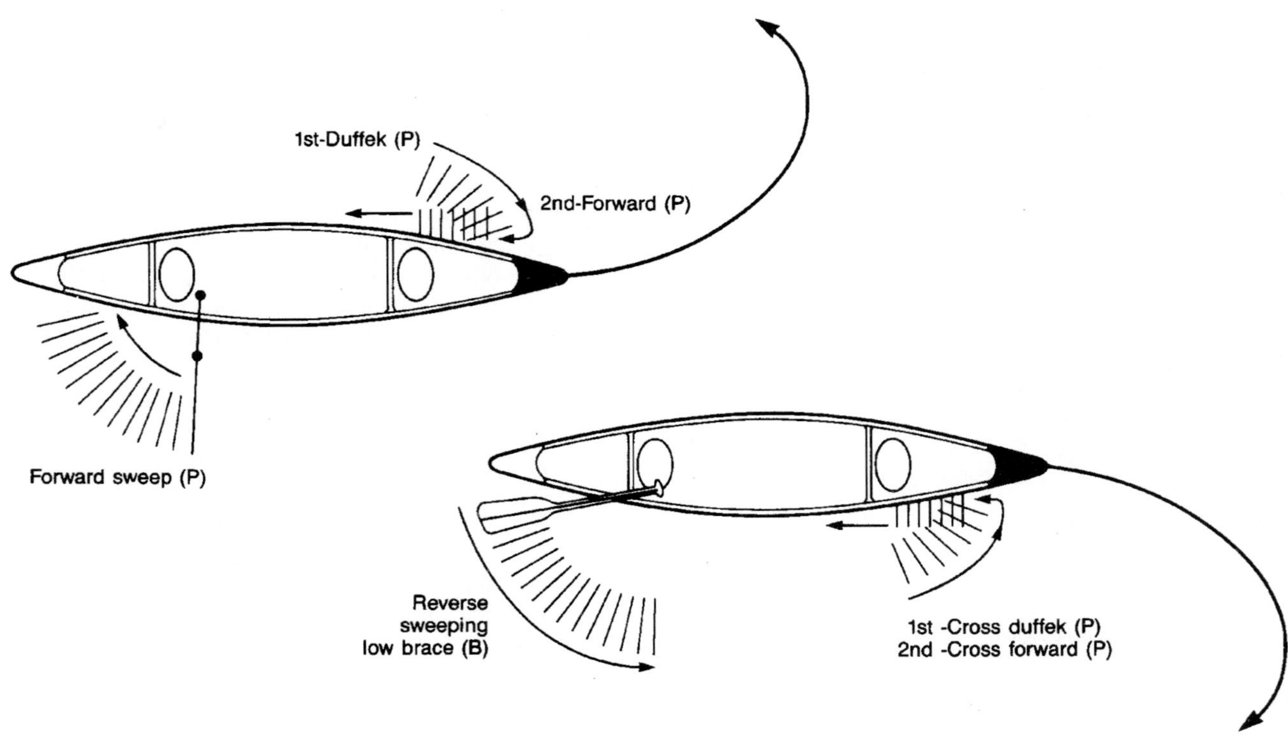

Figure 19-45. Tandem canoe U-turns.

water flows back in. These techniques rarely get all the water out of the canoe. The paddler then must decide what to do with the partially submerged boat. The choices are to reenter the boat and paddle to shore or to bail the boat to empty it further. Swamped boats can be paddled, though progress is slow and unbalanced.

Group rescue

Where other boats are available to assist in the rescue, the process changes. Swimming paddlers move to a position where they can help. This may be at the end of the overturned boat, where they can push, or at the ends of the rescue boat, where they can stabilize. With the boat upside down and perpendicular to the rescue boat, one end is lifted and pulled over the craft. The tipped craft is moved up and over the rescue craft until it is balanced, rolled upright, and slid back into the water (figure 19-46). The boat is then moved into position beside the rescue craft and held so that the swimmers can reenter the craft.

Figure 19-46. Group rescue.

SAFETY

Canoeing and kayaking are challenging, adventurous activities with inherent risks. Therefore, it is important to develop an awareness of safety and develop skills that promote safe paddling. Risks in boating cannot be eliminated, but they can be managed to an acceptable level. It is highly recommended that instructors be certified to teach canoeing and/or kayaking by an organization and that participants enroll in certified courses.

The recent increase in popularity of canoeing and kayaking has brought with it an increase in accidents and fatalities. Much can be learned from accident reports compiled by the U.S. Coast Guard. They reveal that most accidents are the result of ignorance. The majority of small-craft fatalities involve unknowledgeable, inexperienced boaters. Accident reports indicate five common problems.

1. Paddlers are often not wearing lifejackets, which are either forgotten or used for other purposes, such as padding, sitting on, or kneeling on.
2. Cold water or cold weather is present. Hypothermia inhibits reasoning abilities, including the ability to paddle effectively, and the ability to self-rescue.
3. Most victims are inexperienced, having had no formal instruction or practice.
4. Alcohol is a contributing factor. Drugs and alcohol affect coordination and judgment. Slow response time and poor decisions in hazardous conditions make accidents predictable.
5. Victims often cannot swim. The ability to be at ease in or around water increases the ability to perform well in stressful situations.

INTERNATIONAL SCALE OF RIVER DIFFICULTY

The American Whitewater Affiliation's International Scale of River Difficulty is a useful tool to determine the severity of sections in a river. These guidelines offer a general classification for rivers, but be aware that the system is not exact. Rivers do not always fit neatly into the various classifications. Regional interpretations of the classification system can create misunderstandings. In addition, if rapids on a river generally fit into one of the following classifications, but the water temperature is below 50°F or the trip is an extended trip in a wilderness area, the river should be considered one class more difficult than normal.

There is no substitute for a cautious approach to rivers with which a paddler is unfamiliar.

Moving water has three classifications:

1. Class A—Flowing under 2 mph
2. Class B—2 to 4 mph
3. Class C—Greater than 4 mph

Whitewater has six classifications:

Class I: Easy

- Few obstructions—all obvious and easily missed.
- Fast-moving water with riffles and small waves.
- Risk to swimmers is slight.
- Self-rescue is easy.

Class II: Novice

- Straightforward rapids with wide, clear channels that are obvious without scouting.
- Occasional maneuvering may be required, but rocks and medium-size waves are missed easily by trained paddlers.
- Swimmers are seldom injured, and group assistance, while helpful, is seldom needed.

Class III: Intermediate

- Rapids with moderate, irregular waves that can be difficult to avoid and capable of swamping an open canoe.
- Complex maneuvers in fast current, and frequent narrow passages requiring good boat control.
- Large waves, holes, and strainers might be present but are easily avoided.
- Strong eddies and powerful current effects can be found, particularly on large-volume rivers.
- Scouting is advisable for inexperienced parties.
- Chances of injury while swimming is low, but group assistance may be required to avoid long swims.

Class IV: Advanced

- Intense, powerful rapids requiring precise boat handling in turbulent water.
- Depending upon the character of the river, there may be long unavoidable waves and holes or constricted passages demanding fast maneuvers under pressure.
- A fast, reliable eddy turn may be needed to negotiate the drop, scout rapids, or rest.
- Rapids may require "must" moves above dangerous hazards.
- Scouting is necessary the first time.
- Risk of injury to swimmers is moderate to high, and water conditions can make rescue difficult.
- Group assistance is often essential but requires practiced skills.
- A strong Eskimo roll is highly recommended.

Class V: Expert

- Extremely long, obstructed, or violent rapids that expose the paddler to above-average risk of injury.
- Drops may contain very large, unavoidable waves and holes or steep, congested chutes with complex, demanding routes.
- Rapids often continue for long distances between pools or eddies, demanding a high level of fitness.
- What eddies exist may be small, turbulent, or difficult to reach.
- Several of these factors may be combined at the high end of this class.
- Scouting is mandatory.
- Rescue is extremely difficult even for experts.
- A very reliable Eskimo roll and above-average rescue skills are essential.

Class VI: Almost Impossible

- Difficulties of Class V are carried to the limits of navigability.
- Nearly impossible and very dangerous.
- Risks are high and rescue may be impossible.
- For teams of experts only at favorable water levels, after close study and with all precautions.
- The frequency with which a rapids run should have no effect on this rating, as there are a number of Class VI rapids that are regularly attempted.

TEACHING CONSIDERATIONS

1. Always consider the teaching site. Pools, ponds, lakes, and calm places in a river are acceptable. Make sure the site will be free from such distractions as loud noises and groups of other people and free from the danger of trees, branches, debris, broken glass, or other objects.
2. Initial instruction can occur onshore or at the side of the water or pool. It is then possible to work on technique with the paddle and walk about freely to give feedback to people who need correction.
3. Use visuals—such as miniature boats and paddles, charts, or mock drawings of boats in the sand—to help illustrate points about stroke technique and maneuvers.
4. Move from simple to complex. Boats can actually be paddled by hand to see the action and reaction of strokes on water. With this simple understanding, paddles can be added early and you can then proceed with more-complex drills.
5. Teach spins and turning strokes first so the group can stay close to you. Then teach power and bracing strokes when the group has beginning control and knowledge of the paddle.
6. Teach and refine for good technique and stroke mechanics. For example, if a stroke is intended to turn the boat, it must be applied away from the center at an angle that creates torque. If a stroke is intended to propel a boat in a straight line (forward, backward, or sideways), the paddle must be vertical in the water and pulled in a line opposite the intended motion.
7. Allow students to gain expertise paddling on one side or position before asking them to change. Then, to create versatile paddlers, encourage them to transfer their learning to paddle on the opposite side, to change positions (bow to stern), to paddle with a different person, and to switch from tandem to solo paddling.
8. After students have learned strokes and simple maneuvers, develop drills in which they have to respond automatically. For example, have them respond to verbal commands to turn right, turn left, sideslip right, sideslip left. Mix the commands so their responses become second nature.
9. Move from simple singular maneuvers to combining several maneuvers. Make up a course on a flat-water pond, lake, or river using obstacles such as bleach bottles or milk carton buoys to be negotiated. For example, enter the vessel, sideslip away from shore, paddle forward, turn left around a bend (obstacle), back up, go between two rocks (obstacles), turn right, paddle forward, etc.
10. Move from a more controlled obstacle course to a natural setting where students negotiate moving between two rocks, around a tree or bend, laterally beside a dock, and so on.
11. Learn all strokes and maneuvers on flat water before proceeding to moving water.
12. Help students to learn to read river signs in a classroom setting before encountering them on the water. For example, upstream and downstream Vs, strainers, hydraulics, standing waves should all be discussed before practicing on a river.
13. Practice map and compass reading and discuss trip-planning procedures before going on any day trips.
14. Practice safety and rescue procedures along with a paddling sequence. For example, paddle out with another boat and have one capsize (stay near shore). Follow rescue procedures and then paddle back to shore.
15. Instructors should be certified to be aware of standards of practice.
16. If having enough boats is a problem (one boat for every two students), consult local outfitters, YMCAs, canoe clubs, etc. They are often willing to help.

GLOSSARY

amidships The area midway between the bow and stern. Often shortened to "midships."

astern Behind the canoe, kayak, or other craft.

back paddle Paddling backward to slow or check forward motion.

bail To remove water from a craft.

bar An accumulation of sand, gravel, or rock, usually located along the inside bend of a river.

beam The width of a craft measured at its widest point.

blade The broad, flat section of a paddle.

bow The area in the forward end of a watercraft.

bow person Person who tandem paddles from the bow, front thwart, or front seat.

bracing stroke Paddle stroke providing stability against the capsizing force of a lateral current. May also be used for turning.

broach To turn a craft broadside to oncoming waves or obstructions.

capsize To overturn.

closed boat Boats having the deck as an integral part of the craft.

combination stroke A blended stroke maneuver consisting of two or more simple strokes.

confluence The point where two or more rivers flow together.

control hand The upper hand on a canoe paddle, which controls turning of the paddle blade.

cross draw A stroke used to move the canoe, or part of the canoe, to the paddler's normal offside.

current General movement of water in a river caused by gradient differentials.

deck On a traditional open canoe, the triangular piece found at bow and stern to which the gunwales attach at their ends; often called "deck plates." On a closed canoe or kayak, a covering for the entire hull.

double blade Paddle with a blade at each end; usually used in a kayak and sometimes in an open or decked canoe.

downstream V A clear deep-water path for canoes or kayaks to negotiate through between two rocks.

draw stroke A paddle stroke designed to move the craft to the onside of the paddler or toward the power face of the blade.

Duffek stroke A high bracing stroke first used in the kayak by Milovan Duffek of Czechoslovakia. Using mainly to enter or leave an eddy as an eddy turn (entering) or a peel-out (leaving).

eddy Place where the current either stops or moves upstream below obstructions and on the inside of bends.

eddy turn A dynamic technique used by boaters to enter an eddy.

feather Returning the paddle to the "catch" position (ready for a propulsive action) with one edge leading, thus reducing resistance by water or air.

flotation Material placed in a canoe to keep it floating high when upset or swamped.

forward stroke The standard propulsion stroke used in paddling a canoe directly ahead. Also called "basic forward" or "power forward."

freeboard The shortest distance from the waterline to the top of the gunwale of a canoe or to the seamline of any decked boat.

gunwale Strips along the top of a canoe's sides, extending from bow to stern, where the deck and topsides meet.

hull The frame, or body, of a craft, exclusive of rigging and flotations systems.

hydraulic A water formation caused by a sudden drop of the river over a dam, rock, or ledge, causing an upstream current on the surface of the water, which tends to hold or spin boats.

hypothermia A serious, life-threatening physical condition caused by a lowering of the body's core temperature.

inside bank In a river bend, the edge of the river with the slower, shallower water.

inverted J A reverse J stroke, used by the tandem bow or solo paddler when canoeing in reverse.

J stroke Stroke used by tandem stern or solo paddler to correct the characteristic swing of the craft to the offside when only a forward stroke is used.

K-1 A kayak with one paddler who sits on his or her buttocks, keeps the legs extended forward, and uses a double-bladed paddle.

keel A thin projecting strip of material running down the exact center of the outer hull of a craft from bow to stern.

lee, leeward, leeway A protected area downwind or downstream of an obstruction that breaks the normal direction and force of the wind or water. Leeward means "downwind." Leeway means "the drift of a boat downwind."

life vest Personal buoyancy device that is worn like a vest; provides upper-body protection and warmth. Also called a "PFD" (personal flotation device).

low brace Brace stroke in which the entire paddle is nearly flat on the surface of the water.

mouth Area where a river joins another body of water.

nonpower face The face of a paddle blade opposite the power face.

offside Side of the canoe on which the paddler is not usually paddling.

paddle The tool used to propel the boat in the desired direction.

painter A length of rope attached to an end of a canoe.

pillow A smooth bulge on the river's surface created by water flowing over an underwater obstruction.

port The left side of a craft when facing toward the bow.

portage The act of carrying a canoe and gear around an obstacle. Also, the place where the canoe has to be taken from the water and carried on land around an obstruction or dangerous spot in the river.

power face The face of the paddle blade that bears against the water.

pry A type of stroke that uses the craft as a fulcrum to move the boat away from the blade.

recovery The component of a stroke preparing for the next propulsive action.

rocker The upward sweep of the keel line toward both ends of a canoe.

ruddering Holding the paddle blade stationary in the water at a fixed angle to steer.

scull, sculling To propel or align a craft by moving a paddle side to side in a continuous figure-eight pattern using the same power face throughout.

sideslipping Situation in which a canoe's center of gravity continues in the initial direction of movement even though the boat is turning.

skirt Garment worn around the waist of closed-boat paddlers. It attaches around the coaming (a raised frame to keep out water) to make the cockpit water tight.

standing wave A wave formed at a right angle to the flow of the current. Usually occurs in several sets and most often indicates a deep-water channel.

starboard The right side of a craft when facing the bow.

stem The curved section at the ends of a canoe that slices through the water when paddling forward or backward.

stern The rear section of a watercraft.

strainer A solid object in the water (such as a fallen tree) that allows the water to pass but prevents boats and people from continuing down stream.

swamp When a canoe fills with water but does not capsize.

sweep canoe The last canoe in a group, usually containing experienced paddlers, extra equipment, rescue lines, and a first-aid kit.

sweep stroke A wide, shallow stroke used for turning or pivoting the canoe.

tandem Two paddlers in a canoe.

throat The flare of the paddler's shaft where it starts to form the blade.

thwart Cross braces, running from gunwale to gunwale, which provide reinforcement for the gunwales. Also known as a "spreader" or "crossbar."

track Paddling in a straight line.

trim The manner in which a canoe rides on the water.

through The low point, or hollow, found between the crests of two standing waves.

tumblehome The inward-curving upper portion of a canoe that produces a narrowing of the beam at the deck level.

upstream VA single rock in the river that deflects water to both sides of the downstream current, creating a current differential behind which is often created an eddy pool.

yoke A cushioned shoulder harness that clamps to the gunwales of a canoe permitting the canoe to be carried upside down on the paddler's shoulders.

SUGGESTED READINGS

Bechdel, L., and Ray, S. 1989. *River rescue.* 2d ed. Boston: Appalachian Mountain Club. Focuses on safety and rescue techniques. A must for those intending to paddle whitewater.

Burch, D. 1993. *Fundamentals of kayak navigation.* 2d ed. Old Saybrook, Conn.: Glove Pequot. A definitive work on ocean navigation in small boats. Covers navigation fundamentals, potential risks posed by natural events in the coastal environment, and consequences of self-propulsion limitations.

David, J. 1988. *Sea kayaking.* 3d ed. Seattle: University of Washington Press. This comprehensive manual goes beyond techniques and equipment to give a thorough analysis of navigation, weather, ocean currents, tides, storms, rescues, survival situations, and expedition planning.

Evans, E., and Evans, J. 1988. *The kayaking book.* New York: Viking Press. Traces the history of the sport and includes information on kayaking in all types of water.

Ford, K. 1995. *Kayaking.* Springfield, Va.: American Canoe Association. Beautifully photographed, clearly illustrated, and well written. For beginning students in both whitewater and coastal kayaking.

Foster, T., and Kelly, K. 1995. *Catch every eddy, surf every wave.* Springfield, Va.: American Canoe Association. A thorough explanation of the concepts that are the backbone of contemporary whitewater paddling, including playboating.

Gullion, L. 1987. *Canoeing and kayaking: Instruction manual.* Newington, Va.: American Canoe Association. This instruction manual for certified canoe and kayak instructors is a must for anyone planning to instruct others.

Gullion, L. 1994. *Canoeing.* Springfield, Va.: American Canoe Association. Elaborate photographs and illustrations. An ideal introduction to quietwater canoeing.

Gullion, L. 1996. *Kayak and canoe games.* Springfield, Va.: American Canoe Association. Starts with lighthearted paddling games and adds suggestions to develop additional games that build solid skills, knowledge, and excitement while maintaining safety.

Price, B. 1991. *Fundamentals of coastal kayaking: Manual for instructors.* Springfield, Va.: American Canoe Association. The ACA's instruction manual for kayaking on open and coastal waters, from the Great Lakes to the Florida Keys.

Ray, S. 1992. *The canoe handbook.* Harrisburg, Pa.: Stackpole Books. Begins with a clear, thoughtful discussion on the basic hydrology, currents, and behavior of rivers, followed by paddling techniques, maneuvers, boats, equipment, and safety.

Rowe, R. 1993. *White water kayaking.* Harrisburg, Pa.: Stackpole Books. A concise, comprehensive, clear guide to everything you need to know for whitewater kayaking technique and river running. Especially good for beginners.

Seidman, D. 1992. *The essential sea kayaker.* Camden, Me.: International Marine. Fully illustrated, the best beginning kayak manual available. Covers boats, gear, paddle strokes, maneuvers, braces, rolls, and general paddling information.

Wallbridge, C., and Sundmacher, W. 1995. *Whitewater rescue manual.* Springfield, Va.: American Canoe Association. Practical guidance for whitewater canoeists, kayakers, and rafters of all levels.

Washburn, R. 1989. *The coastal kayaker's manual.* 2d ed. Old Saybrook, Conn.: Globe Pequot. Focuses on stability, capsizing, righting, paddle strokes, bracing, rescue skills, navigation methods, and planning for trips. Intended for intermediate-level kayakers.

RESOURCES

Magazines

American Canoeist, 7432 Alban Station Blvd., Suite B226, Springfield, VA 22150.

American Whitewater, American Whitewater Affiliation, 1343 N Portage, Palatine, IL 60067.

Canoe, American Canoe Association, Webb Co., 1999 Shepard Rd., St. Paul, MN 55116.

Paddler, Paddling Group, 4061 Oceanside Blvd., Suite M, Oceanside, CA 92056.

River World, World Publications, 1400 Stierlin, Building C, Mountain View, CA 94043.

Organizations

American Canoe Association, 7432 Alban Station Blvd., Suite B226, Springfield, VA 22150. Membership plus a complete book and film library.

American Red Cross, 17th and D Sts. NW, Washington, DC 20006. A good source for courses, books, and films.

Canadian Recreational Canoeing Association, P.O. Box 500, Hyde Park, Ont, Canada N0M1Z0.

National Paddling Committee, 1750 E. Boulder St., Colorado Springs, CO 80909. Videotapes and training manuals on Olympic flat-water techniques.

Sierra Club, 530 Bush St., San Francisco, CA 94108.

There are many local and state canoe clubs. Consult a phone book under River Outfitters to obtain locations and contact persons.

Films and Videotapes

Cold, wet, and alive, videotape. Nichols Productions,17000 Carwell Rd., Silver Springs, MD 20904. This video follows a group of early season paddlers down a cold-water stream and documents their encounter with the silent killer hypothermia.

Fast and clean, videotape. Nichols Productions, 17000 Carwell Rd., Silver Springs, MD 20904. Preparations of the U.S. whitewater slalom team for the 1984 national and world competitions.

Heads up! River rescue for river runners, videotape. Russ Nichols/Walkabout Productions, American Canoe Association, 7432 Alban Station Blvd., Springfield, VA 22150. Fundamentals of river rescue, from simple self-rescue techniques to technical group rescues.

The kayaker's edge, videotape. Whitewater Instruction, 160 Hideaway Rd., Durango, CO 81301. For kayakers looking for instruction on how to begin whitewater paddling or for seasoned veterans wanting a tune-up on their skills.

Margin for error, 16 mm film; also available on videotape. Nichols Productions, 17000 Carwell Rd., Silver Springs, MD 20904. How to plan for and run a trip down a whitewater river.

Path of the paddle: Quiet water, videotape. Blue Heron Enterprises, 6212 W Cermak Rd., Berwyn, IL 60402. Bill Mason demonstrates basic paddling strokes for solo and tandem paddlers; filmed in rugged Canadian Shield country.

Path of the paddle: Whitewater, videotape. Blue Heron Enterprises, 6212 W Cermak Rd., Berwyn, IL 60402. How to read the rapids, plan a course, and follow it while in complete control of the boat.

Performance sea kayaking, videotape. American Canoe Association, 7432 Alban Station Blvd., Springfield, VA 22150. This video demonstrates and explains paddling, rescue and surf technique, and basic seamanship.

Sea kayaking: Getting started, videotape. American Canoe Association,7432 Alban Station Blvd., Springfield, VA 22150. A comprehensive, indexed reference for both beginning and experienced paddlers, with clear demonstrations of strokes, rescue, basic navigation, and general knowledge, this video provides an excellent overview of the diversity of sea kayaking.

Solo playboating, videotape. Whitewater Instruction, 160 Hideaway Rd., Durango, CO 81301. Intermediate whitewater open-canoe paddlers who are ready for advanced skills will find this fast-paced video an excellent learning tape.

Uncalculated risk, 16 mm film; also available in videotape. American Red Cross, General Supply Office, 17th and D Sts. NW, Washington, DC 20006. Concentrates on the risk and dangers of river running.

Whitewater self-defense: The Eskimo roll, videotape. Nichols Productions, 17000 Carwell Rd., Silver Springs, MD 20904. Slow motion and stop action, using underwater cameras, help demonstrate the skill and clearly show components of the Eskimo roll.

Wild Americans, videotape. Watershed Films, P.O. Box 551, Lotus, CA 95651. Big action, obligatory wipeouts, original music, and outrageous humor combine to make this an instant boating classic. Catch a glimpse of California's wet and wild side!

Lacrosse

After completing this chapter, the reader should be able to:

- Appreciate the history, development, and values of lacrosse
- Understand the rules of both the men's and women's versions of lacrosse
- Be aware of considerations of equipment selection and care
- Demonstrate the basic lacrosse skills of cradling, catching, throwing, scooping, shooting, and dodging
- Understand basic offensive and defensive strategies
- Instruct a group of students in the basic skills of lacrosse

HISTORY

With a history that is centuries old, lacrosse is the oldest sport in North America. The sport is rooted in Native American religious ceremony, in which it is referred to as *baggitaway*. Early explorers of North America found different forms of lacrosse widely played by the Indians. French missionaries gave the game its present name because the sticks the Indians used resembled the crosier (*la crosse*) carried at religious ceremonies by a bishop as a symbol of his pastoral office.

The first use of the word *crosse* in reference to the game was made in 1636 by the Jesuit missionary Jean de Brébeuf, who saw the Hurons play the game near Thunder Bay, Ontario, and mentioned it in a report to his ecclesiastical superiors. Indian lacrosse was a mass game, played not only for recreation but also as a means of training warriors. Most teams were made up of about a hundred players, sometimes nearly a thousand. The distance between goals was usually between 500 yards (457 m) and half a mile (805 m), but occasionally the goals were several miles apart! Games lasted as long as three days, starting at sunup and ending at sundown.

French pioneers began playing the game avidly in the early 1800s. On the same day in 1867 that the Dominion of Canada was created, lacrosse was declared its national sport. In 1861 Dr. W. George Beers, a Montreal dentist, formed the Canadian National Lacrosse Association and drew up the first set of written rules for the game. Later that year an Indian team traveled to England to play, and as a result of interest aroused in the game there, the English Lacrosse Association was formed in 1868. The sport was introduced into Australia in 1874 and has been played there ever since.

Development of the Men's Game

A group of Indians from Canada demonstrated lacrosse at the Sarasota Springs, New York, fairgrounds during the racing season in 1867. This event brought the first mention of lacrosse in American newspapers, and soon there were club teams in the Midwest, North, and East. In New York City, in the fall of 1877, intercollegiate lacrosse began when New York University played Manhattan College. The Intercollegiate Lacrosse Association was formed in 1882, and the development of the game in the United States was underway.

Lacrosse on the high school and college levels in the United States took great strides forward beginning in the late 1950s. At that time there were 80 high schools and 40 colleges playing the game. By 1997 there were 890 high schools and 179 colleges playing lacrosse on the varsity level. There are also approximately 250 high schools and 200 colleges that support lacrosse on the club level.

The international Lacrosse Federation sponsors a World Championship Series every four years, with teams from the United States, Canada, England, Australia, the Iroquois Nations, Japan, Germany, Sweden, Wales, Scotland, and the Czech Republic. Emerging modified lacrosse programs are also being developed in Denmark, France, Ireland, New Zealand, Singapore, and Hong Kong, vying for the world championship. The United States has won the gold medal in every competition—except in 1978, when Canada achieved a big upset.

Development of the Women's Game

By the 1870s lacrosse had been transported to England, where the rules were modified to eliminate roughness and body contact, and in 1890 St. Leonard's and St. Andrew's Schools of Scotland played the first women's game. The success of this game was immediate, and soon women's lacrosse was being played throughout England.

In the early 1900s women's lacrosse recrossed the Atlantic with English teachers who introduced the game at Bryn Mawr and Sargent Colleges. Women enjoyed the game so much that it spread into the other women's colleges, and the demand for qualified instructors kept England's Constance M. K. Applebee, Joyce CranBarry, and Joyce Riley in the United States for years as coaches.

The game continued to expand in popularity on both the college and high school levels so that in 1932 the United

States Women's Lacrosse Association (USWLA) was formed to promote its growth and to prepare rules and standards. By 1933 the first USWLA National Tournament was held in Greenwich, Connecticut. This tournament continues to be held each year with schoolgirls, club, and, as of 1994, masters divisions.

Collegiate tournament play was introduced in the late 1970s by the Association for Intercollegiate Athletics for Women (AIAW) and continues today through the National Collegiate Athletic Association (NCAA), with tournaments for Division I, II, and III.

Worldwide, women's lacrosse is played in England, Scotland, Wales, Australia, Japan, Canada, the Czech Republic, Sweden, France, Germany, Ireland, and the United States, with programs being developed in New Zealand and Denmark. The international game is governed by the International Federation of Women's Lacrosse Association, and a World Cup competition is held every four years.

VALUES

Lacrosse is one of the great team games on the American sports scene. Nearly everyone who has played it or watched it loves the game. Lacrosse gets in your blood because it is such a fast-moving and exciting sport. It has been accurately characterized as "the fastest game on two feet."

Lacrosse is a beautiful game, too—above all, for the skill of the stick handlers in throwing and catching either long, looping passes or bulletlike short passes. But that is just the beginning. There are frequent changes in the action: The defensive team gets possession of the ball and dashes downfield; the dodging and the stick checking; the quick pass to an attacker on the crease and an equally quick shot at the goal; the amazing saves of a good goalie; and the sudden body checks that are so different from the constant pounding of bodies in football. Also in contrast to the often obscured contact in football, all action takes place in the open, so that the knowledgeable spectator can follow and appreciate the fine points of strategy and tactics.

This wide-open, action-packed game presents many scoring opportunities. In fact, one of the foremost reasons for the popularity of lacrosse is the high number of climactic plays that occur during a game. In a typical college game, a combined total of 70 or more shots will be taken at the goal by the two teams and as many as 25 goals will be scored. This makes for excitement, geared to the action-loving players and fans of today.

Lacrosse is played in the spring, and in most areas this means green grass, budding leaves, and blooming flowers. Except in areas that have a year-round warm climate, this provides a refreshing change from the winter season, when most sports are played indoors. How invigorating it is to leave the heated gymnasium and get outside to the beautiful spring weather to play or watch lacrosse! There is a certain magic to springtime, and those who have been exposed to lacrosse know there is a touch of magic in this great American game.

Authors' note: It is interesting to watch the evolution of sports and their rules over the years. In the past many sports have had different sets of rules for men and women, and in some cases these rules have begun to merge (e.g., basketball and, in this book, the rules for speedball). In lacrosse, however, the rules for the men's and women's games are still considerably different, so we will present each game separately in this book. We will begin by noting the major differences between men's and women's lacrosse:

1. There are no boundary lines in women's lacrosse. Men's lacrosse is played within a lined, rectangular field.
2. The men's center draw starts on the ground. The women's center draw starts from a standing position.
3. Men's lacrosse is a body contact sport. Body contact is strictly forbidden in women's lacrosse.
4. Field players in the men's game are heavily padded. Women do not wear heavy gloves or helmets, due to the noncontact nature of the game.
5. Women's field sticks must be woven with four or five vertical thongs, and they do not have a loose pocket. Men's sticks have a very loose pocket and are often made of a mesh material.

Men's Lacrosse

RULES

Field and Goals

The playing area of a lacrosse field is bigger than that of a football field. It is 110 yards (about 100 m) long and 60 yards (about 55 m) wide. The goals are 80 yards (about 73 m) apart, and there is a playing area of 15 yards (13.8 m) behind each goal, which permits considerable behind-the-goal action. The length of the field is divided in half by a center line. A circle with a 9-foot (2.76 m) radius is drawn around each goal and is known as the *crease*. A rectangular box, 35 yards × 40 yards (32 m × 36.6 m), surrounds each goal and is called the *goal area* (see figure 20-1 for field markings).

The goal consists of two vertical posts joined by a top crossbar. The goalposts are 6 feet (1.84 m) apart, and the top crossbar is 6 feet from the ground. A goal line is drawn between the goalposts to indicate the plane of the goal. Attached to the goal is a pyramidal cord netting, which is fastened to the ground at a point 7 feet (2.15 m) in back of the center of the goal.

Players

There are 10 players on a team, plus a number of substitutes for each of the four positions: goal, defense, midfield, and attack. The goalkeeper, or goalie, protects the goal and receives primary support from three defensive players.

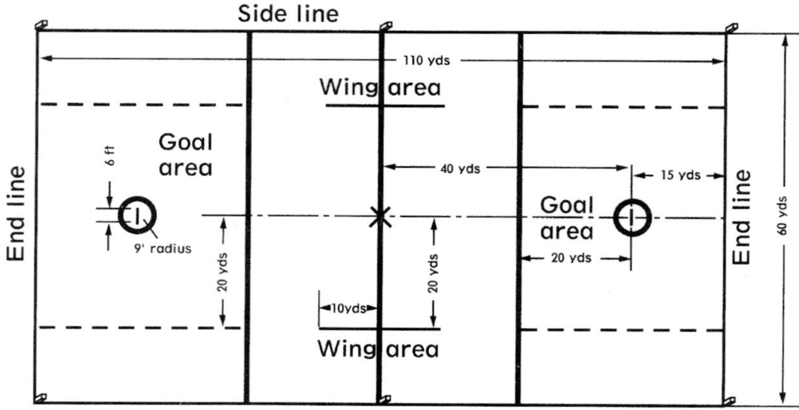

Figure 20-1. Lacrosse field. (To convert yards to meters, multiply by 0.91.)

Because they are normally near the goal, they are known as the *close defense*. Three midfielders cover the entire field, operating as both offensive and defensive players. One of the midfielders handles the face-offs and is called either the *center* or the *face-off player*. Three attackers spend most of their playing time around the opponent's goal and are referred to as the *close attack*.

Ball and Sticks

The lacrosse ball is solid rubber and white, yellow, or orange. It is slightly smaller than a baseball and just as hard. When dropped from a height of 6 feet (1.84 m) on a concrete floor, it must bounce 43 to 51 inches (1.1 to 1.3 m). The ball may not be touched by the hands except by a goalie while in the crease. Although it is legal to kick the ball with the foot or bat it with the stick, most of the action takes place with the ball being controlled in the pockets of the player's sticks.

The lacrosse stick—or *crosse*, as it was originally called—may have an overall length of 40 to 72 inches (1.02 to 1.84 m). The inside measurement of the head of every stick, except the goalie's, is between 6.5 and 10 inches (16.6 and 25 cm). Attackers normally use sticks with the smallest heads to aid them in ball control and dodging.

The stick is made of wood, plastic, or any other synthetic material. The net of the stick is constructed of gut, rawhide, clock cord, linen, nylon, or any other synthetic material and is roughly triangular in shape. A guard stop, which is made of a rubberized material, is located at the throat of the stick, a minimum of 10 inches (25 cm) from the outside edge of the head. The pocket of the stick may not sag to such a depth that it becomes unreasonably difficult for an opponent to dislodge the ball. This is determined by placing a ball in the pocket: If the top surface of the ball is below the bottom edge of the wall, the pocket is too deep and must be adjusted. This ruling does not apply to the goalie's stick.

Personal Equipment

The rules require all players to wear a pair of gloves and a helmet equipped with a face mask. A chin pad is secured to the mask and acts as a cushion to keep the mask from being pushed into the face. A cupped chin strap must be fastened on both sides of the helmet to keep it in the proper position. A lacrosse helmet is considerably lighter than a football helmet because the amount of physical contact in lacrosse is minimal compared with that in football. The lacrosse helmet mainly provides protection from the ball and, from blows by the opponent's stick. Gloves are worn for the same reason. They are similar to ice hockey gloves but more flexible.

Arm or elbow pads and a shoulder pad are worn for protection from stick checks, and are also required by rule. The remaining pieces of equipment worn by the lacrosse player are shoes, a jersey, and shorts. The cleated shoes worn for football or soccer are used for lacrosse. The jerseys are similar to football jerseys, and the shorts are similar to those worn in soccer or basketball.

PLAY OF THE GAME

Time

The regulation playing time of a college varsity game is 60 minutes, divided into four periods of 15 minutes each. High school teams play four 10-minute periods. In the event of a tie score at the end of a regulation game, sudden-victory play will begin, with the winner being the team scoring the first goal.

Officials

The game is controlled by two officials: a referee and an umpire. If both teams agree, a third official, designated the field judge, may be used. The referee has the final word in all decisions. The officials start the play at the beginning of each period and after each goal with a face-off.

Offside

The offside rule, which is peculiar to the game of lacrosse, requires each team to have three players located on its attack half of the field (between the center line and the endline) and four players on its defensive half of the field (between the center line and the endline). This rule prevents all 10 players from jamming in front of the goal in an effort to prevent a score, as is done at times in the game of soccer. It enables lacrosse to be a wide-open, freewheeling game with ample opportunity for scoring attempts.

Out-of-Bounds

When a player throws or carries the ball out-of-bounds, the opposing team gets possession. This is a basic rule for all team sports, but in lacrosse there is one exception to this rule: When a loose ball goes out-of-bounds as a result of a shot taken at the goal, it is awarded to the team whose player is closet to it at the exact time it crosses the boundary line. This gives the offense the opportunity to maintain control of the ball after a missed shot goes out-of-bounds.

Substitutes

There are two methods of substituting players in lacrosse. The regular method allows players to enter the game whenever play has been suspended after the ball has gone out-of-bounds at any point along either sideline. The other method is similar to ice hockey's substitution of players while the game is in progress. One player at a time may enter the game when a teammate leaves the playing field. This takes place at a special substitution area at the center line.

Penalties

Although the uninitiated spectator often thinks lacrosse is a wild, stick-swinging game, it is not nearly as rough as it appears. There is physical contact in lacrosse, but not nearly as much as in football, with its continuous hitting on every play. Injuries in football are more numerous and more serious. Even though body and stick checks are part of lacrosse, there are definite limitations on them, which prevent injuries. In addition, the protective equipment worn by the lacrosse player minimizes injuries. Body checking of an opponent is legal as long as the opponent either has possession of the ball or is within 5 yards (4.6 m) of a loose ball and the contact is from the front or side and above the knees. A player can check the opponent's stick with his own stick when the opponent has possession of the ball or is within 5 yards (4.6 m) of a loose ball. The opponent's gloved hand on the stick is considered part of the stick and can be legally checked. However, no other part of his body may be checked.

Lacrosse is similar to ice hockey in that a player who violates the rules must spend time in a penalty box. This forces the violator's team to operate with one less player than its opponent—or even more, if other penalties occur at the same time or while a player is already in the penalty box. The team that has been fouled then plays with one player more than the other team and usually ends up taking a close-range shot at the goal. There are two types of fouls: personal and technical.

Personal fouls, the more serious type, consist of illegal body checking, slashing with the stick, tripping, unnecessary roughness, and unsportsman-like conduct. The penalty for a personal foul is suspension of the offending player from the game for 1 to 3 minutes, depending on the official's judgment of the severity and intention of the foul. Most personal fouls call for only a 1-minute suspension.

Technical fouls are those of a less serious nature, and they consist of interference, holding, pushing, offside, and stalling. The penalty for a technical foul is suspension from the game for 30 seconds if the offending team does not have possession of the ball at the time the foul is committed.

A player who has committed a violation of the playing rules must serve time in the penalty box. The player must remain there until substituted for or informed by the timekeeper that it is time to reenter the game. The player is also released from the penalty box when the opposing team scores a goal. Expulsion fouls and unsportsman-like conduct fouls, however, are such serious violations that they require that the full time always be served.

If a defending player commits a foul against an attacking player who has possession of the ball, a slow-whistle technique, similar to that used in ice hockey, is enacted. The official drops a signal flag and withholds his whistle until a scoring play is completed. The scoring play is considered to have been completed when the attacking team loses control of the ball, takes a shot, or the ball leaves the attack-goal area.

FUNDAMENTAL SKILLS AND TECHNIQUES

Holding the Stick

The player must hold the stick properly to control the ball effectively in the pocket. Figure 20-2 shows a right-handed player with the proper grip of the stick. The left (lower) hand, with the palm facing down, grasps the stick at the end of the handle for protection. Failure to do so, resulting in a portion of the stick (even just 1 or 2 inches) being exposed, gives the defender a good chance of making a successful poke check on the end of the handle and dislodging the ball. The right (upper) hand, with the palm facing up, is placed on the handle about 12 inches (30.7 cm) from the left hand. Both hands are in front of the hips or slightly outside them.

Beginners often feel more comfortable grasping the stick with the upper hand closer to the head of the stick, giving them more control in catching and cradling the ball. However, they lose a considerable amount of leverage and power when releasing the ball with their hands too far apart on the stick. More-advanced players like to shoot the

Figure 20-2. Grip and two-hand front cradle.

Figure 20-3. Two-hand upright cradle.

ball with their hands about 6 inches (15.4 cm) apart, giving them greater leverage. As a general guide, the hands are placed in the basic position of about 12 inches (30.7 cm) apart when catching, throwing, cradling, shooting, and scooping the ball.

The fingers hold the stick with a firm but not tight grip. Beginners often make the mistake of "squeezing the stick to death" with a viselike grip and consequently lose the feel for controlling the ball. The stick rests more in the fingers than in the palm of the upper hand. The thumb is on top of the handle. The elbow of the upper arm is pointed toward the ground and not out to the side. These points allow for a free and easy motion to cradle the ball and keep it in the pocket.

Cradling

Cradling is probably the most difficult technique for the beginner to learn, and it is obviously the most important. Each player must be able to run at top speed, often surrounded by opponents, and still control the ball in the pocket of the stick. The key to cradling is the looseness of the upper hand and wrist. The loose wrist motion of the lacrosse player's upper hand while cradling can be compared to the symphony conductor's handling of the baton. When conducting the maestro moves the entire arm as well as the hand, and so does the lacrosse player when cradling.

Most youngsters have played around with either a table tennis paddle or tennis racquet, trying to keep the ball on the flat surface of the paddle or racquet by moving their arms and turning their wrists in a swinging motion. This technique is similar to cradling a lacrosse ball, and it may be helpful for the beginner to hold the stick in front of the body with only one hand and cradle the ball this way. The ball is not shaken or jiggled around in the pocket of the stick by the wrist action alone; it is rocked back and forth with a smooth, rhythmic motion of the entire upper arm as well as the hand. If the wrists are not locked but are allowed to move with the swinging motion of the arms, which results normally from running, the ball will come to a more positive rest in the pocket. Both hands are involved with the cradling, although the upper hand carries the bulk of the load. The lower hand has to have a loose enough grip to allow the stick to be turned in it. Beginners can look at the ball when cradling just to make sure it is under control in the pocket. As confidence is gained in handling the ball, the player does not need to look at it because he has a feel for its position in the stick.

There are different types of cradles, but each has the same basic motion. Figure 20-3 shows the two-hand upright cradle, which is used when a defender is playing the opponent with the ball. This cradle gives good protection of the ball and keeps the stick in a position to release the ball quickly and accurately. The one-hand cradle (figure 20-4) gives excellent protection because the lower hand is placed in front of the body to prevent the defender's checks from getting to the stick.

Figure 20-4. One-hand cradle.

Throwing

The techniques used in throwing a football or baseball are the same ones used in throwing a lacrosse ball with the stick. Figure 20-5 shows a right-handed player in the three phases of the throwing motion. The body is turned to the side and the feet are staggered. The upper hand is even with the shoulders or slightly above, and it controls the stick throughout the throwing motion. When one throws a football or baseball, the upper hand is well above the shoulder. However, the lacrosse player uses the stick to place the ball in this position, and therefore the upper hand remains at shoulder level or slightly above. The upper hand is primarily responsible for accuracy, but it also shares in providing the power with the lower hand, which is about 6 to 8 inches (about 15 to 20 cm) from the body. The stick is held at about a 45-degree angle from the horizon and with the head of the stick facing in the direction the ball is to be thrown. The ball rests in the pocket, and the thrower should have a feel for it.

In the actual throwing motion, the following takes place:

1. The body weight is drawn back first to the rear leg and then transferred to the front leg.
2. The upper body is turned from a side position to one facing directly to the front. The whipping of the shoulders gives added power.
3. The upper hand is drawn back several inches and then follows through with a snapping motion. This wrist snap is the key to throwing with the lacrosse stick, just the same as it is in throwing the football or baseball, because it gives both accuracy and power.

Figure 20-5. Three phases of the throwing motion.

4. The lower arm is bent at the elbow, which places the lower hand in a position closer to the body than the upper hand.
5. The lower hand pulls down on the end of the handle, making a small arc toward the middle of the body.
6. The ball leaves the stick from the center of the pocket.
7. The ball is aimed for the head of the receiver's stick.
8. The stick ends up pointing directly at this target in a nearly horizontal position.

To emphasize the similarity between throwing a baseball or a football and a lacrosse ball with the stick, the beginner can throw with just one hand, the upper hand, on the stick. The wrist snap is of primary importance, and the throw can be made with the identical motion used by a pitcher or quarterback. The accuracy and power with one hand on the stick are obviously more limited, but it is easy to feel the similarity in the throwing techniques.

The most common error the beginner makes is pushing the ball out of the pocket rather than throwing it. This is caused either by the failure to draw the stick back several inches just prior to the forward motion or by a failure to snap the wrist when making the throw. When the ball is pushed out of the stick, it has limited power and control. The beginning thrower also tends to use primarily the pull-down move by the lower hand to release the ball instead of using the joint action of both the upper and lower hands.

Catching

When a player catches the ball, the positions of both the body and the stick are important (figure 20-6). The upper body squarely faces the ball in its flight. The feet are about shoulder width apart and on line rather than staggered. This position allows the receiver to move quickly to either the left or the right, depending on where the ball is thrown. The stick is placed slightly above the head as a target for the pass. The pocket of the stick is positioned so that is completely faces the ball. The catch is made in front of the body, with the head of the stick reaching out for the ball, much the same as a baseball player using a glove to catch the ball. The baseball player doesn't catch the ball when it is even with the body or with the arm completely straightened out in front of the body. Rather, the player reaches out with the gloved hand as the ball approaches and then cushions the ball into the glove, actually making the catch about 6 inches in front of the body.

The lacrosse player uses the same techniques in catching the ball with the stick. The idea of catching in lacrosse is also much the same as trying to catch a thrown tennis ball with a tightly strung racket. The stick must be withdrawn or the ball will rebound. The receiver cushions the ball in the pocket by bringing the head of the stick back toward the body and making use of a quick but soft wrist action. This cradle motion controls the ball in the pocket and keeps it from bouncing out.

Catching the ball on the backhand side—that is, the side opposite the receiver's stick—requires a different maneuver. The receiver swings the stick across the front of the body into the backhand position (figure 20-7). The entire stick is moved to the backhand side, not just the head of the stick. Beginners will often move just the head of the stick and leave the butt end on the forehand side. This makes for a very awkward catch. The wrist or cradle action is the same, except that it is done in the backhand position. The receiver will either sidestep or cross over to get to a ball

Figure 20-6. Three phases of the catching technique.

Figure 20-7. Backhand catch.

thrown to the backhand side. If the ball is close to the body, a right-hander will sidestep with the left foot. Figure 20-7 shows a right-hander who has pivoted on the left foot and made the crossover with the right foot because the ball was not near the body. The crossover step provides extra reach.

Once the catch is made, the receiver always turns into a position with the body between the stick and the nearest opponent. This gives the best possible protection of the stick. Beginners—even some advanced players—often make the mistake of turning the wrong way and bringing the stick in front of the body, where the opponent can check it.

Scooping

Control of the ball is a significant factor in a team's success. Because the ball is on the ground for a portion of every game, it is vital for a team to try to gain possession of it more than 50 percent of the time. Scooping a ground ball that is being contested by as many as five players requires not only mastering the basic skills of actually scooping the ball, but also a determination and fierce competitiveness. A team's mental attitude is usually reflected in its play of the ground ball, and in most cases the team controlling the ground ball wins the game.

Maintaining the proper body and stick position is essential for the scooper. Starting within several yards of a ground ball, the scooper bends the knees and upper body in a semicrouch position. If holding the stick right-handed, then the right foot is forward on the scoop to give a free-flowing scooping motion with the arms (figure 20-8). The

Figure 20-8. Scooping the ball.

left (lower) arm determines the angle that the stick makes with the ground in the scoop. The angle will vary according to the size of the player, but a general guideline of approximately 30 degrees can be established. The lower arm will be slightly bent in the scoop. If the angle approaches 60 degrees, it is going to place the stick at too steep an angle, which minimizes the effectiveness of controlling the ball in a fast-moving pressure situation. Instead of getting their nose down near the ground to play the ball, players will often take the lazy approach: scooping the ball with the body in an upright position and with the stick at a sharp angle. This technique, referred to as *spiking* the ball, should be avoided.

The end of the handle is held to the side of the body rather than in front, where the stick could dig into the ground and force the butt end of the handle into the scooper's groin or midsection. The head of the stick hits the ground 1 to 2 inches (2.6 to 5.2 cm) from the ball. A common mistake is for the scooper to try to place the head of the stick right next to the ball, which may cause it to hit or go over it. The scooper must keep his or her eyes on the ball until it has been scooped into the stick with a shovel-like motion and should keep moving. Do not flip the ball into the air as it is scooped. If a player is completely ambidextrous, the ball may be scooped either left- or right-handed. However, if one hand is obviously stronger than the other, the stronger hand should be used to scoop the ball in a pressure situation, not the weaker hand.

Stress should be placed on the importance of scooping the ground with both hands on the stick. It may seem easier to scoop with just the lower hand gripping the stick at the butt end of the handle, but the percentages are not good with the one-handed scoop. The one-handed scoop using just the upper hand should also be avoided, because the end of the handle is exposed to the opponent's check. The chance for error is far less in the two-handed scoop because the scooper gets the body closer to the ground and can control the stick better.

Once the ball is in the stick, the scooper's primary concern is protecting it. There are several courses of action, depending on the circumstances. Determine the location of the opposition as soon as the ball is scooped. If surrounded, tuck the stick close to the body and try to dodge out of trouble. This maneuver is referred to as the *scoop and tuck*. If, after the scoop, an open area is available, regardless of whether it's toward the offensive or defensive half of the field, burst full speed for daylight. If pressure comes from the side once on the run, the player can hold the stick with one hand and protect it with the other.

INDIVIDUAL OFFENSE

Dodging

Every player on the team must strive to master the face, roll, and bull dodges. These three dodges gives the player with the ball the capability of going by an opponent and advancing the ball toward the goal. Most dodges occur as a result of an opponent's mistake or overcommitment. Incorrect body or stick position by the defender can also encourage the dodge. The ball carrier can initiate the dodge by baiting the opponent into making a mistake and then taking advantage of it.

Protection of the stick by the dodger is probably the most important factor in completing a successful dodge. A simple rule to achieve this protection is: Keep your head between and in direct alignment with the head of your stick and the opponent. If you maintain this head-on-head position, the defender cannot check the ball carrier's stick without hitting him on the helmet and committing a foul.

Face Dodge

The face dodge is best used when an opponent delivers a check at the ball carrier's stick. The ball carrier pulls his own stick across the front of the body when he sees the stick coming. Actually the stick goes in front of the face—hence the name *face dodge*. The ball carrier can help set up the face dodge by faking a pass to a teammate. Use a head-and-eye fake, looking in the direction of the anticipated pass and even calling a player in that area by name. Have two hands on the stick when faking the pass to make it more realistic. If the opponent raises the stick in the air to block the faked pass, this will open up the opportunity for the face dodge just as well as the opponent's using an aggressive slap check.

Figure 20-9 shows a right-handed player executing the face dodge. In one simultaneous motion the player pushes off with the right foot, sidesteps to the left with the left foot, and pulls the stick across the face. When the face dodge is done with quickness and agility, the dodger gains at least a step on the opponent in the new direction.

Roll Dodge

Of all the dodges, the roll dodge is probably used most frequently. It is effective when the opponent is very aggressive with stick checks, especially with a horizontal thrust that almost turns or pushes the ball carrier in the opposite direction. The check actually helps to roll away from the pressure. The roll dodge can be done in either a slow-moving or

Figure 20-9. Two phases of the face dodge with a side step.

a fast-moving situation. It is not necessary to keep two hands on the stick because the success of the dodge is dependent more on footwork than on the handling of the stick. Figure 20-10 shows a right-handed attacker who, while driving toward the goal, has reacted to the check of the defender with a roll dodge. The roll dodger pivots on the left (lead) foot, then pushes off the left leg and takes a step with the right foot in the direction opposite the original path. This step is sizable, 2 to 3 feet (0.6 to 0.9 m), and is the key to the roll dodge. It should be as close to the defender as possible to facilitate rolling by in the new direction. If the dodger rounds out on the first step, moving away from the

Figure 20-10. Three phases of the roll dodge.

defender, no advantage will be gained because the defender will have a chance to recover position.

When taking the first step on the roll dodge, the ball carrier faces away from the opponent and throws his hips into him. The head of the stick stays even with the player's own head while making the pivot. If the head of the stick is kept well above the head, the defender may be able to check it. If the head of the stick is trailed, the defender can reach around and also make the check. However, if it is even with his own head, the stick is well protected and the defender will either jeopardize his positioning by making a reckless swing with his stick or foul him.

Bull Dodge

Whereas both the face dodge and roll dodge have the dodger changing direction and going in a direction opposite to the original path, the bull dodge starts one way and climaxes in the same direction. The name of the dodge indicates brute strength overpowering the defender, but in many cases it is the burst of speed that gives the dodger the advantage. Because the dodger has the advantage of knowing when the burst of speed is going to start the burst, the dodger will be able to beat even a defender who is as fast. If the defender is slower, the attacker should have no trouble gaining the advantage by running at full speed throughout the dodge.

If the defender has similar or greater speed and size than the attacker, the attacker can make use of change-of-pace maneuvers, head fakes, and stick fakes to throw the defender off balance. By driving hard and using one of these techniques, then by bursting full speed in the original direction, one can gain a jump on the opponent.

There are other dodges that are for the most part combinations of the basic three: face, roll, and bull. Master of these three, however, will give a player all the weapons needed to dodge the opponent. This applies to players on all levels, from "little league" to college varsity. The dodges can be used by players in all positions, goalies and defensive players as well as midfielders and attackers.

Shooting

Because games are won by the number of goals scored, shooting plays a vital role in any team's success. Although being able to shoot the ball with power is important, the crucial factor in effective shooting is accuracy. One of the shocking statistics in lacrosse is the high percentage of shots that miss the goal completely. Emphasis must be placed on taking only good shots and keeping them on target, or on the goal. Shots can be classified in two general categories: outside shots and close-range shots.

Outside Shots

Outside shots are those normally taken approximately 12 to 18 yards (11 to 16.5 m) from the goal. A shot taken past the 18- to 20-yard (16.5 to 18.3 m) mark is considered to be too long and not very effective against a good goalie. Outside shots should be bounced, because they are harder for the goalie to follow than are shots thrown into the air. The shooter should aim the outside bounce shot at the center of the goal, anticipating it to go about 8 to 12 inches (20.5 to 30.7 cm) to either side of center and thus inside the pipes of the goal. Aiming for a spot just inside the pipes is asking for trouble, because the margin of error will cause the ball to go outside the pipes too many times.

Close-Range Shots

Any shot taken between the 12-yard (11 m) mark and the crease can be considered a close-range shot. These shots are high-percentage scorers because of the proximity to the goal. The shooter keys on the body and stick position of the goalie and tries to place the ball where the goalie is most vulnerable. If the goalie's stick is high, the shooter can direct the ball low, and vice versa. The shooter also has the option of bouncing the ball or firing it in the air. But most important, the ball should be shot hard and accurately for an open area. Because the shooter is close to the goal, the ball should be aimed about 6 to 12 inches (15 to 30.7 cm) inside the pipes. Trying to place the ball just an inch or two inside the pipes usually results in hitting the pipe or missing the goal completely.

Shooting Technique

The same basic techniques that apply to throwing the ball also apply to shooting it. The upper hand of the shooter is in a position over the shoulder, in much the same way that most baseball pitchers and football quarterbacks hold their arms when throwing. This over-the-shoulder shot is the most effective of shots because it is the most accurate. The upper hand follows through in a vigorous throwing motion with a snap of the wrist as the lower hand pulls down hard on the butt end of the handle. The body weight transfers from the rear to the front leg in much the same fashion as an outfielder in baseball catches a fly ball and fires to home plate to put out a runner trying to score from third base. The head of the stick actually ends up pointing to the ground because the body follow-through is so complete.

TEAM OFFENSE

The structuring of a team's offense is vital to its success. Games are won by scoring goals, and a team must utilize the talents of its ballplayers to give them the opportunity to score. This requires detailed organization by the coach and a thorough understanding of the offensive strategy by each attacker and midfielder. A disorganized offense can completely demoralize a team. Confusion will reign if there is little coordination between the attack and midfield units and players are allowed to freelance and "do their own thing" without their teammates' awareness and cooperation.

A team usually scores nearly half its goals on unsettled play: intercepting a clearing pass, taking the ball away from the goalie or a defensive player, dodging an over aggressive defender who forces the attacker to dodge, gaining possession of a ground ball after a big scramble and pressing for the goal, and fast breaks initiated at the defensive end of the field. The goals scored in these situations are easy because the defense is not settled and ready to meet the attack. The more goals a team can score this way, the better its chances of winning.

The other half of a team's goals come from settled, all-even play. A team has to work persistently and patiently to score in this situation. Some offenses are attack-oriented; others are midfield-oriented. The capabilities of the players determine the emphasis. In any offensive play, all six players are involved if it is to be successful. Some players may have to be good "actors" while others are carrying out the primary effort to score. However, no player can just stand around and watch play and consequently allow a defender to help stop the play.

There are different styles of offense, and most teams make use of a combination of them. Dodges and flip-offs when double-teamed, the cutting game, set plays, inverts, and a fast-break, move-the-ball offense are the basic ways to score in the settled situation. Regardless of the style, discipline is a key factor. Each player must know his responsibilities within the system and carry them out to the letter.

INDIVIDUAL DEFENSE

A complete understanding of the basic skills of defending against an opponent with the ball is essential to every player on the field. Each defensive player and midfielder obviously becomes involved with the primary responsibility of neutralizing the opponent when in possession of the ball. Attackers make use of the same principles when they play an opponent who is attempting to clear the ball. The goalie must know the defensive techniques to assist defensive teammates with positive verbal instructions.

The techniques for playing one-on-one defense in lacrosse are identical with those used in basketball, although the lacrosse player has the advantage of using a stick. However, it is imperative the stick be handled more like a foil than a bludgeon. Too many defensive players feel they must be extremely aggressive with the stick and show their superiority over their opponents by pounding them with the stick and trying to gain possession of the ball. They believe that this style is more challenging to them personally and that it gives them more notoriety than the patient, position-conscious defensive game. A defender who has an easy time handling a weak attacker might run into trouble when playing against one who is an equal or better. The take-the-ball-away approach will often lead the defender to committing a foul or being dodged. Therefore, the conservative style of defense (play your position, apply pressure, and be patient) should be emphasized.

Stance

The stance of the defensive player is vital to effectiveness in defending the player with the ball. Control of the body and readiness to move in any direction are essential. The feet should be spread a little wider than shoulder width and staggered in a heel-to-toe alignment. The defender must maintain balance by keeping most of the weight on the balls of the feet. The heels should make contact with the ground to provide stability. Knees should be flexed and the upper body bent slightly forward. This semicrouch position resembles that of a boxer (figure 20-11).

Eyes

The defender's eyes do not center on any one thing, but rather look through the attacker's hands, stick (pocket), and eyes, as each of these can give a tipoff. If the attacker has only one hand on the stick, he normally will not be able to shoot or feed effectively. Therefore, the defender can concentrate primarily on maintaining proper position and getting ready to execute a poke or slap check (discussed later) when the attacker puts the other hand on the stick. However, the defender can use the poke check to annoy an attacker who is carrying the stick in one hand. When the attacker has two hands on the stick, the defender should be ready to apply pressure. The attacker's eyes will often betray when and where the ball will be thrown. Only the best attacker will look one way and then throw the other way. Most players look exactly where they are going to throw the ball, and their faces will almost light up when they spot the open player and prepare to release the ball. The defender must be ready for the clever attacker who fakes with the eyes and then makes a countermove.

Positioning

Being in the proper position when the offensive player gets the ball is extremely important for the defender. The defender assumes a squared-up position with the body in a direct line with the ball carrier's stick side and the center of the goal. The alignment of the feet is also determined by the attacker's stick position. If the attacker has the stick in a right-hand position, the defender should have the left foot back and right foot forward in a staggered alignment (figure 20-11). The feet are reversed when the attacker has the stick in the left hand. This allows the defender to move quickly in the direction the opponent is facing.

Footwork

The speed at which the offensive player moves will determine the footwork of the defender. A "shuffle" with short, choppy steps and no crossover steps is used when the opponent moves at a slow to half-speed pace. When shuffling,

Figure 20-11. Defensive position (player on right).

the feet should remain spread about shoulder width to provide a solid base. They should never come closer than about 8 to 10 inches (about 20 to 25 cm) apart. This footwork is similar to a boxer's maneuvering in the ring. The body is squared off and facing the opponent when using the shuffle. When the attacker increases speed to the point where the defender would not be able to keep up using the shuffle, the defender should change to a hip-to-hip running position (figure 20-12). The defender's body is turned in the same direction as the opponent's body, and the hips are even with those of the offensive player. This allows the defender to maintain the proper defensive position between the opponent and the goal. If the attacker slows up, the defender can resume shuffling.

Handling the Stick

Proper handling of the stick by the defender when playing the ball is almost as important as proper footwork. If using a stick of attack or midfield length, the hands should be about 12 inches (30.7 cm) apart. If using a long-handled stick, the hands should be farther apart to better control the bigger stick. With either stick, the lower hand should be at the butt end of the handle and the upper hand should be the proper distance up the handle, never at the throat of the stick. Placing the stick across the chest or on the number of the opponent's jersey can be most disconcerting. From this position the defender can execute any check.

A player who is basically a right-hander should play right-handed when on defense—vice versa for the left-hander. It is not a good idea to change hands when on defense because the switching of the hands will result in less than complete control of the stick. Trying to change hands every time the attacker changes direction will place the defender at a decided disadvantage. Another reason for not changing hands is to ensure that the defender will be holding the stick with the stronger hand when the ball is on the ground. This will allow scooping the ball more easily if he does check it out of the opponent's stick. The extra second or two of delay to change hands for the scoop in this situation could cause the ball to be lost.

It is debatable whether the forehand or backhand stick position is stronger on defense. The forehand position can be defined as that used by a right-handed defender who is guarding a left-handed driver. The backhand position (figures 20-11 and 20-12) is used when a right-hander plays against a right-handed driver. There are two important advantages to the backhand position:

1. The stick rests across the chest of the opponent and acts as a natural deterrent to his taking a shot at the goal. If the attacker is forcing his way into a good shooting area, the defender can use a backhand hold to stop penetration and turn him back. The arms of the defender and the stick act as a natural "hook" on the attacker.
2. When the attacker runs toward the goal at full speed, the defender can keep pace and still keep the stick resting across the attacker's body and deliver checks that will interfere with shooting. It is extremely

Figure 20-12. Hip-to-hip running defensive position (player on right).

difficult, if not impossible, for the defender to do this when holding the stick in a forehand position and moving at full speed.

Basic Checks

Poke check

The poke check is one of the most effective checks because the opportunity to dislodge the ball from the opponent's stick without overcommitting is greater than in the other checks. The poke check consists of a thrust of the stick, propelled through the upper hand by the lower hand. This technique is similar to the billiard player's handling of a cue stick. The lower hand draws the stick back slightly just prior to the stroke to provide additional power. It is important for the upper hand to remain in contact with the handle as it slides through the fingers to provide control. If the upper hand loses its grasp, the lower hand will not be able to control the stick, thereby giving an advantage to the attacker. If the attacker is holding the stick with one hand, the thrust can be directed at any part of the handle that is showing. If he has two hands on the stick, it can be aimed at the cuff of the glove holding the butt end of the stick. The defender must guard against an overaggressive poke that will cause him to step into the opponent, resulting in an opening to roll by on the side opposite the check.

Slap check

The *slap check,* as the term implies, is merely a short, slapping blow directed at the attacker's lower, gloved hand or the handle of the stick just above it. It is used mainly when the attacker either has both hands on the stick or is about to put his lower hand on it. The slap check will not be effective if the attacker is holding the stick in one hand and protecting it well with the other. The wrist action of the upper hand on the stick delivers the check, and it should be as quick as possible. The head of the stick will be directed at the target anywhere from a horizontal position up to an angle of approximately 45 degrees above horizontal. The check should not cover a distance any greater than about 18 inches (46 cm). In fact, the shorter the check, the less it is "telegraphed." When the defender hauls back with the stick as if to bludgeon the opponent, not only is the maneuver tipped-off, but also this usually results in a check that generates so much power it gets out of control and exposes the defender to a face or roll dodge. The head of the defender's stick should not go beyond a position horizontal to the ground when it is in the downward motion. If it does, it can cause a foul by tripping or hitting the attacker on the lower part of the body. When making the slap check with the stick moving in a horizontal path, the defender must guard against using too vigorous a check, which will give the attacker an easy roll dodge.

Over-the-head check

The over-the-head check is a risky one, and it requires extreme caution. If it does not knock the ball out of the opponent's stick, the defender is in a vulnerable position and will probably be dodged. There are various techniques for executing the over-the-head check:

1. The defender takes the upper hand off the stick and raises the lower hand over the opponent's head. The defender's arm will be straightened out, and with a

quick flick of the wrist the stick will swing like a pendulum, checking the head of the opponent's stick.

2. The defender takes the lower hand off the stick and raises the upper hand over the opponent's head. The arm is straightened out, and with a quick snap of the wrist the butt end of the stick will make the pendulum swing and check the opponent's stick. This technique is best used when the attacker is facing the defender.
3. The defender can make the over-the-head check with both hands on the stick and directing them over the opponent's head. The arms almost straighten out completely, and the check is made by snapping both wrists. This check is not as popular as one-hand checks.

Wraparound check

The wraparound check is almost as dangerous as the over-the-head check because it is a one-handed maneuver and the defender does not have complete control of the stick. However, it can be effective if the attacker has worked his way into a good shooting position close to the goal. The defender takes the lower hand off the stick, straightens the other arm, and directs the stick in a horizontal position toward the opponent's stick. This check is more effective when a right-handed defender is playing against a left-handed attacker who is going to the left, and, vice versa, when a left-handed defender is playing against a right-hander going to the right.

TEAM DEFENSE

Defense is the most important phase of team play in lacrosse. The goalie, three defensive players, and three midfielders must blend together into a well-coordinated group that presents a solid, unified front to the opposition. Defensive players must be concerned not only with guarding their opponents but also with assisting each other. If the game were strictly a series of one-on-one confrontations, the defense would lose out most of the time because the offensive player would find it easy to get a close-range shot at the goal given the liberty to maneuver the defender over the entire field without interference from any other defensive players. It is reassuring for each member of the defense to know that the strong support of teammates is available.

The mission of the defense is obviously to prevent the opponent from scoring. The philosophy for team offense follows the pattern established for individual defense. Position and patience are the watchwords, as opposed to an aggressive, take-the-ball-away approach.

The goalie is the backbone of the team defense and directs all the action. The defensive players and midfielders have definite responsibilities concerning both the opponents and their defensive teammates. Even attackers must know defensive strategy because they may find themselves at the defensive end of the field when they are forced to go over the center line in a riding situation.

There are three types of team defense: one-on-one, zone, and a combination of one-on-one and zone. If a team plays more than one defense in a game, it is imperative that each player knows which defense is being used at a given time.

TIPS TO REMEMBER

1. Keep your hands approximately 12 inches (30.7 cm) apart on the stick when throwing, catching, scooping, and shooting the ball.
2. When throwing the ball, snap the upper hand/wrist and follow through with a motion similar to that used in throwing a baseball or football.
3. Throw the ball to a teammate on the stick side and at a height that is slightly above the head.
4. When cradling the ball; move the entire upper arm and keep a loose wrist.
5. When scooping the ball, keep two hands on the stick and bend at the knees.
6. A defender's mistake or overcommitment will normally dictate the type of dodge to be used by the ball carrier.
7. When dodging, the ball carrier should keep his head between and in direct alignment with the head of his stick and the opponent's stick.
8. Stress accuracy in shooting rather than power. Don't try to place the ball just inside the pipes of the goal because this will frequently result in missing the goal completely or hitting the pipe.
9. When defending against the ball carrier, handle the stick like a foil and don't bludgeon the ball carrier with stick checks that could result in a foul. Keep the stick across the numbers of the opponent's jersey and use short, quick, 6-inch (15 cm) checks.
10. Repetition is the key to learning. Be sure to execute all the fundamental skills on the run. Move your feet!
11. Remember that lacrosse is a team game and must be undertaken with enthusiasm, fair play, and a positive attitude.
12. While playing the game, respect everyone (opponents, teammates, coaches, and referees) and you will gain self-respect, which is most important.

TEACHING CONSIDERATIONS

1. Handling the stick should dominate practice sessions for beginners. Catching, throwing, and cradling drills will enable players to feel comfortable in controlling the ball in their sticks.
2. Learning the three basic dodges will enable players to gain more confidence with stick handling and their ability to maneuver with the ball.
3. Players enjoy shooting at a goal, and emphasis should be placed on teaching proper, accurate shooting techniques.

4. Team offense can be developed by first working with three-on-three maneuvers for both attack players and midfield players. Then all six offensive players can be coordinated in a basic pattern of offense.
5. When teaching the techniques for playing one-on-one defense, stress should be placed on proper positioning, footwork, and use of the various stick checks.
6. The natural progression is to follow one-on-one defensive play with three-on-three, and finally team defense, which is six-on-six.
7. Developing a team defense and a team offense should not be too difficult to teach because lacrosse, with its six-on-six play, is very similar to basketball's five-on-five play. Making sure that each player understands his offensive and defensive responsibilities is most important. There must be organized and controlled play at both ends of the field.

Women's Lacrosse

RULES

General

Women's lacrosse is played by two teams of 12 players on a grass field or artificial surface. The goal cages are placed 100 yards (91.4 m) apart, and technically there are no boundary lines. There are no restrictions as to player movement (other than related to specific strategy and safety considerations in front of the goal area), and play may continue behind the goal cage area.

The game is played in an upright position, and the ball is thrown from a stick through the air from player to player. The aerial nature of the game combined with the freedom of movement makes lacrosse a dynamically creative and fast-moving game. Players generally match up player to player; and because no body contact is permitted, it often becomes a game of quickness and interceptions, with the focus on scoring goals. The only player with special equipment and privileges is the goalkeeper.

Young players may be introduced to the game through keep-away games with just a few players per side or the game of seven-on-a-side lacrosse. These games enable each player to maintain a maximum amount of activity time through the learning phases.

Ball and Sticks

Ball

The ball is solid rubber, with a circumference of not less than 7.75 inches (19.8 cm) nor more than 8 inches (20.5 cm). It must weigh not more than 5.25 ounces (150 g) and not less than 5 ounces (143 g). It must have a bounce of not less than 43 inches (1.1 m) and not more than 51 inches (1.3 m). Although white and orange balls are readily available, yellow balls must be used for formal competition on the high school and college levels.

Sticks

Field player. Field players propel the ball through the air with a *crosse*, or stick. The stick may be constructed of wood (figure 20-13) or with a plastic head (figure 20-14) and wooden or aluminum handle. The head of the stick resembles a woven basket in which the ball is carried, or cradled, and thrown. This pocket must consist of four or five thongs laced through the top of the stick with stitches cross-lacing the thongs. Mesh is not allowed. The pocket must be kept tight at all times so that when the ball is placed in a horizontally held stick it does not lie below the sidewall of the stick. The head of a field player's stick may range from 7 to 9 inches (17.8 to 22.9 cm) wide.

Goalkeeper

Goalkeepers may use a stick with a 12-inch (30.7 cm) head. Most goalkeepers use a plastic-headed stick that is allowed to have a deep mesh pocket. Although some goalkeepers still prefer a traditionally strung head (woven with thongs and cross-stitches), most goalies have moved toward a mesh pocket.

Personal Equipment

Clothing

For play on grass or turf, cleated shoes may be worn. The cleats may be rubber or plastic but not metal. For play on turf, players may wish to wear turf shoes. Uniforms are

Figure 20-13. Wooden lacrosse stick.

Figure 20-14. Plastic lacrosse stick.

usually short skirts, kilts, or loose-fitting shorts. The shirt should fit loosely enough to allow the arms full movement. Some teams wear knee socks, but because the playing season tends to be in warm weather, many wear short socks.

Gloves

Field players may choose to wear thin, close-fitting gloves for warmth or knuckle protection. These gloves have padding on the back that still allows for maximum flexibility. Many players do not wear gloves, as they are not required.

Goalkeeper's Equipment

Helmet

Because the ball is shot directly at the goal face, where the goalkeeper stands, head protection is required. Lightweight, close-fitting helmets are manufactured specifically for women's lacrosse goalkeepers. The face is covered with a mask that comes down below the chin.

Throat protector

Throat protection is required. The protector may be attached to the bottom of the face mask and be made of plastic or foam, or a protective collar may be worn around the neck.

Chest protector

Although a body pad covering the upper body and continuing down along the thighs may be worn, more movement and greater flexibility are achieved by wearing a separate chest protector. Several styles of compressed foam are available that cover the chest, clavicle area, and stomach.

Thigh protection

Slip-on pants with built-in pelvic protector and foam padding covering the thighs and hip bone area are recommended.

Leg protection

With the use of the large-headed stick, many goalkeepers elect to keep their legs free to allow maximum speed and ease of movement. When protection is used, it generally consists of a slip-on foam shin guard. Occasionally knee pads are worn.

Gloves

Large padded gloves similar to men's lacrosse gloves are worn by goalkeepers. Rules require that the padding should not be excessive and not exceed 1 inch (2.5 cm).

Dimensions of the Field

The field for women's lacrosse consists of two goals 6 feet by 6 feet (1.8 m by 1.8 m) placed 100 yards (91.4 m) apart. The goals sit in the middle of a circle with a radius of 8.5 feet (2.6 m) called the *crease*. Coming off of the crease are two fan-shaped areas of 8.75 yards (8 m) (arc) and 13.1 yards (12 m) (fan) that demark the critical scoring area. The center of the field is marked by a large circle, with a radius of 10 yards (9.14 m) and a center line of 3.3 yards (3 m) drawn horizontally to the goal lines. Although there are no boundary lines, there must be at least 10 yards (9.14 m) of free playing space behind each goal and the entire playing area must be at least 60 yards (54.4 m) wide (figure 20-15).

Rules

Women's lacrosse is played by two teams of 12 players each with one being designated as goalkeeper. Although players may move into any area of the field, the game is started with three line-attack players (first home, second home, third home), five midfield players (two attack wings, one center, two defense wings), and three line-defense players (third person, cover point, point). The goalkeeper completes the defense line (figure 20-15). Time of play is generally 25-minute halves with a 10-minute halftime. Some college play has recently gone to 30-minute halves, while younger groups may elect a 20-minute half.

Draw

The game is started by a center draw. The opposing centers toe the center line facing their attacking goal and place their sticks back to back horizontally at a level above their waists. The ball is placed between their sticks, not resting on the sidewalls but cushioned between the pocket weave. At the umpire's command "Ready," the players remain

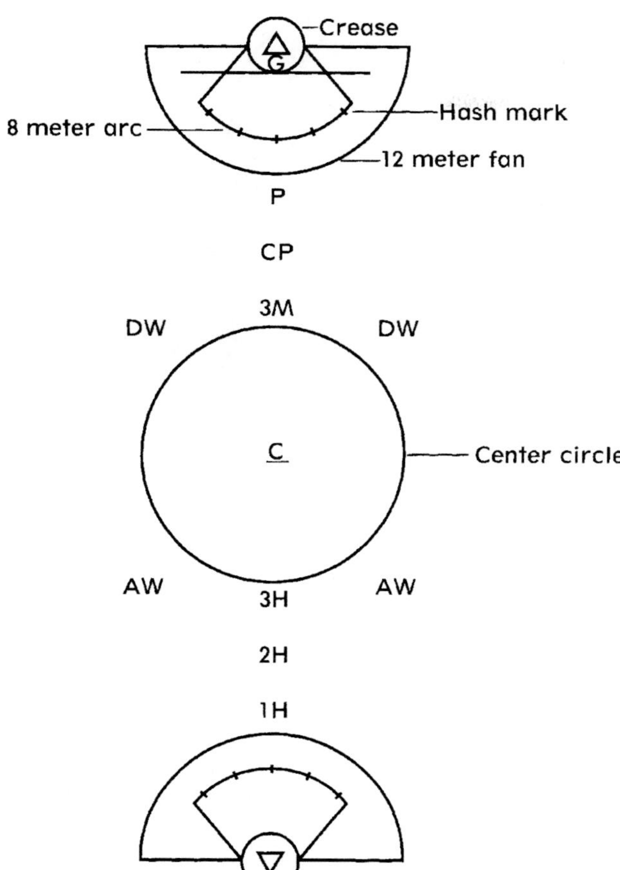

Figure 20-15. Women's lacrosse field dimensions and playing positions.

motionless until the umpire blows the whistle, when they push their sticks up and away in an effort to raise the ball above their heads and out of the circle to one of their teammates. All other players must remain out of the center circle during the draw. Midfield players usually position themselves around the circle in anticipation of the drawn ball and move into the circle toward the ball when the umpire blows the whistle.

Scoring

The ball may be shot from any position on the field. The whole ball must cross the goal line for a goal to count. For safety reasons, a ball shot directly at the goalkeeper's body is disallowed, and the attacking player's body or stick may not enter the crease at any level during a shot or its follow-through. When a goal is scored, play is restarted at the center draw. If the ball does not cross the goal line or if an attacking player has entered the crease, the goalkeeper may place the ball in her stick and, within 10 seconds, pass the ball out of the crease to a teammate.

Stand

One of the unique rules in women's lacrosse is the stand: When the umpire blows the whistle, the ball is considered dead and all players are required to "stand" in the position they were in when the whistle blew. They may not move until the umpire restarts the game. Any player who moves after the whistle has blown, either intentionally or by the momentum of her original movement, is returned to her original position before play is restarted.

Throw

When the game needs to be restarted without giving an advantage to either team, a throw is taken. One player from each team, standing at least 1.1 yard (1 m) apart and on the side nearer to the goal she is defending, faces the umpire, who is about 6 yards (5.5 m) away. On the whistle, the umpire throws the ball in the air a little higher than head height and between the players so that they may move toward it and into the game. All other players must be 4 yards (3.7 m) away from these players and may move (stop standing) on the umpire's whistle.

A throw is taken when:

1. The ball goes in the goal off a nonplayer
2. The ball goes out of the established boundaries (natural boundaries) and it cannot be determined which player was closer to the ball as it went out of bounds
3. Simultaneous fouls occur
4. The ball lodges in the clothing of a field player or umpire

Fouls

Major fouls. A player may not:

1. Dangerously or roughly check or tackle another player's stick.
2. Slash or touch another player with the stick or body.
3. Hold the stick within the space (sphere) around another player's face or throat.
4. Reach across with the stick in front of or across the shoulder from behind another player.
5. Block or move in front of an opponent without giving the opponent a chance to move out of the way.
6. Place the body between the opposing team's ball carrier and the goal, blocking the free space to goal (figure 20-16) unless closely guarding an opponent.
7. While defending within the 8.75 yards (8 m) arc, remain in that area for more than 3 seconds, unless closely guarding an opponent. There may only be one defender per opponent.
8. Use the body to stop an opponent's movement, or, if the ball carrier, use the body to force one's way.
9. While carrying the ball, keep the head of the crosse so close to the head as to make an opponent's check illegal.

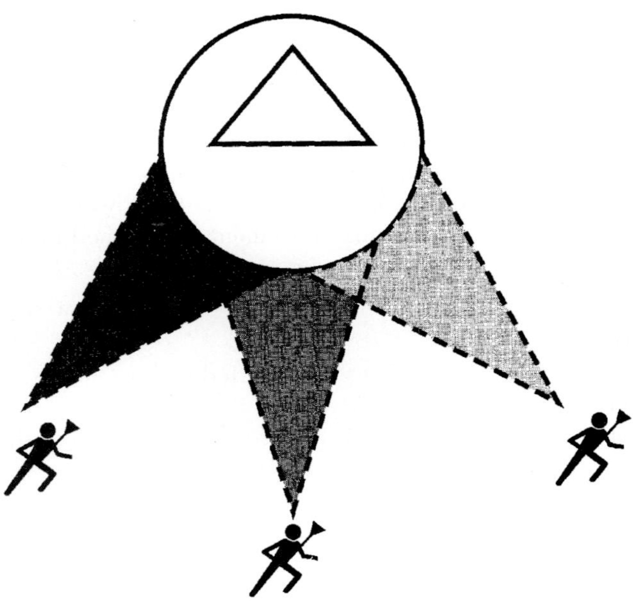

Figure 20-16. Free space to the goal.

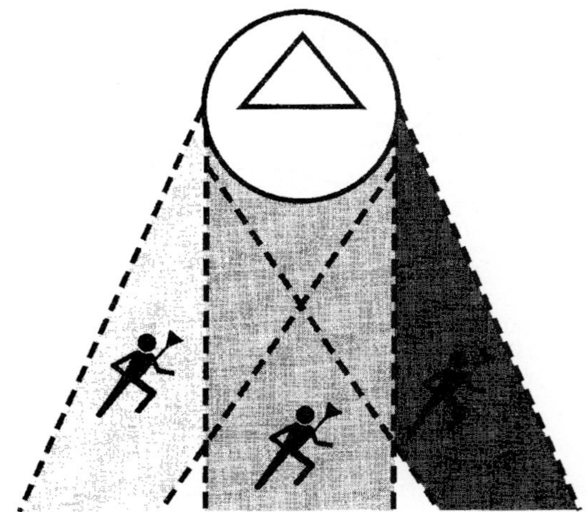

Figure 20-17. Penalty lanes.

Minor fouls. A player may not:

1. Cover a ground ball with the foot or stick.
2. Check an opponent's empty stick.
3. Guard one's stick with the hand or elbow.
4. Touch the ball with the hand.
5. Allow the ball to play off the body, unless the player is the goalkeeper and is inside the crease.
6. Throw the crosse.
7. On the center draw, step into the circle until the whistle blows.
8. Play with a crosse that does not meet measurement and pocket requirements.

Goal circle (or crease) fouls. Field players may not enter or have any part of their stick or body in the goal circle.

Goalkeepers may not:

1. Allow the ball to remain in the crease longer than 10 seconds.
2. Play the ball outside of the circle with the hand.
3. Step back into the crease while in possession of the ball.
4. Place one foot outside of the goal circle and drag the ball inside.
5. Score a goal with a crosse that does not meet specifications for field players.

Penalty for major and minor fouls. The penalty for fouls is the *free position*. On the umpire's whistle, all players stand. The umpire than awards the ball to the fouled player while moving all other players 4.4 yards (4 m) away. For major fouls the offending player is moved 4.4 yards (4 m) behind the player awarded the free position. Play is restarted by the umpire's arm signal and whistle.

Penalty for major fouls inside the 13.1 yards (12 m) fan. The penalty for a major foul by a defensive player awards a free position to the fouled attack player on the spot where the foul occurred. All other players and their crosses must be moved sideways out of the penalty lane (figure 20-17). The goalkeeper may remain within the goal circle.

Penalty for major fouls inside the 8.75 yard (8 m) arc. Major fouls committed by the defense within the 8.75 yard (8 m) arc result in a free position to the fouled attack player, who is placed on the closest hash mark on the 8.75 yard (8 m) arc. All other players are cleared from the 8.75 yard arc and penalty lane, and the offending defense player is placed on the 13.1 yard (12 m) fan, directly behind the fouled attack player. If a major foul occurs to the side of the 8.75 yard arc, the fouled player is positioned 8.75 yards from the goal, and all other players must be moved from the penalty line (figure 20-17).

Penalty for minor fouls inside the 13.1 yard (12 m) fan. Minor fouls by the defense within the 13.1 yard (12 m) fan result in an *indirect free position* awarded to the fouled attack player, who is placed on the nearest spot on the 12-meter fan. The ball must be touched by another player before a shot on goal is attempted. The offending defense player is placed 4.37 yards (4 m) behind the fouled player. All other players may remain in their positions, as long as they are 4.37 yards (4 m) away from the player taking the free position.

Basic Skills

Cradle

The cradle allows a player to move with the ball remaining securely within the laced pocket of the stick. Because the rules require the stick to have a tight pocket, continuous movement is required to keep the ball in place. Cradling is a natural movement that mirrors the body's movement while running. To teach a natural cradle, the following progression should be used:

Figure 20-18. Learning the cradle.

1. Have players run 20 yards with their arms in a natural pumping movement.
2. Focus players' attention on the natural movements of their arms.
3. Have players clasp their hands in front of the body, elbows bent, with the hands held slightly above the waist (figure 20-18).
4. With clasped hands players should run 20 yards again, overemphasizing the arm-pumping movement. This results in the arms moving together from one side of the body to the other, which is the movement of a natural full cradle.
5. Players should hold the stick in a vertical position, with the middle of the stick clasped in both hands. Remind players to keep their arms bent at waist level.
6. Have players run 20 yards with the stick remaining vertical and moving naturally from one side of the body to the other as the arms pump during the running motion (figure 20-19).
7. Players should gradually spread their hands apart on the stick (figure 20-20) and continue to reinforce the natural arm-pumping motion until they have one hand just below the head of the stick and one hand at the bottom (figure 20-21). Both arms should still remain above waist level. Teach players to be comfortable with either the right hand or the left hand at the top of the stick.

Figure 20-19. Learning the cradle: hands together.

Figure 20-20. Learning the cradle: hands spread.

Figure 20-21. Learning the cradle: final position.

Figure 20-22. Ready to throw.

Figure 20-23. Adding the stick.

8. Once players are comfortable with the full cradle, teach them the half-cradle, which has the stick movement coming from mid-body to one side and back again.

Grip during cradle (figures 20-13 and 20-14). Lay the stick, with the open pocket facing up, on the ground. While looking at the back of the hand, spread the thumb away from the other fingers to form a V between the thumb and index fingers. Wrap this hand around the stick just below the pocket with the V and back of the hand on the same side of the stick as the open pocket. Place the other hand at the bottom of the stick and bring the stick to a vertical position, with the bottom hand slightly above waist level. With this grip and relaxed shoulder and arm movements, the cradle will keep the ball in the pocket.

Throw

Lacrosse is a passing game, which means that players must have several ways in which to throw the ball. The most common are the overarm throw (a lever-type action when not closely guarded or a punch-type throw when closely guarded) and the underarm throw. To teach the overarm throw, the following progression should be used:

Overarm: lever style

1. Without a stick, the player should throw the ball to another player.
2. Focus player's attention on taking back the hand, opposite foot forward, shoulder rotation, and follow-through, as in the softball throw.
3. Freeze the player in the position of "hand back and ready to throw the ball" (figure 20-22).
4. Place a stick in the throwing hand with the pocket facing toward the sky and the end of the stick pointed toward the target. Remember to maintain the body's correct throwing position.
5. With only the throwing hand holding the stick, throw the ball toward the target, making sure that the stick face remains open toward the target, the bottom of the stick moves in a lever action under the arm, and a correct body rotation position is maintained.
6. Repeat this process, adding the second hand to the bottom of the stick (figure 20-23).
7. Start cradling while walking. As the cradle comes to the side of the body, move into the throwing position and throw the ball while walking through the throwing action. The stick moves in a lever action and finishes with the throwing arm straight toward the target and the bottom hand in the armpit (figure 20-24).
8. Gradually increase speed from a walk to running and throw on the run.

Figure 20-24. The throw.

Overarm: punch style

1. The punch style is very similar to the lever style, but limit the upper-hand preparation of the throw to a position in front of the throwing shoulder instead of behind the shoulder.
2. Body position and motion remain the same. Because of the starting position, there is a much smaller lever action. The power loss is compensated for by a push from the upper arm and hand.

Grip during overarm throws. When throwing overarm, the grip is relaxed to allow the stick face to open up toward the target. This results in the hand moving around the stick, where the back of the pocket is. As the ball is thrown, the hand should be firm on the stick. Immediately after the throw, the hand should return to the cradling position.

Underarm throw. When another player is guarding the ball carrier, there are times when the carrier must be able to throw the ball when the stick is on the wrong side of the body for an overarm throw. To accomplish a throw, either switch hands—placing the other hand on the top of the stick—or use an underarm throw. If the thrower is trying to throw under the opponent's stick, the underarm throw is the better choice. A description of this movement follows.

Body position. The body is turned sideways, with the shoulder aimed at the target. Both feet can be turned sideways. The arms are pulled across the body away from the target, the hand of the aiming shoulder on top, in a cradle position (figure 20-25). At the start of the throw, the stick is held in a vertical position.

Arm and stick movement. In one continuous movement, the stick is turned almost upside down and moved in a shovel/sweep across the body, ending with the top of the stick pointed at the target and the arms extended. The foot closest to the target may step toward the target during the movement (figure 20-26). The stick movement simulates a canoe stroke or snow shoveling.

Grip during underarm throw. The grip during the underarm throw remains the same as during the cradle, with the V positioned just below the open pocket face of the stick.

The catch. (figure 20-27) The catch is an extension of the cradle. The player must make sure that the pocket on the stick face is open toward the oncoming ball and must continuously watch the ball move into the pocket of the stick. As soon as the ball enters the pocket, the player should absorb its shock with a "soft give," as in baseball, and continue into a cradle. The feeling of the give is an important skill because most catches are made while moving toward an oncoming ball.

Grip during the catch. The V of the top hand may be slightly relaxed during the catch. However, this should result in a minimal amount of repositioning of that hand. Once the ball enters the stick, a natural wrap into a continuous cradle will keep the ball in place. If the V is moved too far out of the cradle position, it will be difficult to move

Figure 20-25. Underarm throw (side view).

Figure 20-26. Underarm throw (front view).

smoothly into a cradle, with the result of the ball bumping out of the pocket.

Ground ball pick-ups

Because passing and catching are skills that require some practice to consistently be successful, it is inevitable that the ball will sometimes hit the ground. Because players may not touch the ball with their hands, ground balls must be picked up with the stick.

Body position. The body is turned sideways (as in throwing) when executing a ground ball pick-up. Which side turns, or opens up, is determined by where and how closely one is being defended. The player who is picking up the ground ball should position the body between the opponent and the ground ball. As the ball is approached, the player should slowly move into a crouch position by bending the knees and lowering the hips (figure 20-28). As the front foot outdistances the ball, the player should already be low enough to scoop the stick through it as it moves toward the front foot (figure 20-29). As the player scoops, she continues to run through the ball and gradually assumes an upright cradling position (figure 20-30).

Figure 20-27. The catch.

Figure 20-28. Approach for picking up a ground ball.

Stick position. The stick is lowered and scrapes the ground with the lip of the stick moving under the ball. As the ball enters the stick, a gradual cradle is immediately started and continues as the player slowly moves into an upright position.

Grip. The grip is the same as with the cradle, with the V of the hand positioned just below the open pocket. This position enables a smooth transition into the cradle.

Figure 20-29. The scoop.

Figure 20-30. Moving from the scoop to the cradle.

Body checking

No matter what strategy is used, lacrosse always comes down to a level of one player competing against another. When playing against an opponent who possesses the ball, it is critical to maneuver into a safe playing position before making an attempt to dislodge the ball. This skill is called body checking. There is no body or stick contact. The player who is body checking positions her body about a stick's length away from the opponent and moves with her in an effort to slow her down, keep her from moving in the desired direction, or move her into a position where she or a teammate can legally check her stick.

Double-teaming

Double-teaming refers to two defense players who, through their body-checking skills, maneuver their opponent into a position where one of the defense players has a clear opening to the attacker's stick and is able to legally check her stick.

Stick checking

The ball may be dislodged from a player's stick by the opponent's stick. There are strict rules on how this should be accomplished. The stick checker must be in a position where she can reach the opponent's stick without crossing the body or reaching from behind. When the checking stick makes contact with the ball carrier's stick, all stick movement must be away from the ball carrier's body and must never occur within the imaginary sphere around her head. The checking movement must also be combined with a short jab-and-release motion.

Cutting

As the ball is moved down the field, it is each player's responsibility to maneuver herself into a position that gives the ball carrier a passing option. Each player accomplishes this by first eluding the defense and then timing a movement, or "cut," toward the ball carrier. If the cutter does not receive the ball, she should then pull away from the play, reposition, and cut again. Sometimes this is accomplished by making one cut and immediately following it with a second cut.

Cutting practice. Place the ball carrier at one corner of a square. Place the cutter at the corner diagonally across from the passer. As the passer turns toward the cutter, the cutter runs toward one of the other corners, showing with her stick where she wishes to receive the ball. A double cut can be practiced by using two sides of a square. Be sure to time the cut based on the passer's readiness to throw.

This pattern can then be transferred to any position on the field. When a defensive player is added, the cutter should execute a fake before making a cut.

Attack Movement

Attack movement is generated by moving the ball down the field in twos, then in threes, and then by adding interchanging movements. The next step would be a two-on-one situation, along with a continuous "give-and-go" passing formation. This is built upon to create situations of three-on-two and three-on-three. Small games with these formations can then be played in any area of the field.

A popular small game used to practice ball movement up and down the field is to create a three-on-three or four-on-four formation in a line. Each player stays with her opponent while the ball is passed up and down the line. Each time the ball is intercepted by an opponent, the direction of play is changed.

In lacrosse, when your team has the ball you are an attack player. Although some positions are known as attack positions, this distinction arises due to their proximity to the goal.

The ball is moved down the field through a series of cutting and passing movements. Although players are constantly repositioning after a cut and interchanging their positions, there are general areas of the field for each posi-

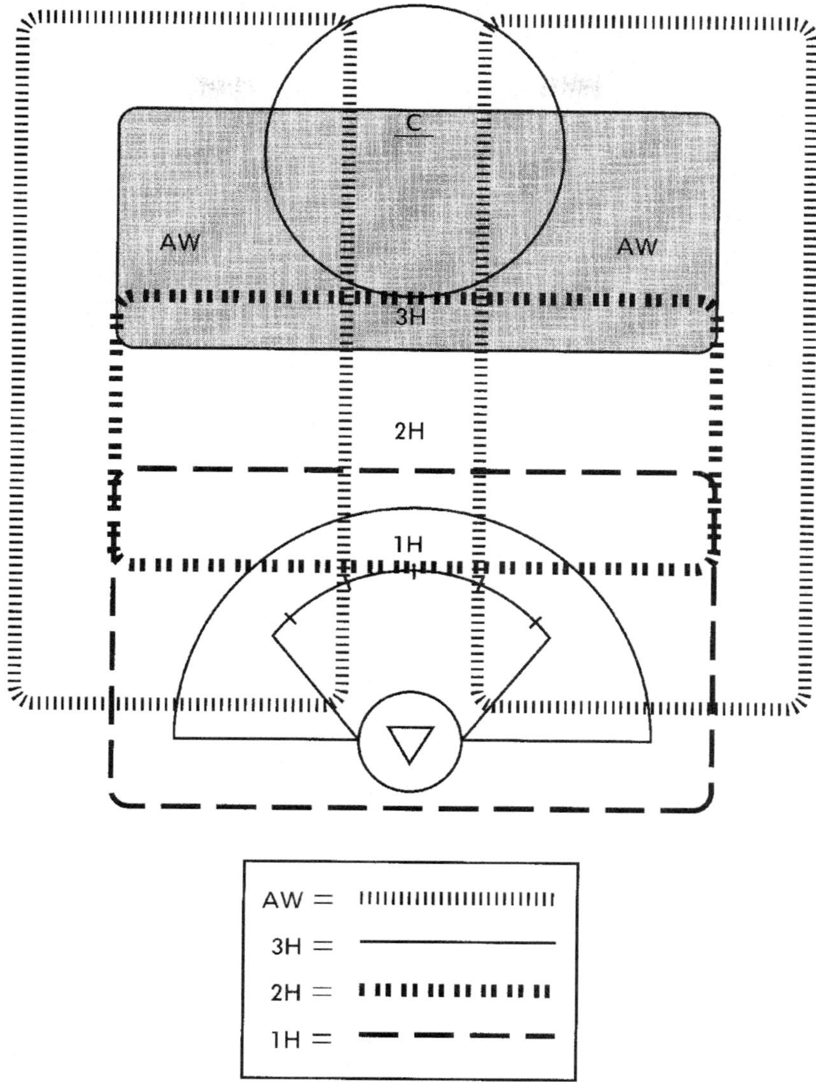

Figure 20-31. Playing areas of the homes and attack wings.

tion. The following are general guidelines only and are not meant to restrict movement.

As the goalkeeper clears the ball, the line defense—point (P), center point (CP), and third man (3M)—the defense wings (DW) and the center (C) cut in order to give the goalkeeper passing options. The line defense players' roles are to move the ball away from their defensive goal and to either the midfield players (wings or center) or into the attack. The role of the midfield players—defense wings (DW), attack wings (AW), center (C)—is to act as connectors between the defensive end of the field and the attacking end of the field.

The attack wings cover the outside of the field from the center area to the goal (figure 20-31). Occasionally they will cross over to the other side of the field. When this occurs, the other wing often crosses to keep the field balanced. Each of the homes covers the width of the playing area and approximately one third of the area between the center of the field and the goal area.

An example of this kind of movement is shown in figure 20-32, where the DW receives a clear, turns and passes to the third home (3H), who has made a movement toward the outside of the field in order to make the space for a cut directly to the DW. The AW has also cut to receive the ball, but the DW chose to pass to the 3H. The 3H turns and passes to the second home (2H), who has moved out and down to make space and then cut toward the ball. The 2H then turns and passes to the first home (1H), who has repositioned herself away from the goal so that her cut enables the 2H to pass directly to her. The 1H then turns and has an opportunity to shoot at the goal or pass off to the opposite AW, who has repositioned herself below the

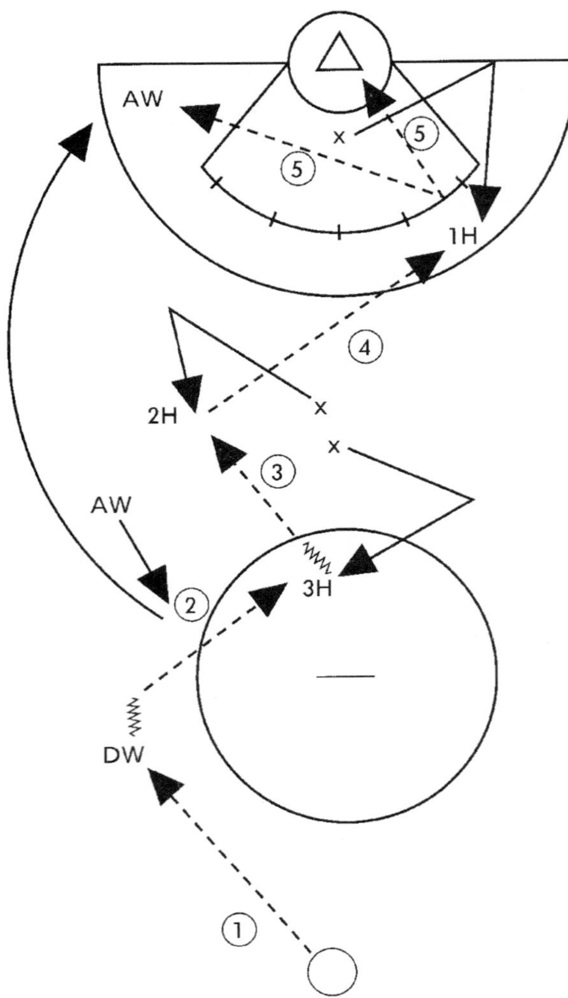

Figure 20-32. Passing during an attack.

ball. Another option would be a pass to the ball-side AW or the 2H, who would be repositioning in an attempt to be available should the 1H need an outlet pass.

Once the ball has reached the attacking end and a goal has not been scored, the attack players need to reposition themselves while keeping the ball in motion. They should continuously send cutters through the attacking area in an attempt to gain a position that would allow a shot on goal. Teams devise numerous plays to cover this situation.

Defense Movement

All defense movement starts with the ability to effectively and safely body-check. After the initial skill is learned, players should begin in one-on-one situations and build into two-on-one situations. At this point, double-teaming concepts can be introduced and continued into three-on-two situations.

When a member of the opposing team has the ball, all players become defense players and play in a one-on-one formation until the ball crosses the center of the field. At this point, some teams elect to continue to play with one-on-one formations, while others choose to create a zone formation. A common zone using five players, four in boxed areas and one chaser, is shown in figure 20-33.

Teams who play a one-on-one formation often have a plan to account for fast breaks. The one shown in figure 20-34 shows the DW who is not on the ball side (weak side) dropping off to cover the center of the field and often picking up the 2H or 3H. The 3M or the CP may pull off and pick up the ball-carrying AW, who has lost her opposing DW. If the opposing DW has stayed with the attacking AW, the 3M may still pull off and, along with her DW, create a double-team situation that should lead to a turnover.

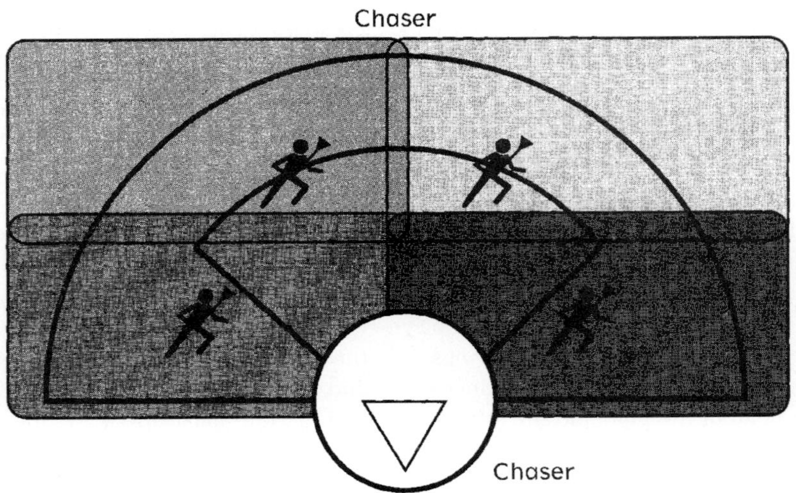

Figure 20-33. A zone formation with a chaser.

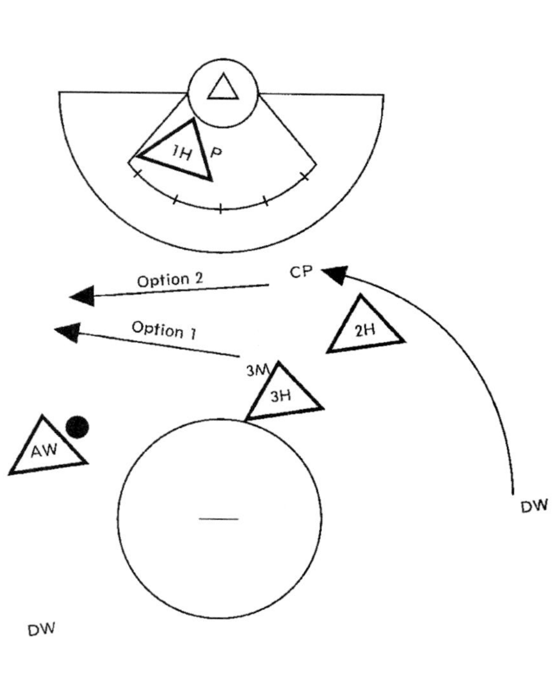

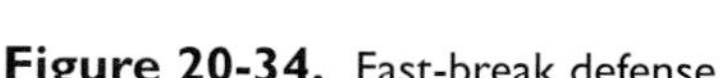
Figure 20-34. Fast-break defense.

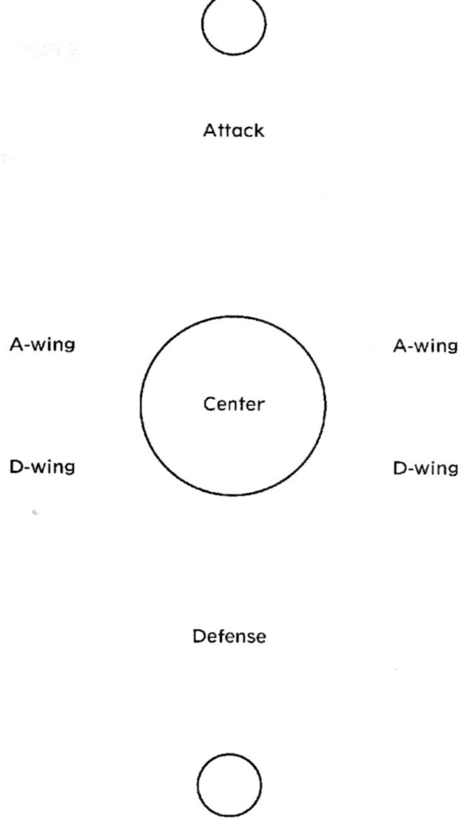

Figure 20-35. Positions for a seven-a-side lacrosse.

Seven-a-Side Lacrosse

A great small game and lead-up to full field lacrosse is seven-a-side lacrosse. Each team has one attack, two attack wings, a center, two defense wings, and one defense player (figure 20-35). All play is person-to-person, with no restrictions on where players may move. However, keeping a balance to the playing area is an important concept and should be constantly stressed.

The game can be played outdoors in a small area or indoors on a court similar to a basketball court. Goals could be basketball backboards or official goals, which are basketball-type hoops placed 5 feet off the ground on a standard and angled 45 degrees toward the floor, with the open face toward the playing area. The hoop has a net with a closed bottom.

Play is started for the center circle when the official blows the whistle. Only one player, usually the center, may be in the center circle with the ball. She has 10 seconds in which to pass the ball out of the circle to a teammate after the whistle has blown. Play is continuous and follows all the field game rules until a foul occurs or a goal is scored. When a goal is scored, play is restarted from the center circle with a center throw by the nonscoring team.

Any player may attempt to score a goal from any space within the playing area. The ball carrier may also run to the goal and place the ball in the goal while making contact with the goal rim or standard. Because there are no goalkeepers, full field game rules pertaining to the crease, arc, and fan do not apply.

TEACHING CONSIDERATIONS

1. Cradling, throwing, and catching can be taught immediately and practiced in small game-type activities. From the start, encourage all skills to be practiced on the move and with either hand at the top of the stick.
2. Ground ball pick-ups should be taught next, combined with throwing in different directions on the run.

3. Introduce small keep-away games with no resistance, slowly building to passive resistance. Slowly build the numbers of players within these games.
4. Be sure that players are aware of their body space and stick space as they work with and compete against other players.
5. Emphasize the importance of safe body checking before introducing stick checking.
6. Once stick checking has been introduced, apply the rules of the game tightly and consistently in practice and game situations. In some environments, stick checking may be eliminated.

GLOSSARY— MEN'S

attackmen The three offensive players that operate around the goal area.

ball stop A piece of foam rubber that adheres to the throat of the stick and facilitates holding the ball in the pocket.

body check A deliberate bumping of an opponent from the front—above the knees and below the neck—when the opponent is in possession or within five yards of the ball.

checking Attempting to dislodge the ball from your opponent's stick.

clear Running or passing the ball from the defensive half of the field to the attack goal area.

cradling The rhythmical coordinated motion of the arms and wrists that keeps the ball secure in the stick and ready to be passed or shot.

crease The circle with a nine-foot radius around each goal.

cross check An illegal check or hold using the area of the stick handle between the hands.

cutting A movement by an offensive player without the ball, toward the opposition goal and in anticipation of a feed and subsequent shot.

dodges Ball-carrying maneuvers used for eluding defenders.

ground ball A loose ball anywhere on the playing field. Opposing teams fight for possession using body and stick checks as well as scooping techniques.

handle An aluminum or wooden pole connected to the head of a stick; the part of the stick that players grasp when executing any maneuver with their sticks.

head The plastic part of the stick connected to the handle.

holding A technical foul committed either by grabbing an opponent or by hindering a ballcarrier's progress with one's stick.

interference A technical foul committed by preventing the free movement of an opponent who is neither in possession of the ball nor within five yards of a loose ball.

midfielders The three players who play in the center of the field and play both offense and defense.

offside A technical foul in which the offending team has either fewer than three players in its offensive half of the field or fewer than four players in its defensive half of the field.

pocket The strung part of the head of the stick that holds the ball.

riding The act of preventing a team from clearing the ball.

throat The part of the head of the stick where the plastic meets the handle.

GLOSSARY—WOMEN'S

blocking Occurs when a player moves into the path of the ball carrier and creates contact without giving the ball carrier time to change direction

body checking When a defender moves with an opponent and causes the opponent to slow down, change direction, or pass.

bridge In a wooden stick, the area on the bottom of the pocket made of heavy gut or nylon the connects the woven sidewall to the wooden wall.

charging When a player with the ball pushes through the opponents by using the body

cradle The arm and stick movements used to keep the ball in the stick

crease The circle around the goal cage. Sometimes called the "goal circle."

crosse A lacrosse stick is often called a *crosse*.

cutting A movement made into a space on the field toward the ball carrier in order to recieve a pass.

gut Sticks made of wood are often woven with a fine gut thread. Bridges may also be woven of a thicker gut.

sidewall The side edge of a stick. In wooden sticks, one sidewall is woven from a stiff nylon material.

slashing Recklessly swinging a stick at or across opponent's body.

stick checking A controlled tap on an opponent's stick designed to dislodge the ball.

thongs, or leads Leather or synthetic strips that run vertically in the pocket of the crosse and around which the pocket is woven.

SUGGESTED READINGS

Burbank, A. 1994. *Beyond X's and O's: A women's lacrosse playbook*. Northampton, Mass.: Smith College.

Kurtz, A., and Green, T. 1989. *Modern women's lacrosse*. Hanover, N.H.: ABK.

Marino, M. 1994. *On attack*. Glassboro, N.J.: Rowan College.

National Collegiate Athletic Association. Current ed. *NCAA lacrosse rule book*. Overland Park, Kan.: NCAA.

United States Women's Lacrosse Association. Current ed. *Official lacrosse rules*. Hamilton, N.Y.: USWLA.

Urick, D. 1988. *Lacrosse: Fundamentals for winning*. New York: Time.

RESOURCES

Videotapes

On the attack; Defense, the long sticks; Goalie, the last defense; and *The middie* are available from the Lacrosse Foundation, 113 W University Parkway, Baltimore, MD 21210.

Skills and techniques and *The goalkeeper* are available from the United States Women's Lacrosse Association, Hamilton, N.Y.

21 Mountaineering

After completing this chapter, the reader should be able to:

- Explain the importance of physical conditioning and weather considerations in mountaineering
- Select proper mountaineering equipment
- Recognize what backpacking, camping, and other skills are necessary to lead a mountaineering trip
- Demonstrate proper hiking skills for various types of terrain and conditions
- Apply rock-climbing principles
- Practice various rock-climbing holds and descending techniques
- Understand the management and use of ropes in climbing and descending

Mountaineering as a sport evolved from a desire to fulfill the need for adventure, to satisfy curiosity for scientific study, and to test abilities and limits. Now that the earth's highest points have been attained, the dream has been extended to space, but even those limits are being reduced. The challenges of earthbound adventurers can be successfully met with the knowledge of the dangers involved and with the training necessary to handle them. A mountaineer shares and appreciates the beauty of nature and, at the same time, learns to venture into the mountains with respect.

Increasing numbers of people are expressing interest in a variety of outdoor recreation sports that relate to the wilderness, mountains, rivers, and oceans. These would-be adventurers must be made aware of the responsibilities that accompany this interest. The skills discussed in this chapter are necessarily very basic, and the reader should note that proper instruction and experience are required to properly employ them in the field.

HISTORY

Examples of famous climbs include the biblical account of Moses receiving the Ten Commandments on Mount Sinai and Hannibal crossing the Alps with his elephants. Military conquests long provided the strongest reasons for passage through and over mountains. One may conjecture that when military needs no longer existed, peoples' adventurous spirit turned in peacetime to the mountains and to the pursuit of climbing, with scientific or geographical reasons given for the activity.

According to Ronald W. Clark's book *Men, Myths and Mountains*, in 1492, as Columbus set sail on his history-making first voyage, a group of men in France started an assault on a rock bastion that had long been considered inaccessible and inhabited by evil spirits. That this climb was made for the challenge it offered, not for necessity, might mark it as the beginning of climbing as a sport. Actually, climbing was not recognized as a sporting pastime until a century or so later.

In the mid 1500s, Josias Simler, a naturalist professor at Zurich University, published *Concerning the Difficulties of Alpine Travel and Methods by Which They May Be Overcome*. In the same era the clergy and monks played a significant part in the development of mountain travel.

Climbing has never been confined to men. Clark states that women began to join climbing groups early in the 1800s. In 1809 Marias Paradis, from Chamonix, France, became the first woman to climb Mont Blanc. Recent history has also recorded an attempt on Mount Everest by an all-female team.

Military mountaineering in the Alps played a large and tragic part in World War I. After the war, interest in climbing the world's highest mountains intensified. Membership in long-established mountain clubs, such as the Appalachian Mountain Club and Sierra Club, grew quickly, as did the outing clubs of schools and colleges of the United States.

After World War II the U. S. Army Tenth Mountain Division, with many famous skiers and mountaineers in its ranks, sponsored climbing schools and made many climbs themselves that helped rekindle interest in mountaineering among the youth of the United States. Today, with the advent of worldwide trekking companies, professional guiding, and indoor rock-climbing walls, mountains are even more accessible.

PHYSICAL CONDITIONING

One should not engage in mountaineering without first attending to one's physical condition. Cardiovascular and respiratory conditioning exercises are appropriate for mountaineers. Stamina and an intense desire to persist are important qualities to possess in difficult situations. A mountaineer living in the city should consider the many training facilities available. Running and weight training are the two main exercises for the climber preparing for the mountains. Using stairs instead of elevators and practicing fingerhold chin-ups on the casing over doorways are simple but effective conditioning activities.

WEATHER CONSIDERATIONS

No hiker or climber can afford to disregard the weather. Forecasts are essential, and the normal weather patterns should be known. Local inhabitants may sometimes be helpful, and a rudimentary knowledge of weather signs is necessary. As a general rule the temperature drops 3 to 5°F for every 1,000-foot (305 m) gain in elevation. Marginal weather at lower elevations may mean storms at higher elevations. Thunderstorms produce highly dangerous conditions. Lightning follows the ridges along exposed mountain tops. The difference between temperatures in the sun and the shade or in the wind and out of the wind can be as great as 50°F. These facts are essential to hikers and climbers in determining their route or abandoning it.

EQUIPMENT

Boots

A well-fitted pair of leather hiking boots is suitable for both hiking and rock climbing. Sneakers are preferred by some hikers, but are suitable only in dry conditions and do not provide the protection or support of leather boots and are not suitable for exposed rock climbs. Lightweight hiking shoes are popular on trails and are kind to both the environment and hikers' feet. Plastic climbing boots are currently state of the art for glacier travel and for snow and ice climbs. They are used almost exclusively on climbs of big mountains. Specialized rock-climbing shoes provide the greatest sensitivity for technical climbing and come with sticky rubber soles (figure 21-1).

Figure 21-1. Assorted boots and shoes for climbing.

Clothing

A layering system is most comfortable for the ever-changing conditions of the mountains. Synthetic thermals and fleece provide warmth and at the same time wick moisture away from a perspiring body. They also dry much faster than natural fibers, vastly reducing the risk of hypothermia in extreme cases. A final wind- and waterproof layer is essential even on the most hopeful of days in the mountains. Hats and gloves are also important for some local conditions. Sunblock is advisable when venturing to higher elevations, and a helmet is crucial when scrambling or rock climbing in the mountains.

FUNDAMENTAL SKILLS AND TECHNIQUES

Backpacking and camping skills should be acquired and should include knowledge of how to:

1. Make a fire
2. Use gasoline, alcohol, and kerosene compact mountain stoves
3. Read a map and use a compass
4. Use and care for tents
5. Construct an improvised shelter
6. Know first aid
7. Be aware of problems that might be encountered so that the consequences of poor decisions can be avoided

DUTIES OF THE TRIP LEADER

1. Inspect the group's equipment.
2. Make health check: allergies, prior injuries, and physical limitations.
3. Group information:
   a. Objective
   b. Direction being taken
   c. Route or trail markers being followed
   d. Return route if different
   e. Time starting and expected return
   f. Weather report and forecast
   g. Orientation via map or guidebook
   h. Action if separated
4. On the trail:
   a. Determine the hiking order and assign numbers so the order can be maintained.
      (1) Place weak hiker between two strong hikers.
      (2) Be about second or third place for best observation and control.
   b. Assign first-aid person and assistant leader to the rear and establish that *no one* be behind them. This must be a hard-and-fast rule.
   c. Establish water policy.
      (1) Drink on a regular basis, thirsty or not.
      (2) Do not limit the water intake, as each hiker may have different needs.

(3) Only exception: When refills are not available, practice conservation.

d. Do not force stragglers to hurry to catch up. Slow the pace for them.

e. Execute a shakedown break after first 15 minutes on the trail.

f. Inspect at the rest halts: red face, blueness from cold, possible foot problems, temperament problems between hikers.

g. Coordinate trail procedures.
   (1) Maintain about 5 feet (1.5 m) between hikers; do not close up tight when column slows down or stops for minor obstacles.
   (2) Avoid accordion action.
   (3) When head of column passes through a difficult area, slow down until the whole column has passed the obstacle.

5. Trail discipline:
   a. Establish trail communications policy.
      (1) Use voice instructions and hand signals.
      (2) Whistle only in emergencies.
      (3) Check off by calling for a numbers count.
   b. Establish behavior policy.
      (1) Get off the trails during rests.
      (2) Put feet up and take packs off.
      (3) Do not litter.
      (4) Purify water that is not obtained from an approved source.
      (5) Conserve energy; restrain excess exuberance.
      (6) Take rest halts often, but limit duration to 5 minutes every 30 minutes.
6. Other leader responsibilities:
   a. Make all decisions related to safety of party.
   b. Do not let people climb alone even to reconnoiter.
   c. Know the point of no return.
   d. Know when and where help is available.
   e. Know when to stop and make improvised camp in emergencies.
   f. Keep together.
   g. Send no one alone for help.
   h. Be sure all of the group members eat; all need the energy, especially if fatigued.
   i. Keep control in poor visibility; keep in visual or physical contact with the person ahead.
   j. Know when to push on, when to turn back, and when to stop and take shelter.
7. Objective dangers:
   a. Lightning
   b. Rain
   c. Hail
   d. Snow
   e. Ice
   f. Falling rock
   g. Falls
   h. Injuries
   i. Poor visibility
   j. Difficult terrain
   k. Altitude sickness
   l. Cold or heat
8. Subjective dangers:
   a. Fatigue
   b. Indecision
   c. Disorientation with surroundings
   d. Hunger
   e. Fear
   f. Lack of necessary knowledge

MOUNTAIN WALKING

The principles of mountain walking evolved from the need to conserve energy on long, steep climbs. The normal stride on level ground involves most leg muscles, but especially the muscles of the calf. When a hiker walks naturally, he or she plants the leading foot, then rises on the ball of that foot, lifting the heel as the rest of the body moves through and bringing the other foot forward. Thus, the calf muscles are used continually to help lift the weight at each step. This technique on steep terrain overworks these muscles and is unnecessarily tiring.

The mountain walking technique uses predominately the larger thigh muscles and allows a rest at each step. Keep the foot flat and use the full sole; that is, do not step off on the ball of the foot or raise the heel. Straighten the leg completely at each step. Lock the knee momentarily. This places the weight on the skeleton of the body and allows the muscles to relax. This full-sole technique—combined with a slow, steady pace, straight back, and body weight over the ball of the foot—is the true mountaineer gait. It requires fewer rests, saves time, covers more ground, and results in arrival at the objective with reserves of energy for other tasks.

A normal pace on flat land for day hikes is about 106 steps a minute or 2½ to 3 miles (4 to 4.8 km) per hour. This rate can be kept up for long periods. In the mountains, distance and time are figured in terms of elevation to be gained or lost. The climb over hard ground, following trails with relatively few obstacles, should take about 1 hour for every 1,000 feet (305 m) gained in elevation. This is true whether the climb is straight up or on a series of switchbacks, or traverses. Climbing straight up is tiring, so the pace is slower. The pace may be from 50 to 90 steps a minute, depending on the steepness of the climb, the weight of the pack, and the condition of the climber. At high altitudes (above 12,000 feet [3,660 m]), lack of oxygen becomes a problem. For some, this problem is noticed at elevations as low as 6,000 feet (1,830 m) above sea level. Descent rates should be about 2,000 to 2,500 feet (610 to 762 m) of elevation per hour.

TYPES OF TERRAIN

Hard Ground

Compact earth or gravel may be mixed with small to medium-size rocks on well-used trails.

Grassy Slopes

Mountain meadows of varying steepness and length are found on the route to many climbs, especially in the Rockies. These slopes are covered with long grass that grows in clumps, with a flat spot on the uphill side of each clump. In the climb, place the full sole of your foot on this flat spot. Climb on a traverse, and switch back and forth for a change. When changing direction, point the lower foot in the old direction and the uphill foot in the new direction to avoid crossing the legs and losing balance. This is the standard herringbone position. A short, steep pitch can be climbed with the herringbone step, but this is tiring and should be used only for short stretches. On all types of terrain avoid the tendency to lean into the slope, no matter how steep. Roll the ankles out to help keep the feet flat (figure 21-2).

Descent on grassy slopes

Descend on a traverse, often in a jog (depending on the weight of the pack and the condition of the climber). Use a hop-skip technique: weight on the downhill foot and skip with the uphill foot, using it for balance. Drag the uphill foot as if injured. With a little practice a very rapid descent can be made safely. Keep the momentum under control, change direction carefully, keep knees bent and hands low, and keep the weight at a right angle to the slope, not forward or back. Do not run straight down grassy slopes, one foot in front of the other. This will result in loss of control. The slope may be taken safely straight down, but at a much slower pace. Keep weight back, dig in with the heels, turn toes out, and do a slow skip.

Scree Slopes

Scree is a form of loose gravel and small rocks ranging from the size of a pea to stones the size of a fist. Scree is found at the base of high cliffs and forms long scars down mountainsides. Scree may be found in old avalanche paths of either snow or rock and mud slides that took off the top layers down to the gravel, or it may be caused by natural erosion and water runoff. Because of the looseness of the gravel, which rolls under the feet, scree slopes are very tiring and awkward to climb.

Ascent on scree

Use the full-sole, locked-knee technique. Dig in the toe of the uphill foot and the heel of the lower foot. If everyone in the group steps in the same place, a staircase will be

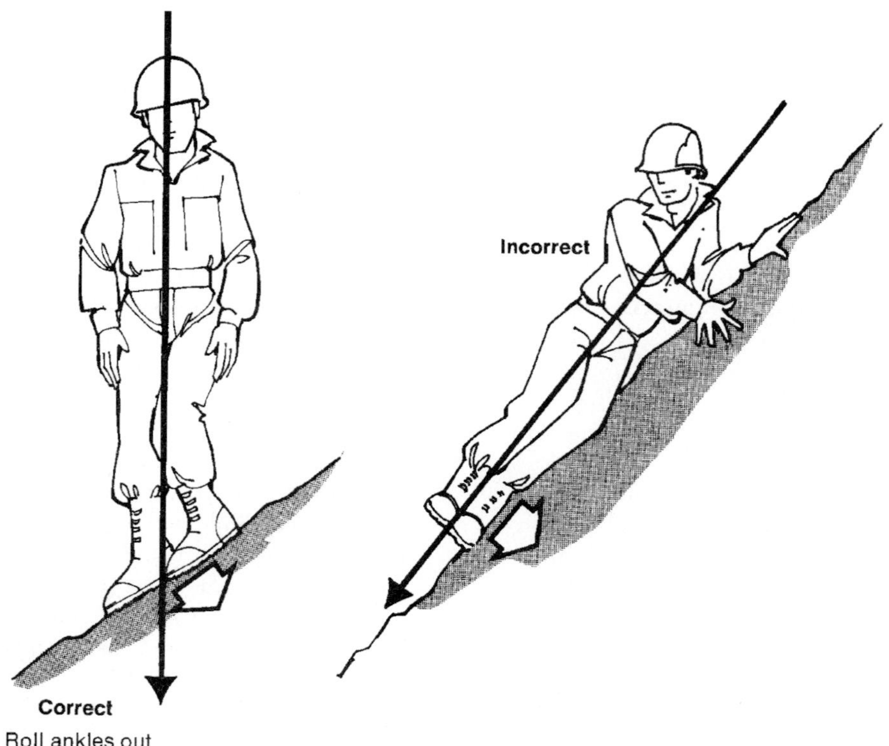

Figure 21-2. Grassy slope ascent.

formed. Traverse as often as the width of the slope permits. If the terrain is steep, keep a greater distance between climbers to avoid their being hit by dislodged rocks.

Descent on scree

Allow extra space between climbers. Use the hop-skip technique on traverses. Straight-down routes are preferred as long as large rocks are not a danger. Hop down, keep the feet shoulder-width apart, knees bent, hands low, and shift the weight from one foot to the other, alternating as in a snowplow position. Keep the weight slightly back and dig in the heels, and hop down in low bounds, but not with both feet at once like a rabbit. Be careful to keep your speed under control; slow down gradually before you reach the bottom.

Talus Rock

Talus is rock lying loose over hard ground. It is composed of boulders of many sizes, from rocks the size of a fist to boulders the size of boxcars. Talus is found at the base of cliffs and above the timberline on mountains. It is deposited through years of erosion and the effects of freezing and thawing; some talus is the result of the Ice Age's ravages. Talus may be strung over many acres. This loosely anchored rock is often not stable. Great care should be taken when working up, down, or across talus fields. On all types of terrain always step on the uphill side of the rock. This presses the rock down into the material below and usually stabilizes it. Being careless and stepping on the downhill edge of any loose rock may send it tumbling down the slope, endangering anyone below or resulting in the climber losing balance and twisting an ankle. This use of force applied directly over and down on loose rock must become second nature to climbers. The principle applies to handholds as well.

Low-Angle Rock

Low-angle rocks are small cliffs with pitches not over 40 to 60 degrees. These usually can be climbed safely with normal precautions, proper technique and careful route selection, without the aid of climbing ropes. Exposure should be kept to a minimum if possible. Study the rock strata carefully to see which way the slabs run. Layers tilted upward usually offer better handholds and footholds than strata inclined downward.

High-Angle Rock

High-angle rocks are cliffs with steep pitches and rock faces, some small but others many hundreds of feet high. These rock faces require careful study, expert climbing techniques, and the use of ropes, along with trusted partners and mechanical protection. Formerly, pitons driven into the rock were the only form of man-made protection. These have been replaced by a range of hand-placed devices that are removed by the last member ascending in the team. They do not scar or permanently deface the rock, as pitons do. Some of the newer devices are solid, while others have movable parts so that their size can be changed for use in different-sized cracks (figure 21-4).

Slab Rock

Slab rock is smooth and ranges in steepness. It can be climbed without using the hands for balance with proper footgear and technique if the slab does not slope more than 45 degrees and is dry.

ROCK-CLIMBING PRINCIPLES

The techniques of safe rock climbing apply to all degrees of steepness and types of rock. The cardinal rules are:

1. Keep three appendages on the rock at all times: one hand and two feet or two hands and one foot.

A

B

Figure 21-3. A, Proper form—upright, not leaning in, maximum friction from shoe soles. **B,** Poor form—leaning into rock, little friction from soles.

Figure 21-4. Rack of protection.

2. Move one hand or one foot at a time.
3. Test all holds.
4. Let the legs do the lifting. (They are five times as strong as the arms.) Use the hands for balance.
5. Try to keep handholds between the shoulders and the waist.
6. Yell "Rock" if you dislodge one and it falls or you drop a piece of equipment. This warns anyone below to hug the cliff and avoid being hit. If you are below and hear that cry, do not look up; something may hit you in the face.
7. Avoid leaning in and hugging the rock when climbing.
8. Roll the ankles out to get as much of the sole on the rock as the holds permit. Friction is what holds the feet in place when there is no discernible edge on which to stand.
9. Avoid root and brush holds. They are usually shallow and not safely anchored.
10. Move the head slowly if you have to look down, to avoid getting dizzy.
11. Avoid using your knees, elbows, or stomach. Their use limits our maneuverability.
12. Do not pass over small foot- or handholds just to find a larger one father away. Try to move the feet and hands up at a similar rate to avoid getting overextended.
13. Move loose rock to a safe place. If this is not possible, yell "Rock" before tossing it down, thus giving others a change to protect themselves.
14. Execute a little jump step and change feet if you find that your legs cross when shifting holds, but make sure you have secure handholds before you hop.
15. Keep a buffer zone between what you know you can climb and what you would like to climb. Call this your margin of safety.
16. Stay low and move away from the edge before you straighten up and look down when arriving at the top of a cliff that may be on a ridgeline. The wind may be blowing strongly and knock you back over the cliff.
17. Watch out for scree over hard rock. When stepped on, it acts like ball bearings, and the feet slip out from under you in an instant. This is also dangerous if there are ledges or hard rock under a thin layer of scree on what looks like a true scree slope. Keep the soles and tread free of rocks and debris for safe climbing.
18. Use the edge of the sole by turning the inside of the foot to the rock to get more of the foot on the rock when traversing a face.

HOLDS

The following holds and all combinations of them will eventually be used by experienced rock climbers (figure 21-5).

Pull Holds

Pull holds are handholds using the fingers. They must be tested carefully. Dig out any loose sand or gravel around the hold. Keep the hands dry.

Friction Holds

Footholds or handholds depend on the climber's weight being forced down on the rock; so the more of the hand or foot on that surface, the safer the hold. A combination of pull and friction holds for the feet works best when the body is kept away from the rock. Lean back as far as the hands and feet allow so that the body weight pushes the feet against the rock, making friction overcome gravity.

Push Holds

Push holds are important because they work well even on loose rock. As long as the push is directly down and over the rock, the friction generated can support a lot of weight. Push holds in which the hands are palms-down and the fingers are pointed down the rock are often used when climbing down. The weight of the body is then held back by friction and muscles.

Pinch Holds

Very small projections of rock can be used as pinch holds by using the very ends of the fingers. Pinch holds are true

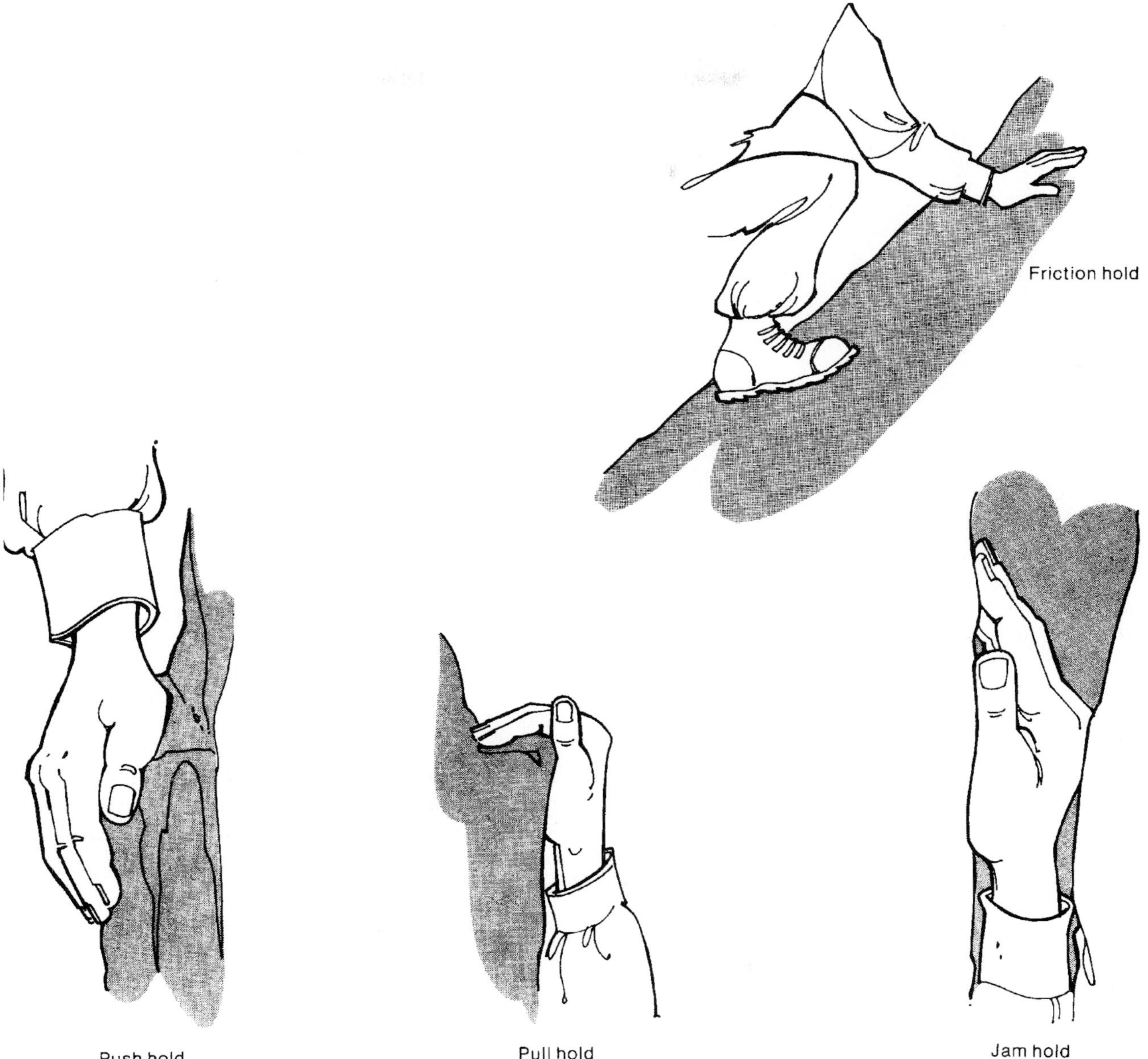

Figure 21-5. Holds.

balance holds, but should only be considered intermediate holds as the body moves to larger holds. The two feet and the other hand must have stronger and larger holds, but pinch holds can be depended on momentarily for balance as the body moves on up or across to a better position. When pinch holds are used, the body is usually in motion, moving to larger holds.

Jam Holds

Sometimes a fissure is found in the rock where angles come together or the rock changes direction and small cave-type apertures appear, often only large enough for the hand. Slide the hand into this opening and try to make a fist, which will act as a chockstone, preventing the hand from being withdrawn as long as the fist is kept clenched. This opening can sometimes be used for the feet. The foot is jammed into the opening as far as it will go. This is a temporary hold, and care must be taken that the angle of climb allows the foot to be withdrawn safely without disturbing balance as the climb continues.

Cross Pressure

Cross pressure, or chimney technique (figure 21-6), is used whenever there are opposing surfaces or rock walls that

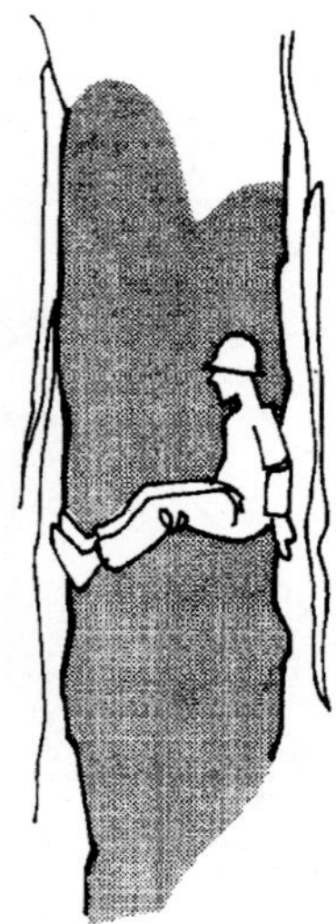

Figure 21-6. Chimney technique.

allow the back and hands to be pressed against one side and the feet against the opposite wall. The body can be inched up as long as the space remains close enough to hold this cross pressure. Friction and the muscle power of the back, legs, hands, and feet will hold the climber in place. One body part is moved at a time, with the hands, back, and feet working together, moving and releasing pressure. Be sure that you do not have gear or equipment around your waist, such as a canteen, to catch on projections and disturb your balance. The key to many spectacular climbs has been the use of the chimney technique.

DESCENDING TECHNIQUES

On rock faces, the same route used in climbing up often is followed to climb down, as long as exposure is kept to a minimum. The climb down is more difficult than the ascent because of limited vision. When the climb is relatively easy, face out and climb down. Keep all the techniques in mind. Move the hands down before moving the feet. Make full use of push holds to hold the body back as you feel for the footholds. If the climb is only moderately difficult, move down sideways; and if it is difficult, face in and move down backward. It is important to always move your hands down first to avoid a stretched-out position. Look between your legs for the footholds. The hands can usually use the hold where the feet were placed. Keep in mind the route you used in climbing up. Again use palm push holds to the fullest, with fingers pointed down. Be sure to brush off any debris from the rock and from the soles of your boots before moving up or down.

Descent on Slab

Well-treated boots or sneakers should be able to hold on slab rock that slopes up to 45 degrees, without your using the hands. To test your footgear, crouch down on the steepest slope on which you feel safe. Then with your feet flat and your weight over the balls of the feet and the knees forward of the feet, try balancing on one foot. You should find that your position is stable and that you can balance there securely. This will add to your confidence in your footgear. It is important to know at what angle you can depend on the feet to hold and when they will not. Perform these tests where there is little or no danger in case you are wrong.

SCRAMBLING

Scrambling is the step between the mountain walking and technical rock climbing, where the terrain dictates the use of all limbs. Often the ground is not continually difficult or over-exposed, but a rope and protection should be applied as necessary. Scrambling routes follow the natural lines of a mountain (ridges and gullies) and are most likely to be the easiest paths of ascent.

Scrambling in Groups

The best climber usually leads and selects the route. The leader may be stationed at trouble spots to help the weaker climbers, trying to find spots that afford rest and relative safety at intervals during the climbs. Encourage climbers to help each other, with a boost here and there or a friendly hand grasp from above. Keep the group disciplined enough that they do not crowd each other and that no one steps back on someone else's hands. Always watch for falling rock. Discourage jumping down from rock to rock shelves; loose stones may cause a loss of balance. Have an alternate route in case weather or injury requires it. Keep the climb within the limits of the weakest climber.

USES OF CLIMBING ROPES

The safe use of climbing ropes depends on a knowledge of rope strengths, knots, and rope management. A form of nylon rope is best because of its durability, resilience, and strength. Climbing ropes are used to limit the distance a climber will fall, to aid in rapid descents, and to make routes safer.

The decision to climb roped up is made whenever the leader believes there is too much risk of a fall or when any member of the party asks to be roped.

For a two-party climb the leader climbs until a suitable spot for a belay is found. The distance away from the partner should be no more than a standard rope length. A belay is a hold in which by use of the rope and a braking method of handling the rope, the lead climber can stop the partner from falling more than an acceptable distance (figure 21-7). The lead climber places protection while ascending and is thus belayed from below. If the lead climber falls, he or she would fall twice the distance to the last piece of protection.

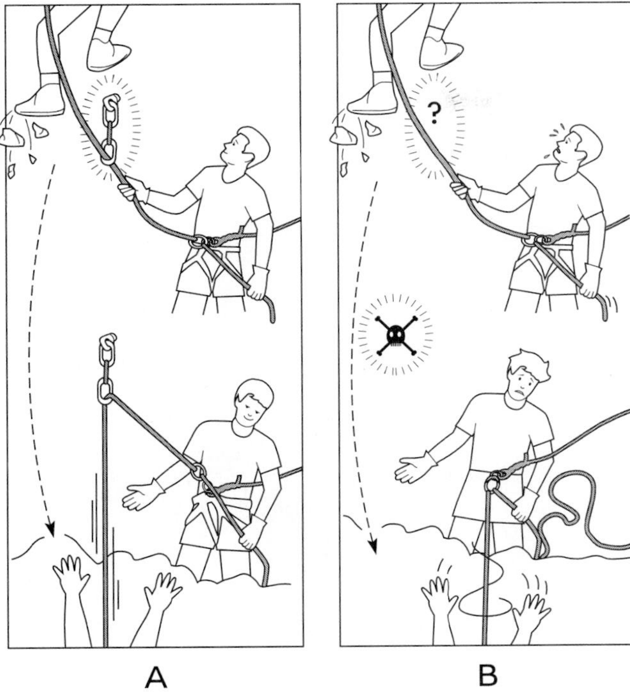

Figure 21-7. A, Proper belay. **B,** Improper belay.

After proper commands, signals, and testing of the position, the leader then safeguards the partner's climb up to the spot. This sequence is repeated, or they can leapfrog, letting the number-two climber pass and then lead, as long as both partners have equal ability. Each climber has to be able to climb without pulling or depending on the rope for direct aid. The exception would be if the climber above on belay is notified by the partner climbing up that help is needed. Then the belayer would take up any slack between them. The belayer would actually provide tension on the rope so that the climber who is feeling insecure can depend on the belayer to prevent a fall.

There are techniques to be used for most situations in rock climbing, including how to fall safely. These procedures must be practiced over and over until the reactions of the climbers become reflex actions. Mechanical aids (called "protection") such as carabiners and slings may be placed and used as intermediate anchor points for the climbing rope to pass through on the way up a rock face that does not provide belay spots (figures 21-8 and 21-9). Protection has a ring or an eye to which the carabiner is attached and through which the climbing rope is snapped. These anchor points limit the distance a climber will fall. If above the protection, the climber will fall only the distance to the protection and the same distance below it plus any distance the belayer allowed. The belayer has a variety of choices. One option is to place protection (figure 21.10) with a sling rope anchor to the rock to make it impossible to be pulled off.

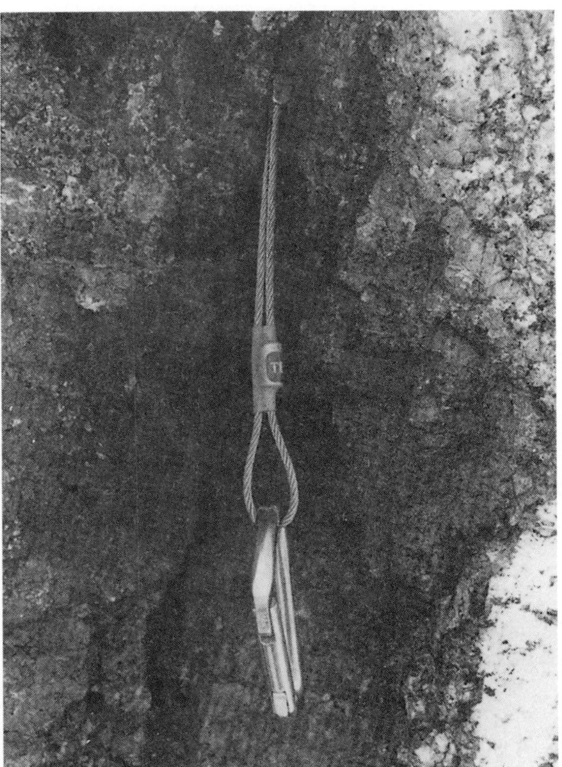

Figure 21-8. Protection placed in a crack.

Figure 21-9. Protection: spring-loaded cramming device.

Figure 21-10. Placing protection.

Figure 21-11. Body rappel.

Another possibility is to snap the climbing rope into protection placed above so that the climbing rope leading to the climber above will pull the belayer into the rock in the case of a bad fall. The alternative selected depends on the terrain. Climbing teams develop a feel for the rope running between them and can tell what their partner is doing even when the partner is not in sight. When the climb up is finished, the climbing ropes should be inspected as they are recoiled and the route down is determined.

RAPPELLING

Rappelling is a technique of using ropes to slide down steep rock faces or very steep, dangerous ground slopes. It is a quick but safe way to descend. The two basic rappel techniques are body rappel (figure 21-11) and rappelling with equipment.

Common characteristics of all rappels include some of the following.

First, an anchor point must be established. Three anchor points are preferred in case one fails. The anchor can be a strong tree or a secure rock around which the rappel rope can run free. It can be established with sling ropes around the anchor point and carabiners to run the rappel rope through. Piton anchors are used on difficult areas by experienced mountaineers. The anchor point must not obstruct the rope nor contain sharp edges that could cut the rope or create excess friction that might weaken the rope. The anchor must be solid. The construction and evaluation of an anchor is extremely important and should be done very carefully. The rope must be retrievable from below. Climbing ropes are marked in the center, and the rappel rope is doubled around the anchor point and centered. Both ends are dropped down the face to be climbed. Both ends of the rope must be together and reach the ground. If rappelling to a dismount point, where another rappel is to be established, the ends of the rope must be tied together in the correct manner to prevent the possibility of rappelling off the end.

Second, rappellers should wear gloves to prevent rope burns. The first person down is responsible for clearing the rope and the route down of any obstructions, such as loose rock, brush, or tree limbs. This person dismounts at the bottom, frees the rope of any tangles, steps away, and yells "Off rappel" loudly so that everyone at the top can hear that it is safe for the next person to come down. The last person down makes sure that the rope at the anchor point can be pulled down when she or he gets to the bottom.

Body Rappel

This method should only be used on relatively gradual slopes and only in an emergency situation, because it is not as safe as using equipment. After the anchor point is established, face the anchor point with your back to the cliff edge. Straddle the rope, reach behind with the right hand, and grasp both ropes and bring them around and across the right hip, Next, pass the ropes across the chest and over the left shoulder (for right-handed people). Grasp the rope that is leading to the anchor point loosely in front with the left hand. This is the guide hand. Next, reach behind your body again with the right hand and grasp the rope that is running down behind your back. Make sure that the rappel rope does not touch the bare skin at any place—neck, shoulder, or legs. The right hand is the brake hand. Grasp the ropes with the back of the hand out and the thumb and forefinger next to the hip. To stop at any point, bring the hand tight to the hip, keeping the back straight, knees bent, and feet apart. Look over the downhill shoulder as the body is turned slightly down the face. To descend, allow slack for the rope to slide around the body as you lean back and walk down the face. Keep your feet flat against the rock if the face is vertical. Lean back at about 75 to 80 degrees, but not at right angles on the body rappel. This is a slow, controlled rappel. The rope must be flipped free as the brake hand moves away from the hip and the fingers loosen enough to allow the rope to slide through. Body weight and gravity should do the rest. the rappeller can stop anytime, but must not let go of the rope in the brake hand. The guide hand may be released if needed to adjust clothing, remove loose rock, or whatever, but *never* the brake hand. When the rappeller is down, the rope should be unwrapped from around the body, untangled, and checked to see that it is free. The rappeller should then step away and yell "Off rappel."

Equipment Rappel

It was once common to make seats from lengths of nylon webbing, but today it is standard practice—safer and far more comfortable—to use a manufactured sit harness. The harness is linked from the climber to the rope via a locking carabiner and a figure-eight descending device (figure 21-12). With the friction created by the figure eight, the climber can make a fast, safe, and comfortable descent (figure 21-13). Speed is controlled by adjusting the grip on the brake hand, the one gripping the rope below the descending device. The other hand holds the rope above the device to guide the rope and give the climber balance.

To begin the descent, merely move the brake hand away from the hip, relax the fingers around the rope, and lean back; gravity will do the rest. To stop, place the hand back on the hip and squeeze the rope.

Keep the feet apart so as not to swing to and fro. The knees should be bent to absorb shock. Keep the feet flat against the rock face, keep the back straight, and keep looking down the route being followed. Relax the guide hand so that the descent is not hindered by excess friction.

A minimum friction on the body makes for a smooth, fast, safe descent completely controlled by the climber. An experienced instructor should be on hand to watch every

Figure 21-12. Figure eight.

Figure 21-13. Rapelling with a figure eight.

move and correct mistakes immediately as the climbers first learn on a moderately steep ground slope.

Climbers should practice on a short face, about 10 feet (3 m) high, with a safe landing. Beginners will find that the first step down is the hardest. When practicing on vertical rock, there are two safety measures that should be adopted until expertise is acquired. A belay rope is attached around the waist of the rappeller with either a two-loop bowline or a simple bowline. If using equipment, it should be tied into the harness. The belay rope is attached to a safety person who is on belay above and who can put tension on the rope if needed, at a signal from the instructor. The instructor should be *beside* the student rappeller. The instructor makes the last check and signals the belayer when ready.

The other safety check is to a have a person at the bottom who holds the ends of the rappel ropes in both hands. If the rappeller needs to be stopped from any reason, this person can pull on the ropes and the rappeller will brake to

Figure 21-14. Climbing rope.

a stop. To recover, the rappeller resumes position and signals "OK" and the safety tension is released.

The instructor must insist on a no-nonsense attitude and strict attention during all rock-climbing classes. Inattention and carelessness can quickly lead to serous injury.

Rappelling is not a sport in itself, despite the tendency of some clubs or schools to classify it as a separate activity. It is just one phase of mountaineering.

ROPE MANAGEMENT

General Principles

Careful inspection of the rope (figure 21-14) for cuts, excess wear, weak spots, and burns must be made constantly. Ropes should not be left with knots in them. Avoid stepping on the rope because this may grind small pieces of rock into the rope, which will act as an abrasive and eventually weaken and cut the fibers. Rope should be dried carefully if wet, but not near an open flame, as nylon ropes melt. Rope should not be hung across sharp objects or nails. If run over rough cliff edges, the edges should be padded with packs or clothing. Also avoid long-term exposure to direct sunlight and any contact with harmful chemicals (gasoline, oil, etc.)

Knots

Many manuals cover in detail all manner of knots and how they are tied and used. Familiarity with such skills is obviously a prerequisite for the mountaineer.

TEACHING CONSIDERATIONS

Do not attempt to instruct in mountaineering unless you have completed a qualified program of training and have had a great deal of experience.

GLOSSARY

altitude Same as "elevation," but usually used in connection with height attained and normally expressed when the elevation is above 12,000 feet (3.66 km).

balance climbing Climbing using only the feet, depending on body position for balance. Done on comparatively easy rock.

belay A method of anchoring a climber with the use of rope for protection against falling.

bivouac A temporary camp-out, usually planned but of short duration (one or two nights).

body or sit harness Web nylon belts that are fastened to the climber that act as seats for support of the body when rappelling or when suspended in space while anchored to the rock and maneuvering for new positions. The climbing rope is attached or hitched to a ring on the seat.

carabine A metal alloy or aluminum oval ring with a hinged gate that allows a rope to be snapped in at any spot. Gates may have a locking screw for extra safety.

chocks; nuts Small blocks of steel with a cable loop embedded in them. Chocks are stuffed in the cracks, or fissures, to serve in the same manner as the pitons. Carabiners are snapped to the cable sling. These chocks, or nuts, can be removed, whereas pitons are usually so well driven they cannot be removed without damage.

climbing rope Rope 165 feet (50.3 m) in length, 7⁄16 inch (11 mm) in diameter, nylon test about 6,200 pounds (2,800 kg), tensile strength/150 feet (45.7 m), 9 mm in diameter, test strength 3,500 pounds (1,580 kg).

crampons Steel-tooth foot harnesses, attached to the sole of the climbing boots, used on snow and ice climbs.

elevation Usually expressed in feet (meters) above sea level and used in connection with the number of feet (meters) in height to be climbed.

free climbing Climbing with protection but without aid.

frostbite Freezing of exposed flesh or lack of circulation to the extremities; may be superficial or deep, can be severe, and may result in gangrene and amputation if not properly treated.

glissade A technique of sliding down steep, hard-packed snow using ice ax or even ski poles to control the speed. The body faces out from the slope, and the slide is feet-first.

grassy slopes Mountains covered with grass that grows in clumps.

high-angle rock Steep rock faces of 70 to 90 degrees.

hypothermia Lowering of the body temperature that, if severe, results in death; usually a result of exposure to cold or wet conditions, not a result of freezing.

ice ax An ax with a head of two parts: a horizontal blade and an end graduating to a point. The shaft is made of metal or a composite, the blade of high-alloy steel. The end of the shaft is a pointed spike for probing and digging into solid snow-packed crevasses or slopes. The ice ax is used to chop steps for footholds. It can be used as an anchor for the belay. It also is used as a brake to stop a falling climber or a roped team of climbers.

low-angle rock Rock where balance climbing is sometimes practiced; it is not steep.

overhangs Protruding pieces of rock that hang out over the rest of the rock face; they require extreme care and skill to negotiate.

piton A steel-alloy shaft with a ring, or eye, at the head. Pitons come in varying lengths and shapes. They are driven into cracks, or fissures, in the rock and used with snaplinks to act as anchor points for ropes.

piton hammer A short-shafted hammer, blunt on one end and pointed on the other, for driving pitons into the rock cracks. The pointed end is for cleaning out the fissures or testing holds.

rappel A method of sliding down an anchored climbing rope; means of fast descent down a cliff.

scree slopes Gravel and loose rock scars running down a mountainside.

shakedown break The first rest halt on a hike or mountain walk, used to adjust packs, clothing, and so on. It is usually of slightly longer duration than subsequent rest halts.

slab rock Smooth, sloping rock faces of varying steepness and length.

sling rope Pieces of rope (Perlon or nylon) in 10- to 15-foot (3 to 4.6 m) lengths, used in various rope installations and for anchoring climber or material; can be used as seats for rappelling.

spread eagle A position resulting when a climber has both feet and arms too far apart for safety. It is difficult to recover from this position.

talus Loose rock, often unstable, lying on mountain slopes.

timberline The elevation on a mountain at which trees cannot grow because of high wind, poor soil, and inability to establish anchoring roots. The timberline varies in different parts of the United States and the world.

verglas A thin icy coating over rock caused by cold, moist air condensing and freezing on the surface.

SUGGESTED READINGS

Appalachia. Published semiannually. Boston: Appalachian Mountain Club.

Long, J. 1993. *How to rock climb*. 2d ed. Evergreen, Colo.: Chockstone Press.

Luebben, C. 1993. *Knots for climbers*. Evergreen, Colo: Chockstone Press.

Orienteering

After completing this chapter, the reader should be able to:

- Appreciate the development, values, and objectives of orienteering
- Use maps and a compass for navigation
- Organize a cross-country orienteering event
- Teach others map- and compass-reading skills
- Conduct orienteering lead-up games
- Organize orienteering variations
- Set an appropriate orienteering course

The sport form of land navigation is called orienteering. It is a cross-country race in which participants use a map and compass to navigate between checkpoints along an unfamiliar course. The activity can be a means of enjoying other outdoor pursuits or as a sport complete with competition, rules, and organizational structure. Both aspects of orienteering qualify its inclusion in the "environmental sports" family, along with running, cross-country skiing, hiking, kayaking, and similar activities.

VALUES

Orienteering has many appealing attributes for modern physical education and recreation. People from 10 to 70 years old can participate in this lifetime sport with no extraordinary physical or mental abilities. Orienteering can be conducted as a coeducational activity; it is appropriate for males and females. Groups, pairs, or individuals can navigate an orienteering course in a competitive or cooperative fashion, involving the participants in a wide range of commitment and challenge. Finally, orienteering can be organized on commonly found, accessible tracts of land. Schoolyards, parks, and town forest preserves are all adequate.

HISTORY

Orienteering began when humans first ventured from their familiar environs into an unmapped world, seeking new horizons. Organized orienteering, however, is a relatively new addition to the sports world, particularly in the United States. The first time an event was labeled an orienteering race was in 1900 at a meet organized by Club Tjalve in Oslo, Norway. By 1919 orienteering meets were attracting as many as 200 people, with Capt. Ernst Killander organizing these meets outside of Stockholm and generally being credited as the father of orienteering.

The sport's next boost came in the early 1930s with the invention, by Bjorn and Alvar Kjellstrom, of the one-piece protractor compass, or orienteering compass, which provided a simple tool for land navigation. By 1942 orienteering was a compulsory activity in Swedish physical education programs. Orienteering continued to grow, rivaling soccer as the most popular sport in Sweden and spreading to other Scandinavian countries.

In 1946 Bjorn Kjellstrom, now living in the United States, sponsored the first orienteering meet in the United States at the Indiana Dunes State Park. However, the sport remained relatively unpracticed in North America until 1965, when Geoffrey Dyson and John Disley introduced orienteering in Canada, where it steadily gained popularity. Since 1967 the sport has grown in the United States, beginning with permanent orienteering groups centered at the Marine Physical Fitness Academy in Quantico, Virginia, in the Delaware Valley, and in New England. The United States Orienteering Federation, which now represents more than a hundred clubs and has a membership of 2,500, was founded in 1971.

Today some orienteering meets rank as the largest participative athletic events in the world; the Oringen in Sweden attracts over 10,000 competitors for 5 days of competition.

Before organizing an orienteering event, a physical educator or recreation leader should have experience and solid understanding of the following components of the sport: equipment, techniques using map and compass, instructional games, safety precautions, teaching methodology, and sources of information.

OBJECTIVES

Orienteering in whatever setting it might be offered can provide the unique contribution of fostering the attitude that the outdoors is a safe and interesting place. The following objectives are considered outcomes of an orienteering program. The participant will:

1. Gain the basic skills of land navigation using a map and compass
2. Improve his or her physical fitness
3. Learn to be self-reliant in the outdoors
4. Acquire an increased awareness of the environment

EQUIPMENT

Maps

The map serves as the primary tool of navigation to the participant and to the trained eye can yield an enormous amount of information. The most common maps used for orienteering are topo (topographic) maps and are published and distributed by the United States Geological Survey, which is a division of the U.S. Department of the Interior. The two most common series are the 7.5-minute series (scale of 1:24,000) and the 15-minute series (scale of 1:62,500). Some areas are mapped at scales of 1:250,000 and 1:1,000,000. The 7.5-minute series is definitely best for orienteering and land navigation. Many sporting goods stores, bookstores, and camping stores stock government topographical maps of the local area. An index of maps from which one can order is available from the Map Information Office, U.S. Geologic and Geodetic Survey, Washington, DC 02042.

As competitive orienteering becomes more popular, specialized orienteering maps (figure 22-1) containing greater detail and accuracy are being produced in active areas of orienteering throughout the country. These maps differ from the government topographical maps in that they have a larger scale, usually 1:10,000 or 1:15,000; contain four or five colors: and are drawn from recent, precise aerial photographs. The added detail and accuracy allow course setters to design more demanding orienteering courses and remove the element of luck from the competition.

Both types of orienteering maps contain much the same kinds of information:

Location. Each map has a title describing a location and contains longitude and latitude coordinates that locate the area on the earth's surface.

Date. The map must be up-to-date; many parts of the United States have dramatically changed during the past 10 years, and government maps may not reflect these changes.

Distance. Topo maps contain two types of scales: bar scales and ratio scales. The bar scales are given in miles, feet, and kilometers. The ratio scales are given as a ratio of units of distance on the map to the actual landscape. For example, a map with a 7.5-minute series has a ratio scale of 1 unit on the map equaling 24,000 units on the actual landscape.

Direction. The top border of topographical maps represents the northerly direction, or true geographic north. The top of the specialized orienteering maps indicates magnetic north, because such maps are used exclusively by orienteers using magnetic north-seeking compasses. In either case, the righthand border is east, the bottom is south, and the lefthand border is west.

Elevation. The unique feature of topographical maps are their description of elevation in the land mass. This is shown by contour lines in the form of concentric rings. The distance between each contour line, termed the *contour interval*, represents a vertical change in elevation of the terrain. The center of the rings is the high point of elevation, and the broader circles show progressive lower areas.

Natural-terrain features. Important natural features of mappable size are shown. Examples of such features are bodies of water, including lakes, streams, marshes, and swamps; cliffs; woods; and fields. Orienteering maps contain detailed information of this nature.

Other features. Houses, roads, bridges, and power lines are among the other features symbolically displayed on the map. The explanation for each symbol is contained in the map's legend or, in the case of USGS maps, the symbols are explained in a separate pamphlet.

Compass

The compass, second only to the map among the orienteer's tools, serves to supplement and confirm information given on the map. The most commonly used compass in orienteering is the protractor compass. The important difference between the protractor, or orienteering, compass and others is the rectangular base plate that serves as a protractor and assists in determining direction of travel. Protractor compasses are available in the United States from several commercial sources. Models featuring a liquid-filled compass housing that dampers and stabilizes movement of the magnetic needle are well worth the additional expense.

Types of compasses

A variety of compasses are available, each having features designed for different functions:

Plain watch compass. This compass appears as a pocket watch and is suitable for general travel that requires limited accuracy.

Wrist compass. Similar to a plain watch compass, the wrist compass has a wristband, allowing the wearer free use of both hands. This is a popular ski orienteering compass, but, like the watch compass, it does not afford the accuracy required for regular orienteering.

Lensatic compass. Also commonly called the army or the prismatic compass, the lensatic compass features excellent sighting devices but lacks a protractor base, so it cannot be used to take a compass bearing. Because of its high accuracy, it is popular in map-making.

Mirror compass. The mirror compass is similar to an orienteering compass, but it also has a sighting device that uses a mirror for added precision. The mirror compass is used for course setting, map-making, and backpacking, but it is considered too heavy for conventional orienteering.

Protractor, or base-plate, or orienteering, compass. The following are the main components of the orienteering compass (figure 22-2).

Base plate. The Plexiglas rectangle under the compass itself is referred to as the base plate, or protractor, and serves two purposes: measures distance using the scale (in

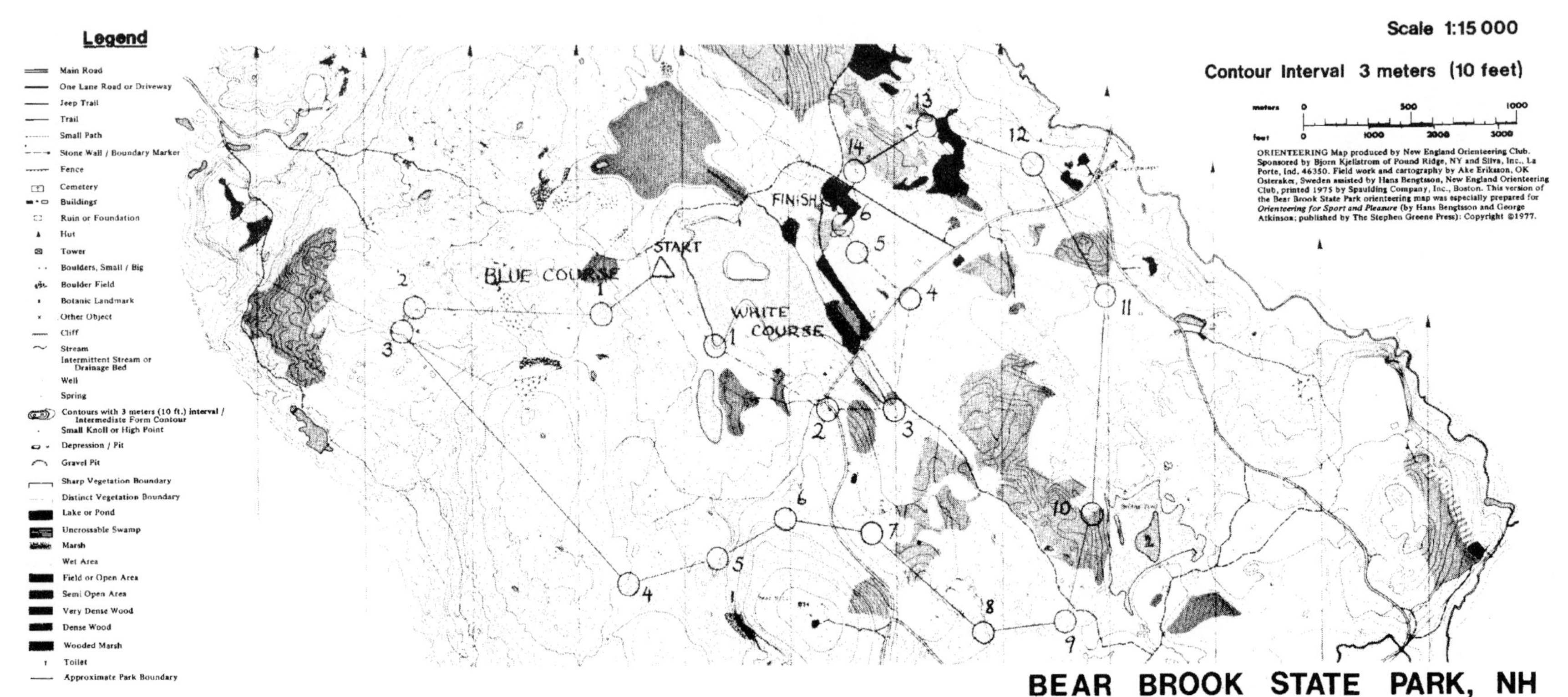

Figure 22-1. Orienteering topographical map. (Figures 22-1, 22-2, and 22-4 to 22-7 from *Orienteering for Sport and Pleasure,* copyright by Hans Bengtsson and George Atkinson. Reprinted by permission of the Stephen Greene Press, a wholly owned subsidiary of Viking Penguin, Inc.)

millimeters or inches) on the edges and assists the orienteer in determining a course of travel.

Compass housing. The compass housing is mounted on the base plate and appears as a basic watch compass. It must rotate freely on the protractor and should have a transparent bottom.

Direction-of-travel arrow. The only arrow on the base plate, located in the center of the long end of the protractor, is the direction-of-travel arrow.

Orienting, or north, arrow. The north arrow is drawn on the bottom of the compass housing. This arrow is flanked by a series of parallel, orienting lines.

Magnetic needle. Suspended in the compass housing is a freely rotating, floating needle. The red end of the needle points to magnetic north when not influenced by nearby iron objects.

Strap. Although not shown in the figure, a strap attached to a compass with a slip knot at the distal end provides the best protection in the event of a fall.

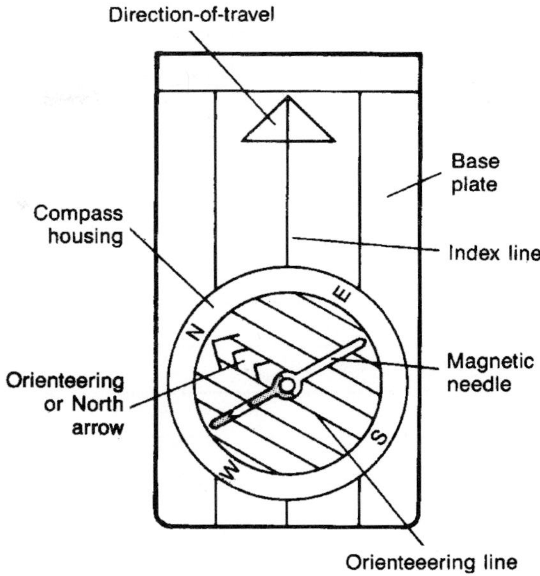

Figure 22-2. The protractor or base-plate compass.

Other Equipment

Personal equipment required in orienteering, in addition to the map and compass, simply amounts to functional clothing to be worn in the woods. Hiking boots are used by beginners; "knobby" orienteering shoes are the footwear of experts. Weather dictates the type of clothing necessary, but generally it is the same as that worn for a hike.

In organizing a meet, several items of equipment (aside from maps and compasses) are indispensable: scorecards, control markers, punches, plastic map cases, red pens for copying courses from master maps onto individual maps, and clipboards.

CHARACTERISTICS OF A CROSS-COUNTRY ORIENTEERING EVENT

The most commonly practiced form of orienteering is the cross-country event resembling a car rally or treasure hunt. The event occurs in an area of 75 to 2,000 acres, ideally consisting of wooded acreage with varied terrain. The meet organizer, using a topographical map (figure 22-1), places from 6 to 15 markers, or "controls," in the field at distinct terrain features, such as trail junctions or hilltops. The positions of the controls are precisely drawn on a master map, numbered sequentially, and connected with a straight line, forming a course or a string of controls for the event. Participants in the cross-country event are then assigned the task of copying the control locations on a personal copy of the map.

Individuals are started in a staggered fashion and proceed to locate the markers in the correct sequence, using their skills of navigation in moving from one control to the next in the most efficient or fastest manner. Controls are not hidden but are visibly placed at the listed control description to eliminate the element of luck as much as possible. Route choice, navigational techniques, and rate of travel (running versus jogging) are at the discretion of each participant. Codes or punches at the controls, marked by the competitor on a scorecard (figure 22-3), ensure presence at each control. The elapsed time of the orienteers is computed and then placed in rank-order, with the fastest declared the winner. Because of the challenge of locating all the controls on a course, most orienteers consider completion of the race a satisfying goal and position in the meet of secondary importance.

BASIC ORIENTEERING TECHNIQUES

Map Reading

The map is the primary tool of navigation, with the compass used as a supportive tool to verify and confirm the course when needed (figure 22-4). To get the most information from a topographical map, use the following basic techniques of map reading:

1. Before going into the field, be familiar with the map's scale, contour interval, and symbols.
2. Beginners should always keep the map "oriented," that is, keep the top facing north regardless of your direction of travel. This will keep the map properly aligned with the terrain. This might not be necessary for advanced land navigators. Maps can be read sideways or upside down if necessary, but always keep the map pointing toward north. This can be accomplished in three steps:
   a. Place the compass on the map with its magnetic needle adjacent to a north line on the map.

CLASS | COURSE | NO.

NAME

CLUB

ATTACH HERE ONLY

CLASS | COURSE | NO.

NAME

CLUB

competition | date | compass

Orienteering ® Control Point Cards

FINISH

START

TIME

1	2	3	4	5
6	7	8	9	10
11	12	13	14	15

Figure 22-3. Orienteering scorecard.

Figure 22-4. Getting a bearing with a map and compass.

   b. Turn both the compass and the map together until the magnetic needle is parallel to the map's north lines, being certain that the north end of the magnetic needle points toward the north edge of the map.
   c. Remove the compass without turning the map, and the map is oriented—that is, the map now corresponds to the surrounding terrain.
3. Fold the map to a readable, holdable size. Concentrate on the part of the map you are using; the remainder will only confuse you. Walking or running is best accomplished with a small, neatly folded map that will not get caught on tree branches. Pinch the map between the first two fingers, using the thumb to trace your progress.
4. When reading the map, visualize the terrain through which you will soon be passing. Try to imagine the ground level view that will soon be coming over the horizon, including the slope of the hills, vegetation, and other terrain feature. Visualize these things in your mind before seeing them in the field.

Travel by Compass

On some occasions the compass must be heavily relied on to determine a direction of travel, usually when adequate terrain features for navigating are lacking or if the orienteer simply wishes to be absolutely certain of the course of action. This procedure is called taking a compass bearing, and it is accomplished in four steps.

Establishing direction. Place the long side of the compass protractor along the line of intended travel by connecting your present location and your destination with the compass edge. Be sure that the direction-of-travel arrow is pointing from your location to your destination (figure 22-5).

Setting the north-south lines. While pressing the protractor firmly to the map with your thumb, turn the compass housing around so that the north-south lines of the compass are parallel to the north lines of the map. Be sure that the

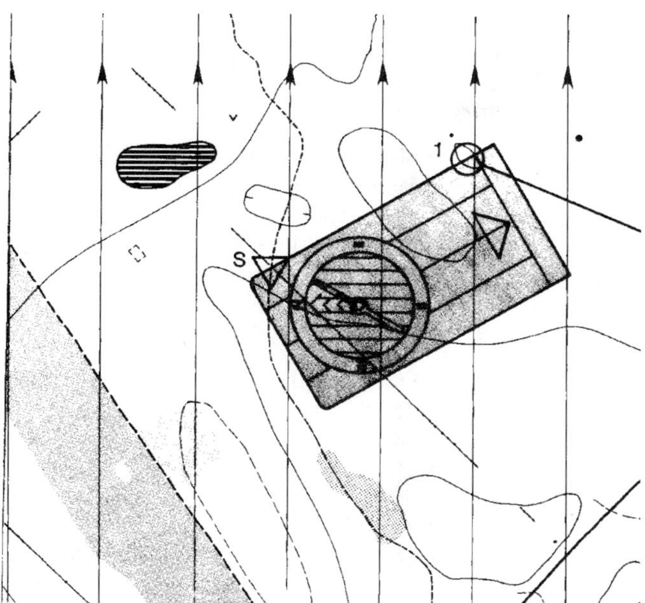

Figure 22-5. Establishing direction from *S* to *1*.

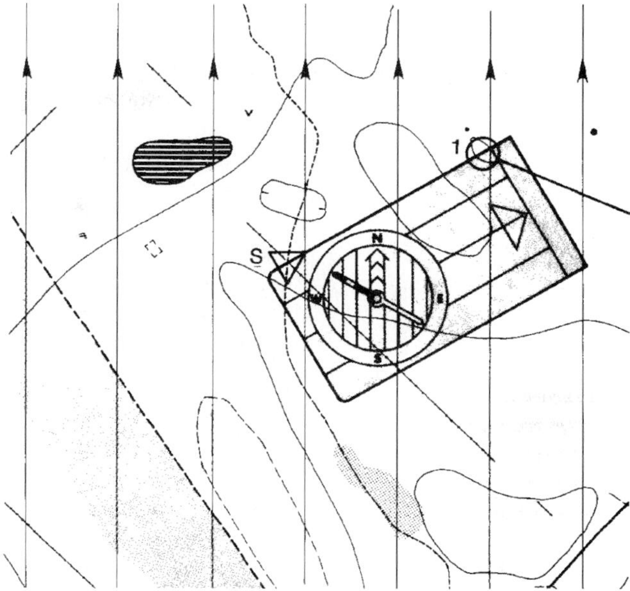

Figure 22-6. Setting the north-south lines.

north arrow of the compass housing is pointing to the north of the map (figure 22-6).

Reading the bearing. Remove the compass from the map. If the north lines of the map point to geographic north, as in most topographical maps, then an adjustment must be made in the bearing, because there is a difference between geographic north and magnetic north. This difference is called the angle of declination, which measures the amount that magnetic north deviates east or west from geographic north. If the declination is west, add the angle of declination to the compass bearing. If the declination is east, subtract the angle of declination from the compass bearing. An easy-to-memorize aid states: "Declination west, compass best. Declination east, compass least." If the north lines, or meridians, point toward magnetic north, as in orienteering maps, then no adjustment is necessary. To correct a standard topographical map to magnetic north-south lines, draw new meridians reflecting the angle of declination for that particular map. Draw a series of parallel lines tilted at the proper angle of declination from the north-south borders of the map. Now both map and compass speak the same language: magnetic.

Now hold the compass level in your hand with the direction-of-travel arrow pointing away from you. Turn around so that the north end (red) of the magnetic needle coincides with the north arrow of the compass housing. The direction-of-travel arrow is now pointing toward the destination.

Running the bearing. Look down at the compass and focus on the direction-of-travel arrow. Slowly lift your head, sighting directly in line with the direction of travel arrow. Pick out a prominent landmark, which can be a rock or tree about 100 to 200 feet ahead of you in this direction. Take the easiest route to the landmark, avoiding obstacles, and then repeat this step again by sighting new landmarks until you reach your destination.

If there are no prominent landmarks and you are team orienteering, a technique called leapfrogging—where a teammate is sent out to act as a sighting point—can be used.

Remember that the compass is used to supplement the map; so while running on a bearing, consult the map to recognize your progress (figure 22-7).

Route Choice

Route choice is the essence of successful orienteering and must be learned by experience. The fastest route around an orienteering course is different for every individual and is based on fitness, orienteering skill level, and experience. Overriding these factors, however, is the terrain of the course, which ultimately dictates route decision. Commonly, one must make decisions concerning path versus woods travel, elevation gain versus distance, and open fields versus woods.

Aiming Off

When taking a compass bearing toward a control located on a linear feature, such as a path across your direction of travel, you have a 50–50 chance of arriving at the path either to the right or the left of the control. You will not know in which direction your bearing is off, so many orienteers purposely aim slightly to one side of the control and when arriving at the path—knowing the direction of their "error"—they move down the path to the control. The orienteer knows for certain in what direction to turn to seek the marker.

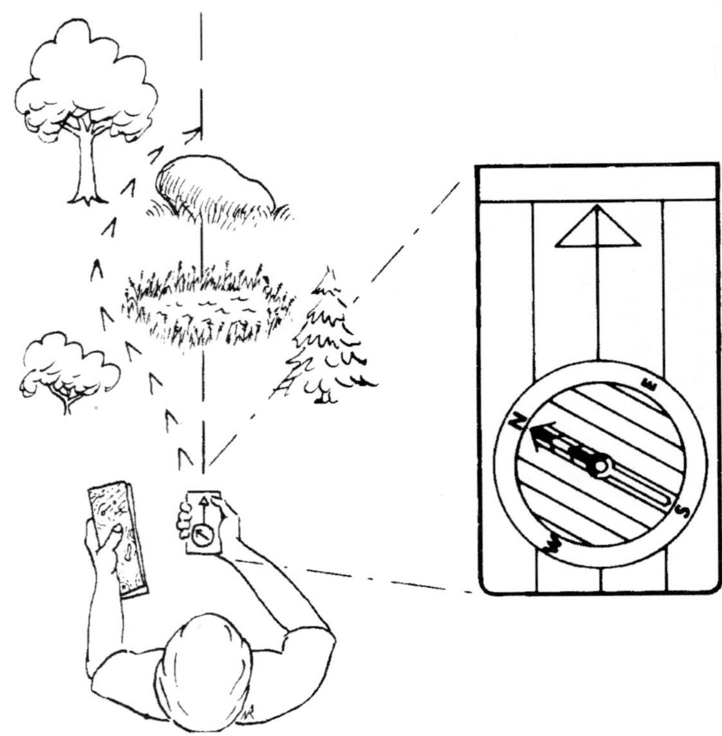

Figure 22-7. Running the bearing.

Attack Point

Within 165 yards (150 m) of a control, the orienteer should identify an obvious or visible feature to use as the last relocation point on the path to the marker. The larger and more definite the feature and the nearer its location, the more desirable the attack point. Path junctions, corners of fields, and the like provide excellent reference points on the orienteer's last 165 yards (150 m) or less of navigating to a control. Often a course does not provide such luxuries, and the orienteer must adopt another technique.

Precision Compass

Precision compass is the precise application of the four-step method of taking a compass bearing cited earlier. Extreme accuracy is required in this technique, which is often employed while traveling form the attack point to the control. This method is time consuming but necessary in those parts of the course containing difficult navigation problems and should be used in conjunction with the technique of pace counting.

Precision Map Reading

Precision map reading is commonly referred to as aggressive map reading and is used in areas containing numerous detailed terrain features that can confuse the competitor. The thumb is accurately passed over the map as the orienteer moves through the terrain, checking off each feature along the route. This technique results in slow travel, but it produces consistency over time.

Control Finding

Once in the immediate locale of the control marker, the orienteer must use cautious awareness to quickly find the control. Good skills in this area can save minutes:

1. Always read the control description carefully before searching for its location. Knowing what you are looking for—for example, the knolltop, the marsh.
2. Choose a good attack point.
3. Slow down as you near the control.
4. Concentrate on your task, ignoring other orienteers in the area.
5. Use extra caution on the first and last control of the course because both are critical in finishing the course.

Traffic Lighting

Each competitor's pace throughout a course should be controlled by an imaginary traffic light in the mind. Through experience, the participant learns the appropriate light for existing terrain conditions, but the following can serve as a general guide:

1. Green light: Go. Travel at the fastest speed possible while still maintaining navigational control. This

technique is used when traveling long open linear features, such as trails, roads, and stone walls.

2. Yellow light: Proceed quickly but cautiously under more difficult conditions. More-precise navigating is employed. This technique is often used in arriving at an attack point.
3. Red light: Stop or go slowly. This technique is used when temporarily lost or disoriented, when a control has been missed, or during particularly critical navigational portions of the course. Good orienteers can sense when to use this light and to slow down, avoiding a major mistake. While traveling from the attack point to the control using precision map reading and compass, use this light.

Collecting Features

Any distinct feature across the direction of travel that will aid in navigation is termed a collecting feature. It can be used effectively to funnel the orienteer toward an attack point.

Handrails

Terrain features that are parallel to the direction of travel serve as "handrails" to a control. Paths, roads, streams, or ridges that orienteers can travel beside serve as excellent handrails.

Rough Compass

Frequently an orienteer must travel quickly to get to a large collecting feature or handrail that will be easy to locate. A rough compass bearing coupled with a sense of direction will lead one to the feature. The standard four-step method is used in taking the compass bearing, but it is done quickly. Sightings with the compass along the direction of travel are done less frequently and often on the run.

Distance Judging

This essential skill is done with varying degrees of accuracy but is accomplished so that the orienteer knows his or her location at all times. Distance judging requires a two-step approach, first measuring the distance and then pace counting while traveling. To measure the distance to be traveled, place the edge of the protractor along the direction of travel and calculate the number of millimeters on the map between the current location and the destination. Then refer to the map's scale to translate millimeters on the map to meters on the terrain. This gives the distance to be traveled, but if additional precision is required, this can be translated into the orienteer's paces. By taking repeated trials over a 110-yard (100 m) course in varying terrain, the orienteer should know the number of paces (a double stride) required to cover 110 yards. This personal yardstick of pace counting takes time to develop but is indispensable in precise compass and map-reading situations. Some typical measures for pace count per 110 yards for adults are:

Hiking	60 paces
Running in dense woods	45 paces
Running in flat woods	40 paces
Running on open trails	36 to 38 paces

Orienteers should develop their own pace-count values in using this technique.

INSTRUCTIONAL GAMES

Orienteering teachers rely on their ingenuity to devise orienteering lead-up games, so imagination is the limit. Following are some popular instructional activities that, when done at high speeds, become training exercises for competition.

Follow the Leader

There are two main variations of this activity: (1) both leader and followers have a map, and (2) only the leader has a map. In the first case, the leader chooses a point without telling the group where it is. Starting from a known location, the leader orienteers to the point and the rest follow, trying to determine the route on their map. Periodically the leader stops along the route to quiz the group on their location and how they got there. When the destination is reached, the process is repeated with a new leader. The second variation of this game, where only the leader has a map, is similar, but the distances of travel are reduced to 110 to 220 yards (100 to 200 m), and map memory ability is critical. Groups of up to six persons are appropriate. Both activities develop map reading and terrain memorization.

Figures

The purpose of this exercise is to encourage precision compass and accurate pace counting. The game should initially be played in a flat, open field and on a small scale; but as students become more proficient, the game can be moved into wooded areas and the distance increased.

The task of each student is to walk on an assigned three- or four-sided course and to achieve "closure" at the end, or to finish at the starting point. As an example, the figure of a rectangle will be used (figure 22-8). The student is assigned the following compass bearings and distances:

Side 1: Go 100 paces at 10 degrees
Side 2: Go 50 paces at 100 degrees
Side 3: Go 100 paces at 190 degrees
Side 4: Go 50 paces at 280 degrees

A small marker left at the individual's starting point serves as a reference. Instructors can vary both the figures and the distances. Four-sided figures require increments of 90 degrees from the initial compass bearing. Squares require an equal number of paces for all four sides; triangles use only three compass bearings and increments of 120 degrees on each of the two subsequent bearings. Instructors can invent many elaborate courses,

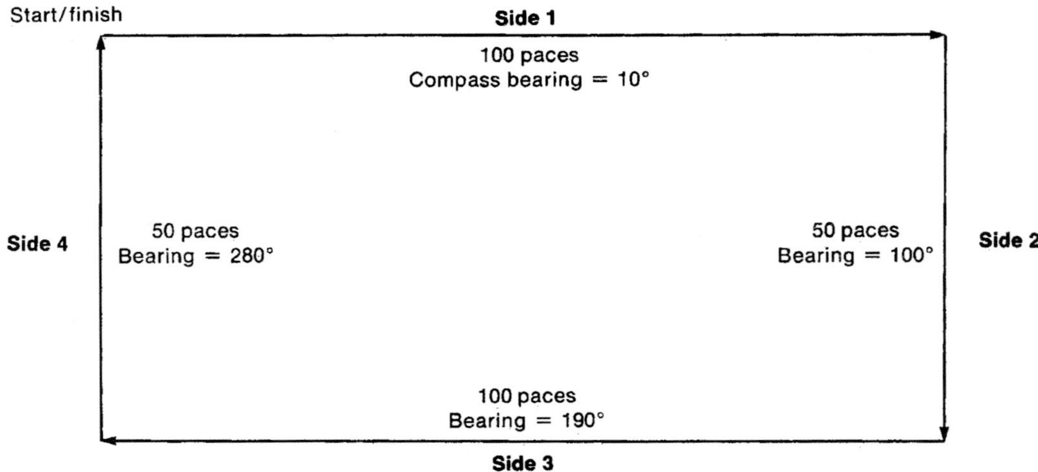

Figure 22-8. Instructional game diagram for a figures exercise.

but they should test them for closure before implementation. This exercise can be done individually or in pairs, with one person using the compass and the other measuring each side.

Map Walks

This informal activity is instructive for beginners in groups of up to a dozen people with one leader and resembles a slow-paced version of Follow the Leader. At the start, the leader teaches map orienting and basic elements of map reading, such as scale, elevation, and symbols. After this brief lecture the group, armed with the preceding skills, goes for a walk in an area containing many terrain features. During the walk, map orienting and thumbing are stressed and appropriate items discussed as terrain features appear along the route. The length of the walk should be adjusted to the group's attention span and physical abilities. This activity is most successful with novices.

Score Orienteering

This activity resembles an Easter egg hunt and is a variation of the cross-country event cited earlier. Ten to 20 controls are placed at terrain features in an area by the instructor prior to the activity. Each control is assigned a point value form 5 to 30, depending on its difficulty and distance from the start. The purpose of the event is for each individual to accumulate points by locating as many high-valued controls as possible within an allotted time. Controls can be located in any order. Whoever accumulates the most points within the time limit wins.

This activity has a number of benefits:

1. Students are encouraged to work efficiently and quickly, making this the sprint race of the orienteering world.
2. The time limit is helpful in working within a class schedule. All participants will be at the finish at a determined time.
3. It is conducive to parks and even schools yards because many controls can be placed in a small area.

Trim Orienteering

This is the most educational of all orienteering variations. The activity is simply score orienteering done on a larger scale without a time limit and without competition. Fifty to 100 controls are placed in the woods on a semipermanent basis. Because the markers will remain out in the elements for 1 to 6 months, special small aluminum or wood markers that can be attached to trees are required. Maps are printed showing all the control locations and are made available at local schools, banks, sporting goods stores, or newspaper offices, for example. The course organizer promotes the course and distributes maps.

The advantages of trim orienteering include the following:

1. People can try orienteering at their convenience and at their own pace.
2. Families can enjoy orienteering in a noncompetitive fashion.
3. Schools can use parts of the course for instruction.
4. Competitive orienteers can use the course for training.

TRAINING

Orienteering requires mental and physical abilities, so it follows that training should develop one's capabilities in both areas. Unfortunately, in the United States few devote adequate preparation to the mental and technical aspects of orienteering, but many concentrate on the physical training. This deficiency can be corrected by keeping in mind the unique demands of orienteering while planning a conditioning program.

Technique Training

The basic techniques previously mentioned can be sharpened through a variety of activities, including:

1. Map making
2. Course setting
3. Instructional games (including those previously mentioned)
4. Cross-country orienteering training meets

All of these training activities can produce physical benefits when done at a sufficiently high work load.

Physical Training

Orienteering places three distinct physical requirements on the participant: cardiovascular endurance, agility, and running speed. Physical training should be molded to meet these demands.

Cardiovascular endurance can be improved in a variety of methods—most commonly, walking, running, jogging, bicycle riding, and cross-country skiing. This is the most overly trained aspect of all orienteering's components, so keep in mind that the objective of such training tools is the ability to maintain a high work level for 60 to 90 minutes in an orienteering race.

Agility is probably the most ignored physical requirement for successful orienteering. Running at high speeds in the woods places different demands on the body than running at a similar pace on a track. Increased agility can be obtained by training, over the same terrain that orienteering meets use—woods, paths, boulder fields, meadows, and hills—adapting the running stride to the undulating, varied footing of the outdoors. Training runs should simulate the specific demands of an orienteering course.

Assignment Orienteering

This interdisciplinary approach can incorporate many school subjects into an orienteering format. A standard cross-country orienteering course is used, but once an individual or group arrives at a control, an assignment must be accomplished. The task can be related to other school subjects or to orienteering and may require an instructor at the control.

SAFETY PRECAUTIONS

A few precautions when organizing an orienteering event can eliminate most safety problems:

1. Check the area to be used. Mark on the map all barbed-wire fences, rivers, and cliffs. Avoid running courses over cliffs or across deep rivers.
2. Always employ a check system to register participants. Standard orienteering scorecards contain a stub with the entrant's name, which the organizer retains. On finishing, the orienteer picks up the stub. At the end of the event, the organizer should be left without any stubs. Competitors are reminded to report to the finish regardless of whether they complete the course.
3. Establish a closing time for each course, at which time participants must return to the finish.
4. Place a safety compass bearing on each map or course description that leads from any point on the map to a large collecting feature on the map's border. For example, if a road borders the south edge of the meet area, the safety bearing would be 180 degrees, bringing anyone in need of help to a civilized area.
5. Respect private property and cultivated fields. Always request permission from landowners before designing courses on their property.

COURSE SETTING

For orienteering meets to take place, an organizer or leader must prepare a course and place orienteering markers in the woods. The skill of the course setter along with the quality of the map play a major role in the success of an orienteering meet. The course setter's task is to test the orienteer's running and navigational skills at the appropriate level. Toward this goal, the course setter follows three important rules:

1. Keep the competition fair. The quality of the map should be adequate for orienteering competition and verified by field checking on the part of the course setter. Controls should be correctly placed and not hidden, thus eliminating the element of luck.
2. Design a course to meet the skill level of the orienteers. If a diverse population of orienteers is to attend the meet, several courses must be designed to meet the needs of all levels of orienteers. The difficulty of a course can be controlled by varying the number of controls, course distance, and difficulty of controls (control placement).
3. Design a course that measures both physical and mental skills. Every part of a good orienteering course presents navigational problems that require the orienteer's concentration and awareness. Distances that require merely running skills are a waste.

The course setter should always establish the course well in advance of the competition and preferably have the course checked in the field by another individual. The satisfaction of watching participants enjoy his or her creation is the course setter's reward.

Varied running speeds are developed by changing the pace of training runs or using instructional games that force the participant to travel using the traffic-lights system. Varied-pace training runs can include interval training, fartlek, and hill climbing. Instruction games such as Follow the Leader and Score Orienteering also encourage the ability and knowledge of varying running speed.

ORIENTEERING VARIATIONS

Night Orientating

Only orienteers with experience should participate in this event. A few modifications of the basic cross-country orienteering format will provide safety:

1. Use a relatively civilized area, such as a park or athletic field.
2. Place controls at readily distinguishable features, such as path junctions or fence corners.
3. Shorten the course to a maximum of 3 kilometers (1.86 miles) (less for young participants).
4. Use track relay batons, for example, wrapped with reflective tape as control markers.
5. Insist on everyone checking in at the finish regardless of whether they complete the course.
6. Require flashlights and whistles for all participants.
7. Avoid meet sites containing cliffs, rivers, or busy highways.

Ski Orienteering

This is an approved but yet-to-be-implemented Olympic sport that combines orienteering with cross-country skiing. Ski orienteering differs from orienteering primarily in the placement of control markers (nearer paths in the winter version). The meet organizer ensures a number of routes between each control, making route choice the primary navigational problem.

Bicycle Orienteering

Requiring road maps instead of topographical maps, this variation of the orienteering theme can be an enjoyable activity. Relatively traffic-free roads are necessary, and participants should be able to find controls without leaving the pavement. Distances of 15 to 30 kilometers (9.3 to 18.6 miles) are not uncommon. Like ski orienteering, several possible route choices should be allowed per control.

TEACHING CONSIDERATIONS

1. Orienteering is best learned by doing. Encourage beginners to experience navigational problem solving as soon as possible.
2. Limit the amount of lecture time each period to allow sufficient time for practice of techniques.
3. Use a part-whole approach. Reduce the total activity to three aspects: the map, the compass, and the map and compass together.
4. Begin activities in a familiar setting with a simple orienteering course for group. Later, have individuals attempt more-difficult courses in less-familiar surroundings.
5. Allow time at the end of each lesson for discussion of route choices, techniques, and strategies.

GLOSSARY

aiming off Plotting a bearing wide of the precise target to avoid false turns near the mark.

angle of declination The angle representing the difference between geographic north and magnetic north.

attack point A feature form which an orienteer begins to navigate carefully to a control.

bearing A direction to travel, usually measured in degrees from north and determined by a map and compass.

beeline Straight line.

checkpoint An easily identifiable feature.

collecting feature A distinct feature that is relatively easy to find and recognize.

contour interval The vertical distance between contour lines on a topographical map.

control A prism-shaped, usually red-and-white marker placed in the field prior to an orienteering event and corresponding to a known map point; to be located during the event.

control extension Plotting a course to a larger adjacent feature rather than to the easy-to-miss, smaller actual target.

draw A shallow valley with steep sides.

fartlek Swedish word meaning speed play; a form of running training incorporating increased efforts over various distances at different paces.

handrail A feature running parallel to one's direction of travel and thereby serving as a handy navigational aid.

interval training Repeated fast-paced runs of 100 yards to three quarters of a mile interspersed with recovery walks or jogs.

knoll A small hill.

meridians Imaginary lines running true north to true south on a map or the terrain.

pace count The number of steps traveled.

precise compass The following of the compass reading.

reentrant An elongated, sloping valley.

rough compass The following of a general compass route.

saddle A low point on a ridge connecting two summits.

spur A narrow, sloping ridge.

topographical map The graphic delineation of natural and fabricated features showing their relative position and elevation.

SUGGESTED READINGS

Garrett, M. 1996. *Orienteering and map games for teachers.* Forest Park, Ga.: U.S. Orienteering Federation. A stimulating set of orienteering lesson plans and game ideas especially for elementary grade school teachers.

Kjellstrom, B. 1994. *Be expert with map and compass.* 5th ed. New York: Macmillan. Basic handbook on participation and event organization.

Lowry, R., and Sidney, K. 1989. *Orienteering skills and strategies.* 3d ed. North York, Ontario: Orienteering Ontario. A textbook intended for middle to high school ages, but good for all levels.

Mcneill, C., et al. 1998. *Teaching orienteering.* 2d ed. Doune, Scotland: Harveys. Encyclopedic collection of orienteering lesson plans and exercises.

Randall, G. 1989. *The Outward Bound map and compass handbook,* New York: Lyons & Burford.

Seidman, D. 1995. *The essential wilderness navigator.* Camden, Me.: Ragged Mountain Press.

Stott, W. 1992. *Armchair orienteering.* 3d ed. Vol. 1. Winnipeg: Manitoba Orienteering Association. Workbook on reading topographical maps.

RESOURCES

Films and videotapes

Jones, K. 1990. *Finding your way in the world.* Minneapolis, The Richard Diercks Company, Inc.

International Film Bureau, 332 S. Michigan Av., Chicago, IL 60604.

Orienteering Service/USA, P.O. Box 547, North La Porte, IN 46350.

Silva, 2466 State Road 39 N, North La Porte, IN 46350.

Organizations

Map and Information Office, U.S. Geological and Geodetic Survey, Washington, DC 02042. USGS topo maps can be ordered from this agency. For areas west of the Mississippi River, write to Western Distribution Branch, USGS, Building 41, Box 25286, Federal Center, Denver, CO 80225. For areas east of the Mississippi River, write to Eastern Distribution Branch, USGS, 1200 S. Ends St., Arlington, VA 22209.

United States Orienteering Federation, P.O. Box 500, Athens, OH 45701.

Web site

U.S. Geological Survey: http://www.usgs.gov/index.html

Racquetball, Paddleball, and Handball

After completing this chapter, the reader should be able to:

- Understand the similarities of and differences among racquetball, hardball, and paddleball
- Select equipment properly
- Recognize the court markings for these sports
- Understand the rules and scoring procedures for games involving two, three, or four players
- Execute the basic skills, including court positioning and various shots and serves
- Display a knowledge of offensive and defensive strategies
- Recognize and use racquetball, handball, and paddleball terms correctly
- Instruct a group of beginning players in the fundamentals of the sports

The popularity of racquetball as a recreational activity increased significantly in the mid 1960s and has been a popular pastime ever since. The game is a variation of handball and paddleball, activities that have long been popular. The popularity of racquetball can be partially explained by the fact that even beginners can achieve early success in contacting and placing the ball using a stringed racquet, whereas the skills are more difficult to master in handball and paddleball. Although the rules for all three activities are similar, each has its advocates, claiming their favorite to be the best of the three.

HISTORY

Handball

There is evidence that handball originated in Rome and that it is one of the oldest of sports. Ireland is credited with first developing the game and holding the first championship tournament. John Kavanagh of York, England, was the leading player and champion in 1840, the same year handball was introduced to the United States.

The first international match was played in 1887 for a purse of $1,000. The match was between Phil Casey of Brooklyn, and John Lawler, the Irish champion. Casey won 7 straight games and the championship. The matches were played on a four-wall court. Casey retained the championship for many years and was called the father of the game in the United States. In 1897 the Amateur Athletic Union (AAU) sponsored the first American tournament, won by Michael Egan.

In the early years of the game, four-wall courts were used. Later, around 1913, a one-wall court game on the beaches of New York became popular. This was a modification of the four-wall game. The use of one wall brought the game outdoors. A three-wall court is sometimes used for play in which abbreviated side walls abutting the front wall permit corner shots and some sidewall shots.

The first four-wall championship was held in Los Angeles in 1919, and the first one-wall AAU Championship was held in New York in 1924. The first YMCA National Championship was held in Cleveland in 1925.

The AAU, the YMCA, the United States Handball Association (formed in 1951), and the Jewish Community Recreation Association hold joint regional and national championships. Now, the USHA holds annual state, regional, and national tournaments for the open and age-group divisions for juniors, males, and females.

Paddleball and Racquetball

The game of paddleball is generally believed to have been formulated at the University of Michigan in the early 1920s. The rules are similar to those for handball except that a wooden paddle is used instead of the hand and a different type of ball is used. Racquetball, which developed from paddleball around the late 1940s, has rules similar to paddleball except that a stringed racquet is used. Racquetball is a much faster game than paddleball. There is more emphasis on the serve, and the rallies are shorter in racquetball. However, paddleball is still popular because its longer rallies provide excellent physical conditioning and there is an emphasis on control and placement of the ball. The USRA conducts annual state, regional, and national tournaments for the open and age-group divisions for juniors, males, and females in racquetball.

NATURE OF THE GAMES

A rubber ball is batted alternately by the players against the front wall of a one-, three-, or four-wall court. The object is to cause the ball to rebound to such a position and in such a manner that the opponent cannot return it before the second bounce. The ball may be played either on the fly from the front wall or after one bounce from the floor or ground. It is put in play by a serve that must first hit the front wall. A point is scored only by the player or team serving.

VALUES

One of the best of the many features of these great recreational sports is that they combine a vigorous workout in a short time with a great deal of fun. The proper ball, a pair of gloves (or a paddle or racquet), and suitable clothing and shoes are the only equipment needed. Most YMCAs, recreation centers, and athletic clubs have courts. The popularity of these activities grew so fast that commercial racquetball and handball facilities have been built all around the United States. A one-wall court can be marked off in any gymnasium or erected outdoors on a tennis court or similar playing area. The rules are simple and can be learned in a short time. These games require only two, three, or four persons to play, so it is easy to play a game almost anytime without getting a lot of people together.

These games can be played at any age, However, because they require fast reactions, quick reflexes, and good eye-hand coordination, it is important to play with partners and opponents of comparable ability.

EQUIPMENT

Balls

The balls used for paddleball and racquetball are about the size of a tennis ball. They are manufactured by several companies and come in different colors and degrees of "liveliness." The ball used in paddleball is much slower than the ball used in racquetball. The official racquetball is 2¼ inches (5.7 cm) in diameter and weighs about ¼ ounces (40 g). The official handball is black, 1⅞ inches (4.8 cm) in diameter, and weighs 2¼ ounces (65.7 g). It is often suggested that beginners use a softer, larger ball, such as a tennis ball, until some of the basic footwork and shot fundamentals are mastered.

Gloves

In handball, gloves must be worn. The gloves may be made of leather or a soft material and must be light in color. The fingers of the gloves cannot be webbed, and no foreign substance (tape, rubber bands, or the like) can be worn on the gloves. Padded gloves are available and are recommended for beginners. After the hands become toughened and the player's skill increases so that batting the ball does not result in sore hands, tight-fitting, unpadded gloves are recommended to allow increased control of the ball. Gloves are sometimes worn by paddleball and racquetball players as well, but their purpose is to improve the grip on the paddle or racquet.

Racquet

With the increase in popularity of racquetball has come an increase in the number, types, and sizes of racquets available. The phenomenon is similar to the proliferation of types of tennis racquets. The USRA rules now state that the racquet length is limited to 22 inches (58.9 cm). Frames are made of fiberglass, graphite, and various kinds of metals, plastics, and compositions of differing shapes. The racquet strings may be made of gut, nylon, monofilament, graphite, plastic, metal, or some combination of these.

Of course, prices vary considerably. For the beginner, a lightweight frame has advantages. Most importantly, the racquet should feel comfortable when gripped. When selecting a racquet, it is important to grip the handle with the safety thong attached in the correct manner.

Paddle

The paddle, although much the same size as the racquet, is made entirely of wood. Some models have a leather-wrapped handle similar to that of the racquet, and all paddles should have a safety thong attached to the handle. Most paddles have regularly spaced holes drilled through the face to reduce air resistance.

Eyeguards

Because of the possibility of eye injury, special eyeguards have been introduced and are highly recommended for both novice and advanced players. In fact, in many tournaments and recreational facilities, lensed eyewear is required. Because the ball travels at such a high rate of speed, if it hits a player directly in the eye, it is possible to injure the eye seriously. The wearing of eyeguards is especially important for beginning players because of their tendency to turn the head to look for the ball.

COURTS

One-Wall Court

The one-wall court is 20 feet (6.10 m) wide, 34 feet (10.36 m) long, and 16 feet (4.88 m) high, with at least 6 feet (1.83 m) of clear space beyond the side and long lines. (The 34-foot line is called the "long line.") There are no official specifications for playing surfaces. The surface is usually wood, cement, or clay (figure 23-1).

The short line is drawn across the court 16 feet (4.88 m) from the front wall and parallel to it. The service line is drawn across the court 9 feet (2.74 m) behind the short line and parallel to it. The space between the service line and short line is the service zone.

Four-Wall Court

The four-wall court should have a hardwood floor, and sidewalls should be constructed of smooth plaster, tile, concrete, glass, or brick. The court should measure 20 × 20 × 40 feet (6.10 × 6.10 × 12.19 m) (figure 23-2).

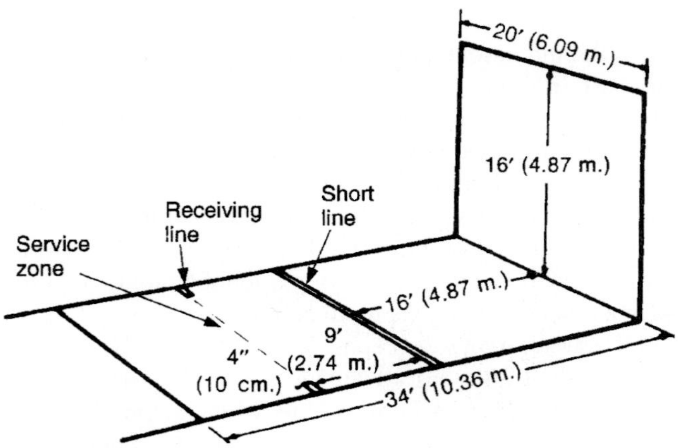

Figure 23-1. One-wall court.

Three-Wall Court

Three-wall courts are occasionally used and are identical to four-wall courts in dimensions, except that there is no back wall.

RULES

One-Wall Court

The rules for the four-wall court also apply to the one-wall court, with the exception of those rules pertaining to sidewalls, back wall, and ceiling plays where there is no ceiling adjoining the front wall, and with the following other considerations.

Serving. The server drops the ball to the floor within the service zone and on the first bounce strikes it in such a manner that it hits the front wall and returns to the floor beyond the short line and in front of the long line. The opposing side must make a legal return by striking the ball after the first bounce or on the fly.

Following are terms that pertain to serving:

long ball A long ball passes over the long line on the serve.
short ball A short ball does not pass over the short line on the serve.
out An out results from serving two short balls, two long balls, or one short ball and one long ball; serving the ball out-of-bounds; or hitting the floor before the wall.

Special rules for paddleball

1. Loss of 3 points for throwing the paddle
2. Loss of 2 points for dropping the paddle
3. Loss of 3 points and serve for throwing the paddle while serving
4. Loss of 5 points and serve for hitting any player with the paddle
5. In paddleball doubles, the server's partner must stand off the court in the extension of the service area while the teammate is serving. Violation will be a fault. In addition, the server's partner must not enter the court until the served ball has passed. Violation will be a fault.
6. A striker must call "Block" whenever there is danger of hitting the opponent while taking a normal swing. Upon the block call, the striker must refrain from hitting the ball. The point is then replayed. An opponent may call "Block" if he or she foresees danger. If the game if being refereed, the referee will either confirm or deny legitimacy of the call.

Four-Wall Court

1. The game may be played by two (singles), three (cutthroat), or four players (doubles).
2. In handball, a game consists of 21 points. A match consists of two games of 21 points with a tiebreaker of 11 points if the first two games are split.

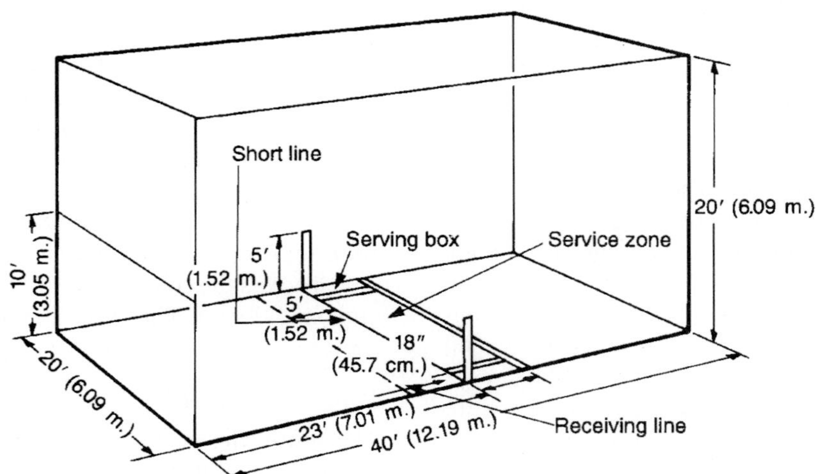

Figure 23-2. Four-wall court.

3. In racquetball, a game consists of 15 points; a match, two games of 15 points, with a tiebreaker of 11 points if the first two games are split.
4. Only the racquet, paddle, or one hand may be used to strike the ball. The use of the foot or any other portion of the body to return the ball is not permitted.
5. In attempting to return the ball, a player cannot strike it more than once.
6. Serving:
   a. To make a legal service, the server drops the ball to the floor within the service zone and strikes it on the bounce, so that it hits the front wall first and on the rebound lands on the floor back of the short line, before or after striking one of the sidewalls.
   b. Drive-serve zones in racquetball. The drive-serve lines are 3 feet (0.91 m) from each sidewall in the service box, dividing the service area into two 17-foot (5.18 m) service zones for drive-serves only. The player may drive-serve to the same side of the court on which he or she is standing, so long as the start and finish of the service motion take place outside of the 3-foot line. The referee watches the 3-foot line to see that none of the server's body passes over the line and prevents the receiver from plainly seeing the served ball. Violation is an out (figure 23-3).
   c. The three types of serve are legal serve, out serve, and fault serve. If the serve is legal, play continues; if the serve is an out serve, the server is retired; if the serve is a fault serve, another serve is permitted. What constitutes each of these types of serve is explained under "Playing Regulations."
   d. After the ball has been legally served, the opposing side makes a legal return by striking the ball on the fly or the first bounce, causing it to hit the front wall before hitting the floor. The ball may hit the ceiling, back wall, and either one of or both sidewalls before it hits the front wall.
   e. The serving and receiving sides alternate in attempting to make legal returns until one side fails. If the serving side fails, it scores an out; if the receiving side fails, a point is scored for the server.

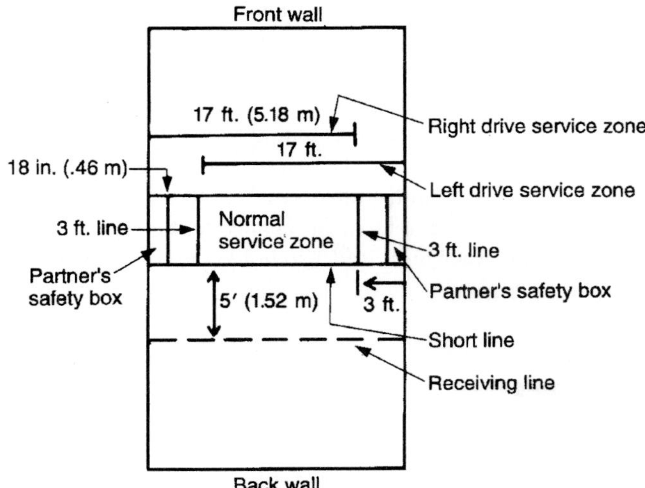

Figure 23-3. Drive-serve zones in racquetball.

Three-Wall Court

Three-wall handball is played similarly to four-wall, with the exception of the back wall. In place of the back wall, a line is drawn on the floor parallel to the front wall and is called the "long line." A ball in play striking behind the long line is a point or a handout depending on the side last to hit the ball. A served ball that lands behind the long line is a long ball. Hitting two long balls or one long and one short ball in succession puts the server out.

PLAYING REGULATIONS

Service

1. The choice for the right to serve is decided by a coin toss, and the player winning the toss has the option of serving or receiving the first game. The player who wins the most points in the first two games has the option of serving first for the third (tiebreaker) game. In informal matches a common procedure to determine who serves is to see which player can rebound the ball off the front wall and come closest to the short line.
2. With the exception of the racquetball drive-serve, the server may start serving from any place in the serving zone.
3. In serving, the server must start and stay within the service zone; while serving, neither the ball nor any part of either foot may extend beyond the service line or short line. Stepping on (but not over) either line is permitted. For stepping over a line once, a fault is charged. Stepping outside the service zone twice in succession retires the server and counts as an out. "Stepping over" is the act of putting any part of the foot past the short or service lines. On a lob serve, the server may not back out of the service zone until the ball has passed the back service line.
4. In serving, the ball must be bounced on the floor and struck on the rebound from the floor. The server is out if the attempt to hit the ball on this rebound fails. Not more than three bounces may be used in making a service. Bouncing of the ball by a server in any part of the court before serving is counted as a bounce within the meaning of this rule. Violation of this rule retires the server.
5. A served ball that first hits the front wall and on the rebound passes so closely to the server (or the server's

partner, in doubles) that it prevents the receiver from having a clear view of the ball is played over. Two in a row results in an out.

6. In singles, when the server loses the service, the server becomes the receiver; the receiver then becomes the server, and so on alternately in all subsequent services of the game.
7. In doubles, only one player on the team that serves first is allowed to serve in the first inning. When this player is put out, each of the opponents is allowed to serve until put out. On resuming service, the player who served first serves again until put out, and then the partner serves.
8. The server may not serve until the opponent has had a chance to get placed or the referee calls play.
9. In handball and racquetball doubles, the server's partner must stand within the service zone until the ball passes the service line on each serve. Two consecutive violations of this rule retire the server.
10. If a player's partner is hit by a served ball while standing in the service box, the serve counts as a dead ball without penalty, but any short or fault preceding the service partner being hit with the ball is charged.
11. In doubles, each partner must serve in the regular order of service. Failure to do so counts as a handout, and the points scored on the illegal serve do not count.
12. Every effort should be made to keep the ball dry, particularly on the service. Deliberate violation of the spirit of this rule results in forfeiture of serve. The ball may be inspected at any time during a game, and the referee puts a new ball in play if advisable.

Receiving Service

1. In handball, paddleball, and racquetball the receivers must stand at least 5 feet (1.52 m) in back of the short line, as indicated by the service or restraining line.
2. In handball the receiver can hit the ball after it passes the short line.
3. In racquetball and paddleball the receiver may not enter the safety zone (the 5-foot [1.52 m] area between the short line and receiver's line) until the served ball bounces or crosses the receiver's line.
4. A receiver may play the service either on the fly or after the first bounce. In making a fly return, the receiver must play the ball after it passes over the short line in handball and receiver's line in racquetball and paddleball.

Faults

1. Two consecutive faults retire the server.
2. A serve is considered short when the served ball hits the front wall and fails to strike back of the short line on the fly.
3. A short also occurs when a served ball hits the front wall and two sidewalls before striking the floor back of the short line.
4. A serve is considered long when the served ball rebounds from the front wall and touches the back wall before touching the floor.
5. A serve is also considered a fault if the ball rebounds from the front wall and touches the ceiling.
6. Stepping over the outer edges of the service or short line with any part of the foot in the act of service is considered a fault.
7. Serving the ball in handball and racquetball doubles when the server's partner is not in the service box with his or her back against the wall is considered a fault. It is a fault in paddleball when the serve is made before the server's partner is out of the court.

Hinders

1. A returned ball that strikes an opponent on its way to the front wall is considered dead, even if it continues to the front wall before striking the floor.
2. Dead-ball hinders: A dead-ball hinder occurs when (1) a ball takes an irregular bounce as a result of contacting a rough surface or wet spot, (2) an opponent is hit by the shot in flight, (3) there is body contact sufficient to stop the rally, (4) any ball rebounding from the front wall is close to the body of the defensive player and prevents the offensive play from having a clear view of the ball, or (5) any body or racquet contact occurs during the backswing.
3. Avoidable hinders:
   a. An avoidable hinder results in the loss of the rally. It does not necessarily have to be an intentional act.
   b. A player's unintentional interference in such a way as to prevent the opponent from having a fair chance to return the ball is considered a hinder.
   c. In doubles, both players on a side are entitled to a fair and unobstructed chance at the ball. The referee should be alert in rendering decisions under this rule to discourage any practice of playing the ball where an adversary cannot see it until too late to get into position. It is no excuse that the ball is "killed" or that the adversary "could not get it." A player is entitled to a fair chance to recover any ball.
4. The principles just cited also hold true in singles. It is the duty of the side that has played the ball to get out of the way of the opponent.
5. It is the duty of the referee to decide all hinders and covered balls.
6. When a player is interfered with by her or his partner, a hinder cannot be claimed.
7. When, in the opinion of the referee, a player is hindered intentionally, the referee decides the point against the offending player.

8. In four-wall play a ball off the front wall on the fly or a bounce that goes into the gallery or an opening in the sidewall is a hinder, but if it goes into the gallery or opening after a player has touched it (a ball caroming off a racquet, paddle, or hand), it counts as a point or an out against the player attempting the return.

Outs

1. A player intentionally interferes with an opponent.
2. A partner serves out of turn.
3. A served ball touches the server in singles or doubles.
4. In handball or racquetball a served ball strikes the server's partner when the latter is outside the service box.
5. A legally returned ball strikes the partner of the player returning the ball.
6. A player fails to play a ball properly returned from a service.
7. A served ball hits the ceiling, floor, or sidewalls before striking the front wall.
8. A served ball hits the front wall and sidewall, front wall and floor, or front wall and ceiling at the same time (crotch ball).
9. The server makes two successive faults.
10. The ball bounces more than three times on the serve.

SPECIAL POPULATIONS

Rule modifications have been made in these sports to accommodate special populations, such as wheelchair athletes and athletes with visual or hearing disabilities. In general, the standard rules governing the sports are followed, except for some modifications. For example, there is typically a two-bounce or multibounce rule in effect. In wheelchair play, rules referring to feet are adapted to indicate where the wheels touch the floor. Players with visual disabilities may make multiple attempts to strike the ball until the ball has been touched or has stopped bouncing (USRA 1997, Rules 8, 9, and 10).

SAFETY

Novice paddleball or racquetball players should be careful to avoid swinging wildly at the ball because the paddles and racquets can injure a partner or opponent. In fact, paddles and racquets have a thong attached to the handle that must be secured to the player's wrist to prevent a paddle or racquet from slipping from the hand. For this reason, it is illegal to switch the paddle or racquet from hand to hand during play.

FUNDAMENTAL SKILLS AND TECHNIQUES

The beginner watching an experienced player soon learns that there are fundamentals common to most sports. The beginner is often out of position, off-balance, and unable to get a good, accurate shot, while the more experienced opponent seems to always be in the correct position. The beginning student should work on these fundamentals.

Position on Floor

Study the possible angles that a ball can travel and rebound within the four rectangular walls of the court as you would in studying angles while playing billiards. Throw or hit the ball at the walls at different angles and heights and observe the rebounds. Try to move to that spot where the ball is expected to be best played (figure 23-4).

Footwork

The fundamental skill of correct footwork is essential for proficiency and accuracy in these activities. For a right-handed player the left foot and side should be toward the front wall when a forehand stroke is called for; if a backhand or a left-hand stroke is called for, the right foot and side should face the front wall. While waiting between shots, the front of the body should face the front wall, the feet should be about shoulder-width apart, the weight should be evenly distributed on both feet, and the player should be ready to move in any direction. While waiting and when contacting the ball, the knees are usually bent and the body is crouched (figure 23-5).

Accuracy of Playing Shots

Accuracy depends on proper footwork, good balance, and keeping the eyes on the ball with correct arm action and follow-through. The player, by experience, should gain the ability to choose the angle and spot that is desirable to hit without looking at the spot. (The player should be watching the ball.)

Practice low corner shots that have little or no rebound. These shots are called "kill shots." The sidearm stroke is most accurate for this shot.

The Hand

Snug-fitting gloves should be worn for handball. The tips of the fingers should be slightly squeezed together, and the entire hand should be slightly cupped like a swimmer's hand. The wrist and elbow should be flexible to accommodate a wrist-snap shot or an overarm stroke similar to that of throwing a fast ball. In stroking the ball, the hand should follow through toward the spot where the ball is directed before the arm swings across the body to complete the follow-through. The hand can also be held in a tight fist for certain kinds of shots (figure 23-6).

Strokes

The arm strokes used in all three activities are similar except that in racquetball and paddleball a backhand stroke is often employed, whereas in handball the player must develop the ability to use the nondominant hand in striking

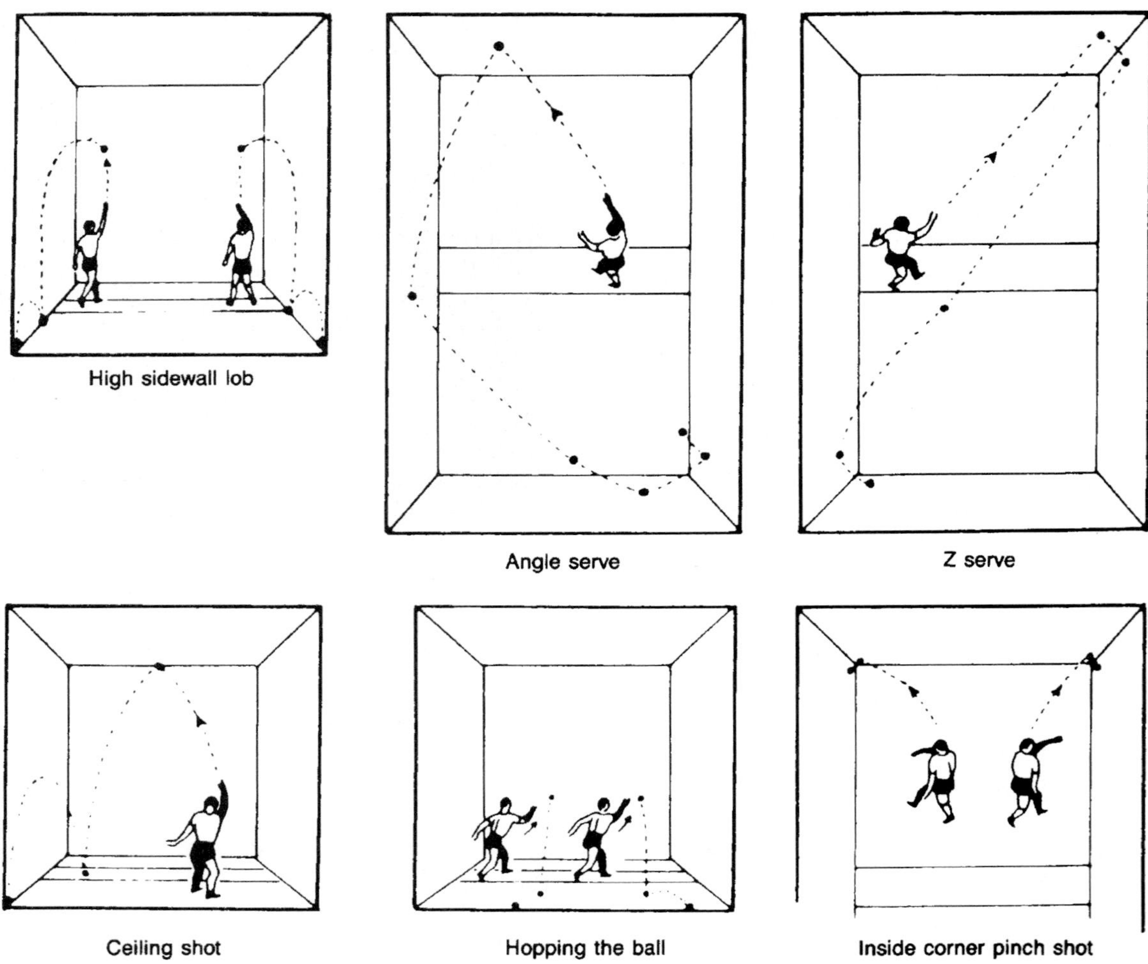

Figure 23-4. Floor positions and ball placement.

the ball. In all three activities the overarm, sidearm, and underarm strokes are used.

Overarm. The body position for the overarm stroke is similar to that in throwing a ball fast, for example, from a catcher to second base. The arm swings back so that the racquet or the hand begins the stroking action from behind the ear. If a ball is hit from a high reach, the arm is usually held almost straight while stroking. A quick, flexible wrist snap is desirable.

Sidearm. The sidearm stroke on the dominant side of the body is similar to a sidearm throw except that the elbow is tucked in for the forehand stroke. If the player is right-handed, the left foot should be in front of the right, and vice versa. Often the stroke is made without changing feet and with a quick, flexible wrist snap. However, the feet should always be ready to react if a more accurate stroke can be delivered by shifting the feet.

Underarm. This stroke is not as common in racquetball or paddleball as it is in handball. In all three activities the underhand stroke is usually less effective than bending low at the knees and waist and using the sidearm stroke.

In handball, where power is desired, the ball may contact the heel of the hand, which is strong and muscular and can withstand repeated contact with the ball.

In all three activities the use of the wrist to impart speed to the ball is critical. Because of the velocity with which the ball travels, often a player will not be able to get in the proper position to effectively use the proper body, leg, and arm movements, and the wrist snap in these situations is the only remaining movement to achieve a decent return. In racquetball and paddleball this motion is aided by the use of light racquets and paddles. In handball it is helpful to contact the ball toward the tips of the fingers, when possible. This permits a longer leverage to the hand, and a wrist whip gives the ball added speed and accuracy. To master this stroke requires a great deal of practice. The ball can be hit with the palm of the hand, but this shot is not very accurate, nor can speed or power be obtained from it.

Figure 23-5. Stance for an open-hand shot in handball.

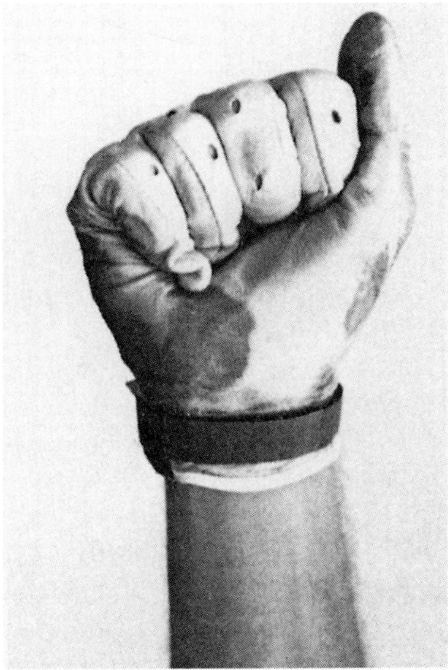

Figure 23-6. Handball fist shot.

Kill Shots

A kill shot is one that hits the front so close to the floor that there is practically no bounce before an opponent can reach the ball and play it. There are many varieties of kill shots.

Straight kill shot. The straight kill is a shot to the front wall that does not touch either sidewall, but hits the wall low.

Outside-corner pinch shot. In the outside-corner pinch shot, the ball first hits the sidewall, bounces to the front wall, and then bounces to the floor. Either the right or left corner may be used.

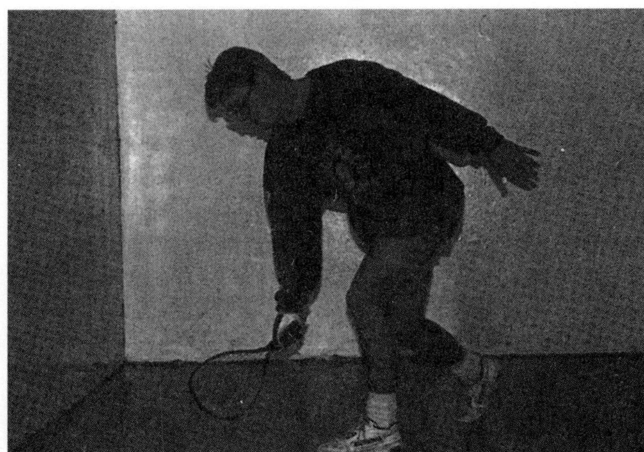

Figure 23-7. Racquetball forehand kill-shot position.

Inside-corner pinch shot. In the inside-corner pinch shot, the ball first hits the front wall, bounces to the sidewall, and then bounces to the floor. Again, either the right or left corner may be used.

Fly kill shot. In the fly kill shot the ball is hit on the fly from a front wall rebound so fast that the opponent has no opportunity to play the ball.

A player should constantly strive to direct a ball into an area or at such an angle into the sidewalls that the opponent has no opportunity to play the ball. This is a skill that can be mastered only by practice and experience.

Back-Wall Shot

A hard shot that hits moderately high on the front wall will often rebound all the way to the back wall without hitting the floor. A player sensing such a situation should move into a position to return the ball as it comes off the back wall (or floor) and is moving toward the front wall. By waiting until the ball is near the floor, the player can execute a kill shot (figure 23-7).

Occasionally a player may not have time to get into the proper position to return a back-wall shot. It may be possible to hit the ball hard and moderately high against the back wall to cause it to rebound to the front wall before hitting the floor. This shot should be used only in desperation because it often results in an easy return for the opponent. The shot should be used only when the player is out of position and needs to buy time to regain proper court position.

Ceiling Shot

The ceiling shot is basically a defensive pass shot used when a player is out of position or when a change of pace is needed. It may also be used offensively to move an opponent out of the center-court position. It is executed by hitting the ball relatively hard and directing it toward the ceiling a few feet in back of the front wall. The intent

Figure 23-8. Racquetball drive serve.

should be to cause the ball to bounce on the floor approximately in the serving area and then come down in a back corner near a sidewall. By hitting the ceiling and front wall, the ball develops an overspin and bounces higher than normal, possibly causing the opponent to misplay the ball.

Pass Shot

A shot directed in such a way that it travels along the sidewall that is farthest away from the opponent is a pass shot. It should not be hit with so much force that it rebounds off the back wall, but instead it should drop into one of the back corners.

Serve

There are many types and variations of serves, such as the drive serve (see figure 23-8). A serve is begun by dropping the ball on the floor behind the service line. On the first bounce, the server hits it with the racquet, paddle, or hand. To be a legal serve, the ball must hit the front wall; it can then either rebound directly back behind the server or from the front wall onto the sidewalls, as long as it rebounds to the floor behind the short line. The server is permitted another serve if a fault is committed. Two faults retire the server.

Drive serve. In the drive serve the player, while standing in the drive-serve zone (figure 23-3), contacts the ball close to the floor so that it hits the front wall close to the floor and rebounds just behind the short line. It is usually directed at an angle so that when it reaches a receiver it is near a sidewall.

Z serve. In the Z serve the player serves from the side so that the ball rebounds from the front wall to the sidewall opposite the server at such an angle that the ball lands behind the short line. This serve can also be hit high so that the ball rebounds to the back wall and corner behind the server.

Direct high lob. The server stands close to the right or left sidewall and serves the ball high up on the front wall and close to the sidewall, so that the ball rebounds far back in the court but is very close to the sidewall on its entire flight. This type of serve often drops dead in the back corner and is difficult to return. Some of these serves may just touch the sidewall on their rebound flight, causing the ball to drop dead.

Two-wall serve to back corner. The server takes a position close to the right wall and serves the ball about head high and about 4 or 5 feet (1.5 m) from the left sidewall. The ball rebounds to the left sidewall just back of midcourt, rebounds to the floor and on back to the right corner, and hits the back wall and then the right wall before hitting the floor.

The flight of this serve causes the receiver to run around, following the ball and looking for an opportunity to play it, which is difficult.

HINTS ON PLAY AND STRATEGY

1. Throughout a game, keep in mind that situations like those described in the various serves may arise, and the ball can be directed and played like a serve. In these situations there is a need to quickly size up an

opponent's weaknesses and strong points and play to the weaknesses.
2. Keep your eyes on the ball. Follow it constantly.
3. Protect your eyes by wearing lensed eyeguards.
4. Watch your opponent's feet and position. He or she will usually telegraph the return shots.
5. Avoid rushing the ball. It is important to wait before attempting the return shot.
6. Concentrate on your serve, when you have complete control of the ball.
7. Develop several different serves. Analyze your opponent's return of various serves. Concentrate on the serve that is most difficult for your opponent to return.
8. Change from fast play to lob shots and runaround plays to keep an opponent off balance. Strive to place shots accurately.
9. Be constantly on the alert for balls that can be contacted close to the floor or for the opportunity to hit corner kill shots.
10. Constantly work for a desirable position on the court. A good spot is usually the "hole," or "well," near the center of the court and service area. This is also known as the "offensive spot," and the backcourt is known as the "defensive spot." Try to keep the opponent out of the well.
11. Strive to think ahead and set up a series of plays that will keep the opponent off balance and therefore at a disadvantage.
12. Continue to practice your weakest strokes. In handball it is usually necessary to practice hitting with the nondominant hand. In racquetball and handball, regularly practice hitting backhand strokes. On either a serve or rebound, concentrate on hitting a spot on the front wall, but keep the eyes on the ball until it is hit. After a serve, come quickly to midcourt. Continue to maneuver for the offensive position throughout the game.

SKILLS TO PRACTICE ALONE

Serving Drills. Drive Serve

Purpose. To develop accuracy in the drive serve and be able to drive-serve to a variety of court positions.

Method. From the center of the service zone, hit three drive serves to each of the four designated court positions. Repeat the circuit three times. Score 1 point for each correct placement. Total points possible = 36. (Note: You can total points scored to each designated area to indicate your most accurate placement. Total points to each area = 9) (Norton and Bryant 1991, p. 96).

Defensive Shots. Lob, Ceiling, High Z, Around-the-Wall

Purpose. To practice hitting a defensive shot from two court positions and develop accuracy in ball placement.

Method. Using a dropped ball, hit each defensive shot ten times, from center and backcourt positions (five to each corner). Use the same target area as designated for the lob and high Z serves. Total points possible for each serve from each position = 50. To vary this drill, begin the defensive shot with a side wall toss (Norton and Bryant 1991, p. 96).

30-Second Drill

Purpose. To learn to react quickly to the ball's court position and improve movement time, and to work on ball control.

Method. Begin in a center-court position. Drop the ball and return it to the front wall. Continue to return the ball off the rebound, counting the number of times the ball is returned in 30 seconds. Count only shots that would be legal returns in a game. Do this drill at least every other practice session. Try to improve by one to three shots each time (Norton and Bryant 1991, p. 95).

Forehand and Backhand Shots from Side-Wall Toss

Purpose. To practice hitting forehand and backhand shots to the back corners of the court from a ball bouncing off the side wall.

Method. Stand with your hips pivoted and facing the side wall appropriate for either a forehand or backhand stroke. Toss the ball into the side wall. After the rebound, hit the ball to a back corner of the court. Hit eight balls from each of the three court positions, four to each corner, then repeat eight shots each from the same court positions with the other stroke (Norton and Bryant 1991, p. 94).

Suicide Drill

Purpose. To develop muscular endurance and anaerobic capacity, and to practice moving to the ball and returning it to the front wall.

Method. Begin in the center court, drop the ball, and hit it to the front wall. Continue to return the ball as quickly as you can, moving to hit all balls after one bounce. Work at positioning yourself correctly for each hit. Continue this drill for 2-minute intervals, allowing yourself to rest 30 to 60 seconds after each hitting session. Repeat the drill ten times. Record the number of balls hit during each 2-minute interval (Norton and Bryant 1991, p. 94).

Ceiling Ball Rally

1. Stand in the rear court and direct the ball to the ceiling.
2. As the ball rebounds toward the back court, adjust your court position to strike the ball, attempting to repeat the ceiling ball return.
3. Continue executing ceiling ball returns until either the ball bounces twice or the return does not contact the ceiling.
4. During the return, the ball can hit either the ceiling or the front wall first (although ceiling first is

preferred), as long as the ball contacts both the ceiling and the front wall.

5. The score is determined by the number of successful returns made before the ball either bounces twice or fails to contact the ceiling or the front wall on the return.
6. A good score for a beginner is ten successive returns in a row in any one of five repetitions of the test (Kozar and Catignani 1997, p. 58).

Off-the-Back-Wall Kill

1. Using masking tape or other temporary marking material 1 to 2 inches wide, make a line along the width of the front wall 1.5 feet up from the floor.
2. Stand 5 feet from the back wall in the center of the court and toss the ball about waist high against the back wall.
3. As the ball strikes the back wall, pivot into a forehand (or backhand) striking position and slide toward the front wall with the ball as it rebounds off the back wall and contacts the floor.
4. Slide your feet and adjust your body position while waiting for the ball to drop to knee height or lower near the lead leg, which is the prime striking position.
5. Strike the ball and direct it so that it contacts the front wall between the floor and the marked area.
6. A good score for a beginner would be five successful attempts out of ten trials.

Once you are able to consistently hit directly to the targeted area on the front wall, attempt to improve your accuracy by hitting either side wall before the ball contacts the marked area on the front wall (Kozar and Catignani 1997, p. 57).

Deep Lob Serve

1. Using masking tape or other temporary marking material 1 to 2 inches wide, outline a 5-foot-square area on the side wall in each rear corner.
2. Assume the appropriate position in the service zone for the lob serve.
3. Execute the lob serve so that it contacts the front wall three-fourths of the way up, rebounding in a slow arc to the left or right rear corner.
4. Note the number of times the ball hits the targeted 5-foot-square area on the side wall before contacting the floor.
5. A good score for a beginner would be three successful attempts out of ten trials (Kozar and Catignani 1997, p. 56).

Drive and Short Lob ("Garbage") Serve

1. Using masking tape or other temporary marking material 1 to 2 inches wide, outline a 3-foot-square area in each of the rear corners of the court.
2. Assume the appropriate position in the service zone for the drive or garbage serve.
3. Execute either a drive or a garbage serve and attempt to land the ball on the second bounce in one of the outlined target areas.
4. Note the number of successful attempts after ten trials. Be sure to attempt both serves an equal number of times to each corner targeted area.
5. A good score for a beginner in attempting each of these serves would be a total of five successful attempts out of ten trials (Kozar and Catignani 1997, p. 55–56).

COURT COURTESY

If there is any doubt about a play, it should be played over. It is not fair play to deliberately hit an opponent with the ball in order to get a hinder on the play. An opponent is entitled to a fair, unobstructed opportunity to play the ball.

TEACHING CONSIDERATIONS

1. Many school situations will be limited to games on one-wall courts. Taped lines on the walls and floor can be used to mark off playing areas.
2. Teach students basic sidearm and underarm patterns, beginning with tapping the ball easily against the wall rather than hitting strokes requiring maximum force. Start with forehand strokes before introducing backhand strokes. Emphasize action of the wrist and open stance as well as returning to a ready position in the play area. Emphasize getting the racquet in proper position.
3. Use partners to practice alternating hits in a cooperative way before introducing competitive strategies. Emphasize interference rules as soon as you introduce partner work. When two players can keep the ball going fairly consistently (at least six hits) without losing control of the ball, begin to increase the demand for greater force levels by increasing the distance of the players from the wall.
4. When players can consistently keep the ball going against the wall, encourage them to begin placing the ball to make their partners move to unused spaces in the playing area. Teach for changing the level of the ball against the wall, changing the angle of the shot, and changing the force level of the ball as offensive strategies. Name the shots and teach for form.
5. Introduce the serve and game rules as players begin to need more formal regulation of play (after some consistency is developed in ability to return the easier shots).
6. Modify and develop rules as necessary to meet the needs of the facilities available.
7. Require all players to wear lensed eyeguards. Emphasize eye safety in early instruction. Insist that

players wear a wrist thong on racquets and paddles at all times and constantly remind them about racquet safety.

GLOSSARY

ace A serve that completely eludes the receiver.

avoidable hinder A hinder that results in the loss of a rally. It may be intentional or unintentional.

crotch ball A ball hitting at the juncture of the front wall and the floor or the ceiling, sidewall, or corner.

dead ball A ball out of play, following a fault not played, a penalty, or a hinder.

fault An infraction of the rules that involves a penalty other than an out.

first service In doubles, only the first player serves to start the game.

handout A handout occurs when a side loses the serve.

hinder An accidental interference or obstruction of the flight of the ball not involving a penalty.

kill A ball returned to the front wall in such a manner that it rebounds from the front wall or sidewall so close to the floor that it is impossible to return.

long ball A ball that, on the serve, either hits the back wall directly or passes over the long line (three wall).

match Winning two out of three games.

out Sometimes called a "handout." It is scored against the serving side when the server fails to serve legally. In a doubles game, when each of the two partners has been put out, it is a sideout. In a singles game, retiring the server retires the side.

point Scored only by the serving side and made when an opponent fails to play a legal serve or a legally returned ball.

receiver The player or players to whom the ball is served; also called the "receiving side."

receiving line The line running parallel with and 5 feet (1.52 m) in back of the short line.

receiving zone The back court is the receiving zone for the serve.

screen serve A served ball that passes so close to the server (or partner) that the receiver is unable to get a clear view of the ball.

server The person serving the ball.

service line The line running parallel with and 5 feet (1.52 m) in front of the short line.

service zone The space between the outer edges of the short and service lines in which the server must remain while serving the ball.

short line The line running parallel with the front wall and dividing the court into two equal parts.

SUGGESTED READINGS

Allsen, P., and Witbeck, A.: *Racquetball,* ed. 6, Dubuque, Iowa, 1996, WC Brown. Contains sequential photographs depicting critical movements of various strokes, games strategy, racquetball terminology, questions for self-evaluation, and practice drills.

Clark, J: *Seven lifetime sports,* Dubuque, IA, 1991, Eddie Bowers Publishing. One of the lifetime sports presented in this book is racquetball and the chapter contains information on history, benefits, terminology, rules, equipment, skill fundamentals, error corrections, drills, games and skills tests.

Edwards, L. R. 1992. *Racquetball*. 2d ed. Scottsdale, Ariz. Gorsuch Scarisbrick. Discusses rules, equipment, terminology, tournament competition, and strategy.

Fabian, I., et al. 1988. *Racquetball: Ten beginning keys to success*. Dubuque, Iowa: Eddie Bowers. Features a section on stretching, over 100 pictures and diagrams, and teaching aids and drills.

Hiser, J: *Racquetball,* Dubuque, IA, 1998, WCB/McGraw-Hill. Covers basics, warming up, strokes, serves, shots, strategy and conditioning among other topics.

Isaacs, L., Lumpkin, A., and Schroer, D. 1992. *Racquetball everyone*. 2d ed. Winston-Salem, N.C.: Hunter Textbooks. Covers the basics from beginning to advanced. Contains chapters on rarer information, such as goal setting, mental preparation, injuries, and tournament play. Especially helpful to instructors who teach large groups of students with various levels of skill.

Kittleson, S: *Teaching racquetball: steps to success,* Champaign, IL, 1993, Human Kinetics.

Kozar, A., and Catignani, E. 1997. *Beginning racquetball*. Winston-Salem, N.C.: Hunter Textbooks.

Liles, L., Neimeyer, R: *Winning racquetball,* 1993, WCB/McGraw-Hill. Contains sections on the basics, essential skills, advanced skills, game strategy and winning racquetball.

Lowy, C. 1991. *Handball*. 2d ed. Boston: American Press.

Moore A, Scott T, Portfield W: *Three-Wall Racquetball, Everyone,* ed. 3, Winston-Salem, N.C. 1993, Hunter Textbooks. Grips, swings, and shots are presented step-by-step with numerous photos. Two chapters are devoted to the standard and the modified three-wall game. Each Chapter is followed by an evaluation and assessments of knowledge and skills.

Norton, C., and Bryant, J. 1997. *Beginning racquetball*. 4th ed. Englewood, Colo.: Morton. Contains more than 200 photographs illustrating basic skills. Includes chapters on safety, strokes, serves, strategy, drills, etiquette, and interpreting rules.

Official racquetball rules. 1997. Colorado Springs, Colo.: American Amateur Racquetball Association.

Official rules for one-wall paddleball. 1997. New York: American Paddleball Association.

Racquetball: Steps to success. 1992. Charleston, W. Va.: Cambridge Physical Education and Health. Combines the knowledge and experience of master teacher Stan Kittleson with the latest research on learning racquetball.

Turner, E., Clouse, W: *Winning racquetball: skills, drills and strategies,* Champaign, IL, 1996, Human Kinetics.

The new and official U.S. Handball Association handball rules. 1997. Tucson: U.S. Handball Association.

Verner, B. 1991. *Racquetball: Basic skills and drills*. Mountain View, Calif.: Mayfield. Contains a comprehensive introduction to the game, material on strategy, drills following each discussion of a shot or strategy, and boxed information on common faults, hints for improvement, and problem areas.

RESOURCES

Films and videotapes

Anderson, B., and Anderson, J. *Racquetball and handball stretches chart*. Drawings and instructions. Stretching, P.O. Box 767, Palmer Lake, CO 80133.

Chassard, A. *Racquetball*, videotape. Cambridge Physical Education and Health, Dept. PE9, P.O. Box 2153, Charleston, WV 25328. Al Chassard shares his insider's expertise in the basics of a strong all-around game. The video uses slow motion to show the proper grip and how to execute the forehand and backhand strokes.

Fancher, T., et al. *Sports techniques films*. American Alliance for Health, Physical Education, and Dance. 1900 Association Dr., Reston, VA 22091. Ten-minute films on racquetball fundamentals, shots, serves, service returns, and strategies of singles, doubles, and cutthroat racquetball.

Lodi, N. J. Carmel Productions, 1994. Presents highlights from the last half century of handball. 1 videocassette (60 min.).

Keeley, S. *Racquetball lessons made easy*, audiocassette and booklet course. Russell Productions. 1845 Gardinig Place, San Diego, CA 92110.

Peck, D. 1991. *Perfect form racquetball*. Master the sport of racquetball with unique SyberVision role-model learning method. Sybervision Perfect Form Series. 1 videocassette (60 minutes).

Racquetball. 1978. This three-part program gives instruction in grips, forehand, backhand, overhand and underhand shots, various serves, pass shots, alley passes, angle passes, and "kill" shots. 26 minutes. C: Dr. John Reznik, Pr: Champions on Film. Dist: SyberVision Systems, Inc., 1 Sansome Street, Suite 810, San Francisco, CA 94104, 800-606-8255.

Racquetball. 1992. Learn the basics of the sport. Slow-motion photography brings the action down to a pace that will let you follow and learn. Different strokes are introduced, and special attention is paid to the bank shots how to use the confines of the court to your own strategic advantage. 25 minutes. Dist: Cambridge Educational.

Racquetball for all ages. 1991. Al Chassard demonstrates winning form, proper stride, and game strategy for a great game of racquetball. 25 minutes. Pr: Champions on Film, Dist: SyberVision Systems, Inc., 1 Sansome Street, Suite 810, San Francisco, CA 94104, 800-606-8255.

Racquetball fundamentals. 1980. Various ways of gripping the racquet, basic strokes, court position, and serving are some of the topics covered in this program. 11 minutes. Dist: AIMS Multimedia, 9710 Desoto Avenue, Chatsworth, CA 91311, 800-367-2467.

Racquetball: Learn your lessons. 1990. Fran Davis and Stew Hastings share tips on the basics and the equipment of the game. 30 minutes. Athletic Institute, 200 Castlewood Dr., North Palm Beach, FL 33408.

Racquetball with Dave Peck. 1984. All of the fundamentals you need to play masterful racquetball are demonstrated in this SyberVision neuromuscular programming video. Includes four video cassettes. 60 minutes. Pr: SyberVision Systems. Dist: SyberVision Systems Inc., 1 Sansome Street, Suite 810, San Francisco, CA 94104, 800-606-8255.

Reznik, J. *Introduction to racquetball*. 16 mm film. Champions on Film, Division of School Tech Corp, RQ. Box 1941, Ann Arbor, MI 48106.

Reznik, J. *Racquetball basic shots*. 16 mm film. Champions on Film, Division of School Tech Corp, RQ. Box 1941, Ann Arbor, MI 48106.

Reznik, J. *Racquetball swing*. 16 mm film. Champions on Film, Division of School Tech Corp, RQ. Box 1941, Ann Arbor, MI 48106.

The following videos are available from The United States Handball Association, 1-800-BUY-USHA:

Instructional Video
1990 Atlanta Nationals
1991 Lakewood Nationals
1991 Dallas Pro/World
1992 Lancing Nationals
1993 Pro Singles
1993 Open Doubles
1993 Open Doubles
1994 Minneapolis Nationals
1994 Houston Nationals
1995 One-Wall Singles
1995 One-Wall Doubles

Yellen, M., and Adams, L. *Playing smart*. Features team Ektelon's top-ranked professional players demonstrating racquetball game strategies and tips. 1 videocassette (31 minutes, 15 seconds). Dist: Ektelon, 1 Sportsystem Plaza, Bordentown, NJ 08505, 800-283-2635.

Rugby

After completing this chapter, the reader should be able to:

- Appreciate the development and values of the game of rugby
- Select rugby equipment and lay out a rugby field
- Describe the rules and scoring procedures of the game
- Practice the fundamental techniques of rugby
- Explain the skills and duties required of the various positions
- Use lead-up activities and other suggestions to teach the fundamentals of rugby

HISTORY

Ball games resembling football have been played for well over two thousand years. Many descriptions, paintings, and drawings surviving from the Middle Ages show that the game has been played in the British Isles for centuries.

Rugby football was devised accidentally at Rugby School in England in 1823, when one of the players on Rugby's team, William Webb Ellis, tucked the ball under his arm and ran across the goal line, an act recognized as unsportsman-like conduct. However, this form of the game gained tremendous popularity over the next 40 years, and when the word *football* was used, some people asked, "Which kind?" Separate rules for rugby and football were formulated in the latter half of the nineteenth century.

Some twenty years after the division from football, a group of clubs in northern England formed what eventually became known as Rugby League. Rugby Union and Rugby League now support two totally distinct games.

Rugby has been played in the United States since the late nineteenth century but has been overshadowed by gridiron football and soccer, both of which developed from a rugby framework. Walter Camp, a halfback from Yale, changed the course of rugby to gridiron with two basic suggestions. One was to reduce the number of players from fifteen to eleven. The second was to guarantee possession so that appropriate plans of attack and defense could take place. By 1888 blocking and tackling below the waist were legalized. By 1900 the line-out was abolished, and, after a threat by President Theodore Roosevelt to ban the game if it was not cleaned up, the forward pass was introduced and rugby was almost gone. Rugby was an official Olympic sport four times from 1896 to 1924. U.S. teams won the gold medal twice (1920 and 1924), defeating the French team both times.

During the 1950s interest was rekindled, and today there are more than 250,000 players and over 15,000 clubs in the United States. In 1975 the American governing body, now known as USA Rugby, was formed. It is composed of seven territorial unions—the Northeast, Mid-Atlantic, Southeast, Midwest, West, Pacific, and Southern California Rugby Football Unions. USA Rugby sponsors thirteen different national championships.

In 1997, fourteen of the traditionally successful clubs formed the Super League, rugby's answer to the NFL.

There are five American national teams (Men, Women, Collegiate Men, Collegiate Women, and Under-19s) altogether. The men's senior team is known as the Eagles and they compete every spring in the Pacific Rim Championship, played between the United States, Canada, Japan, and Hong Kong. The women's senior side have met with impressive international success. In 1991 they won the first Women's World Cup, and they were finalists in 1994.

Once a strictly amateur sport, rugby began to go professional with the advent of the men's World Cup in 1987, held ever four years. At first payment to players was covert, but following the 1995 World Cup the game became officially "open."

VALUES

Rugby is a team game that requires players to use their skill in conjunction with others to achieve success. It is a running game that requires active involvement of each player for the duration of the game. It develops team spirit and cooperation and affords a high level of satisfaction for the participants.

Because players are moving continually, rugby helps develop cardiovascular endurance. The basic skills of the game require speed, balance, coordination, and strength, important in any physical development program. By virtue of the structure of the game, greatest enjoyment in rugby comes as a result of being fit. In fact, many sports physicians consider rugby second only to such events as long-distance cross-country skiing and running as the most cardiovascularly demanding activity today. It is a contact sport, and players should physically equip themselves to meet this requirement. Fitness and strength training are recommended, and with an organized group, most of this can be done using a ball. When training for any sport, it is important to use the tools of that sport—in this case, the ball—as much as possible.

Preseason conditioning involves building endurance and strength, with emphasis on development of individual skills. During the season much of the time is spent building the team, developing and coordinating plays, and sharpening basic and individual skills. Keeping the body fit and flexible helps prevent injury. Stretching is extremely important before and after training; 10 to 15 minutes should be allowed for gradual loosening up of the major muscle groups in the neck, chest, lower back, arms, abdomen, thighs, hamstrings, and calves.

EQUIPMENT

Clothing

Rugby can be played by persons of all ages and requires little equipment. Proper shoes are most important. They should be high-laced and have leather, rubber, plastic, or aluminum cleats to give the player a secure grip on the ground. It is strictly prohibited for rugby boots to have a single stud in the middle of the toe. Socks, shorts, and a rugby shirt make up the rest of the basic uniform. It is advisable to wear a mouth guard to protect the teeth. Some players (mainly the forwards, who experience a great deal of physical contact) wear shin guards, scrum caps, and headbands. Recently soft shoulder padding has been allowed.

Ball

The rugby ball is oval and made of four panels of leather or other approved material. It weights 13½ to 15½ ounces (378 to 434 g).

FIELD

Rugby is played on a rectangular field not exceeding 110 × 75 yards (100.6 × 68.4 m) (figure 24-1). It is often played on a shorter and narrower field, depending on the space available and the age of the players. A line drawn across the center, the halfway line, divides the field. The goal-posts, placed in the center of the goal line, consist of two uprights exceeding 3.7 yards (3.4 m) in height and a crossbar 6.1 yards (5.6 m) wide. The crossbar is attached to the uprights 3.3 yards (3 m) from the ground. The in-goal area between the goal line and the dead-ball line must not exceed 24 yards (22 m).

Throughout the rugby playing world, the field is referred to as the "pitch," and sidelines are called "touchlines." Kicking or running the ball out of bounds is called "putting the ball into touch."

A 24-yard (22 m) line is marked in each half of the field between the goal line and the halfway line. The significance of the 24-yard (22 m) line is that a player may kick the ball directly into touch (out of bounds) from inside his or her own 24-yard (22 m) line and the goal line, thus stopping play where the ball, still in the area, crosses the touchline (sideline). If a player kicks the ball directly into touch in front of the 24-yard (22 m) line on the fly, the out-of-bounds play (or lineout) must begin on the sideline perpendicular from where the player kicked the ball, not where it went out of bounds. The two lines marking the side of the field, the touchlines, mark where the ball goes into touch (out of bounds). The dotted 5.5-yard (5 m) lines shows the point where the front player in the line-out stands, and the 16.4-yard (15 m) mark denotes the point beyond which the line-out may not extend. A dotted 10.9-yard (10 m) line drawn across the field enables the referee to decide whether the kickoff has gone the required 10.9 yards (10 m).

A 5.5-yard (5 m) mark in front of each goal line is used for 5.5-yard (5 m) scrums when the defending team brings the ball over its own goal line and touches it down. Touch flags are placed on each corner where the goal line and touchline meet. Flags are also placed at points along the outside of the touchline to mark the halfway line and both 24-yard (22 m) lines.

RULES

Officials

One referee has control of the game and enforces the rules. Two line judges (touch judges) watch the sidelines and signal the referee when the ball has gone out of bounds. They also assist the referee where possible regarding infringements of the rules.

The referee keeps the time and the score. Players must obtain permission from the referee to leave and reenter the field during play.

Duration of Game

The game is made up of two periods, each 40 minutes in duration. There is a 5-minute interval between periods (10 minutes in international play), during which the teams change ends.

The referee may add on time at the end of each period if necessary. For example, play may be stopped because of injury to a player. With an injury, the referee would add on to the half the amount of time the injured player used to collect him- or herself or to leave the pitch.

Players and Positions

Rugby is played by two teams of 15 players each: eight forwards—two props, one hooker, two locks, two flankers, one No. 8—and seven backs—one scrum half, one fly half, two center three-quarters, two wing three-quarters, one fullback.

Substitutes

In the past, substitutes were only allowed in international games and certain specific games. A maximum of two

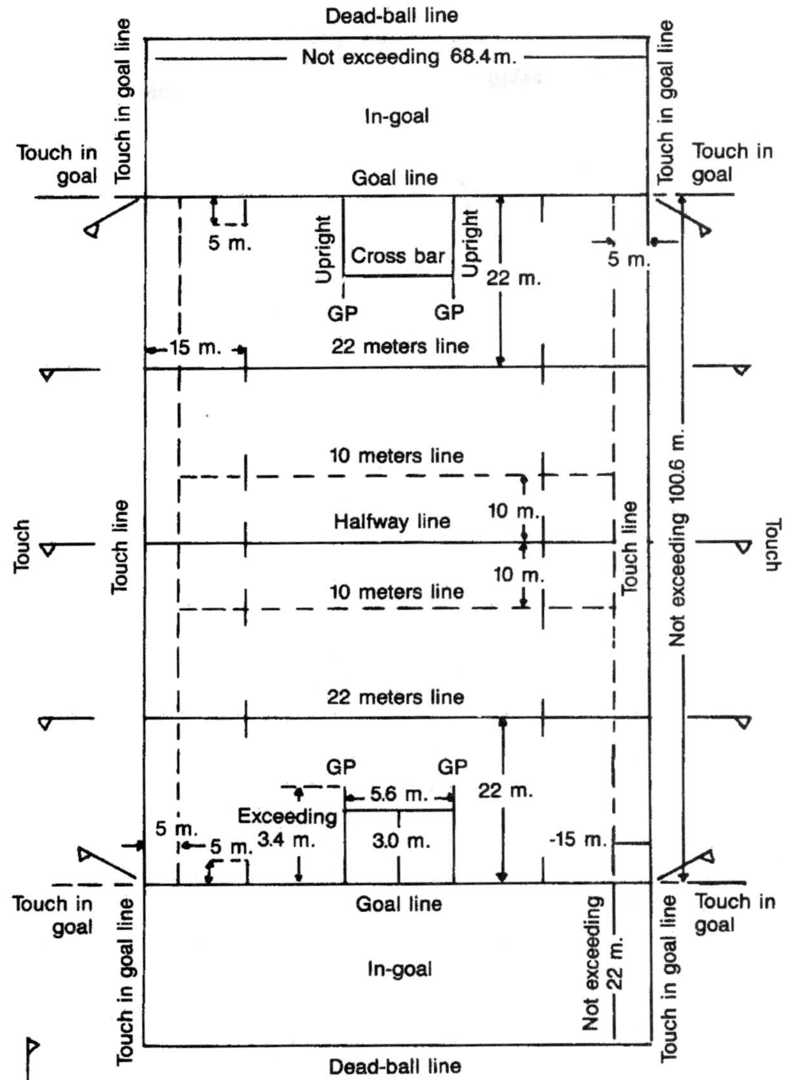

Figure 24-1. The rugby field.

injured players could be replaced. However, now, due primarily to the increased levels of intensity with which the game is played, the International Rugby Board (IRB) has authorized up to six (seven in international play) substitutions for injury or tactics; however, four of these must be experienced front-row players. The USARFU allows this type of substitution in all matches. Players who are substituted for may not rejoin the match.

Basic Playing Privileges of Players

1. A player may catch or pick up the ball and run with it.
2. A player may kick the ball while in possession of it.
3. A player may pass the ball to another player provided the ball is not thrown forward.
4. A player may tackle a member of the opposition who has possession of the ball. A tackled player must pass the ball or release the ball and get up and move away immediately.
5. A player may not interfere with a member of the opposition who is not in possession of the ball.
6. A player caught in possession of the ball may attempt to transfer it to a teammate provided the player does not come in contact with the ground.
7. A player may not advance forward in front of the ball.

Starting the Game

The captain of the team successfully calling the referee's coin toss has the option of either kicking off or receiving, or defending one goal or the other. The other captain has the choice in the area not selected by the first captain.

For the kickoff, the ball is normally placed on a round tee in the center of the halfway line. (Some international matches still use little mounds of sand that are provided on an as-needed basis by "sand boys" from the sidelines.) At the sound of the referee's whistle, the ball is kicked forward so it travels at least beyond the opposition's 10.9-yard (10 m) line. The same procedure is used to start the second period. All other kickoffs used to restart play after scores must be drop kicks.

On the kickoff, opponents must stand behind their 10.9-yard (10 m) line, over which the ball must cross. If the ball crosses the touchline without bouncing, opponents may accept the kick, have it retaken, or scrummage or lineout at the center.

Although most kickoffs are aimed to travel only 10.9 to 16.4 yards (10 to 15 m), with the aim of rewinning the ball, kicking the ball deep into an opponent's territory is also an option. However, if the ball crosses the goal line, the opposition gets a scrum at midfield.

Scoring

Try. A try is scored when a player carries the ball over the opposition's goal line and touches the ball on the ground in the goal area.

Try = 5 points

Conversion. After a try is scored, the successful team has the opportunity to gain 2 additional points (conversion) by kicking the ball between the posts above the crossbar from a point in line with where the try was scored. The ball may be place-kicked or drop-kicked. Team members must be behind the kicker; the opponents must remain behind the goal line until the kicker motions toward the ball, when they may charge or jump. If a try is successfully converted, it is called a goal.

Goal = 7 points

Goal = Try (5 points) + Conversion (2 points)

Penalty goal. A penalty is awarded for a major infringement of the rules of the game, such as a high tackle, dangerous play, or obstruction. This allows the team to whom the penalty is awarded an opportunity to score 3 points by kicking the ball through the posts above the crossbar from the point where the infringement occurred. The ball may be drop-kicked or placekicked.

Penalty goal = 3 points

Drop goal. A drop goal is scored when a player drop-kicks the ball from anywhere on the field. The ball, as in a penalty, must still travel between the posts over the crossbar during the continuous flow of play. (Interestingly, drop goals are still allowed in gridiron, however as American football has evolved the "art" of drop-kicking has all but vanished.)

Drop goal = 3 points

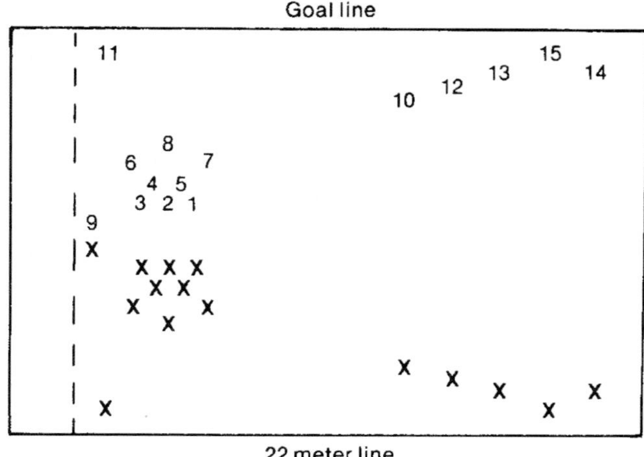

Figure 24-2. Set scrum position. *X*, Position. Numbers, player's number in each position: *1*, Loose head prop; *2*, Hooker; *3*, Tight head prop; *4, 5*, Locks; *6, 7*, Flankers; *8*, No. 8; *9*, Scrum half; *10*, Fly half; *12, 13*, Center three quarters; *11, 14*, Wing three quarters; *15*, Fullback.

Set Scrum

When play is halted unintentionally by a minor infringement of the rules, such as an unintentional offsides or forward pass, a set scrum is called. The eight forwards form a scrum, with three forwards (a loose-head prop, a hooker, a tight-head prop) in the front row, two forwards (locks) in the second row, one (the No. 8) in the third row, and the two remaining forwards (flankers) on the sides. The eight forwards bind closely together and push against the opposition. This is called the "set scrum" (figure 24-2). The scrum half puts the ball into the tunnel made where the two front rows of forwards meet, and the hookers from each team try to "hook" the ball back through the scrum onto their side. If the ball goes straight through the tunnel and out the other side, it must be put into the scrum again. No player may handle the ball in the scrum.

Ruck

A ruck occurs most frequently in free or open play after a player has been tackled to the ground and when one or more players from each team close around and contest for the ball when it is on the ground. This is done primarily by trying to drive the opposing players away from the ball. Players must remain on their feet and may not handle the ball while it is still on the ground and between and beneath the opposing players who are bound onto each other. The ball is made available from a ruck by players channelling the ball free backwards with their feet.

Maul

A maul occurs in free or open play when one or more players from each team close around a player who is carrying

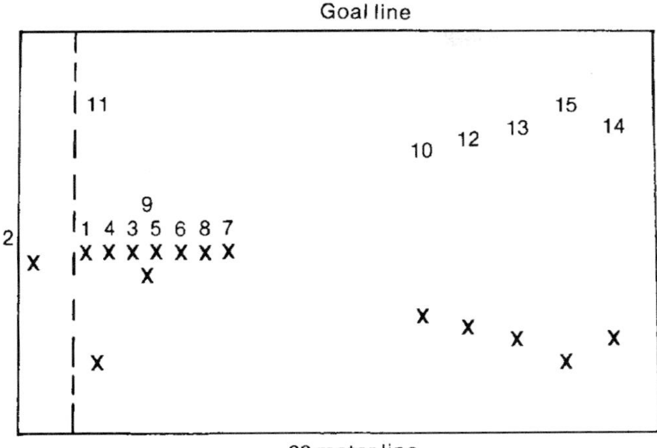

Figure 24-3. Line-out position.

the ball and is not taken to the ground. This is commonly referred to as a standing tackle. A maul ends when the player with the ball breaks loose from the other players or when the ball is released and channelled (handled backwards toward one's own teammates) free. If the ball does not become available, a set scrum is called by the referee.

Line-Out

If the ball or the player carrying it touches or crosses the touchline, the ball is "in touch" (out of bounds), and play is restarted by a line-out (figure 24-3). The ball is thrown in at right angles to where it went into touch between the forwards of both teams, who line up to receive the ball. The two "packs" of forwards line up opposite each other in a line at right angles to the touchline (figure 24-3). The team that last touched the ball before it went out of bounds is considered responsible for the stoppage, and the opportunity to restart the game by throwing the ball into the line-out is given to the other team. The scrum half may stand beside the line-out, but all other backs must remain 10.9 yards (10 m) back from the line-out. If the ball is not thrown straight into the line-out, the referee offers the other team the choice of a set scrum in 16.4 yards (15 m) or another line-out. Players must not push, charge, bind, lift, or move within 5.5 yards (5 m) of the touchline or beyond the farthest player not more than 16.4 yards (15 m) from the touchline until the ball has been thrown in. Players must also maintain a free channel through the line-out. A line-out is completed when players involved move beyond the center line of the line-out.

Fouls

Players may not:

1. Strike, hack, kick, or trip an opponent
2. Make a dangerous tackle or tackle with a stiff arm
3. Charge, obstruct, or grab an opponent who does not have the ball
4. Obstruct or deliberately waste time
5. Deliberately knock or throw the ball forward

It is not a foul if:

1. The ball bounces forward after hitting the ground or a player
2. A player shoulder-charges a player in possession of the ball and attempts to wrap up the opposing player with the arms
3. The ball is knocked forward in an attempt to catch the ball, but is retrieved before it hits the ground

Offside

A player in front of the ball when a teammate is playing it is offside. A penalty may be called if the offside player plays the ball or obstructs or tackles an opponent. Offside is penalized by a penalty kick at the point of infringement, or in free play the option of a scrum is given at the point where the offender last played the ball.

An offside player may be put onside if a teammate carries or kicks and pursues the ball past him or her. No penalty is given if the offside position is unavoidable and the player retires immediately and without interfering with an opponent. If contact cannot be avoided, the player is "accidently offside," and a set scrum is formed.

FUNDAMENTAL SKILLS AND TECHNIQUES

All players should practice the fundamental skills of passing, running with the ball, kicking, rucking, mauling, and tackling. Once proficient at these, it is important to practice the particular skills needed for the position of choice.

Passing

Passing the ball requires a combination of timing, balance, accuracy, and control. The object is to transfer the ball to a teammate as smoothly as possible. It is important to pass in front of the receiver so the teammate can catch the ball easily (figure 24-4).

1. Hold the ball in front of the body, in both hands.
2. Look in the direction of the pass and swing the hands across the body, while rotating the upper torso. This helps guide the ball accurately in front of the receiver. When passing to the left, transfer the weight from the right foot to the left.
3. As the ball is released, run toward or behind the player you just passed to, in order to support your pass.

Receiving a Pass

A good pass should be delivered in front of the receiver. The receiver, with hands outstretched, should watch the ball until it reaches the hands. This allows an early catch and quick transfer.

Figure 24-4. Passing.

Catching a Kick

When catching the ball out of the air, it is important to get the body behind the ball. Keeping the eyes on the ball at all times, cradle the arms and pull it into the chest. It is good form to turn the shoulders parallel to the touchline, so as not to knock-on if the ball is fumbled.

If a player is standing behind the 22 meter line, then a fair catch, known as a "mark," may be called for. The ball must be caught cleanly, and the player must have at least one foot on the ground while simultaneously calling "Mark!" The referee has discretion as to whether the mark is valid and will blow the whistle to indicate that the mark was given. A free kick is then awarded. If the referee does not blow the whistle, play continues. This is a very important distinction from the gridiron fair catch. Marks are usually called tightly in defensive situations when a team is trying to slow the opponent's momentum. A player can also call for a mark if the ball is caught on the fly from an opponent's knock-on.

Running with the Ball

When running with the ball it is as important to be aware of the position of teammates as it is to be aware of the position of the opponents. Be ready to pass the ball to a teammate or to kick where necessary. Try not to run too far off alone, because, when tackled by the opposition, there will be no support nearby. Run parallel to the touchline when possible. When running and passing, try to create a situation where more teammates than opponents are nearby (overlap), and then exploit this position to score.

Side Step

The side step is a means of beating an opponent one-on-one by sending the opponent in the opposite direction. It can be done from either side by a combination of transfer of weight and body movement.

1. For a side step to the right, approach the opponent in a straight line.
2. With the weight on the right leg, drive to the left, taking the opponent with you.
3. Now firmly place the left foot on the ground and drive back to the right, leaving the opponent running in the opposite direction.

Handoff (Stiffarm)

When there is not time to side step, a handoff might be executed.

1. While approaching the opponent, place the ball under the arm farthest from the tackler.
2. Bend the nearest arm and place it on the opponent's shoulder.
3. Using the opponent's shoulder, move away by straightening the arm and pushing the tackler away.

Kicking

Kicking the ball requires timing, balance, and control. The three basic types of kick are the punt, the dropkick, and the placekick.

Figure 24-5. Punt.

The punt

1. Hold the ball with both bands, the left hand under and on the side of the ball and the right hand on top at the back of the ball.
2. Drop the ball while stepping forward with the left foot.
3. Transfer the body weight to the left foot.
4. Keep the head over the ball, and bend the right knee.
5. Swing the right foot forward to contact the ball, keeping the weight on the left foot.
6. Land the ball on the boot at the same angle as it leaves the hand.
7. While following through, the toe should be pointing away. Keep the weight on the left leg and lean backward (figure 24-5).

Dropkick

1. Hold the ball upright with one hand on each side of the ball.
2. As the ball is dropped in front of the body, step on the left foot and look at the ball.
3. As the ball comes in contact with the ground, strike it with the right instep, keeping the toe pointed.
4. Follow through, keeping the head down and the eyes on the ball. It is important to keep the right foot pointed.
5. While completing the follow-through, keep the weight on the left leg. Some players like to drop the ball slightly on the side. When doing so, keep the same basic principles in mind as in the straight-on dropkick, and swing the leg through in a full arc.

Placekick

As with the dropkick, there are different types: straight-on, round-the-corner, and torpedo.

Straight-on.

1. Place the ball upright on a round rugby tee and steady the right foot directly behind the ball.
2. Retire about 4 to 6 steps and hold steady.
3. Start to run, keeping the head down and the eyes on the ball.
4. Put the left leg down just short of and slightly to the left of the ball.
5. Swing through with the right leg, straightening it on impact and contacting the ball with the toes.
6. Follow through the line of flight of the ball (figure 24-6).

Round-the-corner.

1. Approach the ball from an angle, with the left foot coming down just short of and slightly to the left of the ball.
2. Swing the right foot through in an arc.
3. With the weight on the left leg and the eyes on the ball, swing the leg through.

Torpedo.

1. Place the ball on the ground at an angle pointing toward the goalpost.
2. Use the straight-on method of kicking.

Scrummaging

Pushing position

The hips should be below the shoulders and the chin held forward to straighten the back. There should be approximately a 90-degree angle between the trunk and thighs and also between the thigh and lower legs. The knees should be near the ground. The legs should be wide (figure 24-7).

Power

The power of the push comes almost exclusively from the legs.

Figure 24-6. Straight-on placekick. **A,** Front view; **B** and **C,** side views.

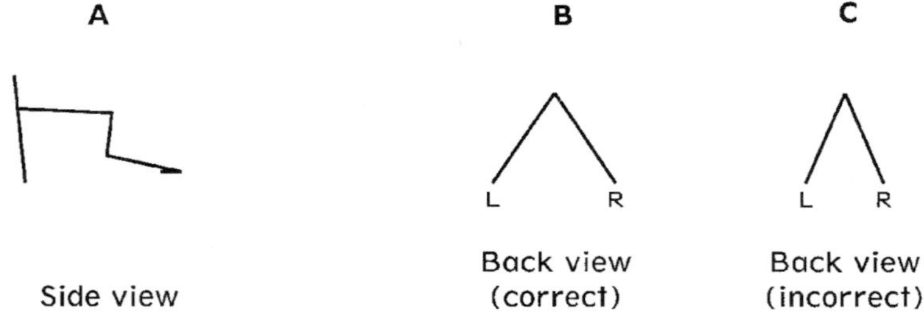

Figure 24-7. Scrummaging: the pushing position. **A** and **B,** Side view and back view of correct positioning; **C,** back view of incorrect positioning.

Traction

Maximize foot-ground contact at the instant of the drive. Turning the toes outward can help.

Transferring the power

It is important, if you are pushing on one of your own teammates, to push as directly as possible on the line of the spine. The player being pushed must be sure that the knee of the leg being pushed is behind the hips. If the player being pushed in the loose head prop does not do this, it will result in being popped out (figure 24-8).

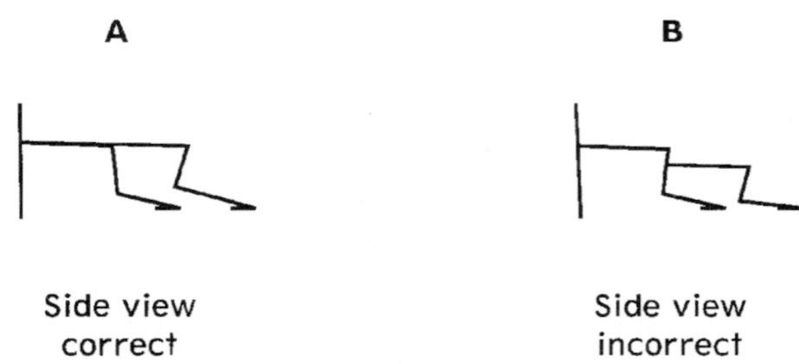

Figure 24-8. Transferring the power. **A,** Side view of correct positioning; **B,** side view of incorrect positioning.

Getting low

The lower a drive is, the more effective. Keep the hips below the shoulders and get the trunk lower by moving the feet back and the knees near the ground.

Drive

At the instant of the drive, drop the knees a little, pick up the head and drive forward with both legs.

Locking

On your own ball it is often best to just try not to go backward—lock your knees (figure 24-9).

Crabbing

As soon as the scrum goes down, get the weight to your right foot, bring the left foot in slightly, shift the right foot to the right, and continue these steps. This shifts the whole

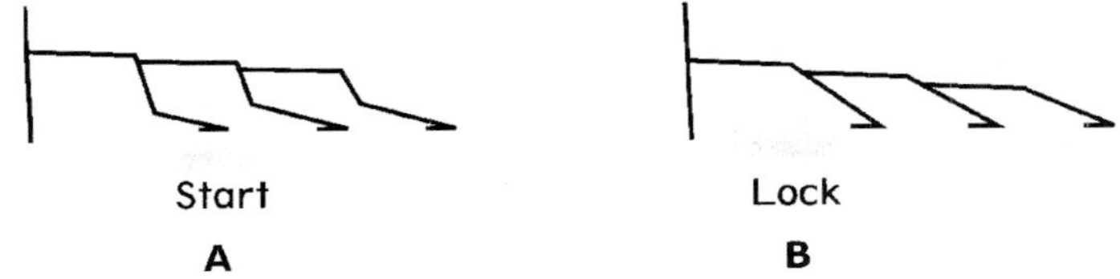

Figure 24-9. Locking. **A,** Starting position; **B,** locking position.

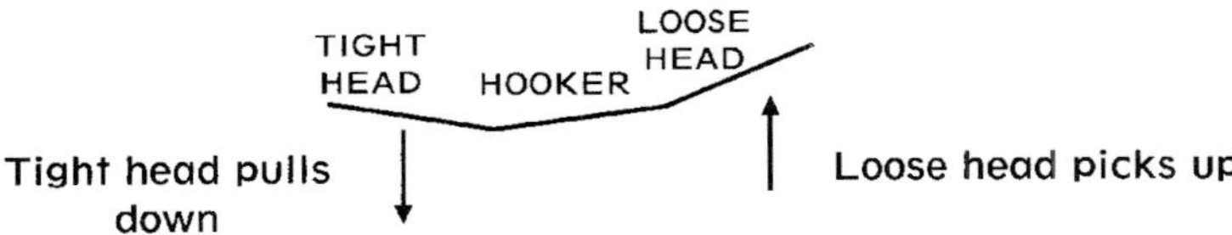

Figure 24-10. Opposing players' shoulders should look like this.

scrum to the right, making it difficult for the opposing team to set up an 8-person drive or wheel.

Front row

As seen by the opponent, the front row players' shoulders look like figure 24-10. Excessive picking up or taking down will prevent your pack's power from being transmitted directly to the opposition, so stay as horizontal as possible on the 8-person shove.

Tackling

Tackling requires a combination of ability, concentration, timing, and confidence. Many top coaches also stress that tackling is as much attitude as it is skill. After ball handling, tackling is the next most necessary skill. The best way to learn how to tackle is to practice one step at a time and build up confidence. With the correct technique it is possible to knock down the opponent without getting hurt. The three basic types of tackle are head-on, side-on, and from behind. A fourth type, smothering, is sometimes used. In this tackle the arms are wrapped around an opponent to prevent him or her from advancing or passing the ball.

Head-on tackle

1. Judge the approach of the opponent so as to make contact with the shoulder and body weight.
2. As the opponent approaches, drive into the tackle from one leg.
3. Contact the opponent at about waist height, keeping the head to the side. Close the arms tightly around the opponent's legs.
4. Follow through using momentum to bring the opponent to the ground (figure 24-11).

Figure 24-11. Head-on tackle.

Side-on tackle

The basic principles for the head-on tackle apply for the side-on tackle.

1. Line up the opponent.
2. Drive in off one leg and contact the opponent just above the knees.
3. Keep the head behind the opponent's back and wrap the arms around the opponent's legs.
4. The momentum and the arm lock will cause the opponent to fall.

Tackle from behind

1. Drive in off one leg, keeping low.
2. Keeping the head clear, contact the opponent above the knees and close the arms tightly around the legs.
3. The locked legs and momentum will cause the opponent to fall.

PLAYING POSITIONS

Forwards

The eight forwards—known as "the pack"—play as a unit. They are the platform from which the backs play. The forwards are in the front line of attack and are the main source through which their team gains possession of the ball. On gaining possession of the ball, the forwards have the option of trying to advance the ball forward among themselves or of transferring the ball to the backs. Physical makeup and natural ability often determine the position one plays.

Although different skills are required for each forward position, forwards as a group need to be strong, powerful, and mobile. They are generally larger and more physical than the backs. The back row of the scrum needs to be fast and aggressive, whereas the front five forwards provide much of the power. The hooker must be quick with the feet in the scrum, and the two locks, usually the largest players on the team, provide useful targets in the line-out, as well as the power behind the push in the set scrums.

Backs

Each back position has its particular skills, but in general backs must learn to handle, run, pass, tackle, and kick a ball with ease. Speed, coordination, and ability to read the play are important. The scrum half is the link between the forwards and backs and must be able to transfer the ball to the back line when it is made available by the forwards. The fly half marshals the back line, determines the play, and keeps the backs in position. The back-line players have an important role in halting an opposition attack, because they present the main line of defense.

Offense or Attack

The offense should advance forward as a unit, creating gaps in the opposition defense. This may be done by beating the opposition in a one-on-one situation, by creating an extra player situation, or by driving the opposition back by strength. The offense tries to maintain possession of the ball while advancing and to support the player with the ball. They should vary the attack and prevent the defense from organizing.

Defense

Organization and pressure are the two keys to defense. The defense tries to maintain position and to halt the advancing team before they can mount a full attack. Strong decisive tackling, support for the tackler, quick thinking, and ability to adapt to the situation presented will make things difficult for the advancing team.

LEAD-UP ACTIVITIES

Mini-rugby

Mini-rugby is used as an introduction to the 15-a-side game. Its advantages are that it requires a much smaller playing area and fewer players, and it is simple yet exciting and an ideal game for beginners. Participants are afforded an opportunity to play many of the positions of the full game.

The playing area is 75.4 × 41.5 yards (69 × 38 m). Each team has nine players: four forwards—two front row, one lock, one flanker—and five backs—one each scrum half, fly half, center, wing, fullback.

The game may be played on a full-sized rugby pitch, using only one half from touchline to touchline. The game is started from the center and "drop outs" from the existing 16.4-yard (15 m) line.

The adapted rules include the following:

1. There are no line-outs.
2. Kicking is not encouraged.
3. Direct kicking to touch is only allowed inside the 16.4-yard (15 m) area.
4. There are no kicks at goal for penalties.
5. When a try is scored, a kick at goal is taken from in front of the posts.

When penalties are awarded, the opposition retires 7.6 yards (7 m) and the attacking team "taps the ball" and plays on. Tackling is unrestricted. The rules for offside, on-side, knock-on, throw forward, and so on apply as usual. Each period lasts 20 minutes. The objectives of this type of training are to work on and improve straight running, good tackling, creating quick overlap situations in attack, and pressure defense.

Touch Rugby

Touch rugby may be played during training. The size of the field should correspond to the number playing. The idea of the game is to score a try by touching the ball down behind the opposition's goal line. Players advance the ball by passing and running with the ball.

Tackling and kicking are not allowed. The opposition attempts to touch the player with the ball. Each team has four plays in which to advance the ball. A play is considered finished when a member of the opposition touches the advancing player in possession of the ball. After four plays the other team has four plays in which to score. Each play is started by touching the ball on the foot and passing it to a teammate.

There are no line-outs or scrums, but knock-ons and offsides result in the ball being automatically turned over to the other team. The goals for players in touch rugby are improving ball handling skills, recognizing attack situations quicker, and practicing continuous support running.

Grids

Teams of 2 to 10 players oppose each other in a playing area approximately 5.5 yards (5 m) square. The objective is to develop fundamental skills in a simulated situation. Games in the grids may be organized for drill in a particular skill, such as passing. For example, with five players, three players can attempt to score a try and the other two attempt to stop them. This develops skills for tackling, decision making, passing, using the extra player, and running with the ball. The number of players and rules of the games can be modified to suit the objective of practice.

TEACHING CONSIDERATIONS

1. Because of safety considerations involved, tackling should probably not be part of the game taught to younger students. Touch rugby, with teams of 3 to 10 players, and modified rules, is probably more appropriate.
2. The weight and shape of the ball make rugby a unique activity, requiring different ball handling and kicking than in soccer and football. Experience in other field sports such as speedball, soccer, and football will help. However, practice time with the rugby ball is a necessity.
3. Practice in ball handling skills should be designed for maximum participation. In most instances this means passing, catching, and kicking skills should be practiced with partners. Distances, directions, and force level requirements should vary as they do in actual games.
4. Offensive and defensive play can be introduced in two-on-one situations. Additional offensive and defensive players may be added as strategies are improved. Actual game play can begin in two-on-two situations.
5. Add scoring options and out-of-bounds rules gradually as the need arises. Maintain offside rules to differentiate rugby from football.
6. Stay with the game long enough for skill and appreciation of it to develop.
7. Some suggested drills are:
   a. Passing drill "pass at pace." In rugby, passing is the most fundamental of all skills. The rugby pass must combine the elements of rhythm, speed of pass, speed and acceleration of the run, and length and accuracy.
      (1) Group of four players separate about 4.4 yards (4 m) apart. They begin by quickly passing from 1 to 2, to 3, to 4.
      (2) Once the ball is in 4's hands, 4 sprints ahead to a cone 22 yards (20 m) in front. The other three must sprint to keep up with 4.
      (3) At the cone 4 passes back to 3 who sprints 11 yards (10 m) to the next cone.
      (4) At this cone 3 passes to 2 who likewise sprints 11 yards (10 m) to the next cone.
      (5) At this cone, 2 passes to 1, who then ensures the line is realigned for the final quick hands passing 1 to 2 to 3 and finally to 4.

      This drill encompasses all of the techniques necessary to pass properly in a game: accuracy, pace, length, alignment, and, if done with a great deal of repetition, fitness.
   b. Loop or outside support drill. One of the most important skills a rugby player needs to develop continually is support of the ball carrier.
      (1) As in the preceding drill, 4 players about 4.5 yards (4 m) apart begin by passing the ball laterally 1 through 4. After each player passes, he or she sprints to the outside of the last player in support.
      (2) Each player "loops" once as this is accomplished, and it should be done within 33 yards (30 m). At the 33-yard (30 m) mark, 4 places the ball on the ground, waits for a realignment of the other three players, and then begins the drill again going in the same direction.
      (3) The width of the drill should be no more than 16.7 yards (15 m). This forces all players to step into each pass, creating space on the outside.
      (4) As the drill is completed the players have traveled 55 to 66 yards (50 to 60 m), so again these handling drills can also be used for fitness.
   c. Standing tackle drill. Since rugby is a contact support, a ball carrier must know what to do when hit. In many cases a defensive player will try to hold up a ball carrier. This is called a "standing tackle." This is done to help strip the ball carrier of the ball. To prevent this is obviously an important objective for the offense.
      (1) Four players line up across a similar grid as in preceding drills *a* and *b*. Either player 2 or player 3 runs the ball forward, with the other 3 players behind. This player runs about 11 to 16.5 yards (10 to 15 m), places the ball on the ground and retreats 5.5 yards (5 m) and faces the others.
      (2) One of the trailing players shouts "ball," scoops up the ball (using the proper technique of stationary hand in front of the ball and scooping hand coming in from behind), and then drives into the stationary player.
      (3) After contact, and while keeping in balance, the charging player abruptly rotates the shoulders perpendicular to the tackler, keeping *both* hands on the ball.
      (4) The next player drives into the teammate ball carrier, utilizing the outside shoulder. This player drives the shoulder into the ball carrier with a ripping motion over the ball to help secure it from the tackler.

(5) The last player stands off at depth and, when he or she sees the ball re-won, shouts for the pass and takes it a pace, runs up 11 to 16.5 yards (10 to 15 m), places the ball on the ground, and retreats. The entire process is repeated 3 to 4 times in this 66-yard (60 m) grid.

GLOSSARY

accidental offside A player is offside unintentionally.
attacking team Team that has possession of the ball.
conversion Attempt to gain 2 extra points by kicking the ball over the crossbar after a try has been scored.
dead-ball line Line at the end of the field of play.
defending team The team that is attempting to stop the attacking team from scoring while also trying to gain possession of the ball.
drop goal The ball is drop-kicked over the bar during the continuous flow of play.
drop-kick Kicking the ball on the half volley.
24-yard (22 m) drop-out Dropkick from the 24-yard (22 m) line to restart the game after the ball has been touched down in the end zone by the defending team or when the ball has crossed the dead-ball line.
foul An infringement of the rules.
goal Obtained by scoring a try and a conversion. Worth 7 points.
halfway line Line that marks the center of the field.
in-goal area Area between goal line and dead-ball line; end zone.
in touch A ball that goes out of bounds is said to be in "touch."
kickoff Used to start the game at the beginning of each period and after a team has scored a try.
knock-on The ball is knocked forward during an attempt to catch it.
line-out Used to restart the game when the ball goes out of bounds.
mark Given to a player who catches the ball cleanly while standing still; player must call, "Mark."
maul One or more players from each side surround and hold the player with the ball and start to struggle for it.
pack The eight forwards.
penalty goal Worth 3 points when a player placekicks or drop-kicks the ball over the crossbar after a penalty given by the referee for an infringement of the rules of the game.
ruck One or more players from each side in the field of play are on their feet and shoving each other, with the ball on the ground between them.
set scrum Used to restart the game after an unintentional infringement of the rules.
throw-in A means of putting the ball into the line-out to restart the game after the ball has gone out of bounds.
try Score when a player carries the ball over the opposition goal line and touches the ball on the ground. Worth 4 points.

SUGGESTED READINGS

Greenwood, J. 1993. *Think rugby*. London: A+C Black.
Greenwood, J. 1991. *Total rugby*. London: A+C Black.
Handbook and laws of the game of rugby. 1993. Albany, Calif: Lampa Printing and Lithograph.
Honan, B. 1992. *Rugby skills training*. Queensland, Australia: Queensland Rugby Union.
Prusmack, A. J. 1979. *Rugby: A guide for players, coaches, and spectators*. New York: E. P. Dutton.
Robertson, I. 1980. *Success in rugby*. London: John Murray.
Walker, P. 1980. *The love of rugby*. London: Octopus Books.

RESOURCES

Films and videotapes

Focus on rugby, Trace Videos, Reedswain, Inc, 62 Byers Rd., Chester Springs, PA 19425.
Mini rugby barbarians style, Rugby Football Union, Twickenham, Middlesex, England.
1991 World Cup Final, England vs Australia, Soccer Learning Systems (Telephone: 1-800-762-2376) Pickwick Video Ltd., London.
This is mini rugby, Welsh Rugby Union, 28 St. Marys St., Cardiff, Wales.
Film of the United States—International Games may be obtained through *Rugby* (newspaper), published by Rugby Press, Ltd., 527 Madison Ave., New York, NY 10022.
Rugby skills training, Queensland Rugby, Union, Australia, On Set Production (Telephone: 07 875-1651).
Video films of international games may be obtained through Trace Video Sports Club, c/o Brandon Hall, Box 1167, Natchez, MS 39120.
Running passing power, Close contact leap, and *Thinking boot*. Three rugby videotapes available from "How To" Sports Videos, Box 5852, Denver, CO 80217.

Wall charts

Wall charts may be obtained from the Welsh Rugby Union, 28 St. Marys St., Cardiff, Wales.

Web sites

International Rugby Board (Rules, regulations, etc) www.irfb.com
Rugby Magazine (Monthly News - US) www.inch.com/~rugby
Rugby Today (daily news - international) www.rugbytoday.com

Self-Defense

After completing this chapter, the reader should be able to:

- Explain the basic principles and strategies of self-defense
- Appreciate the importance of the accuracy, force, speed, and follow-through of self-defense moves
- Demonstrate and execute releases, kicks, and strikes employed in self-defense
- Explain to a group of students when and how to use the techniques described in this chapter

HISTORY

Every society has a history of combat. When the working class does not have the advantage of weapons, they tend to devise some method of unarmed self-defense and pass it down from generation to generation. One art of self-defense was developed by Chinese monks in the twelfth century. By monastic rules the monks were forbidden to use weapons in combat. Because they were constantly being attacked by roving bandits, they were forced to devise a defense that did not depend on weapons. During the last half of the twelfth century the Japanese discovered this art, copied it, claimed it as their own, and called it "jiu jitsu." *Jiu* means "gentle"; *jitsu* means "art" or "practice." Many systems of jiu jitsu were developed by the Japanese. In 1882 Jigora Kano, a Japanese instructor who had spent years practicing the many systems of jiu jitsu, established the Kodokan, *a school for studying the way*, and labeled his system "judo," which means "the way" or "the principle."

One branch of the Kodokan was established in 1921 in New York City. However, because this system was mainly competitive, Americans were not interested. In 1925 a group of young Americans developed its own system of self-defense and called the organization the American Judo Club. They produced a system of self-defense that, during World War II, proved to be very effective. After the war, interest in judo as a competitive sport started to grow, and today it is recognized throughout the world.

Many school systems throughout the United States are including self-defense against violent crime in the physical education curriculum in junior and senior high schools, colleges, and universities. Classes are also being included in the curricula of various local agencies, such as recreation centers, YMCAs, YWCAs, and others.

Modern self-defense is not a martial art. Judo, karate, aikido, and other martial arts require years of training and continual practice, plus speed, balance, coordination, agility, and disciplined mental training. Modern self-defense is simply street fighting combined with common sense. It can be learned in a short time by any person, young or old, weak or strong, coordinated or uncoordinated, and it can be retained for life.

FACILITIES AND EQUIPMENT

No special facilities or equipment are needed for self-defense classes; they can be offered in any room or on any playing field. Football dummy bags, rolled gymnastics mats, and volleyballs can be used for kicking, punching, and jabbing. If such equipment is not available, students can bring pillows and cushions from home.

CLOTHING

Students should wear comfortable, loose-fitting clothing. Tennis shoes are preferred footwear. However, inasmuch as students may not be wearing gym clothes if attacked, during the last weeks of class they should wear regular street clothing. During practice of self-defense techniques, it is recommended that jewelry be removed.

BASIC PRINCIPLES

Self-defense skills should meet the following criteria:

1. They must be so simple that every student can perform them proficiently. Self-defense, unlike tennis or basketball, is a life-and-death skill. If you teach a skill that even one student cannot master, the student may be seriously injured or killed attempting to use it.
2. They must be easily mastered in a short time. Most self-defense classes last between 5 and 15 weeks. In most cases this is the only instruction time the students will ever receive in self-defense.
3. They must be easy to remember without much practice. It is unlikely that students completing a self-defense course will continue to practice the skills. Yet they must be capable of performing them if attacked in 10 days or in 10 years.
4. They must be designed to totally incapacitate, not merely hurt, the assailant. There is only one round in self-defense—the first one. If the first round is lost, the entire fight is lost.

STRATEGIES

There are three strategies in self-defense. The first two require no skill or ability, just common sense.

1. Eliminate the potential of danger before it begins.
2. Recognize and avoid danger.
3. Fight only when necessary.

Eliminate the Potential of Danger

Most potential danger can be eliminated by learning to "think safety." Below are listed a few of the hundreds of ways to "think safety."

1. Never hitchhike or pick up a hitchhiker.
2. Have secure locks on all doors and windows and use them.
3. Change all locks when you move into a home or apartment.
4. Keep blinds closed at night.
5. Do not hide keys outside your home or in your car.
6. When walking to your home or car, have your key in hand so that you can enter quickly.
7. Be cautious when entering your car, when you are usually looking down and are vulnerable. Look in the back seat before entering a car alone.
8. Walk in well-lighted areas; do not take shortcuts down alleys.
9. If you are a single woman, do not list your first name on your mailbox or in the telephone book. Use two initials plus your last name for identification.

Recognize and Avoid Danger

Even if you eliminate all of the possible dangers you can imagine, you are not totally safe. Therefore, learn to be aware of your surroundings, the dangers that exist, and how to react when necessary. Examples of some ways to recognize and avoid danger are listed here.

1. If confronted by a robber with a weapon, it is almost always best to give up your valuables. Do not fight! Material things can be replaced, but your life and health cannot. However, because many rapes and killings begin as simple robberies, in some cases early and effective resistance may prevent assault.
2. If you are on the street and believe you are in danger, do not stay around to find out. Change your direction and run. If followed, holler "Fire, fire, fire!" Noise of any kind that draws attention to you or your assailant is an effective deterrent. If the assailant continues to chase you, drop your purse or wallet. If that is what the person is after, you are safe.
3. If you receive an obscene phone call, hang up. If the calls continue, tap on the mouthpiece with your fingernail and say, "Officer, this is the call I have been expecting. Now you can trace it." Then hang up.
4. Verify the identify of all visitors before you allow them into your home.
5. If you return home and find your door open or windows broken, do not go in. Telephone the police.
6. If you see anything suspicious in your neighborhood, do not investigate it yourself. Call the police.
7. If you are followed by another car while driving, do not go home and do not try to outrun the car. Rather, pretend to ignore the driver, keep your hand on the horn, and drive at a safe speed to a gas station, police station, or market.
8. If approached by an exhibitionist, pretend to ignore the person and immediately telephone the police.

Fight Only When Necessary

The only time you should fight is when your life or health is in danger. There are two major reasons for this:

1. You can lose. There is no assurance that every time you fight, you will win. Therefore, if you fight for a few valuables and lose, you are very foolish, because you may lose your life or health.
2. You must incapacitate, not simply hurt, the aggressor. Therefore, if you are merely verbally insulted and in anger you incapacitate the aggressor, you expose yourself to a lawsuit.
3. Fight to escape. Escape is your primary objective.

BASIC TECHNIQUES

Over the years the approach to self-defense has shifted from the learning of rather formal movements to a less structured and "whatever works" philosophy. The techniques presented here attempt to mirror this progression. The initial movements have as their basic objective to "turn the tables," allowing the person attacked to gain the upper hand on the assailant. These are followed by techniques primarily for situations in which the assailant is much more powerful than the victim. The goal of these movements is to incapacitate the aggressor. Remember, the primary objective is to escape from danger.

Self-defense has four elements: accuracy, force, speed, and follow-through.

Accuracy

Your self-defense blow must be accurate. Do not aim for the nose and hit the chin. That will only hurt your assailant, and you may not have an opportunity to strike again.

Force

Although a physically fit person will deliver the most effective blow, strength is not necessary for self-defense skills. An 80-year-old person can successfully deliver a groin pull or eye gouge. Nevertheless, the more force you can generate, the safer you will be. Therefore, fight with 100 percent effort.

Speed

Speed is an element of good timing. Because the assailant will most likely be larger and stronger than you, the element of surprise is necessary. This does not mean that you must always react immediately. If you can talk to the assailant, ask "What do you want?" Then pose no threat, and pretend to cooperate. Wait until you can react properly, then employ some of the techniques described later with all the speed you can generate. If you panic and cannot remember what to do, do nothing. Do not struggle. Simply wait until you remember.

Follow-Through

If you must fight, plan to follow through with kicks, blows, and jabs until the assailant is totally immobile. If attackers are not incapacitated, they become enraged and more vicious than before. Remember, the primary objective is to escape from danger.

Screams

A scream can accomplish three purposes:

1. It can attract attention.
2. It can unnerve even the most determined assailant.
3. It can make you feel much more powerful and aggressive. Any type of noise is a deterrent; the last thing an assailant wants is attention. However, do not rely on noise to bring help. The assailant does not want attention and may leave, but help may not come, and if someone does investigate, he or she may he cautious.

When running from danger, do not scream "Help!" Unfortunately, people may not come to your rescue. Rather, scream "Fire!" When people hear "Fire!" they feel they have a vested interest: their house or car may be on fire. However, when under attack, scream karate-type sounds, like "Seiha, ahhh!" Scream as loudly and forcefully as possible throughout the entire attack. When the assailant is incapacitated, run for the police, screaming "Fire!" Once again, never scream "Help!"

Vulnerable Areas and Bodily Weapons

Six vulnerable areas on a person's body are recommended as targets (figure 25-1). A blow to any of these will incapacitate, not just hurt, an attacker. Seven body weapons are recommended for use (figure 25-2).

Defense Against Women

Self-defense against a female attacker is exactly the same as against a man, with the exception of using the groin as a vulnerable area. A hit to the groin or breasts of a woman will hurt, but will not incapacitate. Therefore, when fighting with a woman, strike her knees, nose, throat, solar plexus, and eyes.

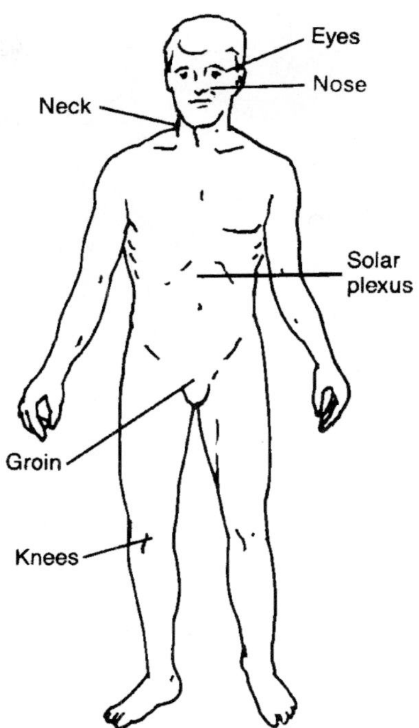

Figure 25-1. Vulnerable areas.

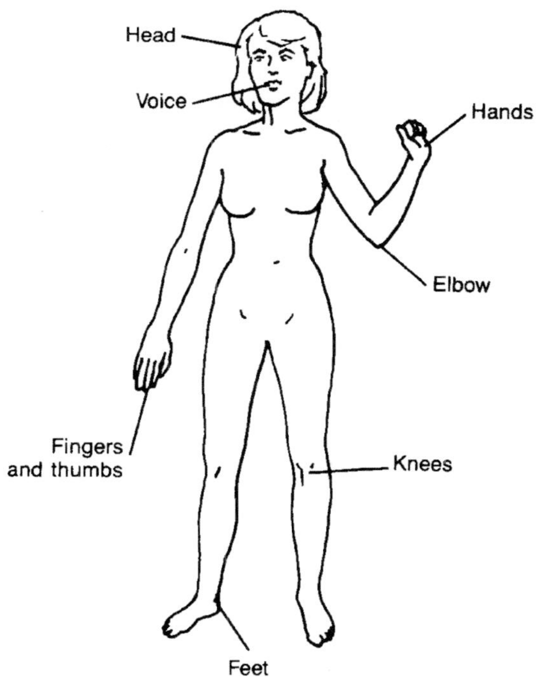

Figure 25-2. Seven body weapons.

Figure 25-3. Chest push.

SKILLS

Release from Grips

Chest push (figure 25-3). The assailant puts a hand on the victim's chest. The victim immediately places both hands on top of the aggressor's hand at the base of the fingers. Holding the hand tightly against the chest, the victim then flexes sharply at the waist and knees, sending the aggressor to the ground.

Front two-hand choke (figure 25-4). The aggressor places the hands around the victim's throat. The victim clasps the hands together, spreads the elbows, and then drives the arms up against the aggressor's arms, forcing them free. If the aggressor has established a firm grip or if the victim is considerably smaller and weaker than the aggressor, this move should be preceded by a knee lift or kick to the groin or leg (described later). This defense may also be used while lying on the floor.

Another defense against the front choke is the two-hand thumb-grab and twist (figure 25-5). The victim reaches up with one hand and grasps the aggressor's wrist, then with the other hand grabs the aggressor's thumb and rotates the hand toward the forearm.

Attack from the rear (figure 25-6). If a defender is grabbed from the rear, several defensive moves may be made. The victim may be able to drive an elbow into the aggressor's neck, solar plexus, or groin.

Kicks

The legs are the strongest part of the body. A small person can immobilize a larger person with a kick of only 40 pounds of pressure. Kicks should be directed to the front

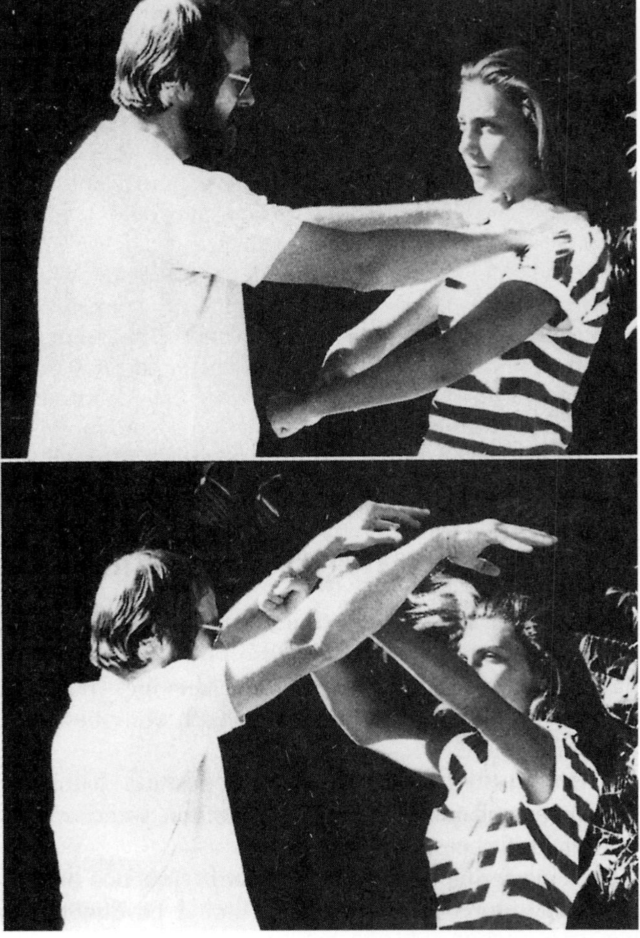

Figure 25-4. Front two-hand choke.

Figure 25-5. Second defense against the two-hand choke.

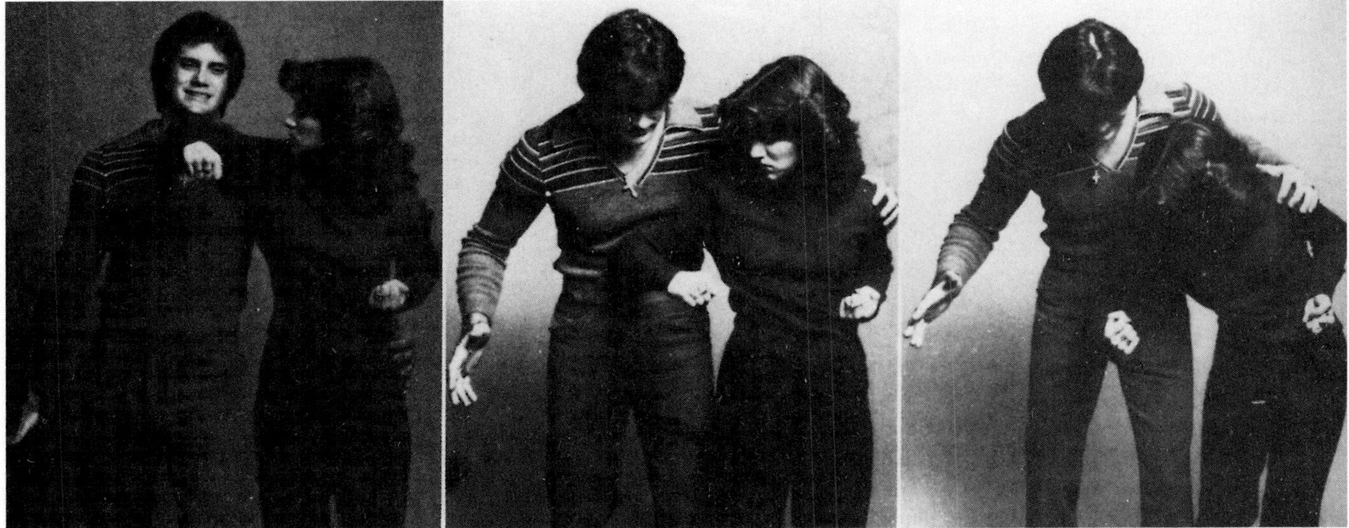

Figure 25-6. Attack from the rear. **A,** Neck, **B,** Solar Plexus, **C,** Groin.

and side of the assailant's knees, groin, and to the head, once the assailant is on the ground.

Front kick (figure 25-7). A front kick is used to defend against an assault from the front. Practice this kick in three steps:

1. Lift your knee toward your chest, flex your foot, and bend your supporting leg.
2. Extend your leg straight out, keeping your foot flexed, and contact the target with your heel, not your toes.
3. Bring your leg back to the first position, with your knees still raised. From this position you may kick again if necessary.

After mastering these individual steps, practice delivering them to a single count. They should be directed so quickly that they can hardly be seen. Remember, kick through the target, not just at it.

Side kick (figure 25-8). A side kick is used when you are attacked from the side. Practice it in three steps:

1. Lift your leg directly sideward and flex your foot. Keep the supporting leg slightly bent, and lean slightly away from the direction in which you intend to kick.
2. Extend your leg out, keeping your foot flexed, and kick through the target with your heel.

Figure 25-7. Front kick.

Figure 25-8. Side kick.

3. Bring your leg back to the first position so that you can kick again if necessary.

Rear kick (figure 25-9). If attacked from the rear, use the rear kick. Learn the rear kick in three steps:

1. Flex your striking leg, turn the foot outward, and flex at the ankle. Bend your supporting knee.
2. Extend your leg backward, with the ankle still flexed, and kick through the target with your heel.

Figure 25-9. Rear kick.

Figure 25-10. Supine kick.

3. Flex your leg back to the starting position so that you can kick again if necessary. Be sure to look at the target (knee) to aim your kick. Do not aim for the shin or instep, as this will only hurt rather than incapacitate your assailant.

Supine kick (figure 25-10). If you are thrown to the ground, roll onto your back and execute supine kicks. Lift your

Figure 25-11. Knee lift.

Figure 25-12. Groin pull.

head and shoulders slightly off the ground. Bring your knees to your chest, and kick into the assailant's knee or groin. If the attacker moves away, save your energy and stop kicking. Jump to your feet as quickly as you can.

Strikes

Knee lift (figure 25-11). A knee lift into the groin will incapacitate a man. This blow has limited value, because the man must be standing directly in front of you. To execute this blow, drive your knee forcefully upward and forward, between the man's legs and into his groin.

Groin pull (figure 25-12). One of the most simple, effective, and efficient techniques is a groin pull. It is simple because the only action necessary is a squeeze and a pull. It is effective because it will instantly force a male assailant to the ground in pain. It is efficient because with only one hand you can easily grab your target from many positions. To execute a groin pull, simply reach between your assailant's legs, grab the genitals, squeeze, and pull. Unlike the knee in the groin, the groin pull will not be expected by the assailant. This technique works effectively almost any time a person has one hand free. The only time the groin pull is difficult is when a man is wearing tight pants. Then a groin hit must be used.

Groin hit (figure 25-13). The groin hit is more difficult than a groin pull because you can miss the target. Use a groin pull whenever possible. To execute a groin hit, double your hand into a tight fist, bend your arm slightly, and forcefully drive the bony portion of your arm up and through the assailant's groin. Bending your knees will give you additional balance and power. The groin hit can be used when you are attacked from the front or rear.

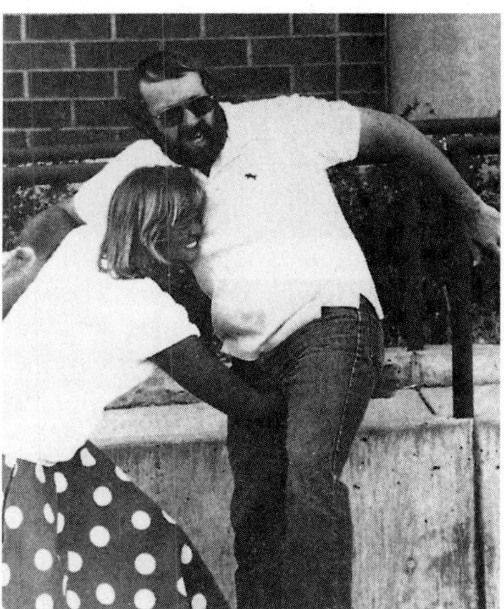

Figure 25-13. Groin hit.

Single-hand blow (figure 25-14). The nose, point of the chin, and even the eye sockets are targets for the single-hand blow. Curl your fingers back to the cushioned part of your hand, and hold your thumb at the side of your index finger. Flex your wrist backward, and do not clench your entire fist. Bring your hand to your chest, heel up, and thrust your

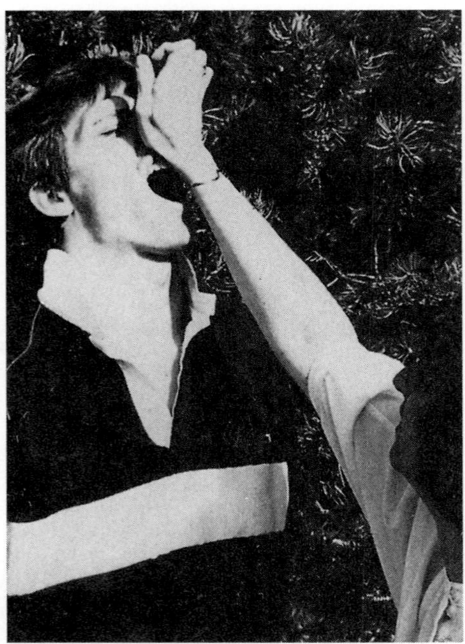

Figure 25-14. Single-hand blow.

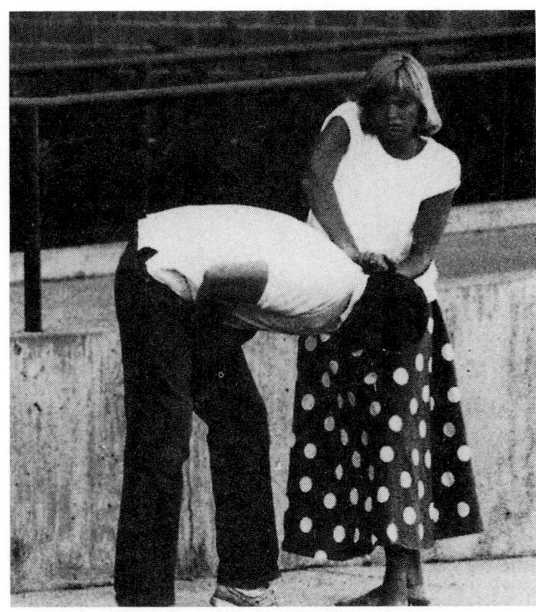

Figure 25-15. Double-hand blow.

hand up, striking your target at the base of your assailant's nose, contacting the nostrils with the base of your hand. Once again, aim through your target, not at it, to achieve maximum power. Retract your hand to the starting position at your chest so that you can hit again if necessary. You should become equally proficient with both your right and left hand.

Double-hand blow (figure 25-15). To achieve the correct hitting position for the double-hand blow, clasp your hands together, palms facing inward, as though clapping. Do not intertwine your fingers. This blow is delivered into the assailant's throat or to the back of the neck once the assailant has doubled over from a kick, groin pull, or knee lift.

Thumb gouge (figure 25-16). When your life is threatened and both hands are available, execute a thumb gouge. To deliver the thumb gouge, place your hands firmly on either side of your assailant's head to stabilize it, and gouge your thumbs deeply and directly into the assailant's eyes. If the assailant is wearing glasses, the technique is exactly the same but inside the glasses. This technique is used most effectively against strangulation with the hands or with an object, such as a scarf, nylon stocking, or necktie. If you are being strangled from behind with an object, both of the assailant's hands must be on that object. This allows you to turn (believe it or not) in either direction and perform a thumb gouge. Depending on the amount of pressure that you apply, this technique will temporarily or permanently blind an assailant.

Finger jab (figure 25-17). A finger jab should be used when you have only one hand free. Any time both hands are free, execute a thumb gouge. To perform a finger jab, round all four fingers slightly and gouge all fingers into the assailant's eyes. Jabbing with four fingers rather than two fingers will increase your chances of contacting the eyes. If the assailant is wearing glasses, direct your fingers to the upper cheeks, just under the lower rim. On striking the cheeks, continue your fingers under the glasses and into the eyes.

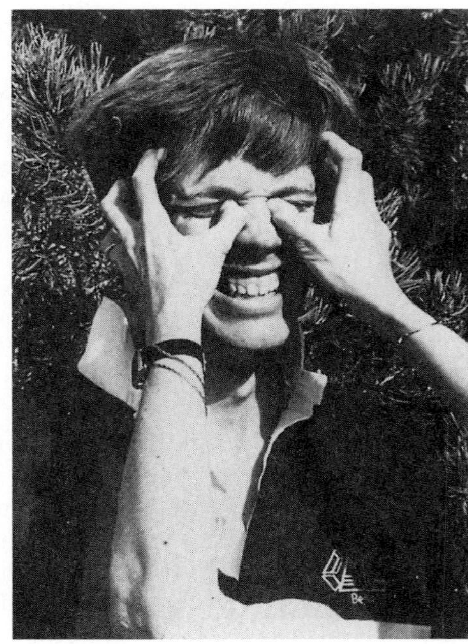

Figure 25-16. Thumb gouge.

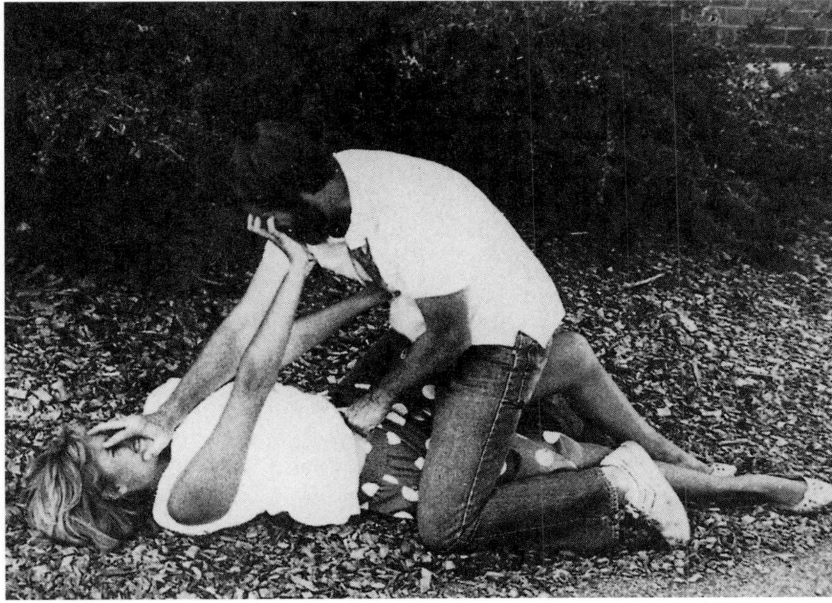

Figure 25-17. Finger jab.

TEACHING CONSIDERATIONS

1. Only teachers who have received special training themselves should attempt to teach self-defense.
2. If you do not have time to teach the techniques until the students master them, do not teach self-defense. Students may gain a false sense of security about their abilities that may endanger their lives.
3. Organize class for practice primarily in partners (victim and attacker). Change partners often so that students get an opportunity to work with different people and to play both roles.
4. Initial practice of techniques should include walking through the action with a partner slowly until correct body position is established. Speed and force characteristics can be practiced using objects such as stuffed bags or rolled mats. It is desirable to eventually use mannequins as instructional aids so that accuracy as well as force can be practiced.
5. Space work on strategies throughout the lessons and repeat ideas often. Use situational examples to practice decision making.
6. Combine moves by having the attacker respond to the victim's moves to simulate an extended fight. Do this in slow motion first and then increase speed.
7. Include short review sessions throughout the curriculum to reinforce skills.
8. Each student will have unique talents and limitations. Develop a strategy to fit each student.

GLOSSARY

accuracy The self-defense maneuver must be "on target."

American Judo Club A club established in 1925 by a group of young Americans.

chest push To shove or push the attacker on the chest with one or two hands.

finger jab To push the fingers into the assailant's eyes, nose, or throat.

follow-through To continue a movement to the point of incapacitating the attacker.

front choke To attack the windpipe.

front hug To approach the victim and wrap the arms around the body.

groin hit To punch the attacker in the groin or genitals.

groin pull To grab the genitals and pull.

jiu jitsu *Jiu* means "gentle"; *jitsu* means "art."

kick To use the feet and legs to incapacitate.

knee lift To forcibly lift the knee to the groin or face of the assailant.

modern self-defense This is not a martial art but street fighting combined with common sense. It can be learned in a short time by any person.

potential danger Not to "hit the target."

rear attack The attacker grabs the victim from behind.

scream A basic offensive to alert someone for assistance. Yell "Fire" throughout the attack.

speed To react with expedience to surprise the attacker.

supine kick A kick to the groin when one has been wrestled to the ground.

thumb gouge To use the thumbs to gouge the eyes.

vulnerable areas The areas of the body recommended as targets: eyes, nose, neck, groin, solar plexus, and knees.

SUGGESTED READINGS

Lavergne, C. 1989. *Self-defense*. Boston: American Press.

Nelson, J. 1991. *Self-defense: Steps to success*. Champaign, Ill.: Human Kinetics. Written as a course text or as a self-instruction guide, this book uses a skills progression to (1) develop awareness and vigilance, (2) sharpen observational skills, (3) learn communication skills to defend against volatile situations, and (4) acquire physical self-defense tactics.

Nelson, J. 1994. *Teaching self-defense: Steps to success*. Champaign, Ill.: Human Kinetics.

Peterson, S. L. 1989. *Self-defense for women: How to stay safe and fight back*. Englewood, Colo.: Morton. A practical, well-illustrated guide on how women of all ages can defend themselves in a variety of situations.

RESOURCES

Films and videotapes

Family self defense, available from MediaMart, 155 A Moffett Park Dr., Suite 103, Sunnyvale, CA 94059

Instant self-defense guide for women; The woman "how to" of self-defense; Women's self defense; Save your kids, save yourself; Protect yourself; and *Fight back! Emergency self-defense for women* are all available from Cambridge Physical Education and Health, P.O. Box 2153, Charleston, WV 25328.

Self-defense and *Self-defense for women*, videotapes. "How To" Sports Videos, P.O. Box 5852, Denver, CO 80217.

Shattered. MTI Teleprograms, 3710 Commercial Ave., Northbrook, IL 60062.

This film is about rape. Canadian Filmmakers Dist. Centre, 406 Jarvis St., Toronto, Ontario N44 2G6.

Vulnerable to attack. Professional Arts, P.O. Box 8003, Stanford, CA 94305.

Web sites

http://galaxy.tradewave.com/editors/weiss/BooklistSD.html
http://www.cs.utk.edu/~bartley/index/prevention/selfDefense/
http://www.middlebury.edu/~jswan/martial.arts/pages/sd2.html

26 Skiing: Alpine

After completing this chapter, the reader should be able to:

- Appreciate the development of skiing and its recent popularity
- Recognize the importance of the selection and care of equipment
- Describe and execute beginning skiing techniques
- Understand intermediate and advanced techniques
- Describe the various types of skiing competitions and techniques
- Recognize and use skiing terms correctly
- Instruct a group of students in basic skiing techniques

HISTORY

Skiing started as a form of travel in hunting and war during the Stone and Bronze Ages. Snowshoelike skis have been found in the bogs and marshes of Finland, Norway, Sweden, and Russia, as well as on rock-wall carvings in Norway and Russia. The primitive toe-strap bindings were too loose for any real control, but a single solid pole acted as a downhill brake and a "pusher" on the flats. The short ski, 6 to 7 feet (182 to 213 cm), for pushing off, and the long ski, 9 to 12 feet (274 to 366 cm), for gliding, were the first skis commonly used in Scandinavia. As the sport spread to the Alps, skis of equal length evolved.

Skiing as a modern recreational and competitive sport owes much to Sondre Norheim, Mathias Zdarsky, and Sir Arnold Lunn. Norheim, a Norwegian, invented the "stiff" binding in the early 1800s. Zdarsky, in Austria, developed the first dynamic ski technique and started the first ski school. It took a British scholar, Sir Arnold Lunn, to devise slalom and downhill racing. Later he devised the Arlberg-Kandahar races and was knighted for his contribution to skiing and mountaineering, and for the improvement of Anglo-Swiss relations.

Although Americans did not have great ski techniques during the 1850s, they are credited with the first professional races. The gold rush in the snow-covered California Sierras attracted many Scandinavians, who could get around on snowshoes easily. Skiing became instantly popular and was even used in delivering mail in winter. Records show that in 1855 a ski competition was held in Onion Valley, California, for a prize of $25,000 in gold nuggets.

The first ski club in the United States, formed in 1872 in New Hampshire, was called the Nansen Ski Club. In 1904 seventeen ski clubs met in Michigan to form the National Ski Association. Since then, skiing has become a major American sport and industry (figure 26-1). The U.S. Ski Team is now considered one of the best in the world. Phil Mahre of the U.S. Ski Team attained the highest goal in competitive skiing by winning the World Cup in 1981, 1982, and 1983. His 1981 win was the first ever by an American skier.

Once Phil Mahre broke through this barrier, individual members of the U.S. Ski Team continued to do well in international competition. Some of the most memorable accomplishments include Tamara McKinney's winning of the World Cup in 1983; Steve Mahre's winning of the giant slalom at the World Ski Championships in 1983; Bill Johnson, Phil Mahre, and Debbie Armstrong's winning of gold medals in the downhill, slalom, and giant slalom, respectively, in the 1984 Olympics; Diane Roffe's winning of the giant slalom at the 1985 World Ski Championships, and Tamara McKinney's winning of the gold in the Alpine

Figure 26-1. Downhill skiing is a popular wintertime activity.

combined and the silver in the slalom at the 1987 World Championships.

At the 1992 Olympics in Albertville, France, the U.S. Ski Team captured two silver medals (Hilary Lendh in the women's downhill and Diane Roffe in the women's giant slalom). Eva Twardoken and Julie Parisien also skied well, with Twardoken placing seventh in the giant slalom and eighth in the super-G and Parisien finishing fourth in the slalom and fifth in the giant slalom.

In 1994 the U.S. team brought home two gold and two silver medals. Tommy Moe captured both the gold in the men's downhill and the silver in the super-G. For the women, Diane Roffe-Steinnrotter won the gold in the super-G, and Picabo Street took the silver in the downhill.

Science and technology now make skiing available without an abundance of natural snow. Artificial snow has allowed ski areas to extend their season and provide consistently good surfaces. Snow-making capabilities have been a boon to the industry, especially for skiers living away from the snow belt.

PRESEASON CONDITIONING

To enhance the enjoyment of skiing, to speed up the learning process, and to prevent injury, it is important to implement a conditioning program. Perhaps the most enjoyable way to enhance fitness is by participating in activities that incorporate the elements of fitness beneficial to alpine skiing. Alpine skiing is an anaerobic activity. However, the skier must first establish an aerobic base upon which anaerobic fitness can be established. Bicycling, swimming, mountain hikes, and jogging/running/sprinting can be used for aerobic and anaerobic conditioning. Strength and power are best trained in a weight room, preferably using free weights. Tennis, racquetball, squash, volleyball, basketball, and soccer can be enjoyable, in addition to contributing to general athletic ability. Waterskiing, wind-surfing, trampolining, rollerblading, ice skating, and gymnastics help develop balance, agility, coordination, and ski-specific motor skills.

Due to modern technological advances in equipment design, producing greater speed and forces in the turns, alpine competitive skiing has become an extremely strenuous sport. A highly structured strength-training program has become a dominant part of year-round preparation. Conditioning the abdominal area, hips, buttocks, thighs, and lower legs will greatly increase the quality of an alpine skiing experience.

Summer

Flexibility
Aerobic
Endurance strength
(higher repetitions/ lower weight)
Sport activities
Motor skills

Early Fall

Flexibility
Aerobic/anaerobic
Strength
(higher weight/lower repetitions)
Sport activities
Motor skills

Late fall

Flexibility
Anaerobic
Power
(medium weight/medium repetitions, explosive moves)
Sports activities
Motor skills

Winter (ski season)

Flexibility
Maintenance
Sport activities
Motor skills

Prior to any sports or conditioning activity (including skiing) it is important to warm up the body. Slightly elevate the heart rate by bicycling or jogging lightly, then stretch with a full complement of flexibility exercises.

EQUIPMENT

Boots

Boots are a primary equipment item, demanding a combination of lateral stiffness and proper fit to ensure good control of the skis and happy feet.

Because the price of boots is relatively high, the beginner should first rent a pair of buckle boots carefully fitted at the ski shop. The boots should feel snug, with one thin pair of nylon or silk socks plus one pair of thermal socks. If it is possible to lift the heel inside the boot, if the buckles are not tight enough, or if the boots are too soft, turns will lack precision, regardless of how good the skier. Boots that are too small will cut off circulation, causing numbness and possible frostbite. For maximum comfort, it is a good idea to loosely fasten buckles while riding the lifts, then tighten them before the descent. Buy a comfortable pair of plastic buckle boots because they retain their stiffness, comfort, and appearance longer than do leather boots. A boot press is often used to hold and carry the bulky boots about.

The technological advances in ski boots have been great during the past few years (somewhat like those in the running shoe). Foam liners in combination with standard plastic shell boots help to accommodate the anatomical differences of the foot of an individual athlete and therefore provide the best control over the direction of the ski and reasonable comfort. It is difficult to imagine contemporary alpine racing without foamed boots. Because of these developments and because so many companies now manufacture ski boots, it is wise to consult a reputable ski equipment retailer to ensure proper fit and appropriate boots for your skiing ability.

Skis

Most modern skis are constructed of a wood laminate. The core is often reinforced with Kevlar, carbon fiber, or ceramic. Fiberglass is used to enclose the construction. Solid-wood and metal skis are basically gone from the market.

Proper ski length is determined by several factors: height, weight, ability, aggressiveness, and attitude (how

Table 26-1. CHARACTERISTICS OF SKIS

Type of ski	Characteristics	Recommended length
Sport/Racing	Tracks well but only turns well if precisely controlled	Women: height plus 15–20 cm (5.9–7.9 in) Men: height plus 20–30 cm (7.9–11.8 in)
All-around compact, mid-length	Turns easily and tracks well	Women and men: height plus 5–15 cm (2–5.9 in)
Short	Turns very easily but does not track well	Women and men: height minus 5–10 cm (2–3.9 in)

badly do you want to improve?). In general, when the skis are held vertically the tips should be about face height for a novice skier. The curve of the ski should wrap around the top of the head for advanced or aggressive skiers.

Most ski shops allow the skier to try various lengths and models prior to purchase. Otherwise, rental skis will give the skier an opportunity to find the correct length and model suited for his or her needs (see table 26-1).

When planning to purchase new skis, expect to pay approximately $300 to $500. Most shops carry used equipment, and ski swaps abound during the fall.

Whether buying used or new skis, the bases should be tuned up, and the edges should be sharpened and beveled. Today's ski bases and edges are so hard, it is difficult for a recreational skier to do the job by hand. It is better to choose a quality ski shop where the employees are skillful and technicians are available to stone-grind the base.

Waxing

Most skis made in recent years incorporate a polyethylene or graphite running surface. Polyethylene and graphite have somewhat minimized the need for waxing because these surfaces reduce friction.

Snow temperature, air temperature, humidity, and snow texture affect the amount of friction between the ski base and the snow surface. Racing almost always requires preparation of the ski bases with wax. Very cold, dry conditions or extremely warm, wet situations will call for even recreational skiers to wax the ski bases to enjoy the sport.

Prior to waxing, imperfections in the base should be repaired and the edges sharpened and beveled. It is best to iron the wax onto a warm, dry, clean ski base. The wax should be left on the ski base as long as possible, but scraped off prior to skiing. After the wax has been scraped down to a thin layer (thicker for warm, wet conditions), the base should be brushed or rilled depending on conditions.

Wax companies usually color-code waxes for specific snow/air temperatures and snow textures. It is best to buy one brand of wax, read the directions, and then experiment. Staying with one brand of wax and learning to use it correctly will allow the skier to make educated choices under varying conditions.

Bindings

Release bindings disengage boots from the skis in a hard fall. They do not guarantee against serious injury, but they do reduce risks. Step-in bindings with the direct release at the toe and heel are the most up-to-date. Be absolutely sure to have the bindings adjusted and tested by a ski shop mechanic. Do not swap skis with friends until the skis have been inspected. Bindings that are too loose or too tight are dangerous. They should not release unless the skier lunges forward or puts an extreme torque to the bottom of the leg. The bindings should be mounted in accordance with the manufacturer's specifications.

Ski brakes should be used to prevent runaway skis when bindings release. Binding systems using brakes are preferable to those incorporating safety straps. In fact, ski straps are no longer an acceptable safety device. Except in backcountry skiing, ski brakes are without exception required in ski areas worldwide.

Derby-Flex

An aluminum plate mounted between the ski and the binding improves the flex pattern of the ski during a turn (giant slalom). The ski carves more smoothly on the smaller radius. All racing giant slalom skis are outfitted with Derby-flex without exception. A side effect is that the additional distance between the boot and the bottom of the ski increases the distance of the edge and the center of the mass inside the turn, allowing a very efficient execution of the carved turn.

Lifters

These are additional plastic spacers mounted on the top of the Derby-flex. This combination brings the skier approximately 1 inch (2.5 cm) higher than standard bindings. Besides enhancing turning actions, as described above, the ski boot is elevated well above the snow, even in the extreme angle, and therefore the danger of "dragging" the boot on the snow is minimal. Some racers have taken the lifter notion to an extreme by building the distance between the bottom of the ski and the bottom of the boot to 70 mm. For safety reasons, FIS now limits this practice to no more than 55 mm for adult racers and 50 mm for

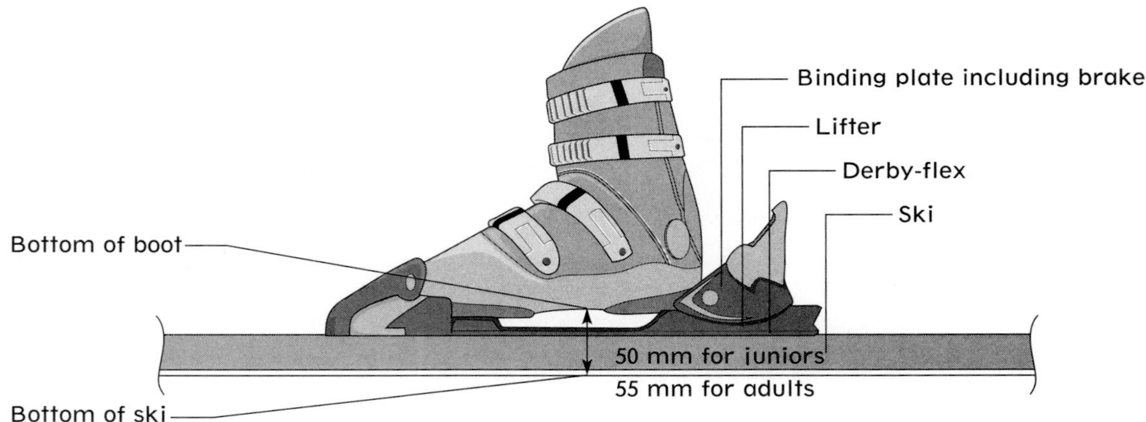

Figure 26-2. Maximum lifter distances.

junior racers. This distance includes the thickness of ski, Derby-flex, lifter, and binding plate. See figure 26-2.

Poles

Ski poles are built with handles, wrist loops, and metal alloy, fiberglass, Kevlar, or bamboo shafts. The rings, or baskets, attached near the pointed tips of poles prevent the shafts from sinking into the snow too deeply. Prices range according to quality, weight, and flexibility of poles. The expensive thin-walled steel poles with adjustable grips are light and easy to manipulate, but can break at the end of their flexibility. The cheaper poles, made of aluminum alloys, are heavier and nonadjustable, but usually bend rather then break.

When one is standing on hard ground with boots on and grasping the pole, the elbow should form a right angle with the forearm parallel to the ground. Poles that are too long get in the way and cause bad habits in technique. Ski shops can easily cut down poles to a suitable length.

Ski pole grips

To get the most out of the pole action and to prevent dropping it, the loop of the pole must be in the correct position. With the loop facing you, slip the palm of the hand underneath and entirely through the strap (figure 26-3), close the fist around the handle and strap, and slide the hand down so that the loop is snug around the wrist. When skiing, hold the pole firmly in this position.

Ski poles help a skier maintain balance, walk or glide, climb, make turns, get up from falls, and ski faster.

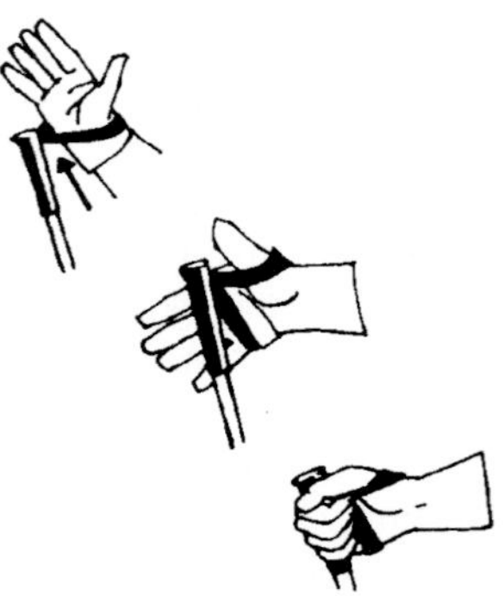

Figure 26-3. Ski pole grip.

BEGINNING TECHNIQUES

Walking and Gliding

Walking on skis is the same motion as walking without skis, except for the sliding tendency. Here poles are used for stability and pushing. The change of weight from one ski to another "sets" the ski, making it easy to push off for the next step. Following the natural inclination of the arms, the skier extends the arm and pole opposite the extended leg and pulls against it. As the skier brings the other leg forward, he or she braces against the opposite pole. The weight is kept on the balls of the feet so the knees can bend properly (figure 26-4).

The exaggerated form of walking is *gliding*. The skier lunges forward and upward from a slight crouch and pulls against the poles to create the momentum for a gliding movement.

Side Step

When a hill becomes too steep to walk up, the side step is recommended (figure 26-5). With skis pointing across the hill, place the uphill ski a foot above the next, then draw up the lower one. For very steep slopes put pressure on the edges and poles.

Falling and Getting Up

The best way to fall is to one side. Remember, even the best skiers fall. If you start to lose your balance, try to stay

Figure 26-4. Wallking and gliding.

Figure 26-5. The side step.

up as long as possible. But if gravity gets the best of you, try to relax.

The best way to get up is to place the skis across the hill on the downhill side of the slope. Next, tuck the legs up under the hips on the uphill side and push your body up with the hands or poles.

Downhill Schussing (Tucking)

The keys to the downhill schuss are correct body position and the ability to relax (figure 26-6). Build confidence by starting with a ski teacher on a gentle slope. The run-out should be sufficient to stop safely. Find a fairly flat area and

Figure 26-6. Downhill schussing (tucking).

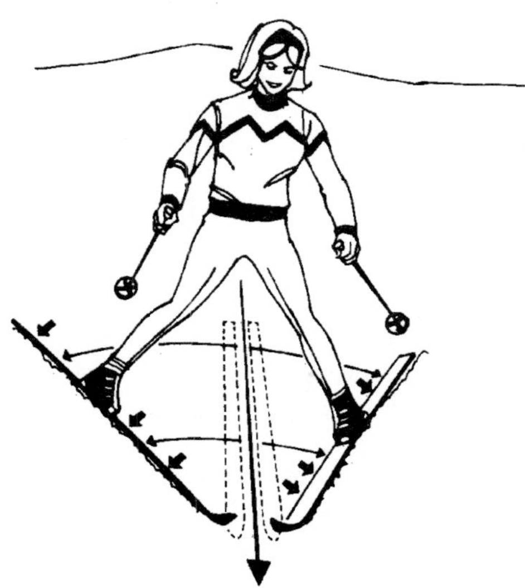

Figure 26-7. Wedge braking technique.

point the skis straight down the fall line. Skis should be parallel and about a foot apart, with weight evenly distributed on them. Lean slightly forward, bending at the ankles, knees, and hips. Do not bend forward at the waist. Let the legs absorb bumps by leaning forward and tucking the legs up as you go over the bumps.

Remember, when schussing from deep snow to a hard surface or from packed snow to ice, lean farther forward so that the ski cannot run away with you. In contrast, to schuss from hard snow to powder, lean slightly back.

Wedge

The wedge (figure 26-7) is the basic braking technique used by beginners. Facing down the fall line in the downhill schuss position, push off with a brushing motion into a V ski position, with the ski tips together and the tails wide apart. The wider the V, the slower the speed. Intermediate skiers brake by sliding both skis to one side.

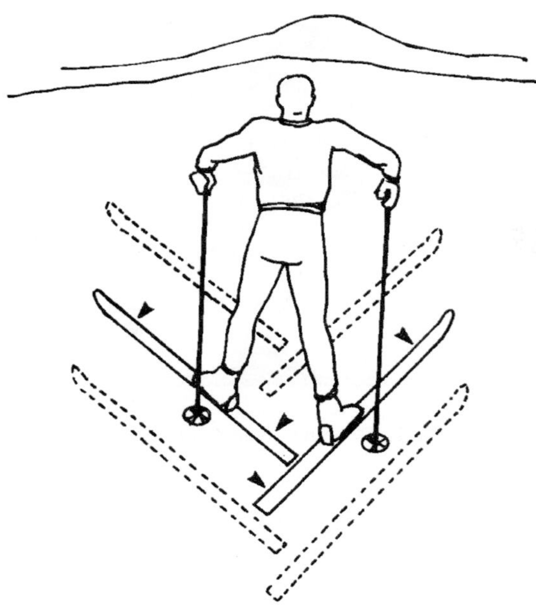

Figure 26-8. The herringbone.

Figure 26-9. Kick turn.

Herringbone

The herringbone is a faster means of climbing a hill than is the side step, provided the hill is not too steep (figure 26-8). Face directly up the hill with skis in a V position, with the tips wide apart and the tails close together. Weight is on the inside edges, and the poles are used to propel upward and prevent backslip as the weight is shifted from one ski to the other.

Kick Turn

The kick turn is used not only as a fine balance exercise on flat ground, but also for changing direction on dangerous terrain (figure 26-9). The turn is actually a stationary 180-degree change of direction. Starting with the skis parallel, poles halfway between boots and ski tips, and weight on the left ski, kick up the right ski high enough for the ski to stand on its tail. Next, rotate the raised ski to face in the opposite direction, and bring the pole around as a brace. Transfer your weight to the right ski as the left ski and pole shift around next to the right ski. On a steep slope with skis facing across the fall line, the lower leg is always the kick-up leg.

SKIING SAFETY AND ETIQUETTE

1. The best assurance against first-day injury is a lesson from a ski instructor.
2. Have a ski shop mechanic or instructor adjust and check bindings while you are wearing the skis and boots. Do not swap skis with friends without the same adjustment.
3. Do not ski on unmarked trails or where avalanche warnings have been placed, even though the snow looks sensational.
4. Do not ski alone.
5. To avoid frostbite on subzero days, wear thermal underwear or warm-up pants, an insulated parka, goggles, and a mask or scarf. If a white spot appears on your face, place a bare hand on the spot for a minute, but do not rub, and then head for shelter.
6. Do some loosening-up exercises before the first run. Warming up prevents strained muscles and may prevent injury.
7. Be a patient learner. *Ski in control* and build up confidence.
8. Be cognizant of the safety of others. Offer your assistance to anyone who needs help.
9. Ski on slopes appropriate to your skill.
10. Obey all the rules of the skiing area.
11. Inform slower skiers you are approaching from behind by calling out “On your left (right).”
12. Do not “cut in” in lift lines.

INTERMEDIATE TECHNIQUES

Traversing

Skiing in a straight line other than the fall line is *traversing* (figure 26-10). Skis are parallel and slightly apart, weight is

Figure 26-10. Traversing.

over the balls of the feet, with two thirds of the weight on the lower ski and one third on the upper ski. Ankles and knees are rolled into the hill, causing the inside edges of the skis to bite into the snow without slipping. To compensate for this, the upper body leans slightly downhill, but essentially square over the skis. The amount of the bending motion, *angulation*, depends on the steepness of the slope and the radius of the turn. During the traverse the arms should be slightly forward and about at waist level.

Stem Christie Turn

The stem turn (stem christie), which combines the wedge turn with the traverse, is useful for a slow turn (figure 26-11). The skier enters the turn from a regular traverse position, then stems the uphill ski into a half-V. As the weight transfers, the body angulates over the ski, causing both skis to come around in the turn. As the new direction is established, the skis can run back into the parallel position. Problems in turning usually result from insufficient weight shift to the uphill ski.

Figure 26-11. Stem christie turn.

ADVANCED TECHNIQUES

Parallel Turn (Christie)

The parallel turn is a progressive form of stem christie, but is more complex because of its dependence on *up-unweighting* and precise edge control (figure 26-12). The turn starts from the *traverse* position, standing square over the skis. The skier sinks slightly and plants the pole lightly in the snow on the downhill side between boot and ski tip in anticipation of the turn. As the skier explosively up-unweights, the pressure on the *inside edges* transfers to the *outside edges* and the ankles and knees power the skis around in the turn, ending in a traverse position. The upper torso should be kept as still as possible throughout the turn.

Figure 26-12. Parallel turn (christie).

Hop Turn

The hop turn is an exercise for coordinating the parallel turn. To execute, thrust the heels of the skis in the direc-

Figure 26-13. Wedeln.

tion of the turn, either in quick rhythmic thrustings or subtle hops between long traverses.

Wedeln

The wedeln is an advanced form of parallel skiing in which the ankles and knees manipulate a series of rhythmic half-turns (figure 26-13).

Stepping

Inside-outside (at the end of a turn)

1. Traversing on downhill ski in lowered (knee-bent) position on inside edge. Extend downhill knee and transfer weight to uphill ski and back to downhill ski.
2. Same as exercise one; now more weight to uphill ski and transfer to outside edge.
3. Same as exercise two; now extend uphill leg (knee and hip) and glide on outside edge of uphill ski across the slope.
4. Same as exercise three; glide extended for a few yards; roll ski (apply either inclination, angulation, or leap) on inside edge; make turn.
5. Same as exercise four in various turns (long, short, wide, tight).
6. All exercises repeated, but stepping (gliding) on a flat ski.
7. Emphasize exercises three and four with a step (glide), not only laterally, but also forward. Foot, however, should not move in *front of knee*.
8. Exercise four after gliding (stepping) on uphill ski; incline body and roll uphill ski on inside edge; start turn. Careful, you need some speed. (If too slow, application of angulation is necessary.)
9. Same as exercise three; extend uphill knee through a leaping movement and change edges while in the air; touch-down is combined with the start of the turn. Actually, the body starts to rotate into the turn in the air.
10. Link turns together; completion phase and preparation phase of turn almost become one unit.

Inside-inside (at the beginning of a turn)

1. On flat or easily descending terrain, with packed snow, standing in wedge position, transfer weight from one ski to the other (inside edge).
2. Wedge position leaping from one ski to the other (weight transfer).
3. Wedge position (stationary), unweighted ski matches pressurized ski and leg.
4. Same as exercise two and three in slow speed (plow-hops).
5. Plow-hops, keeping pressure a little longer on the inside edge to allow the ski to turn.
6. Same as five; make complete turns.
7. In a traverse, skiing on inside edge of downhill ski, lift uphill ski and bring in wedge position and back to parallel.
8. Same as seven; transfer half of weight to wedged uphill ski; let uphill ski glide on inside edge with most of the weight still on inside edge of the downhill ski.
9. Same as eight; transfer weight completely to wedged uphill ski and start turn.
10. Same as nine; change weight and skis and edges while leaping.
11. Tighten up turning radii and put emphasis on leaping movement to shift weight. Touch down to new ski and edge must be smooth (catlike), executed with a lot of absorbing motion (lowering knee and bending in all three leg joints).
12. Vary turning radii and ski in different terrain.
13. At especially high speeds, try to make weight change without a leap.
14. Same as 13, while extending bring body in position for new turn. Use varied speed inclination and hip or knee angulation.

Uphill ski to inside ski (outside-outside: at the beginning of a turn)

1. Standing on a small bump, weight on the uphill ski, scissor downhill.
2. Same as one; move weight from uphill ski to scissored downhill ski and glide down small bumps. Prior uphill ski (outside ski) will be matched to new uphill ski (inside ski).
3. Same as two; move with small leap; weight to new inside ski (scissored), but to outside edge; absorb and

pressurize. Ski turns on outside edge. Match outside ski and leg.
4. Same as three; leap onto outside edge of inside ski. Ski down small bump; let ski turn. Bring outside ski (this was the ski you leaped from) alongside the turning inside ski. Shift weight to the inside edge of this ski and continue turning.
5. Make moves to right and left.
6. Try to link turns together (skating step downhill); moderate speed, not too slow.
7. Apply this move in tactical rhythm changes from long into short turns.
8. Ski out of the start and around the first gate, if turn to second gate is not too long.

ALPINE COMPETITION

Slalom

The slalom is a course with a vertical drop of 394 to 722 feet (120 to 220 m) for men and 394 to 591 feet (120 to 180 m) for women. The course should be set on a slope with a gradient of 20 to 30 degrees. A slalom course consists of a minimum of 42 gates and a maximum of 63 gates for women and 75 gates for men. The gates are set 13.1 to 19.7 feet (4 to 6 m) in width and successive gates may not be less than 2.5 feet (0.75 m) and not more than 49.2 feet (15 m) apart. Quickness, power, and agility are prerequisites for a good slalom skier. Slalom skis are usually a little shorter than giant slalom or downhill skis.

Giant Slalom

The giant slalom is contested on a longer course than the slalom and has fewer gates. A giant slalom course should have a vertical drop of 820 to 1,312 feet (250 to 400 m) for men and 820 to 1,148 feet (250 to 350 m) for women. Giant slalom speeds are higher than those in slalom. The number of gates in giant slalom is figured by computation of 12 to 15 percent of the course's vertical drop.

Ideal giant slalom terrain is undulating. Strength, agility, and fearlessness are required characteristics of the giant slalom skier. Although the slalom is an athletic event, many consider the giant slalom to be more technical.

Downhill

Downhill is the fastest and considered by some to be the most exciting event. Speeds up to 90 mph (145 km/h) are reached. Many courses are over 3 miles (4.8 km) in length. Gates and terrain are used by the course setter to control the racer's speed. The racer has limited protection other than a helmet and the netting that lines the trail.

Super Giant Slalom

The super giant slalom combines some of the speed of downhill with the more technical turning aspect of the giant slalom. Speeds are very high in this exciting event.

NORDIC COMPETITION

Nordic competition includes cross-country skiing and jumping.

SCORING COLLEGIATE MEETS

The events in a collegiate ski meet may include the giant slalom, slalom, individual cross-country and cross-country relay for both men and women. Approved cross-country distances for both men and women are 3.1 to 18.6 miles (5 to 30 km).

1. A men's and women's alpine and cross-country meet consists of four to eight events, equally distributed by sex and discipline.
2. A men's and women's alpine or cross-country-only meet consists of two to four events.
3. A men's and women's alpine or cross-country-only meet consists of one to four events.

The final score of a team in the meet shall be the sum of the points earned in each of the events. If two or more teams receive the same score, that position shall be declared a tie.

SKI ORGANIZATIONS GOVERNING COMPETITIONS

Fédération Internationale de Ski

All races are run according to the rules of the Fédération Internationale de Ski (FIS). This representative body supervises the Olympic Games, which are held every 4 years; and the World Championships, which follow 2 years after the Olympics.

United States Ski Association

The United States Ski Association (USSA) is the governing body for the sport of skiing in the United States. There are eight geographical divisions, each with its own membership, classification of racers, and schedule of competitions, ranging from juniors through veterans. National, Olympic, and World Championship teams are selected on the basis of qualifying races.

National Collegiate Athletic Association

The National Collegiate Athletic Association (NCAA) is the governing body of intercollegiate ski racing. The top teams and individuals compete at NCAA Championships. The individual winners of the various events, including both alpine and Nordic competitions, are named to the All-American Ski Team at the end of each season.

National Standard Race

National Standard Race (NASTAR) operates on a handicap system, as in golf, using a simple giant slalom course especially designed for recreational skiers of all ages. With the aid of computers and professional pacesetters, skiers can compare their skiing with that of other skiers throughout the country.

TEACHING CONSIDERATIONS

1. Ensure that students are provided with safe equipment, properly fitted. The safety aspects of equipment should be a first priority of instruction.
2. Teach students how to grip poles and maintain the proper stance; emphasize a relaxed, balanced position over the skis.
3. Teach how to fall and how to get up. Have students practice several times.
4. Teach walking and side-step patterns. Combine with falling and getting up. Provide enough practice time for students to begin to feel comfortable with problems encountered with the length of the skis.
5. Start downhill schussing on a slight incline, allowing students to come to a natural stop at the end. Add the snowplow braking technique as students increase speed.
6. Gradually increase the slope of the hill when students become confident in schussing, keeping the skis under control. Use the side-step pattern and the snowplow for both braking on the slope and for stopping.
7. Introduce the stationary kick turn and practice often as a lead-up into more-advanced turns. Begin traversing skills as soon as students have control of skis in beginning skills. Start instruction on the side of an incline going across the slope so that you can give continuous cuing on weight distribution.
8. Add the stem christie turn to the traversing skills, encouraging quick recovery from turn to traversing position.
9. Increase slope and conditions gradually as students master intermediate skills; alter them to techniques used to accommodate changes in conditions.
10. As new techniques are introduced, decrease the difficulty of the practice conditions.
11. Keep instructional sessions active so that students are not standing still in cold weather.

GLOSSARY

angulation When edges bite into the snow from pressure exerted by the ankles and the knees being rolled into the hill, the upper body leans slightly downhill to compensate.

camber Arch of the ski as seen from the side.

canting Adjustment to achieve ideal balance between the inside edge of the ski and the direction of the pressure.

carved turns A form of advanced skiing following the christie turn in which turns are made using the edges without skidding the skis.

chatter Undesirable vibrations of edges while skiing on ice or hard-packed snow.

christie A turn without skidding; carved turn.

edge control Adjusting the angle between the snow and the running surface of the ski.

fall line The imaginary line of gravity straight down a slope.

groove Indentation running nearly the full length of the bottom of the ski; it helps in control.

inside edges Edges of the skis that grip the snow on the inside of the arc of the turn.

linked turns A series of turns in alternating directions.

moguls Mounds of snow.

outside edges Edges of the skis on the downhill side of the slope, which do not grip the snow.

ruade Movement made by lifting the tails of the skis off the ground and turning, with the ski tips acting as pivots.

schuss boom Skiing dangerously out of control.

sitzmark Indentation in the snow made by a skier falling down.

torsion The amount of lengthwise twist in a ski.

traverse Skiing on inside edges at an angle to the fall line.

tuning Adjustment of original base and edges to fit individual needs of the skier.

up-unweighting A down-up movement of the ankles and knees to reduce weight on the skis before turning; it facilitates changing of edges.

wedeln A series of rhythmic half-turns in alternating directions.

SUGGESTED READINGS

Cottrell, J. 1993. *Skiing everyone*. 2d ed. Winston-Salem, N.C.: Hunter Textbooks. Includes hundreds of photos to illustrate equipment, exercises, proper techniques, and rules of the slopes. Gives tips on how to correct errors, dos and don'ts for the slopes, and drills for practice. A wealth of useful information; especially good for programs where location or time limits actual slope experience and time is spent on conditioning and preparation.

Gullion, L. 1990. *Ski games*. Champaign, Ill.: Human Kinetics. This book is focused on teaching children to ski using a games approach.

National Collegiate Athletic Association. Current ed. *Official skiing rules*. Washington, D.C.: National Collegiate Athletic Association.

Yacenda, J. 1987. *High-performance skiing*. Champaign, Ill.: Human Kinetics. Contains advice for skiing in steep terrain in all types of weather and snow conditions.

Yacenda, J. 1992. *Alpine skiing: Steps to success*. Champaign, Ill.: Human Kinetics. Can be used as a course text or as a self-instruction guide. Contains specific performance goals, drills, and checklists for evaluation.

RESOURCES

Films and videotapes

The great ski chase. Summit Films Productions, Denver.
Incredible skis. Summit Films Productions, Denver.
The moebius flip. Summit Films Productions, Denver.
NASTAR. Joseph Schlitz Brewing, Milwaukee.
Ski country USA. Summit Films Productions, Denver.
Ski the outer limits. Summit Films Productions, Denver.

Breakthrough basics of downhill skiing with Hank Kashiwa, West One Video, 1995 Bailey Hill Rd., Eugene, OR 97405. Covers the fundamentals of skiing, the importance of conditioning and stretching, and provides a workout program to begin at home.

Downhill skiing basics, alpine skiing with Jean-Claude Killy. Sports Video, 745 State Circle, P. O. Box 1941, Ann Arbor, MI 48106.

Alpine Ski School: *Distinctive skiing, Black diamond skiing*, and *Fundamentals of skiing*. Karol Video, 22 Riverside Dr., Wayne, NJ 07470.

Fifteen different videos, including *Learn to ski, Advanced ski tuning guide*, and *Olympic gold workout*. "How To" Sports Videos P.O. Box 5852, Denver, CO 80217.

Skiing for the future. Vic Braden. Available from Human Kinetics, P.O. Box 5076, Champaign, IL 01825-5076.

Skiing: Cross-Country

After completing this chapter, the reader should be able to:

- Appreciate the development of cross-country skiing
- Select and care for cross-country skiing equipment
- Practice proper skiing techniques on various terrains
- Suggest appropriate off-season conditioning activities
- Identify correct cross-country skiing clothing
- Be aware of safety concerns

HISTORY

The history of skiing is deeply meshed with the history of all lands that are seasonally covered with snow. The earliest pictorial representation of skiing shows man hunting elk on skis. This picture dates back to approximately 2500 B.C. and was found on the island of Rödöy, off the coast of Norway. The earliest known skis date back to the same era and were found in a bog near Hoting, Sweden. It appears that the early skis were made of bone and were used in Scandinavia for hunting and later for warfare.

Two events in the Middle Ages demonstrate the importance of skiing to the military in the northern countries. In 1206 in Norway, two members of the king's guard carried the king's son, Haken, on skis over the Dovre mountains away from enemy forces. The child later became one of Norway's greatest kings, and the event is now celebrated in the famous Norwegian Birkebeiner race. In the 1500s, a similar event occurred in Sweden when Gustav Vasa was leading the battle against Danish rulers. Sensing defeat, Vasa left the town of Darlarna and headed for the Norwegian border. He was later persuaded by skiers to return to fight the Danish army, and the route of his triumphant return on skis is followed in today's most famous cross-country ski race, the Vasaloppet. Gustav Vasa went on to become the founder of modern Sweden.

Interest in skiing spread internationally in the late 1800s as the British discovered skiing in the European Alps and started formal ski competitions. The exploits of Norwegian explorer Fridthjof Nansen, written in *The First Crossing of Greenland* fueled British interest in skiing. Gradually, skiing in the Alps acquired its own techniques and style and evolved into the current discipline of alpine skiing. At the same time, cross-country skiing continued to grow in popularity and technical development. The use of metal bindings appeared at the end of the nineteenth century near Telemark, Norway, and the use of two ski poles of equal length was substituted for the traditional long single pole at about the same time.

Skiing was brought to the United States by Scandinavian immigrants and flourished in the 1800s. Pictures of the California mining camps of the 1840s and 1850s show well-organized ski racing. The most well-remembered American skier of this era was John "Snowshoe" Thompson, who, beginning in 1856, carried mail from Nevada to California over the mountains on skis. Thompson's legendary trips covered 90 miles (144 km) in about three days while he carried 60 to 90 pounds (27 to 40 kg) of mail.

Interest in skiing in the United States focused in those geographic areas with large concentrations of Scandinavian settlers. By 1872, the first ski club in the United States was formed in Berlin, New Hampshire, and named the Nansen Ski Club. Other clubs soon followed in the Midwest. The 1932 Winter Olympics in Lake Placid, New York, further heightened interest in skiing because it was the first Olympiad with Nordic (cross-country and jumping) and Alpine (downhill) skiing competitions. The previous Olympics had featured only Nordic events. Recent Olympic media coverage has heightened people's awareness of the sport of cross-country skiing and the sport of biathlon (cross-country skiing and marksmanship) as well. Events in which the men compete are 10, 15, 30, and 50 km races, alternating techniques between classic and skating. The women compete in the 5, 10, and 30 km events.

Interest in cross-country skiing was sustained in the early twentieth century by a small group of clubs, Eastern colleges and universities, and preparatory schools. Competitions accompanied winter carnivals at many colleges and universities in the Northeast, with ski jumping attracting more spectators than cross-country skiing. At the same time, alpine, or downhill, skiing was growing rapidly in popularity in the United States, led by Hannes Schneider and his distinctive Austrian Alborg technique, with its Christina turns.

Skiing in the United States was greatly advanced by the onset of World War II and the formation of the country's first ski troops, the Tenth Mountain Division. The ski troops proved to be one of the most effective and decorated units of the war, combating German forces in the Battle of Italy. A lasting side effect of this wartime activity was that a cross-section of American men—and not just those graduating from certain Eastern colleges—was exposed to the latest skiing and survival techniques. After the war, many of the soldiers of the Tenth Mountain Division continued to follow their interest in skiing by working in the ski industry.

Despite the expanded base for cross-country skiing, participation in the sport remained relatively small through the 1960s, obscured by its downhill relative. This status was dramatically changed by the "discovery" of cross-country skiing in the early 1970s, resulting in the recent boom in the sport. Cross-country ski sales in the United States amounted to about 14,000 pairs in 1966 and exploded to about 277,000 pairs by the winter of 1971–72. This twentyfold increase can be partially attributed to the American public's growing interest in fitness and the environment. Cross-country skiing appealed to people who participated in other cardiovascular fitness pursuits, such as jogging and cycling, and seemed consistent with their sense of concern for the environment. In short, the sport took on the image of being health- and fitness-enhancing as well as environmentally sound.

Recent Historical Developments

Cross-country skiing has continued to grow in popularity since 1972, but at a reduced rate. Sales of cross-country skis currently exceed 400,000 pairs annually. Helping this growth has been increased media attention and books such as John Caldwell's *The Cross-Country Ski Book*. First published in 1964, the volume provided much-needed technical information for first-time skiers. Bill Koch's silver medal in the 1976 Olympics in Seefield, Austria, and his subsequent overall World Cup Title in 1982 brought cross-country skiing further attention.

With the increased popularity of cross-country skiing, the public now has a wider range of skiing opportunities. Backcountry skiing in wilderness parks and on undeveloped lands is still available. In addition, well-developed commercial ski touring centers now exist in most parts of the country with adequate winter snow cover. Cross-country skiing facilities can provide prepared and groomed trail systems, trail maps, and systematic markings, and usually some kind of ski patrol for safety support. This kind of skiing simply was not available in the United States before 1972 and widens the base of appeal to those who would not explore wilderness areas on their own. Now the skier can choose his or her level of involvement in skiing.

In addition, more ski organizations now sponsor and support cross-country ski events. The U.S. Ski Association traditionally sponsors ski races and ski touring opportunities. Ski touring clubs now appear in or near most urban areas of the Snow Belt to provide instruction, tours, and racing experiences for the public.

With the dramatic improvements in snow grooming of cross-country ski trails, the skating technique has become increasingly feasible and practical. Bill Koch popularized the technique in North America with his World Cup victory in the winter of 1981–82. The skating technique on cross-country skis closely resembles a speed skater using long ski poles. Skating is considerably faster than the traditional skiing technique that has been used for centuries, but it requires different waxing, equipment, and conditioning.

EQUIPMENT

Recent interest in cross-country skiing has led to more changes in ski equipment in the past twenty years than in the previous century. Touring skis have become lighter and more responsive; fiberglass and other synthetic fibers have all but replaced traditional hickory and other hardwood skis; ski bottoms either are waxable in the old skiing tradition or have special "no-wax" synthetic bases; ski boot and binding combinations have become more diverse and provide more support. Today's cross-country skiers must become good consumers to purchase the appropriate equipment for their needs, locale, and budget. In sum, the recent advances in cross-country ski technology provide for safer and more enjoyable skiing.

Skis

Cross-country skis are longer, lighter, and thinner than their alpine counterparts. They are designed primarily to allow the skier to slide forward over the snow with a minimum of resistance and effort. Cross-country skis have traditionally been made of thin laminated strips of wood, but in the past two decades the trend has been toward fiberglass skis with wood and fiberglass cores and various types of plastic running surfaces. Cross-country skis can be categorized into four distinctive types (figure 27-1):

Ski	Width	Purpose
Telemark	65–80 mm	Downhill lift service skiing
Backcountry/ mountaineering	60—70 mm	Off-trail skiing and exploration
Touring	50–60 mm	Groomed and ungroomed trail skiing
Racing	44 mm	Classic and skate skiing on groomed trails

Beginners are advised to use touring or light touring skis depending on their use. The other two types of skis and their usage go beyond the scope of this chapter. Skis for adults are sized in terms of the skier's height and weight.

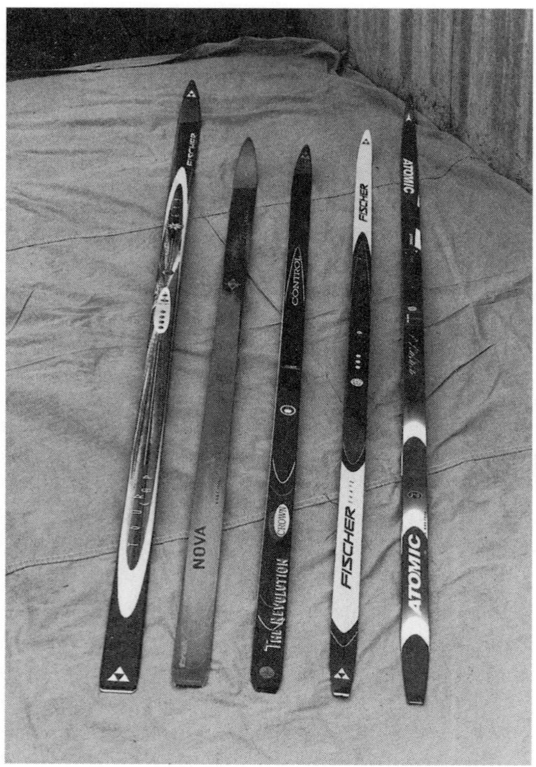

Figure 27-1. Cross-country skis. From left: Telemark, mountaineering, touring, race skating, and race touring.

Ski sizes for adults currently range from 165 cm to 210 cm. Cross-country skis are built with a degree of camber, or bow, in the running surface.

The camber of both skis in a pair should match, and the user should be able to flatten out the entire length of the skis when he or she stands on them on a smooth, hard floor. Bottom camber helps propel the skier forward when flattened on the snow.

Perhaps the most difficult decision when purchasing the first pair of skis is whether to choose waxable or waxless skis. Cross-country skis with machined bottoms have eliminated the necessity of applying wax to the bottom, or running, surface of the skis. Such waxless skis have gained popularity with beginning and recreational skiers because of their convenience. The disadvantage of waxless skis lies in their performance. They cannot adjust to the variety of snows and temperatures that the skis will face and as a result will not slide as easily as well-waxed cross-country skis. However, improved technology has narrowed the gap between the performance of waxable and waxless skis.

With the evolution of the skating technique, "skating" skis are now available. They are about 2 to 4 inches (5 to 10 cm) shorter than classical skis; have a stiffer bottom camber, particularly in the tail of the ski; and feature reinforced sidewalls to withstand stress.

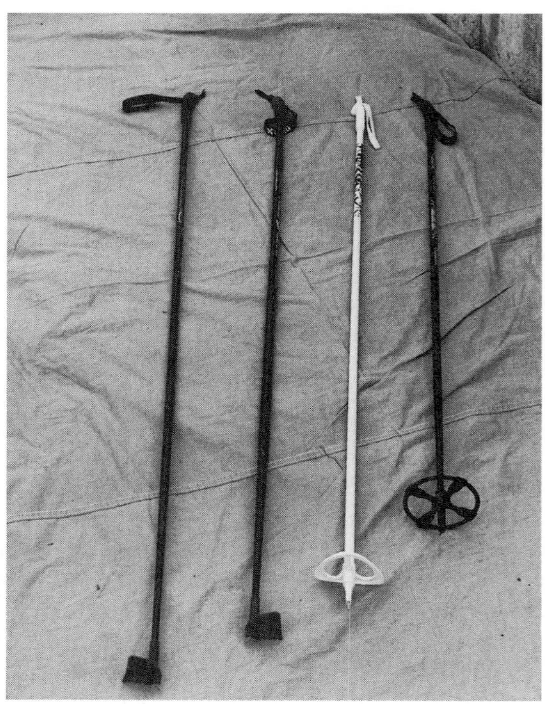

Figure 27-2. Cross-country ski poles.

Poles

Ski poles (figure 27-2) are important for a cross-country skier because they are used for both balance and pushing the skier forward. Beginners will quickly learn that downhill ski poles are not adequate for skiing cross-country. Cross-country poles are made of aluminum or carbon fiber and have three distinctive features. They are quite long and should fit comfortably under the skier's armpit while she or he is standing on a floor. Second, the tip of a cross-country ski pole is bent forward to allow for easy removal from the snow when the pole is well behind the sliding skier. Third, cross-country poles have a comfortable grip with an adjustable strap that allows the pole to stay attached to the skier's wrist even when not tightly gripped.

Poles come with a variety of baskets that are appropriate for different skiing conditions. Wide baskets can support the pole in deep, soft snow, while smaller, sometimes triangular baskets work well in packed, prepared-track ski conditions.

Skiers who intend to do much of their skiing using the skate technique should purchase ski poles that come up to their upper lip with the tip of the pole on the floor (90 percent of height). Longer poles are mandated by the increased stride length of the skate. The added length of the poles requires them to be much stiffer than traditional poles. Common skating-pole materials are aluminum or a graphite fiberglass blend.

Figure 27-3. Cross-country ski boots.

Boots

Cross-country ski boots (figure 27-3) vary to be compatible with the types of skis previously cited, with touring and light touring boots the preference for most recreational skiers. Although cross-country boots have long been made of leather uppers with leather or rubber soles, they are now also commonly made with synthetic soles and nylon, plastic, and even Gore-tex uppers. Despite these changes, several rules remain:

1. The ski boot should fit like a comfortable hiking boot or running shoe with the socks of the skier's choice.
2. Higher ski boots should be used because they provide more support and warmth than low-cut models.
3. The ski boot should be compatible with the type of ski and should tightly match the ski binding.
4. Cross-country ski boot soles should allow for maximum heel-to-toe flexibility while minimizing side-to-side movement.

Light touring boots suffice for most recreational usage because they provide a compromise among support, warmth, and flexibility. Skiers with unique podiatric or circulatory conditions should seek ski boots to accommodate their requirements. Fortunately, a wide variety of quality ski boots is available today.

Boots designed for skate skiing have stiffer soles and increased ankle support, yet are lightweight. They feature more lateral support and have less sole flexibility to absorb the demands of skate skiing.

Bindings

The modern advances of ski technology are also evident in cross-country ski bindings (figure 27-4). Traditional cable and three-pinned "Nordic norm" bindings have been challenged. As in many sports, the changes originated in racing skis and later were used in recreational skis. The changes have complicated a once simple decision. Modern bindings appear to work well when matched with the correct boot sole. The skier should carefully examine the compatibility of boots and bindings and check for lateral play between the two. The best boot-binding combinations feature a tight, positive attachment.

Many new bindings extend the entire length of the ski boot sole. They provide a heel plate or locator that keeps the boot stable when flattened to the ski.

CLASSICAL SKI TECHNIQUES

Getting Started

Correct cross-country skiing technique allows the skier to cover a wide variety of terrain in an effective and efficient manner. Technique is discussed here to help the skier make the sport more enjoyable and safe. First, the skier should practice putting on the skis and then simply walking about for a short distance with or without poles. Second, while on flat ground the skier should fall, if the snow is soft enough, and practice getting up. This exercise demonstrates the relative safety of cross-country skis. With the skis attached to the ski boots only at the toe, the skier should have little fear of slow-motion falls. Relaxation plays a major part in all ski techniques. The skier should take some time to become comfortable both walking and getting up from a fall.

Flat-Terrain Techniques

Diagonal stride

The basic stride of cross-country skiing is called the "diagonal stride" (figure 27-5), and it is the hallmark of sound cross-country ski technique. Besides being used on flat

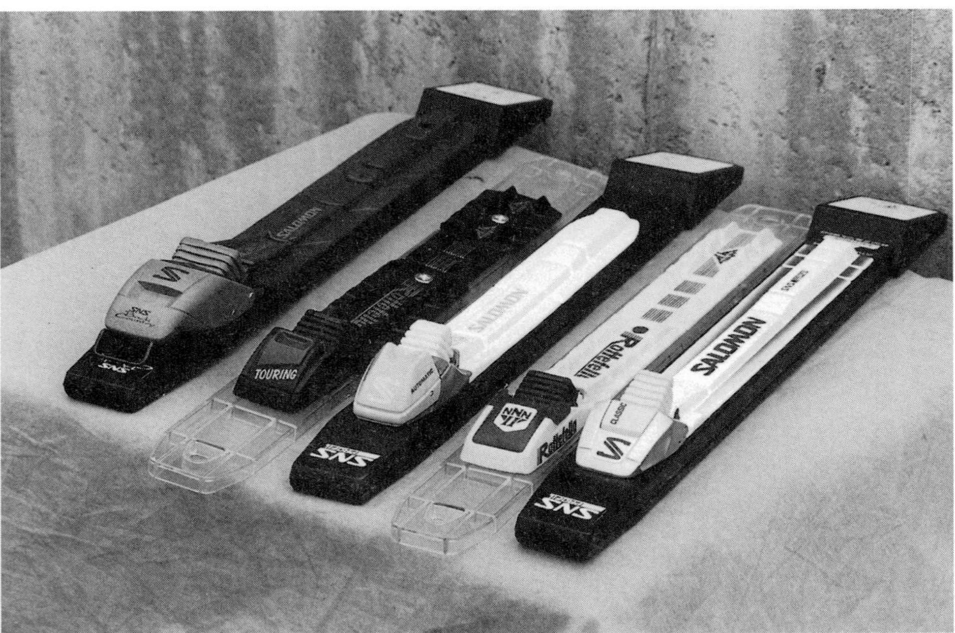

Figure 27-4. Cross-country ski bindings.

terrain, it can be adapted, depending on the skier's strength and ability, to uphill sections. The diagonal stride can be broken down into three distinct but overlapping phases: the kick, glide, and pole.

The kick phase begins with one leg kicking, or pushing, down against the snow and the opposite leg sliding or shuffling forward. The body leans forward from the hips as the skier's weight transfers to the bent front leg. The glide phase extends from this weight transfer until the time the pole in the skier's opposite hand is planted out in front. Remember that the left arm and right leg will be forward at the same time, just as in walking or running. The poling phase continues until the opposite leg begins to kick, beginning the next cycle. This rhythmic stride allows the skier to shuffle, using arms and legs for propulsion forward. The kick should be down, as well as backward, into the snow. The poling motion should markedly contribute to extending the skiers already initiated glide ahead and will require considerable effort with the arms for the beginner. The diagonal stride, seen as a whole, requires strength, balance, and coordination.

Double pole

Double poling (figure 27-6) can be used to maintain forward motion on slight downhills or on flat terrain as an alternative to the diagonal stride. The double pole can be defined as having two phases: the poling phase and the recovery-free glide phase. In the initial poling phase, the poles are planted as far forward as pole length and strength will allow and with the arms in a rigid but flexed position. Then the upper body flexes at the waist, propelling the skier forward. The arms push the poles back behind the skier, leaving the skier bent over almost horizontal to the ground with both arms extended behind. In the recovery phase, the poles are retracted from the snow and the body should come back up to the vertical as the arms prepare to reach ahead to begin the next pole. Much of the poling force should be provided by the upper torso—by the abdominal muscles in particular—rather than only by the arms.

Double pole with kick

This maneuver (figure 27-7) combines the upper-body motion of the double pole with a single kick, or "scooter push," of one leg, as in the diagonal stride, and serves as an efficient way to change pace while skiing. Practiced skiers mix these three techniques, depending on their level of fatigue and the demands of the terrain.

The double pole with kick is initiated by simultaneously reaching forward with both arms and pushing backward or kicking with one leg as described in the diagonal stride. The skier's body weight is now all on the forward ski, and the rear, or kicking, leg is extended. While the skier glides on one ski, both poles are planted as far forward as possible. The glide is now maintained by a double pole. The kicking leg returns to the snow as the body flexes over the poles.

The recovery phase is the same as in double poling. The double pole with kick requires some coordination and practice before mastery, but it is a relaxing technique to use

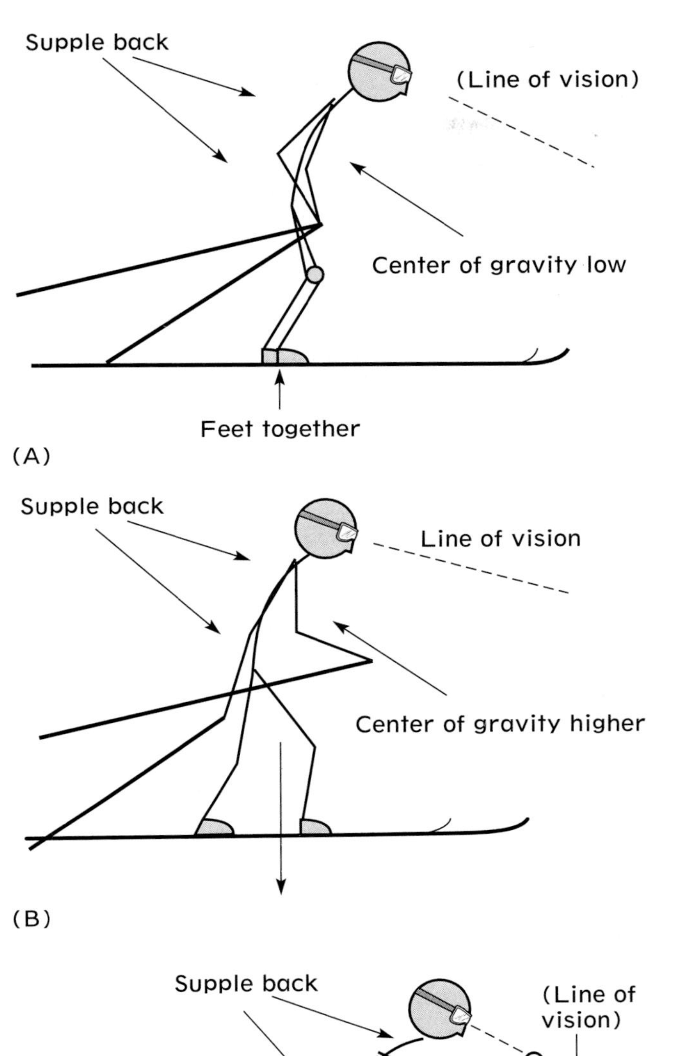

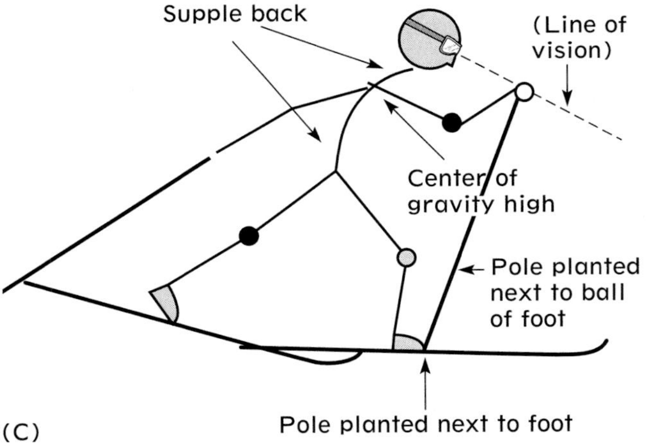

Figure 27-5. Diagonal stride. **A,** Middle phase. **B,** Kick initiation. **C,** Glide phase.

on flat or rolling terrain. The difference between the double pole with kick and the pure double pole is that in the pure double pole the kicking phase is excluded and only the poling motion provides the power to propel the skier down the track.

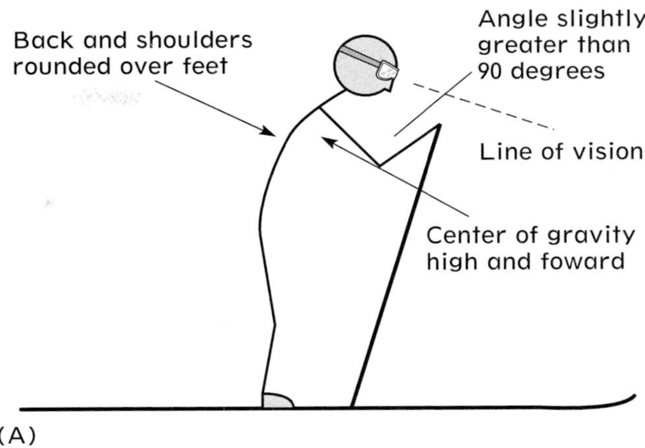

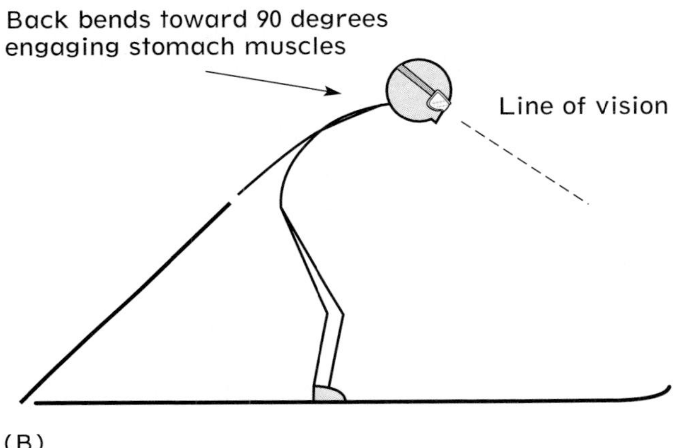

Figure 27-6. Double poling. **A,** Initiation. **B,** Follow-through.

Uphill Techniques

With practice and strength, all of the previously described techniques used on flat terrain can be applied to gradual uphills. Some adaptations must be made, particularly in the diagonal stride, in which the free-glide phase becomes shorter and the pole is planted back further than on the flats. Stride length decreases, and the gliding foot is pushed further ahead of the knee. Again, skiers should measure their capabilities and match them to the terrain. Other techniques exist for steep or otherwise difficult uphill stretches.

Herringbone

Here the skier uses the basic diagonal stride but angles both skies out (figure 27-8) to reduce the angle of the hill. The arms are kept low, with the poles forcefully pushed into the snow behind the skier. To help grip the snow, the inside edges of each ski are angled into the snow. A common error that occurs when executing the herringbone is to bend forward at the waist, so the skier should be aware of keeping the head looking up the hill and the heel down on the forward ski.

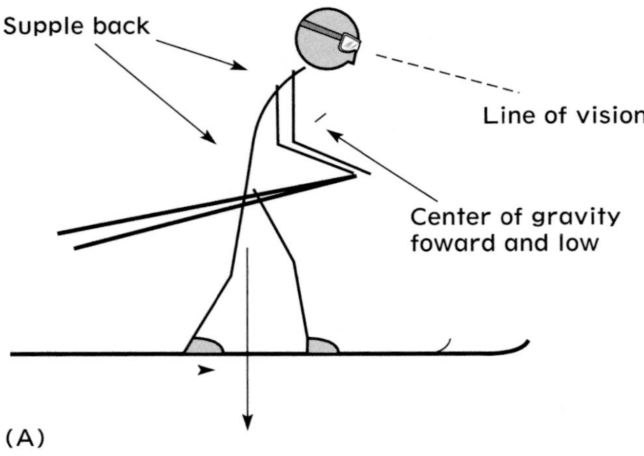

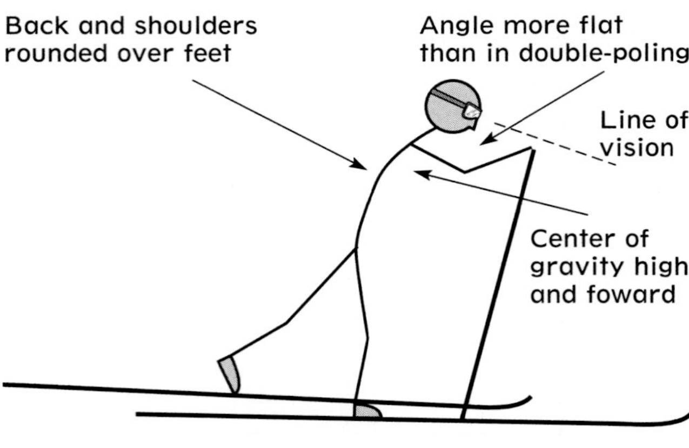

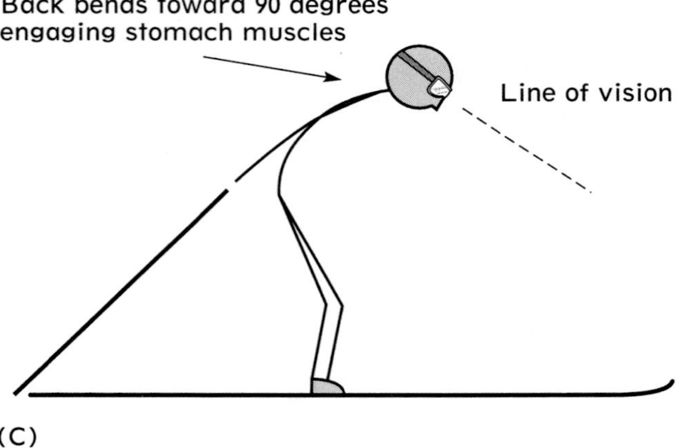

Figure 27-7. Double pole with kick. **A,** Kick initiation. **B,** Kicking phase. **C,** Follow-through.

Side step

On even steeper hills, the side step (figure 27-9) is a slower but certain way for beginners to get up. The skier stands with the skis going across (at a right angle to) the fall line of the hill (the imaginary line down the hill's steepest slope). The skier angles the skis into the hill and lifts the uphill ski, stepping up the hill about 1 foot (30 cm). The downhill ski follows, and the action is repeated. The skier should be certain that the skis remain perpendicular to the fall line and that the uphill edges of the skis are rolled into the hill.

Downhill Techniques

Straight downhill

Cross-country skis are designed to cut through the snow in a straight path with a minimum of resistance and therefore cannot be turned and maneuvered as readily as alpine skis on downhill situations. Velocity and direction can be controlled on cross-country skis using several simple techniques.

The basic downhill position of the skis should be a relaxed position with the weight evenly distributed on both skis. The skier must be conscious that the ski-boot heel is not attached to the ski and must keep his or her body weight pushing down on the heels. The term *soft knees* has been developed to explain the skier's relaxed, flexible stance that is needed to absorb the bumps in the terrain. The wedge (figure 27-10) serves as the basic technique used to control the skier's downhill descent. As the skier descends the hill, the tips of the skis are moved together as the tails are spread apart, forming a V-shaped ski position. To brake from this position, the skier wedges out the ski tails and pushes on the inside edges of both skis.

Wedge turn

From the controlled position just described, the skier can initiate a turn by shifting weight onto one ski, which turns the skier in the opposite direction. A good sign of a strong weight shift to one ski will be the shoulder of that same side rotating forward as the skis turn. Wedge turns can be linked together to form a controlled method of traversing and descending a hill.

Step turn

The step turn is the basic maneuver for changing direction on cross-country skis. The technique appears to be a simple movement, but requires the skier to commit almost all body weight to one ski and then to regain balance. While in the basic downhill position, the skier picks up the ski in the direction of the turn. The skier then plants that ski in the new direction and shifts the body weight to that ski. The trailing ski is then brought alongside the first ski to regain the basic downhill position. Emphasis should be placed on a smooth, complete weight transfer from one ski to the other. Several quick, small step turns are preferable to one wide-angle step adjustment, particularly at higher speeds.

Advanced downhill turns

Once the skier masters these basic downhill maneuvers, she or he can acquire other, more advanced downhill turns.

Figure 27-8. Herringbone on uphill. (From *Cross-country skiing today,* by John Caldwell. © 1977 by John Caldwell. Reprinted by permission of The Stephen Greene Press, a wholly owned subsidiary of Viking Penguin, Inc.)

Figure 27-9. Side step on gradual uphill. (From *Cross-country skiing today,* by John Caldwell. © 1977 by John Caldwell. Reprinted by permission of The Stephen Greene Press, a wholly owned subsidiary of Viking Penguin, Inc.)

(Refer to chapter 26 for an elaboration of other downhill turns that can also be done on cross-country skis.) In addition, the time-honored telemark turn still remains as a classic advanced cross-country ski maneuver.

SKATING TECHNIQUES

Skating requires different rhythms, skills, and strengths from the classical technique previously explained. Many beginners, particularly children, find skating to be more natural and easier to learn than the older kick-and-glide approach. Keep in mind that the movements explained here require adequate equipment (particularly longer poles) and skis without cross-country kick wax.

Marathon Skate

Skating (figure 27-11), a recent addition to cross-country ski technique, was popularized in ski racing by Bill Koch in his 1981–82 World Cup victory. The skate has revolutionized cross-country ski racing and has been adopted by most successful ski racers. The effects of this revolution are filtering down to citizen ski racers and ski tourers. Skating can be used as a replacement for the double pole with kick and the diagonal stride in situations where the skier wishes to maintain a relatively high velocity. This is most effective on crusty snow or on well-prepared ski tracks.

The skate is initiated with a double pole followed by a single kicking action of one leg. The poling motion is

Figure 27-10. Wedge on gradual downhill. (From *Cross-country skiing today,* by John Caldwell. © 1977 by John Caldwell. Reprinted by permission of The Stephen Greene Press, a wholly owned subsidiary of Viking Penguin, Inc.)

initiated at the time of the skate kick. The kicking ski is angled out at about 40 degrees, and the skier pushes out to the side by exchanging weight onto the kicking ski. The tails of the skis will slightly cross before the kick, and at the end of the kick the leg will be extended. In the recovery phase, the kicking leg is brought back completely over the ski track and followed by a glide phase. As a new technique, the skate has many variations, but the skier should practice skating with either leg and mixing it into the other, more traditional techniques. While learning the technique, use existing ski tracks on a level or slightly downhill trail. Practice the marathon skate using both feet as the skating foot.

V-1 Skate

Now the skier does not need set ski tracks, but just packed snow. The V-1, or asymmetric, skate gains its name from the V pattern that the skis etch on the snow. Here the skier steps out onto one ski and adds a double-pole motion. But instead of returning the ski into the track as in the marathon skate, the skier skates off onto the other foot as the arms recover. In total, this looks like a speed skater's motion with the lower body combined with a strong double pole. This creates a strong side action with one ski and the double poling motion. The skier should strive to get full weight exchange to both sides of the body. Try this on level terrain before moving to slight uphills. Common problems with beginners include not committing their full weight to the skating ski and allowing the skis to drift farther and farther apart when initiating the skate step. The two boots almost touch one another as they pass in their strides. Strength and coordination are required to use the V-1 on steeper and longer uphills.

Notice in figure 27-12 how the skier stays fairly erect and straightens the skating leg as he rides over the flat skating ski.

V-2 Skate

As the skating technique evolves, the V-2, or symmetric, skate appears to be the technique of the future. Now mostly used on flat or slightly downhill terrain by ski racers, future skiers will be strong enough and have enough balance to V-2 on the uphills.

The V-2 is performed in the same fashion as the V-1 except that the skier double poles on every skating step. Instead of having a strong and weak side, as in the V-1, the V-2 has a bilateral motion with a poling action on the left and right strides. The leg tempo must slow down to allow the arms to recover, and the poling motion is shorter and quicker.

Summary

Skating is a relatively new technique in cross-country skiing. In cross-country ski-racing events, classical and skating events exist side by side, in much the same way that different swimming strokes have their own events. They are just variations of self-propulsion on snow. Skating requires more strength, particularly in the upper body, yet it provides more freedom of motion. Beginners are encouraged to try both versions for the full enjoyment of all skiing techniques.

GUIDELINES FOR THE CROSS-COUNTRY COURSE

A cross-country course must be laid out to be a technical, tactical, and physical test of the skier. The degree of difficulty should be in accordance with the ability of the competitors.

Figure 27-11. Marathon skate at the end of the kick. (From *The cross-country ski book,* by John Caldwell. Reprinted by permission of The Stephen Greene Press, a wholly owned subsidiary of Viking Penguin, Inc.)

Figure 27-12. V-1 Skate. **A,** Front view. **B,** Rear view.

The cross-country course should consist of:

1. One-third uphill section with a climb between 9% and 15% plus some short climbs that are steeper (10% slope = 45 degrees).
2. One-third undulating terrain using all terrain features, with short climbs and downhill sections, and height differences of 5½ to 11 yards (5 to 10 m).
3. One-third varied downhill section demanding competence in all downhill skills.

Number of Competitors

Four men and four women from a team may compete in the individual event for the team score, with the highest finishing three in each to count in the team scoring. A relay team consists of three competitors.

WAXING

Cross-country ski wax is a unique chemical compound that allows cross-country skiers to get a grip, or purchase, on uphills. When properly selected and applied, cross-country, or kicker, wax alternately grips the snow crystals when weight is put on the ski and slides when the weight is released from the ski as in the glide phase of the cross-country ski technique. There is both an art and a science to cross-country ski waxing. It requires matching the ski and the skier's weight and technique to the snow conditions and temperature.

Before the revolutionary changes in skis from wood to synthetic-base surfaces and from straight bottoms to patterned or mohair no-wax surfaces, ski waxing was a reasonably straightforward procedure. Charts matching snow conditions to ski wax color were simple. Now, with the wide variety of skis and ski bottoms and wax and no-wax surfaces, waxing has become specific to each type of cross-country ski. (Written procedures go beyond the scope of this chapter.) Some suggestions will prove helpful for the beginner:

1. Follow the manufacturer's ski base preparation and waxing recommendations. These should come with the skis or be available from the retailer.
2. Adjust these basic waxing rules to your personal technique, needs, and local snow conditions.
3. Consistently use one or two brands of cross-country and alpine wax until you have mastered their entire range of waxes before moving on to other brands.
4. Even "no-wax" skis can perform better with the application of gliding, or alpine, wax on the nongripping portion of the ski bottoms. This will protect the ski against wear and damage as well as improve its gliding capabilities.

The skating technique simplifies cross-country ski waxing. Because the skier gets more power on the snow using the edge of the ski, no cross-country, or kick, wax is necessary. New silicon-based products can be applied to the full length of waxless skis for improved performance.

OFF-SEASON CONDITIONING

Because cross-country skiing is a winter sport, most cross-country skiers turn to other sports and recreational activities for the remainder of the year. Most cross-country participants engage in other outdoor pursuits that are in the same endurance-based, aerobic family of sports. The purpose of off-season conditioning should be to adapt the skier to the physical demands of skiing, allowing the skier to enjoy skiing when snow arrives. Cross-country skiing can be a demanding experience for those who have been dormant in the off-season. Keep in mind that ski tours, cross-country pursuits, and citizen ski races can extend for a matter of hours or an entire day, depending on the fitness and skills of the skier, so the skier's off-season conditioning should focus on gradually adapting the skier's conditioning for such adventures. Specifically, the skier should prepare for the demands (cardiovascular, muscular, and technical) required for his or her level of involvement. Some conditioning guidelines to remember are as follows:

1. Make cross-country training as enjoyable as possible. Find off-season pursuits that are fun. If possible, find other people to train with. This will provide companionship and a support system to maintain a training program.
2. Train in the off-season at the same level of intensity that you will use when skiing. Higher levels of conditioning for skiers require more-formal training programs and time. Be realistic in the goals for a cross-country ski season.
3. Conditioning that approximates cross-country skiing is more effective than general conditioning. Gear off-season training specifically to cross-country skiing if you are serious about ski fitness. An example of this is to train on terrain similar to that which will be skied in the winter.
4. Cross-country skiing is a total-body sport in terms of the demands placed on the skier. No individual can excel in all dimensions of skiing. Conditioning programs should place emphasis on the skier's weaknesses to produce more balance.

Cardiovascular Endurance Training

Cross-country skiing is a member of the cardiovascular endurance family of activities. For that reason, participating in any other endurance-producing activity in the off-season can be beneficial for skiing performance. Bicycling, jogging, orienteering, hiking, skulling, and rowing are common off-season alternatives. Canoeing, kayaking, and swimming, although not as commonly used, are also beneficial to off-season recreational skiers. The use of roller skis (figure 27-13) or roller blades is the most sport-specific form of off-season cardiovascular training. The use of a heart-rate monitor is strongly urged for skiers of all levels of ability. This allows the athlete to be aware of the stresses on his or her body.

Muscular Strength and Endurance Training

Cross-country skiing places demands on the strength and endurance of all the major muscle groups of the body. Besides the weight-lifting, weight-training, and circuit-training methods cited in chapter 41, the use of Universal and Nautilus exercise devices is helpful. The skier should not overlook hard physical labor, such as wood splitting, gardening, and chain sawing, as a means for developing muscular endurance. Cross-country trail clearing in the late autumn can be a foundation to snow-skiing fitness.

Figure 27-13. Off-season conditioning on roller skis. (From *The cross-country ski book,* by John Caldwell. Reprinted by permission of The Stephen Greene Press, a wholly owned subsidiary of Viking Penguin, Inc.)

The skating technique places a premium on muscle endurance and strength. Therefore, skaters should place emphasis on strength and muscle endurance training relative to their cardiovascular fitness.

Skill Training

As previously mentioned, off-season conditioning should closely approximate snow skiing. Skill training is a component that helps the skier master the technical aspects of skiing while in the off-season. Skill training minimizes the difficulty of the transition from off-season or dry-land training to snow skiing. Many ingenious forms of skill training have been developed by ski racers. Some are appropriate for the recreational athlete (such as roller skiing or roller blading). The simple addition of ski poles in hiking or jogging can improve both endurance and technique. Ski bounding and ski striding on gradual uphill slopes are other examples of excellent skill-training activities.

Roller skis are the most sport-specific tool relative to cross-country ski training. They provide excellent skill, cardiovascular, and muscle endurance training.

CLOTHING

The correct clothing for cross-country skiing can vary as widely as skiing and weather conditions. Few formal rules can be stated, but several guidelines are offered:

1. Dress in the same clothes you would wear if hiking in similar weather.
2. Wear loose fitting, nonbinding clothing, which will allow a wide range of motion.
3. Wear several light and warm layers, which provide more ventilation than a few heavy bulky layers (e.g., a ski parka). Next to the skin layers should be synthetic such as polypropylene, which allows for the transport of moisture away from the skin.
4. Always remember that hats, ear band, and gloves or mittens are essential.
5. Bring a change of dry shirts, socks, and footwear for after a ski tour.

Many ski tourers have found some of the new synthetic fibers that can provide warmth and windproofing to be ideally suited for the sport. A small backpack or fannypack can hold additional clothing and a trail snack.

SAFETY CONCERNS

Although cross-country skiing is a relatively safe sport, the participant should exercise caution, ski within his or her limits, and use common sense. When on a day-long tour, the following equipment should be included:

Small backpack	Screwdriver
Extra ski wax	Matches
Spare ski tip	Map and compass
Adhesive tape	Ample fluids
Knife	Extra food

Injuries are rare in cross-country skiing, but two emergency situations should be recognizable to all skiers: frostbite and hypothermia. Frostbite is the freezing of the surface layers of skin cells on exposed extremities of the body—usually ears, nose, chin, fingers, or toes. Frostbite can be prevented by keeping hands and feet—and face, in extreme cold—properly covered. Partners can check each other's faces to reveal any area lacking in circulation and appearing white or gray. Frostbite victims should be removed from the wind and cold as quickly as possible. Treatment for serious frostbite requires medical personnel.

Hypothermia is the gradual lowering of the core temperature of the body and can occur when a person is exposed to much wind, cold, and wetness. Hypothermia is most likely to occur when a skier is hungry, tired, and inexperienced about how to behave outdoors in the winter. Symptoms of hypothermia include lethargy, slurred speech, poor coordination, and shivering. Efforts must be made immediately to warm the person both by removing her or him from the cold and feeding hot fluids, if the person is conscious. Medical care is advised in serious cases. Hypothermia can be avoided by proper clothing, adequate feeding, and traveling within one's limits.

Cross-country skiers venturing away from prepared trails in the wilderness of Western states should be aware of and prepared for avalanches. These circumstances mark where cross-country skiing borders on ski mountaineering and demands particular respect and training for unstable snow conditions. Skiers who anticipate going into such environments—usually found in the Rocky Mountains and the Sierra Nevada—need information beyond the scope of this chapter. Skiers traveling in these conditions must carry special equipment, such as beepers and avalanche chords, for avalanche protection. Most cross-country skiers will avoid such steep terrain and deep-snow conditions.

TEACHING CONSIDERATIONS

1. Initial practice should include walking with skis on flat terrain. Practice lowering the body to the ground in a slow fall and getting up again until the skier is comfortable maneuvering the length of the skis.
2. Instruction should be consistent with the perceived purposes of the learner. Beginning recreational skiers will need only basic skills to make their initial experiences safe and satisfying. Do not attempt to teach all techniques in one period. Come back to more advanced techniques after participants have had an opportunity to use what they have learned. If possible, teach techniques on a need-to-know basis as students encounter conditions needing more advanced techniques. Consider the endurance level of participants when planning lessons. Beginners use more energy than skilled participants. Make beginning trails short.
3. Begin with flat-terrain techniques. The diagonal-stride and double-pole techniques should be sufficient for the beginner to enjoy a flat-terrain experience. Later lessons can incorporate the double pole with a kick or marathon-skate technique for students who are interested in speed.
4. Most cross-country experiences require only minor adjustments to the basic cross-country skiing techniques, which can be taught and practiced quickly on the appropriate terrain. Skiers who will experience steeper slopes will need basic instruction in how to get up and down a hill safely on their skis. The side step and herringbone should be taught as methods of getting up a steep hill. The straight-downhill ski technique will be sufficient for moderate inclines, but the wedge technique will need to be mastered to control speed on steeper inclines. These skills are not easily performed without practice or instruction on sloped terrain, and beginners should be encouraged not to attempt downhill skills on large slopes. The side step can be taught as a safety skill to get down a slope that is beyond the skier's skill level.
5. Keep instruction sessions short. Minimize listening time; maximize practice and opportunity to participate in a cross-country experience right away.

GLOSSARY

cardiovascular fitness The ability of the body to process oxygen to do work using the heart, lungs, blood vessels, and muscles.

citizen ski races Ski races designed for mass participation by recreational skiers. Citizen ski racers are considered skiers between elite ski racers and recreational ski tourers.

glide wax Sometimes referred to as "alpine, or speed, wax"; it can be applied to the tips and tails of skis to enhance ski speed. Used exclusively in skating.

kicker wax Sometimes referred to as "cross-country wax"; it is applied to a waxing zone of varying length in the middle of the ski. Kicker wax produces the grip allowing the skier to move uphill.

ski bounding An uphill running exercise designed to simulate the movement of skiing uphill. This is done in the off-season for skill and cardiovascular training.

SUGGESTED READINGS

Endestad, A., and Teaford, J.K. 1987. *Skating for cross-country skiers*. Champaign, Ill.: Human Kinetics. Combines the technique and training principles of skiing and speed skating.

Gaskill, S. 1997. *Fitness cross-country skiing*. Champaign, Ill.: Human Kinetics.

Gullion, L. 1990. *Ski games*. Champaign, Ill.: Human Kinetics. Designed for both Nordic and alpine skiing, helps children learn basic skills in a carefree, noncompetitive environment.

Gullion, L. 1993. *Nordic skiing*. Champaign, Ill.: Human Kinetics. A primary resource for students in a beginning-activity class or as a self-instruction guide.

National Collegiate Athletic Association. Current ed. *NCAA men's and women's skiing rules book*. Mission, Kan.: NCAA.

RESOURCES

Films and videotapes

Cross-country skating techniques for beginners with Bill Koch and Kari Swenson and *Cross-country skiing for beginners with Bill Koch* are both available from West One Video, 1995 Bailey Hill Rd., Eugene, OR 97405.

Cross-country skiing, Nordicross, Performance skiing-cross country skiing advanced, Telemarking and *World of cross-country skiing for beginners*. "How To" Sports Videos, P.O. Box 5852, Denver, CO 80217.

Cross-country skiing: The ultimate fitness sport. Sport Imaging, 562 Montague Rd., Amherst, MA 01002.

Gaskill, S. *Classic drills and techniques*. Eagle River Nordic, P.O. Box 936, Eagle River, WI 54521.

Skating and striding: Cross-country skiing and *Skiing cross-country with Jeff Nowak*. Karol Video, 22 Riverside Dr., Wayne, NJ 07470.

Reference

United States Ski Association, 1726 Champa St., Denver, CO 80202.

Skin and Scuba Diving

After completing this chapter, the reader should be able to:

- Appreciate the development of skin and scuba diving
- Understand the need for preliminary safety precautions
- Describe features of the equipment used in skin and scuba diving
- Understand the principles of diving physics and diving medicine
- Recognize the need for completing a nationally recognized scuba training program before attempting to scuba dive

The underwater world is relatively unexplored and filled with beauty beyond description. It is a world of greater depths than the highest mountain peaks and covers nearly seven tenths of the surface of the earth. It is inhabited by uncountable varieties of animal and plant life. It is a restless, dynamic, changing world possessing rhythm, design, movement, and power. Humans are inexplicably drawn to this underwater world. They must, however, proceed with care and skill. This underworld can be very dangerous. For these reasons the following information, though brief, is explicit, definite, and important for those who venture below the water's surface. In addition, completion of a nationally recognized scuba training program is required before attempting to scuba dive.

HISTORY

Exploration of the land surface and surfaces of the world's water masses dates from the beginning of human history, but exploration of the underwater world is a relatively recent adventure. Although Aristotle wrote about diving devices as early as 360 B.C., and the great historian Pliny in A.D. 77 described the use of breathing tubes for underwater activity, real opportunity for extended underwater movement and investigation did not occur until introduction of the scuba regulator in 1943 by Jacques-Yves Cousteau and Emile Gagnan of France.

The forerunners of modern methods of underwater exploration and sport are many. Early Greek and Roman strategists, in an effort to perfect the art of warfare, trained and equipped soldiers of strong swimming ability to approach enemy craft from below the water's surface. They were supplied with air through a short length of hollow reed. Soldiers of the fifteenth and sixteenth centuries were fitted with surface-breathing bags connected to the diver by means of a hose and leather hood arrangement and wore weighted shoes. These divers were restricted to the shallow depths because of their crude equipment. In his autobiography Benjamin Franklin described his development of hand and foot fins to facilitate faster swimming. In the early 1800s William Forder developed a metal helmet that covered half of a diver's body and was supplied with air from the surface by a hand-operated bellows. In 1837 Augustus Siebe developed a full dry diving suit with a rigid helmet. In the latter part of the 1800s the French developed a rubber diving suit and mask, supplied with air from a metal canister carried by the diver. A mechanical regulator was employed to control the flow of air. An American, C. J. Lambersten, patented a successful closed-circuit rebreathing unit in 1942. This unit was adopted by the U.S. Navy for underwater demolition teams, because with this equipment the diver's expired air did not bubble to the surface to reveal his position as he worked underwater.

Recently the design of the scuba has been refined and sophisticated, but the basic principle remains the same as the Cousteau-Gagnan design.

PRELIMINARY CONSIDERATIONS

The term *skin diving* is used to describe diving activity in which the diver uses mask, snorkel, and fins and holds his or her breath while swimming underwater. The term *scuba* is the acronym for "Self-Contained Underwater Breathing Apparatus" and refers to underwater swimming in which the diver adds to the basic skin diving items equipment designed to take an air supply beneath the surface. *Sport diving* is commonly used to refer to both skin and scuba diving activities.

Prerequisites

The student who wishes to learn scuba diving should locate a scuba instructor who holds *current certification from a recognized national agency* (NASDS, NAUI, SSI, PADI, or YMCA). Qualified instruction and subsequent certification in scuba diving are mandatory for the diver who wishes to purchase compressed air from a dive shop or diving resort. In addition, the student benefits from the experience of a qualified instructor.

Swimming test

One needs to be a reasonably proficient swimmer who is comfortable and relaxed in the water. The following swimming skills represent the minimum the student must be able to do before becoming certified.

1. Swim 200 yards (183 m) using any stroke desired
2. Tread water for 10 minutes

Medical examination

In addition to being a reasonably proficient swimmer, the student must be in sound medical health. The student will be asked to fill out a medical questionnaire prior to taking a class. The questionnaire will contain medical questions regarding the following areas:

1. Cardiovascular system
2. Pulmonary system
3. Neurological system
4. Otolaryngological system
5. Gastrointestinal system
6. Metabolic and endocrinological function
7. Hematological properties
8. Orthopedic considerations
9. Behavioral health

If any problems are indicated by the student, a physician will be required to approve the student for participation in scuba diving.

In addition, because venous gas emboli formed during decompression can result in fetal malformations, women should not dive during any stage of pregnancy.

SKIN DIVING

General Skills

Skin diving courses are taught by several different certifying organizations, such as PADI (Professional Association of Diving Instructors), NAUI (National Association of Underwater Instructors), and the YMCA. The performance requirements for these courses vary, but some of the common skills taught are:

1. How to examine, prepare, adjust, wear, and remove basic snorkeling equipment, including mask, fins, snorkel, booties, thermal protection, weight belt, and buoyancy control device.
2. How to safely enter and exit the water in a variety of conditions.
3. How to attain proper weighting.
4. How to breathe through and clear a snorkel. Clearing a snorkel is done through the blast or displacement method.
5. How to inflate and deflate the buoyancy control device.
6. How to swim and make surface dives using snorkeling equipment.
7. How to maintain direction underwater and use proper ascents.
8. How to communicate with and stay with a buddy.
9. How to remove and replace the weight belt at the surface in water too deep to stand.

Equipment

Items essential for skin diving are the mask, snorkel, and fins (figure 28-1). When diving in cold water, a diver should wear a neoprene wet suit or a dry suit. When a wet suit is worn, a weight belt must also be used to overcome the suit's buoyancy. Diving authorities insist that a personal floatation device, such as an inflatable vest or belt, is absolutely essential for safe diving.

Supplementary items of equipment are the surface float, such as a tire tube or paddle board, knife, game and collecting bags, diver's flag, compass, depth gauge, pressure gauge, watch, and photographic equipment. Some of these items are required by law in some states.

Mask

The mask keeps water from coming in contact with the eyes and eliminates distortion, thereby enabling the diver's vision to be limited only by the light and clarity of the water. It also prevents water from being inhaled through the nose. The mask should fit the face with comfort and provide a watertight seal when the diver is submerged. The lens should be made of safety glass, not plastic. The mask's adjustable strap should attach on or near the front of the mask to assure a snug watertight fit. Some models have a one-way purge valve for clearing water from the mask, but water is easily cleared from the mask without a purge. Required are masks with molded depressions that permit the diver to close off the nostrils by pressing with the fingers, facilitating easy clearing of the ears.

Snorkel

The snorkel is a tube that is held in the diver's mouth and extends above the surface of the water. It enables a diver to swim and breathe without lifting the head from the water. Although several types are available, a J-shaped semirigid rubber or plastic tube is the most advisable and popular among experienced divers. Those with ping-pong valves and rubber flutter valves are inefficient and not recommended for sport diving. A rubber or silicone mouthpiece allows the diver to maintain control of the tube and breathe with the head submerged for easy underwater viewing. The snorkel should have a soft rubber or silicone mouthpiece that is comfortable in the diver's mouth, permitting extended use without undue mouth fatigue.

Fins

Fins are mainly of two types: open-heeled and full-footed. Either is satisfactory, depending on the diver's preference, but an adjustable-strap model is usually preferred. The

Figure 28-1. Snorkels, masks, and fins.

adjustable-strap model requires the wearing of a neoprene "bootie" to ensure proper fit. The bootie increases comfort and makes beach walking much easier than having an unprotected foot. The purpose of the fins is to give extra power in swimming, not to increase speed. The fin should fit comfortably to allow circulation and prevent the feet from cramping, but it should be snug enough to be secure when going through the surf. Fins of extra-large design can cause undue fatigue, particularly when used by an untrained diver. Beginning divers should use a medium-sized fin of medium flexibility.

Exposure dress

Wet suits made of cellular-foam neoprene and designed to fit snugly over the whole body are preferred for most water temperatures. A small amount of water enters the wet suit, is quickly warmed by the diver's body, and then serves as insulation between the body and the surrounding water. For very cold water or long exposure times, a dry suit is required. Dry suits prevent water from entering by using latex seals at the neck and wrists. Both dry suits and wet suits increase the diver's buoyancy significantly, so weights must be worn to enable the diver to submerge and swim with ease.

Weight belt

The weight belt deserves special attention. Lead weights attached to a web belt or a padded weight belt with pockets are used to overcome buoyancy. Most important is the quick-release buckle, which must be capable of being operated with one hand. When any situation that could possibly lead to an emergency occurs, the diver must be able to release the weight belt and allow it to fall away free and clear.

Accessory equipment

Information about other equipment for skin diving may be found by consulting the references at the end of the chapter. However, no one should dive without a personal flotation device, such as an inflatable vest, in addition to a surface float. A good automobile inner tube with attached line makes a practical surface float for resting. A canvas or burlap bag tied to it serves to carry the diver's equipment.

Skin Diving Skills

All basic swimming strokes except the breast stroke are used for diving; however, the open, enlarged flutter kick with very loose knee action is the most common source of propulsion. Many divers alternate the dolphin kick with the flutter kick to help prevent fatigue. A strong kick allows the diver freedom for the hands and arms to carry equipment, take pictures, and pick up interesting objects. When the diver is swimming, the arms are usually trailed in a comfortable position at the sides and are not specifically in use (figure 28-2). This position allows for maximum balance and relaxation. However, when swimming in turbid (murky) water with poor visibility, the diver should extend both arms forward at full length to ward off undetected obstructions. When underwater, the diver should always swim as effortlessly as possible, conserving oxygen and thereby extending the length of "down time."

Figure 28-2. Skin divers in proper underwater swimming position.

Diving down

When in open water, the diver should use either the tuck or pike surface dive to submerge. If the dive must be made through kelp or other plant life or into unfamiliar water, a feet-first dive should be executed.

Hyperventilation

Some divers extend their down time by means of rapid and deep breathing with exceptionally full exhalations just before submerging. This practice, called "hyperventilation," combined with the exertion of swimming under water and a change in the normal regulatory responses of carbon dioxide and oxygen caused by the pressure changes, can cause anoxia (lack of oxygen) and result in blacking out or even possibly drowning. Instead, the diver should take two or three deep breaths and hold the final one at about two-thirds capacity to start the dive.

Clearing

When the diver submerges, the snorkel will be filled with water, but the air pressure in the diver's mouth prevents the water from entering it. Upon surfacing, the diver can blow out the water in the tube by a short forceful exhalation while keeping the face submerged.

Sometimes a small amount of water seeps into the face mask during the dive. To clear the mask, the diver should roll to one side, press the upper edge of the faceplate inward, and exhale through the nose into the mask. The water pooled in the bottom side of the mask is forced out by the air pressure. Care should be taken not to release hand pressure on the mask while still blowing; otherwise, water will flood into the mask through the released seal. Another method is for the diver to tilt the head back, press on the top of the mask, and exhale through the nose.

If the mask has a purge, make it the lowest point, seal the mask against the face, and exhale through the nose (figure 28-3A, B).

Equalizing pressure

To provide for comfort and prevent injury, it is essential that pressure inside and outside the eardrum always be equal. When the diver descends, pressure on the eustachian tube side of the drum and that developed by increasing pressure of water on the outside must be equalized. Swallowing and sliding the jaw from side to side will sometimes accomplish this. Pinching the nose while blowing gently against the closed nostrils can also equalize the pressure. However, other methods should be tried first because mucus can be forced into the middle ear with this technique. The diver must never use earplugs or place anything in the ears while diving.

A

B

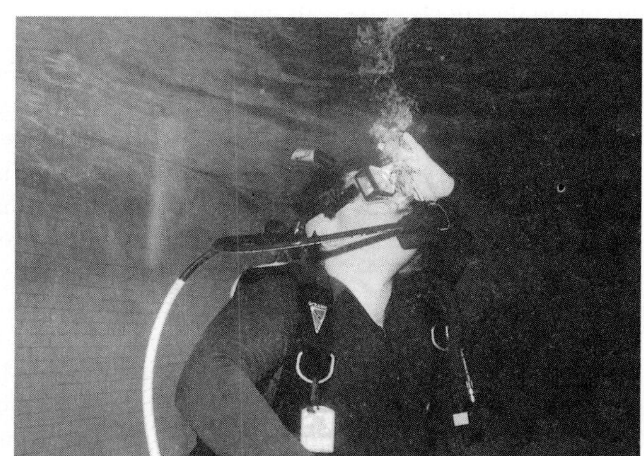

Figure 28-3. Clearing mask: head tilted back. **A,** Front view. **B,** Side view.

Entries

Always enter the water from as close to the surface as possible. When the entry is from a point well above the surface, such as the side of a boat that is not equipped with a diving platform, the entry should be made with a giant-stride feet-first jump. When executing this entry, cover the face mask with one hand to prevent it from being dislodged by the impact of the water. Keep other gear, such as a camera, well away from the body. Take a giant stride well away from the takeoff point, keeping the body erect and eyes looking forward. After settling in the water, level off and make an approach swim to the diving area.

Ascending

When ascending, extend one hand and arm overhead, look up, and keep turning 360 degrees. This method should always be used to ensure that the diver does not come up headfirst under another diver's tank, a boat, a floating object, or any obstruction that could cause injury.

Performance techniques

When beginning a dive, you should snorkel on the surface, pushing a tube in front with the face submerged until reaching the diving location. Swim easily, conserving energy and strength for the dive. The dive should be planned so that both buddies know the intentions of the other. A well-planned dive is the first step toward a safe dive.

Buddy diving

Never dive alone. Diving together and staying together take practice between partners, but must be done to ensure enjoyable and safe diving. You enter the water together, dive together, and leave the water together.

DIVING PHYSICS

As the diver goes beneath the water surface, he or she is aware of an increase in the surrounding pressure. This has an important effect on parts of the diver's body and the air the diver breathes.

The air mixture compressed in a scuba tank is atmospheric air, never pure oxygen, and contains the same gas percentages (78.62% nitrogen, 20.84% oxygen, 0.04% carbon dioxide, and 0.5% water) as atmospheric air. When these gases are breathed under pressure, as in scuba diving, several basic laws of physics must be carefully considered.

Boyle's law states that if temperature is constant the volume of a gas will vary inversely with the absolute pressure, while the density varies directly with the pressure. If the pressure of a gas is doubled, the volume is decreased by one half, but the density is doubled. This simply means that when a skin diver is descending, the air in the lungs is compressed; and as the diver surfaces, it expands. This phenomenon is important only to the skin diver diving to exceptional depths. If the scuba diver, breathing air at the ambient pressure (pressure equal to the surrounding water), does not exhale and breathe normally when ascending, the volume of air taken into the lungs at depth is going to expand as the pressure of the surrounding water is lessened during the ascent. This gas expansion can cause serious medical problems or result in a fatal injury.

Henry's law states that the quantity of gas that goes into solution in any liquid is directly proportional to the partial pressure of the gas. This means that if a quantity of liquid is capable of absorbing 1 quart of gas at 1 atmosphere of partial pressure, the same quantity of liquid would absorb 2 quarts of gas at 2 atmospheres. An understanding of gas absorption by the blood while diving is important to the diver in appreciating the need for computing a decompression dive.

Generally, we live under a constant pressure of 14.7 pounds per square inch (1.013×10^5 N/m^2), or 1 atmosphere (pressure decreases slightly as altitude increases); but when we dive beneath the surface of the ocean, we add about 0.445 pound per square inch for every foot (0.3 m) depth. When we reach the 33-foot (10 m) depth, we have added another 14.7 pounds per square inch (1.013×10^5 N/m^2) and are at 2 atmospheres of absolute pressure. For each additional 33 feet (10 m) we add another atmosphere of pressure. The diver must understand and appreciate the effects of this pressure of water and atmospheric pressure above the water. It is this pressure that causes pain in the diver's ear during descent, drives gas into solution, and presses the face mask against the face.

Sight and hearing are dramatically affected by the water. Because of the water's refraction and absorption of light, underwater objects appear to be about one third closer than their actual distance and about one fourth larger than their actual size. Sound travels much more rapidly in water than in air. When a tank is struck with a hard object such as a knife, the noise can be easily heard for quite a distance; however, it is more difficult to determine the direction from which the sound came in water than it is in the atmosphere. Communicating by voice underwater is very unsatisfactory, so divers must develop a system of hand signals that all divers in the party understand and are able to use.

SCUBA DIVING

Several types and arrangements of self-contained underwater breathing apparatuses enable the diver to take a supply of air below the surface. Scuba has been the greatest advance in the effort to explore the underwater world. Assuming a consumption rate of 0.5 cubic feet per minute, such equipment extends diving time to 140 minutes on the surface, 70 minutes at 33 feet (10 m), or 20 minutes at 99 feet (30.2 m). Scuba also frees the diver to swim with relatively complete freedom and to roam the depths at will. Although time and depths can be extended dramatically over skin diving limits, the novice scuba diver is cautioned to restrict depth of his or her first 25 or 30 dives to 60 feet (18.3 m). For normal sport diving a limit of 100 feet (30.5 m) should be used and the absolute limit of 130 feet (39.6 m) is recommended. However, no diving should be done without consulting U.S. Navy standard decompression tables (or their equivalent, such as PADI). These may seem to be unduly restrictive diving limits, but it is interesting to note that many amateur and recreational divers find their most interesting and enjoyable diving in about 35 feet (10.7 m) of water. Remaining within this depth limit enables the diver to stay down longer on each tank, have better light, reduce the chance of decompression sickness, and witness a greater variety of coral and animal life.

Equipment

Two general classifications are recognized: the closed-circuit, or rebreather, scuba and the open-circuit scuba. Although other equipment is sometimes used, only the open-circuit scuba means that all exhaled air is exhausted into the water and none is reused. In closed-circuit scuba the breathing gas is recirculated; the carbon dioxide is absorbed by granulated chemicals and the oxygen is added to a breathing bag as needed from a high-pressure supply tank. Open-circuit scuba uses compressed atmospheric air and never pure oxygen, as in closed-circuit scuba, because 100 percent oxygen becomes toxic when breathed under pressure greater than 29 pounds per square inch (even less for some people). This pressure is reached when diving deeper than 33 feet (10 m). The three main components of open-circuit scuba are the regulator, the tank, and the valve (figure 28-4).

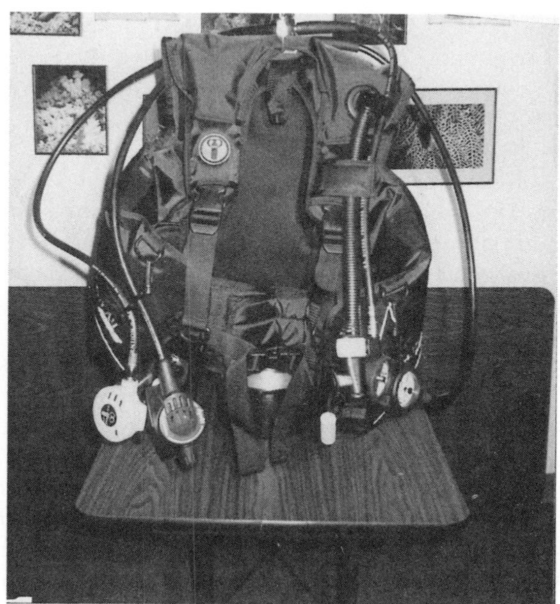

Figure 28-4. Open-circuit scuba gear.

Regulator

The regulator (figure 28-5) is the heart of the scuba. It is responsible for delivery of the diver's air at exactly the correct pressure whenever the diver inhales. For this reason the regulator is often referred to as a *demand* regulator, because it permits air to flow into the diver's mouth each time the diver demands it by the slightest inhalation. This inhalation causes a drop in the pressure on one side (dry side) of a rubber diaphragm. The water pressure on the other side (wet side) of the diaphragm is then able to push the diaphragm inward, which in turn activates a lever that opens a valve and allows air to flow through the diver's air hose. When the pressure on both sides of the diaphragm again becomes equal, the valve closes and the air flow is shut off. This pressure balance is regained when the diver discontinues inhaling.

Modern regulators are designed with a single hose. A detailed reference for specifications should be consulted to

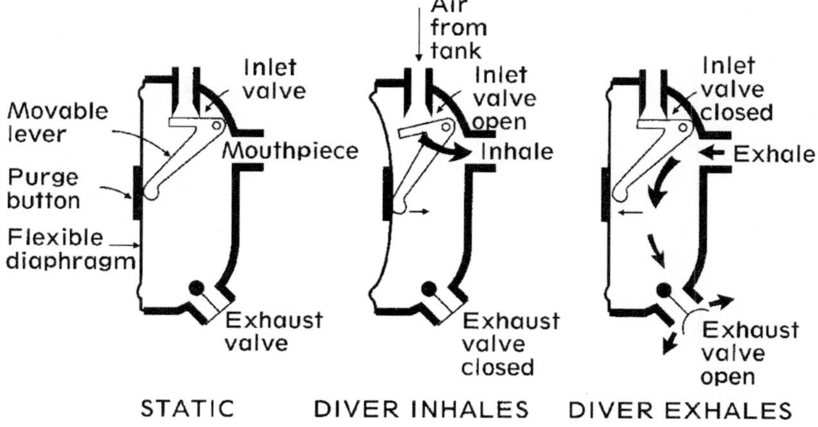

Figure 28-5. Regulator.

become familiar with their operation. At present the two-stage, single-hose regulator is the most widely used because of its reliability, ease of repair, and ease of breathing with it.

Valve

The valve is located between the tank and the regulator (figure 28-6). Basically, there are two types of tank valves: the constant reserve (J type) and the nonreserve (K type). The J valve mechanism (no longer very popular) is preset to provide air as long as tank pressure remains above 300 pounds per square inch (20.67×10^5 N/m^2), but below this pressure a spring-activated piston restricts the diver's air and breathing becomes difficult. This is a signal to the diver that the air supply is low and the serve lever should be pulled to open the reserve valve and allow the last 300 pounds of air to flow freely. The diver should end the dive at this time by returning to the surface station for another tank and rest period. Never continue diving when on reserve air, and always check to make sure the reserve lever is in the up, or loaded, position before entering the water.

The nonreserve, or K-type, valve has no reserve feature and is simply an on-off valve control. Divers using this valve usually attach an air pressure gauge to their regulator to keep themselves constantly informed about the air remaining in the tank. The K valve with a pressure gauge is the most widely used type.

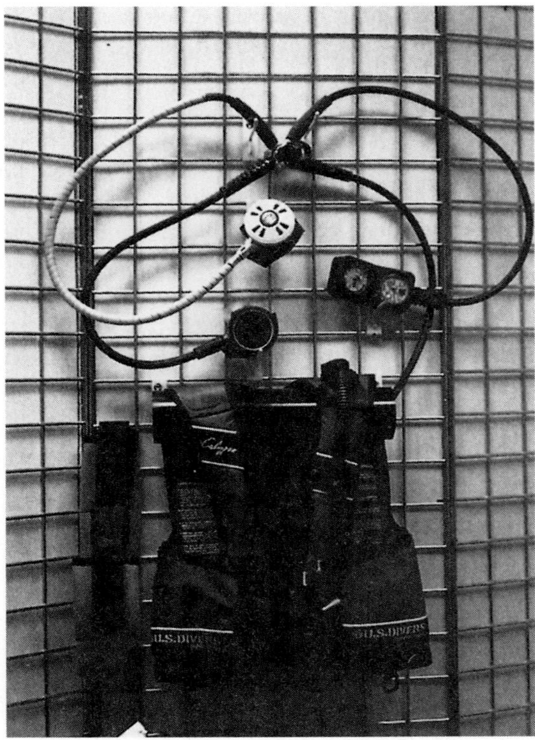

Figure 28-6. Scuba diving equipment—BC, valve and pressure gauge.

Tank

Air cylinders for diving are available in many sizes and in single, double, and triple units. The size and air pressure of the tank generally determine the time a diver can remain submerged. However, breathing rate, water temperature, depth, and working rate are also important determinants of underwater time. The tank size usually recommended is the "standard 80." This means the tank contains 80 cubic feet of air when filled to 3,000 pounds per square inch.

Backpack

The backpack must be fitted with quick-release buckles or safety hitches and must never impede removal of the weight belt. The backpack must secure the scuba to the diver with comfort and allow freedom of movement in all positions.

Scuba Diving Skills

Scuba diving skills are taught by several different certifying organizations. Skills are learned in the swimming pool and then later applied in the open-water check-out dives. The performance requirements for scuba courses vary, but some of the common skills taught are:

1. How to examine, prepare, adjust, wear, use, and remove scuba equipment. Scuba is an equipment-intensive sport, and proper usage of and care for the equipment are very important.
2. How to enter the water (figure 28-7), check and adjust buoyancy, and perform a proper descent and ascent. These are skills that are used every time a diver goes diving. Following appropriate techniques when entering and descending, achieving neutral

Figure 28-7. Giant stride standing entry.

buoyancy while diving, and ending the dive with a correct ascent are important to the enjoyment and safety of the diver.

3. How to breathe through a regulator and how to relocate and clear a regulator that comes out of the diver's mouth. Proper breathing is easy because it is not too different from breathing on land.
4. How to remove water from a mask, remove and replace the mask, and swim and breathe underwater without a mask. It is common for small amounts of water to come into the mask, so the diver must know how to easily remove it. Also, in the unlikely event that the mask becomes dislodged, the diver needs to know how to replace it and remove the water.
5. How to respond to an out-of-air situation. Five options are taught: Normal ascent, alternate air ascent, emergency swimming ascent, buddy breathing, and emergency buoyant ascent are all methods for a diver to return to the surface low on or out of air. The one to choose is dependent on the situation.
6. How to deal with leg cramps or tiredness. Oversized fins can cause cramping, and overexertion can be caused by a number of situations.
7. How to navigate underwater using a compass. Principles of navigation are generally taught in specialty classes, but new divers need some exposure to navigation techniques.
8. How to remain at a given depth through proper buoyancy control. Buoyancy is one of the most important skills a diver can learn. Proper buoyancy conserves air, reduces exertion, and protects the reef from misplaced hands and fins.

The following skills should be mastered under the observation of a trained instructor before attempting to scuba dive.

Entries. When entering and exiting through the surf while wearing a scuba, the diver must remember that, although carrying a supply of unrestricted air, he or she is more vulnerable to wave action in the surf and can be easily tumbled and thrown about when attempting to stand. When exiting through the surf, the diver should remain in an extended swimming position until well up on the beach before attempting to stand, then quickly turn about and shuffle backward until clear of all surge and water action.

When entering from an elevated point, boat dock, or land, the diver should use a feet-first entry, but never into unknown water. The diver should grasp and protect the mask with one hand, as in the skin diving entry, and with the other hand hold the weight belt buckle to prevent it from releasing accidentally.

When entering unknown water, the diver should make a feet-first drop or slide-in entry. Other methods, such as forward and backward rolls, may be used when appropriate for conditions.

Submerging and swimming without a mask. Replace and clear the mask without surfacing. (See skin diving skills for clearing.)

Mouthpiece clearing. Remove the mouthpiece underwater. Return it to the mouth, give a short, sharp exhalation to clear it of water, and resume breathing. Use the purge valve if available. Always take the first breath slowly after clearing the snorkel or mouthpiece of the regulator.

Buddy breathing. Two divers share one air supply. The diver with air passes the regulator mouthpiece to the buddy, who receives and clears the mouthpiece and takes two breaths before returning it. The diver with the air supply always retains control of the mouthpiece. The second diver uses the hands to help swim and keep the two divers close together. Buddy breathing is no longer required to be taught, because most divers now have an octopus setup on the regulator (see figure 28-4) that allows an out-of-air diver to breathe through an auxiliary second stage.

Free ascent. Practice of this skill will help the diver remain calm if his or her air supply is lost. In this situation the diver looks up, starts a controlled ascent with one arm extended over the head, and exhales continuously for entire ascent. The diver's instructor, with air functioning and mask in place, must always accompany the free-ascending diver to the surface.

Buoyancy testing. Buoyancy testing is essential because the addition of scuba equipment adds several pounds of weight that tends to overcome the buoyancy of the diver. Weights should be added or subtracted to allow the diver to float at eye level with a normal breath of air.

DIVING MEDICINE

Most diving disorders or medical problems in diving are classified as barotrauma, or a change in normal conditions because of changing pressure. Usually it is an injury resulting from unequal pressure between a space inside the body and the outside water pressure. The cavities of the middle ear and the sinuses are most susceptible to changing pressure, but serious problems can also develop from pressure on the breathing gas. Nitrogen narcosis, oxygen toxicity, and carbon monoxide poisoning are examples of these disorders. Some of these problems and their causes, symptoms, and treatment appear in table 28-1.

TWELVE BASIC RULES

1. Be in top physical condition and have an annual medical examination.
2. Be comfortable in the water.
3. Secure certified training in the use of scuba from a recognized agency.
4. Use safe, time-proven equipment from reputable manufacturers.
5. Be familiar with the diving area *before* diving.
6. Know the basic laws of diving physics and physiology.

(continued on p. 421)

Table 28-1 DIVING DISORDERS

Disorder	Cause	Symptoms	Treatment
Drowning	Physical exhaustion; running out of air; loss of mask or mouthpiece; flooding of apparatus; entanglement	No respiration; blueness of skin	Immediate artificial respiration, preferably by mouth-to-mouth method; start at once
Air embolism	Failure to breathe normally or holding breath while ascending results in blockage of circulatory system by excessive pressure rupturing lung tissues and allowing air to enter bloodstream	Weakness; dizziness; loss of speech; paralysis of extremities; visual disturbances; staggering; bloody, frothy sputum; unconsciousness; death can occur within seconds after reaching surface, if not before	Recompress immediately to 74 pounds per square inch (165 feet or 50 m); medical care; provide oxygen immediately
Decompression illness (bends or caisson disease)	Bubbles of nitrogen expand in bloodstream and tissues of body from inadequate decompression following exposure to pressure; nitrogen absorption depends on depth, time, and working rate; nitrogen more soluble in fatty tissues	Skin rash; itching; pain deep in joints, muscles, and bones; choking; visual disturbances; dizziness; convulsions; weakness in arms and legs; loss of hearing or speech; paralysis; unconsciousness; death	Recompress by Navy treatment tables; if caught early, there are usually no serious aftereffects; provide oxygen immediately.
Nitrogen narcosis	Intoxicating effect of nitrogen when breathed under pressure; no prevention except to avoid deep diving; occurs usually at about 130 feet (39.6 m), though reported at 30 feet (9.1 m)	Loss of judgment and skill; feeling of intoxication; slowed mental activity; fixation of ideas; similar to alcohol intoxication	Stop work; reduce pressure; effects disappear when ascending; no aftereffects
Oxygen poisoning	Using pure oxygen; depends on carbon dioxide tension and work rate; not probable on compressed air until about 132 feet (40.2 m)	Nausea; dizziness; headache; twitching of muscles around mouth and eyes; disturbance of vision (tunnel vision); numbness; unconsciousness	Surface; rest; medical care; never dive below 30 feet (9.1 m) on pure oxygen; use only compressed air in tanks
Carbon monoxide (CO) poisoning	Contaminated air supply from internal-combustion engines; improperly lubricated compressors; carbon monoxide combines with blood, causing internal asphyxiation; improper exhalation	Lips and mouth are bright cherry red; 10% in blood causes headache and nausea; 30% causes shortness of breath; 50% causes helplessness; may seem to be all right on bottom but lose consciousness on ascent	Surface; artificial respiration if not breathing; oxygen; medical care
Apnea	Hyperventilation and extended dives in skin diving	No true warning symptoms (except moment of blackness before total unconsciousness)	Fresh air; artificial respiration; do not hyperventilate excessively
Squeeze	Pressure differential over concerned area; middle ear and sinuses usually first place where pain felt; also face mask, suit, lung (thoracic) squeezes	Usually sharp pain due to stretched or damaged tissues; damage can occur without pain, however	Equalize pressure on affected areas

7. Always use a float with surface identification, usually a diver's flag.
8. Join a reputable diving club.
9. Never dive alone.
10. Practice skin diving frequently *before* scuba diving.
11. Heed all pains and strains as warning symptoms.
12. Know basic first aid.

TEACHING CONSIDERATIONS

1. Scuba diving should not be taught by anyone who does not hold current certification as an instructor by a recognized national agency. Information needed goes beyond that described in this text.
2. Scuba diving cannot be taught to anyone who cannot pass the swimming test or medical examination.
3. Beginning skin diving skills can be taught in a pool. Students should be cautioned, however, that practice in the pool is not adequate for skin diving in large bodies of water.
   a. Maintain the buddy system.
   b. Familiarize students with use of equipment before diving. Practice using the equipment on the surface.
   c. Practice dives using proper ventilation techniques.
   d. Practice diving, clearing and equalizing pressure, and ascending techniques.
   e. Practice surface snorkeling, diving, clearing and equalizing pressure, swimming to a point, and ascending.

GLOSSARY

absolute pressure True pressure; gauge pressure plus 14.7 pounds.
air embolism Air bubble in the bloodstream that occurs when the diver attempts to surface while holding his or her breath.
anoxia Oxygen deficiency.
aqualung Tank containing compressed air.
atmospheric pressure Air pressure at sea level is 14.7 pounds per square inch (1 atmosphere). It increases at the rate of 0.444 pounds per square inch for each foot (0.31 m) of depth in seawater.
BCD Buoyancy control device.
bends Too much nitrogen in the bloodstream. It expands as the diver ascends.
Boyle's law At a fixed temperature, the volume of a given quantity of gas varies inversely with its absolute pressure.
buoyancy Upward force exerted on the immersed or floating body by a fluid.
compressor Used to fill scuba tanks with air.
decompression Release from pressure.
dry suit Waterproof neoprene exposure suit used by divers.
face mask A mask equipped with faceplates to increase a diver's vision.
fins Devices worn on the feet to increase kicking power.
hyperoxia Too much oxygen in body tissue.
hyperventilation Respiratory activity in excess of that required to meet the body's normal requirements.
nitrogen narcosis Diving ailment resulting when a diver goes too deep and the nitrogen in the air supply begins to have a narcotic effect.
recompression Treatment of decompression sickness or air embolism by use of a recompression chamber.
regulator Device used for the adjustment and automatic control of air flow.
scuba *S*elf-*C*ontained *U*nderwater *B*reathing *A*pparatus.
skin diving Diving without the use of underwater breathing apparatus.
snorkel J-shaped tube that projects above water at one end and terminates with a mouthpiece underwater.
tank Air cylinder used by divers.
tidal volume Volume of air inhaled and exhaled normally.
toxic Poisonous.
weight belt Belt of lead weights used to overcome buoyancy.
wet suit A close-fitting suit constructed to trap a thin layer of water against the body to retain body heat when diving in cold water.

SUGGESTED READINGS

Graver, D. 1993. *Scuba diving*. Champaign, Ill.: Human Kinetics.
Navy Department. Current ed. *United States Navy diving manual*. Washington, D.C.: U.S. Government Printing Office.
Pierce, A. 1985. *Scuba life saving*. Champaign, Ill.: Human Kinetics.
Professional Association of Dive Instructors. Current ed. *PADI open water diver manual*. Santa Ana, Calif.: PADI.
Robinson, J., and Fox, A. 1987. *Scuba diving with disabilities*. Champaign, Ill.: Human Kinetics.

Periodical

Skin Diver Magazine, 8490 Sunset Blvd., Los Angeles, CA 90069.

RESOURCES

Videotapes

Ghost fleet, How to use dive tables, Learn snorkeling, and *Scuba refresher course*. These four programs available from "How-To" Sports Videos, P.O. Box 5852, Denver, CO 80217.
Scuba and snorkeling classes, Scuba Joe Dive and Travel Center, 3156 28th St., Boulder, CO 80301.

Soccer

After completing this chapter, the reader should be able to:

- Appreciate the history and sociocultural values of the most popular sport in the world
- Understand the rules and spirit of the game
- Demonstrate proper technique associated with the fundamental skills of the game
- Understand the game's basic offensive and defensive principles
- Understand effective teaching progression involved with skill acquisition
- Demonstrate a thorough knowledge of soccer terminology

HISTORY

The roots of soccer are grounded in antiquity. Some believe that soccer's origins can be traced to the ancient (2500 B.C.) Chinese game of tsu-chu, or kickball. The Egyptians (2000 B.C.), Japanese (600 B.C.), ancient Greeks (Episkyros), and Romans (Harpastum) have also been intimately linked with the evolution and spread of the game. The Roman legions under Emperor Claudius (A.D. 43) are credited with carrying the game to Britain; where it was integrated into the local games and evolved, grew, and developed from the Middle Ages through the industrial revolution.

The modern form of soccer gained its renowned shape and identity in October 1863, in London's Freemason's Tavern, where the first football association (English Football Association) was established and the laws of the game were formulated. The laws served to separate association—"assoc" football (soccer)—and rugby. The kick-in was replaced by the throw-in (1863); offsides (1866), corner kick (1872), and referees (1874) were added, as were the whistle (1878), the penalty kick (1891), and various numbers of substitutions. Thus, the modern game of soccer was off and running, and wherever England's ships gained port, soccer was soon to follow.

Contemporary soccer is truly an international game, with the Fédération Internationale de Football Association (FIFA), established in 1904, representing approximately 170 nations. Soccer was introduced to the Olympic Games in Paris in 1900, and the inaugural World Cup was played in 1930 in Montevideo, where the Uruguayan hosts defeated Argentina. Since then, such luminaries as Pele, Charlton, Cruyff, Beckenbauer, Maradona, Romanrio, Ronaldo, and Roberto Baggio have served to spread the passion of the game around the world.

The United States Soccer Federation (USSF), founded in 1913, serves as the governing body for most U.S. soccer interests. Since 1972, the USSF has offered coaching certification, as does the National Soccer Coaches Association. The United States Youth Soccer Association (USYSA), formed in 1974, is charged with the development and promotion of the game for those under age 19. Each of these affiliated organizations is attempting to build positive links to all communities by offering bilingual coaching courses, to promote not only the sport but also community solidarity. Today soccer is one of the most popular participatory sports for young boys and girls and has emerged as an intercollegiate favorite, with over 1,200 teams competing each year. The U.S. women's team captured the inaugural Women's World Cup in Beijing, China, in 1992, and in 1994 the United States opened its doors to the global soccer community to host the World Cup for the first time. It was won by the team from Brazil. The 1998 World Cup was won by France. In the 1996 Olympic Games in Atlanta, the United States women's team won the gold medal, and the men's team held its own with the rest of the world. Nigeria won the men's gold medal.

The impact of the United States' hosting the 1994 World Cup led to the emergence of the Major League Soccer (MLS), which initiated play in the summer of 1996.

THE NATURE AND SPIRIT OF THE GAME

Soccer is the most popular sport in the world, and it is also one of the most demanding. Soccer's intricacies have been described as playing chess at 30 miles per hour—referring to its cardiovascular, cognitive, competitive, and psychomotor challenges. Soccer can be played in industrial and less developed nations, by young and old, by boys and girls, by elite and physically or mentally challenged, and on beaches or in massive stadiums. All that is needed is a ball and willing participants, and the spirit of the game (unwritten laws of fair play and honor).

THE GAME, BALL, AND PLAYERS

A soccer match is contested by two teams of 11 players each (with an appropriate number of substitutes), one of which is designated the goalkeeper. The object of the game is to score by propelling the 14- to16-ounce (400 to 457 g) no. 5 ball (27 to 28 inches [69 to 71 cm] in circumference) completely across the goal line and within the confines of the 8 × 24-foot (2.44 × 7.32 m) goalposts and crossbar. The game is begun—after one team has won the coin toss and has elected to defend a goal—by a kickoff from the center of the field (the ball must move or be touched before it can be played by another player). The game is restarted in a similar fashion after each goal and at each half, or period. The duration of the game consists of two 45-minute halves and typically a 10- to 15-minute half-time break, after which the teams exchange ends. High schools and colleges have adopted an overtime procedure for those games ending in a tie score. The high schools play two 10-minute periods, while the colleges play two 15-minute periods. All phases and dimensions of the game may be modified to accommodate the individual needs of the participants. Examples of game durations, ball and field sizes, and age modifications are shown in table 29-1.

Once play has been legally initiated, each team attempts to gain possession, and through planned and creative combinations of the fundamental skills (passing, shooting, heading, trapping, dribbling, tackling and marking, and goalkeeping) attempts to place the ball in the back of the opponent's net. It is hard to believe that these seemingly simple skills placed in a competitive environment have captured the hearts of hundreds of millions of players and spectators. Indeed, more people watched the World Cup than watched man take the first step on the moon!

FIELD OF PLAY (Figure 29-1)

The field, sometimes referred to as a pitch, is rectangular, typically 120 × 70 yards (110 × 64 m). International FIFA-sanctioned matches must be played on grass fields that are between a minimum of 110 × 70 yards (100 × 64 m) and a maximum of 120 × 80 yards (110 × 73 m). The field is bounded by lines no more than 5 inches (12.7 cm) in width running the length of the field (touchlines), as well as the field's two goal lines. The field is divided into two equal parts by a halfway line, upon which is centered a circle with a 10-yard (9.1 m) radius, where play is started at the beginning of each half or after a goal is scored. There is a penalty area at each end of the field that begins 18 yards (16.5 m) beyond each goalpost on the goal line and extends at right angles another 18 yards (16.5 m) into the field. The capstone line (44 yards [40.2 m]) enclosing the box designates where the goalkeeper can legally handle the ball, as well as the area where a penalty kick may be awarded. Within the penalty area is the penalty kick mark, located 12 yards (11 m) from the center of the goal line. The goal area is also found within the penalty box, extending 6 yards (5.5 m) from each goalpost and boxed in with a 20-yard (18.3 m) capstone line paralleling the goal mouth line. Goal kicks are taken within this rectangular area. At each corner of the field, an arc (quarter circle) with a radius of 1 yard (0.9 m) is drawn where corner flags at least 5 feet (1.5 m) high are placed and corner kicks are taken.

GOALS

The goals, centered on each goal line, consist of two upright posts 8 feet (2.44 m) high and 24 feet (7.32 m) apart, joined at the top by a horizontal crossbar measuring 24 feet (7.32 m). Goalposts are typically made of wood, tubular metal, or plastic, not exceeding 5 inches (12.7 cm)

Table 29-1. GAMES MODIFICATIONS FOR AGE

Player age	Game length	Overtime periods
Adults	Two 45-minute halves	Two 15-minute halves
Under 16	Two 40-minute halves	Two 15-minute halves
Under 14	Two 35-minute halves	Two 10-minute halves
Under 12	Two 30-minute halves	Two 10-minute halves
Under 10	Two 25-minute halves	Two 10-minute halves
Under 8	Two 25-minute halves	Two 5-minute halves
Player age	**Ball number and weight**	**Ball circumference**
Under 14	No. 5, 14–16 ounces (400-457 g)	27–28 inches(69-71 cm)
Under 12	No. 4, 11–13 ounces (314-371 g)	25–26 inches (64-66 cm)
Under 8	No. 3, 8–10 ounces (229-286 g)	23–24 inches (58-61 cm)
Player age	**Goal size**	**Field size**
Under 12	7 × 21 feet (2.13 × 6.40 m)	90 × 50 yards (64 × 46 m)
Under 8	6 × 18 feet (1.83 × 5.49 m)	70 × 35 yards (73 × 50.3 m)

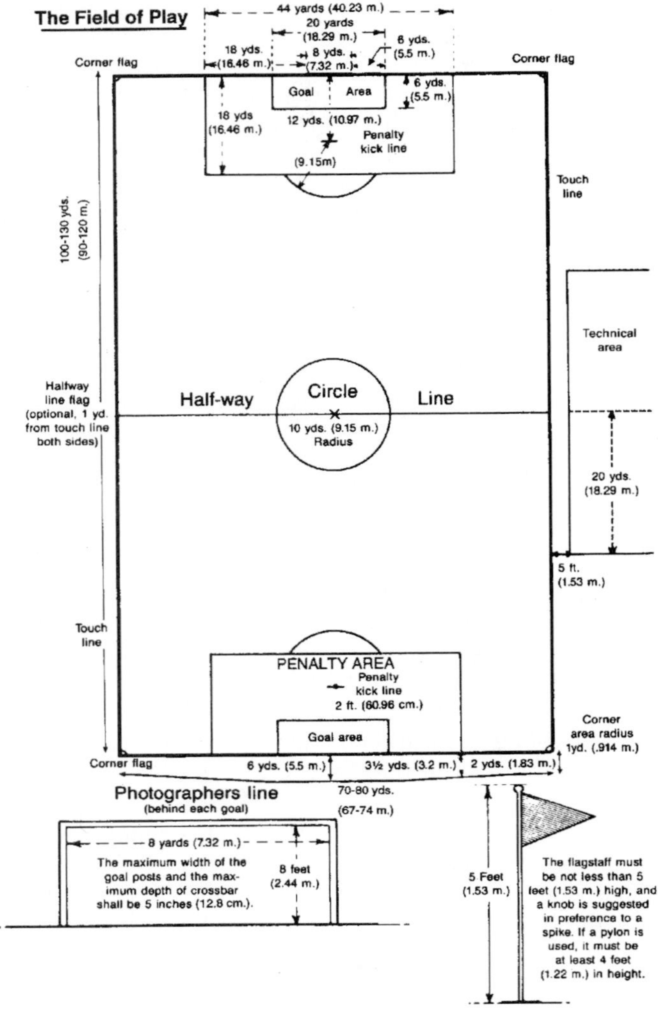

Figure 29-1. Soccer field.

in width or depth. Nets are made of hemp, jute, or nylon, and they should be attached to the back of the crossbar and goalposts, extending behind the goal so as not to interfere with the play of the goalkeeper.

TECHNICAL AREA

The technical area (coaching box) can be helpful in the management of the game. A box is marked at least 5 feet (1.53 m) from and parallel to the touchline and extending 20 yards (18.29 m) in both directions from the halfway line. Coaches and players should remain inside the technical area, except when players are warming up in preparation to substitute, which typically occurs with permission of the referee at the halfway line of the field.

EQUIPMENT

Soccer is one of the most economical team sports played. The only requirements are a ball, appropriate footwear (flats or spikes), shin guards, mouth guard, athletic supporter (for males), shorts, shirt (in different color for the goalkeeper), and socks, along with the field equipment consisting of goals, nets, corner flags, and a lining machine. Cones are also very useful for practice sessions and are a solid investment. Rings, jewelry, and glasses should be left at home or with a friend!

OFFICIALS

Soccer matches are presided over by a referee and two assistant referees. The two assistant referees run the touchlines

Figure 29-2. Official soccer signals.

(opposite sides and halves) and signal when a ball completely crosses the touchline (throw-in), goal line (goal kick or corner kick), or goal. They also may indicate fouls and offside infractions, usually by snapping their flags in the direction of the team that is to maintain ball control (figure 29-2). In all cases, however, it is the referee who calls (whistles) or does not call the infraction and awards possession of the ball or goal. The assistant referees serve as "advisors" in this regard. The referee usually keeps the official time on the field, at least for the last several minutes of the game to allow for injury or extra time. The officials' objective is to allow play to be free-flowing and within the spirit of the game while maintaining optimal safety for the participating players.

OUT OF BOUNDS (RESTARTS)

Once the ball completely crosses (either in the air or rolling) the touchline or goal line or a violation is whistled, the referee will designate by hand signal the team that is awarded possession of the ball. Depending on the situation, any number of restarts may occur. Restarts can be direct (can be scored without touching another player) or indirect (must be touched by another player, even the opposition, before a goal is awarded). Direct restarts included the following:

Penalty Kick

A penalty kick is taken from the penalty kick, or 12-yard (10.97 m), mark. All players—with the exception of the penalty kicker and the goalkeeper—must be outside the penalty area and at least 10 yards (9.14 m) from the ball until the ball is struck forward. The goalkeeper may move on the goal line with his or her feet until the ball is kicked. The ball remains in play if it rebounds off the goalpost or the goalkeeper. The penalty kicker, however, may not play the rebound until the ball is touched by another player. A penalty kick is awarded when deliberate handling of the ball, holding, charging, tripping, pushing, or striking occurs inside the penalty area by the defending team.

Corner Kick

When the ball crosses the defender's goal line and is last played by a defender, a corner kick is awarded from within the 1-yard (0.9 m) arc of the corner of the field (by the flag) closest to where the ball crossed the goal line. Players defending the corner kick must be 10 yards (9.14 m) from the corner kick when it is taken.

Direct Kick

Whenever any of the infractions cited in the "Penalty kick" or "Fouls and misconduct" sections occur, but are outside the penalty area or are committed by the offensive team in the defensive penalty area, then ball possession via a direct kick is awarded. The referee will signal the direct-kick violation by a tilting arm pointed in the attacking direction of the team that is to be awarded the ball. Defending players must always be 10 yards (9.14 m) from the ball before it is played or a retake may be awarded.

Indirect restarts identified by the referee's straight, upraised arm signal include the following:

Goal Kick

When the ball crosses the defensive goal line and is last touched by the attacking side, the ball is awarded to the defending team. The goal kick is taken from the goal area and must clear the penalty area before being touched by either team. If such a violation occurs, the goal kick is retaken.

Throw-In

When the ball crosses completely over the touchline, a throw-in is awarded to the team that last touched the ball. A throw-in is a two-handed overhead movement that must be taken with both feet on the ground. An improper throw-in results in loss of possession and a throw-in for the opponent. If a throw-in fails to enter the field of play, a retake results.

Indirect Free Kick

An indirect free kick is offered to the opposing team following a technical infraction, such as offsides, obstruction, dangerous play, or delay of game (see "Fouls and misconduct" section). The indirect-kick restart is similar to that for the direct kick in that opposing players must be 10 yards (9.14 m) from the ball; however, another player must touch the ball before a goal can be awarded directly off a shot.

Offsides

A player is in an offsides position if he or she is nearer to the opponent's goal line than the ball at the moment the ball is played or passed by a member of his or her team unless:

1. The player is in his or her own half of the field.
2. There are two opponents (including the opposing goalkeeper) nearer to their own goal line than the attacking player.
3. The ball was last played by the attacker.
4. The attacking player receives the ball directly from a goal kick, corner kick, throw-in, or drop ball.
5. An offensive player even with the second-to-last defender is on-side.

Drop Ball

A drop ball is called for after the referee stops play due to an injury or emergency or when a call is unclear or in doubt. The ball is usually dropped in a nonthreatening or neutral territory and must hit the ground before being played. If the ball is played before hitting the ground (a violation), it is dropped again.

FOULS AND MISCONDUCT

When a player commits a foul or some other form of misconduct or illegal behavior, the opposing team is awarded a direct or indirect free kick. A direct free kick is awarded for intentionally fouling an opponent in any of the following ways (referred to as penal fouls):

- Kicking or attempting to kick an opponent
- Tripping
- Jumping at an opponent
- Charging in a violent or dangerous manner
- Striking or attempting to strike
- Holding
- Pushing
- Handling the ball (except by goalkeepers in their own penalty areas)
- Spitting at an opponent

If a defending player intentionally commits one of the penal offenses within his or her penalty area, a penalty kick is awarded from the 12-yard (10.97 m) mark to the opposing team.

Indirect free kicks are awarded to the opposing team when a player commits one of the following technical infractions:

- Playing in a dangerous manner, such as high kicking
- Charging with the shoulder when the ball is not within playing distance of the players involved (playing the opponent rather than the ball)
- Intentional obstruction of an opponent when not playing the ball
- Charging the goalkeeper, except when the goalkeeper is holding the ball, is obstructing an opponent, or has passed outside the goal area
- When the goalkeeper has taken more than four steps without releasing the ball or has used tactics with the intention of delaying the game
- Offsides

CAUTIONS AND GAME EXPULSIONS

When, in the judgment of the referee, a player is not playing within the laws and spirit of the game by committing

Figure 29-3. Passing drill.

any number of serious violations, the referee may issue to the player a caution, or yellow card. Any repeat offense (flagrant violation) shall result in ejection from the game. If the referee finds a player guilty of any of the following:

- Violent conduct or serious foul play
- Abusive language
- Persistent misconduct after receiving a yellow card

a red card is awarded and immediate expulsion results. The player who is expelled may not be replaced, thus placing his or her team at a serious disadvantage.

FUNDAMENTAL SKILLS AND TECHNIQUES

Soccer is a game of movement, speed, physical and mental control, space, timing, flow, creativity, improvisation, and imagination. To safely play and enjoy the game, the acquisition, practice, and mastery of certain basic fundamental skills are required.

Passing

Passing (figure 29-3) is the foundation of the game. Most short passes are made with the inside of the foot (figures 29-4, 29-5, and 29-6), although the outside of the foot, the "touch" of a toe, and even the heel are often used during a match. Longer passes are either chipped, by placing the foot under the ball, or struck with force, while leaning the body backward to create the desired loft. During a match, the ball is passed to teammates at various angles, including a square pass made at a right angle to the attacker in the hope that the passer will continue the momentum and receive a return pass (wall pass, or give and go). The through pass is the most direct forward pass in the game because the ball is thrust behind the opponents into their defensive space as your teammate runs onto the ball. Of course, when thwarted or attempting to delay the game, or to create a planned opportunity, the ball can be passed

Figure 29-4. Instep kick instructions.

Figure 29-5. Instep kick, close up.

Figure 29-6. Instep kick in action.

backward, laterally, or "around," including to your own goalkeeper, who in this case may not play the ball with his or her hands.

Shooting

Shooting is obviously a key element of soccer. The basic technique can be described as a powerful instep blast, although, like the pass, any surface of the foot or body can be employed. If the shot is struck forcefully with the right instep, the shooter's right foot will also hit the ground first as full force, momentum, and low follow-through are enacted. The skill of shooting is very difficult, and it often seems that the potential scorer is "never in the right position." Sometimes the ball is rolling; sometimes it is up in the air, and a volley shot (figure 29-7) must be used; and sometimes the ball must be taken after a "quick bounce," or half-volleyed. The technique of shooting includes accuracy, deception, discipline, and optimal concentration; and practice in all game situations is paramount.

Figure 29-7. Volley kick.

Heading

Heading is used by the player to pass or to shoot the ball. The proper technique for safe heading is crucial, and injury to the neck area should always be a consideration when warming up, teaching, and practicing the skill. The ball should be attacked by the header with the frontal bone of the forehead near the hairline and directed to a teammate or space that will permit a teammate to collect the ball or afford time to reorganize, especially in the defensive third of the field. Heading technique includes concentration, awareness of players around you, proper body posture and positioning, including the use of the arms as a protective shield, and keeping your eyes on the ball as it is directed.

Trapping and Collecting

Trapping and collecting the ball from a teammate's pass or opponent's miscue is the technique necessary for bringing the ball under complete control. Various parts of the body may be used, depending on the ball position upon arrival. The chest (figure 29-8), thigh (figure 29-9), and instep (figure 29-10) are often employed to control the ball if it arrives in flight, while the sole of the foot, or the inside or outside of the foot trap, is often used for ground balls. The key to control is knowing and using your immediate space to gain possession of the ball. Another key to successful trapping and collecting is to utilize muscular control and bodily momentum-absorption techniques (give and take) to ease the ball into your control space. Concentration and knowing the opponents' whereabouts are mandatory so that the ball can be collected, protected, and distributed to a teammate.

Dribbling

Dribbling (figure 29-11) is one of the most exciting and creative elements of the game and should be encouraged. Dribbling requires the player to use a series of soft

Figure 29-8. Chest trap.

Figure 29-9. Thigh-high trap (with marker).

touches, or pushes, as the ball is dribbled into appropriate space. Effective dribbling is done with both feet employing feints, or fakes; change of pace; and rapid, deceptive moves. Dribbling technique also requires proper body position because the ball often needs to be shielded, screened, and protected from a defender or marker (figure 29-12). Dribbling can be used to advance the ball, move into position to get off a quick shot, delay the game, or to take the ball into open space. Dribbling is also a great warm-up and aerobic and anaerobic conditioner. All practices should include dribbling.

Tackling and Marking

Tackling (figure 29-13) is a defensive technique that is designed to dispossess an opponent from the ball so that you or your teammate can gain ball possession. It involves marking (figure 29-14), or playing the opponent with the ball until the optimal time (usually just after the opponent has touched the ball) to make your tackling move. Tackling is usually accomplished by blocking, poking, or sliding in a calculated effort to win the ball. It requires sound judgment, assertive play, mental toughness, and teamwork.

Goalkeeping

The goalkeeper, or goalie, is unique in that he or she may legally use the hands (the W position, connecting the two

Figure 29-10. Collecting the ball with inside of foot trap.

A

B

Figure 29-11. Dribbling.

Figure 29-12. Shielding.

Figure 29-13. Tackling drill with coach.

Figure 29-14. Marking.

Figure 29-15. Goalkeeping with W grip.

Figure 29-16. Goalie smother.

Figure 29-17. Goalkeeping in a crowd.

thumbs for high balls, and palms open, fingers down for low shots) to stop, control, and catch a ball within the penalty area if it is not intentionally passed to him or her by a teammate (figure 29-15). Upon collection of the ball (figure 29-16), the goalie is also permitted to clear the ball or initiate "instant offense" by throwing (distributing), drop-kicking, or punting the ball. Defensively, the goalkeeper must know when and how to challenge, come off the line, and cut down the attacker's angle and effectively smother and deflect shots. Often sound judgment, common sense, and coolness under pressure (mental ability) are as important as physical skill when selecting a solid goalkeeper (figure 29-17).

SYSTEMS OF PLAY

A system, or style, of play (figure 29-18) describes the organization and configuration of the players on the field, as well as their responsibilities within the team structure. The beauty of soccer is that it is fluid, spontaneous, and

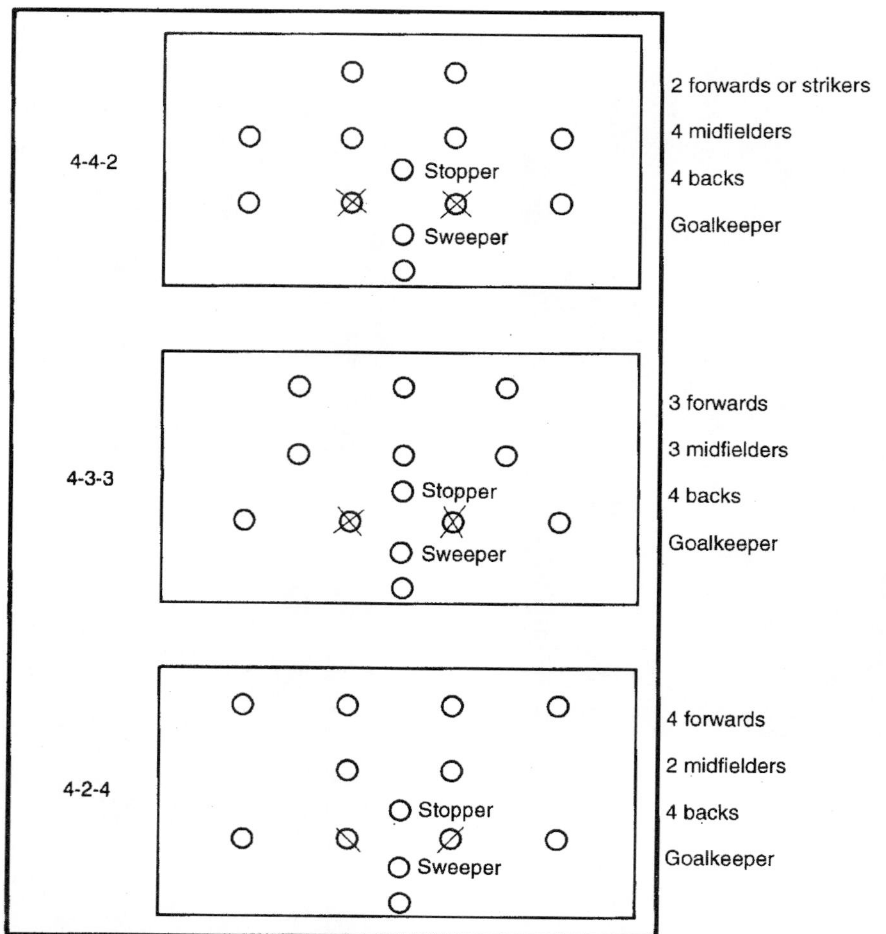

Figure 29-18. Sample systems of play.

constantly changing pace and configuration. Current systems of play have evolved from the original English 2–3–5 offensive set of the early 1990s to the Arsenal Football Club's 3–2–5 WU system of the 1930s, from the famous Brazilian World Cup 4–2–4 formation to Italy's more defense-minded Catenaccio, or 5–4–1, system to "total futbol," where total interchangeability is the optimal objective and weapon.

Regardless of the system of play, numbering begins from the defensive posture and works its way through the midfield to the most forward players. It is interesting to note that all the great systems of play had players like Pele, Cruyff, and Beckenbauer to carry them to prominence. Typically, the team's players and the skill and style of the opponent determine how a coach chooses to implement a particular style of play.

OFFENSIVE AND DEFENSIVE PRINCIPLES

The basic principles of soccer appear to be simple, but they take a great deal of practice, communication (verbal and nonverbal), discipline, and dedication. One primary principle often overlooked is that when your team is in possession of the ball, everyone attacks; and when the ball is lost, everyone becomes a defender.

Attacking Principles (Moving, Support, Penetration, Finishing)

Ball possession dictates who is the attacker and who is the defender. A good attacking player must be able to move without the ball, not only to create space, but also to receive a pass from a teammate. These moves, or runs, often take the form of near- and far-post runs, corner-flag runs, and runs away and off the ball, as well as overlapping runs, where a player, usually from the midfield position, runs forward past the ball being held by a teammate and into open space behind the defense. The pass is then fed to the penetrating overlapper, who collects the ball and goes to the goal.

Also critical to the team and the player who possesses the ball is support from teammates (at least two should always be 10 to 15 yards from the teammate with the ball). With proper support (depth and width) and communication, combination play, such as wall passing and "give and goes," can be initiated and space can be created and exploited for penetration (via passing and dribbling) behind the defense. After the defense has been penetrated and a scoring opportunity has been created (usually by improvising a combination of runs, passing, and dribbling), the principle of finishing, or scoring, must be effectively applied. Shooting is the only way to score, and functional practice makes perfect.

Defensive Principles (Chase, Delay, Support, Balance and Concentration, Challenge, Counterattack)

Defense is soccer's great equalizer. A team well schooled in defensive principles and sound judgment should have a chance to be competitive in every match. Defense begins as soon as the ball is lost to the opposition. Immediate chase and pressure should be applied to the player who has taken control of the ball. The objective is to delay the player with the ball and force him or her to the nearest touchline, thereby preventing a quick penetration toward the goal. This delay permits the defense time to retreat, organize (find, mark, track), or regroup to support the defender playing the ball. This support involves balance, depth, and cover in order to restrict the amount of space that the opponent has to exploit. This is especially crucial in the defensive third of the field, where the defensive team must concentrate to force the attacking team to its least desirable offensive options (usually away from the center of the field, where the shooting angle is most favorable).

Once proper defensive support and cover are implemented, the defender playing the ball can challenge, or tackle, the ball. Often the ball is won by the cover person after the ball is challenged by the primary defender. When the ball is won, a counterattack (quick offensive penetration) or more deliberate offensive buildup is constructed, depending on where the ball is won. Thus, the game of soccer is a 90-minute, continuous series of attacks, defensive destroys or offensive breakdowns, counterattacks, combination passing and buildups, and creativity.

TEACHING CONSIDERATIONS

Teaching the game of soccer should be an enjoyable and positive experience for all. It is important to note that teaching/coaching responsibilities first and foremost include the health and safety of the player, so a thorough medical examination should be required and placed on record and the instructor should possess first-aid and CPR certification. All involved should be made aware "in print" of the emergency medical considerations involved in both practice sessions and matches.

Seasonal and practice plans should include the appropriate fitness level to be attained before strenuous practice and games are conducted. Practices should be conducted in a safe learning environment, and the instructor should always check the facilities (field, locker rooms, and security) before and after practice.

Practice should be fun, fast paced, and well organized and should begin with an informal "get to know each player" before a more structured 7- to 10-minute warm-up (dribbling, jogging, passing, static flexibility). The warm-up should include both individual (e.g., ball juggling) and cooperative group activities (e.g., cooperative stretching). Practices can be divided into a table of specifications, where each component can be manipulated by the instructor depending on the age, fitness and skill levels, season, and the particular goals to be accomplished daily or long range. A sample hour-long table of specifications looks like the following:

Warm-up	7 to 10 minutes
Functional fitness	7 to 10 minutes
Aerobic endurance (circuit-training course)	
Anaerobic (speed)	
Strength (power)	
Individual skill instruction and evaluation	5 to 10 minutes
Small-sided games	5 to 10 minutes
Tactical considerations and economical training	5 to 10 minutes
Scrimmage (small grid, half or full field)	5 to 10 minutes
Cool-down (static stretching)	5 minutes

INSTRUCTIONAL STRATEGIES

It is important that each player master both the skills and the tactics (strategy) of the game. The skills should be introduced with varying degrees of time, space, pace, rest, and opposition being progressively adapted and manipulated in the following order:

- Individual instruction (foundational stage)
- Individual feedback and mastery
- Individual versus single opponent (1v1, 2v1, 3v1, passive resistance)
- Small groups (2v1, 2v5, 2v3, at progressively faster rates)
- Small sided related games (6v4, 5v4)
- Small grid, half- or full-field game conditions (7v7 or 8v8 continuous pressure and opposition)

At all phases of the progressive instructional plan, players should receive concise hands-on instruction, positive feedback, and accurate evaluation. Although soccer skills are individually taught, they must eventually be placed into the ever-changing game environment (opposition, pace, flow, timing), and these often neglected concepts must be effectively integrated into all practice sessions. Fun, mastery of skill, confidence, and individual and team self-worth must also be emphasized at every practice. The teaching of soccer is an ongoing process, and there is nothing more rewarding than watching a player develop in all phases of the game and become part of the most popular sport in the world.

GLOSSARY

attacking team The team that possesses the ball.
banana shot A shot or pass that curves.
blocking Tackle using the inside of the foot to block the ball from an opponent who is dribbling.
chip To lift or lob the ball into the air and over another player.
clear To send the ball by foot or head away from the goal.
collecting A technique of receiving and gaining control of the ball.
CONCACF Confederation of North American and Caribbean Association Football, of which the United States is a member and must win the CONCACF title to gain a World Cup berth.
corner kick A restart after the ball crosses the opponent's goal line when last touched by the opponent.
cover To provide defensive support for teammates, especially when marking or tackling.
cross To kick the ball from the wings (outside) toward the goal area or to a teammate cross-field.
defending team The team that is trying to gain possession of the ball.
defensive concentration The defending team overloads the middle of the field, usually in the defensive third of the field.
depth Proper support of teammates on attack or defense.
diagonal run A run designed to penetrate the defense while drawing defenders from the middle of the field.
direct free kick A free kick from which a goal may be scored directly.
dribbling A succession of forward pushes or touches in which the player keeps the ball under control.
drop ball Ball held waist high and dropped by a referee.
dropkick A ball that is dropped on the ground by the goalie and kicked just after it bounces.
economical training Practice sessions involving at least two of the four components of the game: fitness, technique, tactics, psychology.
far post Goalpost furthest from the ball and the target of attacking runs.
functional training Repeated skill work under matchlike conditions.
grids The use of confined space for practice and small-sided games.
holding Impeding the progress of a player by placing the hand or extended arm in contact with the player.
indirect free kick A free kick from which a goal cannot be scored unless touched by another player.
man-on Popular term used to signal a teammate that defensive pressure is approaching, suggesting an immediate touch or pass to a teammate.
mark To stay close to an opponent for defensive purposes.
offsides Usually a player that does not have two defensive players between him or her and the goal when receiving the ball from a teammate.
own goal A goal scored by the defending team.
poke tackle Use of the defender's toe to push the ball away from an attacker.
restart The starting of play whenever the ball is out of play or the game is stopped. Also referred to as "dead ball."
shielding When the dribbler stays between the ball and the marking opponent.
square pass A pass played laterally to a teammate or space.
stopper The central defender located in front of the sweeper.
striker The most forward attacking player(s).
sweeper The last defender.
target player Usually a striker, who receives the ball a large share of the time.
through pass A pass that goes between and past defenders.
throw-in To put the ball in play from the touchline by a two-hand overhead throw.
touchline Side boundary of the field.
trapping A technique used to gain possession and control of the ball. Usually accomplished by the sole of the foot, thigh, or chest.
volley Meeting the ball in the air with some part of the body and directing it to a teammate or on goal.
wall Defensive tactic in which several players line up 10 yards (9.14 m) from a direct or indirect kick in the defensive third of the field.
width Attacking team's attempt to spread the defense in the attacking third of the field.

SUGGESTED READINGS

Albus, B. 1993. *Intercollegiate Soccer Association of America guide.* St. Louis: Event Management.
Brown, E. W. 1990. *Youth soccer: A complete handbook.* Carmel, Ind.: Benchmark Press. For volunteer coaches. Provides detailed descriptions of how soccer should be taught to children of all ages.
Caligiuri, P., with Herbst, D. 1997. *High-performance soccer: Techniques and tactics for advanced play.* Champaign, Ill.: Human Kinetics. Filled with technical advice, insightful tips, and practice exercises for players and coaches who want to excel on the field.
Coaching youth soccer. 1995. Champaign, Ill.: Human Kinetics. Part of the American Coaches Effectiveness Program. A basic book for the parent-coach or the first-time coach. Follows a step-by-step teaching progression for most skills.
Fédération Internationale de Football Association. Current ed. *FIFA laws of the game.* Zurich: FIFA.
Garland, J. 1997. *Youth soccer drills.* Champaign, Ill.: Human Kinetics. Provides coaches and parents of youth players ages 5 to 12 with progressive drills for optimal learning and having fun.
Hargreaves, A. 1990. *Skills and strategies for coaching soccer.* Champaign, Ill.: Human Kinetics. Includes drills for beginning, intermediate, and advanced players.
Luxbacker, J. 1995. *Soccer practice games.* Champaign, Ill.: Human Kinetics. Details enjoyable games to develop fitness, skills, and tactical awareness in players of all ages.
Luxbacker, J. 1995. *Soccer: Steps to success.* Champaign, Ill.: Human Kinetics. A primary resource for students in beginning activity classes and a self-instruction guide.

Luxbacker, J. 1996. *Teaching soccer: Steps to success.* Champaign, Ill.: Human Kinetics. Features management and safety guidelines, rating charts, 84 drills, teaching cues, suggestions for identifying and correcting errors, and test questions.

Luxbacker, J. 1997. *Soccer: Winning techniques.* 3d ed. Dubuque, Iowa: Eddie Bowers. Contains more than 80 photographs and diagrams illustrating basic concepts.

Luxbacker, J., and Klein, G. 1993. *The soccer goalkeeper.* 2d ed. Champaign, Ill.: Human Kinetics. Provides information on equipment, tactics, mental and physical skills, and drills for the goalkeeper.

National Collegiate Athletic Association. Current ed. *NCAA soccer rules manual.* Shawnee Mission, Kan.: NCAA.

National Collegiate Athletic Association. Current ed. *Official NCAA soccer guide.* New York: NCAA.

Negoesco, S. 1993. *Soccer.* Dubuque, Iowa: Wm. C. Brown.

Pronk, N., and Gorman, B. 1991. *Soccer everyone.* Winston-Salem, N.C.: Hunter Textbooks.

Rees, R., and van der Meer, C. 1997. *Coaching soccer successfully.* Champaign, Ill.: Human Kinetics. Discusses the factors that must be considered to build and maintain a winning soccer program.

Reeves, J., and Simon, J. 1991. *Select soccer drills.* Champaign, Ill.: Human Kinetics. Features 125 drills covering every aspect of the game.

Rookie coaches soccer guide. 1991. Champaign, Ill.: Human Kinetics. Part of the American Coaches Effectiveness Program. Explains the essential skills for coaching soccer.

Schmidt, C. 1997. *Advanced soccer drills.* Champaign, Ill.: Human Kinetics. Soccer drills for advanced players.

Simon, J., and Reeves, J. 1994. *Soccer restart plays.* Champaign, Ill.: Human Kinetics.

Smith, M., and Johnson, M. 1991. *Soccer.* Boston: American Press.

U.S. Soccer Federation. 1998. *FIFA laws of the game: A guide for referees.* Hitzigweg, Switzerland: FIFA.

Yeagley, J. 1994. *Winning soccer.* Indianapolis: Masters Press.

RESOURCES

Videotapes

Forty soccer videotapes covering all aspects of the game. "How To" Sports Videos, P.O. Box 5852, Denver, CO 80217.

Puma videocoach soccer series with Hubert Vogelsinger. West One Videos, 1995 Bailey Hill Rd., Eugene, OR 97405.

Soccer on video, Soccer Learning Systems, San Ramon, California 94583.

Soccer refereeing series (2 tapes) and *Winning at soccer with Bobby Charlton* (6 tapes) are available from Cambridge Physical Education and Health, P.O. Box 2153, Charleston, WV 25328.

Soccer series: *Juggling, Dribbling and passing, Shooting, Goal keeping.* NCAA instructional video tapes. Karol Video, 22 Riverside Dr., Wayne, NJ 07470.

Soccer series: *Laws of the game, Fair and unfair challenges, Unsporting behavior.* United States Soccer Federation, U.S. Soccer House, 1811 S. Prairie Ave., Chicago, IL 60616.

Soccer series: *The world's greatest goals, Great goals, The world's greatest saves, The world's greatest players.* HIJ Coerver Goal Series. ACME, One Acme Plaza, P.O. Box 811, Carrboro, NC 27510.

Computer software

Davis, C. 1996. *The coaches edge player visualization software.* Lawrence, Kan.: The Coach's Edge.

Let's play soccer: ESPN soccer, Multimedia PC CD-Rom. Champaign, Ill.: Human Kinetics.

The Complete 1996/1997 Major League Soccer CD-Rom Yearbook. Major League Soccer Communications Department, 110 East 42nd Street, 10th Floor, New York, NY 10017.

Softball

After completing this chapter, the reader should be able to:

- Appreciate the development of softball and the popularity of its many variations
- Know the basic rules of the game and some of their modifications
- Demonstrate the basic softball skills of throwing, catching, batting, pitching, and baserunning
- Execute effective offensive and defensive softball strategy
- Modify the game of softball to meet local conditions and needs
- Teach softball skills and strategies to a group of students

HISTORY

The YMCA perhaps did more than any other organization to inaugurate softball by transferring the game of baseball from outdoors to indoors about 1900. Softball is an adaptation of baseball. Because of limited indoor space and the hardness of the baseball, the YMCA directors originally made the softball softer, the bat smaller, and the baselines and pitching distances shorter. They also changed the delivery of the pitch to an underhand motion.

Several years later the Playground Association of America, now known as the National Recreation and Park Association, needed a game that could be adapted to small outdoor spaces and could be played by all ages, especially by young boys and girls. The game acquired different names at different times, such as "playground ball," "kitten ball," "recreation ball," and "ladies' ball," but in 1933 "softball" was adopted as the official name by the Amateur Softball Association. That year a national tournament was held at the world's fair in Chicago. At the same time, this organization set up and standardized rules that are the basis for rules today. During the Depression, when thousands of people were unemployed, the game was a great source of recreation at community centers.

Before World War II, public interest in softball grew so much that teams were organized into leagues all over the country, and it was estimated that well over 5 million people engaged in this popular American game. Because of its great appeal to all ages and because little equipment is needed and any ordinary playground is adequate, softball has become one of the most popular of all activities. It is now played by over 35 million Americans. The game has even been modified for the blind by use of a ball that emits a beeping sound.

Modifications of the basic rules have produced many types of games and leagues, such as fast pitch and slow pitch; leagues for men's teams, women's teams, and coed teams; games using the regulation-size softball (12 inches, or 30.5 cm, in circumference), games using a much larger ball, and games for women using a softball 11 inches (27.9 cm) in circumference; rules forbidding the use of gloves; and many other interesting variations. Presented here are the abridged rules and techniques of fast-pitch softball, followed by a common set of rules for slow-pitch. As mentioned, many variations are enjoyed in different parts of the country.

EQUIPMENT AND FIELD

The bat should be round and made of hardwood or aluminum, no more than 34 inches (86.36 cm) long, 2¼ inches (5.72 cm) in diameter at its largest part, and weighing no more than 38 ounces (1.08 kg).

The ball should be a smooth-seamed, leather-covered sphere containing yarn and kapok, measuring no less than 11⅞ inches (30.16 cm) and no more than 12⅛ inches (30.8 cm) in circumference (although some women's leagues now use an 11-inch [27.94 cm] ball) and weighing from 6¼ to 7 ounces (178.6 to 200 gm).

The home plate should be made of solid rubber or other suitable material (figure 30-1). The distance to the pitcher's box is 40 feet (12.19 m) for women and 46 feet (14.02 m) for men for fast-pitch. For both men's and women's slow-pitch the distance from home plate to the pitcher's plate is 50 feet (15.24 m).

Gloves may be worn by any player, but mitts are limited to first basemen and catchers. The pitcher's glove may not be white or gray and must be a solid color. Other players may use multicolored gloves.

A mask, throat guard, and chest guard must be worn by catchers in fast-pitch and are recommended in slow-pitch. Spikes or any other type of sharp projections on the shoes are usually prohibited, except in higher levels of competition.

All players on a team must wear identical uniforms (e.g., color, trim, style), including caps. Helmets may be worn by catchers, batters, and baserunners; under some local rules, they must be worn.

Playing field dimensions are given in figure 30-1.

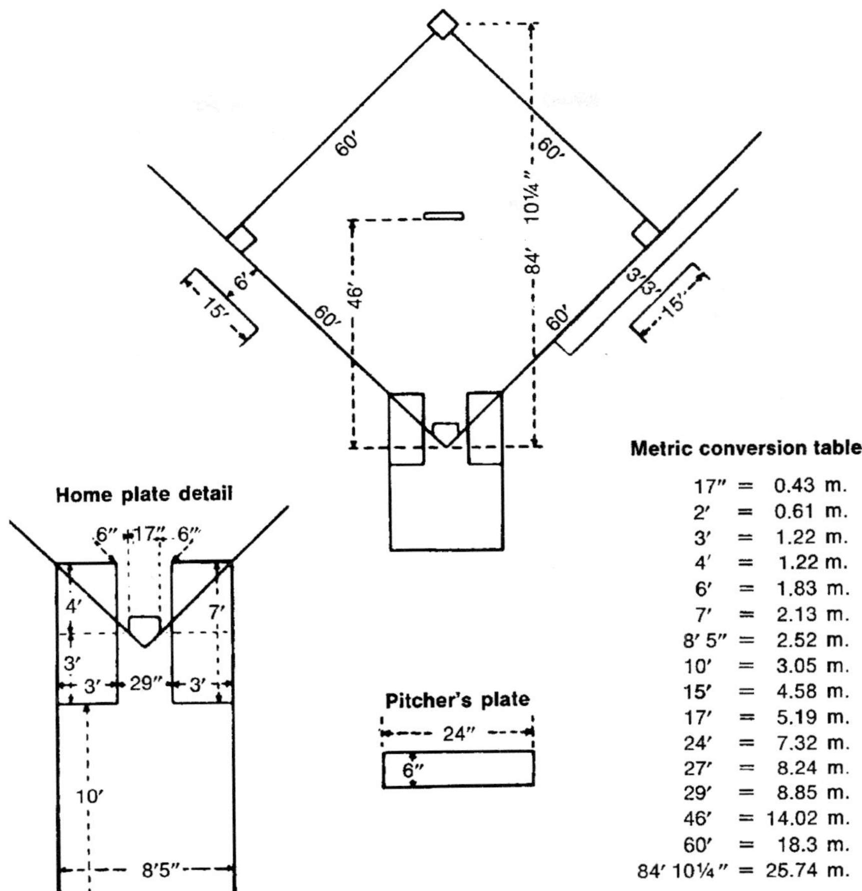

Figure 30-1. Softball playing field for men. Pitching distance for women's fast-pitch is 40 feet (12.19 m). The bases are 65 feet (19.81 m) apart for men's and coed slow-pitch. Official distances from home plate to the fence are 225 feet (68.58 m) and 200 feet (60.96 m) for men's and women's fast-pitch, respectively. In slow-pitch the official distances are 275 feet (83.87 m) for men and 250 feet (76.2 m) for women.

ABRIDGED RULES (FAST-PITCH)

Teams, Players, and Substitutes

A team shall consist of nine players, whose positions shall be designated as pitcher, catcher, first baseman, second baseman, third baseman, shortstop, left fielder, center fielder, and right fielder. Ten players are allowed if a designated batter is used. Except for the pitcher (who must be positioned as defined in the pitching rules), the catcher (who must be within the lines of the catcher's position), and the designated hitter, players in the field may be stationed at any locations on fair ground.

A substitute may take the place of a player whose name is in the team's batting order. Any starting player (except the designated hitter) may be withdrawn and reentered one time as long as the player remains in the same position in the batting order. A player other than a starting player may not reenter the game after being removed. The designated hitter may bat for any player provided it is made known before the start of the game. The designated hitter must always occupy the same position in the batting order, cannot enter the game on defense, may be substituted for by a player who has not yet been in the game, but may not reenter the game once replaced.

The Game

1. A regulation game consists of seven innings, unless the team second at bat scores more runs in six innings than the team first at bat has scored in seven innings.
2. It is a regulation game if the team last at bat in the seventh inning scores the winning run before the third player is out.
3. It is a regulation game if it is called by the umpire because of darkness, rain, or other cause, provided five or more innings have been played by each side or

the team second at bat has scored more runs at the end of its fourth inning or in any part of its fifth than the team first at bat has scored in five complete innings.

4. When a game is called in any inning after the fifth, the score is what it was at the time the game was called if the team second at bat has more runs than the first team at bat. Or, if the team second at bat has fewer runs than the team first at bat when the game is called, the score is that of the last inning completed by both sides.

Pitching

1. Preliminary to pitching, the pitcher must come to a full stop for at least 1 second but not more than 10 seconds, facing the batter with the ball held in both hands in front of the body and with both feet on the ground and in contact with the pitcher's plate.
2. The pitcher is not considered in pitching position unless the catcher is in position to receive the pitch.
3. In the act of delivering the ball to the batter, the pitcher may not take more than one step, which must be forward and toward the batter. The step must be taken simultaneously with the delivery of the ball to the batter.
4. A legal delivery is defined as a ball delivered to the batter underhand and with follow-through of the hand and wrist past the straight line of the body before the ball is released. The pitcher may use any windup desired, provided no motion to pitch is made without immediately delivering the ball, no rocker action is made, there is no stop in or reversal of the forward motion, no more than one revolution of the arm is made in the windmill motion, and the windup is not continued after the forward step is taken as the ball is released.
5. At no time during the progress of the game may the pitcher use tape or other substance on the pitching hand or fingers or on the ball. Powdered resin may be used to dry the hands.
6. "No pitch" is declared whenever the pitcher pitches during a suspension of play or when a quick return of the ball is attempted before the batter has taken position or when the batter is off-balance as the result of a previous pitch.

Illegal Pitches

An illegal pitch, entitling all base runners to advance one base, is called by the umpire as follows, and in each of the cases cited a ball is also called in favor of the batter:

1. Any delivery of the ball to the batter without the pitcher's previously taking position as defined in the pitching rules
2. Taking more than one step before releasing the ball
3. Final delivery of the ball to the batter with the hand above the hip and the wrist of the pitching arm farther from the body than the elbow as described in point 4 of the pitching rules
4. Failure to follow through with the hand and wrist past the straight line of the body as described in point 4 of the pitching rules
5. Rolling the ball along the ground or dropping the ball while the pitcher is in pitching position
6. Making any motion to pitch without immediately delivering the ball to the batter
7. Delivery of the ball to the batter when the catcher is outside the lines of the catcher's position
8. Continuing the windup after taking the step described in point 3 of the pitching rules
9. Taking a pitching position on or near the pitcher's plate without possessing the ball

In each of these cases the ball is considered dead and not in play until again put in play at the pitcher's box. If, however, the batter strikes at and hits into fair territory any of the illegal pitches just mentioned, there is no penalty for such illegal pitch; the ball remains in play, and the base runners may run bases or be put out as though the ball had been legally pitched.

Foul Tip

A foul tip is a ball that is batted by the batter while standing in the lines of the batter's position and that goes sharply and directly to the hands of the catcher and is legally caught. A foul tip caught is a strike and the ball remains in play. A foul hit ball that rises higher than the batter's head is not a foul tip under this rule.

Out

Besides grounding out, flying out, or being tagged out, a player is declared out if any of the following occur:

1. The batter makes a foul hit other than a foul tip as just defined and the ball is caught by a fielder before touching the ground, provided it is not caught in the fielder's hat, cap, protector, pocket, or other part of the uniform or does not strike some other object before being caught.
2. The ball is batted illegally.
3. A bunt is fouled after the second strike.
4. The batter attempts to hinder the catcher from fielding or throwing the ball by stepping outside the lines of the batter's position or in any way obstructs or interferes with that player; the exception to this rule is that if a base runner attempting to steal is put out, the batter is not out.
5. Immediately after three strikes, whether there are no outs, one out, a runner on first base, runners on first

and second bases, runners on first, second, and third bases, or runners on first and third bases.

6. The third strike is swung at and the ball does not touch any part of the batter's person.
7. Before two players are out, while first and second bases or first, second, and third bases are occupied, the batter hits a fair fly ball that is handled or, in the opinion of the umpire, could have been caught by an infielder with reasonable effort.
8. The batter steps from one batter's box to the other while the pitcher is in position ready to pitch.

FUNDAMENTAL SKILLS AND TECHNIQUES

The basic skills of softball, like those of any other sport, must be learned and practiced often. The techniques necessary for good performance are given here.

Catching

Fielding fly balls

There are two methods for fielding fly balls: (1) with the thumbs of both hands together and the fingertips up (overhead catch, figure 30-2) and (2) with the little fingers of both hands together and letting the ball drop into the nested hands (basket catch).

The advantage of the first method is that a throw following a catch can be made faster. The overhead catch is preferred to the basket catch whenever possible. The ball is visible, and if it spins it is more likely to remain in the hands. The fielder should be at the spot at which the ball is descending to get set for it.

Figure 30-2. Overhead catch of a fly ball.

If the ball is hit deep over the head, the fielder should turn and run (never run backward) to the spot where the ball is expected to drop, glancing over the shoulder while running.

When the ball drops into the hands, let them give slightly with the impact. Shield the eyes from the sun with the gloved hand. Do not hold the ball after catching it. Be careful that revolving balls do not spin out of the glove.

Provide backup for other fielders when possible.

Fielding ground balls

A bouncing ground ball should be fielded at the height of its bounce. For quick play, advance to meet the ball. Time the speed of advance with the speed and bounce of the ball. The success of this play lies with the fielder's judgment and timing with the moving ball.

If the bouncing ball is above the waist, catch it with the fingertips turned up. The waist-high ball can be caught either way, depending on whether the ball is dropping or coming up. If the ball is below the waist, it is fielded with the fingertips pointing toward the ground and cupped so the ball rolls into the glove.

To maintain balance when running in for a ball, run with the legs and feet apart. Meet the ball out in front of the body, with the foot on the glove side of the body slightly advanced. Keep the eyes on the ball until it is in the hands.

A ground ball may take unexpected hops to the right or left, and these should be fielded with the feet apart, the knees slightly bent, and the body crouched. In fielding fast and hard-hit balls, it is allowable to block balls by closing the feet or dropping on one knee.

Throwing

Although throwing is a natural activity, some skills in throwing the ball in softball differ from the natural way of throwing.

Overhand throw

In the overhand throw (figure 30-3), the ball is grasped with two fingers on the top (a small hand may require three fingers on top) and the thumb underneath. The hand is swung down, ending well behind the shoulder below shoulder height. The left side of the body is turned in the direction of the throw. The left foot is in front, the toe touching the ground. The weight of the body starts on the right foot and is brought forward with the forward motion of the arm. While the elbow is leading the arm movement, the wrist is cocked to increase the range of motion of external rotation. The ball is released with a downward snap of the wrist, which increases the speed the ball receives from the arm motion.

Figure 30-3. Overhand throw.

Underhand windmill pitch

The windmill pitch starts below the shoulder with the arm fully extended. The hand is turned with the palm down at the start and then is brought forward with a pendulum swing of the arm to the front. The elbow is slightly flexed throughout and then straightens just prior to the release. The follow-through brings the hand, with the palm up, about chest high (figure 30-4).

From this underhand throw, several kinds of pitches can be made: drop, curve, change-up, rise, and knuckle.

Figure 30-4. Underhand windmill pitch.

Batting

Good batting ability and clever baserunning are the keys to successful offensive softball. It is therefore essential that beginners practice and observe the following skill fundamentals. (Because this is written for beginners, it is assumed that the player throws and bats with the same side of the body; therefore, switch-hitting is not described.)

1. Select a bat that feels comfortable in weight, grip, and balance.
2. Use a finger grip (not palms) that best controls the bat.
3. Assume a natural and comfortable position at the plate, with the feet slightly further apart than shoulder width and with the nondominant side of the body toward the pitcher. The elbows should be out and away from the body to allow for freedom in swinging the bat. The nondominant elbow is on a level with the hand and slightly below the shoulder. It will point slightly toward the ground.
4. Start the swing with a relatively short stride forward and by rotating the hips. This is followed immediately by swinging the bat and following through. The swing is best described as throwing the hands or throwing the bat at the ball.
5. If the ball is coming into the strike area, keep the bat poised at shoulder height, ready to swing. Never rest the bat on the shoulder while waiting for the pitch (except in slow-pitch).
6. Keep the eyes on the ball from the moment the pitcher starts the windup until the ball reaches the plate.
7. Observe pitches carefully, and swing only at pitches in the strike zone.
8. Swing the bat forward on a horizontal plane. Do not swing too hard.
9. Drop the bat and run quickly to first base as soon as the ball is hit.
10. Good vision, muscle control, strong forearms, and quick wrist action are the keys to good hitting.

Power and choke hitters

A power hitter stands farther back from the plate, with the feet well apart and parallel to the sides of the batter's box. The power hitter grips the bat near the small end with the dominant hand above the other hand.

A choke hitter stands closer to the plate than the power hitter when first learning. The trunk should be slightly inclined toward home plate. The choke hitter grips the bat several inches from the small end of the bat.

Bunting

Bunting is an effective offensive weapon in softball. The arms and elbows are held well out from the body; the nondominant hand holds the bat near the small end, and the other hand holds the bat loosely and guides it. The bat recoils slightly when it meets the ball.

There are two kinds of bunts: (1) the sacrifice and (2) the push bunt, directing the ball between the pitcher and first base. As the pitcher lets go of the ball, the hitter should run the dominant hand about halfway down the bat. Hold the bat loosely to deaden the bunted ball and at an angle to lay the ball down either the first- or third-base line.

Catching

The catcher should be in a half-squat position to move quickly and reach to the sides or to jump up and move forward for a throw. Practice a quick snap throw. Work as close under the bat as possible. Keep the eyes on the ball.

Pitching (Fast-Pitch)

Assume the pitching position with both feet on the rubber plate. Throw an underhand pitch to the batter (figure 30-4). Preliminary movements may be taken by the pitcher as long as the final delivery to the batter is underhand.

The pitcher should develop a wrist snap and a finger flip with a complete follow-through. A pitcher should be able to throw a slow ball for a change of pace.

Practice putting spin on the ball to create a curve that will cause the batter to hit a pop-up. (See figures 30-5 to 30-8 for various pitches.)

To prevent a successful bunt, pitch high in the strike zone.

Baserunning

In fast-pitch softball the runner must maintain contact with the base until the ball leaves the pitcher's hand. Readiness to start for the next base requires assuming a stance facing the next base with the left foot touching the side of the base and the right foot forward, ready to sprint for the next base the instant the pitcher releases the ball. If the ball is hit to the right side of the field, a runner leaving first base should watch the third-base coach to determine whether to stop at second base or try for third base. The base coach has a better view of the entire field of play and can make a better judgment than the runner. Run straight at the base until you are 10 to 15 feet (3 to 4.5 m) from it. If it appears you might be able to go on to the next base, move out to the right and curve in, in order to push off and run straight toward the next base. If it appears the base you are heading for will be as far as you can advance, continue on a straight line and slide if necessary.

A runner must be able to slide correctly. An excellent slide is the hook slide. This is performed by sliding on the thigh and hip and hooking the bag with the toe of the foot or sliding past the base and tagging it with the hand, depending on the position of the defensive player. The runner slides to the right of the bag, making it difficult to be tagged. The slide should be started soon enough in front of

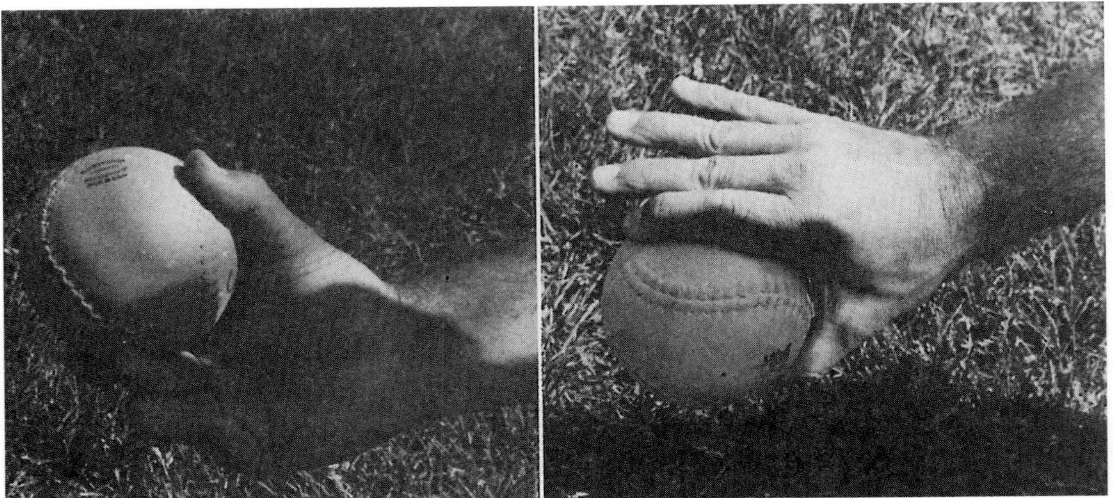

Figure 30-5. In-curve and out-curve releases.

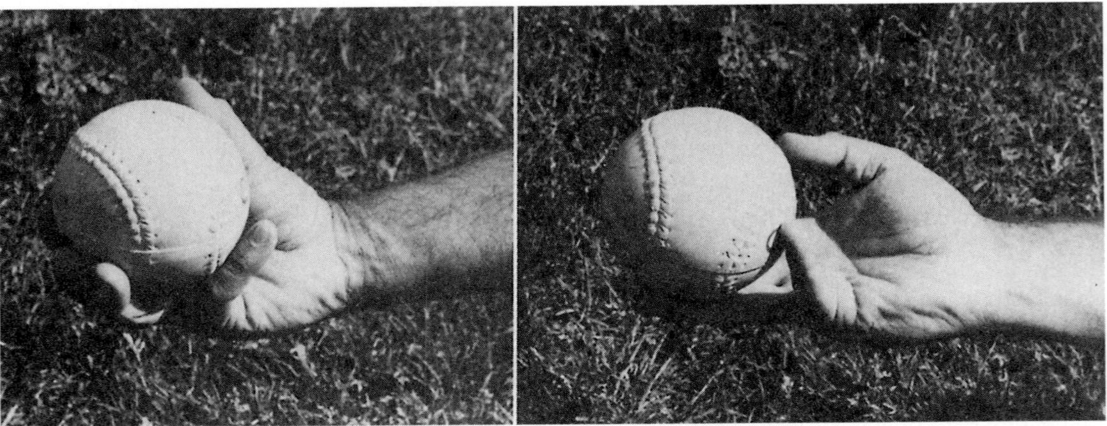

Figure 30-6. Drop grip and drop release.

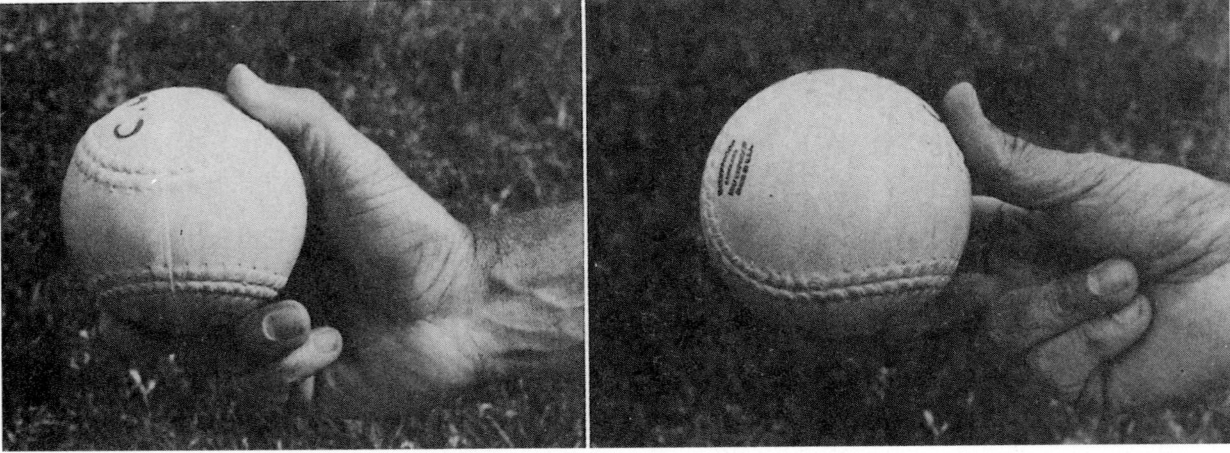

Figure 30-7. Grip and release for fast ball in-curve and out-curve.

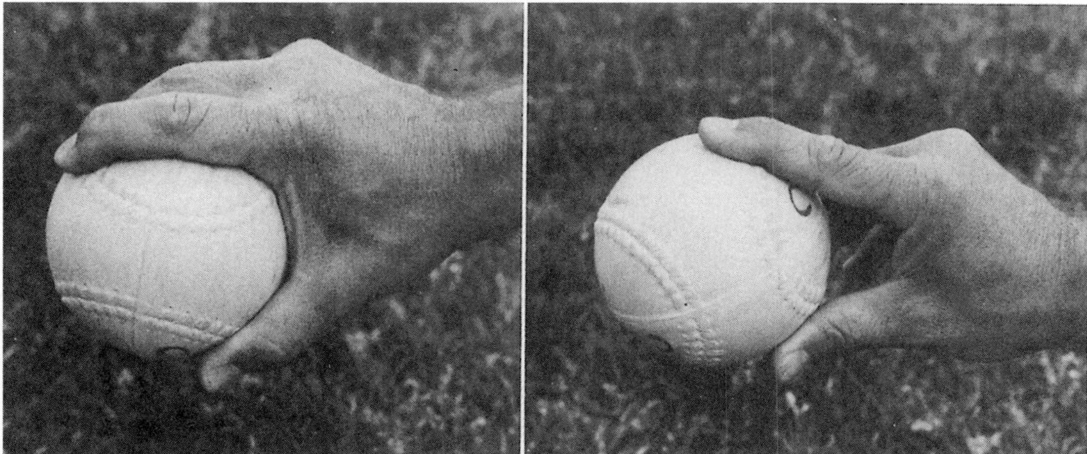

Figure 30-8. Grip and release for rise.

the bag so that the runner can slide to the bag and not plunge onto it.

The Infielders

First base

The person playing first base should cover the base in a way that does not cause interference with the runner, but allows balls from all directions to be played. This person should be able to catch high and low throws. The person playing first base should play the base on the inside when receiving throws from the infield. If no runner is on the base, the player normally stands about 6 feet (1.83 m) off the base and a few feet toward home plate. (In slow-pitch the player should play a few feet behind the line between first and second base.) In softball the distance from home to first base is relatively short, making the bunt an effective offensive weapon. The first-base player must always be ready to charge forward in case of a bunt.

Second base

The person playing second base must have the ability and agility to run to the left or right for ground balls. The best position is a little nearer second base than first and back of the baseline. It is important for this player to back up other infielders when possible.

Shortstop

The shortstop should play about 10 to 12 feet behind the baseline and approximately halfway between second and third base. A shortstop must be agile, quick, and able to move equally comfortably to the left or right. Generally the shortstop covers second base when the ball is hit to the right side of the infield and covers third base when the person playing third base is fielding the ball. Another important function of the shortstop is to be the pivot on a normal double play. This involves covering second base, taking the throw and touching the base for the forceout, then quickly throwing the ball to first base to put out the batter. When not fielding a ground or fly ball, the shortstop has many assignments as a backup or relay person, depending on the game situation.

Third base

The person playing third base should play about 6 feet (1.8 m) from the base inside the diamond and in front of the baseline toward home plate. (In slow-pitch the player should play a few feet behind the line between second and third base.)

Keep any runners close to the base, but do not leave an opening in your position. The third-base player should compete with outfielders for flies until shouted off by the outfielder.

The Outfielders

Outfielders must have running speed, be able to accurately judge the flight of a fly ball, and be able to throw accurately and hard. A throw must be long (or to a cut-off), with smooth execution of a full arm action rather than a wrist snap. Outfielders should study hitters to know where they hit. An outfielder should watch every pitch and be ready to move in any direction at each pitch. In playing a ground ball, the outfielder should place the body in front of the ball to block it.

Team Offensive Strategy

Players should sacrifice individual record performances for team success. A batter should sacrifice getting on first to move a runner to second so that a hit can possibly score the runner on second.

In fast-pitch softball, the hit-and-run play is good offensive team strategy. Also, the squeeze play is an offensive weapon that may be used with a runner on third. The hit-and-run is used primarily with a runner on first base, less than two outs, and the batter ahead in the count. In the hit-and-run the runner breaks from the base with the pitcher's release of the ball while the batter tries to hit a ground ball through an open spot in the infield. The batter's main objective is to advance the runner to the next base. The squeeze bunt is used with a runner on third base, less than two outs, and the batter ahead in the count. In the "suicide squeeze," the runner breaks from third with the pitcher's release of the ball while the batter tries to bunt the ball on the ground. When the game is in the late stages and there are fewer than two outs, it is good strategy to bunt in an attempt to score the runner. The runner starts for home as the pitcher releases the ball and the batter bunts.

The double steal is another excellent offensive play used to catch the defensive team off balance. This play can be attempted with runners on first and second, but most often is attempted with runners on first and third, the idea being to score the runner on third if the catcher throws the ball to second base in an effort to retire the runner coming from first base.

Almost any offensive or defensive strategy that is effective in baseball is also good for softball.

Defensive Strategy

Good defense involves meeting any crucial situation that may arise. For example, to break up a double steal, the shortstop or second-base player may run over behind the pitcher and in front of second base, receives the throw from the catcher, and throws it back to the catcher.

The infield can draw in for a play at the plate. A double play is always an excellent defense if it can be executed.

When runners are on base, always try to put out the lead runner when possible. If this is not possible, be sure to get at least one runner out. When a runner is on third, hold this runner and then get the batter or another runner out. Good team defense requires that infielders help the other infielders.

An intentional pass or a pitchout to make a play at second or first can be good defensive strategy in the proper situation.

SLOW-PITCH SOFTBALL

Slow-pitch softball is very popular in high school, college, and city recreation programs. In fact, there are probably more participants now in slow-pitch than in fast-pitch softball.

Playing Field

The playing field is basically the same as that for fast-pitch softball. Differences between slow-pitch and fast-pitch field dimensions are noted in figure 30-1.

Equipment

Equipment specifications for the bat and ball are identical to fast-pitch, although many local leagues have begun using 14-inch (35.56 cm) and 16-inch (40.64 cm) softballs. Although not required and seldom used, catcher's masks are recommended. Spikes are prohibited.

Players

A team consists of 10 players: pitcher, catcher, first baseman, second baseman, third baseman, shortstop, left fielder, center fielder, right fielder, and short fielder. Sometimes the four outfielders spread out across the whole outfield.

A starting player may reenter the game in the same position after being substituted for. A substitute may not reenter the game. A starting player may reenter once. Some slow-pitch rules allow for more than ten batters when the team is up to bat.

Game

A regulation game consists of seven innings. In case of a tie game more innings are played. A forfeited game is awarded to the team that is ready to play.

Pitching regulations

The pitching arm must come to rest holding the ball in front of the body, with one or both feet in contact with the rubber. This position cannot be held longer than 10 seconds. The pivot foot must remain in contact with the pitcher's plate until the ball leaves the hand. It is not necessary to take a step, but if taken, it must be toward the batter and must be within the area bounded by the edges of the pitcher's plate. The pitch must be released at moderate speed (umpire's judgment), and at the release the hand must be below the hip. The ball must be delivered with a perceptible arc of at least 6 feet (1.83 m) from the time it leaves the pitcher's hand until it reaches home plate. The pitched ball may not be higher than 12 feet (3.66 m) from the ground during its flight to home plate.

In slow-pitch, a batter may be walked by notifying the home plate umpire.

Batting

The batter shall take a position within the lines of the batter's box. The batter has 1 minute to be set after the umpire calls "Play" or the batter is *out*. All batters must bat in their batting order or an out is called on the person at bat. However, if this error is discovered in time, the correct batter can replace the incorrect batter, while assuming the ball, and strike count of the incorrect batter.

A *strike* is called (1) for each legally pitched ball passing through the strike zone, (2) for each pitched ball missed by the batter, (3) for each foul tip (the batter is out if the tip is on the third strike), (4) for each pitched ball struck at and missed that touches any part of the batter, and (5) for hitting a batter positioned in the strike zone.

A *ball* is called for a pitched ball that does not enter the strike zone. The strike zone is over any part of home plate between the highest shoulder and the knees of the batter when in a natural batting stance.

A *fair ball* is one that (1) lands in fair territory (between first and third bases), (2) lands on any one of the bases, with the exception of home base, (3) falls on fair ground beyond first or third base, or (4) bounds over first or third base but then lands in foul territory. It should be noted that home base is in fair territory.

The batter is out when an *infield fly* is hit with base runners on first and second or first, second, and third, with less than two outs and in the judgment of the umpire the ball could be caught. This is called the infield-fly rule.

A *foul ball* is a legally batted ball that (1) settles on foul ground outside the first or third baseline or behind home plate or (2) bounds past first or third base on foul ground, or outside of bases. *If a foul fly is caught, the batter is out.* The batter is out if there are two strikes and the next batted ball is a foul. A foul tip is a batted ball that goes from the bat, not higher than the batter's head, to the catcher's hands and is legally caught. A legally caught foul tip on the third strike is a dead ball. Base runners may not advance.

The batter is out under the following circumstances:

1. On three strikes
2. When the ball is bunted or chopped downward
3. When a fly ball is legally caught
4. On an infield-fly rule
5. When the batter interferes with the catcher
6. When the batter is tagged or thrown out at first base

Intentional interference puts a runner out plus the batter who hit the ball.

Baserunning

1. All bases must be touched in order.
2. If two base runners are on the same base, the last runner on can be tagged out.
3. The batter becomes a base runner when four balls are called.
4. When a fair ball bounds or rolls into a bleacher or over, under, or through a fence or other obstruction marking the boundaries of the playing field, the ball is dead and all base runners are awarded two bases from the time of the pitch.
5. There is no base stealing. Only after the pitched ball has passed home plate and has been batted can the base runner leave a base.
6. The base runner is out if running outside the 3-foot (0.91 m) line and interfering with the play. But the base runner is not out if it is necessary to run around a fielder taking the batted ball.
7. The base runner is out if he or she passes another base runner.
8. The base runner is out if off base and struck by a fair batted ball before it passes a fielder.

TEACHING CONSIDERATIONS

1. Establish a reasonable level of consistency in fielding and throwing skills before using these skills in game or gamelike conditions.
   a. Consider beginning with a softer ball.
   b. Start with fielding slow balls thrown directly to the fielder. Increase the speed gradually and cause the fielder to move to either side, forward, and back to receive the ball.
   c. Include throws of different distances and directions from the fielder. Acknowledge appropriate throwing patterns for different situations.
   d. Include fielding of batted balls as soon as learners are ready for balls coming with more force.
2. The basics of the game can be taught without batting a pitched ball (by replacing batting with a throw or batting off a tee) and with a smaller number of players. There are many lead-up and modified games that permit more practice and have much higher levels of participation than the official game. Teachers should consider using these. Baserunning and defensive strategies are best taught without batting to permit more offensive play opportunities.
3. Practice pitching as a separate skill. Give all students opportunities to play all positions. Do not permit weak players to be "left out in the field."
4. Teach the windmill style of pitching using the following sequence:
   a. Have partners stand facing each other approximately 6 feet (1.83 m) apart, with their gloves on the ground.
   b. Have partners grip the ball with their fingers perpendicular to one of the four large seams and with fingertips on the seam.
   c. Have partners use their nondominant hand to grip their throwing forearm just below the elbow and hold it against their side.
   d. One partner then pitches the ball to her or his partner using a flip of the wrist.
   e. The partners continue flipping the ball back and forth about 10 times each, using only their wrists.
   f. The partners repeat the same drill, except that they grip their upper arms just above the elbow and hold the upper arm against their side. The partners flip the ball back and forth 10 times using elbow flexion and a strong wrist snap.

g. After this is mastered, the partners put their gloves on and flip the ball back and forth 10 times at each step, using this progression:
   i. Starting with the pitching arm parallel to the ground behind the player and bringing it forward to release the ball.
   ii. Starting with the pitching arm perpendicular overhead and bringing it down in back and then forward to release the ball.
   iii. Starting with the pitching arm parallel to the ground in front and taking it up and overhead before bringing it forward to release the ball.
   iv. Starting with the pitching hand and ball in the glove at belt level and taking that ball up and overhead before bringing it forward to release the ball.

Throughout the above steps, the partners should *not* try to pitch the ball fast, but they should strive to develop proper technique (i.e., use a strong wrist snap and elbow flexion while moving the arm in the sagittal plane) and direct the ball at their partner's belt buckle. The pitcher should not move the feet during steps a–f. In step g, the pitcher should stride forward with the leg on the opposite side of the pitching arm. The distance between the partners should gradually be increased from the initial 6 feet (1.83 m) to approximately 15 feet (4.57 m) as they progress through these steps. As partners become more competent with the windmill technique, the distance between them can gradually be increased until they reach the official distance, while still maintaining good form and pitching the ball in the strike zone with some consistency.

5. For less skilled batters, have the teacher bat, slow down the pitching, or give the batter the option of throwing the ball up to himself or herself or batting off a tee. To teach batting, consider using aspects of the following progressions:
   a. Use whiffle balls and bats.
   b. Bat off a tee.
   c. Bat a ball suspended on a rope or string with Velcro.
   d. Use bigger bats and bigger balls.
   e. Slow down the pitching and place pitches accurately to the batter.
6. Start with only basic rules. Add more-technical rules as learners are ready for them.
7. Give students the responsibility for leadership (being captain or in charge of equipment), but teach them what is expected of these people and maintain those expectations.
8. Keep safety in mind (e.g., playing especially weak players where they will receive many thrown balls could result in injuries).

GLOSSARY

appeal play A play on which an umpire cannot make a decision until requested by a player. The request must be made before the next play.

assist Throwing or deflecting, by a player, of a thrown or batted ball by which an out is made.

base on balls Reaching first base after four balls are called.

base path An imaginary line 3 feet (0.91 m) to either side of a direct line between bases.

battery The pitcher and catcher.

batting average The number of hits made by a batter divided by the times at bat. Walks, sacrifices, and being hit by a pitch are not counted as a time at bat.

batting order The official listing of the sequence of the players to bat.

beanball A ball thrown at the batter.

bunt A ball softly touched by the bat that lands within the infield.

designated hitter A player who does not take the field defensively but bats in place of another player.

double play A play in which two players are legally put out on the same hit ball.

error A play that fails to cause the out of a runner or that allows advancement of a runner.

fair territory The part of the playing field within or including the first- and third-base foul lines from home plate to the bottom of the extreme playing-field fence and perpendicularly upward.

foul tip A ball that goes directly from the bat to the catcher's glove.

hit-and-run The hit-and-run is an offensive tactic in which a runner breaks from a base as the pitcher releases the ball while the batter tries to hit the ball through an open spot in the infield.

infield That portion of the field within the baselines.

infield-fly rule The batter shall be declared out when hitting an infield fly with runners on first and second or first, second, and third, with fewer than two outs.

inning That portion of a game in which a team plays both offense and defense, starting with the first team at bat.

passed ball Failure of the catcher to hold a pitched ball and the runner advances. An error is charged against the catcher if the third strike is dropped and the runner reaches first base.

pivot foot The foot that the pitcher must keep in constant contact with the pitcher's plate until the delivery of the ball.

play "Play ball" means to begin the game or resume play.

sacrifice bunt A bunt for the purpose of advancing a runner.

sacrifice fly A fly ball hit to the outfield, allowing a runner to score after tagging up when the ball is caught.

stolen base A player on base advances to the next base without the ball being hit.

strike zone The area between the batter's knees and armpits and over the plate.

"suicide" squeeze play An offensive tactic in which the runner on third breaks from the base as the pitcher releases the ball while the batter tries to bunt the ball on the ground.

switch hitter A batter capable of batting both right-handed and left-handed.

Texas leaguer A looping ball that lands safely between the infield and outfield.

wild pitch A pitched ball thrown in such a way that the catcher cannot catch it.

SUGGESTED READINGS

Craig, S., and Johnson, K. 1997. *Softball*. Dubuque, Iowa: WCB/McGraw-Hill. The authors present up-to-date analysis of fast-pitch softball fundamentals.

Elliot, J. 1990. *Youth softball: A complete handbook*. Carmel, Ind.: Benchmark Press. Contains information on fundamental skills, safety, equipment, facilities, legal liability, conditioning, coaching, nutrition, injuries, and motivation.

Kneer, M.E., and McCord, C. L. 1995. *Softball: Slow and fast pitch*, ed. 6. Dubuque, Iowa: WCB/McGraw-Hill. Covers equipment, rules, and techniques for both fast- and slow-pitch softball.

Pagnoni, M., and Robinson, G. 1992. *Softball*. North Palm Beach, Fla.: Athletic Institute. Emphasizes physical conditioning, hitting, fielding, throwing, baserunning, fast- and slow-pitching, and strategies of coaching.

Petroff, T. 1992. *Softball hitting*. North Palm Beach, Fla.: Athletic Institute. Stresses hitting techniques—stance, grip, stride, and bunting—as well as mental approach.

Potter, D., and Brockmeyer, G. 1989. *Teaching softball: Steps to success*. Champaign, Ill.: Human Kinetics. Contains management and safety guidelines, rating charts, drills, teaching cues, error detection, and written test questions.

Potter, D. L., and Brockmeyer, G. 1989. *Softball: Steps to success*. Champaign, Ill.: Human Kinetics. In 25 chapters the authors identify the keys to correct technique, describe common errors, provide practice drills, and suggest performance goals for softball skills.

Reach, J., Schwartz, B., and Van Wyk, K. 1989. *Softball everyone*. Winston-Salem, N.C.: Hunter Textbooks. Coverage of both slow- and fast-pitch softball. Includes history, equipment, terminology, scoring, rules, and building skills. Individual and team offensive and defensive skills are presented.

Rikli, R. 1991. *Softball skills test manual*. Reston, Va.: American Alliance for Health, Physical Education, Recreation and Dance. Contains skills tests with national norms, instructions for administration, and suggestions for their use.

RESOURCES

Videotapes

Five individual videotapes and one series of seven videotapes available from Cambridge Physical Education and Health, P.O. Box 2153, Charleston, WV 25328.

Fast-pitch series (five videotapes: *Hitting and bunting, Offensive strategies, Pitching mechanics, Pitcher development*, and *Team defense*) available, along with four others from "How To" Sports Videos, P.O. Box 5852, Denver, CO 80217.

Pitching and Hitting, Karol Video, 22 Riverside Dr., Wayne, NJ 07470.

Slow pitch softball: Reflex hitting system with Ray DeMarin, West One Videos, 1995 Bailey Hill Rd., Eugene, OR 97405.

Softball hitting and a series of three videotapes (*Basic skills in softball, Better hitting and baserunning*, and *Better pitching and defense*), Athletic Institute, 200 N. Castlewood Dr., North Palm Beach, FL 33408.

Speedball

After completing this chapter, the reader should be able to:

- Appreciate the wide variety of skills that can be developed in this game, which is a combination of basketball, touch football, and soccer
- Understand scoring procedures and rules for the game
- Demonstrate the many physical skills involved in speedball
- Modify the game to fit specific circumstances
- Instruct a group of students in the fundamentals of speedball
- Be familiar with the sport's terminology

HISTORY

Before 1920 the main team sports used for fall outdoor participation in physical education classes and intramural programs were touch football and soccer. Many recreation directors, physical education teachers, and coaches felt the need for a vigorous outdoor game through which participants could develop many basic skills. After much experimentation, Elmer D. Mitchell of the University of Michigan developed the rules for speedball, combining many of the fundamental elements and skills found in basketball, touch football, and soccer. Because speedball is designed to permit all players on a team to participate in all phases of the game, including catching, throwing, and kicking, it developed rapidly and is now widely used in recreation and physical education classes and in intramural programs throughout the United States.

Speedball gradually became popular with both sexes. However, because basketball and soccer rules for women differed from those for men, in 1933 the National Section of Women's Athletics of the American Association for Health, Physical Education, and Recreation revised and adapted speedball rules for girls and women.

As rules for men's and women's basketball and soccer become increasingly similar and with the passage of legislation mandating coeducational physical education classes, two sets of speedball rules are now considered unnecessary by the authors of this text. As with any physical activity, recreation leaders, physical educators, or coaches should select and modify the rules, field dimensions, and player positions to best fit their needs. We present here a version of speedball that no longer divides the activity into men's and women's games. This is a sport that lends itself well to coeducational situations.

GENERAL DESCRIPTION

Speedball is played by two teams. Although 11 players constitute a regulation team, the game can be played with fewer members. A variety of techniques are used in speedball, including kicking and dribbling the ball with the feet as in soccer, catching and throwing the ball as in basketball, and punting and passing the ball as in football. Because speedball combines the elements of basketball, soccer, and touch football, generally the soccer rules apply when the ball is on the ground, basketball rules apply to aerial or fly balls, and football rules usually apply in the forward passing of the ball and in scoring. The playing positions are listed in table 31-1 and shown in figure 31-1.

Table 31-1. PLAYING POSITIONS

Playing positions
Left wing
Left inner
Center
Right inner
Right wing
Left halfback
Center halfback
Right halfback
Left fullback
Right fullback
Goalkeeper

The object of the game is for the team in possession of the ball to advance the ball down the field toward the opponent's goal line and score. The opponents of the team in possession of the ball try to intercept and obtain possession of the ball to move it toward the opposite goal line in an attempt to score.

FIELD AND EQUIPMENT

Although fields of varying sizes can be used for speedball, the one most commonly used is the size of a football field. Figure 31-1 shows the dimensions of a speedball field. A middle line divides the playing area in half. Two restraining lines run parallel to the middle (halfway) line. There is a penalty area at each end of the field that extends the width of the field. The end-zone penalty area is 10 yards (9.14 m). The ball used for speedball is slightly larger than a soccer ball. Although the regulation ball is recommended for use, many schools prefer to use a soccer ball. The goalie should

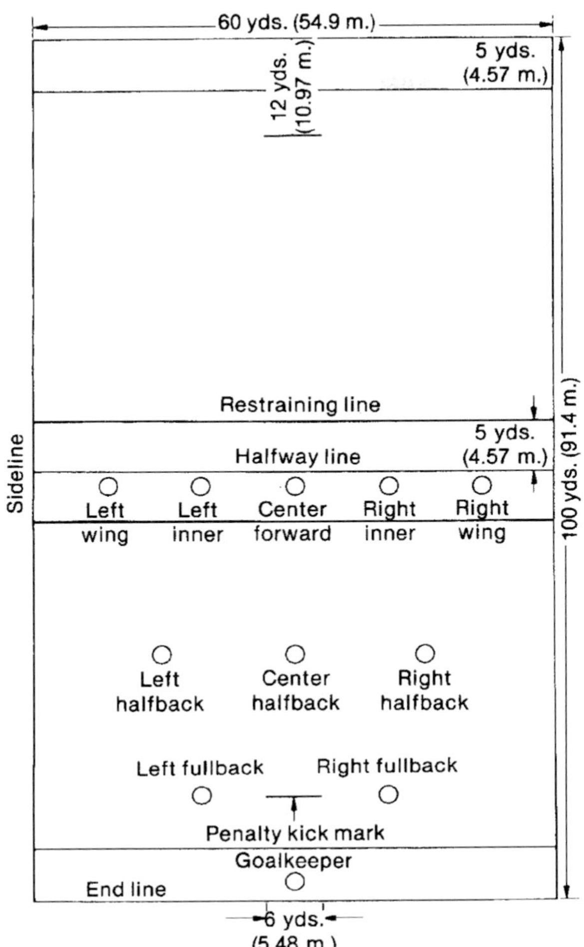

Figure 31-1. Speedball field and lineup.

be provided with gloves, shin guards, and, if desired, knee pads. All other players may wish to also use shin guards and soccer/cleated shoes for better traction.

SCORING

Points may be scored as follows.

Field goal. A field goal is scored when a ball that has been kicked or legally played with any part of the body passes between the goalposts and under the crossbar. A field goal counts 3 points.

Dropkick. A dropkick is made when the ball passes over the crossbar after having been drop-kicked from the field of play outside the penalty area. A dropkick counts 2 points.

Touchdown. A touchdown is scored when an offensive player passes the ball to a teammate who catches it behind the opponent's goal line. A touchdown counts 1 point.

Penalty kick. A penalty kick is scored when the player awarded the try kicks the ball between the goalposts and under the crossbar. A penalty kick counts 1 point.

Table 31-2. VALUES OF DIFFERENT TYPES OF SCORING

	Points
Field goal	3
Dropkick	2
Touchdown	1
Penalty kick	1
End goal	1

End goal. An end goal is scored when an offensive player who is in the end zone legally causes the ball to pass over the endline but not between the goalposts. An end goal counts 1 point.

The values of different types of scoring are given in table 31-2.

FUNDAMENTAL REGULATIONS

Officials

The officials for a game of speedball consist of two umpires, two timekeepers, and two scorers. The umpires have final authority in all decisions pertaining to the conduct of the game. Two linespersons may assist.

Duration of Game

A regulation speedball game consists of four 12-minute quarters with a 10-minute rest period between halves and a 2-minute interval between quarters. Each team is allowed three time-outs during a game. Each additional time-out taken by a team constitutes a technical foul.

Beginning the Game

The game and each quarter are started by having one team kick off (placekick) into its opponent's territory from the center of the field. The members of the kicking team line up on the middle, or halfway, line. They remain behind the ball until it is kicked. The opponents of the kicking team must remain behind their restraining line until the ball is kicked. The kickoff must travel the length of the circumference of the ball and may be lifted by the foot to a teammate. It may not be touched by the kicker until another player has touched it. Goals are changed at halftime. After a score, the team that did not score kicks off.

Playing the Game

Aerial, or fly, ball

A ball that has been kicked into the air is referred to as a fly ball or an aerial ball. A fly ball that has been caught may be passed from one player to another, as in basketball, or moved by a forward pass, as in football. It can continue to be played in this manner until it again touches the ground, becoming a ground ball. A player catching a fly ball is allowed to take one step in making a pass if the ball is caught while the player is standing still; two steps, if the player catches the ball while running.

Ground ball

A ball that is in contact with the ground is called a ground ball, whether it is stationary, rolling, or bouncing. The ball remains a ground ball, even though it may bounce into the air, until it is lifted into the air by a direct kick or a kick-up. A ground ball can be kicked, headed, or played with any part of the body except the hands and arms.

Dribbling the Ball

A player may dribble a ground ball with the feet using a succession of short kicks. A player may use one overhead dribble; that is, after catching the ball, the player may toss it into the air and catch it again. The player may toss it in any direction and run to catch it before it strikes the ground. Any number of steps may be taken before catching the ball after tossing it. Only one overhead dribble is permitted before passing to another player. A touchdown cannot be scored by an overhead dribble.

Goalkeeper

The main work of the goalkeeper is to keep the ball from going through the goal. The goalkeeper has no privileges or restrictions, but is governed by the same rules as other players.

Illegal Play

Although defensive play is allowed in speedball, blocking and tackling (as in football) are illegal. A player must attempt to secure the ball legally and without undue body contact or roughness.

Tie Ball

A tie ball is called when two opposing players catch the ball simultaneously, hold the ball without gaining possession, or commit a double foul, or when the officials are in doubt as to which side last touched the ball before it went out-of-bounds. In case of a tie ball, the official puts the ball into play by a jump ball (as in basketball). All players must remain at least 5 yards (4.57 m) from the spot where the ball is being put into play as a jump ball until it is touched by one of the jumpers. Following a jump ball, the ball may be played as a fly ball. A score may not result from a jump ball that is caught in the end zone, even though the ball is still in play. The jump ball is used at the spot of the foul in the case of a double foul. If the ball drops to the ground after the jump, either jumper can kick it.

Out-of-Bounds

When a player causes the ball to go out-of-bounds over the sidelines, it is put into play with a pass by a player of the opposing team. In returning the ball to the field of play, the player can use either an underhand or overhand pass and can use one or both hands. In the case of a double foul over the sideline, a jump ball is used 5 yards (4.57 m) in from where the foul was committed. When a player causes the ball to go over the end line without scoring, the opponents put the ball into play by a pass or a kick.

Penalty Kick

A placekick is used in making a penalty kick. A penalty kick is awarded as the result of a foul. The kick is made from the 10-yard (9.14 m) line. The defensive players may be behind the goal or in the field, as long as no one is within 5 yards (4.57 m) of the kicker.

RULES

Violations

The following infractions of rules are considered violations:

1. Traveling with the ball
2. Touching a ground ball with the hands or arms
3. Dribbling overhead more than once
4. Kicking or kneeing a fly ball before catching it
5. Causing the ball to go out-of-bounds
6. Interfering with a kickoff or jump ball
7. Illegally interfering with a penalty kick
8. Illegally interfering with a player returning the ball from out-of-bounds

Violation penalties

The penalty for a violation committed on the field of play outside of the end zone is that the opponents are awarded the ball out-of-bounds for a throw-in. If a violation is committed within the penalty area, one penalty kick is given to the opponents. If the penalty kick is missed, the ball continues in play.

Technical Fouls

The following infractions are considered technical fouls:

1. Illegal substitutions
2. Unsporting conduct
3. Unnecessary delay of the game
4. Taking more than three time-outs
5. Having more than 11 players on the playing field at one time

Technical-foul penalty

A penalty kick is awarded for a technical foul committed outside the penalty area. Any member of the team may make the penalty kick. If the penalty kick is not successful, the ball is dead and a touchback is awarded to the opponents.

Personal Fouls

Personal fouls include the following infractions:

1. Pushing, holding, kicking, tripping, charging, or blocking an opponent
2. Unnecessary roughness

Personal-foul penalties

If a personal foul is committed by a player within the penalty area, the offended team is given two penalty kicks. If the second kick is missed, the ball remains in play. If a player commits a personal foul outside the penalty area, the opponents are given one penalty kick. If the penalty kick is not successful, a touchback is declared.

Team Fouls

Team fouls include the following infractions:

1. Taking more than three time-outs
2. Having more than 11 players on the field of play at one time
3. Failing to report to the officials before going into the game

Penalties for team fouls

One penalty kick is awarded for each team foul. In the case of a double foul, two opposing players jump for toss-up.

FUNDAMENTAL SKILLS AND TECHNIQUES

Dribbling with the Feet

Dribbling with the feet is used in moving the ball toward an opponent's goal line, most often in situations where it is not advisable to kick up or kick to a teammate. In dribbling the ball it is extremely important to control the ball at all times, which means that it must not be kicked with force. In most cases the inside surface of the foot should be used for best control, although experienced players may use the outside of the foot along the area of the little toe. Ordinarily, for best control the ball should be kicked from an even run about every third step.

Instep Kick/Pass

This type of kick is the most accurate because the individual generally has better control of the ball. The player should place the nonkicking foot next to the ball and then the kicking foot strikes the ball along the arch area of the inside of the foot.

Outside-of-the-Foot Kick/Pass

This kick, performed with the outside of the foot, is used to push/pass the ball to a teammate.

Passing

Many types of basketball passes may be used. Any kind of one- or two-hand throw is acceptable depending on the particular situation. The baseball-type pass is used extensively in speedball because of the wide playing field available. A player with the ball may pivot as in basketball if one foot is stabilized. This sometimes helps in finding a teammate open to receive a pass.

Overhead Dribble

Only one overhead dribble is allowed. The overhead dribble is made by tossing the ball into the air and running to catch it before it strikes the ground. There is no restriction on the number of steps that may be taken after tossing the ball and before catching it again. The overhead dribble is particularly useful when a closely guarded player tosses the ball over the head of the opponent to get free.

Placekicking

The placekick is used in an attempt to score after a foul. The ball is placed on the 10-yard (9.14 m) line. The object is to kick the ball past the goalkeeper, between the goalposts, and under the crossbar. The goalkeeper is the only player on the opposing team who is permitted to defend against the placekick.

Drop-Kicking

For the best control of the ball in drop-kicking, hold the ball just above the knees, flex at the waist, drop the ball to the ground, and kick it just as it bounces; take one step with the left foot and kick the ball with the right foot, or vice versa (figure 31-2).

Punting

Punting in speedball is used to advance the ball toward the opponent's goal line as quickly as possible. Techniques of punting in speedball are similar to those in football. The ball should be kicked with the upper surface of the instep. Take one step forward with the left foot, drop the ball from extended arms, and kick the ball with the right foot. The ball should be dropped as the foot starts its upward swing. If the player kicks with the left foot, the reverse technique should be used.

Catching

The ball should be caught with the entire hand, because many passes are vigorously thrown. After the catch, the ball should be held with the fingers. Inasmuch as catching a speedball is similar to catching a basketball, the same technique should be practiced in perfecting this skill.

Trapping

Trapping with the feet

In trapping the ball with the foot, the player extends the leg forward toward the ball with the heel 4 to 5 inches (10 to 13 cm) above the ground and the toe pointing upward. The sole of the foot is presented to the ball as it approaches. When the ball comes within reach of the foot, the player presses down and traps the ball between the sole of the foot and the ground.

Figure 31-2. Drop kick.

Trapping with the legs

In trapping the ball with the right leg, the player slightly advances the left leg diagonally forward and outward and flexes the right leg as though intending to kneel. The flexion should be inward over the right toe. The ball should be trapped between the lower leg and the ground. In double-leg trapping, the feet are close together as the rolling ball approaches from the front. The player traps the ball by kneeling on it. However, the weight of the body should remain over the feet. More advanced players may stop a rolling ball by rotating either leg outward, contacting the ball with the inside of the foot, and "giving" as contact is made.

Trapping with the body

Any part of the body, except the hands and arms, may be used to stop or slow the ball. To prevent the ball from rebounding too vigorously off the body, the player should move back slightly at the instant of impact.

Kick-Up

In many situations a ground ball may be played more advantageously by converting it into an aerial ball. A player may convert a ground ball into a fly ball by kicking it into the air.

Kick-up with two feet

With the ball held firmly between the insides of the feet and ankles, the player jumps into the air, lifting the ball upward (figure 31-3). After releasing the ball from the ankles and feet, the player catches it before it touches the ground. Because the kick-up is one of the easiest ways to pick up a ground ball, players should practice and develop considerable skill in its use.

Kick-up with one foot

This play can be made on a rolling ball by flipping the ball into the air with the foot and catching it after it leaves the foot but before it touches the ground. As the rolling ball approaches, the player should extend the leg forward with the pointed toe touching the ground. As the ball rolls onto the instep of the foot, the player flips the ball into the air and catches it.

The one-foot kick-up can be made on a stationary ball by placing the foot on top of the ball and drawing it backward to start the ball rolling toward the player. Then the toe is quickly placed under the ball so that it will roll onto the instep. When it rolls onto the instep, the player quickly flips the ball into the air and catches it before it touches the ground (figures 31-4 and 31-5). The kick-up technique on both a rolling ball and a stationary ball can also be used to lift the ball to a teammate.

OFFENSIVE PLAY

In moving the ball down the field, the forward line should be spread out and the players should attempt to stay in front of the ball. As the ball approaches the goal line, the wings should go across the endline to receive a forward pass. The halfbacks should remain in a position to back up the forwards or try to score if an opportunity presents itself. Also, the halfbacks should be ready to guard against

Figure 31-3. Kick-up with two feet.

Figure 31-4. Kick-up with one foot (side view).

the opposing team if the ball is intercepted and lost. A long kickoff deep into the opponent's territory usually is best. The kicking team should move rapidly down the field after the kickoff to prevent the opponents from returning the ball toward their goal line. In a game comprised of novice players, a long kickoff downfield is not always the best strategy. The best strategy often is to keep control of the ball by dribbling it along the ground or converting it into an aerial ball or to gain possession of the ball by a kick-up or by using a short control pass.

DEFENSIVE PLAY

One-on-one player defense is most often used. Fullbacks, guards, and halfbacks guard the opposing forwards. The goalkeeper may leave position to assist in stopping a touchdown play when necessary.

Figure 31-5. Kick-up with one foot (front view).

TEACHING CONSIDERATIONS

1. Decide on the rules applicable for coed situations. Most students will have had some experience with basketball, soccer, and football; teach speedball as a combination of these sports. Be clear about how to score and how to legally play aerial and ground balls. Use a modified soccer ball for young learners.
2. If soccer is part of the school curriculum, less time need be spent on dribbling and passing skills with the feet. If soccer is not a part of the curriculum, this part of the game will need more work than passing and throwing skills using the hands.
3. Teach students how to move the ball down the field (both aerial and ground balls) and how to convert ground balls to aerial balls. Practice until these skills are developed with some consistency. Work with executing the punt and catching punts as a way to move the ball down the field. Help students to understand that dribbling with the feet is the slowest way for groups to move the ball. Use small groups of partners or groups of three to practice moving the ball.
4. Add defensive players only after students have some control of both aerial and ground balls. Start with two-on-one, three-on-one, and three-on-two situations to introduce defensive and offensive play of both aerial and ground balls. Gradually add additional offensive and defensive players. Practice the types of scoring possibilities first without defense and then with defense, again initially giving the offense the advantage.
5. Use smaller fields and fewer players (four, six, or eight) on a team when play begins. For example, divide the length of the field to make three fields of 60 by 33⅓ yards (54.9 × 30.3 m) and play widthwise with 6 to 8 players per team. This will allow offensive and defensive strategies to be better understood and practiced and will give students more practice opportunities with basic skills.
6. Introduce penalty kicks only after continuous play has been achieved.
7. Some examples of lead-up game activities might include:
   a. Keep away
   b. Dribble, kick-up, and pass to a teammate
   c. Toe pick-ups to a teammate while running down the field
   d. Punting and punt receiving
   e. Minigames (smaller fields, fewer players)
8. Circuit station probabilities might include:
   a. Dribble through or around obstacles
   b. Conditioning activities
   c. One-foot lift to a target area
   d. Volleying with partners
   e. Goal shooting and goalkeeping

GLOSSARY

aerial ball A ball that has been raised into the air by either a one- or two-foot kick; a punt, dropkick, kick-up, or thrown ball that has not touched the ground. Also called a "fly ball."

air dribble A ball that is tossed or tapped into the air and caught by the same player.

attackers The team in possession of the ball.
blocking the ball Intercepting the ball with any part of the body. A player cannot block a ground ball with the arms or hands unless a ground ball is in contact with the body.
closely guarded Being guarded within 3 feet (0.9 m).
dead ball A ball no longer in play; out-of-bounds, after a score, after a foul, during time out, or a tie ball.
defenders The team not in possession of the ball.
double foul Fouls committed at the same time by both teams; a toss-up is awarded.
dribble Advancing the ball by a series of kicks.
dropkick Dropping the ball to the ground and kicking it just as it bounces from the ground.
end goal Passing the ball over the endline but not between the goalposts; counts 1 point.
field goal Passing the ball between the goalposts and under the crossbar; counts 3 points.
foul An infringement of the rules for which a free kick, free throw, or penalty kick is awarded the opponents.
free kick A placekick from which a goal can be scored directly.
free throw A throw taken by any player on the team that has been fouled during the play of an aerial ball.
goalkeeper A player whose duty it is to defend the goal.
ground ball A stationary, rolling, or bouncing ball that is in contact with the ground.
handling the ball Putting the hands or arms on a ground ball.
indirect free kick A free kick from which a goal cannot be scored directly.
kick-up The play converting a ground ball into an aerial ball.
own goal The goal one's team is defending.
own half The half of the field in which one's own goal is located.
passing Means of moving the ball by passes or batting with the hands to another player.
penalty kick A free kick awarded as the result of a foul; a placekick from the 10-yard (9.14 m) line, and the ball must go under the crossbar.
placekick A stationary ball kicked by a player.
punt A play in which a player drops a caught ball and kicks it before it touches the ground.
trapping Stopping the motion of the ball by placing the sole of the foot on it, by kneeling on it, or by catching it between the front of the legs and the ground.
volley A play in which a player fields a fly, or aerial, ball with some part of the body, such as the head, hip, or shoulder.

Springboard Diving

After completing this chapter, the reader should be able to:

- Describe the origins of diving and the few standardized diving rules
- Be cognizant of safety precautions for springboard diving
- Be familiar with a progression of activities to be used as a lead-up to springboard diving
- Recognize the groups of dives and the fundamental skills of the approach, hurdles, and entry
- Teach, in a logical progression, jumping from the diving board, the basic required dives, and a few more-difficult optional dives

HISTORY

Diving is a form of aerial acrobatics. It is an outgrowth of gymnastics. Instead of landing on a mat, the diver dives into water, either headfirst or feetfirst.

Originally, diving into water was more or less a stunt, such as a high dive from a bridge, from flying rings suspended over a pool, or from a rope suspended from a branch to swing the performer far out over the water.

The competitive sport of diving is believed to have originated in the early 1900s in England, Germany, and Sweden. At that time only a few simple dives were perfected. The dives were named after their originators, such as "the Mollberg," which was later changed to "full gainer" and is now known as the "reverse somersault." The half reverse was first called the "flying Dutchman," later the "half gainer," and now is known as the "reverse dive."

During the past 40 years, competitive diving has developed into one of the most beautiful, thrilling, and spectacular of aerial acrobatics. It is both fun and great sport.

Men's springboard and platform diving have been dominated by divers from the United States. The gold medal in the springboard event has been won by a U.S. diver in 15 of the 20 Olympics since it was introduced in 1908, and in the platform event 12 of the 22 times since 1904. Although not quite as dominant, the U.S. women divers have also enjoyed great success. They have captured the gold in the springboard event in 11 of 18 Olympics, and in the platform event 8 of 19 times.

In fact, between 1920 and 1976 the United States won 106 of a possible 156 Olympic medals in men's and women's springboard and platform events. (The United States boycotted the 1980 Olympics.)

Greg Louganis continued domination in the sport by U.S. men by being the first male diver in 56 years to win the gold in both the springboard and platform events in 1984, and then topped this achievement by being the first male ever to repeat this performance at the 1988 Olympics. Chinese divers have improved, however, and in 1988 captured the silver and bronze in both springboard and platform diving in the men's event and dominated the women's events, with the exception of U.S. diver Kelly McCormick's bronze in the springboard event.

In 1992 at Barcelona (with Greg Louganis retired) the United States still fared well with Mark Lenzi winning the gold in springboard and Scott Donie winning the silver in platform. Mary Ellen Clark captured the bronze for the United States in women's platform, and Julie Ovenhouse finished fifth in springboard. Once again the Chinese divers continued to improve, winning three of the four gold medals, as well as a silver and a bronze.

In 1996 the Chinese divers repeated this performance by again winning 3 of the 4 gold medals as well as a silver and a bronze. For the United States, Mark Lenzi captured the bronze in men's 3-meter and Mary Ellen Clark brought home the bronze in the women's 10-meter.

SAFETY

Although springboard diving is an exciting activity, it requires close attention to the following precautions to make it safe:*

1. Make sure the water is deep enough for diving. No matter how shallow you intend your dive to be, remember that diving from the deck into water shallower than 9 feet (2.75 m) could cause a head or spinal injury or even death. The only exception to this rule is supervised racing starts done by trained swimmers who are under direct supervision. For racing starts, the American Red Cross recommends that the water be at least 5 feet (1.52 m) deep. (United States Swimming, the National Collegiate Athletic Association, and the National Federation of High School Associations require a minimum depth of 4 feet [1.22 m] below a standard 30-inch [76 cm] starting block.) Diving into above-ground pools is never safe.

*Adapted from American Red Cross: *Swimming and diving*, St. Louis, 1992, Mosby.

2. When you dive from a deck or diving board, make sure there is enough room to maneuver and that the water is free of obstructions. Because some people need more room to maneuver than others, be sure you have enough room for yourself. Always dive directly forward from a deck or diving board. When you dive from a deck, the area of entry should be free from obstructions (such as lane lines and kickboards) for at least 4 feet (1.22 m) on both sides. For dives from a 3.3-feet (1 m) diving board, you need 10 feet (3.05 m) of clearance on both sides.
3. Make sure you are physically capable of doing a dive and psychologically ready to try it.
4. In a headfirst dive, extend your arms with your elbows locked alongside your head. Keep your hands together with thumbs touching (or interlocked) and palms facing toward the water. Keeping your arms, wrists, and fingers in line with your head helps you control the angle of entry. This reduces the impact of the water on the top of the head and helps protect you from injury. Keep your body tensed and straight from the hands to the pointed toes.
5. For springboard diving, use equipment that meets the standards set for competition.

Figure 32-1. Dive in pike position.

RULES

A few simple rules are now standardized internationally:

1. A dive is executed from either a standing, running, or handstand position.
2. It is executed from either a backward or forward starting position.
3. It can be performed from either a rigid platform or a springboard.
4. It must be executed in one of four body positions:
   a. Tuck, in which your body is flexed at both hips and knees.
   b. Pike, in which your body is flexed at the hips (figure 32-1).
   c. Straight, in which your body is held straight throughout the dive (figure 32-2).
   d. Free, which is some combination of the other positions (usually pike and straight) and is used only in certain twisting dives.
5. Your legs must be held together at all times, with toes pointed.
6. Entry can be either headfirst or feetfirst.
7. Competitive springboard diving must be performed from either a 3.3- or 9.9-foot (1 m or 3 m) height from the water.
8. Platform diving must be performed from a height of 32.8 feet (10 m).
9. A springboard must be either 14 or 16 feet (4.27 or 4.88 m) long by 20 inches (50.8 cm) wide. It must be 16 feet (4.88 m) for championships.

Figure 32-2. Dive in straight position.

ELEMENTARY DIVING TECHNIQUES (PROGRESSIVE LEARNING FOR BEGINNERS)

Before attempting springboard diving, the beginner should start in the water at the shallow end of the pool, pushing off from the sidewall and gliding as far as possible on the surface, with the entire body stretched out straight, arms and legs held together, head down between the arms, and toes pointed. By experimenting, the beginner will discover how some positions are more streamlined than others. This principle applies to entering the water following a dive.

Undersurface Dive

Push off as described, but direct your arms and head at a shallow angle toward the bottom. When nearing the bottom, turn your hands and head upward and your body will again glide to the surface.

Deep-Water Surface Dive: Pike

This dive requires considerable skill in the use of your hands and arms, inasmuch as one cannot push with the feet from the bottom of the pool as in the shallow-water dive. But it is not too difficult for the beginner. It teaches you to pike with your legs straight at the knees and with your ankles stretched and held together. This is a swimming and lifesaving skill. It is performed from the surface of the water in a breaststroke swimming position.

Take a deep breath, duck your head sharply, pull your arms laterally to your hips as in the breaststroke, face your palms down and press the water downward, and sweep your arms forward. When your trunk is vertical, or upside down, your body is in a pike position with your legs lying on the surface. Now lift your legs vertically above your hips as your arms sweep forward. The weight of your legs above the water will push your body down toward the bottom. Tuck, rotate, place your feet on the bottom, and push up to the surface, with your arms trailing at your sides. Repeat several dives continuously, getting a breath above the surface between each dive.

Deep-Water Surface Dive: Tuck

The tuck is performed exactly like the pike, except that your knees as well as your hips are bent. This teaches a closely bunched tuck for somersault dives. Note that your body turns down more easily than in the pike position.

ELEMENTARY DIVING FROM POOL DECK

The steps for learning a simple dive from the pool deck will provide self-confidence and a feeling of success. Remember to move through the steps at your own pace. Some steps might require more practice than others. If you have good coordination and kinesthetic awareness, you may be able to move through them quickly. This progression may also be used to learn to dive from a dock.

Figure 32-3. Kneeling position.

Kneeling Position

Kneel on one knee while gripping the pool edge with the toes of the other foot (figure 32-3). The foot of your kneeling leg should be in a position to help push from the deck. Extend your arms over your head as shown. Focus on a target either on the bottom about 4 feet (1.22 m) out from the side or on the surface of the water 1 to 2 feet (0.3 to 0.6 m) from the side. The objective is to dive deep. Focusing on a target helps you enter the water at the right place and at the correct angle, avoiding a belly flop. Lean forward, try to touch the water, and when you start to lose your balance, push with your legs. As you enter the water, straighten your body and extend both legs. Practice this skill until you feel comfortable with it and can do it without error.

Compact Position

You do this dive in much the same manner as a dive from the kneeling position. Put one foot forward and one back, with the toes of your leading foot gripping the edge of the deck (figure 32-4). Start in the kneeling position. Then lift

Figure 32-4. Compact position.

Figure 32-5. Stride position.

Figure 32-6. Standing dive—start.

up until both knees are off the deck and flexed so that you stay close to the water. Extend your arms above your head. Focus on a target the same distance from the deck as in the dive from a kneeling position. Bend forward and try to touch the surface of the water with your hands. When you start to lose your balance, push off toward the water. Bring your legs together as you enter the water.

Stride Position

After several successful dives from the compact position, you should be ready for a dive from the stride position. Stand upright with one leg forward and one leg back. The toes of your forward foot should grip the edge of the pool. Extend your arms above your head. Focus on a target on the bottom of the pool 5 to 6 feet (1.5 to 1.8 m) out from the side or on the surface 3 to 4 feet (0.9 to 1.2 m) out. Bend your legs only slightly as you bend at the waist toward the water. Try to touch the surface of the water and, as you lose your balance, lift your back leg until it is in line with your torso (figure 32-5). Your forward leg should stay as straight as possible.

Standing Dive

The final dive from the deck is the standing dive. Stand with your feet about shoulder-width apart, with the toes of both feet gripping the edge of the deck. Extend your arms above your head. Focus on a target at the same distance as in a dive from the stride position. Bend at the knees and angle your hands down toward the target (figure 32-6). Push off the deck, lift your hips, and extend your legs so they are in line with your torso (figure 32-7). As you gain confidence, you may move your feet closer together.

Figure 32-7. Standing dive—finish.

TECHNIQUES OF SPRINGBOARD JUMP DIVES

The beginner should progressively advance to the next category of elementary dives, the jump dives. In all of these, the diver enters the water feet first. The dives are first executed from a standing position at the takeoff end of the board to give the student the sensation of a springing takeoff from slightly higher than the side of the pool.

Front Jump: Straight

As your body leaves the board, reach your arms upward, shoulder-width apart, fingers and thumbs squeezed together. Press your head and shoulders slightly backward to keep your body from falling forward and to keep it

Figure 32-8. Standing or running front jump—straight position.

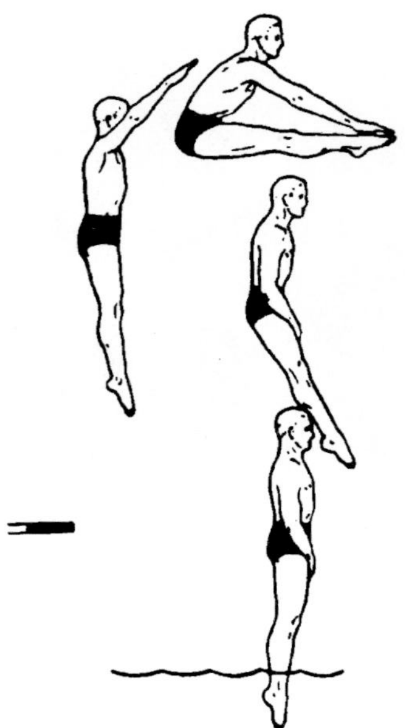

Figure 32-9. Standing or running front jump—pike position.

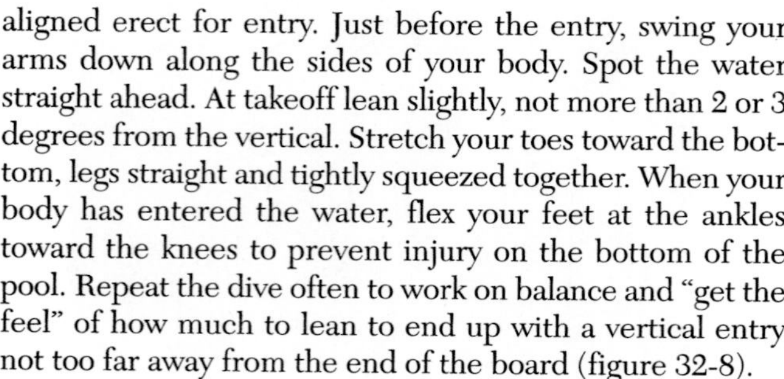

aligned erect for entry. Just before the entry, swing your arms down along the sides of your body. Spot the water straight ahead. At takeoff lean slightly, not more than 2 or 3 degrees from the vertical. Stretch your toes toward the bottom, legs straight and tightly squeezed together. When your body has entered the water, flex your feet at the ankles toward the knees to prevent injury on the bottom of the pool. Repeat the dive often to work on balance and "get the feel" of how much to lean to end up with a vertical entry not too far away from the end of the board (figure 32-8).

Front Jump: Pike

Reach your arms toward the ceiling as in the straight front jump. Just before your body reaches maximum height, with your legs held together straight at the knees and toes pointed, flex your body at the hips. Hold your head erect and spot with your eyes straight ahead. Lower your arms to your legs, hands touching your toes. Unpike immediately and slide your hands along your legs to the side of your body for the entry. Entry is the same as in the straight front jump. Considerably more skill, balance, and control are required to achieve a vertical entry when performing a front jump pike than when performing a front jump straight (figure 32-9).

Front Jump: Tuck

This dive is easier to perform than the pike, but it teaches the fundamentals of tucking and untucking. The diver reaches high at the takeoff and, instead of piking, tucks the body. To execute this dive, the knees are brought up to the chest, and the knees and ankles are held together and the ankles extended. The arms are lowered, the hands grasping the lower legs and pulling them in so that the heels are brought toward the buttocks in a tight tuck. The hip and knee joints must be relaxed. The head is held erect throughout the dive, with eyes directed forward. The tuck is held until after the diver has passed the peak of height. As legs are untucked, they shoot downward and are pressed backward in line with the trunk. The hands slide down to the sides of the body. On all foot-entry dives, the arms are to be held at the sides of the body, not overhead (figure 32-10).

Back Jump

As the diver jumps from the board, the arms swing up in front of the body, while kept straight, to an overhead position. The arms are stretched upward. As the diver jumps upward and backward from the board, the head and body must be held erect to avoid a falling takeoff. As the diver descends from the peak, the hands are lowered to the thighs, and a vertical entry is made. The eyes should remain focused on a spot on the wall at eye level at the rear wall or on the anchored end of the diving board. The eyes then aid the body to control itself during the dive. The back jump may also be executed in pike and tuck (figures 32-11 to 32-13).

Figure 32-10. Standing or running front jump—tuck position.

Figure 32-12. Standing backward jump—pike position.

Figure 32-11. Standing backward jump—straight position.

Figure 32-13. Standing backward jump dive—tuck position.

FUNDAMENTAL TECHNIQUES OF SPRINGBOARD DIVING

Forward Approach

There are many different skills to be learned in the art of diving. Two of the most essential are good body control and coordination. This means proper movement of arms in the hurdle and proper handling and straightening of knees and ankles in dropping on and springing from the board. Obtaining adequate height above the water is one of the prerequisites for becoming a good diver. The trampoline is an excellent training apparatus for developing height in dives, for losing the fear of height, and for learning to maintain balance. A trampoline should only be used under direct supervision of a diving coach or instructor.

The approach is a skill consisting of the stance, walk, hurdle, and takeoff.

Stance

Assume an erect position, with your chest and chin up, stomach drawn in, and arms along the sides of your body, feet together. (See figures 32-14 and 32-15 for the progressive stages of the approach.)

Walk

The forward approach must consist of at least three steps. The hurdle is not a step. Most competitive divers prefer four or five steps and a hurdle. The steps should be of moderate speed and natural. The last step should be a little

Figure 32-14. Series of ideal forms for executing standing takeoff.

Figure 32-15. Series of ideal forms for executing three-step run, hurdle, and takeoff.

longer than the others. During the walk, focus your eyes on the tip of the board until just before your feet land on the board; then raise your eyes to a focal point on the water several feet in front of the board.

The steps in your walk should be normal walking steps rather than long ones.

Hurdle and takeoff

The hurdle for adults should be approximately 2 feet (0.6 m) long for adults, shorter for children. If using the four-step approach, and assuming that your left foot is the best takeoff foot, start the approach with your right foot. As you step onto the takeoff foot, your shoulder girdle and head should pull up erect from the forward lean of your walk, eyes focused on the end of the board. Your hands are slightly behind your hips, fingers and thumbs straight and squeezed together. From this position your arms swing forward and are lifted above your head. The knee opposite your takeoff leg is sharply raised to aid your takeoff leg and arm to reach maximum height in the hurdle for a longer drop onto the end of the board. During the drop, your body is stretched straight with both legs together. Just as your feet are about to contact the board, raise your toes slightly to drop onto the balls of your feet and bend your knees. Your arms are now moving downward and backward toward your hips in preparation for the landing. As you land and the board bends for your body weight, your arms swing past your hips, as straight as possible, and up in front of your body to an overhead position at the point of takeoff. As your arms swing up, your legs extend against the board, and both of these actions aid in depressing the diving board. Finally, the board recoils, sending you into the air. You must stay in contact with the board until it is through bending down and until it rebounds. The takeoff should not be hurried. A great deal of practice is required to acquire an accurate hurdle and line of flight from the takeoff.

Height and Line of Flight

Height in diving is the vertical distance of the highest peak reached by the body's center of motion in the line of flight. The line of flight is the path described by the center of body weight from the takeoff to the entry. Height and correct line of flight are a natural result when the walk, hurdle, and takeoff are well controlled and timed. Too much effort or muscular power in the walk and takeoff will result in inconsistency for the takeoff.

Entry

The point of entry of a dive should be at a spot on the surface directly under the center of body weight, on a line with the descending flight of the body, and projected downward to the bottom of the pool. The diver should follow the line of flight well below the surface of the water. Arching the body upward too soon under the surface can result in a bad back sprain.

For headfirst entries, your arms should be sharply closed several feet above the surface and held in line with your spine. Your head is held between your arms so that the water hits your hands instead of your head upon entry. Your legs must be stretched and closed tightly, your ankles and toes stretched and pointed in line with your legs. Your feet should pass into the same hold on the surface that your head entered. Your body should not be arched at entry.

On foot-entry dives, your body is held erect, your arms are closed snugly along the sides of your body, and your head is held erect.

Back Approach

Dives in the back and inward groups and some dives in the twisting groups require the diver to start from a position on the end of the diving board with the back facing the water.

Approach

You take the initial position on the board as if doing a forward approach. However, after a momentary pause, you walk confidently to the end of the board. The walk to the end of the board should end approximately 18 to 24 inches (46 to 61 cm) from the end of the board with your left foot leading (the following directions can be reversed if you prefer to pivot in the opposite direction). Your right foot is then crossed in front of your left leg and placed at the end of the board. As your weight is shifted to the ball of your right foot, you simultaneously raise both arms so that they extend directly forward from the shoulder (parallel with the diving board) and execute a one-half turn to the left. This movement results in a position with the front part of your right foot on the board and the back part of your right foot off the board over the water. Then your left foot is brought into place next to your right foot, and with your arms still extended your feet are adjusted to secure proper balance with your heels parallel to the water. Finally, your arms are lowered to the sides. You must keep your center of gravity over the relatively small base of support (front half of your feet), and there is a slight feeling of leaning forward. For inward dives your center of gravity should be slightly more forward than for backward or backward twisting dives.

Takeoff mechanics

The first motion is to lift your arms (extended) laterally and slightly forward from the sides of your body (figure 32-16). Your arms may be raised to shoulder height or above, depending on your preference. As your arms move upward, your body is also raised up on your toes. This action causes a reaction by the board, and it is important to time the rest of the takeoff with the rhythm of the board. Most divers take a deep breath during this initial movement.

Figure 32-16. Series of ideal forms for executing the back takeoff.

Your initial arm movement is crucial to the success of the takeoff. If done too forcefully, the movement can cause your entire body to lose contact with the board (called a crow-hop) and destroy the rhythm of the takeoff.

Next, your arms circle back as your knees bend to push the diving board down. The driving action of your arms continues until the hands are slightly below the hips, where it quickly changes direction and your arms begin to move upward again. Just before your arms change direction from downward to upward, your knees and ankles extend against the board and your arms reach up into the intended line of flight of the dive.

Except for the time your arms are changing from downward to upward, they should remain fairly straight during the takeoff movement. During the downward phase of the takeoff, your hips actually move slightly down and back to compensate for your knees and shoulders bending slightly forward. It is important to keep your shoulders over your knees and your hips over your heels.

GROUPS OF DIVES

Competitive dives are categorized into five groups:

Group I—Forward dives
Group II—Backward dives
Group III—Reverse dives
Group IV—Inward dives
Group V—Twisting dives

All are combinations of the forward or backward dive with either a somersault or a twist in one of the straight, pike, tuck, or free positions. The dives described here are listed in group order, but the following sequence is recommended for teaching them to beginning divers:

1. Forward dive: tuck
2. Forward dive: pike
3. Forward dive: straight
4. Backward dive: straight
5. Inward dive: tuck
6. Inward dive: pike
7. Forward dive: half twist
8. Backward somersault: tuck
9. Forward somersault: tuck
10. Reverse somersault: tuck
11. Reverse dive
12. Forward one-and-one-half somersault

Group I: Forward Dive: Tuck

As your feet make contact with the board at the end of the hurdle, your eyes focus straight ahead. After the lift into the air, focus on the water directly below. After the reach into the air, your head goes down and your hips go up. Keep looking at the water during this maneuver. Bend at the knees and hips and grab your legs midway between your ankles and knees. Hold on to your legs until you have rotated enough to straighten out for a vertical entry. This dive is a good skill to use while learning to dive or for practicing head-first entries.

Group I: Forward Dive: Pike

The takeoff is made with your hands held close together in an overhead reach. The pike is started at the end of the reach. Your feet are pressed forward, your arms are moved downward, and your hips are lifted above your head as your body rises into the peak of the dive. Your eyes are spotted on the surface of the water below you. As the peak of the dive is reached, your hands are brought into contact with your feet. Your legs at this point are in a vertical position, with your toes pointing downward.

As your body drops below the peak of the dive, it has rotated slightly forward, so that its position resembles an inverted V. Your legs are then lifted slowly as your body starts to open up, and the continued rotation of your body places it in a vertical position for the entry. As your legs lift upward, your arms reach forward to a position along the sides of your head, and your hands are held close together at the entry.

Group I: Forward Dive: Straight

This dive is commonly known as the "swan" or "plain front dive." It is, in reality, a half somersault. The difficulty of this dive lies in the amount of body control required to

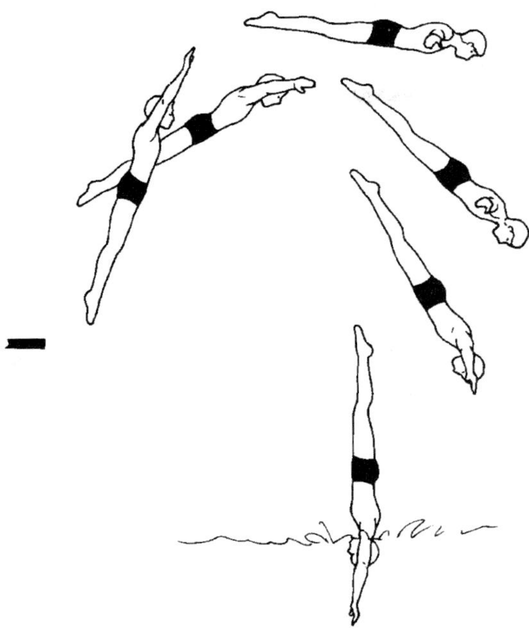

Figure 32-17. Forward dive—straight position.

maintain the body in good alignment while in the air. As your feet come in contact with the board at the end of the hurdle, your eyes are lifted from the board and are focused straight ahead. Your face is held directly forward until after the peak of the dive has been reached. When you leave the board, your body should be stretched. Your hands are lifted from your hips and are spread out straight from your shoulders with a slight forward angle. A line across your upper back should follow along the top of your arms when your body is in the straight position. From the head down, your body should be straight and your legs held close together with your toes pointed.

As the peak of the dive is reached, your body rotates forward around its center of mass, which is just above your hip joint. This rotation lifts your legs upward and levels your trunk, so that your heels are just above your head level when your body is at its peak.

The rotation continues as your body falls from the peak, and your head is slowly dropped between your arms as your eyes are shifted to the point of entry. Your hands are brought close together as the vertical entry is made.

You should reach for the bottom as the entry into the water is made (figure 32-17).

Group II: Backward Dive: Straight

Although the backward takeoff dives are blind dives, they are easy to perform in that the body is simply levered backward and additional movements are then made.

As your body lifts from the board in the dive, your eyes are first focused overhead. Your arms reach upward and slightly backward and are spread in line with the back of your spine. At the height of the lift, when your head is about at the peak of the dive, your head is stretched backward and your eyes begin to look for the entry spot in the water behind you.

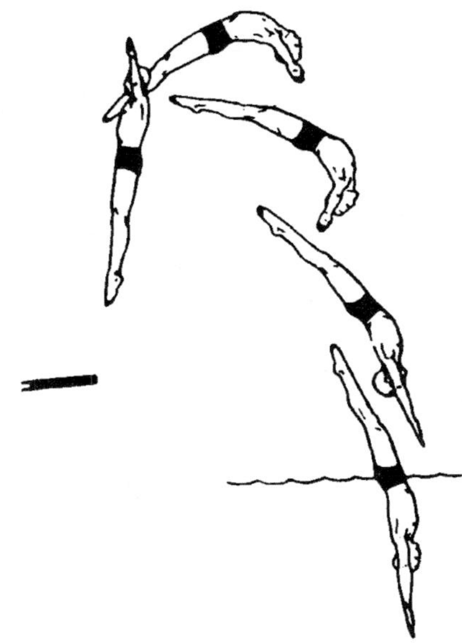

Figure 32-18. Back dive—straight position.

During this head and arm action, your hips and legs should be lifted and your knees and ankles must be stretched. Your arms are brought together when your body has dropped to a point opposite the board, and the entry is made with your hands close together and your head between your arms (figure 32-18).

Group III: Reverse Dive: Straight

As your body drops onto the board preliminary to the takeoff for this dive, your weight should remain over your toes, and you should not shift your weight backward as your heels contact the board. As the board lifts you, the center of body weight (in your hips) should be shifted just in front of your base of support (balls of feet), so that your body is easily projected forward and upward.

The reverse dive is one of the most graceful of all dives. It is essentially a backward dive from a forward takeoff. You actually gain distance in a forward direction, thus the name "gainer" or "reverse dive."

At takeoff, your arms lift to an overhead position, then spread laterally to shoulder level as your eyes look upward and your head is tilted back. When your body reaches the position at the end of the lift from takeoff, your head, arms, and shoulders are levered backward and your chest, hips, and legs are lifted as well as stretched. When your body reaches the horizontal position at the peak, your legs remain lifted as if anchored, because backward rotation causes your

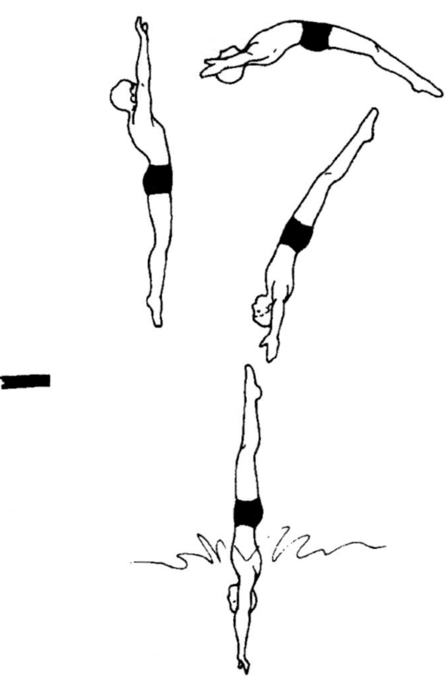

Figure 32-19. Reverse dive—straight position.

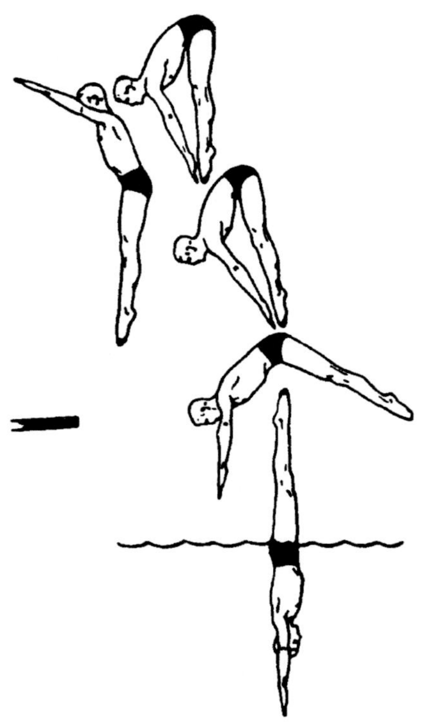

Figure 32-20. Inward dive—pike position.

head and shoulders to drop. Your arms are closed, your head is brought between your arms, and your body is straightened as it drops in a vertical entry (figure 32-19).

Group IV: Inward Dive: Pike

While your body is poised over the end of the board, your center of mass is over the balls of your feet. During the preliminary arm movements of the takeoff, your center of mass moves vertically but should not move forward or backward.

At the time of takeoff from the board, your arms are straight and reaching overhead and slightly forward of a vertical line with the palms facing forward.

At the end of the reach, your hips are flexed and raised, your arms are brought forward and downward, and your hands touch the front of your feet at the peak. Your hips have lifted above your head to the peak of the dive. Your legs are vertical when the pike is completed. Your eyes sight over your toes to the entry point as the touch occurs. After you touch your feet, your body begins to straighten as your arms are moved laterally to an overhead position in preparation for the entry (figure 32-20).

Group V: Forward Dive, Half Twist: Straight

The takeoff is similar to the forward dive: straight with the twist initiated just before leaving the board by turning your shoulders in the desired direction of the twist. The arms are spread to a T position at your body lifts to the top of the dive. To twist to the right, as you are ascending, your left arm and shoulder are rotated forward while your head remains stationary with your eyes focused forward. As you rotate in a somersaulting direction, the water should come into view directly below your left hand. (See second position in figure 32-21.) Your arms move as in turning a large steering wheel counterclockwise. Your legs constantly bear upward during the twist and the drop of your trunk.

Your head should not resist the downward movement of the dive by pulling backward, but should be allowed to follow the downward rotation movement. Once the eyes focus on the entry point at the peak of the dive, they should not lose sight of it during the rest of the dive. Following this rule aids in obtaining the necessary arch to rotate your body.

Your hands are closed slowly above your head, and your arms are pressed to your ears as your body is straightened for the headfirst vertical entry (figure 32-21).

Group I: Forward Somersault: Tuck or Pike

Your body leaves the board in the same manner for both the forward somersault tuck and pike except that more rotational force is needed to successfully complete the pike somersault. Somersaulting rotation is achieved by throwing your head, trunk, and arms outward and downward just before leaving the board.

In the tuck, your heels are brought toward your buttocks while you bend at your knees and waist and grab your legs with your hands. When your back is approximately parallel

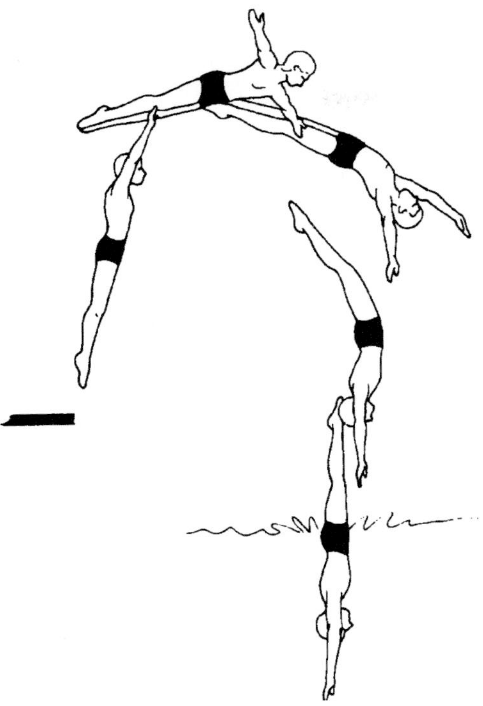

Figure 32-21. Forward dive, half twist—straight position.

Figure 32-22. Forward somersault—tuck position.

with the water, your legs are extended. This produces a "sitting in air" appearance. (See fourth position in figure 32-22.) Complete extension follows, with the same entry as for all feetfirst dives.

In the pike, the actions are the same except that the body is bent at the waist only. The pike should be held

Figure 32-23. Forward somersault—pike position.

slightly longer than the tuck, because the velocity of the rotation is slightly less.

The angle of entry can be adjusted in both dives by remaining either tucked or piked or by opening. This adjustment is learned quickly with practice (figures 32-22 and 32-23).

Group II: Backward Somersault: Tuck

The tuck is started just after the upward and backward swing of your arms on takeoff and is done by lifting your thighs to your chest and drawing your heels toward your buttocks while grabbing your shins with your hands.

During the somersault you should maintain the tuck position while looking upward to sight the water at approximately one-half revolution. The focus should remain on the entry point until the opening from the tuck begins, when you can look at the water under the tip of the board or at the tip of the board itself.

Because the motions of the backward somersault push you in the direction of the board, it is important that when springing the board your balance is moved backward to ensure the dive is accomplished at a safe distance from the board.

When your chest is horizontal to the surface and well above the board, your legs are thrust to full extension and your toes are kept pointed. Your head and shoulders are

Figure 32-24. Back somersault—tuck position.

held erect so that your body is perfectly aligned at the entry.

As your body is opened your hands simply slide from your shins to the front of your thighs (figure 32-24).

Group III: Reverse Somersault: Tuck

At the takeoff, your eyes are focused upward and your reach is made slightly in back of vertical. Your arms will move forward slightly in reaction to your legs' coming toward your chest when going into the tuck position. (See first position of figure 32-25.) The tuck is held until your chest is parallel to the water, at which time your legs are thrust out, your hands ride up your legs to your thighs, and your body is readied for a feetfirst entry (figure 32-25).

Group I: Forward One and One-Half Somersault: Tuck or Pike

This dive is very similar to the forward somersault–tuck, except an additional half forward somersault rotation is made while your body is in the tuck or pike position.

The tuck or pike is started just after takeoff and performed the same as in the forward somersault described previously. Opening from the spin begins at approximately the one and one-quarter somersault position by extending your legs and reaching for the entry with your arms while your eyes focus on the entry point.

Your arms reach for the point of entry, and your body slides down the parabolic line of trajectory and into the water (figures 32-26 and 32-27).

TEACHING CONSIDERATIONS

1. Students should feel secure in deep water before attempting diving skills.
2. Before teaching springboard diving, work on surface dives and dives from a pool deck. Stress form (clear body positions) in all beginning diving experiences. Make clear the desired form by demonstrating and practicing position on the deck.
3. The approach and hurdle are essential skills for springboard diving. Practice them on the deck and then on the board without an actual dive. As students begin this practice on the board, they should continue into the water with a feetfirst entry rather than attempting to stay on the board. After students start on the board, focus on essential beginning points and visual spotting techniques. Work for an integrated, natural production of force in the takeoff.
4. Begin springboard diving with jump dives (feet entering first). Students can have more opportunities to practice control and good form if they practice jumping onto mats into the desired body position (with or without the use of a minitramp or trampoline) rather than only diving into the water.
5. Start with basic dives in each of the five groups of dives. Work for good form and consistency before moving to more-advanced dives. Divers should have a clear idea of takeoff, flight, and entry positions. Use audiovisual aids to freeze the critical parts of the dive and to stress learning cues. Provide learners with videotaped and verbal feedback if possible after some consistency is established.
6. Organize large-group instruction for maximum practice. Avoid long lines at the board. Include review and repetition of work. Do not permit students to move to more-advanced dives unless a

Figure 32-25. Reverse somersault—tuck position.

Figure 32-26. Forward one and one-half somersault—tuck position.

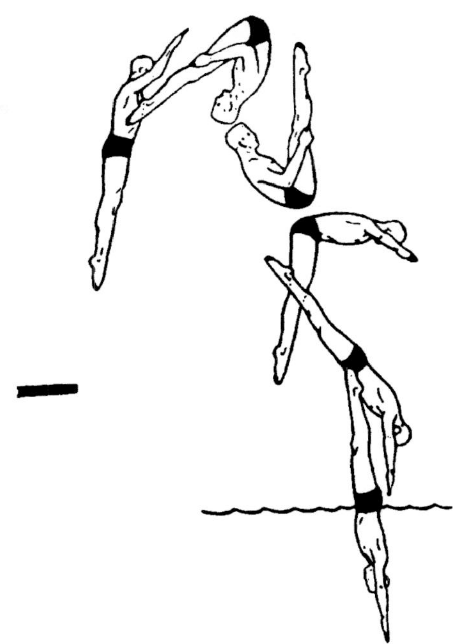

Figure 32-27. Forward one and one-half somersault—pike position.

high level of consistency is established with the less difficult ones.

GLOSSARY

approach The stance, three or more steps, and hurdle taken before the takeoff.

award A score ranging from 0 to 10 given by each judge signifying how well the dive was performed.

balk Beginning the approach but stopping before leaving the board.

center of mass The point around which the weight of the body is evenly distributed.

degree of difficulty A number assigned to each dive that ranks the dive according to difficulty.

final score The sum of the scores awarded for each dive.

free position Any combination of the layout, pike, and tuck positions used in executing twisting dives.

fulcrum The bar located near the middle of the board that is usually adjustable to permit varying the amount of spring obtained from the board.

hurdle The jump during the approach just preceding the takeoff.

low board The 3.3-foot (1 m) board.

long Rotating past a vertical line of entry.

optional dive Any official dive performed in a competition that is not required by the rules governing the contest.

peak The place in a dive where the diver's center of gravity reaches its highest point.

pike position A diving position in which the body is bent at the hips but not at the knees.

save A movement made during the entry of a dive to cause the legs to enter the water vertically even though the dive was long or short.

score The number obtained when the sum of the judges' awards is multiplied by the degree of difficulty for a dive.

short An expression denoting that a diver entered the water before the desired amount of rotation was achieved.

straight position A diving position in which the body is straight or slightly arched, not bent at the hips or knees.

takeoff The period of a dive between the end of the hurdle and the time the diver loses contact with the board.

tuck position A diving position in which the body is bent at the hips and the knees and is as compact as possible.

SUGGESTED READINGS

Gabriel, J. 1990. *U.S. diving safety manual.* Indianapolis: U.S. Diving.

NCAA men's and women's swimming and diving rules. 1998. Mission, Kans.: National Collegiate Athletic Association.

O'Brien, R. 1992. *Ron O'Brien's diving for gold.* Champaign, Ill.: Human Kinetics. Contains over 700 illustrations that present the fundamentals of diving.

Swimming and diving rule book. Current ed. Kansas City, Mo.: National Federation of State High School Association.

Vickers, B. 1989. *Springboard diving.* Boston: American Press.

RESOURCES

Videotapes

Diving my way, Ron O'Brien, The Athletic Institute, 200 Castlewood Dr., North Palm Beach, FL 33408 1-800-933-3335.

Diving techniques, Karol Video, 22 Riverside Dr., Wayne, NJ 97470.

Swimming

After completing this chapter, the reader should be able to:

- Be familiar with the evolution of swimming and the various strokes
- Orient a group of students to being in water
- Instruct novice swimmers in basic swimming skills, such as floating, gliding, and beginning propulsion
- Teach beginning and advanced swimming strokes
- Recognize the proper progressions for teaching beginning, intermediate, and advanced swimmers

HISTORY

Early humans probably learned swimming by observing animals that used a running motion to move about, on, or in the water. Water is an unnatural medium for humans because it interferes with the breathing mechanism; animals are usually better equipped anatomically for swimming. Humans cannot easily keep the nose above water while horizontal.

Carvings showing people swimming have been found dating as early as 9000 B.C. In the Middle Ages, accounts in the Greek, Roman, Anglo-Saxon, and Scandinavian classics dealt often with great feats of swimming of the heroes of the day.

In 1538 Nicolaus Wynman, a German professor of languages, wrote the first book on swimming. In 1696 a Frenchman named Thevenot wrote a more scientific treatise.

The strokes listed here are still fundamental and seaworthy for utility purposes, but have been considerably refined for competitive swimming.

These strokes evolved in the following order:

1. The "doggy" or human paddling strokes.
2. The breaststroke (sailor stroke), the first scientific stroke taught.
3. The underarm sidestroke. This stroke was still too slow for speed because both arms recovered under the water as they did in the breaststroke. The kick was scissorslike.
4. The side, or English, overarm stroke. This stroke was faster than either the breaststroke or the side underarm stroke because the uppermost arm recovered above the surface and thereby reduced undesirable resistance.
5. The trudgen stroke. This stroke was discovered in South America in 1860 by an Englishman, John Trudgen. It employed the method of recovering both arms above the water hand-over-hand. It further reduced resistance to water and created greater speed. It was similar to the side overarm stroke except that the body turned over to permit the under arm to lift out of the water for recovery. In this stroke the scissors kick was used.
6. The Australian crawl. Introduced to England by Richard Cavell of Australia in the 1902 championships, this was the first true hand-over-hand stroke with alternating vertical movement of the legs. Cavell explained the stroke as "crawling through the water." The scissors kick was eliminated for speed swimming because the leg recovery caused great resistance.
7. The American six-beat leg-kick crawl. The Australian stroke was scientifically refined by American coaches. This style broke all existing freestyle records in speed swimming and became known as the fastest human stroke in water.
8. The inverted breaststroke (elementary backstroke). This is the breaststroke executed while swimming on the back.
9. The back crawl. About 1910 the crawl was turned onto the back and was much faster in competition than the inverted breaststroke. Since there was no recovery of arms or legs underwater as in the inverted breaststroke, it minimized resistance and created faster speed on the back.
10. The butterfly breaststroke. This stroke began to make its appearance in competition about 1934. The kick remained the same as in the breaststroke, but both arms recovered above the water simultaneously. They lifted out of the water at the hips and were swung laterally forward to the entry, resembling a butterfly in flight, thus the name.
11. The butterfly (dolphin) stroke. The newest of all the swimming strokes was created by D. A. Armbruster through the ability and skill of Jack Sieg. The purpose of this stroke was to obtain greater speed with the breaststroke by eliminating the recovery underwater of the legs in the kick. This was accomplished by moving the legs up and down in unison from the hips.

This kick actually created greater speed when used without arms than did the alternating flutter kick. It synchronized beautifully with the butterfly arm stroke and created greater speed.

All of these strokes been developed and refined, and have been put to practical use by the average swimmer. They are used in many different water activities usually called aquatics. Some of the aquatic activities are these:

1. Recreational swimming
2. Lifesaving
3. Competitive swimming
4. Synchronized swimming or ballet
5. Springboard and platform diving
6. Water games: polo, basketball, baseball, and similar activities
7. Water safety
8. Water survival
9. Skin diving and scuba diving

Most of these aquatic activities use the fundamental skill strokes.

It is strongly recommended that the beginner be taught all of the basic strokes to gain self-assurance in the water and experience the joy and relaxation of recreational swimming. To accomplish this, the beginner must know the fundamental skill strokes. This method of learning is the "all-stroke method for beginners" (figure 33-1).

UNITED STATES OLYMPIC SWIMMING HISTORY

Men

In the 1896 Olympic competition at Athens, there were only two swimming events. They were held in a lake, and competitors could use any stroke. Over the years competitions have become increasingly organized in terms of distances, strokes, and facilities. By 1912 there were six men's swimming events and two women's swimming events. In addition there were two men's and one women's diving events.

Early outstanding U.S. swimmers were Charles Daniels, who won four golds in 1904, 1906, and 1908, and Duke Kahanamoku, who won the 100 m freestyle in 1912 and again in 1920. His new style of kicking (the flutter kick) was later adopted by most freestyle swimmers. In 1924 Johnny Weissmuller, the next dominant U.S. swimmer, emerged. He was the first person to swim the 100 m freestyle in under a minute, and he won a total of five gold medals at two Olympiads.

In 1932 the Japanese men won five of six events, and three of six events in 1936. The years that followed, the Australian men became the swimming power.

Then in 1964, Don Schollander of the United States matched Johnny Weissmuller's feat of five gold medals by winning four in 1964 and one in 1968. Schollander's gold medal in 1968 was in the 4 × 200 m relay. Mark Spitz, a team member on that relay team, was destined to win seven gold medals in 1972. It is still the most gold medals ever won at a single Olympic Games in any sport, and each medal involved a world record (four were individual events and three were relays).

One of the most dominating team performances occurred at the 1976 Olympics when the U.S. men's team won 12 of 13 possible golds and 10 silvers in the 11 individual events. In 1980, when the United States boycotted the Olympics, the Soviet men's team dominated by winning seven of the 13 gold medals. In 1984, when the Soviets boycotted, the U.S. men returned to dominance by winning gold medals in 8 of 13 swimming events, plus both gold medals in diving.

In 1988 a record 21 different nations earned medals in swimming (both men's and women's), but the men's events were once again dominated by a U.S. swimmer. Matt Biondi gathered five golds, one silver, and a bronze, for a performance eclipsed only by Mark Spitz.

The Unified team (formerly the Soviet Union) and the Hungarian team were surprisingly strong at the 1992 Olympics in Barcelona, but the U.S. men's team brought home seven gold medals and six silver or bronze medals.

In the 1996 Olympics at Atlanta, the Centennial Olympic games, the Russian men's swim team ruled the pool. They won gold in six individual events and were the only team other than the United States to win gold in the relays. The Russians won 7 of the 16 events and the United States won four gold medals.

Women

The first Olympic women's swimming events were held in 1912, and the next several Olympics were dominated by swimmers from Australia, Great Britain, and the United States.

In 1920 Ethelda Bleibtrey of the United States won the 100 m freestyle, the 200 m freestyle, and anchored the 4 × 100 m freestyle relay to sweep all three events at the Antwerp Olympics. In 1932 the U.S. women's swim team, led by Helene Madison, won six of the seven swimming and diving events, but it won only three bronze medals in 1936.

After World War II (in 1948–1960) the U.S. women's teams won 14 gold medals in four Olympic Games. The women's team from Australia emerged as a power at this same time, winning 10 golds including five in 1956 and four in 1960. The U.S. women began to reemerge as a swimming power in 1968 when Debra Meyer won three gold medals. In 1972, when Mark Spitz was winning seven golds, the dominant woman swimmer was Shane Gould of Australia with four golds, one silver, and one bronze. However, Melissa Belote of the United States also won three golds in two individual events and a relay.

In 1972, when the U.S. men had the great team performance, the U.S. and Australian dominance in the women's events continued, but it came to an end in 1976 as

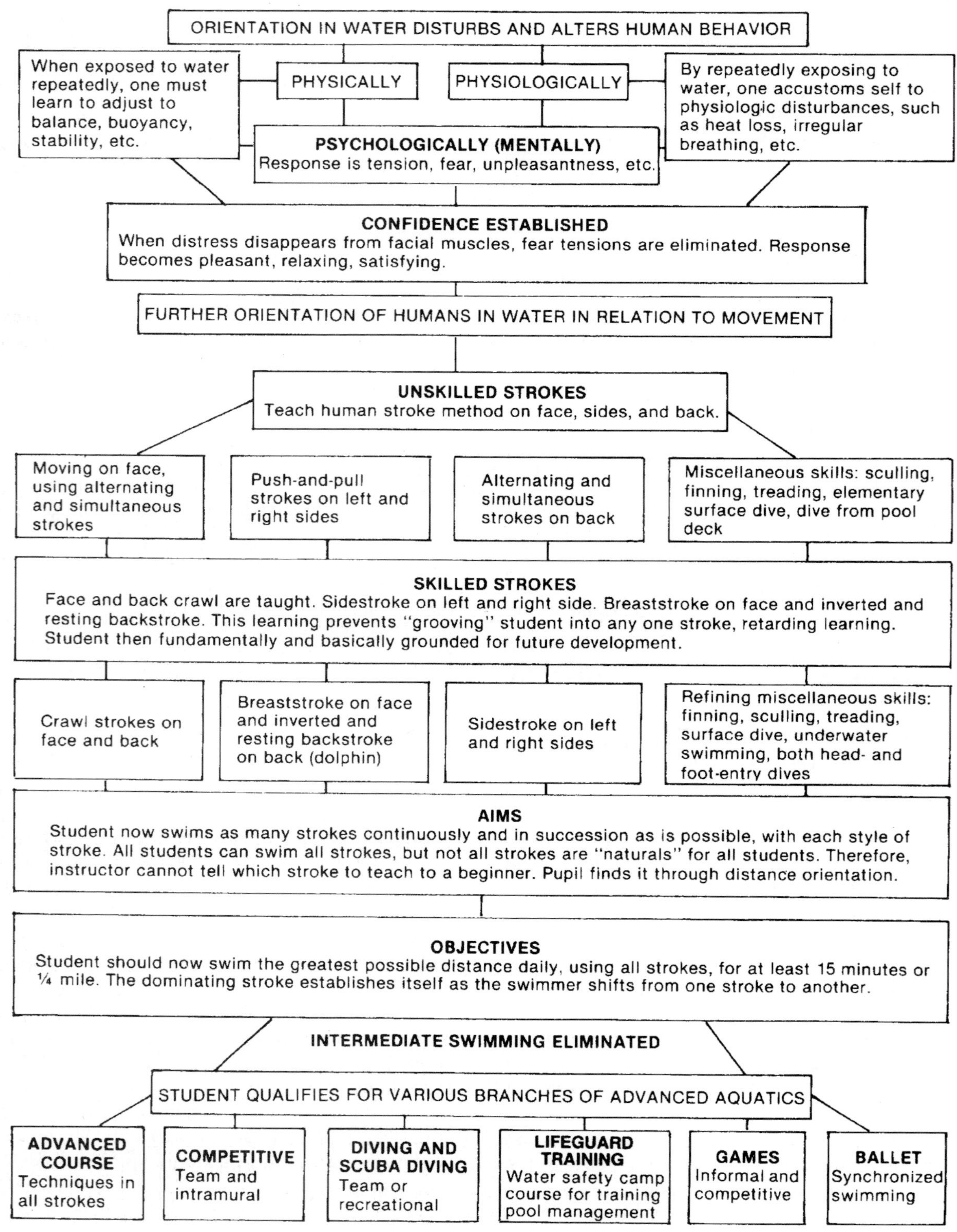

Figure 33-1. The all-stroke method—a progressive learning procedure chart for swimming.

the East German women won 11 of the 13 golds. Shirley Babashoff of the United States did manage a gold and three silvers, giving her eight Olympic medals in her career and establishing her as one of the United States' great female swimmers.

When the United States boycotted the Olympics in 1980, the East German women repeated their feat of garnering 11 golds. In 1984, when the East Germans boycotted, the U.S. women swimmers returned to power with 11 of the 13 individual events and one relay.

In the 1988 Olympics the stars of the women's swimming competition were Kristin Otto of East Germany and Janet Evans of the United States. Otto's six gold medals broke the record for most golds won by a woman in any sport at one Olympics. Seventeen-year-old Janet Evans won the 400 m individual medley, the 800 m freestyle, and the 400 m freestyle in a world record time of 4:03:85.

The U.S. women's team remained a world swimming powerhouse with 14 medals, although the Chinese women's team was surprisingly strong at the 1992 Barcelona Olympics. Janet Evans again won the 800 m freestyle and took the silver in the 400 m freestyle.

At the 1996 Olympics in Atlanta, seven countries won gold medals in the women's swimming events. The United States won 6 of the 16 gold medals. The star woman swimmer was Michelle Smith from Ireland, who won three individual gold medals. Amy Van Dyken was the bright star for the United States with a gold and a silver medal in individual events and two more golds in the relays.

SWIMMING SAFETY RULES

Indoor Swimming Pools

1. Do not enter the pool or swim unless a lifeguard or qualified instructor is present.
2. Do not run on the pool deck.
3. Do not engage in horseplay in the pool or pool area.
4. Do not eat, drink, or use glass bottles in the pool area.
5. People with communicable diseases or infectious conditions such as open sores, eye infections, etc., will not be allowed in the pool.
6. Never swim near the diving area when diving boards are being used.
7. Only one person at a time is allowed on diving boards.
8. Before using diving boards, be familiar with the depth of the pool and configuration of the bottom of the pool.
9. Diving boards are to be used only for diving.
10. Diving into the pool from the deck is prohibited.
11. All swimmers must wear bathing suits. T-shirts, cutoffs, or other clothing will not be allowed.
12. All people with long hair should wear a swim cap.

Open Swimming Areas

13. Do not remain in the water during an electrical storm.
14. Before participating in any aquatic activities—such as canoeing, boating, sailing, skin diving, scuba diving, and water skiing—understand all safety rules and procedures.
15. Air-filled flotation devices will not compensate for lack of swimming skills.
16. Never dive into water of unknown depth or into water that has not been checked for floating or partially submerged foreign objects.
17. Always be aware of the temperature of the water. Do not remain in cold water for excessive periods of time. Do not enter the water if you are chilled.

THE ALL-STROKE METHOD FOR TEACHING BEGINNERS

The all-stroke method begins by adjusting students to water. When the student is comfortably adjusted to water, the basic skill strokes can be learned quite rapidly.

Beginners make reasonable progress learning all strokes; however, not everyone can swim all strokes equally well. (People differ anatomically.) Therefore, by teaching all of the students all of the strokes, each one will naturally find the stroke most comfortable and suitable through a distance orientation program after the stroke skills are learned. The stroke that takes the least effort will naturally be selected most often, even though the students are basically "grounded" in every stroke. This also prepares students for advanced swimming, lifesaving, or any other form of aquatic interest. This may eliminate the intermediate level of swimming.

The secret of the all-stroke method is to really work the legs by drilling them in different kick skills. Legs are composed of big muscles that in everyday living are used only to walk, run, jump, and perhaps dance. To get legs to relax in water and to move in new patterns the swimmer must train them.

Correct breathing habits are the next essential skill to teach. Water interferes with a human's breathing mechanism. Humans have to learn to exhale completely under the surface and inhale above the surface. They must develop breathing patterns for different strokes.

Instructors should emphasize skill learning by progressive drills and action. Action creates interest and results in interested students who will work hard if they know they are learning. Swimming taught progressively and intensively accomplishes that. If students become fatigued (not exhausted) from constant exercise, they will naturally take it easy, and when they take it easy, the response is relaxation. Relaxation is learned through constant repetitions.

OBJECTIVES

1. To orient students to water, a medium that disturbs a person physically, physiologically, and psychologically and produces:
   a. Instability
   b. Apparent loss of body weight
   c. Loss of sense of balance
   d. Change in body position for locomotion
   e. Change in heat-regulatory mechanism
   f. Change in respiration
   g. Change in normal muscle tonus
2. To develop confidence, using drills that have the following goals:
   a. To eliminate mental barriers to bring in the water
   b. To learn the proper techniques of inhalation and exhalation
   c. To relax in the water
   d. To enjoy swimming
3. To teach self-reliance for self-preservation
4. To teach an appreciation of distance over water no matter how short or long
5. To teach respect for water while swimming
6. To impart confidence in skill and techniques
7. To teach strokes in such a way as to motivate persistent practice
8. To encourage swimming as a source of lifelong pleasure and fitness
9. To teach distribution of effort and conservation of strength
10. To teach how to delay fatigue
11. To teach how to dive into water

BASIC SKILLS AND TECHNIQUES

Adjustment to Water

1. Examine the pool markings to know its depth at all locations before entering the water
2. Wade waist deep into the pool and submerge repeatedly to chin level, rinsing up and down and splashing the face.
3. Hold onto the overflow gutter and allow water to lift the legs and body to the surface. Stay relaxed.

Breath Control

Depending on the level and maturity of swimmers, the following activities can be performed while holding onto the pool gutter, holding onto a partner, or without support:

1. Standing in waist-deep water with the body inclined forward, practice breath holding: Inhale through the mouth, close the mouth, shut the eyes, and submerge the face flat beneath the water; hold for 3 seconds and recover. Repeat several times, lengthening the time underwater.
2. Inhale through the mouth, submerge the face with the eyes closed, exhale slowly through the nose, and recover. Repeat several times.
3. Inhale through the mouth, submerge the face with the eyes closed, and exhale through the nose, mouth, or both, steadily but as slowly as possible. Recover and repeat several times.

Use of Eyes Underwater

Inhale, close the eyes, submerge, open the eyes, count the number of fingers visible on a partner's hand, and recover. Repeat.

Balance and Control of the Body

The following activities are designed to aid the student in developing confidence in the water. To ensure that fear is not reinforced, it is important to discuss and practice (with partners) the procedures of returning to a stable position before assuming the various floating and gliding positions.

Jellyfish float. This float may be performed in either the pike or tuck position. Take a deep breath, submerge the face, raise the knees to the chest or extend the legs, and hold with the arms for 3 seconds. Release the hold, elevate the back and head, allow the legs to extend to the bottom of the pool, let the arms float up a little, and then push them down and toward the hips while at the same time raising the head. The instructor should pay close attention to the swimmer in these initial floats as individual differences, especially in amount of leanness and fat, will result in large differences in ability to float (figure 33-2). Repeat.

Streamline (prone) float position. (Water must be at least waist deep.) The streamline float is done on the stomach. The position is taken by lifting and extending the arms forward beyond the head beneath the surface, with the head held low in the water, and extending the legs (figure 33-3). To recover to the standing position, pull the knees to the chest, round the back, then simultaneously press firmly downward with the extended arms, extend the legs to the bottom of the pool, and lift the face from the water. With the legs extended downward, the feet will settle on the pool floor. Keep the eyes open. After recovery, exhale through the nose, open the mouth, inhale, and flutter the eyes open.

Streamline (prone) glide and stand. For the streamline glide, bend forward at the waist, with the arms extended forward. Lay the upper body and arms in the water, just under the surface. Take a deep breath, bend the knees, and roll the face under the surface. Straighten the knees, push the feet off the bottom, glide into the prone position and glide. At the end of the glide, draw the knees into the chest and recover, as in the prone float.

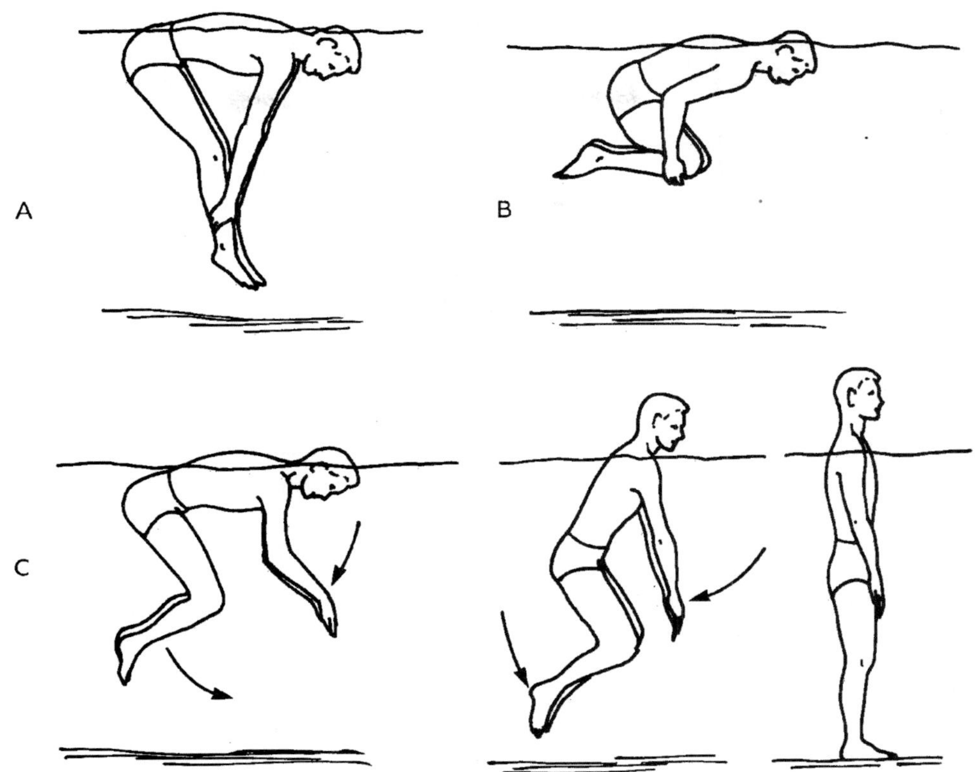

Figure 33-2. **A,** Jellyfish float, pike. **B,** Jellyfish float, tuck position. **C,** Recovery from jellyfish float.

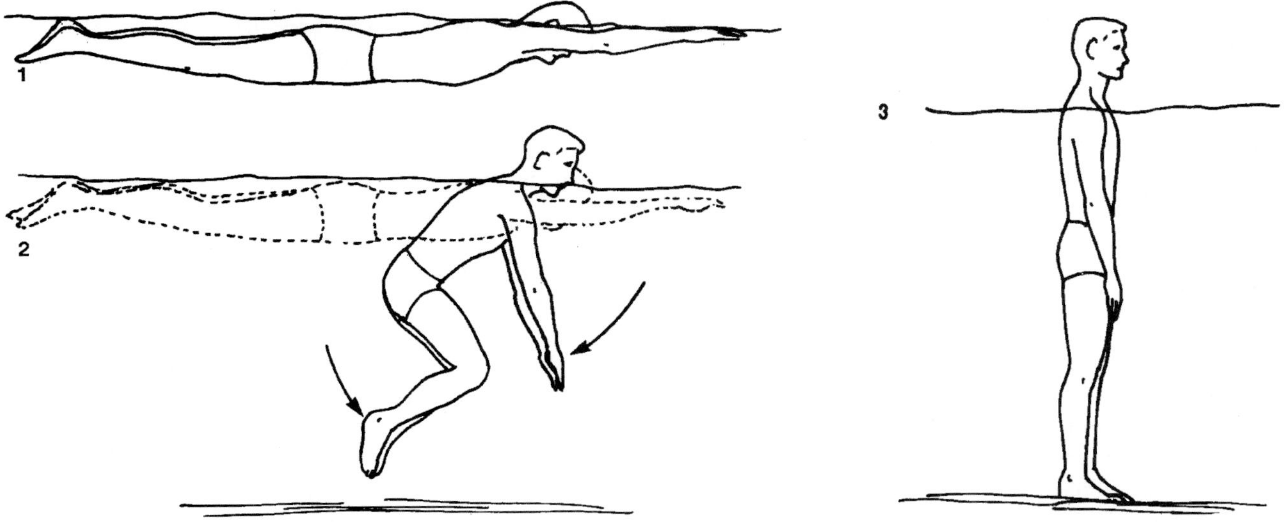

Figure 33-3. Streamline float and recovery.

Back floating position. With a partner standing directly behind, assume a back floating position by submerging to the chin and, with the partner supporting the back of the neck with one hand and the small of the back with the other, lift the hips and extend the arms sideward. The ears will be under water. The partner gradually removes support, first from the small of the back and then from the neck. The body will not necessarily stay horizontal in the water. Some swimmer's legs have a tendency to sink. The important elements are to relax, keep the arms

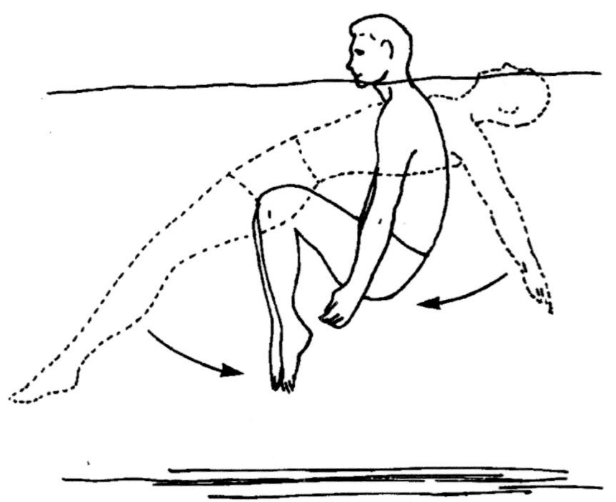

Figure 33-4. Back float and recovery.

extended, and hold the neck back to keep the face above water. The partner should help in the recovery the first few times. To gain recovery from the back float, move the arms downward and forward in the water, round the back, bring the knees to the chin, and lift the head slowly forward. When the body moves to a vertical position, extend the legs to the bottom and stand (figure 33-4).

Back glide and stand. For the back glide, crouch until the shoulders are submerged, lie back until the ears are submerged, push off with the feet, and glide until forward motion stops. Recover by bringing both knees up toward the chest and the head forward. At the same time bring both arms forward. During the glide, keep the arms at the side and the legs straight and together.

Simple Leg Movements to Keep Body Horizontal and to Aid Propulsion

Kick glide, streamline position. For the kick glide, streamline position, start with the streamline glide, but as the body straightens out on the surface, move the legs alternately up-and-down with the knees and ankles fairly loose; continue to the limit of breath-holding ability. (For additional practice, hold onto the splash gutter or a kickboard and kick the legs as above.)

Kick glide, back position. In the kick glide, back position, assume a back floating position but with the back flat, the chin tucked well into the throat, and the arms kept by the sides. Move the legs in a slightly bent-kneed flutter kick. Snap each knee into extension when finishing the kick. (For additional practice, hold onto the splash gutter and execute the flutter kick.)

Simple Arm Movements for Support, Propulsion, and Balancing of Body

Arm stroke on the front. For the arm stroke on the front (dog paddle or human stroke), assume the prone position in the water and extend the arms alternately forward and downward, following with a press backward under the body. Cup the hands slightly on the pull backward. In the recovery forward of each arm, straighten the hand, draw it up under the chin, and extend it to a forward position; cup the hand and repeat the stroke.

Arm stroke on the back. The arm stroke on the back (finning) is a paired movement of the hands and arms in a back position. The arms are first extended by the sides and then drawn up about 1 foot (30 cm), extended outward so the hands are perpendicular to the body, then push water backward toward the feet using a fishtail flip of the hands and wrists.

Coordination of Breathing with Leg and Arm Movements

Combined stroke on the front. The combined stroke on the front is composed of up-and-down alternating beats of the legs and the dog paddle with the arms, with breathing done entirely above the surface or alternately inhaling above and exhaling below the water. Two or more beats of the legs should accompany each cycle of arm strokes.

Rotary breathing should be done with the head rotated to the side. If the head is rotated to the left to get air, inhale when the right arm is extended forward. Rotate the head into the water on this cycle, and when the left arm is extended, exhale underwater through the mouth. To inhale to the right side, the left arm should be extended, and on this cycle, as the right arm is extended, rotate the face into the water and exhale.

Combined stroke on the back. The combined stroke on the back consists of finning with the hands and flutter kicking with the legs. Assume the back floating position with the back flat and the chin tucked well into the throat. First, the leg beat is started using greater speed and more flexibility than is used in the front kick. The thrust of the hands (finning) is put into the stroke at regular intervals. Breathe naturally.

Turning, right and left. Begin the front stroke (human stroke), maintaining the body nearly horizontal, and execute a right turn and then a left turn in the middle of the pool. Try executing a complete turn. Extend the hands and pull in the opposite direction of the turn.

Change positions. In changing position or turning over from the front to the back, start swimming, keep the body nearly horizontal, and at the point of changing positions, roll the body either right or left to a back floating position. Keep the shoulders and head low in the water. The head, arms, hips, and legs will aid in rolling the body. In changing from a back float to the front, roll in a similar manner to a front position and resume the stroke.

SAFETY AND SURVIVAL STROKES

The first three strokes are presented for their use as water safety and survival strokes. They require the least amount of energy and skill. They are not competitive strokes.

Resting Backstroke

The resting backstroke (figure 33-5) should be the first stroke taught to beginners. It requires little coordination and gives the student a sense of security. This is principally a resting stroke for an emergency or for easy swimming while resting, and it lays a sound foundation for the breaststroke and elementary backstroke as well as for treading water. The face is never underwater, and thus breathing is not a disturbing factor.

Whip kick (inverted breaststroke kick)

The recovery is executed by spreading the knees to about approximately hip-width while holding the heels together. Keep the heels down as they are drawn toward the buttocks so that the knees do not lift out of the water, and at the same time lift the hips to prevent the drop. Separate the heels and cock the feet outward toward the knees Start the drive by sweeping the legs out and pushing against the water with the soles of the feet, extending the feet as they kick. During this kick, when the knees are not quite straightened, squeeze the thighs together forcefully with the knees relaxed to give a whiplike motion to the foreleg and feet, resulting in increased propulsion. This stroke can also be introduced using a flutter kick first, because the whip kick can be difficult for some students to master.

Arm stroke

The arm recovery starts from the sides of the thighs by turning the palms downward and slightly at an angle in the direction of recovery, the little-finger side of the hand leading and knifing through the water. The arms are held straight. The arms move outward away from the thighs to a point just above the shoulders.

The arm pull is executed by turning the palms to the rear and slightly downward and moving the straight arms forcefully to the sides of the thighs.

At no time during either the recovery or the pull of the hands or arms should they be above the surface.

Whole stroke

This stroke is easy to execute because the arms and legs work in unison. The arms and legs recover at the same moment and kick and pull at the same moment. When the stroke is closed, stretch out straight and pause until the momentum is spent. Repeat.

Elementary Backstroke

This stroke (figure 33-6) should be taught after the resting backstroke has been mastered. This style affords a little more speed than does the resting backstroke, but is still restful and easy to learn. However, more coordination is required to execute it because the arms are partly recovered before the legs recover.

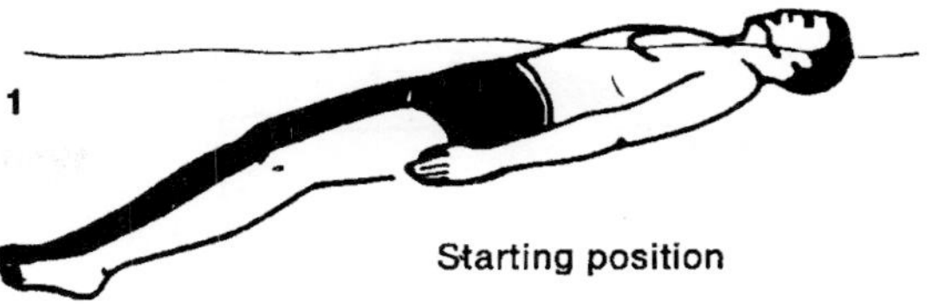

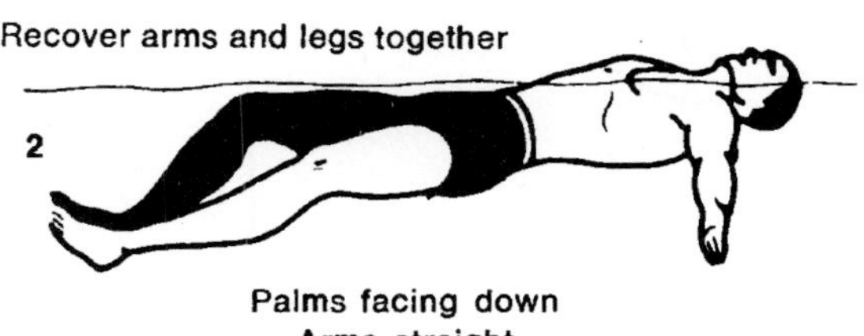

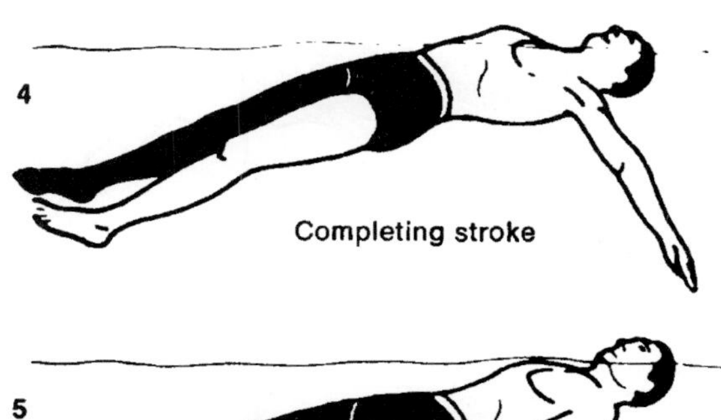

Figure 33-5. Progressive steps in the resting backstroke—the first skill stroke to learn.

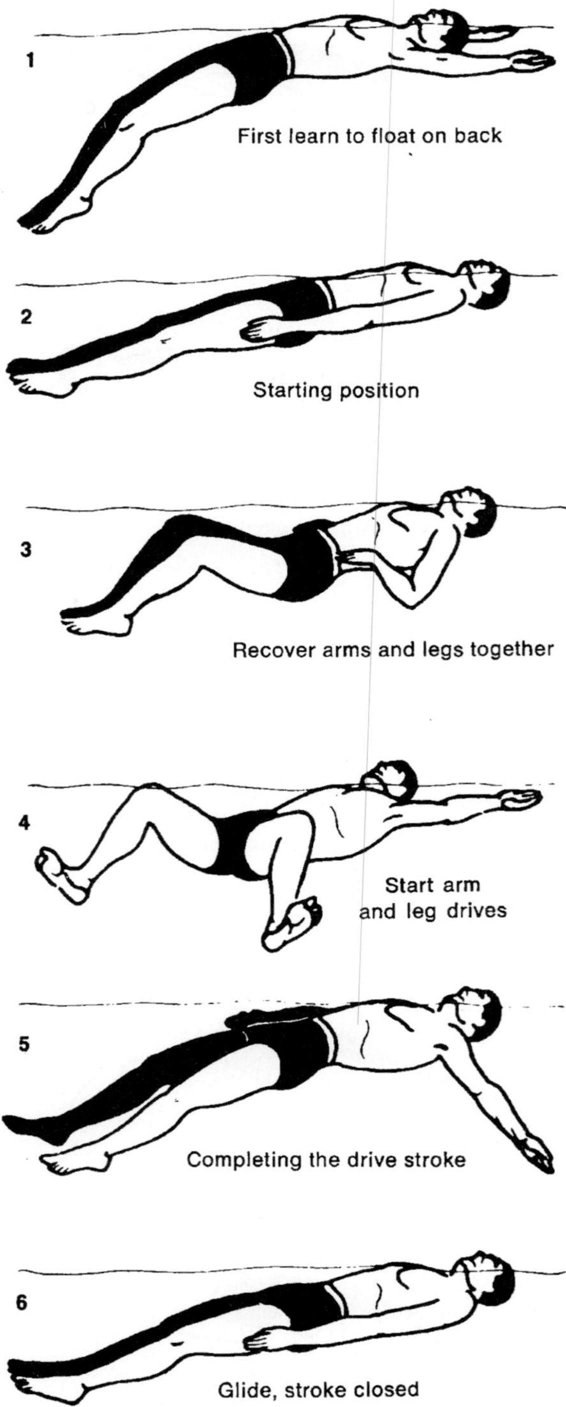

Figure 33.6. Progressive steps in swimming the elementary backstroke.

Whip kick

The whip kick is executed exactly the same as in the resting backstroke kick.

Arm stroke

The arm recovery in the elementary backstroke differs from that in the resting backstroke. The arm recovery is executed by bending the elbows downward and sliding the hands from the sides of the thighs up along the sides of the body toward the shoulders. Then the hands, palms facing up, reach out diagonally from the armpit under the water until the arms are straight. Turn the palm facing backward and pull, straight-armed; to the sides of the thighs. Pause until the momentum from the pull subsides.

Whole stroke

In the propulsive phase the arms and legs start at the same time, although the legs will usually finish before the arms because of a shorter range of motion. Stretch the body and legs straight, though relaxed, and pause until the momentum is spent. In the recovery phase, hold the legs straight while the arms recover to about armpit level; then start the leg recovery at the same slow speed as the arms recover. When the arms have reached the pulling position, the legs have recovered to the kick position; that is, the knees and heels are apart, feet pointed outward. Breathe regularly.

Underarm Sidestroke

The underarm sidestroke (figure 33-7) is easy to learn. It is the basic stroke for lifesaving. Breathing is not difficult because the nose and mouth are turned to the rear and water passes by the side of the face.

Scissors kick

The scissors kick is perhaps the most powerful of all kicks in the water, which is why it is used so much in lifesaving.

First the kick is learned on both sides by holding onto the side of the pool. The body is held straight on its side, legs straight, feet extended, and one leg on top of the other. The legs remain parallel with the surface of the water throughout. To start the recovery movement, flex at the knees and slowly draw the heels backward with both legs together and moving simultaneously. This drawing of the heels backward gives just the proper amount of flexion at the hip joint. In this position, if an imaginary line were passed through the midpoint of the shoulder and hip joints, it would project out over the legs at a midpoint between the knees and ankles when the legs are in a full recovery position. The scissors is now opened by moving the bottom leg back and the top leg forward, still maintaining the fully flexed knees. The foot of the top leg flexes toward the knee. The under foot remains extended. From this position the legs start the drive, sweeping outward and together by extension of the knees and the foot of the top leg. The

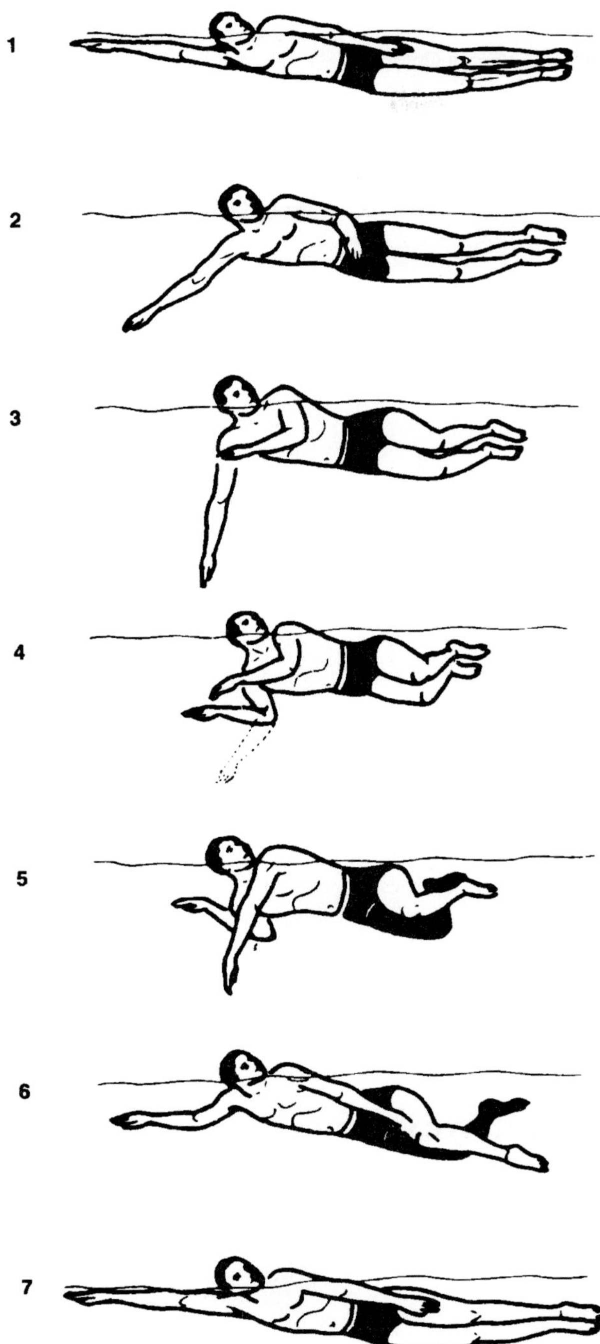

Figure 33-7. Progressive steps in swimming the underarm sidestroke.

under leg hooks the water like it is kicking a ball. The top leg uses a whip motion similar to a horse's pawing. With a powerful yet smooth movement, the legs come together stretched straight and relaxed and pause long enough for momentum to be spent in the glide.

Arm stroke

While the body is on its side, with the shoulders in a true vertical plane, the under arm is extended forward directly under the head, with the palm facing down and the hand just under the surface. The upper arm pulls back, hugging closely along the upper front part of the body with the palm of the hand resting on the front side of the upper leg—never on the top of the leg.

The learner should first get a clear mental picture of the arm stroke from the starting position—that is, both arms moving simultaneously along the longitudinal plane of the body. They meet just under the head, change direction, and simultaneously extend again to their starting position. The under arm moves forward; the upper arm moves backward. As the upper arm slides forward to meet the under arm, the under arm should pull diagonally downward and backward to a line under the head. Here it changes direction and starts the recovery movement, with the hand and fingers pointing forward to its starting position. Even though the hands move in and out together, the under arm is always pulling on the "in" movement, while the upper arm is pulling on the "out" movement.

Whole stroke coordinated in four steps

It is recommended that each of the following four steps be learned thoroughly before advancing to the next step (figure 33-8).

Step 1: scissors kick only. Take a deep breath and lie on the side floating position with the body straight and the under arm extended in a line with the body. Turn your face into the water on top of the under arm and hold your breath. The upper arm is in front of the upper thigh. Take at least four kicks in succession and pause between each stroke for the glide. After at least four kicks, switch sides. The upper hand is in front of the upper thigh and remains on it during these kick exercises. This trains the upper arm to work in unison with the kick, as it must do in the whole stroke.

Step 2: the kick and upper arm. The body is positioned as in step 1. To execute step 2, the upper hand and arm recover at the same time as the legs. The hand moves forward beyond the face, with the elbow and hand submerged to a point beyond the face. The arm pull starts at the same time as the kick. The upper arm and legs recover at the same time and the kick and pull occur at the same time.

Step 3: the kick. upper arm, and underarm. The body and face are still in the same position as in step 1. To execute step 3, press—do not pull—the under arm diagonally down and backward to a point under the face. At the same time

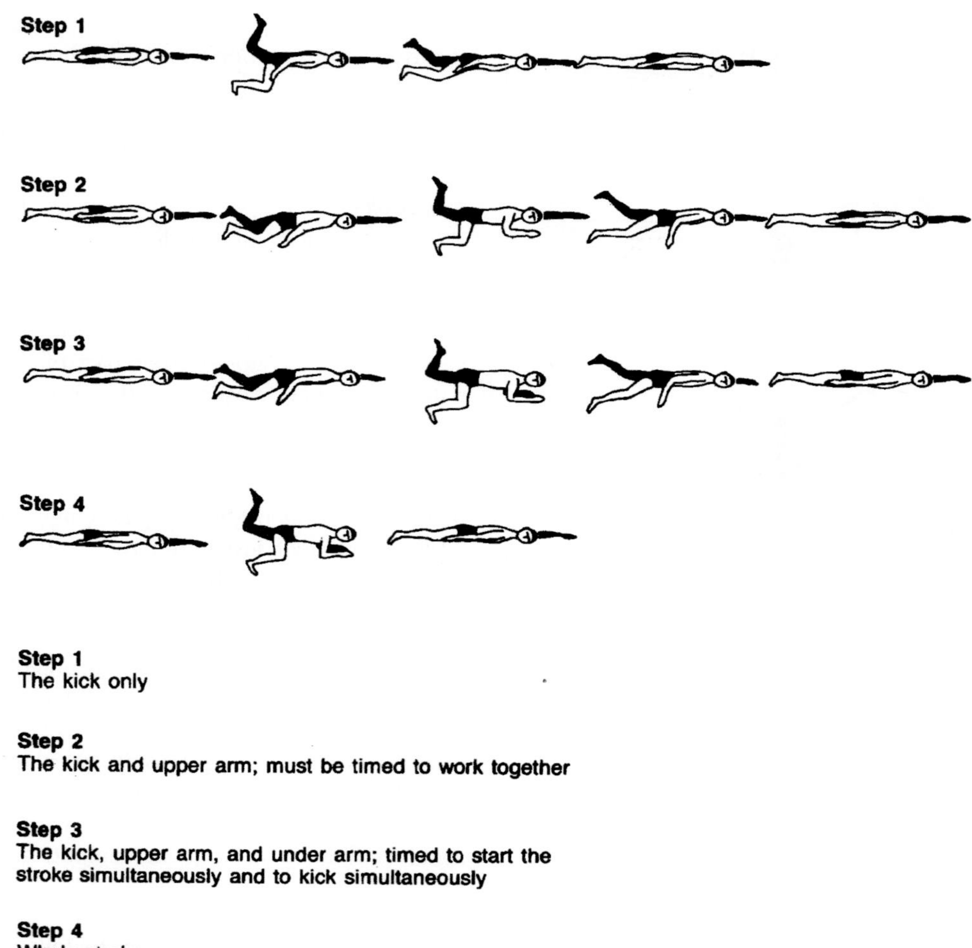

Figure 33-8. Progressive steps in learning the sidestroke (as seen from above).

that the under arm starts its press, the legs and upper arm are recovered. The hands meet, cross over, and repass as the under-arm hand recovers and thrusts forward to guide the glide. At the same time the under arm recovers, the upper arm and legs start the pull and kick. Pause and glide. This makes it easy for the arms and legs to coordinate into the whole stroke. Repeat at least four strokes before stopping for air.

Step 4: breathing. Take one or two strokes in the step 3 position and then turn your face out of the water and face to the rear, with the chin in line with the upper shoulder. Breathe in as the arms and legs come in; breathe out as the arms and legs go out. Now repeat the same four-step procedure on the right side. The water level should remain constant at your face, leveling at the corner of the lower eye and lower corner of the mouth.

Note: These four-step procedures can also be performed with flotation devices, such as kickboards.

COMPETITIVE STROKES

Breaststroke

The breaststroke was the first competitive stroke and is still used in competitive events. It is also an excellent utility stroke and is used in lifesaving.

Kick

There have been many modifications of the breaststroke kick in order to increase the speed of the entire stroke. In general, the main characteristic of these modifications has been to reduce unwanted resistance by narrowing the knee spread and increasing the desired resistance by adding a slightly downward thrust in the propulsive phase of the kick. However, for the beginner the traditional kick is probably easiest to learn initially.

The breaststroke kick (whip) is almost the same as used in the inverted or the resting backstroke. The body is prone, arms extended, face below the surface of the water with the

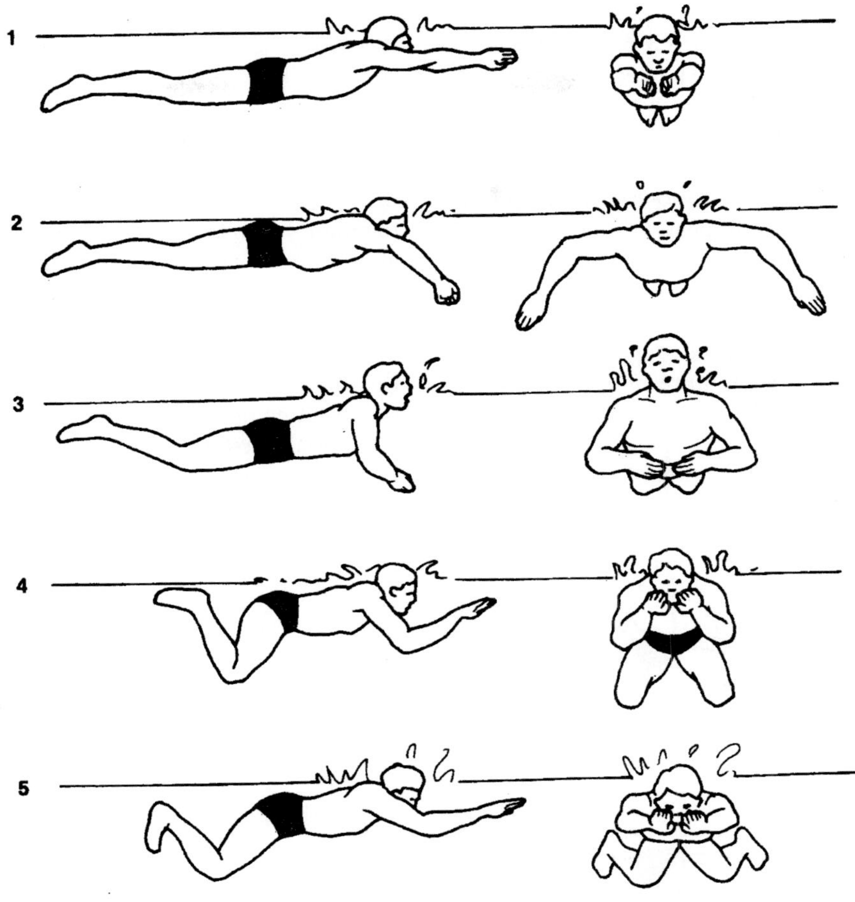

Figure 33-9. Progressive steps in swimming the breaststroke.

water line at the top of the forehead, and the heels close together. The recovery begins by drawing the heels forward toward the buttocks and then separating them to hip width with the angle of the thighs to the upper body slightly greater than 90 degrees. The thighs should not go as far as to be directly under the pelvis (figure 33-9.) The heels are then flexed in preparation for the drive. The drive is made forcefully but smoothly by pressing the feet first outward and then backward and inward until they are together, with the toes pointed. Glide with the legs fully extended until momentum from the kick is spent. During the propulsive phase of the kick, water is pushed backward by the soles of the feet. Then the legs whip together by driving the thighs in toward each other before the knees have fully extended. This movement gives the powerful whiplash kick.

Arm stroke

In the streamline position, the arms are extended forward, hands close together, palms facing away from each other. The arms press outward and downward simultaneously until the hands are slightly wider than the shoulders. The elbows then bend and the hands press downward so the palms face the feet. The hands then press inward together until they are under the chin. This part of the arm pull is the power phase of the pull. At the chin the hands release the water and immediately begin to recover by pushing them from the chin until the arms are extended forward. Pulling too wide removes the support from under the shoulders and head, causing them to drop and sink, which disturbs the body balance. As the arm pull is being completed, the face is lifted to breathe and the knees begin their flexion for the kick recovery. The recovery of the arms begins under the chin as the hands join each other and are thrust forward to the starting position. At this point pause to allow for a glide. The entire arm stroke is a continuous, uninterrupted movement. Practice walking across the pool without the breathing action first. Then coordinate the breathing with arm action technique.

Whole stroke

Push off from the side of the pool with the body prone on the surface, fully extended, the face underwater. The arms pull as just described, the breath is taken as the arms begin their recovery and the legs are recovered with the feet spread and cocked for the drive. The legs begin their recovery and then perform the propulsive kick when the arms are fully extended.

The legs then pause for the glide when they have closed at the end of the drive. The body is now fully extended. Exhale slowly during the glide. Repeat several strokes to time the movements smoothly and continuously from the start of the stroke to the end of the leg drive (figure 32-9). The breaststroke can be executed with the face out of the water, as may be required in some lifesaving situations. The glide is shortened and the stroke requires more effort.

Crawl Stroke

The crawl stroke, usually called freestyle in competition, (figure 33-10) is the fastest of all swimming strokes. Engineering and mechanical principles have been applied to this activity and have made it one of the most refined of all sports skills.

Flutter kick

The body is prone, with arms and legs fully extended, face under, and ankles stretched and feet and toes close together. From this position the flutter kick is executed by alternately moving the legs vertically from the hips, forcefully and regularly. On each downward beat the foot turns inward (pigeon-toed). This occurs naturally if the ankles and feet are held loosely. This increases the surface area of the foot. In the upward beat the foot is extended with the sole pushing up against the water, not pigeon-toed. Beginners should first attempt this kick with the legs straight yet not rigid in order to move from the hips. Then the knee action can be learned, which is similar to pedaling a bicy-

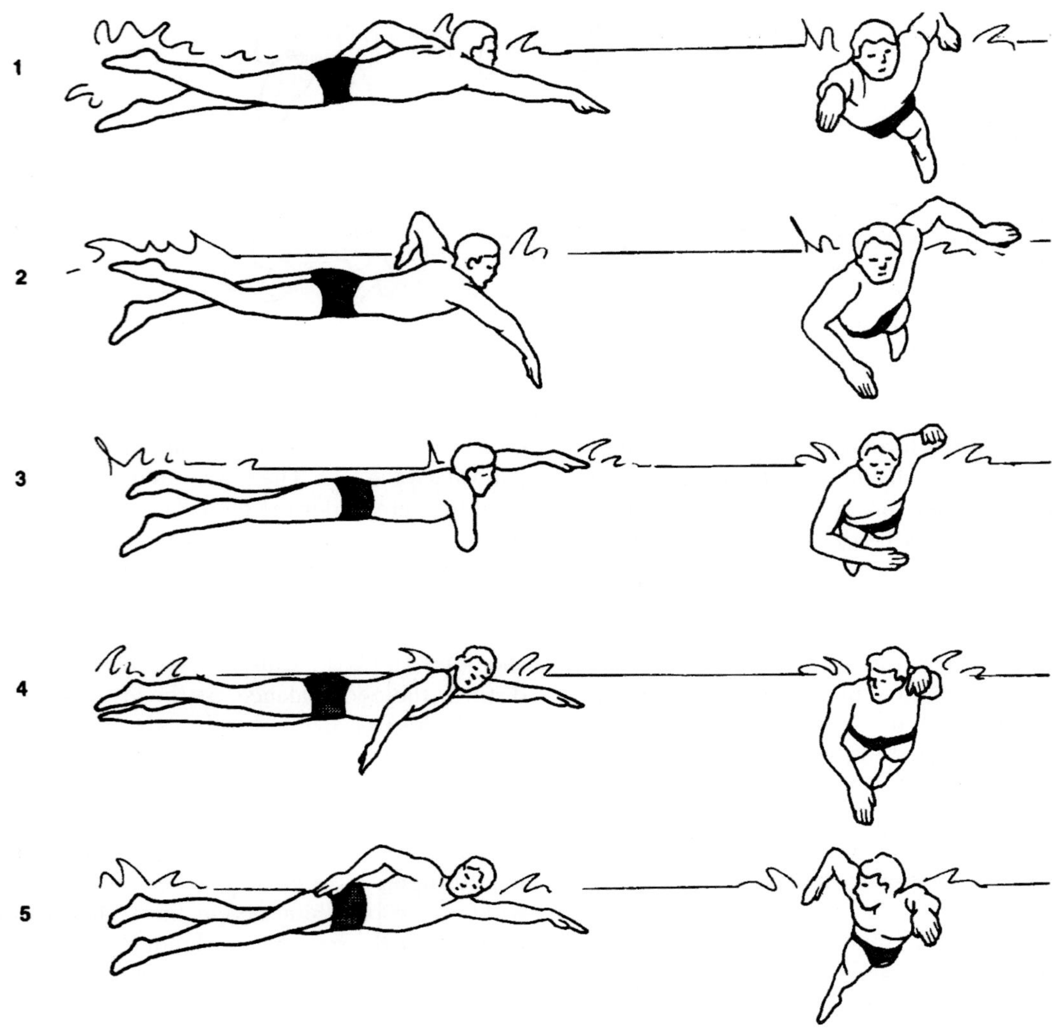

Figure 33-10. Progressive steps in timing the arms and legs with breathing in the crawl stroke.

cle. As the leg drives up, the sole of the foot pushes upward with the knees slightly flexed and remains there until the knee is almost straight on the downward beat. (See action of right leg in figure 33-10, 1 through 3.) This movement results in a quick down-up whip of the foreleg and foot at the end of the downbeat, the same principle used in the breaststroke kick. This skill can be learned by daily drills with the aid of a kickboard.

Arm stroke (alternating)

This stroke is executed by alternately reaching hand-over-hand forward into the water and pulling the body forward. The arm stroke has seven components: (1) entry, (2) support, (3) catch, (4) pull, (5) push, (6) release, and (7) recovery.

For the entry, place the hand in the water at a natural arm's length, directly in front of the shoulder. The fingers should enter the water before the elbow or shoulder. A comfortable reach should be made; never overreach. (See figure 33-10, 1 through 3.)

An opposition-rhythm type of stroke is maintained. This means that the arms are nearly opposite each other at all times.

The catch (the position the hand assumes when it is in the optimal position to begin propulsion) and pull should start first in the wrist and then in the elbow, bending slightly for good leverage (figure 33-10, 2). The pull shifts into a push as the arm passes under the side of the chest toward the hip. Then the push continues the drive to the release with the forearm and hand. (The release of one hand coincides with the catch of the other hand.) At this point the shoulder begins to lift in preparation to recover the arm until the hand clears the surface at the hip.

The arm is then recovered to the entry by lifting the shoulder, bending at the elbow, and turning the hand so that the palm faces to the rear and gradually faces the water at entry. The arm recovery movement is up and forward with the elbow high. The hand enters the water first, followed by the forearm. The hand reaches forward as the shoulders and hips rotate. The desired high elbow position on the recovery, entry, and catch is made easier if the shoulders and hips are allowed to roll to both sides during a complete stroke. The rolling action should be symmetric, with the head held in a relatively stable position (figure 33-10).

Whole stroke

While the arms execute a complete revolution, the legs complete some number of evenly measured beats. In walking, the arms and legs move in a 1:1 ratio, an opposite-arm-and-leg counterbalancing movement. In swimming the crawl, a preferred leg-to-arm ratio is 3:1; that is, the legs perform three beats to each armstroke, or six beats to each complete cycle of both arms. If speed is desired, the fundamental mechanics of the stroke become quite complex and highly technical in obtaining the ease and balance necessary for good performance as well as speed.

Breathing

Breathing in the crawl stroke is executed as follows: just as the arm opposite the breathing side has entered the water and is stretching for the catch, the hips are rotating and the arm on the breathing side has completed two thirds of the pull, the head is rotated to inhale and then immediately follows the roll of the body back into the water. When rotating the head for air, keep the chin close to the throat and the mouth inside the trough of the bow wave formed by the head. Take a quick breath as the mouth is opening; do not pause after opening the mouth. Curl the lips out away from the teeth when opening the mouth (figure 33-10, 4 and 5).

Back Crawl Stroke

The back crawl stroke (called the backstroke in competition) (figure 33-11) is the fastest stroke done on the back.

Inverted flutter kick

Essentially the kick is the same as the flutter kick in the crawl stroke. The body is extended on its back, legs held closely together and ankles and toes pointed. The legs move alternately up and down with action originating from the hips. On the upward beat the toes turn in. At the end of the upward beat the kneecap should not break the surface. The foot should throw some water above the surface without breaking the surface of the water. To accomplish this skill, the thigh, as in other styles of kicks, forcefully drives down just before the knee has straightened. This action gives the foreleg and foot an effective propulsive up-down whip. The ratio of leg kicks to one complete cycle of arm (left and right) stroke revolution is 6:1, the same as in the crawl stroke.

Arm stroke

The arms move in opposition to one another as in the crawl stroke. The hands exit the water thumb-first and enter the water with the little finger first.

The arm is bent slightly at the elbow at the beginning of the recovery phase, but it is straightened for the entry. The arm recovers to the entry with an upward swing and continues to the entry at a point not more than 6 inches (15 cm) outside the shoulder line. The hand and forearm should not be slowed as they near the point of entry, but should accelerate so that they are in the water before the shoulder can sink under.

The power, or pull, phase of the stroke can be done with either a bent or straight arm. The bent-arm stroke is used by high-level competitive swimmers and is more difficult to learn than the straight-arm pull. In the initial part of the straight-arm pull, the arm is shallow, about 2 to 6 inches (5 to 15 cm) underwater. As the arm reaches a

Figure 33-11. Progressive steps in swimming the back crawl showing the six leg beats and one revolution of the arm cycle.

point directly out from the shoulder, the depth should be about 6 to 10 inches (15 to 25 cm). From here, the arm continues until it reaches the leg and begins the recovery phase (figure 33-11).

The bent-arm pull is initiated with the hand entering the water, little finger first, palm out, facing away and slightly backward, with the arm straight. Body roll is crucial to perform the bent-arm stroke. At the point of entry, the body rolls onto the side of the arm entering the water. The hand enters the water and presses outward and downward until it catches the water. The catch with one hand and release with the other hand should coincide. The catch is made 12 to 18 inches (30 to 45 cm) below the surface. As the pulling hand presses downward, outward, and backward, the elbow bends. Next the hand presses upward, backward, and inward toward the hip and surface. The arm will have a maximum bend of about 90 degrees at this point and will be about 6 inches (15 cm) below the surface. The hand now increases its pulling speed and presses downward and outward. The moment the arm has finished its pull along the side of the thigh, the hand gives a final downward press as the shoulder is lifted out of the water and the hand is turned to face outward. The final push downward is probably the most propulsive part of the stroke. In both types of pulls the arm stroke should be smooth and relaxed throughout. A slight hip roll and a more pronounced shoulder roll permit an easier recovery and catch, as well as more efficient action of the opposite arm.

Breathing and head position

Breathing should be continuous and rhythmic. The chin is always lined up on dead center, and the head should never move from side to side. The ears should be below the water surface. The head should be propped up as if it were on a pillow. The swimmer should be able to see his or her toes. The body stretch will prevent sagging at the hips (figure 33-11).

Butterfly (Dolphin) Stroke

The butterfly stroke was created in 1935 by David A. Armbruster, the swimming coach at the University of Iowa, with the aid of one of his swimmers, Jack Sieg. The legs in this stroke move in unison in an up-and-down wavelike action that resembles the movement of a dolphin. The arms also move in unison. The arms recover bilaterally, low above the surface; are held nearly straight; and resemble the wings of a butterfly in flight.

The stroke is definitely dominated by the kick. This wavelike kick by the legs has become the fastest means of kicking through water. It is even faster than the alternating flutter kick.

The butterfly stroke is very exhausting to the untrained individual, but it provides a learning challenge. The dolphin kick can also be used with the crawl and back stroke turns for increased speed and power. Except for use as a competitive swimming stroke, it has little, if any, value to humans . It is certainly not a survival stroke due to the high energy demands it requires of the swimmer. However, the stroke is included here because many students desire to learn it, if for no other reason than for its rugged, challenging action and for the satisfaction of being able to perform it.

Kick

As practice progresses, the student should first practice the kick on the surface of the water, with the hands finning at the sides of the hips. As a final step of conditioning and training, and before the whole stroke is attempted, the student should submerge and practice the kick underwater during breath-holding intervals. The hands should be finning at the sides of the hips rather than extended in front of the head. By practicing the kick underwater, the student is able to assure forward progress. It is also essential while performing underwater to relax the entire spine from the shoulders through all the joints to the end of the toes. Swim fins help beginners become familiar with this movement. When the true shortened up-and-down beat of the kick and the up-and-down action of the hips have been mastered, the student can progress to the arm action.

Downbeat. Both legs sweep downward simultaneously. The hips flex, the knees flex, and the thighs move downward at the beginning of the downbeat. At the end of the downbeat the legs are fully extended, with the toes pointed and the hips flexed. At the completion of the downbeat, the feet are pressing downward with the most velocity and force in the entire kick. Loose ankles provide the whipping action necessary to be propulsive.

Upbeat. Hip extension moves the legs toward the surface while the legs are still straight. Gradually the knees start to flex as the legs move toward the surface, and the hips drop lower in the water.

Arm stroke

The student should first practice the arm stroke by walking across the swimming pool, bent at the hips, chin at water level, stroking with the arms. The stroke can also be practiced while stationary, in the same position.

During the arm stroke the hands trace the shape of an hourglass underwater. The arms start the stroke from the point of entry, in front of the head, pressing downward into a short lateral spread. The hands and forearms continue the pull backward with a quick inward action, with the hands coming very close together, elbows bent until they reach a point just under and ahead of the shoulders. From this point the power drive is completed backward and outward past the hips until the arms and hands have cleared the surface of the water. This final emphasis is delivered by straightening the elbows until shoulders, arms, and hands have cleared the surface of the water. This action forces the arms to swing laterally forward with the hands just above the water and the elbows slightly bent through the recovery phase to the correct point of entry. During the recovery the arms are held nearly straight, palms facing the surface. The recovery should be executed without hesitation at the end of the power phase. The hands and forearms should enter the water slightly ahead of the upper arms and shoulders, with the wrists slightly flexed. The catch of the next stroke is started without breaking momentum.

When walking or swimming across the pool practicing the arm stroke, the student should imagine the body moving toward the face of a large clock; the left arm should enter the water pointing to 11 o'clock and the right arm should point to 1 o'clock.

There is no pause in the entire stroke turnover. This is what is known in swimming terms as a *fast turnover stroke;* that is, the moment the arms complete the power drive, they go into the recovery to start the next stroke. Not only must the arms recover quickly, but the power drive of the arms must also be rapidly executed. It is this fast turnover cadence that makes the stroke so strenuous, especially if the beginner is poorly conditioned. However, most students skilled in other strokes can learn the challenging, complex skills involved in performing this stroke.

Whole stroke

The stroke is started with one or two kicks with the head submerged and the arms in streamline position. The hands enter the water just outside the shoulders simultaneously, pointing to the 11 and 1 o'clock positions, respectively. As the hands execute the catch, with a slight spread and downward press, the first downward beat of the kick takes place (figure 33-12, 1 and 2). This downbeat of the kick is a natural counteraction caused by the powerful downward catch and pull of the forearms, similar to the counterswing of the arms and legs in walking or running. While the hands and arms execute the inward drive or pull to a point just ahead of under the shoulders, the first upbeat of the kick takes place (figure 33-12, 3 and 4). From this point the arms continue to complete the final power drive as the second downbeat of the kick takes place (figure 33-12, 4 and 5). This action is again a natural counterbalancing movement of legs and arms. As the arms drive out of the water at the hips and move into the recovery phase, the legs execute the second upbeat (figure 33-12, 6 through 8). Note that during the entire arm recovery phase there is only one beat of the legs, which is up, and none supporting the body. For this reason it is essential that the swimmer move the arms quickly from the end of the drive to the entry. This quickened movement will prevent the body from sinking below swimming level. The most troublesome part in learning the stroke is this latter phase. If the arms move too slowly or hesitate at any point between the final drive and the entry, rhythm and timing are lost.

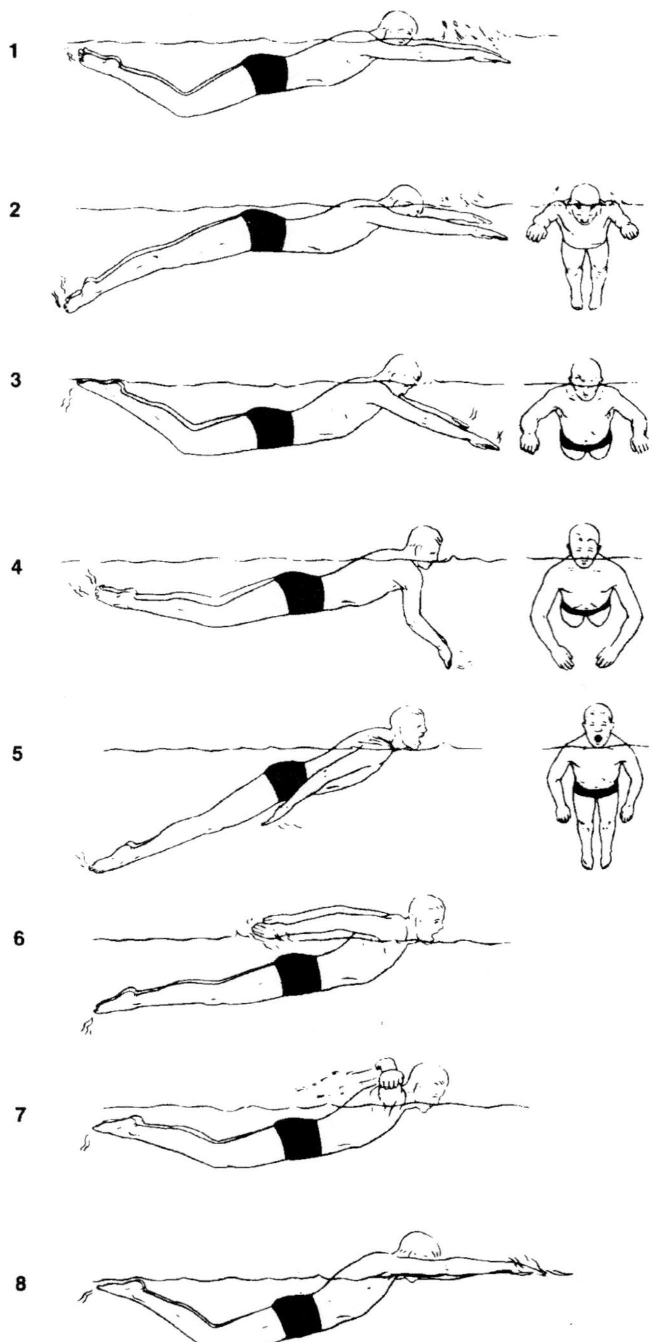

Figure 33-12. Progressive steps in swimming the butterfly (dolphin) stroke.

In executing the entry, the arms plunge lightly into the water and immediately go into the catch to start the next stroke. The stroke should first be practiced without breathing until reasonably satisfactory timing is attained. Beginners often make the mistake of starting the recovery of the arms prematurely, before the arms and hands have cleared the surface of the water well back of the hips and straightened elbows (figure 33-12, 5 and 6).

Breathing

Correct breathing in the butterfly (dolphin) stroke is not too difficult, providing the beginner does not develop a tendency to lift the head too high or back. In learning this skill, the student should again walk the arm stroke across the swimming pool with the face submerged while executing the breathing and correct timing action of the head in the arm stroke cadence. Taking a breath every stroke should be practiced. Correct breathing habits in this stroke are essential to obtain ease of performance of the entire stroke.

To inhale, the swimmer should lift the head up and out just far enough for the mouth to clear the surface of the water. This action takes place just as the arms have passed backward under the shoulders and are completing their drive. Air is actually taken just as the arms clear the water and move into the recovery phase (figure 33-12, 4 through 6). Note how the finishing "kick" of the arm stroke gives the head the necessary lift to inhale. The head drops quickly but not deeply into the water after inhalation, before the arm recovery has reached the point of entry (figure 33-12, 7 and 8). A quick recovery of both the head and the arms gives support to the body during this phase of the stroke. Both the head and the arms are above the surface of the water during the second upward beat of the kick. If this phase of the stroke is not well timed and executed, the torso and hips will tend to sink too deep in the water to continue forward. With practice, proficiency is acquired and the tiring, unnecessary movements are minimized.

LEARNING PROGRESSION FOR BEGINNERS

1. Study pool sanitation and personal health and hygiene
2. Provide the opportunity to orient and adjust to water in order to overcome the loss of body weight, loss of balance, and loss of body heat, all of which disturb the beginner psychologically, physiologically, and physically using the following exercises:
   a. Submerge the face, opening the eyes underwater, and hold the breath
   b. Bobbing exercises, where the swimmer pushes him or herself down toward the bottom. Once the head is submerged push off the bottom to go back to the surface.
   c. Floating, tucked and body straight, on both the face and back
3. Adjustment of the hands and feet to paddling in shallow water
   a. Sculling with and without the feet
   b. Finning with and without the feet
   c. Treading water with and without the feet
4. Unskilled strokes on the face, sides, and back
5. Skilled strokes
   a. Kicks
      (1) Flutter
      (2) Scissors (both sides)
      (3) Whip
      (4) Dolphin
   b. Arms strokes
      (1) Alternating stroke with breathing
      (2) Sidestroke with breathing
      (3) Breaststroke
      (4) Resting inverted breaststroke
      (5) Butterfly
6. Synchronize action of arms and legs in all strokes by using part-whole method, that is, breaking down each stroke from the whole into its component parts and by progressive stages building it again into the whole stroke
7. Orientation in distance swimming

LEARNING PROGRESSION FOR INTERMEDIATE SWIMMERS

Instruction in intermediate swimming is given to those who have taken and passed the beginner's course; those who have never had instruction but can pass the beginner's test, although they have no knowledge of stroke technique; or those who can swim in deep water.

1. Review swimming pool landmarks regarding pool depths, any unique features of the natatorium, and personal safety rules.
2. Review strokes, and review techniques of proper breathing.
3. Drill on stroke techniques.
4. Start orientation to distance swimming, emphasizing relaxation and natural breathing.
5. Practice fundamental dives from the springboard.
6. Learn and practice safety factors for self and others, such as recognizing tired-swimmer's stroke, use a simple rescue, simple carries in towing, and resuscitation.
7. Swim distances, stressing ease in breathing, relaxation, and the distribution of effort over distance comfortably.

LEARNING PROGRESSION FOR ADVANCED SWIMMERS

Instruction in advanced swimming is open to those who have passed the intermediate course or have achieved the ability to swim ¼ mile (0.4 km) and demonstrated all of the standard strokes.

1. Practice timing the strokes to develop ease of performance with added power and speed, thereby gaining confidence.

2. Swim each stroke 100 yards (91 m) with correct technique and timing of breathing with strokes.
3. Kick 25 yards (22.9 m) on each side, holding the upper arm out of the water fully extended.
4. Kick 25 yards (22.9 m) on the back, holding both hands out of the water.
5. Swim ¼ mile (0.4 km) mile in 8 minutes or less.
6. Learn a good racing start and good technique in turning at the end of the pool.
7. Be able to do at least three dives from the springboard in good form.
8. Learn safety procedures and operations of small craft.
9. Swim safely for 20 minutes.
10. Learn how to wade properly in water of unknown depth.
11. Learn how to swim out of a swift current.
12. Learn how to assist another person temporarily in distress in deep water.
13. Learn how to swim for two people.
14. Swim under water for a distance of 25 yards (22.9 m).
15. Learn how to conserve strength.
16. Learn how to rest while tired in deep water.
17. Learn boatmanship:
    a. Paddling and rowing.
    b. What to do when capsized.
    c. How to land safely when capsized.
18. Be able to teach others how to swim.
19. Learn how and when to make a safe rescue.
20. Be able to demonstrate proper resuscitation.

TEACHING CONSIDERATIONS

1. Skilled lifeguards should be on duty in the pool for all instructional sessions.
2. Beginning classes should contain fewer students than intermediate or advanced classes. All classes should be ability grouped as specified in the chapter.
3. All sessions should include introduction, practice, and summary.
4. Basic stroke technique is easier to understand if demonstrations and initial practice take place out of the water.
5. Consider using a "buddy" system for safety and skill feedback.
6. Work first for technique and then use strokes for distance and conditioning.
7. With intermediate and advanced swimmers, identify why students are taking the course. Competition, endurance, and recreational goals require different teaching techniques.

SUGGESTED READINGS

Colwin, C. 1992. *Swimming into the 21st century*. Champaign, Ill.: Human Kinetics. Presents an overview of every phase of competitive swimming, swimming research, practical coaching advice, and training schedules.

Costill, D., Maglischo, E., and Rishardson, A. 1992. *Swimming*. Champaign, Ill.: Human Kinetics. Part of the *Handbook of sports medicine* series.

Counsilman, R. 1994. *New science of swimming*, 2d ed. Needham Heights, MA, Allyn and Bacon. This is a classic reference on the science of swimming by the "father" of modern competitive swimming.

Cryer, W. 1991. *Swimming*. Scottsdale, Ariz.: Gorsuch, Scarisbrick.

Intercollegiate and interscholastic swimming guide: Official rules of swimming and diving. Published annually. New York, National Intercollegiate Athletic Bureau.

Leonard, J. ed. 1992. *Science of coaching swimming*. Champaign, Ill.: Human Kinetics. Applies sports science principles to the art of coaching swimming.

Maglischo, E. 1993. *Swimming faster: A comprehensive guide to the science of swimming*. 2d ed. Mountain View, Calif.: Mayfield. Brings together recent research on the biomechanics of stroke technique and the physiology of swimming. Extensively illustrated.

Messner, Y. J. 1992. *Swimming everyone*. 2d ed. Winston-Salem, N.C.: Hunter Textbooks. Coverage for beginning through advanced swimming classes, including step-by-step presentation of skills, background of the activity, equipment used, safety, injury prevention, self-evaluation techniques, and values of the sport.

Official NCAA swimming and diving guide. Current ed. Shawnee Mission, Kans.: National Collegiate Athletic Association.

Shea, E. 1986. *Swimming for seniors*. Champaign, Ill.: Human Kinetics.

Thomas, D. G. 1990. *Advanced swimming: Steps to success*. Champaign, Ill.: Human Kinetics.

Thomas, D. G. 1996. *Swimming: Steps to success*. 2d ed. Champaign, Ill.: Human Kinetics.

Vickers, B. J., and Vincent, W. J. 1994. *Swimming*. 6th ed. Dubuque, Iowa: WCB/McGraw-Hill. Contains illustrated material on elementary diving, special water activities, competitive swimming and diving, cardiopulmonary resuscitation, and artificial respiration.

Periodicals

Aquatics International (quarterly), Communications Channels, P.O. Box 5111, Pittsfield, MA 01203.

Fitness Swimmer (monthly), Rodale's Fitness Swimmer, P.O. Box 5307, Pittsfield, MA 01203-5307.

Journal of Swimming Research (quarterly), 304 SE 20th St., Fort Lauderdale, FL 33316.

Swim Magazine (monthly), Sports Publications, Inc., 228 Nevada St., El Segundo, CA 90245.

Swimming Technique (quarterly), Swimming World Publications, P.O. Box 45497, Los Angeles, CA 90045.

Swimming World (monthly), Sports Publications, 155 S. El Molino, Suite 101, Pasadena, CA 91101.

RESOURCES

Videotapes

American Red Cross: *Swimming and diving skills*, American Red Cross, 17th & D Street, Washington, DC 20006.

Freestyle techniques and *Starts, turns and individual medley*, Karol Video, 22 Riverside Dr., Wayne, NJ 07470.

Gambril, D.: *Don Gambril's gold medal series: Breaststroke; Backstroke; Butterfly; Freestyle and coach's drills* and *The fundamentals of swimming* (5 videos), Swimming World, P.O. Box 91870, Pasadena, CA 91109.

Getting better: Championship swimming with John Naber; *Swimming strokes: Olympic style swimming*; and *Excellence in swimming stroke technique* are available from Cambridge Physical Education and Health, P.O. Box 2153, Charleston, WV 25328.

Naber, J., and Fletcher, J.: *Teaching kids swimming with John Naber and Joy Fletcher*. West One Video, 1995 Bailey Hill Rd., Eugene, OR 97405. Takes the viewer through a thorough program that acquaints youthful swimmers with the water.

Swimming, Different strokes, and *Getting better* are among several videos available from Sports Videos, 745 State Circle, P.O. Box 1941, Ann Arbor, MI 48106.

Thomas, D.: *Water is friendly: The first step in learning to swim.* Human Kinetics, P.O. Box 5076, Champaign, IL 61825.

Thirteen videos, including several on the various strokes, drills, and baby water safety. "How To" Sports Videos, PO. Box 5852, Denver, CO 80217.

Web site

The Yellow Pages of Swimming: http://www.tcd.net/swimlinx.html

Table Tennis

After completing this chapter, the reader should be able to:

- Appreciate the historical development and social values of table tennis
- Select the proper equipment for the game
- Properly apply the rules for singles and doubles play
- Demonstrate and execute proper grips, footwork, and shots
- Understand singles and doubles strategy

HISTORY

The exact origin of the sport now called table tennis is in question. Most experts can narrow it down only to the late nineteenth century, although there are lithographs suggesting an origin as early as 1810. It is believed to have originated in England. At one point in history, table tennis was known as "ping-pong." It is believed that this name was derived from the sound of the ball hitting the table ("ping") and the ball hitting the hollow vellum battledore, which was the paddle at the time ("pong"). Now the title *Ping-Pong* is usually reserved for the recreational version of the activity, and *table tennis* is the name used for the sport. The sport has also been known as Gossima, Flim-Flam, and Whif-Whaf. After a brief period of popularity in the United States, table tennis fell into obscurity. It was revived around 1920 and gradually gained in popularity around the world. The International Table Tennis Federation (ITTF) was established in Berlin in 1926, and the United States Table Tennis Association (USTTA) was established in 1933. The latter changed to USA Table Tennis (USATT) in 1994.

Table tennis is now considered to be the world's second largest participation sport and is a major sport in Asia and Europe. It is the number one racquet sport in the world, with over 10 million playing competitively each year.

Although world championships have been held in table tennis since 1926, it did not become a full-medal Olympic event until 1988 in Seoul. Early years of international competitions were dominated by Central European countries, especially Hungary and Czechoslovakia. In the 1950s the dominance in table tennis shifted to Japan. In the 1960s, 1970s, and 1980s China dominated the sport. China captured six of the possible seven titles at the world championships in New Delhi in 1987. South Korea spoiled the sweep by winning the women's doubles. In the 1988 Olympics, the Chinese and the South Koreans split the four gold medals, with China winning the women's singles and the men's doubles and South Korea winning the men's singles and the women's doubles.

At the 1992 Barcelona Olympics the four table tennis events (men's and women's singles and doubles) were dominated by the Chinese teams. They won six of the possible 12 medals including three of the four gold medals.

At the 1996 Summer Olympics in Atlanta, Georgia, the four table tennis events (men's and women's singles and doubles) were all won by China. Today, China, Korea, and Sweden are regularly recognized as the world's powerhouses.

VALUES

Table tennis is an excellent club or home game for everyone because it requires a minimum of equipment, is relatively inexpensive, and can be played almost anywhere by all age groups. It is very popular at recreation and community centers. Many table tennis tournaments are held each year. Table tennis causes little or no damage or injury because a small racquet and light-as-a-feather ball are used.

Finding opponents to play singles or doubles is usually easy. If unequal in ability, the better player can spot an opponent a few points to increase the competitive enjoyment of the game.

EQUIPMENT

Any type of clothing allowing freedom of movement and comfort is acceptable. Rubber-soled shoes that facilitate safe side-to-side movements should be worn. However, in tournament play USATT rules specify that clothing may be of any color, except that the main color shall be clearly different from that of the ball in use. Whenever an orange ball is used, white but not orange clothing is allowed.

Racquet (Blade)

A variety of satisfactory racquets are available from commercial sources. The racquet blade should be made of wood but may be reinforced with fibrous material such as carbon fiber, glass fiber, or compressed paper. The striking surface (racquet covering) of the racquet blade must be covered with a pimpled rubber with the pimples facing

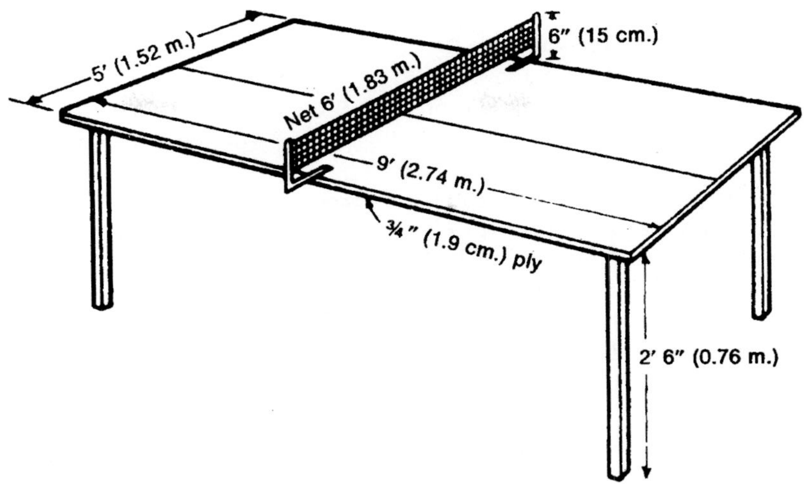

Figure 34-1. Table and net.

inward or outward. A single layer of cellular (sponge) rubber is located underneath the rubber surface. The two surfaces of the blade may have different striking surfaces, but must be different colors, namely black and red.

Ball

The ball is small, celluloid, spherical, matte in color, 1½ inches (38 mm) in diameter and ⅞ ounces (2.5 g) in weight. It is fragile but quite hard to break unless stepped on. The USATT-approved standard ball has a uniform bounce. If it is dropped from a height of 12 inches (30.5 cm) on an approved table, it should bounce 8¾ to 9¾ inches (22 to 25 cm).

Table

The table is usually constructed of ¾-inch (1.9 cm) material, commonly plywood or particle board, and must be 9 feet (2.74 m) in length and 5 feet (1.52 m) in width. The playing surface should be dark (usually green or blue) and nonreflecting and should lie on a horizontal plane 2 feet 6 inches (76 cm) above the floor. The sidelines and endlines are white and should be ¾ inch (1.9 cm) wide. The centerline is also white, but only ⅛ (3 mm) wide (figure 34-1). It is best to use tables approved by either USATT or ITTF. There should be sufficient room around the table to permit players to "go after" the ball without running into obstructions. Official rules state that the minimum playing space for each table is 40 feet (12 m) long, 20 feet (6 m) wide, and 11.5 feet (3.5 m) high.

Net

The net is lightweight. It is stretched taut across the center of the table and attached to the outside by supporting posts. The top of the net should be 6 inches (15 cm) above the table and extend to attached posts 6 inches (15 cm) outside of the sidelines. The bottom of the net should be as close to the table as possible and the ends of the net as close to the supporting posts as possible.

RULES (ABRIDGED)*

Singles

A game is won by the player who first scores 21 points, unless both players have scored 20 points, in which case the one who first scores 2 points more than the opponent is the winner.

The choice of playing position at the table and order of service are determined by the toss of a coin. If the winner of the toss prefers to have first choice of playing positions, the opponent then has the choice of whether to serve first or receive first, and vice versa.

The change of service takes place after 5 points have been scored. A point is normally awarded when the play of a service is concluded. The receiver then becomes the server and the server becomes receiver, and so on, after each 5 points until the end of the game or the score is 20-all. Whenever the score becomes 20-all, the receiver becomes the server and the server the receiver, and so on, after each point until the end of the game.

In the start of a new game, the player who served first in the previous game becomes receiver and the receiver becomes server, and so on, alternating after each game.

The players also exchange ends after each game, and if play consists of more than one game, in the deciding game of the match the players change ends when one player reaches a score of 10. A match is the majority of three (or five) games.

**The Laws of Table Tennis* (latest edition), USA Table Tennis, 1 Olympic Plaza, Colorado Springs, CO 80909-5769.

Service

A good service is delivered by projecting the ball from the free (nonserving) hand, which must start from above the playing surface. The ball must be resting in the palm of the free hand, which is flat and the thumb free of the fingers. Without imparting spin to the ball, it is projected near vertically upward at least six inches. As it starts to descend, the ball is struck so that it touches the server's court first and then, passing directly over or around the net, touches the receiver's court. At the instant of contact of the racquet on the ball in service, both handle and ball must be behind the endline of the server's court, but not farther back than the part of the server's body, other than his or her arm, leg, or head, whichever is farthest from the net.

A good return of a served ball must be struck by the receiver on the first bounce so that it passes directly over or around the net and touches the opponent's court.

Points

Unless the rally is a let, a point is awarded to the opponent in the following circumstances:

1. Failure to make a good service
2. Failure to make a good return
3. If the player, the racquet, or anything that the player wears or carries touches the net or its supports while the ball is in play
4. If the player, the racquet, or anything that a player wears or carries moves the playing surface while the ball is in play
5. If the player's free hand touches the playing surface while the ball is in play
6. If, after being struck by the opponent, the ball comes in contact with the player or anything the player wears or carries before it has passed over the endlines or sidelines, not yet having touched the playing surface on the player's side of the table
7. If at any time the player volleys the ball—that is, before the ball hits the table top—except as provided in number 1 under "Let" (below)
8. If a player strikes the ball twice in succession

Let

A let ball, which is then replayed, is called in the following cases:

1. If the served ball, in passing over or around the net, touches it or its supports, provided that the service would otherwise have been good or is volleyed by the receiver
2. If a service is delivered when the receiver is not ready, provided always that the receiver may not be deemed unready if an attempt to strike the ball is made
3. If either player is prevented by a disturbance not under his or her control from serving a good service or making a good return
4. If either player gives up a point, as provided in number 3 to 7 under "Points," owing to an accident not within his or her control
5. If a game is interrupted for correction of an error in order or ends

Scoring

A point is scored by the side that makes the last successful return prior to the end of a rally. An unsuccessful return occurs whenever the ball is missed, struck with the side of a racquet blade having an illegal surface, hit off the table, sent into the net, or hit onto the player's own half of the court on the return. Failure to make a good serve also scores a point for the opponent unless it is a let.

In play

The ball is in play from the moment it is projected from the hand in service until the rally is decided as a let or a point.

Doubles

Good service

The service is delivered as previously described, except that it must touch first the right half of the server's court and then, passing directly over or around the net, touch the right half of the receiver's court. The centerline is considered part of each right-hand court.

Choice of order of play

The official rules specify that the team winning a coin toss has the choice of ends or the right to receive or serve. After the choice is made, the other team makes the remaining choice.

The pair who have the right to serve the first five services in any game decide which partner shall serve, and the opposing pair decide similarly who will first be the receiver.

Order of service (figure 34-2)

The first five services must be delivered by the selected partner (1) of the pair who have the right to do so and must be received by the selected partner (3) of the opposing pair (figure 34-2A). The second five services must be delivered by the receiver of the first five services (3) and received by the partner of the server (2) of the first five services (figure 34-2B). The third five services must be delivered by the partner of the first five services (2) and received by the partner of the receiver (4) of the first five services (figure 34-2C). The fourth five services must be delivered by the partner of the receiver (4) of the first five services and received by the server (1) of the first five services (figure 34-2D). The fifth five services must be delivered in the same manner as the first five services, and so on in sequence until the end of the game or a score of 20-all, at which point each player serves only one service in turn until the end of the game.

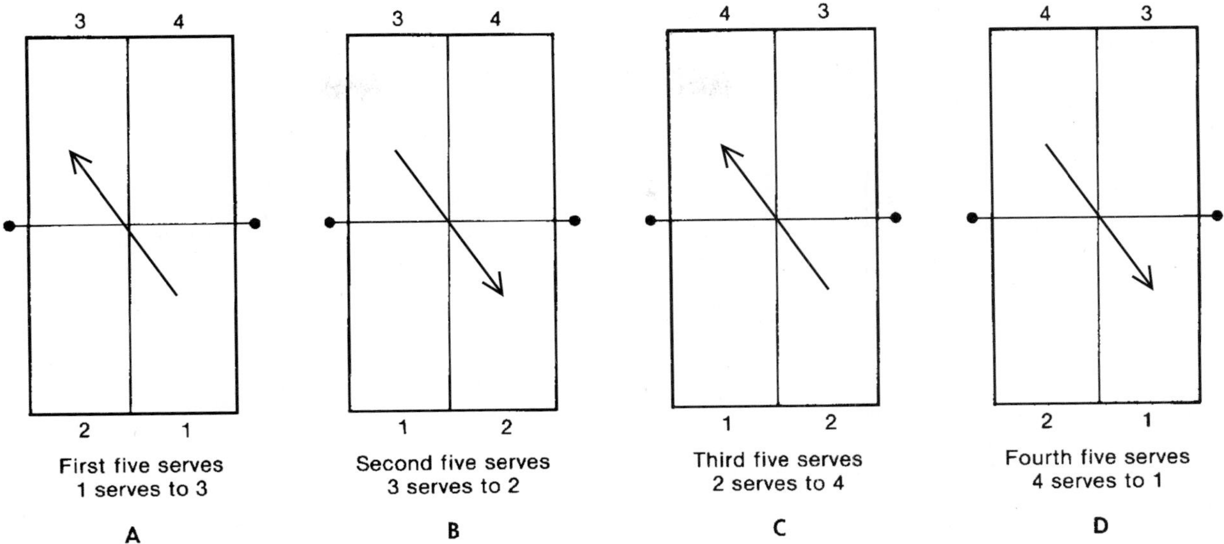

Figure 34-2. Order of service for doubles.

The team (or player in singles) who served first shall receive first in the next game. In each game the initial order of serving is the opposite of the preceding game.

In a one-game match or in the deciding game of a match of more than one game, the pair that served the first five services has the right to alter its order of receiving or that of its opponents at the first score of 10.

FUNDAMENTAL SKILLS AND TECHNIQUES

Shake-Hands Grip

Shake-hands grip is both highly versatile and popular. With the blade perpendicular to the floor, the racquet is grasped as if shaking hands with it. The index finger is pointed along the bottom of the blade surface with the thumb on the surface of the other side.

Forehand grip

In the forehand grip the short handle of the racquet is gripped very closely to the blade, with the blade itself partially held in the hand and the forefinger and thumb bracing opposite sides of the blade (figure 34-3A). Rotate the top of the racquet toward the body (upward) to obtain a stronger forehand.

Backhand grip

The backhand grip is the same as for the forehand, except that the side of the thumb rests on the back of the blade (figure 34-3B).

Penhold Grip

The same side of the blade is almost always used for both backhand and forehand shots. Thus, the grip position remains unchanged unless the racquet is deliberately rotated between rallies in order to use the striking surface on the other side of the blade. With the racquet pointing down, hold the racquet where the handle meets the blade with the thumb and index finger. This is similar to holding a pen. Either curl up or straighten the remaining fingers. Figure 34-3C, D depicts the penhold grip.

Points to Remember

1. Do not grip the racquet too tightly; relax.
2. Hold the wrist firmly and rotate the forearm as needed to obtain the correct blade angle.
3. Whenever possible, angle your body toward the ball when making forehand and backhand shots in order to move forward when striking the ball.
4. Constantly check the racquet head, making sure that it is not dropped because the wrist is bent.
5. Regularly check the thumb and index finger to keep them in the proper place.

Serving

For a topspin serve with either a forehand or backhand stroke, the ball is put into play by projecting it upward from the flat free hand. (See figure 34-4.) As the ball is descending, it is met by the racquet, which is swung forward and upward and the racquet face is closed (facing toward the table top and net).

For a backspin (chop) serve, the ball is struck with a downward, forward motion of the racquet. (See figure 34-5.) The racquet face is open (facing upward from the table top and net). The player will need to practice adjusting the angle of the racquet to find the most effective one. More advanced players might want to work on the forehand and backhand side-spin serves.

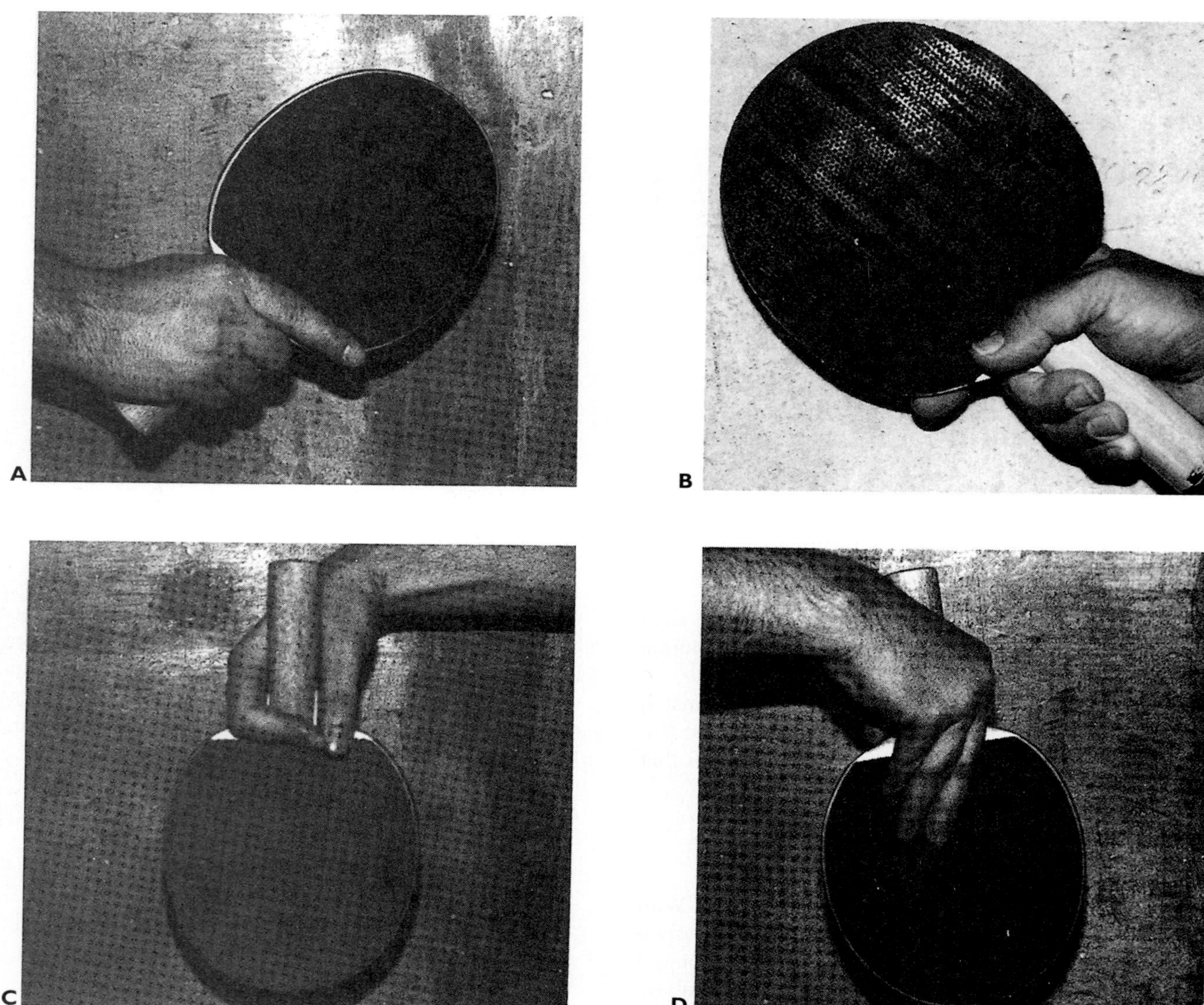

Figure 34-3. Grips (as seen from behind the player). **A,** Forehand; **B,** Backhand; **C,** Penhold, striking-surface side; **D,** Penhold, backside.

For a forehand side-spin serve, the racquet is brought across the ball from right to left (if right-handed) just as the racquet strikes the ball, with the racquet head moving to a nearly vertical position and the ball being struck in front of the server.

For a backhand side-spin serve, the racquet is swung across the ball from left to right and (if right-handed) the ball is released from the left hand just as the racquet passes in front of the server. Effective spin serves require giving the ball considerable spin.

In putting the ball into play, the server must keep the fingers straight and together and the thumb free. No cupping or pinching of the ball is permitted. If this rule is violated, a let is called and the server warned. If the violation is repeated, a point is awarded to the opponent.

Footwork and Stance

Proper stance and footwork in serving or receiving are just as important in learning table tennis as they are in tennis, badminton, or any sport that requires a constantly alert player. See figure 34-6 for two excellent examples of the stance that is often called the "ready position."

A good beginner's stance in serving the ball is a position where your playing elbow is about 1½ to 2 feet (45 to 60 cm) directly behind the centerline of the table. Face slightly to the right side with the feet well apart and the left foot forward (for a right-handed player). Remember the service rule stating that at the moment of impact, both the racquet and ball must be behind the endline on the table. In addition, the service toss must start at table height or above.

Figure 34-4. Start of the forehand topspin serve.

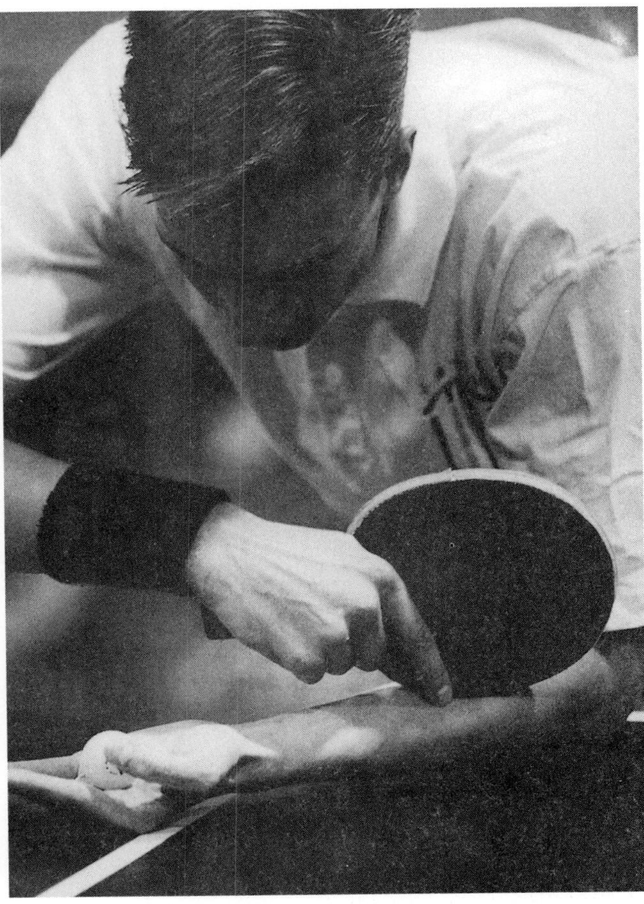

Figure 34-5. Backhand serve.

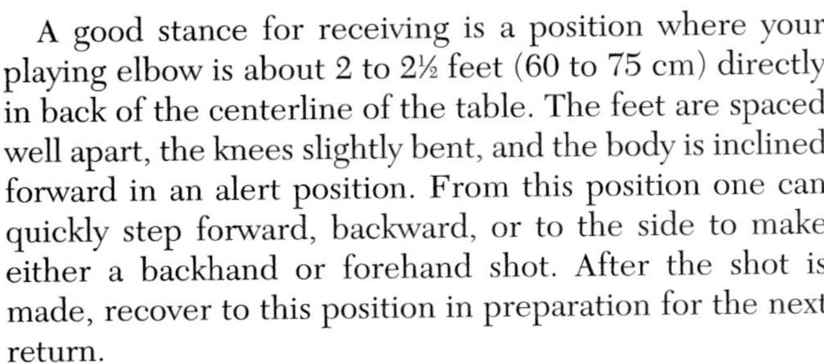

A good stance for receiving is a position where your playing elbow is about 2 to 2½ feet (60 to 75 cm) directly in back of the centerline of the table. The feet are spaced well apart, the knees slightly bent, and the body is inclined forward in an alert position. From this position one can quickly step forward, backward, or to the side to make either a backhand or forehand shot. After the shot is made, recover to this position in preparation for the next return.

For a forehand or backhand return, the feet should be placed, at the moment of contact of the racquet with the ball, so that they are perpendicular to the line of flight of the ball. The feet should be well spread in order to shift weight forward and backward in delivering a shot.

Whenever possible, attempt to be moving forward when striking the ball. In going after a ball for an effective shot, remember to face the ball as you play it. Also remember to return quickly to midcourt after the shot is made. Watch the ball at all times as demonstrated in the backhand return shown in figure 34-7.

Figure34-6. Stances, or ready positions.

Figure 34-7. Watching the ball.

Stroke Techniques

Push shot

The push shot is the easiest way to return a backspin serve or shot. A backhand push is accomplished by meeting the ball as it touches the table and gently hitting it back over the net with a racquet that is rotated toward the body and is slightly down. This lifts and carries the ball forward at the same time. The backhand push occurs in front of the body while the forehand push occurs to the forehand side of the body.

In addition, by holding the racquet almost motionless when contacting the ball, it will rebound back over the net. This is called a "block shot," and it resembles a miniature drive shot, which is described next.

Forehand top-spin shot

The forehand top-spin shot (figure 34-8) is the basic offensive drive shot. It is accomplished by striking the ball with a vigorous upward forward motion. The ball should be struck in front of and to the right side of the body (if right-handed) when it is at or just past its maximum bounce. The racquet is tilted forward at the point of contact with the ball. The upward motion imparts the overspin. This shot, at first, is best played on deep or high-bouncing returns because it requires both skill and accuracy. Shifting the body weight forward adds power to the shot, as does rotating the arm backward at the elbow.

Forehand and backhand loop shots

Loop shots begin with the knees bent and the racquet pointing downward and below tabletop height. A long, high, looping, striking, or grazing of the ball when it is dropping allows considerable topspin to be placed on the ball. In turn, it will bounce high and deep off the table. Finish with the racquet head held high. Snapping the wrist at contact increases the spin and speed placed on the ball. The emphasis during the stroke may be either upward or forward, depending on the kind and amount of spin on the incoming ball.

Backhand drive

The backhand drive is similar to the forehand drive, except that it is often shorter because the arm may cross in front of the body if not turned sideways. The ball is hit in front of and slightly to the left side of the body (if right-handed) and preferably as it is rising. The wrist may be snapped at contact, but the racquet continues forward in the direction of the new ball path. The racquet is held nearly perpendicular; and as the ball is struck, the racquet rotates downward (clockwise) toward the tabletop.

Forehand chop

The forehand chop is primarily a defensive stroke. It is executed with a hatchet-chopping motion. The stroke starts from nearly shoulder height, whenever possible, hitting forward and downward with the top of the racquet blade open (tilted back away from the ball). The stroke is finished with the arm almost fully extended in front of the body. Cutting with the blade down behind and under the ball gives the ball a backspin as it leaves the face of the racquet. This stroke should be executed with considerable speed. Chop shots are primarily defensive returns.

Figure 34-8. Completion of forehand drive.

Backhand chop

The backhand chop also requires that the racquet be tilted backward (open). It is like the forehand chop, except that it is a shorter stroke and employs stronger use of the forearm and wrist. The stroke is started at about chest height and ends at about waist height. This shot, like most shots, requires a great deal of practice to acquire a worthwhile degree of control and accuracy.

Drop shot

The drop shot is executed by moving the racquet as if beginning a drive, but stopping the forward motion of the racquet and opening its face just before hitting the ball and letting the ball hit the racquet, returning the ball just over the net. This shot should be used only occasionally as a change of pace, to catch an opponent off guard, or when an opponent has moved back from the table on a preceding shot.

Smash shot

The smash shot is what its name suggests. It is used on a higher-than-net bounce—the higher the better. It is hit straight forward and downward, with little or no spin, onto the opponent's court. Attempt it only when an advantageous situation presents itself. Play it accurately and put weight behind the smash. It is a kill, or point-making shot. Remember to avoid contact with the table.

Points to Remember

1. Vary your shot and strategy; make your opponent guess what stroke you will make.
2. Exploit your opponent's weakness and work toward eliminating yours.
3. Practice spins for control and accuracy.
4. Do not smash when a drive is more desirable and safer.
5. Concentrate on the ball.
6. Do not smash too soon or be overanxious.
7. Do not telegraph your intentions or your shot.
8. If shots are hitting the net too often, try an upward, lifting motion instead of a straightforward swing.
9. In a drive, be sure to follow through.
10. Vary your serves and returns.
11. Do not hit harder than your form justifies.
12. Always strive to perfect form.
13. Always assume that the opponent will return the ball.
14. Adhere to form and do not sacrifice it for speed or power; speed and power will naturally follow well-executed form and good technique.

Strategy

It is very important to recognize as early as possible the kind and amount of spin imparted to the ball by the opponent. Different shots produce different spins; consequently, the appropriate countershot must take this into account. Becoming skilled in this facet of the game requires considerable study and practice.

For singles play

Probably the safest strategy for both the defensive and the offensive games is similar to that of tennis: rely on the opponent to commit an error. Concentrate on returning

Figure 34-9. Positioning for doubles play.

the ball safely to the opponent's court. Vary the speed of returns. Try different shots and study the opponent's weaknesses and strong points. Size them up quickly and play to an opponent's weaknesses. Keep the opponent guessing, and avoid setting up easy shots. Keep the ball in play.

For doubles play

Essentially, strategy in doubles play is the same as in singles play. Alternating successive shots between team partners makes doubles play actually a singles game. Offensive strategy therefore consists of keeping the opponents running and off balance, as in tennis. Do not drift into a slow, deliberate game, but mix the type of shots and tempo of the game.

If one wins the toss at the start of the game, it is sound strategy to choose to receive first. This causes the opponents to determine who is to serve first, and the receiving team can then choose wisely who is to receive (the same player must receive from the same opponent throughout the game). Receiving first puts one in a strategic position in the possibly crucial closing moments of a close game.

Keep your eyes on the ball. Learn to react quickly in choosing which type of shot to make in each game situation. Use cross-court angling shots and keep opponents off balance. Constantly strive for a versatile, deceptive attack and defense to keep opponents from anticipating your shots in advance.

It is especially important to assume the correct playing position between shots. Ordinarily, a player, after hitting a shot, moves back away from the table to avoid blocking the partner's pathway to the ball while also remaining as close to the playing area as possible (figure 34-9). Moving to one side or the other often results in being out of position when it is your turn to hit the ball.

TEACHING CONSIDERATIONS

1. Have students first practice bouncing the ball up and down on the forehand, backhand, and alternate sides of the racquet. In addition, hitting a ball off a wall from various distances, as well as having two students volley back and forth in the air without a table, is helpful practice.
2. Begin practice with two students at a table when possible.
3. Teach the grip and a simple courtesy serve (hitting the dropped ball as it bounces up from the table) to beginners. The objective is to be able to put the ball into play. Later teach the legal serve and spin.
4. Teach the ready position and forehand and backhand racquet positions. Let beginning students practice hitting the ball back and forth in a cooperative way before introducing specific offensive strokes. When the ball crosses the net at least eight times consecutively, students should be ready to begin keeping the ball low to the net and placing the ball at various spots on the table in game situations.
5. After basic ball control has been mastered, teach specific offensive and defensive shots and introduce spin shots.
6. Teach singles rules before doubles rules.
7. Include an opportunity for game or gamelike play in each lesson. Give game play a focus in the beginning

of the unit by changing the scoring or rules to encourage skill development (e.g., "Keep ball less than 6 inches [15 cm] above the net" or "The ball must bounce in the alternate side of the opponent's court").

8. Match students of equal ability for game play. In large groups, play for time rather than points so that games finish at the same time for rotation.

GLOSSARY

ace A point scored on a shot that is impossible for the receiver to return.

ad Advantage.

angle shot Moving a shot diagonally across the table, also called a crosscourt shot.

backhand Hitting the ball with the back of the hand facing the direction of movement.

backspin Revolving the ball the opposite way of its flight (counterclockwise spin); mainly used on defensive shots.

blade The racquet face minus any covering.

block A quick return performed by holding the racquet directly in the ball's path and blocking it soon after it bounces.

chop Hitting the ball downward on the back of the ball, giving the ball a backspin. Used primarily on defense when not close to the table.

closed racquet A position of the racquet where the top edge is pointing away from you.

dead A ball with no spin.

deep A ball that bounces very close to the endline.

deuce A tie game at 20-all; 2 points scored consecutively are needed to win.

drive Giving a stroke topspin by turning the racquet slightly forward as the ball is hit; hitting the ball with a closed racquet face.

drop shot A shot that barely crosses the net. It is most effective when an opponent is away from the table.

flat A ball without any spin, usually travelling very fast.

flip, or flick A return striking the tabletop near the net that is produced with considerable wrist action and has topspin.

follow-through Continuing the swing after hitting the ball.

forehand Hitting the ball with the palm of the hand facing the direction of movement.

kill shot See "smash."

let Playing the ball over; occurs when the ball hits the top of the net and passes over it on the serve, when the receiver is not ready, or when an accident prevents a good service or return.

loaded A ball imparted with a lot of spin.

loop A long sweeping upward motion that just grazes the ball and puts tremendous spin on it.

match A 2-of-3 or 3-of-5 games contest.

mixed doubles A game in which each team consists of one male and one female.

open racquet A position of the racquet where the top edge is pointing toward you.

penhold One of two major racquet grips. It is similar to holding a pen.

pips Small conical bits of rubber located on one side of a sheet of table tennis rubber.

playing surface The tabletop, including the edges.

points Games are to 21 points and must be won by two points.

push A backspin return of a backspin shot.

rally The serve and all intervening legal returns; it ends when a point is won.

rating A number assigned to competitive players that changes based on personal match results. The higher the number, the better the player.

rubber The generic term for the material used as a racquet covering.

score The server's score is always called first.

serve Used to put the ball in play.

shakehands One of two major racquet grips. It is similar to shaking hands.

smash Executing a high-speed shot, usually after receiving a high bounce.

spin The rotation of the ball.

topspin A forward-rotating ball (clockwise spin).

two-step footwork This starts with a short step taken with the foot facing the direction one is moving followed by a step with the other foot so that both feet move together.

USATT USA Table Tennis; the National Governing Body for the sport of table tennis in the United States.

volley Illegal stroking of the ball while it is in the air before it hits the table.

SUGGESTED READINGS

Gurney, G. 1994. *Table tennis: The early years*. 53 London Road, St. Leonards-on-Sea, East Sussex, TN37 6AY, England, International Table Tennis Federation.

Hodges, L. 1993. *Table tennis: Steps to success*. Champaign, Ill.: Human Kinetics. Contains over 120 drills and 140 illustrations.

Preiss, S. 1991. *Table tennis: The sport*. Dubuque, Iowa: WCB/McGraw-Hill.

Seemiller, D., and Holowchak, M. 1996. *Winning table tennis: Skills, drills and strategies*. Champaign, Ill.: Human Kinetics.

Periodical

USA Table Tennis Magazine. Published by USA Table Tennis, One Olympic Plaza, Colorado Springs, CO 80909.

RESOURCES

Videotapes

Get hot with Scott and *Table tennis* are both available from Cambridge Physical Education and Health, P.O. Box 2153, Charleston, WV 25328.

Play table tennis with the Swedish national team. "How To" Sports Videos, P.O. Box 5852, Denver, CO 80217.

Web sites

USATT-Net: http://www.usatt.org

ITTF Web Site: http://www.ittf.com

Team Handball

After completing this chapter, the reader should be able to:

- Appreciate the evolution, development, and values of an activity that is gaining popularity in the United States
- Construct a team handball court
- Demonstrate knowledge and understanding of handball rules
- Execute the fundamental skills of passing, running, dribbling, and shooting
- Demonstrate offensive and defensive principles of the game
- Teach a group of students how to play team handball

HISTORY

Team handball, as it is called in the United States to distinguish the fast-paced and popular Olympic sport from the four-wall court sport that is played in the United States, developed in Europe (Bohemia, Germany, Denmark, and Sweden) during the early 1900s. Handball, as it is known in the rest of the world, evolved from combining several middle-European games, including German raffball and torball and Danish handbold, which resulted in a new sport (field handball), that could be contested across international boundaries.

In 1928, the Amateur Handball Federation was formed by the representatives of 11 countries with the inaugural rules calling for 11 players on a side and for the sport to be played outdoors on soccer fields. In 1933, this version of handball, "field handball," was included in the events in the 1936 Berlin Olympics. This was the only time that this version of handball was included as part of the Olympic program. When the Olympics were resumed in London in 1948, field handball was not included, and the sport, for the most part, laid dormant until the Games returned to Munich in 1972.

At the 1996 Summer Olympic Games, Denmark won the women's gold medal while the United States women's team finished last out of eight teams. Croatia won the men's team gold. The United States men's team finished ninth.

Handball, as it is played today, developed in the Scandinavian countries, where the sport moved indoors to escape the severe winters of northern and eastern Europe. Due to a lack of indoor facilities that would accommodate the 11-person teams, the number of players on each team was reduced to seven—a goalkeeper and six court players. This is the version of handball that the International Handball Federation (IHF) embraced at its seminal meeting in 1946. At that time the IHF was comprised of 54 nations representing almost 3 million players. Handball was recognized as an international sport by the International Olympic Committee in 1965 and was included as a new Olympic event for men in 1972 at Munich and for women in 1976 at the Montreal Games.

In general, the most powerful handball teams have been from the Eastern European countries and the Soviet Union. Since 1972, the gold medal in men's handball has been won by Yugoslavia (1972), the Soviet Union (1976), East Germany (1980), Yugoslavia (1984), the Soviet Union (1988), and the Unified team (1992). The women's handball gold medal has gone to the Soviet Union (1976 and 1980), Yugoslavia (1984), and South Korea (1988 and 1992). Asian countries, notably China and South Korea, are beginning to serve notice in the sport, as indicated by South Korea's gold medals in the 1988 and 1992 women's competition and silver in the men's competition at the 1988 Seoul Olympics.

The United States Team Handball Federation (USTHF) was formed in 1959 and is a member of the IHF and the Pan-American Handball Federation. The USTHF falls under the jurisdiction of the USOC and has its administrative offices at the U.S. Olympic Training Complex in Colorado Springs, Colorado. It publishes *Team Handball–USA*, the official publication of the federation.

While rapidly expanding into more than 80 countries worldwide, team handball has grown at a modest but steady rate in the United States. During the past decade, it has gained a large number of participants and enjoys its most avid following on the East Coast. Team handball's growing popularity is due to its fast, exciting action and low cost of participation in comparison with other team sports.

VALUES

Team handball is an excellent sport for physical education and recreation programs. The equipment required is minimal and relatively inexpensive. Existing facilities such as basketball courts, can be modified to accommodate the sport.

Team handball is a fast-moving sport that can provide an intense cardiovascular workout. It requires motor skills common to other popular sports, including running, jumping, throwing, and catching. The rules are simple and when played competitively, it ranks as one of the fastest and most demanding of team sports.

The sport may be played with as few as five and as many as seven players on each team. It is similar in concept to basketball, lacrosse, soccer, and water polo. The objective is to score a goal by moving the ball past the defensive team and throwing the ball past the goalkeeper into the goal. Dribbling, passing, and defensive techniques are similar to those used in basketball. A goal counts as 1 point.

Team handball can be modified to be played by 5 to 15 players on a team, depending on available space. It can be played by elementary school students (where it lends itself well to coed activity) as well as those at the junior high, secondary, and collegiate levels. Additionally, it is a tremendous intramural, collegiate, and recreational sport.

In summary, team handball is a sport for all seasons, ages, and those who are enthusiastic to participate in a vigorous and exciting game. It is easily learned, may be played indoors or outdoors, is adaptable to almost any location or environment, and can be modified to meet the needs of special populations.

EQUIPMENT

The equipment required is minimal. A basketball-type shoe may be used for indoor and outdoor play, and a cleated shoe may be used on grass. Team uniforms with special identification for the goalkeepers are necessary. Players may wish to wear knee and elbow pads, and mouth guards, and goalkeepers may want to wear additional protective equipment.

The only other piece of equipment needed is a ball. The USTHF ball requirements for men are a weight of 15 to 17 ounces (.43 to .48 kg) and a circumference of 23 to 24 inches (58 to 60 cm), while, for women and juniors, the ball must weigh 11½ to 14 ounces (.33 to .40 kg) and have a circumference of 21 to 22 inches (54 to 56 cm). Balls may be constructed with 12, 18, or 32 panels. At least two balls should be available at the beginning of a game. (When handballs are not available for physical education and recreational use, appropriately sized playground balls can be substituted.)

THE FIELD OR INDOOR COURT

The following discussion of the playing area reflects dimensions established by the USTHF, which allows for variation from the standard IHF rules. Precise international measurements can be found in the IHF rules, which may be obtained from the IHF or USTHF.

The official indoor or outdoor field may be not more than 147 × 75 feet (44 × 22 m) and no less than 126 × 60 feet (38 × 18m) (figure 35-1). The field for international competition is 131 feet 4 inches × 65 feet 8 inches (40 × 20 m). An indoor basketball court can be modified without difficulty (figure 35-2).

Located centrally on each goal line is a goal 6 feet 8 inches (2 m) high and 10 feet (3 m) wide. The goal is usually made of 3 × 3-inch wood and pipe, fitted with a nylon net tensioned so that the ball cannot immediately rebound (figure 35-3). In front of each goal are two semicircles. The inside arc (the goal area line or the 6 m line) identifies the goal area and is a solid line drawn at a radius of 20 feet (6 m) from the goal. The next arc is the free-throw or 9 m line. It is drawn as an interrupted line parallel to and outside the goal area line, 3 m farther from the goal. Two marks are drawn directly in front of each goal—the penalty mark is at a distance of 23 feet (7 m) from the goal while the other mark lies between the penalty mark and the goal at a distance of 13 feet (4 m) from the goal. When a player is awarded a penalty throw, the mark at 13 feet (4 m) identifies the closest the goalkeeper may approach toward the penalty shooter. Midway between the goal lines a centerline is drawn, and on the sideline closest to the players' benches each team's substitution area is delineated by a 6-inch (15 cm) hash mark that is 14 feet 7 inch (4.45 m) from the centerline. The width of all the lines in marking the court is 2 inches (5 cm). A complete diagram of court dimensions with all markings is illustrated in figure 35-1.

RULES

Officials

There are two referees who are in charge of the game. Both have the right to warn and disqualify players, and their decisions are final. The most frequently used referee signals are illustrated in figure 35-4.

The field referee is stationed behind the play. The field referee's duties are to announce penalties, give warnings, and order suspensions. The field referee concentrates on the player with the ball and that player's opponent or marker. Responsibilities also include checking the proper distance of the defense on free throws. The decision of the field referee prevails over the goal referee on contradictory decisions.

The goal referee's positioning should be ahead of the play and on the goal line. His or her duties include enforcing goal area rules; whistling penalty throws, goals scored, and corner throws; and supervising throw-offs and throw-outs.

In addition to the two referees, a scorekeeper and a timekeeper are required. These officials are responsible for controlling time, monitoring substitutes entering and leaving the field of play, keeping the time for suspensions, and generally helping the referees by keeping them abreast of these concerns.

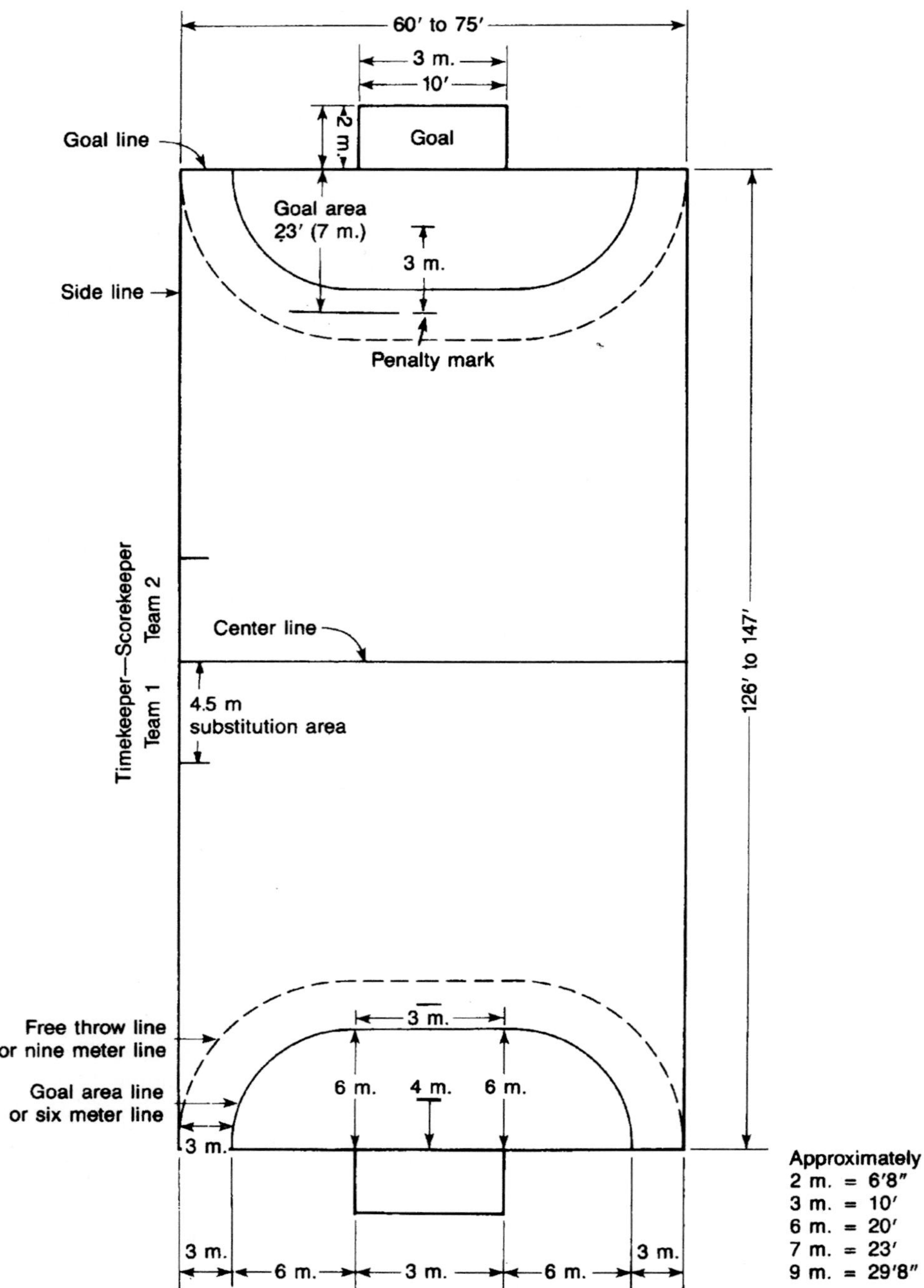

Figure 35-1. Team handball field dimensions and markings.

Duration of Game

Game duration can be adjusted to accommodate age, gender, and competitive variables. Competitive conditions include official USTHF games and tournament competitions play. Time periods for official USTHF games are as follows: Men play two 30-minute periods with a 10-minute halftime; junior males play two 25-minute periods with a 10-minute halftime, and all other teams play two 20-minute periods with a 10-minute intermission. In competition, where teams may play several games during a one- or two-day tournament, rules allow for games without intermissions—men play two 15-minute periods, while junior males and all other teams play two 10-minute periods.

In case of a tie at the end of regulation play, there is a provision for two 5-minute periods for overtime. If, before the start of the game, it was determined that there should

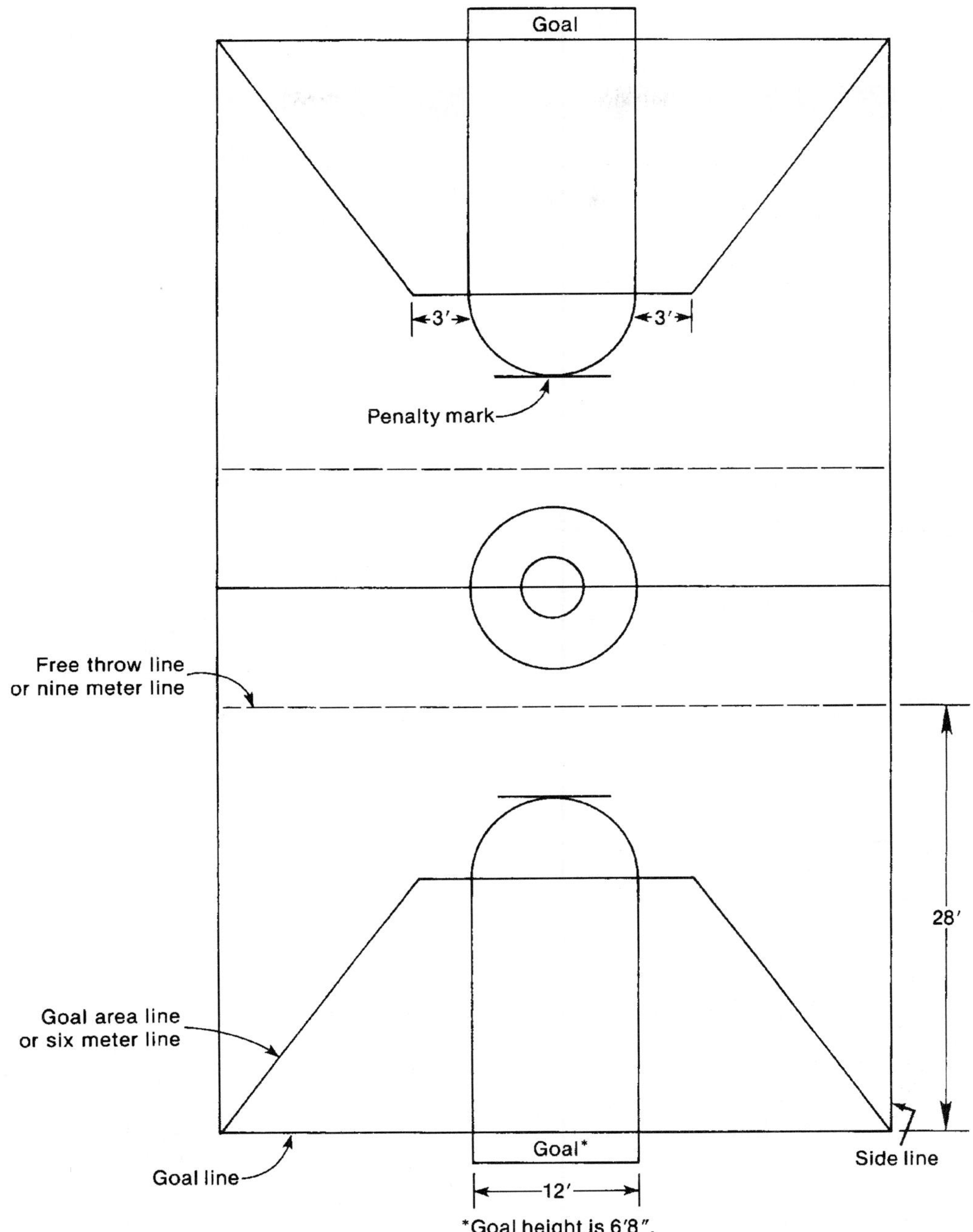

Figure 35-2. Basketball court modifications for use as team handball court.

not be a time, then overtimes shall continue until a winner is determined. No players may be added to the roster for the overtime periods.

Number of Players, Substitutions, and Suspension

The game may be played with 5 to 15 players of either or both sexes. An official USTHF team has 12 players—10 court players with only 6 playing at a time, and 2 goalkeepers with only 1 playing at a time. The positions of the players are goalkeeper, center halfback, right and left backs, center forward, and right and left wings.

Substitution is from the bench area near midcourt. Once a court player is off the playing field, a substitute may enter. Substitutes need not notify the timekeeper. The procedure is the same for the goalkeeper, but the goalkeeper substitute must have a distinctive uniform. Illegal

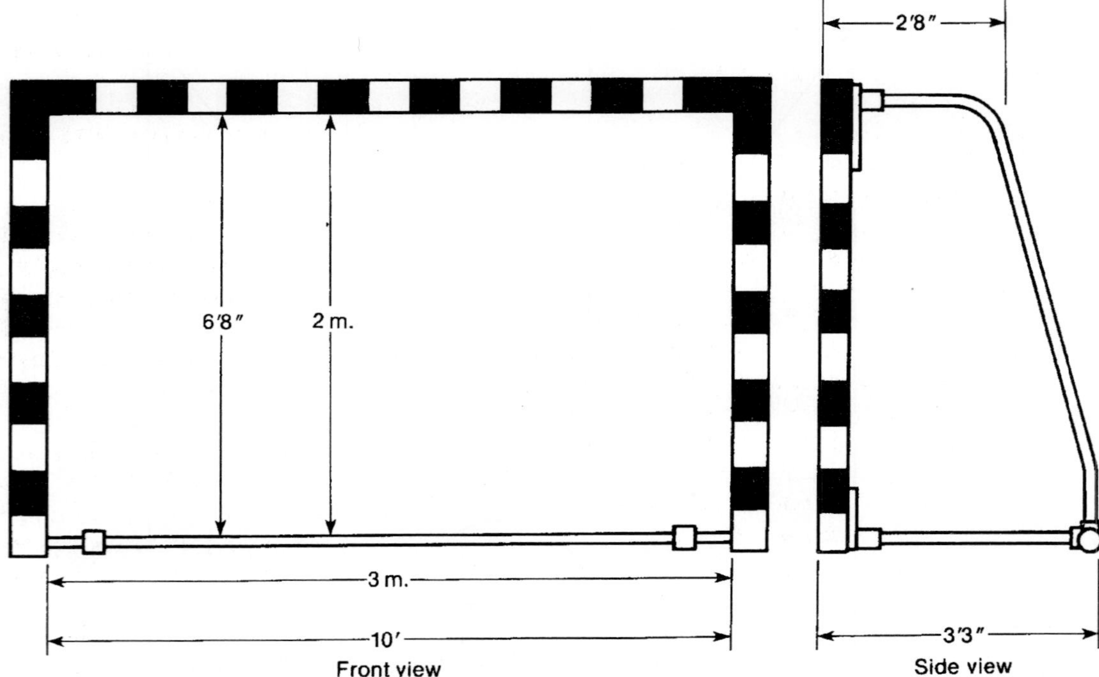

Figure 35-3. Team handball goal specifications.

substitution may result in a free throw or penalty throw for the opponent.

Players may be suspended from play for 2 minutes, 5 minutes, or permanently, depending on the severity of the foul. With suspension, the opposing team receives a penalty throw.

Playing Privileges of Court Players

1. A player may hold the ball for up to 3 seconds, pass, shoot, dribble, or run three steps with the ball.
2. Players may not double dribble, hold the ball for more than 3 seconds, kick the ball, or travel (take more than three steps with the ball) (penalty: free throw).
3. Stalling is not permitted (referee's judgment).
4. A defensive player may obstruct an opposing player by using the body or arms. A player is not permitted to strike, grab, or tackle an opponent, and the ball must be the object of attack by the defensive players.
5. No player except the goalkeeper may dive for a ball lying or rolling on the ground.

Playing Privileges of Goalkeeper

1. The goalkeeper may defend the goal in any way using the hands, feet, and body.
2. Usual time and step restrictions are placed on the goalkeeper with possession of the ball.
3. The goalkeeper is free to move outside the goal area anytime without the ball, but must then abide by the rules for other players.
4. The goalkeeper is prohibited from leaving the goal area when in control of the ball (penalty: free throw).
5. When the goalkeeper recovers a blocked or missed shot for a throw-out, opponents can block it from outside the 6 m line, a goal can be scored directly from it, and the goalkeeper cannot touch the ball again until it has been touched by another player.
6. The goalkeeper is prohibited from picking up a ball outside and carrying it into the goal area (penalty: penalty throw).
7. A court player substituting for a goalkeeper must notify the official before entering the goal area (penalty: penalty throw). This court player cannot enter the goal area until the goalkeeper is off the court (penalty: penalty throw).
8. The ball may not be thrown to a player's own goalkeeper while the goalkeeper is in his or her goal area (penalty: penalty shot).

Start of Play

The game officially must be started with seven players per team: six court players and one goalkeeper. A coin toss determines the option of side or throw-off, which places the ball into play. The game starts within 3 seconds after

Figure 35-4. Team handball referee signals.

Figure 35-5. Player taking a corner throw.

the referee blows the whistle. All players must begin on their own half of the court. A goal cannot be scored from a throw-off.

A throw-off is taken from the center of the field in any direction typically to one's own team. All players must be in their respective halves of the field when the throw-off is taken, the opposing players being at a distance of at least 10 feet (3 m) from the ball. Whenever a goal is scored, play begins again at center court with the team that conceded the goal taking a throw-off. When taking a throw-off, throw-in, free throw, or penalty throw, the thrower must keep part of one foot in constant contact with the ground. The player may, however, repeatedly lift and put down the other foot.

Ball Out-of-Bounds

A ball is not out-of-bounds until the entire ball crosses the goal line or sideline. A ball crossing the sideline is put back into play with a throw-in by the team that did not last touch the ball before it went out-of-bounds. A throw-in must be executed from outside the sidelines, with one foot remaining stationary during the throw. The ball may be thrown with one or two hands. A goal cannot be scored from a throw-in.

A ball crossing the goal line outside the goal and last touched by the offensive team, or touched by the goalkeeper on a shot on goal when the goalkeeper was the only defender touching the ball, results in throw-out. The goalkeeper executes the throw-out from within the goal area in whatever manner is desired. A goal cannot be scored directly from a throw-out. Opposing players must stay behind the 9.9-yard (9 m) line on a throw-out.

When a ball crosses the goal line outside the goal, and was last touched by a member of the defensive team other than the goalkeeper, a corner throw is awarded to the offensive team (figure 35-5). The ball is placed in play similar to a throw-in from the intersection of the goal line and sideline.

Fouls—Common (Penalty: Free Throw)

Common fouls are called for such violations as faulty substitution, faulty throw-in, intentionally playing across goal line or sideline, and body contact or striking an opponent that results in loss of possession or failure to complete the play. Furthermore, the defender must be between the player and the goal. These violations result in the fouled team being awarded a free throw. If contact is not too blatant or the defender had good defensive position, a foul is not always called. Free throws are also awarded for double dribbling; taking more than three steps; holding the ball more than three seconds; offensive player charges; illegal picking, holding, or pushing; or unnecessarily rough play.

Fouls—Flagrant (Penalty: Penalty Shot)

Flagrant fouls are called for violations, such as taking the ball away from a player; obstruction with arms, hands, or legs; grabbing an opponent; pushing or forcing an opponent into the goal area; and shooting or throwing the ball at an opponent intentionally. These fouls result in the awarding of a penalty shot to the opponent. If the foul is severe, by the referee's judgment, the player may be suspended from the game.

Free Throw

In a free throw the ball is put into play at the point of the infraction. If the foul occurs between the 6.6- and 9.9-yard (6 and 9 m) lines, however, the ball is put into play from the 9.9-yard (9 m) line closest to the point of infraction. All offensive players must be outside the 9.9-yard (9 m) line, and all defensive players must be at least 10 feet (3 m) from the ball. A direct shot at the goal or a pass are the options for a free throw.

Penalty Shot

This is a free shot at the opponent's goal from the penalty mark, with only the goalkeeper defending and being at least 10 feet (3 m) from the thrower until the shot is taken. Any player may take the shot, and one foot must be stationary at all times. The shot must be taken within

Figure 35-6. Player taking a penalty shot.

3 seconds after the referee blows the whistle. All other players must be outside the 9.9-yard (9 m) line (figure 35-6).

Referee's Throw

Although rarely used, the referee's throw is warranted in certain game situations. If there are simultaneous infractions or interruptions to the game, such as from an injury, a referee's throw is the only fair way to put the ball back into play. The referee stands in the area where the double foul was committed and bounces the ball back into play. All players must remain at least 10 feet (3 m) away until the ball has been bounced.

Goal Area

Legal entry

1. Goalkeeper is legal in the goal area.
2. A court player may not enter the goal area except after playing the ball when no advantage is gained.

Penalties for illegal entry

1. A court player in possession of the ball in the goal area (penalty: free throw).
2. A court player not in possession but gaining an advantage (penalty: free throw).
3. A court player gaining defensive advantage (penalty: penalty throw).

FUNDAMENTAL SKILLS AND TECHNIQUES

Inasmuch as team handball is similar to basketball in terms of running, dribbling, passing and taking shots on goal, many of the basic skills that should be practiced parallel those of basketball.

Passing

Passing is basic to the game and is a good skill with which to begin a program. Passes may be made with one hand or two. Beginners should master the chest or push pass, bounce pass, overhead pass, shovel or underhand pass, baseball pass, reverse pass, and hook pass. A handball is about the size of a softball, and beginning players tend to want to grip the ball, which is an incorrect technique for control. The ball should rest in the hand on the fingertips, and considerable wrist snap should be used in passing. Players should be reminded to make short, crisp passes, and to pass frequently. Just as in basketball, a good passing team will have a distinct advantage over a group of individuals.

Shooting

Although team handball shots are for the most part different than those in basketball, there are many similarities and several of the shot names are the same. Shots that are similar to those in basketball and may be practiced with some technical changes are jump shots, dive shots, lob shots, underhand shots, and any of the twisting moves that might be used with dunk shots. Changes in technique include not gripping the ball, and using a great deal of wrist snap and strong lower arm moves similar to those used in throwing a softball. It is preferable for players to learn to shoot with one hand rather than two in order to shoot with optimal power. Furthermore, jump shots following a run are desirable. Finally, players should learn to shoot at the high and low corners of the goal (figure 35-7) and to utilize bounced shots.

Dribbling

Dribbling is basically the same as in basketball. It is important to keep the body low for protection and ease of movement, while keeping the ball low and the head up to watch for an opening in which to pass or shoot. Remember that a pass can move the ball down the court much faster than a dribble, so one should look for the pass before taking the dribble (figure 35-8).

Running

Running and being in sound condition are key components of team handball. The player able to help the team with or without the ball is the best kind of team player. Agility drills

Figure 35-7. Player taking a shot at the goal.

Figure 35-8. Player driving toward the goal in a team handball game adapted as a class activity.

for quickness in changing directions and lateral movement are important, but time should also be devoted to promote aerobic and anaerobic endurance, as well as overall strength, power, and flexibility.

Offensive Play

The three basic offensive player positions in team handball are the wing player, circle runner, and back-court player. Each position has responsibilities.

The wing player (usually two) should be quick and agile and able to lead the fast-break attack. This player attacks the goal when shooting and should be able to protect the ball. The circle runner is usually the biggest and strongest player on the court and is generally a blocker, setting picks for the wing players and back-court players. The circle runner (usually only one) needs strength to handle the ball in heavy traffic and coordinate moves with the other players. The back-court players (usually three) should be strong, hard throwers who can pass, run, dribble, and shoot well. These players should be the best all-around athletes on the court and usually provide most of the team scoring.

Just as in basketball, there are set plays in team handball, and it relies heavily on players setting screens and picks for one another to take shots at the goal. Offensively, players should focus on total team movement, remain spread out, think pass before dribble, move the ball quickly, and always pose a scoring threat.

Because defensive teams employ either a one-on-one or zone defense and follow many of the principles of basketball defense, the offensive team should practice against both of these defensive sets of systems.

Defensive Play

Most defensive effort in team handball involves the positioning of defenders between the free-throw line and the goal area line. The basic defense patterns are the one-on-one defense and the zone defense. In one-on-one defense, each player is responsible for one opponent. In zone defense, each player is responsible for a zone or area on the court. A zone defense is designed to give the opponent longer shots and prevent close shots at the goal. Team members must continually communicate to make each system successful.

In summary, each defender should strive to stay between the goal and his or her designated opponent; the defense should shift as a unit; no defense will fit all offensive systems; the defender should not jump too soon when

Figure 35-9. A defensive block.

attempting to bock a shot or pass (figure 35-9); and constant communication between defenders is necessary.

Goalkeeping

Goalkeeping is probably the most important and difficult position in team handball. A goalkeeper should be quick, unafraid of the ball, possess good hand-eye and foot-eye coordination, and be able to throw the ball to start the fast break. The goalkeeper should not catch the ball unless thrown directly at him or her, but should block shots by knocking them down, to the side, or over the goal line. The team that has a talented and well-trained goalkeeper has a great advantage during match play (figure 35-10).

BEGINNING ACTIVITIES AND DRILLS

1. Practice dribbling with each hand; dribble while moving; dribble in and out of cones or around classmates; play tag while dribbling.
2. Practice throwing and catching: overhand throws, underhand flick passes, reverse passes, bounce passes.
3. Position students in pairs approximately 30 feet (9 m) apart to combine the above throws and catches with step movements (within the 3-step limit). Thrower jogs forward to throw, then retreats before catching partner's return throw. Increase the distance between partners as students' proficiency and strength increase.
4. Position two groups of three to four students approximately 40 to 50 feet (12 to 15 m) apart in lines facing the other group. First player in line 1 performs 3-step jog toward the other line, jumps and throws to first player in line 2, then continues to the end of line 2. First player in line 2 catches the thrown ball, then performs footwork, jump, and throw to student in line 1 and continues to the end of line 1. The drill continues with students moving from line to line—catch the ball, execute the 3-step footwork, jump and throw, and continue to the end of the line.

TEACHING CONSIDERATIONS

1. The basic skills of team handball are essentially those of basketball with the exception of shooting. Shooting strategies are more similar to those of soccer, as are some field placement strategies. See the chapters on basketball and soccer for additional teaching suggestions.
2. Students should practice footwork in combination with passing and shooting. They must also learn to jump before shooting.
3. Keep team size small for maximum opportunity for practice and play. Use several small courts (or outside areas) with fewer players rather than a large area with many players.
4. Since the ball is lighter and smaller than a basketball, more students will be able to throw longer and harder

Figure 35-10. Goalie blocking a practice shot on goal.

passes than in basketball. Practice passing ahead of moving players and moving into open spaces to receive a pass in consort with two or three players. Stress the pass (rather than the dribble) as the quickest way to move the ball down the court.

5. Gradually add defensive players to practice moving the ball down the court (three-on-one and three-on-two situations). Initially, scoring can include passing the ball across the endline or into an undefended goal. Later a goalkeeper should be included, and three-on-three and four-on-four games can be played.
6. Supplement goaltending practice with play around the goal area line. Students must become familiar with the unique skills and strategies that are required by the sport.
7. When teams get above four-on-four players, introduce specific player roles (other than goalkeeper) if they have not begun to emerge from four-on-four play (wing, circle runner, and back-court player).
8. Introduce zone defense (particularly on larger courts) after students have mastered the basics of person-to-person play. Place as much emphasis on defense as on offense.
9. Provide opportunity for gamelike play each lesson (modified in the beginning). Encourage skill and strategy development by modifying the rules to reinforce the lesson content (e.g., no dribbling, or scoring from the sides only).
10. Match-condition scrimmages should be frequent with positive feedback on each player's technique and tactical understanding of the game.

GLOSSARY

common foul Violations such as illegal substitutions, illegal throw-in, illegal body contact, double dribble, and more than three steps with the ball (penalty: free throw).

corner throw A throw taken by an offensive team player after a ball crossed over the goal line last touched by a defensive player other than the goalkeeper, except when a shot was taken, to put the ball back into play.

court player A team player other than the goalkeeper.

defensive player A player whose team does not possess the ball.

flagrant foul Violation such as rough body contact and unsportsman-like play (penalty: penalty throw and possible suspension).

free throw Results from a common foul and is used to put the ball back into play from the point of the infraction, unless infraction occurs between the 6.6- and 9.9-yard (6 and 9 m) lines, in which case the ball is put in play on the 9.9-yard (9 m) line nearest the point of infraction

goalkeeper The only person who can legally play the ball in the goal area and use the feet.

held ball A ball held more than 3 seconds.

offensive player A player whose team possesses the ball.

penalty throw Results from a flagrant foul and is a free shot at the goal from the penalty mark with one foot remaining stationary during the throw and only the goalkeeper in the goal are defending.

referee's throw Does not occur often, but is the result of simultaneous infractions of disruptions to the game and is executed by the referee's bouncing the ball back into play from the point of infraction while all players are at least 10 feet (3 m) away.

throw-in Used by the team that did not cause the ball to go across the sideline to put the ball back into play.

throw-off Taken from the center of the field to start the game.

throw-out When the goalkeeper blocks or catches a shot that does not cross the goal line, he or she uses the throw-out to put the ball back into play.

traveling Illegal progression in any direction with the ball.

SUGGESTED READINGS

Clanton, R., and Dwight, M.: 1997. *Team handball: Steps to success,* Champaign, IL. Human Kinetics.

Hamil B., and LaPoint J: *Team handball, skills, strategies and training,* Dubuque, Iowa. 1994. Eddie Bowers Publishing.

Klussow, NP: *Handball,* Berlin. 1956. Taktik.

Team handball rules and regulations. Waterford, Conn. 1993. Jayfro Corporation.

Team handball: Rules of the game. 1992. United States Team Handball Federation.

Toomey B., and King B: *The Olympic challenge.* Costa Mesa, Calif, 1988. HDL Publishing.

Trosse, H.D.: *Handball training,* ed 2. Reinbek, Germany, 1988. Taktik.

Trosse, H.D.: *Trainingslehre handball.* Berlin, 1985. Bartels and Wernitz.

36 Tennis

After completing this chapter, the reader should be able to:

- Have a basic knowledge of the historical development of tennis
- Understand the proper selection of equipment
- Know the rules and scoring of tennis and understand the etiquette of play
- Perform and demonstrate the fundamental skills for effective playing technique
- Know the principles of strategy for competitive play
- Teach others by using sound instructional and practice techniques

HISTORY

There is evidence that a form of tennis was played in the ancient Greek and Roman Empires and that a game in which a ball was batted back and forth with a type of racquet may have been played in the Orient more than 2,000 years ago. Still other indications are that tennis may have begun in Egypt or Persia 500 years before the Christian era.

Despite these obscure ancient origins, there is no doubt that a tennislike game was played in thirteenth-century France. Called *jeu de paume* (literally, "game of the hand"), it was first a bare-handed game of hitting a stuffed cloth bag over a rope. When paddles, and later racquets, were added, the game grew steadily in popularity. By the close of the fourteenth century it was also well established in England.

It is believed the game received its present name when English visitors heard French officials call *tenez*, which means to resume play, an expression similar to "play ball" used by baseball umpires. The English thought *tenez* was the correct name for *le paume*. In time the English word *tennis* was substituted.

At the beginning of the fifteenth century there were 1,400 professional players in France, and yet the first standardized written rules of tennis did not appear until 1599. The game reached a peak of popularity in England and France during the sixteenth and seventeenth centuries; but soon after, the game almost disappeared due to the civil war in England and the French Revolution.

What remnant of the game was left in England seems next to appear at a garden party given in 1873 by British Army Major Walter C. Wingfield. His guests were introduced to a game called "sphairistike," later to become more descriptively referred to as "lawn tennis." In attendance at the party was an army officer who took the game with him to Bermuda as a diversion for the British garrison stationed there. Miss Mary Outerbridge, who was vacationing on the island during the winter of 1873–74, became intrigued with the game and took equipment with her upon returning to her New York home.

As a member of the Staten Island Cricket and Baseball Club, Outerbridge received permission to lay out a court in an unused corner of the grounds. Within a few years tennis was included as an activity at nearly every major cricket club in the East, and soon it became a sport of the masses. But the rules were diverse, so in 1880 Outerbridge's brother called a meeting in New York to establish a standard code. An outcome of that meeting was the establishment of the United States Tennis Association (USTA), still the ruling body of American tennis today.

Later that same year the first tournament for the National Championship of the United States was held at Newport, Rhode Island. The site was moved in 1915 to Long Island, and in 1978 it was relocated to its present site at the National Tennis Center in Queens, New York City. This tournament is now called the U.S. Open. The U.S. Open, the Australian Open, the French Open, and Wimbledon are the four "grand slam" events on the professional tour.

In 1988, tennis returned to the Olympics for the first time since 1924, and was open for the first time to professional players. At the 1996 Olympics, held in Atlanta, Georgia, Andre Agassi of the United States won the men's tennis gold medal in singles by defeating Sergi Bruguera of Spain, 6–2, 6–3, 6–1. Leander Paes of India won the bronze medal, earning India's first Olympic medal in any sport since 1980. In men's doubles, Todd Woodbridge and Mark Woodforede of Australia won the gold medal by defeating Neil Broad and Tim Henman of England, 6–4, 6–4, 6–2. In the semifinals, Woodbridge and Woodforde played the longest men's doubles set in Olympic history, defeating Jacco Eltingh and Paul Haarhuis of Holland 6–2, 5–7, 18–16 in 3 hours and 16 minutes. Lindsay Davenport of the United States won the gold medal in women's singles by upsetting Arantxa Sanchez Vicario 7–6 (8–6), 6–2. Jana Novotna won the bronze by beating Mary Joe Fernandez 7–6 (8–6), 6–4. Americans Gigi Fernandez and Mary Joe Fernandez won their second gold medal in women's doubles by defeating Jana Novotna and Helena Sukova of the Czech Republic 7–6 (8–6), 6–4. Conchita Martinez and Arantxa Sanchez Vicario of Spain won the bronze medal for women's doubles by besting Brenda Schultz-McCarthy and Manon Bollegraf of the Netherlands 6–1, 6–3.

VALUES AND REASONS FOR POPULARITY

Tennis is a popular lifetime sport throughout the world for the following reasons:

1. It can be played by able-bodied individuals as well as many individuals with disabilities. The United States Tennis Association has a division devoted to the promotion of wheelchair tennis that offers instruction, league play, and tournaments.
2. It can be played by both men and women and is well suited for mixed-gender competition.
3. It requires only two or four players.
4. It can be played indoors and outdoors.
5. It can provide a strenuous physical workout, requiring cardiovascular endurance, quick movement, and good flexibility.
6. Public and private courts are widely available.
7. Tennis lessons are widely available for players of all skill levels.
8. Organized leagues and tournaments for recreational players are available in most communities.
9. Equipment costs are relatively low.
10. It can be played both as an individual and team sport.

EQUIPMENT

Clothing

Historically, tennis attire has been both fashionable and functional. For many years tennis attire was distinguished by its "all white" quality and its ability to signal the wearer's social status. Today, there is a much greater emphasis on the functional aspect of tennis apparel; clothes are made from microfibers designed to wick away perspiration, keeping the player more comfortable, and shoes are designed to fit well, absorb shock, and resist wear.

Ball

Tennis balls are made of two rubber cups molded together, covered with a colored felt, and inflated to a specific pressure. Most manufacturers produce a normal and a high-altitude ball. The high-altitude ball is inflated to a lower pressure than the standard ball for better playing characteristics at elevations above 4,000 feet (1,219 m). Manufacturers have experimented with a variety of tennis ball colors; of these, optic yellow is most widely available and is the color used on the professional tour.

Racquet

For many years, tennis racquets were made of wood and there was little variation in the size or shape of the frames. By the late 1970s, metal racquets began to replace wood racquets, and soon, frames made of composite materials began replacing metal. Today, most tennis racquets are made from fibers such as graphite, Kevlar, or fiberglass.

With the introduction of the radical Profile widebody racquet in the mid 1980s, Wilson Sporting Goods started a revolution in frame design and development. The main advantage of the widebody racquet is that it is more rigid longitudinally, and therefore more powerful than a standard racquet design. The main disadvantages of widebody racquets are that they transfer more shock to the arm when striking the ball and strings tend to wear out quickly. Thus, these racquets were popular with recreational players, but less so with professional players. The latest innovation in racquets is to have an extra-long head-to-heel length with a more traditional cross-section. Today most manufacturers market racquets in a traditional 27 inch (68.5 cm) length and the new, extra-long (28 to 32 inches, 71.1–81.3 cm) length.

Strings

Tennis racquet strings are measured by the thickness of their diameter. Strings range from 14 (thick) to 18 (thin) gauge diameters, with 16 gauge being the most popular for recreational players. Strings are made from two basic materials: natural gut (cattle intestines) or synthetics. Professional players still primarily use natural gut strings; however, most recreational players use synthetic strings, which are more durable and cost less than gut. Most tennis racquets are strung with 55 to 70 pounds (25 to 32 kg) of tension. Higher tensions work well for players who hit the ball hard, while midrange tensions are best for most recreational players. Because tennis racquet strings lose resiliency and wear out over time, they need to be replaced occasionally. The need to replace strings depends on frequency and level of play. In general, strings should be replaced annually, although some players have the strings replaced several times a year.

Grip

The area on the racquet where the player places his or her hand is called the *grip*. Adult tennis racquet grips range from 4 to 5 inches (10.2 to 12.7 cm) in circumference, measured in steps of ⅛ inch (0.32 cm). For adult males, common grip sizes are from 4½ to 4¾ inches (11.5 to 12.1 cm). For adult women, 4 to 4½ inches (10.2 to 11.5 cm) are most common. The grips on children's racquets are smaller, typically from 3 to 4 inches (7.65 to 10.2 cm). A good way to determine correct grip size is to hold a racquet using an Eastern forehand grip (see figure 36-1); the thumb should just touch the top knuckle of the second finger. A proper grip is important because a grip that is too small can cause the racquet to twist in the hand when the ball is struck off-center, whereas a grip that is too large can make it difficult to hold on to the racquet while hitting the ball.

A

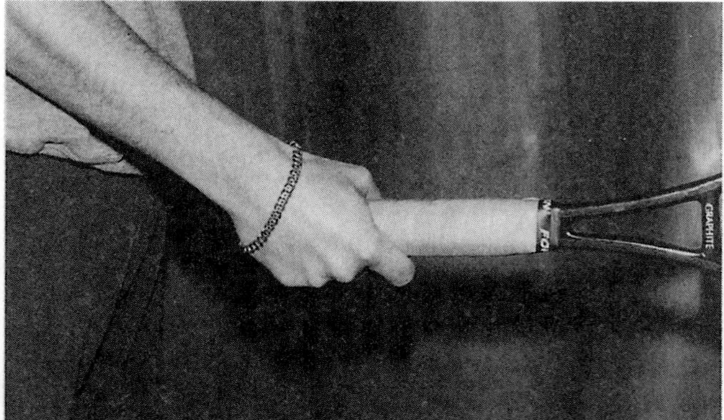

B

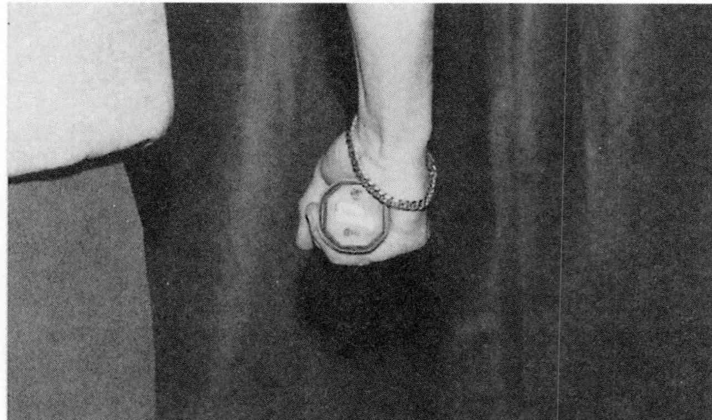

Figure 36-1. Eastern forehand grip. **A,** Side view; **B,** Back view.

Courts

Most tennis court surfaces are constructed from one of four types of material: clay, grass, cement or asphalt, and synthetics. In the United States, public courts are generally cement or asphalt owing to the durability and low maintenance costs of these surfaces. Clay courts are still common in Europe, South America, and in the southeastern United States. In recent years, clay courts have regained some popularity in other regions of the United States as well because they are less stressful on the body and easier on tennis balls and shoes than hard courts. In addition, clay is particularly suited for match play because the ball tends to bounce rather high, allowing a player more time to get in position to play a return. As a result, rallies are longer and more involved than on faster courts. Grass courts have the advantage of providing a cool and soft surface that is easier on the body and equipment; however, high maintenance costs and low durability limit the availability of these courts. Grass courts are most often found at private clubs and resorts. Synthetic court surfaces are primarily used for professional tournaments conducted indoors.

Most tennis courts are constructed and lined for both singles and doubles play. A few tennis courts are lined for singles play only. Some professional tournaments, primarily indoor events, also use singles-only courts.

Dimensions

1. Singles court: 78 × 27 feet (23.8 × 8.23 m)
2. Doubles court: 78 × 36 feet (23.8 × 10.97 m) (4½ foot [1.37 m] alley added to each side)
3. Height of net at center: 3 feet (0.914 m), commonly measured by taking the length of the racquet plus the width of the racquet head (using a normal-size racquet)
4. Height of the net at the singles sideline: 3½ feet (1.07 m)
5. Height of the posts: 3½ feet (1.07 m)
6. Distance of the posts away from the sidelines: 3 feet (0.914 m)
7. Distance between the baseline and the service line: 18 feet (5.49 m)
8. Distance between the service line and the net: 21 feet (6.40 m)

The endlines are called "baselines," and the sidelines are called "sidelines." The forecourt is near the net, and the backcourt is near the baselines (figure 36-2).

RULES AND SCORING

Singles Game

The United States Tennis Association (USTA) sets the rules for tennis, along with the International Tennis Association (ITA). The USTA booklet "Friend at Court" is a complete guide to the rules of tennis, the tennis code of conduct, USTA regulations, solutions to common rules problems, and officiating techniques and procedures. Many serious recreational players keep a copy of "Friend at Court" in their gear bags. The booklet is available from USTA Publications, 70 West Red Oak Lane, White Plains, NY, 10604. The USTA address on the World Wide Web is http://www.usta.com/.

1. One player remains the server for all points of the first game of a match, after which the receiver becomes the server for all points of the second game, and so on alternately for subsequent games of the match.
2. To start a match, the player who wins a "toss" may choose (*a*) to serve or to receive for the first game, whereupon the other player shall choose the end of the court on which to start, or (*b*) the end, whereupon the other player shall choose to serve or to receive. The "toss" is typically a spin of a racquet where one player guesses if an identifying mark will land up or down.

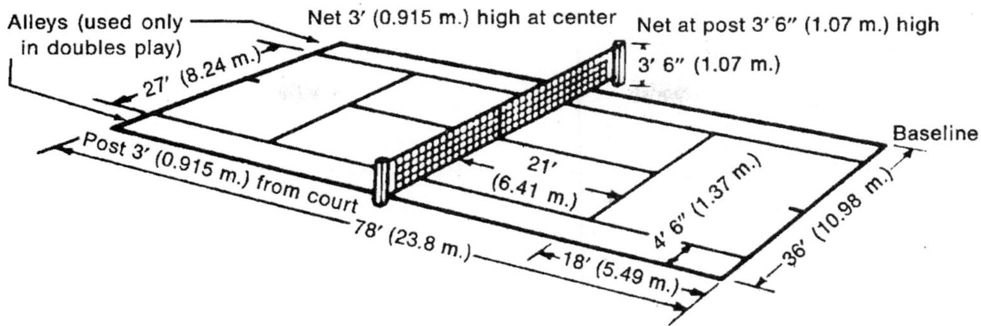

Figure 36-2. Tennis court.

3. The server must take up a position behind the baseline, without touching that line, and between an imaginary extension of the center mark and the singles sideline. From that position the server must project the ball into the air by hand and strike it in any fashion (an underhand serve is legal) before the ball hits the ground.
4. For each point the server is given two opportunities to make one good service into the proper court. To start a game, the server stands to the right of the center mark and attempts to deliver the ball diagonally across the net into the receiver's right service court. When the first point has been completed, the server then stands to the left of the center mark and serves diagonally. Thus, when the total number of completed points is an even number, service attempts are made from the right of the center mark; service attempts are made from the left when the completed points are an odd number. If a player inadvertently serves from the wrong side of the center mark, play resulting from that service is to be counted, but the improper position of the server must be corrected as soon as it is discovered.
5. A fault is an invalid serve and is counted as a service attempt. The *foot fault* occurs when the server steps on the baseline or into the court before the racquet contacts the ball or when the server is in contact with the imaginary extension of the center mark or singles sideline. However, the serve may legally be made while the server is completely in the air. Another service fault occurs when the server swings with the intent of hitting the ball but misses (although the ball may be tossed and then caught without penalty, so long as no serve is attempted). Finally, the service is a fault if the delivered ball does not land in the proper service court or on a line bounding that court. If the ball touches the net and then lands within the proper service court (including its lines), it is not a fault but a *let.*
6. Any service that is a let does not count as an attempt and is retaken. In addition, a let may be called by a receiver who was not ready to receive the serve, unless the receiver makes an attempt to return the ball. Any other interruption in normal play from an outside source is also a let and the point is replayed. For example, if a ball from a neighboring court interrupts a rally or either of the services, the entire point is replayed, including the two service opportunities for the server.
7. There are no rules that govern the position of the receiver; a station may be taken anywhere, including within the service court. However, the receiver may not strike the served ball until after it has bounced.
8. With the occurrence of a legally served ball, play is continuous as long as the players succeed in making legal returns, even though a returned ball may strike another ball lying within the boundaries of the court. As is true with the service, a ball that lands on a line is considered to have landed in the court bounded by that line. After the service, it is not necessary for either player to allow the ball to bounce before making an attempted return.
9. After the service, a player has made a good return and play continues:
   a. When the ball lands from flight within the proper court.
   b. If the ball strikes and passes over the net and then lands within the proper court.
   c. When a player strikes a ball on his or her side of the net, even though the follow-through carries the racquet over the net without touching it. Note, however, that if a ball has bounced on a player's side of the net and the spin of the ball causes it to rebound or it is blown back over the net again, that player may then reach over the net to strike the ball, provided the player does not touch the net or the opposing court.
10. The server wins a point when a legal service is not returned or when a service hits the receiver or the receiver's racquet before it touches the ground. The receiver wins a point when the server commits two

consecutive faults (double fault) or otherwise delivers the ball in an illegal manner. After the service, a player loses a point:
   a. When the ball bounces twice before the player strikes it.
   b. When a returned ball lands outside the opposing court.
   c. When a ball lands within a player's court and then strikes a permanent fixture before its second bounce.
   d. Any time a player strikes a ball before it has bounced and fails to make a good return, no matter where the player was standing when the ball was struck.
   e. If the player or the player's clothing or racquet touches the net or net post while the ball is in play.
   f. If the player hits a ball from flight before it has passed to that player's side of the net.
   g. If the ball in play touches a player or anything the player wears or carries except the racquet. A return may legally be made off any part of the racquet.
   h. If the player throws the racquet at and hits the ball.
   i. If the player intentionally interferes with an opponent.
11. Players change sides of the court at the end of the first, third, and every subsequent odd game of each set and at the end of each set, unless the total number of games in a completed set is an even number, in which case the change is not made until the end of the first game of the next set.

Scoring

A player must win at least four *points* to win a game, then at least six games to win a set, and usually at least two sets to win a match. When a player has no points in a game, the score is called *love*; the first point is called 15; the second point, 30; the third point, 40; and on winning the fourth point, that player has won the game, provided that the player is ahead by at least two points at that time.

When both players have won one point, the score is called 15-all, and when both players have won two points, the score is 30-all, but when both players have won three points, the score is called *deuce*. A score of deuce means that one player must win two consecutive points to win the game. The first point won by a player after a deuce score is called *advantage* for that player (often shortened to *ad*). If that point is won by the server, it is called *ad in*; and if that point is won by the receiver, it is called *ad out*. If the same player who won the advantage point also wins the next point, the game is won by that player. However, if the other player wins the next point, the score returns to deuce, and so on until one player wins two consecutive points after a deuce score.

When a player wins six games and has at that time a lead of at least two games, that player wins the set. If a player wins six games and the opponent has won at least five games, traditional scoring requires that the set be extended until one player has a two-game lead. However, this custom has been replaced by playing a tie-breaker game if the set becomes tied at six games each. In this game the first player to win seven points with a two-point advantage wins the set. To start the tie-breaker game, if it is player A's turn to serve the thirteenth game (with the set tied at six games each), that player serves for the first point. Then, player B serves for points 2 and 3. Note that player B serves from the left of the center mark for point 2, then from the right of the center mark for point 3. Next, player A serves points 4 and 5, left then right of the center mark. Player B then serves point 6, the players change sides, and player B serves for point 7. The game continues with players alternately serving for two points each until one player has won at least seven points with the necessary two-point advantage. Players continue to change sides whenever the total number of points played is any multiple of six.

Points won in a tie-breaker game are called by their numerical value rather than the traditional scoring. After the tie-breaker game, player B becomes the server for the first game of the next set, and the players stay on their sides of the court for that game (see table 36-1).

Doubles Game

1. The server may stand anywhere between an extension of the center mark and the doubles sideline, behind the baseline. One player serves for the first game of the set, then a player on the opposing team serves for the second game. The partner of the player who served for the first game then serves for the third game, and the partner of the player who served the second game then serves for the fourth game, and so on for all subsequent games of the set, each player serving every fourth game. A team may elect to change its order of service for the next set.
2. Should a partner serve out of turn, a correction must be made as soon as the mistake is discovered, but play that has been completed before the discovery must be reckoned. If a game has been completed before the erroneous serving order is discovered, the order as altered must then remain for the continuation of the set.
3. One player of each team must receive all serves in the right service court, and that player's partner must receive all serves in the left service court for the entire set. At the end of any set a team may change its order of receiving for the next set. The order of receiving is not determined by the order of serving.

Table 36-1. TENNIS SCORING

Scoring				
Points	**Games**	**Sets**	**Tie-break**	**Match**
Love, 15, 30, 40, deuce, ad in, ad out. Either the server or receiver can win points. The server's score is announced first, followed by the receiver's score, prior to each point.	First player or team to win 4 points with a 2-point margin. When the score is tied 40–40, it is called *deuce*. The first player to win 2 consecutive points wins the game.	First player or team to win 6 games with a 2-game margin. When a set is tied at 6–6, a tie-break is played to determine the winner of the set. The server's score is announced first, followed by the receiver's score, prior to each game.	First player or team to win 7 points with a 2-point margin. The player or team that wins the tie-break wins the set 7–6. The server's score is announced first, followed by the receiver's score, prior to each point in the tie-break.	The first player or team to win 2-out-of-3 or 3-out-of-5 sets. Most matches are played using the 2-out-of-3 set format. Some men's professional tournaments use a 3-out-of-5 set format.

4. Should a team receive out of turn, the altered receiving order must remain as is until the end of the game in which the discovery is made, whereafter the partners must resume their original order for the next game they receive.
5. If a served ball strikes the server's partner (including that partner's racquet), it is a service fault; but if a served ball strikes the receiver's partner or racquet before it touches the ground, it is a point for the serving team.
6. If both partners strike the ball for any return, it is a point for their opponents.
7. To play a tie-break game, the player whose turn it was to serve for the thirteenth game of the set (with the score tied six games each) serves for the first point of the game. Thereafter each player serves for two points, holding to the same rotation as was used in the set and following the same change of ends after every six points, as is true for singles.

ETIQUETTE

There is a code of etiquette in tennis that obliges every player to maintain a certain spirit within the rules, including giving an opponent the benefit of the doubt on line calls, avoiding foot faults during serving, never intentionally distracting an opponent, never stalling in an effort to upset an opponent, and always conducting oneself in a fashion that makes the game enjoyable for everyone. Specific situations are:

1. Any call of "out" on an opponent's ball must be made as soon as possible, before you have sent the ball back across the net.
2. You cannot ask for replay of a point where you are unable to make a sure call. The rules do not allow it, so the doubt must be resolved in favor of your opponent.
3. You may, however, ask your opponent to make the call on a ball that lands on your side, but that you did not clearly see.
4. If you hit a point-ending shot that you see as clearly out but your opponent thinks is good, you should make the correct call. This applies also to your own serve.
5. However, if you hit a first serve that you saw as out and the receiver, nevertheless, returns the ball for a point-winning placement without making an out call, you must assume the receiver made the return in good faith; therefore, the point counts and you cannot make an out call (which would then allow for your second serve).
6. Whenever a player realizes he or she has committed a violation, that player should make the call immediately. This includes such things as hitting the ball after two bounces, touching the net, or hitting the ball before it has crossed over the net.
7. The server should announce the score of the game prior to serving each point, always calling the server's score first and the receiver's second.
8. If there is a disagreement as to the score and it cannot be resolved, the score should revert back to the last score on which there was agreement.
9. The server should never hit a serve until the receiver has had time to assume a ready position.
10. A serve that is clearly out should not be returned by the receiver.
11. After a point has been played, you should return balls directly to the server; do not hit them back carelessly.
12. If your ball goes into the adjoining court, wait until the players on that court finish their point before calling for the ball.
13. If a ball from an adjoining court comes into your court, return it to the owners as soon as possible. If it interferes with your point, play a let.
14. In doubles, call service faults for your partner when he or she is the receiver.
15. Try for every point. Tossing points and playing to the audience are insulting to your opponent.

16. In nontournament play, insist on furnishing the balls half of the time—perhaps more often if you are much the inferior player.
17. Do not damage the court unnecessarily.

FUNDAMENTAL SKILLS AND TECHNIQUES

All strokes in tennis depend on a solid foundation of hitting techniques that give substance to every shot. These are the basic skill performances that should become automatic for any court situation, as follows:

Stay relaxed. Tense muscles produce rigid shots that are scattered and faulty. The first requisite for smooth, coordinated hitting is to remain relaxed—not lethargic, but calm. Stay loose, yet alive and energetic.

Think rhythm and timing. Give each swing a fluid motion with an unhurried start, a solid middle, and an unrestrained finish.

Be ready to respond. Between shots, maintain a ready-to-react position with a low center of gravity, feet shoulder-width apart, knees bent, weight mostly on the toes, and buttocks down. Relax your shoulders, and ease your grip in the racquet.

Pivot the whole body. From the ready-to-respond position, as soon as you sight the oncoming ball, begin to rotate your entire body by turning shoulders, arms, and hips, all together in a neat, packaged backswing that coils the body ready for uncoiling into the foreswing. This is especially critical for hitting a backhand, in which the shoulders play an important power role.

Go forward at impact. At contact with the ball, your weight should be going forward, toward the direction of the intended shot. Bring everything (racquet, arm, shoulders, hips, and knees) forward with the stroke. Feel the energy of your body driving the ball where you want it to go.

Hit the ball early. Contact the ball in your groundstrokes diagonally in front rather than alongside or behind your body. Intercept the ball early in its flight during a volley. Reach up and forward for serves.

Hit through the ball. Make sure the racquet is not quitting its forward speed as it meets the ball. Keep your racquet alive, actively moving through the hitting zone for all shots, including a volley or a lob.

Bend your knees. Never lock your knees when hitting, waiting to hit, serving, or receiving the serve, or playing the net. Flexed knees will allow a smooth shift of weight and provide a uniform, rhythmical swing.

Keep your eyes on the ball. Focus on the ball as it leaves your opponent's racquet, then refocus again after the bounce. Notice how much the ball slows down from its bounce, giving you time to clearly set your sights and organize the coordination of your swing. And on the serve, keep your chin up to see the actual contact.

Coil and uncoil. Every swing is a continuous motion of winding and unwinding—coiling into the backswing, then uncoiling for the foreswing. No matter how strong the swing, every shot should be flowing coil-uncoil of effortless energy in motion.

GRIPS

How a tennis player grips the racquet might not seem like an important aspect of the game, yet in fact the grip plays a vital role in a player's ability to hit the ball effectively. The function of the grip is to help the player maintain control of the racquet while orienting the racquet face with the ball. This is important because if the racquet face is angled down just slightly, the ball will not clear the net. Because of the mechanical differences between forehand and backhand shots, many players find that using different grips for different shots improves their game. Experimenting with different grips will help players find the grips that best suit their game.

Forehand Grips

Eastern forehand grip

The eastern forehand grip is sometimes called the "shake-hands" grip because the hand is positioned on the grip of the racquet in the same way as the hand is positioned when shaking hands. Notice in figure 36-1A that the palm of the hand is in contact with the right surface of the grip and in figure 36-1B that the heel of the hand is in contact with the top-right bevel. The eastern forehand is a good grip for the beginner and intermediate level players because the angle of the racquet face can be effectively controlled when hitting groundstrokes. In addition, the eastern forehand can also be used when serving and playing forehand volleys.

Western forehand grip

The western grip is often preferred by advanced players who hit forehand groundstrokes with topspin. Notice in figure 36-3A that the hand is rotated to the right so that the palm is in contact with the bottom-right bevel of the grip. Figure 36-3B shows that the hand is, in effect, positioned *under* the racquet. The main disadvantage of the western forehand grip is that it requires a relatively large shift in the position of the hand when playing either backhand groundstrokes or volleys, and it cannot be used for serving.

Continental grip

The Continental grip is very similar to the eastern forehand, with the main difference being that the hand is rotated slightly to the left on the grip. Notice in figure 36-4A that the palm is in contact with the top-right bevel of the grip. In figure 36-4B the heel of the hand is essentially in the same position as the Eastern forehand grip. The continental grip is an *all-purpose* grip and can be used for forehand and backhand groundstrokes, serves, and volleys. The main disadvantage of the continental grip is that it might not be the most effective grip for any of these shots

A

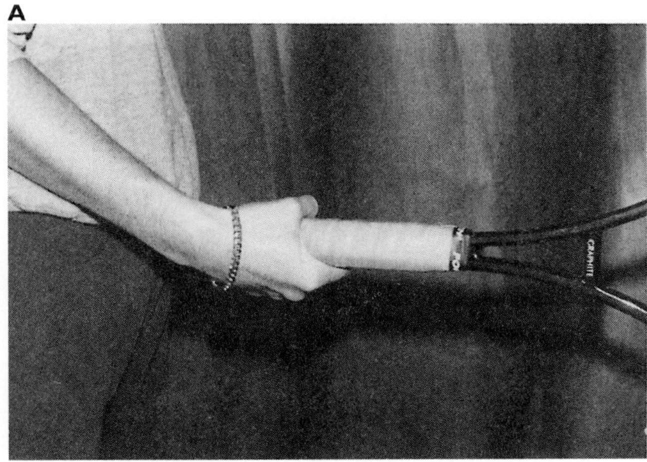

B

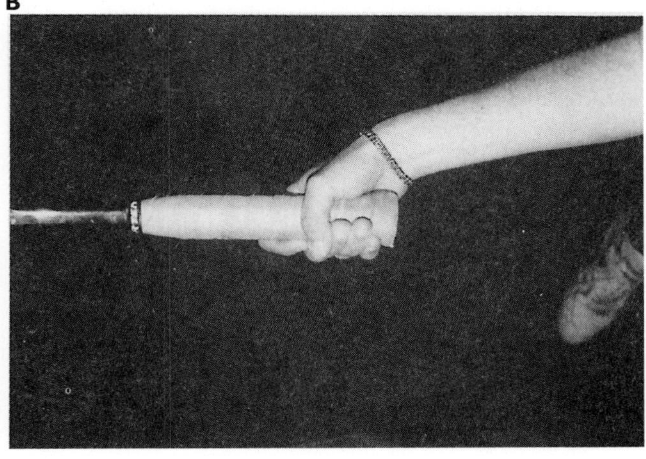

Figure 36-3. Western forehand grip. **A.** Side view; **B.** Top view.

A

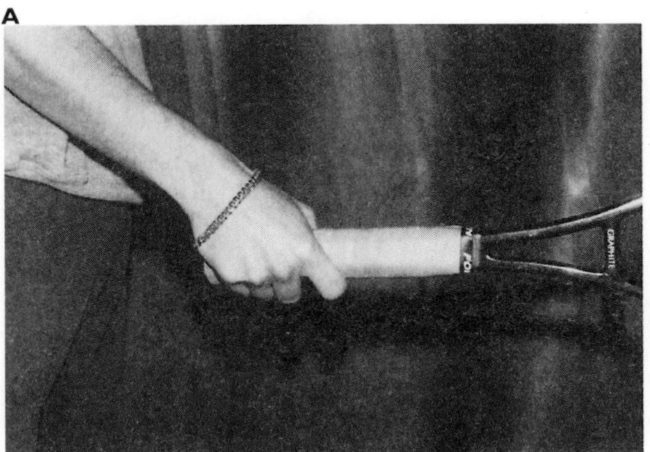

B

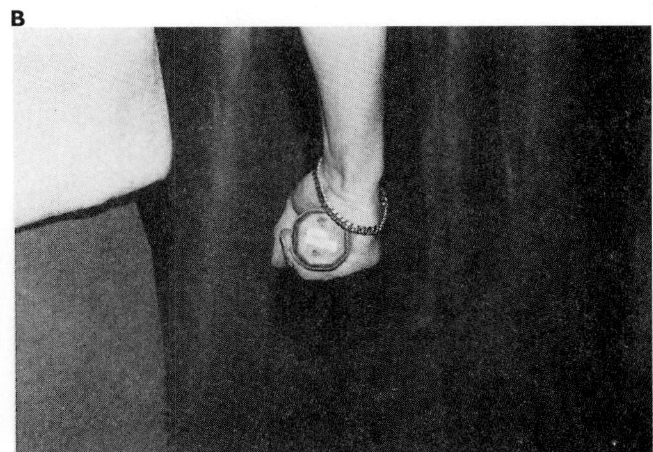

Figure 36-4. Continental grip. **A.** Side view; **B.** Back view.

individually. As a result, few players today use the Continental grip except perhaps for a volley or serve.

Backhand Grips

Eastern backhand grip

The eastern backhand is the most commonly used grip for the one-handed backhand groundstroke. Many advanced players also used the Eastern backhand for the serve. Figure 36-5A shows that the palm of the hand is in contact with the top bevel of the grip. Notice in figure 36-5B that the palm of the hand faces the surface of the court. The eastern backhand is the best one-handed grip for hitting topspin groundstrokes, although most recreational players find this shot difficult to master. The main disadvantage of the eastern backhand grip is that it requires a very strong forearm and hand to control the racquet at impact with the ball. Another potential disadvantage is that the eastern backhand can lead to tennis elbow in players who lack the strength necessary to play groundstrokes with this grip.

Two-handed backhand grip

The two-handed grip is the most common and effective alternative to the eastern backhand grip. Notice in figure 36-6A that the right hand is positioned on the grip with an Eastern forehand or continental grip and the left hand is positioned up the grip toward the head of the racquet with essentially a western grip. Figure 36-6B shows that the thumb of the right hand is in contact with the heel of the left hand. The two-handed backhand grip is a much stronger grip than the eastern backhand, and for some players it is easier to use and more effective than a one-handed grip. There are two disadvantages to using a two-handed backhand. First, it can be difficult to play very low

A

B

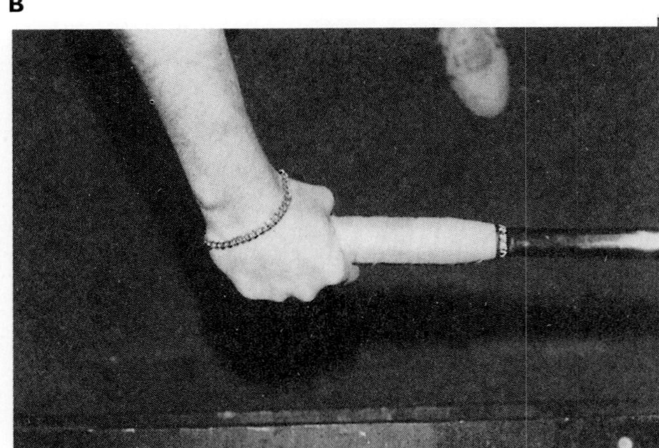

Figure 36-5. Eastern backhand grip. **A.** Back view; **B.** Top view.

A

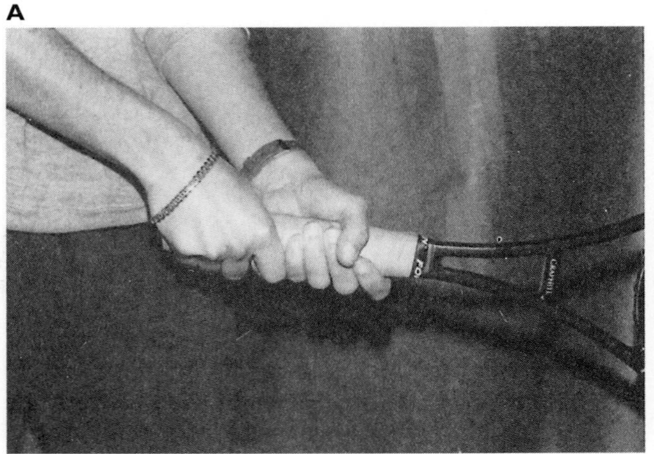

B

Figure 36-6. Two-handed backhand grip. **A.** Side view; **B.** Top view.

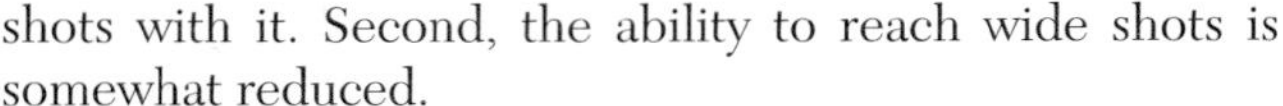

shots with it. Second, the ability to reach wide shots is somewhat reduced.

Continental grip

As discussed in the section on forehand grips, the Continental grip is an *all-purpose* grip that can be used for hitting forehands and backhands. The main advantage of the Continental grip (figure 36-4) is that changes in hand position are not needed when playing different shots. Also, the continental backhand is a good grip for hitting backhands with underspin. One disadvantage to using this grip is that it is difficult to hit topspin. Another disadvantage is that, like the eastern backhand, this grip requires good forearm and hand strength.

GROUNDSTROKES

Backhands (figure 36-7) and forehands (figure 36-8) are collectively called "groundstrokes." They are the framework upon which all other aspects of the game are built. To produce effective groundstrokes, you should do the following:

1. Keep the trip loose to start, firm to hit. Between shots, ease your grip. You will automatically squeeze the racquet harder as you come into the ball.
2. Get a good shoulder turn for the coil into the backswing, especially for backhand shots, and emphatically if hitting a two-handed backhand.
3. When coiling for a backhand, look over the forward shoulder to sight the approaching ball. Pretend that an arrow extending through both shoulders would point at the ball. Bring the front shoulder down low for a low ball, high for a high ball.
4. Watch the ball all the way into the hitting zone. You do not need to see the ball actually hitting the strings, but keep a keen focus on the ball as it approaches the area of contact.

(continued on p. 523)

Figure 36-7. Backhand drive.

Figure 36-8. Forehand drive.

Figure 36-9. Two-handed backhand drive.

5. Take your weight off your front foot as you coil into the backswing so that you can step forward into the shot.
6. Point the handle of the racquet at the target (the area you want to hit the ball into) in your backswing.
7. Get all your weight into the shot. Accelerate the racquet into the contact point and have your weight going toward the target.
8. On two-handed backhands, keep the trailing arm directly behind the handle at contact, not lifted up with a hunched shoulder (figure 36-9).
9. Extend your swing fully through the ball without hesitation, easing up only after contact.
10. Try to carry the ball on the strings as long as you can. Imagine that each ball has three other balls behind it. Try to thread the racquet through all four as you swing.

THE SERVE

Serving is a truly enthralling part of tennis. It is enlivening, arousing, and catalytic of the rest of one's game. However, the act is hardly more difficult than throwing a ball (figure 36-10).

1. Serving is a dynamic, whole-body act. Start with an attitude of mental and physical freedom. If you hold

Figure 36-10. Service.

back, you tighten your muscles and the swing has a cement-arm feeling. Instead, relax your whole body. Let your arm go limber.

2. To prepare for the serving motion, take up a throwing stance behind the baseline. Stand as if you are going to toss a ball over the net.
3. Imagine the spot, in the air, where the racquet will meet the ball. Hold the ball in your tossing hand directly beneath that spot. Cradle the ball in your fingers, not in your palm, and point your thumb toward the imagined spot of contact.
4. Hold the ball and racquet in front of you, together, more-or-less pointed toward the target service court.
5. Start the serving motion with both arms, then continue into the windup without pause. There is no hurry at the start, but there is no static halt at any point in the windup.
6. Lift the ball up unhurriedly, using your thumb as a guide to point toward the final destination of the toss.
7. Coil your body, similar to preparing for a forehand, and bring the racquet around behind you with the handle pointing toward the tossed ball.
8. Most or all of your weight should come to the back foot as you toss and wind up. Add some bend to your knees.
9. Start your foreswing into the ball from the ground up; that is, the knees rebound from their bend, the backbone uncoils, the hitting shoulder catapults toward the ball, and the arm thrashes up and over with the elbow unbending and the wrist adding a final vigorous snap that makes the racquet feel like a whip.
10. Build speed as you go. At the moment you hit the ball, your swing should still be gaining momentum. The whole swing is upward and forward in a clean arc that starts slow and finishes fast.

RETURN OF SERVE

There is no more neglected phase of tennis than the return of serve. Yet the techniques for success are surprisingly simple:

1. Stand in the middle of the widest possible area into which the server can hit, as far in as you can be and still feel confident in being able to hit under control.
2. Hold the racquet loosely, directly in front of you, with your body flexed and your weight on the front of your feet.
3. Go to meet a wide serve by moving diagonally forward, on a path 90 degrees to the flight of the ball. Move toward the ball, not away from it.
4. The harder the serve, the more the swing for the return must be compact, with less backswing, but with no restriction on the follow-through.
5. Keep a solid, firm wrist as you come into the ball, especially on hard serves.
6. Have a "scrambling" attitude. Do anything to get the ball back.

PLAYING THE FORECOURT

The liveliest tennis occurs at the net. Go up to the net often, not only for the tactical advantage it presents, but also because it adds dimension to the game. However, approach the net only after your opponent hits a ball that lands shallow in your court or when you hit a ball that you believe will force your opponent to reply with a weak return. Once at the net, your two offensive weapons are the volley and the overhead.

Doubles are played almost exclusively at the net. A good serve, volley, and overhead are essential to play competitive doubles.

Volley

1. A volley is a short stroke (figure 36-11). It is a compact and firm block of the ball—a punch rather than a swing.
2. However, the weaker the opponent's return is, the more your volley stroke can resemble a regular groundstroke.
3. The ball should be contacted early, before it gets to the side of your body.
4. Generally, use the continental grip so that both forehand and backhand volleys can be played.
5. Reach for a wide ball by quickly turning your shoulders and pushing into a short step with your lead foot and, if necessary, following with a crossover step with your trail foot
6. Stay ready with your racquet head chin-high, in front of you.
7. Defend the net like an ice hockey goalie. Attack the ball! Hit every ball you can reach, aggressively when you can.

Overheads

1. You must get under and *in back* of the lofted ball. Skip-step into position. Keep your legs limber, with knees unlocked, for last-minute adjustments.
2. The overhead is like a serve, but the windup is more compact. Forget any fancy windup. Just get the racquet up and over your shoulder, like you were an archer reaching back to pull an arrow out of the quiver.
3. Turn sideways as you arrive at your hitting place and rivet your eyes on the ball.
4. Make contact with the ball more in front of you than for a serve.
5. Hit the ball with as much power as you can control. The overhead is not a push or a punch, so crack off a point winner.

Figure 36-11. Forehand volley.

LOB

Use a lob to loft the ball over an opposing net player or when you need time to recover court position.

1. Let the racquet do the work. There is no need to lift your whole body into the shot.
2. Shorten the backswing. Get the racquet *under* the point of contact, then hit upward and forward in the same plane as the height you want to give to the ball.
3. Try to hold the ball on the strings as long as possible, and follow through into the path of the ball.
4. Maintain a firm wrist for the stroke.
5. Whenever you can, hit the ball just over the reach of your opponent's racquet. Always provide enough clearance—hit too high rather than too low.
6. When under pressure, do anything to get the ball up and give it extra height.

HALF VOLLEY

This is a difficult shot and should be avoided by playing either at the net or in the backcourt. When this shot is necessary, use the following techniques:

1. Bend the knees to get down to the ball.
2. Watch the ball all the way to the racquet.
3. Use no preliminary swing, but execute a full follow-through, hitting with a great deal of lift to make the ball drop into the court.
4. Stop and balance the weight forward at contact.
5. Use a firm, rigid twist and get the proper angle to the racquet. This angle is somewhat over the ball.
6. After hitting the shot, move to the net rather than remain in the middle of the court.

SPIN

A topspin (forward spin) causes the ball to drop rapidly and hence may be hit hard and fairly high above the net and still fall into the court.

A cut, or slice (backward spin), causes the ball to float or sail; it has a short, low, slow bounce. It may cause the net player to hit the ball into the net or out-of-bounds.

On service, a right-hand slice bounces to the left and curves to the left. An "American" service curves to the left and down, but bounces to the right and high.

GENERAL REMINDERS

At any level of play, there are on-court behaviors that are important parts of quality play:

1. Think positively about your game. Be in command of your physical responses.
2. Think of the racquet as part of your body, as an extension of your hitting arm.
3. Make every stroke a continuous, rhythmical, fluid action.
4. Hit the ball with your entire body, not just your arm.
5. Keep your style somewhat free and not bound by a compulsion to have perfect, picture-book form.
6. Focus your attention on the ball in play, not your opponent, the net, the baseline, or a previous errant shot.
7. Play dynamic, aggressive, spontaneous tennis.
8. Relish every chance to hit the ball. Enjoy the sheer physical pleasure of playing the game.

EFFECTIVE PRACTICE

Practice is the basis of improvement. It is the time to discipline your muscles so that in the next match your mind can focus on the enjoyment of the game instead of the mechanics of your swing.

Create muscle memory. If there is no structure to practice, it becomes too easy to slip into lazy habits such as not bending the knees or failing to transfer the weight properly. Keep your thoughts on the fundamentals of the game, looking first at your grip, then checking your pivot and backswing. Give special attention to accelerating the racquet into the ball. Try to train your muscles with free-flowing strokes.

Rehearse offense and defense. Offensive tennis is built around hitting the ball consistently deep into your opponent's court and hitting powerful serves. Practice these by trying to land every groundstroke behind the opponent's service line and hitting serves with extra effort. But also rehearse the defensive shots you'll need in competition, such as a well-lofted lob and returns of strong serves.

Make practice like a game. Part of every practice should simulate the game or segments of the game so that practice is not merely hitting the ball back and forth without purpose. Creating gamelike circumstances makes practice more interesting and gives incentive to do well.

Practice specific shots. Have a partner feed you the type of shot you want to practice. For instance, if you want to rehearse overheads, ask to have lobs hit to you. Often it is better if your partner hits a bucket of balls to you, without attempting to return your shots. After the bucket is exhausted, switch roles so that you can aid your partner's practice.

Play specific points. Try to stage playing situations. Be inventive with these drills, but make them as close to reality as possible. For example, you can play a three-ball rally whereby your partner feeds a ball to you that you hit for a deep shot and then follow with a charge to the net. Your partner, not bothering to flag down your shot, hits another ball to you that you can volley and then lifts another ball for you to hit as an overhead. Or, while your partner is practicing serves, you could practice returns by attempting to return every serve, in or out, while your partner does not chase your returns but attends only to serving.

Include aerobic conditioning. Practice can be arranged to incorporate rehearsal of skills and aerobic conditioning for tennis play. A good drill is an all-court scramble where your partner has a bucket of balls and hits a variety of placements to any part of your court. You chase down and return every ball you can, and your partner continues to act as a feeder without retrieving shots.

Practice in logical sequence. Warm up properly, then hit easily for the first few minutes. Next, give your shots plenty of depth, then try for placements into a particular area of the court. Play some "rapid fire," when you and your practice partner stand across the net from each other, just inside the service line, and hit volley after volley to each other. Then hit serves and returns of serve. Play match situations. Then do drills that include aerobic conditioning, and finish off the session with free hitting, in which you focus solely on rhythm and form.

Make practice fun. Add variety to the sessions. Experiment with different techniques or add spin to the ball. Or, play some points when the only rule is that the ball must cross over the net. Let practice be therapeutic and spark renewed interest in the game. Remember that tennis is a game. Its purpose should be to add enjoyment to your life.

USING A BACKBOARD OR BALL MACHINE

Practicing against a backboard or with a ball machine is an effective way to refine groundstrokes, serves, and volleys. Because the ball returns consistently from a wall or machine, a player can concentrate on proper stroke mechanics, movement, and positioning rather than on returning the ball to another player. In addition, an hour or two of backboard or ball machine practice can provide a vigorous physical workout. Backboards can often be found at public parks, schools, and private tennis facilities, some of which may also provide the use of ball machines.

Most backboards are 10 to 12 feet high and have a 2-inch-wide horizontal line painted 3 feet above the ground to simulate a net. Some good practice drills include hitting forehand and backhand groundstrokes crosscourt and down the line, hitting groundstrokes with underspin and topspin, and hitting first and second serves. As you alternate crosscourt and down-the-line strokes, you will learn to distinguish among the subtle differences in the timing of your swing and body positioning, allowing you to better play these shots. By practicing hitting the ball with spin, you will learn the difference between a low-to-high stroke used for topspin and the high-to-low stroke used for underspin. Backboard practice is also an effective way of learning forehand and backhand grip changes. As you practice, you will learn to automatically, without conscious effort, shift hand position on the grip when changing from forehand to backhand. The main disadvantage of backboard practice is that there is no way to tell whether a given shot would actually land in play on a real court. When practicing with a backboard, it is best to think about actually hitting the ball into a tennis court, and not just hitting the ball hard.

Ball machines are even more effective than backboards because they allow for practice on an actual court. These machines are designed to "throw" tennis balls to a player in a consistent manner, using either pneumatic pressure or spinning wheel mechanisms. Sophisticated machines can throw tennis balls with different spins, at different speeds, and at different angles.

Like backboards, ball machines can provide effective practice for forehand and backhand groundstrokes, such as hitting crosscourt and down-the-line groundstrokes, and for hitting with spin. Machines are more effective than backboards for volley practice, and some machines can also be used for overhead practice, which is not possible with a backboard. Although the serve cannot be practiced with a ball machine, some machines can be used to practice the return of serve. The main disadvantage of ball machines is that they do not simulate actual play because human opponents are less predictable and hit with more variability than a machine. The ability to successfully play the wide variety of shots hit by human players is difficult to learn with machines.

PRACTICE VERSUS PLAY

People participate in sports for many reasons: for example, for the pleasure of the activity, for exercise, for the competition, for social interaction, and to test and improve motor skills. One reason why tennis is so popular is because it is both physically and mentally challenging to master the many varied skills needed to play well. Many enthusiastic players become proficient enough to play tennis in a relatively short time with some instruction and practice, but they are generally quick to realize that continued practice and play are necessary to improve their overall game.

Many players assume that playing a match serves as practice, and indeed a player can learn things during a match that are not well learned during practice, such as how to apply strategy. However, during match play, the goal is to win points and games, so players tend to rely on their strengths and avoid their weaknesses. Although practice might not be inherently enjoyable, because it requires physical and mental effort, the best way to correct weaknesses and improve overall performance is through deliberate practice. In contrast to playing games, deliberate practice involves specific activities designed to improve skills and performance during matches.

Practice Drills

The following drills can be used to practice tennis fundamentals. A playing partner or ball machine is needed to practice groundstrokes, approach shots, and volley drills, whereas the serve drill can be practiced alone.

Deep rally practice

Two players (P1 and P2) hit groundstrokes with the objective of hitting consecutive shots into the shaded areas.

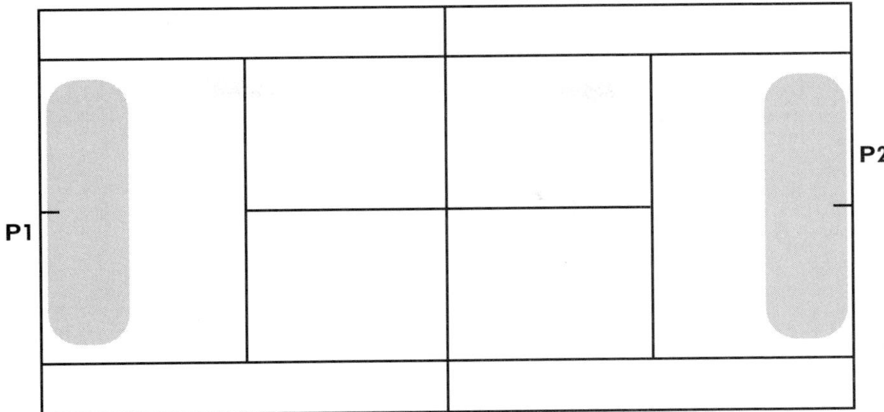

Figure 36-12A. Deep rally practice.

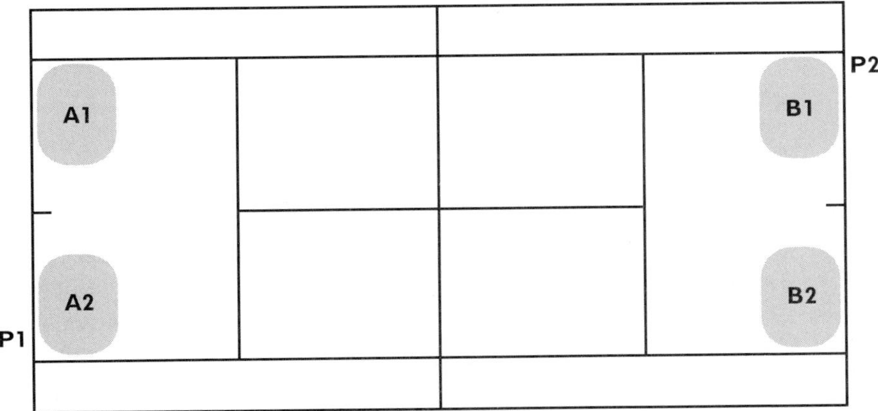

Figure 36-12B. Cross-court practice.

Players can hit forehands, backhands, or a combination of the two (figure 36-12A).

Cross-court practice

Two players (P1 and P2) hit groundstrokes with the objective of hitting consecutive cross-court shots into the shaded areas. For example, players exchange forehands from areas A2 to B1 or backhands from A1 to B2 (figure 36-12B).

Down-the-line practice

Two players (P1 and P2) hit groundstrokes with the objective of hitting consecutive down-the-line shots into the shaded areas. Players hit forehands to the right side of the court only and backhands to the left side only (figure 36-12C).

Approach shot practice

Two players (P1 and P2) rally two or three groundstrokes deep (GD), then P1 hits a short ball (GS), P2 moves forward and plays an approach back to P1. P1 plays a return shot that P2 volleys from the net position (figure 36-12D).

Volley practice—1

The net player (V) practices forehand and backhand volleys by returning balls hit by the player at the baseline (B). Forehand volleys are hit to area A1 and backhand volleys to area A2 (figure 36-12E).

Volley practice—2

Both players take a position near the net and practice forehand and backhand volleys (figure 36-12F).

Serve practice

The player (P) practices four types of serves. Wide serves (A1) and down-the-center serves (A2) to the deuce court, and down-the-center serves (B1) and wide serves (B2) to the ad court. More-advanced players should practice hitting first and second serves to the targets (figure 36-12G).

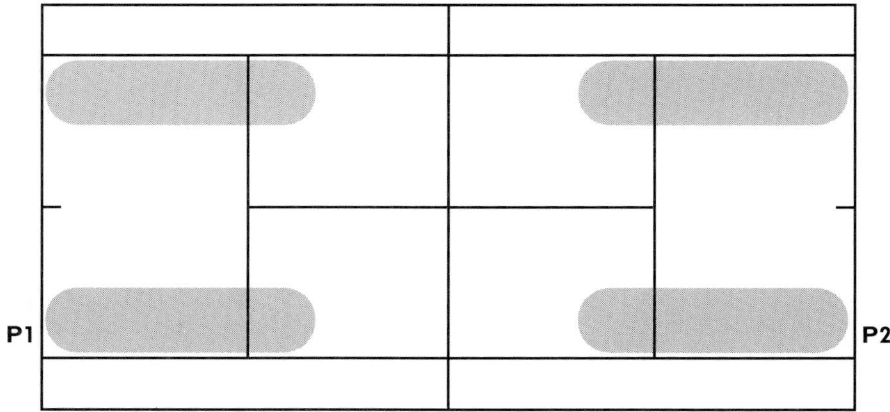

Figure 36-12C. Down-the-line practice.

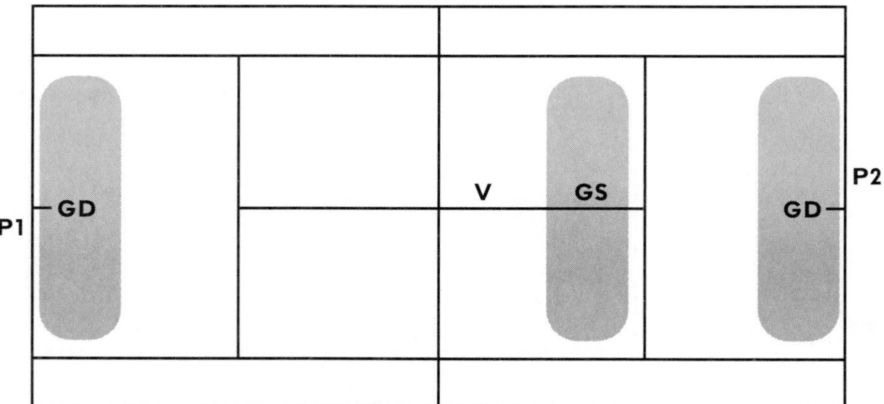

Figure 36-12D. Approach shot practice.

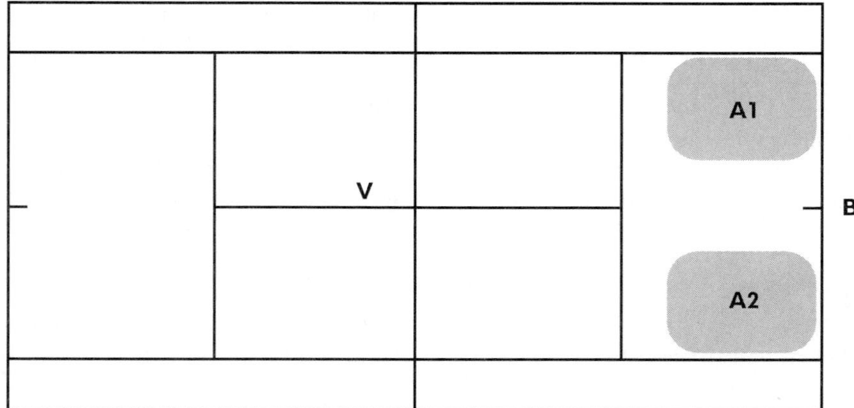

Figure 36-12E. Volley practice—1.

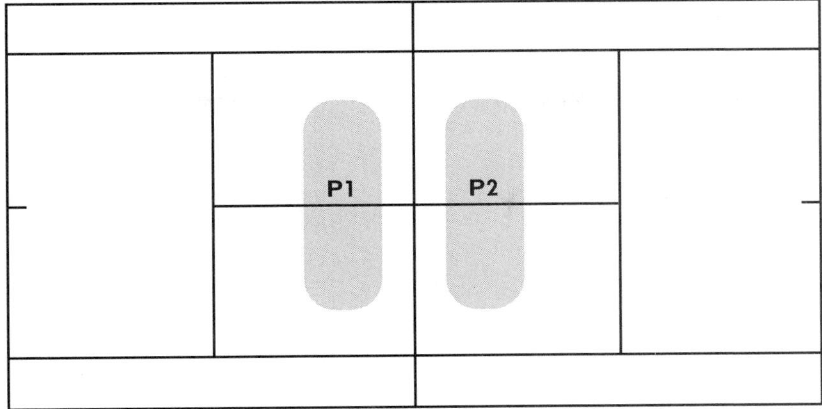

Figure 36-12F. Volley practice—2.

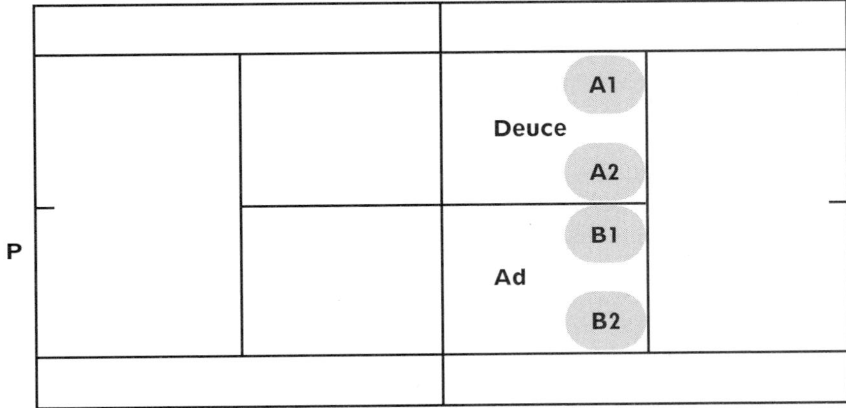

Figure 36-12G. Serve practice.

STRATEGY

The strategy for effective play in tennis is remarkably uncomplicated. Most situations in a game have automatic answers or, at least, sensible responses.

Singles

Keep the ball in play. The first rule of tennis strategy is to hit the ball over the net, land it inbounds, and do this one more time than an opponent on each point. The worst mistake is to hit the ball into the net. It is a dead loss, never giving an opponent a chance to commit an error. Rather than trying constantly for point winners, loft the ball with enough room to clear the net by several feet. Give your opponent opportunities to misplay the ball.

Keep the ball deep. An associated tactic is to consistently place the ball deep. This will compel an opponent to stay back, hitting incessantly from behind the baseline, with little chance to come up to the net to hit point winners. You will also give yourself more time between points as the longer returns from your opponent allow you to move into a better hitting position on each ball and to collect yourself for a rhythmical, free-flowing swing.

Know when to use angles. When your opponent offers a shallow ball, take advantage of the expanded angles for placing your return. The further inside the court you can move to hit, the greater the potential is for hitting an angled shot toward either sideline. If you are also pulled off to one side of your court for this shallow ball, the situation then becomes more favorable for hitting a cross-court return.

Use the forecourt often. Go up to the net as often as you can, even if you are still uncertain about your ability. Your presence alone may be enough to force a jittery opponent into committing errors. And once at the net, finish the point off as quickly as possible. Try to hit every ball out of your opponent's reach.

Get the first serve in. Too often players assume they should bash away at the first serve and, upon failure, push the second. Instead, slow down the pace of the first serve and increase the pace of the second. This makes first serves successful more often and keeps your opponent from stepping up to hit winners off your second serve.

Play percentage tennis. An overall guide is to ask (1) What do you do best? And (2) Where is your opponent weakest? Use your strengths. Note what an opponent cannot do well and play to that flaw often. That way you will win instead of trying to avoid losing.

Doubles

Take the net. Doubles is a net game. The basic and overriding objective is to gain control of the net, from where most points are won. Both players should get into the forecourt at every opportunity to take command of the point.

Hit high-percentage serves. Control the pace of your serve. If you can, hit it mostly to the receiver's backhand side, where it will generate a softer return, giving your net-playing partner more time to reach the ball and volley a winner.

Hit away from a net player. When one opponent is at the net and the other back, hit the ball past the net player. It is especially important to return a serve back toward the server as deep as you can. Alternatively, lift a lob over the net player.

Exploit open space. Doubles teams are often overprotective of the alleys and thus play too far apart. Send the ball up the middle often, where the two of them may hesitate an instant due to uncertainty over who will take the ball. However, when given a chance to hit crosscourt, take advantage of the wide doubles court. Use the angle opportunity, but provide a margin of error by aiming to land the ball on the singles sideline.

Cover the empty space. Tie an imaginary rope between you and your partner. If your partner is forced off the side of the court, let the rope pull you over to cover the now wider area of return space that is presented to your opponents. Always stay in the middle of the court space that is left over when your teammate is pushed out of position.

TEACHING CONSIDERATIONS

1. The techniques of skilled hitting have a common denominator of physics. Regardless of how contradictory different players' styles appear to be, at the critical microsecond when racquet and ball are in contact, everyone must impart the same force to achieve the same end. Learn the physics that apply to hitting a tennis ball, then help students to understand those laws and evaluate how well they are doing in relation to them.
2. Keep instructions simple. It is easy to become overloaded with instructional facts about each stroke. At some point a learner will no longer handle all the information while simultaneously trying to organize commands about what the muscles should do. The best method is often the simplest. Focus on only the most important aspects of hitting.
3. Attend mostly to the rhythmical patterns of the swing. Encourage learners to first develop smooth, flowing motions for each swing, without necessarily judging their swings on the basis of where the ball goes. Emphasize the coiling and uncoiling and the position of the body relative to the ball. Have them think of the *art* of tennis. Make them "look good" as they hit. Focus their attention on the sensation of rhythm and timing for every swing.
4. Play lots of "minitennis" games to emphasize rhythm and proper position. Have one partner stand at the net and toss the ball on one bounce to the hitter; then switch roles. Or have partners stand on opposite sides of the net at the service lines and rally the ball, trying to keep it within the boundaries of the service court. Provide students with games in which they can have instant success by making it possible to develop a feel for the game.
5. Become target oriented. Introduce rallying for specific targets. For example, to improve the depth of everyone's shots, stretch a piece of cord across the court several feet inside the baseline to act as an aiming point for deep groundstrokes. For the serve, stand a ball can (as a target) inside each corner of the service court. Or exchange groundstrokes using the alley as in the inbounds area.
6. A common mistake is to turn one's head prematurely, looking up to see where the ball is going before it is hit. Have players attend to all the dimensions of the ball as they follow it into the hitting zone. Focus on the spin, trying to actually see the seams of the ball. Or note the color of the ball and try to heighten its hue as it approaches. Create the habit of refocusing on the ball after its bounce. Then play "Bounce-and-hit," whereby both partners say "bounce" every time the ball bounces (including on the opposite side of the net), and "hit" every time a player strikes the ball. This will help players to refocus after the bounce and to concentrate on the ball rather than on mechanical parts of the swing.
7. The service toss is a major headache for many players. Too often they throw it into the air with an exaggerated lift of the knees. Isolate the toss by practicing it alone, perhaps starting with the tossing hand resting against the inside of the forward thigh, then lifting and releasing the ball as if settling it on a shelf at hitting height. Place a racquet on the ground, the head in front and inside the forward foot. Toss the ball to the proper height and allow it to drop to see if it will land on the racquet face.
8. Teach beginners to serve with a four-part but continuous sequence, as follows: (1) start with both hands held together, elbows bent, racquet pointed in the direction of the target court; (2) drop both hands

down at the same time, toward the forward thigh; (3) bring both arms up together to release the ball, and arc the racquet behind the hitting shoulder; then (4) deliver the racquet into the back of the ball with an accelerating forward swing. Have students say "down-together, up-together, swing" as they practice the motion of the serve.

9. Arrange variants of the game to encourage certain skills. For example, play a groundstroke game without the serve, in which each point begins with one player hitting a groundstroke and the ball crossing the net three times before a point can be scored (this will encourage controlled rallies). Or practice second serves by playing games in which only one serve is allowed. Or play games in which the server hits half-speed and only backhands are allowed thereafter.
10. Make practice fun. Add variety to the sessions, sometimes doing such things as hitting the ball with the racquet held in the nondominant hand. Play some points where the only rule is that the ball must cross over the net and land in front of the fence. Or have a rule that after every shot players must run up and touch the net with their racquets. Try a game in which, on each side, a player hits a shot and then hands the racquet off to another player for the next shot.

GLOSSARY

ace A point-winning serve that is hit beyond the reach of a receiver.

ad court The left service court; also that court into which the serve is hit when the total number of points played in a game is an odd number.

ad in When the server has a score of advantage.

ad out When the receiver has a score of advantage.

advantage The next point after a deuce score. The player who wins the point is said to have the "advantage"; and if that player also wins the following point, the player will have won the game; if not, the score returns to deuce.

alley The area on either side of the singles court that is included as inbounds for doubles play.

approach shot A groundstroke hit by a player to prepare the way for an approach to the net.

backcourt An undefined area in the vicinity of the baseline.

backhand A stroke used to play a ball on the opposite side of a player's dominant hand.

baseline The line marking the end of the court.

break (service break) To win a game that the opponent serves.

center mark A short line extended inward from the baseline as a continuation of the center service line that marks the two halves of the court and indicates the sides of the court in which the server must stand.

chop stroke A forward, downward motion giving the ball backspin.

cross-court shot Hitting the ball from one side of the court across the net to the side diagonally opposite.

deuce An even score in a game after six or more points have been played or an even score in games after 10 or more games have been played.

deuce court The right service court; also that court into which the serve is hit when the total number of points played in a game is an even number.

double fault Failure of a player to get either of the two service attempts into the proper service court.

down-the-line shot A ball hit across the net parallel to a sideline.

fault A served ball that does not land within the proper service court or any other violation of the rules of service.

foot fault A service delivery that is illegal because the server stepped on the baseline or into the court before the racquet contacted the ball.

forecourt That area of the court between the net and the service line.

forehand A stroke used to play a ball on a player's dominant side.

game A unit of a set completed when one side wins four points before the other side wins three or, if both sides have won three points, when one side thereafter gains a two-point margin.

groundstroke A forehand or backhand stroke used to hit the ball after it has bounced.

let Any point that must be replayed. Most often it refers to a serve that hits the top of the net, then lands in the proper service court.

lob A high, arcing shot that lands near the opponent's baseline.

love A score of zero. In a love game, one side wins no points; in a love set, one side wins no games.

match A contest between two or four players in which one side must win a predetermined number of games or sets to be declared the winner.

match point Term used when a side needs only one more point to win the match.

overhead (smash) A free-swinging stroke used for a ball that is over the player's head.

rally The exchange of shots between opponents after the serve, usually referring to prolonged play.

serve The stroke used to put the ball into play at the start of each point. The more inclusive term *service* applies to the right to be the server and the served ball itself.

service break A game won by the receiver.

set A unit of a match completed when one side wins six games or when one side wins the tie-breaker game.

set point When a side needs only one more point to win the set.

sideline The line that marks the outside edge of either the singles or the doubles court.

tie-breaker A scoring system designed to eliminate prolonged sets in which one player must win seven points with a two-point advantage to win a set. Played when a set becomes tied at six games each.

topspin A forward rotation of the ball that causes the ball to drop to the court surface more rapidly than a ball hit without spin.

underspin A backward rotation of the ball that causes the ball to sail farther than it would without spin (see **chop stroke**).

volley A short punch stroke used to hit the ball before it bounces.

SUGGESTED READINGS

Barton, J., and Grice, W. 1994. *Tennis*. 5th ed. Boston: American Press.

Brown, J. 1995. *Tennis: Steps to success*. 2d ed. Champaign, Ill.: Human Kinetics.

Bryant, J. E. 1997. *Game-set-match*. 4th ed. Englewood, Colo.: Morton. Written especially for first-time tennis players.

Contains sections on learning experience suggestions, elimination of errors, mental aspects of competition, and physical aspects of the game.

Chu, D. 1995. *Power tennis training.* Champaign, Ill.: Human Kinetics.

Clark, J. 1992. *Seven lifetime sports.* Dubuque, Iowa: Eddie Bowers. The chapter on tennis discusses history, benefits, terminology, rules, equipment, skill fundamentals, error corrections, drills, games, and skills tests.

Claxton, D., and Faribault, J. 1992. *Tennis.* 2d ed. Scottsdale, Ariz.: Gorsuch Scarisbrick. Includes a task-mastery workbook and learning sequences for tennis skills.

Gensemer, R. 1994. *Tennis for the experienced player*. 2d ed. Englewood, Colo.: Morton. Using more than 150 photographs, concentrates on the advanced tennis course participant by describing such skills as spin and power for the serve, returning the serve, playing the lob, strategy, and realistic practices.

Gould, D. 1992. *Tennis anyone?* 5th ed. Mountain View, Calif.: Mayfield. Includes material on the background of tennis, basic strokes, serve, net play, receiving the serve, rules, scoring, etiquette, singles and doubles strategy, drills, and conditioning activities.

Gropel, J. L., et al. 1992. *High-tech tennis*. 2d ed. Champaign, Ill.: Human Kinetics. A collaborative work to combine the sciences of biomechanics, motor learning, exercise physiology, and sport psychology as they apply to tennis.

Hensley, L., ed. 1989. *Tennis skills test manual*. Reston, Va.: American Alliance for Health, Physical Education, Recreation and Dance. Designed to improve teaching and evaluation of tennis skills. Contains a series of skills tests with national norms for boys and girls (grades 9–12) and college.

Johnson, J., and Xanthes, J. 1996. *Tennis*. 7th ed. Dubuque, Iowa: WCB/McGraw-Hill. Contains basic descriptions of tennis skills, information on where to play, a section on wheelchair tennis and conditioning and preparation for play.

Johnson, M. L., and Hill, D. L. 1995. *College tennis.* 5th ed. Winston-Salem, N.C.: Hunter Textbooks. Emphasizes stroke mechanics, presented through line drawings and text.

Moore, C., and Chafin, M. B. 1990. *Tennis everyone.* 5th ed. Winston-Salem, N.C.: Hunter Textbooks. Contains hundred of photos and covers practice drills, officiating, development of the sport, the National Tennis Rating Program, the two-handed backhand, and an up-to-date listing of films and where to obtain them.

Smith, S. 1995. *Coaching tennis successfully*. Champaign, Ill.: Human Kinetics.

Stolle, F., and Knight, B. 1992. *Tennis: Let's analyze your game*. Englewood, Colo.: Morton. Describes techniques for individual and group instruction at all levels. Discusses equipment, tennis tips, preventing injuries, skills tests, and coaching tips.

U.S. Tennis Association. Annual. *Official tennis guide and yearbook with official rules.* New York: A. S. Barnes.

U.S. Tennis Association. Annual. *USTA publications*. Princeton, N.J.: U.S. Tennis Association.

Van Collie, S. 1992. *Tennis: The lifetime sport*. San Leandro, Calif.: Briston. Especially valuable for seniors who are just taking up tennis or those who are returning to the game.

Zebas, C. J., and Johnson, H. M. 1997. *Tennis: Back to the basics.* 3d ed. Dubuque, Iowa: Eddie Bowers. Includes more than 100 photos and diagrams and a chapter on how to analyze the basic tennis strokes.

RESOURCES

Videotapes

Fourteen tennis programs available from Sports Video, 745 State Circle, P. O. Box 1941, Ann Arbor, MI 48106.

NCAA tennis videos (4 tapes); *ESPN's teaching kids tennis; Visual tennis; Tennis, spin and you; Warm up to attack; Tennis by Vic Braden* (4 tapes); *Tennis our way; The tennis teaching methods of Dennis Van Der Meer* (4 tapes), and *Tennis talk* (12 tapes) are available from Cambridge Physical Education and Health, P. O. Box 2153, Charleston, WV 25328.

Nine videotapes available from Human Kinetics, P. O. Box 5076, Champaign, IL 61825-5076: *Advanced footskills for tennis; Fitness testing for tennis; Movement training for tennis; Playing better tennis under pressure; Strength training for tennis; Tennis biomechanics; The science and myths of tennis; The serve; Women's doubles*.

Series including *Serve and return of serve, The volley, The forehand,* and *The backhand*. Karol Video, 22 Riverside Dr., Wayne, NJ 07470.

Six series of tennis videotapes. *Complete tennis from the pros* (4 programs), *Dennis Van Der Meer* (12 programs), *How to win at doubles and stay the best of friends* (2 programs), *New Dennis Van Der Meer* (3 programs), *Play your best tennis* (2 programs), and *Tennis to win* (2 programs) plus 7 miscellaneous programs. "How To" Sport Videos, P. O. Box 5852, Denver, CO 80217.

Thirteen videotapes, many about famous tennis professionals. Corbin House, 227 Corbin Place, Brooklyn, NY 11235.

Web sites

Association of Tennis Professionals: http://www.atptour.com/
The Davis Cup: http://www.daviscup.org/
Tennis Online: http://www.tennisonline.com/
The Tennis Server: http//www.tennisserver.com/
United States Professional Tennis Association: http://www.uspta.org/
United States Tennis Association: http://www.usta.com/
Women's Tennis Association: http://www.corelwtatour.com/

Touch Football and Flag Football

After completing this chapter, the reader should be able to:

- Appreciate the historical development of touch and flag football
- Know the rules for each of these activities
- Demonstrate the basic skills of blocking and touching (removing flags), kicking, passing, and receiving a football
- Understand the fundamentals of offense and defense for touch and flag football
- Correctly execute several offensive and defensive formations used in the two activities
- Teach the fundamentals of touch and flag football to a group of novice players

Touch and flag football are similar to regulation rugby football and to American football except that the ball carrier is downed differently. In touch football the ball carrier is stopped by being touched with both hands rather than being tackled. Flags being removed will down a ball carrier in flag football versus tackling or touching. In addition, noncontact blocking (screen blocking) is utilized in both flag and touch football. These changes lessen the danger of injury and encourage a more open game. Forward passing is usually the principle offensive weapon, with all players eligible to receive a pass.

With the exception of a few rules, flag and touch football in all aspects are virtually the same (e.g., equipment, field of play, scoring). Therefore, they will be discussed together, and any differences will be noted in the text.

HISTORY

Football as it is played today is derived from soccer and rugby. Harvard, Yale, Princeton, and Rutgers universities were early players of the game, which at the time was not much more than a gang fight over a round ball.

However, since 1869 rules have been formulated, equipment has been adopted and qualified, and coaches and members of the medical profession have worked toward making football a relatively safe game.

Touch football is a modification of football that can be safely played without pads. Playing the game without costly equipment has enabled children and young adults to participate. Touch football is an interesting and beneficial game for all who desire competition and fun.

In 1932, the Intramural Sports Section of the College Physical Education Association adopted rules for school and college play.

The National Touch and Flag Football Rules were first developed after considerable study of the variations of the game played in colleges and universities throughout the United States and Canada by a National College Touch Football Rules Committee of the College Physical Education Association. In 1950 this committee, in addition to an advisory committee and subcommittees, submitted questionnaires to more than 100 schools concerning the rules and recommended their standardization. The recommendations were then approved by the Intramural Section of the College Physical Education Association. Through cooperation with the Athletic Institute, the first rule book was published in 1952. The latest version of these rules is located in the second edition of the Official U.S. Flag and Touch Football Rules published in 1992. Even though official rules exist for these sports, local custom, available facilities, and tradition often dictate the rules used.

EQUIPMENT

Playing field. The field is 40 yards (36.6 m) wide by 100 yards (91.4 m) long (figure 37-1). It is suggested to modify the size of the field to fit the needs of the class. For example, if the class is very large and there is a desire to provide maximum time on task and increase participation, a field may be divided into two smaller fields with four teams.

Ball. A regulation American football is used for men, and a junior-sized football is used for women.

Uniforms. No special uniform is necessary, and a gym uniform is adequate. Teams should be equipped with distinctively colored jerseys. However, two groups of different-color flag belts will suffice. Cleated shoes are recommended; however, basketball, tennis, and gym shoes are suitable. Cleated shoes have some restrictions covered in the rules and regulations section.

THE GAME

Length of Game

The length of the game is up to the discretion of the instructor, based on class size and time limit. However, the

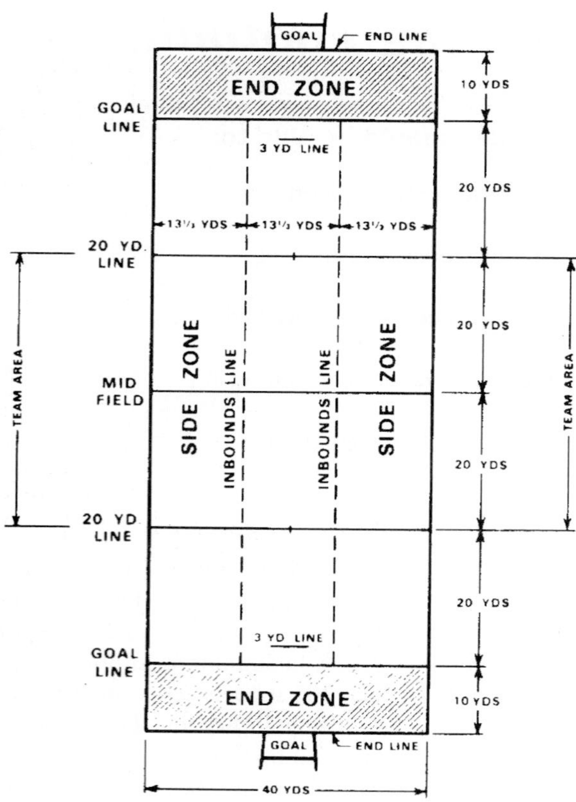

Figure 37-1. Football field.

following time frame is suggested: A game with two 20-minute halves on a running clock with 10-minute halves. The clock will start when the ball is legally snapped or the kickoff is legally touched. It will run continuously for 20 minutes unless stopped for a:

1. Score; starts when the kickoff is legally touched.
2. Team time-out; starts on the snap.
3. Referee's time-out; starts on the ready-for-play signal.

At the end of the 20-minute period six additional plays will be executed without the game clock. The clock will only be used during this period to monitor the time allowed between plays. When the official announces that regulation time has expired and that only six plays remain, the play continues normally. During this time each down will count as one play of the six. If a penalty occurs and causes the down to be repeated, the play number will be repeated. (For example: On the last play of the game there is a defensive penalty and the offense accepts. The offense gets to repeat the last down.) If a team scores, the extra point attempt does not count as one of the six plays. In addition, a punt counts as a play.

Overtime

An overtime period is played in case of a tie. There are two common methods of playing an overtime period:

1. Each team is given four downs from the first 20-yard (18 m) zone line heading away from the nearest end zone; the team advancing the ball the farthest in the four downs is the winner. If both teams score, repeat the procedure.
2. Each team is given four downs from the same 10-yard (9.1 m) line heading into the nearest end zone. The team that scores is the winner. If the score is tied or there is no score after the four downs, the procedure is repeated.

One additional option is to award the win to the team with the most 20-yard (18 m) zone line penetrations during the game. If penetrations are also tied, one of the overtime procedures mentioned previously may be employed.

Time-Outs

Many leagues and flag/touch football organizations limit the number of time-outs per game to speed up play. It is recommended to limit each team to two or three time-outs per game.

Scoring

1. Touchdown: 6 points
2. Safety: 2 points and possession of the ball by punt
3. Forfeited game: 1 point
4. Point after touchdown: 1 point from the 3-yard (2.7 m) line and 2 points from the 10-yard (9.1 m) line.

If there are goalposts available, there may be kicks for extra points from the 3-yard (2.7 m) line for 1 point. Two points are awarded for running or passing. In addition, a team may be allowed to attempt a field goal for 3 points. Many leagues and organizations do not use kicks because of the lack of goalposts. If kicks are used, the defense should not be allowed to rush the kicker, for obvious safety reasons. To have kicks without a defensive rush would give the offense an unfair advantage; therefore, kicks are rarely used.

Players and Substitutions

1. A team consists of 7 to 11 players. The offensive team must have at least three players on the line of scrimmage.
2. It is advised, for safety and maximum participation, to keep the number of players to 11 or below. Having four teams of 5 players each is better than two teams of 10.
3. Any number of substitutions may be made during the game. Substitutes must report to the referee before entering the game.

Playing Regulations

1. Start of the game: The game is started by the following procedures:
   a. A coin is tossed, and the winner gets the choice of which goal to defend and whether to receive the ball or defer the choice until the second half.

b. Putting the ball into play: The ball is put into play at the beginning of the game, at the beginning of the second half, and after a score by one of two ways depending on league or organization requirements. The ball may be put into play by a kick, a dropkick, or a punt from the 20-yard (18 m) line. If kicks are not allowed, the team that would normally receive the ball puts the ball into play by starting its offensive series from its own 20-yard (18 m) line.

c. Recovery of a kickoff or punt: A punt or kickoff is only a live ball for the receiving team. If the receiving team touches the ball in the air but does not catch it, the ball becomes dead when it touches the ground. If the ball hits the ground before a receiving player touches it, it is still a live ball and can be picked up and advanced by the receiving team only. If a kicking-team player touches a ball that is live on the ground or in the air, the ball becomes dead and the receiving team remains in possession. No member of the kicking team may interfere with a receiving-team player's attempt to catch the ball.

2. Ball kicked or punted over opponent's endline (back of the end zone): If the ball goes through the opponent's endline, it goes to the opponents for scrimmage on their own 20-yard (18 m) line.
3. Ball kicked or punted out of bounds: If the ball goes out of bounds, the receiving team gets possession of the ball where it went out of bounds.
4. Fumbled ball: If a ball is fumbled and touches the ground, it is a dead ball and the offense retains possession of the ball.
5. A down: A down is a unit of the game that starts with a legal snap or legal free kick and ends when the ball next becomes dead. "Between downs" is any period when the ball is dead.
6. Series of downs: A team in possession of the ball shall have four consecutive downs to advance to the next zone by scrimmage. Any down may be repeated or lost if provided by the rules.
7. Zone line-to-gain: The zone line-to-gain in any series shall be the zone in advance of the ball, unless distance has been lost due to penalty or failure to gain. In such cases, the original zone in advance of the ball at the beginning of the series of downs is the zone line-to-gain. The most forward point of the ball, when declared dead between the goal lines, shall be the determining factor.
8. Awarding a new series: A new series of downs shall be awarded when a team moves the ball into the next zone on a play free from penalty; or a penalty against the opponents moves the ball into the next zone; or an accepted penalty against the opponents involves an automatic first down; or either team has obtained legal possession of a ball as a result of a penalty, free kick, protected scrimmage kick, touchback, pass interception, or failure to gain the zone in advance of the ball.
9. Failure to advance: If in four consecutive downs a team fails to advance the ball to the next zone, the defense receives the ball. If on the fourth down the offense elects to punt, it must declare that intention to the officials. Quick kicks are not allowed. On the punt the offense must have every player except the punter on the line of scrimmage. No offensive player may move until the ball is kicked. The defense must have at least three players on the line of scrimmage, and they may not move until the ball is kicked. All punts must be announced. The defense is not allowed to attempt a punt block.
10. Downed ball: The player is downed in touch football when touched by an opposing player with both hands anywhere between the offensive player's knees or shoulders. In flag football a player is downed when one or both of the flags are removed by an opposing player. If the offensive player's flags fall off inadvertently, a defensive player may down the offensive player by the rules of touch football.
11. Passing:
    a. All players on the offensive team are eligible to receive a pass. Any member of the defensive team may intercept a pass.
    b. Only one forward pass may be thrown per down. Any forward pass must be executed behind the line of scrimmage. There is no limit to the number of laterals a team may use on any given down. A lateral is any ball thrown or tossed parallel or backward from the line of scrimmage.
12. Snapping: The snapper shall pass the ball back between her or his legs from its position on the ground with a quick and continuous motion of the hand(s). Any player may receive the snap as long as he or she is a minimum of 2 yards (1.83 m) back from the line of scrimmage.
13. Motion: One offensive player may be in motion during the snap as long as three other offensive players are on the line of scrimmage. The player in motion must not be moving toward the line of scrimmage before the ball is snapped.
14. Mercy rule: If a team is 17 or more points ahead when the referee announces the 2-minute warning or that there are six plays left in the game, the game shall end.
15. Scoring:
    a. Touchdown: A touchdown shall be scored when a legal forward pass is completed or a fumble or backward pass is caught on or behind the

opponent's goal line or when a player who is legally in possession of the ball penetrates the vertical plane of the opponent's goal line.

b. Extra points: An opportunity to score 1 point from the 3-yard line or 2 points from the 10-yard line shall be granted the team scoring a touchdown. If the league has goalposts, a successful kick will be 1 point and running or passing into the end zone from the 3-yard line will be 2 points.

c. Safety: A safety results when a runner carries the ball from the field of play to or across his or her own goal line, and it becomes dead there in his or her team's possession. Exception: When a defensive player intercepts a forward pass in his or her end zone and downs the ball, it is not a safety. If the interceptor attempts to run the ball out of the end zone and the ball becomes dead, it is a safety.

Fouls and Penalties

1. Ball in play; dead ball; out-of-bounds:
   a. A dead ball becomes alive when it is snapped or kicked. A ball is declared dead when:
      (1) It goes out-of-bounds.
      (2) A player catches a free kick and then drops it on the ground.
      (3) A backward pass or fumble touches the ground.
      (4) A runner is legally tagged (touched or flag pulled).
      (5) An official sounds a whistle.
   b. Out-of-bounds: A player is out-of-bounds when any part of the body touches anything other than another player or a game official that is on or outside the sideline or endline.
2. Fair-catch interference: While any free kick is in flight beyond the kicking team's scrimmage line, no kicking-team player shall touch the ball or receiver nor obstruct the receiver's path to the ball. Penalty: Fair-catch interference; 10 yards (9.1 m) from the previous spot, and replay the down.
3. Encroachment: Following the ready-to-play signal and until the snap, no player on the defense may encroach (enter the neutral zone) nor may any player contact opponents or in any other way interfere with them. After the center has placed his or her hands on the ball, it is encroachment for any player to break the scrimmage line plane. Penalty: Encroachment; 5 yards (4.6 m) from the previous spot.
4. Snap: A player may pick up the ball and advance it to a player at least three yards deep in the offensive backfield. The ball does not have to be snapped between the legs.
5. Minimum line players: The offensive team must have three players on the line of scrimmage prior to the snap. Penalty: Dead ball foul, illegal procedure; 5 yards (4.6 m).
6. Motion: More than one player in motion during the snap or a motion player moving toward the line of scrimmage during a snap is illegal. Penalty: Illegal motion; 5 yards (4.6 m).
7. Illegal forward pass: A forward pass is illegal if:
   a. The passer's foot is beyond the line of scrimmage when the ball leaves the hand.
   b. There is more than one forward pass.
   Penalty: 5 yards (4.6 m) from the spot of the foul and a loss of down.
8. Pass interference: Contact that interferes with an eligible receiver who is beyond the line of scrimmage is pass interference unless it occurs when two or more eligible receivers make a simultaneous and bona fide attempt to reach, catch, or bat a pass. It is also pass interference if an eligible receiver is deflagged or tagged prior to touching the ball. Penalty:
   a. Offensive pass interference: 10 yards (9.1 m) from the previous spot and loss of down.
   b. Defensive pass interference: 10 yards (9.1 m) from the previous spot and automatic first down. If it is ruled intentional or unsportsman-like, an additional 10 yards (9.1 m).
9. Unsportsman-like conduct and personal fouls. These are left to the instructor's discretion. Any player displaying conduct that is deemed harmful to players or is unsportsman-like should be penalized. Penalty: Unsportsman-like conduct; 10 yards (9.1 m). If the action is flagrant, the offender shall be disqualified.
10. Roughing the passer: Defensive players must make a definite effort to avoid charging into a passer after it is clear the ball has been thrown. Penalty: 10 yards (9.1 m); automatic first down.
11. Blocking: The offensive screen block shall take place without contact. The screen blocker shall keep the hands and arms at the side or behind the back. Any use of the hands, arms, elbows, legs, or body to initiate contact during a block is illegal. Penalty: Personal foul; 10 yards (9.1 m).
12. Use of hands or arms by the defense: Defensive players must go around the offensive player's screen block. The arms and hands may not be used as a wedge to contact the opponent. Penalty: Personal foul; 10 yards (9.1 m).
13. Runner:
    a. Guarding the flag or deflecting a touch: Runners shall not flag-guard or guard their body by using their hands, arms, or the ball to deny the opportunity for an opponent to tag or remove a flag belt. Penalty: Guarding or flag guarding; 10 yards (9.1 m).

b. Stiff-arm: The runner shall be prohibited from contacting an opponent with extended hand or arm. Penalty: Personal foul; 10 yards (9.1 m).

Officials

1. The referee has absolute charge of the game, and decisions made by the referee are final.
2. The umpire pays particular attention to holding and interference on forward-pass plays.
3. The line judge measures distance and reports offside and personal fouls, such as holding and roughness. The line judge may also be the timekeeper if no special individual is assigned this duty. (See figure 37-2 for official football signals.)

FUNDAMENTAL SKILLS AND TECHNIQUES

Stance

The player must be positioned within 1 foot (30.5 cm) of the scrimmage line in a 2-point stance.

Offensive-line stance. The stance used by players on the offensive line must enable them to move forward, backward, and laterally; therefore, it must be a position with the feet comfortably apart and staggered, knees bent, with the body in balance to facilitate a quick movement in the desired direction.

Defensive-line stance. This stance is similar to the offensive stance, but the body is closer to the ground. Weight must be forward so a lineperson can charge forward.

Offensive-backfield stance (2-point stance)

1. The feet are about shoulder-width apart, with the toes pointed straight ahead.
2. Weight is equally distributed on the balls of both feet, and the knees are slightly flexed.
3. The hands or elbows are on the knees, arms are slightly flexed, thumbs are on the inside of the knees, the head is up, and the eyes are straight ahead.

Defensive-backfield stance. Players should stand in a natural but alert posture, feet apart and staggered. A semierect body position facilitates quick movements yet affords an effective position to observe movements of the offense.

Blocking

The object of blocking is to stop or deter a defensive rusher's attempt to reach the quarterback on a pass play. It may also be used to obstruct the path of the defender on a running play. Screen blocking is utilized in that the player on the line attempts to stay in front of the defensive player without making contact (figure 37-3A, B).

Blocking techniques

1. Assume a 2-point stance.
2. Feet are parallel with the knees, which are bent to achieve a low center of gravity and afford maneuverability in any direction.
3. Keep your head up and concentrate on the defender's midsection.
4. Arms and hands are held behind the back or at the sides.
5. If pass blocking, take an inside-position step with the foot nearest the center to take away the inside rushing lane. Attempt to make the rusher take an outside path that will allow a pocket for the passer to throw from. If the blocker gets past, the blocker should immediately turn and face the passer while retreating backward and alert the passer or the oncoming rusher. This allows two things: (*a*) it does no good for the blocker to follow the rusher to the passer, which reduces the traffic the passer must scramble through, and (*b*) it gives the passer a safety valve to throw to if pressured. At worst, the blocker will get to the original line of scrimmage.
6. If blocking for a run, attempt to maneuver between the rusher and the running lane.

Blocking strategies

1. If the passer wishes to stay in the pocket, the blocker should line up as near the offensive center as possible without interfering with the snap. This virtually takes away the inside path toward the passer. The blocker needs to be patient, protect the inside, and let the rusher commit to the outside rush. Once the rusher starts outside, pivot on the inside foot, staying low, and attempt to run with the rusher on an inside-out path past the passer. Blockers should also be careful not to become overly anxious and step outside to an outside fake, thus leaving an opening to the inside.
2. If the passer wishes to sprint (roll) out to one side, the blockers should block as follows:
   a. Play-side blockers should line up wider than normal to entice the rusher to the inside. The passer can help entice the rusher by taking an initial step in the opposite direction of the rollout. The blockers then attempt to hook (reach) the rusher and make him or her take an inside path to the passer. This block can be assisted by lining up a receiver near the outside of the rusher. On the snap, the blocker and the receiver double-team the rusher.
   b. Off-side blockers should line up very tight to the center to make sure the rusher cannot take an inside path toward the rollout. Getting the rusher to take an outside path complements this type of play.
3. If the passer wishes to run to the outside or run an option, the blockers would block the same way as on a sprint-out pass. Exception: If the team runs an option attack, the quarterback may option off the rusher instead of the defensive back. In this case the

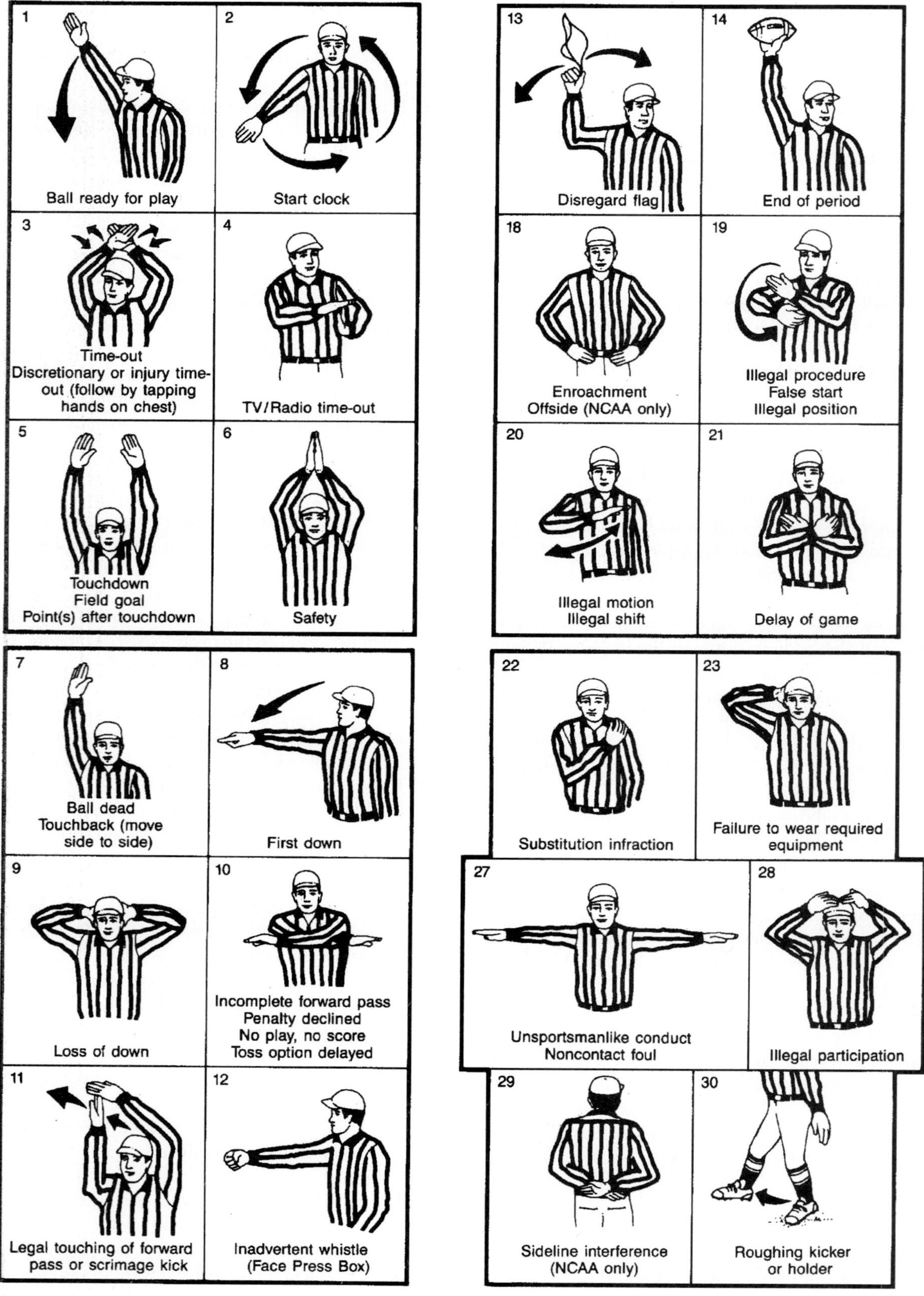

Figure 37-2. Men's and women's touch and flag football signals.

Figure 37-2—*cont'd.* Men's and women's touch and flag football signals.

A

B

Figure 37-3. Screen block. **A,** Arms behind back. **B,** Arms at sides.

blocker would not attempt to block the rusher and would release and block downfield.

Touching (Touch Football)

Touching is used as a substitute for tackling. The location of the ball carrier when touched by a defensive player will determine the location for start of the next play. Touch the opponent between the knees and the shoulders.

Flag Removal (Flag Football)

Pulling flags is used as a substitute for tackling. The flags are located on a belt around the runner's waist. If close enough, it is good strategy to use both hands to grab at the flags to reduce the chances of an unsuccessful grasp.

Kicking

Punting. The punt is one of the most important plays in football. It can determine the outcome of the game. The punt is used to gain yardage or to better a team's position on the field. Punting is highly specialized, and constant practice is necessary to develop into a good kicker.

1. Stand with the feet slightly apart and staggered, legs flexed at the knees, and weight equally distributed on the balls of both feet.
2. Incline the body forward from the waist, arms and hands extended in front of the body, fingers spread, and palms up.
3. Have the kicking foot ahead at the start of the kick.
4. Follow the ball with the eyes from the center and after the ball is caught; keep the eyes on it until it has been kicked.
5. Hold the ball with both hands, laces up and with the long axis of the ball cocked slightly to one side.
6. Hold the ball on the kicking-foot side just below the chest.
7. Take a maximum of three steps before contacting the ball.
8. Keep the kicking foot plantar-flexed (pointed) at and through the impact with the ball.
9. Release the ball so that it remains in its long axis until after being kicked and before the nonkicking foot touches the ground.
10. Contact the ball between the toe and upper part of the kicking foot.
11. Swing the leg from the hip through the perpendicular arc, the center of the long axis of the ball meeting the instep approximately 2 feet (60 cm) above the ground.

12. As the foot meets the ball, extend the lower leg and lock the knee joint. The kicking motion should follow a path slightly across the ball (for a rightfooter, the kicking leg goes slightly left), which imparts spin on the ball.
13. The follow-through extends along this line and should end up slightly across the body and as high as the kicker's flexibility allows. A higher follow-through will create a higher apex of the punt. A high punt allows for better punt coverage.
14. When advantageous, kick out-of-bounds.

Punting Drills

1. Drop drill. One of the most common errors of punting is a poor drop. If dropped correctly the ball will not tumble or turn and should land on the kicking foot in the same position as when dropped.
   a. Assume the normal starting position.
   b. Extend arms to the position used in a normal punt.
   c. Release the ball with both hands simultaneously.
   d. Do not attempt to kick the ball, but let it hit the ground.
   e. Watch the patch of the ball to see if it turns or tumbles.
   f. If the ball is dropped properly, it will bounce straight up or back toward the kicker.
2. One-step drop drill. This incorporates a stepping motion with a drop.
   a. Assume a normal starting position or one with the kicking leg slightly forward.
   b. Take an elongated stride with the nonkicking leg and drop the ball before the foot touches the ground. Do not take another step.
   c. Concentrate on the ball, and observe whether the ball tumbles or turns and how it bounces. Both of these drills work to improve the drop and can be done alone or with partners who can help watch for mistakes.
3. One-step drop, punch (pass). This works on the drop and proper foot contact. Have kickers choose partners and face each other approximately 5 to 7 yards (4.5 to 6.5 m) apart.
   a. Same as *a* in one-step drop drill above.
   b. Same as *b* in one-step drop drill above.
   c. Swing kicking leg through the correct motion but at one-quarter speed, and stop the motion after contact is made with the ball. Make sure the kicking foot is plantar-flexed at impact.
   d. If contact is made correctly, the ball should spiral. The objective is to kick the ball to the partner with a spiral.
   e. The distance between partners as well as the speed of the kicking motion can be gradually increased. Distance and speed of the kicking motion should not be increased unless the kicker is making correct contact with the ball and consistently spiraling the ball. This drill can be expanded by adding one step and then another until the desired number of steps is achieved. In addition, kickers should be reminded to attempt a full motion and not a full-speed motion until their level of skill allows it.
4. Coffin corner drill. This is a buildup drill that concentrates on technique and accuracy.
   a. Line up on a hash mark on the 20-yard (18 m) line and face the nearest corner of the end zone.
   b. Kick five punts and attempt to land in or near the corner out-of-bounds.
   c. After five punts, increase the distance by 10 yards (9.1 m) and repeat.
   d. Continue to increase the distance as the kicker's strength allows.
   e. This drill makes kickers use less force and concentrate on accuracy because the starting distance is short. In addition, it is an excellent warm-up for kickers.

Receiving Punts

1. Concentrate on the ball from the time it leaves the kicker's foot until it is safely caught.
2. Sprint to the point just below the ball and assume a good football position. This allows movement in any direction if the ball drifts.
3. Form a basket with the hands (fingers spread), arms, and forearms nearly parallel, and give with the arms and legs as the ball impacts.
4. The eyes should follow the ball into the arms, while making a nodding motion with the head.
5. Do not attempt to run upfield until the catch is ensured.

Punt-Receiving Drills

1. Throwing the ball
   a. Partner up by twos, start at 20 yards (18 m) apart, and throw the ball high in the air.
   b. Receivers position themselves under the ball and attempt to catch it.
   c. Gradually increase the distance between partners, but always attempt to throw the ball high.
   d. When possible, throw the ball sometimes so the nose turns over and sometimes with the nose staying up. This will change how the ball descends and help the receiver work on judgment.
2. Punt drill. Have partners actually punt the ball to each other. As with the previous drill, start rather close and gradually increase the distance between partners.

3. Concentration drill
   a. Put players in groups of three: one punter, one receiver, and one distracter.
   b. The punter lines up approximately 35 to 40 yards (32 to 36.5 m) away from the receiver and punts the ball to the receiver.
   c. The receiver attempts to catch the ball.
   d. The distracter waits until the ball almost makes contact with the receiver and then screams or lightly touches the receiver as a distraction.
   e. After the kicker kicks five balls, have the partners rotate positions.
   f. This drill is an excellent concentration builder.

Placekick

The traditional and soccer styles of placekicks may be used. The soccer-style kick is a popular form that has evolved in recent years.

Traditional style

1. The kicker should stand so that the path of the kicking leg will be in line through the point of the kick and over the center of the crossbar.
2. A spot slightly below the center of the ball should be picked in advance and the eyes kept focused on this spot throughout the kicking action.
3. The feet should be comfortably spread, knees slightly bent, and body slightly inclined forward from the hips.
4. For the kickoff, any number of steps may be taken in the approach to the kick, but for a field goal or point after touchdown, only two- or three-step approaches are valid.
5. The nonkicking foot should be planted slightly to the side and far enough back of the ball to allow contact to be made below the middle of the ball. Both side and back positions should be within 6 to 12 inches (15 to 30 cm).
6. As the nonkicking foot is planted, the kicking lower leg should reach a position at least parallel to the ground. The higher the back swing, the more force that can be imparted to the ball.
7. The eyes should remain focused on the ball from the start of the approach until contact is made with the ball. The kicker should actually see the foot contact the ball.
8. On impact, the foot should be locked in a dorsal-flexed position of about 90 degrees. This allows a consistent point of impact and solid impact (figure 37-4A, B, C).
9. The follow-through of the kicking leg is toward the intended line of flight.
10. If greater height is needed, the kicker should start the approach slightly closer to the ball. This makes the impact point lower, which achieves a higher trajectory. If more distance is needed, the kicker should move further away. This causes the impact position to be higher, so that the ball will travel further but with less trajectory.

Soccer-style kick

1. The approach should have the same number of steps as the conventional kick, except from a different angle. The kicker should approach from approximately a 45-degree angle.
2. On the last step, the nonkicking foot should land in approximately the same spot as in the conventional style. The plant foot might land slightly wider in this style due to the approach.
3. On the last step, the backswing of the kicking lower leg should reach a position at least parallel to the ground. The higher the backswing, the more force that can be imparted to the ball.
4. The downswing should be made down and slightly across the kicker's body, so that the foot makes contact behind the ball in line with the intended line of flight.
5. At impact, the kicking foot should be plantar-flexed and make contact slightly below the middle of the ball (figure 37-5A, B).
6. The eyes remain focused on the ball from the start of the approach through the kicking motion.
7. The follow-through finishes close to the intended line of flight.

Note: In both styles of kicks, the follow-through does not have to be very high.

Drills for Kicking (Both Styles)

1. No-step wall drill. Position partners 10 feet (3 m) away from a wall with a target taped to the wall 3 feet (90 cm) high. Partners take turns holding for each other and kicking.
   a. Conventional: Stand directly behind the ball with the feet parallel and the plant foot in the desired position. Soccer: Stand in the same manner but at a 45-degree angle to the intended line of flight.
   b. Lift kicking lower leg up past parallel to the ground and down into the ball slightly below the center.
   c. On impact, soccer-style foot is plantar-flexed and conventional style is dorsal-flexed.
   d. Follow-through is short, about 12 to 18 inches (30 to 45 cm), and toward the target.
   e. The object is to use good form, keep the head down, and hit the target.
2. One-step partner drill
   a. Drill is exactly like the preceding drill, except that the kicker stands in the same starting position and takes one elongated stride backward.

A

B

C

Figure 37-4. Conventional style kick. **A,** Backswing (ankle locked). **B,** Downswing/foot position. **C,** Dorsi-flexed position.

b. From this position, the kicker takes a stride toward the ball and pulls the lower leg up past parallel in the backswing and then down through the ball.
c. The follow-through is short to emphasize technique, not direction.
d. The kicker attempts to kick the ball to the partner 10 yards (9.1 m) away.
e. The distance can gradually be increased between partners. The kickers will find that they can kick the ball a great distance with only one step if done correctly.
f. This drill can also be expanded by increasing the number of back steps taken by the kicker until the desired number of steps is reached.

Note: Kickers may have a problem when taking back steps and then approaching the ball. Typically, they take normal steps backward but elongated steps toward the ball. Therefore, they will be too close to the ball at contact.

A

B

Figure 37-5. Soccer-style kick. **A,** Body and foot position. **B,** Plantar-flexed position.

Most kickers use a 3:1 ratio when determining how far back to go—for example, if using a one-step kick, the kicker would position himself or herself behind the ball in the desired plant position and take three normal steps backward from the ball. A conventional kicker would start here, and a soccer-style kicker would then take one or two lateral steps. It is important for soccer-style kickers to remember as they take lateral steps not to go directly lateral (parallel) to the line of scrimmage. This would put them further away from the ball than they marked off. Therefore, the lateral steps should be slightly less than parallel to the line of scrimmage.

3. Accuracy and progression drill
   a. Position the ball at the extra-point mark and have the kickers attempt to make five in a row.
   b. If they are successful; have them move back 5 yards (4.6 m) and attempt to make five more.
   c. As long as they are successful, they can continue to move in 5-yard (4.6 m) increments.
   d. Once a kicker misses, the partners switch.
   e. This builds concentration, leg strength, and is an excellent warm-up.

Passing

The forward (overhead) pass is an offensive technique used to advance the ball and to hold secondary defensive players deep enough to make the running game function.

Grip

1. Grip the ball slightly behind the middle with two to three fingers on and across the lace. How far behind the middle a player grips the ball depends upon the passer's hand size. Typically, throwers with smaller hands grip the ball near the back of the ball (figure 37-6).
2. The fingers and thumb should be relaxed and well spread, but not to a point where the passer's palm is on the ball. Keep the ball in the fingers, not in the hand.
3. In the event that the front part of the ball fails to drop in flight, the index finger should be extended toward the rear point of the ball.

Ready position (stance and position before the throw)

1. The stance should be such that the line of the shoulders are perpendicular to the line of scrimmage.

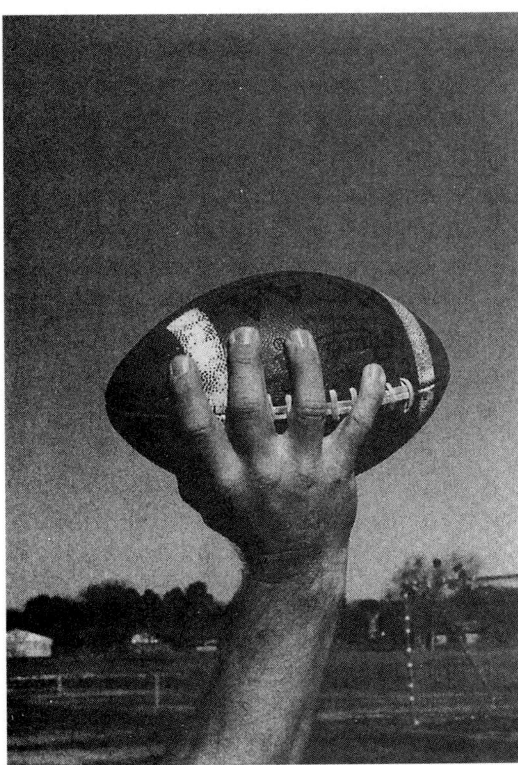

Figure 37-6. Passing grip.

Figure 37-7. Upper-arm and ball position for throwing.

2. Feet should be slightly less than shoulder-width apart.
3. The throwing hand is positioned on the ball as mentioned above, and the nonthrowing hand is placed lightly and on the opposite side for control.
4. The ball is held near the head and shoulder area. This allows the passer to deliver the ball as quickly as possible.

Throwing motion

1. The ball is raised toward the throwing shoulder with both hands. The nonthrowing hand releases the ball as the throwing hand is pulled back with the ball to a position behind the ear with the upper arm parallel to the ground (figure 37-7).
2. As the forward throwing motion begins, the passer should take a large stride with the lead foot.
3. As the passer steps, the nonthrowing arm is pulled back sharply in the direction opposite to the pass. This aids shoulder rotation and promotes a stronger throwing motion.
4. As the nonthrowing arm is pulled back, the throwing hand is led by the elbow and moved directly over the shoulder in a sharp downward motion, with the thumb rotating down toward the knees. The thumb-down position promotes the proper spiraling effect.

Follow-through

1. The majority of the thrower's weight should be shifted to the front foot as the ball is delivered.
2. The throwing hand should finish across the body over the opposite knee.

Additional coaching points

1. A common error passers make is stepping toward the receiver instead of toward where the receiver will be when the ball arrives. This typically causes the ball to end up behind the receiver. Therefore, the passer should always step toward the point where the ball is intended to meet the receiver. The step also transfers momentum, allowing more force in the throwing motion.
2. The passer should concentrate on that point where the ball is intended until the ball reaches the receiver. Concentrating on the receiver during the throwing motion or ball during its flight will inhibit accuracy.

Lateral pass

The lateral pass is one of the most successful methods of producing touchdowns, provided a few general rules are followed.

A

B

Figure 37-8. Centering. **A,** Two-handed snap. **B,** One-handed snap.

1. Use for passes under 5 yards (4.6 m).
2. Use when you are prevented from breaking away.
3. Do not wait for a lateral pass when you are in a position to block for the ball carrier.
4. Use a lateral pass as late as possible.
5. Do not throw lateral passes indiscriminately.
6. Practice either the basketball-type lateral or the one-handed underhand lateral pass.
   a. Basketball pass:
      (1) The ball is delivered by both hands with arm and wrist action, so that it turns relatively slowly end over end.
      (2) There is very little arch on the ball.
   b. One-hand underhand pass:
      (1) The ball rests in the right hand and is held there by the left hand until the toss is made, the ball rolling off the fingertips with a slight spiral action.

Centering

Centering is much like a forward pass, but upside down.

1. Hold the ball on the ground with the dominant hand.
2. Place your fingers on the laces.
3. Use the nondominant hand to guide the ball, if necessary. A center may use a one- or two-handed snap (figure 37-8A, B).
4. Spread the feet wider than shoulder-width.
5. With the quarterback right behind the center, pass the ball with the dominant hand only.

Pass Receiving

1. Concentration is the most important teaching point. The receiver should watch the ball from the time it leaves the thrower's hand until the catch is tucked away.
2. Whenever possible, the receiver should reach forward to meet the ball as it approaches and give with the arms and hands on impact. This will cushion the impact and reduce the chances of the ball bouncing off the hands.
3. The arms and hands should be relaxed.
4. The fingers should be spread, with the palms facing the ball.
5. The hands should be very close together and if:
   a. chest high or higher, the rule is "thumb to thumb."

b. below chest high, the rule is "little finger to little finger." Keeping the hands close together and fingers spread creates a natural pocket for the ball.
6. As the ball is caught, the receiver should tuck the ball away into a protected position, with the arm close to the body.
7. In the protected carrying position, the front nose of the ball is covered with the hand with the fingers spread. The back point of the ball is locked into the elbow joint. The arm is then held closely and tightly to the body for added protection.

Pass-receiving drills

The following drills may also improve throwing.

1. Target drill
   a. With a partner, starting at 10 yards (9.1 m), the receiver makes a target with the hands above, below, or to the side. The arms are extended and the hands form a pocket. The passer attempts to hit the target, and the receiver catches the ball, concentrating on technique.
   b. The partners throw the ball back and forth, alternating targets and gradually increasing the yardage.
2. One-handed drill
   a. Partners face each other from 10 yards (9.1 m) and lightly throw the ball with a slight loft.
   b. The receiver attempts to catch the ball using one hand.
   c. The receiver may use the body to assist, but not the other hand or arm.
   d. As the receivers become adept at this speed, the passer may increase the speed of the throw.
   e. This drill teaches receivers to reach and give with the ball as well as to improve concentration.
3. Ball drill
   a. Partners set up 15 yards (13.7 m) apart.
   b. The receiver turns his or her back on the passer.
   c. The passer throws a soft, lofted pass about the shoulder height of the receiver and to the outside (right or left).
   d. As the ball is released, the passer yells "Ball!"
   e. The receiver turns as quickly as possible and attempts to catch the ball.
   f. The passer should never throw the ball *at* the receiver, but can increase the difficulty by increasing the ball speed or yelling "Ball" later.
   g. This drill teaches the receiver to turn the head around quickly on a route to locate the ball and then make an adjustment to the ball's flight.
4. Toe dance drill
   a. The passer lines up on a sideline.
   b. The receiver lines up 10 yards (9.1 m) away on a yard line approximately 10 yards away from the sideline. For example, the passer stands on the intersection of the 10-yard line and the sideline facing the 20-yard (18 m) line. The receiver stands on the 20-yard line, 10 yards away from the sideline and facing it.
   c. The receiver jogs toward the sideline, and the passer attempts to throw the ball so the receiver and the ball meet at the intersection of the yard line and the sideline.
   d. Once there, the receiver tries to get possession of the ball before going out-of-bounds.
   e. As the receivers become proficient at this task, the passer can widen the throw out-of-bounds, forcing the receiver to stretch to catch the ball and attempt to keep at least 1 foot (30 cm) inbounds.
   f. This drill can also be used in the end zone. The passer sets up on the endline, while the receivers run toward the endline.
   g. This drill promotes concentration and body awareness in relation to the sideline and endline.

LEARNING SEQUENCE

1. Practice all the physical skills related to the game:
   a. Throwing
   b. Receiving
   c. Kicking/punting
   d. Blocking
   e. Pass coverage
   f. Deflagging
   g. Lateral passing
   h. Running with the ball and fakes
   i. Pass rushing
2. Learn the positions, including duties and common formations
3. Learn kicking formations and assignments involved:
   a. Getting down field quickly and keeping the runner inside
   b. Kicker as safety
4. Practice offensive plays:
   a. Routes
   b. Blocking schemes
   c. Defensive-formations recognition
   d. Audibles
5. Practice defensive formations:
   a. Player to player
   b. Zones:
      (1) Two-deep straight
      (2) Two-deep rotation
      (3) Three-deep
   c. All defensive formations change depending on how many players rush the passer

6. Practice the kicking game:
   a. Punt return
   b. Punt coverage
   c. Extra point
   d. Kickoff
   e. Kickoff return
7. Playing suggestions
   a. Assignments should not be tipped off by players' leaning or pointing the eyes, head, or body or by changing facial expression.
   b. Remember that the passer is a ball carrier as long as the ball is in his or her hands.
   c. Vary your style of defensive play when flanked by an offensive player. Move out and set, move out and come back in motion, and move and dart through the split if it is wide enough.
   d. Early in the game discover which defensive players are weak in covering passes.
   e. Set up plays by sacrificing one or two downs to make future plays function properly.
   f. Plays should be set up in a sequence, including both passing and running plays.

DEFENSE

With the rule changes that eliminated contact blocking, offensive football is almost exclusively passing. Therefore, the type of defense employed must be set up to stop the pass first. With any of the following defenses, a few adjustments will control any running attack.

There are three key factors for a successful defensive team:

1. A strong pass rush: The pass rush is not typically the primary focus of a defense. Mistakenly, teams put slower, weaker players in this position. However, just like all levels of football, pass rushing is the most important aspect of defending the pass. Nothing helps the defensive backfield more than a quarterback who is under tremendous pressure. The more time a quarterback has, the more difficult it is to cover the receivers.
2. Team speed: Rarely will an offensive team be completely stopped. Therefore, overall team speed allows maximum pursuit of the ball in all situations. Three vital positions where team speed and ability are needed most are pass rusher, linebacker, and safety. The three best athletes on the team should play in these positions. Team speed is also more vital if the defense runs a player-to-player defense.
3. Communication and cohesion: No matter what the skill level, if players are not communicating, there will be missed assignments and lack of unity in the defense. Therefore, players may line up incorrectly, and, by mere position alone, set themselves up to be beaten by an offensive player. For example, the defense is in a two-deep rotational zone that ends up in three-deep coverage if the quarterback rolls out. If the corner who is supposed to drop back as a safety does not, then one third of the deep zone is uncovered. Therefore, the defense must never line up in a position where it cannot cover.

Player-to-Player Pass Coverage

Eligible receivers are covered by a single defensive player who follows the receiver wherever he or she goes.

Coverage rules

1. Concentrate on the receiver, not the quarterback.
2. Concentrate on the receiver's midsection, not the head.
3. Never let a receiver get behind you. Therefore, the initial distance between a receiver and a defensive back should be determined by the receiver's speed.
4. Never leave your player unless you see the ball has been thrown.

General strengths

1. Allows tighter coverage, especially in short-yardage situations.
2. Makes the receiver work harder to get open and catch a pass.

General weaknesses

1. Requires more-skilled, faster athletes to perform properly than do other defenses.
2. Requires more physical effort than the zone, so fatigue may become a factor. This is especially true if players are playing both offense and defense.
3. Overloads by receivers (three to one side) make it difficult to cover.
4. Crossing patterns by multiple receivers may cause a defender to be screened and not be able to pursue the receiver.
5. One new offensive innovation, lines up without any blockers and two or more receivers lined up on each side. A player-to-player defense would have a difficult time defending this offense, especially if the receivers run crossing patterns.

Player-to-Player Formations and Strategies

The following illustrations are for seven-player teams. For eight- or nine-player teams, use the additional player(s) to cover players where needed. For example, if the offense uses another wide receiver, cover this player with another defensive back. If the player lines up as a blocker or in the backfield, the extra defensive player may rush, take the back one-on-one, or play a rover and help where needed.

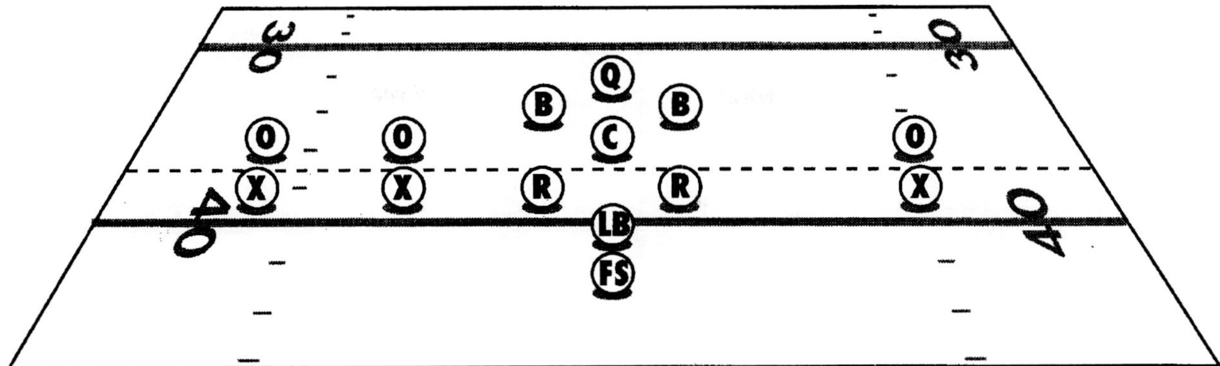

Figure 37-9. Two rushers, one free safety, one linebacker (player to player no. 1). (B: blocker; C: center; FS: free safety; LB: linebacker; O: receiver; Q: quarterback; R: rusher; X: secondary defender).

Two rushers, one free safety, one linebacker (figure 37-9)

Player responsibilities

1. Rushers only have rushing responsibilities. They attempt to sack or pressure the quarterback.
2. The linebacker takes center or first blocker to release for a pass. If no release, linebacker reads the quarterback and plays a shallow (8 to 10 yards; 7 to 9 m) middle-zone coverage.
3. The free safety typically lines up in the middle of the field, favoring the strong receiver side (side with two or more receivers). The free safety plays like a center fielder, reading the quarterback's eyes, and breaks on the ball when it is released. The free safety has no one-on-one responsibilities, so he or she must alert the other defensive backs if there is a run.
4. The remainder of the backs each pick a receiver and run with him or her wherever he or she goes. These players cannot concern themselves with the run or other receivers. They must focus on the receiver and not the quarterback. Defenders should attempt to stay between their player and the end zone and never get beat deep. They should line up with enough distance between the receiver and defender to enable deep coverage.

Strengths and weaknesses

1. Excellent for short-yardage plays. Allows tight coverage on receivers.
2. Allows free safety to help out on deep patterns or speedy receivers.
3. Allows maximum pressure on the quarterback.
4. If the quarterback gets outside of the rushers, the free safety must come up and make the play. Because of the distance the safety must travel, this usually results in a substantial gain.
5. If the center releases and is picked up by the linebacker and a second blocker releases, the free safety is again responsible for the play.
6. If both blockers and center release, one of the players will be uncovered.

Strategies

1. Have rushers line up wide and rush from the outside and keep the quarterback in the pocket to stop the quarterback from running.
2. Not much can be done about multiple blockers releasing in this defense. Switching to a single-rusher defense would be the best tactic.

Two linebackers, two rushers, no free safety (figure 37-10)

Responsibilities

1. Rushers and pass-coverage backs are the same.
2. With two linebackers, one is designated to take the first blocker to release. If another blocker releases, the second linebacker covers this player. If another blocker does not release, the linebacker plays a shallow middle zone and takes the quarterback if he or she runs.

Strengths and weaknesses

1. Allows maximum pressure on the quarterback.
2. Excellent for short-yardage plays. Allows tight coverage on receivers.
3. Reduces the success of the quarterback running.
4. Reduces the success of short passes to the second blocker releasing.
5. There is no free safety to help cover deep. Therefore, if a defensive back is beaten deep, it usually results in a long gain or a touchdown.

Strategies

1. Defensive backs must play a little softer and not be fooled by a short fake, allowing the receiver to get behind the defender.

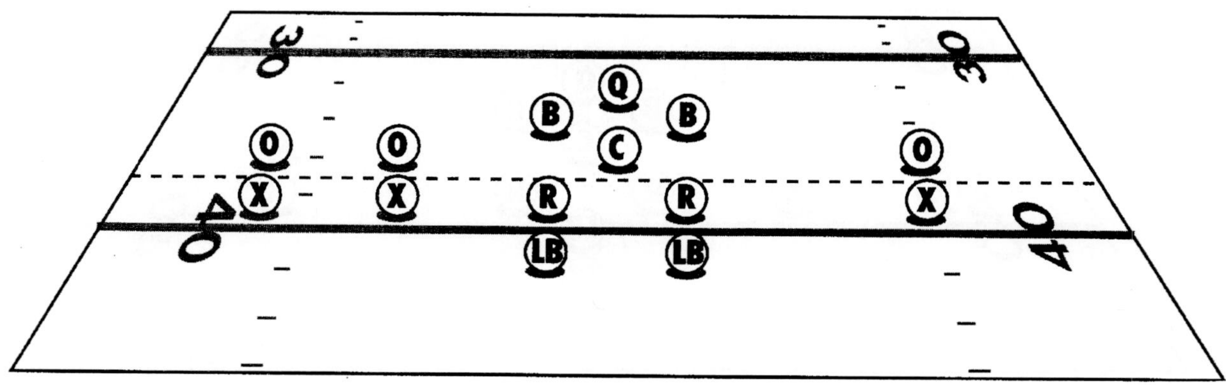

Figure 37-10. Two linebackers, two rushers, no free safety (player to player no. 2). (B: blocker; C: center; LB: linebacker; O: receiver; Q: quarterback; R: rusher; X: secondary defense).

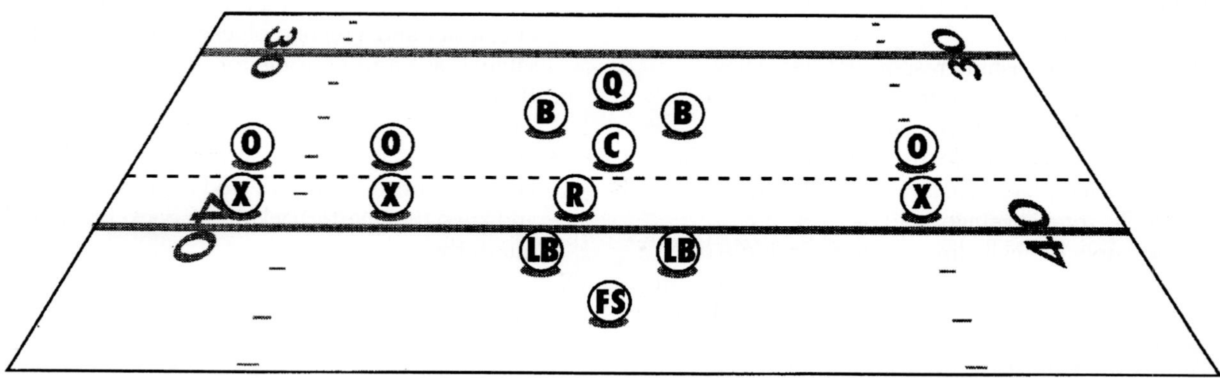

Figure 37-11. One rusher, two linebackers, one free safety (player to player no. 3). (B: blocker; C: center; FS: free safety; LB: linebacker; O: receiver; Q: quarterback; R: rusher; X: secondary defense).

2. Rushers can take an inside or outside path to the quarterback, allowing more pressure.

One rusher, two linebackers, one free safety (figure 37-11)

Responsibilities

1. Defensive backs and two linebackers play the same as the defense above.
2. Free safety plays the same as in the first player-to-player defense.

Strengths and weaknesses

1. This defense has all the strengths of the aforementioned defenses save one: Because there's only one rusher, the quarterback will have additional time to throw and the receivers will have additional time to get open.

Strategies

1. Defensive backs can play tighter.
2. Have one of the linebackers line up like a rusher and drop back into position on the snap of the ball. This will keep the lone rusher from being double-teamed by the blockers.
3. In this defense, the lone pass rusher *must* be an aggressive, fast player to pressure the quarterback.

Zone Coverage

With the exception of pass rushers, each defensive player is assigned an area (zone) to be responsible for covering. Receivers entering their zone should be guarded by release as the receiver enters another zone.

Coverage rules

1. Stay at home. Never follow a receiver into another zone.
2. Keep the receiver in front of you.
3. Safeties must stay as deep as the deepest player in the zone and wide as the widest player.
4. When the ball is released, all defensive backs attempt to break on the ball and/or pursue.

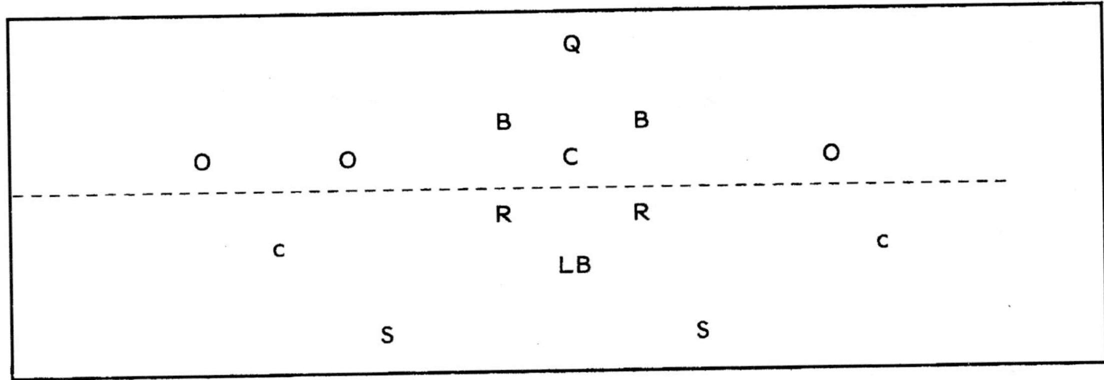

Figure 37-12. Two safeties, corners, and rushers; one linebacker (zone no. 1). (B: blocker; C: center; c: corner; LB: linebacker; O: receiver; Q: quarterback; R: rusher; S: safety).

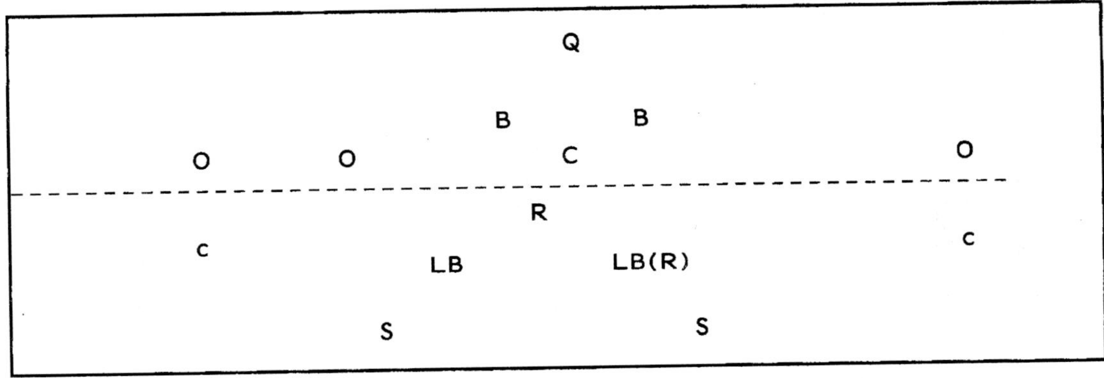

Figure 37-13. Two safeties, linebackers, and corners; one rusher (zone no. 2). (B: blocker; C: center; c: corner; LB: linebacker; O: receiver; Q: quarterback; R: rusher; S: safety).

General strengths

1. Does not require exceptionally gifted athletes.
2. Is not as fatiguing as player-to-player defense.
3. Good at preventing the deep pass.
4. Has more players breaking on the ball than player-to-player defenses.

General weaknesses

1. Does not allow tight coverage in short-yardage plays.
2. Is weak in the seams between zones.
3. Is susceptible to the zone being flooded by multiple receivers.
4. Is typically weak in the flat area.

Zone Formations and Strategies

Two safeties, corners, rushers; one linebacker (figure 37-12)

Player responsibilities

1. Rushers pursue quarterback.
2. Corners have the flat area on their side. The flat area is approximately 10 to 12 yards (9 to 11 m) deep, from the near sideline to the linebackers' hook/curl zone.
3. Linebacker has the hook/curl zone. This zone is about 10 to 12 yards deep and approximately 10 yards on either side of the linebacker.
4. Each safety has one half of the field, behind all of the other zones.

Strengths and weaknesses

1. Allows maximum pressure on the quarterback.
2. Excellent against the run.
3. Can be hurt in the seams between zones.
4. Flooding the zones makes it difficult to cover.

Strategy. Have defenders line up with a player-to-player look and on the snap of the ball go into their zones. This may confuse the quarterback and not tip off the weak areas of this defense.

Two safeties, linebackers, corners; one rusher (figure 37-13)

Player responsibilities

1. Strong-side rusher pursues the quarterback.
2. Weak-side rusher drops into linebacker position and plays the hook/curl zone on his or her side.

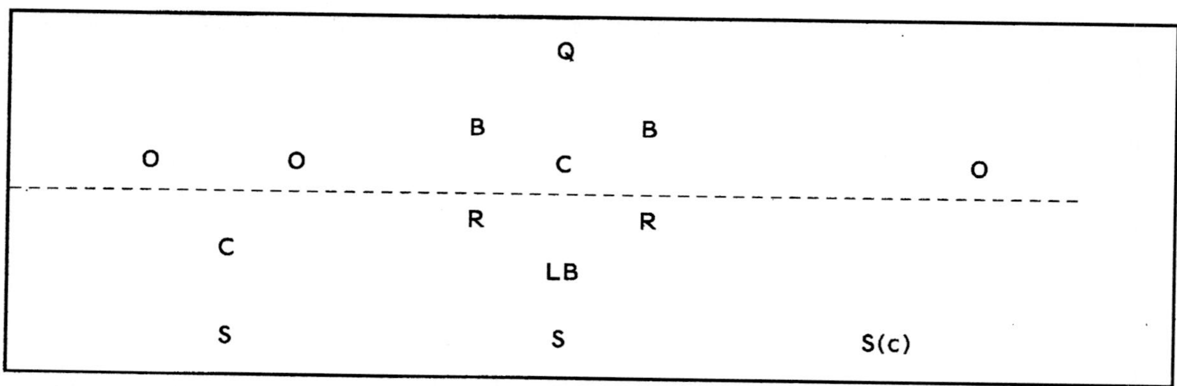

Figure 37-14. Three safeties, one corner, one linebacker, two rushers (zone no. 3A). (B: blocker; C: center; c: corner; LB: linebacker; O: receiver; Q: quarterback; R: rusher; S: safety).

3. The linebackers widen to the strong side and play the hook/curl zone. Having two linebackers cover this zone helps the corners by decreasing their flat coverage.
4. Corners have flats. The flats will not be as wide due to the two-linebacker set.
5. Safeties play halves.

Strengths and weaknesses

1. Excellent short-pass coverage, which allows more players to break on short passes.
2. Deep passes are more difficult to throw because the ball typically has to pass over one of the shallow defenders to a receiver. This helps the safeties because the ball is in the air longer and allows them additional time to pursue a pass.
3. Excellent against the run.
4. With only one rusher, the quarterback will have additional time to find a receiver, especially one on a deep route.

Strategy. Have the weak-side rusher move to the linebacker position on that side on the snap of the ball. This will help the single rusher from being double-teamed.

Three safeties, one corner, one linebacker, two rushers (figure 37-14)

Player responsibilities

1. Rushers pursue quarterback.
2. Linebacker covers hook/curl zone.
3. Strong-side corner (corner on the two-receiver side) plays the flat.
4. Weak-side corner (corner on the one-receiver side) lines up in the flat zone and sprints to the deep, outside one third of the field on that side.
5. Both safeties line up in halves and rotate toward the offense's strong side and play thirds. Therefore, in the above illustration, the right corner plays the right outside one-third; the right safety plays the middle one-third; and the left safety plays the left outside one-third.

Strengths and weaknesses

1. Excellent against the deep throw.
2. Puts maximum pressure on the quarterback.
3. Weak-side flat is uncovered.

Strategy. Have safeties and corners line up in Cover I prior to the snap and move to the new coverage on the snap of the ball. This will prevent the opponents from identifying an uncovered area. It may also lure the quarterback into throwing deep.

Three safeties, two corners, one linebacker, one rusher (figure 37-15)

Player responsibilities

1. Strong-side rusher pursues quarterback.
2. Weak-side rusher lines up to rush and drops into the corner position on the snap of the ball and plays the flat.
3. Linebacker covers hook/curl zone.
4. Corners and safeties rotate toward the offensive strong side and play thirds, as in zone 3A (figure 37-14).

Strengths and weaknesses

1. Only one rusher allows the quarterback additional throwing time.
2. Excellent against the deep pass.
3. Does not give up the weak-side flat, as does zone 3A.

Strategies. As in zone 3A, line up in zone 1 and switch on the snap of the ball.

OFFENSE

Even though speed is an asset for an offensive team, it is not as important as for the defense. A team can have a very productive offense with receivers who run good routes and are excellent possession receivers.

There are two major factors for an effective offense:

1. A good quarterback is the most important individual in the offense.
2. Everyone on the offensive unit should have decent quickness and must be able to catch the ball.

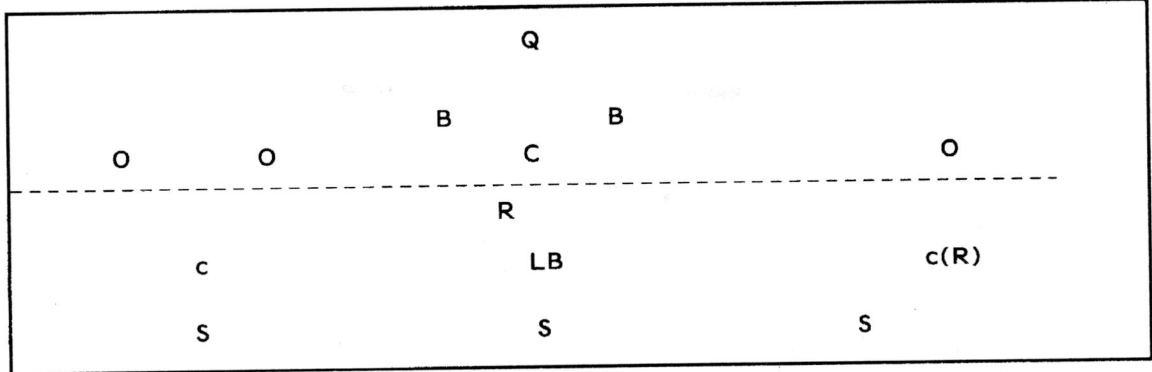

Figure 37-15. Three safeties, two corners, one linebacker, one rusher (zone no. 3B). (B: blocker; C: center; c: corner; LB: linebacker; O: receiver; Q: quarterback; R: rusher; S: safety).

Offensive Considerations

1. Types of offense:
   a. Drop back: Quarterback stays in the pocket to throw.
      (1) Quarterback needs a strong arm.
      (2) Must be excellent blockers for maximum protection.
      (3) Receivers must be fast to allow the deep pass.
   b. Sprint out: Quarterback rolls to one side of the field to throw.
      (1) Quarterback must be mobile and have decent throwing ability.
      (2) Do not need strong blockers.
   c. Option: Quarterback sprints out to one side of the field and throws or pitches to the option back. Option back may run or throw.
      (1) Must have a quarterback with excellent mobility, and would be very effective if he or she can throw on the run.
      (2) Option back needs good speed, lateral movement, and throwing ability.
      (3) Need quick blockers to slow the rush.
   d. One- or no-blocker set.
      (1) Quarterback must be quick and have a strong arm.
      (2) Receivers need to run hard, quick routes and move with the quarterback if he or she scrambles.
2. Personnel: Dictates what style of offense will be utilized. This is especially true with the quarterback.
   a. Quarterback:
      (1) If the quarterback is not very mobile but has a good arm, he or she should stay in the pocket formed by the blockers to throw.
      (2) If the quarterback is very mobile but does not have a strong arm, an option or sprint-out attack may be preferred.
      (3) If the quarterback has both mobility and throwing ability, the offense may utilize any attack.
   b. Receivers:
      (1) If they are not very fast, the offense must rely on short, quick passes and attempt to have a ball-control type offense.
      (2) If they have excellent speed, they can be used in all offenses.
   c. Blockers:
      (1) If they are slow, they would be better suited for the straight drop-back pass.
      (2) If they are quick, they can work in any offense, but would be excellent for the option and sprint-out style.

Offensive Formations

The following formations are composed of seven-person teams. If additional players are used, they may be lined up as receivers or blockers depending on the style of offense and the defense played against.

Option sets (figure 37-16)

Strengths and weaknesses

1. This is a good ball-control offense.
2. There are fewer chances for interceptions.
3. Forces the defense to commit to cover the run, which opens up passing lanes.
4. It is excellent for running out the clock.
5. It is difficult to catch up when down by several points.
6. Limits the amount of field the offense can attack. Because the quarterback is running in one direction, it makes it very difficult to throw back to the other side of the field. This enables the defense to give up an area and use that player to help stop the run.

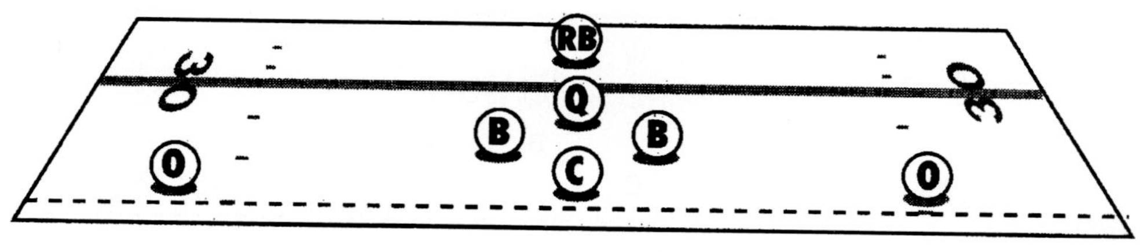

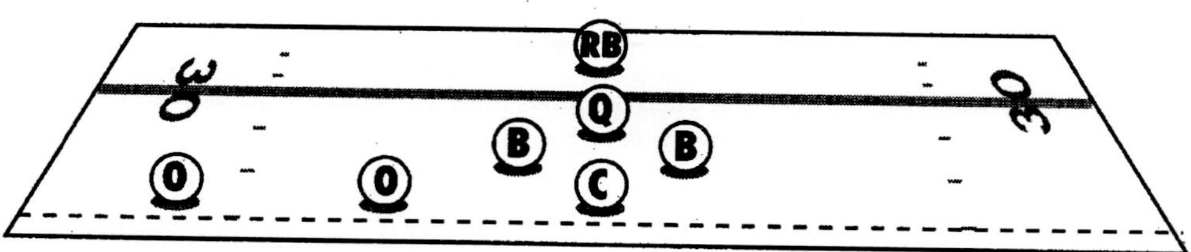

Figure 37-16. I. Option sets. (B: blocker; C: center; O: receiver; Q: quarterback; RB: running back).

Strategies

1. Do not always line up the running back in the backfield, but have him or her line up as a receiver and go in motion to start the option.
2. Do not always run the option. Mix the running plays with some passing plays to keep the defense from stacking up to stop the run.

Note: Sprint-out and drop-back formations may use motion with receivers and/or an option for formation.

Sprint-out and drop-back pass formations (figure 37-17)

Strengths and weaknesses

1. Provides more opportunities for interceptions.
2. May not provide as much ball control unless many short passes are thrown.
3. It is easier to catch up from a large deficit.

Strategies

1. Alternate formations to confuse the defense.
2. Alternate the side receivers line up on, to confuse the defense by showing it something different almost every play.
3. Use motion to identify player-to-player coverage and to flood a zone.

One- or no-blocker formations (figure 37-18)

Strengths and weaknesses

1. Allows maximum number of receivers into the pass pattern, which puts a tremendous strain on the coverage.
2. Excellent against player-to-player defense because so many receivers are releasing and many receivers are lined up on the same side.
3. Excellent for short-yardage passes.
4. Hard to make a long pass unless the quarterback can avoid the rush.
5. If the defense is in player-to-player coverage and the quarterback avoids the rush, there is no player left to guard the quarterback and the run becomes a viable option.

General Offensive Strategies

1. Take what the defense gives you.
   a. Player-to-player defense.
      (1) Have many crossing patterns.
      (2) Put many receivers on the same side. This makes it very hard to cover if the receivers cross.
      (3) Find the weakest defender and let the receiver he or she is covering line up alone to allow more room to get open.
      (4) Use the one- or no-blocker offense.
      (5) Clear out an area with the receivers, release a blocker there, and throw to him or her.
      (6) Quarterback should run if the rush can be avoided.
   b. Two-deep zone with two corners, one linebacker, and one rusher.
      (1) Flood zones with several receivers.
      (2) Throw passes between the seams of the zones.
      (3) Quick-outs and quick-ins with the wide receivers are difficult to stop if done correctly.
      (4) If the quarterback has time, flood the deep areas with receivers because each safety has to cover half the field.
   c. Two-deep zone with one rusher, two corners, and two linebackers.

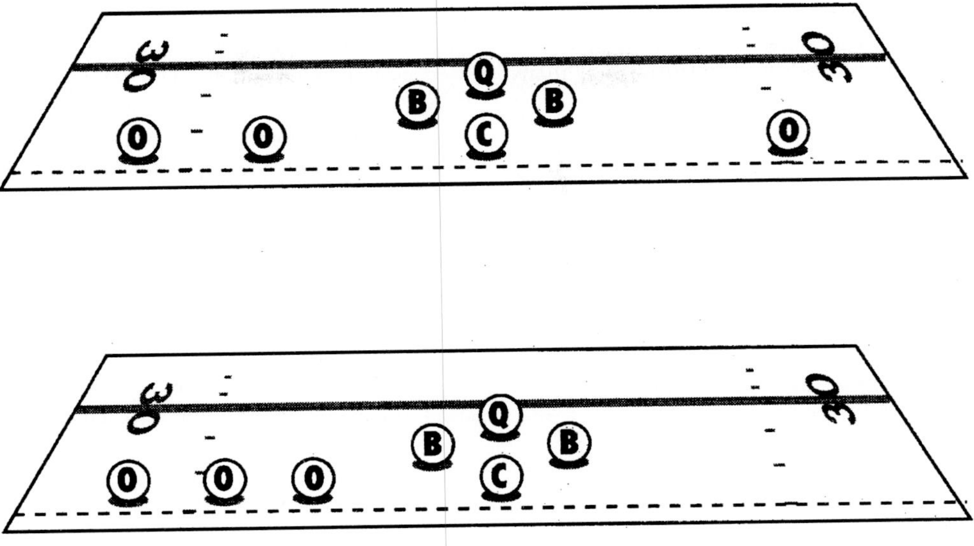

Figure 37-17. II. Sprint-out and drop-back pass formations. (B: blocker; C: center; O: receiver; Q: quarterback).

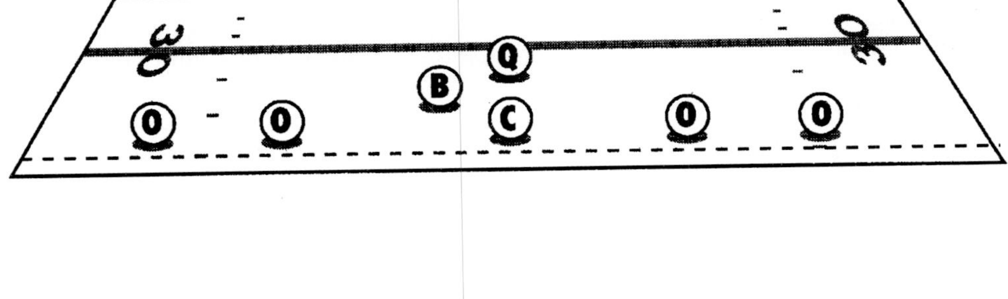

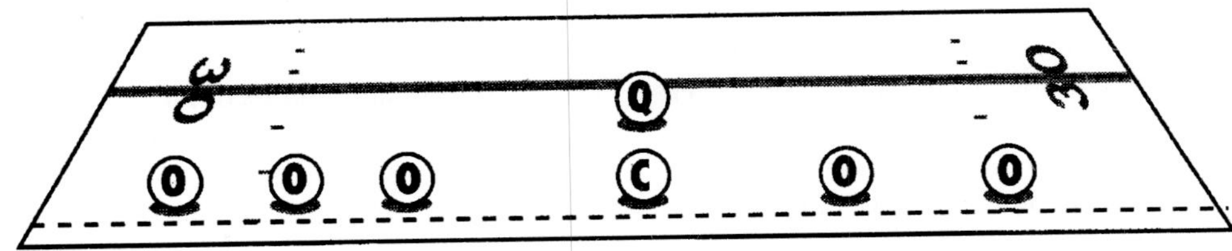

Figure 37-18. III. One- or no-blocker formations. (B: blocker; C: center; O: receiver; Q: quarterback).

(1) Short patterns are going to be very difficult to defend.
(2) Any medium-distance pattern that is between the linebackers is good.
(3) Flood the deep safeties.

d. Three-deep zone with two corners, one linebacker, and one rusher.
(1) Throwing deep will be difficult, so concentrate on short patterns.
(2) Flood the short patterns with several receivers.
(3) Because there is only one rusher in this formation, the quarterback should have more time to throw and may run if the rush can be avoided.

2. Give the defense a different look as often as possible.
3. Build plays on one another—in other words, set the defense up. Throw to one area with a pattern of two or more receivers. On the next play, run the same pattern but throw to a different receiver.

4. All receivers must run their routes as if they were the primary receiver.
5. The quarterback should attempt to throw to as many receivers, including the lineman, as possible. This keeps the defense from keying on any one player.

SAFETY PRECAUTIONS

1. Inspect all equipment to ensure safety and minimize injuries.
2. Provide competent officials.
3. Inspect the field and clear it of all obstacles that might cause injuries.
4. Give immediate medical attention to injured players.

TEACHING CONSIDERATIONS

1. Use a modified ball (smaller, lighter) for young learners and women. Consider using a foam or plastic ball to establish skills.
2. In most school programs, contact blocking or tackling of any sort should not be permitted for safety reasons. Flag football is an acceptable substitute.
3. Passing and receiving skills should be taught first. Partner work can be used, first with stationary receivers at short distances and then with moving receivers at longer distances.
4. Two-on-one play can begin a player's introduction to defense. Encourage players to break up passing plays by staying with the receiver between the goal and receiver.
5. All players should practice kicking skills. This can be done in partners, with one partner kicking and the other receiving the ball.
6. When passing, kicking, and receiving skills have become somewhat consistent, modified games can be played, beginning with two-on-two and moving toward more players on each side. Having six players is adequate for the game and encourages more participation. Teach a few basic offensive and defensive plays and then encourage students to design their own plays.
7. Increase the size of the playing field as the number of players increases. Add centering and specific positioning as students begin to understand, through their play, the need for differentiated positioning. Keep rules at a minimum. Enforce no-contact rules consistently.

RULE MODIFICATIONS

The following sample rule and/or game modifications are used to increase time on task and participation and improve the chances for learning and success.

1. Favor more teams with smaller numbers of students per team. The field sizes might have to be modified, but smaller numbers of students increases the number of opportunities for each player to touch the ball and be a more active participant.
2. Use smaller balls. The smaller balls will be more developmentally appropriate for students with smaller hands and weaker students.
3. Use nontraditional balls (e.g., Nerf, softcover balls, balls of various shapes that are easier to catch) to improve motivation and increase success.
4. If field goals are used, construct goals that are larger than normal to increase success.
5. If more adept players tend to "hog" the ball, change the rules to promote cooperation of typically weaker or excluded students. For example, though it is erroneous thinking, girls are typically avoided because they are thought to be not very good. The following coed rules could be applied to increase participation by the girls:
   a. Any boy-to-boy touchdown equals 6 points. Any boy-to-girl or girl-to-boy touchdown equals 9 points.
   b. After a successful boy-to-boy play (completed pass), the next play is deemed "closed" and must include a girl. This could entail a girl throwing to a boy, a girl throwing to a girl, or a boy throwing to a girl. This play must be successful, in that at least one yard is gained. If the play is unsuccessful, the next play is also deemed "closed."
   c. Award extra points at the end of the game (6 or instructor's choice) if all players on a team attempted to throw a pass or made an attempt to catch a pass. If all team members were part of a completed pass (either the thrower or receiver) the team is awarded double the extra points for attempts (12 or teachers choice).
6. The actual game could be structured like a scrimmage. For example, for two teams of 8 players:
   a. Each team has 8 consecutive offensive plays.
      (1) Normal zone-line-to-gain rules apply. If the team makes a first down, they continue to score.
      (2) If a first down is not made after the first four plays, the team returns to the original zone line and continues until all 8 plays have been attempted.
      (3) If a score is made on the first play, the team returns to the original zone line and continues until all 8 plays have been attempted.
   b. Each player has a chance to be the quarterback. The participants can determine the order, but after the first quarterback calls and executes a play, another player gets a chance to do the same. This way of playing the game effectively moves the ball around. For example, students who typically do not get the ball thrown to them

typically choose another avoided player to throw a pass to.

c. During the offense's 8 plays, the defense also rotates positions; therefore everyone is afforded the chance to play each position and its players are not relegated to positions they do not want to play.

d. Once the offense has completed 8 plays, the ball is turned over to the defense.

7. Invoke a "secret play" rule into your game. For example, each team is allowed one secret play per half. Rules:

   a. At any given time the quarterback may elect to punt the ball instead of throwing a pass.

   b. Wherever the ball lands is where the opposing team must start their next offensive series.

   c. If the ball goes into the end zone or beyond, the opposing teams starts on the first zone line.

   d. However, to award the defense for being alert and thinking, if they catch the punt, the offense is charged with an incomplete pass, must proceed with the next down, and lose their secret play for this half.

GLOSSARY

backfield The players behind the line, who usually handle the ball.

backward pass A pass that travels toward the goal line a team is defending; may be made by any player.

balanced line Same number of players on each side of the center.

block Using the shoulder, but not the arms, to intercept a defensive player or to stop a defensive player from touching the ball carrier.

bootleg play Faking a handoff or a pass to another player, then running with the ball shielded with the body from the defensive team's view.

button hook A pass route in which the receiver turns and runs back to catch the ball.

centering The act by the center of putting the ball in play from the ground by handing or passing the ball between the legs to a backfield player.

clipping Landing on the back of the leg(s) of a player not carrying the ball.

cross-back An offensive play in which two backs cross, one of them taking a handoff from the quarterback.

cut back To change direction; usually done by the receiver or ball carrier.

disqualifying foul Unnecessary roughness, for which a player is removed from the game.

double wingback An offensive formation: two backs are placed about 1 yard (0.9 m) outside of their ends, one back is placed either to the right or left behind a guard, and the tailback is about 5 yards (4.5 m) behind the center.

down A unit of the game that starts with the entering of the ball and ends when the ball is declared dead.

end zone The 10-yard (9 m) area between the goal line and end-line.

fair catch A catch designated by the player receiving a kicked ball by raising the hand.

flag guarding Using the hands, arms, or clothing or spinning more than once to prevent another player from pulling the flag. Penalty: 15 yards (13.7 m) and loss of down.

flanker An offensive player lining up closer to the sideline than the team.

handoff A play in which one back hands the ball to another back.

lateral pass Passing the ball backward or sideways.

line of scrimmage An imaginary line marking the position of the ball at the start of each play.

offsides Advancement of a player beyond the line of scrimmage before the ball is snapped.

safety A score made when a free ball, or one possessed by a player defending his or her own goal, becomes dead behind the goal, provided the impetus that caused the ball to cross the goal was supplied by the defending team.

shotgun offense A formation, used primarily for passing, in which the quarterback lines up 5 to 6 yards (4.5 to 5.5 m) behind the center.

SUGGESTED READING

Flagball for the nineties. 1990. Reston, Va: American Alliance for Health, Physical Education, Recreation and Dance.

Renner, B. 1998 *Kicking the football*. Champaign, Ill.: Human Kinetics.

The United States Flag and Touch Football League. Current ed. *The United States flag and touch football rules*. Mentor, Ohio: USFT Football League.

RESOURCES

Videos

NIRSA: Flag and touch football rules and *First and twenty* are both available from NIRSA, 850 SW 15th St., Corvallis, OR 97333.

Soccer-style placekicking: techniques and fundamentals and *All-pro punting techniques* are both available from Cambridge Physical Education and Health, P.O. Box 2153, Charleston, WV 25328.

Web sites

United States Flag Football League www.c-sports.com/usftl/

National Touch Football League www.ntfl.com/

Track and Field

After completing this chapter, the reader should be able to:

- Become familiar with the events included in a track and field competition and the equipment and facilities required
- Understand the various skills involved in the running, jumping, vaulting, and throwing events
- Be aware of the rules governing competition in these events
- Teach basic skills in these events to a group of students

HISTORY

Track and field events originated almost with the beginning of humanity. To survive, humans had to be gymnasts, sprinters, hunters, and warriors. Survival depended on the ability to outperform the challenger, human or animal. When not being pursued or in search of sustenance, early humans kept physically fit by engaging in running, jumping, or throwing activities with families or other groups.

Games involving the fundamentals of track and field were formulated by the Greeks during their Golden (Homeric) Age. The most famous of these games were the Olympics, which began in 776 B.C. and were held every 5 and then 4 years until A.D. 392, when they were abolished by the Romans. In 1894 they were reorganized by Pierre de Frédy, Baron de Coubertin, and since then they have been conducted in different countries as an international festival.

The U.S. men's Olympic track and field teams have done well since the first modern-era Olympic games, held in Athens in 1896. They have been one of the dominant teams, with strong competition coming from the Soviet Union, Great Britain, East Germany, and West Germany. The breakup of the Soviet Union and other Eastern European countries has weakened these teams. The U.S. women's Olympic track and field teams have also fared well since their first competition in the 1928 games, where they won 1 gold, 2 silver, and 1 bronze. The Soviet Union and German women's teams dominated the competition through 1976. In 1980 the women's team began to improve, and in 1984 it became a world contender with 16 medals. In the 1992 Olympics at Barcelona the U.S. track and field team won 30 medals, 20 by the men and 10 by the women. This total included 12 of the possible 43 gold, 8 silver, and 10 bronze medals. The U.S. team won both of the men's relay events, and the women took a gold and silver in their two relays. Nineteen of the 30 medals were in track events (11 men and 8 women). Carl Lewis, Mike Powell, and Joe Greene swept the men's long jump while Jackie Joyner-Kersee was the only double medal winner in individual events (bronze in the women's long jump and gold in the heptathlon).

The U.S. track teams continued their dominance in the 1996 Olympic games in Atlanta, winning 13 gold, 5 silver, and 5 bronze for a total of 23 medals. The men won 16 and the women won 7 medals. Russia was second with 10 total medals, and Germany finished third with 7 total medals. The U.S. total of 23 medals was down from the 30 medals won in the 1992 games, but the 1996 games had the largest participation in history. Over 100 countries competed, with 45 countries winning medals. The memorable moments of the 1996 games were Carl Lewis and Jackie Joyner-Kersee's long jump performances, Canada's Donovan Bailey's 100-meter victory, France's Marie-José Pérec's 200-400 double victory, and Michael Johnson's remarkable double in the 200-400 with a 200 world record of 19.32, (0.50 seconds) under the old world record.

Research continues to have an impact on improving performances with the application of scientific principles. Improvements in training techniques, nutrition, and psychological preparation are helping athletes achieve their goals of faster sprint and endurance times, longer distances in the horizontal jumps and throws, and higher heights in the vertical jumps. Humans have not yet reached their limits. Records will continue to fall in the future.

EVENTS

Track and field events involve running, jumping, and throwing activities. The running activities make up the *track* events; the jumping and throwing events make up the *field* events. The track events are sprints, hurdles, relays, middle distances, and long distances. The field events are the long jump, triple jump, high jump, pole vault, shot put, discus, javelin, and hammer throw. Below is an example of an outdoor high school competition and order of events.

Track Meet

A track meet consists of contests in a presented number of races of different length, called track events, and of contests in jumping and/or throwing called field events. Competition is by individuals except in the relays, which involve competition of teams consisting of four individuals.

One-Session Meets Order of Events

When no preliminary flights or heats are required.

Boys

4 × 800 (3200 m) relay	400 m dash
110 m high hurdles	300 m intermediate hurdles
100 m dash	800 m run
4 × 200 (800 m) relay	200 m dash
1600 m run	3200 m run
4 × 100 (400 m) relay	4 × 400 (1600 m) relay

Girls

4 × 800 (3200 m) relay	400 m dash
100 m high (33″) hurdles	300 m low hurdles
100 m dash	800 m run
4 × 200 (800 m) relay	200 m dash
1600 m run	3200 m run
4 × 100 (400 m) relay	4 × 400 (1600 m) relay

Field Events

Should begin at least 30 minutes before first track event

Boys	Girls
Long jump	Long jump
High jump	High jump
Shot put	Shot put
Javelin	Javelin
Pole vault	Pole vault

Immediately following the long jump and shot put

Triple jump	Triple jump
Discus	Discus

Running Events

Sprints

Outdoor sprints include 100-, 200-, and 400-meter dashes. Indoor sprints vary with the facility and range from 50 to 400 meters. These events are 80 to 100 percent anaerobic in nature (maximum intensity).

Middle distances

Outdoors or indoors, any race between 600 and 1,000 meters is considered middle distance. These distances require approximately 50 percent aerobic and 50 percent anaerobic power (speed and endurance). The most common races are 800 meters (half mile) and 1,500 meters (1 mile equivalent).

Long distances

The long-distance running events in both indoor and outdoor competition are the 3,000 meters (just short of 2 miles) and the 5,000 meters (3.1 miles). Additional events run outdoors are the 10,000 meters (6.2 miles), the 3,000-meter steeplechase, and the marathon (26 miles, 385 yards). Racing walking is included in some competitions, with common distances of 10k to 20k.

Hurdles

A confusing array of races are run over varying hurdle heights and race distances. The heights of hurdles, the distance between them, and the total distance run, vary among men, women, youth, master, and senior athletes. The outdoor hurdle sprint race for the men is the 110-meter high hurdles. They are 42 inches high (1.07 m) and 39 inches high (1.01 m) for high school boys. The hurdle sprint endurance race is the 400-meter hurdles, also called the intermediate hurdles. The hurdles are 36 inches high (0.91 m). The high school boys run 300-meter hurdles which are 36 inches high (0.91 m). The women run the 100-meter short sprint distance with hurdle heights of 33 inches (0.84 m) for open and collegiate women and for high school girls. The women's sprint endurance hurdle race is 400 meters for open and collegiate women with hurdles 30 inches high (0.76 m) and 300 meters for high school girls (30 inches high also). The indoor races vary between 50 to 55 and 60 meters or yards for both men and women. The indoor hurdle heights are 42 inches for open and collegiate men, 39 inches for the high school boys, and 33 inches for open, collegiate, and high school girls (figure 38-1).

Figure 38-1. Hurdle.

Relays

Relay teams consist of four members (except in the shuttle hurdle relays). Each runner carries a baton a specific distance, passing it to the next runner within a marked zone until the last runner carries it across the finish line. The relays include 4 × 100 meters, 4 × 200 meters, 4 × 400 meters (mile relay), 4 × 800 meters (2-mile relay), and 4 × 1500 or 1600 meters (4-mile relay). The sprint medley relays consist of two types: (1) 100, 100, 200, and 400 meters; and (2) 200, 200, 400, and 800 meters. The women run both sprint medleys and the men run only the 200, 200, 400, 800. The distance medley consists of 400, 800, 1200, and 1600 meters. Both the men and women run this race.

Steeplechase

The steeple is a 3,000-meter event for men and women. This is a relatively new event for the women (1996). It includes 28 hurdle jumps and 7 water jumps. The hurdles and the water jump barrier are 3 feet high (0.917 m), 13 feet wide (3.96 m), and the top bar should be 5 inches square (12.7 cm). The water jump is 12 feet square (3.66 m) with a regular downward slope resulting in a depth of 2.29 feet (0.70 m). The water jump pit is filled with water to track level and has a 3-foot barrier in front of it. The competitor must go over the barrier and over or through the water. They may jump, vault, or place a foot on each hurdle or water barrier (figure 38-2).

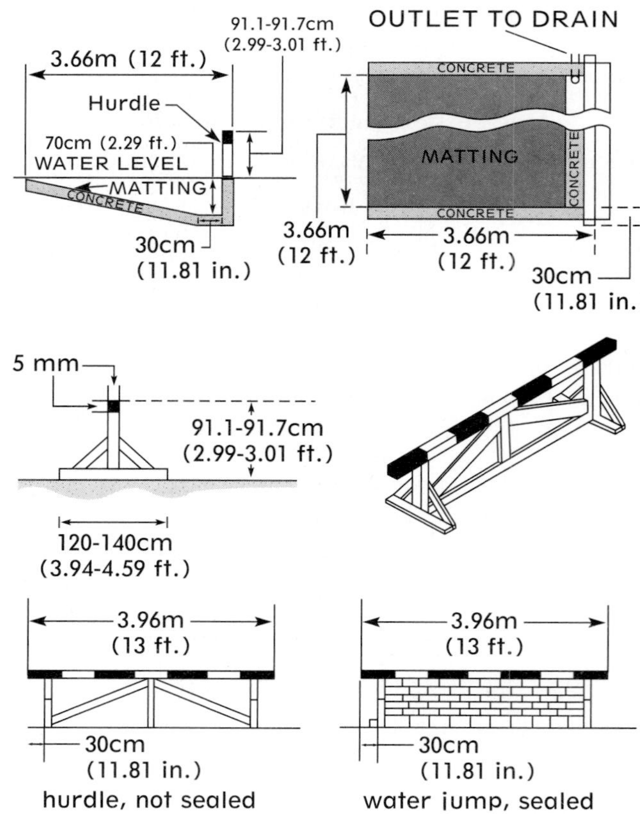

Figure 38-2. Water jump and hurdle measurements.

Jumping Events

Long jump and triple jump

The runway generally varies from 120 to 160 feet (36.6 to 48.8 m) for men and 90 to 140 feet (27.4 to 42.7 m) for women. The takeoff should be from a board made of wood or other suitable rigid material 7.8 to 8 inches wide (19.8 to 20.32 cm) and at least 4 feet long (1.22 m) and not more than 3.94 in. thick (10 cm). The landing area must not be less than 9 feet in width (2.74 m) and identical in elevation with the takeoff board. The area shall be filled with sand. The styles of long jump used are the sail, hitch kick, and hang (figure 38-3). The triple jump has three phases, previously known as the "hop, step, and jump." The jumper must make the first jump (sometimes called the hop) by landing on the takeoff foot, the second jump (sometimes called the step) by landing on the nontakeoff foot, and the third jump into the landing pit.

Figure 38-3. Long jump.

High jump

The two primary styles of jumping are the straddle and the "Fosbury Flop" (figure 38-4), named after Dick Fosbury, who used a back layout technique with a curved approach. This back layout style dramatically increased high-jump performances by allowing the athlete to use more speed in the approach and provided for a very efficient bar clearance.

Figure 38-4. The flop.

Pole vault

The modern pole vaulter must have exceptional speed and strength and the agility of a gymnast. The combination of speed, strength, and coordination makes this a spectacular event. The introduction of the fiberglass pole has revolutionized this event. Tremendous increases in performances have resulted since its introduction. Records have moved from 16 feet to over 20 feet (4.9 to over 6.1 m). The runways vary from 125 to 140 feet (38.1 to 42.7 m) in length. The poles have increased in length from 14 feet to over 16 feet.

Throwing Events

Shot put

The 16-pound (7.26 kg) shot is used for college, U.S.A. Track and Field (USATF), and Olympic men's competition. High school boys use a 12-pound (5.45 kg) shot. College, USATF, Olympic women, and high school girls use an 8 pound 13 ounce (4 kg) shot. The shots are made of a cast-iron, bronze, or brass shell with a lead center. The indoor shot has a plastic or rubber shell. The shot is thrown from a circle 7 feet (2.13 m) in diameter with a stop board in front.

Discus

The discus is usually made of wood with a metal rim. Some are made of rubber, but these are not legal outside of high school competition. Collegiate and open men's discus must have a minimum weight of 4 pounds 6.55 ounces (2 kg) with a diameter of 8.67 inches (219–221 mm). The high school boy's discus weight is 3 pounds 9 ounces (1.62 kg) with a diameter of 8.2 inches (209–211 mm). For high school, college, and open women, the discus must weight no less than 2 pounds 3.25 ounces (1 kg) with a diameter of 7.1 inches (180–182 mm). All divisions throw the discus from a circle 8 feet 2.5 inches (2.5 m) in diameter.

Hammer

The hammer consists of a round weight attached to a triangular handle by a wire. The men's collegiate and open hammer weighs 16 pounds (7.27 kg). The high schools boy's hammer weighs 12 pounds (5.45 kg). High school girls, open, and collegiate women all throw the 8 pound 13 oz. (4 kg) hammer. The hammer may not exceed 48 inches (1.22 m) in length for the men and high school boys and 47 inches (1.195 m) for women and high school girls. The hammer is thrown from a circle 7 feet (2.13 m) in diameter. The indoor equivalent of the hammer is the 56 lb (25.4 kg) weight, the 35 lb (15.88 kg) weight, the 25 lb (11.34 kg) weight, the 20 lb (9.08 kg) weight, the 16 lb (7.26 kg) weight, or the 12 lb (5.45 kg) weight. These weights are thrown with a shorter handle than the hammer and the weight used depends upon the level of the competition. The women and high school athletes throw the lighter weights.

Javelin

The javelin consists of three parts: head, shaft, and cord grip. The shaft must be constructed of metal and should have fixed to it a metal head terminating in a sharp point. The grip should be about the center of mass and shall not exceed the diameter of the shaft by more than 0.3 inches (8 mm) with uniform thickness. The length of the men's and boys' javelin is 8.7 feet (2.7 m). The weight must not be more than 1 pound 12 ounces (800 g) with a cord grip of 6 inches (16 cm). The women's and girls' javelin is 7 feet 4 inches (2.3 m) long with a minimum weight of 1 pound 9 ounces (600 g) and a cord grip of 5.7 inches (15 cm).

Other Track and Field Events

Some Olympic events are not always standard in U.S. competitions (e.g., 20 kilometer walk).

Race walking

Race walking is advancing through a progression of steps so taken that unbroken contact with the ground is maintained. The advancing leg must be straightened (i.e., not bent at the knee) from the moment of first contact with the ground until the leg is in the vertical upright position. Failure to adhere to this rule can lead to a warning and then to disqualification. The race walk is generally conducted over a distance of 3 to 10 kilometers (1.86 to 6.2 miles) on the track and 10 to 50 kilometers (6.2 to 31 miles) on the road.

Decathlon and heptathlon

The tests of all-around skill and ability are the decathlon for men and the heptathlon for women. The participants in these events are often considered the "world's best athletes."

The decathlon consists of 10 events that are run over 2 days in the following order: first day: 100-meter dash, long jump, shot put, high jump, and 400-meter dash; second day: 100-meter hurdles, discus, pole vault, javelin, and 1500-meter run. The heptathlon consists of seven events that are scheduled over 2 days in the following order: first day: 100-meter hurdles, high jump, shot put, and 200-meter dash; second day: long jump, javelin, and 800-meter run.

FACILITIES

Building a track-and-field facility can be a very difficult task. Many complicated factors must be considered in the planning and construction phases. Some of the considerations include the unique needs of each track program, site selection and analysis, choice of surface, amenities and accessories, markings and specifications, and hiring a qualified contractor and consultant.

Specifications

A track site will require an area of approximately 5 acres (600 feet long, and 300 feet wide). Additional area will be needed for grading, curbs, draining, grandstands, bleachers, lighting, fences, walkways, and so on. A 400-meter oval track is the standard size for all levels of competition. Some tracks are built around a football or soccer field; this provides for multipurpose usage. Some high school tracks don't have curbs. Curbs are required for NCAA, national and international competition. Most tracks have 6 to 8 lanes (36–42 inches wide), and some affluent programs have the more expensive 9- to 10-lane tracks. The two most common shapes for tracks are (1) an oval equal-quadrant track with two 100-meter straightaways and two 100-meter curves, and (2) a nonequal oval quadrant track where the straightaways are larger or smaller than the curves. The oval is slightly stretched or slightly compressed in these tracks (figure 38-5).

Choice of Surfaces

There are many types of surfaces to choose from. Financial resources, type of usage, geographical location, maintenance capability, durability, and performance characteristics all influence the special needs and circumstances.

Types of Surfaces

1. Natural material track systems (cinder and clay): These tracks are relatively inexpensive to construct, but they have two major disadvantages: They have constant and costly maintenance, and rain usually causes soggy conditions, cancellations, or postponements.
2. All-weather (rubber-asphalt emulsion): A combination of rubber with asphalt emulsion and sand. These were popular in the 1960s. These tracks were durable and unaffected by ordinary weather. However, summer heat softens the surface, and winter cold hardens the surface. It also becomes harder as it ages. These disadvantages no longer make this surface cost-effective.
3. Rubber-latex/polyurethane: Most tracks today are constructed with rubber particles bound with latex or polyurethane. These surfaces are installed on top of asphalt, concrete, or some other existing surfaces. The depth of these surfaces is ⅜ to ½ inches. The rubber used may be black or colored. Natural rubber, styrene-butadiene rubber (SBR), and ethlene-propylene-diene rubber (EPDM) are the standard choices. The rubber may be virgin or recycled. Virgin rubber is more expensive than recycled rubber, and colored rubber is more expensive than black rubber.

Consultants and Contractors

It is highly recommended to hire experienced consultants (i.e., architect, landscape engineer, contractors) who are trained and specialize in building tracks. Colleagues who have recently completed a project should be contacted

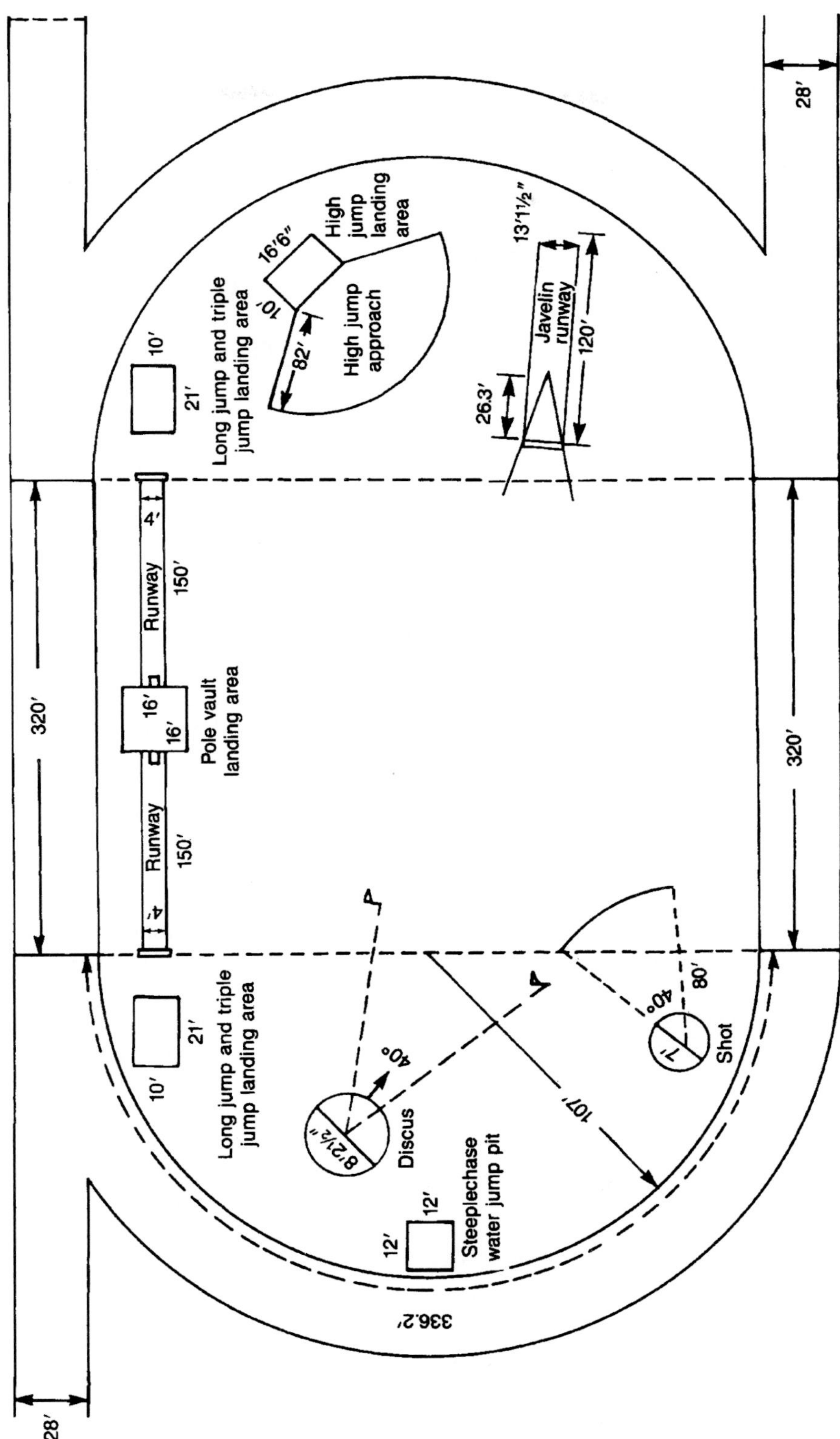

Figure 38-5. Track and field facility.

to check a contractor's references, business, and work performance.

SHOES

With the advent of new training and racing surfaces in the past few years, many types of shoes have been introduced. There now seems to be a specific shoe for every event in the sport of track and field. Most shoes have interchangeable spike plates and are built for protection and comfort as well as style and fit. The type of shoe worn can make a great difference in terms of traction on a racing surface and therefore can represent the winning edge.

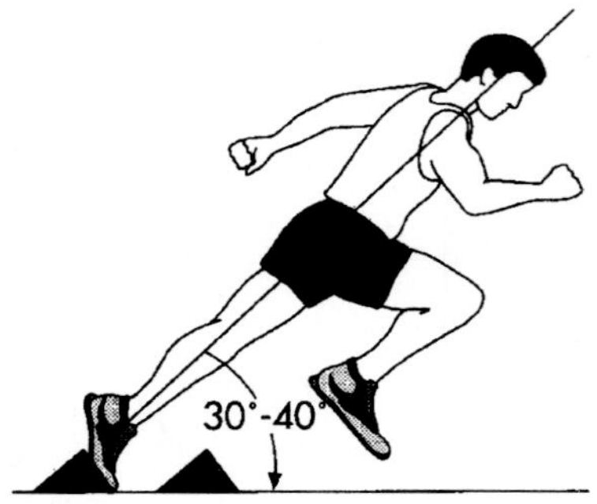

Figure 38-6. A well-balanced starting position for maximum acceleration.

BASIC TECHNIQUES

Sprinting

The basic components of sprinting are:

1. Start: incorporates reaction time, block clearance time, and velocity out of the blocks
2. Accelerations: the ability to reach maximum velocity in the shortest time
3. Velocity maintenance: the length of time or distance the maximum velocity can be maintained
4. Mental and psychological aspects: relaxation, coordination, rhythm, concentration, and self-confidence

Sprint start

Starting blocks are essential to the sprinter. They provide a solid base from which to push off and prevent slipping or injury to the runner. Adjustable blocks that can be used either indoors or outdoors are the most effective.

1. Reaction times can have a positive effect on sprint times by providing a winning margin measured in hundredths of a second. However, this is only 1 percent or less of the racing distance. The most important factor is that the runner leaves the blocks with the greatest possible velocity in a balanced position that sets up a maximum acceleration pattern. There is a pronounced forward lean in this position, with force being applied against the blocks in a straight line drawn from the head through the shoulders, hips (center of mass), drive leg, and lead foot. The angle of this line should be between 30 to 40 degrees (figure 38-6). Size, strength, flexibility, and agility dictate this angle.
2. Selection of block spacings significantly affects block clearance time and velocity out of the blocks. Studies have shown that the bunch start (10 to 12 inches [25 to 30 cm] between the blocks) provides the fastest block clearance time, including reaction time, but produces the slowest velocity and momentum out of the blocks. Research by Franklin Henry on acceleration patterns indicates that velocity out of the blocks appears to be more important than block clearance time. The medium start (14 to 21 inches [35 to 53 cm] between blocks) provides the most efficient spacing for maximum velocity and block clearance time.

   These findings can be used as guidelines in selecting block spacing. However, they do not allow for individual differences of body type, size, and comfort. Research on angles of flexion in related body joints of the knee, hips, ankles, and the like suggest optimal starting positions based on these angles. To find the optimal starting position for each athlete, the following procedure should be used:
   a. Place the athlete in the set position and establish an angle of 90 degrees in the knee joint of the front leg. The greatest amount of force can be exerted in the shortest amount of time in this position. The front leg should be the athlete's stronger leg, but he or she should use whichever is more comfortable.
   b. Establish an angle of approximately 120 to 135 degrees in the rear knee. This facilitates a fast, forceful drive of the rear leg. Pulling the rear leg off the rear block results in a loss of power. The rear leg should push forcefully against the rear block for maximum force.
   c. Elevate the hips and establish a forward lean to provide a forward horizontal component. The hips should be slightly above the shoulders, and the forward lean should not place too much pressure on the hands.
   d. The starting blocks are placed under the runner while maintaining these angles. The block spacings are established at this point. Application of the medium-start principles supplements these spacings, and adjustments are made to fine-tune the start (figure 38-7).
3. Starting fundamentals:
   a. "On your mark": The runner moves in front of the blocks and backs into position, carefully placing

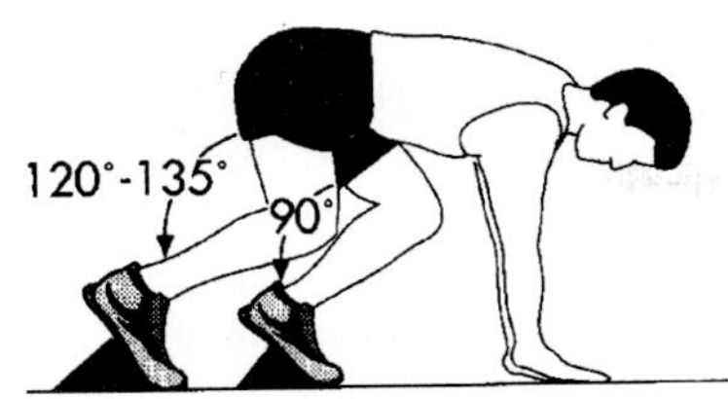

Figure 38-7. Recommended leg angles and block spacings while in the set position.

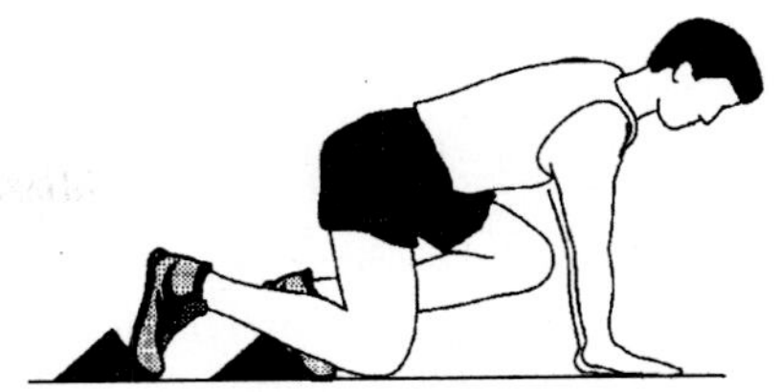

Figure 38-8. "On your mark" position.

the feet in the blocks one at a time. The feet should be straight, with the toes in contact with the surface of the track. The hands are placed directly under the shoulders, with the fingers and thumbs bridged just behind the starting line about shoulder width apart. The arms are fully extended, with the weight evenly distributed between the hands, rear knee, and foot. The front knee is relaxed, extending just inside the forearm. The head is in natural alignment with the trunk, and the eyes are focused just about a yard in front of the starting line (figure 38-8).

b. "Set": The runner raises the hips to the desired level and extends the knee joints to the appropriate angles. The shoulders move slightly forward in front of the hands to provide a horizontal component. In competition the runner should focus on a sensory response to the gun (figure 38-7).

c. "Go": The starting action is initiated by reacting immediately to the sound of the gun. Movement is initiated by picking up the hands and driving the lead arm forward and up, the other arm backward. Simultaneously, force is applied against both blocks as the legs extend against the blocks. The rear foot clears the blocks first as it is driven into the first stride. The shoulders gradually rise as the front leg fully extends. The body is now placed in the appropriate driving angles (30 to 45 degrees) to prepare the runner for maximum acceleration (figure 38-6).

4. Acceleration: Studies have shown that elite sprinters reach their maximum velocity between 60 and 70 meters (66 and 77 yards). Less talented sprinters may reach maximum velocity in 50 to 60 meters (55 to 66 yards). The main objective of sprinting is to accelerate over the longest possible distance in the shortest possible time. Clearing the blocks with maximum force in a balanced position sets up the acceleration pattern.

a. Speed is the product of stride length and stride frequency. The actual stride length is the distance between the touchdown of the toes for each stride. Top sprinters have an average stride length of 7 feet 2½ inches to 7 feet 9¾ inches (2.20 to 2.38 m). Stride length will vary because of individual muscle strength, leg length, flexibility, speed of running, and/or any injuries.

The foot strike should be less than 12 inches (30 cm) in front of the athlete's center of mass to prevent overstriding. The sprinter should develop a stride length that combines with stride frequency to produce the fastest time because increasing actual stride length results in decreased stride frequency.

The effective stride length is the distance the center of mass is projected with each stride. Increasing strength and flexibility in the relative muscle groups can increase the effective stride length by applying additional force to the ground. This increases stride length without decreasing stride frequency.

b. Stride frequency is the number of strides per second. For the best sprinters it is four-and-a-half to five strides per second for both sexes. Research seems to indicate that vary little improvement can be made in stride frequency, although improving strength, conditioning, technique, and relaxation can result in some gains. Improving stride frequency has a positive effect on maximum velocity, but this must be achieved without reducing effective stride lengths. This can be produced by an effective combination of stride length and stride frequency that meets the individual skills of each runner.

5. Maintenance of maximum velocity: After reaching maximum velocity (about 50 to 70 m [55 to 75 yards]), the runner can only maintain maximum velocity for a few strides (about 15 to 25 m [16 to 27 yards]) before fatigue causes a gradual deceleration. Deceleration can be minimized by relaxation, conditioning, and concentration on proper technique.

6. Basic running mechanics for sprinters: Running mechanics are influenced by the distance run and the speed required for each distance. Long- and middle-distance runners require running mechanics that place an emphasis on economy of motion, pace

judgment, and relaxation to conserve energy. Sprinting requires a more vigorous and explosive action that produces a greater stride length and stride frequency;.

a. Posture: The initial body position is a product of acceleration. During the start, the forward lean is greatly exaggerated to provide maximum horizontal forces through the center of mass. As the sprinter continues to accelerate, the body becomes more erect until maximum velocity is reached. Only a slight forward lean is required at this point to counter wind resistance. The forward lean comes from the ground up, not from the hips. The hips must stay tucked to prevent flexion at the waist and loss of driving force. A backward lean is a product of deceleration and should be avoided or controlled. Fatigue and a lack of strength cause the runner to gradually lean backward. The runner should focus on maintaining the forward lean throughout the race. This prevents the foot from striking too far in front of the body, causing additional deceleration.

b. Leg action
   (1) Takeoff (driving) phase: This phase is characterized by the supporting leg driving through the athlete's center of mass and pushing the body into a flying trajectory. The athlete should keep this flight angle small. The lower the flight angle, the less time spent in the air and the sooner the return to the ground. This increases strike frequency. During this phase the support leg should be maximally extended at the hip joint, but not completely extended at the knee. This incomplete knee extension reduces ground contact time and increases stride frequency and horizontal velocity (figure 38-9A).
   (2) Landing (ground contact) phase: The foot should be placed no more than 12 inches (30 cm) in front of the body at impact. The foot and lower leg should have a negative acceleration (moving backward) with a pawing action. This reduces the breaking force at impact. The sprinter lands on the outside ball

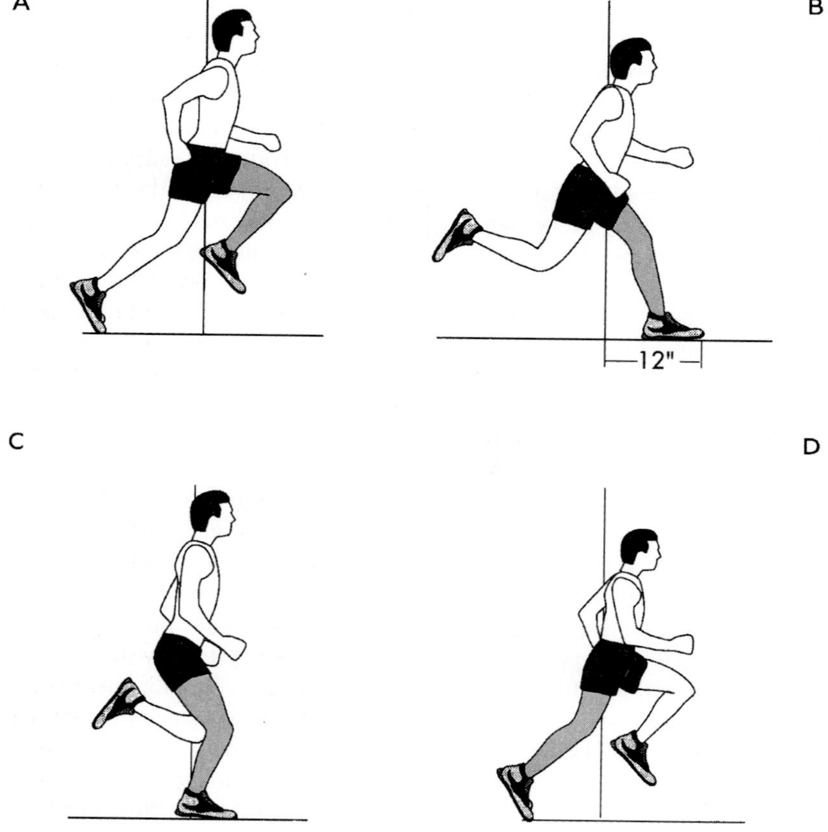

Figure 38-9. **A,** The takeoff or driving phase. **B,** The landing phase. **C,** The amortation phase. **D,** The recovery phase.

of the foot, rolls to the heel, rolls to the ball of the foot, and pushes off with the big toe (figure 38-9B).

(3) Amortation phase: This phase is responsible for absorbing the impact forces and resisting the gravitational force. The center of mass (hips) moves over the supporting leg and prepares for another takeoff phase. The breaking forces at the hip, knee, and ankle should be minimized to prevent a mushing out, which increases ground time and results in a loss of velocity. These joint angles should be kept as straight as possible. The free leg should be kept completely folded up, with the heel tight against the buttocks. This tight leg position shortens the lever and allows the thigh to rotate through faster (figure 38-9C).

(4) Recovery phase: This phase begins immediately after the amortation phase and ends with a new takeoff phase. The ankle should be flexed, and the foot should pass over the knee of the supporting leg as it moves forward. This high-thigh position increases the rotational speed of the thigh and increases the range of motion to apply force to the ground (figure 38-9D).

(5) Arm action: The arms are primarily used for absorbing twisting forces created by the thrust of the legs. They also balance the body and assist in maintaining stride rhythm. The elbow joint should remain at approximately 90 degrees to facilitate a fast rotation through the arm-swing cycle. The hands are driven to the shoulder or chin level on the *forward swing* to the midline of the body. The runner should focus on keeping the shoulders down and square and take care not to cross the midline.

The *backswing* is the most neglected technical aspect of the arm action, with many athletes producing incomplete backswings. This results in less driving force and reduced stride length. The hands should be driven past the hips, with the elbows driven to shoulder height while maintaining the 90-degree elbow flexion. This produces maximum driving force on the backswing. The hands should be relaxed and slightly cupped using a "bird-in-the-hand" concept (i.e., not too tight, not too loose). Some runners also extend their fingers, but this is an individual choice.

200 Meters

The 200-meter runner must be able to run the curve efficiently and then carry the speed for an additional 100 meters. The runner must run as close to the lane line as possible on the curve to cut down the distance run, without running on the lane line. Technically you can run less than 200 meters by doing this. Also, to maintain balance and fight the centrifugal force that tends to push the athlete outward, the athlete should look inside, lean inside, and drive the outside arm across the body to help maintain balance. 400-meter runners should practice this curve-running technique also (figure 38-10).

Training

In addition to developing explosive speed and power, the 200-meter runner must develop speed endurance. *Long-speed endurance* can be developed by running three to six 300- to 600-meter runs at 80 to 100 percent effort. Full recovery of 5 to 10 minutes should be used for quality runs. Shorter recoveries of 90 seconds to 2 or 3 minutes trains the lactate tolerance system. A high level of lactic acid is developed with these workouts. These are for your 200–400-type athletes and are very tough anaerobic workouts. *Short-speed endurance* can be developed by running three to six 150- to 300-meter runs at 80 to 100 percent effort. Again, full recovery is used for quality work, and short recovery for a lactate workout. These are for your 100–200-type athletes. The athletes are exposed to a low or moderate level of lactic

Figure 38-10. 200-meter curve-running technique.

acid with these workouts, so a higher quality of speed endurance can be done at these distances.

400 Meters

The basic mechanics of sprinting also apply to the 400-meter race. The primary goal of a 400-meter runner is to distribute speed and energy over the total racing distance in the most efficient manner. It is not physiologically possible to run the 400 meters all-out. Pace judgment and effort distribution are critical skills.

Good 400-meter runners must be good sprinters. They must be capable of maintaining 90 to 95 percent of their best 200-meter velocity while running the 400 meters. Outstanding 400-meter runners have approximately a 1-second differential between the first and second 200 meters (e.g., 21½ + 22½ = 44 seconds). The first 150 meters should be run in as relaxed and smooth a manner as possible while trying to maintain the rhythm and velocity with the least effort. At the 200-meter mark, the runner must gradually start to increase the arm drive and knee

Figure 38-11. A, Nonvisual baton pass—underhand upward pass. **B,** Nonvisual pass-up sweep push pass.

lift. This controlled pickup will allow the runner to come off the final turn with good momentum and in good position. In the final 100 meters the runner must stay as relaxed as possible and try to maintain form and technique. Success in this event requires maximum development of the anaerobic capability energy system. Training in a high state of lactic acid buildup will develop this capacity (40 to 45 seconds of near-maximum effort). The mental aspects of 400-meter runners are just as important: They must be aggressive and able to withstand pain and fatigue.

Relays

The relays are a popular and exciting event. They require teamwork and timing. Relays employ two types of baton passes: the nonvisual and the visual pass. The *nonvisual (blind) pass* is one not seen by the receiver, and it is used in sprint relays. The baton must be passed in a 20-meter (22-yard) zone, and the outgoing runner has an additional 10-meter (11-yard) zone in which to accelerate. Sprint relay runners usually alternate hands, with the first and third runners carrying the baton in the right hand and the second and fourth runners carrying the baton in the left hand.

The *visual pass* is a pass that is seen by the receiver. It is primarily used in long (1600 m and above) relays, when fatigue may lessen coordination, decreasing the runner's ability to pass accurately. The pass must be made in a 20-meter (22-yard) zone.

Nonvisual pass technique

The outgoing runner should accelerate maximally into and through the passing zone as the incoming runner hits the go mark. Start with 18 to 20 feet (5.5 to 6 m) for the go mark and gradually increase to 20 to 30 feet (6 to 9 m) as the timing and conditioning improve. Visual or vocal cues can be used to initiate the pass. Some teams still use the upsweep-V technique (figure 38-11A). However, the extended arm position of the outgoing runner—with the open-palm, thumb-down hand position—is a much more efficient technique (figure 38-11B) because it provides a bigger target, a natural hand-baton fit, better control, and a longer free distance between runners. (The arms are completely extended by both runners.) The incoming runner uses an upsweep push into the target hand of the outgoing runner. The main objective is to keep the baton moving through the passing zone at top speed.

Visual passing technique

The outgoing runner should turn and go as the incoming runner hits the go mark (about 10 to 15 feet [3 to 4.5 m]). The outgoing runner accelerates into three to five fast strides and turns about 10 meters (11 yards) into the zone. The outgoing runner reaches back with the left hand, chest facing the curb. The hand should reach high into the face of the incoming runner. This provides a good target, with the fingers extended and the thumb open in a natural reaching position (figure 38-11C). The incoming runner places the baton in the target hand of the outgoing runner.

Figure 38-11—*cont'd.* **C,** Visual passing technique.

Figure 38-12. 1600-meter relay visual pass..

As the outgoing runner turns, she or he must judge the strength and speed of the incoming runner. The outgoing runner has about 10 meters (11 yards) to slow down or speed up to complete the pass. As soon as the pass has been completed and the runner is clear of traffic, the baton should be switched to the right hand, and the runner should sprint hard through the first turn and establish position (figure 38-12).

Hurdles

Hurdling is an event that requires outstanding sprinting ability to be successful. The best hurdlers are excellent sprinters. Other necessary physical characteristics are rhythm, flexibility, coordination, balance, and efficient technique.

Technique

The start is basically the same as for sprinting, but adjustments must be made to achieve the correct stride number to the first hurdle. Eight strides is the most common pattern to the first hurdle, but some taller athletes may use seven strides. The lead leg should be placed in the rear block in preparation for eight strides to the first hurdle, in the front block for seven strides. The takeoff distance from the hurdle is important to establish an efficient flight path over the hurdle. The hurdler's size, speed of approach, and lead-leg action determine the proper takeoff distance for each hurdler. The average distance is 6½ to 7½ feet (2 to 2.3 m) for men and 6 to 6½ feet (1.8 to 2 m) for women

Hurdle clearance

Efficient hurdle clearance depends on a proper takeoff and lead-leg action. The takeoff should be high on the balls of the feet, with a highly flexed lead knee and a large split between the legs. This lifts the center of gravity high into an efficient flight path over the hurdle while minimizing vertical forces. The lead leg should not swing up with a straight or locked leg, which slows down the action significantly. The lead leg should not swing to the inside or the outside, which can create balance problems during landing. The lead leg should be directly in front of the hip, with the toe straight up (figure 38-13A). The takeoff (trailing) leg is driven up and around to the side of the body in a tightly folded position. The toe of the trailing leg is turned out. This should be a fast, continuous action.

Arm action

The single-arm action is the most efficient technique because it simulates the running action. The lead arm is driven forward about shoulder level, with a bent elbow. This balances the lead leg. The trailing arm swings backward for balance and rhythm. The hurdler leans forward with the shoulders square. This gets the hurdler down to the ground quicker.

Landing

The hurdler should land on the ball of the foot with the center of mass (hips) over or slightly in front of the landing foot. The trailing leg comes through with a high knee action and flows into a full sprint stride (figure 38-13B). The hurdler takes three sprint strides between hurdles, with the last stride being shorter. Hurdling is sprinting, so the hurdler should sprint through the first hurdle out of the blocks, between the hurdles, and off the last hurdle through the finish line.

Technique for women

Women require some different techniques because their hurdles are lower. The center of mass does not have to be lifted as high. The technique is closer to sprinting, and the hurdling action is less pronounced. The lead-leg action is quicker and more explosive. The female hurdler leads with a bent knee, then explosively kicks out the lower leg. This is immediately followed by a quick snap of the leg down and under the body for landing (figure 38-13C).

The trailing-leg action is also less pronounced for women. It is not brought around, as it is for male high hurdlers. It is kept tight under the body, with the toe turned

Figure 38-13. A, Takeoff, lead-leg action, and hurdle clearance technique. **B,** The landing and sprint off of the hurdle. **C,** The women's 100-meter hurdle technique.

out to clear the hurdles. Women do not have to lean as much as men do; they are very close to their sprint posture throughout the race. Some smaller women may need to lean somewhat. The other technical aspects are similar to those in men's hurdling.

Endurance Events

Whether you are training for health, fitness, or competition, the training systems are basically the same. The goals, training intensities, and workloads will dictate the specific differences. Modern training systems utilize many of the old systems, but mix and modify them to meet individual needs, abilities, events, and local environmental conditions. With the exception of a few philosophical differences regarding how much, how fast, and how far to run, the main emphasis is on development of the aerobic metabolic oxygen transport system (the lungs, heart, and vascular systems). There is a strong correlation between a high aerobic capacity (VO_2 max) and success in endurance events.

Training methods

Middle-distance runners are more balanced in their use of the aerobic and anaerobic systems in their training, they use about a 50 percent to 50 percent ratio. 5K and 10K runners and marathoners use from 70 to 80 percent of their training from the aerobic energy systems. Long continuous runs, fartlek, interval training, and various types of speed work (anaerobic) make up most programs.

Long continuous runs. This is the major part of endurance runners' training programs where they build a strong aerobic base first. The runs will range from 3 to 10 miles for the middle-distance runner, and 10 to 20 miles for longer-distance runners. These runs may average a pace of 5 to 7 minutes per mile for men and 6 to 9 minutes per mile for women, depending on the level of competition and fitness.

Interval training. Interval training was developed by Drs. Hans Reindell, and Woldemar Gerschler with their world-record-setting athlete Rudolph Harbig in the 1930s. They used alternating measured runs of 200 to 400 meters on a flat track, at a measured pace with easy recovery jogs for a measured length of time. Precise measurement of each phase of work is essential to get the specific training effect to produce the developmental heart stimulus. These are the basic elements: (1) *The distance run:* Groups of 100, 200, or 400 m, etc. (2) *The recovery interval:* 30, 60, or 90 seconds. Heart-rate recovery of 120 beats/minute have also been used. (3) *The pace* of the run. How fast each interval is run depends on the fitness of the athlete and the race pace desired. (4) *The number of repetitions:* The number of times the run is repeated depends on the planned workload. **Example:** 20 × 200 m run at a pace of 30 seconds, with a 90-second jog recovery.

Fartlek. This was developed by the great Swedish coach Goster Homer in the 1940s. Homer trained the great distance runner Gunder Haegg. Fartlek alternates hard and easy running over varied and interesting terrains. It takes the athlete away from the confines of a track to a more natural setting. However, fartlek can be done on the track. Fartlek means "speed play." The runners usually run fartlek in pine-needled forest, parks, golf courses, and in the hills. The runner can develop speed and endurance at the same time in a fun and stimulating environment. It is a flexible and wide-ranging system.

Training plans

With a basic understanding of the various training systems, coaches and athletes must develop a training plan to meet their special needs and situation. The following are basic principles of training:

1. A medical evaluation should precede each year's training.
2. Workloads should be increased gradually over days, weeks, and years.
3. A strong aerobic base should be developed first, with long continuous runs.
4. Gradually reduce the resting heart rate and raise the steady state (an increase in pace without an increase in lactic acid).
5. Develop anaerobic power (speed). All distance races need some training done at race pace or faster. Even the marathon.
6. Use variety in the terrains, training runs, environment, and competitions.
7. Training systems must adapt to the individual.
8. Develop a periodation training plan with specific phases, goals, and objectives.
9. Training must be consistent with regularity of workouts, diet, rest, recovery, and mental development.
10. Training should include some work on running mechanics, and pace judgment.
11. Fun and enjoyment should be a major part of the training program. Variety and clear expectations play a part in these goals.

Running the Steeplechase

The key to the steeplechase lies in mastering the barriers. Running workouts combining long distance, intense distance intervals, and speed work are necessary, but the method for jumping the barriers deserve special attention. The key to jumping the barriers is momentum. It is important not to slow down in front of the hurdles or the water jump. Lack of momentum causes landing with the center of gravity far behind the lead leg and coming to a near halt on the far side of the barrier. The usual method for attacking the water jump is to place the lead leg on the barrier, allow momentum to move the body across the barrier, push off the barrier, and land in the water on the other foot far enough out so that the leg that pushed off the barrier can land next on the track beyond the water. It is important to get back to proper running form as quickly as possible.

Jumping Events

Long jump

Approach. The distance of the run-up is determined by strength, skill, conditioning, and the acceleration pattern of the jumper. Young jumpers may need only 14 to 16 strides, although more-experienced jumpers may require 18 to 23 strides. The main objective of the approach is to develop maximum controllable speed at takeoff. Many techniques have been used to achieve this goal: a gradual buildup, an explosive buildup, or a two- to four-step walk-in to the first check mark. All have been effective, but the key factors are a fast, relaxed, consistent stride pattern. One or two check marks are the most commonly used number. One check mark is placed at the start, and one is placed four to six strides from the takeoff board. The jumper should establish the takeoff foot and starting mark by "running through" the jump a few times to check for accuracy.

Takeoff. Speed down the runway is more important than jumping ability by a 2:1 ratio. Jumping ability is important, obviously, but not at the expense of losing horizontal velocity at takeoff. The most efficient takeoff action is one that allows the jumper to get lift at the appropriate angle with a minimum loss of horizontal velocity.

The position of the takeoff foot and the center of mass at takeoff are the most important technical considerations for successful jumps. If the foot is too far in front of the body at takeoff, the jumper will get good lift but lose horizontal velocity; and if the hips are too high, the jumper will not get enough lifting force. The jumper should use a long/short stride pattern in the last two strides because this lowers the center of mass on the next-to-last stride and catches the hips on the rise in the final stride. This provides an efficient transfer of horizontal velocity at takeoff. A short/long final two strides may place the foot too far in front of the body, resulting in a loss of velocity and shorter jumps. The takeoff action should be fast, with a short duration on the board. A foot plant that is too far in front of the body with a long duration on the board should be avoided (figure 38-14A).

Flight in the air. Long jumpers have traditionally used three types of in-the-air styles: the sail, the hang, and the hitch kick (running in the air). All three styles have been used effectively, and each has its strengths and weaknesses. All styles are basically used to counter forward rotation created at takeoff. They allow the athlete to maintain balance and prepare the legs for an efficient landing.

Figure 38-14. **A,** The hitch kick takeoff. **B,** The hitch kick flight pattern. **C,** The landing.

The hitch kick is the most difficult to learn, but it is the most efficient. It is a natural extension of the run; it puts the athlete in a better landing position; and it can effectively reverse or delay forward rotation. The hitch kick is divided into one-and-a-half and two-and-a-half strides. The two-and-a-half hitch delays forward rotation longer and has the most potential for longer jumps, but it requires great strength, skill, and coordination.

Regardless of the style used, once the athlete leaves the ground, there is nothing he or she can do to change the parabolic flight curve of the center of mass (figure 38-14B).

Landing. The most effective landing position is with the feet as far as possible in front of the center of mass (hips) without falling backward into the pit. Arriving in the landing position too early will result in a premature entry into the pit because of forward rotation. Stomach muscles or leg strength cannot hold the legs up once in this position because forward rotation causes the legs to rotate down into the pit.

The landing action is initiated by extending the legs parallel to the pit or slightly above parallel, with the toes up. The head, chest, and arms are thrust forward. The arms sweep down and back, then forward, as the heels contact the sand. At this point the knees flex and allow the hips to move forward. The athlete can fall forward into a tight tuck position or execute a sit-out technique that employs a pivot to the side with a hip thrust that strikes the sand with the buttocks near or past the feet (figure 38-14C).

Figure 38-15. **A,** Phase I of the triple jump. **B,** Phase II of the triple jump. **C,** Phase III of the triple jump.

Triple jump

As in the long jump, horizontal velocity is a very important factor for success in the triple jump. This is a speed event. The major differences between these events are the lower takeoff angle and three jumps that require an even distribution of effort and conservation of horizontal velocity on each jump. The triple jumper must take off and land on the same foot in the first jump; on the second jump the jumper must land on the opposite foot; and on the third jump the jumper may land in any manner. The triple jumper must also possess balance and a high level of leg strength and power.

Approach. The approach is essentially the same as for the long jump, but it requires additional control. The jumper may have to slow down the approach if he or she does not have the skill or leg strength to handle a faster speed. The takeoff in the first phase is characterized by a single- or double-arm action. The latter provides lifting force and balance, but it disrupts or decreases takeoff velocity. The single-arm action is recommended because it is a more natural extension of the run. The stronger leg should be used for this phase.

First jump. The jumper runs off the board with a single-arm action and pulls the takeoff leg tightly through under the buttocks to a thigh-thigh position in front of the hips. The foreleg is extended slightly forward, and the ankle is cocked (dorsal-flexed). The arms are simultaneously extended backward into a double-arm position (figure 38-15A). The jumper is now prepared to execute the second phase.

Second jump. This is initiated by a forward swinging of the arms, an explosive firing and pawing action by the extended takeoff leg and flexed ankle into the ground under the body, and a forward drive of the opposite knee into a high-thigh position. The jumper must hold this position as long as possible to achieve the greatest distance possible in this phase (figure 38-15B). The jumper must again extend both arms backward, and the foreleg of the lead leg

Figure 38-16. The straddle takeoff, bar clearance, and landing.

extends forward, with the ankle cocked. The jumper is now prepared to execute the final phase.

Third jump. This jump also begins with the forward swing of the arms, the driving, pawing action of the lead leg under the body, and the forward and upward drive of the opposite knee. The flight path and landing of the third phase is similar to the long jump. Triple jumpers usually use a sit-out landing technique because of a lack of momentum to carry them over the legs in the traditional tuck position (figure 38-15C).

High jump

The two basic styles of high jumping that have produced the highest jumps are the flop and the straddle. Currently, the flop is the more popular and has produced the best jumps. The flop allows the jumper to use a faster approach, which has resulted in higher jumps.

Straddle. The approach is from a 20- or 30-degree angle to the plane of the uprights. A proper approach should provide enough speed to allow the jumper to transfer this energy into maximum vertical velocity. The jumper should take off at the appropriate takeoff angle to allow for an efficient rotation around the bar. The approach is from 10 to 14 strides out. The jumper uses a gradual buildup, and the last three strides are the fastest and the longest. The arms and the free leg swing upward explosively together toward the bar. This creates takeoff momentum that adds to the forces created by the speed of the approach and the drive of the takeoff foot. The straddle jumper takes off on the inside foot. After takeoff, the outside arm reaches around the bar, and the head and shoulders dive down below the bar as the hips rise. The takeoff leg flexes and the body rotates around the axis of the bar. During the bar clearance the flexed takeoff leg abducts (opens up) at the hip, and the jumper continues to rotate and lands on the back (figure 38-16).

Flop (back layout). Because the movements are simple and natural, the flop seems to be easier to learn than the straddle. The approach is J-shaped. It begins with a straight line and gradually curves into the takeoff. The flopper uses 8 to 12 strides with two check marks. The marks are placed at the start and the beginning of the curve (the turn mark). The turn mark can only be used in practice; it is not allowed in competitions. At the curve the jumper gradually leans into the inside of the curve and accelerates into the plant and takeoff. The inside lean is critical in placing the jumper in an efficient takeoff position to take advantage of proper takeoff angles and centrifugal force (figure 38-17).

Plant and takeoff. The jumper should plant the outside foot almost parallel to the bar, 3 to 4 feet (0.9 to 1.2 m) directly in front of the near standard (figure 38-18). The jumper plants with the heel and rotates to the toe. The ankle and the knee extend fully to the toe for maximum drive. The inside knee is driven up and across the body at takeoff. This rotates the body into a back-to-the-bar

Figure 38-17. The flop takeoff, accent, layout, leg clearance, and landing.

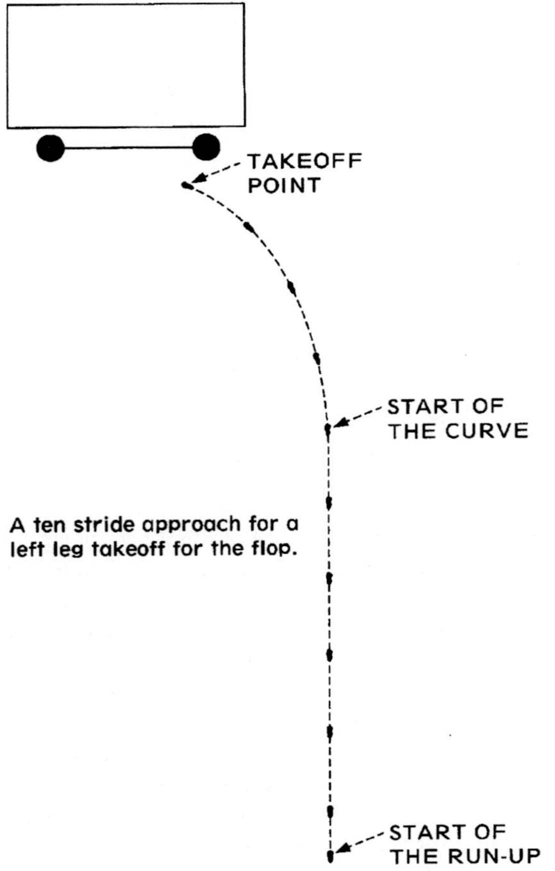

Figure 38-18. A ten stride approach for a left-leg takeoff for the flop.

position. The lead knee must be driven away from the bar, and the body must be perpendicular to the ground at takeoff. This ensures maximal takeoff force with the most efficient takeoff angle to clear the bar. Both the single- and double-arm action have been used effectively. The single-arm action facilitates a faster takeoff with a short, quick takeoff impulse. The double-arm action uses a greater backward lean, a deeper drop (lower center of mass), and a longer takeoff impulse.

Bar clearance. The jumper prepares to clear the bar as soon as he or she leaves the ground. From the back-to-the-bar position the jumper drops the head back and lifts the hips to clear the bar. This places the jumper in a back-layout position around the bar. Spreading the knees with the heels kept close together facilitates flowing into this position. The arms and hands generally rest on the thighs (figure 38-17). Once the hips clear the bar, the jumper drops the hips and lifts the arms and legs to clear the feet (action-reaction). The jumper lands on the shoulder and back in the pit.

Pole vaulting

With the advent of the fiberglass pole, pole vaulting performances improve markedly, requiring new coaching techniques. The fiberglass pole does for the vaulter what the parallel bars and the horizontal bar do for the gymnast. In both cases the resiliency of the apparatus actually aids the performer. There are five phases in vaulting.

Approach. The vaulter should use an approach allowing the greatest buildup of controlled speed. The handhold should be slightly wider than shoulder width (figure 38-19).

Pole plant. The pole should be planted early and out in front of the body. The upper arm is extended as straight as possible over head or slightly in front of the head. The vaulter should continue to drive into the pole. The plant foot should be directly under or slightly behind the upper hand at takeoff.

Swing. After the takeoff the lower arm should be locked. This aids in the transfer of linear velocity to angular velocity. The knee opposite the plant foot should be driven up, whereas the plant foot is left hanging until the next phase: the rollback.

Rollback. During the rollback phase the hips should be brought higher than the head and the knees flexed into the chest. The vaulter should remain in the rollback position until the pole is well into its recoil.

Pull-up/push-up/push-off. The final phase starts with a pull-up, which should be done when the pole is almost straight for maximum efficiency and greatest height potential. The

Figure 38-19. The pole vault approach.

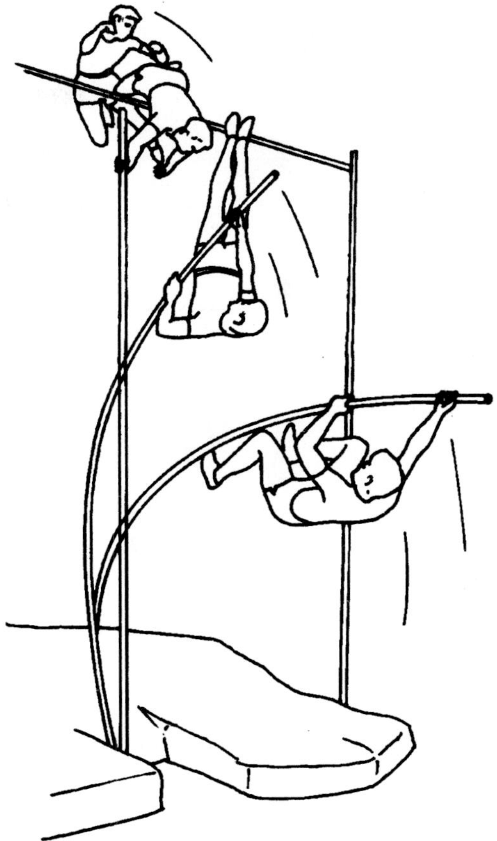

Figure 38-20. Flexibility of fiberglass pole.

push-up is done much like the handstand push-up. After maximum height is realized, the vaulter pushes off, dropping the legs and rotating around the bar (figure 38-20).

Throwing Events

All throwing events are described for a right-handed individual.

Shot put

The technique for throwing the shot is a putting action (elbow and forearm extension). A legal put must be made from the shoulder with one hand only so that, during the attempt, the shot does not drop behind or below the shoulder. There are currently two basic techniques being used effectively: the glide and the spin.

The glide. The glide technique is a modified version of the Perry O'Brien shift, named after the man who used it. It is slowly being replaced by the spin, but it is still a very effective technique. The thrower starts at the back of the circle facing the opposite direction of the sector (figure 38-21). The shot is held at the base of the first three fingers and is placed in the neck under the chin (figure 38-22). The knees should be flexed and the trunk leaning forward over the right leg. The hips and shoulders are square to the back of the circle at this point, and the weight is over the right foot. The throw is started by driving the left leg in the direction of the throw. This action causes a falling backwards in the direction of the throw. At the same time the right leg should begin a driving action. The line of movement is nearly horizontal during this phase. *The landing and throw:* The right foot lands near the center of the circle, and the left foot makes contact with the inside edge of the toeboard. The hips and the body begin to rotate in the direction of the throw. The forearm and elbow of the right arm should remain directly behind the shot. The throwing arm extends explosively and chases after the shot, and the wrist is snapped. The release angle should be about 40 to 42 degrees. During the follow-through and reverse, the thrower should lower the center of mass and extend the arms and legs to maintain balance and stay in the circle (figures 38-21A, B, and 38-23).

The spin. The current men's world record holder and leading throwers are using this technique. This technique seems to be easier to master, and greater speed or velocity of release can be achieved with the spin. Balance, and control of direction may be difficult for some throwers to master. Multi-event athletes have been very successful with this technique. The spin or rotational style of throwing is

Figure 38-21. O'Brien shot put technique. **A,** Glide and landing. **B,** Throwing positions.

Figure 38-22. Starting position at the back of the circle.

Figure 38-23. The release angle and position.

Figure 38-24. The spin.

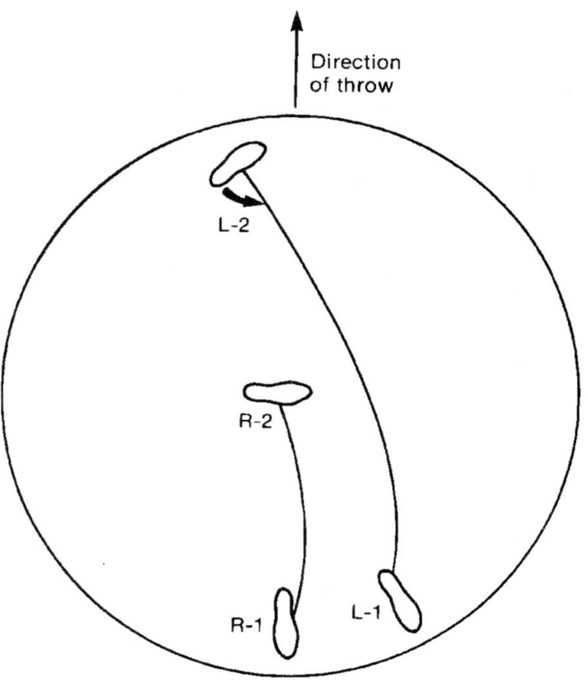

Figure 38-25. Foot movement for shot put.

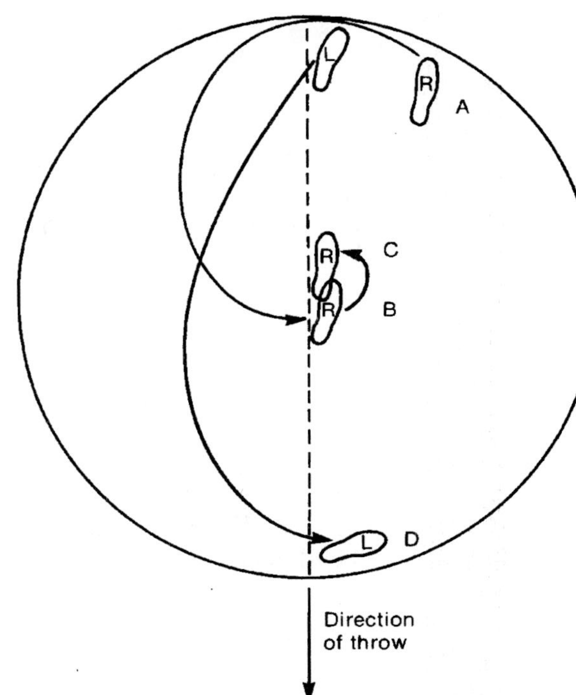

Figure 38-26. Foot movement for discus.

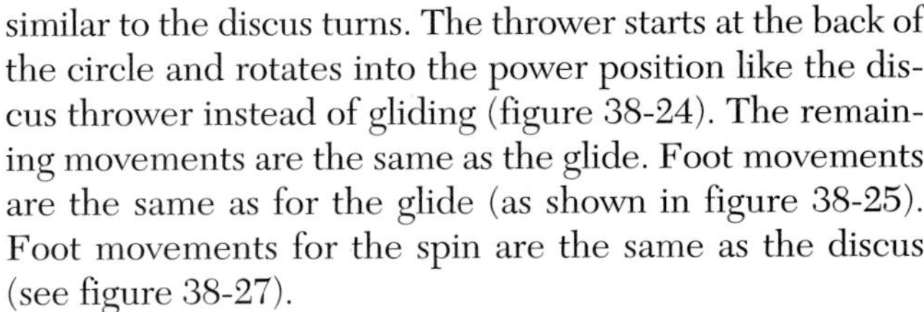

similar to the discus turns. The thrower starts at the back of the circle and rotates into the power position like the discus thrower instead of gliding (figure 38-24). The remaining movements are the same as the glide. Foot movements are the same as for the glide (as shown in figure 38-25). Foot movements for the spin are the same as the discus (see figure 38-27).

Discus

Most beginners are under the mistaken impression that the discus is thrown with the arm. Actually, the force is generated primarily by the hips, legs, and trunk.

The hand is placed on the discus with the fingers slightly separated and the first joint of each finger curled slightly over the rim. The thumb rests on top of the discus, and the wrist is slightly cocked toward the little finger. At the release the discus should spin clockwise (for a right-handed thrower); the index finger is the last finger to lose contact with the discus.

To achieve the greatest force the thrower starts in the extreme back position of the circle and will eventually complete one-and-three-quarters turns before the release. The beginning of the spin is usually preceded by a few preliminary swings of the discus back and forth to establish a rhythm. The beginning position of the spin should be with the feet slightly wider than shoulder width and the top part of the body rotated more than 180 degrees to the right. (See figure 38-26A for position of feet.)

Figure 38-27. A, The discus turn. **B,** The discus throwing action.

The spin is then initiated by the legs and the hips as the weight is shifted to the left. The upper body remains relaxed, and the throwing arm trails behind with the discus at shoulder height. A key here is to keep the feet in contact with the ground as long as possible.

As the weight continues to shift to the left, the right foot will be lifted off the ground and driven forward toward the center of the ring to establish a new support. Before the right foot contacts the ground, the thrower will face the front of the ring, pass through this position, and again face the back of the ring. Once the right foot contacts the ground, the performer pivots on this foot. The left foot comes off the ground to eventually be placed at the front of the circle a little past the centerline. Once the left foot makes contact, the thrower enters the explosive part of the throw.

With the right foot now planted at the center of the circle and the left foot planted at the front of the circle, the thrower explodes and accelerates the turning of the upper body against the firmly anchored lower body. The discus at the beginning of this explosion should be at about shoulder height, dropped to hip height, and then released at shoulder height (figure 38-27A, B).

Javelin

The most important aspect of the javelin throw is the velocity of the release. Velocity is developed in the run-up, the torque created by the thrower's body, and the transfer of these forces over the thrower's plant leg.

Approach. The approach covers 110 to 130 feet (33.5 to 40 m), with crossover steps in the final five or six strides. The crossover steps allow the thrower to place the body in a strong throwing position.

Plant. The thrower plants the leg opposite the throwing arm in front of the body with a long last stride. The javelin is pulled back, and the shoulders are rotated back to create torque in the body (figure 38-28A).

Throw. The throw is initiated by an explosive push by the rear leg that drives the body over the plant leg. The shoulders and the arms follow the leg drive as they rotate into the throw. The final wrist flick and body follow-through further accelerate the javelin at release (figures 38-28B, 38-29).

The javelin's flight path is affected by aerodynamic factors. Because of the design of the javelin, air resistance causes it to follow a nonparabolic curve. Recent design changes that move the center of mass forward have been made to reduce the danger of the javelin traveling too far. Javelin distances initially declined, but they have recently increased again as throwers have learned to throw the new javelin. The angle of release is dependent on the ability of the thrower. The beginner thrower releases at approximately 33 degrees, and the advanced thrower releases at 28 degrees.

Grip. Many varieties of grips are used, but for all of them the hand must be in contact with the cord grip (figure 38-30). The palm should face upward, and the thrower should pull straight through the shaft to the tip into the proper release angle and direction. The final wrist

Figure 38-28. **A,** The javelin crossover and plant. **B,** The javelin throw and follow-through.

Figure 38-29. The power position in the javelin.

Figure 38-30. **A,** Acceptable method of holding the javelin. **B,** Preferred method of holding the javelin. The first finger aids javelin rotation, which stabilizes the line of flight.

and finger drive should be against the cord grip and through the tip, to impart spin on the javelin and stabilize its flight.

Hammer throw

The hammer throw is a very complex event, requiring a high degree of skill, as well as balance, strength, power, speed, and very specific motor patterns. To be successful, the thrower's training must provide specific input that develops the correct motor patterns. Incorrect training patterns can lead to injury and slow development. The hammer is a rhythm event, and many hours of drills are needed to coordinate the balanced movements of the body. The basic parts of the throw are: preliminary swings, entry, turns, low and high points of the swings, and the release. The throw must be viewed as a whole, linked by its various parts.

Figure 38-31. The hammer's three-and-a-half turn sequence.

Technique. The thrower begins from a position facing the opposite direction of the throw and toward the edge of the circle. The thrower begins with the feet approximately shoulder width apart, arms extended, and body weight over the leg on the side of the hammer. The throw is initiated with one or two preliminary swings around the head while facing the starting position in the back of the circle. The thrower then accelerates into three-and-a-half complete turns with the hammer. The hammer thrower attempts to build maximum velocity in the hammer head during the turns. While rotating through the three-and-a-half turns, the hammer moves progressively from a low point to a high point and reaches a final angle of approximately 45 degrees at the release. The most successful hammer throwers can move the feet, hips, and shoulders progressively faster and further ahead of the hammer to maximize the muscular forces acting to increase the hammer's velocity (figure 38-31).

BASIC RULES

Sprinting

1. A false start may be called if the runner does not comply with the command "On your mark" or "Set."
2. A false start is declared if the runner jumps the gun. In NCAA competitions, one false start disqualifies the runner. In IAFF/international competitions, a runner is disqualified after the second false start.
3. If starting blocks are used, they must be set in the athlete's lane and must be made without devices that could provide artificial aid.
4. A competitor who cuts in front of another runner without proper clearance or one full stride on the curve line shall be disqualified.
5. In all races run in lanes, runners shall start and finish in their assigned lanes.

Hurdling

1. The entire body must pass over each hurdle.
2. The hurdler cannot run around a hurdle.
3. The hurdler must stay in the lane.
4. Disqualification shall be ruled by the referee when a competitor deliberately knocks down any hurdle by hand or foot, or does not attempt every hurdle.

Relay Races

1. Disqualification of one runner disqualifies the entire team.

2. The baton must be passed inside the 20-meter passing zone.
3. The baton must be carried in the hand.
4. If the baton is dropped, it must be recovered legally.
5. The last runner of the race must have the baton.
6. After passing the baton, the runner must not interfere with the opponent.

High Jump

1. A legal high jump is one in which a competitor jumps from one foot.
2. The crossbar must be cleared without displacement.
3. It is a failed attempt when after clearing the bar and landing in the pit, the jumper stumbles against the uprights and displaces the crossbar.

Pole Vault

1. The crossbar must be cleared without displacement caused by either the body or the pole.
2. It is a failed attempt if the vaulter leaves the ground in an attempt to vault and fails to clear the bar.
3. It shall not be counted as a trial or failure if a vaulter's pole breaks during an attempt to clear the bar.
4. The pole may be of any material or combination of materials, and it may be of any size and weight.
5. The landing pad measured beyond the vertical plane of the stopboard shall be a minimum of 16 feet wide and 12 feet deep (4.88 m and 3.66 m).

Long Jump and Triple Jump

1. The jumper's shoe must extend over the foul line.
2. The jumper must leave the pit under control beyond his or her mark made in the sand.
3. The triple jumper must take off and land on the same foot in the first jump; he or she must land on the opposite foot in the second jump; and any landing is permissible following the final jump.
4. In attempting a jump in the long jump and triple jump, it is a foul jump if the jumper runs beyond the foul line extended.

Shot Put

1. A legal shot must be used.
2. The shot must land within the sector.
3. The put must be made from within the circle.
4. The competitor must exit from the rear of the circle under control.
5. A legal put must be made from the shoulder with one hand only so that during the attempt the shot does not drop behind or below the shoulder.

Discus

1. The throw must land within the sector.
2. The competitor must stay within the circle until the distance is marked.
3. The complete throw must be from within the circle.
4. A proper discus must be used.

Javelin

1. The throw must land within the sector.
2. The javelin must be held by the cord grip.
3. A regulation javelin must be used.
4. It shall be a foul and not measured if during an attempt to throw, the thrower touches with any part of the body, any surface of the foul line, the run-up lines, or the area outside of the foul line or run-up lines.

Hammer Throw

1. The throw must land within the sector.
2. During the throw the competitor must not leave the circle.
3. The hammer must be legal.
4. Gloves may be used.

SAFETY PRECAUTIONS

1. Warm up with a few flexibility and conditioning exercises before practice or competition to prepare the body and prevent injury.
2. Wear shoes that are suitable for the individual events, and make sure they fit properly.
3. Take proper care of equipment.
4. Use caution in all throwing events. Carry the implements back to the thrower and make sure the throwing area is clear.
5. Check all jumping surfaces for stability and firmness. Take special precautions for wet, slippery conditions.

TEACHING CONSIDERATIONS

In teaching or coaching track and field, the first considerations is to have a basic understanding of the physical and mental responses to training. A general knowledge of exercise physiology and biomechanical principles should be used as guidelines in planning training programs. These guidelines should include the following principles:

1. Specificity of training: Training should be specific to the requirements of the event in terms of the development of strength, power, speed, flexibility, and the aerobic and anaerobic energy systems.
2. Training loads: The appropriate intensity, frequency, and duration of training should be well planned. The principle of gradual progressive overloads should be followed to allow for training adaptation.
3. Individuality: Each individual has unique abilities and skills. A sensitivity to genetic and acquired differences should be considered when planning training programs. Body size and composition and muscle type should be evaluated. Individual temperament and tolerances should also be considered.

4. Adaptation to stress: Adequate rest and recovery cycles should be included in the training to allow for positive adaptation. The "hard day, easy day" principle is a good policy to follow. Overtraining can lead to injury, staleness, and burnout. The athlete needs regular recovery periods, both physically and psychologically.

Class or Team Management

Management requires careful planning to achieve the various training goals. The following tasks should be considered:

1. Setting individual and group goals
2. Designing daily, weekly, and monthly practice times
3. Providing for equipment needs
4. Staffing and teaching strategies
5. Proper selection and grouping of athletes into appropriate events
6. Testing and evaluation of performances
7. Motivational techniques and strategies

Teaching Specific Events

In teaching specific event skills, athletes should be divided into the appropriate event groups with similar carryover value. This provides efficient use of time for skill development.

Group I: sprints, hurdles, relays

The movement skills for these events are very similar. Drills that emphasize arm action, rhythm and relaxation, posture, increased stride length and frequency, starting skills, and maximum acceleration patterns are excellent for these events. Hurdlers require additional work to develop the technical aspects of stride patterns and the hurdling technique and rhythm. Relays can also be worked in with this group. Relay practice should focus on the skills of taking and passing the baton through the passing zone. A variety of standing, jogging, and running drills can be used to improve passing skills.

The conditioning for this group is primarily anaerobic, but some aerobic work is done for general fitness and cardiovascular efficiency. The development of strength, explosive power, and flexibility are important training components of these events. Sprint, hurdling, and relay drills can also be incorporated in warm-up sessions.

Sprint drills. The objectives of these drills are to teach anticipation of the correct sequence of muscular firing and coordination (recruitment of fast-twitch fibers) to teach correct posture for optimal force application in the support phase, and to specifically strengthen muscles throughout the support, landing, and driving phase.

1. A-skip drill: High knee drills done by driving the right or left knee waist-high every other step for 20 to 30 yards. Do 1 to 2 sets with the right and 1 to 2 with the left.
2. B-skip drill: Drive the knees up as in the A-skip, followed by extending the foreleg out and then snapping it explosively under the body. Do 1 to 2 sets with the right leg and with the left.
3. Butt kicks: Drive 20 to 30 yards down the track with quick armswings, and rapidly pull the heels to the butt and extend back down to the track on alternate steps. Do 1 to 2 sets.
4. Straight-leg bounding: With the knees locked out, extend the legs and feet out forward and pull the body down the track with a backwards clawing action. Do 1 to 2 sets of 20 to 30 yards.
5. Ins-outs: Speed control drills from 30, 60, or 100 meters. *Example:* For 60 meters, accelerate for 20 m, relax without slowing down for 20 m, and accelerate for 20 m. Do 8 to 10 repetitions.
6. 4 to 6 repetitions—standing long jumps, to work on timing and landing.
7. 4 to 6 repetitions—standing triple jump, to work on timing, phases, and landing.
8. 4 to 6 repetitions bounding up hills or stairs (20–60 yards)
9. Starts: 6 to 8 repetitions 30-, 40-, or 60-meter starts with a gun. Work on reaction time and starting mechanics.

Hurdle drills

1. Practice 7- to 8-stride rhythm to the first hurdle, with and without starting blocks and the gun.
2. Run 5-step rhythm between the hurdles to work on form, balance, and quickness. Move the hurdles an extra 2–3 yards apart. Do 6 to 10 repetitions 5 to 10 hurdles.
3. Place the hurdles 1–3 yards closer and work on the three stride rhythm and quickness.
4. Focus on the lead leg, trail leg, and arm action.
5. Hurdling is sprinting, so follow the same drills and workouts as the sprinters.

Relay drills

1. *4 × 100 relay drill:* Stand in the alternate pass position and pass the baton between the runners focusing on getting the hand back in a high position, and placing the baton firmly in the target hand. Do this at slow, medium, and fast speed. This can also be done while jogging.
2. *4 × 100 relay drill:* Run through each 20-meter passing zone checking the timing of the go marks of the outgoing runners, the technique of receiving and making the pass, and the time through the zone. Run easy, medium, and fast.
3. *4 × 400 relay drill:* Work with the outgoing runner getting out fast through the first 10 meters, turning to adjust to the incoming runner, taking the pass in the middle of the zone and running aggressively into the curve.

4. Incorporate both the blind and visual passes in the workouts focusing on smooth efficient passes.

Group 2: horizontal jumps (long jump, triple jump)

The horizontal jumps require excellent sprinting ability. They are speed events, and thus the speed component of the training should be with the sprinters. An equal portion of their training for individuals interested in the long and triple jumps should also be used for specific skill development. Training patterns and drills for these events should include the following:

1. Visual aids are used to illustrate the technical phases of the jumps.
2. Run-up drills are used to develop consistency and accuracy in the approach. Check the touchdown pattern on the takeoff board and make any necessary adjustments.
3. Pop-up drills: Use 6- to 10-stride short-approach jumps to practice the technical aspects of takeoff, flight, and landing phases of the jumps.
4. Strength and power development: In addition to weight training, use plyometrics (bounding and box drills), hills, and harness pulls to supplement power development.

Group 3: vertical jumps (high jump, pole vault)

These two events are quite different and require individual approaches. The physical requirements of these events are similar to the sprints and horizontal jumps. The pole vault requires upper-body strength and flexibility, agility, and gymnastic skills.

High jump. The high jump requires a slower, more controlled run-up than vertical jumps. Ninety percent of the jumping height is determined by what the jumper does in the run-up and takeoff. Therefore, most technical training should be focused on developing these skills. Emphasis should be placed on a fast, smooth approach that the jumper can control, and placing the body in a sound takeoff position that efficiently transfers horizontal velocity into maximum vertical lift. Bar clearance is only 10% of the jumping height, but time should be spent on drills that develop timing and efficient rotation around the bar.

Training tips

1. Use soft (plastic or rope) crossbars and the required landing pits to reduce injury and the fear of being hurt.
2. Teach both the straddle and the flop, and allow athletes to choose the style they would like to develop.
3. Determine the takeoff foot and work out an 8- to 10-stride approach. Use the athlete's strongest leg and a straight or curved approach, depending on the style used.
4. Take 10 to 15 approaches and jumps, one or two times a week, at a comfortable height to establish consistency, rhythm, and confidence.
5. Use 1- to 3-step jumps for bar clearance drills. Ramps or boxes can be used for easy takeoff action, but make sure they do not move or slide.
6. Use 3- to 5-step jumps, working on takeoff and bar clearance.
7. Use backward double-leg takeoffs, working on bar clearance.

Pole vault. Executing a pole vault requires speed, strength, flexibility, and agility. The basic technical skills are the approach, plant, takeoff, swing-up, timing of the pull-turn, bar clearance, and landing.

Training tips

1. Teaching progressions
   a. First, teach the grip and pole-carry.
   b. Second, teach the 3- to 5-step pole-planting action.
   c. After the planting action is established, allow the athlete to take off, swing up, and ride the pole into the pit, landing in a sitting position (assisted and unassisted).
   d. When comfortable with these skills, the vaulter is now ready to develop the pull, turn, bar clearance, and landing.
   e. At this point, the approach distance and speed are gradually increased and the full movements are executed.
2. Two check marks are used in the approach, one at the start and one at the takeoff point. Practice run-throughs to establish consistency in hitting the takeoff mark.
3. Full jumps are practiced one or two times a week. Start at a comfortable height and gradually move the bar higher. Take 10 to 15 jumps in a session. Placing the bar 2 feet (60 cm) over the vaulter's best height and attempting to get the ankles over the bar help the vaulter get into a vertical, inverted position.
4. Gymnastic work on the rings and other apparatus has great carryover value for vaulting skills.
5. Use 3- to 5-step pole-plant drills, working on the rhythm of the pole-plant preparation, plant, and takeoff.
6. Pole carry drills. 8 to 10 × (20–40 yard) runs on the track with the pole.

Group 4: throwing events (shot put, discus, javelin, hammer throw)

These events all require maximum development of speed of release of the implement. An increase in the speed of release generally produces an increase in distance. All throwers must exert maximum force against the ground with the entire body (action-reaction) to produce optimal release velocity. The legs and hips initiate these movements (importance of the lower body), and the back, shoulders, arms, wrist, and fingers further accelerate the implements. The greater the forces transferred to the ground, the greater the force potential available to accelerate the implements.

Training tips

1. Use drills that simulate the sequential, coordinated movements of the legs, hips, back, shoulders, arms, wrists, and fingers. They have great carryover value for all throwing events.
2. The use of implements that are slightly lighter or heavier than the standard weight can be used to develop speed or power in specific throwing events.
3. The specific technical skills vary with each throwing event, but they all require the development of very high levels of strength and power in the specific muscle groups. The bench press, incline press, leg squats, power cleans, and other dynamic, explosive exercises are essential for these events.
4. Start beginners from the power position or half circle. Gradually add the glide, turns, or steps in the approach. Hammer throwers should learn the foot movements and weight shifts with and without the hammer. Practice the turns, glides, and foot movements down a line, keeping the weight over the landing leg. Add the complete movement.

Shot put drills

1. Half-circle throws from the power position, with and without the reverse (10–20 throws).
2. Execute 8 to 10 repetitions—glides or spins into the power position and the tow board.
3. Execute throws from the kneeling position with emphasis on shoulder rotation and wrist flick.
4. Execute 10 to 20 full throws, some for easy rhythm and control, and some for speed and explosive power.

Discus drills

1. *Release drills*: Toss the discus in the air with proper spin and catch it, and roll the discus on the ground to a partner.
2. *Half-circle throws*: In the power position, from the front of the circle with and without the reverse.
3. *Spin drills*: Into the power position down the track 10 to 20 yards.
4. *Full throws*: some for control, some for maximum effort, 10 to 20 throws.

Javelin drills

1. One step: Release drills with throws into the ground emphasizing pulling through the tip.
2. 1- to 3-step throws: Emphasis on driving up and over the plant leg.
3. 5-step throws: Emphasis on speed and explosive power.
4. Throwing balls and stubby javelins into nets.
5. Approach: Runs with crossover steps and full throws.

Hammer drills

1. The most important skill to teach beginning hammer throwers is the correct legwork and footwork.
2. During the turns, the left foot (for a right rotation) rotates from the heel to the ball of the foot, but it never looses contact with the ground. The right foot however, is always on the ball of the foot when on the ground, during the turns.
3. Proper grip and starting position.

First part

Drill 1: Start without the hammer in a standing position with the legs shoulder-width apart, slightly flexed at the knees. The left foot is placed on the heel and the right foot is placed on the ball. Perform 90-degree turns to the left (right-hand throwers). At 90 degrees, place the ball of the foot on the ground. Repeat for rhythm and control.

Second part

Drill 2: Start with the finish position of Drill 1. Lift the right foot off the ground and step around 270 degrees using an active rotation on the ball of the left foot. Continue the rotation on the ball of both feet from 270 to 360 degrees.

Full turns

Drill 3: With and without the hammer, start with the left foot forward. Make continuous turns without stopping. It is not important at this point for the left foot to move from heel to ball of the foot absolutely correctly. The correct movement will occur when using the hammer due to its pull.

Drill 4: Progress when ready by completing the turns holding a stick, broomhandle, weighted bags, and finally the hammer.

Throwing

The athlete is now ready to throw.

Drill 5: Start with preliminary swings. Make two swings, the first slightly to the right, and the second to the front and turn and throw.

Drill 6: Use two preliminary swings, execute 1, 2, or 3 turns and throw.

Drill 7: Carry out as many turns as possible with the hammer, without throwing. Four to 5 sets of at least 4 turns. Work up to 5 to 10 sets of 15 to 20 turns.

Group 5: endurance running (800 m, 1500 m, 3 km, 5 km, 10 km)

The basic running mechanics of endurance running are similar to those for sprinting, but, depending on the distance, they are less vigorous and more economical. The main training objective is to develop aerobic endurance and the speed required for the race distance.

1. General training: Include a proper warm-up and warm-down, flexibility exercises, light strength training, and hill work.

2. Specific training: Include hard endurance runs of 3 to 10 miles, speed work, fartlek, slow-recovery runs, and interval training. These should all be worked into the training schedule with the proper rest and recovery.
3. Tactical considerations: Include pace work, surge training, drafting, running in groups, and preparing for environmental factors.

Group 6: special events

Multievents (pentathlon, heptathlon, decathlon)

1. The multievents require a well-balanced training program with an emphasis on maximizing the athlete's strong events and improving the weak events. The scoring tables will also influence event training priority.
2. The pentathlon and heptathlon are speed-oriented events, while the decathlon requires more balance in the development of speed, strength, and endurance. However, all multievents require the development of speed, endurance, strength, power, flexibility, aerobic endurance, and specific technical event skills.
3. The athlete must be patient and develop sound fundamental skills for each event. The athlete must view multievents as one event, with 5, 7, or 10 individual parts.
4. Maintaining emotional control and mental concentration is critical for consistency and maximum performance.

Race walking (10 k, 20 k, 50 k)

1. Training for race walking is similar to the endurance events: The main objective is to increase cardiovascular (aerobic) capacity. The development of legal walking speed is also a consideration.
2. The development of strength and flexibility in the arms, shoulders, hips, trunk, and legs is important for race walking.
3. Start the athlete out by walking normally; then gradually increase the speed without breaking into a run. The elbow angle is nearly 90 degrees, and the heel touches the ground first. The walker pushes off on the toe, and the leg tends to land straight at the knee.
4. Posture should be between vertical and a slight forward lean. A posture too far forward causes the knees to bend and leads to disqualification. Leaning too far backward results in a loss of power.
5. The athlete should walk on a straight line, with one foot over the other. Any other foot placements result in a loss of power and distance.
6. Proper hip rotation allows the walker to gain extra distance without overstriding. The walker must simultaneously rotate the hips in a horizontal and vertical direction. Walking on a line and crossing the left foot over the right side of the line, the right foot over the left side, helps to develop proper hip rotation.

GLOSSARY

AAF/CIF The Amateur Athletic Foundation of Los Angeles, and the California Interscholastic Federation.

acceleration zone An area the width of one lane, 11 yards (10 m) long, which may be used by a relay runner to begin running before receiving the baton in the exchange zone.

aerobic activity Activity of moderate intensity that uses large muscle groups and requires oxygen to produce energy while a person is working.

alley May consist of two or three lanes used as a single lane for running the 800-meter run or 3200-meter relay from a one-turn stagger when more runners are competing than the number of lanes available.

amortation The absorption or loss of force due to flexion at the ankle, knee, and hip during the ground-contact phase of running.

anaerobic activity High-intensity activity in which the energy produced to perform work is done without the presence of oxygen.

anchor The last runner on a relay team.

approach Run used by the competitor before the actual takeoff in the jumps and the javelin throw.

apron Area in front of the high-jump pit.

artificial aid Any object, equipment, or device used illegally to enhance performance. Not legal by the rules of competition.

backswing Driving the arms back past the hips to improve stride length and frequency.

baton The stick carried and passed on by the runners of a relay team.

blind pass A sprint relay passing technique where the outgoing runner does not look back to take the baton.

breaking for the pole Cutting over to the inside lane of the track.

butt kicks Sprint drills designed to improve heel recovery and stride frequency.

cardiovascular system Related to the ability of the heart, lungs, and blood vessels to deliver oxygen and other nutrients to the cells for energy production.

center of gravity Also known as the center of mass. The center of a body's mass. In the human body and all objects, the point which all parts are in balance with each other, and the axis of rotation.

continuous runs Long aerobic runs for 10 minutes to an hour or longer.

cord grip The middle part of the javelin where it is grasped.

course Path of the runner.

crossbar Bar over which high jumpers and pole vaulters jump.

curb Inside border of the track.

curved starting line An involuted (waterfall) starting line used in 1500-, 3000-, 5000-, and 10,000-meter races.

dead heat A race in which two or more runners cross the finish line at exactly the same moment.

dorsal flex A vertical cocking or flexion of the ankle or wrist.

exchange zone An area the width of one lane, 22 yards (20 m) long, used in relay races. The baton must be passed from one runner to a teammate while they are in this zone. Also called the "passing zone."

false start Leaving the starting blocks or starting line before the gun sounds, or making a movement from the set position.

fartlek A system of endurance training that alternates strenuous runs and easy runs over varied terrain. Also known as "speed play."

finish line A line drawn on the track, the edge nearest the runner marking the legal completion of the distance raced.

finish posts Posts on each side of the finish line to which the finish yarn or tape is attached.

finish yarn or tape The cord stretched across the track directly above the finish line to aid the finish judges in determining the winner of a race.

flight The breaking down of a large field of competitors into smaller competitive groups. Used in the horizontal jumps and the throwing events so that competitors may warm up and compete with a reasonable time. Also refers to a lane or row of hurdles.

foul jump or throw A jumper throw counted as a trial but not measured because of some violation of the field event rules.

glide The backward explosive push-off, or shift from the back of the circle to the toe board, in the shot put.

grip The handhold on a baton, discus, shot, or javelin; or, specifically, the cord wrapping on the middle of the javelin.

heat A preliminary round of a race from which the designated places advance to the next round.

high-jump standards Uprights used to hold the crossbar for the high jump.

horizontal velocity The rate of speed in a forward or linear direction.

IAAF International Amateur Athletic Federation.

interval training A fitness workout that alternates hard work with light recovery work.

ins-outs Sprint training drills that alternate fast runs with easy runs for 20, 30, 40, 60, or 100 meters (tempo changes).

jostle To run against or to elbow; a form of crowding or bumping together that may hamper or impede a runner.

Kelly pool balls Small numbered balls used in drawing for lanes; also called "shake balls."

kilometer A metric unit of measuring distance, equal to 1,000 meters (1,093 yds.).

lactic acid A by-product of anaerobic metabolism known to cause localized muscle fatigue (lactate workouts).

lane The path marked on the track for a race or that part of a race during which a runner must stay in a prescribed path.

lap One complete circuit of the track.

leg of a relay The distance over which one member of a relay team must run.

mechanics Biomechanics; the physics of the human body in motion; the forces produced by the body and the forces acting on the body in temporal (time) and spacial (space) dimensions.

medley relay A relay race in which the members of the relay team run different distances.

metabolism The process of physical and chemical changes by which energy is produced for the maintenance of life.

meter A metric unit of measuring distance, equal to 3 feet 3½ inches.

multi-events The decathlon, heptathlon, and pentathlon.

NCAA National Collegiate Athletic Association. The governing body for collegiate athletics.

nonvisual exchange A blind relay pass, used in the short sprint relays.

pass Voluntary giving up of one of a competitor's preliminary or final jumps or throws. Also refers to the actual exchange of a baton or the overtaking of one runner by another in a race.

passing zone See **exchange zone.**

periodation plan A training plan that divides the training stimulus into days, weeks, months, and years. The training phases gradually manipulate the training intensities, loads, and other factors.

pole Inside, or curb, lane of the track.

power position The dynamic throwing position in the shot put, discus, and javelin where the shoulders are parallel to the back of the circle (closed), the hips are perpendicular to the front of the circle (opened), and the weight is back over the rear foot. Produces torque and rotational momentum.

qualifying round Competition in which performances qualify athletes for positions in the trials, but times or distances are not considered for final placing. Marks can be considered for record purposes.

recall Calling back of runners after a false start.

recovery period The rest interval between runs to allow the athlete to recover and return to a resting or normal state.

reverse The switching of the feet in the air as part of the follow-through in the shot put, discus, and javelin. The thrower lands on the non throwing leg for balance and control to stay behind the foul line.

scratch Decision not to compete in an event after confirmation or declaration.

scratch line Curved or straight line behind which throws must be made.

sector lines Boundary lines within which a throw must land to be a fair throw.

shuttle hurdles A relay race where hurdler 1 runs 100 or 110 meters in one direction, hurdler 2 runs back in the opposite direction, hurdler 3 runs back as hurdler 1 did, and hurdler 4 runs in the same direction as 2 to finish the race.

staggered start Start of a race in which runners do not start on a straight line. Used in races run around a curve up to and including 800 meters.

starting block A device against which runners may place their feet in order to get a faster start at the beginning of a race.

straightaway Straight area of the track between one curve and the next.

stride Distance covered by one step.

takeoff board A board from which a long jumper begins the jump.

takeoff mark A spot at which a competitor leaves the ground, as in the high jump and long jump.

toeboard A curved piece of wood or metal used as a foul line for the shot put and the javelin throw.

trailing leg Takeoff (rear) leg in hurdling.

trial An attempt in a field event.

turn Curved portion of the track. A standard 400-meter track has two turns, or curves, in one lap.

USATF USA Track and Field. The national governing body for competition in track and field, road racing and race walking in the United States.

vertical velocity The rate of speed in an upward direction.

visual exchange A baton exchange in which the receiver watches the incoming runner until the pass is completed.

VO_2 max The maximum oxygen used by the body during a hard work. A measure of stamina and endurance.

warm-up Preparation of the body through light exercise for more vigorous exercise.

SUGGESTED READINGS

Bompa, O., and Tudor, P. H. D. 1994. *Theory and methodology of training.* 3d ed. Dubuque, Iowa: Kendall/Hunt.

Bowerman, W., and Freeman, W. 1991. *High-performance training for track and field.* 2d ed. Champaign, Ill.: Human Kinetics. Contains training schedules for 15 events.

Carr, G. 1991. *Fundamentals of track and field.* Champaign, Ill.: Human Kinetics. Includes 13 chapters on specific track and field events, focusing on safety, techniques, teaching steps, common errors, and standards and assessment.

Chu, D. 1991. *Jumping into plyometrics.* Los Altos, Calif.: Tafnews.

Ecker, T. 1986. *Basic track and field biomechanics.* Los Altos, Calif.: Tafnews.

Jacoby, E., and Fraley, B. 1995. *Complete book of jumps.* Champaign, Ill.: Human Kinetics.

Martin, D., and Coe, S. 1991. *Training distance runners.* Champaign, Ill.: Human Kinetics. Contains information on the biomechanics and biochemistry of running and on goal setting, strategies, and stress management.

National Collegiate Athletic Association. Current ed. *Official collegiate track and field guide.* New York: NCAA.

Noakes, T. 1991. *Lore of running.* Champaign, Ill.: Human Kinetics.

Zarnowski, F. 1989. *The decathlon.* Champaign, Ill.: Human Kinetics.

RESOURCES

Track and Field News, 2570 El Camino Real, Suite 606, Mountain View, CA 94040 (415-948-8188). Makes available the following books: *Basic Track and Field Biomechanics,* by Tom Ecker. *Coaching Mental Excellence,* by Ralph Vernacchia, Rick McGuire, and David Cook. *Complete Book of Jumps,* by Ed Jacoby and Bob Fraley. *The Throws Manual,* by George Dunn, Jr., and Kevin McGill. *Train Hard, Win Easy, the Kenyan Way,* by Toby Tanser. *Steve Scott: The Miler,* with Scott Bloom. *Sports Speed,* by George Dintiman, Bob Ward, and Tom Tellez. *Running Trax a Computerized Training Program,* by J. Gerry Purdy.

TF News has many other books and videos. Their *World Class Video* series includes John Smith, sprints: Renaldo Nehamiah, hurdles; Larry Myricks and Ernie Gregiore, long jump; Dick Booth, triple jump and high jump.

Videotapes

Cambridge Physical Education and Health, P.O. Box 2153, Charleston, WV 25328. Makes available the following tapes: *Track and field techniques* (13 tapes), *Bill Dellinger's championship track and field* (17), *Sprinting with Carl Lewis, Coaching men's track and field* (9), *Coaching women's track and field* (9), a track and field series (9), *Running great with Grete Waitz,* and *Bill Rodger's running for fun and fitness.*

Championship Video Production, Tafnews, 2570 El Camino Real, Suite 606, Mountain View, CA 94040. Distributes the World Class Track and Field series, featuring the United States' best athletes and coaches: *Spints and relays* (John Smith, Mike Marsh), *High hurdles* (Renaldo Nehemiah, Jean Poquette), *Long jump* (Larry Myricks, Ernie Gregoire), *Triple jump* (Mike Conley, Dick Booth), *High jump* (Hollis Conway, Dick Booth), *Pole vault* (Earl Bell), *Shot put* (Ron Backes, Steve Forseth), *Discus* (Mike Buncic), and *400 meter hurdles* (Danny Harris, Steve Lynn). Also makes available *Speed dynamics* (Kevin O'Donnell, Loren Seagrave), which includes sprint and hurdle drills and demonstrations by world-class athletes, with detailed training programs.

"How To" Sports Videos, P.O. Box 5852, Denver, CO 80217. Makes available videotapes by the following experts: Bill Dellinger (6 programs), Ken Foreman (6), and Meg Ritchie (2).

Karol Video, 22 Riverside Dr., Wayne, NJ 07470. Tapes available include *Sprinting techniques, Hurdling techniques, The long jump, The triple jump,* and *The discus.*

Sports Video, 745 State Circle, P.O. Box 1941, Ann Arbor, MI 48106. Makes available 30 track and field videotapes.

USATF Development Project makes available a comprehensive list of instructional videotapes and videos of major competitions from the 1988 to 1996 Olympic Games, Olympic Trials, and World Cup Championships. Contact Dr. Lyle Knudson, Director of USATF Development Projects, P.O Box 4805, Dubuque, IA 52004-1840.

Volleyball

After completing this chapter, the reader should be able to:

- Appreciate the development of volleyball and describe the general rules and equipment used
- Practice the fundamental skills of passing, setting, spiking, serving, and blocking
- Explain aspects of team play and offensive and defensive strategies
- Teach the fundamentals of volleyball

HISTORY

Volleyball was invented in 1895 by William J. Morgan, who was physical education director of the YMCA in Holyoke, Massachusetts. He developed the game to provide an indoor game for the winter months in which relatively large groups of men could participate in a small gymnasium. The principal features of tennis were employed, but the net was raised and the players struck the bladder of a basketball with their hands instead of racquets.

The YMCA is chiefly credited with promoting this very fine game throughout the United States and in many foreign countries. In the United States volleyball is played regularly on playgrounds and in recreation centers, camps, and school and college classes and intramural programs. It recently has become one of the most popular sports in high school and college women's athletic programs. Also, it has become an excellent recreational game in the armed services and was played in both World War I and World War II.

The YMCA held its first National Volleyball Championships in 1922. The annual YMCA tournament and the addition of the United States Volleyball Association (USVBA) Open Championship in 1928 further popularized the game, not only as a pleasurable sport but also as a competitive game.

Volleyball was adopted as an Olympic sport in 1964 at Tokyo. Although at the time it was a sport played around the world, it was the Soviets and Japanese who took it most seriously. The Japanese women's teams introduced tenacious defense and increased the level of play by scraping and diving for every ball hit by an opponent. The Soviet's contribution to the game was the power offense. With the exception of 1976, when the Polish men's team defeated the Soviets for the gold medal, the Soviets or the Japanese won every men's and women's volleyball gold medal through 1980 (Soviet men three gold, women three gold; Japanese men one gold, women two gold). In fact, in the women's competitions from 1964 through 1980 the only time the gold or silver medal failed to go to the Soviets or Japanese was in 1980, when the Japanese boycotted the Olympics (silver to East Germany).

Until 1984 the highest finish by a U.S. men's team was seventh in 1968, and the highest placement by a U.S. women's team was eighth in 1968. But in 1984 (when the Soviets boycotted) the U.S. men won the gold and the U.S. women won the silver (China won the gold). In 1988 the Soviet women's team regained the gold by beating Peru (with China capturing the bronze), but the U.S. men's team repeated its gold medal performance, this time by beating the Soviets 13–15, 15–10, 15–4, and 15–8. Both the men's and women's U.S. volleyball teams took the bronze medal at the 1992 Barcelona Olympics. The men's gold was won by Brazil and the women's gold by Cuba. In the 1996 Olympic Games neither U.S. team medaled. The men's gold was won by the Netherlands, and the women's gold was captured by Cuba.

Today the game of volleyball requires team strategies involving offensive and defensive plays and highly refined individual skills. Another modification that has become popular, especially on sand courts and beaches, is played with just two players on each side. Most recently four-person volleyball has become popular across the nation.

DESCRIPTION AND EQUIPMENT

Volleyball for men and women is played on a rectangular court divided by a tightly stretched net. The top of the net is 7 feet 11⅝ inches (2.43 m) from the floor for men and 7 feet 4⅛ inches (2.24 m) from the floor for women (figure 39-1). A backcourt spiking line is drawn across the court 9 feet 10 inches (3 m) from and parallel to the centerline. At a point 8 inches (20 cm) behind and perpendicular to each end line, two lines, 6 inches (15.2 cm) wide, are drawn to mark the service area for each team. These lines are extensions of the sidelines. Six players constitute a team: three frontline players and three backline players.

An inflated leather ball 25⅝ inches (65 cm) in circumference and weighing between 9 and 10 ounces (260 to 280 g) is used. It is somewhat smaller than a basketball and resembles a soccer ball or water polo ball in size. Knee pads are not required equipment although they are highly recommended for safety purposes.

The play begins with a serve by the right back player. The server stands with both feet in the service area, which must be at least 6 feet 6 inches (1.98 m) deep and is designated as the entire end line. The right boundary line of this area is an extension of the right sideline and the left boundary line is an extension of the left sideline of the court. The serve consists of hitting the ball with the hand (open or closed) or any part of the arm so that it goes clearly over the net and within the boundaries designated by vertical extensions of the sidelines called the "net antennae." The receiving team must return the ball over the net before it touches the floor. Each team may hit the ball a maximum of three times in returning it across the net (a block is not considered one of the three hits). The ball is returned back and forth until one team makes an error. Only the serving team may score points except during rally play, whereby a point is scored on every legally served ball by either the receiving team or the serving team. Rally point scoring is reserved for tie-breaker games in 3-of-5 game matches. If the receiving team commits a fault, a point is scored. If the serving team makes the error or commits a fault, side-out is called and the other team serves following the rotation of players.

The ball must be cleanly hit in volleyball; it may not come to rest momentarily in the hands or on the arms. A player may not hit the ball twice in succession (*exceptions:* blocking rule and successive contacts are allowed on the first attempt to play the ball when coming from the opponents' court. This now includes any overhead or use of finger action, as in setting, during the attempt). The server continues to serve until loss of serve or completion of the game. Following a side-out, the opposite team must rotate clockwise one position before serving. This rotational system is used so that every player rotates not only in serving but in position on the floor. Both teams must be in correct rotation order at the time the ball is served. However, after the serve players may exchange court positions.

ABRIDGED RULES AND REGULATIONS

USVBA rules and regulations are described here.

Playing Area and Court Specifications

The height of the net is the only difference between court specifications for men and women. For the official measurements of the court and playing area for men see figure 39-1.

Officials and Their Duties

1. The first referee is the superior official and decides whether the ball is in play or dead and when point or side-out is made and imposes penalties for rule infractions. The first referee is in full control of the match and any judgement decisions rendered by the first referee are final.
2. The second referee assists the first referee wherever possible but is primarily responsible for net and centerline violations, supervision of substitutions, and overlap violations of the receiving team. This referee stands outside the court behind the standard, constantly changing positions as the ball changes sides of the court and should be positioned on the side of the net opposite the ball.
3. The scorer, seated on the side of the court opposite the referee, keeps the record on points scored,

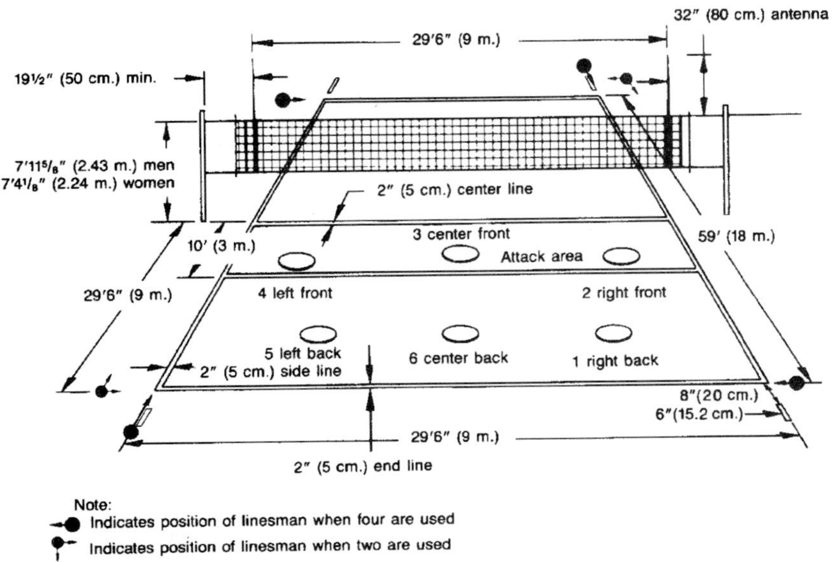

Figure 39-1. Volleyball court.

substitutions made, and time-outs called and supervises rotations of servers.

4. When two line judges are used, they are stationed diagonally opposite each other (figure 39-1). They are responsible for decisions concerning boundary plays and serving errors.

Players and Substitutes

1. In official matches each team must consist of only six players. Player positions along the net are designated right front, center front, and left front; those in the backcourt are called right back, center back, and left back.
2. When the ball is served, players must be in their rotational order. Side-to-side and front-to-back relationships of players must be maintained until the serve is contacted. In the frontline the center front must be between the right and left front. In the backline the center back must be between the right and left backs. Also, back-row players may not overlap with their corresponding frontline player. In other words, the left back must be deeper in the court than the left front. However, the left back does not need to be deeper in the court than the center forward because they do not have a side-to-side or front-to-back relationship. As soon as the serve is contacted, players may move anywhere on their side of the court.
3. A substitute may replace any player when the ball is dead, provided the player has reported to the scorer and received permission of the referee. A player taken out of a game may reenter once, but must return to the original position in the serving order.
4. In international rules, a substitute who enters the game and is then removed cannot reenter until the next game. In high school rules a player is permitted three entries into a game, with starting the game counting as one entry. Effective in 1998 in collegiate rules a maximum of 12 team substitutions are allowed with no entry limitations per player.

Service and Rotation of Positions

1. Choice of playing area or service at the start of a match is determined by the toss of a coin. After each game the teams alternate who serves first. When teams are tied in the number of games won, the first serve in the deciding game is determined by a coin toss.
2. The player in the right back position makes the serve and continues as the server until side-out is called. After side-out is called, an opponent becomes the server.
3. Each member of a team, on receiving the ball for service, rotates clockwise one position and remains in this new position until side-out has been called on an opponent's serve.
4. When a game is completed, teams change courts, and alterations in rotation of players must be made at that time. During the deciding game of a match the team captain may decide to change courts when one team reaches 8 points unless it is mutually agreed to remain on the same side of the court throughout the final game for the match.
5. The server must stand entirely outside the court and anywhere behind the end line until the ball is struck. The server must bat the ball with one hand clearly over the net so that, if untouched, it will land within the opponent's court. A serve is good if it clears the net and is touched by an opponent, regardless of where it might have fallen.

Returning the Ball

1. A return may be hit in any direction. A player may use any part of the body above (and including) the waist to hit the ball. Inadvertent play of the ball below the waist is permitted. For example, a hand-driven spike that rebounds unintentionally off a player's foot would be a legal play on the ball. However, if the defensive player stuck his or her leg out to block the ball and it rebounded off the foot, it would be illegal.
2. A return that passes over that part of the net between the net posts or their imaginary extensions is in play even if it touches the top of the net while in flight.
3. A return may be recovered from the net, provided the player avoids contact with the net.
4. After once contacting the ball, a player may not touch it again until it has been touched by some other player. (*Note:* After the ball has been blocked at the net, any of the blockers may make the next contact.)

Restrictions in the Play of Backline Players

1. Backline players may not participate in the action of blocking.
2. Backline players may not spike from the attack area, but may from behind the attack line.
3. Inasmuch as the attack line extends indefinitely, a backline player may not hit a ball into the opponents' court from above the height of the net while outside the court and within such limits of the attack area.

Infractions

If any member of the receiving team commits any of the infractions listed, 1 point is credited to the serving side; if the infraction is made by the serving team, side-out is called.

1. Serving illegally or serving out of turn.
2. Catching or holding the ball or failing to make a legal return.

3. Touching the ball twice in succession with any part of the body, unless the attempt is on the first hit over the net from the opponent, including a blocked ball.
4. Contacting the net. A player is not considered to have contacted the net if a hard-driven ball causes it to touch him or her. (*Note:* Should two opponents contact the net simultaneously, both are called for a violation; however, neither team is penalized and the serve is repeated. Insignificant net contact by a player not involved in an action of playing the ball is not an infraction. This includes any contact made by a player's hair. Players attempting to play the ball, or attempting to fake attack on the ball, or attempting to block the ball are considered to be involved in the action of playing the ball, and net contact during these examples would be an infraction.
5. Touching the ball when it has already been played three times without passing over the net.
6. Completely crossing the centerline when not directly involved in a play on the ball is permitted. For example, a setter in attempting to push off from the net position could step across the centerline and not be called for this action. Another example, is if the setter is running in from the back row to the net and in planting the feet, he or she crosses the centerline, this is legal. However, if a player is across the line before beginning a jump, or lands from a set and crosses the line, this would be illegal because it was part of the play on the ball. Note that anytime the player crosses the centerline, whether involved in the play of the ball or not, and makes contact with an opponent, an infraction will have occurred.
7. Reaching under the net and intentionally or unintentionally interfering with the opponent's play of the ball.
8. Changing player positions before the serve has been made. Until the serve is made, players on each team must be in their relative court positions.
9. Violating substitutions or time-out regulations.
10. Unnecessarily delaying the game.

Time-Out

1. Time-out can be called only by the referee on request of a team captain or coach when the ball is dead.
2. Time-out for substitutions is not charged against a team, provided play is resumed immediately.
3. Time-out for rest is limited to twice in each game, and play must be resumed in 45 seconds, except that if a player has been injured but is to remain in the game, the rest period may last 3 minutes.
4. Time-out between games is 2 minutes.

Scoring

1. Failure of the receiving team to return the ball legally over the net into the opponent's court scores 1 point for the team serving.
2. A game is won when either team scores a 2-point lead with 15 or more points.
3. The score of a forfeited game is 15–0.
4. A match is won by the team that first scores two of three or three of five games. The three-of-five format is most common among college and international matches. Courts are changed in the middle of the third or fifth game.
5. Some local rules may put a 17-point cap on the first four games of a five-game series with no cap on the deciding game.
6. NCAA rules require rally scoring (eliminates side-out and thus a point is scored every serve) in the fifth game of a match. However, often home teams in dual matches decide the method of scoring to be used.

FUNDAMENTAL SKILLS AND TECHNIQUES

Volleyball is a game that challenges the participant's skill in the use of the hands and agility in jumping, twisting, reaching, and hitting. Hitting motions that require the use of proper body control and muscular coordination are constantly demanded.

Passing

The most fundamental skill to be learned is the ability to pass the ball to a teammate, which is required on almost all plays.

Forearm pass

A forearm pass should be used to receive serves, low balls, and spikes (figure 39-2). The forearm pass used to recover the opponents' attack is called a "dig." The official rules do not permit carrying the ball, which occurs during any open-handed hit below the chest. If the ball is hit underhanded, the player should clasp the hands together in any one of three methods: (1) clenched fist, (2) curled fingers, or (3) thumb over palm (figure 39-3).

When possible the passer should move quickly to a position behind the ball, with knees bent, feet shoulder-width apart, and trunk slightly forward. The hands and arms should be extended and together and parallel, with the elbows locked during contact. The hands should point toward the floor, and the ball should be contacted on the forearm above the wrist. The arm movement should be an arc from the shoulders, with the legs actively involved.

Setting

The setter moves to a position so that the forehead is in line with the descending ball and faces the direction of the intended set. The setter's hands "form a window" 6 inches

Figure 39-2. The forearm pass.

in front of the face, with the upper arms nearly horizontal, wrists cocked, and fingers spread. The ball should be contacted with the inner surface of the thumb and fingers. A synchronized springing action of the fingers, wrists, and arms, as well as extension of the legs, pushes the ball forward (figure 39-4).

Spiking

Spiking is the act of striking the ball with great force in a downward direction into the opponent's court. To accomplish this powerful offensive skill, the player must learn to coordinate the approach, takeoff, and arm movements. The outside spiker's preliminary position is near the sideline and attack line. Three or four steps are taken during the approach, with the last step taken with the stronger leg.

The step-close takeoff is one method of transferring the momentum of the body into a vertical direction.

During the last steps the heels of both feet contact the floor, and then the weight is shifted forward to the toes. Both arms swing backward to shoulder height when the heels contact the floor. The arms are swung forward and upward during the takeoff. The left arm extends directly

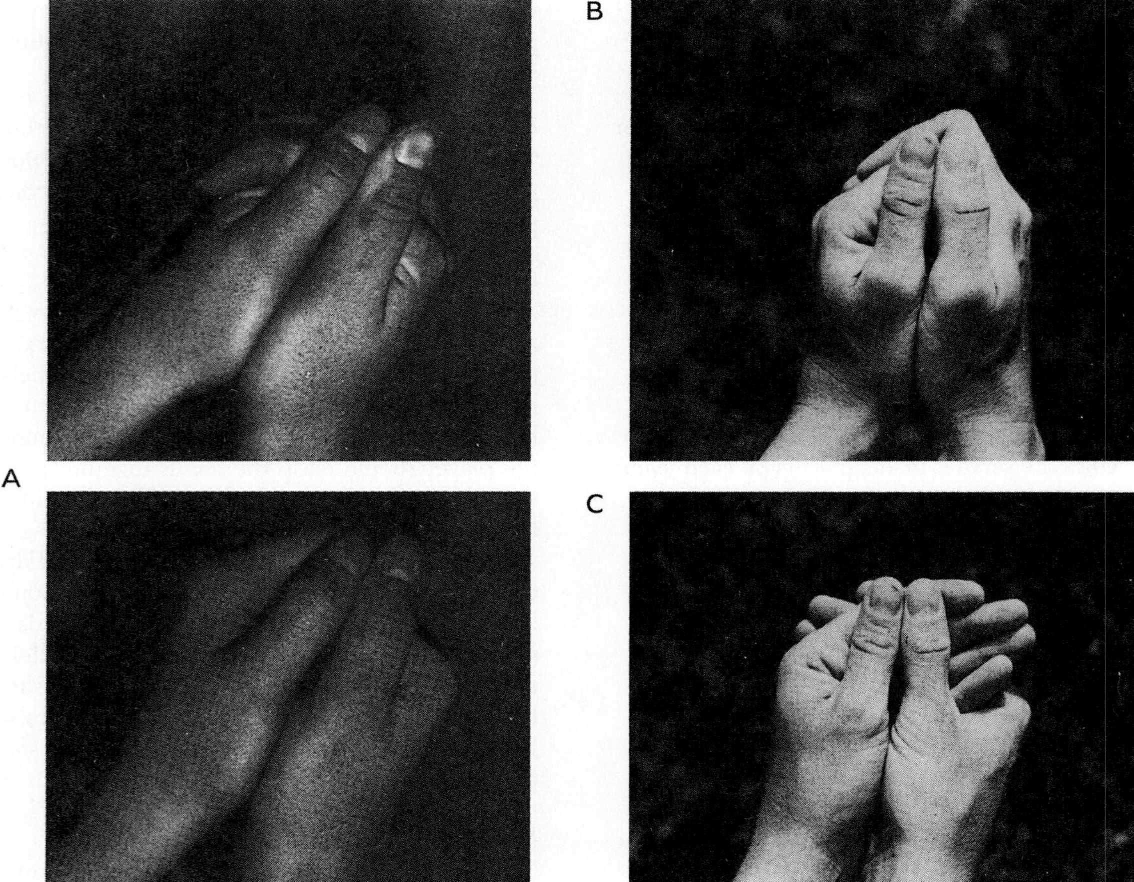

Figure 39-3. Hand positions for the forearm pass. **A,** Clenched fist. **B,** Curled fingers. **C,** Thumb over palm.

Figure 39-4. The set.

upward above the shoulder, and the right arm bends into a throwing position. The left elbow leads the swing, followed by an extension of the spiking arm, contacting the ball with the heel of the open hand. The wrist should snap quickly over the ball to impart a topspin (figure 39-5).

Tip

A tip is a soft shot contacted with the fingertips. The arm action is similar to the spike, but the attacker reduces the speed of the swing. The ball is contacted high above the net so that the tip is just over the opponent's attempted block.

Serving

Serves should never be missed at the beginning of a game, after a time-out or substitution, or near the end of a close game. Players should study the opposing team and serve to deep corners, weak players, areas between players (seams), and substitutes. Players should always concentrate on keeping the serve inbounds.

A player should learn to serve accurately and carefully, avoiding trick serves, because a team cannot score unless the serve is made good. The success of a serve therefore depends primarily on accuracy, control, and consistency. Regardless of the type of serve used, the server should attempt to place the ball in the opponent's backcourt, preferably in the corners or to the opponent's weakest receivers or to serve short, just over the net, to cause the front-row spikers to pass the ball.

Types of service

The underhand serve is the easiest to learn and control. The use of the overhand serve can give greater speed to the served ball as well as a floating line of flight deceptive to the opposing receivers. Sidearm serves can also be made.

Underhand serve. The underhand serve is the easiest and simplest for beginners to use to start play.

In executing this serve, the player faces the net with the left foot in front (if right-handed) of the right, rests the ball in the left hand at about knee height, and hits the ball just after releasing it off the holding hand. The hitting arm swings as in bowling a ball. The hand follows the ball straight through in the direction of the flight of the ball (figure 39-6A).

Overhand serve. There are two types of overhand serves: the floater and the topspin. The chief asset of the floater is its speed and its weaving line of flight, making it difficult for opponents to return. The topspin serve, while resulting in a more predictable path than the floater, tends to dive toward the floor after it crosses the net.

The overhand serve is executed by tossing the ball 2 or 3 feet (about 0.8 m) in the air above and in front of the right shoulder. The left side of the body faces the net, with the feet in a stride position. As the ball falls to the desired hitting spot, the arm extends from a cocked position to contact the ball. The heel of the hand should be used. Contacting the ball momentarily at its midpoint and with little follow-through results in a floater, while contacting the ball on its lower midsection, snapping the wrist, and rolling the hand over the top of the ball imparts the topspin. The overhand serve is the one most used by players participating in power volleyball (figures 39-6B and 39-7).

Sidearm serve. The sidearm serve is infrequently used. Its chief assets are its deceptive curves and the twist that the line of flight often has. Accurate use requires practice, but the serve can be used as a change of pace.

The ball is held at about hip level and is tossed about a foot into the air while the arm swings parallel to the floor. The left side of the body faces the net, left foot forward as in a forehand stance in tennis, and the swing of the arm is similar to the forearm swing.

Jump serve. Hitting the serve while jumping allows the server to contact the ball at a higher point, thus permitting a steeper angle. The similarity of the body actions of this serve to the spike (except the angle of contact with the ball) makes this serve a natural, and its use is increasing in high-level competition.

Figure 39-5. Spiking.

Receiving the serve

The ball should be advanced from the backcourt to the frontline in preparation for either spiking or placement in the opponent's court. The success of the receiving team depends on anticipating the flight of the serve and then on accurate passing.

Because the overhand serve is such a potent offensive weapon, formations for receiving the serve are necessary. An effective approach called "the W formation" is for the two frontline outside players to move back and toward their respective sidelines and the frontline center player stay near the net with the right shoulder turned slightly toward the net. The backline center player becomes the primary serve returner by being positioned in the center of the court approximately 12 feet (3.7 m) ahead of the backline. The backline outside players move back to about 6 or 7 feet (about 2 m) from the backline. In this formation the receiving team is best prepared to react to the rebound from the center back player, whose job is to nullify the effects of the opponent's serve.

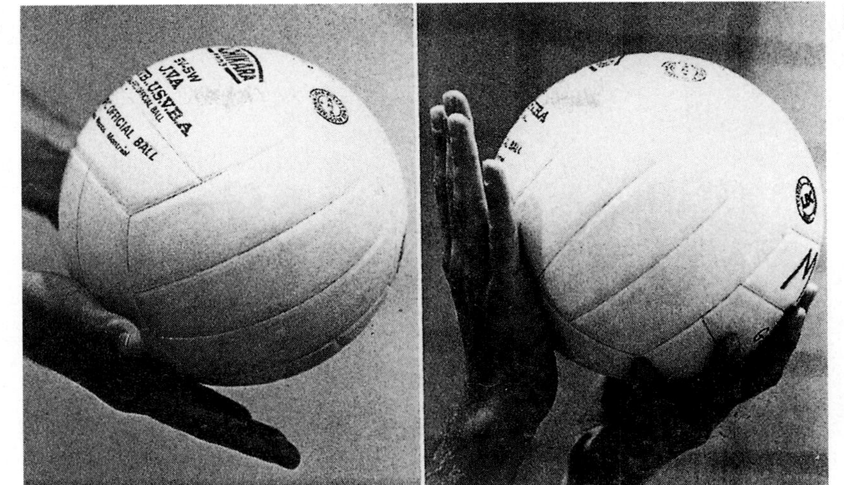

Figure 39-6. Contact for the underhand **(A)** and overhand floater serve **(B).**

Figure 39-7. Overhand serve.

Blocking

Blocking is a defensive play by a player or players against the spike or any other placement play near the net. Essentially, the block consists of a defensive player or players jumping into the air directly in front of the spiker, with arms extended in an effort to block the ball and at the same time to rebound it off the arms back into the spiker's court (figure 39-8). This results in the receivers forming into a W arrangement as shown in figure 39-9. To block effectively, one should time the jump with that of the spiker. Multiple

Figure 39-8. Blocking.

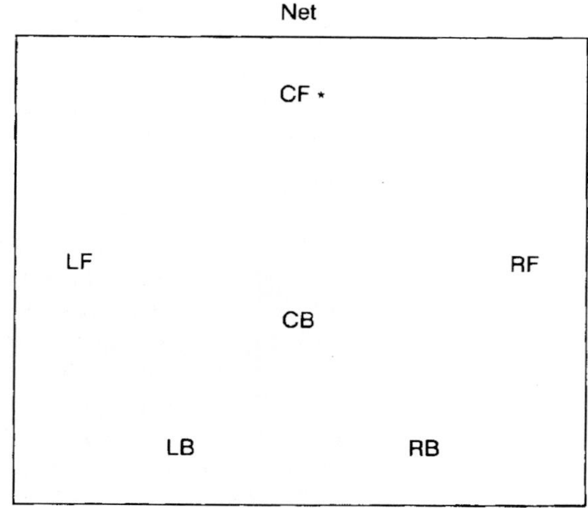

Figure 39-9. Formation for receiving a volleyball serve (back toward net).

contacts by a player(s) participating in a block are legal, provided they are during one attempt to intercept the ball.

Retrieving the Ball from the Net

To play the ball from the net, crouch low, legs spread and bent, with the body facing the sideline. As the ball rebounds from the net, use a forearm pass and an upward-backward striking motion so that a teammate may be able to play the ball. If the ball hits the net near the top, it will drop almost straight down. If it hits low in the net, it may rebound several feet, and the retriever must be stationed accordingly.

Team Play

The idea of the game of volleyball is not merely to hit the ball back and forth over the net. Essentially, the game offers many opportunities for team play, both offensive and defensive. When these skills are smoothly developed and executed, a real sense of enjoyment is derived by all players.

Offense

The basic offense consists of passing the ball from the backline to a setter at the net. The setter delivers the ball above and within 2 or 3 feet (about 0.8 m) of the net to the spiker for the attack plays selected to take advantage of the opponent's weaknesses.

The attack is used to develop and establish a playing situation that will deliver to the opponent an unplayable ball. This requires team play. The spiker should aim the ball into an unguarded area of the opponent's court. Sometimes as a surprise play the spiker tips the ball just over the blockers' heads or directs it to either side of the blockers' hands.

The four-two is a simple, basic offense. Four players are designated as attackers and the two best ball handlers as setters. In this system a setter always switches to the center of the frontline. Success depends on the ability of the five remaining players to pass the ball to the designated setter. The service order should be arranged so that the two setters and two best spikers are diagonally opposite each other.

Defense

Primarily, good defensive methods are formation plays to most effectively block or recover a hard-hit or well-placed ball. A block is usually set up by grouping two (or occasionally three) frontline players. The backline players are the secondary line of defense. The diggers must crouch low with hands held waist high, ready for a low, fast spiked ball.

Return quickly to original position when drawn out on a play. The server should assume position immediately after a serve.

TEACHING CONSIDERATIONS

1. The overhead set is the basic skill upon which continuous play can be built. Therefore, it should be the first skill taught. Teach the set using the following guidelines:
   a. Begin teaching the fundamentals of the set in partners off of simple tosses. Once a basic degree of skill is accomplished, move into a triangle formation.

^^^^^^^^^^net
T. S

Th.

T.—Target with ball
Th.—Thrower with ball
S—setter
P—pass

Drill sequence is throw, set to target (positioned at net where the spike should occur) and T. catches the ball.

A variation of this drill would be to position the target behind the setter, and the setter can then practice the back set.

b. To create a more gamelike drill, change the formation as follows:

^^^^^^^^^^net Th. S P	Th. throws (tosses) the ball to P, who passes the ball to S (setter), who sets a high outside set to Th. (who is also the target for the set). The drill can be repeated with a backset and by positioning the Th. on the back side of the setter.

c. To create a more gamelike drill, use a group of 4 and change the formation so that the Th. is across the net on the other side. The formation would look as follows (use 2 balls):

Th. ^^^^^^^^^^net T. S P	Th. throws over the net to P (passer), who passes to S (setter), who sets the high outside set to the target. The drill can be varied to put T. on the back side of the setter to practice back sets.

Use a group of 5 and position a second target on the backset side at the right sideline. The setter can then front set or backset the ball off the pass.

2. Once the set is established one-on-one, two-on-two, and four-on-four, cooperative and competitive play can be introduced to teach positioning and basic offensive and defensive strategy. Offensive strategy includes:
   a. Playing the ball to an empty space on the opponents' court (back and to the sides).
   b. Changing the direction of the ball.
   c. Changing the dynamics of the hit (tip or spike).
   d. Defensive strategy for beginning players includes primarily returning to home base to cover space.
3. The serve can be introduced as court size increases. Introduction of the serve requires introduction of the forearm pass. Progression for teaching the forearm pass is as follows:
   a. Establish a proper body position and rebounding surface with which to play the ball. The feet should be slightly wider than shoulder width, with one foot slightly advanced. The shoulders are tipped forward at the hip and should be out in front of the knees. The arms are extended out and the elbows are in full extension to create a firm rebounding platform for ball contact. Think of the pass as a rebounding skill first. As the students become more familiar with the correct body position, add a slight armswing from the shoulders to direct the ball to the target.
   b. Utilizing a partner and a ball. Assume the correct position and simply rebound the ball off of the passing platform. Add slight movement to position behind the ball and rebound.
   c. Add the slight armswing to give impetus up to the setting target (this can still be done in partners). Then begin adding greater movement for positioning prior to contact.
   d. Utilizing groups of three in volleyball as quickly as possible is a valuable teaching concept. The game is really a game of triangles in many instances. Using three people and two balls, create a triangle for practicing the pass.

^^^^^^^^^^net Th. T. P	Th.—Thrower P—Pass T.—Target . —Ball	Using two balls increases the pace of the drill and the number of repetitions for the player. Increase difficulty and create a more gamelike drill by placing the thrower on the other side of the net.

4. Combine practice of the forearm pass with the set and serve until students can receive a serve with the forearm pass from different directions and can set it in different directions.
5. Introduce the spike and dig only after consistency with the set and forearm pass is established.
6. Build new skills into the basic game gradually. Provide opportunities to play the game in modified form through the unit, gradually increasing the number of players, size of the court, and skills used as students develop consistency. Do not permit students to swing at the ball with one hand (make it illegal in game play if necessary). Modify rules to encourage good play (e.g., must be three hits on a side, or use as many hits as needed).

GLOSSARY

ace A serve that lands in the opponent's court without being touched.

actual playing time Time from the service to dead ball; 8 minutes constitutes a timed game.

blocking A defensive play; attempting to block or stop the returning ball over or near the net.

carrying the ball It is illegal to hold the ball. It must be batted.

catch Allowing the ball to come to rest on any part of the body.

cover Being positioned behind a spike or a block to field a ball glancing off a team member.

dead ball Ball that is out of play.

defaulted game Game in which one team does not have six players to start.

delaying the game Deliberately slowing down the game.

dive A defensive maneuver to recover a ball by extending to a prone position to contact it.

double foul Simultaneous fouls.

foot fault To step on or over the endline before or during the serve, or to step completely over the centerline.

game point The last point in the game.

held ball The ball coming to rest momentarily in the hands or arms.

kill A spike that is impossible to return.

match To win two of three or three of five games.

point Awarded the serving team for any infringement of the rules by the receiving team or for an unreturned shot.

roll A defensive maneuver to recover a ball. Rolls may be executed in all directions for recovery.

rotation Clockwise movement of the players following a side-out and prior to a team's term of service.

run-through A passing skill used to play a dropping ball while remaining on your feet.

service Putting the ball into play by the right back.

service area Area 6 feet 6 inches (2 m) deep and anywhere behind the end line.

set A high pass that is generally the second play by a team to relay the ball for a spiker.

side-out Ending of a team's right to serve because of an infringement of a rule.

spike A ball hit forcibly from a height above the net.

switch A change of playing positions on the court for strategic reasons.

term of service Serving the ball until side-out is called.

time-out Stopping the game for rest, substitutions, or injuries.

tip A change-of-pace attack.

violation A foul, such as a lift, double hit, or four hits on one side.

SUGGESTED READINGS

Bertucci, B., and Peterson, J. 1993. *Volleyball drill book: Game action skills*. Indianapolis: Masters Press.

Bertucci, B., and Peterson, J. 1993. *Volleyball drill book: Individual skills*. Indianapolis: Masters Press. Written for all competitive levels. Presents 200 drills and includes chapters on serving, receiving, digging, passing, spiking, and blocking.

Davis, K. 1992. *Advanced volleyball skills*. Winston-Salem, N.C.: Hunter Textbooks. Covers specialization of positions, court movement, individual strategy, gamelike drills, rules, evaluations, rating scales, and resources.

Herbert, M. 1991. *Insights and strategies for winning volleyball*. Champaign, Ill.: Human Kinetics. Covers how to play as a team, game planning, using scouting reports and statistics, and other coaching hints.

Kluka, D. A., and Dunn, P. J. 1996. *Volleyball*. 3d ed. Dubuque, Iowa: Wm. C. Brown. Presents the unique characteristics of volleyball with clear photos of sequential movements, visual skill enhancements, a chapter on officiating, and a discussion of volleyball's history.

McGowan, C. 1994. *Science of coaching volleyball*. Champaign, Ill.: Human Kinetics.

Mills, B. 1995. *Mental training and performance enhancement: Guide for volleyball coaches and players*. Dubuque, Iowa: Eddie Bowers. Covers nontraditional areas of performance enhancement.

Mills, B., and Asher, K. 1997. *Volleyball: Keys to success*. Dubuque, Iowa: Eddie Bowers. Contains contributions by some of volleyball's finest experts.

Neville, W. 1990. *Coaching volleyball successfully*. Champaign, Ill.: Human Kinetics. Explains how to demonstrate and direct the practice of basic skills and strategies.

Neville, W. 1992. *Serve it up: Volleyball for life*. Mountain View, Calif.: Mayfield. Contains information on history, facilities, equipment, rules, skills, defense, physical training, strategies, and game variations.

Stokes, R., and Haley, M. 1992. *Volleyball everyone*. 3d ed. Winston-Salem, N.C.: Hunter Textbooks. Contains hundreds of illustrations, teaching/learning aids, checklists, quizzes, resources, defensive and offensive strategies, drills, and a section on playing on sand.

U.S. Volleyball Association. 1998. *Official volleyball reference guide*. Colorado Springs: U.S. Volleyball Association.

Viera, B. L., and Ferguson, B. J. 1996. *Volleyball: Steps to success*. 2d ed. Champaign, Ill.: Human Kinetics. A primary resource for students in a beginning volleyball class.

RESOURCES

Videotapes

Coaching women's volleyball (7 programs) and *Gold medal volleyball* (10 programs). "How To" Sports Videos, P.O. Box 5852, Denver, CO 80217.

NCAA volleyball videos (2 videos), *USA volleyball, Do it better volleyball, Coaching women's volleyball* (9 videos), *Beginning girls volleyball* (3 videos), and *Coaching boys volleyball* (8 videos) are available from Cambridge Physical Education and Health, P.O. Box 2153, Charleston, WV 25328.

Serving, blocking, and individual defenses and *Passing, setting, and spiking*. Karol Video, 22 Riverside Dr., Wayne, NJ 17470.

Volleyball and *Volleyball drills*. Sports Video, 745 State Circle, P.O. Box 1941, Ann Arbor, MI 48016.

Water Polo

After completing this chapter, the reader should be able to:

- Describe the history of and equipment and facilities for water polo
- Explain rules and officiating practices
- Execute the swimming skills required of a water polo player
- Demonstrate defensive and offensive skills and tactics
- Teach a group of students how to play water polo using proper drills and teaching techniques

HISTORY

Bored with conventional swimming races and stunts, a group of British aquatic athletes created a new type of game during the 1860s. Played originally in lakes, with 11 players per side and rafts as goals, water polo has undergone numerous refinements. Today it ranks as perhaps the most demanding of all aquatic sports.

Introduced to the Olympic Games in 1900, water polo has always appealed to swimmers throughout the world, especially in Europe. Until recent years, however, it remained a rather obscure sport. Great Britain and Belgium dominated early Olympic competition (Great Britain won four gold medals in the five Olympics between 1900 and 1920, and Belgium won four silver medals and a bronze medal in the six Olympics between 1900 and 1924). Incredibly, beginning in 1928, Hungary won a medal in every Olympics through 1980, amassing six golds (1932, 1936, 1952, 1956, 1964, and 1976), three silvers (1928, 1948, and 1972), and three bronzes (1960, 1968, and 1980).

With the increase in the number of swimming pools and the availability of well-trained professional swimming coaches, resulting in the tremendous increase in the number of competent swimmers around the world, water polo is one of the fastest growing sports. In fact, of the 30 sports on the Olympic agenda, the U.S. Olympic Development Committee rated water polo as the third fastest growing sport in the United States.

In the past, for various reasons, the United States did not conform to the rules used by most other nations, that is, the FINA (International) rules. Now, however, water polo in the United States follows almost exactly the FINA rules so that its teams can gain experience to enable them to do well in international competition.

Earlier in this century the United States promoted what was called "softball" water polo, in which a soft, semi-inflated ball was used; the ball could be taken underwater, and much of the action occurred beneath the surface. This game attracted few spectators because no one could see what was happening underwater. Furthermore, the referee, who was situated at poolside, could not see what was taking place, and, therefore, an increasing number of underwater injuries occurred.

In the late 1940s and throughout the 1950s, a small group of California swimming coaches brought U.S. water polo back to the surface of the water and created a style of play that appealed to California high school and college swimmers and that, during the 1960s, spread rapidly across the country.

Until 1984 the United States had managed only three bronze Olympic medals (1924, 1932, and 1972) in water polo. The United States did win the gold, silver, and bronze medals in 1904, but the only foreign team (Germany) withdrew because of the "strange" rules adopted in St. Louis. In both 1984 and 1988, however, the U.S. teams finished with the silver medal, losing in both cases to Yugoslavia in close games. The 1984 final score was 5–5, but the gold medal went to Yugoslavia because they had scored more total goals in the tournament. In 1988 the Yugoslavian team defeated the U.S. team 9–7 in the first overtime game in Olympic history.

In July 1991 the U.S. men's water polo team defeated Yugoslavia 7–6 in overtime to win the first gold medal for the United States in major international competition since 1904. This was in the FINA World Cup tournament in Barcelona, Spain. In the 1992 Olympics Italy won the gold, with Spain taking the silver and the United States fourth place. In 1996 Spain captured the gold medal with Croatia winning the silver and Italy the bronze.

In June 1991 the U.S. women's water polo team won a bronze metal at the FINA World Cup. Women's water polo is not an Olympic event.

EQUIPMENT

Each team must have two sets of caps—one white set and the other set a dark, contrasting color, except they cannot be yellow/orange caps. The visiting team shall wear white caps and the home team dark caps. Plastic ear guards shall be worn on all caps and must match the caps (e.g., dark

Figure 40-1. Swim caps with guards.

guards on dark caps and white guards on white caps) (figure 40-1).

Goalkeepers may wear solid-red caps or caps quartered with two contrasting colors. The goalkeeper's ear guard shall be the same color as the field players on his or her team. Goalkeepers' caps shall be numbered 1 or 1A.

The ball is rubber fabric composition, yellow/gold in color, waterproof, four-ply, with a self-closing valve. The ball shall be inflated to a maximum 15 pounds per square inch (6.82 kg), measure 27 to 28 inches (69 to 71 cm) in circumference, and weigh 15 to 17 ounces (429 to 486 g). A smaller ball is available and recommended for women's and youth's games.

NCAA RULES

Play is based on two popular sports: swimming and lacrosse.

The game is played on the surface of the water by teams of seven players each. NCAA water polo is now considered legal in both 100-foot (30.5 m) and 75-foot (22.9 m) pools, with the 100-foot field preferred and championships played in a 100-foot by 75-foot pool. The deeper the water, the better. If the entire playing area is deep—6½ feet (2 m) or more—it is ideal, but most indoor pools have a shallow end. The goalposts must be 10 feet (3.05 m) apart, and the crossbar must be 3 feet (0.91 m) above the water surface when the water depth is 5 feet (1.52 m) or more; when the water depth is less than 5 feet, the crossbar must be 8 feet (2.44 m) from the floor of the playing area. Canvas backing and sides must enclose the goal area. The depth of the goal space must be a minimum of 18 inches (46 cm). The boundaries of the penalty throw zone extend along the 4-yard (3.66 m) line a distance of 22 feet (6.7 m).

At the start of the game each team consists of six field players and a goalkeeper, each wearing a swimsuit and a cap with ear protectors. The captain of each team can be any player on the team. Substitutions may be made only during time-outs or dead time.

The goalkeeper is the only player on a team who can stand or jump from the bottom (if the water is shallow enough to permit this), catch and pass the ball with both hands at the same time, or hit the ball with a clenched fist, provided he or she is inside the 4-yard (3.66 m) line.

The guards and forwards on each team may swim freely up and down the pool as they see fit, interchanging positions as often as they wish. They may not stand on or jump from the bottom, nor may they touch the ball with more than one hand at a time when catching, passing, or shooting it, nor may they enter inside the opposing team's 2-yard (1.83 m) line unless preceded by the ball.

Over the years water polo rules have changed frequently because of influences of the NCAA, AAU, and FINA. The rules are beginning to stabilize, as demonstrated by the fact that the AAU and NCAA rules are now identical, except for a few minor differences for the goalkeeper. A current rule book from both organizations and the appropriate state high school rule book should be consulted to ensure that players are familiar with the differences.

PLAYING TIME

In intercollegiate competition the game consists of four 7-minute quarters, the teams changing ends after every period of play. In high school competition the game consists of four 5- or 6-minute quarters, depending on whether the participants are varsity, junior varsity, or frosh-soph, and the teams change ends after every period. There is a 2-minute interval between each quarter and a 5-minute interval between halves.

STARTING THE GAME

At the start or restart of a game, one player (usually the goalkeeper) must be in position between the goalposts and the field players must take up their positions at least 1 yard (.91 m) apart on their respective goal lines. They may grasp the wall of the pool, ready to push off (figure 40-2).

The game is started with a blast of the whistle by the referee, who then drops or throws the ball at the halfway line into the lane closest to the referee. If the ball is not dropped or thrown properly, it may be done again. If a player on one team jumps the whistle, the ball is given to the opposing team on the 2-yard (1.83 m) line where the infraction occurred.

OFFICIALS

The head referee walks along one side of the pool, watching for infractions, and is aided by the assistant referee, who patrols the opposite side of the pool. The referees are both equipped with shrill whistles.

Whenever one of the referees sees an infraction committed by a player, the referee blows the whistle and uses hand signals to indicate what has occurred. For example,

Figure 40-2. Lineup and start of a game just after referee's whistle.

two thumbs up signals a jump ball, and an extended hand with 4 fingers held up indicates a 4-meter shot.

Anticipation is the name of the game, and unless there is obvious doubt as to whose ball it is, which requires the players to look up to see which color flag is being extended, the players must react to change of possession almost instinctively.

In addition to the two referees, other necessary officials include a timer and a scorer, both of whom should be seated at the scorer's table at poolside. For important competition, there should be goal judges, situated at each end of the pool, whose primary duty is to help the referees determine whether the shots taken by the players enter the goal for a score.

As in all sports, it is important that the officials be skilled and competent. This is especially true in water polo, in which the players are somewhat submerged and out of sight, thus inviting underwater holding and kicking unless the referees are adept at interpreting what is happening beneath the surface.

TECHNICAL FOULS

The following are common technical fouls:

1. Starting before the referee blows the whistle to begin the quarter
2. Holding onto or pushing off from the sides of the pool during play
3. Taking or holding the ball underwater when tackled by an opposing player ("tackled" meaning to have made body contact)
4. Swimming inside the opposing team's 2-yard (1.83 m) line unless preceded by the ball
5. Touching the ball with both hands at the same time (goalkeeper excepted)
6. Standing on, walking on, or jumping from the bottom when taking an active part in the game (goalkeeper excepted)
7. To cause the ball to go out-of-bounds. Should a player cause the ball to go out-of-bounds, a player of the opposing team puts it in play with a free throw. If the ball in flight strikes the side of the pool above the water line or goes out of the pool, it is out-of-bounds and play is restarted by a free throw awarded to the opposing team at the point the ball went out.

When a technical foul occurs, the referee blows the whistle and by proper extension of the flags awards possession of the ball to the team against which the infraction was committed. The player on the team awarded possession who was nearest the point of infraction then has 3 seconds to put the ball back into play; this may be done by passing to a teammate or by dropping the ball into the water and swimming with it. The ball must visibly leave the hand.

PERSONAL FOULS

The following are personal fouls:

1. Pulling back a player who does not have the ball
2. Any penalty-shot foul
3. Interfering with a free throw
4. Entering the water incorrectly
5. A dead-time technical foul

Each personal foul is accompanied by a 20-second ejection for the offending player (except for making a foul resulting in a penalty shot). The ejected player must swim to the ejection area and exit the water. The player should be ready to reenter the water correctly when the 20-second ejection flag of the player's color is raised and waved from the scorer's table. To enter the water correctly, the ejected player shall reenter from the ejection area 2 yards (1.83 m) from the corner of the field on the side of the pool opposite the scoring table, under his or her goal line. The reentry, if from the pool deck, shall be to slip into the water feet first. Play can continue immediately after the foul is called, but if the offending player interferes or is too slow in leaving the pool, another personal foul may be charged at the referee's discretion. The player who is ejected may be substituted for at the coach's discretion or must be substituted for if it is the third foul. Accumulating three personal fouls results in fouling out of the game.

FACE-OFF

1. A face-off shall be used to put the ball back in play after the following situations:
   a. A poorly thrown ball to start the game
   b. A ball strikes or lodges in an overhead obstruction
   c. A double foul is committed
2. Method of face-off

One player from each team closest to the area where the infringement occurred shall be selected by the referee to engage in a face-off. When the two opposing players are ready, the referee will toss the ball into the water between them. Play is restarted when one of the players touches the ball. In a face-off the ball may be played before it hits the water. Therefore, it is an advantage to have the player with the highest eggbeater (described later) to take the face-off. Two players must play the ball after the face-off before a try for a goal can be made.

PENALTY SHOT

A penalty shot can be awarded by either of the referees when (1) an offensive player inside the opponents' 4-yard (3.66 m) line but not touching the ball is held, sunk, pulled back, kicked, or struck, and (2) a player other than the goalie uses two hands to block a shot. When one of these infractions occurs, the head or assistant referee should immediately blow the whistle and extend the hand with four fingers extended, signaling that a penalty shot has been awarded.

A penalty shot is taken from the 4-yard (3.66 m) line in front of the goal. All players except the defending goalkeeper must leave the 4-yard line until the shot is taken, and no player can be within 2 yards (1.83 m) of the shooter.

After ascertaining that the shooting player is on the 4-yard line and ready to shoot and that the goalkeeper is on the goal line, the referee gives a sharp, quick blast of the whistle. At the whistle, the shooter must shoot without delay and without faking at the goal. The goalkeeper may try to block the shot; if the shot is blocked or is otherwise missed, the ball is immediately in play and action continues.

WHEN A GOAL IS SCORED

A shot must be attempted within 35 seconds from the time a team obtains the ball. The goal counts if it is made after the 35-second whistle blows but the ball left the player's hand before the whistle blew. The offensive team loses possession of the ball if a shot is not taken within the 35-second time period.

When a goal is scored, either from a shot taken by a player out in the field or by virtue of a penalty shot, all players must move back to their respective sides of the pool. The player whose team has just been scored on and who is closest to the center throws the ball back to either the goalkeeper or another player at the referee's signal. Both teams should be ready to play almost immediately after a goal has been scored; there should be no letup in the action. It is the referee's decision when the game is to resume.

SWIMMING SKILLS

The better one can swim, the better chance one has at becoming a competent water poloist. It is practically impossible for a swimmer of limited ability to play a respectable game of water polo because the rules place a premium on speed and continual action.

The ordinary *freestyle*, or *crawl, stroke* is used most commonly in water polo. However, because each player must remain alert to the positioning of other players and the location of the ball, it is necessary to swim with the head raised. This results in a type of crawl stroke in which the arms are a bit higher and the legs a little lower than normal, but by and large, there is not much dissimilarity to the regular racing crawl stroke used by competitive swimmers; basically the same muscles propel the body through the water.

The second most important stroke for the water poloist is a specific version of the *breaststroke* in which a whip, or frog, kick is used. This type of kick, especially when refined into the eggbeater kick, does the best job of enabling the player to raise the body high out of the water. The higher a player rides in the water, the more advantageous it is.

To perform the *eggbeater kick* the poloist simply uses the familiar breaststroke frog kick, but moves the legs alternately rather than simultaneously; in short, when one leg is bent in the frog position, the other is extended, and vice versa. This kick, when mastered, enables the player to raise the body several inches—sometimes as much as a foot—out of the water.

The *sidestroke kick* is also important because a single sidestroke or scissors kick, done from a prone, stationary position, will quickly provide momentum with which the player may get started, after which the crawl stroke is usually used.

The *backstroke* is useful because there will be times in every game when the player is sprinting downpool ahead of, the ball. By turning over on his or her back, the player can look and see where the ball is while continuing to swim down the pool.

The *butterfly stroke* is not used much in actual water polo competition, but many coaches use it during practices to help players build up their shoulder and arm muscles.

Normally the first 30 or 40 minutes of every water polo practice is devoted to the swimming skills just discussed because a poloist must be able to perform several different strokes with finesse and speed. Inasmuch as a game lasts 20 or 24 minutes in high school competition and 28 minutes in college competition, not including the time used for changing ends after each quarter or for time-outs, during which time the player remains in the water either swimming or treading water, a high degree of stamina is necessary. A poloist participating in a water polo game from start to finish will usually be in the water twice as long as a swimmer competing in a mile-long race! Furthermore, the necessity for making continued stops, pivots, and directional changes in midpool adds to the requirement for stamina.

Many champion swimmers have used water polo for conditioning purposes, and an increasing number of swimmers are finding that they enjoy the tactics provided by water polo more than mere swimming up and down the pool.

DEFENSIVE SKILLS AND TACTICS

Recent rule changes have resulted in changes in defensive tactics. For example, the full-pool press is seldom employed now because of the new method of starting the game after each goal is scored (all players moving to the center of the pool). Because the goalkeeper can now throw the ball anywhere in the pool, the offensive team has increased forward mobility. The standard defense is the half-pool one-on-one, but with the new ejection rule (personal fouls), the zone defense must be employed at times as well.

Half-pool one-on-one. The defensive team members fall back into their half of the pool area whenever the opponents capture possession of the ball. As soon as the opponents swim past midpool, the defenders pick them up and guard them one-on-one. The half-pool one-on-one is effective at shutting off the opposing team's fast break, but it allows the opponents to take their time setting up their attack, and it also removes all defensive players from the opposing team's goal area and, therefore, eliminates a quick counterattack in case the ball is intercepted or stolen.

Zone defense. The defensive team members fall back into a cluster around their goal and defend a particular segment of the goal area rather than a player on the opposing team. Thus the defensive team shuts off almost all close-in shots that the attacking team might want to take, but challenges the attackers to shoot freely from far out. This necessitates good goaltending by the defensive goalkeeper.

Personal fouls committed by the defensive team shall result in the removal (ejection) of that player immediately from the playing area by the quickest way for 20 seconds, until a goal is scored by either team or that player's team regains possession of the ball or restarts play after a stoppage of play, whichever occurs first.

When an ejection occurs, the zone defense becomes a necessity because of the six-on-five situation. The typical defense for an ejected-player situation is a 3-2. Three players shift back and forth on the 2- or 3-yard line while the ball is passed back and forth. The two outside players guard the two outside offensive players and sluff (leave their assignments and move toward the ball) when the ball goes inside.

Slow-swimming teams have used the zone defense successfully to stop faster-swimming opponents, but it places an emphasis on defense rather than offense and does not lend itself well to much scoring by the team relying on it.

No matter what tactics are used by a team defensively, each player must possess individual skills. Guarding an opponent is not easy. Each player when guarding must determine whether the opponent likes to swim around a lot or remain in one position, handles the ball with the right or left hand, is intimidated by close breathing-down-the-neck guarding, or uses illegal underwater tricks to gain an advantage.

Guarding. Guarding is defined as when a defensive player from one team makes bodily contact with any offensive player from the other team. This maneuver is only permitted when the offensive player has possession of the ball. Holding, striking at the ball with the open hand, pulling, and sinking an opponent are permitted while the opponent has the ball. When the ball is released, no bodily contact is allowed.

A good player stays close to the opponent, prepared to guard whenever possible. It may be permissible to guard an opponent by impeding the arm or leg movement, by swimming over, or by sinking the opponent, *provided the opponent is touching the ball.* This makes water polo a rough sport at times.

Many beginning water poloists are competent swimmers and have enough ball-handling ability to do a good job offensively at the start, but good guarding is a separate skill that must be practiced often. The poloist who can keep a particular opponent from scoring while causing some bad passes to be thrown and some good passes to be fumbled is an asset to any team.

GOALTENDING

As in soccer, field hockey, and other sports, the goalkeeper in water polo has special privileges and restrictions. The goalkeeper's position in the field of play and duties are unique.

In water polo the goalkeeper should play about 2 or 3 feet (0.6 or 0.9 m) in front of the goal being defended. A good goalkeeper can block at least half the good shots taken at the goal. In short, a skilled goalkeeper's value cannot be underestimated; the goalkeeper is the backbone of the team, always being in position to compensate for errors being made by teammates and often positioning teammates when on offense.

The goalkeeper may stand on or jump from the pool bottom (shallow pool), may go up to the centerline, but not beyond it, and may use two hands or strike the ball with clenched fists.

It is true that a goalkeeper needs swimming speed less than the other players, but there will come times when a loose ball falls in front of the goal, and the goalkeepers speed in swimming to it might save a score by the opposition. Furthermore, the goalkeeper must tread water (in a deep pool) throughout the entire game. Inasmuch as a game can last as long as 45 minutes, including between-quarter breaks and time-outs, stamina is necessary.

From the position in front of the goal, the goalkeeper can see all that is taking place in the pool and should not hesitate to shout directions to teammates.

The goalkeeper should be able to move quickly from side to side across the goal when opposing players swim in from various angles to shoot and should also be able to stand up to strong shots without flinching. More than any other player, the goalkeeper's ability to execute the eggbeater kick and raise the body high out of the water is important; a goalkeeper who is high in the water, with outstretched arms and a confident expression, can be an intimidating sight to a player swimming in and preparing to shoot.

The goalkeeper should be an adept ball handler. The goalkeeper is the only member of the team allowed to catch and pass the ball with both hands at the same time, and poor ball handling is inexcusable.

To summarize, the goalkeeper should have some swimming speed and stamina, a good eggbeater kick, the ability to "talk it up" to teammates, fast reactions, better than average ball-handling skill, courage, and enough strength to withstand a degree of physical contact, because the goalkeeper, like any other player, can be tackled when touching the ball.

Goalkeeper is a demanding position to play, and only the best athletes can succeed at it.

OFFENSIVE SKILLS AND TACTICS

The team in possession of the ball has one objective: to advance the ball down the pool by dribbling and passing and then to score by shooting the ball into the opposing team's goal.

Dribbling is done by controlling the ball between the arms while swimming the crawl stroke with the head raised. The arms are carried a bit higher than normal in the recovery to protect the ball from opponents. Proficient poloists can dribble with amazing speed, but a better way to advance the ball is by passing. This seemingly simple skill is actually difficult to perform. The passer can pick up the ball with only one hand, but when doing so can immediately be tackled by an opponent. Therefore, the passer must first assume a position to make the pass without being grabbed, ducked, or otherwise impeded; this requires adroit body maneuvering.

Because players are usually low in the water, the passer frequently has a tough time seeing a teammate to whom to pass with all the splashing that is taking place, so sharp eyesight is helpful (figure 40-3).

Finally, the passer must lift the body up out of the water with a powerful kick so that the passing arm clears the surface of the water and the thrown ball clears the outstretched arms of the opposing team.

It is essential that the pass arrive on target; if it is even a foot or two off target, the receiver may have trouble catching it, because just one hand can be used and the catch must be made in a manner so as to avoid being tackled.

If the pass receiver is stationary in the water and has secured an advantageous position over an opponent, the pass thrown to the receiver should be a dry pass, one that travels from the passer to the receiver entirely in the air without touching the water (figure 40-4).

If the pass receiver is swimming down the pool or is closely guarded by an opponent, the pass thrown to the receiver should be a wet pass, one that lands in the water in front of the receiver if the receiver is swimming or at the side away from the opponent if the receiver is closely guarded.

Whether wet or dry, the pass must be thrown with accuracy and must then be caught and handled adeptly. The mark of a good water polo team is its ability to advance the ball down the pool with accurate passes and without losing control or possession.

As with defensive tactics, offensive play in water polo has recently changed dramatically because of the new rules. Two commonly used attacks involve the fast break and a motion type of offense.

Fast break. If all players on a team are in top physical condition, the team is likely to use a fast-break offense. When the team gains possession of the ball, all the players break as swiftly as possible toward the opposing team's goal. This takes some practice and coordinated effort so the players do not swim into each other. But when these techniques are executed properly, one or two players are almost

Figure 40-3. Water polo game in progress.

Figure 40-4. Passing into the hole.

Figure 40-5. Fast break (white caps) after an intercepted pass.

assured of breaking into the open and will have a good shot at the goal if given an accurate pass.

A fast-breaking team can often run up many goals against an inferior opponent, but this type of attack requires a whole team of swift, well-conditioned athletes, much practice, and accurate passing. Furthermore, if the attack does not result in a score, the team members will have to use their speed to get back on defense hurriedly (figure 40-5).

Motion offense. In the motion offense, one or two players drive to the 2- or 3-yard line. They set the "hole." When the ball comes to them, a foul usually occurs. Then the other players make a break to get free for a shot. If a good shot does not result, the ball is returned to the hole and worked again for a foul, pass, and shot. The hole guard's fouls often result in an ejection and a six-on-five situation. To a great extent, the offense works off of the fouls.

Whether a team uses a fast-breaking offense, depends on a single shooter stationed near the opposing team's goal to do most of the scoring, or uses two or three players breaking in and around the player on the 2- or 3-yard line, no scores can be recorded without some strong, accurate shooting.

SHOOTING SKILLS

The goal at which the players are shooting is large: 10 feet (3.05 m) across, with the crossbar 3 feet (0.91 m) above the water surface when the water is 5 feet (1.52 m) or more in depth and 8 feet (2.44 m) from the floor of the playing area when the water is less than 5 feet deep. Yet when a goalkeeper is positioned in front of the goal, with the body held high and the arms outstretched, the goal looks surprisingly small to the attacking player. Furthermore, whenever the attacker touches the ball or lifts it up in preparation for taking the shot (figure 40-6) opponents can tackle the attacker.

It takes much practice to become a good shooter, one who can handle the ball easily with one hand, outmaneuver opponents to avoid being tackled, and shoot past a waiting goalkeeper. A player who under these conditions can score on 50 percent or more of shots over a season of competition is doing well.

Water polo players should take at least 50 practice shots daily and should learn to master as many different shots as possible. Every player should be able to score through hard, accurate shooting when the opportunity presents itself.

Frequently Used Shots

Power shot. When unguarded and unhurried, the shooter can simply assume a vertical position in the water, rear back, and shoot as hard as possible toward the goal.

Bounce, or skip, shot. From the same unguarded and unhurried vertical position, the shooter can throw the ball

Figure 40-6. Attacker preparing to shoot at goal.

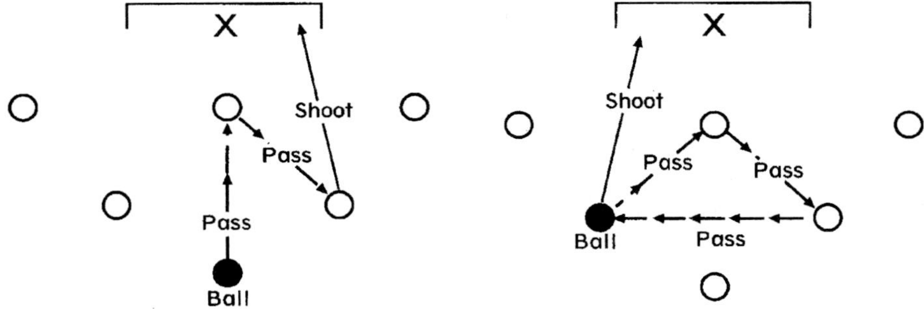

Figure 40-7. Two shooting drills.

so that it hits the water in front of the goal and bounces up into the goal.

Lob shot. Taken from almost any position facing the goal, the lob shot is designed to be thrown high into the air so that it sails gently over the goalkeeper's outstretched arms into the corner of the goal in the rear.

Pop shot. When swimming in toward the goal and closely pursued, a player often cannot stop and shoot without being caught from behind and tackled; therefore, from the swimming position the player can lift the ball a few inches into the air with the underwater arm and then slap or hit the ball goalward with the other arm as it swings forward on the recovery.

Shooting Drills

Two shooting drills are shown in figure 40-7. These drills should be practiced without defensive players in position and with the players in the drill changing position. As skills develop, the same drills may be practiced with defensive players in position.

PASSING DRILLS

Circle Drill

The circle drill is excellent for practicing the dry pass. Catching the ball softly with the fingers spread wide should be emphasized. All players should practice with both the left and right hands. If the group is large enough for two or more circles, competition can be easily established by having each circle count the number of good passes and receptions without the ball touching the water.

A keep-away drill could also be used by having three or four defenders in the center of the circle try to intercept the ball. Such a drill emphasizes sharp, quick passes to the open player on the part of the offense and quick reaction and hustle on the part of the defense.

Three-Player Passing Drill

The three-player passing drill is good for practicing the wet pass (figure 40-8). Leading the receiver should be emphasized, but not so much that the defense has a chance at the ball. Have all players vary positions and use both hands.

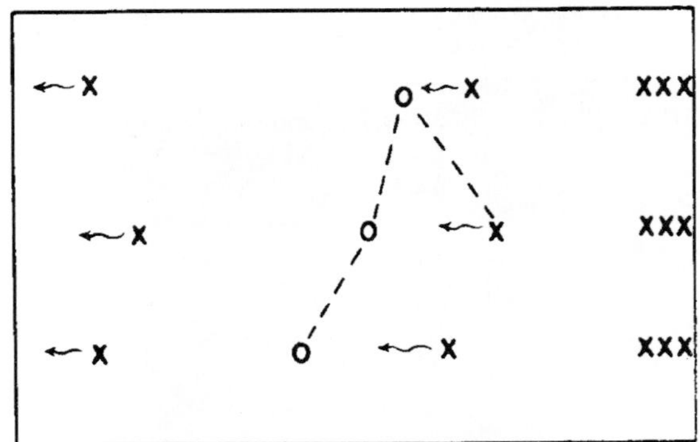

Figure 40-8. Three-player passing drill.

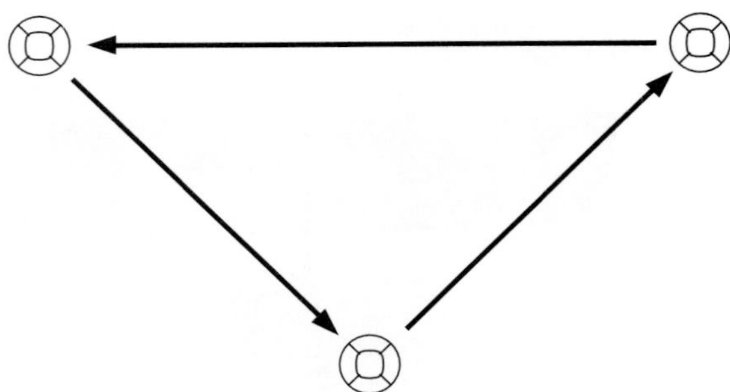

Figure 40-9. Triangle passing drill.

Triangle Passing Drill

Three players form a triangle and continuously pass in one direction. Switching direction every so often allows work on the cross-face pass (figure 40-9).

TEACHING CONSIDERATIONS

1. Water polo requires highly conditioned players with skilled swimming techniques. If students do not have the stamina to participate with official rules, consider modifications that permit resting on the side of the pool, two-handed ball handling, or no guarding. Excessive fatigue in an unconditioned or unskilled swimmer can be dangerous.
2. Include conditioning and practice of the basic swimming strokes used in water polo as a large part of all classes (crawl, breaststroke, sidestroke kick, and backstroke).
3. Teach passing as a basic individual skill in shallow and then deep water, first to stationary receivers and then to moving receivers. Add a passive defender (no guarding) and a moving receiver as soon as basics are established. As the technique becomes consistent, give guarding privileges to the defender.
4. Teach guarding as a separate skill, first with a passive offensive player and then with an active offensive player.
5. Combine practice of dribble and pass, dribble and shoot, and receiving a pass and shooting, first without defense, next with passive defense, and then with active defense. Move from practice situations using one individual moving the ball to a partner and then three players moving the ball. When adding defensive players, give the offense the advantage initially.
6. Teach shooting skills first without a goalkeeper, then with a goalkeeper, and then with a defender.
7. Teach player-to-player defense initially as the basic defense. Later teach zone defense around the goal and zone defense as a basic defense.
8. Begin game play in two-on-one, three-on-two, and three-on-three situations using a smaller play area.
9. All practice situations should be organized to permit maximum ball-handling opportunities. Waiting for a turn should be avoided.
10. Skills involving positioning in game play should be gradually integrated into practices as defense is added and the number of players increases. Because swimmers can tire easily and cannot quickly recover from poor positioning, strategies on player movement in the play area are critical and should be taught specifically.

GLOSSARY

backing Canvas backing to enclose goal space.

caps Each team must have two sets of caps, one white and the other a contrasting color. The visiting team wears white. All caps must have plastic ear guards.

corner throw A throw taken by the offensive team when the defense causes the ball to go over its goal line.

ejection Penalty accompanying a personal foul. Offending player must swim to ejection area, exit the water, and remain out for 20 seconds (or less, if a goal is scored).

ejection area The space in the comer of the pool opposite the scorer's table where an ejected player waits until signaled back into the game after his or her first or second personal foul.

face-off A procedure used when the referee cannot determine which team should put the ball back into play. One player from each team is positioned side by side, facing the referee at the side of the pool, each toward his or her defensive end, and races for the ball when it is dropped by the referee into the water.

free throw A throw used to put the ball in play after a foul, goal, ball out-of-bounds, or any other situation in which one team is directly given the ball. The free throw is later taken at the point of infraction. The player has 3 seconds to get rid of the ball. It may not be thrown directly at the goal.

game 28 minutes of actual play, in four periods of 7 minutes each. There should be 2-minute intervals between quarters and a 5-minute period at the half.

goal throw A free throw taken by the goalkeeper after the offensive team causes the ball to go over the goal line outside the goal.

guarding When a defensive player from one team makes bodily contact with an offensive player from the other team. This maneuver is only permitted when the offensive player has possession of the ball. Holding, striking at the ball with the open hand, pulling, and sinking the opponent are permitted. When the ball is dropped or released, no contact is permitted.

hole The area in front of the goal at the 2-yard (1.83 m) line.

illegal player A player who has committed a third personal foul or has been ejected for the entire game.

impeding When a player intentionally hinders or slows the progress of an opponent by swimming on the back, legs, or shoulders of the opponent or swims under any swimming opponent with or without the ball.

penalty throw A throw taken by any member of the offended team from the penalty line. A one-handed, over-the-shoulder shot is taken.

pop shot, or tee shot Executed by a player swimming in with the ball (dribbling) toward the goal, she or he, without stopping, lifts the ball slightly out of the water with one hand and hits it with the other hand.

signals The flag positions used by the referee to denote the game situations.

technical fouls Infractions committed that are not of a personal nature, such as stalling, striking the ball with the fist, or being within 2 yards (1.83 m) of the opponent's goal line.

35-second clock The visible digital timer used to indicate how long any team may have possession/control of the ball before attempting a shot at the goal. A shot must be attempted within the 35-second time limit or the offensive team loses possession.

35-second possession It is a technical foul for a team to retain a ball for more than 35 seconds without shooting the ball at the opponent's goal.

time-outs There may be three time-outs of not more than 2 minutes each per team in the first four quarters. In overtime each team may have one time-out.

SUGGESTED READINGS

Cicciarella, C. 1994. *Water polo*. 2d ed. Boston: American Press.

H_2O polo. 1993. Waterford, Conn.: Jakro.

How to coach water polo when you don't know anything about it. 1992. Indianapolis: American Water Polo Coaches Association, 201 S. Capitol Ave., Suite 500, Indianapolis, IN 46225.

NCAA official water polo rules. Current ed. Kansas City, Mo.: NCAA.

Swimming, diving, and water polo rules. Annual. Kansas City, Mo.: National Federation of State High School Associations.

Periodical

Water Polo Scoreboard (monthly), U.S. Water Polo, 201 S. Capitol Ave., Suite 520, Indianapolis, IN 46225.

RESOURCES

Videotape

Water polo, Karol Video, 22 Riverside Dr., Wayne, NJ 07470.

Weight Training

After completing this chapter, the reader should be able to:

- Describe the history of weight lifting and distinguish the differences among the activities in this chapter
- Set up a personal weight training and circuit weight training program
- Recognize the importance of safety in these activities
- Identify appropriate exercises for various parts of the body
- Explain the competitive lifting events
- Teach basic weight lifting techniques to a group of beginning students

OVERVIEW

Weight training is an exercise that utilizes progressive resistance movements, typically with free weights or weight machines, to build strength or muscle endurance. The activity of weight training has become very popular, with several different purposes. Some perform weight training for sport; that is, they participate in weight lifting, powerlifting, or bodybuilding competitions. Athletes of other sports, such as football or track and field, use weight training to enhance their performance in their own sports. Many people also use weight training for general fitness; they just want to look and feel better. Although these reasons for lifting stem from different goals, all those who participate in a weight-training program expect the program to produce benefits such as increased strength, increased muscle size, and an improvement in the ratio of fat-free mass to body fat.

HISTORY

The exact period in history when weight training became a practice or part of a training regimen is not known. Strongmen such as Samson, Hercules, and the Greek warrior Milo are part of ancient myth and folklore.

In its earliest form, weight lifting was a part of everyday life. Weight training also played an important role in preparing soldiers for battle in the days of the Greeks, Egyptians, and Romans. During the Middle Ages, Romans trained their soldiers by marching them over long distances with heavier-than-normal loads. Throughout the seventeenth to nineteenth centuries, most of the empires and armies of Europe followed the Greek and Roman examples and trained with overloaded packs.

Weight "lifting" was introduced to the United States between 1859 and 1872, when Dr. G. B. Winship toured the United States and Canada, giving lectures and presenting exhibitions.

Weight "lifting" soon found its way into carnivals and circuses and onto vaudeville stages, where men and women performed unbelievable feats of strength that in fact were tricks—which probably was responsible for most of the myth and mystery that has surrounded weight lifting until recent times. Weight training survived this era and went on to find its way into YMCAs and athletic health clubs. With these organizations promoting the activity, evidence of the value of weight training began to grow.

Through most of the early 1900s, weight training was practiced, almost exclusively, by those who competed in one of the weight-lifting sports.

The sport of weight lifting has been included in the Olympic Games since 1896. At first there were two events, a one-handed lift and a two-handed lift, and the lifter's body weight was not considered. In 1920 the press, snatch, and clean and jerk were introduced, and this system remained until 1972, when the press was eliminated. In the United States, organized competition began in 1929 when the Amateur Athletic Union (AAU) held its first national championship. In 1932 the United States entered its first team in Olympic competition.

The sport of bodybuilding first began in the United States in 1938 when the Amateur Athletic Union held the Mr. America contest. This was the only group to organize national contests until 1950 when the National Amateur Bodybuilders Association (NABBA) began the Mr. Universe Competition. The International Federation of Bodybuilders formed in 1946, and it began the Mr. Olympia contest in 1965. Today this is the biggest and most prestigious bodybuilding competition. In 1965 the NABBA held its first Miss Universe competition. In 1980 women began competing in the Miss Olympia contest.

The sport of powerlifting involves three lifts: the squat, deadlift, and bench press. In recent years it has been the most popular form of competitive lifting in the United States. In less than ten years the sport grew to the extent that more than forty nations compete in the International Powerlifting Federation World Championships. Although a comparatively new form of competition, the sport of powerlifting is now being considered as an additional event in Olympic competition.

Using weight training for other sports was not done until the late 1960s when the San Diego Chargers and the University of Hawaii both had strength coaches and had successful seasons. The University of Nebraska followed suit and won national championships in 1970 and 1971. They credited their success to their strength program. Strength and conditioning quickly became popular for the sport of football. Today strength and conditioning for sport is done for most all sports and is being used even at the high school level.

Medical doctors began experimenting with strength exercise for injury rehabilitation and muscle rebuilding soon after World War II. Their efforts were successful, so they encouraged physical educators to include weight training in gym classes. Magazines devoted to weight lifting and bodybuilding also helped to make the public more aware of the benefits of this activity. More gyms opened up throughout the country, but they were still used by mostly hardcore lifters. In the 1970s, weight machines were introduced into many gyms and weight training became more popular amongst the general population.

Weight training and bodybuilding are constantly increasing in popularity in colleges and health clubs throughout the country. It is not uncommon to find a set of barbells or other weight-training equipment in the recreation room of many American homes. In an age that has provided us with countless labor-saving devices, weight training has provided the much needed vigorous exercise that our push-button lifestyle has taken away.

GENERAL CONSIDERATIONS

When it comes to weight training, the goals of lifters are different. Weight lifters and powerlifters are concerned with strength, bodybuilders are concerned with size and definition, and athletes are concerned with improving their performance. Goals for noncompetitive lifters are numerous. With lifters having different goals as well as different levels of experience, how lifters train will vary also. The following guidelines are to help beginners with starting a weight-training program.

Frequency. One common lifting schedule amongst beginners and people lifting just "to keep themselves in shape" is to lift three times per week. This gives them 1 or 2 days off between lifting days, and makes for an easier schedule to follow. More advanced programs often follow different weekly schedules, concentrating on specific areas on set days during the week.

Logical order. Exercises should progress from large muscle groups (legs, back, chest) to smaller muscle groups (shoulders, triceps, biceps) and usually go from multi-jointed lifts (hip-knee-ankle or shoulder-elbow) to single-jointed lifts (knee, ankle, or elbow). Example: a leg press (which involves movement around the hip, knee, and ankle joints) is done before leg extensions (which involve movement around the knee joint).

Beginning poundage. By trial and error one selects starting amounts of weight that can be lifted with proper form for a determined number of repetitions (e.g., 10 to 12 reps).

Rest and recovery. The amount of rest needed depends on the lifting intensity of the individual. For beginners 1½ to 2 minutes between each set is a good starting point.

Sets and repetitions. Again it depends on the level and goals of the individual. A basic program usually consists of three sets of 10 to 12 repetitions, with proper recovery between sets.

Weight Training

GENERAL TECHNIQUES FOR ALL LIFTS

Stretching. Basic overall stretching should precede any lifting, with particular attention to the muscle groups to be exercised. For example, before the bench press you should concentrate on stretching the chest, shoulders, and triceps. Many experts suggest that stretching activities should be used at the end of a workout as well.

Warm-up. Warm-up activities should be specific to the exercise; for example, a light bench press should be done in preparation for the bench press exercise. Usually a warm-up consists of 10 repetitions with a light, comfortable weight.

Breathing. One should inhale during the negative, or lowering, phase of all lifts and exhale during the working, or positive, phase. One should never hold the breath during any part of a lift.

Full range. One should always complete the full range of motion during any lift, and never do any partial or half movements while learning basic exercises.

Spotting. For any exercise culminating with the lifter in a fatigued state and still supporting the weights, a spotter should be used. See figure 41-1 for an example of the correct spotting technique.

Figure 41-1. Free-weight bench press—starting position.

FUNDAMENTAL SKILLS AND TECHNIQUES

Exercises for the Upper Body

Free-weight bench press (for chest, shoulders, and upper arms)

Starting position. Lie on the bench with feet flat on the floor and arch the back slightly. The spotter lifts the weight from the rack and gives it to the weight lifter, who should take the weight with the arms extended and the hands slightly wider apart than the shoulders (figure 41-1).

Movement. Lower the bar to the middle of the chest (figure 41-2). Then recover to the straight-arm starting position.

Technique and safety tip. Once the bar is pressed up approximately 12 to 14 inches (30 to 35 cm) from the chest, strive to angle the bar slightly back toward the head and shoulders. This places the bar at an advantageous angle for the shoulders and triceps to finish the lift. Always have a spotter behind your head to assist returning the bar to the rack.

Figure 41-2. Free-weight bench press.

Universal gym bench press

The technique for this exercise is the same as for the free-weight bench press, but no spotter is required. The body should be positioned so that handles cross the middle of the chest.

Universal gym lat pull (for upper back, biceps, and posture muscles)

Staring position. Grasp the bar with a wide overhand grip. Sit on the seat with the leg pad snug against the thighs. Keep your head up and the back straight (figure 41-3).

Movement. Pull the bar down behind the head until the bar reaches the base of the neck (figure 41-4). Return the bar to the starting position.

Technique and safety tip. Return the bar slowly to avoid any loss of control or stabilization. No spotter is necessary.

Figure 41-3. Universal gym lat pull—starting position.

Free-weight bent rowing (for posture muscles, biceps, and upper back)

Starting position. Stand with the feet shoulder-width apart and the toes pointed out slightly. Bend over until the torso is nearly parallel to the floor, and bend the knees slightly. Grasp the barbell with an overhand grip, with the hands at about shoulder width.

Movement. Pull the barbell up until it reaches the lower rib cage (figure 41-5). Then return it to the starting position.

Technique and safety tip. Concentrate on raising the elbows as high as possible. No spotter is necessary. Always keep the knees bent and use relatively light weights to avoid lower-back injury.

Free-weight overhead press (for shoulders and upper arms)

Starting position. Stand with the feet shoulder-width apart and the toes pointed out slightly. Keeping the head erect, squat down and grasp the barbell with an overhand grip, with the hands also shoulder-width apart. Return to the standing position and lift the barbell shoulder high (figure 41-6).

Movement. Push the barbell straight up until the arms are fully extended (figure 41-7). Return to the shoulder-high position. The knees should remain straight.

Technique and safety tip. Never bend or arch the back. Always look straight ahead or down during the lift to pre-

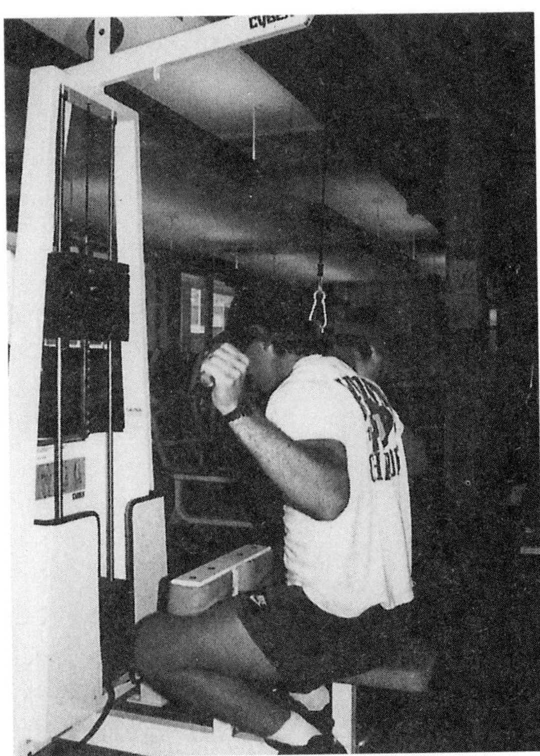

Figure 41-4. Universal gym lat pull.

Figure 41-6. Free-weight overhead press—starting position.

Figure 41-5. Free-weight bent rowing.

Figure 41-7. Free-weight overhead press.

Figure 41-8. Free-weight arm curl—starting position.

Figure 41-9. Free-weight arm curl.

vent lower-back arching. A spotter should be used (as shown) to prevent the lifter from losing control when the bar is at its peak height.

Free-weight arm curl (for biceps)

Starting position. Stand with the feet shoulder-width apart and the toes pointed out slightly. Bend at the knees, grasp the bar with an underhand grip, then return to the standing position (figure 41-8).

Movement. With the elbows tucked tightly against the rib cage, flex the arms at the elbows and pull the bar up to the chest, and return to the starting position (figure 41-9).

Technique and safety tip. To avoid arching the back, keep the head down and the eyes on the bar, or stand with the back against the wall with the feet slightly out from the wall for balance. This exercise can also be accomplished using dumbbells.

Parallel-bar dip (for lower chest, shoulders, and upper arms)

Starting position. Use an overhand grip on the parallel bar, and jump up to an arms-extended position (figure 41-10). Cross the legs and arch the back slightly.

Movement. Bend or "dip" until the chest touches the crossbar or the elbow is bent 90 degrees (figure 41-11). Push back up to the starting position.

Figure 41-10. Parallel-bar dip—starting position.

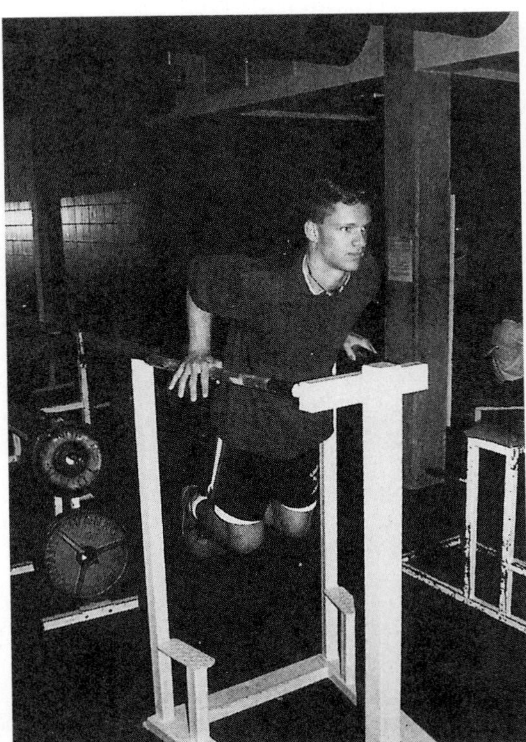

Figure 41-11. Parallel-bar dip.

Figure 41-12. Side lateral raise—starting position.

Technique and safety tip. Keeping the back arched and the eyes forward helps prevent swinging and rocking during the movement.

Side lateral raise (for upper arms, shoulder, and upper back)

Starting position. Stand with the feet shoulder-width apart. Use overhand grip on dumbbells held beside the thighs.

Movement. At the same time, raise both dumbbells sideways and upward (keeping arms straight) until arms are extended just above shoulder height. Lower dumbbells to starting position and repeat (figures 41-12 and 41-13).

Technique and safety tip. Keep head erect and back straight. This exercise can also be done with the trunk bent at the waist (figures 41-14 and 41-15).

Exercises for the Lower Body

Free-weight parallel squat (for thighs, hips, lower back, and buttocks)

Starting position. Stand with feet shoulder-width apart and the toes pointed out slightly. Grasp the bar with a comfortable, wide overhand grip. (The distance between the hands will vary with the individual.) Position the bar across the shoulders just below the base of the neck (figure 41-16).

Movement. With the head up and the back slightly arched, squat until the tops of the thighs are parallel to the floor (figure 41-17). Then extend the legs and return to the starting position.

Figure 41-13. Side lateral raise.

Technique and safety tip. To avoid rounding the back, keep the head up and the eyes focused ahead. The knees should be aligned directly over the toes while in the squat position. The rate of descent should be slow and controlled. Never

Figure 41-14. Bent lateral raise—starting position.

Figure 41-15. Bent lateral raise.

try to bounce out of the squat position. Always use at least one spotter when doing this exercise. If it is difficult to keep the feet flat on the floor, use a heeled running shoe or stand with a 2- by 4-inch board under the heels. Straddling

Figure 41-16. Parallel squat—starting position.

Figure 41-17. Parallel squat.

a bench during the exercise is one way to avoid squatting too far down.

45-degree leg sled (for thighs and buttocks)

Starting position. Sit on padded seat and place the feet high up on the metal platform. Push up on platform and move safety catch. Grasp the handles on the sides of the chair (figure 41-18).

Movement. Flex at the hips and knees to lower the weight. Push weight back up smoothly until legs are almost straight, leaving only a slight bend in the knees (figure 41-19).

Technique and safety tip. Position the seat so that the knees are flexed at least 90 degrees at the start of the exercise. Control the weight in the extended position. Return slowly to the starting position. Push smoothly keeping the weight on the heel of your foot.

Figure 41-18. Leg press on 45° leg sled—starting position.

Figure 41-19. Leg press on 45° sled—movement.

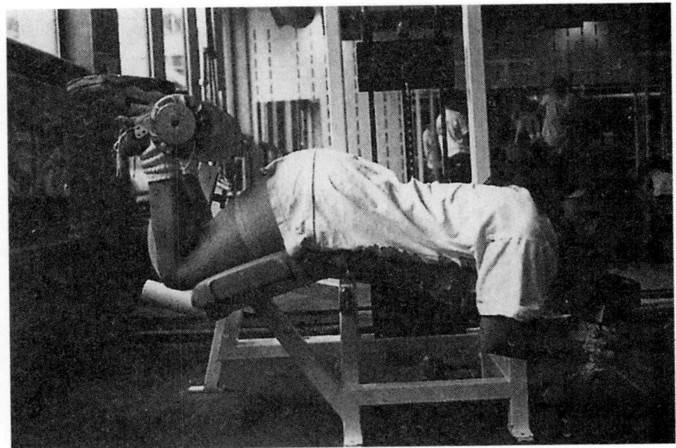

Figure 41-20. Universal gym leg curl.

Universal gym leg curl (for hamstrings)

Starting position. Lie face down on the knee flexion table with the back of the ankles touching the carriage pads. The knees should be extended over the edge of the table.

Movement. Pull the carriage as far up toward the buttocks as possible (figure 41-20). Then return to the starting position.

Technique and safety tip. The hips and buttocks have a normal tendency to rise during the movement, but this can be corrected by using a flexed table.

Free-weight heel raise (for calves)

Starting position. Grasp a dumbbell in each hand and position the balls of the feet over a board or stair step.

Movement. Stretch the calves by lowering the body until the heels are lower than the toes, then extend to a "tip-toe" position (figure 41-21).

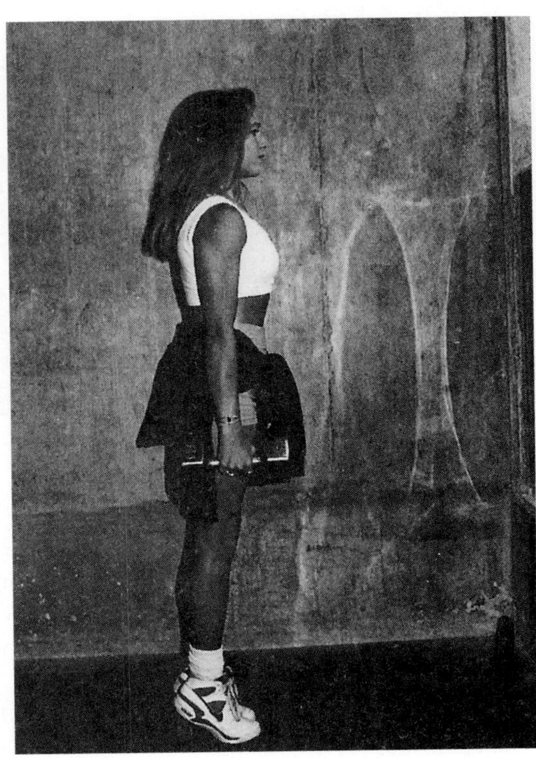

Figure 41-21. Free-weight heel raise.

Abdominal crunches (for abdomen, upper leg)

Starting position. Lie on the back on an incline board with knees bent. Place hands behind the head or fold across the chest. To increase difficulty, a weight may be held behind the neck.

Movement. Roll shoulders up and bring your elbows toward your knees. Return to original position (figures 41-22 and 41-23).

Figure 41-22. Abdominal crunch.

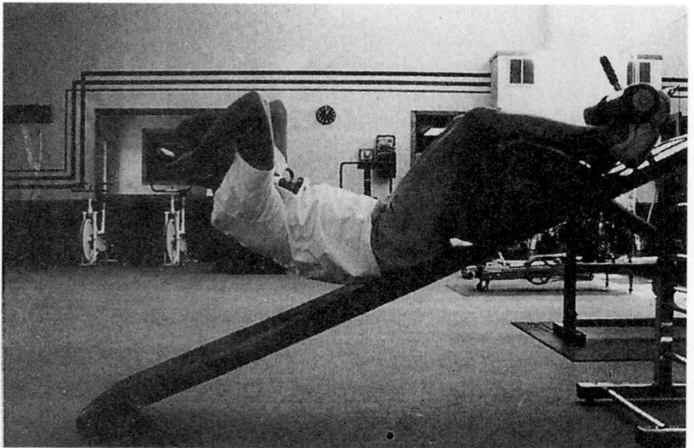

Figure 41-23. Abdominal crunch.

Technique and safety tip. Resistance can be increased or decreased by raising or lowering the board and/or by increasing or decreasing the weight used. If hands are placed behind the head, do not pull on neck with arms.

Back hyperextension (for back extensors and hamstrings)

Starting position. Lie prone on a bench with the end of the bench at the waist.

Movement. With hands behind the neck, arch the back slowly, hold, relax, and repeat (figures 41-24 and 41-25).

Technique and safety tip. Resistance can be increased by holding a weight behind the neck.

Leg extension (for quadriceps)

Starting position. Sit on the bench of a leg extension machine with feet behind the pads. Lean back slightly and hold the bench.

Movement. Raise the legs to a position parallel with the floor, lower slowly, and repeat (figures 41-26 and 41-27).

Figure 41-24. Back hyperextension—starting position.

Figure 41-25. Back hyperextension.

Figure 41-26. Leg extension—starting position.

Technique and safety tip. Resistance can be increased or decreased by adjustment of the machine. If legs cannot reach a parallel position, reduce the weight resistance.

Figure 41-27. Leg extension.

Pull-up (for upper body)

Starting position. Hang from a horizontal bar using a wide overhand grip (palms away from the face) (figure 41-28).

Movement. Starting from a straight hanging position, pull up until the chin is above the bar (figure 41-29), then return to the down position, straightening the arms completely.

Technique and safety tip. To increase the resistance, a hanging weight can be strapped to the waist.

Shoulder shrug (for upper body)

Starting position. Start from a normal standing position while holding the barbell in front of the thighs (figure 41-30).

Movement. Raise the shoulders as high as possible while keeping the arms straight (figure 41-31).

Technique and safety tip. Keep the back straight and avoid the temptation to lean backward. If heavy weights are used, a spotter should stand behind to prevent loss of balance.

Circuit weight training

Circuit weight training has become an increasingly popular form of exercise because it is believed to be one of the best forms of total body conditioning. Circuit weight training involves aerobic (using oxygen) as well as anaerobic (not using oxygen) work capacities. Normally, circuit weight training consists of 8 to 12 stations, with different weight training exercises at each. The participant moves from one station to another continuously. This provides the aerobic phase, with only enough time to get ready for the next exercise. Usually 10 to 15 repetitions are completed at each station. This provides the strength and local muscle endurance components. Rest time between stations is normally 10 to 15 seconds. The exercises should progress from the large, major muscle groups to the smaller groups and alternate between the upper and the lower body.

Figure 41-28. Pull-up (wide overhand grip)—starting position.

Figure 41-29. Pull-up.

Figure 41-30. Shoulder shrug—starting position.

Figure 41-31. Shoulder shrug—movement.

TYPICAL CIRCUIT PROGRAM

1. Frequency: Program should be done 3 days per week on alternate days.
2. Intensity: 30 to 45 seconds at each station, doing as many repetitions as possible or 10 repetitions at each station.
3. Rest time: 15 seconds between stations
4. Order of exercises:
   a. Abdominal crunch (figures 41-22 and 41-23)
   b. Back hyperextension (figures 41-24 and 41-25)
   c. Parallel squat (figures 41-16 and 41-17)
   d. Bench press (figures 41-1 and 41-2)
   e. Leg press (figures 41-18 and 41-19)
   f. Universal gym lat pull (figures 41-3 and 41-4)
   g. Overhead press (figures 41-6 and 41-7)
   h. Leg curl (figure 41-20)
   i. Arm curl (figures 41-8 and 41-9)
   j. Leg extension (figures 41-26 and 41-27)
   k. Side lateral raise (figures 41-12 and 41-13)

After the circuit has been completed, the individual should fully recover before starting another cycle.

SETTING UP A PERSONAL CIRCUIT

Below are a few stations, listed by body part. When setting up a circuit, choose one or two exercises from each section. (Be sure to choose exercises that can be done with available equipment.) Next, decide time intervals to be used; and finally, determine how many repetitions will be used at each station.

Another technique is to complete as many repetitions as possible in a chosen time limit (e.g., 30 to 45 seconds). If this procedure is adopted, items 2, 3, and 4 above change to (2) Intensity: desired time limit; (3) Repetitions: maximum; and (4) Rest time: longer than 15 seconds to accommodate recovery. Also, only one cycle may be necessary when using this technique.

Section 1: Lower Body (Large-Muscle Group)

1. Free-weight parallel squat
2. Universal squat
3. Squat jump (figures 41-32 and 41-33); remember, do not bounce or sag in the squat position; jump as high as possible; alternate which foot is forward in the squat portion of the exercise

Section 2: Upper Body (Large-Muscle Group)

1. Bench press
2. Incline-bench press
3. Resistance push-up (figures 41-34 and 41-35); done like a normal push-up, but with partner supplying resistance by pushing on the back

Figure 41-32. Squat jump—starting position.

Figure 41-33. Squat jump.

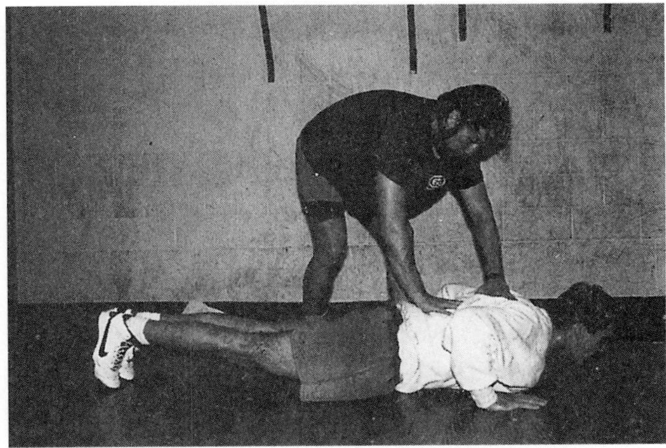

Figure 41-34. Resistance push-up—starting position.

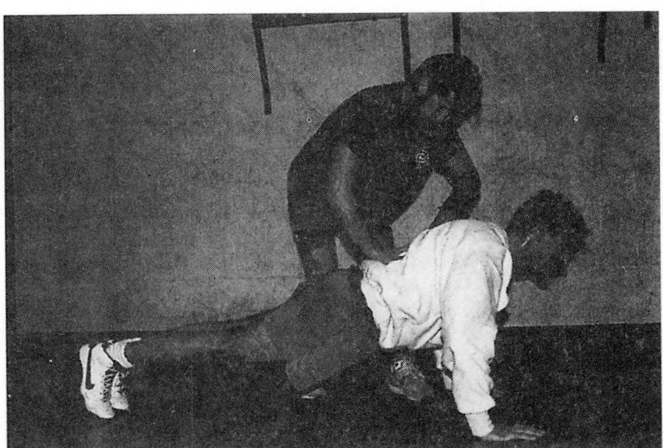

Figure 41-35. Resistance push-up.

Section 3: Lower Body (Small-Muscle Groups)

1. Back hyperextension
2. Universal leg press

Section 4: Upper Body (Small-Muscle Groups)

1. Overhead press
2. Parallel bar dip
3. Bent rowing
4. Lat pull-down
5. Pull-up

Section 5: Lower Body (Single Muscle Group)

1. Leg extension
2. Calf raise
3. Leg curl

Section 6: Upper Body (Single Muscle Group)

1. Arm curl
2. Sit-up
   a. Unanchored
   b. Standard bent-knee sit-up
3. Side lateral raise
4. Shoulder shrug
5. Bent lateral raise

KEEPING A RECORD

When beginning a weight training or circuit training program, write down your goals and chart your progress toward them. Fancy charts and printed graphs are not necessary. However to keep track of current status and future plans, a diary or log is often helpful.

Most diaries start with the date and personal observations, such as body weight and current condition (for example, tired, energetic, strong, weak). This is followed by a renewal of goals (e.g., "Add two more repetitions to every exercise this week"). Next entered are the exercises to be done, and finally, the number of sets, number of repetitions, and amount of weight used for each exercise. Use one page for each workout session. When doing circuit weight training, list the exercise to be done and the heart rate at the completion of each circuit.

Competition lifts

The following descriptions are for the lifts used in competitions. This section is meant to familiarize you with how the lifts are performed in their respective competitions and not as instructions for doing these lifts. Because these lifts are much more advanced, they should be done with instruction and supervision from a weight-lifting coach (Olympic lifts) or powerlifting coach.

OLYMPIC LIFTS

Snatch

Place the bar horizontally in front of the legs. Grip the bar with both hands and pull it in one motion from the floor to the end of the arms vertically above the head, either splitting or bending the legs. The bar should pass with a continuous nonstop movement along the body, of which no part other than the feet may touch or graze the floor during execution of the movement. The lifted weight must be held in the final motionless position, arms and legs stretched and feet on the same line, until the referee gives the signal to lower the weight (figure 41-36).

Clean and Jerk

Place the bar horizontally in front of the legs. Grip the bar with both hands and pull it up in a single, distinct motion from the ground to the shoulders while splitting or bending the legs. While resting the bar on the chest or arms, bring the feet back to the original position, that is, on the same line. Bend the legs, then extend the legs and the arms suddenly, thus jerking the bar to arm's length above the head. The weight must be held in the final motionless position until the referee's signal to replace the bar on the platform (figure 41-37).

POWER LIFTS

Squat

Place the bar horizontally across the back of the shoulders. Assume an upright position with the hands gripping the bar and the feet flat on the platform. After the referee's signal, bend the knees and lower the body until the surface of the legs at the hip joint is lower than the tops of the knees. Then recover to the standing position (see figures 41-16 and 41-17).

Bench Press

Assume a supine position on the bench, with the feet flat on the floor. The proper lift does not officially start until the bar is brought down and is absolutely motionless on the chest. When the referee's signal is given, the bar must be pressed vertically to arm's length (see figures 41-1 and 41-2).

Dead Lift

Place the bar horizontally in front of the feet. Bend at the knees, grip the bar with both hands, and lift it upward with one continuous motion, with the arms remaining extended until standing erect with the knees locked and shoulders thrust back.

LIFTING EQUIPMENT

There are several pieces of weight-training gear that can be used to make lifting weights safer or more comfortable.

Weight belts. Weight belts provide some support for the lower back. A belt should be used for lifts that involve the lower back (squats, dead lift) or when lifting weights over the head (shoulder press, clean and jerk).

Lifting gloves. Lifting gloves are used to make gripping weight bars more comfortable. They help to prevent or minimize calluses on the hands.

Wrist straps. Wrist straps are used to improve the lifter's grip. They are helpful with most lifts for the back (pull-ups, pull-downs, rows) where you pull the weight toward your body.

Wraps. Wraps (knee, elbow) provide support and stabilization for joints.

TEACHING CONSIDERATIONS

1. The decision to include weight training in a program should be based in part on the availability of equipment in relation to the number of students involved. A vigorous workout two or three times a week for a minimum of 4 weeks can provide gains for

Figure 41-36. Snatch.

Figure 41-37. Clean and jerk.

Figure 41-37—*cont'd.* Clean and jerk.

each student in both strength and muscular endurance.

2. For a school program, consider circuit weight training because of the total body effect. For units with specialized training goals, teach students the principles and possible effects of both weight training and circuit weight training.
3. Individual pretesting to assist with individual programs should be conducted before a full program is begun. Students can design their own programs if they are taught the principles of program design and if the teacher checks the programs before the students begin. Goal setting should be part of each program, with periodic checks of progress in relation to goals.
4. Partner work is almost a necessity for many exercises and is necessary for spotting.
5. Proper form and safety need to be taught and emphasized. Partners can be used to check form and weight room mirrors are also beneficial for this purpose.
6. If students are kept off the equipment when they are not using it for exercising, accidents are less likely to occur.

GLOSSARY

barbell A specialized steel bar 4 to 7 feet (1.2 to 2.1 m) long with one or more disks of various weights.

cheat Do an exercise improperly.

circuit weight training A type of weight training done in a continuous manner until an entire cycle of exercises is completed.

clean Raise the barbell in one explosive motion to the standing bent-arm press position.

dumbbell A short-handled barbell used in one hand.

isokinetic exercise A type of resistance exercise in which the amount of resistance offered is regulated by a mechanical device to be proportional to the effort applied.

isometric exercise A type of exercise involving the static contraction of a muscle or muscle group. Resistance is greater than force applied.

isotonic exercise Exercise involving muscle contraction that produces movement through a partial or complete range of motion. Resistance remains constant.

Olympic lifts Snatch and clean and jerk.

power lifts Squat, bench press, and dead lift.

press Push a barbell or dumbbell to arms' length.

repetitions (reps) Number of times an exercise is repeated without stopping.

resistance Amount of weight or pressure the muscles work against.

set A specific number of repetitions.

spotter Person responsible for assisting the lifter if needed for safety.

weight lifting A competitive sport; Olympic weight lifting or power lifting.

weight training A form of exercise in which muscle groups are worked against resistance. Apparatus is usually a barbell, dumbbell, or weight machine.

SUGGESTED READINGS

Baechle, T., and Groves, B. 1992. *Weight training: Steps to success.* Champaign, Ill: Human Kinetics. Presents a self-paced program and the knowledge to design a customized weight-training program.

Berger, E. 1992. *Introduction to weight training.* 2d ed. Needham Heights, Mass.: Allyn & Bacon. Discusses the principles and tools of weight training.

Fahey, T., and Hutchinson, G. 1991 *Basic weight training for women.* Mountain View, Calif.: Mayfield. Along with instructions for designing a training program, includes topics of special interest to women, such as osteoporosis, amenorrhea and dysmenorrhea, pregnancy, anorexia, and sport injuries common among women.

Field, R., and Roberts, S. 1998. *Weight training.* Dubuque, Iowa: WCB/McGraw-Hill.

Hesson, J. L. 1998 *Weight training for life.* 4th ed. Englewood, Colo.: Morton. Presents a lifetime approach to weight training. Topics include goal setting, stretching, guidelines for all ages, exercises for women, setting up a personal program, and advanced techniques.

Johnson, M. 1997. *Weight lifting and conditioning exercises.* 3d ed. Dubuque, Iowa: Eddie Bowers. Presents a wide variety of exercises for all major body parts.

Kraemer, W., and Fleck, S. 1993 *Strength training for young athletes.* Champaign, Ill.: Human Kinetics. Designed to assist strength trainers, coaches, physical educators, and parents in designing strength-training programs for all major muscle groups and 16 sports, especially for kids age 7 to 18.

Pauletto, B. 1991 *Strength training for coaches.* Champaign, Ill.: Human Kinetics. Discusses strength-training exercises and principles, testing, and evaluation.

Rasch, P. J. 1990 *Weight training.* 5th ed. Dubuque, Iowa: Wm. C. Brown. Includes material on weight training for men and women, safety precautions, and the physiology of weight training.

Signorile, T., Tuten, R., Moore, C., and Knight, V. 1993 *Weight training everyone.* 4th ed. Winston-Salem, N.C.: Hunter Textbooks. Covers free weights and Universal and Nautilus equipment for women and men at all levels of training.

Silvester, L. J. 1992 *Weight training for strength and fitness.* Boston: Jones & Bartlett. Includes a brief history of strength training, scientific findings applied to strength training, and information about bodybuilding.

Stone, W. J., and Kroll, W. A. 1991 *Sports conditioning and weight training.* 3d ed. Dubuque, Iowa: Wm. C. Brown. Contains nearly 20 photos; shows how to apply strength and conditioning exercises to most major sports for women and men. Scientific principles, in-depth training programs, flexibility, warm-up, stretching, and sport nutrition are covered.

U.S. Weightlifting Federation. Current ed. *Official rules.* Colorado Springs: U.S. Weightlifting Federation.

Wescott, W. L. 1991 *Strength fitness: Physiological principles and training techniques.* 3d ed. Dubuque, Iowa: Wm. C. Brown.

Periodical

National Strength and Conditioning Association Journal (bimonthly), National Strength and Conditioning Association, 300 Old City Hall Landmark, 920 O St., Lincoln, NE 68508.

RESOURCES

Videotapes

Personal training from Gold's gym (2 tapes), *Strength training for women athletes, Keys to weight training, Esquire great body series* (9 tapes), and *Building the body beautiful* (3 tapes) are available from Cambridge Physical Education and Health, Charleston, WV 25328.

Strength training techniques, Circuit strength training, Training for speed, Plyometrics training, Strength program design for football and *Strength program design for basketball* are available from Sports Video, 745 State Circle, P. O. Box 1941, Ann Arbor, MI 48106.

Wrestling

After completing this chapter, the reader should be able to:

- Display a knowledge of the various forms of wrestling and the equipment and facilities used
- Explain the rules of the sport and the differences that exist between high school and college wrestling
- Demonstrate fundamental skills, including starting positions, takedowns, escapes, reversals, and pinning holds
- Teach a beginning group of students the fundamental skills of wrestling
- Explain safety and scientific principles of wrestling

HISTORY

Wrestling is the most natural and, therefore, one of the oldest forms of combat in which two individuals can engage. Even today children left to their own devices and without instruction do not hesitate to take hold of each other and wrestle about, so it is not surprising that wrestling is one of the oldest known sports.

At the dawn of civilization wrestling was an art of war. Even before written history, we are reasonably sure, people of the Stone Age developed a form of wrestling that bordered on the scientific. They had to provide for themselves by means of strength and cunning, so physical combat was essential, not only between individuals but with animals.

Carvings and drawings found on cave walls in France, estimated to be between 15,000 and 20,000 years old, illustrate combatants in holds and leverage positions similar to many present-day wrestling positions.

An ancient double vase from about 2800 B.C. featuring two wrestlers in action was discovered by archeologists in Mesopotamia, near present-day Baghdad, Iraq. And from paintings, reliefs, vases, mosaics, and writings we know that wrestling was important in Egyptian culture. For example, more than 200 pictographs of wrestlers from approximately 2500 to 3000 B.C. were discovered on the walls of the temple-tombs of Beni Hasan, a village on the Nile in central Egypt, indicating that wrestling had already reached a high stage of development in Egypt 5,000 years ago. It was competitive, with definite objectives, and it was controlled by strict rules that determined the winner, with successful performance requiring know-how, strength, and endurance.

Wrestling as combat was an ancient method for settling disputes. Many references are made to wrestling in the Bible—e.g., "And Jacob was left alone; and a man wrestled with him until daybreak" (Genesis 32:24). Wrestling progressed through the ages until it developed into a sport in the modern sense of the word.

Heroes of antiquity—such as Gilgamesh, Jacob, Ulysses, and Milo—all earned a certain degree of fame as wrestlers, but it was the Greeks who raised wrestling to its zenith as a sport. It flourished not only as exercise in athletic training, but as an integral part of national life, rooted in the need to prepare citizens for war and in Greek ideals of beauty and harmony. Wrestling was the heart of Greek sport and formed the chief event of the pentathlon. The Greeks believed that wrestling displayed strength, agility, and grace better than any other activity, and their language is full of expressions borrowed from the terminology of the wrestling match.

Although Greek tradition ascribed wrestling's invention and original rules to Homer's legendary hero Theseus, it is generally accepted now that wrestling in its systematic and scientific form was probably introduced into Greece from Egypt or Asia. Historians are quick to point out that Homer's description of holds corresponds closely with the Beni Hasan figures in Egypt.

It was not until the last quarter of the second century B.C. that wrestling was introduced into Rome, but it never attained the same degree of popularity as in Greece. Wrestling was also popular in the Orient, particularly Japan. The first recorded wrestling match in Japan took place in 23 B.C. In China, many famous wrestlers were produced during the period of the Five Dynasties (A.D. 907–960).

During the later Middle Ages, wrestling bouts were frequently held between English towns, and almost every village festival included this sport as part of its entertainment. One of the more notable contests reported in the sporting annals was held in 1520 between Henry VIII of England and Francis I of France, the so-called Cloth of Gold meeting. At the time of this match, the English and French kings were the foremost monarchs in Europe. Unfortunately, although records document the contest, they do not clearly describe the outcome.

Long before Christopher Columbus set foot in the new world, the Indians of North and South America were holding wrestling matches as sport. Later, wrestling matches were popular entertainment at social gatherings of the early European settlers. George Washington was well known as the colonial champion in the collar-and-elbow style of wrestling, long before he led colonists against the British in the Revolutionary War. Abraham Lincoln, best known of all presidents for his wrestling skills, was famous for his success in free-for-all and catch-as-catch-can competitions. Even though America's wrestling heritage dates back to the days of the Revolutionary War and was popular among Union soldiers during the Civil War, the first organized American national tournament was not held until 1887.

Although wrestling is one of the oldest sports, it did not come into prominence as an amateur sport in the United States until the last fifty or so years. The first organized intercollegiate wrestling meet was held between the University of Pennsylvania and Yale in 1900. Perhaps the greatest single influence on the development of amateur wrestling in this country was the formation of the Wrestling Rules Committee by the National Collegiate Athletic Association (NCAA) in 1927. Before 1900 it was necessary for coaches to agree on the rules, weights, length of matches, etc., before engaging in any meet or tournament. Dr. R. G. Clapp, head of the Physical Education Department, University of Nebraska, served as the chairman of this committee for many years. Dr. Clapp's background, insight, and dedication provided the guidance for this committee in establishing the rules that greatly aided the development of amateur wrestling in American universities and colleges. With an official set of rules in place, college wrestling held its first national (NCAA) tournament in 1928. The new rules, a variation of international freestyle wrestling, led to the American style of wrestling, referred to as catch-as-catch-can, or folkstyle, wrestling.

Today, the value of wrestling is universally recognized. Wrestlers are among the best-conditioned and best-disciplined athletes. By its very nature, amateur wrestling invites a wider range of individuals to participate, from 100-pound dynamos to behemoths weighing well over 200 pounds. Both boys and girls participate in wrestling at the secondary school level and receive instruction together in physical education settings. Vision- and hearing-impaired people and those with other physical disabilities find wrestling an excellent sport in which to participate.

Wrestling is basic stuff: speed, strength, intelligence, and courage. There are several distinct styles of wrestling, including catch-as-catch-can, freestyle, Greco-Roman, judo, and sumo. Both freestyle and Greco-Roman are international styles of wrestling and are contested in the Olympic games. The American interscholastic and intercollegiate styles are really modifications of international freestyle wrestling and are commonly referred to as folkstyle, or catch-as-catch-can wrestling. In international freestyle and Greco-Roman, the emphasis is on executing throws or takedowns that lead to immediate pins. In freestyle no points are awarded for time advantage or escapes. The action is much faster than in folkstyle and requires three officials. The Greco-Roman style has the same basic rules and scoring as freestyle, but unlike freestyle and folkstyle wrestling it does not allow for the use of the legs in holds nor application of any holds below the waist. On the other hand, the American style places a greater emphasis on the ability to gain control over the opponent after he or she has been brought to the mat. From this position on the mat, the contestant in control attempts to work the opponent into position for a fall. In judo, a style used in Japan, the objective is to throw the opponent cleanly or pin the back to the mat for a period of 30 seconds. Sumo, another Japanese style, has become a national sport in Japan. The primary requisite is great strength.

From the first modern Olympic games until 1924, wrestling rules varied greatly, usually favoring the country hosting the event. In Paris in 1924 some order was achieved, and both freestyle and Greco-Roman events were contested. Over the years many countries have produced great Olympic individual wrestlers and wrestling teams. Turkey, Sweden, the United States, West Germany, and the Soviet Union all were successful until around 1960. Since then the sport has been taken more seriously by the former Eastern Bloc countries than by other parts of the world. With a total of 20 gold medals (10 categories in each of the two styles), it is a sport worth concentrating on to gain international attention.

In the 1972 Olympics held in Munich 15 of the gold medals were won by Eastern Bloc wrestlers (nine by the USSR). The United States won three golds, including one by Dan Gable, who did not give up a point in six matches. Between 1972 and 1980 the Soviet wrestlers continued to dominate the sport. In 1984 in Los Angeles the U.S. wrestlers put together a competitive team and did well (Seven golds and two silvers in freestyle and the first-ever golds [two] in Greco-Roman events), but the performance was somewhat tainted by the Soviet boycott. In 1988 the United States captured only two gold medals and five medals overall. The USSR captured nine medals, four of them gold.

In 1992 in the freestyle events, the U.S. Olympic team picked up six medals, including three gold, two silver, and one bronze. John Smith (136 lbs), Kevin Jackson (180 lbs), and Bruce Baumgartner (286 lbs) were all Olympic champions. In the Greco-Roman events the United States captured only one silver (Dennis Koslowski at 220 lbs) and one bronze (Rodney Smith at 150 lbs).

In the freestyle events in the 1996 Olympics, the U.S. team captured five medals—3 gold, a silver, and a bronze. Kendall Cross (125.5 lbs), Tom Brands (136.5 lbs), and Kurt Angle (220 lbs) were Olympic champions. Townsend Sanders (149.5 lbs) brought home a silver, and Bruce

Baumgartner (286 lbs), a bronze. In the Greco-Roman events Brandon Paulson (114.5 lbs), Dennis Hall (125.5 lbs), and Matt Ghaffari (286 lbs) all won silver medals.

A new development in American wrestling is the inclusion of women in both folkstyle and freestyle wrestling. In fact, one of the fastest-growing areas of wrestling in the United States is women's freestyle wrestling.

Title IX of the 1972 Education Amendments Act is a federal law that requires high schools and colleges that receive federal funds to not discriminate on the basis of gender in the provision of any educational activity—including athletics. Since the passage of Title IX, young women have competed on male teams against males but until recently women have not competed against other women in the sport of wrestling. Women's freestyle wrestling features the exact same rules as men's freestyle, except that matches are 4 minutes instead of 5.

Women's wrestling is growing very rapidly at all levels. Today both genders participate in wrestling at the junior high, senior high, and college levels and receive instruction together in the physical education setting. In 1997, the state of Michigan sponsored the first-ever women's state high school championships. A total of 120 female wrestlers competed in ten weight classes. In 1998 this tournament drew 272 girls representing 38 states. Even the women's collegiate movement is growing. In 1993, the University of Minnesota–Morris was the first college in the nation to sponsor women's wrestling as an official varsity sport. Since that time, women's programs have been developed at New York University, Cumberland (Kentucky), the University of Wisconsin–Stevens Point, and Central Washington University. A countless number of women have also joined their collegiate men's programs.

USA Wrestling, the national governing body, has sponsored the women's freestyle national team and has been participating in the Women's Freestyle World Championships since 1989. As the national governing body, USA Wrestling is responsible for the development of amateur wrestling in the United States and has been a major contributor in the growth of women's wrestling. USA Wrestling is providing new opportunities for young women to participate and grow as athletes in the sport.

THE MAT

The wrestling area of the mat is no less than 32 feet (9.7 m) square or, if circular, 32 feet in diameter, and not more than 42 feet (12.8 m) square or a circular area 42 feet in diameter. There should be at least a 5-foot (1.52 m) width of mat around this area. The mat should have the shock quality of a 2-inch (5 cm) thick hair felt mat. In the center of the mat there should be painted a circle 10 feet (3.04 m) in diameter.

Two 1-inch (2.54 cm) starting lines are placed in the center of the mat. One of the lines lies on the diameter of the 10-foot circle, and the other starting line is parallel to the first line and 10 inches (25.4 cm) from it. One-inch (2.54 cm) lines close the ends of the starting lines, forming a box in the center of the mat. One starting line should be green (toward the home team) and one red (toward the visiting team) (figure 42-1).

EQUIPMENT

The uniform (figure 42-2) consists of full-length tights, close-fitting outside trunks, and a sleeveless shirt without fasteners at the shoulder and fastened down at the crotch. A properly cut one- or two-piece uniform is optional. A minimum 4-inch (10 cm) inseam is required. Lightweight over-the-ankle wrestling shoes, without heels and laced through eyelets, must be worn, and a protective earguard is required. In addition, contestants must be clearly identified by some means (such as red or green anklets).

ABRIDGED RULES

The rules for wrestling are among the most variable of any sport. It is not uncommon for the point values assigned for various moves to change frequently. The rules presented here may need to be compared to a current rule book for the most recent changes.

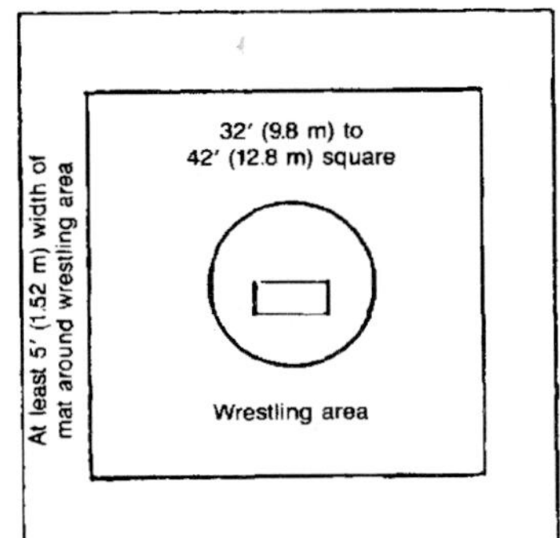

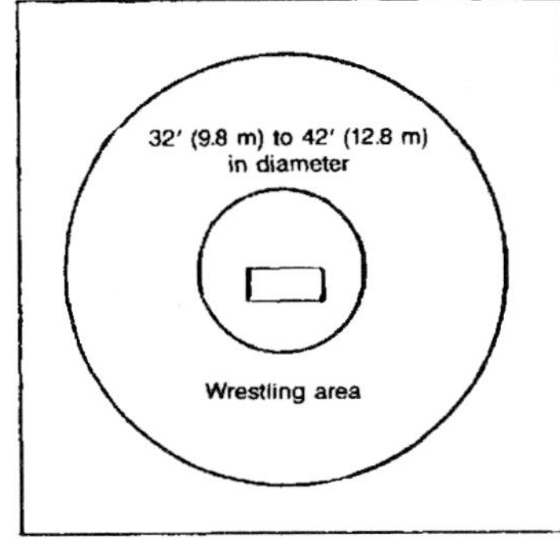

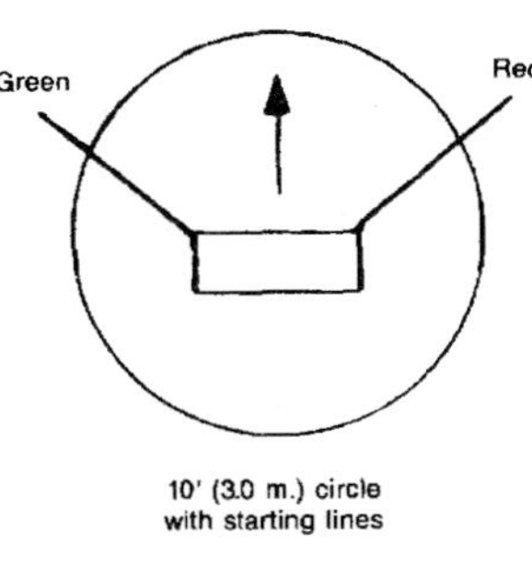

Figure 42-1. Recommended mat sizes.

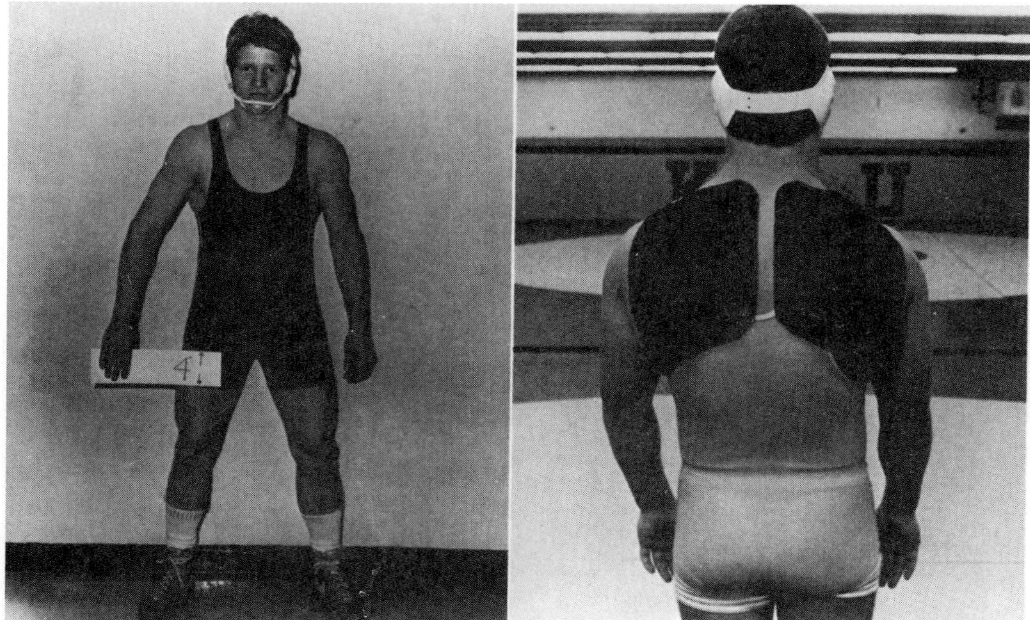

Figure 42-2. Font and rear views of official uniform. Front view shows 4-inch inseam. Rear view shows pinning area.

Weight Classification

Intercollegiate

The classes for intercollegiate wrestling are as follows:

125 pounds (56.7 kg) and under
133 pounds (60.3 kg) and under
141 pounds (63.9 kg) and under
149 pounds (67.6 kg) and under
157 pounds (71.1 kg) and under
165 pounds (74.8 kg) and under
174 pounds (78.9 kg) and under
184 pounds (83.4 kg) and under
197 pounds (89.3 kg) and under
285 pounds (129.2 kg) and under

In all dual college meets there is no weight allowance at weigh-in.

High school modification

103 pounds (46.7 kg) and under
112 pounds (50.8 kg) and under
119 pounds (54.0 kg) and under
125 pounds (56.7 kg) and under
130 pounds (59.0 kg) and under
135 pounds (61.2 kg) and under
140 pounds (63.5 kg) and under
145 pounds (65.8 kg) and under
152 pounds (68.9 kg) and under
160 pounds (72.6 kg) and under
171 pounds (77.5 kg) and under
189 pounds (85.7 kg) and under
215 pounds (97.5 kg) and under
275 pounds (124.7 kg)

High school competition is governed by the National Federation of State High School Athletic Associations.

One of the many problems facing wrestlers, their coaches, and their parents is the practice of dieting and dehydrating in order to wrestle at a lower weight class. In no other sport are we so consistently determined to have our athletes weigh in at a weight considerably below their usual weight. The extent to which wrestlers diet and dehydrate in order to compete at a lower weight class becomes a serious medical problem for many. The overwhelming medical evidence indicates that this practice is both physically dangerous to the contestant and completely illogical from the standpoint of improved performance.

From a health standpoint, crash diets designed to produce rapid or extreme weight loss are to be condemned. Disturbing the fluid balance of the body by dehydrating also has serious health hazards. These dangers are intensified in the immature organism of the growing, adolescent athlete.

Because rapid weight reduction ("cutting weight") through caloric restriction, dehydration, and excessive exercise in heated environments exposes wrestlers to decreased performance, heat-related trauma, and hazard to health and life, USA Wrestling has adopted the following rules:

1. With regard to the practice of dehydration, the use of hot rooms, hot showers, hot boxes, saunas, steam rooms, heating devices, diuretics, laxatives, excessive

food and fluid restriction, and self-induced vomiting is prohibited.
2. Regardless of purpose, the use of vapor-impermeable suits (e.g., rubber or rubberized nylon) is prohibited.
3. Violation of these rules shall cause the individual(s) in question to be suspended from the competition for which use of the prohibited methods were intended.

Major Differences Between Scholastic and Collegiate Rules

Injury time

HIGH SCHOOL: Three minutes to recover.
COLLEGE: Two minutes to recover.

Riding time

HIGH SCHOOL: No riding time.
COLLEGE: One point for 1 minute or more accumulated time advantage more than opponent.

Fall

HIGH SCHOOL: Two seconds.
COLLEGE: One second.

Number of matches

HIGH SCHOOL: No wrestler shall compete in more than five full-length matches in any day.
COLLEGE: No similar rule.

Weight allowance

HIGH SCHOOL: 2 pound allowance in January.
COLLEGE: No allowance.

Weigh-in

HIGH SCHOOL: Maximum of 1 hour and minimum of 30 minutes before dual meet is scheduled to begin.
COLLEGE: Maximum of 1 hour and minimum of 30 minutes, before dual meet is scheduled to begin.

Duration of bout

HIGH SCHOOL: Three 2-minute periods (tournaments—overtime, two 1-minute periods; consolation—three periods: first period, 1 minute; second and third periods, 2 minutes each).
COLLEGE: Three periods: first period, 3 minutes; second and third periods, 2 minutes (tournaments—overtime, three 1-minute periods, consolation—three 2-minute periods).

Sweatbox, sauna, rubber suit

HIGH SCHOOL: Prohibited.
COLLEGE: Prohibited.

Weight class restriction

HIGH SCHOOL: May wrestle one weight class above actual weight at time of weigh-in; unlimited contestant must weigh a minimum of 184 pounds (83.4 kg).
COLLEGE: May wrestle any weight class above actual weight; unlimited contestant must weigh a minimum of 177 pounds (80.3 kg).

Conduct of Match

The first period starts with the wrestlers opposite each other on their feet, one standing on the green area and the other on the red. The wrestlers will first come forward and shake hands and then go back to their 3-foot starting lines. When the referee blows the whistle, they begin wrestling. A fall during this or one of the other periods terminates the match. If no fall occurs in the first period, a coin is tossed and the winner of the toss chooses either the bottom or top position to start the second period. The third period starts with the wrestlers in the alternate positions. The referee starts all wrestling with the whistle. If during the match no falls occur, the winner is decided by the point system. Wrestlers must return to and remain in their respective areas until the winner is declared or a penalty (table 42-1) will be imposed. In case of a tie in tournaments, there will be three overtime periods of 1 minute each. Wrestlers' positions will be the same as when beginning a match and decided in the same way, by the toss of a coin. If there is still a tie at the end of overtime, criteria are applied to the overtime periods to determine the winner. These include (in the following order) abusive and unsportsman-like conduct penalties, near falls, takedowns, reversals, escapes, riding time, stalling, illegal holds, technical violations and unnecessary roughness, time advantage. Then these criteria are applied to the normal match. If none of these criteria produce a winner, the referee shall determine the winner by deciding the superior wrestler.

In college and high school wrestling, if the wrestlers go off the mat, they are brought back to the center of the mat with the wrestler that had advantage on top. If neither had control, they start again on their feet.

Scoring for High School and College

Point-scoring system for matches in which no fall occurs

1. For takedown, or bringing the opponent to the mat from standing: 2 points
2. For escaping from a defensive position on the mat: 1 point
3. For reversal of position from a defensive position on the mat: 2 points
4. For a near fall or a situation in which the offensive wrestler has control of the opponent and a fall is imminent: 2 points when near-fall criterion is held for 2 seconds, 3 points when held for 5 seconds
5. For 1 minute or more of superior, accumulated time advantage behind an opponent: 1 point, 1 point being the maximum awarded for the match

Table 42-1. INFRACTION PENALTY TABLE*

Infraction	Rule, section	Warnings, cautions	First penalty	Second penalty	Third penalty	Fourth penalty
Unnecessary roughness†	6-5	No	1 match pt.	1 match pt.	2 match pts.	Disqualify
Illegal holds†	6-8	No	1 match pt.	1 match pt.	2 match pts.	Disqualify
Technical violations‡	6-10, 6-18	See Note B and Summary	1 match pt.	1 match pt.	2 match pts.	Disqualify
False starts and incorrect starting positions§	6-17, 6-18	Yes (two)	1 match pt.	1 match pt.	1 match pt.	1 match pt.
Unsportsman-like conduct‖ Nonparticipating team personnel; Contestants before and after match	6-4	No	1 team pt.	1 team pt.; disqualify, remove from premises		
Unsportsman-like conduct‖ contestants	6-4	No	1 match pt.	1 match pt.	2 match pts.	Disqualify
Flagrant misconduct	6-6	No	Disqualify; 1 team pt.; remove from premises¶			
Foreign substances on skin or illegal uniform or equipment	6-7	No	Disqualify if not removed or corrected within contestant's remaining injury time**			
Control of mat area and Questioning the official#	4-11, 4-13, 8-5	Yes (verbal)	Warning	1 team pt.	2 team pts.	2 team pts.; remove from premises

*Note A: Any combination of four penalties, excluding false starts and assuming in correct starting positions, accumulated during a regular match or during an overtime match will result in disqualification.

Note B: Disqualification due to technical violation, illegal holds, unnecessary roughness, or unsportsman-like conduct does not eliminate a contestant from further tournament competition. Disqualification for flagrant misconduct eliminates that contestant from further competition in that tournament, and the contestant forfeits all points and placement earned in the tournament.

†Points for unnecessary roughness, technical violations, and illegal holds will be awarded in addition to points earned by the offended wrestler.

‡Stalling (including delay of match) is a technical violation with penalties awarded for such action being preceded by a visual warning.

§The first two violations will result in visual cautions.

‖The penalties are cumulative throughout a dual meet or a tournament session for coaches, trainers, managers, and physicians. They are cumulative for a contestant for a match or dual meet. These penalties are cumulative per institution.

¶Removal is for the duration of the dual meet or tournament in which it occurs.

#A verbal warning and a warning precede the first penalty. These offenses are cumulative per institution throughout each dual meet and for the duration of triangular meets, quadrangular meets, and tournaments.

**Referee may declare an official's time-out to correct equipment or uniform that becomes illegal or inoperative during use.

SUMMARY OF TECHNICAL VIOLATIONS

Stalling (6-10-a)
Holding legs (6-10-b)
Delaying match (6-10-f)
Interlocking hands (6-11)
Figure-four scissors (6-12)
Leaving mat without permission (6-13)
Going off wrestling area (6-14)
Toweling off (6-15)
Grasping clothing, etc. (6-16)
False starts (6-17)
Incorrect starting position (6-18)

Dual-meet scoring (team points)

1. Fall (any part of both shoulders held in contact with the mat for 2 seconds in high school and 1 second in college competition): 6 points
2. Decision
   a. Five points if winning wrestler has 15 match points more than losing wrestler (technical fall)
   b. Four points if winning wrestler has between 8 and 14 match points more than the losing wrestler
   c. Three points if winning wrestler has 7 or fewer match points than losing wrestler
3. Draw: 2 points for each team
4. Forfeit: 6 points

5. Default: 6 points
6. Disqualification: 6 points

Because of the many levels of American folkstyle wrestling and the numerous organizations involved with the sport, there has been a tendency for repeated annual changes in rules, match scoring, tournament scoring, and weight classifications. Therefore, it is important for anyone using this text to secure the current NCAA, National Federation of State High School Athletic Association, and the USA Wrestling rule and interpretation guides.

Illegal Holds

The following holds are illegal: hammerlock above the right angle, the twisting hammerlock, front headlock, headlock without the arm, the straight head scissors, over scissors, full nelson, strangle holds, all body slams, toe holds, twisting knee lock, key lock, overhead double-arm bar; bending; twisting, or forcing of the head or any limb beyond its normal limit of movement; locking the hands behind the back in a double-arm bar from a neutral position; full back suplay from a rear standing position; and any hold used for punishment alone. Illegal holds are signaled by the referee. See figure 42-3 for this and other signals.

Figure 42-3. Official wrestling signals.

FUNDAMENTAL SKILLS AND TECHNIQUES

Descriptions are given from one side only. However, the techniques may be applied from the other side by changing the approach from right to left and left to right.

Wrestling Positions

Square stance

Feet should be comfortably spread and turned out, with the weight centered on the balls of the feet and distributed evenly on both feet so that movement is free and easy. The knees should be bent, back rounded, head up, and arms extended forward but elbows close to the body (figure 42-4).

Starting position on the mat (referee's position)

Defensive wrestler. The defensive wrestler must be kneeling with hands in the center of the mat. The wrestler must keep both knees on the mat and must not spread them more than the width of the shoulders. The legs must be parallel, with the toes turned neither out nor under in an exaggerated position. The heels of the hands must be on the mat and not less than 12 inches (30 cm) in front of the knees (figure 42-5).

Offensive wrestler. The offensive wrestler may be kneeling or on one knee with a foot at the side of the opponent and the head along the midline of the opponent's back. The palm of the right (or left) hand must be placed loosely against the defensive wrestler's navel at the waistline, and the left (or right) hand must be placed loosely on the back of the opponent's left (or right) elbow. The knee or leg must not touch the near leg of the opponent and must be even with or ahead of the defensive wrestler's foot.

Optional offensive starting position. The offensive wrestler may be positioned on either side or to the rear of the opponent, with all weight supported on both feet, one knee, or both knees. The offensive wrestler must place the hands on the opponent's back with thumbs touching. Only the hands can touch the defensive wrestler's back. The defensive wrestler must be positioned as described above (figure 42-6).

Wrestling Objectives

Offensive

1. Takedown: to take the opponent to the mat
2. Controlling: to keep the opponent under control on the mat
3. Breaking: to force an opponent off-balance when down on the mat
4. Pinning: to bring the opponent's shoulder blades in contact with the mat for 2 seconds

Defensive

1. Reverse position: to change from a defensive position on the mat to an offensive position
2. Escaping: to free oneself from the grasp of an opponent while in a defensive position on the mat

Figure 42-4. Square stance.

Figure 42-5. Basic starting position on the knees.

Takedown skills

In preparation for a takedown, the wrestlers move around, tie up, and use various set-ups to gain an advantage. The eyes should be focused ahead but past the opponent so that one can be aware of anything that moves in the range of vision. An example of a tie-up is to hook the back of the opponent's head with your right hand and at the same time put your left hand on the opponent's bicep. Pull with the right hand and push with the left hand. A set-up is any movement or act that distracts the opponent to make him or her vulnerable to a takedown move.

The drop step is a penetration move for a takedown attack. Bend the knees to lower the hips, drive off the inner edge of the back foot, and step as far forward as possible while keeping good balance. Keep the head up and the arms in, close to the body. Concentrate on getting your hips close to the opponent (figure 42-7).

Duck under. From the standing position, grasp the opponent's right elbow with the left hand, drop to the right knee, and force the arm up. Grasp one or both of the opponent's legs and force the opponent off-balance (figure 42-8).

Figure 42-6. Optional offensive starting position.

Figure 42-7. Drop step.

Counter. Defensive wrestler resists by moving the feet back, dropping to the knees, and forcing the opponent's head to the mat.

Arm drag and go-behind. Start from the standing position. The objective is to get behind the opponent while standing. Grasp the opponent's left wrist with the right hand, and then with the left hand grasp opponent's left arm above the elbow and pull with both hands to the left until the opponent is partly turned. Then slip the right arm around the opponent's waist and with the right foot step behind the opponent. Lock the hands around the opponent's waist (figure 42-9).

Counter. Resist and keep facing the offensive wrestler when the opponent attempts to pull your arm.

Drop with leg trip. The objective is to take the opponent down from a position behind. Lock your hands with your arms around the opponent's waist and your head resting on the opponent's left hip. Drop to the left knee and grasp the opponent's left ankle with the left hand. Place your right leg in front of the opponent's right leg. Then force your right shoulder to the opponent's buttock and force the opponent forward while pulling the opponent's ankle.

Counter. Open the body lock by tearing the opponent's hands apart.

High-crotch to single-leg takedown. From a tie-up position, lift the opponent's elbows and simultaneously step in quickly. Once in close, duck the head and shoulder under the opponent's left arm, reach behind the opponent's back with your right arm, and bring it between the opponent's legs. Grasp your right hand with your left hand and pull up. This is the high-crotch position (figure 42-10). This can be followed by a single-leg takedown by moving down on the opponent's left leg while dropping to the mat on your right knee. By pulling the opponent's left leg and foot toward you and pushing forward with your shoulders, the opponent can be dumped backward for the takedown (figure 42-11).

Counter. Keep the leg the attacker is trying to control between the opponent's legs to prevent him or her from lifting it.

Figure 42-8. Duck under and takedown.

Figure 42-9. Armdrag and go-behind.

Figure 42-10. High-crotch position.

Fireman's takedown. From the collar-biceps tie-up, move the left hand from the biceps to the opponent's triceps. Step the right foot between the opponent's legs and drop to the left knee. Move your head under the opponent's right arm and pull down (figure 42-12). Move your right hand from the opponent's neck and go between the legs and reach up the back. Drop your left hip to the mat, pull down with your left hand or arm, and lift the opponent's body with the right arm. Pull your head out and reach across the opponent's body with your right arm to hold under the left shoulder with your right hand (figure 42-13).

Counter. Free up the right arm (being held at the tricep by the attacker) and cross face and get the left arm under the attacker's midsection or between the legs to avoid being lifted off the mat.

Breakdowns and rides

To break a wrestler down means to put the wrestler on hands and knees on the mat from the starting position. Because of the low center of gravity and the four points of support, this is difficult. The technique is to disengage one of the points of support.

Bar arm and waist lock. From the starting position, pull the near arm out from under and force the opponent to the mat by pulling the opponent down with the arm that is around the waist (figure 42-14).

Counter. After the tie-up, the bottom wrestler rolls toward the top wrestler. Then the bottom wrestler takes the left arm, which is free, wraps it over and around the top wrestler's arm, and grasps the top wrestler's wrist and pries it loose.

Far ankle and far arm. The object is to quickly reach under the wrestler and grasp the far arm above the elbow. Now pull this arm to you, and at the same time grasp the far ankle with the other hand. Turn the opponent over by applying body leverage (figure 42-15).

Counter. The best way to counter this move is for the bottom wrestler to pull the right arm away (or the left arm if the approach is from the other side).

Figure 42-11. Single-leg takedown.

Figure 42-12. Fireman's takedown—initial move.

Figure 42-13. Fireman's takedown—completion.

Figure 42-14. Bar arm and waist lock.

Figure 42-15. Far ankle and far arm.

Grapevine and arm bar. This can be accomplished only if the top wrestler is extremely fast. The top wrestler must quickly move on the bottom wrestler's back and wrap the right leg between the bottom wrestler's arm and leg. The top wrestler then places the body across the bottom wrestler. While in this position the top wrestler grasps, from above, the bottom wrestler's arm.

Counter. The bottom wrestler should expect this and not allow the top wrestler to place a foot between arm and leg. However, if the top wrestler's leg does go through, the bottom wrestler should push it through farther than the opponent wanted it to go (figure 42-16).

Head pry and near arm. To execute this breakdown, the top wrestler moves the right knee to a position between the bottom wrestler's legs. The top wrestler then slides the left hand down to the wrist of the bottom wrestler. While lifting the bottom wrestler's arm up and slightly to the side, the top wrestler places the head in back of the bottom wrestler's arm and applies pressure. This pressure and the pressure forward of the right thigh force the bottom wrestler to the mat (figure 42-17).

Counter. The bottom wrestler should try to pull the arm forward as the top wrestler moves the hand from the elbow to wrist.

Grapevine and bar nelson. Execute a grapevine as previously described, placing the right forearm behind the opponent's neck, pushing the left arm under the opponent's left arm, and locking the hands (bar nelson).

Grapevine and half nelson. Execute a grapevine as described previously, placing the left arm under the opponent's left arm and the forearm behind the opponent's neck (half nelson).

Body scissors and half nelson. Place the right foot between the opponent's right arm and right thigh with the left foot

Figure 42-16. Grapevine and arm bar.

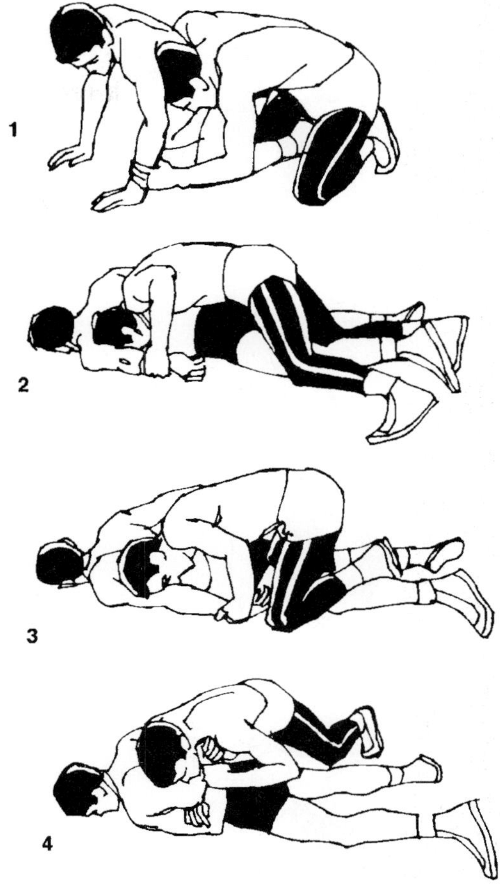

Figure 42-17. Head pry and near arm.

in a similar position, locking the feet (body scissors). Execute a half nelson as before.

Spiral breakdown. The top wrestler moves the right hand to inside the bottom wrestler's right thigh and pries outward. The top wrestler also moves the left forearm behind the bottom wrestler's left forearm and pushes forward. At the same time, the top wrestler is circling in a clockwise direction.

Escapes and reversals

Stand-up. The wrestler in the defensive position pushes off the mat with both hands, brings the elbows back and toward the ribs, raises the head and trunk, and steps out with either foot. By sitting on the rear foot and leg, which are still on the mat, the wrestler prevents the opponent from grasping this ankle or stepping over the near leg. Next, the defensive wrestler grabs the opponent's hands, pulls them apart, and pushes back with the back. The opponent is forced to resist this action (which helps the bottom wrestler to stand) or else be pushed over backward. Finally, when both wrestlers are standing, the defensive wrestler continues to pull the opponent's hands apart and then turns to face the opponent (figure 42-18).

Counter—far ankle pick-up. The offensive wrestler releases the arm that is around the defensive wrestler's wrist and moves this arm to grasp and lift the far ankle of the bottom wrestler (figure 42-19).

Counter—forward jam. Remaining in the referee's position, the top wrestler jams the defensive wrestler forward and down to prevent a standup (figure 42-20).

Counter—near-ankle pick-up. The offensive wrestler releases the near arm in the referee's position, moves behind, and grasps and lifts the near ankle of the bottom wrestler (figure 42-21).

Counter—body lock and forward trip. If the defensive wrestler gets to a standing position, the offensive wrestler should keep the hands tightly clasped around the defensive wrestler's body, step outside and in front of the bottom wrestler's leg, and push forward, thus tripping the defensive wrestler back to the mat (figure 42-22).

Side roll. The wrestler in the defensive position locks the opponent's right wrist by pressing the arm close to the body, then rolling to the right, bringing the opponent over and under (side roll) or holding the right arm between the opponent's legs (crotch hold).

Sit-out. Step the right foot forward first. Then shoot the left foot out and forward. At this point (figure 42-23, 2) the

1

2

3

Figure 42-18. Stand-up.

defensive wrestler can turn out (to the right) by pushing down with the right elbow to break the offensive wrestler's grasp around the waist and swinging the left arm forcefully forward, or turn-in (as illustrated).

Counter. The top wrestler should break the left arm down as the bottom wrestler attempts to execute the kick-out with the left leg.

The switch. Begin the switch by crossing the right hand over the left (if the referee's position is on the right side). Now place the weight on the left foot. Kick the right foot forward and to the left. Keep the hips off the mat. With the left arm, reach over the top wrestler's left arm and grasp the left thigh from the inside. Lean back and apply force to the opponent's shoulder. Now pivot on the right foot and grasp the top wrestler around the waist (figure 42-24).

Counter. Break down the bottom wrestler's right arm as the opponent attempts to pivot just after kicking out.

Figure 42-19. Far-ankle pick-up.

Figure 42-20. Forward jam.

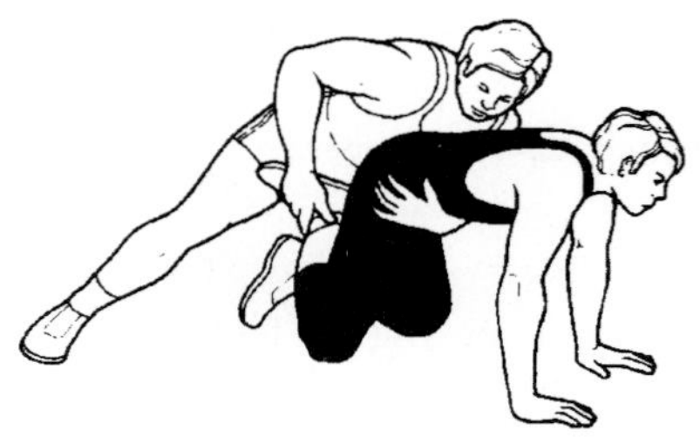

Figure 42-21. Near-ankle pick-up.

Figure 42-22. Body lock and forward trip.

Pinning holds

Side roll. This move is executed from the referee's position (figure 42-25). The bottom wrestler straightens the left leg and at the same time grasps the top wrestler by the wrist (right). The bottom wrestler then brings the right leg to the left, drops on the right shoulder, and rolls the top wrestler over. As the top wrestler hits the right side, the bottom wrestler turns to face the opponent. The bottom wrestler now places the left arm over the top wrestler's

Figure 42-23. The sit-out and turn-in.

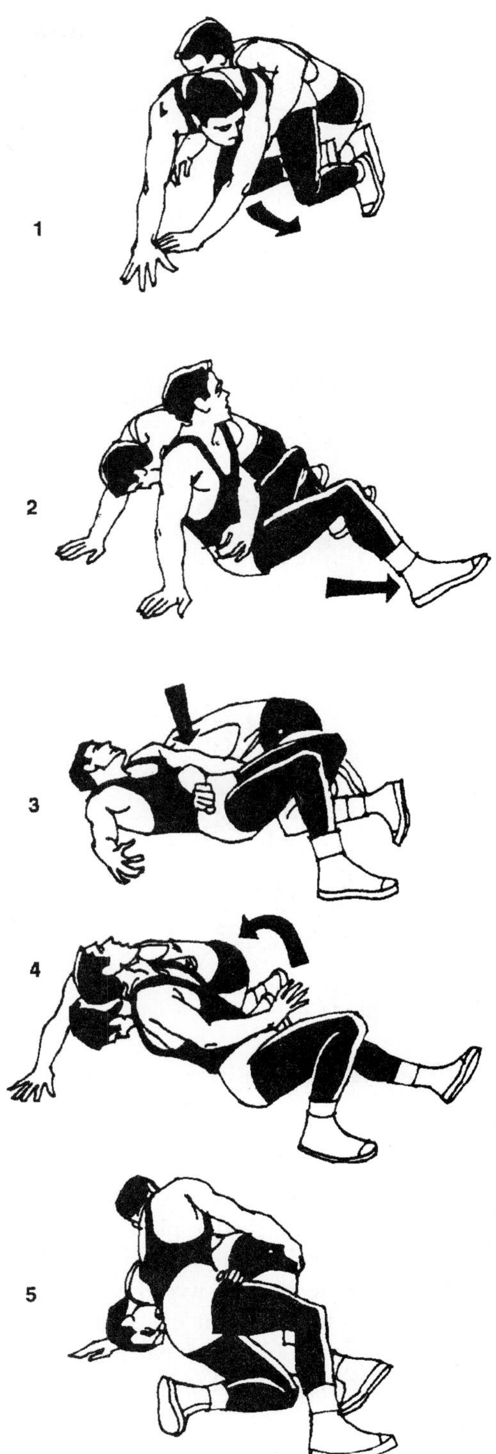

Figure 42-24. The switch.

right shoulder and around the head to a half nelson. Finally, the bottom wrestler inserts the right arm between the opponent's legs, raises the left leg, and then locks the hands. Locking the hands or arms around the opponent's leg and head is called the cradle.

Arm bar and half nelson. The top wrestler uses the near-arm breakdown described earlier. Then bring the left hand up and put it on the bottom wrestler's back. Apply a half nelson with the right hand, move to the right side and "sink" the half nelson in as far as possible. Circle counter clockwise on your knees to turn the bottom wrestler on his back. This combination of moves is called the "chicken wing" (figure 42-26).

Figure 42-25. Side roll.

Three-quarter nelson. This also is executed from the referee's position. The top wrestler places the right knee behind the bottom wrestler. The top wrestler then moves the right arm from the bottom wrestler's waist, reaches under the wrestler with the right hand, and locks hands over the back of the wrestler's head. Next, the top wrestler pulls the bottom wrestler's head under and moves to the left. To keep the bottom wrestler from rolling out, the top wrestler retains control of the bottom wrestler's leg with the right leg (figure 42-27).

Half nelson and crotch hold. Starting in the referee's position and using a breakdown, the offensive wrestler puts the defensive wrestler flat on the mat. The offensive wrestler then secures a half nelson on the bottom wrestler by moving the arm closest to the bottom wrestler's head under the near arm and behind the neck. With the other arm, the offensive wrestler grasps the defensive wrestler's top leg, lifts it up, and pushes the bottom wrestler over to the back. The top wrestler continues to maintain a half nelson with one arm and an inside crotch hold with the other (figure 42-28).

Near cradle. Assume the wrestlers are in the referee's position, with the top wrestler on the left side of the bottom wrestler. If the bottom wrestler tries to stand up by raising the left knee off the mat, the top wrestler should release the right arm from around the bottom wrestler's waist and move that arm behind the opponent's left knee. At the same time, the top wrestler should shift to a position in front of the bottom wrestler and move the left arm from the bottom wrestler's left elbow to a position around the head and try to lock hands under the wrestler's chest. By pulling the hands together and pushing the wrestler to the right and forward, the top wrestler should be able to move the opponent into a pinning position (figure 42-29).

Guillotine. This is done from either the kneeling or the referee's position. Starting from the cross-body ride, the top wrestler reaches over the body of the bottom wrestler and places the right hand on the mat for support. Then the top wrestler grasps the bottom wrestler's left wrist with the left hand. The top wrestler then lifts the bottom wrestler's left arm up over the head and falls back, pinning the bottom wrestler's shoulders (figure 42-30).

Counter. The bottom wrestler should not allow the top wrestler to lift the left arm.

SAFETY

All possible precautions should be used to ensure the safety of the participants. The rules in wrestling are continuously being altered to help prevent injuries and to make the sport safer and more rewarding for the participants. Wrestlers should be monitored continually and reminded regularly regarding the use of illegal holds, including slam, headlock, head scissors, twisting knee lock, neck wrench, and figure-four overscissors (refer to current rule book). In one of the very early class periods the instructor should explain and demonstrate all illegal holds, as well as potentially dangerous situations, including guillotine, chicken wing, standing front headlock, and takedown with arms tied up.

It has become traditional to begin wrestling instruction by first teaching those skills that can be employed as takedowns. It seems only natural that instruction should begin with standing techniques (takedowns) because regulation matches begin from the starting positions. However, one of the most overlooked safety concerns in the teaching of wrestling is the well-known fact that a vast majority of injuries occur during the early stages of instruction and are often the result of falling to the mat from a standing posi-

Figure 42-26. Chicken wing.

tion. Too often it is assumed the primary cause of injury is the failure to warm up properly. The fact that the first stage of a wrestling match is conducted in a standing position is commonly ignored. The novice wrestler is more susceptible to injury as a result of a tenseness that accompanies a fall to the mat because of a lack of experience and/or confidence.

A safer method of teaching wrestling skills is to depart from the conventional approach and begin teaching skills from a down position on the mat. This method will accomplish three major objectives: (1) allow the participants time to gain confidence in performing basic skills, (2) provide the participants time to develop a certain amount of mat sense, and (3) cut down on the number of injuries from the standing position due to changes of landing (*a*) on another wrestler, (*b*) off the edge of the mat, or (*c*) into an awkward landing position.

In addition to proper instruction and knowledge of the rules prohibiting dangerous holds, the following are some general safety suggestions:

1. Have a telephone available in an area near the wrestling room. Emergency number(s) should be posted in a conspicuous place near the telephone.
2. A well equipped first-aid room should be maintained near the wrestling room.
3. A supply of accident record forms should be kept in the wrestling room. The teacher/coach should complete the accident form in detail within 24 hours following any accident.
4. A daily record of each wrestler's weight before and after each work-out should be kept adjacent to the weighing scale. A careful monitoring of each wrestler's weight is one step toward maintaining the well-being of the wrestler.

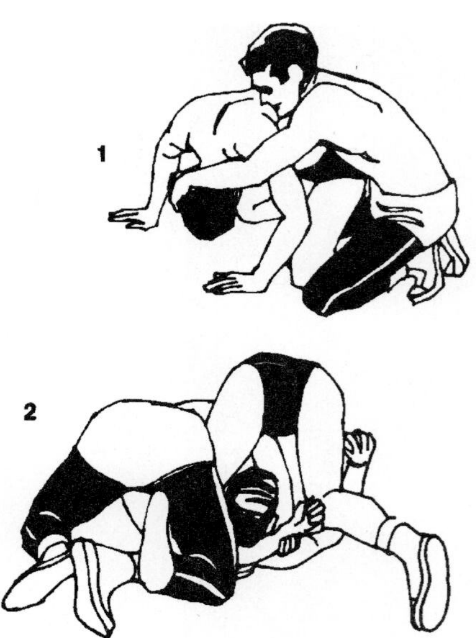

Figure 42-27. Three-quarter nelson.

5. Participants should not be permitted to wrestle without a proper warm-up. Only semiresistance should be allowed when practicing new holds.
6. Pair the contestants, as nearly as possible, according to weight, height, and athletic temperament.
7. Place spotters around the edges of the mats to prevent the participants from going off the mats and onto the floor.
8. Condition wrestlers gradually.
9. Trim fingernails and toenails short.
10. Participants should not be permitted to wear rings or other jewelry when wrestling.
11. Participants should keep all personal equipment clean.
12. Begin teaching holds from the referee's position first.
13. All lacerations or abrasions should be treated immediately.
14. All mats should be checked at least once a year to be sure they have adequate resiliency.

Communicable-disease control procedures should be followed, including those to protect against the spread of blood-borne pathogens.

1. Be certain that mats are cleaned and disinfected.
2. Wrestlers should take hot, soapy showers after each workout and clean their equipment and clothing. This practice will help prevent skin infections.
3. Wrestling mats in a high-use facility should be disinfected after each class. In a facility that does not have high use, the mats can be cleaned at the end of each day. The frequency of use, the temperature and humidity of the room, and the type of activity are significant factors in determining how often mats should be cleaned.

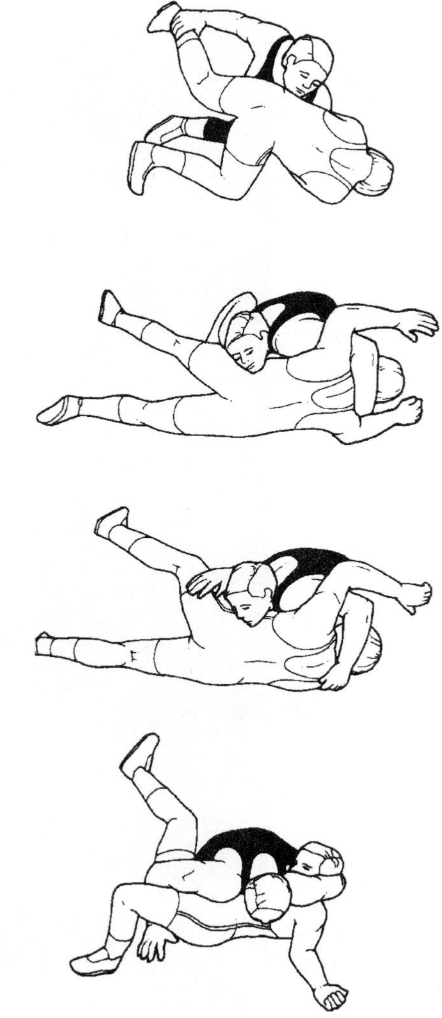

Figure 42-28. Half nelson and crotch hold.

4. There are two commercial disinfectants recommended for mats that are OSHA approved: O-Syl Disinfectant and Amphyl Disinfectant. Both disinfectants are super concentrates that must be mixed with water; they are available from Baxter Scientific Products. The Nevada Department of Environmental Health and Safety suggests that laundry bleach—i.e., a solution of sodium hypochloride—should be used to clean and disinfect mats.
5. If regular laundry bleach is used, be certain to dilute it by mixing one part bleach with nine parts water. The bleach should be mixed daily and put into spray bottles for application. Following the application of disinfectant, the mats should be dried with towels. Contaminated towels should be properly disposed of or disinfected.

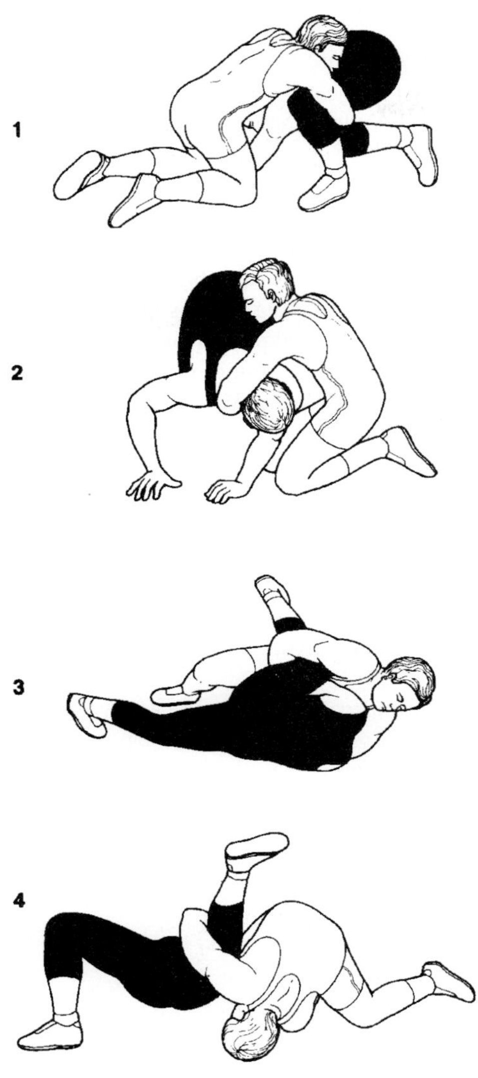

Figure 42-29. Near cradle.

Figure 42-30. Guillotine.

6. Mats should be periodically removed from the floor so that the floor can be cleaned. Mats should be cleaned and dried on both sides before being replaced. Under no circumstances should mats be cleaned with mops and pails of water; this practice is a source of mold, mildew, and other microorganisms.
7. To clean up blood, use paper towels to cover the soiled area, spray cleaning solution onto paper towels, wait one minute and then clean up the wet towels and dispose of them in a medical waste bag. Spray the mat area again with the cleaning solution and wipe dry with a towel. Latex gloves should always be worn when coming in contact with blood.
8. All human blood and certain body fluids should be treated as if they are known to contain HIV, HBV, or

other bloodborne pathogens. (Check your institution's bloodborne pathogen policy and procedure.)

9. All individuals who are responsible for cleaning mats should be directed to wear rubber gloves and approved eye and respiratory protection.
10. Although saliva has not been implicated in HIV transmission, mouthpieces, resuscitation bags, and other ventilation devices should be available for use to minimize the need for emergency mouth-to-mouth resuscitation.

PERSONAL STRATEGY

1. *Live right.* Watch how you eat, drink, and party. Consistently maintain your class weight. Retain your maximum strength by not undertraining or overtraining. Get sufficient rest. Keep clean even when just working out.
2. *Train right.* Challenge your coach. Set up a training schedule and follow it. Always attempt to practice with a superior wrestler. You should hurt sometimes during your training program.
3. *Watch and ask.* Do not fool around when not wrestling. Try to pick up new skills. Get into the middle of the action. Ask questions about new moves that you see and then learn them.
4. *Be prepared.* Know the scientific principles involved in wrestling. Know all the skills of wrestling so you can successfully counter them. Know the method of scoring points. Be aware of the penalty system.
5. *Wrestle.* Plan ahead what move you are going to make and what you will do if your opponent successfully counters it. Try to outguess your opponent. Watch your opponent's center of weight and move quickly.
6. *Shake hands.* Be courteous when the match is over, whether you win or lose.

SCIENTIFIC BASIS OF WRESTLING

On what basis does a teacher or coach make sound judgments on training, practice, and skill analysis? The answer is via the study of the sciences of exercise physiology, biomechanics, and motor learning. The reader may wonder why these sciences are important. In brief, a working knowledge of the scientific bases of motor learning equips a teacher or coach to make sound judgments concerning methods of instruction and length, frequency, and nature of practice. A knowledge of exercise physiology equips one to make sound judgments concerning the amount and type of training to prescribe in a given case. A knowledge of biomechanics equips one to choose appropriate techniques and to detect the root cause of faults that may arise in performance. These sciences are not always able to provide immediate solutions, but they do offer the means whereby an answer can ultimately be obtained.

Biomechanical Principles

Wrestling coaches are concerned with the forces that act on the human body and the effects that these forces produce during the performance of the various skills comprising the sport. Their ability to understand and/or teach the various wrestling techniques (takedowns, breakdowns, reversals, escapes, counters, and pinning combinations) depends largely on their appreciation of both the effects they are trying to produce and the forces that cause them.

The wrestler, in applying various holds, takes advantage of the fundamental principles of biomechanics. An example of this knowledge is an understanding of the principle of mechanical advantage. Mechanical advantage for a wrestler is the application of a comparatively small force (f) acting through a comparatively long distance (D) that produces a large force (F) acting through a comparatively short distance (d). The common automobile bumper jack offers us an everyday example of the application of this principle. You must push the jack handle up and down many times (a small force); consequently, through a distance of several feet, you are able to lift the car a few inches.

Wrestlers want to maximize their mechanical advantage so that they can get a large resulting force from a much smaller applied force. The main principle used by the wrestler to gain this mechanical advantage is the lever. For the wrestler the lever is generally a portion of the leg or arm free to turn on some fixed point (axis), which is called the *fulcrum*. The point of the fulcrum is usually established by the wrestler applying the hold.

Conditioning Principles

Many people have suggested that amateur wrestling is one of the most rugged sports because of its great requirements of physical conditioning. It is generally agreed that attaining a high level of physical conditioning is one of the necessary components leading to successful performance in wrestling.

The general overriding principles that are considered necessary for any individual who hopes to attain improvement in physical performance and upon which all athletic training and conditioning should be based are:

1. *Overload.* This principle states that all organs or systems in the human body must he taxed beyond their accustomed loads to increase their physical capacity. The body tends to adapt to the various demands imposed upon it as a result of prolonged muscular activity. Workouts need to be of such frequency, intensity, and duration that the level of stress is near its maximum for the present level of conditioning.
2. *Progression.* Training should begin at a comfortable level and over time systematically progress to much higher levels. This can be accomplished by

manipulating the variables of frequency, intensity, duration, or a combination of these variables.

3. *Retrogression*. Training on an almost daily basis is necessary to improve the state of conditioning. Several consecutive days of complete inactivity may intrude on the overall performance, and longer periods of inactivity lead to retrogression.
4. *Recovery*. Sufficient periods of recuperation must be included in both the daily and the overall training programs. Schedule hard workouts only every other day.
5. *Principle of diminishing returns*. The closer one gets to maximum performance, the greater the time and effort must be exerted in terms of training and conditioning in order to gain even slight improvement in performance.
6. *Individual differences*. Even when athletes receive the same conditioning program, each individual's rate of improvement and level of development may be different.
7. *Specificity*. Training must be specific to the particular requirements and strategies of that sport.

Aerobic and Anaerobic Training

During the course of a wrestling match all of the physiological systems of the body are taxed. As such, planning a training program for the wrestler that will ensure a high level of sport-specific conditioning requires an understanding of physiological training principles, an awareness of which parameters are called upon during the course of a match, and an appreciation of the relationship between general physical condition and sport-specific conditioning.

During a match a wrestler will use two basic energy pathways to furnish the required energy for the required performance. The contribution made by each pathway is dependent upon the intensity and duration of the activity. If the activity is intense and prolonged up to 60 seconds, the anaerobic pathway will prevail in energy delivery. If the activity persists beyond 60 seconds, the energy will start to be produced by the aerobic pathway. Although this system is more efficient, it does not produce the same quantity of energy as the anaerobic pathway, and subsequently a reduction in intensity will result.

Wrestling is an activity characterized by short-duration, high-intensity bursts of action that use great amounts of explosive strength and are repeated intermittently during the course of a 6- or 7-minute match. It is a sport requiring high levels of training for each of the energy pathways mentioned above.

The aerobic system is considered the basis of all athletic conditioning. Before engaging in any sport-specific training, a well-established aerobic base should be developed. Attaining this base will provide for higher levels of sport-specific conditioning to be achieved and subsequently, higher-level performances. Additionally, a highly developed aerobic system will allow for more rapid recovery from anaerobic work and for quicker resynthesis of the high-energy phosphate during the easier, submaximal phases of the bout.

During training, the aerobic energy pathway the teacher/coach must be concerned with has two components: the ability of the cardiovascular system to deliver oxygen to the working muscles, and the ability of the muscle tissue to extract and use the oxygen delivered. Exercise physiologists suggest that continuous training is the best method to increase this oxygen transport component, whereas interval training appears to be the best means to increase oxygen utilization at the muscle cell level. In the first training component, training specificity is important but sport specificity is not—that is, continuous activity at a heart rate level of 75 percent of the maximum for periods of 20 minutes or more is necessary, but the activity producing the increased heart rate can be jogging, cycling, swimming, cross-country skiing, etc. However, for the second component (oxygen utilization) adaptation occurs only in the working muscles, so training must be sport-specific and must utilize muscle groups, movements, and resistance patterns encountered during the performance of specific skills. To improve the extraction and utilization rate of oxygen in the muscle tissues, the wrestler must follow an interval training system using specific wrestling movements.

Anaerobic capacity refers to the maximum amount of energy that can be produced and made available for use in the first 30 to 90 seconds of all-out effort. Training for the anaerobic energy pathway is similar to the second component of aerobic training in that it requires both training and sport specificity. The major limitation of anaerobic capacity is the accumulation of lactic acid in the working muscles. The effect of training is to increase the muscles's tolerance to lactic-acid accumulation. The result is that the wrestler will be able to sustain an all-out effort for a longer period of time. It is this repeated exposure to high levels of lactic-acid accumulation that produces training adaptation.

Coaches do not agree on the best method of training for this pathway. However, some exercise physiologists have indicated that any of the following approaches will produce a significant training effect:

1. Maximal effort for 1 minute followed by a rest period of 4 to 5 minutes, or an exercise-to-rest ratio of 1:4 or 1:5.
2. Maximal effort ranging between 30 to 80 seconds, with an exercise-to-rest ratio of 1:2 or 1:3.
3. Ninety to 100 percent effort at maximum aerobic capacity for 2 to 3 minutes, with an exercise-to-rest ratio of 1:1.

Motor Learning Principles

Teachers and coaches need to understand the general nature of the processes involved in learning and performing various motor skills. With a foundation in motor learning, coaches/teachers will be able to develop appropriate methods for conducting practice and for teaching specific wrestling skills. The following is a list of some general principles related to practice:

1. The amount of practice affects the quality of learning, although the effect is not always proportional.
2. The spacing or distribution of practice appears to affect performance and/or learning (massed practice, distributed practice).
3. Practicing while being physically fatigued appears to affect performance to a greater degree than learning does.
4. The decision to practice a motor skill as a whole or by parts should be made on the basis of the complexity and organization of the skill (task organization, task complexity).
5. Variability of practice is important for motor skills where novel responses must be made.
6. Practice that occurs mentally can be beneficial to the acquisition of a new motor skill and to the performance of a well-learned skill.

TEACHING CONSIDERATIONS

1. Match students for weight.
2. Begin with holds from the referee's position before the standing position.
3. Walk through beginning holds with a passive defense until proper technique is established. Increase resistance gradually.
4. Combine offensive and defensive moves in practice. Give both offense and defense a choice of several moves in drill-like practices, focusing the wrestlers on the decision-making process involved in selecting a move.
5. Introduce illegal holds as they may occur in drills, and be firm about calling them.
6. As soon as several offensive and defensive skills have been developed, provide opportunities for minimatches in each lesson. Use these times as opportunities to teach rules and scoring. Structure the matches to require or encourage the use of particular moves as part of the lesson (e.g., give more points for a particular move).
7. Go back to basics when students revert to poor technique. Provide for repetition. Continually return to earlier moves as you introduce advanced moves.
8. Modify the rules as needed to make illegal any move beginners cannot perform safely, either because of skill level or conditioning.
9. Changed matched partners as often as possible within a weight class.

DRILLS

Wrestling drills should emphasize the proper wrestling mechanics. Use of these drills can be a real timesaver because they are an effective way to integrate the teaching and perfecting of wrestling skills with physical and mental conditioning. Take care that the drills do not become too complicated or tedious. Here are some suggestions for the teacher/coach to keep in mind when developing and using wrestling drills:

1. Proper administration of the drill is of paramount importance.
2. An explanation of the drill should be accompanied by a demonstration of how it is to be performed.
3. Drills are beneficial if characterized by disciple, order, and good management.
4. Drills should be programmed from the simple to the complex.
5. All drills should reinforce proper wrestling mechanics.
6. Drills should not be allowed to drag along after interest is lost.

Warm-Up Drills

Run, sprawl, cuddle, and recover drill

Many outside of wrestling see this drill as four separate drills, but in teaching wrestling it is considered a single drill. This drill is designed to (1) teach basic wrestling skills (sprawl, cuddle), (2) introduce chain wrestling, and (3) provide warm-up.

Wrestlers begin by running in place, on the whistle they are asked to *sprawl* (drop hands straight to the mat, throw legs back with feet spread and back arched); immediately they should *cuddle* left or right (roll to left or right and take a fetal position, raise and throw leg toward the head to the defensive starting position and then *recover* to the neutral standing position. Recovering includes bringing both knees to the mat, shifting the weight back over the feet, pushing off the mat with the hands to return to the standing position, and continue to run. The circuit is repeated as often as the teacher or coach feels appropriate for the state of training and experience for the class or team.

Preliminary Mat Drills

Passive-resistance drill

The wrestlers are paired off. One member of each pair is designated as being the offensive wrestler. The designated wrestler executes setups, takedowns, rides, breakdowns, pins, escapes, reversals, and counters as directed by the coach. The other wrestler offers only token resistance. This wrestler is not to be completely submissive, but rather sufficiently resistant to require the move to be correctly applied for it to work. After a reasonable period of time the position of the two wrestlers is reversed.

Point-of-contact drill or "floating drill"

From the referee's position, the top wrestler places the chest on the opponent's back but does not use the arms or legs to secure a wrestling hold. The underneath wrestler attempts to displace the top wrestler by moving, turning, sitting out, twisting, or rolling about the mat, but is not permitted to use any lock, grip, or wrestling hold. It should be the purpose of the wrestler to expend a minimum amount of effort while maintaining the position of advantage.

Spinning drill

Spinning is an excellent conditioning activity and also contributes to effective wrestling skills. One wrestler assumes the down defensive position. The other wrestler assumes the floating position by placing the chest on the back of the underneath wrestler. The top wrestler spins to the right or left on command, keeping the chest on the bottom wrestler's back. The top wrestler pivots on the chest and moves in a circular motion around the bottom man who remains stationary. The spinning wrestler should attempt to travel 180 degrees on each move, completing the entire circle (360 degrees) in two moves. The wrestlers reverse positions every 20 to 30 seconds.

Change-of-Pace Drills

Challenge drill

This game-type drill gets it name from the fact that both sides or teams are challenged. The game or drill begins by dividing the class or team into two groups. The teacher/coach assigns one group a challenge. The other group is told to prevent it. Examples are as follows:

1. The members of one group are told to remain standing on their feet. The other group is given the task (challenge) of taking them down and keeping them from regaining a standing position.
2. One group is told to remain prone while the other is told to turn them over onto their backs and hold them there.
3. One group is told to maintain at least some part of their bodies in contact with a line on the mat while the other group is to prevent this action.

At the conclusion of the assigned challenge, wrestlers are instructed to remain in their last position in order to be counted. Scores are totaled at the end of each challenge. The roles of each group are then reversed. In this way each group has to accomplish and prevent the same tasks. The number of tasks that can be assigned is only limited by the coach's imagination and creativity.

WRESTLING LEAD-UP STUNTS/GAMES

Here is a description of a few stunts and games that can be used in classes and wrestling programs as lead-up games. It is suggested that several stunts might be used during each physical education class in leading up to the unit on wrestling.

Chicken or rooster fighting

Contestants grasp their own ankle from behind and while balancing on the opposite foot attempt to knock the opponent off balance.

Dog wrestling

Two contestants face each other on hands and knees, with a strap or towel tied in a circle placed behind each of their heads. The heads are kept up and back. Each contestant attempts to pull the other over a line on the mat.

Foot push

Contestants sit on the floor or mat facing each other. The feet are placed in contact and the knees bent. Contestants support themselves with their hands behind the their back with fingers pointing away from the back. The object is to straighten the legs against the pressure exerted by the opponent.

Hand wrestle

Contestants grasp left or right hands and stand with right or left foot against the outside of the opponent's right or left foot. The object is to make the opponent move either foot from the starting position.

Hop and pull

Divide the class or team into two sides. Each side forms a line facing each other. Contestants from both sides advance and grasp the right hand of the opponent and lift their own left foot. At a signal, contestants attempt to pull the opponents to their goal line. If the left foot touches the floor or mat, that contestant loses.

GLOSSARY

arm drag A preliminary move to execute a takedown from behind.

breakdown From the referee's position, the wrestler on top forces the bottom wrestler off the hands and knees to a position flat on the mat.

bridge A position on the mat in which the wrestler is supported on the head and feet with the back arched.

counter Stop a move made by the opponent.

cradle A move made to force the opponent's head and knees together.

decision If no fall occurs in a match, the wrestler with the greater number of points is declared the winner.

default Winning a match through the inability of an opponent to continue the match.

disqualification A situation in which a contestant is banned from participation in accordance with the Infraction Penalty Table (Table 42-1).

escape Gaining a neutral position by the defensive wrestler while the supporting points of either wrestler are within the wrestling area.

fall Holding both of an opponent's shoulders to the mat simultaneously for 1 or 2 seconds; also termed a *pin*.

folkstyle The popular form of wrestling found in American schools and universities. Similar to but not the same as freestyle.

forfeit Winning a match through failure of an opponent to appear.

freestyle An international form of wrestling that emphasizes domination by taking the opponent to the mat and turning the opponent with the intent to pin.

Greco-Roman An international form of wrestling that has its roots in ancient Greece. This form of wrestling allows no holds below the waist, and the legs cannot be used for any purpose other than standing.

half nelson A hold executed from the rear by reaching either the left or right arm under the opponent's corresponding arm and using the hand behind the head to apply pressure.

hammerlock Holding the opponent's arm behind the back. This is illegal if the hand is pulled away from the body or if the angle at the elbow is less than 90 degrees.

judo A recent (1850) alteration of the ancient Japanese martial art of jujitsu. Judo emphasizes defensive tactics, physical training, and character development.

near fall Position in which the offensive wrestler holds the opponent's shoulders or the scapula area in contact with the mat for a designated time, less than that required for a fall.

neutral position Position in which neither wrestler has control.

out of bounds The supporting parts of either wrestler outside the boundary lines.

pin Synonymous with *fall*.

position of advantage Having control of an opponent.

reversal Act of moving from a defensive position to an offensive position.

riding time or time advantage The offensive wrestler who has control in the advantage position is gaining time advantage. If a contestant has one minute or more of net time advantage, that wrestler is awarded one point.

sit out A maneuver executed from the referee's position in which the bottom wrestler throws the legs forward to a sitting position.

stalemate Neither wrestler is able to improve the situation; the referee stops and restarts the match.

stand-up A breakaway (escape) move resulting in getting up to the feet quickly.

starting position on the mat Position in which the defensive wrestler is kneeling with hands in the center of the mat. The offensive contestant is kneeling at the side of the opponent, with the nearest arm around the opponent's body perpendicular to the long axis with the palm of the hand placed on the navel and the other hand placed on the back of the opponent's nearest elbow.

sumo The national sport of Japan. The object of the event is to force your opponent out of the ring or make any part of his body, except for the soles of his feet, touch the floor. The emphasis is on strength and gargantuan size. Many of the sumo wrestlers weigh 350 to 400 pounds.

sweatbox or hot box An illegal device consisting of a confined heated space or box that wrestlers use to facilitate weight loss through sweating.

takedown Bring an opponent from a standing position to the mat and keep under control.

technical fall Occurs when a wrestler has earned a 15-point advantage over an opponent.

time advantage Accumulated time during which a wrestler is in a position of advantage over the opponent; no more than 1 point may be awarded in any one match. (Not used in high school.)

SUGGESTED READINGS

Amateur Athletic Union of the United States. Current ed. *Official wrestling guide*. New York: AAU.

American Coaching Effectiveness Program. 1992. *Rookie coaches wrestling guide*. Champaign, Ill.: Human Kinetics. Provides beginning coaches with detailed information on the responsibilities of a coach and explains the essential skills for coaching wrestling, including how to teach wrestling techniques and strategies.

Barry, D., and Simpson, B. 1994. *Winning wrestling moves*. Champaign, Ill.: Human Kinetics. Provides high school and college wrestlers and their coaches with all the fundamentals and latest refinements in wrestling techniques.

Chapman, M. 1990. *Encyclopedia of American wrestling*. Champaign, Ill.: Human Kinetics. A detailed chronicle of the people and places that have made wrestling history.

Costell, D., and Willmore, J. 1993. *Training for sport and activity: The physiological basis of the conditioning process*. 3d ed. Champaign, Ill.: Human Kinetics. Provides the practitioner with information of practical value regarding the training and conditioning of athletes.

DeVries, H., and Housh, T. 1994. *Physiology of exercise for physical education, athletics and exercise science*. 5th ed. Dubuque, Iowa: Wm. C. Brown. Part of this book pertains to the physiology of training and conditioning of athletes.

Keith, A. 1990. *Successful wrestling*. Champaign, Ill.: Human Kinetics. Step-by-step instructions for 30 wrestling techniques, from simple to complex.

Johnson, D. 1991. *Wrestling drill book*. Champaign, Ill.: Human Kinetics. A unique feature of this book is an index that lists drills by area of emphasis.

Martell, B. 1993. *Greco-Roman wrestling*. Champaign, Ill.: Human Kinetics. Presents championship techniques that will help Greco-Roman wrestlers increase their expertise and help traditional folkstyle and freestyle wrestlers be more competitive.

Mysnyk, M., Davis, B., and Simpson, B. 1994. *Winning wrestling moves*. Champaign, Ill.: Human Kinetics.

National Collegiate Athletic Association. Current ed. *Official wrestling guide*. New York: NCAA.

RESOURCES

Videotapes and Computer Software

Escapes and reverses, *Riding and pinning*, and *Takedowns* (3 videos). Karol Video, 22 Riverside Dr., Wayne, NJ 07470.

Fundamentals, Advanced, and *Free style* (3 videos). "How To" Sports Videos, P.O. Box 5852, Denver, CO 80217.
Fundamentals of wresting with Greg Shoemaker (2 videos). Includes stances, various set-ups, bridging the gap, takedowns, defensive takedowns, escapes, reversals, and pins.
Takedowns with Bobby Douglas of Arizona State (2 videos). Demonstrates the stance, penetration, tieup, double-leg tackle, set-up, second moves, and breakdowns from behind. Wrestling videos (11 videos). Live-action videos feature past and present NCAA and Olympic champions in their finest form. Cambridge Video, P.O. Box 2153, Charleston, WV 25328.
Granby System videos. Grandby System Wrestling, 4817 Admiration Dr., Virginia Beach, VA 23464.
Kid's wrestling: A complete guide to kid's wrestling. This is a series of three videos that are excellent for beginning teachers and coaches.
Mat-stats: A computerized statistics system for wrestling coaches (video). Statmaster, Hyland Enterprises, P.O. Box 7847, Colorado Springs, CO 80933.
Part I: Organizing a kid's wrestling club. This video is 45 minutes long and presents all steps needed to organize and run a youth wrestling program.
Part II: The key to fitness, nutrition, and safety. This video is 45 minutes long and is designed to promote both physical and mental well-being in the young wrestler and reduce the risk of injury.
Part III: Basic skills and better techniques. This 45-minute videotape presents wrestling's seven basic skills. This tape not only demonstrates the skills to be taught but also provides methods on how to teach those skills.
These three videotapes are available from The Athletic Institute, 200 Castlewood Dr., North Palm Beach, FL 33408 (800-933-3335).
Two-part videotape series illustrating more than 25 basic moves, Sports Video, 745 State Circle, P.O. Box 1941, Ann Arbor, MI 48106.
Wrestling classic and *Wrestling's greatest heroes* (2 videos). Corbin House, 227 Corbin Place, Brooklyn, NY 11235.
Wrestling for the 90's (video). National Federation of State High School Associations, 11724 NW Plaza Circle, P.O. Box 20626, Kansas City, MO 64195.
Wrestling tournament manager (DOS software). Athletic Director Systems, 2904 SE 173rd Ct., Camas, WA 98607.

Sources of Additional Information

USA Wrestling
6155 Lehman Dr.
Colorado Springs, CO 80918
719-598-8181
Fax: 719-598-9440

USA Wrestling, Women's Wrestling Committee
6155 Lehman Dr.
Colorado Springs, CO 80918
719-598-8181
Fax: 719-598-9440

Web sites

The Mat: The home of amateur wrestling
http://www.themat.com
USA Wrestling
http://www.usawrestling.org/
Athletics—University of Minnesota, Morris—Women's wrestling. A new look at the future of our sport
http://cda.mrs.umn.edu/~wrestle/wexpect.html
NCAA Press Releases
http://www.ncaa.org/releases/makepage.cgi/rules/1998041301ru.htm

Appendix **A**

Miscellaneous Field and Court Dimensions

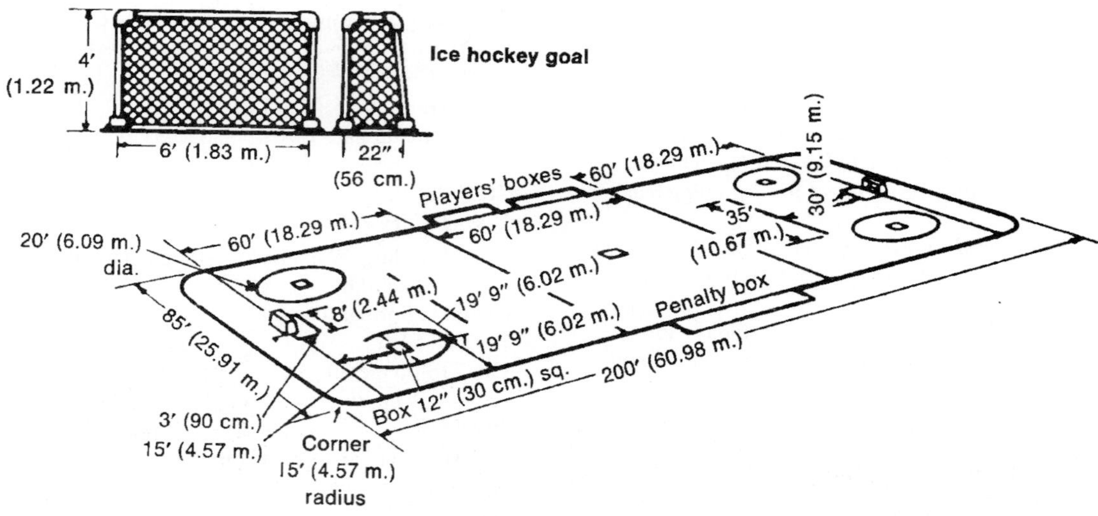

Figure A-1. Ice hockey rink.

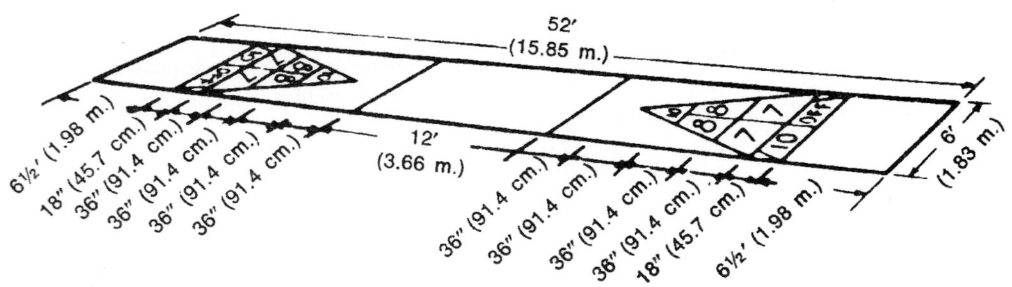

Figure A-2. Shuffleboard court.

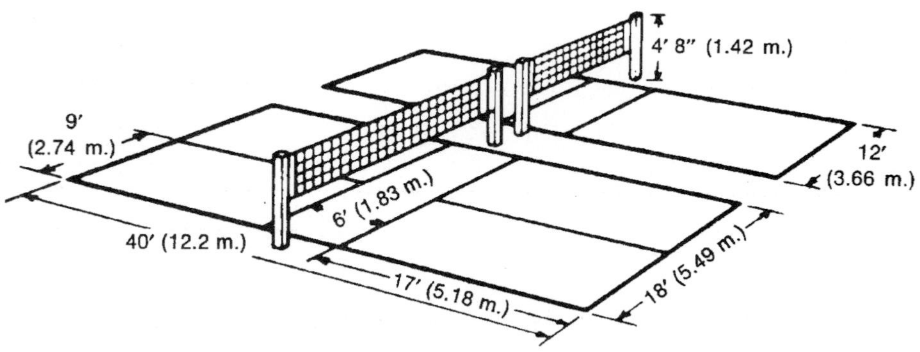

Figure A-3. Deck tennis (double and single) courts.

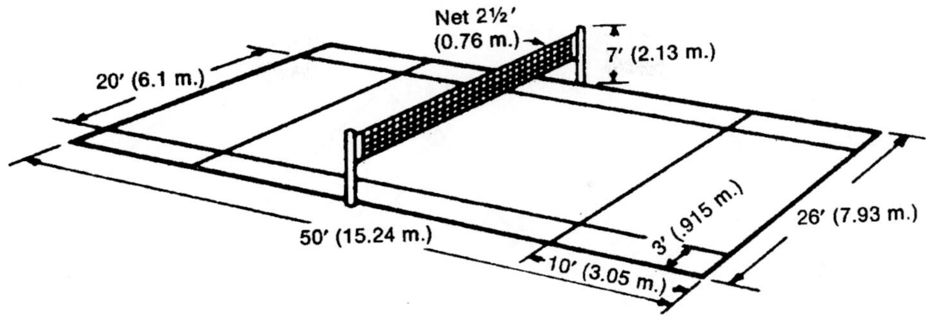

Figure A-4. Aerial tennis court.

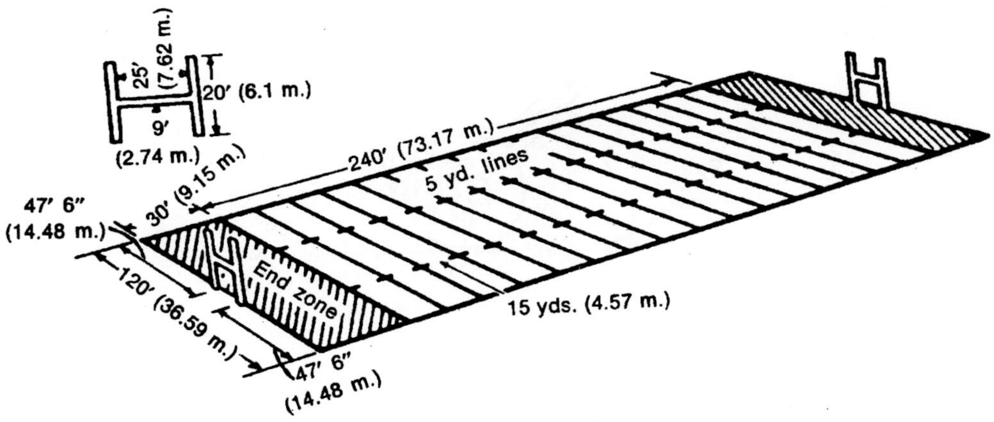

Figure A-5. Six-person football field.

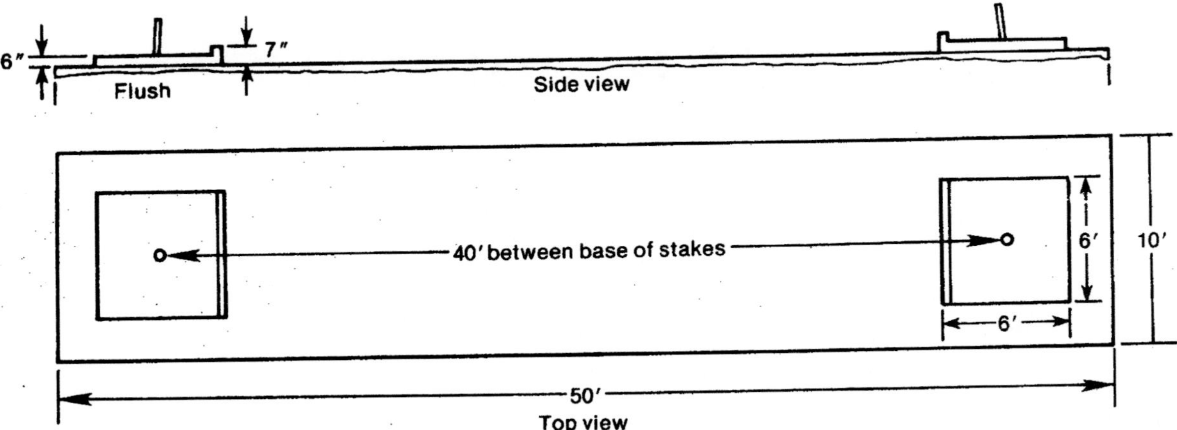

Figure A-6. Horseshoe pit. The 1-inch × 3-foot stakes extend 14 inches above ground and incline 3 inches toward each other. Stakes are 30 feet apart for women and boys under 16 years.

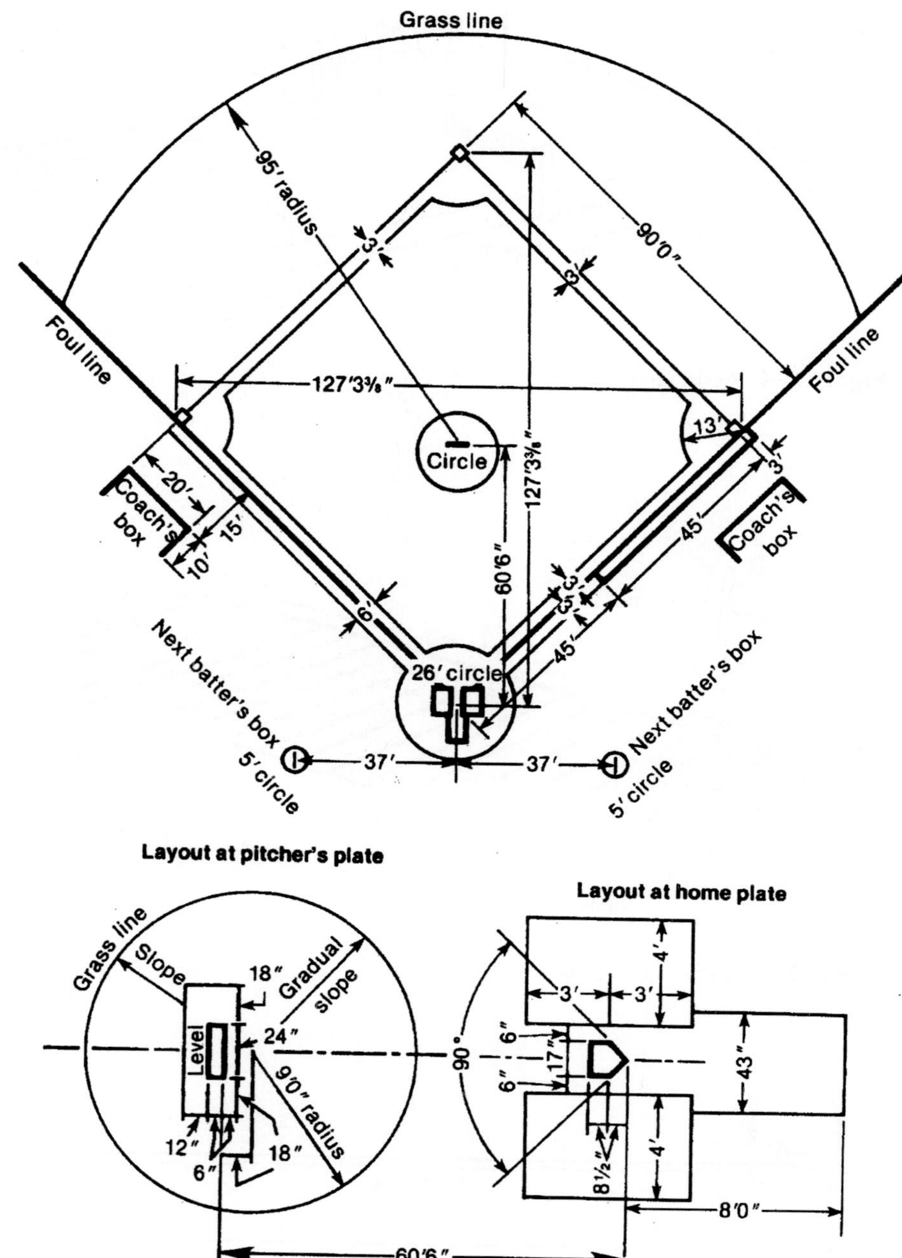

Figure A-7. Baseball diamond.

Appendix **B**

Metric and English Equivalents

Table B-1. CONVERSION

Length	
1 millimeter (mm)	= 0.04 inch
1 centimeter (cm)	= 10 millimeters = 0.4 inch
1 meter (m)	= 39.4 inches = 3.3 feet = 1.1 yards
1 yard (yd)	= 0.9 meter
1 foot (ft)	= 30 centimeters
1 inch (in)	= 2.5 centimeters
Distance	
1 meter (m)	= 39.4 inches = 3.3 feet = 1.1 yards
1 kilometer (km)	= 1,000 meters = 0.62 mile
1 mile (mi)	= 1.6 kilometers
Weight	
1 gram (g)	= 0.035 ounces
1 kilogram (kg)	= 2.2 pounds
1 ounce (oz)	= 28 grams
1 pound (lb)	= 0.45 kilogram

Table B-2. UNITS OF LENGTH IN TRACK AND FIELD EVENTS

Track events						
Meters	**Miles**	**Yards**	**Feet**	**Inches**	**Yards**	**Meters**
1	0	1	0	3.37	40	36.58
2	0	2	0	6.74	50	45.72
3	0	3	0	10.11	60	54.86
4	0	4	1	1.48	70	64.01
5	0	5	1	4.85	75	68.58
10	0	10	2	9.70	100	91.44
20	0	21	2	7.40	110	100.58
30	0	32	2	5.10	120	109.73
40	0	43	2	2.80	220	201.17
50	0	54	2	.50	300	274.32
60	0	65	1	10.20	440	402.34
70	0	76	1	7.90	600	548.64
80	0	87	1	5.60	880	804.67
90	0	98	1	3.30	1000	914.40
100	0	109	1	1.00	1320	1207.01
110	0	120	0	10.70		
200	0	218	2	2.00	**Miles**	**Meters**
300	0	328	0	3.00	1	1,609.3
400	0	437	1	4.00	2	3,218.7
500	0	546	2	5.00	3	4,828.0
1000	0	1093	1	10.00	4	6,437.4
1500	0	1640	1	3.00	5	8,046.7
2000	1	427	0	8.00	6	9,656.1
2500	1	974	0	1.00	7	11,265.4
3000	1	1520	2	6.00	8	12,874.8
5000	3	188	0	2.00	9	14,484.1
10000	6	376	0	4.00	10	16,093.5
26 Miles − 385 yards = 42 kilometers − 195.1 meters						

Field Events							
Feet	**Meters**	**Feet**	**Meters**	**Feet**	**Meters**	**Feet**	**Meters**
1	0.305	6	1.829	20	6.096	70	21.336
2	.610	7	2.134	30	9.144	80	24.384
3	.914	8	2.438	40	12.192	90	27.432
4	1.219	9	2.743	50	15.240	100	30.480
5	1.524	10	3.048	60	18.288	200	60.960

Relation of metric to English scale. For measuring or checking courses where no metric tape is available the following table is acceptable: 1 meter = 39.37 inches = 3.2808 feet = 1.0936 yards. 1 kilometer = 1,000 meters = 0.621370 miles.

Credits

Fig. 1-1. PhotoDisc/Sports & Recreation.
Figs. 1-2, 1-5. Photos by Raili Filion.
Figs. 1-3 and 1-4. From Lumpkin A: *Physical education and sport*, ed 3, St. Louis. 1994, Mosby.
Fig. 2-1. Reprinted with permission from *Research Quarterly for Exercise and Sport,* Vol. 67, No. 2, 193–205. Copyright 1996 by the American Alliance for Health, Physical Education, Recreation, and Dance, 1900 Association Dr., Reston, VA 20191.
Table 2-8. Adapted by permission from E. T. Howley and B. D. Franks, 1997, *Health Fitness Instructor's Handbook*, 3rd ed. (Champaign, IL: Human Kinetics), 308.
Table 2-10. Reprinted with permission from *Research Quarterly for Exercise and Sport,* Vol. 63, No. 1, A52. Copyright 1992 by the American Alliance for Health, Physical Education, Recreation, and Dance, 1900 Association Dr., Reston, VA 20191.
Table 2-15. Reprinted with permission from American Society of Contemporary Medicine and Surgery. Michael L. Pollack, Ph.D; Donald H. Schmidt, MD; and Andrew S. Jackson, PE. Measurement of Cardio-respiratory Fitness and Body Composition in the Clinical Setting. *Comp. Ther.* 1980; 6 (9): 12–27.
Table 2-16. Reprinted from *Y's way to physical fitness* with permission of the YMCA of the USA, 101 N. Wacker Drive, Chicago, IL 60606.
Table 2-17. Based on norms from *The Physical Fitness Specialist Manual,* The Cooper Institute for Aerobics Research, Dallas, TX, revised 1988, used with permission.
Table 2-18. Reprinted from *Y's way to physical fitness* with permission of the YMCA of the USA, 101 N. Wacker Drive, Chicago, IL 60606.
Table 2-21. Reprinted by permission from J. F. Sallis and K. Patrick, 1994, "Physical Activity Guidelines for Adolescents: Consensus Statements." *Pediatric Exercise Science*, 6 (4): 306–308.
Figs. 3-1, 3-3, 3-4, 3-5, and 3-6. Photos by Lorna Francis.
Fig. 3-2. Photo by Raili Filion.
Fig. 4-6. From Archery & Fencing Rules by NAGWS of the American Alliance of Health, Physical Education, Recreation, and Dance. Copyright 1960.
Fig. 4-7. Photo by David C. Tyndall.
Figs. 4-9, 4-10, and 4-11. From Bear F: *Fred Bear's world of archery*, New York, 1979. Doubleday & Co., Inc. Photos by George Bing.
Fig. 6-4. Redrawn from *Badminton*, Sports Techniques Series, Chicago, 1969, The Athletic Institute.
Fig 6-7. From *Badminton*, Sports Techniques Series, Chicago, 1969, The Athletic Institute.
Figs. 7-1 and 7-2. Reprinted with permission of The National Collegiate Athletic Association.
Figs. 7-9 through 7-14. Reprinted with permission of James LaPoint.
Fig. 8-1. From Lemond G., Gordis K: *Greg Lemond's complete book of bicycling*, New York, 1987, Putnam Publishing Group.
Figs. 8-2 through 8-7. Photos by Tom Swensen.
Fig. 9-4. Photo by Raili Filion.
Figs. 9-5 through 9-10. Photos by Marlee Stewart.
Figs. 10-7 and 10-8. Photos by Cynthia Noble.
Figs. 11-1 and 11-2. Harold Duvall, Innova Champion Discs, East Coast Sales Office, Rock Hill, SC 29732.
Fig. 11-3. Adapted from Frisbee Sports and Games, Charles Tips and Dan Ruddick.
Figs. 11-4 through 11-12 and 11-14 through 11-16. The Discourse, Dan Ruddick.
Figs. 11-13 and 11-15. Frisbee Sports and Games, Charles Tips and Dan Ruddick.
Fig 12-1. Reprinted by permission of The American Alliance for Health, Physical Education, Recreation, and Dance, 1900 Association Dr., Reston, VA 22091.
Figs. 12-2, 12-5, 12-6, and 12-8 through 12-11. Photos by Anne Klinger.
Figs. 13-1, 13-2, 13-6, and 13-11. Photos by Raili Filion.
Fig. 14-1. From *Rules of golf* by United States Golf Association, P.O. Box 708, Far Hills, NJ 07931.
Figs. 14-8B, 14-14, and 14-15. Photos by Raili Filion.
Fig. 15-41. Photo by Raili Filion.
Figs. 16-1, 16-7 through 16-11. Photos by Daniel R. Kibler.
Figs. 16-2 through 16-6. Liz Miller, *Get Rolling*, Ragged Mountain Press, copyright 1998. Reprinted by permission of the McGraw-Hill Companies.
Fig. 17-1. From Klafs CE, Lyon MJ: *The female athlete*, ed 2, St. Louis, 1978, Mosby.
Fig. 17-6. Courtesy of Washington University assistant track coaches.
Figs. 18-2 through 18-5. Photos by Rick Schmidt.
Figs. 20-2 through 20-12. Photos by Robert Scott.
Figs. 20-13, 20-14, and 20-18 through 20-30. Photos by Polly Keener.
Figs. 21-1, 21-3, and 21-4. Photos by Norman Gilchrest.
Figs. 21-9, 21-10, and 21-12 through 21-14. Photos by Tresa Gilchrest.
Figs. 22-1, 22-2, and 22-4 through 22-7. From *Orienteering for sport and pleasure*. Copyright 1977 by Hans Bengtsson and George Atkinson. Reprinted by permission of The Stephen Green Press, a wholly owned subsidiary of Viking Penguin, Inc.
Fig. 22-3. Courtesy of Silva Company, Orienteering Services, U.S.A., Box 547, LaPorte, IN 46350.
Fig. 23-8. Photo by Raili Filion.
Fig 25-6. From *Seven days to self-defense*. Copyright 1980 by Ted Gambordella. Used with permission of Contemporary Books, Inc., Chicago.
Fig. 26-1. Photo by Raili Filion.
Figs. 27-8 through 27-10. From *Cross-country skiing today* by John Caldwell. Copyright 1977 by John Caldwell. Reprinted by permission of The Stephen Greene Press, a wholly owned subsidiary of Viking Penguin, Inc.
Fig. 27-13. From *The cross-country ski book* by John Caldwell. Copyright 1984 by John Caldwell. Reprinted by permission of The Stephen Greene Press, a wholly owned subsidiary of Viking Penguin, Inc.
Figs. 27-11 and 27-12. Photos by George Atkinson.
Figs. 27-5 through 27-7. Drawn by S. Fjeldleim, head ski coach at University of Northern Michigan.
Fig. 28-6. Photo by Raili Filion.
Figs. 29-3 through 29-17. Photos by March Krotee.
Fig. 30-4. From The Athletic Journal.

Figs. 31-2 through 31-5. Photos by Laura deGhetaldi.
Figs. 32-1 and 32-2. Photos by Gerald DeMers.
Figs. 32-3 through 32-7. Photos by Raili Filion.
Fig. 34-3. Photo by Raili Filion.
Figs. 34-4 and 34-5. Courtesy USATT, Photos by Allsport.
Fig. 35-4. From United States Team Handball Federation: *Rules of the game*, 1981–1985 edition, Colorado Springs, Colo, USTHF.
Figs. 36-1, 36-3 through 36-8, and 36-11. Photos by Randy Hyllegard.
Fig. 37-2. From Grambeau RJ: *The official national and touch football rules*. North Palm Beach, Fla. 1986. The Athletic Institute. Used with permission of the Athletic Institute.
Figs. 37-3 through 37-8. Photos by Randy Bonnette.
Figs. 38-1 through 38-3. Photos by Al McDaniels.
Figs. 38-10, 38-12, 38-19, 38-22, 38-23, and 38-29. Photos by Kirby Lee.
Figs. 39-4 and 39-8. Photos by Brian Lewis, Media Relations, Intercollegiate Athletics, University of Colorado.
Figs. 40-2 through 40-6. Photos by George Weiny.
Figs. 41-1 through 41-35. Photos by Raili Filion.
Fig. 41-36. From *The clean and jerk lift*, Colorado Springs, Colo, United States Weightlifting Federation.
Fig. 41-37. From *The snatch lift,* Colorado Springs, Colo, United States Weightlifting Federation.
Fig. 42-2. Permission to reprint granted by the National Collegiate Athletic Association. From *NCAR wrestling rules and interpretations*, Mission, Kan, 1989, NCAA. Specifications subject to revision annually.
Figs. 42-4 through 42-13 and 42-26. Photos by Raili Filion.